# MENTAL HEALTH ACT
# MANUAL

# MENTAL HEALTH ACT MANUAL

*by*

Richard M. Jones M.A. (Kent and Brunel),
Solicitor, C.Q.S.W.

*Consultant, Morgan Cole, Solicitors*
*Honorary Professor of Law, Cardiff University*

Thirteenth Edition

**SWEET & MAXWELL**

 THOMSON REUTERS

Published in 2010 by Thomson Reuters (Legal) Limited
(Registered in England & Wales, Company No 1679046.
Registered Office and address for service:
100 Avenue Road, London, NW3 3PF) trading as Sweet & Maxwell

*For further information on our products and services, visit
www.sweetandmaxwell.co.uk*

Typeset in Great Britain by Hobbs the Printers Ltd, Southampton
Printed in the UK by CPI William Clowes, Beccles NR34 7TL

*No natural forests were destroyed to make this product;
only farmed timber was used and re-planted.*

A CIP catalogue record for this book
is available from the British Library

ISBN 978-0-414-04451-7

# PREFACE

One of the major reasons why this edition follows so quickly from the last is the significant amount of caselaw that the Upper Tribunal has generated on the terms of the Mental Health Act and the Tribunal Procedure (First-tier Tribunal) (Health, Education and Social Care Chamber) Rules 2008. Particularly noteworthy is the decision in *RM v St Andrew's Healthcare* where the First-tier Tribunal made a direction under r.14(2) of the 2008 Rules to prohibit disclosure to the patient of the fact that he was being covertly medicated. On hearing an appeal against that decision, the Upper Tribunal was satisfied that disclosure would be likely to cause the patient serious harm, even to the point where the patient's life would be at risk, but allowed the appeal on the ground that it was in the interests of justice for the patient to be able to challenge his detention effectively.

Given the current economic climate, could amendments be made to the Act which save the taxpayer significant amounts of money without prejudicing the interests of patients? One obvious area to target is the operation of the Second Opinion Appointed Doctor system which is expensive to run and is operating under great strain due to the increased demand that is being placed upon it by the need to provide certificates for community treatment order patients. Having reviewed relevant research, Peter Bartlett and Ralph Sandland concluded that "the SOAD system has done little to protect patients from overenthusiastic treatment regimes or abuses of their legal rights" (*Mental Health Law: policy and practice*, 2007, p.332). This finding is supported by the fact that only a tiny minority of SOAD interventions results in a significant change in patients' treatment plans. Rather than have a system which requires a SOAD visit on every occasion when a certificate is required, would it not be more sensible for Responsible Clinicians to submit treatment plans to the Care Quality Commission (in Wales, Health Inspectorate Wales) and for SOAD visits to be confined to those cases where a clinical scrutineer considers that the plan reveals an issue that requires further investigation? Such a procedure would eliminate futile SOAD visits while retaining the main benefit of the SOAD system which is the peer review of clinicians' treatment decisions.

In this edition, I have attempted to assist practitioners in Wales by making appropriate references to the Mental Health (Hospital, Guardianship, Community Treatment and Consent to Treatment) (Wales) Regulations 2008 and to the statutory forms that are used in Wales. The distinctive nature of the legislative landscape in Wales is likely to become starker if the proposed Mental Health (Wales) Measure, which is being considered in the National Assembly for Wales, becomes law. The Measure, which comprises no less than 51 sections and two Schedules, places new duties on Local Health Boards and local authorities in Wales and makes amendments to the 1983 Act as it applies in Wales. The Measure is doubtless a product of the expectation shared by many legislators that the passing of legislation inevitably leads to improved outcomes for citizens. Professor Phil Fennell, in his evidence to the Legislative Committee which considered the Measure, succinctly explained why more legislation for Wales is likely to be counter productive:

"It is noteworthy that England, which currently has the same legislative framework as Wales, has mental health services which are generally recognised to be far superior to those available in Wales. What is needed is the political will to develop these services in Wales, to fund and to staff them adequately, and to use existing policy levers and legislation to the full, not to introduce more legislation which is distinctive mainly for its complexity and volume. Far from enabling Wales to lead the way, this Measure may simply allow the time frame for the introduction of better services to slip further behind."

In preparing this edition, I have taken account of material that was available to me on September 1, 2010.

*Richard Jones*
*e-mail: richard.jones2@morgan-cole.com*

# CONTENTS

## APPENDIX D
Mental Health Act 1983 Approved Clinician (General) Directions 2008 1069

# Table of Cases

# Table of Cases

# Table of Cases

# Table of Cases

xiv

## Table of Cases

## Table of Cases

# Table of Cases

# Table of Cases

# Table of Cases

# PART 1

## MENTAL HEALTH ACT 1983

### (1983 c.20)

ARRANGEMENT OF SECTIONS

SECTION

PART I

APPLICATION OF ACT

1

PART VI

REMOVAL AND RETURN OF PATIENTS WITHIN UNITED KINGDOM, ETC.

*Removal to Scotland*

# Mental Health Act 1983

Part X

Miscellaneous and supplementary

*Miscellaneous provisions*

*Supplemental*

Schedules

An Act to consolidate the law relating to mentally disordered persons.

[May 9, 1983]

GENERAL NOTE

The origins of modern mental health legislation lie with the Mental Health Act 1959 **1–002** which repealed all existing legislation dealing with mental illness and mental deficiency.

It was based on the Report of the Royal Commission on the Law Relating to Mental Illness (Cmnd. 169) and incorporated the principles that no one should be admitted to hospital if care in the community would be more appropriate, and that where admission to hospital was required compulsion, which was to be a medical instead of a judicial matter, should if possible be avoided. In January 1975, the Labour Government announced its intention to review the 1959 Act in the light of the many changes which had taken place in treatment and care, in the patterns of services for the mentally disordered, and in public attitudes. An interdepartmental committee of civil servants was set up to undertake the review and it considered a number of suggestions for amending the Act including comprehensive reviews which had been carried out by the Royal College of Psychiatrists and by MIND in Vol. 1 of its publication, *A Human Condition*. It also considered that part of the "Report of the Committee on Mentally Abnormal Offenders" (Cmnd. 6244) (The Butler Report) which reviewed Pt V of the 1959 Act which is concerned with offenders. The Committee's suggestions were set out in a consultative document, "A Review of the Mental Health Act 1959" (HMSO, 1976), and comments were invited from interested bodies and individuals. Following the publication of the consultative document, two further major contributions to the debate came in the form of the second volume of MIND's, *A Human Condition*, on offender patients and the British Association of Social Workers' document, "Mental Health Crisis Services—A New Philosophy."

In 1978, the Government published its response to this consultative exercise in a White Paper, "The Review of the Mental Health Act 1959" (Cmnd. 7320). Some of the proposals in the White Paper were set out in a tentative form because they were either not put forward in the consultative document or were not fully developed at that time. Comments on these proposals were invited but before the Government could translate its proposals into an amending Bill a change of government took place. Further consultations then took place and the Conservative Government's conclusions were embodied in a Bill which was published in November 1981, together with an accompanying White Paper, "Reform of Mental Health Legislation" (Cmnd. 8405). The Bill, which was scrutinised by a Special Standing Committee of the House of Commons, was enacted in October 1982 as the Mental Health (Amendment) Act 1982. It made substantial amendments to the 1959 Act as well as introducing new powers relating to the treatment and discharge of mentally disordered patients. In Cmnd. 8405 the Government announced its intention to introduce a consolidation measure soon after the Royal Assent had been given to the 1982 Act and a Consolidation Bill was introduced in the House of Lords on January 20, 1983. This was referred to the Joint Committee on Consolidation Bills which reported on February 9, 1983 (HL 81, HC 193). The Bill was enacted as the Mental Health Act 1983 on May 9, 1983.

**1–003**     In October 1998, the Labour Government appointed a group of experts (the "Expert Committee") to advise on the degree to which the 1983 Act needed updating "to support effective delivery of modern patterns of clinical and social care for people with mental disorder and to ensure that there is a proper balance between safety (both of individuals and the wider community) and the rights of individual patients" (*Review of the Mental Health Act 1983*, 1999, App.A). The Parliamentary Under-Secretary of State made it clear to the Committee at its first meeting that the Government would not accept any recommendation that would enable a patient who was subject to compulsory powers to be non-compliant with medication when "appropriate care in appropriate settings is in place" (*Review of the Mental Health Act 1983*, 1999, App.C, para.11). The Expert Committee published its report in November 1999. Fundamental to the Committee's approach was a desire for new legislation to promote the principle of non-discrimination on the grounds of mental health. This inevitably led the Committee to emphasise the place of patient autonomy. As the Committee stated, "in the context of physical health a patient with capacity is free to choose whether or not to accept treatment: his or her autonomy is respected." However, the Committee adopted a pragmatic approach in its recommendations. Although the Committee accepted that the safety of the public must be allowed to outweigh the individual autonomy of a capacitated mentally disordered person "where the risk is great", it provided no adequate explanation as to why the principle of patient autonomy should not lead to such a person being dealt with through the criminal justice system. The Committee divided on whether a capacitated mentally disordered person should have the same "right" as a capacitated physically disordered person to self-harm or whether such patients should be protected from themselves through mental health legislation. The Committee concluded that the choice between the two approaches was a "moral" one that should be taken by politicians and not the Committee.

Given the nature of the Committee's approach to the principle of patient autonomy, it was hardly surprising that when the Government published its response to the Committee's proposals in the form of a Green Paper (*Reform of the Mental Health Act 1983: Proposals for Consultation*, Cm. 4480) it rejected the introduction of a notion of capacity into the criteria for compulsory intervention. The Government's view was that it "is the *degree of risk* that patients with mental disorders pose, to themselves or others, that is crucial to [the decision on whether a patient should be made subject to a compulsory order]. In the presence of such risk, questions of capacity—while still relevant to the plan of care and treatment—may be largely irrelevant to the question of whether or not a compulsory order should be made" (p.32*)*.

The Green Paper was followed in December 2000 by a White Paper, "Reforming the Mental Health Act" (Cm. 5016). This confirmed the Government's emphasis on risk: "Concerns of risk will always take precedence, but care and treatment provided under formal powers should otherwise reflect the best interests of the patient" (para.2.16). The theme of risk was further emphasised by the Government's concern that existing legislation had "failed to provide adequate public protection from those whose risk to others arises from severe personality disorder" (Foreword, p.1).

A Draft Bill was published in June 2002 (Cm. 5538). The Bill was scrutinised by the Joint Committee of the Houses of Commons and Lords on Human Rights, which reported in November 2002 (HL Paper 181; HC 1294). The Draft Bill did not cover everything that was intended to be in the final version of the Bill to be introduced in Parliament but was accompanied by a consultation document seeking views about a number of policy areas. Following the consultation process, the Government published a new version of the Bill in September 2004 (Cm. 6305). The revised draft Bill was subject to pre-legislative scrutiny from a Joint Committee of the House of Commons and House of Lords. Having considered a great deal of evidence, much of it hostile to the Government's proposals, the Committee reached the view that "the Government should proceed with the Bill, but only with significant amendments, as proposed in our report" (HL Paper 79-1; HC 95-1, p.5). The Government published its response to the Joint Committee's report in July 2005 (Cm. 6624). On March 23, 2006, the Secretary of State for Health announced that the Government had abandoned its plans to proceed with the draft Bill and would instead proceed to "introduce a shorter, streamlined Bill that amends the [1983] Act".

The Mental Health Bill, which was given its first reading in the House of Lords on November 16, 2006, was scrutinised by the Joint Committee on Human Rights which published its report in February 2007 (HL Paper 40; HC 288). A progress report was published by the Joint Committee in June 2007 (HL Paper 112; HC 555). The Parliamentary debates on the Bill, especially those in the House of Lords, largely focused on the Government's response to amendments proposed by Conservatives, Liberal Democrats and crossbenchers who were advocating on behalf of the Mental Health Alliance, an organisation which stated that it "is a coalition of 79 organisations working together to secure humane and effective mental health legislation" (the Alliance lost five of its members in May 2007 over the issue of which professional groups should have the power to renew the detention and supervised community treatment of patients). Opinions regarding both the alleged inadequacy of the current state of the law and the Government's proposals were forcibly expressed. A disinterested bystander would have been surprised to learn that although the 1983 Act was clearly in need of reform, it is generally thought to provide a legislative structure which works reasonably well in practice by striking an appropriate balance between the interests of patients and the public. The main innovation in the Bill was the introduction of supervised community treatment. The Mental Health Act 2007 received the Royal Assent on July 19, 2007.

For fuller accounts of the convoluted process that led to the passing of the 2007 Act, see Paul Bowen, *Blackstone's Guide to the Mental Health Act 2007* (2007), pp.6–18 and Phil Fennell, *Mental Health: the New Law* (2007) pp.2–12. The history of mental health legislation up to and including the 1983 Act is considered by Paul Unsworth in *The Politics of Mental Health Legislation* (1987) and by Phil Fennell in Ch.1 of *Principles of Mental Health Law and Policy* (2010).

*Transfer of functions to Welsh Ministers*

**1–004**    Subject to a number of exceptions that are noted in the annotations to the relevant sections, the functions of the Secretary of State under this Act were transferred to the National Assembly for Wales by the National Assembly for Wales (Transfer of Functions) Order 1999 (SI 1999/672, art.2 Sch.1) (as amended by SI 2000/253, art.4 Sch.3). These functions are now exercised by the Welsh Ministers by virtue of the Government of Wales Act 2006 s.162, Sch.11 para.30.

*Judicial interpretation*

**1–005**    In *R. v Hallstrom Ex p. W (No.2); R. v Gardner Ex p. L* [1986] 2 All E.R. 306 at 314, McCullough J. said:

"There is . . . no canon of construction which presumes that Parliament intended that people should, against their will, be subjected to treatment which others, however professionally competent, perceive, however sincerely and however correctly, to be in their best interests. What there is is a canon of construction that Parliament is presumed not to enact legislation which interferes with the liberty of the subject without making it clear that this was its intention. It goes without saying that, unless clear statutory authority to the contrary exists, no one is to be detained in hospital or to undergo medical treatment or even to submit himself to a medical examination without his consent. That is as true of a mentally disordered person as of anyone else".

This passage was cited with approval by the Court of Appeal in *St George's Healthcare NHS Trust v S* [1998] 3 All E.R. 673 at 692–693.

*Injunctions to support an authority's performance of its duties under this Act*

**1–006**    In *Broadmoor Hospital Authority v R* [2000] 2 All E.R. 727, the issue before the Court of Appeal was whether a statutory body is entitled to be granted an injunction in civil proceedings to support its performance of its statutory duties. It was held that:

(i) if a public body is given a statutory responsibility which it is required to perform in the public interest, then, in the absence of an implication to the contrary in the statute, it has standing to apply to the court for an injunction to prevent interference with its performance of its public responsibilities and the court should grant such an application when it appears to the court to be just and convenient to do so; and

(ii) conduct outside a hospital can affect what happens within the hospital and if this is so jurisdiction exists in the court to provide protection by injunction. However there would need to be a substantial risk to the hospital's powers being prejudiced for the court to exercise its discretion to issue an injunction. Lord Woolf said at 736:

"If for example an individual was causing interference with the discipline of a special hospital by writing letters to the patients then notwithstanding the ability of the authority to censor correspondence, in the appropriate situation an injunction against the individual could be granted to reduce the risk of discipline being undermined and treatment interfered with."

*Court orders granted against mentally incapable persons*

In *Wookey v Wookey* [1991] 3 All E.R. 365, the Court of Appeal held that an injunction **1–007** ought not to be granted against a person who is incapable of understanding what he or she is doing or that it is wrong, because such a person is incapable of complying with it. The appropriate way of dealing with the problem behaviour of a mentally incapable person is the use of the powers under the Mental Health Act. However, an interlocutory injunction might be appropriate if the court considers that the mental condition of the person against whom the injunction is sought should be investigated. In such cases the Official Solicitor should be approached for advice as to whether or not he would wish to act for the person who was liable to have an injunction made against him. *Wookey* was considered in *Cooke v Director of Public Prosecutions* [2008] EWHC 2703 (Admin); [2008] M.H.L.R. 348, where the Divisional Court held that an anti-social behaviour order (ASBO) should not be made under s.1C of the Crime and Disorder Act 1998 against a person who, by reason of mental ill health, would not have the capacity to understand or comply with the order.

The degree of capacity which an individual must have in order to be subject to the contempt jurisdiction was considered by the Court of Appeal in *P v P (Contempt of Court: Mental Capacity)* [1999] 2 F.L.R. 897 where it was held that it was not necessary for the person to comprehend the meaning or significance of courts or of the legal process. What was required was that a potential contemnor should understand that an order has been made forbidding him to do certain things and that if he did them he may very well be punished.

If, in a borderline case, the judge concludes that the person concerned possesses the required level of capacity to enable an order to be made against him, the person's legal advisers should monitor the situation and if the position deteriorates return to the court with an application to discontinue the order (*Harris v Harris (acting by his Guardian ad Litem, the Official Solicitor)*, CA, April 22, 1999).

*Voting*

The law relating to the right of patients in psychiatric hospitals to vote has been changed **1–008** by the Representation of the People Act 2000. New s.3A of the Representation of the People Act 1983 (as inserted by s.2 of the 2000 Act) essentially excludes those patients who have been detained in psychiatric hospitals as a consequence of criminal activity from voting in parliamentary and local government elections. Other patients, both detained and informal, will be entitled to be registered to vote pursuant to either new s.7 of the 1983 Act (as inserted by s.4 of the 2000 Act) or to new s.7A of the 1983 Act (as inserted by s.5 of the 2000 Act). Section 35 of the Electoral Administration Act 2006 amends Sch.4 to the 2000 Act so that mental health patients who are detained under Pt II of this Act are no longer prevented from voting in person if they are granted leave of absence under s.17. The amended Sch.4 also enables such patients to vote by post or by proxy if registered to do so. Voting rights are considered in *Principles of Mental Health Law and Policy* (2010) at paras 25.25 to 25.34 and by Brenda Hale in *Mental Health Law* (2010), pp.312 and 313.

The blanket disenfranchisement of patients who are subject to orders made by a court under Pt III of this Act breaches art.3 of Protocol No.1 to the European Convention on Human Rights: see *Hirst v United Kingdom* (No.2) (2006) 42 E.H.R.R. 41, and the note on Protocol No.1 in Pt 5.

No-one may vote on behalf of a person who lacks the capacity to do so (Mental Capacity Act 2005, s.29).

*Marriage*

The marriage of patients detained under this Act is provided for under s.1 of the Marriage **1–009** Act 1983. Guidance on the relevant procedure is contained in paras 5 to 7 DHSS Circular No. LAC (84)9:

"The Marriage Act also permits the marriages of patients detained in hospital under the Mental Health Act 1983 to take place in hospital. It does, however, exclude from these provisions those detained under the shorter-term provisions, i.e. sections 2, 4, 5, 35, 36, or 136 of the Mental Health Act 1983.

When a detained person wishes to be married in hospital the notice of marriage required by section 27 of the Marriage Act 1949 must be accompanied by a statement made in the prescribed form by the hospital managers not more than 21 days before the date on which notice of the marriage is given:

    i. identifying the establishment where the person is detained; and
   ii. stating that the hospital managers have no objection to that establishment being specified in the notice of marriage as the place where that marriage is to be solemnised.

A copy of this form is at Annex B. Further copies are obtainable from the local Superintendent Registrar.

Hospitals will wish to arrange careful counselling for any detained patient who wishes to marry, and possibly for their prospective spouses, so that both parties may consider the matter fully."

Anyone, including the doctor in charge of the patient's treatment, who does not believe that the patient is capable of giving a valid consent to the marriage, may enter a caveat with the Superintendent Registrar before the ceremony. The caveat can be in the form of a letter which sets out the grounds for contending that the patient lacks the required capacity. A patient is capable of entering into a marriage if he or she is capable of understanding the nature of the contract of marriage (*Sheffield City Council v E* [2004] EWHC 2808 (Fam); [2005] Fam. 326, para.136). The person concerned must be also able to understand the nature of sexual intercourse and its foreseeable consequences, which is not an onerous test (*Local Authority X v MM (by her litigation friend, the Official Solicitor) and KM* [2007] EWHC 2003 (Fam)).

The Superintendent Registrar will give the person who gave notice of marriage an opportunity to answer the objection and to produce evidence in rebuttal of the grounds alleged. If the Superintendent Registrar is in doubt whether or not the caveat ought to obstruct the issue of a certificate for marriage, he may refer the matter to the Registrar General. There is a right of appeal to the Registrar General against a Superintendent Registrar's refusal to issue his certificate for marriage by reason of a caveat.

The impact of the Human Rights Act 1998 on the marital rights of detained patients is considered in the note on art.12 of the European Convention on Human Rights.

*Civil Partnerships*

**1–010**    Under s.13 of the Civil Partnership Act 2004, any person may object to a proposed civil partnership. The notice of objection, which must be sent to the registration authority, has to state the objector's place of residence and the ground of objection. If the registration authority refuses to register the civil partnership because of the objection, either of the proposed civil partners may appeal to the Registrar General (Civil Partnership Act 2004, s.15).

If two people wish to register as civil partners of each other at the place where one of them is detained under this Act (otherwise than by virtue of s.2, 4, 5, 35, 36, or 136), the notice of the proposed civil partnership must be accompanied by a supporting statement made by the hospital managers which (a) identifies the hospital where the person is detained, and (b) states that the managers have no objection to that hospital being specified in a notice of proposed civil partnership as the place at which the person is to register as a civil partner (Civil Partnership Act 2004, s.19). The statement must be in the form prescribed by the Civil Partnership (Registration Provisions) Regulations 2005 (SI 2005/3176) reg.4(2).

Among the grounds set out in s.50 of the Act under which a civil partnership is voidable are:

(i) either partner did not validly consent to its formation as a result of unsoundness of mind, and

(ii) at the time of its formation either of the partners, although capable of giving a valid consent, was suffering (whether continuously or intermittently) from mental disorder of such a kind or to such an extent as to be unfitted for civil partnership.

*Diplomatic immunity*

By virtue of the Diplomatic Privileges Act 1964 s.2, Sch.1 art.29, "the person of a dip- **1–011** lomatic agent shall be inviolate. He shall not be liable to any form of arrest or detention. The receiving state shall treat him with due respect and shall take all appropriate steps to prevent any attack on his person, freedom or dignity." Article 1(e) defines a "diplomatic agent" as "the head of the mission or a member of the diplomatic staff of the mission" and art.37 extends the provisions of art.29 to "the members of the family of a diplomatic agent forming part of his household" who are not nationals of the receiving state. Diplomats and their families should not therefore be made subject to the provisions of this Act unless the inviolability afforded by the 1964 Act has been lifted.

According to Dr David Pariente, the legal department of the Foreign and Commonwealth Office has advised that such inviolability:

"can only be lifted by the State which the diplomat represents; in normal circumstances the State's consent must be obtained from the appropriate Head of Mission, usually an Ambassador, with whose agreement the provisions of the Mental Health Act can then be exercised. Irreversible and hazardous treatments would require his consent. In cases of extreme emergency, where immediate detention of the diplomat is the only way to protect human safety, such action would be justifiable on the basis of the inherent right of self-defence, or the duty to protect human life. In such a case the Foreign and Commonwealth Office should be informed immediately."

Dr Pariente further reports that the Medical Defence Union has "advised that the consent of the Head of Mission should be sought in writing; and that the issue of breach of confidentiality should not present a problem to a doctor who was clearly acting in the best interests of the patient" ("Diplomatic immunity and the Mental Health Act 1983" (1991) *Psychiatric Bulletin* 15 at 207–209).

An approved mental health professional faced with the possibility of making an application in respect of a person who is covered by the 1964 Act should contact the Foreign and Commonwealth Office which could request the relevant Head of Mission to provide the necessary consent.

*International*

International human rights law is built on the fundamental principle that all people **1–012** should be protected equally under the law. Article 1 of the Universal Declaration of Human Rights (UDHR), adopted by the UN in 1948, provides that "all people are free and equal in rights and dignity". The UN subsequently drafted two binding international human rights conventions to promote the implementation of, and expand upon the rights established in the UDHR. They are the International Covenant on Civil and Political Rights (ICCPR) and the International Covenant on Economic, Social, and Cultural Rights (ICESR). Both conventions entered into force in 1976. Together with the UDHR and the UN Charter, they make up what is known as the "International Bill of Human Rights". The UK has ratified both conventions and is under an obligation, under international law, to ensure that its policies do not conflict with the rights established therein. The ICCPR is particularly relevant to patients who are subject to compulsory powers and a number of its articles are mirrored in the European Convention on Human Rights (EHCR). In 1991, the UK ratified the Convention on the Rights of the Child (CRC) which is relevant to patients who are under 18. Although the rights under the ICCPR and the CRC are not directly enforceable in England and Wales, they can be used as an aid to interpreting the rights under the ECHR. In *Smith v Secretary of State for Work and Pensions* [2006] UKHL 35; [2006] All E.R. 907, para.78, Baroness Hale, cited the CRC, and said obiter:

"Even if an international treaty has not been incorporated into domestic law, our domestic legislation has to be construed so far as possible so as to comply with the international obligations which we have undertaken."

**1–013** The ECHR is not the only relevant human rights instrument emanating from Europe. The Charter of Fundamental Rights of the European Union was proclaimed at Nice in December 2000. The rights set out in the Charter, which are partly based on the on the rights recognised by the ECHR, are divided into six sections: dignity, freedoms, equality, solidarity, citizen's rights and justice. Article 3(2) is of particular interest:

"In the fields of medicine and biology, the following must be respected in particular:— the free and informed consent of the person concerned according to the procedure laid down by law."

The status of the Charter was explained by Munby J. in *R. (on the application of A,B,X and Y) v East Sussex County Council (No.2)* [2003] EWHC 167 (Admin); (2003) 6 C.C.L.R. 194 at para.73:

"The Charter is not at present legally binding in our domestic law and is therefore not a source of law in the strict sense. But it can, in my judgment, properly be consulted insofar as it proclaims, reaffirms, or elucidates the content of those human rights that are generally recognised throughout the European family of nations, in particular the nature and scope of those fundamental rights that are guaranteed by the [ECHR]."

In the absence of an international convention that specifically addresses the needs of people with mental disabilities, it is necessary to identify non-enforceable standards that have been established in international agreements. The UN adopted a "Declaration of the Rights of Mentally Retarded Persons" in 1971. Although the Declaration is in many ways dated, it does establish the important principle that the "mentally retarded person has, to the maximum of feasibility, the same rights as other human beings" (para.1). Also of relevance is the United Nations Convention on the Rights of Persons with Disabilities which was adopted by the General Assembly on December 13, 2006. The UK Government ratified the Convention on June 8, 2009. Among those covered by the Convention are people "who have long term . . . mental [or] intellectual . . . impairments which in interaction with various barriers may hinder their full and effective participation in society on an equal basis with others" (art.1). In 1991, the UN adopted twenty-five principles for "The protection of persons with mental illness and the improvement of mental health care". The principles, which established minimum human rights standards of practice in the mental health field, have been directly incorporated into the mental health legislation of a number of counties. Principle 23.1 requires states to "implement [the] Principles through appropriate legislative, judicial, administrative, educational and other measures, which they shall review periodically".

A "White Paper" on the protection of human rights and dignity of people suffering from mental disorder, especially those placed as involuntary patients in a psychiatric establishment was published by the Council of Europe in 2000 for public consultation with a view to drawing up guidelines to be included in a new legal instrument of the Council. This was followed by "Recommendation No. R(2004)10 of the Committee of Ministers to member

States concerning the protection of the human rights and dignity of persons with mental disorder" which was adopted by the Committee of Ministers on September 22, 2004. The United Kingdom Government has indicated that it reserves its right to comply or not to comply with the recommendations contained in this document.

On February 23, 1999, the Committee of Ministers adopted "Principles concerning the legal protection incapable adults", Recommendation R (99) 4. The European Court of Human Rights has said that although "these principles have no force in law for this Court, they may define a common European standard in this area" (*Shtukaturov v Russia* [2008] M.H.L.R. 238, para.95).

The only international instrument against which UK mental health law can be judicially tested is the ECHR. The rights set out in the Convention are derived essentially from the UDHR. The Human Rights Act 1998 incorporates articles from the ECHR into UK law. In *R. (on the application of SC) v Mental Health Review Tribunal* [2005] EWHC 17 (Admin); [2005] M.H.L.R. 31 at para.54, Munby J. said that the exercise by state authorities of compulsory powers in relation to persons suffering from mental disorder calls for increased vigilance in reviewing whether the ECHR has been complied with. A note on the 1998 Act, together with Sch.1 to the Act, which sets out the relevant articles of the Convention, can be found in Pt 5.

International human rights law applicable to those who suffer from a mental disorder has been extensively reviewed by Lawrence O. Gostin and Lance Gable in "The human rights of persons with mental disabilities: a global perspective on the application of human rights principles to mental health" (2004) 10 Maryland Law Review 1, 20–121 and by Kris Gledhill in Ch.27 of *Principles of Mental Health Law and Policy* (2010).

Most of the materials mentioned above can be accessed on the website of the Human Rights Library of the University of Minnesota (*http://www1.umn.edu/humanrts/*).

*Transitional provisions*

Detailed transitional provisions are set out in Sch.5. General continuity between the **1–014** repealed legislation and this Act is provided for in paras 1 and 3 which specify that periods of time which began under the repealed legislation are to be re-calculated under the corresponding provisions of this Act and that anything done under the repealed legislation, e.g. detention for treatment under the 1959 Act, does not cease to have effect because of the repeal of that legislation.

Transitional provisions that relate to the implementation of the Mental Health Act 2007 are contained in Sch.10 to that Act. They stipulate the extent to which an amendment to the 1983 Act by the 2007 Act applies to or has an impact on a patient who is subject to the 1983 Act when the amendments come into force. Further transitional provisions are contained in the Mental Health Act 2007 (Commencement No.6 and After-care under Supervision: Savings, Modifications and Transitional Provisions) Order 2008 (SI 2008/1210); the Mental Health Act 2007 (Commencement No.7 and Transitional Provisions) Order 2008 (SI 2008/1900); and the Mental Health Act (Commencement No.8 and Transitional Provisions) Order 2008 (SI 2008/2561). The Department of Health published "Implementation of the Mental Health Act 2007: Transitional Arrangements" (July 31, 2008) which can be accessed on its website.

*Extent*

This Act applies to Scotland and Northern Ireland only to the extent provided for in **1–015** ss.146 and 147, respectively. The whole of this Act was extended to the Isles of Scilly on March 12, 1985, by the Isles of Scilly (Mental Health) Order 1985 (SI 1985/149) with the modification that the expression "local social services authority" in the Act shall, in relation to the Isles, mean the Council of the Isles constituted under the Isles of Scilly Order 1978 (SI 1978/1844).

*Abbreviations*

**1–016**    In the annotations, the following abbreviations are used:

Aarvold Committee: Report on the Review of Procedures for the Discharge and Supervision of Psychiatric Patients subject to Special Restrictions (Cmnd. 5191).

AC: Approved Clinician

AMHP: Approved Mental Health Professional

Butler Committee: Report of the Committee on Mentally Abnormal Offenders (Cmnd. 6244).

Code of Practice: The *Code of Practice* published under s.118(4) of this Act.

Commission: the Care Quality Commission

CTO: Community treatment order

ECHR: European Convention on Human Rights

ECtHR: European Court of Human Rights

ECT: electro-convulsive therapy

Explanatory Notes: Explanatory Notes on the Mental Health Act 2007 prepared by the Department of Health and the Ministry of Justice, in consultation with the Welsh Assembly Government

Joint Committee: House of Lords and House of Commons Joint Committee on Human Rights

LSSA: Local social services authority

Mental Health Bill: the Mental Health Bill introduced to Parliament on November 16th, 2006

MCA: Mental Capacity Act 2005

MHAC: Mental Health Act Commission

MHRT: Mental Health Review Tribunal

NR: Nearest relative

Public Bill Committee: Public Bill Committee—Mental Health Bill (Lords)

Memorandum: Mental Health Act 1983: Memorandum on Pts I to VI, VIII and X. Department of Health and Welsh Office, 1998.

The Reed Committee: Review of Health and Social Services for Mentally Disordered Offenders and others requiring similar services, Chairman: Dr John Reed, HMSO, 1992.

Reference Guide: Reference Guide to the Mental Health Act 1983 (2008)

RC: Responsible clinician

RMO: Responsible medical officer

Royal Commission: Report of the Royal Commission on the Law Relating to Mental Illness and Mental Deficiency 1954–1957, Chairman—Lord Percy (Cmnd. 169).

Special Standing Committee: The special Standing Committee which considered the Mental Health (Amendment) Bill.

SCT: Supervised Community Treatment

SOAD: Second opinion appointed doctor

the Tribunal Rules: the Tribunal Procedure (First-tier Tribunal) (Health, Education and Social Care Chamber) Rules 2008 (SI 2008/2699)

the 2007 Act: the Mental Health Act 2007

tribunal: the First-tier Tribunal (Mental Health) or the Mental Health Review Tribunal for Wales

the English Regulations: Mental Health (Hospital, Guardianship and Treatment) (England) Regulations 2008 (SI 2008/1184)

the Welsh Regulations: the Mental Health (Hospital, Guardianship, Community Treatment and Consent to Treatment) (Wales) Regulations 2008 (SI 2008/2439) (W.212).

the Welsh Rules: the Mental Health Review Tribunal for Wales Rules 2008 (SI 2008/2705) (L.17).

## PART I

## APPLICATION OF ACT

**Application of Act: "mental disorder"**
  **1.**—(1) The provisions of this Act shall have effect with respect to the recep- **1–017**
tion, care and treatment of mentally disordered patients, the management of
their property and other related matters.
  (2) In this Act—
      ["mental disorder" means any disorder or disability of the mind;
      and
      "mentally disordered" shall be construed accordingly;] [. . .]
      and other expressions shall have the meanings assigned to them in section
      145 below.
  [(2A) But a person with learning disability shall not be considered by reason of
that disability to be—
  (a) suffering from mental disorder for the purposes of the provisions mentioned
      in subsection (2B) below; or
  (b) requiring treatment in hospital for mental disorder for the purposes of sec-
      tions 17E and 50 to 53 below,
  unless that disability is associated with abnormally aggressive or seriously irresponsible conduct on his part.
  (2B) The provisions are—
  (a) sections 3, 7, 17A, 20 and 20A below;
  (b) sections 35 to 38, 45A, 47, 48 and 51 below; and
  (c) section 72(1)(b) and (c) and (4) below.]
  [(3) Dependence on alcohol or drugs is not considered to be a disorder or disability of the mind for the purposes of subsection (2) above.]
  [(4) In subsection (2A) above, "learning disability" means a state of arrested or
incomplete development of the mind which includes significant impairment of
intelligence and social functioning.]

AMENDMENTS
  The amendments to this section were made by the Mental Health Act 2007, ss.1, 55,
Sch.11, Pt 1.

DEFINITION
  patient: s.145(1).                                                    **1–018**

GENERAL NOTE
  Apart from indicating the extent of this Act, this section defines the term "mental dis- **1–019**
order", excludes dependence on alcohol or drugs from the definition, and makes special
provision for patients who have a learning disability.

*Code of Practice*
  Guidance on the definition and identification of mental disorder for the purposes of this **1–020**
Act is contained in Ch.3. Issues of particular relevance to patients with learning disabilities
and autistic spectrum disorders are considered in Ch.34. Chapter 35 considers issues relating to patients with personality disorders.

*Human Rights Act 1998*

**1–021**    See the cases cited in Pt 5 under "Persons of unsound mind" in art.5(1)

*Subsection (1)*

**1–022**    In *R. v Kirklees MBC* [1992] 2 F.L.R. 117 at 120, Kennedy J., speaking obiter, said that this provision "seems to suggest that the provisions of [this] Act never do apply if the person admitted to hospital for assessment turns out not to be a mentally disordered person". The *Kirklees* case is considered in the General Note to s.131.

MANAGEMENT OF THEIR PROPERTY.    Given the repeal of Pt VII of this Act by the Mental Capacity Act 2005, this phrase is otiose.

*Subsection (2)*

**1–023**    MENTAL DISORDER.    The Mental Health Act 2007 abolished the four categories of mental disorder previously used in the Act, namely mental illness, mental impairment, psychopathic disorder and severe mental impairment. The Minister of State explained the rationale for this change:

> "At present, a patient being treated under the Act often needs to be assigned to one of four separate categories of mental disorder. We wish to replace these with a simpler single definition of mental disorder under which a patient's needs and risks, not the label that happens to be applied to a person's mental disorder, determine when action is taken. This simple single definition will also make the Act easier for clinicians to use and for other to understand. This will not alter the way in which the Act deals with leaning disability" (*Hansard,* HL Vol.687, col.657).

The definition of mental disorder, as substituted by the 2007 Act, is consistent with the interpretation that the European Court of Human Rights has given to the phrase "persons of unsound mind" in art.5(1)(e) of the European Convention on Human Rights. In *Winterwerp v Netherlands* (1979) E.H.R.R. 387 para.37, the court held that this phrase is:

> "not one that can be given a definitive interpretation . . . it is a term whose meaning is constantly evolving as research in psychiatry progresses, an increasing flexibility in treatment is developing and society's attitude to mental illness changes, in particular so that a greater understanding of the problems of mental patients is becoming widespread. In any event, Art.5(1)(e) obviously cannot be taken as permitting the detention of a person simply because his views or behaviour deviate from the norms prevailing in a particular society."

The definition, which is used throughout the Act, provides clinicians with a very wide discretion in identifying which conditions come within its scope. This is, perhaps, worrying given the propensity of some in the psychiatric profession to medicalise normality; see, for example, A. Horwitz and J. Wakefield, *The Loss of Sadness: How Psychiatry Transformed Normal Sorrow into Depressive Disorder* (2007) and the remarks of Longmore L.J. in *R v Deighton*, below. The definition includes some disorders of "sexual preference" such as "paraphilias like fetishism or paedophilia" (Explanatory Notes, para.24). Although the two internationally recognised diagnostic manuals which are widely used by British psychiatrists, the ICD-10 (World Health Organisation) and the DSM-IV (American Psychiatric Association), provide classifications of mental disorder, it "cannot be said that something that is not in any classification is not a mental disorder (Public Bill Committee, col.16, per the Minister of State). The ICD-10 cautions against "social deviance or conflict alone" being categorised as being a mental disorder (p.5), while the DSM-IV states that neither:

"deviant behaviour (e.g. political, religious or sexual) nor conflicts that are primarily between the individual and society are mental disorders unless the deviance or conflict is a symptom of a dysfunction in the individual" (p.xxii).

The Explanatory Notes state at para.17:

"Examples of clinically recognised mental disorders include mental illnesses such as schizophrenia, bipolar disorder, anxiety or depression, as well as personality disorders, autistic spectrum disorders and learning disabilities. Disorders or disabilities of the brain are not regarded as mental disorders unless (and only to the extent that) they give rise to a disability or disorder of the mind as well."

Whether a condition is a disorder or disability of the mind, as opposed to a disability or disorder of the brain is, in the absence of any legislative attempt to distinguish between them, a matter for clinical judgment. A disorder of the brain, such as a brain injury or a brain tumour, which either causes a mental disorder or manifests itself by causing a malfunctioning of the mind, will come within the definition of mental disorder.

Patients who are being treated in a general hospital can suffer from a mental disorder which require their detention under the Act, but which do not come within the clinical experience of most psychiatrists. Dr Eleanor Feldman describes how she:

"encountered a situation where a patient had an acute and severe but reversible brain disorder, in this case limbic encephalitis, and its treatment involved steroids and other very toxic drugs used in immunotherapy. The patient was grossly disorientated and lacked mental capacity to make a decision about his treatment or the need to remain in hospital. Moreover, his behaviour was very disturbed requiring strong and prolonged measures over a matter of up to two weeks to restrain and sedate him, to administer treatment and keep him on the neurology unit." ("The use of the Mental Health Act and common law in non-consenting patients in the general hospital" (2006) Psychiatry 5(3): 107–9).

It is clear that this patient was suffering from a mental disorder and was being deprived of his liberty for the purposes of art.5 of the ECHR.

In *St George's Healthcare NHS Trust v S* [1998] 3 All E.R. 673, 696, Judge L.J. said that the court did not doubt "that reactive depression (not merely a transient sense of being 'a little down' or 'fed up with everything') is capable of amounting to a mental disorder." His Lordship also said, at 957, that a person cannot be characterised as being mentally disordered "merely because her thinking process is unusual, even apparently bizarre and irrational, and contrary to the views of the overwhelming majority of the community at large".

In the context of a criminal trial where the appellant claimed that he failed to appreciate what he was doing was wrong because he was suffering from "avoidant personality disorder", the Court of Appeal said that the courts should "resist the temptation to medicalise normality" (*R. v Deighton* [2005] EWCA Crim 3131 para.14 per Longmore L.J.).

The search for a definition of mental disorder is constrained by the factors identified by Baroness Hale in *R. (on the application of B) v Ashworth Hospital Authority* [2005] UKHL 20; [2005] 2 All E.R. 289 at para.31:

"[P]sychiatry is not an exact science. Diagnosis is not easy or clear cut. As this and many other cases show, a number of different diagnoses may be reached by the same or different clinicians over the years. As this case also shows, co-morbidity is very common. . . . It is not easy to disentangle which features of the patient's presentation stem from a disease of the mind and which stem from his underlying personality traits."

In the context of the criminal law, the difficulties of drawing a distinction between mental distress and symptoms amounting to a recognisable psychiatric illness were identified by Judge P. in *R v D* [2006] EWCA Crim 1139 at para.30:

> "As the Law Commission reports [in *Liability for Psychiatric Illness,* No.249 (1998) HC 525], the distinction 'is not clear', quoting one medical consultee who suggested that the 'overlap between mental health and illness is so large a grey area that it is not suitable for the legal purpose to which the diagnosis is being put'. The classification in DSM-IV and ICD-10 were not themselves always sufficient 'to distinguish those with the greatest impairment of functioning', and several of the consultees commented that it would be unjust to relay on the criteria in these classifications to distinguish psychiatric illness from 'mere mental distress'. It was suggested that some did not 'reflect the complexities of the psychological impact of trauma', and current categorisation might exclude some diagnoses which were generally acceptable. Observations like these confirm that current understanding of the workings of the mind is less than complete".

Also of relevance in this context are Hobhouse L.J's observations in *R. v Chan-Fook* [1994] 2 All E.R. 552 at 559 on the decision of the Court of Appeal in *Attia v British Gas* [1988] Q.B. 304 regarding the position at civil law:

> "[T]he Court of Appeal discussed whether the borderline should be drawn between on the one hand the emotions and distress and grief, and on the other hand some actual psychiatric illness such as anxiety neurosis or a reactive depression. The authorities recognise that there is a line to be drawn and whether any given case falls on one side or the other is a matter for expert evidence."

A similar approach was taken by the House of Lords in *R. v Ireland; R. v Burstow* [1997] 4 All E.R. 225 at 231, a case under the Offences against the Person Act 1861, where Lord Steyn said that neuroses "must be distinguished from simple states of fear, or problems in coping with everyday life. Where the line is to be drawn must be a matter of psychiatric judgment."

In earlier times, Bowen L.J. said that "the state of a man's mind is as much a fact as the state of his digestion" (*Edgington v Fitzmaurice* (1885) 29 Ch.D 459 at 483).

MIND. In the context of the *McNaghten* rules, which set out the test for insanity, Devlin J. said that the term "mind" should be "used in the ordinary sense of the mental faculties of reason, memory and understanding" (*R. v Kemp* [1957] 1 Q.B. 399 at 407). This statement was approved by Lord Diplock in *R. v Sullivan* [1983] 2 All E.R. 673 HL at 677. Lord Diplock's judgment in *Sullivan* suggests that if a disorder severely impairs these faculties it can be categorised as a disorder mind, irrespective of the aetiology of the disorder.

*Subsections (2A), (2B)*

**1–024**   These subsections, together with subs.(4), preserve the way the Act works with regard to people with a learning disability. It provides that for certain purposes of the Act a person may not be considered to be suffering from a mental disorder simply as a result of having a learning disability: the disability must be "associated with abnormally aggressive or seriously irresponsible conduct" on the part of the person concerned. One of the consequences this approach is that it will continue to be impossible to make a guardianship application in respect of a person with a learning disability who is passively enduring the seriously irresponsible conduct of others. An application to the Court of Protection under s.16 of the Mental Capacity Act 2005 for a personal welfare decision could be made if the person was mentally incapacitated.

The preservation of the status quo, which has little to commend it, serves as a monument to effectiveness of the learning disability lobby. The Minister of State responded to an expression of puzzlement about the rationale for the approach adopted by explaining that "there has been a historic attachment to saying that learning disability should be included in the Bill in this way, and I am afraid that there is no getting away from that" (Public Bill Committee, col.43).

LEARNING DISABILITY. See subs.(4).

IS ASSOCIATED WITH. This phrase denotes an association which may not be the result of causation (*P v Mental Health Review Tribunal and Rampton Hospital* [2001] EWHC Admin 876; [2002] M.H.L.R. 250 para.26). The association must be with the learning disability and not with an unrelated physical disorder. Lord Adebowale gave the following example of a case where an association with learning disability was absent:

"Mr S, who has a severe learning difficulty, autism and communication difficulties, lives in a residential setting. He was detained under the 1983 Act because he was becoming increasingly agitated and exhibited aggressive behaviour, banging his head against a wall. It was later discovered—this is shocking but true—that Mr S had a small twig in his ear, which was causing him distress, as it would most people, and which he expressed in his agitated behaviour. This scenario shows how the distress of a person with a learning disability can be automatically attributed to a mental disorder without paying sufficient attention to physical factors. This is about not just lazy diagnosis but making false assumptions" (*Hansard,* HL Vol.668, col.66).

ABNORMALLY AGGRESSIVE OR SERIOUSLY IRRESPONSIBLE CONDUCT. These terms are con-    **1–025** sidered in the *Code of Practice* at paras 34.6 to 34.10. The origin of this phrase, which is taken from the definition of psychopathy in the Mental Health Act 1959, was recounted by Lord Rix:

"These words are very familiar to me because they arrived in the 1983 Act after a long three-way process of negotiation on the telephone between the then Minister, the noble Lord Elton, myself, then in the capacity as secretary general of Mencap, and a copy of *Roget's Thesaurus*. It was the best compromise we could then reach between the Government's position that people with a learning disability should come under the scope of the Act, and my position that people with a learning disability are not ill and should not be treated as if they were" (*Hansard,* HL Vol.687, col.662).

What is "abnormally aggressive" or "irresponsible conduct" must, to a certain extent, depend upon the cultural and social context within which the behaviour occurs. In *R. v Trent Mental Health Review Tribunal Ex p. Ryan* [1992] C.O.D. 157, Nolan L.J. said:

"No doubt whether the conduct is the result of the disorder . . . is a medical question. Whether it amounts to seriously irresponsible or abnormally aggressive behaviour seems to me . . . to raise questions other than of a purely clinical nature".

In *Re F (Mental Health Act: Guardianship)* [2000] 1 F.L.R. 192, the Court of Appeal adopted a restrictive construction of the phrase "seriously irresponsible conduct" by holding that a 17-year-old patient's natural desires to return home, albeit to an inadequate home where she had been exposed to chronic neglect and possible sexual exploitation, could not be categorised as irresponsible conduct. Thorpe L.J. said at 198:

"The urge to return [home] is almost universal . . . The deficiencies of the home are more apparent to other adults than to the young who have known no other. Furthermore, any measure of irresponsibility must depend on an evaluation of the consequences of return . . . Clearly each case must depend on its particular facts and we would not wish to be taken as offering any general guideline."

Although his Lordship emphasised that the court had reached its conclusions "on the special facts of a difficult and unusual case", the court's finding is significant because the urge to return home is not the only "almost universal" urge that might affect a patient. The desire to be member of a family group would also fall into this category. When determining whether a person's conduct falls into the category of "seriously irresponsible conduct", the clinician should pay special attention to the consequences of the conduct (or potential conduct) for the person and/or others. The clinician should refrain from categorising conduct as being seriously irresponsible in the absence of a clear opinion based on reliable evidence that the conduct either would or is resulting in a significant risk to the person's health or safety or to the health or safety of others.

In *Newham LBC v Mr BS and S (an adult represented by her Litigation Friend, the Official Solicitor)* [2003] EWHC 1909 (Fam), Wall J. applied *Re F* and held, rather surprisingly, that a person's total lack of road sense and a tendency to rush into the road without looking did not amount to "seriously irresponsible conduct". However it is not arguable that this decision sets down a general proposition of law that a tendency to rush into the road could never amount to seriously irresponsible conduct (*GC v Managers of the Kingswood Centre of Central and North West London NHS Foundation Trust* (CO/7784/2008)). This case concerned a patient with obsessive compulsive disorder which manifested itself as a compulsion to pick up litter, even if that litter was in the road. The patient had been knocked down by vehicles but considered himself invincible. The hospital managers at a hearing concluded that such conduct could be categorised as being "seriously irresponsible"; King J. found that they were entitled to do so. I am grateful to Alexander Ruck Keene, barrister, for drawing my attention to this case.

There is no requirement for the person to be currently engaging in abnormally aggressive or seriously irresponsible conduct. It is enough that the learning disability caused such conduct in the past and that there is a real risk that, if treatment in hospital is discontinued, it will do so in the future: see *Lewis v Gibson* [2005] EWCA Civ 587; [2005] M.H.L.R. 309, where Thorpe L.J. said at para.31:

> "To make a balanced assessment of the patient's present state some regard must be had to the past history and the future propensity. A conclusion based only on the recent past, which might represent a transient phase of quiescence, would be superficial."

*Subsection (3)*

**1–026**   This provision prevents a dependence on alcohol or drugs from being treated as a mental disorder for the purposes of the Act. In some respects this is an odd exclusion because alcohol and drug dependency are treatable mental disorders, and such dependency may be a ground for detention under art.5(1)(e) of the ECHR. The rationale for the original version of this exclusion as contained in the Mental Health (Amendment) Act 1982 was explained by the Government in Cmnd 7320 at para.1.29:

> "Government advisory bodies have . . . pointed out that that it is incompatible with current thinking on the nature of drug dependence and drinking problems to regard them as mental disorders. These conditions are increasingly seen as social and behavioural problems, manifested in varying degrees of habit and dependency. However it is recognised that alcohol or drug dependency can be associated with certain forms of mental disorder."

The exclusion does not prevent a person being categorised as mentally disordered if, as well as being dependent on alcohol or drugs, he or she is suffering from:

(i)  an unrelated mental disorder, or

(ii) a mental disorder which arises from, or is suspected to arise from, alcohol or drug dependence or from the withdrawal of alcohol or drugs.

Therefore a person who is suffering from a drug or alcohol induced psychosis or from delirium associated with alcohol withdrawal would not be excluded by this provision. It is also the case that a person's alcohol or drug dependency could be treated under the authority of s.63 if the dependency is categorised as being a consequence of the patient's diagnosed mental disorder (*B v Croydon Health Authority* [1995] 1 All E.R. 683 CA).

A person who is not dependent on alcohol or drugs but who is acutely intoxicated following the administration of alcohol or drugs would not be excluded from the definition of mental disorder by this provision.

In his "Review of Homicides by Patients with Severe Mental Illness" (March 2006), Professor Tony Maden states at p.63:

"Substance misuse in the context of serious mental illness and violence may greatly increase risk, yet there is little sign within [the cases studied] of it being considered as an indication for use of compulsory powers. The 1983 Act does not allow detention for substance use alone but it is an important indicator of the nature and extent of mental illness, and the associated risk to others, so it should be included in any assessment for possible detention."

DRUGS. This term, which is not defined, includes medicines and illicit drugs.

*Subsection (4)*

This provision defines "learning disability" for the purposes of subs.(2A). Guidance on **1–027** the definition is given in the *Code of Practice* at paras 34.4 and 34.5.

ARRESTED OR INCOMPLETE DEVELOPMENT OF MIND. This phrase excludes persons whose learning disability derives from accident, injury or illness occurring after the mind has fully developed.

INCLUDES. What follows is not an exclusive list of attributes associated with the disability.

SIGNIFICANT IMPAIRMENT. Whether the impairment is considered to be "significant" is a matter for clinical judgment. ICD-10 states that a patient with mild mental retardation has an IQ score within an approximate range of 50 to 69 (in adults, mental age from 9 to under 12 years). The *Code of Practice*, at para.34.4, cautions against the "application of an arbitrary cut-off point such as an IQ of 70". In *Meggary v Chief Adjudications Officer, The Times,* November 11, 1999, the Court of Appeal held that a high IQ was not conclusive in determining the existence of a "severe impairment of intelligence and social functioning" for the purposes of determining an autistic child's entitlement to disability living allowance. Simon Brown L.J. said:

"In most cases, no doubt, the measurement of IQ will be the best available method of measuring intelligence. But among the dictionary definitions of intelligence one finds the reference not merely to the functions of understanding and intellect but also to the qualities of insight and sagacity. It seems to me that in the case if an autistic child those qualities may well be lacking and to the extent that they are there will be a functional impairment which overlaps both limbs of the regulation, i.e. both intelligence and social functioning".

The significance of the impairment must be measured against the standard of normal persons, not other people with learning disabilities (*R. v Hall (John Hamilton)* (1998) 86 Cr. App. R. 159).

## PART II

## COMPULSORY ADMISSION TO HOSPITAL AND GUARDIANSHIP

GENERAL NOTE

**1–028**   The principles that underpin this Part were identified by Sir Thomas Bingham M.R. in the following extract from his judgment in *Re S-C (Mental Patient: Habeas Corpus)* [1996] 1 All E.R. 532 CA at 534, 535:

> "[N]o adult citizen of the United Kingdom is liable to be confined in any institution against his will, save by the authority of law. That is a fundamental constitutional principle, traceable back to Ch.29 of Magna Carta 1297 (25 Edw. 1 c. 1), and before that to Ch.39 of Magna Carta (1215). There are, of course, situations in which the law sanctions detention. The most obvious is in the case of those suspected or convicted of crime. Powers then exist to arrest and detain. But the conditions in which those powers may be exercised are very closely prescribed by statute and the common law. . . . [Mental patients] present a special problem since they may be liable, as a result of mental illness, to cause injury either to themselves or to others. But the very illness which is the source of the danger may deprive the sufferer of the insight necessary to ensure access to proper medical care, whether the proper medical care consists of assessment or treatment, and, if treatment, whether in-patient or out-patient treatment.
>
> Powers therefore exist to ensure that those who suffer from mental illness may, in appropriate circumstances, be involuntarily admitted to mental hospitals and detained. But, and it is a very important but, the circumstances in which the mentally ill may be detained are very carefully prescribed by statute. Action may only be taken if there is clear evidence that the medical condition of a patient justifies such action, and there are detailed rules prescribing the classes of person who may apply to a hospital to admit and detain a mentally disordered person. The legislation recognises that action may be necessary at short notice and also recognises that it will be impracticable for a hospital to investigate the background facts to ensure that all the requirements of the Act are satisfied if they appear to be so. Thus we find in the statute a panoply of powers combined with detailed safeguards for the protection of the patient."

In *St George's Healthcare NHS Trust v S* [1998] 3 All E.R. 673, the Court of Appeal held that this Act cannot be deployed to achieve the detention of an individual against her will merely because her thinking process is unusual, even apparently bizarre and irrational, and contrary to the views of the overwhelming majority of the community at large. It could only be used to justify the detention of a mentally disordered person who fell within the prescribed conditions.

A patient who is detained under this Act retains all civil rights which are not taken away expressly or by necessary implication by his detention (*Raymond v Honey* [1982] 1 All E.R. 756 HL). The extent to which this Act provides implied authority for staff to override the civil rights of patients is outlined in the note on "act purporting to be done in pursuance of this Act" in s.139(1).

A child can be detained under this Part. Section 25 of the Children Act 1989 which sets restrictions on the use of secure accommodation for children, does not apply to a child who is detained under any provision of this Act (Children (Secure Accommodation) Regulations 1991 (SI 1991/1505) reg.5).

In the "Report by the Committee for Privileges on Parliamentary Privilege and the Mental Health Act" June 18, 1984, HL (254), the Committee for Privileges was of the view that the provisions of this Act override any previously existing privilege of Parliament or peerage so far as it conflicts with the liability of mentally disordered peers to compulsory detention in hospital under ss.2 to 6. The procedure for vacating the seat of a Member of the House of Commons who has been detained under this Act is set out in s.141.

Powers, other than those contained in this Act, that are available to individuals to control and detain patients are set out in Appendix A.

*The "sectioning" of compliant mentally incapable patients*

There is a practice of making applications to detain patients who require medical treat- **1–029** ment for their mental disorder despite the fact that such patients are both mentally incapable and compliant, in that they are not exhibiting dissent to being in hospital or to being treated at the time when the application is made. In particular, it is felt that a compliant mentally ill patient who needs to be given ECT as a treatment for depression must be detained under this Act before the treatment can be given, even though the effect of the depression has been to render the patient mentally incapable. As the provision of medical treatment to a mentally incapable patient who is not being deprived of his or her liberty is authorised under ss.5 and 6 of the Mental Capacity Act 2005 if the treatment is considered to be in the patient's best interests, the "sectioning" of the patient solely for the purpose of providing "authority" for medical treatment for his mental disorder to be given is both unnecessary and unlawful as the statutory criteria for detention cannot be satisfied. An assessment for the sectioning of a mentally incapacitated person who is compliant to being in hospital should be made if the patient is being deprived of his or her liberty as a failure to detain the patient under this Act would violate the patient's right under art.5 of the European Convention on Human Rights (*HL v United Kingdom* (2005) 40 E.H.R.R. 32; [2004] M.H.L.R. 236). If the patient does not satisfy the criteria for detention, an application should be made for the authorisation of the deprivation under Sch.A1 of the Mental Capacity Act 2005. The nature of a "deprivation of liberty" is considered in Part 6.

## Procedure for Hospital Admission

**Admission for assessment**

**2.**—(1) A patient may be admitted to a hospital and detained there for the period **1–030** allowed by subsection (4) below in pursuance of an application (in this Act referred to as "an application for admission for assessment") made in accordance with subsections (2) and (3) below.

(2) An application for admission for assessment may be made in respect of a patient on the grounds that—

(a) he is suffering from mental disorder of a nature or degree which warrants the detention of the patient in a hospital for assessment (or for assessment followed by medical treatment) for at least a limited period; and

(b) he ought to be so detained in the interests of his own health or safety or with a view to the protection of other persons.

(3) An application for admission for assessment shall be founded on the written recommendations in the prescribed form of two registered medical practitioners, including in each case a statement that in the opinion of the practitioner the conditions set out in subsection (2) above are complied with.

(4) Subject to the provisions of section 29(4) below, a patient admitted to hospital in pursuance of an application for admission for assessment may be detained for a period not exceeding 28 days beginning with the day on which he is admitted, but shall not be detained after the expiration of that period unless before it has expired he has become liable to be detained by virtue of a subsequent application, order or direction under the following provisions of this Act.

DEFINITIONS

**1–031**     patient: s.145(1).
hospital: ss.34(2), 145(1).
mental disorder: ss.1, 145(1).
medical treatment: s.145(1), (4).

GENERAL NOTE

**1–032**     This section authorises the compulsory admission of a patient to hospital for assessment (or for assessment followed by medical treatment), and for detention for this purpose for up to 28 days. If, after the 28 days have elapsed, the patient is to remain in hospital, he or she must do so either as an informal patient or be detained for treatment under s.3, if the conditions of that section are satisfied. Patients detained under this section are subject to the consent to treatment provisions contained in Pt IV of this Act (s.56(3)). Admission under this section is unlawful if the patient does not require a period of in-patient care in the hospital named in the application: see *R. v Hallstrom Ex p. W*; *R. v Gardner Ex p. L*, noted in the General Note to s.3.

In *R. v Wilson Ex p. Williamson* [1996] C.O.D. 42, Tucker J. held that an application made under this section:

> "is only intended to be of short duration for a limited purpose—assessment of the patient's condition with a view to ascertaining whether it is a case which would respond to treatment, and whether an [application] under s.3 would be appropriate. It was intended that the assessment should take place within 28 days, without any extension of time unless it was necessary for the purpose of replacing the nearest relative. Although there is nothing to suggest that s.2 is a once and for all procedure, there is nothing in the Act which justifies successive or back to back, applications under this section. . . . The powers under s.2 can only be used for the limited purpose for which they were intended, and cannot be utilised for the purpose of further detaining a patient for the purposes of assessment beyond the 28-day period, or used as a stop-gap procedure."

The *Williamson* case provides authority for the proposition that an application under s.2 cannot be used for an improper purpose. Tucker J. identified two examples of such a purpose: (1) using a second application under s.2 in order to extend the 28-day assessment period (subs.(4) prevents a second application being made under this section during the currency of an existing section); and (2) using an application under s.2 as a "stop-gap" procedure in circumstances where it is not possible to proceed with a s.3 application because of a nearest relative objection (see s.11(4)). The fact that a second use of s.2 was involved in the *Williamson* case is not relevant to (2) as the rationale for finding the use of the section to be improper is that those who had made the decision to use s.3 must have reached the conclusion that the patient does not require detention for assessment. In *C v South London and Maudsley Hospital National Health Service Trust and London Borough of Lambeth* [2001] M.H.L.R. 269, McCombe J., on refusing an application for leave under s.139, said that an application under this section could be made "where at least one of the doctors may have thought informally that s.3 admission might in the long run be desirable". In this case a preliminary decision was made to admit the patient under s.3, but this was aborted when the approved social worker (now the approved mental health professional (AMHP)) reported that the patient's nearest relative would object to the application. An application under this section was made three days later by a different approved social worker, who "may well have known" that an application under s.3 would not be possible. This application was supported by a medical recommendation from one of the doctors who had made the original decision to proceed under s.3. It is clear from the judgment in this case that the McCombe J. considered that the fact that medical recommendations had not been made to support a possible application under s.3 was of particular significance: also see the note on "Section 2 or section 3?", below.

An application for a second s.2 can be made if a significant change in the patient's situation can be said to justify the need for a reassessment. For example, a patient is detained under s.2 in city A, is discharged, and then moves to city B where his mental health deteriorates to the extent that he is subject to a second application under s.2. In these circumstances the second s.2 could be in close proximity to the first s.2.

It is not possible to use the holding powers provided for in s.5 while the patient is liable to be detained (s.5(1)(6)). Neither is it possible to use the holding powers to extend the 28-day period once the s.2 has expired (*Williamson*, above).

An application under this section should be the usual method of detaining a patient who requires to be assessed. An emergency application under s.4 should only be used where the need for the patient's admission is so urgent that it is not practicable to obtain the second medical recommendation that is required for an admission under this section.

An order for the patient's discharge from this section can be made at any time prior to the expiration of the 28-day period by his responsible clinician, the hospital managers or, subject to s.25, his nearest relative (s.23(2)(a)). A discharge cannot be effected by implication, e.g. by an assessment for detention under s.3 concluding that the patient should not be detained under that section. An AMHP may not lawfully apply for the admission of a patient whose discharge has been ordered by the decision of a tribunal of which the AMHP is aware unless that professional has formed a reasonable and bona fide opinion that he or she has information not known to the tribunal which puts a significantly different complexion on the case as compared with that which was before the tribunal: see *R. v East London and City Mental Health NHS Trust Ex p. Brandenburg* [2003] UKHL 58; [2004] 1 All E.R. 400, which is considered in the General Note to s.3 under the heading "The detention of a patient subsequent to a discharge by the First-tier Tribunal (Mental Health) or the Mental Health Review Tribunal for Wales".

There is nothing to prevent a patient who has been detained under this section from being arrested in respect of a criminal offence.

*Human Rights Act 1998*

In *R. (on the application of H) v Secretary of State for Health* [2005] UKHL 60; [2005] 4 **1–033**
All E.R. 1311, it was contended on behalf of the patient that this Act fails to comply with art.5(4) of the European Convention on Human Rights (which is designed to procure the speedy release of someone who should not in fact have been detained in the first place or should not be detained any longer), in that it does not provide a practical and effective right of access to a tribunal for a patient detained under s.2 who lacks capacity to apply to a tribunal by herself. The only way to do this, it was argued, is automatically to refer every such detention to a tribunal. The House of Lords declined to hold that s.2 is incompatible with art.5(4) on the ground that art.5(4) does not require that every case be considered by a court. It requires that the person detained should have the right to "take proceedings" which stops short of requiring judicial authorisation in every case. However, their Lordships said that every sensible effort should be made by the hospital managers to enable the patient to exercise that right if there is reason to think that she would wish to do so.

Also see the note under this heading in the General Note to s.3.

*Section 2 or section 3?*

The advice contained in the 1999 edition of the *Code of Practice* has been interpreted as **1–034**
requiring s.3 to be used as the initial detaining section for patients who are "well known" to the mental health service. This interpretation was reinforced by concern expressed by the Mental Health Commission over the "misuse" of s.2 where s.3 would have been more appropriate to admit such patients (see, for example, para.3.1 of the MHAC's Sixth Biennial Report, 1993–1995) and the widely held, but totally erroneous view expressed by some practitioners that treatment under Pt IV cannot be given to patients detained under s.2. The MHAC subsequently modified its view on this issue and became supportive of the approach adopted here, see para.4.39 of the MHAC's *Twelfth Biennial Report*, 2005–2007.

This Part provides two routes which can be used to detain and treat patients: s.2 which provides for the assessment and treatment of patients for a non-renewable period of up to 28 days, and s.3 which provides for the patient's detention and treatment for a potentially unlimited period. A patient whose current mental health and circumstances require him to be subject to the very significant procedure of compulsory detention surely needs to be assessed however well known he or she might be to the mental health service. Something has happened in that patient's life to justify intervention under this Act and it is the factors that precipitated the detention and their impact on the patient that need to be assessed. The extent of any prior knowledge that might exist about the patient does not deflect from the need to assess the patient's *current* situation. This strongly suggests that the intention of Parliament was for s.2 to be used as the initial section to detain patients, because that section specifically provides for the patient's assessment, and that an application under s.3 be made if the assessment leads the clinical team to conclude that the patient needs a further period of treatment whilst being detained. In any event, practitioners' choice of section should be guided by the least restriction principle which is set out in para.1.3 of the *Code of Practice*. Other factors which support the approach advocated here are:

(i) the finding of Tucker J. in *R. v Wilson Ex p. Williamson*, above, that one of the purposes of s.2 is to ascertain whether an application under s.3 would be appropriate;

(ii) dicta in a number of cases where the judges have assumed that s.2 can be used to admit a well known patient; see for example, *R. v Bournewood Community and Mental Health NHS Trust Ex p. L* [1998] 1 All E.R. 634,641, CA, where Lord Woolf M.R. said that it would have been possible to use s.2 to admit the patient who had been in very close contact with the mental health services for most of his life and *R. v East London and City Mental Health NHS Trust Ex p. Brandenburg*, above, where the Court of Appeal assumed that it could be appropriate to detain a patient under s.2 subsequent to his discharge by a tribunal;

(iii) the fact that s.3(2)(c) states that an application under s.3 should be made if the necessary treatment can *only* be provided under that section suggests that such an application should not be made unless the patient has been assessed as needing treatment under s.2 for a period longer than that provided for in that section. This is because both sections provide clinicians with identical powers to treat the patient;

(iv) section 29(4) allows for the extension of the patient's detention under s.2 if a displacement application is made to the county court on the ground that the patient's nearest relative has "unreasonably objected" to a s.3 application being made, before the s.2 admission expires. This provision, and the absence of any equivalent remedy to an applicant who uses s.3 as an initial detaining section and is then faced with an objection from the nearest relative, is a clear indication that this Act was drafted on the assumption that an application under s.2 would precede an application under s.3; and

(v) the fact that it is not possible to convert an application under s.4 into an application under s.3 in respect of a well known patient (see s.4(4)).

Those who advocate the use of s.3 as the initial detaining section for the well known patient fail to identify the action that an AMHP applicant should take when faced with a s.11(4) objection made by the nearest relative of a patient who has been assessed as being either actively suicidal or as posing an immediate and serious risk to the safety of others. An application under s.2 cannot be made in these circumstances (see the *Williamson* case, above) and although the AMHP would have the option of applying to the county court under s.29 for an interim order displacing the nearest relative on the ground that the objection was unreasonable, such action may be too late to avoid catastrophic consequences for the patient and/or others.

The question of whether s.2 or s.3 should be uses to admit a patient is considered in Ch.4 of the current edition of the Code at paras 4.25–4.27.

*The deteriorating patient*
See the note under this heading in the General Note to s.3.                    **1–035**

*Applications to the First-tier Tribunal (Mental Health) or the Mental Health Review Tribunal for Wales*
The patient may make an application within 14 days of his or her admission (s.66(1)(a),  **1–036**
(2)(a)).

*Code of Practice*
The roles of mental health professionals when undertaking assessments that might lead  **1–037**
to an application for admission to hospital and the criteria for detention under this section are considered in Ch.4. Conflicts of interests that might arise in the assessment process are considered in Ch.7. Guidance on the conveyance of patients can be found in Ch.11.

*Subsection (1)*
MAY BE ADMITTED.   The hospital named in the application is not placed under a legal  **1–038**
obligation to admit the patient: see the note on "to hospital" in s.6(1).

DETAINED THERE.   The patient can be granted leave of absence from the detaining hospital under s.17, but only after the patient has received a period of in-patient treatment at that hospital: see the *Hallstrom* case noted in the General Note to s.3. Making an application in respect of a patient where the intention is to grant the patient immediate leave of absence to enable the patient to be treated at another hospital is unlawful because the application provides authority for the patient to be detained in the hospital named in the application (see s.6(2)), which is where the initial in-patient treatment must take place. Also note the use of the term "there" in this provision.

APPLICATION.   An application under this section can be made by either the patient's nearest relative or by an AMHP (s.11(1)). It will be addressed to the managers of the hospital to which admission is sought (s.11(2)). If the applicant is an AMHP, he or she must inform the patient's nearest relative that the application is to be or has been made (s.11(3)). The nearest relative cannot prevent an AMHP making an application. In deciding whether to make an application an AMHP is required to have regard to any wishes expressed by relatives of the patient (s.13(1)). This does not mean that the AMHP is placed under a legal obligation to consult with the patient's relatives before he or she makes an application. The applicant must have seen the patient within the previous 14 days (s.11(5)) and an AMHP applicant must interview the patient before the application is made (s.13(2)). The patient has to be admitted to hospital within 14 days of the time when he or she was last medically examined prior to the recommendations required by subs.(3) being made (s.6(1)(a)). It is possible to make an application in respect of a person who is already receiving hospital treatment as an in-patient on an informal basis (s.5(1)). An application for the admission of a ward of court cannot be made without the leave of the High Court (s.33(1)).
The effect of an application for admission for assessment is set out in s.6.

*Subsection (2)*

*Paragraph (a)*
IS SUFFERING.   A patient whose symptoms of mental disorder are being controlled by  **1–039**
medication still suffers from that disorder: see the note on "The deteriorating patient" in the General Note to s.3.

In *R. v Kirklees MBC Ex p. C* [1993] 2 F.L.R. 187 at 190 CA, Lloyd L.J., speaking obiter, said that:

> "having regard to the definition of patient in s.145 there is, in my view, power to admit a patient for assessment under s.2, if he or she appears to be suffering from mental disorder, on the ground that he or she is so suffering, even though it turns out on assessment that [he or] she is not. Any other construction would unnecessarily emasculate the beneficial power under s.2 and confine asessment to choice of treatment."

This approach was confirmed in *St George's Healthcare NHS Trust v S* [1998] 3 All E.R. 673, where the Court of Appeal held that the identification of the presence of mental disorder for the purposes of this section cannot be a final concluded diagnosis: the final diagnosis may or may not confirm that provisional view.

MENTAL DISORDER. Unlike the position under s.3, it is possible for a learning disabled person whose condition is not associated with "abnormally aggressive or seriously irresponsible conduct" to be the subject of an application under this section.

NATURE OR DEGREE. The meaning of this phrase is considered in the note on s.3(2)(a).

WHICH WARRANTS THE DETENTION OF THE PATIENT IN A HOSPITAL. This requirement assumes that an assessment has concluded that the patient's need for assessment and treatment cannot be met without recourse to this section; see further para.4.4 of the *Code of Practice*. The patient must need a period of assessment under detention as a hospital *in-patient*: see the note on "detained there", above. The detention must be related to or linked with the patient's mental disorder; the patient's need for treatment for an unrelated physical disorder does not provide the necessary warrant (*St George's Healthcare NHS Trust v S*, above). In the *St George's* case, the Court of Appeal declared an admission under this section to be unlawful because the grounds prescribed in this paragraph were not established. Judge L.J. said at 697:

> "The contemporaneous documents themselves demonstrate that those involved in the decision to make an application for admission failed to maintain the distinction between the urgent need of [the patient] for treatment arising from her pregnancy, and the separate question whether her mental disorder (in the form of depression) warranted her detention in hospital. From the reasoning to be found in them, the conclusion that the detention was believed to be warranted in order that adequate provision could be made to deal with [the patient's] pregnancy and the safety of her unborn child is unavoidable."

ASSESSMENT. An application under this section would be unlawful if the patient was not going to be subjected to an assessment for his or her mental disorder after admission (*St George's Healthcare NHS Trust v S*, above).

The patient's detention under this section does not automatically lapse on the completion of the assessment because: (1) the authority to detain can only end either on the expiration of the 28-day period, an order of discharge being made by a tribunal or an order for discharge being made under s.23; and (2) this section authorises the detention of the patient for assessment "or for assessment followed by medical treatment".

OR FOR ASSESSMENT FOLLOWED BY MEDICAL TREATMENT. Treatment under this section need not be confined to treatment which is an inherent part of the assessment process.

*Paragraph (b)*

**1–040**   There is no requirement for the two recommending doctors to agree on the nature of the risk justifying detention under this section; see further the *Code of Practice*, paras 4.6 and 4.7.

HEALTH. The patient's mental as well as physical health is covered by this term. This interpretation was adopted by the Mental Health Act Commission in its *Second Biennial Report*, 1985–1987, at para.11.3. If the patient's "health" was confined to his or her physical health, this would result in a situation where a patient who was suffering acute mental distress arising from his or her mental disorder could not be made the subject of an application in the absence of self harming or violent behaviour. The opinion that is sometimes heard from practitioners that an application under this section can only be made if the patient is either a danger to himself or others, or is engaging in seriously disruptive behaviour, is incorrect. Also see the note on "the deteriorating patient" in the General Note to s.3.

SAFETY. With the patient being exposed to the risk of being harmed, either through his or her own acts or omissions or through the acts or omissions of others.

PROTECTION OF OTHER PERSONS. The nature of risk evaluation was considered by Stuart-Smith L.J. in *R. v Parole Board Ex p. Bradley* [1990] 3 All E.R. 828 at 836: "... the precise level of risk is not (surely cannot be) spelt out". In his "Review of Homicides by Patients with Severe Mental Illness" (March 2006), Professor Tony Maden states, at p.60:

"Risk assessment alone is not enough and there has to be an effective means of managing that risk. Given the nature of the sample, which is defined by the presence of serious mental illness, it is inevitable that medication and compliance are major issues. Non-compliance was an identified problem in most of these cases."

With regard to intervention, Professor Maden reports, at p.63, that it:

"has become commonplace for CPA meetings to list signs of relapse or deterioration but the missing element seems to be a clear statement of when to intervene. It is pointless to identify early warning signs of relapse unless they lead to action."

In *R. v North West London Mental Health NHS Trust Ex p. Stewart* (1996) 39 B.M.L.R. 105, Harrison J. said:

"The protection of 'other persons' does not necessarily mean the public at large because it could simply relate to an individual person or persons rather than to the public at large, nor is there the requirement that such persons should be protected 'from serious harm.'"

Although the matter is not free from doubt, it is likely that this phrase covers both protection from physical harm and protection from serious emotional harm. The *Code of Practice*, at para.4.8, states that harm includes psychological harm. The protection of the mental health of the main carer of the patient could therefore be the main trigger for "sectioning" the patient. Although this provision does not make explicit reference to the protection of a person's property, actual or threatened damage to a person's property could cause that person serious emotional harm.

Although an unborn child is not a "person" in need of protection, the "health or safety" of the potential mother can be assessed on the basis that she is heavily pregnant: see *St George's Healthcare NHS Trust v S*, above, where Judge L.J. said at 696:

"Those responsible have to deal in realities, and [the patient] was dangerously ill [with pre-eclampsia]. Although the risks were caused by her pregnancy, the potential damage could have fallen within s.2(2)(b)."

It is therefore permissible to detain a pregnant patient whose mental disorder requires assessment in circumstances where a major concern is the likely impact on the mother's physical and/or mental health of an unsupervised birth. Also see the note on "The Human Rights Act 1998" in s.3.

*Subsection (3)*

**1–041**    FOUNDED ON.    The medical recommendations must be perused by the applicant before the application is signed. A medical recommendation which is signed after the date of the application is invalid; also see the note on "on or before the date of the application" in s.12(1)).

The fact that an application has had to be aborted because, for example, the offer of a bed at the hospital named in the application has been withdrawn does not effect the validity of the medical recommendations that were made in support of the application. As long as the time limit set out in s.6(1)(a) is not contravened, the medical recommendations can be used to support a fresh application addressed to a different hospital.

WRITTEN RECOMMENDATIONS.    Made either separately or jointly (s.11(7)).

TWO REGISTERED MEDICAL PRACTITIONERS.    Complying with the provisions of s.12 and the regulations made under s.12A.

*Subsection (4)*

**1–042**    NOT EXCEEDING 28 DAYS.    The patient can be discharged from detention before the 28 days expire by the tribunal or by an order made under s.23. The patient could also be granted leave to be absent from the hospital under s.17. The 28-day period can be extended if an application is made to the county court on specified grounds for an acting nearest relative to be appointed (s.29(4)) or if the patient has gone absent without leave and has been returned to the hospital before the section expires (see the note on "a patient" in s.21(1)).

BEGINNING WITH.    The day on which the patient was admitted is counted as the first day when calculating the 28 day period (*Zoan v Rouamba* [2000] 2 All E.R. 620 CA). The authority to detain the patient will expire at midnight on the twenty-eighth day.

THE DAY ON WHICH HE IS ADMITTED.    This is either the day on which the patient was admitted to the hospital from the community whilst subject to an application under this section, or the day on which the patient who was in hospital informally was made subject to such an application. In both cases, admission only takes effect for the purposes of this provision when the application has been accepted by a person who has been authorised by the hospital managers to accept it: see reg.3(2) of the English and Welsh Regulations.

UNDER THE FOLLOWING PROVISIONS OF THIS ACT.    The use of the term "following" prohibits a further application under this section being made during the currency of an existing s.2 application (*R. v Wilson Ex p. Williamson*, above).

### Admission for treatment

**1–043**    **3.**—(1) A patient may be admitted to a hospital and detained there for the period allowed by the following provisions of this Act in pursuance of an application (in this Act referred to as "an application for admission for treatment") made in accordance with this section.

(2) An application for admission for treatment may be made in respect of a patient on the grounds that—

(a)  he is suffering from [mental disorder] of a nature or degree which makes it appropriate for him to receive medical treatment in a hospital; and

(b)  [. . .]

(c)  it is necessary for the health or safety of the patient or for the protection of other persons that he should receive such treatment and it cannot be provided unless he is detained under this section[; and

(d)  appropriate medical treatment is available for him.]

(3) An application for admission for treatment shall be founded on the written recommendations in the prescribed form of two registered medical practitioners, including in each case a statement that in the opinion of the practitioner the conditions set out in subsection (2) above are complied with; and each such recommendation shall include—

(a) such particulars as may be prescribed of the grounds for that opinion so far as it relates to the conditions set out in paragraphs (a) and [(d)] of that subsection; and

(b) a statement of the reasons for that opinion so far as it relates to the conditions set out in paragraph (c) of that subsection, specifying whether other methods of dealing with the patient are available and, if so, why they are not appropriate.

[(4) In this Act, references to appropriate medical treatment, in relation to a person suffering from mental disorder, are references to medical treatment which is appropriate in his case, taking into account the nature and degree of the mental disorder and all other circumstances of his case.]

AMENDMENTS
The amendments to this section were made by the Mental Health Act 2007, ss.1(4), 4(2), (3), 55, Sch.11, Pt 2.

DEFINITIONS
    patient: s.145(1).                              **1–044**
    hospital: ss.34(2), 145(1).
    mental disorder: ss.1, 145(1).
    medical treatment: s.145(1), (4).

GENERAL NOTE
    This section provides for the compulsory admission of a patient to hospital for treatment **1–045** and for his or her subsequent detention, which can last for an initial period of up to six months (s.20(1)). The authority to detain a patient under this section can be renewed (s.20(2)). Patients admitted under this section are subject to the consent to treatment provisions contained in Pt IV of this Act (s.56(3)). There is no legal rule which prevents: (a) an application under this section from being made at any time after a s.4 admission has been made (*Re Makin* [2000] M.H.L.R. 41) or (b) a patient who has been detained under this section from being subsequently detained under s.2; see further the General Note to s.2 under the heading "Section 2 or section 3?".
    In *R. v Hallstrom Ex p. W; R. v Gardner Ex p. L* [1986] 2 All E.R. 306, McCullough J. held that admission under this section only covered those whose mental condition was believed to require a period of in-patient treatment in the hospital named in the application. (This finding was approved by the Court of Appeal in *B v Barking Havering and Brentwood Community Healthcare NHS Trust* [1999] 1 F.L.R. 106.) His Lordship said, at 315:

"In my judgment, the key to the construction of section 3 lies in the phrase 'admission for treatment'. It stretches the concept of 'admission for treatment' too far to say that it covers admission for only so long as it is necessary to enable leave of absence to be granted [under section 17], after which the necessary treatment will begin. 'Admission for treatment' under section 3 is intended for those whose condition is believed to require a period of treatment as an in-patient. It may be that such patients will also be thought to require a period of out-patient treatment thereafter, but the concept of 'admission for treatment' has no applicability to those whom it is intended to admit and detain for a purely nominal period during which no necessary treatment will be given.

The phrase 'and his mental disorder . . . makes it appropriate for him to receive treatment in a hospital' in section 3(2)(a) also leads to the conclusion that the section is concerned with those whose mental condition requires in-patient treatment. Treatment in a hospital does not mean treatment *at* a hospital as [leading counsel for the defendants], in effect contends. If his construction were correct there would be a distinction between the patient who could appropriately be treated at home and the patient who could appropriately treated at the out-patients' department of a hospital. Such a distinction would be without reason. When it is remembered that the section authorises compulsory detention in a hospital it is at once clear why a distinction should be made between those whom it is appropriate to treat *in* a hospital (i.e. as in-patients) and those whom it is appropriate to treat otherwise (whether at the out-patient department of the hospital or at home or elsewhere)."

These remarks, which equate "treatment in a hospital" with "in-patient treatment", were described as being obiter and were rejected by Wilson J. in *R. (on the application of DR) v Mersey Care NHS Trust* [2002] EWHC 1810 (Admin); [2002] M.H.L.R. 386, which is considered in the note on s.20(4)(c). His Lordship held that the phrase "medical treatment in a hospital" in s.20(4)(a) incorporated treatment *at* a hospital and that the lawfulness of the renewal of the patient's detention did not depend upon a plan to put the patient at times in a hospital bed. His Lordship concluded his judgment as follows:

"Unless and until [the reform of the Mental Health Act] is enacted, the law will remain (if my interpretation of it be sound) that the compulsory administration of medication to a patient can be secured only by making him liable to be detained or renewing such liability; that such may be achieved only if a significant component of the plan is for treatment in hospital; and that, in such an enquiry, the difference between in-patient and out-patient treatment is irrelevant" (para.34).

Although his Lordship was correct in equating the tests in ss.3(2)(a) and 20(4)(a), his judgment in so far as it relates to s.3(2)(a) is obiter and therefore not binding as a precedent. The following factors suggest that it should not be applied to applications for the initial detention of a patient:

1. The sub-heading to ss.2 to 6 of this Act is "Procedure for hospital admission". In order to be admitted to a hospital, a person must become an in-patient of that hospital.

2. The effect of a duly completed application is to provide authority for the patient to be conveyed to the named hospital, to be admitted to that hospital (s.6(1)(2)) and to be detained there (s.3(1)).

3. An approved mental health professional (AMHP) can only make an application if he or she is satisfied that "detention in a hospital" is the most appropriate way of providing for the patient's mental health needs (s.13(2)). In *Hallstrom*, above, McCullough J. said at 316: "Parliament must have been directing the social worker's attention to the patient's need for in-patient treatment".

4. On an application under s.3, the recommending doctors are required to state why "other methods of treatment or care" such as "out-patient treatment" are not appropriate (see Forms A7 and A8).

It is submitted that the correct interpretation of this section is that an application can only be made if the patient is assessed as requiring a period of hospital in-patient treatment for his or her mental disorder.

The "nominal period" in *Hallstrom* was an overnight admission. In *Re Shearon* [1996] C.O.D. 223, the Divisional Court held that whilst an admission for one week is a relatively small part of the initial six-month period of detention authorised by this section, there was no possible reason for stigmatising a genuine initial one week's intended in-patient treatment as "a purely nominal period during which no necessary treatment will be given". The court further held that the fact that the application was made simultaneously with the institution of a parallel Care Plan did not invalidate the admission and render it unlawful.

Where a patient is admitted to hospital under this section, any previous application that had been made in respect of him under this Part of the Act (i.e. an application under s.2 or 4 or a guardianship application under s.7) is automatically cancelled (s.6(4)).

A patient who had been detained under this section after having been released from prison on licence part way through a sentence should not, upon absconding from the detaining hospital, have been returned to prison by the Home Secretary (now the Secretary of State for Justice) using his recall power without reference to or consultation with the hospital doctors. Normally the s.3 would take precedence over a recall (*R. (on the application of S) v Secretary of State for the Home Department and the Parole Board* [2002] EWHC Admin 2424; [2003] M.H.L.R. 114).

An order for the patient's discharge from this section can be made by his responsible clinician, the hospital managers or, subject to s.25, his nearest relative (s.23(2)(a)).

There is nothing to prevent a patient who has been detained under this section from being arrested in respect of a criminal offence. If the patient is subsequently remanded into custody or sentenced under the criminal law, the provisions of s.22 will apply.

Where a patient who has been detained under this section ceases to be so detained and leaves hospital, he or she has an entitlement to after-care services (s.117).

*The re-sectioning of a patient subsequent to a discharge by the First-tier Tribunal (Mental Health) or the Mental Health Review Tribunal for Wales*
In *R. v East London and The City Mental Health Trust Ex p. Brandenburg* [2003] UKHL **1–046** 58; [2004] 1 All E.R. 400, the House of Lords considered the following question: when a tribunal has ordered the discharge of a patient, is it lawful to re-admit him under s.2 or s.3 of the Mental Health Act when it cannot be demonstrated that there has been a relevant change of circumstances?

The only speech of substance was given by Lord Bingham who identified the following "overriding principles":

1. The common law respects and protects the personal freedom of the individual, which may not be curtailed save for a reason and in circumstances sanctioned by the law of the land. This principle is reflected in, but does not depend on, art.5(1) of the European Convention on Human Rights. It can be traced back to Chapter 29 of Magna Carta 1297 and before that to Chapter 39 of Magna Carta 1215.

2. The law may properly provide for the compulsory detention in hospital of those who suffer from mental disorder if detention is judged to be necessary for the health or safety of the patient or for the protection of others. The necessity for such detention in appropriate cases is recognised by art.5(1)(e) of the Convention, and has long been given effect in domestic law.

3. A person compulsorily detained on mental health grounds should have the right to take proceedings by which the lawfulness of his detention may be decided by a court and his release ordered if the detention is not lawful. This right is expressed in art.5(4) of the Convention.

4. The rule of law requires that effect should be loyally given to the decisions of legally constituted tribunals in accordance with what is decided. It follows that no one may knowingly act in a way which has the object of nullifying or setting at nought the decision of a tribunal. It is not therefore open to the nearest relative of a patient or an [AMHP] to apply for the admission of the patient, even with the support of

the required medical recommendations, simply because he or she or they disagree with a tribunal's decision to discharge. That would make a mockery of the decision.

Lord Bingham continued by stating that in applying these principles, account must be taken of certain important considerations:

1. While doctors may be expected to exercise their best professional judgment in diagnosing the condition and assessing the cases of those suffering from mental disorder, and prescribing treatment, their conclusions will rarely be capable of scientific verification. There will often be room for bona fide differences of professional opinion.

2. The condition of many of those suffering from mental disorder will not be static. Episodes of acute illness may be followed by episodes of remission. Thus it does not follow that a tribunal decision, however sound when made, will remain so. Other things being equal, the longer the period since the decision was made the greater the chance that the patient's mental condition may have altered whether for better or worse.

3. The focus of the tribunal's inquiry into the mental health of the patient is on whether he is "then suffering" from mental disorder. "Then" refers to the time of the tribunal's review and the tribunal has no power to consider the validity of the admission that gave rise to the liability to be detained. Although the tribunal cannot ignore the foreseeable future consequences of discharge, it is not called upon to make an assessment which will remain accurate indefinitely or for any given period of time.

4. A conscientious doctor whose opinion has not been accepted by the tribunal will doubtless ask himself whether the tribunal's view is to be preferred and whether his own opinion should be revised. But if, having done so, he adheres to his original opinion he cannot be obliged to suppress or alter it. His professional duty to his patient, and his wider duty to the public, requires him to form, and if called upon express, the best professional judgment he can, whether or not that coincides with the judgment of the tribunal.

5. It is plainly of importance that the [AMHP] is subject to the statutory duty under s.13 to apply for the admission of a patient where he is satisfied that such an application ought to be made and is of the opinion specified in that section.

Lord Bingham, in applying the principles set out above, rejected a change of circumstances test and held that an [AMHP] may not lawfully apply for the admission of a patient whose discharge has been ordered by the decision of a tribunal of which the [AMHP] is aware unless the [AMHP] has formed a reasonable and bona fide opinion that he has information not known to the tribunal which puts a significantly different complexion on the case as compared with that which was before the tribunal. His Lordship gave three hypothetical examples to illustrate the situations where re-sectioning the patient would be justified:

(a) The issue at the tribunal is whether the patient, if discharged, might cause harm to himself. The tribunal, on the evidence presented, discounts that possibility and directs the discharge of the patient. After the hearing, the [AMHP] learns of a fact previously unknown to him, the doctors attending the patient and the tribunal: that the patient had at an earlier date made a determined attempt on his life. Having taken medical advice, the [AMHP] judges that this information significantly alters the risk as assessed by the tribunal.

(b) At the tribunal hearing the patient's mental condition is said to have been stabilised by the taking of appropriate medication. The continuing stability of the patient's mental condition is said to depend on his willingness to take that medication. The patient assures the tribunal of his willingness to continue to take the medication and, on the basis of that assurance the tribunal directs the discharge of the patient. Before or after discharge the patient refuses to take the medication or communicates his intention to refuse. Having taken medical advice, the [AMHP] perceives a real risk to the patient or others if the medication is not taken.

(c) After the tribunal hearing, and whether before or after discharge, the patient's mental condition significantly deteriorates so as to present a degree of risk or treatment or supervision not evident at the hearing.

The following findings were also made:                                                   **1–047**

1. The position of the patient's nearest relative does not in principle differ from that of the [AMHP], although the nearest relative could not in many cases be expected to be familiar with the evidence or appreciate the grounds on which the tribunal had based its decision.

2. An [AMHP] may well learn of the existence of an earlier tribunal hearing when performing his functions under s.13(2) and will then wish to know the reasons for it. However, if no such information comes to light the law does not place on the [AMHP] (or a nearest relative applicant) a duty to make reasonable enquiries to establish whether any decision has been made by any tribunal and, if so, the grounds upon which it was based.

3. If an [AMHP] makes an application to section the patient subsequent to a decision of the tribunal to discharge him, he should be informed why the decision of the tribunal to discharge him is not thought to govern his case if the application is inconsistent in effect with that decision. As the disclosure of such reasons could be potentially harmful to the patient or to others, it may be necessary for the [AMHP] to give them in very general terms.

   [N.B The duty to give reasons is necessary in order to comply with the obligation under art.5(2) of the European Convention on Human Rights to give reasons where a person is deprived of his or her liberty by arrest. Under Convention case law, the sectioning of a patient constitutes an arrest: see the notes on art.5(2). As the statutory forms do not make provision for the giving of such reasons, it is suggested that the reasons given to the patient be recorded and attached to the application form.]

4. In terms of there being a duty to give reasons for taking a different view from the tribunal, while it would doubtless be helpful if a medical recommendation identified any new information on which it was based, a recommending doctor is not required to do more than express his or her best professional opinion.

There will be occasions when the AMHP who is considering making an application will not have attended the tribunal hearing which led to the discharge of the patient. In such a situation, the AMHP should use his or her best endeavours to establish the factual basis upon which the tribunal reached its decision. This could include an examination of the written reports that were submitted to the tribunal, contacting those who gave evidence to the tribunal and a consideration of the written reasons that the tribunal gave for its decision.

In *R. (on the application of Care Principles Ltd) v Mental Health Review Tribunal* [2006] EWHC 3194 (Admin); [2006] M.H.L.R. 365, Collins J. held that:

1. The "new information" test established in *Brandenburg* covers not only what might have happened subsequent to the tribunal's decision, but also material which had not been taken into account by the tribunal, if such material were discovered (para.43).

2. Section 6(3) of this Act enables the hospital managers to act on an application that appears to be "duly made". The extent of their obligations under that provision must depend on the facts of a particular case. If they are aware of the existence of a previous tribunal decision ordering the discharge of the patient, it requires a critical consideration of the justification for the detention in the light of that decision. It is not "sufficient for them simply to say: we were satisfied that the [AMHP] had properly considered it and discussed it, although it is not specifically explained in the application" (para.45).

With regard to point 2, if the hospital managers are aware of the existence of a decision of a tribunal to discharge the patient they should only accept the application if they are satisfied that the "new information" test has been met. The applicant should inform the managers of the existence of a tribunal discharge known to him or her.

The effect of the *Brandenburg* judgment is that if there is simply a disagreement between the tribunal and the mental health professionals about the interpretation of the evidence presented to the tribunal, the decision of the tribunal, assuming that it is lawful (see the *Ashworth Hospital Authority* case, below), must be allowed to stand.

In *R. (on the application of H) v Oxfordshire Mental Healthcare NHS Trust* [2002] EWHC Admin 465; [2002] M.H.L.R. 282, a case which was decided before *Brandenburg*, Sullivan J. confirmed the re-detention of the patient subsequent to his deferred discharge by a tribunal in circumstances where:

  (i)   the patient had refused to co-operate with the arrangements that were being made for his discharge from the hospital;

  (ii)  where, in any event, no suitable arrangements had been identified;

  (iii) the patient was, in consequence, "becoming increasingly agitated, stressed and disturbed as the prospect of release drew closer, to the extent of refusing to discuss the matter with his social workers and doctors and, indeed, throwing a table at the social workers" (para.65); and

  (iv)  those involved in the re-sectioning had given "careful thought" to the decision of the tribunal (para.63).

His Lordship said that in directing discharge "the tribunal could not have proceeded upon the basis that the [patient's] symptoms would deteriorate to such a marked degree as has in fact occurred" (para.67). This decision is consistent with the principle established in *Brandenburg*.

In *R. (on the application of H) v Ashworth Hospital Authority*; [2002] EWCA Civ 923; [2003] 1 W.L.R. 127, the Court of Appeal addressed the question of what steps are open to mental health professionals and the hospital managers if they are faced with a tribunal decision for discharge which they honestly and reasonably believe is perverse or arguably perverse. The Court held that:

1. In the absence of material circumstances of which the tribunal is not aware when it orders discharge (note that the change in material circumstances test was rejected in the *Brandenburg* case, above), it is not open to the professionals to re-section the patient even if they have been legally advised that there are substantial grounds for saying that the tribunal's decision is arguable unlawful.

2. The appropriate action for the authorities to take in this situation is to apply to the Administrative Court for a stay of the tribunal's decision where there was a grant of permission to apply for judicial review. This is the case even if the decision of the tribunal has been fully implemented by the patient being released from the hospital. The effect of a stay is to suspend the tribunal's order, and temporarily to treat it

as being of no effect. The grant of an injunction under s.37 of the Supreme Court Act 1981 would be inappropriate in these circumstances.

3. The grant of permission to apply for judicial review is not a sufficient condition of a stay. The court should usually refuse to grant a stay unless satisfied that there is a strong, and not merely an arguable, case that the tribunal's decision was unlawful. Even in such a case, the court should not grant a stay in the absence of cogent evidence of risk and dangerousness.

4. In a case where a stay is ordered, it is essential that the validity of the tribunal's decision be determined by the court in a judicial review with the degree of speed that is appropriate and usual where a detained person seeks *habeas corpus* (i.e. if at all possible, within days of the order of stay).

5. If the patient refuses to return to the hospital following the grant of a stay, the machinery of the Act can be mobilised to see that he does.

In *R. (on the application of Care Principles Ltd) v Mental Health Review Tribunal*, above, paras 38–40, Collins J. said that:

1. Where an application is made for a stay, the claimant should always, unless there are very exceptional circumstances, give notice both to the patient's solicitors or representatives and to the tribunal.

2. The necessary basis for the grant of any stay must be drawn to the judge's attention. Normally it would be wrong, as the Court of Appeal held in *H*, above, to grant a stay unless there is cogent evidence that, if the patient is released, he will be a danger to himself or the public.

3. The judge must be informed of all the relevant criteria which must be applied in deciding on a stay.

Rather than making an application to the Administrative Court for a stay, an applicant should now apply to the tribunal itself to stay the proceedings or to suspend the effect of its own decision pending a determination by the tribunal or the Upper Tribunal of an application for permission to appeal against that decision: see r.5(3)(j)(l) of the Tribunal Rules and r.5(2)(g)(h) of the Welsh Rules. It is to be hoped that the tribunals establish procedures that enable such matters to be dealt with as a matter of urgency.

*The deteriorating patient*

The "Committee of Inquiry into the events leading up to and surrounding the fatal inci- **1–048** dent at the Edith Morgan Centre, Torbay, on September 1, 1993" examined the issue of the "sectionability" of a patient whose mental health is likely to deteriorate: see *The Falling Shadow: One Patient's Mental Health Care 1978–1993*, 1995, pp.153–169. The Committee disagreed with the view expressed by the *Internal Review of Legal Powers on the Care of Mentally Ill People in Community* that a patient could not be admitted under compulsory powers "simply on the grounds that his or her past medical history suggests that he or she will relapse in the future" (Department of Health, 1993, para.3.2). The conclusion that the Committee reached was that "there is probably no legal impediment to the readmission of a ['revolving door'] patient . . . at the point of loss of insight when he refuse[s] further medication" (p.160). In fact this conclusion does not conflict with the statement made by the *Internal Review* as a patient who has lost insight would not be detained "simply" on the ground of his medical history.

The Committee found the case of *Devon CC v Hawkins* [1967] 2 Q.B. 26, to be "highly pertinent" to the issue. In this case the question before the court was whether a person who was taking drugs which successfully controlled his epilepsy could be said to be "suffering from" that disease. The answer given by the then Lord Chief Justice, Lord Parker, was in the affirmative. His Lordship said that "so long as drugs are necessary to prevent the manifestation of disease, the disease in my judgment remains". In other words, so the Committee stated, what the patient "was 'suffering from' rested on a prognosis of what would occur in the future if medication was withdrawn" (p.155).

Although it might be the case that a person with a history of mental disorder who is being successfully medicated for that disorder can be said to be "suffering from" that disorder, it does not follow that merely because that person stops taking his medication the disorder becomes one of a "nature or degree which makes it appropriate for him to receive medical treatment in a hospital" (s.3(2)(a)) or one of a "nature or degree which warrants the detention of the patient in a hospital for assessment" (s.2(2)(a)). While a patient whose symptoms are being well controlled by medication cannot be said to be suffering from a "degree" of mental disorder sufficient to justify detention, can that patient be detained because of the "nature" of his disorder? This question was considered by Popplewell J. in *R. v The Mental Health Review, Tribunal for the South Thames Region Ex p. Smith*, which is noted under subs.(2)(a).

The course of a patient's mental disorder is never entirely predictable and this Act requires the professionals involved in assessing a patient for possible compulsory admission to exercise their judgment to determine whether the patient's condition and situation at the time of the assessment meet the statutory criteria for admission. If it is the case that a mere failure to continue with medication would be sufficient to satisfy the statutory criteria with respect to a patient who has a history of admissions subsequent to previous failures to continue with medication, this would result in the personal examination of the patient by the recommending doctors under s.12(2) and the interviewing of the patient by the AMHP under s.13(2) being sterile exercises. One of the objectives of the examinations and interview of such a patient would be to identify whether there is any evidence (apart from the cessation of medication) to suggest that it is likely that history will repeat itself in that the symptoms of the patient's mental disorder will reappear. If there is such evidence, the "nature" of the patient's mental disorder could lead professionals to conclude that detention in hospital is either "appropriate" or "warranted" even though there is either no current manifestation of the disorder (the "degree") or if the symptoms of the mental disorder are not yet acute.

It is suggested that the following approach should be taken by those involved in the assessment of a "revolving door" patient who has ceased to take medication for his or her mental disorder:

(i) a withdrawal from medication is a significant, but not a determining factor in the assessment;

(ii) the role of the professionals involved in the assessment is to assess the patient's response to the withdrawal and to identify the reasons for his or her decision to cease taking medication;

(iii) the "nature" test can be satisfied even though there is no evidence that the patient's mental health has begun to deteriorate: see *Smirek v Williams*, which is noted under "of a nature or degree" in subs.(2)(a); and

(iv) although it would not be possible to determine that the provisions of either ss.2(2)(a) or 3(2)(a) are satisfied solely on the ground that the patient has ceased to take medication, an evaluation of the patient's history, and, in particular, of his or her reaction to withdrawal from medication in the past, could lead to a decision that the "nature" of the mental disorder justifies an application being made.

*Section 2 or section 3?*

**1–049**    The question whether it is appropriate to detain a patient under this section or under s.2 is considered in the General Note to s.2 under this heading.

*Human Rights Act 1998*

In *Winterwerp v Netherlands* (1979) 2 E.H.R.R. 387, the European Court of Human **1–050**
Rights held, inter alia, that in order for the detention of a person of unsound mind to be lawful the mental disorder from which the patient is suffering must be of a kind or degree
warranting compulsory confinement. This finding is reflected in the phrase "nature or
degree" in subs.(2)(a). *Winterwerp* also confirmed that in order to achieve compliance
with art.5 of the European Convention on Human Rights, detention under this Act must
be a necessary and proportionate response to the patient's situation. Other less severe
measures must have been considered and found to be insufficient to safeguard the individual or public interest, leaving no alternative to detention (*Withold Litwa v Poland* (2001) 33
E.H.R.R. 53).

The question whether the continued detention of an asymptomatic patient contravenes
art.5 of the Convention was considered by the Court of Appeal in *R. (on the application
of H) v Mental Health Review Tribunal, North and North East London Region* [2001]
EWCA Civ 415; [2001] M.H.L.R. 48, where Lord Phillips M.R. said at para.33:

"The circumstances of the present case . . . are not uncommon. A patient is detained who
is unquestionably suffering from schizophrenia. While in the controlled environment of
the hospital he is taking medication, and as a result of the medication is in remission. So
long as he continues to take the medication he will pose no danger to himself or to others.
The nature of the illness is such, however, that if he ceases to take the medication he will
relapse and pose a danger to himself or to others. The professionals may be uncertain
whether, if he is discharged into the community, he will continue to take the medication.
We do not believe that Article 5 requires that the patient must always be discharged in
such circumstances. The appropriate response should depend upon the result of weighing
the interests of the patient against those of the public having regard to the particular facts.
Continued detention can be justified if, but only if, it is a proportionate response having
regard to the risks that would be involved in discharge".

The finding of the Court of Appeal in *St George's Healthcare NHS Trust v S*, above, that a
unborn child is not a "person" in need of protection for the purposes of ss.2(2)(b) and
3(2)(c) could possibly be challenged on the ground that a failure to protect the unborn
child constitutes a violation of the child's right to life under art.2 of the Convention.
Although the European Court of Human Rights has found in the context of abortion and
fertility treatment that an unborn child does not have a right to life and is not a "person"
within the meaning of art.2, it has not ruled out that, in certain circumstances, safeguards
may be extended to the unborn child (*Vo v France* (2005) 40 E.H.R.R. 12, para.80).

The Court has confirmed that the detention of a patient under art.5 may be justified on the
ground of protecting the public (*Witold Litwa v Poland*, above) in a situation where the
patient needs control and supervision rather than clinical treatment (*Reid v United
Kingdom* (2003) 37 E.H.R.R. 9, para.51).

Although art.5 is not concerned with the suitability of the treatment that the detained
patient receives or the conditions of his or her detention, subject to the requirement that
he be detained in a hospital, clinic or other appropriate institution (*Ashingdane v United
Kingdom* (1985) 7 E.H.R.R. 528 para.44), the medical treatment of a patient can constitute
"inhuman or degrading treatment" under the Convention if it reaches a minimum level of
severity.

If a patient has been assessed as either needing a particular treatment or requiring a
specialist opinion, an excessive delay in providing that treatment or opinion could give
rise to a claim under art.8(1) of the Convention if the delay has a serious impact on the
patient's health: see *Passannante v Italy* (1998) 26 E.H.R.R. CD 153, noted under art.8(1).

A failure or refusal to provide treatment that is discriminatory will be unlawful, either
under art.14 of the Convention or the Disability Discrimination Act 1995.

*Applications to the First-tier Tribunal (Mental Health) or the Mental Health Review Tribunal for Wales*

**1–051**     The patient may make an application within six months of admission (s.66(1)(b), (2)(b)) and during each subsequent renewal period (ss.66(1)(f), (2)(f), 20(2)). Section 66(2A) disapplies s.66(1)(b) for recalled community patients. A reference to the tribunal will be made in the circumstances set out in s.68. The patient's nearest relative may make an application within 28 days of receiving notification that an order for discharge has been barred under s.25 (s.66(1)(g), (2)(d)).

*Code of Practice*

**1–052**     The roles of mental health professionals when undertaking assessments that might lead to an application for admission to hospital and the criteria for detention under this section are considered in Ch.4. Guidance on the application of the "appropriate treatment" test set out in subs.(3)(d) can be found in Ch.6 and, in respect of patients with a personality disorder, Ch.35 at paras 35.8 et seq. Conflicts of interests that might arise in the assessment process are considered in Ch.7. Guidance on the conveyance of patients can be found in Ch.11.

*Subsection (1)*

**1–053**     MAY BE ADMITTED.     The hospital named in the application is not placed under a legal obligation to admit the patient: see the note on "to hospital" in s.6(1).

DETAINED THERE.     The patient can be granted leave of absence from the detaining hospital under s.17, but only after the patient has received a period of in-patient treatment at that hospital: see the *Hallstrom* case, above. Making an application in respect of a patient where the intention is to grant the patient immediate leave of absence to enable the patient to be treated at another hospital is unlawful because the application provides authority for the patient to be detained in the hospital named in the application (see s.6(2)), which is where the initial in-patient treatment must take place. Also note the use of the term "there" in this provision. It would also be unlawful for an application to be made under this section if the motive for making the application was to enable an application for a community treatment order to be made in respect of a patient who did not require in-patient treatment.

THE PERIOD ALLOWED.     An initial period of six months renewable for a further six months and thereafter renewable at yearly intervals (s.20(1), (2)).

APPLICATION.     An application can be made by either the patient's nearest relative or by an AMHP (s.11(1)). It will be addressed to the managers of the hospital to which admission is sought (s.11(2)). If an AMHP makes the application, he or she must consult with the patient's nearest relative if this is practicable and the application cannot proceed if the nearest relative objects (s.11(4)). The positive consent of the nearest relative to the application is not required. The applicant must have seen the patient within the previous 14 days (s.11(5)) and an AMHP applicant must interview the patient before the application is made (s.13(2)). The patient must be admitted to hospital within 14 days of the time when he or she was last medically examined prior to the recommendations required by subs.(3) being made (s.6(1)(a)). It is possible to make an application in respect of a person who is already receiving hospital treatment as an in-patient on an informal basis (s.5(1)). An application for the admission of a ward of court cannot be made without the leave of the High Court (s.33(1)).

The effect of an application for admission for treatment is set out in s.6.

*Subsection (2)*

*Paragraph (a)*

SUFFERING FROM. A patient whose symptoms of mental disorder are being controlled **1–054** by medication still suffers from that disorder: see the note on "The deteriorating patient", above.

MENTAL DISORDER. A patient with a learning disability can only be made subject to an application under this section if the disability is associated with abnormally aggressive or seriously irresponsible conduct on his or her part (s.1(2A), (2B)).

OF A NATURE OR DEGREE. Also see the note on s.72(1)(b)(i). The meaning of this phrase was considered by Popplewell J. in *R. v Mental Health Review Tribunal for the South Thames Region Ex p. Smith* [1998] EWHC 832 (Admin); (1999) 47 B.M.L.R. 104. His Lordship held that:

(i) although the wording of this phrase is disjunctive, in very many cases the nature and degree of the patient's mental disorder will be inevitably bound up so that it matters not whether the issue is dealt with under nature or degree;

(ii) the word "nature" refers to the particular mental disorder from which the patient suffers, its chronicity, its prognosis, and the patient's previous response to receiving treatment for the disorder. In making this finding, his Lordship rejected a submission made by counsel for the patient that the "nature" of a patient's mental disorder is a static condition; and

(iii) the word "degree" refers to the current manifestation of the patient's disorder.

This criterion can therefore be satisfied in respect of a well-known asymptomatic patient who has ceased to take medication for his mental disorder and who has a history of a significant deterioration in his mental health after ceasing to take such medication. This interpretation is supported by the following comment made by Hale L.J. in *Smirek v Williams* [2000] M.H.L.R. 38 at para.19:

"There are, of course, mental illnesses which come and go, but where there is a chronic condition, where there is evidence that it will soon deteriorate if medication is not taken, I find it impossible to accept that that is not a mental illness of a nature or degree which makes it appropriate for the patient to be liable to be detained in hospital for medical treatment if the evidence is that, without being detained in hospital, the patient will not take that treatment".

However, although it might be lawful to make an application in these circumstances, whether it will be clinically and ethically right to do so is a separate question. It is submitted that the crucial factor in determining whether an application should be made in respect of an asymptomatic patient is the assessment of the risk to the patient and/or others following the cessation of medication. This issue is considered further in the note on "The deteriorating patient", above.

APPROPRIATE FOR HIM TO RECEIVE MEDICAL TREATMENT IN A HOSPITAL. It is submitted that this provision can only be satisfied if the patient requires treatment for his mental disorder as a hospital in-patient: see the comment on *R. (on the application of DR) v Mersey Care NHS Trust* in the General Note to this section.

An assessment of the patient's response to being treated can be a part of the medical treatment that the patient receives: see the comment made by Woolf M.R. in *B v Barking Havering and Brentwood Community Healthcare NHS Trust* [1999] 1 F.L.R. 106 CA, noted under "assessment" in s.2(2)(a).

*Paragraph (c)*

**1–055**     There is no requirement for the two recommending doctors to agree on the nature of the risk which justifies detention under this section.

NECESSARY.   A stronger term than "ought" in s.2(2)(b). The necessity must relate to both compulsion and treatment. In *Reid v Secretary of State for Scotland* [1999] 1 All E.R. 481, 504, Lord Clyde said that the standard is "one of necessity, not desirability".

HEALTH.   See the note on s.2(2).

SAFETY.   With the patient being exposed to the risk of being harmed if he or she is not detained.

PROTECTION OF OTHER PERSONS.   See the note on s.2(2).

AND THAT IT CANNOT BE PROVIDED.   By, for example, an informal admission. The use of restraint on a mentally incapable informal patient either to ensure that necessary treatment is given or to respond to a behavioural disturbance in a situation where the patient is not being deprived of his or her liberty is authorised under ss.5 and 6 of the Mental Capacity Act 2005.

UNLESS HE IS DETAINED UNDER THIS SECTION.   See the General Note to s.2 under the heading "Section 2 or section 3?".

*Paragraph (d)*

**1–056**     This paragraph, which should be read with s.145(4), replaces the requirement that the treatment of certain categories patients detained under this section must be "likely to alleviate or prevent a deterioration of his condition" (the "treatability test" which was contained in the repealed paragraph (b)) with a requirement that "appropriate treatment" be available to all patients. The 10th edition of this work stated, at para.1–051, that the interpretation in case law of the treatability test was so broad that "it is difficult to imagine the circumstances that would cause a patient to fail it". A similar comment can be made of the appropriate treatment test, without the need for judicial intervention, given that it will almost always be appropriate to provide the patient with either specialist nursing or care for the purpose of either alleviating or preventing a worsening of the patient's mental disorder or one or more of its symptoms or manifestations so as to satisfy the terms of s.145(4). In any event, it will be difficult to successfully challenge a clinician's claim that he or she either is or will be providing the patient with appropriate treatment. The rationale for the change was explained by the Minister of State:

"We will . . . introduce a new requirement that appropriate treatment must be available for patients subject to detention in hospital for treatment or on supervised community treatment. This will reinforce the fundamental principle that detention and supervised community treatment must always be for a clinical purpose. The test replaces the more selective 'treatability test', whose many drawbacks include contributing to a culture in which certain groups of patients are labelled untreatable and thereby are denied services. That may have been convenient for service providers, but it was not very useful to patients and was sometimes dangerous to the public.

The appropriate treatment test is designed to ensure that no one will be brought or kept under compulsion unless suitable treatment is available for them. It will not be enough for treatment to exist in theory, which in itself is a considerable patient safeguard. The treatment must be not only available and appropriate to the medical condition but appropriate to the circumstances. For instance, factors such as how far the services are from the patient's home or whether those services are culturally appropriate will need to be considered. That is very much in line with the move across the NHS towards more tailored, individual patient-focused services. It is a change that links mental health very much to the mainstream of NHS reform and improvement" (*Hansard*, HL Vol.687, col.658).

The "certain groups of patients" mentioned refer, in particular, to patients who suffer from personality disorder. It was claimed that such patients "are too often simply written off as untreatable without regard to whether potentially effective treatment is available". It was further claimed that the treatability test was a perverse incentive for people not to comply with treatment. The Minister stated that she had been informed that "lawyers have advised their patients not to engage with treatment because if it can be proved that they are not treatable they have to be released" (Public Bill Committee, cols 121, 122). The Government also preferred the appropriateness test because the treatability test "requires clinicians to predict that a particular outcome of a patient's treatment is likely" and that a clinician "may not always truly be able to predict that a particular treatment is likely to work for a particular patient" (*Hansard*, HL Vol.688, col.319, per the Minister of State).

Those who opposed the change were concerned that the new test provides for the possibility of a person being detained simply for preventive purposes without any medical benefit. One of the proponents of this argument, Lord Carlile, called in aid the following extract from the evidence that Professor Nigel Eastman gave to Joint Committee on the Draft Mental Health Bill:

"Therapeutic benefit to the individual is of crucial importance in terms of protecting the boundary of what is the business of mental health professionals. I am not at all against protecting the public, of course not, but it must be in conjunction with some benefit to the individual that goes beyond simply stopping them offending. If you adopt a definition of treatability which is simply the reduction of risk or the avoidance of offending, that means that locking somebody up is treating them" (*Hansard*, HL Vol.688, col.304).

As medicine is the "science and art concerned with the cure, alleviation and prevention of disease, and with the restoration and preservation of health" (Shorter Oxford English Dictionary), it is difficult to see how medical treatment could ever be described as being "appropriate" for the patient if a view had been taken that there was no possibility of the patient ever gaining any therapeutic benefit from it, apart than the benefit that arises from preventing offending in the community. Further, it is unlikely that a doctor could be said to be acting ethically if he or she was involved in the admission of a patient to hospital in the knowledge that the patient would receive no therapeutic benefit from the treatment that was going to be provided. In any event, the concern about the absence of any reference to therapeutic benefit has been partly allayed by the inclusion of s.145(4) by the 2007 Act.

Although it was claimed in Parliament that the new test might not be compliant with the European Convention on Human Rights, the Joint Committee considered that "in terms of the Convention, there would appear to be no obstacle to replacing 'treatability' with 'availability of appropriate treatment' as a condition of detention" (para.20). This conclusion was reached because art.5(1)(e) of the Convention imposes no requirement that detention in a hospital be conditional on the illness or condition being of a nature or degree amenable to medical treatment (*Koniarska v United Kingdom*, No.33670/96, December 10, 2000). In *Reid v United Kingdom* (2003) 37 E.H.R.R. 9 para.51, the European Court of Human Rights held that confinement under art.5(1)(e) "may be necessary not only where a person needs therapy, medication of other clinical treatment to cure or alleviate his condition, but also where the person needs control and supervision to prevent him, for example, causing harm to himself and other persons."

**1–057**   APPROPRIATE.   Not necessarily the most appropriate treatment, or all of the appropriate treatment that could be provided for the patient. What constitutes appropriate treatment for the patient may change over time. To be appropriate, the treatment must attempt to address aspects of the mental disorder from which the patient is suffering. With regard to psychological therapies and other treatments that require the patient's co-operation, a treatment that is considered to be appropriate for the patient is not rendered inappropriate merely because of an absence of co-operation.

In *MD v Nottinghamshire Health Care NHS Trust* [2010] UKUT 59 (AAC); [2010] M.H.L.R. 93, para.31, Judge Jacobs said: "It may be that medical treatment is still available for a patient but, because of the circumstances of a particular case, it is no longer appropriate." In this case the Upper Tribunal rejected a submission that detention without the possibility of reduction of the risk posed by the patient was containment not treatment ("treatment has to be appropriate, but need not reduce the risk" (para.34)) and confirmed the decision of the First-tier Tribunal that appropriate medical treatment was available because there was the *potential* for milieu therapy to benefit the patient (para.35). Judge Jacobs added to his analysis of this issue in *Devon Partnerships NHS Trust v Secretary of State for Justice* [2010] UKHT 102 (AAC), a case where a patient with an antisocial personality disorder was refusing to engage in treatment. Having referred to the NICE publication "Clinical Guidance No.77 on Antisocial Personality Disorder: Treatment Management and Prevention", which states that people "with antisocial personality disorder should have the opportunity to make informed decisions about their care and treatment, in partnership with healthcare professionals", his Honour said at paras 32 to 34:

"This presents a problem when patients refuse to engage in treatment. Some may argue that there is no treatment available. Whether or not they adopt this tactic, Dr Parker [, the patient's responsible clinician,] told the tribunal that historically patients who are not discharged by a tribunal thereafter accept treatment.

This presents a danger for tribunals. It arises from the way that medical treatment is defined in s.145. That definition is sufficiently broad to include attempts by nursing staff to encourage the patient to engage by taking what the NICE Guidance calls 'a positive and rewarding approach [which] is more likely to be successful than a punitive approach in engaging and retaining people in treatment.' This is not difficult to satisfy. That produces the danger that a patient for whom no appropriate treatment is available may be contained for public safety rather than detained for treatment. The solution lies in the tribunal's duty to ensure that the conditions for continued detention are satisfied. The tribunal must investigate behind assertions, generalisations and standard phrases. By focusing on specific questions, it will ensure that it makes an individualised assessment for the particular patient. What precisely is the treatment that can be provided? What discernible benefit may it have on this patient? Is that benefit related to the patient's mental disorder or to some unrelated problem? Is the patient truly resistant to engagement? The tribunal's reasons then need only reflect what it did in the inquisitorial and decision-making stages."

In this case, the tribunal merely recorded: 'We accept the opinion of Dr Parker that continued treatment in hospital provides alleviation or prevention of a deterioration in his condition. Appropriate medical treatment is available on C Ward with the hope that he will begin to engage in treatment.' That is too general to deal with the issue and it ignores evidence to the contrary. It begged the question of whether the patient could be persuaded to engage."

In *R.(on the application of DK) v Secretary of State for the Home Department* [2010] EWHC 82 (Admin); [2010] M.H.L.R. 64, para.7, Collins J. doubted whether a patient's deliberate decision not to co-operate with available treatment was, of itself, a proper basis for the conclusion made by the tribunal that a condition was not treatable for the purposes of the repealed para.(b); also see *R. v Canons Park Mental Health Review Tribunal, ex p.A* [1994] 2 All E.R. 659, 679, CA where Roch L.J. said in relation to the repealed treatability test: "Parliament could not have intended that a patient should be deemed untreatable simply because the patient withheld co-operation".

Even if the treatment is both "appropriate" and "available", it must also satisfy the necessity test set out in para.(c).

The recommending doctors must state on either Form A7 or A8 in which hospital(s) the appropriate treatment will be available to the patient. If the hospital named by both doctors is not the hospital that accepts the application, the application is fundamentally defective and incapable of rectification under s.15.

MEDICAL TREATMENT. This is given a very wide definition in s.145. It could include nursing or care in an appropriate environment under the supervision of an approved clinician.

IS AVAILABLE TO HIM. Some appropriate treatment must be available to the patient on admission. This test would be satisfied even though the patient was indicating a refusal to accept the available treatment.

The *Code of Practice* is misleading when it implies, at para.6.9, that more than one appropriate treatment has to be available for the test is to be satisfied.

*Subsection (3)*
See the notes to s.2(3).                                                  **1–058**

WRITTEN RECOMMENDATIONS. If an application to hospital A is not accepted due to the lack of a hospital bed, the recommendations can be used to support an application to hospital B as long as the recommendations state that appropriate treatment for the patient is available at that hospital.

*Subsection (4)*
NATURE AND DEGREE. See the note on "of a nature or degree", above.         **1–059**

ALL OTHER CIRCUMSTANCES. "All the patient's circumstances must be looked at, including their age and gender, where they live, where their family and social contacts are, and their cultural background" (*Hansard*, HL Vol.688, col.320, per the Minister of State).

## Admission for assessment in cases of emergency

**4.**—(1) In any case of urgent necessity, an application for admission for assess- **1–060** ment may be made in respect of a patient in accordance with the following provisions of this section, and any application so made is in this Act referred to as "an emergency application".

(2) An emergency application may be made either by an [approved mental health professional] or by the nearest relative of the patient; and every such application shall include a statement that it is of urgent necessity for the patient to be admitted and detained under section 2 above, and that compliance with the provisions of this Part of this Act relating to applications under that section would involve undesirable delay.

(3) An emergency application shall be sufficient in the first instance if founded on one of the medical recommendations required by section 2 above, given, if practicable, by a practitioner who has previous acquaintance with the patient and otherwise complying with the requirements of section 12 below so far as applicable to a single recommendation, and verifying the statement referred to in subsection (2) above.

(4) An emergency application shall cease to have effect on the expiration of a period of 72 hours from the time when the patient is admitted to the hospital unless—

(a) the second medical recommendation required by section 2 above is given and received by the managers within that period; and

(b) that recommendation and the recommendation referred to in subsection (3) above together comply with all the requirements of section 12 below (other than the requirement as to the time of signature of the second recommendation).

(5) In relation to an emergency application, section 11 below shall have effect as if in subsection (5) of that section for the words "the period of 14 days ending with the date of the application" there were substituted the words "the previous 24 hours".

AMENDMENT

The words in square brackets in subs.(1) were substituted by the Mental Health Act 2007 s.21, Sch.2 para.2.

DEFINITIONS

**1–061**    application for admission for assessment: ss.2, 145(1).
patient: s.145(1).
approved mental health professional: s.145(1) (1AC).
nearest relative: ss.26(3), 145(1).
hospital: ss.34(2), 145(1).

GENERAL NOTE

**1–062**    This section provides, in a case of urgent necessity, for the compulsory admission of a person to hospital for assessment for a period of up to 72 hours. The Royal Commission expected the equivalent procedure in the 1959 Act to be used only in exceptional circumstances: "It is important that the emergency procedure should not be used except in real emergencies when action to remove the patient must be taken before there is time to obtain the two medical recommendations required under the normal procedure [i.e. admission under s.2]" (Cmnd. 169, para.409). The emergency procedure was used far more frequently than the Royal Commission envisaged, and it became the most widely used form of compulsory admission. This situation caused concern and in 1966, the Ministry of Health instituted an inquiry to try and establish why the procedure was being used so frequently. That inquiry found, inter alia, that, (1) many medical and social work professionals were largely ignorant of the relevant legislative provisions; (2) those involved in compulsory admissions considered that the emergency procedure, being quicker, easier and of shorter duration than the normal procedure, was a more humane method of admitting formally; and (3) the emergency procedure was administratively more convenient than the normal procedure. In 1974 the Hospital Advisory Service added its voice to the disquiet that was being expressed about the emergency procedure, and in 1976 the Royal College of Psychiatrists said that the advantages of the emergency procedure had "led to misuse and abuse in some areas".

Most of the criticism of the emergency procedure has been based upon the frequency of its use but, as Philip Bean has pointed out, one cannot say that the emergency procedure is being misused because there is a high percentage of admissions under this procedure because "it may be that the high percentage of admissions reflects a psychiatric reality, i.e. that there are a large number of emergencies which required short-term admissions" (*Compulsory Admissions to Mental Hospitals*, 1980, p.69). However, the existence of large regional variations in the use of the emergency procedure does suggest that it had been used inappropriately on many occasions.

Pressure from the Mental Health Act Commission was largely responsible for a decrease in both the number and proportion of applications under this section. Such pressure has, on occasions, led to situations where applications under this section have not been made in circumstances where the criteria set out in subs.(2) of this section have been satisfied. This section should be invoked in a psychiatric emergency where the patient's urgent need for treatment outweighs the desirability of waiting for a medical examination by a second doctor.

An application under this section cannot be renewed at the end of the 72 hour period. If compulsory detention is to be continued the application must either be "converted" into a s.2 application under the provisions of subs.(4), in which case the patient can be detained for 28 days beginning with the date of his admission under this section, or an application for treatment should be made under s.3. This Act does not contain a procedure under which a s.4 application can be converted into a s.3 application by the addition of a second medical recommendation as the criteria for admission under each section are different.

As the nearest relative of a detained patient has to give not less than 72 hours' notice of his or her intention to discharge the patient (s.25), only the responsible clinician (RC) and the hospital managers have the power to order the discharge of a patient detained under this section (see s.23).

Patients admitted under this section are *not* subject to the consent to treatment provisions contained in Pt IV of this Act (s.56(3)(a)). If the patient is mentally capable of making a decision about treatment, the common law enables him or her to refuse to be treated for either a physical or mental disorder. However, if the patient is assessed as being mentally incapable of making a decision about treatment, the treatment can be provided under ss.5 and 6 of the Mental Capacity Act 2005 if it is deemed to be in his or her best interests.

*Applications to the First-tier Tribunal (Mental Health) or the Mental Health Review Tribunal for Wales*
The patient may make an application, but if the second medical recommendation pro- **1–063** vided for in subs.(4) is not forthcoming it will lapse (s.66(1)(a), (2)(a)).

*Code of Practice*
Guidance on the making of applications under this section is contained in Ch.5. The **1–064** factors identified at para.5.6 of the *Code* do not have to be present if the patient's urgent need for hospitalisation outweighs the desirability of obtaining a second medical recommendation.

*Subsection (1)*
APPLICATION. An approved mental health professional (AMHP) should have regard to **1–065** any wishes expressed by relatives of the patient before making an application (s.13(1)). The applicant must use Form A9 (for NRs) or Form A10 (for AMHPs) (in Wales, Form HO9 (for NRs) or Form HO10 (for AMHPs)): see reg.4(1) of the English and Welsh Regulations. The applicant must have seen the patient within the previous 24 hours (s.11(5)) and the patient must be admitted to hospital within 24 hours beginning from the time when he was medically examined or when the application was made, whichever is the earlier (s.6(1)(b)). These time limits were introduced by the 1982 Act to help "to prevent [this section] being used for cases other than those of real emergency" (Cmnd. 7320, para.2.6). Although an AMHP applicant is not required to consult with the patient's nearest relative prior to the application being made, it is submitted that the duty of the AMHP under s.11(3) to inform the nearest relative of an application under s.2 is triggered if the application is "converted" to a s.2 application under the provisions of subs.(4). An application for the admission of a ward of court cannot be made without the leave of the High Court (s.33(1)).

The effect of an application made under this section is set out in s.6.

*Subsection (2)*

**1–066**     APPROVED MENTAL HEALTH PROFESSIONAL.   An AMHP applicant must comply with the requirements of s.13.

URGENT NECESSITY . . . UNDESIRABLE DELAY.   The use of this section should be confined to cases of real emergency where the delay that would be caused by waiting for a second medical opinion would be undesirable because of the patient's urgent need for medical treatment in a hospital.

If a patient who has been detained in a general hospital under s.5(2) needs to be transferred to a psychiatric hospital urgently, an application under this section can be made if the criteria in this subsection are satisfied. The statement made by the Mental Health Act Commission in para.3 of its Guidance Note "Use of the Mental Health Act 1983 in general hospitals without a psychiatric unit" (March, 2001) that this section "cannot be used in the case of in-patients" is not correct (see s.5(1)).

The delay involved in obtaining a second medical recommendation could depend, inter alia, on local geography, the administrative procedures adopted locally to respond to crises, or on the hour at which the crisis occurs. If an AMHP is unable to persuade a doctor approved under s.12 to visit the patient with a view to making an application under s.2, an application under this section should not automatically follow as the AMHP would need to be satisfied that it is "necessary or proper" for the application to be made (s.13(1)). If AMHPs consider that they are being forced to make inappropriate use of this section because of difficulties in obtaining the second medical recommendation required by s.2, they should try to resolve the difficulty at local level or, if this turns out to be unproductive, inform the Care Quality Commission or the Welsh Ministers who are required to keep this Act under review (s.120(1)).

It is difficult to envisage a nearest relative applicant being aware of the distinction between an application made under this section and an application made under s.2.

*Subsection (3)*

**1–067**     ONE OF THE MEDICAL RECOMMENDATIONS.   Which must be completed on Form A11 (in Wales, Form HO11): see reg.4(1) of the English and Welsh Regulations. A medical recommendation provided under this section cannot be used to support a subsequent application made under s.3.

IF PRACTICABLE.   The applicant should ascertain whether it is practicable to involve a doctor who has prior knowledge of the patient. There is no legal requirement for the recommending doctor to be approved under s.12.

*Subsection (4)*

**1–068**     PERIOD OF 72 HOURS.   If the application is "converted" into a s.2 application under this subsection, the 28 days period provided for in s.2 will run from the time of the patient's admission to hospital under this section. An AMHP or a nearest relative applicant should not complete an application form for an admission under s.2 if a "conversion" is effected.

SECOND MEDICAL RECOMMENDATION . . . IS GIVEN.   An appropriate second doctor should examine the patient as soon as possible after admission, to decide whether the patient should be detained under s.2. If a second medical recommendation is given, a record should be made in Part 2 of Form H3 (in Wales, Form HO14). If it is decided that the patient should not be detained under s.2, this does not have the effect of automatically discharging the section as a discharge prior to the expiration of the 72 hours can only be effected by a decision to discharge under s.23 being made by either the patient's responsible clinician or the hospital managers.

HOSPITAL.   Local social services authorities must be informed of those hospitals where arrangements are in force for the reception, in cases of special urgency, of patients requiring treatment for mental disorder (s.140).

## Application in respect of patient already in hospital

**5.**—(1) An application for the admission of a patient to a hospital may be made **1–069** under this Part of this Act notwithstanding that the patient is already an in-patient in that hospital or, in the case of an application for admission for treatment that the patient is for the time being liable to be detained in the hospital in pursuance of an application for admission for assessment; and where an application is so made the patient shall be treated for the purposes of this Part of this Act as if he had been admitted to the hospital at the time when that application was received by the managers.

(2) If, in the case of a patient who is an in-patient in a hospital, it appears to the registered medical practitioner [or approved clinician] in charge of the treatment of the patient that an application ought to be made under this Part of this Act for the admission of the patient to hospital, he may furnish to the managers a report in writing to that effect; and in any such case the patient may be detained in the hospital for a period of 72 hours from the time when the report is so furnished.

[(3) The registered medical practitioner or approved clinician in charge of the treatment of a patient in a hospital may nominate one (but not more than one) person to act for him under subsection (2) above in his absence.

(3A) For the purposes of subsection (3) above—

(a)  the registered medical practitioner may nominate another registered medical practitioner, or an approved clinician, on the staff of the hospital; and

(b)  the approved clinician may nominate another approved clinician, or a registered medical practitioner, on the staff of the hospital.]

(4) If, in the case of a patient who is receiving treatment for mental disorder as an in-patient in a hospital, it appears to a nurse of the prescribed class—

(a)  that the patient is suffering from mental disorder to such a degree that it is necessary for his health or safety or for the protection of others for him to be immediately restrained from leaving the hospital; and

(b)  that it is not practicable to secure the immediate attendance of a practitioner [or clinician] for the purpose of furnishing a report under subsection (2) above,

the nurse may record that fact in writing; and in that event the patient may be detained in the hospital for a period of six hours from the time when that fact is so recorded or until the earlier arrival at the place where the patient is detained of a practitioner [or clinician] having power to furnish a report under that subsection.

(5) A record made under subsection (4) above shall be delivered by the nurse (or by a person authorised by the nurse in that behalf) to the managers of the hospital as soon as possible after it is made; and where a record is made under that subsection the period mentioned in subsection (2) above shall begin at the time when it is made.

(6) The reference in subsection (1) above to an in-patient does not include an in-patient who is liable to be detained in pursuance of an application under this Part of this Act [or a community patient] and the references in subsections (2) and (4) above do not include an in-patient who is liable to be detained in a hospital under this Part of this Act [or a community patient].

(7) In subsection (4) above "prescribed" means prescribed by an order made by the Secretary of State.

AMENDMENT

The amendments to this section were made by the Mental Health Act 2007 ss.9(2), 32, Sch.3 para.2.

DEFINITIONS

**1–070**   patient: s.145(1).
hospital: ss.34(2), 145(1).
application for admission for treatment: ss.3, 145(1).
application for admission for assessment: ss.2, 145(1).
the managers: s.145(1).
mental disorder: s.145(1).
approved clinician: s.145(1).
community patient: ss.17A(7), 145(1).

GENERAL NOTE

**1–071**   This section provides for applications for compulsory detention under s.2 or 3 of this Act to be made in respect of mentally disordered patients who are already receiving treatment in hospital as informal patients. It also sets out the procedures, the "holding powers", that can be used if it is considered that an informal patient (except a community patient (subs.(6)) might leave the hospital before there is time to complete an application under either s.2 or s.3.

Patients who are detained under the provisions of subs.(2) or (4) of this section are not subject to the consent to treatment provisions contained in Pt IV of this Act (s.56(3)(b)). If the patient is mentally capable of making a decision about treatment, the common law enables him or her to refuse to be treated for either a physical or mental disorder. However, if the patient is assessed as being mentally incapable of making a decision about treatment, the treatment can be provided under ss.5 and 6 of the Mental Capacity Act 2005 if it is deemed to be in his or her best interests.

A person who has been detained under either subs.(2) or subs.(4) may be retaken if he absents himself from the hospital without leave as long as the 72 hour or six-hour period has not expired (s.18(5)).

An account of further powers that are available to restrain and/or detain mentally disordered persons is contained in Appendix A.

*Code of Practice*

**1–072**   Guidance on the use of the "holding powers" set out in this section is contained in Ch.12. The use of restraint is considered in Ch.15.

*Human Rights Act 1998*

**1–073**   The powers contained in subss.(2) and (4) of this section do not violate the European Convention on Human Rights because the procedural safeguards established under Convention case law do not apply to emergency situations (*Winterwerp v Netherlands* (1979) 2 E.H.R.R. 387, para.39). The use by staff of common law powers to detain and control patients in emergency situations whilst awaiting the presence of either a doctor or a specialist nurse who has the power to act under either subss.(2) or (4) of this section is also allowable under Convention law. However, such powers should only be used as a "safety net" to cover situations were it is not possible to immediately invoke the statutory powers. In other words, to be consistent with the Convention, common law powers should not be used as an alternative to the powers contained in this Act.

Doctors and nurses who use the holding powers contained in this section are exercising "functions of a public nature" and are therefore "public authorities" for the purposes of s.6 of the 1998 Act (s.6(3)(b)).

*Subsection (1)*

IN-PATIENT. The combined effect of this subsection and subs.(6) is that:  **1–074**

   (i)  an application for compulsory admission to hospital under this Part can be made in respect of an informal patient notwithstanding that he or she is already an in-patient in hospital;

  (ii)  an application for compulsory admission cannot be made in respect of community patients or patients who are already in hospital under compulsory powers except that an application for admission for treatment under s.3 can be made in respect of a patient detained under an application for assessment under s.2; and

 (iii)  where an application is made in respect of a patient who is already in hospital, it is treated for the purposes of this Part as if the patient were admitted to the hospital at the time when that application was received by the managers.

*Subsection (2)*

This subsection enables an informal patient (except a community patient (subs.(6)) to be  **1–075** detained for up to 72 hours if the doctor or approved clinician (AC) who is in charge of the patient's treatment reports that an application under s.2 or 3 ought to be made. It cannot be used to prolong the detention of a patient where the authority to detain is about to expire (subs.(6)) or to provide time for an application to be made to the county court pursuant to s.29(4) to displace a nearest relative after the expiration of the 28-day period of detention provided for under s.2 (*McDougall v Sefton Area Health Authority*, April 9, 1987, McNeill J., cited in L. Gostin, *Mental Health Services—Law and Practice*, 1986, at para.10.04). The Mental Health Act Commission reported that it advised a NHS trust "that consecutive applications of s.5(2) are uncommon and hardly every necessary if assessments are carried out promptly" (*Seventh Biennial Report*, 1995–1997, para.3.2). It is submitted that, following the decision in *R. v Wilson Ex p. Williamson* (noted in the General Note to s.2), this practice is unlawful.

The purpose of this holding power is to prevent a patient from discharging himself from hospital before there is time to arrange for an application under s.2 or s.3 to be made. The patient need not have been admitted to the hospital for treatment for a mental disorder. As soon as the power is invoked, arrangements should be made for the patient to be assessed by a potential applicant and potential recommending doctors.

In its *Second Biennial Report* 1985–87, the MHAC said, at para.17.4, that it viewed an application under s.4 as being "inappropriate following use of s.5(2)." In its *Third Biennial Report* 1987–89, the MHAC, at para.14.5, revised its view to the extent that it regarded the use of s.4 in such circumstances as being "inappropriate in most cases". An application under s.4 would be appropriate if the patient who had been detained under s.5(2) needed to be transferred urgently under s.17 to a different hospital: see the note on "urgent necessity ... undesirable delay" in s.4(2).

The "Inquiry into the Care and Treatment of Gilbert Kopernik-Steckel" recommended that the Mental Health Act Commission should produce advice on the use of statements in a patient's file such as "For section 5(2) if he tries to leave", instructions from one clinician to another which were considered by many medical and nursing staff to override professional judgment. Although statements which fetter the discretion of the section 5(2) clinician should be avoided, there is nothing objectionable in the doctor or AC who is in charge of the patient's treatment making a record to the effect that "section 5(2) should be considered if the patient makes an attempt to leave"; also see para.12.17 of the *Code of Practice*.

In his investigation into Case No.E.1161/01–02, the Health Service Ombudsman recommended that the NHS trust implement an advisory statement about what should happen in the event of a voluntary patient taking steps to leave to leave hospital and that this statement is unlawful for the use of the "NTLW" (Not To Leave the Ward) acronym. The Ombudsman said that the existence of such an advisory statement should be made transparent to patients and their consent to its provisions obtained. The Ombudsman did not comment on the consequences of a patient's failure to consent.

There is no procedure for discharging the patient from the holding power. The power will automatically lapse if:

(i) the result of the assessment is a decision not to make an application under s.2 or 3; or

(ii) the power is invoked by a doctor or an AC who has been nominated under subs.(3) and the clinician in charge of the patient's treatment subsequently decides that no assessment for possible detention needs to be carried out, or

(iii) an application under s.2 or 3 is made; or

(iv) the patient is discharged from the hospital before an assessment can be undertaken, e.g. the patient's violent conduct results in an arrest and removal to police custody.

If an approved mental health professional concludes at the assessment that an application in respect of the patient is not required and the assessing doctor holds a contrary view, there is nothing in this provision that prevents the assessment from being prolonged to enable the patient's nearest relative to consider whether he or she wishes to make an application.

Where this power has been invoked by the doctor or AC nominated under subs.(3), there is no need to involve a potential applicant in the assessment if the clinician in charge of the patient's treatment subsequently examines the patient and concludes that an application should not be made.

The Mental Health Act Commission:

"found instances where section 5(2) appears either to be used simply as a three day holding power, or lasts three days by default because the clinician in charge of the patient's treatment has not informed the records officer as soon as a decision is taken not to proceed with assessment for compulsory detention or because the assessment process is not begun as soon as the section 5(2) is implemented."

This finding led the MHAC to recommend that "a record be kept of the date and time of both beginning and end of the holding power under section 5(2)" (*Fifth Biennial Report 1991–1993*, para.3.5(e)).

**1–076**  IN-PATIENT IN A HOSPITAL. The patient could be receiving treatment in a general hospital for a physical condition: see the note on "medical practitioner or approved clinician in charge", below. An in-patient does not include someone who is already liable to be detained or who is a community patient (subs.(6)), but could include a patient who is in hospital by virtue of a deprivation of liberty authorisation granted under Sch.A1 of the Mental Capacity Act 2005.

A patient who is being treated in an out-patient department, in a day hospital or as a day patient cannot be detained under this provision. The second edition of the *Code of Practice* at para.8.4 offered the following definition of "in-patient": "one who has understood and accepted the offer of a bed, and who has freely appeared on the ward and who has co-operated in the admission procedure". In *R. (on the application of DR) v Mersey Care NHS Trust* [2002] EWHC (Admin); [2002] M.H.L.R. 386 para.27, Wilson J. said that the word in-patient "suggests the allocation and use of a hospital bed". His Lordship made no reference in his judgment to the *Code of Practice* definition. In reality there is little difference between the approach adopted by Wilson J. and the *Code of Practice* in that when a patient has accepted the offer of a bed it is available for his or her use. A suggested definition of a mentally incapable informal in-patient is: a compliant patient who has arrived at the ward and who has not provided any evidence of resistance (either verbal or physical) to the admission procedure. In both cases, the availability of a bed for the patient is a precondition to attaining in-patient status. The current edition of the *Code of Practice* considers this issue at paras.12.6 and 12.7.

As the power contained in this subsection only applies if the patient is an informal in-patient, it is necessary to identify how a patient can divest himself of his in-patient status. Can, for example, an in-patient avoid being held under this provision by the simple expedient of saying to the doctor who is about to invoke the power, "I discharge myself?". It is highly unlikely that the courts would find that a patient could end his in-patient status in this manner as such a finding would have the effect of totally subverting Parliament's intention in enacting this provision. It is submitted that a patient does not lose his in-patient status until he has physically removed himself from the hospital. This approach was endorsed by the Court of Appeal, Northern Ireland in *Re McGee* [2007] NICA 38; [2008] M.H.L.R. 216, where it was held that a patient did not cease to be an in-patient for the purposes of the equivalent provision in the Northern Irish legislation when he expressed his desire to leave the hospital an hour after being told of the decision of the tribunal to discharge him from detention. Girvan L.J. said at para.12: "He did not physically remove himself from the hospital [and his] bed was still available to him."

In *R. v Wilson Ex p. Williamson* [1996] C.O.D. 42, the court declared that the patient's detention under s.2 of this Act was unlawful. Counsel for the hospital managers stated that s.5(2) would not be available following the court's decision because it was "designed for the patient who had been a voluntary patient" and that to use the provision in respect of a patient who had been detained in the hospital unlawfully would be to "take advantage of unlawful status" and would make the hospital managers vulnerable to judicial review on the ground that they were "using it for improper purposes". Although counsel's points have some substance, the correctness of his opinion must be doubted because a patient who has been unlawfully detained is clearly an "in-patient" if he has been admitted to the hospital, and it surely cannot be "improper" for the patient's consultant to utilise the only provision that is available to him or her to prevent a patient, who might have been diagnosed as being either dangerous or suicidal, from being discharged from the hospital. In *R. v Birmingham Mental Health Trust Ex p. Phillips*, May 25, 1995 the fact that the patient had been made the subject of this provision immediately after it was discovered that the application under s.2 that had been made in respect of her was invalid was accepted by Tucker J. without comment. However, the use of s.5(2) in this situation would only be lawful if the invalid section had been discharged by either the hospital managers or the patient's RC: see subs.(6) and the General Note to s.15.

MEDICAL PRACTITIONER OR APPROVED CLINICIAN IN CHARGE. Who should only exercise **1–077** the power after having personally examined the patient (*Code of Practice*, para.12.9). For the identity of the person "in charge" of the patient's medical treatment, see paras 12.3 and 12.4 of the *Code*.

If a patient is receiving out-patient treatment for his or her mental disorder at the time of admission to a general hospital for treatment for a physical disorder, it is submitted that the clinician in charge of the patient's treatment for mental disorder has the power to invoke this provision if he or she happens to be on the hospital site when the crisis occurs.

AN APPLICATION OUGHT TO BE MADE. Although the most frequent circumstance leading to the use of this power is an attempt by the patient to leave the hospital, this ground enables a patient to be detained in the absence of such behaviour. For example, the patient could be detained in a situation where he or she had recently returned to the hospital after having left contrary to professional advice and the clinician in charge of the patient's treatment believed that it was likely that the patient would absent himself again in the near future.

This power should not be used merely to justify the intervention of staff in an emergency to respond to an informal patient's disturbed behaviour as such intervention can be justified under the powers outlined in Appendix A.

If an application is made under s.2 or s.3 during the 72-hour period, the application will commence from the time when it was accepted by the hospital managers and not from the time when this provision was invoked. The application need not be addressed to the hospital which is holding the patient under this provison.

REPORT.   Using Form H1 (in Wales, Form HO12): see reg.4(1) of the English and Welsh Regulations.

**1–078**   DETAINED IN THE HOSPITAL.   Although this provision is silent on the point, it is submitted that the patient is detained by the hospital managers. If the patient is an in-patient of a hospital which is managed by more than one set of hospital managers, the patient can be detained in any part of the hospital that is managed by the hospital managers of the ward where the patient is an in-patient. There is, it is submitted, no authority to detain the patient in a part of the hospital that is managed by different hospital managers; see further, David Hewitt, "What is a hospital?", *Journal of Mental Health Law* September 2004, pp.111–128.

A patient who is detained under this provision cannot be transferred to another hospital under reg.7 of the English Regulations and reg.23 of the Welsh Regulations because such a person is not "liable to be detained in a hospital by *virtue of an application*" under this Part (see s.19(1)(a), (2)(a)).

If a mentally capable patient who has been detained by this provision needs to be taken to another hospital for urgent treatment or for security reasons, the transfer can be made if the patient consents to it. However the s.5(2) will automatically lapse when the patient is moved from the hospital named on the Form H1 because the holding power only provides authority for the patient to be detained in "the hospital", i.e. the hospital that was providing in-patient treatment to the patient at the time when the Form was signed. Consideration would have to be given to invoking this provision again if the patient made an attempt to leave the other hospital. If the patient does not consent to the transfer and the urgency of the situation is such that there is not sufficient time to comply with the formalities of an application under s.2, an application under s.4 can be made and the transfer effected under s.19. If the patient is mentally incapable, a transfer to another hospital can be made under the authority of the powers contained in ss.5 and 6 of the Mental Capacity Act 2005 or the common law doctrine of necessity if the need for the transfer is so urgent that there is no time for an application under this Act to be made and the transfer is in the patient's best interests. If it proves to be necessary, a proportionate amount of force could be used to effect the transfer. The holding power could be invoked at the other hospital if the patient made an attempt to leave.

72 HOURS.   This is the maximum period during which a patient can be detained. The authority to detain under this provision is not renewable. However, circumstances could arise where a change in the patient's situation could lead to a second use of this provision being contemplated soon after its first use.

If a patient who has been detained under this provision absconds, he or she cannot be retaken once the 72-hour period has expired (s.18(5)).

TIME WHEN THE REPORT IS ... FURNISHED.   In the Scottish case of *Milborrow, Applicant*, 1996 S.C.L.R. 315 Sh. Ct, it was held that a report is "furnished" to the hospital managers when it is committed to the internal mail system operated by those managers. The *Code of Practice*, at para.12.5, adopts this approach. The period of detention therefore starts at that point or when the report is handed over to a member of staff who is authorised to receive it: see Form H1.

If the patient is intent on leaving the hospital immediately, the powers outlined in Appendix A will usually provide authority for the patient to be detained for the short period that is required to complete Form H1. Once Form H1 has been completed and committed to the hospital's internal mail system or handed to the authorised member of staff, the patient can be detained even though he might have left the ward area. However, if the patient has left the hospital before the completion of Form H1, the hospital managers cannot subsequently detain him and return him to hospital on the authority of that form. This is because by leaving hospital the patient relinquishes his in-patient status which is an essential pre-condition to the use of this subsection. As a patient who is not "liable to be detained", he could not be returned to hospital under the auspices of s.18.

*Subsection (3)*

This subsection is aimed at lessening the pressures on clinicians to contravene the provisions of subs.(2) by, for example, allowing persons other than the "medical practitioner or approved clinician in charge" to sign Form H1 or by blank forms being signed for use when emergencies occur. **1–079**

MAY NOMINATE.   Good practice dictates that the nomination should be put in writing and conveyed to all relevant staff. It is the doctor or AC in charge of the patient's treatment and not the hospital managers who must make the nomination. The nominee should be a doctor or AC who has been assessed as having the knowledge and experience that qualifies him or her to perform the onerous task of deciding whether patients should be deprived of their liberty. The doctor or AC in charge of the patient's treatment should only nominate a class of doctors, such as "the duty doctor", if satisfied that all of the doctors who come within that class have received appropriate training on the use of the holding power; see further the *Code of Practice* at para.12.15. The nominated doctor or AC cannot delegate to another because of the legal principle *delegatus non potest delegare*.

Only one doctor or AC may be nominated to act during any particular period. A nomination "to Dr A or, in Dr A's absence, to Dr B" would be unlawful.

ON THE STAFF OF THAT HOSPITAL.   The doctor or AC must be employed or contracted to undertake clinical responsibilities at the hospital. A medical practitioner nominee must be a fully registered person within the meaning of the Medical Act 1983 (Interpretation Act 1978, Sch.1).

TO ACT FOR HIM.   The nominated clinician should exercise his or her own judgment when exercising the power under subs.(2). He or she can be advised, but not required to consult with a senior colleague before exercising the power.

*Subsection (3A)*

For the purpose of making a nomination under subs.(3), a doctor who is in charge of the patient's treatment can nominate either another doctor or an AC (who need not be a doctor), while an AC who is in charge of the patient's treatment can nominate either another AC or a doctor. **1–080**

*Subsection (4)*

This subsection provides for nurses of a prescribed class (see subs.(7)) to invoke a "holding power" in respect of an informal patient (except a community patient (subs.(6)) for a period of not more than six hours by completing Form A2 (in Wales, Form HO13). During this period the "medical practitioner or approved clinician in charge" or his or her nominated deputy should examine the patient with a view to making a report under subs.(2). A nurse invoking this provision is entitled to use the minimum force necessary to prevent the patient from leaving hospital. It can only be used in respect of patients who are receiving hospital treatment for mental disorder. It is not sufficient for the patient to be merely suffering from a mental disorder. Although this power can be invoked in any hospital where **1–081** the patient is receiving treatment for mental disorder, it is unlikely that a non-psychiatric ward will be staffed with nurses of the "prescribed class". In an emergency, a nurse who is not of the prescribed class, may use the powers set out in Appendix A to restrain a patient who might be a danger to self or others from leaving hospital until a practitioner who has the power to invoke either this provision or subs.(2) attends.

NURSE. Exercising the holding power is the personal decision of the nurse who cannot be instructed to exercise it by anyone else.

DEGREE. The patient cannot be made subject to this power if he or she is not exhibiting any manifestations of mental disorder: see the note on "of a nature or degree" in s.3(2)(a).

IMMEDIATELY RESTRAINED FROM LEAVING THE HOSPITAL. The power to detain the patient takes effect at the time when the nurse makes his or her report. It can only be used if the patient is indicating either verbally or otherwise that he or she wishes to leave the hospital. Where a patient requires restraint but is not showing any inclination to leave the hospital, nurses have to rely on the powers outlined in Appendix A.

IMMEDIATE ATTENDANCE OF A PRACTITIONER. It is submitted that the nurses' holding power need not be invoked if either the clinician who is in charge of the patient's treatment or his or her nominee is in the hospital building and can attend at the ward within a few minutes of the crises occurring. A combination of the powers outlined in Appendix A and the legal maxim de minimis non curat lex (the law does not take account of trifles) would enable the patient to be held during this brief period.

DETAINED IN THE HOSPITAL. See the note on subs.(2).

SIX HOURS. This is the maximum and non-renewable period during which a patient can be detained. If a patient who has been detained under this provision absconds, he or she cannot be retaken once the six hour period has elapsed (s.18(5)).

FROM THE TIME WHEN THAT FACT IS SO RECORDED. On Form H2 or, in Wales, HO13. Although neither Form requires the nurse to give reasons for invoking the power, the *Code of Practice*, at para.12.31, states that these should be recorded in the patient's notes. The record should be made immediately after the nurse has decided to exercise the power. The power will end six hours later or on the earlier arrival of one of the clinicians entitled to make a report under subs.(2). If a decision is made not to exercise the powers under subs.(2), the patient can either leave the hospital or remain as an informal patient.

*Subsection (5)*

**1–082**  This subsection provides that where the "holding power" provided for in subs.(4) is followed by a report made under subs.(2), the period of 72 hours provided for in subs.(2) runs from the time when the record required by subs.(4) is made.

*Subsection (7)*

**1–083**  PRESCRIBED. Regulation 2(1) of the Mental Health (Nurses) (England) Order 2008 (SI 2008/1207) states that for the purposes of this provision a "nurse of the prescribed class is a nurse registered in either Sub-Part 1 or 2 of the register maintained under article 5 of the Nursing and Midwifery Order 2001, whose registration includes an entry specified in paragraph (2).

(2) An entry in the register referred to in paragraph (1) is an entry indicating that the nurses field of practice is either—

(a) mental health nursing, or
(b) learning disabilities nursing."

SECRETARY OF STATE. The functions of the Minister, so far as exercisable in relation to Wales, are exercised by the Welsh Ministers (see the General Note to this Act) who have made a similar order: see SI 2008/2441 (W.214).

### Effect of application for admission

**6.**—(1) An application for the admission of a patient to a hospital under this **1–084** Part of this Act, duly completed in accordance with the provisions of this Part of this Act, shall be sufficient authority for the applicant, or any person authorised by the applicant, to take the patient and convey him to the hospital at any time within the following period, that is to say—

(a) in the case of an application other than an emergency application, the period of 14 days beginning with the date on which the patient was last examined by a registered medical practitioner before giving a medical recommendation for the purposes of the application;

(b) in the case of an emergency application, the period of 24 hours beginning at the time when the patient was examined by the practitioner giving the medical recommendation which is referred to in s.4(3) above, or at the time when the application is made, whichever is the earlier.

(2) Where a patient is admitted within the said period to the hospital specified in such an application as is mentioned in subs.(1) above, or, being within that hospital, is treated by virtue of s.5 above as if he had been so admitted, the application shall be sufficient authority for the managers to detain the patient in the hospital in accordance with the provisions of this Act.

(3) Any application for the admission of a patient under this Part of this Act which appears to be duly made and to be founded on the necessary medical recommendations may be acted upon without further proof of the signature or qualification of the person by whom the application or any such medical recommendation is made or given or of any matter of fact or opinion stated in it.

(4) Where a patient is admitted to a hospital in pursuance of an application for admission for treatment, any previous application under this Part of this Act by virtue of which he was liable to be detained in a hospital or subject to guardianship shall cease to have effect.

DEFINITIONS
    patient: s.145(1).                                           **1–085**
    hospital: ss.34(2), 145(1).
    the managers: s.145(1).
    application for admission for treatment: ss.3, 145(1).

GENERAL NOTE
    This section authorises the applicant or anyone authorised by him or her to take and con- **1–086** vey the patient to hospital within specified periods, and authorises the hospital managers to detain the patient once he or she has been admitted. It also enables the hospital managers to act on statutory documents that appear to be valid and provides for the termination of existing applications subsequent to a patient's admission for treatment under s.3. The courts have held that the power to detain necessarily carries with it a power of control: see the note on "to detain the patient" in subs.(2).

    A duly completed application provides authority for the patient to be taken to the hospital named in the application (subs.(1)) and detained there (subs.(2)). Either ss.17 or 19 of this Act will have to be used if the patient needs to be treated in another hospital.

    The fact that a patient is detained under this Act does not provide the patient's responsible clinician (RC) with the power to demand that the Health Authority gives priority to the care of that patient: see *R. (on the application of F) v Oxfordshire Mental Health Healthcare NHS Trust and Oxfordshire NHS Health Authority*, noted under s.34(1).

The legality of a patient's detention in circumstances where the requirements of this Act relating to applications have not been fulfilled is considered in the following passage from the judgment of Laws J. in *R. v Managers of South Western Hospital Ex p. M* [1994] 1 All E.R. 161 at 176:

"Section 6(1) and (2) confer authority to convey or detain the patient in hospital where the application is 'duly completed in accordance with the provisions of this Part of this Act.' In my judgment this is an objective requirement and means that the application must not only *state* that the relevant provisions (which include the requirements of section 11(4)) have been fulfilled, but also that it be the case that they have actually been fulfilled. Here they were not; section 11(4) was not complied with. It follows, in my judgment, that the managers were not authorised to detain the applicant unless they were entitled to act upon [the approved mental health professional's] application by virtue of section 6(3). The contrast between section 6(1) and section 6(3) is of course between the words 'duly completed' and 'appears to be made.' In my judgment, where an application on its face sets out all the facts which, if true, constitute compliance with the relevant provisions of Part 2 of the Act (again, including section 11(4)) it is an application which 'appears to be duly made' within section 6(3). If any of the facts thus stated are not true, then although the application *appears* to be duly made, it is not duly completed for the purposes of section 6(1) and 6(2). Here, [the approved mental health professional's] application did state all the facts which, if true, constituted compliance with the relevant statutory provisions. Accordingly it was an application which appeared to be duly made. It follows that, although the managers were not authorised to detain the patient by section 6(2) standing alone, they were entitled to act upon the application, and thus to detain the patient, by virtue of section 6(3). Accordingly, the applicant's detention is not unlawful."

In *Re S-C (Mental Patient: Habeas Corpus)* [1996] 1 All E.R. 532, CA, Sir Thomas Bingham M.R. said, at 542, 543, that he:

"would accept almost everything in [the passage quoted above] as correct with the exception of the last sentence. The judge goes straight from a finding that the hospital managers were entitled to act upon an apparently valid application to the conclusion that the applicant's detention was therefore not unlawful. That is, in my judgment, a non sequitur. It is perfectly possible that the hospital managers were entitled to act on an apparently valid application, but that the detention was in fact unlawful. If that were not so the implications would, in my judgment, be horrifying. It would mean that an application which appeared to be in order would render the detention of a citizen lawful even though it was shown or admitted that the [approved mental health professional] purporting to make the application was not an [approved mental health professional], that the registered medical practitioners whose recommendations founded the application were not registered medical practitioners or had not signed the recommendations, and that the [approved mental health professional] had not consulted the patient's nearest relative or had consulted the patient's nearest relative and that relative had objected. In other words, it would mean that the detention was lawful even though every statutory safeguard built into the procedure was shown to have been ignored or violated. Bearing in mind what is at stake, I find that conclusion wholly unacceptable."

The other members of the Court of Appeal agreed with this finding. It should be noted that the decision in *Re S-C* applies to an administrative decision and not to an order of the court (*R. (on the application of A Claimant) v Harrow Crown Court* [2003] EWHC 2020 (Admin), para.24). An irregular order of the court made under this Act is effective and must be obeyed until set aside by the High Court (*South West Yorkshire Mental Health NHS Trust v Bradford Crown Court* [2003] EWHC 640 (Admin)).

In *R. v Central London County Court Ex p. London* [1999] 3 All E.R. 991 CA para.32, Stuart-Smith L.J., in giving the leading judgment, said, obiter, that he understood the Court of Appeal in *Re S-C* to have interpreted the phrase used by Laws J. which they had criticised as meaning that the patient's *continued* detention is not unlawful, rather than the original detention was not unlawful. These observations were followed by Collins J. in *TMM v London Borough of Hackney* [2010] EWHC 1349 (Admin).

In the *London* case, the court said that hospital managers would have acted lawfully in accepting an application that was made subsequent to an order of county court made under s.29 displacing the patient's nearest relative on an interim basis, even if it was subsequently found that the court had no jurisdiction to make the order.

The following propositions can be said to represent the law on this issue:

**1–087**

(i) an application for admission made by an approved mental health professional (AMHP) or a nearest relative setting out all the relevant facts which, if true, constituted compliance with the relevant provisions of this Part of this Act, is an application which "appears to be duly made" for the purposes of subs.(3);

(ii) after having carefully checked (per Neill L.J. in *Re S-C* at 544) the documentation for obvious errors, the hospital managers are entitled to act on the application without further proof of the facts stated therein. In *Re S-C* Sir Thomas Bingham M.R. said at 537:

> "[Section 6] provides protection for a hospital to which a patient is admitted or in which a patient is detained. Such a hospital is not at risk of liability for false imprisonment if it turns out that the [approved mental health professional] does not meet the definition in section 145(1), or if the recommendations which purport to be signed by registered medical practitioners are in truth not signed by such, although appearing to be so. That is obviously good sense. A mental hospital is not obliged to act like a private detective; it can take documents at face value. Provided they appear to conform with the requirements of the statute, the hospital is entitled to act on them."; and

(iii) if, subsequent to having accepted an application, the hospital managers discover that the application is fundamentally defective (e.g. a relative who is not the patient's nearest relative has been consulted under s.11(4)), this has the effect of rendering the continued detention of the patient unlawful. In these circumstances the hospital managers should:

   (a) inform the patient of the situation and of the need for him or her to obtain legal advice;
   (b) make an appropriate note on the patient's file; and
   (c) exercise their power under s.23 to discharge the patient from his liability to be detained. If the patient is not discharged an application for either *habeas corpus* or judicial review could be made: see the General Note to s.65. A report could be issued under s.5(2) or (4) in respect of the patient if the appropriate requirements were satisfied: see the note on "in-patient in a hospital" in s.5(2).

If there is a genuine dispute about whether a provision of this Act has been complied with (e.g. the patient's nearest relative disputes the AMHP's assertion on the application form that the consultation required by s.11(4) took place), the hospital managers should not attempt to resolve the dispute but should leave the patient to consider challenging the detention. In *Re S-C*, above, Turner J., speaking at first instance, said: "There is, in my judgment, no means by which managers can investigate the truth or otherwise of assertions that the form has not been duly made, let alone is there any guidance as to the manner in which they should adjudicate on such issue and come to a conclusion contrary to that which appears on the face of the application form" ([1996] C.O.D. 221). These comments are consistent with the judgments delivered in the Court of Appeal.

A patient who has been lawfully detained cannot through the medium of the tort of false imprisonment complain against the conditions in which he is detained (*R. v Deputy Governor of Parkhurst Prison Ex p. Hague* [1992] 1 A.C. 58). The same principle applies to claims made under art.5 of the European Convention on Human Rights.

*Human Rights Act 1998*

**1–088**   The approach adopted in *Re S-C* to defective applications was implicitly endorsed by the European Court of Human Rights in *Mooren v Germany* (app.no.11364/03), July 9, 2009, where it was held that defects in a detention order did not necessarily render the underlying detention unlawful for the purposes of art.5(1) of the European Convention on Human Rights, unless they amounted to "a gross and obvious irregularity".

*Code of Practice*

**1–089**   The conveyance of the patient to hospital is discussed in Ch.11.

*Subsection (1)*

**1–090**   AN APPLICATION.   Comprises the application form and the medical recommendation form(s).

DULY COMPLETED.   This is an objective requirement. Until the application is duly completed, there is no power in this Act to prevent the patient from leaving the premises where the assessment is taking place.

If, having signed the application form, the AMHP applicant discovers a minor and rectifiable error on one of the medical recommendations and it is not possible to contact the relevant doctor to right the error, it is permissible for the patient to be conveyed to the hospital on the authority of the application and for the error to be rectified within the 14-day period permitted by s.15.

APPLICANT.   Who will be either the patient's nearest relative or an AMHP (ss.4(2), 11(1)). Where the AMHP is the applicant he or she has a professional responsibility for ensuring that all the necessary arrangements are made for the patient to be conveyed to hospital.

ANY PERSON AUTHORISED BY THE APPLICANT.   Such as the police or a member of the ambulance service. The AMHP is not provided with a power to *direct* another person to convey the patient. Where delegation takes place, the AMHP retains ultimate responsibility to ensure that the patient is conveyed in a lawful and humane manner. The delegate can use reasonable force if necessary (*Code of Practice*, paras.11.17, 11.22).

If it is not practicable for the AMHP to attend at the hospital named in the application because it is located far away from the AMHP's home area, the statutory documentation should be handed to the person who has been authorised by the AMHP to convey the patient to the hospital.

TO TAKE THE PATIENT.   If an application is not "duly completed", there is no authority for an AMHP, medical practitioner or authorised person to take the patient to hospital against his or her will. If such persons were asked to leave the patient's home before the application is duly completed they would be trespassers if they remained and the householder would be entitled to use reasonable force in ejecting them: see *Townley v Rushworth*, 62 L.G.R. 95, DC, where an attempt was made to detain a patient on an emergency application before the medical recommendation had been completed. Lord Parker C.J. said at 98:

"Unless it is to be said that a householder is to sit down and submit, not only to his liberty being infringed in his own house, but also to assault by injection, and to his liberty being removed in hospital, I cannot say that to hit out with the fist is an unreasonable use of force."

Professionals would not become trespassers if one co-owner gave them permission to stay, despite the fact that the other co-owner requested that they leave: see the note on "enter and inspect" in s.115.

A duly completed application does not provide authority for the applicant to force entry into the patient's home. If force is required to gain entry after the application has been completed, an application should be made for a warrant under s.135(2).

CONVEY HIM. Either the applicant or the person delegated by the applicant (including ambulance staff) can use such force as is reasonably necessary to achieve the objective of conveying the patient to the hospital named in the application (s.137(2)). If the patient is likely to be violent or dangerous, police assistance should be requested. At common law a policeman may take any reasonable steps necessary to prevent a reasonable anticipated and imminent breach of the peace, or to stop a beach of the peace while it is in progress (the nature of a breach of the peace is considered in Appendix A). A patient who is being conveyed to hospital is deemed to be in legal custody (s.137(1)) and if he escapes he may be retaken within 14 days after the last medical examination for the purposes of a medical recommendation for s.2 or 3 patients, or within 24 hours from the medical examination, or the time when the application was made, whichever is the earlier, for a s.4 patient (s.138).

If a mentally incapable patient requires emergency hospital treatment for a physical disorder and such treatment is deemed to be in the patient's best interests, ss.5 and 6 of the Mental Capacity Act 2005 provide authority for ambulance personnel to use reasonable force to overcome the patient's resistance to being taken to a general hospital for treatment there before being taken to the hospital named in the application. If the patient requires admission to the general hospital, the application should be addressed to that hospital.

TO HOSPITAL. Which will be the hospital named on the application. It is unlawful to convey a patient to hospital on the authority of an application which does not state the name of the potential admitting hospital. It is also unlawful to take the patient to a hospital that is not the hospital named on the application even though the two hospitals are run by the same hospital managers. The named hospital is not under a legal obligation to admit the patient and the duly completed application does not provide authority to convey the patient to another hospital. It is therefore essential for a recommending doctor to have confirmed to the applicant that a bed is available for the patient in the named hospital. Local discussions that take place between local authorities and health bodies about problems concerning the accessing beds for patients who need to be detained under this Act should be influenced by s.82 of the National Health Service Act 2006 which states:

"In exercising their respective functions NHS bodies (on the one hand) and local authorities (on the other) must co-operate with one another in order to secure and advance the health and welfare of people in England and Wales."

In its *Eighth Biennial Report*, 1997–1999, para.4.45, the Mental Health Act Commission suggested that if a patient cannot be admitted to hospital in an emergency for want of a bed "the [AMHP] should complete the application, making it out to a hospital specified to the relevant health authority in the notice required to be given under s.140 of the Act, and convey the patient to that hospital". This advice is subject to the criticism that the managers of the hospital specified in the s.140 notice are not legally obliged to admit the patient and, in any event, it might be clinically inappropriate for the patient to be admitted to that hospital. The action advocated by the MHAC could also place the AMHP applicant in a difficult position in that the application would only provide authority for the patient to be conveyed to, and detained in, the hospital specified in the application. If, subsequent to the refusal by that hospital to admit the patient, another hospital is identified as being willing to admit the patient, a fresh application form would have to be completed which is addressed to the managers of that hospital.

The MHAC returned to this theme in its *Ninth Biennial Report*, 1999–2001 where a "Good Practice Example" is set out at para.2.50. The example states that if no bed is available at the hospital named in the application, the patient can be formally admitted to the hospital by being held in a "holding area" and that if it proves impossible to identify a bed within the hospital, the patient should be granted leave of absence under s.17 to a "temporary bed" in another hospital. While it is perfectly lawful for a patient to be kept in a "waiting" or "holding" area for the short period that is required to prepare a bed that has been allocated to the patient, the practice commended by the MHAC of "admitting" the patient in a situation where no bed has been identified for him is both potentially dangerous and of doubtful legality.

Holding a patient who might be acutely ill in a non-clinical area of a hospital for what might turn out to be a considerable amount of time can be in the interests neither of the patient nor of staff. Assuming that an approved clinician has been found who is willing to become the patient's responsible clinician (RC), it is at the very least extremely bad practice for the risk assessment that must precede a s.17 leave to be conducted in such an environment. It is also difficult to see how the hospital managers can adequately comply with their duties under s.132 of the Act in these circumstances.

The purpose of both ss.2 and 3 is for the patient to be admitted to the hospital named in the application and for him to be "detained there" (ss.2(1), 3(1)), i.e. at the hospital named in the application. To secure this aim one of the responsibilities of the recommending doctor is to ensure that, where there is to be an application for admission, a hospital bed will be available for the patient unless it has been agreed locally that AMHPs will do that (*Code of Practice*, para.4.75). It is arguably unlawful for an AMHP to make an application to detain a patient if it is known that there is no bed available for that patient in the hospital named in the application. In such a situation, can it be said that the patient has been "admitted" to the hospital for the purposes of s.6(2) of the Act if there is no bed to admit him to? If the patient has not been legally "admitted", the hospital managers have no power to detain him and he cannot be granted leave of absence. If a patient can be said to have been "admitted" merely by virtue of being held within the hospital building, he will, by definition, have become an in-patient. This interpretation conflicts with the point at which it is generally considered that a patient achieves in-patient status for the purposes of s.5(2). The 1993 edition of the *Code of Practice* stated, at para.8.4, that such status can only be achieved if the patient appears on the hospital ward to accept an offer of a bed. Even if it could be argued that the patient who is being kept in a "holding area" has been admitted to the hospital, McCullough J. said in *R. v Hallstrom Ex p. W* [1986] Q.B. 1090 that the term "detention" in s.13 "cannot realistically include a purely nominal period before leave of absence is given, after which the treatment which the patient stands in need is to begin". Although the decision in *Hallstrom* was made in the context of a patient who had been granted leave of absence into the community, the finding of McCullough J. is equally applicable to a patient who has been granted immediate leave of absence to another hospital. In both cases, the detention at the hospital named in the application would be a sham. The *Code of Practice* states, at para.4.92, that patients should not be moved unless it is known that the hospital named in the application is willing to accept them. The *Code*, at para.4.99, considers the action to be taken if, on arrival at the hospital named in the application, a bed is no longer available for the patient.

In her speech to the Royal College of Psychiatrist's Annual Meeting at Glasgow in July 2006, the Parliamentary and Health Service Ombudsman, Ann Abraham, spoke of a complaint that her office had investigated which involved the non-availability of a bed for a sectioned patient. The patient, who had been provided with a limited amount of out-patient care, was sectioned at her home but, despite this, her family were told that there were no beds available for her. Faced with this situation, the family agreed to pay for a bed in a private hospital some distance away and the patient was admitted there under s.2. A bed was eventually found in the local psychiatric unit, but it was left for the family to organise a taxi and two private nurses for the transfer. The Ombudsman's investigation found that medical staff had, in fact considered that the patient needed a bed much earlier, but had felt there was little prospect of a bed becoming available and decided to manage her care at home. The complaint was upheld and a recommendation was made that the family be reimbursed.

If the patient requires emergency treatment for a physical injury or disorder he could be taken to and treated in an A. and E. Department under common law powers or, if he was mentally incapacitated, under ss.5 and 6 of the Mental Capacity Act 2005 before being transported to the hospital named in the application. If the patient requires a period of in-patient treatment for a physical injury or disorder, it is likely that a court would find that it would be unlawful for him to be admitted to the psychiatric hospital named in the application and then immediately taken to a general hospital on s.17 leave (*R. v Hallstrom Ex p. W*, above). It is clearly unlawful for the patient to be admitted directly to the general hospital after having been given a "notional" leave of absence from the psychiatric hospital named in the application. If the patient is mentally competent, he could be admitted directly to the general hospital with his agreement and then taken to the psychiatric hospital before the expiry of the 14-day period provided for in para.(a). If the patient is unwilling to be admitted to the general hospital, he could be admitted to that hospital under this Act although any treatment for his physical condition could only proceed with his consent if he had the required mental capacity. In these circumstances, the general hospital would be the hospital named in the application and the patient's RC would be the psychiatrist who is in charge of the treatment of the patient's mental disorder at that hospital. To cater for this situation, it would be advisable for the psychiatric hospital to make a service level agreement with the general hospital for the provision of psychiatric treatment and Mental Health Act administration services at that hospital. To enable the managers of the general hospital to deal appropriately with any application for discharge that such a patient might make, it is suggested that the managers should attempt to appoint the committee that has been established by the managers of the psychiatric hospital to hear such applications to hear applications on their behalf. The Mental Health Act Commission published a guidance note on the "Use of the Mental Health Act 1983 in general hospitals without a psychiatric unit" which can be accessed on the website of the Care Quality Commission.

*Paragraph (a)*

14 DAYS.    This period may be used to test out whether detention is the only alternative **1–091** for the patient: see para.4.87 of the *Code of Practice*.

BEGINNING WITH THE DATE.    Including the date on which the patient was last examined (*Zoan v Rouamba* [2000] 2 All E.R. 620 CA).

LAST EXAMINED BY A REGISTERED MEDICAL PRACTITIONER.    The relevant date is that of the last medical examination and not the day on which the medical recommendation form was signed by the doctor. If the medical practitioners examined the patient separately, not more than five days must have elapsed between the respective examinations (s.12(1)).

The applicant must have seen the patient within the period of 14 days ending with the day of the application (s.11(5)).

*Paragraph (b)*

TIME WHEN THE PATIENT WAS EXAMINED.    Which may not be the same as the time when **1–092** the doctor signed the Form A11.

WHICHEVER IS THE EARLIER. As an emergency application must be "founded on" the medical recommendation (s.4(3); also see Form A10), it should not be signed until the medical recommendation has been received by the applicant.

*Subsection (2)*

**1–093**   In *D'Souza v Director of Public Prosecutions* [1992] 4 All E.R. 545 at 553–554, Lord Lowry said:

> "A person who is detained in hospital under section 6(2) is lawfully detained. If he goes absent without leave, he is then at large ... , and, since he ought not to be at large and is, by virtue of section 18(1), liable to be taken into custody and returned to the hospital, he would inevitably appear to be *unlawfully* at large [within section 17(1)(d) of the Police and Criminal Evidence Act 1984] until he is taken into custody".

The *D'Souza* case is considered in the General Note to s.135.

SUFFICIENT AUTHORITY FOR THE MANAGERS. The application will be served by delivering it to an officer of the managers who will usually be the nurse in charge of the relevant ward: see reg.3(2) of the English and Welsh Regulations. That officer will check the documents for obvious errors and decide whether or not to accept the application. The application should only be accepted if it "appears to be duly made" and is "founded on the necessary medical recommendations"(subs.(3)). If the application is accepted, the documents should be passed to an officer who has been authorised under reg.4(3) of the English Regulations (reg.4(2) of the Welsh Regulations) to scrutinise them for the purposes of possible rectification under s.15. Even if the application has been properly completed, there is no obligation placed on the managers by this Act to accept the application and detain the patient. There is nothing objectionable in the managers making appropriate enquiries as to the circumstances of the application to enable the appropriate officer to be put in a position to make an informed decision on whether to accept the application.

If the application is accepted, a record of admission shall be made by the managers in the form set out in Form H3: see reg.4(4) of the English Regulations (Form HO14 in Wales: see reg 4(3) of the Welsh Regulations). The date of the application for the purposes of calculation of time is the date when the patient is said to have been "formally detained" on the Form H3.

TO DETAIN THE PATIENT. The courts have held that the express power to detain a patient for treatment necessarily implies a power to control that patient: see the note on "Act purporting to be done in pursuance of this Act" in s.139(1).

*Subsection (3)*

**1–094**   In an appeal on a striking out application, Eady J. agreed with the judge's conclusion that the defence afforded to hospital managers under this provision is not incompatible with art.5 of the European Convention on Human Rights (*M v Bradford District Care Trust*, Case No. LS0128A, July 22, 2004, para.30).

In *TMM v London Borough of Hackney* [2010] EWHC 1349 (Admin), Collins J. referred to the following passage in the *Code of Practice*:

> "13.9 This chapter distinguishes between receiving admission documents and scrutinising them. For these purposes, receipt involves physically receiving documents and checking that they appear to amount to an application that has been duly made (since that is sufficient to give the managers the power to detain the patient). Scrutiny involves more detailed checking for omissions, errors and other defects and, where permitted, taking action to have the documents rectified after they have already been acted on."

His Lordship said, at para.29, that is apparent from this passage "that the obligation to scrutinise arises after the admission based check that the documents appear to amount to an application that has been duly made. If, following such scrutiny, it is apparent that there was a defect which cannot be rectified under s.15 because it is fundamental, the detention should be brought to an end"; also see the General Note to this section. In this case, it was held that this provision entitled the hospital managers to rely on the confirmation of the AMHP in her application form that there had been no objection from the patient's nearest relative.

In *R. (on the application of Care Principles Ltd) v Mental Health Review Tribunal* [2006] EWHC 3194 (Admin); [2006] M.H.L.R. 365, Collins J. held that the extent of the hospital managers obligations to scrutinise the application must depend on the facts of a particular case. If they are aware of the existence of a previous tribunal decision ordering the discharge of the patient, it requires a critical consideration of the justification for the detention in the light of that decision; see the note on this case under the heading "The re-sectioning of a patient subsequent to a discharge made by the First-tier Tribunal (Mental Health) or the Mental Health Review Tribunal for Wales" in the General Note to s.3.

*Subsection (4)*

In *R. (on the application of M) v Hospital Managers of Queen Mary's Hospital* [2008] **1–095** EWHC 1959 (Admin) para.18, Underhill J. considered this provision and said, without deciding the point, that an ineffective application under s.3 would not undermine the s.2 application that preceded it, and that the s.2 application would remain in force, or be revived, until it expired.

The ending of the previous application does not effect the continuity of the three-month period provided for in s.58(1)(b). A fresh admission under s.3 provides the patient with a new opportunity to make an application to a tribunal (s.66(1)(b), (2)(b)).

A similar provision relating to the making of a hospital order or a guardianship order by a court under s.37 can be found in s.40(5). For the effect that reception into guardianship has on existing applications, see s.8(5).

## *Guardianship*

## Application for guardianship

**7.**—(1) A patient who has attained the age of 16 years may be received into **1–096** guardianship, for the period allowed by the following provisions of this Act, in pursuance of an application (in this Act referred to as "a guardianship application") made in accordance with this section.

(2) A guardianship application may be made in respect of a patient on the grounds that—

(a) he is suffering from mental disorder [. . .] of a nature or degree which warrants his reception into guardianship under this section; and

(b) it is necessary in the interests of the welfare of the patient or for the protection of other persons that the patient should be so received.

(3) A guardianship application shall be founded on the written recommendations in the prescribed form of two registered medical practitioners, including in each case a statement that in the opinion of the practitioner the conditions set out in subsection (2) above are complied with; and each such recommendation shall include—

(a) such particulars as may be prescribed of the grounds for that opinion so far as it relates to the conditions set out in paragraph (a) of that subsection; and

(b)  a statement of the reasons for that opinion so far as it relates to the conditions set out in paragraph (b) of that subsection.

(4) A guardianship application shall state the age of the patient or, if his exact age is not known to the applicant, shall state (if it be the fact) that the patient is believed to have attained the age of 16 years.

(5) The person named as guardian in a guardianship application may be either a local social services authority or any other person (including the applicant himself); but a guardianship application in which a person other than a local social services authority is named as guardian shall be of no effect unless it is accepted on behalf of that person by the local social services authority for the area in which he resides, and shall be accompanied by a statement in writing by that person that he is willing to act as guardian.

AMENDMENT

In subs.(2)(a), the words omitted were repealed by the Mental Health Act 2007 s.55, Sch.11 Pt 1.

DEFINITIONS

**1–097**    patient: s.145(1).
mental disorder: ss.1, 145(1).
local social services authority: s.145(1).

GENERAL NOTE

**1–098**    The White Paper that preceded this Act stated that guardianship powers are needed for "a very small number of mentally disordered people who do not require treatment in hospital, either formally or informally, [but who] nevertheless need close supervision and some control in the community as a consequence of their mental disorder. These include people who are able to cope provided that they take their medication regularly, but who fail to do so, and those who neglect themselves to the point of seriously endangering their health" (Cmnd. 8405, para.43).

According to the *Code of Practice* the "purpose of guardianship is to enable patients to receive care outside hospital when it cannot be provided without the use of compulsory powers.  [I]t provides an authoritative framework for working with a patient, with a minimum of constraint, to achieve as independent a life as possible within the community" (Paras.262, 26.4). Guardianship is used infrequently; less than 1000 cases are open in England at any one time. It is invoked predominantly for mentally ill people who are over 65 years of age (National Health Act Guardianship: A Discussion Paper, Department of Health, 1994, p.5). The reception of a patient into guardianship does not carry with it resource implications for the local authority (apart from associated administrative costs) because the fact that a patient is subject to guardianship does not provide that patient with an entitlement to receive community care services under the National Health Service and Community Care Act 1990. Guardianship patients are subject to the Care Programme Approach (*Reforming the Care Programme Approach: Policy and Positive Practice Guidance*, March 2008, p.14).

Sections 5 and 6 of the Mental Capacity Act 2005 provides social care professionals who are caring for mentally incapacitated persons with protection against civil and criminal liability for certain acts done in connection with the care of such persons. The powers that staff have under that Act, which include the power to use restraint which does not constitute a deprivation of liberty, will usually be sufficient to ensure that the best interests of a mentally incapacitated person are satisfied. However, the Code of Practice on the 2005 Act, at para.13.20, provides the following examples of situations where staff might feel that a guardianship application would be appropriate:

- "they think it important that one person or authority should be in charge of making decisions about where the person should live (for example, where there have been long-running or difficult disagreements about where the person should live);

- they think the person will probably respond well to the authority and attention of a guardian, and so be more prepared to accept treatment for the mental disorder (whether they are able to consent to it or it is being provided for them under the Mental Capacity Act); or

- they need authority to return the person to the place they are to live (for example, a care home) if they were to go absent."

In cases where there is a significant dispute between the local authority and the patient and/or his or her carers about how best to meet the patient's needs, an application to the Court of Protection for a best interests declaration under s.15 of the 2005 Act might be a more appropriate option than guardianship.

This section specifies the circumstances whereby a patient aged 16 or over may be received into the guardianship of a local social services authority or a person who is acceptable to the authority. A patient shall cease to be subject to guardianship if an order for his discharge is made by his responsible clinician (RC), by the responsible local social services authority or by his nearest relative (s.23(2)(b)). A discharge by the nearest relative cannot be barred by anyone.

The powers of the guardian are set out in s.8. A local social services authority has a duty to ensure that patients received into guardianship are visited: see reg.23 of the English Regulations and reg.10 of the Welsh Regulations. If the patient is hospitalised, the local authority has duties placed upon it by s.116.

Upon a patient being received into guardianship, the local social services authority (LSSA) must take such steps as are practicable to inform the patient and the patient's nearest relative (unless the patient has requested otherwise) of the rights set out in reg.26(3), (4) of the English Regulations and reg.15 of the Welsh Regulations. The LSSA must also take steps to have a patient and the patient's nearest relative (unless the patient has requested otherwise) informed about independent mental health advocacy (s.130D). There is also a duty placed on the LSSAA to inform a patient when his or her guardianship is renewed (s.20(6); also see reg.26(1)(n) of the English Regulations and reg.15(4) of the Welsh Regulations).

If a patient who has been made the subject of an application under this section is remanded into custody or sentenced under the criminal law, the provisions of s.22 will apply.

Under s.19 and regs 7, 8, and 11 of the English Regulations and regs 23, 24 and 27 of the Welsh Regulations detained patients and patients who are subject to guardianship may be transferred between hospitals and guardians or between detention in hospital and guardianship: see the notes to s.19.

It is an offence under this Act to neglect or ill-treat a patient who is under guardianship (s.127(2)).

*The use of guardianship to authorise the deprivation of a person's liberty*
See Part 6.                                                                                      **1–099**

*Applications to the First-tier Tribunal (Mental Health) or the Mental Health Review Tribunal for Wales*
The patient may make an application within six months his or her reception into guar- **1–100** dianship (s.66(1)(c), (2)(c)) and during each period of renewal (ss.66(1)(f), (2)(f), 20(2)). There is no automatic reference of guardianship cases to the tribunal.

*Code of Practice*
Guidance on guardianship is contained in Ch.26. Advice on deciding between guardian- **1–101** ship, leave of absence and supervised community treatment can be found in Ch.28.

*National Assistance Act 1948*

**1–102**     It is possible for persons who are not necessarily mentally disordered to be compulsorily admitted to a hospital or a care home under the provisions of s.47 of the National Assistance Act 1948. The use of this provision is, in practice, usually confined to cases where elderly people, usually living alone, are unable to care for themselves adequately. Under s.47 a district council or London borough council (in Wales, the councils of counties and county boroughs) may make an application to a magistrates' court to remove a person from his or her home on the grounds (i) that the person is suffering from grave chronic disease *or*, being aged, infirm or physically incapacitated, is living in insanitary conditions; *and* (ii) that the person is unable to devote to himself, and is not receiving from other persons, proper care and attention; *and* (iii) that his removal from home is necessary, either in his own interests or for preventing injury to the health of, or serious nuisance to, other persons. Section 47 has been amended by the Mental Health Act 2007 so that it cannot apply in two situations where the Mental Capacity Act 2005 is or may be invoked. The first is where an order of the Court of Protection authorises the managing authority of a hospital or care home to provide the person concerned with proper care and attention. The second is where—

(a)   an authorisation to deprive the person of his or her liberty is in force, or

(b)   the managing authority of a hospital or care home are under a duty to request a standard authorisation in respect of that person.

The local authority can only make an application under s.47 if the community physician has certified to the authority that he is satisfied after "thorough enquiry and consideration" that it is necessary to remove the person from the premises in which he is residing "in the interests" of the person or "for preventing injury to the health of, or serious nuisance to, other persons." The community physician is an employee of the health service and not the local authority. If, after hearing oral evidence, the court finds that the grounds are satisfied, and that it is "expedient" to do so, it may order that an officer of the applicant local authority remove the person to "a suitable hospital or other place". The "other place" is usually a care home. The order, which provides authority for the person's "detention and maintenance" in the specified place, lasts for an initial period of up to three months, with the court having power to extend it for further periods of up to three months. Six weeks after the making of the order the person who was removed, or someone acting on that person's behalf, may apply to the court for the order to be revoked.

If it is thought necessary to remove the person from his home without delay, s.1 of the National Assistance (Amendment) Act 1951 enables the court, or a single justice, to make a without notice under s.47. If granted, the order provides authority for the person to be detained for an initial period of three weeks. An application under s.1 may be made by either the community physician or the local authority. Neither the 1948 Act nor the common law provide authority for medical treatment to be given to a mentally capable person who has been made subject to s.47 without his or her consent.

*Cleansing of Filthy or Verminous Premises*

**1–103**     The action that a local authority can take when satisfied that premises are either (a) in such a filthy or unwholesome condition as to be prejudicial to health, or (b) are verminous is set out in s.83 of the Public Health Act 1936.

*Subsection (1)*

**1–104**     PATIENT.   As a patient under guardianship is not "liable to be detained" for the purposes of s.56(3), he or she is not subject to the consent to treatment provisions contained in Pt IV of this Act.

ATTAINED THE AGE. At the commencement of his or her sixteenth birthday (Family Law Reform Act 1969 s.9(1)). Where on September 30, 1983, a person who was not then 16 years old was subject to guardianship, the authority for guardianship terminated on that day (s.148(1), Sch.5 para.8(1)).

In *Re F (Mental Health Act: Guardianship)* [2000] 1 F.L.R. 192, the Court of Appeal held that wardship should not have been rejected by the judge as a more appropriate remedy than guardianship for a seventeen year old patient. An immediate consequence of wardship would have been the appointment of the Official Solicitor as her guardian ad litem, thereby securing the benefit of separate representation for the child. Thorpe L.J. said at 199: "[Guardianship] is not a child-centred Jurisdiction and the child lacks the benefit of independent representation." An application for guardianship cannot be made in respect of a ward of court (s.33(3)).

Care proceedings under s.31 and Sch.3, para.5 of the Children Act 1989 could be brought in respect of a child under 16 who requires supervision and control in the community as a consequence of mental disorder.

A child is not a privately fostered child for the purposes of Pt IX of the Children Act 1989 while he or she is subject to guardianship (Children Act 1989 Sch.8, para.4).

PERIOD ALLOWED. A patient may be kept under guardianship for an initial period of up to six months from the day on which the application was accepted (s.20(1)). The authority for guardianship may be renewed for a further period of six months, and then for yearly periods (s.20(2)).

AN APPLICATION. The application is addressed to the LSSA and it must be received within 14 days of the second medical examination (s.8(2)). The application does not have to be accepted within that period. The application must be in the form set out in Form G1 (for a nearest relative applicant) or Form G2 (for an approved mental health professional (AMHP) applicant) (in Wales, Form GU1 (for a NR applicant) or Form GU2 (for an AMHP applicant): see reg.5 of the English Regulations and reg.9 of the Welsh Regulations. There is no time limit within which an application must be accepted.

*Subsection (2)*

A GUARDIANSHIP APPLICATION MAY BE MADE. There is no requirement for the patient to **1–105** consent to the guardianship application. The application may be made by either the patient's nearest relative or by an AMHP (s.11(1)). The applicant must have personally seen the patient within 14 days of making the application (s.11(5)). An AMHP cannot make an application if the nearest relative objects (s.11(4)) and he or she must comply with the provisions of s.13(1). The application must either be sent to the LSSA named as guardian or to the social services authority for the area in which the individual named as guardian resides (s.11(2)).

The power of the nearest relative to veto a guardianship application made by an AMHP can cause difficulty as:

"often social workers are concerned not that the patient may act irresponsibly, but that the relatives may act irresponsibly towards the patient. Where there is a caring relative, guardianship may not be needed. It is where there is a nearest relative who is neglectful, exploitive, or unable to care, that guardianship may well be required, but the relative has a power of veto which can only be overridden by the county court in the limited circumstances [set out in section 29]." (Phil Fennell, "The Beverley Lewis Case: was the law to blame" *New Law Journal*, November 17, 1989, pp.1557–1558).

If an AMHP considers that a nearest relative's likely objection to a guardianship application would place his client at risk, the following legal options could be considered. In cases of urgency, an application to a magistrate for a warrant under s.135 could be followed by an application under s.2 for the patient to be detained in hospital for up to 28 days.

Alternatively, an application made under s.2 could be made direct from the community. In both cases it is assumed that the grounds for an s.2 application could be satisfied. A nearest relative does not have the right to veto applications under either s.135 or s.2. Immediately after the completion of the s.2 application, the AMHP could make an application to the county court under s.29(3)(c) for an interim order to displace the nearest relative. An application under that provision has the effect of extending the life of the s.2 order until the application to the county court is disposed of (s.29(4)), although it should be noted that the nearest relative could use his or her power under s.23 to discharge the patient from the s.2 during this period. While this application is pending, the RC could consider granting the patient leave of absence under s.17 to a non-hospital setting. The patient could then be transferred into the guardianship of the local social services authority under s.19 and reg.7(4) of the English Regulations and reg.23(4) of the Welsh Regulations. If the application to the county court was successful the nearest relative would lose his or her power to discharge the patient from the guardianship.

*Paragraph (a)*

**1–106** MENTAL DISORDER. There is no requirement for the patient to be mentally incapacitated. A patient with a learning disability can only be made subject to an application under this section if the disability is associated with abnormally aggressive or seriously irresponsible conduct on his or her part (s.1(2A), (2B)).

The restrictive construction given to the term "seriously irresponsible conduct" by the Court of Appeal in *Re F (Mental Health Act: Guardianship)* [2000] 1 F.L.R. 192, which is noted under s.1(2A), (2B), could lead to a diminution of the use of guardianship for persons with a learning disability because prior to this decision this term had been broadly interpreted to protect patients who are vulnerable and subject to abuse and neglect: see H. Whitworth and S. Singhai "The use of guardianship in mental handicap services" (1995) 19 *Psychiatric Bulletin* 725–727.

NATURE OR DEGREE. The meaning of this phrase is considered in the note on s.3(2)(a).

*Paragraph (b)*

**1–107** It is difficult to see how the requirement contained in this paragraph will be met if the powers that the guardian would enjoy under s.8 are already being exercised responsibly in respect of a mentally incapacitated patient by the donee of a lasting power of attorney of a deputy appointed by the Court of Protection.

INTERESTS OF THE WELFARE OF THE PATIENT. All factors which might affect the well-being of the patient are covered by this phrase, including the need to be protected from exploitation. The wording is wide enough to encompass the need to prevent the patient's welfare being prejudiced at some time in the future. If the concern relates to possible future harm, the recommending doctors would need to be satisfied that there is a real risk of such an eventuality occurring, e.g. an attempt by a relative to remove a mentally incompetent patient from a care setting to accommodation where the patient's welfare might be seriously prejudiced.

PROTECTION OF OTHER PERSONS. It is submitted that "protection" is not limited to protection from physical harm, but could include protection from serious emotional harm.

*Subsection (3)*

**1–108** WRITTEN RECOMMENDATIONS. Made either separately or jointly (s.11(7)) using either Form G3 (joint recommendation) or G4 (in Wales, Form GU3 (joint recommendation) or Form GU4): see reg.5(1)(c) of the English Regulations and reg.9(1)(c) of the Welsh Regulations.

TWO REGISTERED MEDICAL PRACTITIONERS. Complying with the provisions of s.12 and the regulations made under s.12A.

*Subsection (5)*
This subsection provides for the guardian to be either a LSSA or a person who is accepted **1–109** by the authority to act in that capacity. Neither the authority nor the individual is placed under any legal obligation to accept the duties of guardian. In 99.7 per cent of cases in England, the guardian is a local authority (*Guardianship under the Mental Health Act 1983, England, 2007*).

LOCAL SOCIAL SERVICES AUTHORITY. This does not have to be the authority for the area where the patient lives. If the application is accepted, the authority will become "the responsible local social services authority" (s.34(3)). Although a local authority may decline any guardianship proposal, there is a requirement to take over the role of guardian where a private guardianship arrangement has broken down in the circumstances set out in s.10.

Although the relevant social services authority will be named as the guardian, the authority's scheme of delegation will identify an officer who will formally undertake the guardian's legal functions. This officer will usually be the Director of Social Services or the Director of Adult Social Services. He or she will then identify an employee, invariably a social worker, who will perform casework functions in relation to the patient. It is this person who should represent the authority in tribunal hearings. The only function that cannot be delegated to an officer is the power to discharge the patient from guardianship: see s.23(2), (4).

OR ANY OTHER PERSON. The local social services authority should consider the suitability of any proposed guardian before accepting the application: see paras 26.15 and 26.23 of the *Code of Practice*.

If an AMHP considers that a private guardian has performed his or her functions negligently or in any manner contrary to the interests of the welfare of the patient, an application can be made to the county court under s.10(3) for the guardianship to be transferred to another person or to the LSSA.

A private guardian does not have the power to discharge the patient from guardianship.

ACCEPTED. The time limits for accepting an application for a patient's admission to hospital set out in s.6 do not apply to guardianship applications. The acceptance should be recorded on Form G5 (in Wales, Form GU5): see reg.5(2) of the English Regulations and reg.9(3) of the Welsh Regulations.

THE AREA. i.e. the area where the person named as guardian resides.

RESIDES. Temporary absences from the place where a person lives does not affect residence, as long as there is an intention to return (*R. v St Leonard's Shoreditch (Inhabitants)* (1865) L.R. 1 Q.B. 21). Also note Widgery L.J.'s statement in *Fox v Stirk* [1970] 2 Q.B. 463 at 477: "A man cannot be said to reside in a particular place unless in the ordinary sense of the word one can say that for the time being he is making his home in that place."

WILLING TO ACT AS GUARDIAN. The statement that the person is willing to act as guardian must be in the form set out in either Form G1 or G2 (in Wales, Form GU1 or GU2). The duties of private guardians are set out in reg.22 of the English Regulations and reg.11 of the Welsh Regulations.

**Effect of guardianship application, etc.**

1–110　　8.—(1) Where a guardianship application, duly made under the provisions of this Part of this Act and forwarded to the local social services authority within the period allowed by subsection (2) below is accepted by that authority, the application shall, subject to regulations made by the Secretary of State, confer on the authority or person named in the application as guardian, to the exclusion of any other person—

    (a)　the power to require the patient to reside at a place specified by the authority or person named as guardian;

    (b)　the power to require the patient to attend at places and times so specified for the purpose of medical treatment, occupation, education or training;

    (c)　the power to require access to the patient to be given, at any place where the patient is residing, to any registered medical practitioner, [approved mental health professional] or other person so specified.

(2) The period within which a guardianship application is required for the purposes of this section to be forwarded to the local social services authority is the period of 14 days beginning with the date on which the patient was last examined by a registered medical practitioner before giving a medical recommendation for the purposes of the application.

(3) A guardianship application which appears to be duly made and to be founded on the necessary medical recommendations may be acted upon without further proof of the signature or qualification of the person by whom the application or any such medical recommendation is made or given, or of any matter of fact or opinion stated in the application.

(4) If within the period of 14 days beginning with the day on which a guardianship application has been accepted by the local social services authority the application, or any medical recommendation given for the purposes of the application, is found to be in any respect incorrect or defective, the application or recommendation may, within that period and with the consent of that authority, be amended by the person by whom it was signed; and upon such amendment being made the application or recommendation shall have effect and shall be deemed to have had effect as if it had been originally made as so amended.

(5) Where a patient is received into guardianship in pursuance of a guardianship application, any previous application under this Part of this Act by virtue of which he was subject to guardianship or liable to be detained in a hospital shall cease to have effect.

AMENDMENT

    The words in square brackets in subs.(1)(c) were substituted by the Mental Health Act 2007 s.21, Sch.2 para.2.

DEFINITIONS

    local social services authority: s.145(1).
    medical treatment: s.145(1).
    patient: s.145(1).
    approved mental health professional: s.145(1), (1AC).
    hospital: ss.34(2), 145(1).

GENERAL NOTE

1–111　　This section confers specific powers on the patient's guardian. The 1959 Act gave the guardian the power that a father has over a child of 14. These powers were therefore very wide, as well as being somewhat ill-defined, and it was felt that they were out of keeping, in their paternalistic approach, with modern attitudes to the care of the mentally disordered. Subsection (1) replaces these general powers with specific powers limited to interfering with the autonomy of the person under guardianship only to the extent necessary to ensure that various forms of treatment, social support, training, education or occupation are undertaken.

The patient's guardian, who is subject to the duties laid down in Pt III of the English and Welsh Regulations, does not have any power to use or dispose of the patient's property or to carry out any financial transactions on the patient's behalf.

In *R. (on the application of S) v Plymouth City Council and C* [2002] EWCA Civ 388; [2002] 1 W.L.R. 2583, the Court of Appeal was concerned with how the interest of a guardianship patient in preserving the confidentiality of personal information about himself is to be reconciled with his mother's interest, as his nearest relative, in having access to enough information about him to exercise her statutory functions under this Act. The Court held that:

(i) both at common law and under the Human Rights Act 1998, a balance must be struck between the public and private interests in maintaining the confidentiality of information about the patient and the public and private interests in permitting, indeed requiring, its disclosure for certain purposes; and

(ii) striking the balance would not lead in every case to the disclosure of all the information a nearest relative might possibly want, still less to a fishing exercise amongst the local authority's files. But in most cases it would lead to the disclosure of the basic statutory guardianship documentation. In this case it would also lead to the disclosure of relevant social services records. Hale L.J. said at para.50:

"There is no suggestion of any risk to [the patient's] health and welfare arising from this. The mother and her advisers have sought access to the information which her own psychiatric and social work experts need in order properly to advise her. That limits both the context and the content of dislosure in a way which strikes a proper balance between the competing interests."

If a local authority concludes that the powers set out in this section are insufficient to enable it to manage the case of a mentally incapacitated person appropriately, it should consider making an application under the Mental Capacity Act 2005 to the Court of Protection for an appropriate order (*Lewis v Gibson* [2005] EWCA Civ 587; [2005] M.H.L.R. 309 para.29).

### Human Rights Act 1998

Unlike an application for admission to hospital (see s.6(2)), this section does not provide **1–112** explicit authority for the guardian to detain the patient (in Convention terminology, to deprive the person of his or her liberty). However, for the reasons set out in Part 6, it is submitted that the powers available to the guardian could have such an effect. In *Aerts v Belgium* (2000) 29 E.H.R.R. 50, para.46, the Court held that, in principle, the detention of a mentally disordered person will only be lawful for the purposes of art.5 of the European Convention on Human Rights if effected in "a hospital, clinic or other appropriate institution".

Guardianship proceedings must comply with the standards of art.6(1) of the ECHR because such proceedings involve the determination of a civil right. The fact that the initial determination of the guardianship application is made by an administrative body (the local authority) does not contravene art.6(1) provided that there is a right of appeal to a court (the First-tier Tribunal (Mental Health) or the Mental Health Review Tribunal for Wales) which provides the guarantees of that article (see for example, *Le Compte, Van Leuven and De Meyer v Belgium* (1981) 4 E.H.R.R. 1 para.51). The state must ensure that the appeal is heard within a reasonable time (*Buchholz v Germany* (1981) 3 E.H.R.R. 1 para.50).

The patient's private or local authority guardian is exercising functions of a public nature in respect of the patient and is therefore a "public authority" for the purposes of s.6 of the 1998 Act.

As the patient's guardian is likely to exercise powers which will involve an interference with the patient's right to respect for private and family life under art.8(1), a justification for the interference, which must be a proportionate response to the identified risk, will need to be found in art.8(2). In order to justify the proportionality of the power exercised, the guardian should have identified and assessed the potential effectiveness of alternatives to the use of that power.

It has been argued that the charging of those subject to guardianship who are required to reside in accommodation provided by a local authority breaches art.8 of the Convention; see *R. (on the application of Johnson) v Secretary of State for Health* [2006] EWHC 288 (Admin). Judicial comments made in this case suggest that it is unlikely that such an argument would succeed if the issue proceeded to trial.

*The use of guardianship to authorise the deprivation of a person's liberty*

**1–113**     See Part 6.

*Admission to hospital of patients under guardianship*

**1–114**     If a patient under guardianship is admitted for psychiatric treatment as an informal patient he or she will remain subject to guardianship unless he or she is discharged from it (s.23) or transferred to hospital under the procedure set out in reg.8 of the English Regulations and reg.24 of the Welsh Regulations. The guardianship will also remain in force if the patient is admitted for assessment under s.2 or 4, but it will cease to have effect if the patient is admitted for treatment under s.3 (s.6(4)) or is transferred to hospital under reg.8 or, in Wales, reg.24. If the patient is admitted informally he or she could be made subject to the holding powers provided for in s.5(2) and (4).

*Subsection (10)*

A local authority guardian may delegate its functions under this provision to any committee, officer or other body or person to whom they can normally delegate functions under the Local Government Act 1972 (or the Local Government Act 2000, if relevant): see reg.21 of the English Regulations and the note thereto.

**1–115**     SECRETARY OF STATE.  The functions of the Minister, so far as exercisable in relation to Wales, are exercised by the Welsh Ministers (see the General Note to this Act).

TO THE EXCLUSION OF ANY OTHER PERSON.  This provision prevents a person from taking a decision, including a decision made under the Mental Capacity Act 2005, on the matters covered by paras (a) to (c) which conflicts with a decision made by the guardian. The prohibition covers a deputy appointed by the Court of Protection, the donee of a lasting power of attorney and a lay or professional carer purporting to act under the protection granted by s.5 of the 2005 Act.

*Paragraph (a)*

**1–116**     The guardian may exercise powers over the patient in addition to the specific powers contained in this provision. In *R. v Kent County Council Ex p. Marston* (CO/1819/96), July 9, 1997, Owen J. said that he could "find no difficulty in accepting that section 7 of necessity implies a statutory duty to act for the welfare of the patient". His Lordship further stated that:

"the extent and consequences of that duty are not so clear. An example, of no relevance here, would be seen if a patient were to be given a sexually provocative magazine. I would have no difficulty in accepting that the guardian would a duty to monitor the effects and if necessary to remove the magazine."

This finding was endorsed by Simon Brown L.J. who said, in refusing leave to appeal on September 5, 1997, that it is implicit in s.7:

"that the guardian is entitled in certain respects to act so as to promote the welfare of the patient. Owen J. recognised, as I would too, that the precise extent and consequence of such an implicit duty to act for the welfare of the patient is not clear. I envisage that that may well need clarification at some future date. For example, if there were good reason to suppose that an authority was acting in some totalitarian fashion or was not properly having regard to the interests of its patients, then it seems to me clear that someone would have the standing, would have a sufficient interest to bring the case before the court so that the matter could be properly investigated and the true extent of the authority's discretion be clarified".

In *Marston*, Owen J. upheld the decision of the local authority, acting as the patient's guardian, to refuse to disclose to the patient's former foster brother where the patient was living. The foster brother was ultimately intent on taking over the care of the patient and the local authority had received medical advice that this would be contrary to the patient's interests. The patient, who was mentally incapable, had expressed no interest in seeing his former foster brother. His Lordship also said that as the patient needed protection, the guardian had a right to see letters addressed to him and that whether "the guardian would be entitled to censor them would depend what was in them". However, as the patient was unable to read, the right to see the letters would not have to be exercised. The decision in *Marston* suggests that a guardian has an implied power to make decisions concerning the daily living arrangements of patients who are mentally incapable. Such decisions should be "necessary in the interests of the welfare" of the patient (cf. s.7(2)(b)). *Marston* was not cited in *Re F (Mental Health Act: Guardianship)* [2000] 1 F.L.R. 192 where Thorpe L.J. stated obiter that he doubted the legality of the restrictions that the local authority, acting as guardian, has placed on the patient's contact with her parents.

REQUIRE THE PATIENT TO RESIDE AT A PLACE. The power to take the patient to the place is contained in s.18(7). The person taking the patient can use force if this is required (s.137). If the patient leaves the place where he is required to reside without his guardian's consent, he can be taken into custody and returned to that place within the period specified in s.18(4). An application could be made to a magistrate under s.135(2) if it is not possible to obtain access to where the patient is staying. Anyone obstructing a person authorised by s.18(3) to return the patient would be guilty of an offence under s.129. It is an offence under s.128 to induce or knowingly to assist a person under guardianship to absent himself without leave of the guardian.

The Reference Guide states, at para.19.5, that this power "may be used, for example, to discourage people from sleeping rough or living with people who may exploit or mistreat them, or to ensure that they reside in a particular hostel or other facility". There is no power to require that the patient resides with a particular person.

There no prohibition on charging a person who is subject to guardianship for the accommodation in which he is required to reside, as long as the accommodation is not being provided as an after-care service under s.117. Section 21(8) of the National Assistance Act 1948 states:

"Nothing in this section shall authorise or require a local authority to make any provision authorised or required to be made (whether by that or by any other authority) by or under any enactment not contained in this Part of this Act or authorised or required to be provided under the National Health Service Act 2006 or the National Health Service(Wales) Act 2006."

It has been argued that s.21(8) has the effect of prohibiting a local authority from charging for accommodation in guardianship cases. This argument is erroneous as, unlike s.117, neither this section nor s.7 "authorise or require" the provision of accommodation. Requiring a patient to reside in accommodation is not the same as requiring the accommodation to be provided. Also see the note on "The Human Rights Act 1998", above.

The person in control of the premises where the patient is required to reside has the power "under general law . . . to control who is allowed to be there and in what circumstances"; *per* Hale J. in *Cambridgeshire County Council v R (an Adult)* [1995] 1 F.L.R. 50 at 55. Any restriction on access between a relative and the patient would need to be justified under art.8(2) of the European Convention on Human Rights.

In cases where there is a significant unresolved conflict between the local authority and a mentally incapacitated patient's main carer as to where the patient should reside the authority should consider making an application to the Court of Protection under the Mental Capacity Act 2005 for a declaration as the lawfulness of the placement.

Although McCullough J. made the obiter comment in *R. v Hallstrom Ex p. WL; R. v Gardner Ex p. L* [1986] 2 All E.R. 306, 312 that "there is nothing in [the Mental Health Act 1983] which appears to prevent a guardian from requiring his patient to reside in a hospital", this practice is contrary to the intention of the Act if the patient is likely to require long term hospital care: see Cmnd. 7320, noted in the General Note to s.7. In any event, a hospital is a place of treatment, not of residence. Also see para.26.33 of the *Code of Practice*.

There is nothing to prevent a patient who is subject to guardianship from being admitted to hospital for treatment for either a physical or a psychiatric disorder. In the event of such an admission taking place a local authority acting as the guardian of a patient is required to comply with s.116 of this Act. See the note on "Admission to hospital of patients under guardianship", above, for the legal consequences of a patient being admitted to hospital for psychiatric treatment under compulsory powers.

The responsible social services authority must arrange for the patient to be visited at not more than three monthly intervals: see reg.23 of the English Regulations and reg.10 of the Welsh Regulations.

*Paragraph (b)*

**1–117**   REQUIRE THE PATIENT TO ATTEND.   If the patient refuses to attend, guardianship does not provide authority for force to be used to secure attendance.

FOR THE PURPOSES OF MEDICAL TREATMENT.   Neither the guardian, the patient's nearest relative nor any other adult, can consent to treatment on the patient's behalf. In *T v T* [1988] 1 All E.R. 613 at 617 Wood J. said:

"The wording of section 8 will be seen to be much more restricted than the wider powers of the guardian under section 34 of the [Mental Health Act 1959]. One important effect is to remove the guardian's implicit power to consent to treatment on behalf of the patient. In my judgment there is no power to consent to [abortion] to be found in section 8 . . ., and indeed, on a construction of the statute as a whole I am satisfied that medical treatment means psychiatric treatment."

A patient under guardianship is not subject to the Consent to Treatment provisions contained in Pt IV of this Act (s.56(3)). If the patient is mentally capable of making a decision about medical treatment, the common law enables him or her to refuse to be treated for either a physical or mental disorder. However, if the patient is assessed as being mentally incapable of making a decision about treatment, the treatment can be provided under ss.5 and 6 of the Mental Capacity Act 2005 if it is deemed to be in his or her best interests. If a patient's psychiatric condition is deteriorating because a refusal to accept treatment, consideration should be given to admitting the patient to hospital under s.2 (with the guardianship order remaining in force) or to transferring the patient to hospital under reg.8 of the English Regulations and reg.24 of the Welsh Regulations (with the guardianship order ceasing to have effect).

Although guardianship does not provide authority for a mentally capable patient to be treated in the absence of his or her consent, the existence of guardianship can have the effect of influencing the patient to co-operate with treatment. For an example, see L. Blom-Cooper et al., *The Falling Shadow*, 1995, p.90.

The responsible social services authority must arrange for an approved clinician or a s.12 doctor to visit the patient at least once a year: see reg.23 of the English Regulations and reg.10 of the Welsh Regulations.

*Paragraph (c)*

REQUIRE ACCESS TO THE PATIENT.    This provision, which could be used to ensure that the **1–118** patient did not neglect himself, does not include a power to force entry if this is denied. If entry is denied consideration should be given to utilising the procedure set out in s.135(1) of this Act. A refusal to permit an authorised person to have access to the patient is an offence under s.129.

*Subsection (2)*

BEGINNING WITH.    Including the date on which the patient was last examined by a medi- **1–119** cal practitioner (*Zoan v Rouamba* [2000] 2 All E.R. 620 CA).

*Subsection (3)*

APPEARS TO BE DULY MADE.    An incorrect or defective application can be amended **1–120** under subs.(4).

*Subsection (4)*

ACCEPTED BY THE LOCAL SOCIAL SERVICES AUTHORITY.    The authority may authorise an **1–121** officer or class of officer to consent under this provision to any amendment of a guardian-ship application which it has accepted or any medical recommendation given for the purposes of that application: see reg.21 of the English Regulations and reg.37 of the Welsh Regulations.

INCORRECT OR DEFECTIVE.    See the notes to s.15(1). This provision provides a means of righting accidental mistakes that were made when the statutory documentation was com-pleted; it is not a device for overcoming a fundamental defect in the application: see the General Note to s.15. The amended application must comply with the requirements for making an application. Paragraphs 19.58–19.59 of the Reference Guide state:

"An application or recommendation which is found to be incorrect or defective may be amended by the person who signed it, with the consent of the LSSA. In practice, if the LSSA is content for the document to be amended, it should be returned to the person who signed it for amendment. Consent to the amendment should then formally be given by the LSSA. The consent should be recorded in writing and can take the form of an endorsement on the document itself. If this is all done within a period of 14 days starting with the day on which the application was accepted, the documents are deemed to have had effect as though originally made as amended.

Unlike applications for admission to hospital, there is no procedure for obtaining a new medical recommendation if the ones that come with the application originally prove insufficient. In such cases, a new application would have to be made."

Minor mistakes which are not rectified within the 14-day period would not invalidate the application by virtue of the de minimis principle: see *Re E (Mental Health: Habeas Corpus)* noted in the General Note to Sch.1 of the English Regulations. An application which contains an unrectifiable error (e.g. a relative who was not the patient's nearest rela-tive was consulted under s.11(4)) should be discharged under s.23 as soon as the error is discovered.

By whom it was signed. i.e. the applicant or the recommending doctor. An unsigned application or medical recommendation cannot be remedied under this provision.

## Regulations as to guardianship

**1–122**   9.—(1) Subject to the provisions of this Part of this Act, the Secretary of State may make regulations—

(a) for regulating the exercise by the guardians of patients received into guardianship under this Part of the Act of their powers as such; and

(b) for imposing on such guardians, and upon local social services authorities in the case of patients under the guardianship of persons other than local social services authorities, such duties as he considers necessary or expedient in the interest of the patients.

(2) Regulations under this section may in particular make provision for requiring the patients to be visited, on such occasions or at such intervals as may be prescribed by the regulations, on behalf of such local social services authorities as may be so prescribed, and shall provide for the appointment, in the case of every patient subject to the guardianship of a person other than a local social services authority, of a registered medical practitioner to act as the nominated medical attendant of the patient.

DEFINITIONS
**1–123**   patients: s.145(1).
local social services authority: s.145(1).

GENERAL NOTE
**1–124**   This section, which gives power to the Secretary of State (or, in relation to Wales, the Welsh Ministers: see the General Note to this Act) to make regulations for regulating guardianship, applies to patients who have been placed on a guardianship order made by a court under s.37 (Sch.1, Pt I, para.1).

The Mental Health (Hospital, Guardianship and Treatment) (England) Regulations 2008 (SI 2008/1184) and the Mental Health (Hospital, Guardianship, Community Treatment and Consent to Treatment) (Wales) Regulations 2008 (SI 2008/2439) (W.212) have been made under this section.

## Transfer of guardianship in case of death, incapacity, etc. of guardian

**1–125**   10.—(1) If any person (other than a local social services authority) who is the guardian of a patient received into guardianship under this Part of this Act—

(a) dies; or

(b) gives notice in writing to the local social services authority that he desires to relinquish the functions of guardian,

the guardianship of the patient shall thereupon vest in the local social services authority, but without prejudice to any power to transfer the patient into the guardianship of another person in pursuance of regulations under section 19 below.

(2) If any such person, not having given notice under subsection (1)(b) above, is incapacitated by illness or any other cause from performing the functions of guardian of the patient, those functions may, during his incapacity, be performed on his behalf by the local social services authority or by any other person approved for the purposes by that authority.

(3) If it appears to the county court, upon application made by an [approved mental health professional acting on behalf of the local social services authority], that any person other than a local social services authority having the guardianship

of a patient received into guardianship under this Part of this Act has performed his functions negligently or in a manner contrary to the interests of the welfare of the patient, the court may order that the guardianship of the patient be transferred to the local social services authority or to any other person approved for the purpose by that authority.

(4) Where the guardianship of a patient is transferred to a local social services authority or other person by or under this section, subsection (2)(c) of section 19 below shall apply as if the patient had been transferred into the guardianship of that authority or person in pursuance of regulations under that section.

[(5) In this section "the local social services authority", in relation to a person (other than a local social services authority) who is the guardian of a patient, means the local social services authority for the area in which that person resides (or resided immediately before his death).]

AMENDMENTS
The amendments to this section were made by the Mental Health Act 2007 s.21, Sch.2 para.3.

DEFINITIONS
    local social services authority: s.145(1).                            **1–126**
    patient: s.145(1).
    approved mental health professional: s.145(1), (1AC).

GENERAL NOTE
This section provides for the transfer of guardianship in circumstances where the guard-  **1–127** ian of a patient dies, becomes incapacitated, wishes to relinquish his functions, or is found to be performing his functions negligently. It applies to patients who have been placed on guardianship orders made by a court under s.37 (Sch.1 Pt I para.1).

For the responsibility to inform the patient's nearest relative of a transfer of guardianship under this section, see reg.26(1)(k) of the English Regulations and reg.31 of the Welsh Regulations.

It is also possible for a patient to be transferred from one guardian to another under s.19.

*Subsection (1)*
This subsection provides for the automatic transfer of guardianship from a private guard-  **1–128** ian to a local social services authority. Guardianship could subsequently be transferred to another local social services authority or to a person under reg.8 of the English Regulations and reg.4(2) of the Welsh Regulations.

NOTICE IN WRITING TO THE LOCAL SOCIAL SERVICES AUTHORITY.  See subs.(5).

SHALL THEREUPON.  The authority cannot resist a notice of relinquishment.

*Subsection (2)*
This subsection allows the local social services authority, or a person authorised by the  **1–129** authority, to act temporarily on behalf of a guardian who is ill or is otherwise incapacitated.

MAY, DURING HIS INCAPACITY, BE PERFORMED.  The local social services authority is not placed under a duty to take over the functions of an incapacitated guardian.

ON HIS BEHALF.  "The authority or person acting as guardian ... acts as an agent for the permanent guardian and may not go against any wishes or instructions the permanent guardian may express" (Reference Guide, para.19.130).

THE LOCAL SOCIAL SERVICES AUTHORITY.   See subs.(5).

*Subsection (3)*

**1–130**     This subsection empowers an approved mental health professional to apply to the county court for an order transferring the guardianship of the patient to a local social services authority or to a person approved by that authority.

### *General Provisions as to Applications and Recommendations*

**General provisions as to applications**

**1–131**     **11.**—(1) Subject to the provisions of this section, an application for admission for assessment, an application for admission for treatment and a guardianship application may be made either by the nearest relative of the patient or by an [approved mental health professional]; and every such application shall specify the qualification of the applicant to make the application.

[(1A) No application mentioned in subsection (1) above shall be made by an approved mental health professional if the circumstances are such that there would be a potential conflict of interest for the purposes of regulations under section 12A below.]

(2) Every application for admission shall be addressed to the managers of the hospital to which admission is sought and every guardianship application shall be forwarded to the local social services authority named in the application as guardian, or, as the case may be, to the local social services authority for the area in which the person so named resides.

(3) Before or within a reasonable time after an application for the admission of a patient for assessment is made by an [approved mental health professional, that professional] shall take such steps as are practicable to inform the person (if any) appearing to be the nearest relative of the patient that the application is to be or has been made and of the power of the nearest relative under section 23(2)(a) below.

[(4) An approved mental health professional may not make an application for admission for treatment or a guardianship application in respect of a patient in either of the following cases—

(a)  the nearest relative of the patient has notified that professional, or the local social services authority on whose behalf the professional is acting, that he objects to the application being made; or

(b)  that professional has not consulted the person (if any) appearing to be the nearest relative of the patient, but the requirement to consult that person does not apply if it appears to the professional that in the circumstances such consultation is not reasonably practicable or would involve unreasonable delay.]

(5) None of the applications mentioned in subsection (1) above shall be made by any person in respect of a patient unless that person has personally seen the patient within the period of 14 days ending with the date of the application.

(6) [. . .]

(7) Each of the applications mentioned in subsection (1) above shall be sufficient if the recommendations on which it is founded are given either as separate recommendations, each signed by a registered medical practitioner, or as a joint recommendation signed by two such practitioners.

AMENDMENTS
The amendments to this section were made by the Mental Health Act 2007 ss.21, 22(2), 55, Sch.2 para.4, Sch.11 Pt 1.

DEFINITIONS
    application for admission for assessment: s.145(1).        **1–132**
    application for admission for treatment: s.145(1).
    nearest relative: ss.26(3), 145(1).
    approved mental health professional: s.145(1), (1AC).
    the managers: s.145(1).
    hospital: ss.34(2), 145(1).
    local social services authority: s.145(1).
    patient: s.145(1).
    mental disorder: ss.1, 145(1).

GENERAL NOTE
This section contains general provisions relating to applications for admission for assess- **1–133** ment, applications for admission for treatment, and guardianship applications.

Although primary responsibility for checking that the statutory forms have been completed correctly rests with the applicant, hospital managers and local social services authorities should each designate an officer to scrutinise the documents as soon as they have been received and to take any necessary action if they have been improperly completed: see reg.4(3) of the English Regulations and reg.4(2) of the Welsh Regulations.

*Human Rights Act 1998*
The European Court of Human Rights has held that there are positive obligations that are **1–134** placed on public authorities which are inherent in an effective respect for family life under art.8(1) of the European Convention on Human Rights (*Osman v United Kingdom* (2000) 29 E.H.R.R. 245). In particular, the European Commission of Human Rights has recognised that public authorities might have to take particular steps to protect the mentally disordered in order to fulfil their obligations under that article (*X & Y v Netherlands* (1983) E.C.H.R. Ser.B, No.74). If a mentally disordered person is denied the care and treatment that he or she is assessed as needing by virtue of a nearest relative exercising the right to object to an application under subs.(4), it is arguable that the State is failing in its positive obligation under art.8 to protect that person if an application is not made under s.29(3)(c) to displace the relative.

*Subsection (1)*
APPLICATION. By virtue of reg.4(1) of the English Regulations, the following forms **1–135** must be used: applications for assessment—Form A1 (for NRs) or A2 (for AMHPs); applications for treatment—Form A5 (for NRs) or A6 (for AMHPs); emergency applications—Form A9 (for NRs) or Form A10 (for AMHPs); and for guardianship application—Form G1 (for NRs) or G2 for AMHPs). Applications to hospitals in Wales must use the forms set out in the Welsh Regulations which are: applications for assessment—Form HO1 (for NRs) or HO2 (for AMHPs); applications for treatment—Form HO5 (for NRs) or HO6 (for AMHPs); emergency applications—Form HO9 (for NRs) or Form HO10 (for AMHPs) and for guardianship application—Form GUI (for NRs) or GU2 (for AMHPs).

An application in respect of a ward of court cannot be made without the leave of the High Court (s.33(1)).

MAY BE MADE EITHER BY. The approved mental health professional (AMHP) is "usually a more appropriate applicant than the patient's nearest relative" (*Code of Practice*, para.4.28). Although applications made by nearest relatives are rare, the Royal Commission considered the nearest relative to be a more appropriate applicant than a social worker: "Ideally, in our view, the application should be made by a relative of the patient on medical recommendation, with a mental welfare officer available to explain the procedure and provide the application form and to transport the patient to hospital if necessary" (para.403). In practice, applications by nearest relatives are rare. Neither the AMHP nor the nearest relative can prevent the other from making an application. An application which is signed by a person who is neither an AMHP nor the patient's nearest relative is invalid and incapable of being rectified under s.15.

NEAREST RELATIVE. Or an acting nearest relative appointed by the court under s.29. It is possible for a nearest relative to authorise some other person to act for him or her under reg.24 of the English Regulations or reg.33 of the Welsh Regulations.

APPROVED MENTAL HEALTH PROFESSIONAL. Section 13 places a duty on an AMHP to make an application if certain criteria are satisfied.

*Subsection (1A)*

**1–136** REGULATIONS UNDER SECTION 12A. See the Mental Health (Conflicts of Interest) (England) Regulations 2008 which are reproduced in Pt 2. The equivalent Welsh Regulations are SI 2008/2440 (W.213).

*Subsection (2)*

**1–137** THE MANAGERS. Who are the detaining authority (*R. v South Western Hospital Managers Ex p. M* [1994] 1 All E.R. 161). The application shall be served by delivering it to an officer of the managers of the hospital to which it is proposed that the patient shall be admitted: see reg.3(2) of the English and Welsh Regulations. Hospital managers are not obliged to admit patients in respect of whom applications under Pt II of this Act have been made. In Volume 2 of his *A Human Condition* (1977), Larry Gostin refers to the opinion that Sir Geoffrey Howe Q.C., M.P. gave to the North West Thames Regional Health Authority in 1974 on the role of hospital managers in respect of hospital admissions. Sir Geoffrey concluded that a hospital consultant had no right to admit a patient, except with the authority of the hospital managers (*A Human Condition*, pp.53, 59).

HOSPITAL. As the application does not authorise the applicant to take the patient to any hospital other than the hospital specified in the application, the name of the hospital should not be written on the application form until a recommending doctor has confirmed that a hospital bed has been arranged for the patient. The Mental Health Act Commission suggested that if a patient cannot be admitted to hospital in an emergency for want of a bed, the AMHP should complete an application, making it out to the hospital which has been the subject of a notification under this s.140 of this Act, and convey the patient to that hospital. For a criticism of this approach, see the note on "to hospital" in s.6(1).

LOCAL SOCIAL SERVICES AUTHORITY FOR THE AREA IN WHICH THE PERSON SO NAMED RESIDES. A guardianship application does not take effect until it is accepted by the authority. If it is accepted, the authority will become the "responsible local social services authority" for the purposes of this Part (s.34(3)).

PERSON SO NAMED. If it has not been possible to identify the name of the patient by the time the application is made, it is suggested that the phrase "the patient known by the name of John [or Mary] Smith" be entered in the patient name space on the appropriate application form. A note of the real name of the patient should be attached to the application as soon as it is discovered.

RESIDES. Temporary absence from the place where a person lives does not affect residence, as long as there is an intention to return (*R. v St Leonard's Shoreditch (Inhabitants)* (1865) L.R. 1 Q.B. 21). In *Fox v Stirk* [1970] Q.B. 463 at 477, Widgery L.J. said: "A man cannot be said to reside in a particular place unless in the ordinary sense of the word one can say that for the time being he is making his home in that place."

*Subsection (3)*

This subsection, which applies to both s.2 and s.4 (*Re GM* [2000] M.H.L.R. 41), requires **1–138** an AMHP who makes an application for admission for assessment to take such steps as are practicable to inform the patient's nearest relative that the application is either about to be or has been made and of his or her power to discharge the patient.

WITHIN A REASONABLE TIME. Given that an application deprives patients of their liberty, it is unlikely that a court would consider a delay of more than 24 hours to be reasonable in the absence of circumstances that make contacting the nearest relative problematic.

SUCH STEPS AS ARE PRACTICABLE. The impact that contacting the nearest relative might have on the patient's health and well-being will need to be considered when the AMHP determines whether it would be practicable to take steps to inform that relative: see *R. (on the application of E) v Bristol City Council*, noted under "not reasonably practicable" in subs.(4).

The steps taken could include telephoning to inform a nearest relative who resides at some distance from the admitting hospital or asking a social worker from the area where the nearest relative resides to inform him or her of the application. The actual giving of the information need not necessarily be undertaken by the AMHP who made the application (*R. v Managers of South Western Hospital Ex p. M* [1994] 1 All E.R. 161.).

INFORM. The information could be given either orally or in writing.

APPEARING TO BE THE NEAREST RELATIVE. This section does not impose a duty of reasonable enquiry on the AMHP in deciding who is the patient's nearest relative: see the note under this heading in subs.(4). If the AMHP makes a genuine mistake and informs a person who is not the patient's nearest relative, that mistake does not have the effect of invalidating the s.2 application: see *R. v Birmingham Mental Health Trust Ex p. Phillips* (CO/1501/95), May 25, 1995, where Tucker J. refused applications for *habeas corpus* and judicial review that had been made on behalf of a patient who had been detained under s.2 in circumstances where the patient's mother had been incorrectly identified as the patient's nearest relative; for the action to be taken on such a mistake being discovered, see the General Note to s.6. His Lordship said that a subsequent application that had been made to the county court under s.29 of this Act had also not been invalidated by the mistake.

THE POWER . . . UNDER SECTION 23(2)(*a*). Of the nearest relative to order the patients discharge from hospital. It is suggested that the AMHP should also inform the nearest relative of the power of the patient's responsible clinician under s.25(1) to prevent the discharge from taking place.

*Subsection (4)*

This subsection provides that: (1) an application by an AMHP for admission for treat- **1–139** ment or for guardianship must be preceded by a consultation with the patient's nearest relative unless this is impracticable or would involve unreasonable delay, and (2) the application cannot proceed if the patient's nearest relative objects.

If the nearest relative of a patient who is detained under s.2 objects to an application being made under s.3, the patient can continue to be detained beyond the 28-day period provided for in s.2 if an AMHP applies during the currency of the s.2 to the county court for the nearest relative to be displaced under ground (c) or (d) of s.29(3) (s.29(4)). Once formal steps have been taken to make an application under s.3, it is not possible for an AMHP to overcome a nearest relative's objection by making an application under s.2 in respect of the patient (*R. v Wilson Ex p. Williamson*, noted in the General Note to s.2).

*Paragraph (a)*

**1–140**   OBJECTS.   The AMHP must have formed an objectively reasonable belief that there was an objection to the application. In forming an opinion on this issue, the AMHP must consider whether the nearest relative had previously objected to the patient's detention by, for example, exercising his or her power to discharge the patient from detention. The nearer in time the previous events are, the more relevant they become, particularly if they show a state of mind of the nearest relative which is unlikely to be changed (*Re M* [2009] M.H.L.R. 154). However, the lawfulness of detention does not depend on whether the AMHP reasonably believes that there is no objection but on whether in fact there was no objection (*TMM v London Borough of Hackney* [2010] EWHC 1349 (Admin), para.37). In *GD v Edgware Community Hospital and Barnet L.B.C.* [2008] M.H.L.R. 282 para.27, it was accepted that objection was something that might be gleaned from the totality of what was said, including the way in which it was said. In this case, Burnett J. confirmed that the objection does not have to be either reasonable or sensible. The AMHP should provide the nearest relative with sufficient information to enable him or her to form an opinion (*Re Whitbread*, below). The AMHP can proceed if the relative either does not object to the application or "perhaps wishes to sit on the fence" (*R. (on the application of G) v Ealing LBC* [2002] EWHC Admin. 1112 at para.10, per Scott Baker J.). It is not necessary for the AMHP to ask the nearest relative the specific question of whether there is an objection to the application being made (*Re GM (Patient: Consultation)* [2000] M.H.L.R. 41). However, in cases where the AMHP is unsure whether the nearest relative is objecting, the specific question should be asked (*M v East London NHS Foundation Trust*, above). In order to avoid confusion, it is suggested that in all cases the AMHP should ask the nearest relative whether he or she objects to the application being made. The nearest relative is not placed under any obligation to consent to the application.

In *GD v Edgware Community Hospital and Barnet L.B.C.*, above, para.33, Burnett J. said, obiter, that as an application under s.3 is "not made until it is given to the hospital staff", the nearest relative has a right to signify an objection up to that point. A counter argument, which is consistent with the remarks of Phillips L.J. in *Re Whitbread*, below, is that as an application is "duly completed" under s.6 when it is signed by the applicant, the nearest relative's right to object under this provision ends at that point.

If a nearest relative objects to an application being made but subsequently withdraws that objection, it is advisable for the AMHP to obtain a signed written statement to that effect; per Simon Brown L.J. in *Re Shearon* [1996] C.O.D. 223 DC.

Unreasonable objection by a nearest relative to an application is one of the grounds in s.29(3) which enables a county court to transfer the powers of the nearest relative to an "acting nearest relative".

*Paragraph (b)*

**1–141**   CONSULTED.   The AMHP cannot avoid consulting the nearest relative because of a belief that the nearest relative would not object to the application (*R.(on the application of V) v South London and Maudsley NHS Foundation Trust* [2010] EWHC 742 (Admin); [2010] M.H.L.R. 83). In *B v Cygnet Healthcare* [2008] EWHC 1259 (Admin); [2008] M.H.L.R. 106, King J. held that:

1.  The burden of showing that proper consultation has taken place falls on the AMHP.

2.  As a matter of law, there is no obligation for the nearest relative to expressly lodge an objection under this provision. An intermediary who had been nominated by the nearest relative could be used if an appropriate consultation is undertaken with that person: see *R. v Managers of South Western Hospital,* noted below.

In the *Cygnet* case the patient's father, as his nearest relative, told the AMHP to talk to the patient's sister because of his difficulties with English. It is not good practice to consult via an intermediary who will be neither neutral nor disinterested as the AMHP will have no means of knowing whether the views being expressed are actually those of the nearest relative.

In *Re Whitbread (Mental Patient: Habeas Corpus)* (1998) 39 B.M.L.R. 94, the Court of Appeal held that the consultation with the nearest relative can take place before the applicant has seen the patient in accordance with subs.(5). Phillips L.J. said:

"No express provision is made as to when [the] consultation should take place. Counsel for the respondents conceded that a nexus must exist between the consultation and the application that is subsequently made. The consultation must relate to that application. It must place the nearest relative in a position, if so minded, to object to that application . . . Provided that the [AMHP] explains to the nearest relative that he or she is considering making an application and why, the nearest relative will be afforded the opportunity for objecting to the application that the Act requires."

His Lordship also said: "The consultation will have two objectives. The first will be to provide information to the [AMPH] to assist with the decision of whether to apply for admission. The second will be to put the nearest relative in a position to object to an application".

In *Re Briscoe* [1998] C.O.D. 402, Tucker J. said:

"Lest I needed to be instructed as to the meaning of the word 'consultation', counsel thoughtfully provided the ruling of Webster J. in the case of *R. v Secretary of State for Social Services Ex p. Association of Metropolitan Authorities* [1986] 1 All E.R. 164 where at p.167 Webster J. said this: 'But in any context the essence of consultation is the communication of a genuine invitation to give advice and a genuine consideration of that advice.' Therefore merely informing the nearest relative [of the proposed application] will not suffice."

In *GD v Edgware Community Hospital and Barnet L.B.C.,* above, consultation was held by Burnett J. not to have taken place where the [AMHP] and the other professionals involved in the patient's assessment did no more than nod in the direction of consultation by setting in motion:

"a course of events which was designed to leave consultation with [the nearest relative] to the very last moment, and thus seriously inhibit the chances of his having any effective input into the process and the chances of his having an opportunity to make an objection. In those circumstances, what in my judgment they contemplated, could not properly be considered consultation at all" (para.52).

His Lordship said, at para.47, that the:

"duty to consult is one which exists to enable there to be a dialogue about the action proposed in respect of a mentally ill individual. The person concerned is entitled to have his views taken into account and, importantly, the consultation process should enable the nearest relative to object to the proposed course if he wishes. The consultation must be a real exercise and not a token one. If an objection is made, it does not have to be a reasonable one. It does not have to be one which judged objectively is sensible".

The process of consultation might involve the AMHP in divulging confidential information about the patient to the nearest relative. The transmission of such information should only be to the extent necessary to provide the nearest relative with a genuine opportunity to object to the application.

In *R. v Managers of South Western Hospital*, above, Laws J. said at 175, 176, that the AMHP is not prevented in suitable circumstances from carrying out the duty to consult through the medium of another. He developed this point by stating:

"ordinarily, it will clearly be desirable for the consultation to be carried out directly by the [AMHP]. But there may be circumstances in which that will be difficult, or even well-nigh impossible. What is important is that the consultation be full and effective, to ensure that the nearest relative has the opportunity to play his full part in the process. . . . I do not suggest that an [AMHP] has a wholly free hand to appoint, as it were, a delegate for the purposes of consultation. It remains throughout the [AMHP's] responsibility".

As an AMHP will have the knowledge and experience to engage in a "full and effective" consultation with the nearest relative, an attempt should be made to consult through the medium of another AMHP.

Although there appears to be no legal reason to prevent an AMHP undertaking the consultation through correspondence, this practice is unlikely to result in the "full and effective" consultation advocated by Laws J.

(IF ANY). The application can proceed without consultation having taken place if it appears to the AMHP that the patient has no nearest relative. Reasonable steps must be taken by the AMHP in an attempt to ascertain the identity of the patient's nearest relative.

**1–142**    APPEARING TO BE THE NEAREST RELATIVE. These words "cannot in my judgment, embrace a situation where, on the facts known to the [AMHP], the person in question is legally *incapable* of being the statutory nearest relative having regard to the terms of section 26": *R. v Managers of South Western Hospital*, above, per Laws J. at 175.

This section does not impose a duty of reasonable inquiry on the AMHP applicant when identifying the patient's nearest relative; there is no requirement for the AMHP "to don the mantle of Sherlock Holmes" (see *WC*, below, para.28). The test is subjective. A court cannot inquire into the reasonableness of the AMHP's decision, it can only inquire into the honesty of his assertion that it appeared that that relative was the nearest relative (*Re D (Mental Patient: Habeas Corpus)* [2000] 2 F.L.R. 848 CA).

*Re D* was cited by Scott Baker J. in *R. (on the application of WC) v South London & Maudsley NHS Trust* [2001] EWHC Admin 1025; [2001] M.H.L.R. 187 para.27, where his Lordship said that the court will not interfere with the AMHP's conclusion under this provision unless he or she failed to apply the test in s.26 or acted in bad faith, or in some way reached a conclusion that was plainly wrong. *WC* was applied in *GD v The Hospital Managers of the Edgware Community Hospital and Barnet L.B.C.*, above, where it was held that an additional ground for interfering with the decision of an AMHP is misuse of power.

In the absence of action being taken under s.29 to displace the nearest relative or of the nearest relative agreeing to transfer his or her functions to another under reg.24 of the English Regulations or reg.33 of the Welsh Regulations, the AMHP should consult with the person who he has identified as being the patient's nearest relative using the formula set out in s.26, even though, from a professional perspective, it might be inappropriate for that person to be consulted. However, the consultation need not take place if the AMHP considers that it is not "reasonably practicable" to undertake the consultation.

APPEARS TO THE PROFESSIONAL THAT IN THE CIRCUMSTANCES. The "circumstances" are those known to the AMHP or believed by him or her to exist (*R.(on the application of V) v South London and Maudsley NHS Foundation Trust*, above, para.33).

NOT REASONABLY PRACTICABLE. It would clearly not be practicable for an AMHP to consult with a nearest relative who is either mentally or physically incapable of being consulted or who is implacably opposed to being consulted. Neither would it be practicable to consult in a situation where a patient who is not known to the clinical team is either unable or unwilling to give the AMHP information to enable the nearest relative to be identified.

Paragraph 2.16 of the 1999 edition of the *Code of Practice* stated in relation to this provision:

"Practicability refers to the availability of the nearest relative and not to the appropriateness of informing or consulting the person concerned."

This guidance was held to be both "wrong" and "contrary to common sense" in *R. (on the application of E) v Bristol City Council* [2005] EWHC 74 (Admin); [2005] M.H.L.R. 83 because the author of the Code had fallen into the trap of confusing the different concepts of "possibility" and "practicability". It was therefore possible to interpret this provision to include taking account of the patient's wishes and/or her health and well-being. The court, in accepting submissions made by counsel for the patient which were based on the approach advocated in the 9th edition of this work, found that it was not "practicable" to consult (or inform under subs.(3)) the nearest relative of the patient in circumstances where there was credible evidence that if the AMHP consulted the nearest relative this would cause the patient "significant distress". Bennett J. said at para.28:

"Is the [AMHP] really bound to inform/consult the nearest relative of a patient who may intensely dislike a patient and/or would, or might, not act in the patient's best interest? The answer, in my judgment, is of course not and particularly so where the patient, as here, is competent and has strongly expressed her wish that her nearest relative . . . is not informed or consulted."

His Lordship held that although the significant role of the nearest relative is not lightly to be removed by invoking practicability, the AMHP should not consult if this would be detrimental to the patient in that it would result in a breach of the patient's right to respect for private and family life under art.8 of the European Convention on Human Rights. It follows that consultation should not take place if either a mentally capable or a mentally incapable patient is assessed as being likely to suffer emotional distress, deterioration in his or her mental health, physical harm, or financial or other form of exploitation as result of the consultation. It is submitted the AMHP should disregard the fact that the potential distress caused to the patient would be caused by an irrational belief or fantasy that the patient might have of the nearest relative's attitude to him or her. The evidence that the AMHP relied on when deciding that it was not practicable to consult should be noted on the case file. If the decision was made on the ground that consultation would be detrimental to the mental health of the patient, it is suggested that a confirmatory report from either the patient's general practitioner or a psychiatrist be obtained. As it is the potential impact of the consultation on the patient's art.8 rights that should determine the AMHP's decision, a decision not to consult could be made even though a mentally capable patient is not objecting to the consultation. This could happen if it was known that the nearest relative would be likely to exploit the patient's situation; see further the *Code of Practice* at paras 4.60 to 4.63.

If, subsequent to the patient's detention, the nearest relative disputes the decision of the AMHP applicant that it had not been practicable to consult, the hospital managers should not attempt to resolve the dispute: see the General Note to s.6. The appropriate remedy would be for the nearest relative to seek to challenge the legality of the patient's detention by an application for judicial review.

UNDESIRABLE DELAY.   Given the circumstances of most guardianship applications and applications for treatment, it is unlikely that this situation would often obtain. It could occur if tracing the whereabouts of the nearest relative would involve an excessive amount of investigative work on the part of the AMHP.

*Subsection (5)*

**1–143**   PERSONALLY SEEN.   An intermediary cannot be used (*R. v Managers of South Western Hospital*, above).

The relationship between this provision and s.13(2), which requires an AMHP to interview the patient before making an application, was examined in the following passage of Phillips L.J.'s judgment in *Re Whitbread*, above:

> "In my judgment section 11(5) and section 13(2) do not necessarily refer to the same event. The precondition to an application imposed by s.11(5) applies whether the application is made by the nearest relative or by the [AMHP] and thus must be appropriate to either. It seems to me that the object of section 11(5) is to ensure that the view of an applicant that an application is desirable is informed by recent face to face contact with the patient. So far as the [AMHP] is concerned, this may or may not be the occasion upon which the interview required by section 13(2) takes place. I consider that the Act permits an application to follow from an interview that takes place more than 14 days before the application, provided that the [AMHP] has confirmed his conclusion that an application is desirable by face to face contact with the patient within 14 days of the application."

14 DAYS ENDING WITH THE DATE OF THE APPLICATION.   With the exception of an emergency application, once an application has been completed the patient must be taken to the hospital named in the application within 14 days of the second medical examination of the patient being made (s.6(1)(a)).

## General provisions as to medical recommendations

**1–144**   **12.**—(1) The recommendations required for the purposes of an application for the admission of a patient under this Part of this Act [or a guardianship application] (in this Act referred to as "medical recommendations") shall be signed on or before the date of the application, and shall be given by practitioners who have personally examined the patient either together or separately, but where they have examined the patient separately not more than five days must have elapsed between the days on which the separate examinations took place.

(2) Of the medical recommendations given for the purposes of any such application, one shall be given by a practitioner approved for the purposes of this section by the Secretary of State as having special experience in the diagnosis or treatment of mental disorder; and unless that practitioner has previous acquaintance with the patient, the other such recommendation shall, if practicable, be given by a registered medical practitioner who has such previous acquaintance.

[(2A) A registered medical practitioner who is an approved clinician shall be treated as also approved for the purposes of this section under subsection (2) above as having special experience as mentioned there.]

[(3) No medical recommendation shall be given for the purposes of an application mentioned in subsection (1) above if the circumstances are such that there would be a potential conflict of interest for the purposes of regulations under section 12A below.]

AMENDMENTS

The amendments to this section were made by the Mental Health Act 2007 ss.16, 22(3), (4).

DEFINITIONS **1–145**

    patient: s.145(1).

    mental disorder: ss.1, 145(1).

    approved clinician: s.145(1).

GENERAL NOTE

This section specifies the requirements that apply to medical recommendations which **1–146** are made to support applications for the detention of patients and guardianship applications. A recommendation may not be given if a potential conflict of interest arises (subs.(3)). A doctor who makes a recommendation under this section must be a fully registered person within the meaning of the Medical Act 1983 (Interpretation Act 1978 s.5, Sch.1).

A doctor who completes a medical recommendation on a form prescribed by the English or Welsh Regulations is acting in a clinical capacity, often in circumstances of considerable stress and urgency. The doctor is not "obliged to do any more than complete the form according to his or her professional judgment in the prescribed manner." It would be "wholly inappropriate" to treat that part of the form which requires the doctor to state the reasons why detention is required in the same way as a reasoned determination following a tribunal hearing (*R. (on the application of H) v Oxfordshire Mental Healthcare NHS Trust* [2002] EWHC Admin 465; [2002] M.H.L.R. 282 at paras 70, 71, per Sullivan J.).

A conscientious doctor whose opinion has not been accepted by a tribunal will doubtless ask himself whether the tribunal's view is to be preferred and whether his own opinion should be revised. But if, having done so, he adheres to his original opinion he cannot be obliged to suppress or alter it. His professional duty to his patient, and his wider duty to the public, requires him to form, and if called upon express, the best professional judgment he can, whether or not that coincides with the judgment of the tribunal (*R. v East London and The City Mental Health Trust Ex p. Brandenburg*, HL, which is noted in the General Note to s.3).

If a doctor who has been approached with a view to making a medical recommendation decides not to do so on the ground that the statutory criteria are not satisfied, there is nothing to prevent another doctor from making the recommendation as long as the provisions of subss.(1) to (3) are satisfied.

There is no provision in this Act which allows for the withdrawal of a valid medical recommendation after it has been provided to a potential applicant. In a case known to the author, a request for the return of a recommendation was made subsequent to the recommending doctor being subjected to pressure from members of the patient's family. An attempt to withdraw a recommendation would be a factor that the potential applicant would take into account when making a decision about the appropriateness of making an application.

*Human Rights Act 1998*

A doctor who makes medical recommendations under this Act is exercising "functions **1–147** of a public nature" and is therefore a "public authority" for the purposes of the 1998 Act: see *ibid.*, s.6(3)(b) and *R. (on the application of Wilkinson) v The Responsible Medical Officer Broadmoor Hospital, the Mental Health Act Commission Second Opinion Appointed Doctor and the Secretary of State for Health* [2001] EWCA Civ 1545; [2002] 1 W.L.R. 419, per Hale L.J. speaking obiter at para.61. The effect of this is that it is unlawful for a recommending doctor to act in a way which is incompatible with a patient's rights under the European Convention on Human Rights (Human Rights Act 1998 s.6(1)).

The medical assessment must be based on the actual state of mental health of the person concerned and not solely on past events (*Varbanov v Bulgaria*, [2000] M.H.L.R. 263 para.47).

The recommending doctor can be a general practitioner rather than a psychiatrist (*Schuurs v the Netherlands* 41 D. & R. 186, 188–189).

*Code of Practice*

**1–148**    Guidance on the responsibilities of Strategic Health Authorities under this section is given in Ch.4 at paras 4.102–4.103.

*Duty of care owed by recommending doctors*

**1–149**    In *M (A Minor) v Newham LBC* [1995] 3 All E.R. 353, HL, the local authority, in exercising functions under the child care legislation, arranged for a child whom they suspected was being sexually abused to be interviewed by a social worker and a child psychiatrist. The House of Lords held that the social worker and the psychiatrist:

> "did not, by accepting the instructions of the local authority, assume any general professional duty of care to the [child]. The professionals were employed or retained to advise the local authority in relation to the well-being of the [child] but not to advise or treat [the child]"; per Lord Browne-Wilkinson at 384.

As reference was made in both the Court of Appeal and in the House of Lords to *Everett v Griffiths* [1920] 3 K.B. 163 CA; [1921] 1 A.C. 631, a case decided under the Lunacy Act 1890 where the House of Lords assumed that a recommending doctor owed a duty of care to the patient without deciding the point (in *De Freville v Dill* (1927) 96 L.J. K.B. 1056, McCardie J. considered *Everett* and held that such a duty did exist), it could be argued that the decision in the *Newham* case determines the liability of doctors and approved mental health professionals (AMHPs) undertaking assessments under this Act. The legal position of professionals performing functions under the child care legislation and under this Act is, however, quite different.

The question whether there is a duty of care at common law must be profoundly influenced by the statutory framework within which the acts complained of were done (*X (Minors) v Bedfordshire CC* [1995] 2 A.C. 633 at 739 per Lord Browne-Wilkinson). AMHPs and doctors who undertake assessments under this Act are not involved in either reporting to or advising their employer or any other body. The AMHP is undertaking an independent legal function when determining whether to make an application and the role of the recommending doctors is to examine the patient and support the application if it is considered that the statutory criteria are satisfied. It is submitted that the assumption made by the House of Lords in *Everett v Griffiths*, an assumption shared by Lord Atkinson in *Harnett v Fisher* [1927] A.C. 573 at 596 where the House of Lords left the matter open, is correct and that the AMHP and the recommending doctors have assumed personal responsibility towards the patient to take reasonable care to avoid an inappropriate and/ or unlawful detention. It follows that an action for negligence could be brought where the professional fails to exercise such care. Leave for such actions to be perused was given in *Winch v Jones* [1986] Q.B. 296 and *Buxton v Jayne* [1960] 1 W.L.R. 783. As Atkin L.J. pointed out in the Court of Appeal in *Everett* at 212, s.330 of the Lunacy Act 1890 (now to be found in an amended form in s.139 of this Act) assumes that professionals performing functions under this Act consider themselves bound to exercise reasonable care.

Atkin L.J.'s judgment in *Everett* included the following noteworthy passages:

> "Grievous as is the wrong of unjust imprisonment of an alleged criminal, I apprehend that its colours pale beside the catastrophe of unjust imprisonment on an unfounded finding of insanity. Modern organisation has no doubt done much to remove the horrors that were associated with Bedlam in the days when the victims were subject to public

exhibition. Probably even now the insane ward or reception ward is not without its revolting incidents. But it is the effect on the mind sane, even if feeble, that knows itself wrongly adjudged unsound that produces the most poignant suffering" (at 211).

"[I]t is just as it is convenient that the law should impose a duty to take reasonable care that such persons, if sane, should not suffer the unspeakable torment of having their sanity condemned and their liberty restricted; and I am glad to record my opinion, ineffectual though it may be, that for such an injury the English law provides a remedy" (at 233).

At the House of Lords Lord Haldane described this as a "powerful piece of reasoning displaying anxiety to guard against a possible miscarriage of justice" ([1921] 1 A.C. 631 at 652).

In *Clunis v Camden and Islington Health Authority* [1998] 3 All E.R. 180 at 192, the Court of Appeal said that "the question whether a doctor owes a duty of care to a patient in certifying that a patient is fit to be detained under the Mental Health Act was left undecided in *Everett v Griffiths* and still remains open for decision in an appropriate case".

In *TMM v London Borough of Hackney* [2010] EWHC 1349 (Admin), para.36, Collins J. said that that he could see no reason in principle why an AMHP should not owe a duty of care to the patient. Approved Clinicians owe a duty of care to the patient whenever they propose or administer treatment under Pt IV of this Act (*R. (on the application of Wilkinson) v Responsible Medical Officer Broadmoor Hospital* [2001] EWCA 1545; [2002] 1 W.L.R. 419 para.68).

*Subsection (1)*

This subsection provides that medical recommendations must be signed on or before the **1–150** date of the application by doctors who have personally examined the patient and that where the two doctors examine the patient separately not more than five days must have elapsed between the days on which the separate examinations took place.

The detention of a patient under either s.2 or s.3 can take place within 14 days of the date of the second medical examination of the patient (s.6(1)(a)). Although the medical recommendations remain valid during this period, good practice suggests that fresh examinations of the patient should take place if there has been a significant change in the patient's circumstances subsequent to the date(s) of the original examinations. Section 6 does not apply to guardianship applications.

RECOMMENDATIONS. Incorrect or defective recommendations (apart from joint recommendations) can be rectified under s.15. Recommendations must be in the forms prescribed by reg.4(1) of the English Regulations, i.e. Form A3 (joint recommendation) or A4 for applications under s.2, Form A7 (joint application) or A8 for applications under s.3 and Form A11 for applications under s.4. The equivalent forms under reg.4(1) of the Welsh Regulations are: Form HO3 (joint recommendation) or HO4 for applications under s.2, Form HO7 (joint applications) or HO8 for applications under s.3 and Form HO11 for applications under s.4. For which form to use where the patient was medically examined in Wales, see reg.4(2) of the English Regulations.

If doctors who have not examined the patient together incorrectly complete a joint recommendation form, this would not constitute a fundamental defect in the application (see *Re S-C (Mental Patient: Habeas Corpus)* noted under s.6) as the two doctors would have certified that the criteria for detention are satisfied. The continued detention of the patient would therefore be lawful.

ON OR BEFORE THE DATE OF THE APPLICATION. An applicant should not sign an application and then try to obtain the medical recommendation to support it.

PERSONALLY EXAMINED.   The medical examination of the patient is considered in the *Code of Practice* at paras 4.71 et seq. The examination should be accompanied by such further enquiries as are necessary (*Hall v Semple* (1862) 3 F. & F. 337 at 354 per Crompton J.).

A personal examination of the patient must always precede the making of a medical recommendation, even though the patient might be well known to the doctor. A doctor can examine a patient for the purposes of this provision by observing her conduct over a sufficient period of time, even if she refuses, for example, to answer questions or to submit to a physical examination or is otherwise hostile and unco-operative (*R. (on the application of M) v The Managers, Queen Mary's Hospital* [2008] EWHC 1959 (Admin); [2008] M.H.L.R. 303 para.12; approved by the Court of Appeal at [2008] EWCA Civ 1112; [2008] M.H.L.R. 306 para.25 where it was said, at para.26, that there is no set time that must be taken for an examination to qualify under this provision; what is required is a matter for the professional judgment of the doctor). There would appear to be no reason to prevent an examination being conducted via a video link as this would enable to examining doctor be both observe and attempt to interview the patient; see further, P. Yellowlees, (1997) "The use of telemedicine to perform psychiatric assessments under the Mental Health Act", *Journal of Telemedicine and Telecare*, 3(4), 224–226.

An examination of an unconscious or highly intoxicated patient would not enable the doctor to ascertain whether the criteria for admission under this Act were established. Such a patient could be admitted to hospital and treated under the authority of ss.5 and 6 of the Mental Capacity Act 2005.

If the doctor is unable to gain access to the patient, consideration should be given to invoking s.135(1) of this Act.

FIVE DAYS.   i.e. five clear days between the days on which the medical examinations took place. Therefore if, for example, the first examination took place on January 1 the second can take place no later than January 7. The relevant dates are the dates when the examinations took place and not the dates when the medical recommendations were signed.

*Subsection (2)*

**1–151**   This subsection provides for the approval by the Secretary of State or the Welsh Ministers of one of the doctors who provides a recommendation in support of an application for the admission of a patient to hospital or a guardianship application.

A doctor can be approved under this provision without having been approved as an approved clinician (AC). A doctor who is an AC is automatically treated as being approved under this provision (subs.(2A)). See s.142A for the mutual recognition of approvals in England and Wales.

SECRETARY OF STATE.   The function of the Secretary of State under this provision has been delegated to Strategic Health Authorities (National Health Service (Functions of Strategic Health Authorities and Primary Care Trusts and Administration Arrangements) (England) Regulations 2002 (SI 2002/2375) reg.3(3), Sch.2). This function cannot be further delegated to a Primary Care Trust (reg.5(1) Sch.3). Approval shall be given by the Authority:

"only—

(a) after carrying out such consultations, and obtaining such advice, as the Secretary of State may direct; and

(b) for such periods as the Secretary of State may direct" (2002 Regulations reg.7(2)).

The functions of the Minister, so far as exercisable in relation to Wales, are exercised by the Welsh Ministers: see the General Note to this Act. The Welsh Ministers have transferred this function to Local Health Boards (SI 2003/150 and SI 2003/813). The Mental Health

(Mutual Recognition) Regulations 2008 (SI 2008/1204), which are reproduced in Part 2, provide that doctors approved in Wales for these purposes are treated as if approved in England as well (and vice versa).

SPECIAL EXPERIENCE IN THE DIAGNOSIS OR TREATMENT OF MENTAL DISORDER. In *R. v Trent Regional Health Authority Ex p. Somaratne* (1993) 18 B.M.L.R. 143, Potts J. held that the "special experience" referred to in this subsection does no more than provide a minimum threshold required before approval can be granted and is, therefore, not the only matter which the Health Authority can take into account. This finding was reversed by a majority in the Court of Appeal (1994) 31 B.M.L.R. 140 where it was held that "special experience" is the sole criterion for approving a doctor and that having "special experience" requires examination of the doctor's current knowledge and skills in the diagnosis and treatment of mental disorder. The Health Authority has to consider the doctor's qualifications and experience and not his or her overall suitability for appointment. Following this decision the doctor in question made a fresh application for approval to the Health Authority and this application was refused. An application for a judicial review of this decision was made and judgment was given by Latham J. ([1996] C.O.D. 138). In dismissing the application, his Lordship held that:

1. The Health Authority was entitled to take into account the doctor's age because that issue was only considered in the context of the length of the approval that might be granted.

2. The authority was entitled to issue guidance to members of its Mental Health Approval Panel taking into account the number of psychiatrists in any given area and adjusting the standard to be applied in considering "special experience", provided that this was applied generally and that the adjustment was directed to consideration of experience only. In this case there was no shortage of approved doctors in the relevant areas which would justify departing from what would otherwise be considered an appropriate standard of experience.

THE OTHER SUCH RECOMMENDATION. The recipients of a survey undertaken by E. K. Ung questioned the "independence" of the second medical opinion ("Who should act as the second medical recommendation for sections 2 and 3 of the Mental Health Act", *Psychiatric Bulletin* (1993), 17, 466–468). If the doctor who provides the second opinion is neither approved under this provision nor knows the patient, it is difficult to identify the added value that such an opinion brings to the assessment.

SHALL, IF PRACTICABLE. This wording suggests that an application would be unlawful if neither medical recommendation came from a doctor with previous acquaintance of the patient in circumstances where it would have been practicable to obtain such a recommendation. Such an assumption was made by the Divisional Court in *R. v D'Souza* [1992] Crim. L.R. 119.

The word "practicable" was considered in *Owen v Crown House Engineering* [1973] 3 All E.R. 618 at 622, NIRC, where Sir Hugh Griffiths in giving the judgment of the court said:

"It is important not to equate 'practicable' with 'possible'. When considering whether a course of action is possible, it is not permissible to consider the results of that course of action; if it can be done, it must be done. But when considering whether a course of action is practicable it may be permissible to look at the end result. Like so many words of the English language, 'practicable' will take considerable colour from the context in which it is used."

A similar approach to the meaning of "practicable" was taken by the Court of Appeal in *Dedman v British Building and Engineering Appliances Ltd* [1974] 1 W.L.R. 171, and by

Ewbank J. in *Re P (Adoption) (Natural Fathers Rights)* [1994] 1 F.L.R. 771. All three cases were cited to Bennett J. in *R. (on the application of E) v Bristol City Council* [2005] EWHC 74 (Admin); [2005] M.H.L.R. 83, which is noted under "not reasonably practicable" in s.11(4). In *R. (on the application of C) v South London and Maudsley NHS Trust and Mental Health Review Tribunal* {2003] EWHC 3467 (Admin); [2004] M.H.L.R. 280, the judge said at para.11: "Practicability itself is not a black and white concept and lends itself to questions of judgment fact and degree".

In *TMM v London Borough of Hackney* [2010] EWHC 1349 (Admin), there was a disagreement between the psychiatrists who had been treating the patient as to whether he satisfied the criteria for detention. In those circumstances, the hospital trust decided that it would be fairer to approach two forensic psychiatrists both of whom were approved under s.12 (see para.4.74 of the *Code of Practice*) and neither of whom had previous acquaintance with the patient. One was from within, the other from outside the trust. Collins J. held that this arrangement did not breech this provision. His Lordship said at para.33:

> "Thus I think that the decision to use two professionals who came afresh and who, of course, had access to all hospital notes and could question nurses or other doctors was reasonable and a proper exercise of judgment of what was in the [patient's] interests."

Judgments about practicability might also have to be made in the following situations:

(i)  is it practicable to involve a doctor with previous acquaintance with the patient given the time that it will take for that doctor to attend upon the patient; and

(ii)  is it practicable to involve such a doctor given the patient's need for a specialist assessment (e.g. the AMHP might conclude that the patient's disturbed behaviour and violent fantasies require an assessment from both a general and a forensic psychiatrist, neither of whom were previously acquainted with the patient.)

If it is not possible to obtain a recommendation from a doctor who has had previous acquaintance with the patient, the applicant must explain why this was the case: see Forms A1, A2, A5 and A6. In the *TMM* case, above, Collins J. said, at para.24, that that the relevant passages in these forms were misleading as they suggested that the test was one of possibility rather than practicability. It followed that the word "could" should be replaced with "did".

If neither of the recommending doctors know the patient, it is suggested that the "approved" doctor should attempt to consult with the patient's general practitioner over the telephone before signing a recommendation. Although patients' general practitioners are not obliged under their terms of service to undertake an assessment under this Act, the General Practitioner Committee of the British Medical Association has said that "general practitioners may consider that their attendance to provide an assessment . . ., although not a contractural obligation, is the patient's best interests".

PREVIOUS ACQUAINTANCE. In *AR (by her litigation friend JT) v Bronglais Hospital and Pembrokeshire and Derwen NHS Trust* [2001] EWHC Admin. 792; [2001] M.H.L.R. 175, Scott Baker J. held that this phrase did not require the doctor to have had a previous *personal* acquaintance with the patient. His Lordship said, at para.11, that the requirement is for the doctor to:

> "have some previous knowledge of the patient and must not be coming to him or her cold, as it were. There is no indication as to the extent of the previous acquaintance that is necessary, and in my judgment the words 'previous acquaintance' are ordinary English words which have to be interpreted according to the circumstances of the particular case".

In this case his Lordship held that a doctor who (1) had attended a case conference where he learnt a good deal about the background circumstances of the patient; (2) saw the patient for the first time for about five minutes subsequent to that meeting; and (3) had scanned the patient's recently received medical notes immediately before he made his medical recommendation, did have "previous acquaintance" with the patient.

A doctor who had provided a medical recommendation in respect of the patient on a previous occasion would come within this category. Also see the *Code of Practice* para.4.73.

In circumstances where general practitioners have organised themselves into large rotas or co-operatives to provide emergency out-of-hours services, the Department of Health advised the Mental Health Act Commission that the deputising doctor cannot be considered "to have prior knowledge of the patient simply because he has access to the patient's records" and that the G.P.s deputising/answering service should contact the actual G.P. if it appears from the telephone call that a mental health assessment is likely (MHAC, *Sixth Biennial Report*, 1993–1995, para.8.1).

*Subsection (2A)*

This provides that a doctor who has been approved as an AC is automatically approved **1–152** for the purposes of this section.

*Subsection (3)*

See the notes on s.12A and the Mental Health (Conflicts of Interest) (England) **1–153** Regulations 2008 (SI 2008/1205) which are reproduced in Part 2. Only one medical recommendation in support of an application for admission to an independent hospital may be made by a doctor on the staff of that hospital (English Regulations, reg.4(2)). In Wales, neither recommendation may be given by such a doctor (Welsh Regulations, reg.4(3)).

**[Conflicts of interest**

**12A.**—(1) The appropriate national authority may make regulations as to the **1–154** circumstances in which there would be a potential conflict of interest such that—

(a) an approved mental health professional shall not make an application mentioned in section 11(1) above;

(b) a registered medical practitioner shall not give a recommendation for the purposes of an application mentioned in section 12(1) above.

(2) Regulations under subsection (1) above may make—

(a) provision for the prohibitions in paragraphs (a) and (b) of that subsection to be subject to specified exceptions;

(b) different provision for different cases; and

(c) transitional, consequential, incidental or supplemental provision.

(3) In subsection (1) above, "the appropriate national authority" means—

(a) in relation to applications in which admission is sought to a hospital in England or to guardianship applications in respect of which the area of the relevant local social services authority is in England, the Secretary of State;

(b) in relation to applications in which admission is sought to a hospital in Wales or to guardianship applications in respect of which the area of the relevant local social services authority is in Wales, the Welsh Ministers.

(4) References in this section to the relevant local social services authority, in relation to a guardianship application, are references to the local social services authority named in the application as guardian or (as the case may be) the local social services authority for the area in which the person so named resides.]

AMENDMENT
This section was inserted by the Mental Health Act 2007 s.22(5).

DEFINITIONS
**1–155**   approved mental health professional: s.145(1), (1AC).
hospital: s.145(1).
local social services authority: s.145(1).

GENERAL NOTE
**1–156**   The Mental Health Act 2007 repealed s.12(3) to (7) of this Act which set out the circumstances under which a medical practitioner was disqualified from making a medical recommendation in support of an application. The Government accepted that the subsections were "complex provisions and that placing them in secondary legislation would allow more flexibility to ensure provision keeps pace with changes in practice over time" (*Hansard*, HL Vol.688, col.539, per Baroness Royall). This section therefore introduces a power to enable regulations to be made by the Secretary of State (in respect of England) and the Welsh Ministers (in respect of Wales) setting out when, because of a conflict of interest:

>   (i)   an AMHP may not make an application for admission or a guardianship application; and

>   (ii)   a medical practitioner may not provide a medical recommendation supporting such an application.

The Mental Health (Conflicts of Interest) (England) Regulations 2008 (SI 2008/1205), which are reproduced in Part 2, have been made under this section. Regulations in respect of Wales have been made by the Welsh Ministers: see SI 2008/2440 (W.213). It is submitted that an application that is completed in breach of these Regulations is fundamentally defective, and is incapable of rectification under s.15.

*Code of Practice*
**1–157**   The circumstances in which applications by AMHPs or the provision of medical recommendations by doctors should not be made because of conflicts of interest are examined in Ch.7.

*Subsection (1)*
**1–158**   APPROPRIATE NATIONAL AUTHORITY.   See subs.(3).

*Subsection (3)*
**1–159**   RELEVANT LOCAL SOCIAL SERVICES AUTHORITY.   See subs.(4).

### [Duty of approved mental health professionals to make applications for admission or guardianship]

**1–160**   **13.**—[(1) If a local social services authority have reason to think that an application for admission to hospital or a guardianship application may need to be made in respect of a patient within their area, they shall make arrangements for an approved mental health professional to consider the patient's case on their behalf.

(1A) If that professional is—
(a)   satisfied that such an application ought to be made in respect of the patient; and

(b) of the opinion, having regard to any wishes expressed by relatives of the patient or any other relevant circumstances, that it is necessary or proper for the application to be made by him, he shall make the application.

(1B) Subsection (1C) below applies where—

(a) a local social services authority makes arrangements under subsection (1) above in respect of a patient;

(b) an application for admission for assessment is made under subsection (1A) above in respect of the patient;

(c) while the patient is liable to be detained in pursuance of that application, the authority have reason to think that an application for admission for treatment may need to be made in respect of the patient; and

(d) the patient is not within the area of the authority.

(1C) Where this subsection applies, subsection (1) above shall be construed as requiring the authority to make arrangements under that subsection in place of the authority mentioned there.]

(2) Before making an application for the admission of a patient to hospital an [approved mental health professional] shall interview the patient in a suitable manner and satisfy himself that detention in a hospital is in all the circumstances of the case the most appropriate way of providing the care and medical treatment of which the patient stands in need.

[(3) An application under subsection (1A) above may be made outside the area of the local social services authority on whose behalf the approved mental health professional is considering the patient's case.]

(4) It shall be the duty of a local social services authority, if so required by the nearest relative of a patient residing in their area, to [make arrangements under subsection (1) above for an approved mental health professional to consider the patient's case] with a view to making an application for his admission to hospital; and if in any such case [that professional] decides not to make an application he shall inform the nearest relative of his reasons in writing.

(5) Nothing in this section shall be construed as authorising or requiring an application to be made by an [approved mental health professional] in contravention of the provisions of section 11(4) above [or of regulations under section 12A above], or as restricting the power of [a local social services authority to make arrangements with an approved mental health professional to consider a patient's case or of] an [approved mental health professional] to make any application under this Act.

AMENDMENTS

The amendments to this section were made by the Mental Health Act 2007 ss.21, 22(6), Sch.2 para.5.

DEFINITIONS

approved mental health professional: s.145(1), (1AC).     **1–161**
hospital: ss.34(2), 145(1).
patient: s.145(1).
local social services authority: s.145(1), (4).
medical treatment: s.145(1).
nearest relative: ss.26(3), 145(1).

GENERAL NOTE

**1–162**    This section places a local social services authority (LASSA) under a duty to arrange for an approved mental health professional (AMHP) to consider a patient's case on their behalf if:

(i)  the authority has reason to think that an application for admission to hospital or a guardianship application may need to be made in respect of the patient; and

(ii)  the patient is within their area (subs.(1)).

If a patient has been detained for assessment under s.2, and the LASSA that arranged for an AMHP to consider that admission under subs.(1) has reason to think that an application for treatment under s.3 may be needed, subss.(1B) and (1C) place a duty on that LSSA (rather than the one for the area in which the patient is, or where the patient lives) to arrange for an AMHP to consider the patient's case on their behalf. The duties under subss.(1), (1B) and (1C) do not prevent another LSSA from exercising its power to arrange for an AMHP to consider a patient's case if this is felt to be appropriate (subs.(5)).

The AMHP is placed under a duty to make an application in respect of the patient if he or she considers that an application ought to be made and, having considered any wishes expressed by relatives of the patient or any other relevant circumstances, that it is both necessary and proper for the application to made by him or her (subs.(1A)). This is the case even if the application is made outside the area of the LSSA on whose behalf the AMHP is considering the patient's case (subs.(3)). The role of the AMHP is to "arrange and co-ordinate the assessment, taking into account all factors to determine if detention in hospital is the best option for the patient or if there is a less restrictive alternative" (Explanatory Notes, para.71). Nearest relative applicants are not governed by this section.

There is no legal obligation placed upon an AMHP to inform the patient's nearest relative of his or her right to make an application if the AMHP has concluded that the compulsory admission of the patient is not justified. As the imparting of information about the patient's situation to the nearest relative, or any other person, without the patient's consent would be a breach of the patient's right to respect for his or her private life under art.8(1) of the European Convention on Human Rights, as well as being a breach of the patient's right to confidentiality, a justification for taking such action must be found in art.8(2).

There is no requirement for an AMHP to identify a change in the patient's circumstances before proceeding to make an application under ss.2 or 3 in respect of a patient who has been discharged by a tribunal. However, an AMHP may not lawfully apply for the admission of a patient whose discharge has been ordered by the decision of a tribunal of which the AMHP is aware unless the AMHP has formed a reasonable and bona fide opinion that he has information not known to the tribunal which puts a significantly different complexion on the case as compared with that which was before the tribunal (*R. v East London and The City Mental Health Trust Ex p. Brandenburg*, HL, noted in the General Note to s.3).

For the approval of AMHPs by LSSAs, see s.114.

*Wales*

Applications to hospitals in Wales must be made in accordance with the Welsh Regulations i.e. a Welsh application form must be used. For the medical recommendation form to be used where the patient was medically examined in Wales, see reg.4(2) of the English Regulations.

*Human Rights Act 1998*

**1–163**    An AMHP who is performing functions under this Act is exercising "functions of a public nature" and is therefore a "public authority" for the purposes of the 1998 Act (s.6(3)(b)). The effect of this is that it is unlawful for an AMHP to act in a way which is incompatible with a patient's rights under the European Convention on Human Rights (Human Rights Act 1998 s.6(1)).

If an AMHP acts in an arbitrary fashion by, for example, resorting to making an application for detention in bad faith or making an application in circumstances where such action is a disproportionate response to the patient's situation, he or she will have violated art.5(1) of the European Convention on Human Rights: see *Tsirlis and Kouloumpas v Greece* (1997) 25 E.H.R.R. 198 para.56. In *Litwa v Poland* (2001) 33 E.H.R.R. 53 para.78 the court, in reiterating that a necessary element of the "lawfulness" of a detention within the meaning of art.5(1)(e) is the absence of arbitrariness, said that "the detention of an individual is such a serious measure that it is only justified where other, less severe measures have been considered and found to be insufficient to safeguard the individual or public interest which might require that the person concerned be detained. That means that it does not suffice that the deprivation of liberty is executed in conformity with national law but it must also be necessary in the circumstances".

The giving of "reasons" to a nearest relative for a decision not to make an application in respect of the patient (see subs.(4)) could constitute an interference with the patient's right to respect for his private life under art.8(1) if the reasons contained information that was confidential to the patient. Either the reasons should be drafted in a manner which would not constitute such a violation or a justification for the violation must be found in art.8(2).

*Code of Practice*

Guidance on this section is given in Ch.4 at paras 4.48 et seq. The circumstances in which **1–164** applications by AMHPs should not be made because of a conflict of interest are examined in Ch.7.

*Subsection (1)*

This provision places an obligation on a LSSA to arrange for an AMHP to "consider the **1–165** patient's case on their behalf" if the authority has reason to think that a mentally disordered person who is in their area might need to be made subject to an application for detention or guardianship. Although the AMHP is acting on behalf of the LSSA, he or she acts independently when performing functions under this Act: see the note on "that professional" in subs.(1A) below. As an AMHP may be approved by one LSSA but may be authorised to act on behalf of others (see the General Note to s.114), this duty can be performed either by an AMHP approved by the LASSA that has the duty under this provision and who has been authorised by that authority to act on its behalf or by another AMHP if that AMHP has been authorised to act on its behalf by that LSSA. Subsection (5) enables (but does not oblige) another LSSA to perform the function under this provision if that is felt to be appropriate.

PATIENT WITHIN THEIR AREA.   This includes a patient who is temporarily in the area of the LSSA.

*Subsection (1A)*

An AMHP may well learn of the existence of an earlier hearing of the tribunal relating to **1–166** the patient when performing his functions under this provision and will then wish to know the reasons for it. However, if no such information comes to light the law does not place on the AMHP (or a nearest relative applicant) a duty to make reasonable enquiries to establish whether any decision has been made by any tribunal and, if so, the grounds upon which it was based (*R. v East London and The City Mental Health Trust Ex p. Brandenburg* HL, above.).

THAT PROFESSIONAL.   The responsibilities under this provision are placed on the AMHP and not on the employing authority (*Nottingham City Council v Unison* [2004] EWHC 893 para.18). However, as an AMHP acts on behalf of the local authority (s.145(1AC)), that authority will be vicariously liable for any lack of care or bad faith on behalf of the AMHP (*TMM v London Borough of Hackney* [2010] EWHC 1349 (Admin), para.35). The AMHP should exercise his or her own judgment, based upon social and medical evidence, and not act at the behest of his or her employer, medical practitioners or other persons who might be involved with the patient's care; also see the note on s.114(10). The judgment to be exercised applies not only to the decision on whether an application should be made in respect of the patient; it also applies to the question of what section of this Act to invoke. In *St George's Healthcare NHS Trust v S* [1998] 3 All E.R. 673 at 694 CA, Judge L.J. made the following comments on this section prior to its amendment by the Mental Health Act 2007:

> "[The provisions of s.13] make clear that the social worker must exercise her own independent judgment on the basis of all the available material, including her interview and assessment of the 'patient', and personally make the appropriate decision. When doing so she is required to take account of the recommendations made by the medical practitioners".

Speaking of the role of the AMHP's precursor, Devlin L.J., said: "It is the business of the duly authorised officer, rather than that of the doctor, to see that statutory powers are not used for the purpose [of hospital treatment] unless the circumstances warrant it" (*Buxton v Jayne* [1960] 1 W.L.R. 783 at 784).

It is submitted that the AMHP owes a duty of care to those who are assessed for possible admissions under this Act: see the note on "Duty of care owed by recommending doctors" in the General Note to s.12.

The duty placed on the AMHP by this section does not affect the provisions as to consultation with nearest relatives set out in s.11(4) (subs.(5)).

AN APPLICATION. An application for admission to hospital is addressed to the managers of the hospital named in the application. The AMHP should not complete the application by signing the application form in the absence of confirmation that a bed has been allocated for the patient at that hospital. The dangers of not following this advice are set out in the note on "to hospital" in s.6(1).

If the AMHP makes an application, the reasons for taking such action should be recorded. This was the approach taken by the Local Ombudsman in his investigation into complaint 87/B/1308 where a failure by AMHPs to make adequate records of the circumstances of the compulsory admission of a patient was sufficient for the Ombudsman to find that the employing local authority was guilty of maladministration. There is a legal obligation placed on the AMHP to give reasons to the patient if the application is inconsistent in effect with a decision of the tribunal to discharge him or her (*R. v East London and The City Mental Health Trust Ex p. Brandenburg* HL, above).

The AMHP is obliged, as far as he or she is able, to ensure that the medical recommendations upon which the application is founded comply with the provisions of s.12 and the regulations made under s.12A. The AMHP should not make an application and then look for the medical recommendations to support it because the application is "founded on" the medical recommendations: see Forms A2, A6 and A10.

OUGHT TO BE MADE. In the case of an application for admission to hospital, the AMHP can only be satisfied that an application ought to be made if the requirements of subs.(2) have been met.

The AMHP should not challenge the diagnosis set out in the medical recommendations but, because mental disorder alone does not render a person liable to detention or guardianship, he or she is entitled to take the view that it is not appropriate to make an application. The view of the *Royal Commission*, at para.390, was that "medical and non-medical opinions should supplement each other; each person should be expected to contribute to the final decision only what is appropriate to his own knowledge or experience or to his relationship with the patient".

HAVING REGARD TO.    For a dramatic illustration of the need for AMHPs and other professionals to listen to, and to take account of, the views of family members and others with close knowledge of the patient, see Ch.17 of L. Blom-Cooper *et al.*, *The Falling Shadow*, 1995. The patient's nearest relative will usually be involved in applications under s.2 (see s.11(3)) and s.3 (see s.11(4) and with guardianship applications (see s.11(4)).

RELATIVES.    As defined in s.26(1).

OTHER RELEVANT CIRCUMSTANCES.    Which could include the provisions that have to be satisfied before an emergency application under s.4 of this Act can be made.

NECESSARY OR PROPER.    It is neither "necessary or proper" for an AMHP to make an application in respect of a mentally incapable patient who is compliant to being in hospital if the patient is not being deprived of his or her liberty (see the note on "The 'sectioning' of compliant mentally incapable patients" in the General Note to Pt II).

If the AMHP decides not to make an application it would be improper for that decision to be reviewed by another AMHP in the absence of any change in circumstances, fresh evidence or concern that the AMHP had acted unprofessionally. However, if the decision not to make an application was made by an AMHP with little knowledge of the patient, there should be no objection to that decision being reviewed by an AMHP who has an extensive knowledge of the patient's history and current situation. A procedure which allowed for the automatic review of a decision of an AMHP not to make an application, would undermine the independent nature of the AMHP's role. For a contrary view, see "Disagreements between psychiatrists and social workers over compulsory admissions under the Mental Health Act", R. G. Sammut and H. Sergeant, *Psychiatric Bulletin* (1993), 17, 462–465.

In *St George's Healthcare NHS Trust v S*, above, Judge L.J. said at 695: "In deciding whether it is 'necessary or proper' to make an application under section 2, the AMHP has to approach the individual 'patient' as she is, or at any rate as on the best analysis she can make at the time, the patient appears to be." In this case the Court of Appeal held that the fact that the patient was heavily pregnant and adamantly refusing treatment for her pre-eclampsia were, at least potentially, of compelling importance to the AMHP who had to make an informed judgment under this provision. To require the AMHP to make such a judgment by ignoring the reality of the patient's situation "would be absurd". However, the patient's pregnancy was not sufficient on its own to bring the provisions of this section into play.

BY HIM.    The use of the phrase "necessary or proper for the application to be made *by him*" enables the AMHP to conclude that although an application ought to be made, it would be more appropriate for the application to be made by another AMHP.

*Subsections (1B), (1C)*
See the General Note to this section.                                    **1–167**

*Subsection (2)*
It is possible to have a single interview under this provision doubling as a s.4/2 interview **1–168** in the first instance, followed without further interview by a s.3 application: see *Re GM (Patient: Consultation)* [2000] M.H.L.R. 41, where Burton J. said at paras 69, 70:

"It seems to me entirely possible, provided that a necessary and suitable interview is carried out, for the [AMHP] to have acquired the necessary knowledge, either retaining it in her memory or if necessary reflecting back on any notes, so that there is sufficient to justify an initial section 2 or 4 application, but subsequently, when it comes to a section 3 application, for her to be able to draw on that same knowledge when she comes to consider section 3 . . . In those circumstances there is nothing which prevents the use, for the purposes of a subsequent section 3 admission, of any proper information available on an earlier section 2/4 admission, just as there is no prohibition upon the [AMHP] using acquired knowledge prior to the interview for the purposes of the interview itself . . ."

In this case the patient was the subject of an application under s.3 whilst he was being detained under s.4. A fresh interview would be required if the patient attained informal status subsequent to the expiry or discharge of the initial detaining section and before the need for a further period of detention arose. This is because the attaining of informal status should trigger a fresh enquiry, via an interview, as to the appropriateness of a further period of detention.

During the interview, there is no need for the AMHP to indicate under which section of the Act he or she is operating. What is required is for the role of the AMHP and the purpose the visit to be explained to the patient (*Re GM*, above, para.71).

Where a person requests an AMHP to undertake a mental health assessment in respect of a member of that person's family, and the AMHP concludes that an assessment for possible admission under this Act is required, the person who made the request should be informed as to the possible outcomes of the assessment: see the report of the Local Government Ombudsman into complaint No.97/A/2239. In his report into complaint No.97/A/1082, the Ombudsman found maladministration in a case where: (1) a family had been given inadequate notice of a planned assessment of a patient for possible admission under this Act; and (2) no less than three home care staff were present when the assessment took place.

BEFORE MAKING AN APPLICATION. The interview required by this provision can take place more than 14 days before the application, provided that the AMHP has confirmed that an application is necessary by having face to face contact with the patient within 14 days of the application as required by s.11(5): see *Re Whitbread* (*Mental Patient: Habeas Corpus*) 39 B.M.L.R. 94 (1977) CA, which is considered in the notes to s.11(4)(5).

HOSPITAL. This subsection does not apply to guardianship applications. A recommending doctor has responsibility for ensuring that a hospital bed is available for the patient (*Code of Practice*, para.4.75).

INTERVIEW. The AMHP should explain the purpose of the interview to the patient who should ordinarily be given the opportunity of speaking to the AMHP alone (*Code of Practice*, para.4.53). It is submitted that, in the context of this Act, an attempt by an AMHP to communicate with a patient would be sufficient to constitute an interview and that this would be the case even if the patient was either unable or unwilling to respond. This opinion received judicial endorsement by Underhill J. in *R. (on the application of M) v The Managers, Queen Mary's Hospital* [2008] EWHC 1959 (Admin); [2008] M.H.L.R. 303 para.14, who said that the purpose of the interview is "achieved in [a] case where the [AMHP] attempts to communicate with the patient but she fails to respond, or responds inappropriately, in a manner suggesting that she does indeed require treatment." His Lordship's statement that the requirement that the interview be conducted in a "suitable" manner gave a degree of flexibility to those involved was approved by the Court of Appeal at [2008] EWCA Civ 1112; [2008] M.H.L.R. 306 para.25. Richards L.J. said, at para.26, that there is no set time that must be taken for an interview to qualify under this provision; what is required is a matter for the professional judgment of the AMHP.

An interview cannot take place with an unconscious or highly intoxicated patient. In these circumstances the doctor could use the powers contained in the Mental Capacity Act 2005 to treat the patient, with the AMHP intervening only when the patient is capable of being interviewed. If an unconscious patient requires immediate hospital treatment, he or she could be taken to hospital under the authority of ss.5 and 6 of the 2005 Act.

If the AMHP is unable to gain access to premises in order to interview the person, he or she cannot force entry but should consider making an application to a magistrate under s.135(1).

SUITABLE MANNER. These words were added to this section as a result of an amendment moved at the Special Standing Committee by Mr Tom Benyon MP who stressed the need for those who are involved in the management of deaf psychiatric patients having either the use of an interpreter or a fluency in British Sign Language. He also drew the Committee's attention to a number of cases where patients had been compulsorily detained under the 1959 Act in circumstances where a lack of speech had been mistakenly attributed to mental disorder. Other MPs were concerned that applicants should be sensitive to the difficulties faced by members of ethnic minorities who might not speak English or who might not speak it well. The words "suitable manner" should direct the AMHP's attention to the particular needs of all groups, including children, who might have difficulties in communicating effectively.

SATISFY HIMSELF. The AMHP would need to consult with others who have been involved with the patient's welfare. A doctor who has made a recommendation might be reluctant to meet with the AMHP to discuss the case and, if the case is one of sufficient urgency, the AMHP might have to make an application without the benefit of a discussion with the doctor. If an AMHP makes an application in these circumstances he or she should, in the first instance, attempt to resolve the difficulty by involving relevant bodies at the local level. If the difficulties persist, consideration should be given to contacting the Care Quality Commission or the Health Inspectorate Wales who have a duty under s.120(1) to keep matters relating to the detention of patients under review.

ALL THE CIRCUMSTANCES OF THE CASE. In practice, these "might include the past history of the patient's mental disorder, the patient's present condition and the social, familial, and personal factors bearing on it, as well as the other options available for supporting the patient, the wishes of the patient and the patient's relatives and carers, and the opinion of other professionals involved in caring for the patient" (Reference Guide, para.2.32). This phrase includes "medical considerations" such as the "immediate and catastrophic consequences of self neglect" (*GJ v Foundation Trust* [2009] EWHC 2972 (Fam), para.117(a)).

THE MOST APPROPRIATE WAY. The AMHP is placed under an obligation to be satisfied as to the appropriateness of detention in the light of his or her knowledge of the alternative forms of intervention that would be available for the patient: see the note on "All the circumstances of the case", above. This provision reflects the requirement under art.5(1) of the European Convention on Human Rights that detention must be a proportionate response to the circumstances: see *Litwa v Poland*, which is noted under "Human Rights Act 1998", above. AMHPs are not placed under an obligation to actively seek out alternatives before making an application.

A comprehensive knowledge of local resources available for the mentally disordered is essential if an informed judgment is to be made; also see para.2.32 of the Reference Guide. The AMHP's view as to why there was no alternative to compulsory hospitalisation should be recorded in the client's case notes: see the Local Ombudsman's investigation into Complaint 87/B/1308, noted under subs.(1), above.

If a patient vacillates between consenting and refusing to consent to admission to hospital as an informal patient, it is suggested that the patient should be admitted informally if this is possible, with the holding powers contained in s.5 being used if necessary.

CARE AND MEDICAL TREATMENT. This means care and medical treatment for the patient's mental disorder, and not for a medical disorder which is unconnected with her mental condition (*St George's Healthcare NHS Trust v S* [1998] 3 All E.R. 673 CA). It is therefore unlawful for an application to be made in circumstances where there is no intention to either assess or treat the patient's mental disorder. Despite the confirmation of the legal position given in the *St George's* case, it is the author's experience that this Act has been used to "authorise" the removal of mentally incompetent non-compliant patients from their homes where the sole cause of concern is the patient's need for hospitalisation to treat a physical disorder.

*Subsection (3)*

**1–169**    Although an AMHP can only be approved by one LSSA, he or she can perform AMHP functions in the area of another LSSA (or LSSAs) if that authority has authorised the AMHP to perform such functions.

*Subsection (4)*

**1–170**    REQUIRED.    The communication can be either written or verbal. It might not always be clear whether a communication from a nearest relative amounts to a request to a local authority to act under the provisions of this subsection. It is submitted that if a nearest relative indicates concern about the patient by saying, for example, that the patient "ought to be in hospital" or that "something ought to be done" about the patient, the nearest relative should be informed of the power under this subsection and asked whether he or she wishes to exercise it.

NEAREST RELATIVE.    Or acting nearest relative appointed by the court under s.29. It is submitted that this provision should apply if the approach to the local authority is made by someone acting on behalf of the nearest relative, e.g. a general practitioner.

PATIENT.    If the LSSA considers that the person concerned is not "a person suffering or appearing to be suffering from mental disorder," which is the definition of "patient" in s.145(1), the provisions of this subsection will not apply.

TO CONSIDER THE PATIENT'S CASE.    Which does not necessarily mean that the AMHP undertakes an assessment of the patient or even interviews the patient. The effect of a nearest relative's request under this provision is to require an AMHP to consider whether an application under this Act should be made in respect of the patient. The extent and nature of the inquiries made by the AMHP would depend upon the knowledge that the local mental health service has about the patient. If the patient has been the subject of a recent mental health assessment, the AMHP's obligation would be confined to identifying whether there has been a change in the patient's situation that would justify a reassessment. If the patient is not known, the patient's general practitioner should be contacted to ascertain whether the patient is mentally disordered as the obligation under this section only arises if this is the case: see the note on "patient", above. It could be that the nearest relative is the mentally disordered member of the "patient's" family.

HOSPITAL.    The patient could be receiving hospital treatment for mental disorder as an informal patient. This provision does not apply to a nearest relative who wants a guardianship application to be made.

INFORM.    The AMHP should write to the nearest relative immediately after the decision not to make an application has been made. Note that it is the AMHP, and not the LSSA who has to inform the nearest relative. If the AMHP decides not to make an application, the nearest relative could proceed to make an application him or herself if the required medical recommendation(s) had been made. If the nearest relative's application is made under either s.2 or 3 of this Act, an AMHP would be required to provide the hospital managers with a social circumstances report under s.14.

REASONS. Giving reasons need not necessarily involve the AMHP in revealing confidential information because statements of a general nature such as "I took medical advice and was informed that Mr X is not mentally disordered within the meaning of the Mental Health Act 1983," or "Mr X agreed to enter hospital as an informal patient," or "in my opinion it is appropriate for Mr X to continue to receive treatment at home," would constitute a reason for the purposes of this subsection. Also see the note on "The Human Rights Act", above, and para.4.80 of the Code of Practice.

*Subsection (5)*

This provision confirms that nothing in this section (i) effects an AMHP's obligations **1–171** under s.11(4) and the regulations made under s.12A; (ii) prevents a LSSA other than the LSSA that has duties under subss.(1), (1B) and (1C) from arranging for an AMHP to assess the patient; or (iii) can be construed as restricting an AMHP's power to make an application under this Act.

## Social reports

**14.** Where a patient is admitted to a hospital in pursuance of an application **1–172** (other than an emergency application) made under this Part of this Act by his nearest relative, the managers of the hospital shall as soon as practicable give notice of that fact to the local social services authority for the area in which the patient resided immediately before his admission; and that authority shall as soon as practicable arrange for [an approved mental health professional] [. . .] to interview the patient and provide the managers with a report on his social circumstances.

AMENDMENT

The words in square brackets were substituted by the Mental Health Act 2007 s.21, Sch.2, para.6. The words omitted were repealed by the Children Act 2004 s.64, Sch.5 Pt 4.

DEFINITIONS

    patient: s.145(1).  **1–173**
    hospital: ss.34(2), 145(1).
    nearest relative: ss.26(3), 145(1).
    the managers: s.145(1).
    local social services authority: s.145(1).
    approved mental health professional: s.145(1), (1AC).

GENERAL NOTE

This section places a duty on social services authorities to provide hospital managers **1–174** with a report on a patient's social circumstances if the patient has been admitted to an NHS or private hospital pursuant to an application made by his nearest relative under either s.2 or 3 of this Act.

OTHER THAN AN EMERGENCY APPLICATION. It is unclear whether this section requires a social circumstances report to be made where an emergency application has been converted into a 28-day order by the addition of the second medical recommendation required by s.2 (s.4(4)). Good practice suggests that it should be.

NEAREST RELATIVE. Or an acting nearest relative appointed by the county court under s.29. It is presumably assumed that an AMHP applicant would automatically provide the hospital with the information that would be contained in a social circumstances report.

THE MANAGERS. Or a person authorised by them: see reg.19 of the English Regulations and reg.35 of the Welsh Regulations.

AREA IN WHICH THE PATIENT RESIDED. This need not necessarily be the place where the patient was staying immediately prior to his admission, as temporary absences from the place where a person lives does not affect residence, as long as there is an intention to return (*R. v St Leonard's Shoreditch (Inhabitants)* (1865) L.R. 1 Q.B. 21). Also note Widgery L.J.'s statement that "a man cannot be said to reside in a particular place unless in the ordinary sense of the word one can say that for the time being he is making his home in that place" (*Fox v Stirk* [1970] 2 Q.B. 463 at 477).

INTERVIEW THE PATIENT. A person who refuses to grant the social worker access to the patient commits an offence under s.129(1)(b).

REPORT ON HIS SOCIAL CIRCUMSTANCES. This could include an account of the patient's family and social relationships (including the attitude of carers), history of mental disorder, previous contact with the local authority, access to community resources, employment record, financial situation and accommodation. The report should also contain an account of the circumstances of the admission. If the nearest relatives' application was made after an AMHP had refused to make one, it is suggested that that AMHP should prepare the report which should include an account of the reasons for his or her decision.

## Rectification of applications and recommendations

**1–175**     **15.**—(1) If within the period of 14 days beginning with the day on which a patient has been admitted to a hospital in pursuance of an application for admission for assessment or for treatment the application, or any medical recommendation given for the purposes of the application, is found to be in any respect incorrect or defective, the application or recommendation may, within that period and with the consent of the managers of the hospital, be amended by the person by whom it was signed; and upon such amendment being made the application or recommendation shall have effect and shall be deemed to have had effect as if it had been originally made as so amended.

(2) Without prejudice to subsection (1) above, if within the period mentioned in that subsection it appears to the managers of the hospital that one of the two medical recommendations on which an application for the admission of a patient is founded is insufficient to warrant the detention of the patient in pursuance of the application, they may, within that period, give notice in writing to that effect to the applicant; and where any such notice is given in respect of a medical recommendation, that recommendation shall be disregarded, but the application shall be, and shall be deemed always to have been, sufficient if—

(a) a fresh medical recommendation complying with the relevant provisions of this Part of this Act (other than the provisions relating to the time of signature and the interval between examinations) is furnished to the managers within that period; and

(b) that recommendation, and the other recommendation on which the application is founded, together comply with those provisions.

(3) Where the medical recommendations upon which an application for admission is founded are, taken together, insufficient to warrant the detention of the patient in pursuance of the application, a notice under subsection (2) above may be given in respect of either of those recommendations [. . .]

(4) Nothing in this section shall be construed as authorising the giving of notice in respect of an application made as an emergency application, or the detention of a patient admitted in pursuance of such an application, after the period of 72 hours referred to in section 4(4) above, unless the conditions set out in paragraphs (a)

and (b) of that section are complied with or would be complied with apart from any error or defect to which this section applies.

AMENDMENT
In subs.(3), the words omitted were repealed by the Mental Health Act 2007 s.55, Sch.11 Pt 1.

DEFINITIONS                                                                    **1–176**
    patient: s.145(1).
    hospital: ss.34(2), 145(1).
    application for admission for assessment: ss.2, 145(1).
    application for admission for treatment: ss.3, 145(1).
    the managers: s.145(1).

GENERAL NOTE

This section, which does not apply to documents issued by a court, to documents given in **1–177** support of either a patient's transfer under s.19, the renewal of the patient's detention under s.20, or to documents relating to guardianship or supervised community treatment, provides for admission documents which are found to be incorrect or defective to be rectified within 14 days of the patient's admission. A rectified document is treated as if it had been correctly completed at the time when it was signed. If a document which contains a minor error is not rectified under subs.(1) the application is not invalidated by virtue of the de minimis principle, i.e. the error is too trivial to be of any consequence: see *Re E (Mental Health: Habeas Corpus),* noted in the General Note to Sch.1 to the English Regulations.

Rectification is primarily concerned with dealing with inaccurate recording. It cannot be used to enable "a fundamentally defective application to be retrospectively validated" (per Sir Thomas Bingham M.R. in *Re S-C (Mental Patient: Habeas Corpus)* [1996] 1 All E.R. 532 at 537, CA) or to "cure a defect which arises because a necessary event in the procedural chain leading to the detention has simply not taken place at all. It is essentially concerned with correction of errors on the face of the document" (per Laws J. in *R. v South Western Hospital Managers Ex p. M* [1994] 1 All E.R. 161 at 177). If an admission document reveals a fundamental breach of law or procedure which is incapable of rectification under this section, either the hospital managers or the patient's responsible clinician should exercise their powers under s.23 to discharge the patient from the section. If the patient is discharged, he or she could be made the subject of a report under either s.5(2) or (4) and prevented from leaving hospital if it was considered that the appropriate requirements were satisfied: see the note on "in-patient in a hospital" in s.5(2). This advice is reproduced in an extended form in the General Note to s.6.

The Mental Health Act Commission published a Guidance Note on "Scrutinising and Rectifying Statutory Forms for Admission under the Mental Health Act" which can be accessed on the website of the Care Quality Commission. Paragraph 5 of this document states that because "the lawfulness of an application or order is a matter for the courts, Mental Health Act Commissioners must be cautious about expressing an opinion as to the validity of an application. In particular, they may not suggest that a particular patient is entitled to be released forthwith, even if there has been a clear and fundamental breach". If an application is found to be fundamentally defective, authority for the patient's detention can only be obtained through a fresh application: see para.13.13 of the *Code of Practice.*

The hospital managers should nominate an officer to undertake the task of scrutinising admission documents when the patient is admitted or, if the patient is already in hospital, as soon as practicable after the documents have been received: see reg.4(3) of the English Regulations and reg.4(2) of the Welsh Regulations.

As to the use of obsolete or defective forms, see the General Note to Sch.1 to the English Regulations.

A person who wilfully makes a false entry or statement in an application commits an offence under s.126(4).

*Defective Court Orders*

**1–178**   See the note under this heading in the General Note to Part III.

*Code of Practice*

**1–179**   Guidance on the receipt and scrutiny of documents prescribed under this Act is contained in Ch.13.

*Subsection (1)*

**1–180**   BEGINNING WITH.   Including the day on which the patient was admitted to hospital (*Zoan v Rouamba* [2000] 2 All E.R. 620 CA).

ADMITTED TO A HOSPITAL.   Or a registered establishment (s.34(2)).

INCORRECT.   In that, had the facts been correctly stated, the admission would have been justified, e.g. mis-stating dates, names or places. Rectification can only be used to ensure that the relevant form reflects the factual situation that obtained when the form was completed.

DEFECTIVE.   Probably means that incomplete information has been provided, e.g. leaving a space blank, omitting to insert a date or failing to delete one or more alternatives in places where only one can be correct. It does not mean that a completed form which accurately reflects the factual situation can be altered to provide legal justification for detention.

It is submitted that an application that is completed in breech of regulations made under s.12A is fundamentally defective, and is incapable of rectification under this section.

THE APPLICATION OR RECOMMENDATION.   This section does not allow for the rectification of forms used in the exercise of the holding powers provided for in s.5.

AMENDED.   The amended application or medical recommendation must comply with the relevant provisions of this Act.

BY WHOM IT WAS SIGNED.   It is submitted that an unsigned application or medical recommendation cannot be remedied under this section and that an application or medical recommendation which is signed by a person who is not empowered to do so under this Act is also incapable of rectification. A check therefore needs to be made to confirm that the application is signed by someone who appears to be an AMHP, a nearest relative or an acting nearest relative and that the medical recommendations are signed by practitioners who are not excluded by s.12 or the regulations made under s.12A. When performing this task the scrutinising officer can take certain statements at face value: see the note on reg.3(8) of the English and Welsh Regulations.

*Subsection (2)*

**1–181**   This subsection provides a remedy if *one* of the medical recommendations required under s.2 or 3 of this Act is found to be insufficient to warrant the detention of the patient. It could be used if, for example, a doctor who gives a medical recommendation for admission for treatment on Form A8 fails to convince the scrutineer that he or she has considered other methods of care or treatment. The hospital managers must notify the applicant in writing and if a fresh medical recommendation, not necessarily by the same doctor, is received within 14 days of the patient's admission, the application is treated as if it had been validly made from the date when it was completed. The requirement in s.12(1) that no more than five days must elapse between the two medical examinations made by the recommending doctors does not apply if a fresh medical recommendation is made under this provision. A copy of the notification to the applicant should be placed with the detention papers.

ONE OF THE TWO MEDICAL RECOMMENDATIONS.    As Eldergill has pointed out, it seems that neither this subsection nor subs.(3) allows for the remedying of a defective joint medical recommendation (A. Eldergill, *Mental Health Review Tribunals* (1997), p.269).

INSUFFICIENT.    This procedure cannot be used if the signatory is disqualified from making a recommendation by reason of s.12.

THE APPLICANT.    And not to the doctor who signed the recommendation. The Reference Guide, at para.2.105, recommends that the doctor should be informed of the action taken.

*Subsection (3)*
This subsection allows for the procedure set out in subs.(2) to be used when both rec-    **1–182** ommendations are good in themselves but taken together are insufficient.

INSUFFICIENT.    If, for example, neither recommending doctor is "approved," under s.12. The fresh recommendation and the old one taken together must comply with all the requirements of the Act (subs.(2)(b)), except the requirements about the interval between recommendations and the time of the signature (subs.(2)(a)).

*Subsection (4)*
This subsection provides that this section cannot be used to rectify an emergency appli-    **1–183** cation after it has expired unless it has been "converted" under the provisions of s.4(4).

*Position of patients subject to detention or guardianship*

## Reclassification of patients
**16.** [*Repealed by the Mental Health Act 2007, s.55, Sch.11, Pt 1*]    **1–184**

## Leave of absence from hospital
**17.**—(1) The [responsible clinician] may grant to any patient who is for the    **1–185** time being liable to be detained in a hospital under this Part of this Act leave to be absent from the hospital subject to such conditions (if any) as [that clinician] considers necessary in the interests of the patient or for the protection of other persons.

(2) Leave of absence may be granted to a patient under this section either indefinitely or on specified occasions or for any specified period; and where leave is so granted for a specified period, that period may be extended by further leave granted in the absence of the patient.

[(2A) But longer-term leave may not be granted to a patient unless the responsible clinician first considers whether the patient should be dealt with under section 17A instead.

(2B) For these purposes, longer-term leave is granted to a patient if—

(a)   leave of absence is granted to him under this section either indefinitely or for a specified period of more than seven consecutive days; or

(b) a specified period is extended under this section such that the total period for which leave of absence will have been granted to him under this section exceeds seven consecutive days.]

(3) Where it appears to the [responsible clinician] that it is necessary so to do in the interests of the patient or for the protection of other persons, he may, upon granting leave of absence under this section, direct that the patient remain in custody during his absence; and where leave of absence is so granted the patient may be kept in the custody of any officer on the staff of the hospital, or of any other person authorised in writing by the managers of the hospital or, if the patient is required in accordance with conditions imposed on the grant of leave of absence to reside in another hospital, of any officer on the staff of that other hospital.

(4) In any case where a patient is absent from a hospital in pursuance of leave of absence granted under this section, and it appears to the [responsible clinician] that it is necessary so to do in the interests of the patient's health or safety or for the protection of other persons, [that clinician] may, subject to subsection (5) below, by notice in writing given to the patient or to the person for the time being in charge of the patient, revoke the leave of absence and recall the patient to the hospital.

(5) A patient to whom leave of absence is granted under this section shall not be recalled under subsection (4) above after he has ceased to be liable to be detained under this Part of this Act; [ ... ].

[(6) Subsection (7) below applies to a person who is granted leave by or by virtue of a provision—

(a) in force in Scotland, Northern Ireland, any of the Channel Islands or the Isle of Man; and

(b) corresponding to subsection (1) above.

(7) For the purpose of giving effect to a direction or condition imposed by virtue of a provision corresponding to subsection (3) above, the person may be conveyed to a place in, or kept in custody or detained at a place of safety in, England and Wales by a person authorised in that behalf by the direction or condition.]

AMENDMENT
The references to the responsible clinician were substituted by the Mental Health Act 2007 s.9(3). Subss.(2A), (2B), (6) and (7) were inserted by ss.33(2), 39(1).

In subs.(5) the words omitted were repealed by the Mental Health (Patients in the Community) Act 1995 s.3(1).

DEFINITIONS
**1–186**   patient: s.145(1).
hospital: ss.34(2), 145(1).
absent without leave: ss.18(6), 145(1).
responsible clinician: s.34(1).

GENERAL NOTE
**1–187**   This section provides for the responsible clinician (RC) of a patient to grant that patient leave of absence from the hospital in which he or she is liable to be detained for a specified or for an indefinite period and subject to such conditions as are considered to be necessary. Longer-term leave of absence can only be granted if the patient's RC first considers whether the patient should be made subject to a community treatment order (CTO) (subss.(2A), (2B)). The period of leave may be extended without the patient having to return to hospital. The RC should weigh up and record the potential benefits and risks before making a decision about leave of absence (*G v Central and North West London*

*Mental Health NHS Trust* [2007] EWHC 3086 (QB); [2008] M.H.L.R. 24 para.152). There is no legal obligation to obtain the patient's consent to the leave. The RC has no power to grant leave of absence to patients who have been remanded to hospital by a court under ss.35 or 36, or who are subject to an interim hospital made under s.38. The permission of the Secretary of State for Justice is required before leave can be granted to a restricted patient: see the note on s.41(3).

A patient who has been granted leave of absence under this section continues to be "liable to be detained" and is therefore subject to the consent to treatment provisions in Pt IV of the Act (s.56(3)). Although there is nothing in this Act that prevents staff from using force to ensure that a patient on s.17 leave receives medication provided under the authority of Pt IV, this practice could be unsafe for both patient and staff and, in the absence of an emergency, it would be better for the forcible administration of medication to take place after the patient has been recalled to hospital (cf *Code of Practice*, para.21.24). A patient can be recalled to hospital from leave of absence if the RC considers it necessary to do so in the interests of the patient's health or safety or for the protection of others (subs.(4)).

A s.3 patient who has been granted leave under this section can have his or her detention renewed under s.20 if the patient's RC considers that hospital treatment constitutes a significant part of the patient's treatment plan: see the note on s.20(4)(c).

If a mentally incapacitated patient is granted leave of absence either to receive care in a care home or to receive treatment for a physical disorder in a general hospital, the leave can be combined with a deprivation of liberty authorisation granted under Sch.A1 of the Mental Capacity Act 2005. An authorisation can only be granted if there is no conflict between it and a condition of the patient's leave (*Code of Practice*, paras 28.7 to 28.9).

In *R. (on the application of K) v West London Mental Health NHS Trust* [2006] EWCA Civ 118; [2006] M.H.L.R. 89, the question before the Court of Appeal was whether the NHS Trust was obliged to pay the costs of a detained patient's treatment in an independent hospital where leave had been granted under this section by the patient's RC for the purpose of enabling the patient to be admitted to that hospital. In answering the question in the negative, the court held that:

1. The decision whether or not any particular services should be provided under s.3 of the National Health Service Act 1977 is one for the Secretary of State (or his delegate) and not one for the RC. Section 3, so far as material, provides: "It is the Secretary of State' duty to provide throughout England and Wales, to such extent as he considers necessary to meet all reasonable requirements—(a) hospital accommodation . . ." (now see s.3 of the National Health Service Act 2006).

2. When performing his functions under s.3, the Secretary of State (or his delegate) is not bound to accept and act on the clinical judgment of the RC. A decision as to whether to devote resources to a particular treatment depended on many considerations, including the seriousness of the condition, the likely success of the proposed treatment, the cost of the treatment and the competing needs of other patients.

3. A RC has no power to give directions as to how others are to discharge their functions and this section cannot be construed as conferring such a power.

4. The Secretary of State (or his delegate) is not obliged to use his best endeavours to give effect to a decision of a RC under this section.

Further provisions relating to ground access, leave of absence and the escorting of patients from Ashworth, Broadmoor and Rampton Hospitals can be found in the Safety and Security in Ashworth, Broadmoor and Rampton Hospitals Directions 2000 which are reproduced at Appendix B.

A patient who has been granted leave of absence to reside in the community has been discharged *from the hospital* for the purposes of the social security legislation, although he has not been discharged *from the section* that provides the authority for his continued liability to be detained.

The duty to provide aftercare services applies to a s.3 patient on leave of absence (see the note on "cease to be detained" in s.117(1)).

It is an offence to induce or help a patient absent himself without leave or to harbour or prevent a patient being returned to hospital (s.128).

This section applies without modification to patients who have been made subject to hospital or guardianship orders by a court under s.37 (Sch.1 Pt 1 para.1). It also applies, with subss.(1), (4) and (5) modified as set out below and subss.(2A) and (2B) omitted, to patients who are subject to special restrictions (Sch.1 Pt II paras 2, 3):

"(1) The [responsible clinician] may [with the consent of the Secretary of State] grant to any patient who is for the time being liable to be detained in a hospital under this Part of this Act leave to be absent from the hospital subject to such conditions (if any) as [that clinician] considers necessary in the interests of the patient or for the protection of other persons."

"(4) In any case where a patient is absent from a hospital in pursuance of leave of absence granted under this section, and it appears to the [the responsible clinician] [or the Secretary of State] that it is necessary so to do in the interests of the patient's health or safety or for the protection of other persons, [that clinician] [or the Secretary of State] may, subject to subsection (5) below, by notice in writing given to the patient or to the person for the time being in charge of the patient, revoke the leave of absence and recall the patient to the hospital."

"(5) A patient to whom leave of absence is granted under this section shall not be recalled [by the [responsible clinician]] under subs.(4) above after [the expiration of the period of [12] months beginning with the first day of his absence on leave]."

*The transfer of patients between hospitals*

**1–188**   It is lawful to use this section to grant a patient "trial leave" to a hospital other than the one in which he is formally detained (subs.(3)). Such leave can be useful step in a patient's rehabilitation programme. In these circumstances the approved clinician (AC) who is in charge of the patient's treatment at the base hospital continues to be the patient's RC. Although day-to-day functions relating to the care of the patient can be delegated to an AC at the second hospital, the responsibilities of the RC to renew the patient's detention and to issue certificates under Pt IV of this Act cannot be delegated. If the trial leave is successful the patient could then be transferred to the second hospital under s.19.

*Leave of absence to Scotland, Northern Ireland, the Channel Islands or the Isle of Man*

**1–189**   A patient who is granted escorted leave of absence to travel to Scotland will be subject to the Mental Health (Cross-border Visits) (Scotland) Regulations 2008 (SSI 2008/181) which provide that where patients have been granted leave of absence to travel to Scotland, they may be kept in charge of a person who is authorised for that purpose in relation to the leave. In addition, the Regulations make provision for such escorts to have the power to restrain and retake such patients in the event that they abscond.

Paragraph 12.44 of the Reference Guide states:

"Escorted leave to Scotland, Northern Ireland, the Channel Islands or the Isle of Man can only be granted if the law in the jurisdiction in question allows the patient to be kept in custody once there. At the time of publication, this applies only in Scotland."

*The Human Rights Act 1998*

A patient who has been granted leave of absence under this section continues to be **1–190**
"detained" for the purposes of art.5 of the European Convention on Human Rights: see
*L v Sweden*, App. No. 10801/84, noted under the heading "detention" in the note on
art.5(1)(e). In this case the European Commission held that the granting of leave of absence
with a condition that the patient accepts medication will not contravene the Convention if
one of the grounds in art.8(2) is satisfied. In order to satisfy one of the grounds in art.8(2) to
justify the violation, the patient must be informed of both the nature of the conditions and
the likely consequence of breaching the conditions (*Lambert v France* (2000) 30 E.H.R.R.
346). Also see the note on "conditions" in subs.(1).

*Applications to the First-tier Tribunal (Mental Health) or the Mental Health Review
Tribunal for Wales*

Patients on leave of absence may make an application to a tribunal as if they were still **1–191**
detained in hospital.

*Code of Practice*

Guidance on the use of this section is contained in Ch.21. Advice on deciding between **1–192**
guardianship, leave of absence and supervised community treatment can be found in Ch.28.

*Subsection (1)*

THE RESPONSIBLE CLINICIAN MAY GRANT. It is good practice for the authorisation of **1–193**
leave of absence and the imposition of conditions attached to the leave to be recorded
by the RC and for both the authorisation and the conditions to be communicated to key individuals: see para.21.21 of the *Code of Practice*. A sample leave of absence form is attached
to "Leave of absence and transfers under the Mental Health Act 1983", a guidance note
published by the Care Quality Commission. The RC can grant a patient leave of absence
over the telephone in urgent cases.

Leave of absence cannot be granted to a restricted patient without the permission of the
Secretary of State for Justice: see the General Note above. The Secretary of State may
attach conditions to the leave (*R. (on the application of RA) v Secretary of State for the
Home Department* [2002] EWHC (Admin) 1618; [2003] M.H.L.R. 54); see further the
note on s.41(3)(c)(i). The granting of leave of absence for patients detained at Ashworth,
Broadmoor and Rampton Hospitals must be preceded by a risk assessment by the RC
and a recommendation by the hospital's security director (Safety and Security in
Ashworth, Broadmoor and Rampton Hospitals Directions 2000 para.33).

A RC is not under an obligation to request that the Secretary of State gives his consent to
a patient being granted unescorted leave of absence as an alternative to a conditional discharge granted by a tribunal where those conditions are not yet fulfilled (*R. (on the
application of Hurlock) v Dr Page and the Secretary of State for the Home Department*)
[2001] EWHC Admin. 380).

The RC does not have the power to delegate functions under this section and the exercise
of the discretion to grant leave of absence cannot be fettered by either the hospital managers
or the hospital management. If the patient has been granted leave of absence to be a patient
at another hospital, the conditions of the leave could enable: (a) the patient to have periods
of leave for specified purposes from that hospital; and (b) the patient's AC at the other hospital to have discretion to determine when such leave should be taken.

The advice of the Mental Health Act Commission on the procedure to be adopted on the
granting of leave of absence is contained in the following extract from para.9.7 of its *Fourth
Biennial Report*, 1989–1991: "Leave of absence from hospital under s.17 is often a major
component of rehabilitation programmes. Such leave may cover periods of absence from a
single night up to [a year]. Short term absences of only a few hours also feature extensively
in treatment plans and are sometimes regarded as a form of parole arranged at ward level in
the hospital. The Act, however, describes leave of absence without mention of its duration
whilst its granting is the prerogative solely of the [RC]. The occurrence of any untoward

incidents during absence from hospital could raise the question of its planning and authorisation. On the other hand the requirement to obtain [RC] agreement for every activity outside the hospital'would seriously curtail any patient's involvement in the social programme'and other rehabilitative activities which are often arranged at short notice by ward staff. The recommendation of the Commission is that all absences from hospital should be regarded as constituting leave with a need for [RC] authorisation but that such leave should be agreed periodically, the weekly multi-disciplinary conference being an ideal occasion, with a written statement of the maximum licence that is granted for a defined period and with any related conditions. Staff implementing the treatment programme would then be free to arrange absences from hospital within the known limits and without need to obtain further more detailed authorisations." The MHAC has said that the patient's RC "may instruct nursing staff not to implement any authorised leave on medical grounds at their discretion" (MHAC, *Sixth Biennial Report*, para.9.4).

If a detained patient needs to be moved to a general hospital as a matter of urgency for treatment for a physical disorder or injury, legal authority for the move is present if either (1) leave of absence for such a move has been granted by the RC in anticipation of such an eventuality occurring; or (2) the RC has granted leave of absence over the telephone at the time of the emergency. Authority for treating the patient for the disorder or injury must be found in the common law or the Mental Capacity Act 2005 if the disorder or injury is not related to the patient's mental disorder: see the note on "medical treatment . . . for the mental disorder" in s.63. If the urgency of the situation is such that there is no time to contact the RC and anticipatory leave has not been granted, the 2005 Act will provide authority for a mentally incapacitated patient to be moved to the general hospital. A mentally capable patient can be moved to the hospital with his consent. In both cases, the RC should grant the patient leave of absence under this section at the earliest opportunity as the patient is technically absent without leave.

Any patient who is ... liable to be detained. Including a patient who has been detained under s.2. In order to be granted leave of absence, the patient must have become an in-patient of the hospital named in the application (see the note on "in-patient" in s.5(2)) and the hospital must have accepted the application (see the note on "sufficient authority for the Managers" in s.6(2)).

A patient who has been detained under s.5(2) cannot be granted leave of absence because such a patient does not have a RC: see the definition of RC in s.34(1).

From the hospital. Which is the hospital named in the application or order which provides authority for the patient's detention. Every absence from hospital, however brief, requires leave to be given under this section. With the exception of a restricted patient who is detained in a named hospital unit (see the note on "such hospital as may be prescribed" in s.45A(3)) and a patient who moves between high security psychiatric services and other services provided at the same hospital (s.145(1AA)), leave is not required for the patient to move from one hospital building to another or to have access to the grounds of the hospital. A decision to allow the patient to leave the ward area, but not the hospital, is a clinical decision that should be made following a risk assessment. The Mental Health Unit of the Ministry of Justice has issued the following guidance regarding patients who are detained in named hospital units:

"When the Hospital Order or prison transfer warrant names a specific ward/unit within a wider hospital in which a patient must be detained, the [RC]'s discretion to grant the patient ground leave or transfer is limited.

In these circumstances the [RC] can only grant the patient leave in the grounds of that particular unit, not the wider hospital. In addition the [RC] cannot transfer the patient to another unit even if it is within the same hospital. For any leave or transfer outside the named unit the Secretary of State's permission is needed, even if the leave or transfer is within the same hospital. [RC]s should therefore pay close attention to the detail of detention authorities" (MHU Bulletin, Aug, 2007).

A particular difficulty has arisen where a single hospital site contains a psychiatric and a general facility and the two facilities are administered by different NHS Trusts. In this situation, should a detained patient who needs treatment for a physical disorder at the general facility be sent to that facility under the authority of s.17 leave? As this Act was not drafted in contemplation of NHS trusts, the answer to this question is not easy to determine.

An argument against granting the patient formal leave of absence is that leave under this section is leave from the *hospital* and not from the NHS trust. The definition of hospital in s.145 refers back to the National Health Service Act 2006, which in s.275, defines a hospital as, inter alia, "any institution for the reception and treatment of persons suffering from illness". This definition is very broad and it could be argued that a collection of buildings located on a common site which are used for the treatment of patients constitute a single "hospital", even though the buildings might be managed by different NHS trusts. On this argument, how can a patient be granted leave of absence *from* the hospital if he does not leave the hospital site?

A strong argument in favour of granting leave is that if the patient moves from a part of the hospital that is managed by the NHS trust that is detaining him to a part of the hospital that is managed by another NHS trust, the staff of that other trust would not be authorised to detain him. This is because the application for the patient's detention would not have been addressed to the Hospital Managers of that other trust which, for the purposes of the administration of this Act, constitutes a separate "hospital".

Although the Mental Health Act Commission had been of the opinion that a "hospital" for the purposes of this Act could comprise "all the buildings on a site defined by a single perimeter, even though some of those buildings may have different NHS managers than others", it accepted that "this view is no longer tenable in the light of [para.21.5 of the *Code of Practice*]". The MHAC therefore concluded that:

"where buildings on a single 'hospital' site are managed by different NHS Trusts, formal leave of absence will be necessary where a patient is to move between Trusts, but not for a patient to go into grounds shared by both sets of buildings" ("Leave of absence and transfer under the Mental Health Act 1983", C.Q.C., pp.2, 3; see further, David Hewitt, "What is a hospital?", JMHL September 2004, pp.111–128).

It is submitted that the conclusion reached by the MHAC is correct.

CONDITIONS. For example, to live with a particular person or at a specified place, to be a patient at another hospital (see subs.(3)), to maintain contact with the care co-ordinator, to abstain from substance misuse and to accept prescribed medication. Conditions of this nature constitute interferences with the patient's right to respect for family life under art.8(1) of the European Convention on Human Rights and a justification for the interference would have to be found in art.8(2): see the note on "The Human Rights Act 1998", above.

Section 2(3)(b) of the Care Standards Act 2000 requires all establishments that can accept people who are "liable to be detained" under this Act to be registered as an independent hospital under that Act. However, in order to allow patients who have been granted leave of absence under this section to be provided with care and accommodation in a registered care home, s.2(6) of the 2000 Act exempts anyone on such leave from the definition of "liable to be detained". A condition of leave requiring a patient to reside in a care home is therefore lawful.

Authority for conveying the patient to a hospital or other place specified in the leave of absence is contained in s.18(7).

*Subsection (2)*

**1–194**　SPECIFIED OCCASIONS.　Such as visits to the patient's home or shopping expeditions. The RC should consider whether a condition that the patient be escorted should be attached to such leave.

*Subsections (2A), 2(B)*

**1–195**　Supervised community treatment (SCT) is an alternative to the practice of providing the patient with extended s.17 leave. Extended s.17 leave allows for the detention of a patient who has been placed in the community on leave of absence to be renewed under s.20 if a significant component of the patient's care plan is treatment at a hospital: see *R. (on the application of DR) v Mersey Care NHS Trust* [2002] EWHC 1810 (Admin); [2002] M.H.L.R. 386 and *R. (on the application of CS) v Mental Health Review Tribunal* [2004] EWHC 2958 (Admin); [2004] M.H.R.R. 355 which are noted under s.20(4)(c).

Subsection (2A) uses the term "considers" without qualification. It does not state that the RC should consider SCT and go down that route unless he or she has good reason not to do so. The RC is therefore obliged to examine the respective merits of SCT and extended s.17 leave and reach a conclusion as to which is the better option for a particular patient; see further para.21.10 of the *Code of Practice*. This Act does not provide any guidance to the RC on the criteria that should be used when coming to such a decision. RCs might prefer to use the leave option if, for example, there is a need to test out the patient's response to being on leave of absence for a period of longer than seven days before moving on to a CTO or if the patient's needs could be better met by the greater flexibility provided for by s.17. A patient's antagonism to being on a CTO might also be a factor in favour of using the s.17 regime. Both options provide the RC with a power of recall and either option can be used to provide a legal framework for treating a "revolving door" patient in the community. The implication of para.25.6 of the *Code of Practice* is that the RC should only decide to go down the SCT route if a judgment has been reached that it would not be possible to achieve "the desired objectives for the patient's care and treatment" by using extended s.17 leave. The RC's decision, and the reasons for it, should be recorded in the patient's notes (*Code of Practice* para.21.10). Advice on deciding between guardianship, leave of absence and supervised community treatment is given in Ch.28 of the *Code of Practice*.

*Subsection (3)*

**1–196**　This subsection states that the RC may direct that the patient must remain in custody during his leave if it is necessary in the interest of the patient or for the protection of other persons. The purpose of this provision is to provide those who are caring for a high-risk patient during a period of leave with an immediate power to restrain the patient should he or she make an attempt to abscond. Its effect is that the patient may be detained in the named hospital or care home during the period of leave.

A patient who escapes from custody can be re-captured immediately using the power contained in s.18; there is no need to wait for him or her to fail to return to the "base" hospital or for the leave to be revoked under subs.(4). For provisions relating to the powers of the person having custody of the patient, see ss.137 and 138.

THE MANAGERS.　Or a person authorised by them: see reg.19 of the English Regulations and reg.35 of the Welsh Regulations.

OFFICER ON THE STAFF OF THE HOSPITAL.　"Officer" is not defined in this Act and could include an employee who is neither a nurse nor a doctor. If a person other than a member of the hospital staff is to act as the patient's escort, the RC's authorisation must be in writing. If the patient is to be escorted by a friend or relative, see para.21.27 of the *Code of Practice*.

*Subsection (4)*

This subsection provides for the revocation of leave of absence and the return of the **1–197** patient to hospital. Although it is lawful to treat a patient who is on leave under the authority of Pt IV in the absence of his consent, in most circumstances it would be appropriate for the patient to be recalled to hospital for the treatment to be provided there; also see para.21.24 of the *Code of Practice*. Leave of absence may only be revoked when it is necessary in the interests of the patient's health or safety or for the protection of other persons that he or she again becomes an in-patient. It is therefore unlawful to recall a patient to hospital merely to facilitate the renewal of the patient's detention under s.20 (*R. v Hallstrom Ex p. W*; *R. v Gardner Ex p. L* [1986] 2 All E.R. 306). A patient who is on leave of absence can have his or her detention renewed under s.20 if his or her treatment programme contains a significant element of hospital treatment: see the note on s.20(4)(c).

In the absence of an emergency, a patient's leave of absence should not be revoked without up to date medical evidence to demonstrate that he or she remains mentally disordered (*Kay v United Kingdom* (1998) 40 B.M.L.R. 20 ECtHR).

MAY. The RC has discretion as to whether a notice should be issued. It would be unnecessary to issue a notice if the patient either returns to the hospital on his or her own initiative and asks to be re-admitted or has indicated to the RC that he or she would comply with a request to return to hospital without delay. A notice should be issued if the patient fails to comply with the request.

NOTICE IN WRITING. The Mental Welfare Commission for Scotland made the following comment on an equivalent provision in the Mental Health (Scotland) Act 1984: "In practical terms, particularly in emergency situations where the patient's condition has rapidly deteriorated, the staff who are returning the patient may have to deliver the letter of recall at the time they are taking him into custody" (Annual Report 1999–2000, p.23).

REVOKE. Leave of absence can only be revoked if the provisions of this subsection can be satisfied. Before issuing a recall notice the RC should also "consider what effect being recalled would have on the patient" (*Code of Practice*, para.21.31). The Mental Health Act Commission said that it may "be unlawful to resolve leave and recall a patient solely for the administration of treatment without consent or for the procedures under section 58 to be carried out" (*Fourth Biennial Report* 1989–1991, para.6.10). The recall of a patient for the purpose of administering treatment would be lawful in the following circumstances. If receiving treatment is a condition of the patient's leave of absence, a breach of that condition should trigger a review of the patient's situation. A recall could result from that review if the RC considered that the patient needed a further period of in-patient treatment on the ground that such action was in the interests of the patient's health or safety, or was for the protection of other persons.

RECALL THE PATIENT. A patient who refuses to return to the detaining hospital becomes a patient absent without leave (s.18(1)(b)) and may be taken into custody and returned to the hospital by the categories of staff set out in s.18(1).

*Subsection (5)*

This subsection provides that a patient cannot be recalled to hospital after a period of 12 **1–198** months has elapsed since the first day of leave or the authority to detain lapses, whichever is the earlier. In other words, the maximum period of leave that can be granted to a patient is the unexpired term of his current period of detention. Prior to its amendment by the Mental Health (Patients in the Community) Act 1995, this provision limited leave of absence to a maximum period of six months. Although the Department of Health's Internal Review was clear that the removal of the six-month limit "would be a simple change giving useful flexibility to ensure the continuation of care after patients were discharged", it was recognised that "it will not achieve this by itself". It recommended:

"that extended leave is operated (even if the conditions remain formally subject to the [RC's] discretion) in accordance with the principles of the care programme approach. In particular ... there should always be a named key worker and a clear treatment plan negotiated with the patient and agreed with the other professionals and agencies concerned. It can *never* be acceptable for leave to be allowed to lapse without proper provision having been made for follow-up care" (Legal Powers on the Care of Mentally Ill People in the Community, 1993, para.8.9).

A restriction order patient can be recalled by his RC at any time up to 12 months from the first day of his absence on leave. The Secretary of State can recall such a patient at any time (see the General Note to this section).

*Subsections (6), (7)*

**1–199**     The effect of these provisions is explained in paras.31.18 and 31.19 of the Reference Guide:

"A patient can be kept in custody, conveyed to a particular place or detained in a place of safety in England or Wales, if that is a condition of leave of absence from hospital granted under equivalent legislation in Scotland, Northern Ireland, the Isle of Man or any of the Channel Islands.

In each case, section 137 means they are deemed to be in legal custody while being escorted, conveyed or detained in England and Wales. As a result, if they abscond while in England or Wales, they may be retaken, under section 138, by the person authorised to keep the patient in custody in England, by a police officer (or other constable) or by an AMHP, for as long as they could be retaken under the legislation in the jurisdiction from which they are on leave."

## [Community treatment orders

**1–200**     **17A.**—(1) The responsible clinician may by order in writing discharge a detained patient from hospital subject to his being liable to recall in accordance with section 17E below.

(2) A detained patient is a patient who is liable to be detained in a hospital in pursuance of an application for admission for treatment.

(3) An order under subsection (1) above is referred to in this Act as a "community treatment order".

(4) The responsible clinician may not make a community treatment order unless—

  (a) in his opinion, the relevant criteria are met; and

  (b) an approved mental health professional states in writing—

    (i) that he agrees with that opinion; and

    (ii) that it is appropriate to make the order.

(5) The relevant criteria are—

  (a) the patient is suffering from mental disorder of a nature or degree which makes it appropriate for him to receive medical treatment;

  (b) it is necessary for his health or safety or for the protection of other persons that he should receive such treatment;

  (c) subject to his being liable to be recalled as mentioned in paragraph (d) below, such treatment can be provided without his continuing to be detained in a hospital;

  (d) it is necessary that the responsible clinician should be able to exercise the power under section 17E(1) below to recall the patient to hospital; and

  (e) appropriate medical treatment is available for him.

(6) In determining whether the criterion in subsection (5)(d) above is met, the responsible clinician shall, in particular, consider, having regard to the patient's history of mental disorder and any other relevant factors, what risk there would be of a deterioration of the patient's condition if he were not detained in a hospital (as a result, for example, of his refusing or neglecting to receive the medical treatment he requires for his mental disorder).

(7) In this Act—

> "community patient" means a patient in respect of whom a community treatment order is in force;
>
> "the community treatment order", in relation to such a patient, means the community treatment order in force in respect of him; and
>
> "the responsible hospital", in relation to such a patient, means the hospital in which he was liable to be detained immediately before the community treatment order was made, subject to section 19A below.]

AMENDMENT

This section was inserted by the Mental Health Act 2007 s.32(2).

DEFINITIONS

responsible clinician: s.34(1). **1–201**
application for admission for treatment: s.145(1).
approved mental health professional: s.145(1), (1AC).
mental disorder: ss.1,145(1).
medical treatment: s.145(1).
hospital: s.145(1), (4).

GENERAL NOTE

An outline of supervised community treatment, a term that is not to be found in this Act, **1–202** was given by the Minister of State:

"Supervised community treatment is probably the key change in the Bill and is an area of some controversy. It is important not just from a patient and public safety angle but because clinical practice itself has changed. At present most patients detained under the Mental Health Act are detained in hospital. That reflects the fact that, in 1983, most acute mental health services were provided in hospital. However the world has moved on and we now have a wide range of community-based mental health services . . . .. We also know that some form of compulsory community treatment is established in jurisdictions in New Zealand, Australia, Canada, Israel, Sweden, Belgium, Portugal and Scotland.

It is clear that there is now scope for some patients to be treated under compulsory powers but to live in the community, not in hospital. For suitable patients, SCT meets the need for a framework for their treatment and safe management in the community, instead of detention in hospital. That modern approach strikes a balance between individual autonomy and protection of the patient and the public.

I hope that we will not hear arguments in this House that we should go back to the future and reserve compulsion for detention in hospital. We have made it clear that, to be eligible for SCT, patients must have had an initial period of detention and treatment in hospital. This means that their medical condition and treatment needs will be well established before they go into the community. Criteria are set out in the Bill on whether a patient is suitable for SCT. It will be for clinicians, working with AMHPs, to determine against those criteria whether a patient should be put onto a community treatment order.

There is no question of SCT being imposed on people who have not been detained in hospital first.

We know that some patients stop taking their medication or treatment once they leave hospital, and so relapse and end up being readmitted. This detrimental cycle is often referred to as the revolving door. Patients on SCT will benefit from a structure designed to promote safe community living. This will reduce the risk of relapse and re-detention. They will be asked to comply with conditions to help prevent relapse. . . . If, despite all this, a patient's mental health does deteriorate again, there will be scope to take action to prevent crisis. Under SCT, patients can be recalled to hospital, if they need to be, for treatment. This is important because the power of recall provides the means to tackle relapse, and to avoid its potentially adverse consequences for the patient or someone else. Recall to hospital allows patients to be treated quickly and to return to the community straightaway if it is clinically safe to do so.

I recognise that there were some concerns about our proposals for SCT, but we have tried to deal with them. I assure the House that it is not about forcing people to have treatment in the community. If a patient refuses consent to treatment, it can be given only on recall the hospital. Forcible treatment against a patient's will cannot be given in the community where the patient lacks the capacity to consent unless the treatment is immediately necessary—for example, to save the patient's life.

SCT is a new, modern and effective way to manage the treatment of patients with serious mental health problems. It will allow patients, so far as possible, to live normal lives in the community. This will reduce the risk of social exclusion and stigma associated with detention in hospital for long periods of time or with repeated hospital admissions. . . . SCT will be suitable for a minority of patients who have already been detained in hospital. There will be clear criteria for eligibility, safeguards for patients, and strict provisions for review and appeal, exactly as they apply to detained patients" (*Hansard,* HL Vol.687, cols.656,657).

Prior to the Bill being published, the Government commissioned the Institute of Psychiatry to undertake a literature review of the research available in those countries which use different forms of SCT: see R. Churchill, G. Owen, S. Singh, and M. Hotopf, "International experiences of using community treatment order", Department of Health, March 7, 2007. The report concluded that there is very little conclusive evidence to demonstrate that SCT is either effective or ineffective.

A patient who is suitable for SCT will be made subject to a community treatment order (CTO). Such a patient is referred to throughout the Act as a community patient (s.17A(7)). The patient will be subject to the after-care provisions of s.117 as long as he or she is a community patient (s.117(2)). Part IVA of the Act provides for the regulation of treatment for the patient's mental disorder whilst in the community. Unlike guardianship, a CTO is not limited to patients who are over the age of 16.

Making a patient subject to a CTO is an alternative to granting the patient long-term leave of absence under s.17 of the Act and before an RC places a patient on such leave, he or she must "consider" whether the patient should be dealt with under this section: see the note on s.17(2A), (2B). Advice on deciding between guardianship, leave of absence and supervised SCT is given in Ch.28 of the *Code of Practice.*

This section enables an application for a CTO to be made by the patient's RC if he or she is satisfied that all of the criteria set out in subs.(5) are satisfied (subs.(4)(a)), and an AMHP agrees that the criteria are met and that an order is appropriate (subs.(4)(b)). The AMHP and the RC could be members of the same clinical team. There are no time limits that regulate either the lapse of time that may take place between the AMHP stating agreement with the RC's view that a CTO and any imposed conditions are appropriate or the lapse of time between such a statement by the AMHP and the putting into effect of the CTO by the RC. An application can only be made in respect of a patient who has been detained under s.3 or is subject to an order under Pt III without restrictions (or is treated as such after transfer from another jurisdiction) (subss.(1), (2)). Unlike an application for the patient's detention, an application for a CTO is not addressed to the hospital managers. The CTO must be made subject to conditions (s.17B) and the RC is empowered to order the patient's recall to hospital (s.17E). The duration of the CTO is specified in s.17C. Responsibility for a community patient may be assigned to another hospital under reg.17 of the English Regulations or reg.25 of the Welsh Regulations.

Although the patient's consent to the making of a CTO is not a legal requirement, "in practice patients will need to be involved in decisions about the treatment to be provided in the community and how and where it is to be given, and be prepared to co-operate with treatment" (*Code of Practice*, para.25.14). The patient's nearest relative cannot prevent a CTO being made.

Section 132A requires the relevant hospital managers to give information to community patients about the effect of the CTO and their right to make an application to a tribunal. For the responsibility to inform the patient's nearest relative of the assignment, see reg.26(1)(h) of the English Regulations and reg.32(b) of the Welsh Regulations.

Under s.130D, the:

"managers of the responsible hospital must take steps to give SCT patients information about the availability of independent mental health advocacy. Unless the patient requests otherwise (or does not have a nearest relative), the managers must also take whatever steps are practicable to give this information to the person they think is the patient's nearest relative. This must be done as soon as practicable after the CTO is made," (Reference Guide, para.15.29).

Although there is no provision in this Act for the documents relating to CTOs to be rectified, appropriate arrangements should be put in place to check that such documents have been properly completed (*Code of Practice*, paras.13.16–13.17).

This section applies without modification to patients who have been made subject to hospital or guardianship orders by a court under s.37 (Sch.1 Pt 1 para.1).

*Domestic Violence, Crime and Victims Act 2004*
So hospital managers can meet their obligations under the 2004 Act to invite representa- **1–203** tions from victims, RCs must tell the managers if they are considering discharging the following categories of patients by making a CTO:

"[P]atients subject to unrestricted hospital orders, hospital directions whose associated limitation direction is no longer in force, and unrestricted transfer directions (including hospital orders and transfer directions which were originally restricted, but where the restriction order or direction has since ended or been lifted)" ("Guidance on the extension of victims' rights under the Domestic Violence, Crime and Victims Act 2004", Department of Health, 2008, para.1.10).

*Human Rights Act 1998*
If a CTO is made in the interests of the patient's health or to protect the rights and free- **1–204** doms of others, there would be no interference with the patient's rights under art.8 of the ECHR provided that the making of the order is necessary in a democratic society and is done in accordance with the law (*L v Sweden*, App.No.10801/84). Similar considerations would apply to art.11 which provides for a right "to freedom of association with others".

*Applications to the First-tier Tribunal (Mental Health) or the Mental Health Review Tribunal for Wales*
Paragraphs 147 and 148 of the Explanatory Notes state: **1–205**

"A community patient may apply to the [First-tier Tribunal (Mental Health) or the Mental Health Review Tribunal for Wales], under amended s.66 . . . , when a CTO is made, when it is revoked, when it is extended after six months or a year (as appropriate) and when an order is extended after the patient has been absent without leave for more than 28 days. A NR may also apply to the [tribunal] if the NR makes a discharge order which is not put into effect because the RC reports that the patient would be likely to act in a dangerous manner if discharged; or if he or she is displaced by a court order as allowed under s.29(1)(c) or (d) . . . . The hospital managers must refer a patient to the [tribunal] if a CTO is revoked [or if an application to the [tribunal] has not been made within the relevant period; see s.68].

In the case of community patients who were under a hospital order before being made subject to a CTO, the power under s.66 . . . to apply to a Tribunal when a CTO is made or revoked cannot be exercised until six months after the date of the hospital order. The NR of such a patient may apply to the [tribunal] whenever the patient has a right to apply. The Secretary of State can refer a case of a community patient to the [tribunal], in the same way as for detained patients [; see s.67(1)]."

The rights of SCT patients and their nearest relatives to make tribunal applications are also set out in tables 22.8 and 22.9 of the *Reference Guide*.

The power of the tribunal to discharge a community patient is set out in s.72(1)(c),(1A). The tribunal also has the power to recommend that a detained patient be discharged subject to SCT (s.72(3A)). There is no power for the tribunal to vary or discharge the conditions of a CTO.

*Code of Practice*

**1–206**     Guidance of supervised community treatment is contained in Chs 25 and 29. Advice on deciding between guardianship, leave of absence and supervised community treatment can be found in Ch.28.

*Subsection (1)*

**1–207**     BY ORDER IN WRITING.   The order, which is Form CTO1 (see reg.6(1)(a) of the English Regulations), is called a "Community Treatment Order" (subs.(3)). In Wales, the form is Form CP1: see reg.16 of the Welsh Regulations.

A DETAINED PATIENT.   Of any age. If a child patient is a ward of court, see s.33(4).

*Subsection (2)*

**1–208**     LIABLE TO BE DETAINED.   An application for a CTO can be made in respect of a patient who has been granted leave of absence under s.17.

APPLICATION FOR ADMISSION FOR TREATMENT.   Which is suspended during the currency of the CTO (s.17D(2)(a)), apart from when the patient is recalled to hospital when it is reinstated (s.17E(6)). A CTO can also be made in respect of patients who are subject to hospital orders (without a restriction order) and transfer directions (without a restriction direction): see Sch.1, Pt 1 and s.47(3). If the application, order or direction ceases to have effect, the CTO automatically ends (s.17C).

*Subsection (4)*

**1–209**     AN APPROVED MENTAL HEALTH PROFESSIONAL . . . AGREES.   Paragraph 25.26 of the *Code of Practice* provides guidance on which AMHP should perform this role. There is no requirement for the AMHP to interview the patient prior to signing the statement. Although the *Code of Practice*, at para.25.7, states that if the agreement of the AMHP is not forthcoming it "would not be appropriate" for the RC to approach another AMHP for an alternative view, such an approach would not be unlawful. Indeed, it could be argued that the RC has a professional duty to make such an approach in an attempt to achieve an objective that he or she has ascertained to be in the patient's best interests.

*Subsection (5)*

These criteria essentially state that the patient continues to be detainable under s.3 **1–210** (including the requirement that a patient's learning disability continues to be associated with abnormally aggressive or seriously irresponsible conduct), but can be treated in the community if he or she is subject to a power of recall. When determining whether the RC should be able to exercise the power of recall, the factors set out in subs.(6) should be considered.

*Paragraphs (a), (b), (e)*

See the notes to s.3(2)(a),(c) and (d). **1–211**

*Subsection (6)*

This provision requires the RC to "in particular" consider the risk of the patient's con- **1–212** dition deteriorating in the community when deciding whether it is necessary for him or her to be able to exercise the power to recall the patient to hospital. Apart from considering the patient's history of mental disorder, it "is important that a clinician can consider all relevant factors, an obvious example being the patient's current mental state. Other relevant factors might include the degree of recovery of symptoms, any suicidal ideas or feelings of hopelessness, which will be important predictors of likely risk. In addition, a patient's insight and attitude to their treatment, and the protective circumstances into which a patient would be discharged, might be relevant" (per the Parliamentary Under-Secretary of State, *Hansard,* HL Vol.693, cols 847, 848). The *Code of Practice* considers the sharing of information to manage risk at paras.18.14–18.16.

## [Conditions

**17B.**—(1) A community treatment order shall specify conditions to which the **1–213** patient is to be subject while the order remains in force.

(2) But, subject to subsection (3) below, the order may specify conditions only if the responsible clinician, with the agreement of the approved mental health professional mentioned in section 17A(4)(b) above, thinks them necessary or appropriate for one or more of the following purposes—

(a) ensuring that the patient receives medical treatment;

(b) preventing risk of harm to the patient's health or safety;

(c) protecting other persons.

(3) The order shall specify—

(a) a condition that the patient make himself available for examination under section 20A below; and

(b) a condition that, if it is proposed to give a certificate under Part 4A of this Act in his case, he make himself available for examination so as to enable the certificate to be given.

(4) The responsible clinician may from time to time by order in writing vary the conditions specified in a community treatment order.

(5) He may also suspend any conditions specified in a community treatment order.

(6) If a community patient fails to comply with a condition specified in the community treatment order by virtue of subsection (2) above, that fact may be taken into account for the purposes of exercising the power of recall under section 17E(1) below.

(7) But nothing in this section restricts the exercise of that power to cases where there is such a failure.]

AMENDMENT

This section was inserted by the Mental Health Act 2007, s.32(2).

DEFINITIONS

**1–214**   community treatment order: ss.17A(7), 145(1).
responsible clinician: s.34(1).
approved mental health professional: s.145(1), (1AC).
medical treatment: s.145(1), (4).
community patient: ss.17A(7), 145(1).

GENERAL NOTE

**1–215**   This section requires that a CTO specifies the conditions to which a community patient will be subject. It is not possible for a CTO not to have any conditions attached to it (subs.(1)). Although the RC and the AMHP must agree the conditions (subs.(2)), only the RC has the power to vary or suspend them (subss.(4),(5)). The mandatory conditions set out in subs.(3) are directly enforceable by recall to hospital (s.17E(2)). If the patient (or a donee or deputy taking a decision on the patient's behalf; see para.9.5 of the *Code of Practice*) fails to comply with any other condition, the RC may take that into account when considering whether it is necessary to exercise the power of recall under s.17E (subs.(6)). However, if the criteria for recall are met, the power can be exercised even if the patient is complying with the conditions (subs.(7)).

A patient has no right to seek the review of the conditions imposed on a CTO before a tribunal; conditions can only be challenged by judicial review. The Government's view is that for SCT to work, a patient must accept and be ready to co-operate with the conditions of a CTO; see, for example, *Hansard,* HL Vol.693, col.848.

This section applies without modification to patients who have been made subject to hospital orders by a court under s.37 (Sch.1 Pt 1 para.1).

*Domestic Violence, Crime and Victims Act 2004*

**1–216**   Before an AMHP agrees to the imposition of a condition under or an RC either decides to impose or vary a condition, they must consider any representations from victims and the RC must inform the hospital managers if the patient comes within the scope of the 2004 Act: see the General Note to s.17A under this heading and "Guidance on the extension of victims' rights under the Domestic Violence, Crime and Victims Act 2004", Department of Health, 2008, paras.3.1 to 3.8.

*Code of Practice*

**1–217**   Guidance on this section is contained in paras.25.29 to 25.35.

*Subsections (2), (3)*

**1–218**   Subsection (3) does not contain an exhaustive list of conditions that can be attached to the CTO. The RC, with the agreement of the AMHP, may agree to specify other conditions as long as they are "necessary or appropriate" (not "necessary *and* appropriate") for one or more of the purposes set out in subs.(2). This gives a considerable amount of discretion to the RC regarding the nature of the conditions that can be imposed. They could include conditions that the patient resides at a particular place, attends at a specified place for the purposes of receiving medical or psychological treatment, or conditions concerning the "avoidance of known risk factors or high-risk situations relevant to the patient's mental disorder" (*Code of Practice*, para.25.34). In the Government's opinion, it would be inappropriate to impose a conditions that amounts to a deprivation of liberty for the purposes of art.5 of the European Convention on Human Rights (Joint Committee,

Appendix 3, para.38). As one of the effects of a CTO is to suspend the authority of the hospital managers to detain the patient (s.17D(2)(a)), it is submitted that such a condition would be unlawful.

In para.2.88 of its *Thirteenth Biennial Report* 2007–2009, the Mental Health Act Commission addressed the question of whether a condition that the patient resides at another hospital is lawful:

"The revised Act does state that s.17A provides the Responsible Clinician with the power by order in writing to 'discharge a detained patient from hospital' (s.17A(1)). However, the relevant criterion for making an SCT is stated to be that "treatment can be provided without his continuing to be detained in hospital" (s.17A(5)(c)). A situation where a patient who moves from detention in hospital to residence in a hospital under SCT fulfils the literal meaning of "without . . . continuing to be detained in hospital". In the cases explained to us so far, the hospital named as a place of residence is a different establishment to that in which the patient had been detained. As such, the effect of the community treatment order would certainly be to 'discharge a detained patient from hospital', albeit that they are required to take up residence in another. Whilst such a reading of the law might seem perverse, we suggest that it is no more so than a reading which allows a patient to be discharged to a staffed establishment that functions in much the same way as a hospital, provided that it is not officially designated as such. We have raised this matter with the Department of Health, and whilst officials have accepted that our reading may be correct, they did restate that SCT was designed as a mechanism for discharge from hospital, and not for transfer between one hospital and another. We share this concern that SCT should be operated within the spirit as well as the letter of the law, but the precedent of conditional discharge cases suggests that the boundaries of the law will be tested."

It is submitted that a condition that a patient resides in a named hospital would be held not to be lawful on the ground that a hospital is a place of treatment, not residence.

There is no power to take an objecting community patient to the place where he or she is required to be as a condition of the CTO: see the notes on s.18(7).

A CTO patient can be admitted to hospital as an informal patient for treatment for his or her mental disorder without the recall procedure set out in s.17E being invoked.

*Subsections (4), (5)*

The power to vary or suspend a condition enables the RC to respond to changes in the **1–219** patient's circumstances. It could be exercised as a result of a request made by the patient or the patient's carer. The agreement of an AMHP to the variation or suspension is not required; see further para.25.41 of the *Code of Practice*.

An order varying a condition must be made on Form CTO2: see reg.6(2)(b) of the English Regulations (in Wales, Form CP2: see reg.16(2) of the Welsh Regulations).

## [Duration of community treatment order

**17C.** A community treatment order shall remain in force until—　　　　　　**1–220**
- (a) the period mentioned in section 20A(1) below (as extended under any provision of this Act) expires, but this is subject to sections 21 and 22 below;
- (b) the patient is discharged in pursuance of an order under section 23 below or a direction under section 72 below;
- (c) the application for admission for treatment in respect of the patient otherwise ceases to have effect; or
- (d) the order is revoked under section 17F below, whichever occurs first.]

AMENDMENT

This section was inserted by the Mental Health Act 2007 s.32(2).

DEFINITIONS
**1–221**    community treatment order: ss.17A(7), 145(1).
application for admission for treatment: s.145(1).

GENERAL NOTE
**1–222**    This section specifies that a CTO will end:

1. When the period of the CTO runs out and the CTO is not extended under the provisions contained in s.20A. The effect of a CTO being allowed to lapse on the underlying liability to detention is unclear. Although the CTO has clearly come to an end, so has the suspension of the s.3 (or its equivalent) under s.17D(2). In this situation, it is suggested that an order for the discharge of the s.3 should be made under s.23.

2. If the patient is discharged from the powers of the Act by virtue of an order made under s.23 by the RC, the hospital managers or the patient's nearest relative (for Pt II patients), or a direction made by a tribunal under s.72. The patient is also discharged if the application under s.3 (or order under Part III) otherwise ceases to have effect.
   If the patient is made subject to a CTO during a period of deferred discharge granted by the tribunal under s.72(3), the CTO will end on the discharge taking effect. Placing the patient of a CTO in this situation would therefore be a pointless exercise.

3. If the RC revokes the CTO following the patients recall to hospital under s.17F. Revocation does not end the underlying liability to detention (s.17G).

The CTO, and the underlying liability to detention, will also end if the patient is received into guardianship (s.8(5)), on the patient being detained under s.3 if the patient was subject to s.3 before going onto SCT, but not if the patient was subject to an order or direction made under Pt III at that time (see s.6(4) and paras.2.113 and 2.114 of the Reference Guide) and if the patient has been "detained in custody" for more than six months (s.22).
The CTO will not end if the patient is admitted to a hospital either informally or subject to s.2, is detained under s.135 or 136 or is arrested and charged for a criminal offence.
This section applies without modification to patients who have been made subject to hospital orders (Sch.1, Pt 1, para.1).

*Domestic Violence, Crime and Victims Act 2004*
**1–223**    If the RC decides not to renew the CTO, he or she must inform the hospital managers if the patient comes within the scope of the 2004 Act: see the General Note to s.17A under this heading and "Guidance on the extension of victims' rights under the Domestic Violence, Crime and Victims Act 2004", Department of Health, 2008, paras.3.1 to 3.7.

**[Effect of community treatment order**
**1–224**    **17D.**—(1) The application for admission for treatment in respect of a patient shall not cease to have effect by virtue of his becoming a community patient.
(2) But while he remains a community patient—
(a) the authority of the managers to detain him under section 6(2) above in pursuance of that application shall be suspended; and
(b) reference (however expressed) in this or any other Act, or in any subordinate legislation (within the meaning of the Interpretation Act 1978), to patients liable to be detained, or detained, under this Act shall not include him.
(3) And section 20 below shall not apply to him while he remains a community patient.

(4) Accordingly, authority for his detention shall not expire during any period in which that authority is suspended by virtue of subsection (2)(a) above.]

AMENDMENT
This section was inserted by the Mental Health Act 2007 s.32(2).

DEFINITIONS

application for admission for treatment: s.145(1).  **1–225**
community patient: ss.17A(7), 145(1).
the managers: s.145(1).

GENERAL NOTE

This section sets out the effect of a CTO on certain provisions of this Act. They are:  **1–226**

1. Although the application for admission for treatment (or its equivalent: see the note on s.17A(2)) that was made in respect of the patient remains in force during the currency of the CTO, the hospital managers' authority to detain the patient under s.6(2) is suspended. Therefore, the section does not expire and does not have to be renewed. Paragraph 15.21 of the Reference Guide states:

   "A CTO is an order for the patient's discharge from detention in hospital, subject to the possibility of the patient being recalled to hospital for further medical treatment, if necessary. As with any other discharge from detention, the patient does not necessarily have to leave hospital immediately, or may already have done so on leave of absence."

2. Where the Act, any other Act or any subordinate legislation refers to patients who are "detained" or "liable to be detained", this does not include community patients. One of the effect of this is that the authority to treat the patient under Pt IV is suspended. If the patient is recalled to hospital under s.17E: see s.62A.

3. The renewal provisions contained in s.20 do not apply to the patient while he or she is a community patient. This means that the authority to detain the patient does not expire during the time when that authority is suspended by virtue of subs.(2)(a).

The CTO will come into effect from the date and time specified in Pt 3 of Form CTO 1 (or, in Wales, Form CP1). The patient does not have to leave hospital immediately after the CTO comes into effect; he or she could remain in hospital as an informal patient. The provisions of s.133 apply to a patient who is to be discharged from hospital subject to a CTO (s.133(1A)).

See s.22 for the effect of the patient's imprisonment on the CTO.

This section applies to patients who have been made subject to hospital orders with the modification set out in para.2A of Sch.1 (Sch.1, Pt 1, para.2).

**[Power to recall to hospital**

**17E.**—(1) The responsible clinician may recall a community patient to hospital  **1–227**
if in his opinion—

   (a) the patient requires medical treatment in hospital for his mental disorder; and

   (b) there would be a risk of harm to the health or safety of the patient or to other persons if the patient were not recalled to hospital for that purpose.

   (2) The responsible clinician may also recall a community patient to hospital if the patient fails to comply with a condition specified under section 17B(3) above.

(3) The hospital to which a patient is recalled need not be the responsible hospital.

(4) Nothing in this section prevents a patient from being recalled to a hospital even though he is already in the hospital at the time when the power of recall is exercised; references to recalling him shall be construed accordingly.

(5) The power of recall under subsections (1) and (2) above shall be exercisable by notice in writing to the patient.

(6) A notice under this section recalling a patient to hospital shall be sufficient authority for the managers of that hospital to detain the patient there in accordance with the provisions of this Act.]

AMENDMENT
This section was inserted by the Mental Health Act 2007 s.32(2).

DEFINITIONS
**1–228**  responsible clinician: s.34(1).
community patient; ss.17A(7), 145(1).
medical treatment: s.145(1), (4).
hospital: s.145(1).
responsible hospital; ss.17A(7), 145(1).
the managers: s.145(1).

GENERAL NOTE
**1–229**  This section provides that a RC may recall a patient to hospital in the following circumstances:

1. Where the RC decides that the patient needs to receive treatment for his or her mental disorder in hospital and that, without such treatment, there would be a risk of harm to the health or safety of the patient, or to other people (subs.(1)). The recall notice may be issued even if the patient is in hospital informally at that time (subs.(4)). This would cover the situation of a hospitalised patient who, by refusing treatment, places themselves or others at risk. A patient can be recalled even though he or she is complying with the conditions of the CTO imposed under s.17B. Neither the hospital managers nor the patient's nearest relative can order the patient's discharge from hospital during a period of recall, although an order discharging the patient from SCT could be made.

2. Where the patient fails to comply with the mandatory conditions imposed under s.17B(3) (subs.(2)). Recall to hospital would (a) enable the RC to examine the patient to assess whether the CTO should be renewed, and (b) allow a SOAD to examine the patient in order to meet the certificate requirements in s.64B or 64E. There is no requirement to recall a patient who fails to comply with a discretionary condition imposed under s.17B(2).

An RC need not examine the patient before issuing a notice of recall; he or she can act on reports received which provide an account of the patient's current behaviour and situation. A patient's recall must be effected by notifying the patient in writing (subs.(5)). The patient need not be recalled to the hospital where he or she had been detained immediately before the CTO was made (subs.(3)). If the patient is recalled to a different hospital, a formal transfer could be made under s.17F(2). Patients should not be recalled to a particular hospital unless it has been established that the hospital will accept the patient as hospitals are not obliged to admit patients just because a recall notice has been issued. If the patient refuses to accept the recall notice or if the patient cannot be found, the notice should be delivered to the patient's usual or last known address (*Code of Practice*, paras 25.55, 25.58). A recall notice reinstates the power of the hospital managers to detain the patient (subs.(6)) and the patient may be taken into custody and returned to the hospital (s.18(2A)). A patient who fails to respond to a recall notice becomes a patient who is absent from the hospital without leave and the provisions of ss.18, 21, 21A and 21B will apply. If access to the patient is denied, an application for a warrant under s.135(2) could be made. The 72 hour period referred to in s.17F(6) starts on the patient's arrival at the hospital. The powers which apply to the patient on recall are set out in s.17F.

A CTO patient can agree to being admitted informally to a hospital without a recall procedure being used. The treatment of the mental disorder of such patients ("community patients") is governed by Part IVA. The holding powers set out in s.5 cannot be used in respect of a community patient (s.5(6)).

If a child community patient is a ward of court, the usual rule relating to the need to act in conformity with any order made by the court in the exercise of its wardship jurisdiction does not apply during a period of recall under this section (s.33(4)).

The hospital managers must take steps to inform the patient of the effect of the recall: see reg.6(7) of the English Regulations and reg.22(1) of the Welsh Regulations.

This section applies without modification to patients who have been made subject to hospital orders (Sch.1, Pt 1, para.1).

*Code of Practice*
Guidance on the recall of patients is given in Ch.25 at para.25.47 et seq.  **1–230**

*Subsection (1)(a)*
IN HOSPITAL.  The recall could be to a hospital out-patient department (*R. (on the appli-*  **1–231** *cation of DR) v Mersey Care NHS Trust* [2002] M.H.L.R. 386; also see the *Code of Practice* para.25.61). The patient can be transferred to units within the hospital named in Form CTO3 during the recall period.

*Subsection (5)*
NOTICE IN WRITING.  Using Form CTO3: see reg.6(3)(a) of the English Regulations (in  **1–232** Wales, Form CP5: see reg.19(1)(a) of the Welsh Regulations). For service of the notice of recall, see *ibid.*, reg.6(5),(6) (reg.19(4),(5) of the Welsh Regulations). The hospital managers must record the time and date of the patient's detention pursuant to such notice on Form CTO4 (reg.6(3)(d)) (in Wales, Form CP6: see reg.19(1)(d) of the Welsh Regulations).
The Reference Guide states at para.15.38:

"If the patient's responsible hospital is in Wales, recall must be done in accordance with the equivalent Welsh regulations, even if the patient is to be recalled to a hospital in England. That will involve using a Welsh statutory form, rather than CTO3, to give the patient notice of the recall".

If the patient is in hospital informally when it is decided to recall him or her, the holding powers set out in s.5(2) and (4) cannot be used to prevent the patient from leaving the hospital: see s.5(6).

*Subsection (6)*
As the notice provides the authority to detain the patient, a copy should be sent to the  **1–233** hospital to which the patient is being recalled.

**[Powers in respect of recalled patients**
    **17F.**—(1) This section applies to a community patient who is detained in a hos-  **1–234** pital by virtue of a notice recalling him there under section 17E above.

(2) The patient may be transferred to another hospital in such circumstances and subject to such conditions as may be prescribed in regulations made by the Secretary of State (if the hospital in which the patient is detained is in England) or the Welsh Ministers (if that hospital is in Wales).

(3) If he is so transferred to another hospital, he shall be treated for the purposes of this section (and section 17E above) as if the notice under that section were a notice recalling him to that other hospital and as if he had been detained there from the time when his detention in hospital by virtue of the notice first began.

(4) The responsible clinician may by order in writing revoke the community treatment order if—

    (a)  in his opinion, the conditions mentioned in section 3(2) above are satisfied in respect of the patient; and

    (b)  an approved mental health professional states in writing—

        (i)  that he agrees with that opinion; and

        (ii)  that it is appropriate to revoke the order.

(5) The responsible clinician may at any time release the patient under this section, but not after the community treatment order has been revoked.

(6) If the patient has not been released, nor the community treatment order revoked, by the end of the period of 72 hours, he shall then be released.

(7) But a patient who is released under this section remains subject to the community treatment order.

(8) In this section—

    (a)  "the period of 72 hours" means the period of 72 hours beginning with the time when the patient's detention in hospital by virtue of the notice under section 17E above begins; and

    (b)  references to being released shall be construed as references to being released from that detention (and accordingly from being recalled to hospital).]

AMENDMENT

This section was inserted by the Mental Health Act 2007 s.32(2).

DEFINITIONS

**1–235**    community patient: ss.17A(7), 145(1).

hospital: s.145(1).

responsible clinician: s.34(1).

community treatment order: ss.17A(7), 145(1).

approved mental health professional: s.145(1), (1AC).

GENERAL NOTE

**1–236**    This section identifies the following powers that apply to a community patient who has been recalled to hospital under s.17E:

    1.  The patient may be transferred to another hospital under reg.9 of the English Regulations and reg.26 of the Welsh Regulations (s.19A) by a person specified in reg.12. If such a transfer takes place, the patient is to be treated as if he or she had been recalled to, and detained in, that other hospital (subss.(2),(3)). A transfer between hospitals while a patient is recalled does not change the identity of the responsible hospital. Such a change can be effected under reg.17 of the English Regulations or reg.25 of the Welsh Regulations.

2. If the RC decides that the patient meets the criteria for detention as set out in s.3(2), the RC may, subject to an AMHP's agreement, revoke the CTO (subs.(4)). A CTO can only be revoked when the patient is detained in hospital as a result of recall. The requirement to obtain the agreement of an AMHP is unfortunate because, in the absence of such agreement, the patient will continue to be subject to a CTO which the RC no longer considers to be an appropriate response to the patient's situation. Although the *Code of Practice*, at para.25.7, states that if the agreement of the AMHP is not forthcoming it "would not be appropriate" for the RC to approach another AMHP for an alternative view, such an approach would not be unlawful. Indeed, it could be argued that the RC has a professional duty to make such an approach in an attempt to achieve an objective that he or she has ascertained to be in the patient's best interests. The effect of a revocation is set out in s.17G.

3. The RC may release the patient from detention within the period of 72 hours of the patient's recall to hospital, provided that the CTO has not been revoked (subss.(5),(8)). If by the end of the 72 hour period the patient has not been released, nor the CTO revoked, he or she shall then be released (subs.(6)). On release, the patient continues to be subject to the CTO (subs.(7)). Release means release from detention (subs.(8)(b)); there is nothing to prevent the released patient from remaining in hospital informally. The patient's RC also has the option of discharging the patient from the CTO (s.23), which has the automatic effect of also discharging the underlying application for treatment.

A recalled patient can be treated for his or her mental disorder without consent subject to the safeguards set out in either Part IV or Part IVA: see s.62A .

A recalled patient who absconds is absent without leave and the provisions of ss.18, 21, 21A and 21B will apply.

This section applies without modification to patients who have been made subject to hospital orders (Sch.1, Pt 1, para.1).

*Domestic Violence, Crime and Victims Act 2004*
If the RC decides to revoke the CTO, he or she must inform the hospital managers if the patient comes within the scope of the 2004 Act: see the General Note to s.17A under this heading and "Guidance on the extension of victims' rights under the Domestic Violence, Crime and Victims Act 2004", Department of Health, 2008, paras.3.1 to 3.7. **1–237**

*Code of Practice*
Guidance on revoking the CTO is given in Ch.25 at paras 25.65 et seq. **1–238**

*Subsection (2)*
PRESCRIBED IN REGULATIONS.   Form CTO6 provides authority for the patient's transfer: see reg.9 of the English Regulations. The managers of the new hospital should be given a copy of Form CTO 4 or, in Wales, Form CP6 (see the note to subs.(6)). Transfers from hospitals in Wales to hospitals in England must be done in accordance with the equivalent Welsh regulations using Welsh Form TC 6: see reg.26 of the Welsh Regulations. **1–239**

*Subsection (4)*
ORDER IN WRITING.   On Form CTO5: see reg.6(8)(a) of the English Regulations (in Wales, Form CP7: see reg.20 of the Welsh Regulations). **1–240**

*Subsection (6)*
BY THE END OF THE PERIOD OF 72 HOURS.   The start of this period must be recorded on Form CTO 4 (in Wales, Form CP6). The 72-hour period starts from the time when the patient is admitted to the hospital as a result of the recall notice and not from the time **1–241**

when the recall notice was issued. If the patient is absent without leave at the end of that period, the 72-hour period is extended until the patient either returns or is returned to the hospital where he or she ought to be (s.21A(4)).

The 72-hour period cannot be extended by use of the holding powers contained in s.5(2), (4).

## [Effect of revoking community treatment order

**1–242**     **17G.**—(1) This section applies if a community treatment order is revoked under section 17F above in respect of a patient.

(2) Section 6(2) above shall have effect as if the patient had never been discharged from hospital by virtue of the community treatment order.

(3) The provisions of this or any other Act relating to patients liable to be detained (or detained) in pursuance of an application for admission for treatment shall apply to the patient as they did before the community treatment order was made, unless otherwise provided.

(4) If, when the order is revoked, the patient is being detained in a hospital other than the responsible hospital, the provisions of this Part of this Act shall have effect as if—

(a)  the application for admission for treatment in respect of him were an application for admission to that other hospital; and

(b)  he had been admitted to that other hospital at the time when he was originally admitted in pursuance of the application.

(5) But, in any case, section 20 below shall have effect as if the patient had been admitted to hospital in pursuance of the application for admission for treatment on the day on which the order is revoked.]

AMENDMENT

This section was inserted by the Mental Health Act 2007 s.32(2).

DEFINITIONS

**1–243**     community treatment order: ss.17A(7), 145(1).
hospital: s.145(1).
application for admission for treatment: s.145(1).
responsible hospital: ss.17A(7), 145(1).

GENERAL NOTE

**1–244**     This section provides that if a patient's CTO is revoked, the authority to detain the patient under s.6(2) applies as if the patient had never been a community patient (subs.(2)). In addition, all of the provisions of this Act relating to patients who are liable to be detained (or detained) under s.3 apply to the patient as they did before the CTO was made, unless this Act provides otherwise (subs.(3)). If, at the time when the CTO is revoked, the patient is detained in a hospital other than the one where he was detained when the CTO was made, this Act will apply as if he had been detained in that other hospital at the time when the CTO was made (subs.(4)). For the purposes of calculating the renewal periods under s.20 and for applications and references to a tribunal, the patient is to be treated as if he or she had been admitted under s.3 on the day when the CTO is revoked (subs.(5)). The revocation does not effect the calculation of the three month period set out in s.58(1)(b) (s.62A(2)).

Hospital managers must refer the cases of patients whose CTOs are revoked to the tribunal as soon as possible after the revocation (s.68(7)). This duty rests on the hospital managers of the hospital in which the patient is now detained, even if it was not previously the patient's responsible hospital. The tribunal does not have the power to discharge the patient during the 72-hour recall period.

This section applies to patients who have been made subject to hospital orders with the modification set out in para.2B of Sch.1 (Sch.1, Pt 1, para.2).

## Return and readmission of patients absent without leave

**18.**—(1) Where a patient who is for the time being liable to be detained under **1–245** this Part of this Act in a hospital—

(a) absents himself from the hospital without leave granted under section 17 above; or

(b) fails to return to the hospital on any occasion on which, or at the expiration of any period for which, leave of absence was granted to him under that section, or upon being recalled under that section; or

(c) absents himself without permission from any place where he is required to reside in accordance with conditions imposed on the grant of leave of absence under that section,

he may, subject to the provisions of this section, be taken into custody and returned to the hospital or place by any [approved mental health professional], by any officer on the staff of the hospital, by any constable, or by any person authorised in writing by the managers of the hospital.

(2) Where the place referred to in paragraph (c) of subsection (1) above is a hospital other than the one in which the patient is for the time being liable to be detained, the references in that subsection to an officer on the staff of the hospital and the managers of the hospital shall respectively include references to an officer on the staff of the first-mentioned hospital and the managers of that hospital.

[(2A) Where a community patient is at any time absent from a hospital to which he is recalled under section 17E above, he may, subject to the provisions of this section, be taken into custody and returned to the hospital by any approved mental health professional, by any officer on the staff of the hospital, by any constable, or by any person authorised in writing by the responsible clinician or the managers of the hospital.]

(3) Where a patient who is for the time being subject to guardianship under this Part of this Act absents himself without the leave of the guardian from the place at which he is required by the guardian to reside, he may, subject to the provisions of this section, be taken into custody and returned to that place by any officer on the staff of a local social services authority, by any constable, or by any person authorised in writing by the guardian or a local social services authority.

[(4) A patient shall not be taken into custody under this section after the later of—

(a) the end of the period of six months beginning with the first day of his absence without leave; and

(b) the end of the period for which (apart from section 21 below) he is liable to be detained or subject to guardianship [or, in the case of a community patient, the community treatment order is in force] [. . .]].

[(4A) In determining for the purposes of subsection (4)(b) above or any other provision of this Act whether a person who is or has been absent without leave is at any time liable to be detained or subject to guardianship, a report furnished under section 20 or 21B below before the first day of his absence without leave shall not be taken to have renewed the authority for his detention or guardianship unless the period of renewal began before that day.

(4B) Similarly, in determining for those purposes whether a community treatment order is at any time in force in respect of a person who is or has been absent

135

without leave, a report furnished under section 20A or 21B below before the first day of his absence without leave shall not be taken to have extended the community treatment period unless the extension began before that day.]

(5) A patient shall not be taken into custody under this section if the period for which he is liable to be detained is that specified in section 2(4), 4(4) or 5(2) or (4) above and that period has expired.

(6) In this Act "absent without leave" means absent from any hospital or other place and liable to be taken into custody and returned under this section, and related expressions shall be construed accordingly.

[(7) In relation to a patient who has yet to comply with a requirement imposed by virtue of this Act to be in a hospital or place, references in this Act to his liability to be returned to the hospital or place shall include his liability to be taken to that hospital or place; and related expressions shall be construed accordingly.]

AMENDMENT
Subsection (4) was substituted by the Mental Health (Patients in the Community) Act 1995 s.2(1). The words in square brackets were substituted and inserted by the Mental Health Act 2007 ss.21, 32(4), Sch.2 para.7, Sch.3 para.3. The words omitted were repealed by s.55, Sch.11 Pt 5.

DEFINITIONS
**1–246**  patient: s.145(1).
hospital: ss.34(2), 145(1).
approved mental health professional: s.145(1) (1AC).
the managers: s.145(1).
local social services authority: s.145(1).
responsible clinician: s.34(1).
community patient: s.17A(7), 145(1).
community treatment order: ss.17A(7), 145(1).

GENERAL NOTE
**1–247**  This section, which should be read with ss.21, 21A and 21B, identifies the action that can be taken when a detained patient, a community patient or a patient subject to guardianship absents him or herself without leave. It applies to patients who are absent from England and who are found in Wales, and vice versa. Provisions relating to the removal and return of patients within the UK are contained in Pt VI of this Act. There is no power under this Act to require the return of a patient who has left the UK without authority. The Care Quality Commission requires all service providers to notify it of any absence without leave of a person who is either detained or liable to be detained under this Act. A form that must be used for this purpose may be downloaded from the Commission's website (www.cqc.org.uk).

A patient who has been admitted for treatment under s.3 or received into guardianship under s.7 can be taken into custody at any time up to six months from the date on which he or she absconded or, if later, the end of the existing authority for detention in hospital or guardianship. A community patient cannot be taken into custody after the community treatment order (CTO) ceases to be in force, or six months have elapsed since the patient was first absent without leave, whichever is the later (subs.4). A patient who has been detained under one of the short term provisions of this Act cannot be taken into custody after the authority to detain has expired (subs.(5)).

Subsection (1)(a) of this section can be used to return a patient to the detaining hospital following the granting of a stay by the High Court in proceedings to judicially review the lawfulness of the decision of a tribunal to discharge the patient (*R. (on the application of H) v Ashworth Hospital Authority; R. (on the application of Ashworth Hospital Authority v*

*Mental Health Review Tribunal for West Midlands and North West Region* [2002] EWCA Civ 923; [2002] M.H.L.R. 314, noted in the General Note to s.3 under the heading "The re-sectioning of a patient subsequent to a discharge by the First-tier Tribunal (Mental Health) or the Mental Health Review Tribunal for Wales").

Those persons who have the power under subs.(1) to return the absconder to hospital are not provided with a power under this section to force entry onto premises where the abscon-der is staying. If a power of entry is needed, an application should be made under s.135(2) of this Act for a warrant authorising a policeman to enter the premises to remove the patient or, alternatively, the police might be able to use their powers under s.17(1)(d) of the Police and Criminal Evidence Act 1984: see the General Note to s.135.

It is an offence for a person to induce or knowingly to assist a detained patient to absent himself without leave, knowingly to harbour the patient whilst he or she is at large, or to help the patient to avoid being retaken (s.128). A patient who is absent without leave does not thereby commit an offence (*R. v Criminal Injuries Compensation Board Ex p. Lawton* [1972] 3 All E.R. 582 at 584).

It is sensible for a hospital's absconsion policy not to require that a request for police assistance be made where this is not necessary (*Dunn v South Tyneside Health Care NHS Trust* [2003] EWCA Civ 878; [2004] M.H.L.R. 74 para.71).

This section applies to patients who have been placed under hospital or guardianship orders by a court under s.37 with the modification that subs.(5) shall be omitted (Sch.1, Pt 1, paras 2, 4). For patients who are subject to special restrictions, subss.(3), (4) and (5) shall be omitted and in subs.(1) the words "subject to the provisions of this section" shall be omitted (Sch.1, Pt II, paras 2, 4). The effect of this is that restricted patients may be retaken at any time while their restrictions remain in force. This section also applies to patients who have been sentenced and who remain liable to be detained by virtue of s.22 (s.22(2)(b)).

The National Mental Health Development Unit has published "Strategies to Reduce Missing Patients: A Practical Workbook" (2009).

*Patients who abscond to Scotland*

The Mental Health (Absconding Patients From Other Jurisdictions) (Scotland) **1–248** Regulations 2008 (SSI 2008/333) make provision for the taking into custody of a person who is subject to compulsory measures (including community-based orders) under mental health legislation in England and Wales and who is found in Scotland, as a result of their having absconded, or otherwise having failed to comply with the requirements of the order or other measure to which they are subject. It makes such provision by applying to such persons (with some appropriate modification), the sections of the Mental Health (Care and Treatment) (Scotland) Act 2003 (ss.301 to 303) which provide for the taking into cus-tody of absconding patients who are subject to civil compulsory mental health measures in Scotland. SSI 2008/333, along with the Mental Health (Cross-border Visits) (Scotland) Regulations 2008 (SSI 2008/181) (which is noted under s.17), is intended to bring provision dealing with persons in Scotland who abscond or otherwise fail to comply with require-ments imposed under mental health measures applicable in England and Wales within the scope of the Scottish mental health legislation.

*Human Rights Act 1998*

Although it could be argued that, apart from emergency cases or cases where the patient **1–249** is returned to hospital within a short period of the unauthorised absence, the return of an absconding patient to hospital would constitute a violation of art.5(1) of the European Convention of Human Rights in the absence of an up to date medical report which con-firmed that he or she was suffering from a mental disorder (see *Kay v United Kingdom* (1998) 40 B.M.L.R. 20, noted under s.42(3)), it is likely that the procedure for the return of such patients is Convention compliant by virtue of the provisions of s.21B.

*Code of Practice*

**1–250**   Guidance on this section is contained in Ch.22. The conveyance of patients is considered in Ch.11.

*Subsection (1)*

**1–251**   This subsection and subs.(2) identify the action that can be taken when a detained patient goes absent without leave.

TAKEN INTO CUSTODY.   The patient may be taken into custody in, and returned to England or Wales from Northern Ireland (s.88).

RETURNED.   Reasonable force may be used to secure the return of the patient to the hospital or the place where he or she is required to reside (s.137). There is no power to take the patient to any other place.

OFFICER ON THE STAFF OF THE HOSPITAL.   See the notes on s.17(3).

AUTHORISED IN WRITING.   The authorisation can be transmitted by fax.

THE MANAGERS.   Or a person authorised by them: see reg.19 of the English Regulations and reg.35 of the Welsh Regulations.

*Subsection (2)*

**1–252**   This subsection provides that if a patient has been granted leave of absence on condition that he resides in a hospital other than the one in which he is formally liable to be detained, he can be taken into custody by an officer on the staff of the hospital where he is on leave, or by a person authorised by the managers of that hospital.

*Subsection (2A)*

**1–253**   This provision identifies the action that can be taken when a community patient fails to respond to a recall notice or absconds from the hospital after having been recalled.

THE MANAGERS.   Or a person authorised by them: see reg.19 of the English Regulations and reg.35 of the Welsh Regulations.

*Subsection (3)*

**1–254**   This provision identifies the action that can be taken when a patient who is subject to guardianship absents him or herself from the place where he or she is required to reside by the guardian.

TAKEN INTO CUSTODY.   If access to the patient is denied consideration will have to be given to obtaining a warrant under s.135(2): see the General Note to this section.

*Subsection (4)*

**1–255**   This subsection, which is subject to subss.(4A) and (4B), establishes the time limit within which patients who are absent without leave can be returned to the relevant hospital or place of residence. Its effect is that the authority to take the patient into custody will last until at least six months after the first day of absence.

SHALL NOT BE TAKEN INTO CUSTODY.   But see subs.(5). A patient who is subject to restrictions can be retaken at any time: see the General Note to this section.

BEGINNING WITH THE FIRST DAY OF HIS ABSENCE WITHOUT LEAVE.   Including the first day of the patient's absence without leave (*Zoan v Rouamba* [2000] 2 All E.R. 620 CA).

*Subsections (4A), (4B)*

These subsections provide that if a patient's section, guardianship or CTO is renewed or **1–256** extended before the first day of the patient's absence without leave, the renewal or extension is deemed not to have taken effect unless the period of renewal or extension began before that day. This means that the period during which the patient can be taken into custody is not extended by the renewal or extension.

*Subsection (5)*

This subsection provides that a patient cannot be taken into custody under this section if **1–257** the period of his detention under one of the following powers has expired: admission for assessment (s.2(4)), emergency admission (s.4(4)), or the detention of an in-patient by a doctor or AC (s.5(2)) or nurse (s.5(4)).

*Subsection (7)*

This subsection provides a power to take a patient who is subject to guardianship or a **1–258** detained patient who has been granted leave of absence under s.17 to the hospital or place where he or she is required to be. Reasonable force may be used to ensure that the patient is taken to that hospital or place (s.137).

Although there is a power in subs.(2A) to take a community patient to the hospital to which he or she has been recalled, there is no power to take such a patient to a place where he or she is required to be as a condition of the CTO because there is no power to return the patient to that place.

## Regulations as to transfer of patients

**19.**—(1) In such circumstances and subject to such conditions as may be pre- **1–259** scribed by regulations made by the Secretary of State—

(a) a patient who is for the time being liable to be detained in a hospital by virtue of an application under this Part of this Act may be transferred to another hospital or into the guardianship of a local social services authority or of any person approved by such an authority;

(b) a patient who is for the time being subject to the guardianship of a local social services authority or other person by virtue of an application under this Part of this Act may be transferred into the guardianship of another local social services authority or person, or be transferred to a hospital.

(2) Where a patient is transferred in pursuance of regulations under this section, the provisions of this Part of this Act (including this subsection) shall apply to him as follows, that is to say—

(a) in the case of a patient who is liable to be detained in a hospital by virtue of an application for admission for assessment or for treatment and is transferred to another hospital, as if the application were an application for admission to that other hospital and as if the patient had been admitted to that other hospital at the time when he was originally admitted in pursuance of the application;

(b) in the case of a patient who is liable to be detained in a hospital by virtue of such an application and is transferred into guardianship, as if the application were a guardianship application duly accepted at the said time;

(c) in the case of a patient who is subject to guardianship by virtue of a guardianship application and is transferred into the guardianship of another authority or person, as if the application were for his reception into the guardianship of that authority or person and had been accepted at the time when it was originally accepted;

(d) in the case of a patient who is subject to guardianship by virtue of a guardianship application and is transferred to a hospital, as if the guardianship application were an application for admission to that hospital for treatment and as if the patient had been admitted to the hospital at the time when the application was originally accepted.

(3) Without prejudice to subsections (1) and (2) above, any patient, who is for the time being liable to be detained under this Part of this Act in a hospital vested in the Secretary of State for the purposes of his functions under the [National Health Service Act 2006, in a hospital vested in the Welsh Ministers for the purposes of their functions under the National Health Service (Wales) Act 2006, in any accommodation used under either of those Acts] by the managers of such a hospital [or in a hospital vested in a National Health Service trust][, NHS foundation trust] [, Local Health Board] [or Primary Care Trust], may at any time be removed to any other such hospital or accommodation [which is managed by the managers of, or is vested in the National Health Service trust[, NHS foundation trust] [, Local Health Board] [or Primary Care Trust] for, the first-mentioned hospital]; and paragraph (a) of subsection (2) above shall apply in relation to a patient so removed as it applies in relation to a patient transferred in pursuance of regulations made under this section.

(4) Regulations made under this section may make provision for regulating the conveyance to their destination of patients authorised to be transferred or removed in pursuance of the regulations or under subsection (3) above.

AMENDMENTS

In subs.(3) the words in square brackets were inserted and substituted by the National Health Service and Community Care Act 1990 s.66(1), Sch.9 para.24(2), the Health and Social Care (Community Health and Standards) Act 2003 s.34, Sch.4 para.52, the Health Act 1999 (Supplementary, Consequential, etc., Provisions) Order 2000 (SI 2000/ 90) Sch.1 para.16(3), the National Health Service (Consequential Provisions) Act 2006 s.2, Sch.1 para.64 and the Mental Health Act 2007 s.46(2).

DEFINITIONS

1–260    patient: s.145(1).
hospital: ss.34(2), 145(1).
local social services authority: s.145(1).
application for admission for assessment: ss.2, 145(1).
application for admission for treatment: ss.3, 145(1).
the managers: s.145(1).

GENERAL NOTE

1–261    This section empowers the Secretary of State (or, in relation to Wales, the Welsh Ministers) to regulate the circumstances in which detained patients and patients who are subject to guardianship may be transferred between hospitals or guardians or between detention in hospital and guardianship. It only applies to transfers within England and Wales. The Mental Health (Hospital, Guardianship and Treatment) (England) Regulations 2008 (SI 2008/1184) and the Mental Health (Hospital, Guardianship, Community Treatment and Consent to treatment) (Wales) Regulations 2008 (SI 2008/ 2439 (W.212)) have been made under this section.

In (*R. (on the application of T) v Chief Executive of Nottinghamshire Healthcare NHS Trust* [2006] EWHC 800 (Admin); [2006] M.H.L.R. 103, the patient failed in his attempt to challenge his transfer from one high security hospital to another, which was based on a policy decision of the Department of Health that, if certain criteria are met, patients should be transferred to the high secure hospital closest to their postal address. The challenge was made on a number of grounds, including irrationality, breach of art.8 of the European Convention on Human Rights, and procedural unfairness. The court found, inter alia, that the patient had been allowed to express his views as to whether he wished to be moved and that his views had been taken into account.

For the responsibility to inform the patient's nearest relative of a transfer under this section, see reg.26(1)(a)or (i) of the English Regulations and reg.30 of the Welsh Regulations.

This section applies to patients who are subject to hospital or guardianship orders made by a court under s.37, with the modification that subs.(2) shall read as follows:

"(2) Where a patient is transferred in pursuance of regulations under this section, the provisions of this Part of this Act (including this subsection) shall apply to him [as if the order or direction under Part III of this Act by virtue of which he was liable to be detained or subject to guardianship before being transferred were an order or direction for his admission or removal to the hospital to which he is transferred, or placing him under the guardianship of the authority or person into whose guardianship he is transferred, as the case may be]." (Sch.1, Pt 1, paras 2, 5.)

For restricted patients subs.(1), (2) and (3) shall read as follows:

"(1) In such circumstances and subject to such conditions as may be prescribed by regulations made by the Secretary of State—
(a) a patient who is for the time being liable to be detained in a hospital by virtue of an application under this Part of this Act may [with the consent of the Secretary of State] be transferred to another hospital [. . .]
(2) Where a patient is transferred in pursuance of regulations under this section, the provisions of this Part of this Act (including this sub-section) shall apply to him [as if the order or direction under Part III of this Act by virtue of which he was liable to be detained before being transferred were an order or direction for his admission or removal to the hospital to which he is transferred].
(3) Without prejudice to subsections (1) and (2) above, any patient, who is for the time being liable to be detained under this Part of this Act in a hospital vested in the Secretary of State for the purposes of his functions under the National Health Service Act 1977 or any accommodation used under Part I of that Act by the managers of such a hospital or in a hospital vested in a National Health Service trust [or Primary Care Trust], may at any time [, with the consent of the Secretary of State,] be removed to any other such hospital or accommodation which is managed by the managers of, or is vested in the National Health Service Trust [or Primary Care Trust] for, the first-mentioned hospital; and para.(a) of subs.(2) above shall apply in relation to a patient so removed as it applies in relation to a patient transferred in pursuance of regulations made under this section." (Sch.1, Pt II, paras 2, 5.)

The effect of these provisions is that any transfer of a restricted patient between hospitals, even where the hospitals are administered by the same NHS Trust, is subject to the agreement of the Secretary of State for Justice.

Provisions relating to the transfer of patients to and from high security hospitals are also contained in s.123.

*Human Rights Act 1998*

See (*R. (on the application of T) v Chief Executive of Nottinghamshire Healthcare NHS* **1–262** *Trust,* above.

Paragraph 30.15 of the *Code of Practice* states:

"People authorising transfers on behalf of the Hospital Managers should ensure that there are good reasons for the transfer and that the needs and interests of the patient have been considered. Transfers are potentially an interference with a patient's right to respect for privacy and family life under Article 8 of the European Convention on Human Rights, and care should be taken to act compatibly with the Convention when deciding whether to authorise a transfer".

*Applications to the First-tier Tribunal (Mental Health) or the Mental Health Review Tribunal for Wales*

**1–263**    The patient may make an application within 6 months of a transfer from guardianship to hospital (s.66(1)(e), (2)(e)) and during the same periods as a patient admitted under s.3. If this right is not exercised within six months of the transfer, the hospital managers will refer the case to the tribunal (s.68(1)). A patient who is transferred from hospital to guardianship has the same right to make an application as a guardianship patient who is made subject to a guardianship application on the day that the transfer takes effect (subs.(2)(b).

A transfer between hospitals does not affect patients' (or their nearest relatives') rights to apply to a tribunal, nor give them any new right to do so.

*Code of Practice*

**1–264**    Guidance on this section is contained in Ch.30 at paras 30.13 et seq.

*Subsection (1)*

**1–265**    REGULATIONS.    See regs 7, 8, 10 and 11 of the English Regulations and regs.23, 24 and 27 of the Welsh Regulations.

*Paragraph (a)*

**1–266**    PATIENT.    In order to be transferred under this provision, the patient must have become an in-patient of the hospital named in the application (see the phrase "originally admitted" in subs.(2)(a)) and the hospital must have accepted the application (see the note on "sufficient authority for the Managers" in s.6(2)).

As the patient who is to be transferred must be "liable to be detained" in a hospital, a transfer under this provision can be effected at a time when the patient has been placed on leave of absence under s.17.

BY VIRTUE OF AN APPLICATION.    Including a patient who has been detained under s.2. Patients who are detained in hospital but who have not been made subject to an application are excluded, e.g. patients detained under ss.5(2), (4), 35, 36, 38, 135 and 136 or who are detained in a place of safety under s.37(4). Patients who have been made subject to hospital orders or guardianship orders by a court are included: see the General Note, above.

TRANSFERRED TO ANOTHER HOSPITAL.    Including a high security hospital.

TRANSFERRED TO HOSPITAL.    The procedure for effecting such a transfer is very similar to the procedure for making an application under s.3: see reg.8 of the 2008 Regulations.

*Paragraph (b)*

**1–267**    TRANSFERRED INTO THE GUARDIANSHIP OF ANOTHER PERSON.    Transfer from one guardian to another can, in certain circumstances, also take place under s.10.

AT THE SAID TIME.    Which is the time when he was originally admitted in pursuance of the application: see para.(a).

*Subsection (2)*

*Paragraph (a)*

TRANSFERRED.   Using the procedure set out in reg.7(2) and Form H4 of the English **1–268** Regulations and reg.23(1),(2),(3) and Form TC1 of the Welsh Regulations. Transfer to another hospital managed by the same managers is allowed for without formality under subs.(3).

HOSPITAL.   Or registered establishment (s.34(2)). The transfer of a patient between registered establishments where both establishments are under the same management is governed by reg.7(5) of the English Regulations and reg.23(6) of the Welsh Regulations.

*Paragraph (b)*

TRANSFERRED INTO GUARDIANSHIP.   Using the procedure set out in reg.7(4) and Form G6 **1–269** of the English Regulations and reg.23(4),(5) and Form TC2 of the Welsh Regulations. Fresh medical recommendations are not required on such a transfer. Restricted patients may not be transferred into guardianship: see General Note to this section.

If patients refuse to go the place (if any) that the guardian requires them to reside, they are absent without leave and could be taken to that place in accordance with s.18(7).

Although the patient's nearest relative has no statutory right to object to such a transfer, he or she can discharge the patient from guardianship (s.23(2)(b)).

AS IF THE APPLICATION WERE A GUARDIANSHIP APPLICATION.   The original application will have either been for assessment under s.2 or for treatment under s.3 (subs.(2)(a)). Any outstanding tribunal application must proceed using guardianship criteria set out in s.72(4).

AT THE SAID TIME.   This is the time when the application for admission to hospital was made.

*Paragraph (c)*

TRANSFERRED.   Using the procedure set out in reg.8(1) and Form G7 of the English **1–270** Regulations and reg.24(1),(2),(3) and Form TC3 of the Welsh Regulations.

*Paragraph (d)*

If a patient is transferred under this paragraph, it would appear that the three-month **1–271** period relating to the administration of medicine specified in s.58(1)(b) of this Act would commence from the first occasion when medicine was administered to the patient during the period when he or she was subject to guardianship.

TRANSFERRED.   Using the procedure set out in reg.8(2) and Form G8 of the English Regulations and reg.24(4),(5) and Form TC4 of the Welsh Regulations.

AT THE TIME WHEN THE APPLICATION WAS ORIGINALLY ACCEPTED.   The guardian should ensure that this date is communicated to the hospital managers.

*Subsection (3)*

This subsection enables a patient to be transferred to another hospital, or other accom- **1–272** modation managed by the same managers without any special procedure being followed. It is submitted that it does not apply to patients who have been detained under s.5(2) or (4) because: (1) the fact that "paragraph (a) of subsection (2)", which relates to patients who have been made subject to an application, "shall apply" to this provision suggests that its scope is confined to such patients; and (2) the purpose of the holding powers is to prevent the patient from leaving the hospital where he or she is being treated; also see the *Code of Practice*, para.12.40. If, following the use of the holding powers, the assessment of the patient concludes that an application ought to be made in respect of him or her, the application can be addressed to a different hospital.

HOSPITAL.    For transfers between registered establishments where both establishments are under the same management, see reg.7(5) of the English Regulations and reg.23(6) of the Welsh Regulations.

A patient who is transferred under this provision is treated as if he had been admitted to the hospital to which he has been transferred at the time of the original application.

VESTED IN THE SECRETARY OF STATE.    Or in the Welsh Ministers for the purposes of their functions under the National Health Service (Wales) Act 2006 (SI 2000/253, Sch.3; also see the General Note to this Act).

## [Regulations as to assignment of responsibility for community patients

1–273    **19A.**—(1) Responsibility for a community patient may be assigned to another hospital in such circumstances and subject to such conditions as may be prescribed by regulations made by the Secretary of State (if the responsible hospital is in England) or the Welsh Ministers (if that hospital is in Wales).

(2) If responsibility for a community patient is assigned to another hospital—

(a) the application for admission for treatment in respect of the patient shall have effect (subject to section 17D above) as if it had always specified that other hospital;

(b) the patient shall be treated as if he had been admitted to that other hospital at the time when he was originally admitted in pursuance of the application (and as if he had subsequently been discharged under section 17A above from there); and

(c) that other hospital shall become "the responsible hospital" in relation to the patient for the purposes of this Act.]

AMENDMENT
This section was inserted by the Mental Health Act 2007 s.32(4), Sch.3 para.4.

DEFINITIONS
1–274    community patient: ss.17A(7), 145(1).
responsible hospital: ss.17A(7), 145(1).
application for admission for treatment: s.145(1).

GENERAL NOTE
1–275    This section enables the Secretary of State (in respect of a hospital in England) or the Welsh Ministers (in respect of a hospital in Wales) to make regulations which transfer the responsibility for a community patient to a new responsible hospital. If responsibility is transferred, the patient is to be treated as if he or she had been originally admitted to that hospital.

This section applies to patients who have been made subject to hospital orders with the modification that subs.(2)(b) shall be omitted (Sch.1 Pt 1 paras 2, 5A).

*Subsection (1)*
1–276    PRESCRIBED BY REGULATIONS.    See reg.17 of the English Regulations and reg.25 of the Welsh Regulations. Authority for the assignment must be given on Form CTO10 (in Wales, Form TC5).

*[Duration of authority and discharge]*

**Duration of authority**

20.—(1) Subject to the following provisions of this Part of this Act, a patient **1–277** admitted to hospital in pursuance of an application for admission for treatment, and a patient placed under guardianship in pursuance of a guardianship application, may be detained in a hospital or kept under guardianship for a period not exceeding six months beginning with the day on which he was so admitted, or the day on which the guardianship application was accepted, as the case may be, but shall not be so detained or kept for any longer period unless the authority for his detention or guardianship is renewed under this section.

(2) Authority for the detention or guardianship of a patient may, unless the patient has previously been discharged [under section 23 below], be renewed—

(a) from the expiration of the period referred to in subsection (1) above, for a further period of six months;

(b) from the expiration of any period of renewal under paragraph (a) above, for a further period of one year,

and so on for periods of one year at a time.

(3) Within the period of two months ending on the day on which a patient who is liable to be detained in pursuance of an application for admission for treatment would cease under this section to be so liable in default of the renewal of the authority for his detention, it shall be the duty of the [responsible clinician]—

(a) to examine the patient; and

(b) if it appears to him that the conditions set out in subsection (4) below are satisfied, to furnish to the managers of the hospital where the patient is detained a report to that effect in the prescribed form;

and where such a report is furnished in respect of a patient the managers shall, unless they discharge the patient [under section 23 below], cause him to be informed.

(4) The conditions referred to in subsection (3) above are that—

(a) the patient is suffering from [mental disorder] of a nature or degree which makes it appropriate for him to receive medical treatment in a hospital; and

(b) [. . .]

(c) it is necessary for the health or safety of the patient or for the protection of other persons that he should receive such treatment and that it cannot be provided unless he continues to be detained; [and

(d) appropriate medical treatment is available to him.]

[. . .]

(5) Before furnishing a report under subsection (3) above the [responsible clinician] shall consult one or more other persons who have been professionally concerned with the patient's medical treatment.

[(5A) But the responsible clinician may not furnish a report under subsection (3) above unless a person—

(a) who has been professionally concerned with the patient's medical treatment; but

(b) who belongs to a profession other than that to which the responsible clinician belongs, states in writing that he agrees that the conditions set out in subsection (4) above are satisfied.]

(6) Within the period of two months ending with the day on which a patient who is subject to guardianship under this Part of this Act would cease under this section to be so liable in default of the renewal of the authority for his guardianship, it shall be the duty of the [appropriate practitioner]—

(a) to examine the patient; and

(b) if it appears to him that the conditions set out in subsection (7) below are satisfied, to furnish to the guardian and, where the guardian is a person other than a local social services authority, to the responsible local social services authority a report to that effect in the prescribed form;

and where such a report is furnished in respect of a patient, the local social services authority shall, unless they discharge the patient [under section 23 below], cause him to be informed.

(7) The conditions referred to in subsection (6) above are that—

(a) the patient is suffering from [mental disorder] of a nature or degree which warrants his reception into guardianship; and

(b) it is necessary in the interests of the welfare of the patient or for the protection of other persons that the patient should remain under guardianship.

(8) Where a report is duly furnished under subsection (3) or (6) above, the authority for the detention or guardianship of the patient shall be thereby renewed for the period prescribed in that case by subsection (2) above.

(9) [. . .]

(10) [. . .]

AMENDMENTS

The amendments to this section were made by the Mental Health Act 2007 ss.1(4), 4(4), 9(4), 32(4),55, Sch.3 para.5, Sch.11 Pts 1, 2 and 3. The cross-heading was amended by s.32(3).

DEFINITIONS

**1–278**    patient: s.145(1).

hospital: ss.34(2), 145(1).

application for admission for treatment: ss.3, 145(1).

the managers: s.145(1).

mental disorder: ss.1, 145(1).

medical treatment: s.145(1), (4).

local social services authority: s.145(1).

responsible clinician: s.34(1).

appropriate clinician: s.145(1).

appropriate practitioner: s.34(1).

responsible local social services authority: s.34(1).

GENERAL NOTE

**1–279**    This section provides for patients who have been detained for treatment or placed under guardianship to be detained or kept under guardianship for an initial period of up to six months. It also sets out the criteria that have to be satisfied if the authority to detain a patient or keep him or her in guardianship is to be renewed. Renewal can be for one further period of six months and subsequently for periods of one year at a time.

As a restricted patient whose restriction order has ceased to have effect is treated as if he had been admitted to hospital as an unrestricted patient on the date when the restriction order ceased to have effect (s.41(5)), the start date for renewals under this section is that date.

The finding of McCullough J. in *R. v Hallstrom Ex p. W; R. v Gardner Ex p. L* [1986] 2 All E.R. 306, that a decision to renew the authority to detain a patient cannot be made at a time when the patient is on leave of absence was overruled by the Court of Appeal in *B v Barking Havering and Brentwood Community Healthcare NHS Trust* [1999] 1 F.L.R. 106. A renewal can be made while the patient is on leave of absence if the patient's treatment taken as a whole also requires a significant element of hospital treatment: see the note on subs.(4).

For the responsibility to inform the patient's nearest relative of the patient's renewal of detention or guardianship under this section, see reg.26(1)(b) or (l) of the English Regulations and regs.8 and 15 of the Welsh Regulations.

This section applies to patients who are subject to hospital or guardianship orders made by a court under s.37, with the modification that subs.(1) shall read as follows:

"(1) Subject to the following provisions of this Part of this Act, a patient admitted to hospital in pursuance of an application for admission for treatment, and a patient placed under guardianship in pursuance of a guardianship application, may be detained in a hospital or kept under guardianship for a period not exceeding six months beginning with the [date of the relevant order or direction under Part III of this Act] but shall not be so detained or kept for any longer period unless the authority for his detention or guardianship is renewed under this section" (Sch.1, Pt 1, para.6).

*Human Rights Act 1998*

The question whether the continued detention of an asymptomatic patient contravenes **1–280** art.5 of the European Convention of Human Rights is considered in the General Note to s.3 under this heading.

It is has been argued that the lack of any involvement of the hospital managers as detaining authority in the decision to renew the patient's detention (see the *Warlingham Park Hospital* case, noted under subs.(3)) might constitute a violation of art.5(1) of the Convention as interpreted by the European Court in *Winterwerp v Netherlands* (1979) 2 E.H.R.R. 387: see Phil Fennell, "The Third Way in Mental Health Policy: Negative Rights, Positive Rights and the Convention", (1999) 26 *Journal of Law and Society*, 103–127.

Among the functions that a responsible clinician (RC) has is the decision whether to renew the detention of the patient under this section. In *Winterwerp v Netherlands*, above, the European Court of Human Rights (ECHR) held that that in order for a detention on the ground of unsoundness of mind to be lawful it must be established by objective medical expertise that the person concerned suffers from a true mental disorder. During the passage of the 2007 Act through Parliament, the Joint Committee argued that if initial detention must be based on medical expertise to be compatible with art.5, there is an argument, following *Winterwerp,* that the same should apply to the renewal of detention. In support of this argument, the Joint Committee relied on *Varbanov v Bulgaria* [2000] M.H.L.R. 263 where the court held that it would be a breach of art.5 if a person were detained on the basis that they were of unsound mind without first obtaining the opinion of a medical expert. The Joint Committee argued that this case made it clear that that the opinion of a medical expert who is a psychiatrist is necessary and that renewal of detention by a RC who is not a psychiatrist would contravene art.5. The Government, in not agreeing that *Varbanov* requires the necessary medical expertise to be provided every time by a psychiatrist, countered by claiming that: (a) there is no caselaw specifically on what is meant by medical expertise; (b) *Winterwerp* was not seeking to lay down which sort of qualifications available in a national system which would be acceptable and which would not; (c) the ECHR is a "living instrument" that must be interpreted in the light of present day conditions; and (d) within a modern workforce, it is appropriate for Mental Health Act functions to be allocated to those who are competent to perform them. In the light of these considerations, the Government's view is that *Winterwerp* must be broadly interpreted and that what was required is a person who is able to make a decision as to whether or not the person in question is of unsound mind. As the competencies that must be satisfied before a person can become an AC include the ability to identify the presence and severity of mental disorder, the Government argued that such a person will have the objective medical expertise required by art.5. It is likely that the court would support the Government's contention that it is for national authorities to decide which professionals possess the required expertise to perform functions under the Act as this is a matter which is likely to come within the "margin of appreciation" that the court allows national authorities to have when applying the ECHR This issue is considered at paras 21 to 29 of the Joint Committee's Report and at paras 24 to 34 of the Government's response to the Report, Department of Health, April 13, 2007.

A finding by a RC that the patient is no longer suffering from a mental disorder (see subs.(4)(a)) does not require the patient's immediate release from detention if that patient poses a risk to the public: see the note on s.23 under this heading.

*Applications to the First-tier Tribunal (Mental Health) or the Mental Health Review Tribunal for Wales*

**1–281**     The patient's right to apply to a tribunal arises from the date of the renewal of the detention or guardianship (s.66(1)(f),(2)(f)).

*Code of Practice*

**1–282**     Guidance on the renewal of a patient's detention is given in Ch.29.

*Subsection (1)*

**1–283**     SUBJECT TO THE FOLLOWING PROVISIONS OF THIS PART OF THIS ACT.     Note especially the power of discharge granted by s.23.

SIX MONTHS.     A month means a calendar month (Interpretation Act 1978 s.5, Sch.1).

BEGINNING WITH.     Including the day on which the patient was admitted to hospital or the day on which the guardianship application was accepted by the local social services authority (*Zoan v Rouamba* [2002] 2 All E.R. 620 CA). This means that if the patient was admitted on March 3, the six month period would expire at midnight on September 2.

THE DAY ON WHICH HE WAS SO ADMITTED.     This is either the day on which the patient was admitted to the hospital from the community whilst subject to an application under s.3, or the day on which the patient who was in hospital either informally or subject to an application made under s.2 was made subject to such an application. In both cases, admission only takes effect when the s.3 application has been accepted by a person who has been authorised by the hospital managers to accept it: see reg.3(2) of the English and Welsh Regulations.

*Subsection (3)*

**1–284**     This subsection requires the RC to examine a patient detained for treatment during the two months preceding the day on which the authority for his detention is due to expire. If the RC considers that the conditions set out in subs.(4) are satisfied, the authority to detain the patient is renewed when Form H5 (in Wales, Form HO15) has been completed and furnished to the hospital managers: see reg.13(1),(2),(3) of the English Regulations and reg.5 of the Welsh Regulations. The RC's report provides authority for the patient's continued detention (see the note on "furnish", below). This section does not require that the report should have been considered by the managers before renewal can take place, although it is clearly good practice for this to happen: see *R. v Managers of Warlingham Park Hospital Ex p. B* (1994) 22 B.M.L.R. 1 CA, where Sir Thomas Bingham M.R. said at 11:

> "In my judgment it is essential to distinguish between the authority to detain, which section 20 makes dependent on the due furnishing of a report, and the decision whether or not to discharge, assuming that there was a continued authority to detain, which is plainly entrusted, as section 23 makes plain, to the managers."

As Phil Fennell has pointed out, this decision identifies the RC as "effectively the detaining authority, as the mere furnishing of his or her report is enough to renew the detention.

The original detaining authority, the managers, do not have to have considered the report and satisfied themselves that the conditions of detention continue to be met before the current period of detention expires. Nor do they have to have exercised their discretion over whether to discharge before the expiry of the detention" (All E.R. Rev. 1995, p.384).

Two MONTHS.   This time limit applies to the examination of the patient by the RC, the forming of the RC's opinion and the furnishing of the report to the managers of the hospital where the patient is detained.

THE DAY ON WHICH.   The period of detention can be extended by virtue of s.21.

LIABLE TO BE DETAINED.   This covers patients who are actually detained and those who would be detained if they were not currently on leave of absence under s.17 (*B v Barking and Brentwood Community Healthcare Trust*, noted under subs.(4)(c)).

RESPONSIBLE CLINICIAN.   The duty of the RC under this section cannot be delegated.

EXAMINE THE PATIENT.   If a patient refuses to be interviewed or is assessed as being too dangerous to be interviewed, the RC's examination of the patient could comprise: (1) his observations of the patient; (2) a consideration of the patient's medical history and prognosis; and (3) an evaluation of the patient's current condition in a multi-disciplinary case conference.

The examination could take place on an out-patient basis if the patient is on s.17 leave: see the note on subs.(4)(c).

FURNISH.   In the Scottish case of *Milborrow, Applicant*, 1996 S.C.L.R. 315 Sh.Ct, it was held that a report is "furnished" to the hospital managers when it is committed to the internal mailing system operated by those managers: see the note on s.5(2).

The furnishing of the RC's report gives authority for the continued detention of the patient: see subs.(8) and *R. v Managers of Warlingham Park Hospital*, noted above, where Sir Thomas Bingham M.R. said at 11: "If the authorised period of detention expires without there being a report duly furnished ..., any detention after the expiry date will plainly be unlawful and render the managers at risk of successful action."

MANAGERS OF THE HOSPITAL WHERE THE PATIENT IS DETAINED.   If, subsequent to the furnishing of a report under this section but before the hospital managers have had an opportunity to consider it, the patient is transferred to another hospital under s.19, the managers of the hospital to which the patient has been transferred should consider the report: see s.19(2)(a).

A REPORT.   The report (Form H5 in England and Form HO15 in Wales), which should be kept with the patient's admission documents, requires the hospital managers to consider whether they should exercise their power of discharge in respect of the patient.

Forms H5 and HO15 provide for the patient's RC to state his or her reasons why it is not appropriate for the patient to revert to informal status. The fact that a Mental Health Act Administrator might consider the reasons given by the RC to be inadequate would not effect the validity of the renewal. The purpose of the requirement to give reasons is to assist the managers in their task of considering whether they should exercise their power under s.23 to discharge the patient. Unlike an application of detention, there is no requirement for the renewal to be accepted by the managers before it comes into force.

If the patient's situation changes, it is lawful for the RC to discharge him or her from detention after Pt I of the Form H5 (or Form HO15) has been signed, but before the hospital managers have had an opportunity to consider whether they should exercise their power of discharge. Where this occurs, the Form should be endorsed with a statement confirming that the RC's power of discharge was exercised on the date in question.

During the debate on the Mental Health Bill, Baroness Royall, speaking on behalf of the Government, said:

> "Of course we recognise that renewal is not an easy process. Good practice requires an ongoing assessment of the needs of a patient and the input of a multi-disciplinary team together with the patient. That is reflected in the *Code of Practice.* . . . So the report submitted will be the result of a continued dialogue between several professionals and the patient" (*Hansard,* HL Vol.688, col.455)

A Form H5 or Form HO15 which is defective because of a minor error or slip of the pen would not render the renewal unlawful. If the form is fundamentally defective in some way, for example it was signed by a person who is not the patient's RC or it was completed after the authority for the patient's detention had expired, the renewal would be unlawful. Although minor errors cannot be formally rectified under s.15, it would be sensible for an error on the form to be corrected and initialled.

The date of the renewal is the date on which the authority to detain was due to expire and not the date of the report.

UNLESS THEY DISCHARGE THE PATIENT.    Under s.23(2)(a). Where managers are considering whether to order discharge under this provision, it is the conditions for renewal set out in subs.(4), rather than the conditions for the initial admission for treatment set out in s.3(2), that they should address: per Wilson J. speaking obiter in *R. (on the application of DR) v Mersey Care NHS Trust,* below, at para.19. Even if the conditions for renewal are met, the managers have a discretion under s.23(2) to order discharge *(R. v Riverside Mental Health Trust Ex p. Huzzey* (1998) 43 B.M.L.R. 167).

*Subsection (4)*

**1–285**   This subsection specifies the conditions which have to be satisfied if the authority to detain a patient who has been admitted for treatment is to be renewed.

It is not possible to renew the detention of a patient if there is no longer a need for the patient's treatment to contain an element of hospital treatment. In *B v Barking Havering and Brentwood Community Healthcare NHS Trust* [1999] 1 F.L.R. 106, the patient had been granted leave of absence under s.17. At the time of the renewal of her detention under this section the patient was on leave of absence. She had been granted leave for five days a week and for four hours a day on the remaining two days. The patient challenged the legality of the renewal on the ground that it contravened the ruling of McCullough J. in *R. v Hallstrom Ex p. W, R. v Gardner Ex p. L* [1986] 2 All E.R. 206, that a patient's detention could not be renewed whilst she was "liable to be detained" during a period of leave of absence. In overruling McCullough J. on this point, the Court of Appeal held that as long as the patient's medical treatment viewed as a whole involved treatment in a hospital, the requirements of this section could be met. The fact that the patient happened to be away from hospital at the time of renewal did not mean that she was no longer "detained" for treatment. Further, a renewal would be lawful even if the periods of hospital care could be classified as being for the purposes of assessment, rather than actual treatment.

Although Lord Woolf M.R. in *Barking* made an obiter distinction between out-patient and in-patient treatment by stating that if the treatment of the patient viewed as a whole "involves treatment as an *in-patient* the requirements of [this] section can be met" (at 113H; emphasis added), the court in *R. (on the application of DR) v Mersey Care NHS Trust* [2002] EWHC 1810 (Admin); [2002] M.H.L.R. 386 held that: (1) the test laid down in this subsection was whether the treatment plan provided for a patient to receive medical treatment in a hospital; (2) any distinction between treatment at a hospital and in a hospital was too subtle; (3) the hospital treatment must form a significant component of the patient's treatment plan; and (4) it would be an impermissible and illogical gloss on the Act to make the lawfulness of renewal dependent upon a plan to put the patient at times in a hospital bed. With regard to point (2), his Lordship did not follow the obiter remarks of

McCullough J. in the *Hallstrom* case which are reproduced in the General Note to s.3. In *DR*, the treatment plan provided that the patient should attend occupational therapy at the hospital once a week, that she should receive medication for her mental disorder by injection at her home at fortnightly intervals and that she should attend the ward round at the hospital at weekly intervals. The object of the third requirement was to provide for occasions for "attempted dialogue; for monitoring; for assessment; and for review". It followed that a significant component of the patient's care plan was treatment in a hospital and that the conditions for renewal had been satisfied. Given the definition of hospital in the National Health Service Act 2006, clinical contact with the patient could take place at a clinic or out-patient department maintained in connection with the institution: see the note on "hospital" in s.145(1). It is submitted that there must be a clear clinical rationale for the treatment to take place at the hospital rather than at some other location. For example, medical treatment, such an injection of anti-psychotic medication, that could be appropriately undertaken at the patient's home but is provided at the hospital solely for the convenience of staff would not qualify as "treatment in a hospital" for the purposes of this provision. However, a requirement for the patient to attend the ward round at appropriate intervals for assessment and monitoring by staff would meet the test established by this subsection if the assessment and monitoring comprised a significant component of the patient's treatment plan.

*DR* was applied in *R. (on the application of CS) v Mental Health Review Tribunal* [2004] EWHC 2958 (Admin); [2004] M.H.L.R. 355, where Pitchford J. upheld the decision of a Mental Health Review Tribunal not to discharge a patient from detention under s.3 where the patient had been granted leave of absence under s.17 to reside at her home subject to the condition that she attended the hospital for weekly sessions with a psychologist, and for ward round reviews at monthly intervals. The purpose of the ward round reviews were to: (a) discuss with the patient how her leave was progressing, how her medication was suiting her and whether any adjustments were necessary to the dose of her medication; and (b) provide the patient with supportive and motivational interviewing to help her to move out of the hospital-based model of care to community-based care under the Assertive Outreach Service. His Lordship held that:

1. Lawfulness of detention does not depend upon the degree of control over the patient's movements, since the degree of control may be infinitely variable depending upon the patient's precise needs without undermining the concept of treatment in a hospital (para.40).

2. Viewed as a whole, the course of treatment should be seen as a continuing responsive programme, during which the need for treatment at the hospital and on leave was being constantly reassessed depending upon the circumstances, including the patient's response to the Assertive Outreach Service and the ward round. Until such time as the transition was complete, the element of treatment at hospital remained a significant part of the whole (para.44).

His Lordship said at para.46:

"It is clear to me that the [RC] was engaged in a delicate balancing exercise by which she was, with as light a touch as she could, encouraging progress to discharge. Her purpose was to break the persistent historical cycle of admission, serious relapse and readmission. It may be in the closing stages of the treatment in hospital her grasp on the [patient] was gossamer thin, but to view that grasp as insignificant is, in my view, to misunderstand the evidence."

His Lordship commented, at para.48, that the patient's "knowledge of the [RC's] powers was a significant element in her willingness to accept the treatment plan".

The *Barking* case was considered by Sullivan J. in *R. (on the application of Epsom and St Helier NHS Trust) v The Mental Health Review Tribunal* [2001] EWHC Admin 101; [2001] M.H.L.R. 8, a case where the Trust challenged the decision of the Mental Health Review Tribunal to discharge the patient. The tribunal's decision was made on the ground that as the patient was not receiving hospital treatment it was not "appropriate for her to be liable to be detained in hospital for medical treatment" for the purposes of s.72(1)(b)(i). His Lordship held that:

1. *Barking* is authority for the proposition that one has to look at the whole course of the patient's treatment. To do so, one has to look at the past present and future. "It is not enough to say that the patient is not receiving treatment at a particular time. If, for example, it was proposed that the patient should be admitted to hospital for in-patient treatment in the week following the expiration of a six-month period of liability to detention, it would be absurd if the tribunal could not take that fact into account. The timing of in-patient treatment, whether it falls within or outside a particular period of liability to detention might be dictated by factors other than the patient's own state of health, for example, resource availability or the availability of specialised staff, and so forth" (para.47);

2. It would be inconsistent with the scheme of the Act if the mere prospect, that at some unspecified future time in-patient treatment would or might be required, compelled a tribunal to reject a patient's application for discharge. "The matter has to be looked at in the round, including the prospect of future in-patient treatment, but there will come a time when, even though it is certain that treatment will be required at some stage in the future, the timing of that treatment is so uncertain that it is no longer 'appropriate' for the patient to continue to be liable to detention. It is the tribunal's function to use its expertise to decide whether the certainty, or the possibility, of the need for in-patient treatment at some future date makes it 'appropriate' that the patient's liability to detention shall continue" (para.52). His Lordship further stated that the tribunal should look at "the reality of the situation" when making this decision and should not apply "artificial cut-offs" (para.61).

This decision should be read in the light of the decision in *R. (on the application of DR) v Mersey Care NHS Trust*, above, with the term "hospital treatment" being substituted for "in-patient treatment".

### Paragraph (a)

**1–286**  MENTAL DISORDER.  A patient's learning disability must be associated with abnormally aggressive or seriously irresponsible conduct (s.1(2A), (2B)).

APPROPRIATE FOR HIM TO RECEIVE MEDICAL TREATMENT IN A HOSPITAL.  It can be appropriate: (1) for a patient who has been granted substantial leave to be absent from the hospital to receive the required medical treatment at that hospital; and (2) for the medical treatment to be focused on assessing the patient's mental condition and monitoring her progress towards achieving the eventual aim of total rehabilitation into the community (*R. (on the application of DR) v Mersey Care Trust*, above). As this provision refers to *a* hospital rather than *the* hospital, this provision can be satisfied where the patient is receiving treatment for a mental disorder at a hospital where he or she is required to be as a condition of leave of absence.

### Paragraph (c)

**1–287**  HEALTH OR SAFETY OF THE PATIENT OR FOR THE PROTECTION OF OTHER PERSONS.  See the notes on s.3(2)(c).

UNLESS HE CONTINUES TO BE DETAINED.    This term means "unless he continues to be liable to be detained" and not "unless he continues actually to be detained". This ground can therefore be satisfied in respect of a patient who has been granted leave of absence under s.17: see the *Barking* case, above.

This ground could be satisifed in relation to a potentially dangerous patient who is compliant with medication and who is willing to remain in hospital as an informal patient. This is because an essential element of the patient's treatment is his preparation for eventual discharge from the hospital. A key element of such preparation is the granting of leave of absence to the patient. Given that the patient would pose a potential risk to the public, it would not be appropriate to grant leave in the absence of a mechanism that would enable staff to require the patient to return to the hospital should he exhibit a reluctance to do so. Section 17 provides such a mechanism. This ground is therefore satisfied because an essential element of the patient's total treatment programme, the testing out of his readiness for discharge, can only be put in place if he were a detained patient who could be granted leave under s.17.

*Paragraph (d)*
See the note on s.3(2)(d).                                                                          **1–288**

*Subsection (5)*
PROFESSIONALLY CONCERNED.    In respect of a patient who is being treated in hospital, it  **1–289**
is not sufficient for the consultee merely to be working on the ward where the patient is being treated; a particular involvement with the patient's treatment is required.

*Subsection (5A)*
This subsection, which is considered in the *Code of Practice* at paras 29.4 to 29.9,  **1–290**
requires the RC who is renewing the detention of the patient to obtain a written statement from a person from another profession who has been professionally concerned with the patient's treatment that states that he or she agrees that the conditions of renewal are satisfied. The statement must be in the form set out in Pt 2 of Form H5: see reg.13 (2) of the English Regulations (in Wales, Part 2 of Form HO15: see reg.5 of the Welsh Regulations). Subsection (5) requires the RC to consult at least one other person from the multidisciplinary team before he or she furnishes the renewal report and it is likely that this person will provide the written statement.

*Subsection (6)*
This subsection and subs.(8) provide for the patient's appropriate practitioner to renew  **1–291**
the authority for guardianship. "Appropriate practitioner" is defined in s.34(1).

THE DAY ON WHICH.    The period of guardianship can be extended under s.21.

A REPORT.    See reg.13 and Form G9 of the English Regulations and reg.12 and Form GU6 of the Welsh Regulations. The report is not rectifiable: see the note on "report" in subs.(3).

LOCAL SOCIAL SERVICES AUTHORITY.    Which should give the patient a hearing unless he or she does not wish to contest the renewal. The local authority should require the care professional who has lead responsibility for the patient's welfare to provide a report on the patient's response to being subject to guardianship.

*Subsection (7)*
This subsection specifies that the conditions for making a guardianship application have  **1–292**
to be satisfied if the authority for guardianship is to be renewed.

**[Community treatment period**

**1–293**   **20A.**—(1) Subject to the provisions of this Part of this Act, a community treatment order shall cease to be in force on expiry of the period of six months beginning with the day on which it was made.

(2) That period is referred to in this Act as "the community treatment period".

(3) The community treatment period may, unless the order has previously ceased to be in force, be extended—

(a)  from its expiration for a period of six months;

(b)  from the expiration of any period of extension under paragraph (a) above for a further period of one year, and so on for periods of one year at a time.

(4) Within the period of two months ending on the day on which the order would cease to be in force in default of an extension under this section, it shall be the duty of the responsible clinician—

(a)  to examine the patient; and

(b)  if it appears to him that the conditions set out in subsection (6) below are satisfied and if a statement under subsection (8) below is made, to furnish to the managers of the responsible hospital a report to that effect in the pre-scribed form.

(5) Where such a report is furnished in respect of the patient, the managers shall, unless they discharge him under section 23 below, cause him to be informed.

(6) The conditions referred to in subsection (4) above are that—

(a)  the patient is suffering from mental disorder of a nature or degree which makes it appropriate for him to receive medical treatment;

(b)  it is necessary for his health or safety or for the protection of other persons that he should receive such treatment;

(c)  subject to his continuing to be liable to be recalled as mentioned in para-graph (d) below, such treatment can be provided without his being detained in a hospital;

(d)  it is necessary that the responsible clinician should continue to be able to exercise the power under section 17E(1) above to recall the patient to hos-pital; and

(e)  appropriate medical treatment is available for him.

(7) In determining whether the criterion in subsection (6)(d) above is met, the responsible clinician shall, in particular, consider, having regard to the patient's history of mental disorder and any other relevant factors, what risk there would be of a deterioration of the patient's condition if he were to continue not to be detained in a hospital (as a result, for example, of his refusing or neglecting to receive the medical treatment he requires for his mental disorder).

(8) The statement referred to in subsection (4) above is a statement in writing by an approved mental health professional—

(a)  that it appears to him that the conditions set out in subsection (6) above are satisfied; and

(b)  that it is appropriate to extend the community treatment period.

(9) Before furnishing a report under subsection (4) above the responsible clin-ician shall consult one or more other persons who have been professionally concerned with the patient's medical treatment.

(10) Where a report is duly furnished under subsection (4) above, the com-munity treatment period shall be thereby extended for the period prescribed in that case by subsection (3) above.]

AMENDMENT
This section was inserted by the Mental Health Act 2007 s.20(3). **1–294**

DEFINITIONS
community treatment order: ss.17A(7), 145(1). **1–295**
responsible clinician: s.34(1).
the managers: s.145(1).
responsible hospital: ss.17A(7), 145(1).
mental disorder: s.145(1).
medical treatment: s.145(1), (4).
approved mental health practitioner: s.145(1), (1AC).

GENERAL NOTE
This section provides that a community treatment order (CTO) lasts for an initial period **1–296** of six months from the date when the order was made (subs.(1)). This period is referred to as "the community treatment period" (subs.(2)). The community treatment period can be extended for a further period of six months and, following that, it can be extended for further periods of one year at a time (subs.(3)). The community period is extended from the date when it would otherwise expire, and not from the date of the report furnished under subs.(4)(b). If the community treatment period is not extended, the CTO shall cease to have effect (s.20B).

In order to renew the community treatment period, the patient's responsible clinician (RC) must examine the patient in the two months preceding the expiry date, and send a report to the hospital managers confirming that the conditions set out in subs.(6) are satisfied (subs.(4)). If the patient does not attend for examination voluntarily, the RC may recall the patient to hospital for this purpose: see ss.17B(3)(a) and 17E(2). Prior to sending the report, the RC must obtain a written statement from an AMHP confirming that (a) the conditions set out in subs.(6) are satisfied, and (b) it is appropriate to extend the community treatment period (subs.(8)). Before the report is sent, the RC must have consulted with one or more people who have been professionally concerned with the patient's medical treatment (subs.(9)). On receiving the report, the hospital managers must consider whether they should exercise their power under s.23 to discharge the patient from the CTO. If they decide not to discharge the patient, he or she must be informed that the CTO has been extended for the relevant period (subs.(5)). The patient must also be provided with the information required by s.132A. For the responsibility to inform the patient's nearest relative if the patient's period of community treatment is extended under this section, see reg.26(1)(e) of the English Regulations and reg.22(1)(a) of the Welsh Regulations.

This section applies without modification to patients who have been made subject to hospital orders (Sch.1, Pt 1, para.1).

*Applications to the First-tier Tribunal (Mental Health) or the Mental Health Review Tribunal for Wales*
The patient's right to apply to a tribunal arises from the date of the renewal of the CTO **1–297** (s.66(1)(fza), (2)(fza)).

*Code of Practice*
Guidance on the extension of the community treatment period is contained in Ch.29 at **1–298** paras 29.10 to 29.14.

*Subsection (1)*
BEGINNING WITH. Means "including" (*Zoan v Rouamba* [2000] 2 All.E.R. 620 CA). **1–299**

DAY ON WHICH IT WAS MADE. When the patient's RC signs and dates Part 3 of Form CTO1, the RC is asserting that he or she is exercising powers under s.17A to make a CTO and that the CTO will be effective from a specified date. When is the CTO "made" for the purposes of this Act? Is it the date of the RC's signature or the date when the CTO becomes effective? Although the wording of the Form does not provide a straightforward answer to this question, it is suggested that the *Code of Practice* is correct when it states, at para.25.28, that the relevant date is the date when the order becomes effective.

*Subsection (4)*

**1–300**   PRESCRIBED FORM.   Form CTO7: see reg.13 of the English Regulations (in Wales, Form CP3: see reg.17 of the Welsh Regulations).

*Subsection (6)*

**1–301**   These criteria essentially state that the patient continues to be detainable under s.3 (including the requirement that a patient's learning disability continues to be associated with abnormally aggressive or seriously irresponsible conduct), but can be treated in the community if he or she is subject to a power of recall. When determining whether RC should be able to exercise the power of recall, the factors set out in subs.(7) should be considered.

If during a review of the CTO, the RC concludes that the conditions for extending the CTO do not apply, the RC should use the power under s.23 to discharge the CTO.

*Paragraphs (a), (b), (e)*

**1–302**   See the notes to s.3(2)(a), (c) and (d).

*Subsection (7)*

**1–303**   See the note on s.17A(6).

*Subsection (8)*

**1–304**   There is no requirement for the AMHP to interview the patient prior to signing the statement.

STATEMENT.   In the form set out in Part 2 of Form CTO7 or, in Wales, Form CP3.

APPROVED MENTAL HEALTH PROFESSIONAL.   This need not be the AMHP who agreed under s.17A(4)(b) that it was appropriate to make the CTO. If the AMHP who is approached is unwilling to make the statement, the RC could seek the agreement of another AMHP.

## [Effect of expiry of community treatment order

**1–305**   **20B.**—(1) A community patient shall be deemed to be discharged absolutely from liability to recall under this Part of this Act, and the application for admission for treatment cease to have effect, on expiry of the community treatment order, if the order has not previously ceased to be in force.

(2) For the purposes of subsection (1) above, a community treatment order expires on expiry of the community treatment period as extended under this Part of this Act, but this is subject to sections 21 and 22 below.]

AMENDMENT

This section was inserted by the Mental Health Act 2007 s.20(3).

DEFINITIONS

**1–306**   community patient: ss.17A(7), 145(1).
application for admission for treatment: s.145(1).
community treatment order: ss.17A(7), 145(1).
community treatment period; ss.20A(1),(2), 145(1).

GENERAL NOTE

If a CTO expires, this section provides that: (1) the patient is no longer subject to the **1–307** power of recall; and (2) the application for admission for treatment (or its equivalent under Part III) ceases to have effect. In determining whether the CTO has expired, account must be taken of the fact that the community treatment period might have been extended by the provisions of s.21, which apply to patients who are absent without leave, or of s.22, which apply if the patient has been sentenced, or committed or remanded to custody by a court.

This section applies to patients who have been made subject to hospital orders with the modification set out in para.6A of Sch.1 (Sch.1, Pt 1, para.2).

## [Special provisions as to patients absent without leave

**21.**—(1) Where a patient is absent without leave— **1–308**

(a) on the day on which (apart from this section) he would cease to be liable to be detained or subject to guardianship under this Part of this Act [or, in the case of a community patient, the community treatment order would cease to be in force]; or

(b) within the period of one week ending with that day,

he shall not cease to be so liable or subject [, or the order shall not cease to be in force,] until the relevant time.

(2) For the purposes of subsection (1) above the relevant time—

(a) where the patient is taken into custody under section 18 above, is the end of the period of one week beginning with the day on which he is returned to the hospital or place where he ought to be;

(b) where the patient returns himself to the hospital or place where he ought to be within the period during which he can be taken into custody under section 18 above, is the end of the period of one week beginning with the day on which he so returns himself; and

(c) otherwise, is the end of the period during which he can be taken into custody under section 18 above.]

[(3) Where a patient is absent without leave on the day on which (apart from this section) the managers would be required under section 68 below to refer the patient's case to [the appropriate tribunal], that requirement shall not apply unless and until—

(a) the patient is taken into custody under section 18 above and returned to the hospital where he ought to be; or

(b) the patient returns himself to the hospital where he ought to be within the period during which he can be taken into custody under section 18 above.]

[(4) Where a community patient is absent without leave on the day on which (apart from this section) the 72-hour period mentioned in section 17F above would expire, that period shall not expire until the end of the period of 72 hours beginning with the time when—

(a) the patient is taken into custody under section 18 above and returned to the hospital where he ought to be; or

(b) the patient returns himself to the hospital where he ought to be within the period during which he can be taken into custody under section 18 above.

(5) Any reference in this section, or in sections 21A to 22 below, to the time when a community treatment order would cease, or would have ceased, to be in force shall be construed as a reference to the time when it would cease, or would have ceased, to be in force by reason only of the passage of time.]

AMENDMENT

This section was substituted by the Mental Health (Patients in the Community) Act 1995 s.2(2). The amendments to it were made by the Mental Health Act 2007 ss.32(4), 37(2), Sch.3 para.6. The reference to the appropriate tribunal in subs.(3) was substituted by SI 2008/2883 art.9, Sch.3 para.40.

DEFINITIONS

**1–309**   patient: s.145(1).
absent without leave: ss.18(6), 145(1).
hospital: ss.34(2), 145(1).
appropriate practitioner: s.34(1).
community patient: ss.17A(7), 145(1).
community treatment order: ss.17A(7), 145(1).
the managers: s.145(1).
the appropriate tribunal: ss.66(4), 145(1).

GENERAL NOTE

**1–310**   This section extends the authority for detention, guardianship or supervised community treatment of a patient who is absent without leave when or during the week before the detention or guardianship expires or the community treatment order (CTO) would cease to be in force. The detention or guardianship is extended, or the CTO will not cease to be in force, for up to one week after the patient's return to hospital or place where he or she ought to be. This period enables the patient to be examined and a renewal report made if appropriate. If the patient is returned within 28 days of absconding, s.21A applies for the purposes of a renewal. Section 21B applies if the patient is returned more than 28 days after absconding. If patients have not been taken into custody, or have not come voluntarily to the hospital or place where they ought to be, before the end of the period during which they can be taken into custody under s.18, no renewal can take place.

This section applies to patients who have been placed under hospital or guardianship orders by a court (Sch.1 para.1).

*Subsection (1)*

**1–311**   A PATIENT.   Although it has been said that this section does not apply to patients who are detained under s.2, the wording of this subsection, especially the term "apart from the section" and use of the generic term "liable to be detained", does not have such an effect. It is therefore the case that if a s.2 patient is absent without leave during the final week of detention, the authority to detain can be extended for a week beginning with the day of recapture if he or she is recaptured before the expiration of the 28 day period provided for in s.2(4).

THE COMMUNITY TREATMENT ORDER WOULD CEASE TO BE IN FORCE.   See subs.(5).

*Subsection (2)*

**1–312**   RELEVANT TIME.   This allows for the patient's appropriate practitioner to examine the patient and decide whether he or she wishes to make a report renewing the detention or guardianship under s.20(3) or 20(6), or extending the CTO under s.20A(4). The making of such a report is authorised by s.21A(2) (or s.21A(4) for a CTO) and the date of the renewal is provided for in s.21A(3) (or s.21A(5) for a CTO). This provision also allows time for professionals to consider the appropriateness of making an application under s.3 in respect of a patient who has been detained under s.2.

TAKEN INTO CUSTODY UNDER SECTION 18.   Although a s.2 patient cannot be taken into custody after the section expires (s.18(5)), a s.3 or guardianship patient can be taken into custody long after the detention or guardianship has expired (s.18(4)).

*Subsection (3)*

If the hospital managers are due to refer the patient to a tribunal under s.68 at the time **1–313** when he or she is absent without leave, this provision requires the managers to postpone the referral until the patient either returns or is returned to the hospital where he or she ought to be.

## [Patients who are taken into custody or return within 28 days

**21A.**—(1) This section applies where a patient who is absent without leave is **1–314** taken into custody under section 18 above, or returns himself to the hospital or place where he ought to be, not later than the end of the period of 28 days beginning with the first day of his absence without leave.

(2) Where the period for which the patient is liable to be detained or subject to guardianship is extended by section 21 above, any examination and report to be made and furnished in respect of the patient under section 20(3) or (6) above may be made and furnished within the period as so extended.

(3) Where the authority for the detention or guardianship of the patient is renewed by virtue of subsection (2) above after the day on which (apart from section 21 above) that authority would have expired, the renewal shall take effect as from that day.]

[(4) In the case of a community patient, where the period for which the community treatment order is in force is extended by section 21 above, any examination and report to be made and furnished in respect of the patient under section 20A(4) above may be made and furnished within the period as so extended.

(5) Where the community treatment period is extended by virtue of subsection (4) above after the day on which (apart from section 21 above) the order would have ceased to be in force, the extension shall take effect as from that day.]

AMENDMENT

This section was substituted by the Mental Health (Patients in the Community) Act 1995 s.2(2). Subsections (4) and (5) were inserted by the Mental Health Act 2007 s.32(4), Sch.3 para.7.

DEFINITIONS

    patient: s.145(1). **1–315**
    absent without leave: s.18(6), 145(1).
    hospital: ss.34(2), 145(1).
    appropriate practitioner: s.34(1).
    community patient: ss.17A(7), 145(1).
    community treatment order: ss.17A(7), 145(1).
    community treatment period: ss.20A(1)(2), 145(1).

GENERAL NOTE

If a s.3 or guardianship patient who has absconded returns to the hospital or place where **1–316** he or she is required to be not more than 28 days after absconding, or is taken into custody during that period, subss.(1) to (3) enable the patient's appropriate practitioner to renew the detention or guardianship under s.20 without further formality. If the provisions of s.21 apply, the authority to detain the patient (or the authority for guardianship) is extended for up to a week from the date of his or her return to enable the formalities of renewal to be completed.

If a community patient who has gone absent without leave returns, or is returned, to the hospital where he or she ought to be within 28 days of the first day of his or her absence, subss.(4) and (5) give the patient's RC a week after the patient's return to carry out the examination required by s.20A(4) and make his or her report for the extension of the CTO, if the CTO would have otherwise expired.

If the patient returns or is returned to the hospital more that 28 days after the date of the absconding, the provisions of s.21B apply.

This section applies without modification to patients who have been made subject to hospital or guardianship orders by a court under s.37 (Sch.1 Pt 1 para.1).

*Subsection (1)*

**1–317**    BEGINNING WITH.    Including the first day of his absence without leave (*Zoan v Rouamba* [2000] 2 All E.R. 620 CA).

*Subsection (2)*

**1–318**    REPORT.    On Form H5 (in Wales, Form HO15).

*Subsection (3)*

**1–319**    RENEWAL.    The renewal has effect from the date when the authority for detention or guardianship would have expired if it had not been extended by s.21.

*Subsection (5)*

**1–320**    Under this provision, a CTO which has been extended under subs.(4) takes effect from the day when it would have ceased to be in force if it has not been extended by s.21.

CEASED TO BE IN FORCE.    See s.21(5).

**[Patients who are taken into custody or return after more than 28 days**

**1–321**    **21B.**—(1) This section applies where a patient who is absent without leave is taken into custody under section 18 above, or returns himself to the hospital or place where he ought to be, later than the end of the period of 28 days beginning with the first day of his absence without leave.

(2) It shall be the duty of the [appropriate practitioner], within the period of one week beginning with the day on which the patient is returned or returns himself to the hospital or place where he ought to be [(his "return day")]—

(a)  to examine the patient; and

(b)  if it appears to him that the relevant conditions are satisfied, to furnish to the appropriate body a report to that effect in the prescribed form;

and where such a report is furnished in respect of the patient the appropriate body shall cause him to be informed.

(3) Where the patient is liable to be detained [or is a community patient] (as opposed to subject to guardianship), the [appropriate practitioner] shall, before furnishing a report under subsection (2) above, consult—

(a)  one or more other persons who have been professionally concerned with the patient's medical treatment; and

(b)  an [approved mental health professional].

[(4) Where—

(a)  the patient would (apart from any renewal of the authority for his detention or guardianship on or after his return day) be liable to be detained or subject to guardianship after the end of the period of one week beginning with that day; or

(b)  in the case of a community patient, the community treatment order would (apart from any extension of the community treatment period on or after that day) be in force after the end of that period, he shall cease to be so liable or subject, or the community treatment period shall be deemed to expire, at the end of that period unless a report is duly furnished in respect of him under subsection (2) above.]

[(4A) If, in the case of a community patient, the community treatment order is revoked under section 17F above during the period of one week beginning with his return day—
(a) subsections (2) and (4) above shall not apply; and
(b) any report already furnished in respect of him under subsection (2) above shall be of no effect.]

(5) Where the patient would (apart from section 21 above) have ceased to be liable to be detained or subject to guardianship on or before the day on which a report is duly furnished in respect of him under subsection (2) above, the report shall renew the authority for his detention or guardianship for the period prescribed in that case by section 20(2) above.

(6) Where the authority for the detention or guardianship of the patient is renewed by virtue of subsection (5) above—
(a) the renewal shall take effect as from the day on which (apart from section 21 above and that subsection) the authority would have expired; and
(b) if (apart from this paragraph) the renewed authority would expire on or before the day on which the report is furnished, the report shall further renew the authority, as from the day on which it would expire, for the period prescribed in that case by section 20(2) above.

[(6A) In the case of a community patient, where the community treatment order would (apart from section 21 above) have ceased to be in force on or before the day on which a report is duly furnished in respect of him under subsection (2) above, the report shall extend the community treatment period for the period prescribed in that case by section 20A(3) above.

(6B) Where the community treatment period is extended by virtue of subsection (6A) above—
(a) the extension shall take effect as from the day on which (apart from section 21 above and that subsection) the order would have ceased to be in force; and
(b) if (apart from this paragraph) the period as so extended would expire on or before the day on which the report is furnished, the report shall further extend that period, as from the day on which it would expire, for the period prescribed in that case by section 20A(3) above.]

(7) Where the authority for the detention or guardianship of the patient would expire within the period of two months beginning with the day on which a report is duly furnished in respect of him under subsection (2) above, the report shall, if it so provides, have effect also as a report duly furnished under section 20(3) or (6) above; and the reference in this subsection to authority includes any authority renewed under subsection (5) above by the report.

[(7A) In the case of a community patient, where the community treatment order would (taking account of any extension under subsection (6A) above) cease to be in force within the period of two months beginning with the day on which a report is duly furnished in respect of him under subsection (2) above, the report shall, if it so provides, have effect also as a report duly furnished under section 20A(4) above.]

(8) [. . .]
(9) [. . .]

(10) In this section—

[. . .]

["the appropriate body" means—

    (a) in relation to a patient who is liable to be detained in a hospital, the managers of the hospital;

    (b) in relation to a patient who is subject to guardianship, the responsible local social services authority;

    (c) in relation to a community patient, the managers of the responsible hospital; and

["the relevant conditions" means—

    (a) in relation to a patient who is liable to be detained in a hospital, the conditions set out in subsection (4) of section 20 above;

    (b) in relation to a patient who is subject to guardianship, the conditions set out in subsection (7) of that section;

    (c) in relation to a community patient, the conditions set out in section 20A(6) above.]]

### AMENDMENT

This section was substituted by the Mental Health (Patients in the Community) Act 1995 s.2(2). The words in square brackets were substituted and inserted by the Mental Health Act 2007 ss.9(5), 21, 32(4), Sch.2 para.7, Sch.3 para.8. Subsections (8) and (9) and the words omitted in subs.(1) were repealed by s.55, Sch.11 Pts 1 and 3.

### DEFINITIONS

**1–322**
patient: s.145(1).

absent without leave: ss.18(6), 145(1).

hospital: ss.34(2), 145(1).

community patient: ss.17A(7), 145(1).

approved mental health professional: s.145(1), (1AC).

community treatment order: ss.17A(7), 145(1).

community treatment period: ss.20A(1),(2), 145(1).

local social services authority: s.145(1).

appropriate practitioner: s.34(1).

### GENERAL NOTE

**1–323**
If a s.3 or guardianship patient who has absconded is taken into custody, or returns to the hospital or place where he or she is required to be, later than 28 days after absconding, the patient's appropriate practitioner must comply with the provisions of this section within a week beginning with the date of his or her return (the "return date") if the patient's detention or guardianship is to be renewed under s.20. If the provisions of s.21 apply, the authority to detain the patient (or the authority for guardianship) is extended for up to a week from the return date. The renewal takes effect from the day specified in subs.(6). If the patient's detention or guardianship would expire within two months of the subs.(2) report being furnished, the provisions of subs.(7) apply: see the notes on subss.(5) to (7).

If a community patient who has been absent without leave returns, or is returned, to the hospital where he or she ought to be more than 28 days after the patient was first absent without leave, this section provides the patient's responsible clinician (RC) with a week after the day of patient's return (his or her "return date") to examine the patient, and, if the RC decides that the patient meets the criteria for supervised community treatment, prepare for the hospital managers a report extending the community treatment order (CTO) (subs.(2)). However, if the CTO is revoked under s.17F during that week, the report will have no effect (subs.(4A)). If the CTO expired during the patient's absence, or had less than seven days to run on his or her return, s.21 extends it for up to a week from the return date.

Where the patient is liable to be detained or is a community patient, the RC must undertake the consultation process identified in subs.(3) before furnishing the report under subs.(2) to the hospital managers.

If a patient's detention or guardianship would remain in force a week after the return date, the detention or guardianship will lapse in the absence of a report being furnished under subs.(2). The same applies to a CTO which would be in force at the end of that period (subs.(4)).

Where a CTO would (apart from s.21) have expired before the day on which a report is furnished under subs.(2), the report will extend the community treatment period prescribed in s.20A(2) (subs.(6A). The extension will take effect from the day when order would have expired (subs.(6B)(a)), but if that period would have expired before the subs.(2) report is furnished, there shall be a further extension of the relevant s.20A(3) period (subs.(6B)(b)). If the CTO would expire (taking into account any extension under subs.(6A)) within two months of the furnishing of the report under subs.(2), the report shall also be treated as a s.20A(4) report (subs.(7A)). This avoids the need for two reports, one under subs.(2) and the other under s.20A(4), extending the CTO.

For the responsibility to inform the patient's nearest relative if the patient's detention or guardianship is renewed under subs.(7), or is renewed retrospectively under subss.(5) and (6), or if the patient's period of community treatment is extended under subs.(7A), or is extended retrospectively under subss.(6A) and (6B), see reg.26 of the English Regulations and regs 8, 15 and 22 of the Welsh Regulations.

This section applies without modification to patients who have been made subject to hospital or guardianship orders by a court under s.37 (Sch.1 Pt 1 para.1).

*Applications to the First-tier Tribunal (Mental Health) or the Mental Health Review Tribunal for Wales*
The patient's right to apply to a tribunal arises from the date of the renewal of the deten-    **1–324**
tion, guardianship or the CTO (s.66(1)(fa)(faa), (2)(f)(fza)).

*Human Rights Act 1998*
See the note on s.18 under this heading.    **1–325**

*Subsection (1)*
BEGINNING WITH.   See the note on s.21(1).    **1–326**

*Subsection (2)*
RELEVANT CONDITIONS, APPROPRIATE BODY.   See subs.(10).    **1–327**

FURNISH TO THE APPROPRIATE BODY.   Even if the unexpired period of detention or guardianship is longer than the one week provided for in this subsection.

In the Scottish case of *Milborrow, Applicant*, 1996 S.C.L.R. 315, Sh. Ct, it was held that a report is "furnished" to the hospital managers when it is committed to the internal mailing system operated by those managers: see the note on s.5(2).

PRESCRIBED FORM.   Form H6 for a patient who is liable to be detained, Form G10 for a patient who is subject to guardianship and Form CTO8 for a community patient: see reg.14 of the English Regulations. In Wales, the forms are: Form CP4 for a patient who is liable to be detained, Form GU7 for a patient who is subject to guardianship and Form CP4 for a community patient: see regs 13 and 18 of the Welsh Regulations.

*Subsection (3)*

**1–328**    Although the appropriate practitioner, as defined in s.34(1), must take the views expressed by the two professionals into account before making a report under subs.(2), he or she is not obliged to obtain their agreement to this action.

PROFESSIONAL CONCERNED WITH PATIENT'S MEDICAL TREATMENT. The professional could be concerned with the patient's medical treatment in the community.

AN APPROVED MENTAL HEALTH PRACTITIONER. Who need not have been involved in the patient's admission.

*Subsection (5)*

**1–329**    If a patient's liability to be detained or to be subject to guardianship would have expired before the end of the one week period provided for in subs.(2), and a report is furnished under that provision, the period of renewal shall be the period provided for in s.20(2). The date of the renewal is established by subs.(6).

*Subsection (6)*

**1–330**    This subsection provides that where the authority for detention or guardianship of a patient has been renewed in the circumstances set out in subs.(5), the renewal has effect from the day on which the detention or guardianship would have expired. If this renewed authority is due to expire before the day on which the report under subs.(2) is made, a further period of renewal for the prescribed period is authorised by the subs.(2) report.

*Subsection (6A)*

**1–331**    CEASED TO BE IN FORCE. See s.21(5).

*Subsection (7)*

**1–332**    This provision avoids the need for two reports renewing a patient's detention or guardianship, one under subs.(2) and the other under subs.20(3) or (6), if the authority for the patient's detention or guardianship would expire within two months of the report being made under subs.(2).

**[Special provisions as to patients sentenced to imprisonment, etc.**

**1–333**    **22.**—(1) If—

(a) a qualifying patient is detained in custody in pursuance of any sentence or order passed or made by a court in the United Kingdom (including an order committing or remanding him in custody); and

(b) he is so detained for a period exceeding, or for successive periods exceeding in the aggregate, six months, the relevant application shall cease to have effect on expiry of that period.

(2) A patient is a qualifying patient for the purposes of this section if—

(a) he is liable to be detained by virtue of an application for admission for treatment;

(b) he is subject to guardianship by virtue of a guardianship application; or

(c) he is a community patient.

(3) "The relevant application", in relation to a qualifying patient, means—

(a) in the case of a patient who is subject to guardianship, the guardianship application in respect of him;

(b) in any other case, the application for admission for treatment in respect of him.

(4) The remaining subsections of this section shall apply if a qualifying patient is detained in custody as mentioned in subsection (1)(a) above but for a period not exceeding, or for successive periods not exceeding in the aggregate, six months.

(5) If apart from this subsection—

(a) the patient would have ceased to be liable to be detained or subject to guardianship by virtue of the relevant application on or before the day on which he is discharged from custody; or

(b) in the case of a community patient, the community treatment order would have ceased to be in force on or before that day, he shall not cease and shall be deemed not to have ceased to be so liable or subject, or the order shall not cease and shall be deemed not to have ceased to be in force, until the end of that day.

(6) In any case (except as provided in subsection (8) below), sections 18, 21 and 21A above shall apply in relation to the patient as if he had absented himself without leave on that day.

(7) In its application by virtue of subsection (6) above section 18 above shall have effect as if—

(a) in subsection (4) for the words from "later of" to the end there were substituted "end of the period of 28 days beginning with the first day of his absence without leave"; and

(b) subsections (4A) and (4B) were omitted.

(8) In relation to a community patient who was not recalled to hospital under section 17E above at the time when his detention in custody began—

(a) section 18 above shall not apply; but

(b) sections 21 and 21A above shall apply as if he had absented himself without leave on the day on which he is discharged from custody and had returned himself as provided in those sections on the last day of the period of 28 days beginning with that day.]

AMENDMENT

This Section was substituted by the Mental Health Act 2007 s.32(4), Sch.3 para.9.

DEFINITIONS                                                                                          **1–334**
> patient: s.145(1).
> application for admission for treatment: ss.3, 145(1).
> community patient: ss.17A(7), 145(1).
> community treatment order: ss.17A(7), 145(1).
> absent without leave: ss.18(6), 145(1).
> hospital: s.145(1).

GENERAL NOTE

This section provides that if a patient who is the subject of an application for treatment, a **1–335** guardianship application or a community treatment order (CTO) is sentenced, or committed or remanded to custody by a court, the application will cease to have effect if the period spent in custody lasts for more than six months. The CTO will end due to the fact that the s.3 application has ceased to have effect (s.17C(c)). If the patient is detained in custody for less than six months and would, in the ordinary course of events, have ceased to be liable to be detained for treatment or subject to guardianship or to a CTO prior to his discharge from custody, subss.(4) to (8) provide that he does not cease to be so liable or subject until end of the day on which he is discharged, and for the purposes of ss.18, 21 and 21A of this Act he will be treated as if he had absconded himself without leave on that day, i.e. the patient can be taken into custody within 28 days of his release (s.18(4), as substituted by subs.(7) of this section) and there are seven days during which the application can be renewed (s.21) if it is due for renewal at that time. Subs.(8) applies to community patients who have not been recalled to hospital. If the renewal report is furnished after the expiration of the previous period of detention, guardianship or CTO, the report is deemed to have been furnished on the final day of that period (s.21A). The patient's RC can exercise the power of discharge under s.23 while the patient is in custody.

As this section is not listed in paras (a) to (c) of s.56(3), the consent to treatment provisions contained in Pt IV of this Act will continue to apply to the patient during the period spent in custody. Although it could be argued that the use of the term "patient" in s.56 indicates that Pt IV would not apply to persons detained in custody, "patient" is defined very broadly in s.145(1) as "a person suffering or appearing to suffer from mental disorder". It is also the case that s.56 does not require the patient to be detained in a hospital in order for the provision of Pt IV to apply: it requires the patient to be "liable to be detained". An interpretation that does not exclude the operation of this Act from prisons is consistent with the decision in *R. (on the application of the Howard League for Penal Reform) v Secretary of State for the Home Department* [2002] EWHC 2497 (Admin), where Munby J. held that the powers and duties which a local authority would otherwise owe to a child under the Children Act 1989 do not cease to be owed merely because the child is currently detained in a Young Offender Institution. His Lordship further held that the exercise of a local authority's functions under the 1989 Act take effect and operate subject to the necessary requirements of imprisonment. A Young Offender Institution is subject to the Secretary of State's control under the Prison Act 1952.

This section applies to patients who have been placed under hospital or guardianship orders by a court under s.37, with the modification that for references to an application for admission or a guardianship application there shall be substituted references to the order or direction under Pt III of this Act by virtue of which the patient is liable to be detained or subject to guardianship (Sch.1 Pt I paras 2, 7). For restriction order patients the section applies with the modification that subss.(1) and (5) shall be omitted (Sch.1 Pt II paras 2, 6), i.e. the restriction order will not cease if the patient is detained in custody for more than six months.

*Subsection (1)*

**1–336**  QUALIFYING PATIENT.   See subs.(2).

UNITED KINGDOM.   This means Great Britain and Northern Ireland (Interpretation Act 1978, s.5, Sch.1).

RELEVANT APPLICATION.   See subs.(3).

*Subsection (2)*

**1–337**  This subsection covers the situation where a patient is released before he has been in custody for a continuous period exceeding six months: see the General Note to this section.

*Subsection (7)*

**1–338**  The effect of this subsection, as substituted by the Mental Health (Patients in he Community) Act 1995 s.2(3), was explained by the Parliamentary Under-Secretary of State for Health, Baroness Cumberlege (*Hansard*, HL, Vol.564, col.174):

"At present, section 22 of the Mental Health Act 1983 states that when a patient who has been subject to imprisonment is released, he should be treated as though he were absent without leave under section 18 of the 1983 Act. This is a legal device to provide a period of 28 days in which such patients could be returned to detention in hospital. However, as your Lordships know, clause 2 of this Bill [now s.18(4)] extends the period of time in which an absconding patient can be returned to hospital from 28 days to at least six months. An unintentional consequence of this is to extend the period of time within which a released prisoner could be returned to detention under the 1983 Act. I am sure your Lordships will agree that this is undesirable, both in its own right, and because it would be inconsistent with the provisions laid out in the earlier amendments relating to prisoners subject to supervision applications. The effect of the amendment, therefore, is to retain for the purposes of section 22 the period of 28 days within which a person who has been released from prison may be returned to hospital. This is followed by a period of seven days during which the responsible medical officer must examine the patient and determine whether his liability to detention should be renewed."

*Subsections (7), (8)*
BEGINNING WITH.    Means "including" (*Zoan v Rouamba* [2000] 2 All E.R. 620 CA).    **1–339**

## Discharge of patients

**23.**—(1) Subject to the provisions of this section and section 25 below, a patient **1–340** who is for the time being liable to be detained or subject to guardianship under this Part of this Act shall cease to be so liable or subject if an order in writing discharging him [absolutely from detention or guardianship is made in accordance with this section].

[(1A) Subject to the provisions of this section and section 25 below, a community patient shall cease to be liable to recall under this Part of this Act, and the application for admission for treatment cease to have effect, if an order in writing discharging him from such liability is made in accordance with this section.

(1B) An order under subsection (1) or (1A) above shall be referred to in this Act as "an order for discharge".]

(2) An order for discharge may be made in respect of a patient—

(a) where the patient is liable to be detained in a hospital in pursuance of an application for admission for assessment or for treatment by the [responsible clinician], by the managers or by the nearest relative of the patient;

(b) where the patient is subject to guardianship, by the [responsible clinician], by the responsible local social services authority or by the nearest relative of the patient;

[(c) where the patient is a community patient, by the responsible clinician, by the managers of the responsible hospital or by the nearest relative of the patient.]

(3) Where the patient [falls within subsection (3A) below], an order for his discharge may, without prejudice to subsection (2) above, be made by the Secretary of State and, if [arrangements have been made in respect of the patient] under a contract with a [National Health Service trust][NHS foundation trust][, [[Local Health Board], Special Health Authority or Primary Care Trust], by that National Health Service trust, [NHS foundation trust] [[Local Health Board], Special Health Authority or Primary Care Trust].]

[(3A) A patient falls within this subsection if—

(a) he is liable to be detained in a registered establishment in pursuance of an application for admission for assessment or for treatment; or

(b) he is a community patient and the responsible hospital is a registered establishment.]

(4) The powers conferred by this section on any authority, [trust][, board][(-other than an NHS foundation trust)][, board] or body of persons may be exercised [subject to subsection (5) below] by any three or more members of that authority [trust][, board] or body authorised by them in that behalf or by

three or more members of a committee or sub-committee of that authority [trust][, board] or body which has been authorised by them in that behalf.

[(5) The reference in subsection (4) above to the members of an authority, trust[, board] or body or the members of a committee or sub-committee of an authority, trust[, board] or body,—

(a) in the case of [a [[Local Health Board], Special Health Authority or Primary Care Trust]] or a committee or sub-committee of [a [[Local Health Board], Special Health Authority or Primary Care Trust]], is a reference only to the chairman of the authority[, trust or board] [or trust] and [such members (of the authority, trust, board, committee or sub-committee], as the case may be) as are not also officers of the authority[, trust or board], within the meaning of [the National Health Service Act 2006 or the National Health Service (Wales) Act 2006]; and

(b) in the case of a National Health Service trust or a committee or sub-committee of such a trust, is a reference only to the chairman of the trust and such directors or (in the case of a committee or sub-committee) members as are not also employees of the trust.]

[(6) The powers conferred by this section on any NHS foundation trust may be exercised by any three or more [persons authorised by the board of the trust in that behalf each of whom is neither an executive director of the board nor an employee of the trust.]

AMENDMENTS

The amendments to this section were made by the National Health Service and Community Care Act 1990 s.66(1), Sch.9 para.24(3), the Health Authorities Act 1995 s.2(1), Sch.1 para.107(2), the Health Act 1999 (Supplementary, Consequential, etc. Provisions) Order 2000 (SI 2000/90) Sch.1 para.13(4), the Care Standards Act 2000 s.116, Sch.4 para.9(2), the Health and Social Care (Community Health and Standards) Act 2003 s.34, Sch.4 para.53, the National Health Service (Consequential Provisions) Act 2006 s.2, Sch.1 para.65, the Mental Health Act 2007 ss.9(6), 32(4), 45(1), Sch.3 para.10 and SI 2007, 961 art.3, Sch. para.13(2).

DEFINITIONS

**1–341**     patient: s.145(1).
community patient: ss.17A(7), 145(1).
application for admission for treatment: ss.3, 145(1).
the responsible hospital: ss.17A(7), 145(1).
hospital: ss.34(2), 145(1).
application for admission for assessment: ss.2, 145(1).
the managers: s.145(1).
nearest relative: ss.26(3), 145(1).
local social services authority: s.145(1).
registered establishment: ss.34(1), 145(1).
application for admission for treatment: ss.3, 145(1).
responsible clinician: s.34(1).
Health Authority: s.145(1).
Special Health Authority: s.145(1).

GENERAL NOTE

**1–342**     This section provides for the absolute discharge of detained patients, patients who are subject to guardianship and community patients to be ordered by the patient's responsible clinician (RC), the hospital managers (or the responsible local social services authority for guardianship patients) or the patient's nearest relative. It does not apply to patients who have been remanded to hospital by a court under ss.35 or 36, or who have been made subject to an interim hospital order under s.38. The discharge must be ordered: it cannot be effected by implication. In this section, the term "discharge" means discharge from detention, guardianship or from a community treatment order (CTO), not discharge from hospital.

The provisions of s.133 apply to a patient who is to be discharged under this section.

This section applies to patients who have been placed under hospital or guardianship orders made under s.37 with the modification that subs.(2) shall read as follows:

"(2) An order for discharge may be made in respect of a patient—
(a) where the patient is liable to be detained in a hospital in pursuance of an application for admission [...] for treatment by the [responsible clinician], by the managers [...],
(b) where the patient is subject to guardianship, by the [responsible clinician], by the responsible local social services authority [...],
(c) where the patient is a community patient, by the responsible clinician, by the managers of the responsible hospital [...]" (Sch.1 Pt I, para.8).

The effect of Sch.1, Pt 1 is that both the hospital managers and the RC have the power to discharge a hospital order patient during the first six months of his or her detention even though the patient cannot make an application to a tribunal during that period. The patient's nearest relative, who does not have the power to discharge a hospital order under this section, can make an application to the tribunal under s.69(1).

This section also applies to restricted patients with the modification that subss.(1) and (2) shall read as follows:

"(1) Subject to the provisions of this section and section 25 below, a patient who is for the time being liable to be detained [...] under this Part of this Act shall cease to be so liable [...] if an order in writing discharging him from detention [...] (in this Act referred to as "an order for discharge") is made [with the consent of the Secretary of State] in accordance with this section.
(2) An order for discharge may be made in respect of a patient—
(a) where the patient is liable to be detained in a hospital in pursuance of an application for admission [...] for treatment by the [responsible clinician], by the managers [...];
(b) [...]." (Sch.1, Pt II, paras 2, 7.)

The Secretary of State has his own powers to discharge restricted patients under s.42(2).

*Human Rights Act 1998*

In *Winterwerp v Netherlands* (1979) 2 E.H.R.R. 387, the European Court of Human **1–343** Rights held that the validity of the continued confinement of a mentally disordered person depends upon the persistence of such a disorder. In a subsequent decision of the Court, it was held that it does not automatically follow that a finding by an expert authority that the mental disorder which justified a patient's compulsory confinement no longer persists compels his immediate and unconditional release into the community (*Johnson v United Kingdom* (1999) 27 E.H.R.R. 296). The effect of this decision is that if a patient who is deemed to pose a risk to the public is found no longer to be mentally disordered, discharge from detention can be delayed for a limited period until such time as appropriate after-care facilities are put in place. In *Johnson* the Court said, at para.63, that the authority "should be able to retain some measure of supervision over the progress of the person once he is released into the community and to that end make his discharge subject to conditions".

The question whether a decision not to discharge a patient because of a failure to put in place appropriate after-care facilities in the community violates art.5 is considered in the General Note to s.117 under this heading.

The persons and bodies who have the power to discharge the patient under this provision are "public authorities" for the purposes of s.6 of the 1998 Act.

When exercising their power to review the detention of a patient, the hospital managers are not a "court" for the purposes of Art.5(4) of the Convention. This is because the managers are one of the parties to the review (*De Wilde, Ooms and Versyp v Belgium (No.1)* (1979–80) 1 E.H.R.R. 373).

*Code of Practice*

**1–344**     Guidance on the use of the RC's power of discharge is contained in Ch.29 at paras 29.15 to 29.17. The exercise of the hospital managers' power of discharge is considered in Ch.31.

*Subsection (1)*

**1–345**     PATIENT.     Although an order for the discharge of a restricted patient may be made under this section, the discharge can only take place if the consent of the Secretary of State has been obtained: see the General Note, above.

ORDER IN WRITING.     See reg.18 of the English Regulations and reg.7 of the Welsh Regulations.

DISCHARGING HIM ABSOLUTELY.     The Hospital Managers do not have the power to order the conditional discharge of the patient. The *Code of Practice,* at para.31.38, states that it would be lawful to order that the patient's unconditional discharge takes effect on a specified date in the near future. The accuracy of this guidance is open to doubt for two reasons:

  (i) a deferred discharge is not an absolute discharge. If a patient is discharged absolutely, he or she has a right to leave hospital immediately; a patient who is given a deferred discharge has no such right; and

  (ii) the tribunal is provided with a specific power to order the deferred discharge in s.72(3). If Parliament was of the opinion that Hospital Managers have an implied power to order such a discharge, why was it felt necessary to provide the tribunal with a specific power?

If the Managers are concerned about the adequacy of the after-care services that will be available to the patient on discharge, they should adjourn the hearing and reconvene to a date when the relevant information should be available.

*Subsection (1A)*

**1–346**     Discharging the patient from a CTO has the automatic effect of also discharging the underlying application or order.

*Subsection (2)*

**1–347**     In *R. v Riverside Mental Health Trust Ex p. Huzzey* (1998) 43 B.M.L.R. 167, Latham J. identified the criteria that hospital managers must use when considering the continued detention of a s.3 patient where the nearest relative's application for discharge had been subject to a "barring report" made under s.25. His Lordship said:

"[S]ection 23 provides, *inter alia*, a general discretion in the managers to discharge a patient. No criteria are set out as to what should or should not be taken into account by managers when considering decision as to whether or not to discharge. The question of what are the relevant considerations has to be answered by looking at the general scheme of the Act. Clearly the criteria set out in section 3 are of fundamental importance. If the criteria for admission no longer exist, I cannot see how any decision by managers not to discharge could be other than perverse … Section 23 implicitly recognises that managers have a discretion to discharge even if those criteria have been met. Where … a nearest relative has sought to obtain a discharge order but has been confronted by a barring report [made under s.25], those facts must equally be relevant and material considerations. In my view, the managers are not only entitled to, but must, consider whether or not they are persuaded by the barring report that the patient, if discharged, would be likely to act in a manner dangerous to other persons or to himself. For if they are not so persuaded, they will have reached the position that the nearest relative would have been entitled to an order for discharge if the [RC] had not come to what they have decided was an erroneous conclusion as to the danger presented by the patient. That cannot be anything other than a relevant and material consideration, and would be likely, in almost all circumstances, to mean that discharge should be ordered."

In this case Latham J. held that the failure of the managers to apply their minds to the question of the patient's dangerousness meant that their decision not to order discharge was irrational and had to be quashed. *Huzzey* was applied by Jackson J. in *R. (on the application of SR) v Huntercombe Maidenhead Hospital* [2005] EWHC 2361 (Admin); [2005] M.H.L.R. 379 at para.19, where his Lordship said that "if the managers override the [RC's] report certifying dangerousness, this is a strong pointer in favour of discharge. It is not however an inflexible rule that in every case the managers must discharge if they overturn the finding of dangerousness. Mr Justice Latham in *Huzzey* acknowledged that there may be exceptions. Furthermore, para.23.12 of the [1999 edition of the *Code of Practice*] also acknowledges that there may be exceptions". In *SR*, the ordering of the patient's discharge by the hospital managers subsequent to their decision to override the RC's report was quashed partly on the ground that the managers failed to consider whether to exercise their residual discretion not to order discharge. Hospital managers must therefore consider whether to exercise their residual power not to discharge the patient if they have decided to override the RC's certificate. It is submitted that this residual power should only be exercised if the grounds for continued detention are satisfied and there is evidence to suggest that the patient's health would be significantly compromised if he or she were to be discharged. The *Code of Practice*, at para.31.21, states that the residual power should be invoked if there are "exceptional reasons why the patient should not be discharged." The law on this issue contrasts with that which applies to the tribunal: see the notes on s.72(1)(b)(iii).

In *Huzzey* Latham J. held that as the medical reports which had been placed before the managers justified the continued detention of the patient on the basis of his need for further *assessment*, the patient's continued detention under s.3 could not be justified.

Although the *Huzzey* case was concerned with the power of hospital managers, the approach taken by Latham J. is equally applicable to the RC's power to order discharge. In *South West London and St George's Mental Health NHS Trust v W* [2002] EWHC Admin 1770; [2002] M.H.L.R. 392, Crane J. said at para.81: "Section 23 of the Act does not specifically guide the [RC] or the managers in exercising their power of discharge, but plainly it would appropriate for them to consider the same matters as the [tribunal]". Hospital managers and the RC should therefore assess the need for the patient's continued detention by considering whether: (1) the patient is still suffering from mental disorder; (2) the disorder continues to be of a nature or degree which makes assessment or assessment followed by medical treatment (for s.2 patients) or treatment (for s.3 patients) in a hospital appropriate; (3) for s.3 patients, the appropriate treatment test continues to be satisfied; and (4) detention in a hospital is still necessary in the interests of the patient's own health or safety or for the protection of others. For patients who have been granted leave of absence under s.17, the additional question that will need to be considered is whether the patient's RC continues to need to have a power of recall either in the interests of the patient's own health or safety or for the protection of others. The patient should be discharged if any of these questions can be answered in the negative. If the nearest relative's order for the patient's discharge has been confronted by a barring report, the hospital managers must, in addition to considering the admission criteria, also ask themselves whether the patient would be likely to act in a manner dangerous to other persons or to himself if he were to be discharged (*Huzzey*, noted above). For community patients, the managers should consider the criteria set out in s.72(1)(c)(i)–(iv), (1A). With regard to both community and detained patients, managers have a discretion to order the discharge of the patient even if the relevant criteria for detention or a CTO are satisfied. Managers should therefore consider exercising their discretion to discharge in this situation; see further the *Code of Practice* at paras 31.14 to 31.22.

The solicitors for the Trust in the *Huzzey* case have reported that the patient "was awarded £24,000 compensatory damages and £2,000 aggravated damages by way of compensation for his 87 day detention, around £300 per day. This compensation was set by a jury and seems to reflect the fact that the unit was a medium secure unit and that he was detained with fellow patients in circumstances where his treatment and period of detention were being questioned by him. His detention had also been subject to publicity in the press" (Radcliffe's Mental Health Briefing Note No.37).

ORDER FOR THE DISCHARGE.    There are no statutory criteria governing the exercise of this power.

*Paragraph (a)*

**1–348**    APPLICATION FOR ADMISSION FOR ASSESSMENT.    This includes an emergency application made under s.4 because such an application is "an application for admission for assessment" (see s.4(1)) which is founded on a single medical recommendation.

RESPONSIBLE CLINICIAN.    The RC has a duty to discharge a patient from detention if the medical conditions that justified admission cease to be met (*R. v Drew* [2003] UKHL 25; [2003] 4 All E.R. 557 para.10; also see para.29.16 of the *Code of Practice*). If discharge is ordered, the RC must comply with reg.18 of the English Regulations and reg.7 of the Welsh Regulations. The hospital managers have no power to prevent the RC from exercising the power of discharge. The RC, who has a continuing duty to consider whether the admission conditions remain satisfied (*R. (on the application of C) v Mental Health Review Tribunal London South and South West Region* [2000] M.H.L.R. 220, per Scott Baker J., at para.20), can discharge the patient at any time. "There are no statutory criteria governing the exercise of this power. Its exercise is wholly within the [RC's] discretion subject, in my judgment, to the usual restrictions of lawfulness and so forth. [I]f it is exercised for reasons based on error of law it is susceptible to challenge by judicial review" (*R. (on the application of Wirral Health Authority and Wirral Borough Council) v Dr Finnegan and D.E.* [2001] EWHC Admin 312; [2001] M.H.L.R. 66, per Scott Baker J. at para.68).

So hospital managers can meet their obligations under the Domestic Violence, Crime and Victims Act 2004 to invite representations from victims, RCs must tell the managers if they are considering discharging the following categories of patients:

"[P]atients subject to unrestricted hospital orders, hospital directions whose associated limitation direction is no longer in force, and unrestricted transfer directions (including hospital orders and transfer directions which were originally restricted, but where the restriction order or direction has since ended or been lifted). It includes patients who have been discharged from such an order or direction onto SCT" ("Guidance on the extension of victims' rights under the Domestic Violence, Crime and Victims Act 2004", Department of Health, 2008, para.1.10).

A restricted patient may only be discharged with the consent of the Secretary of State for Justice: see the General Note to this section.

THE MANAGERS. Also see the note on "Discharging him absolutely" in subs.(1). In its *First Biennial Report, 1983–1985*, para.8.13, the Mental Health Act Commission said that the hospital managers "have the right and duty to end a deprivation of liberty as soon as it appears not, or no longer, to be justified by the Act". The managers can delegate their power of discharge under subs.(4). The patient's RC has no power to prevent the managers from exercising their powers of discharge, even if he or she considers that the patient is dangerous.

A patient can make an application to the managers for discharge as often as he or she likes during a period of detention. No formal procedure is laid down for the hearing of a patient's application. In fact, there is no explicit requirement that a hearing should take place at all. Having a hearing is not always the most appropriate mechanism for managers to use when exercising their review function. It would be appropriate for managers to conduct a review by (1) considering written reports from relevant professionals, and (2) interviewing the patient, in the following circumstances:

1. Where a patient make frequent requests for discharge from detention in the absence of any relevant change of circumstances.

2. If the patient does not wish to contest the renewal of his or her detention or CTO.

3. The patient makes an application for discharge immediately after an unsuccessful application to a tribunal in the absence of any relevant change of circumstances.

If a patient makes a request for a review and a tribunal hearing in respect of the patient is imminent, the review should be adjourned until after the hearing. The managers should conduct a review if the patient is not discharged by the tribunal. If a relevant change in the patient's circumstances is identified, either a managers' hearing could take place or a request could be made to the Secretary of State to make a reference to the tribunal (see below).

In order to avoid duplication of effort, a managers' hearing should not take place during the currency the patient's detention under s.2 if the patient has made an application to the tribunal. However a hearing should take place if the patient makes an application to the managers after missing the deadline for submitting an application to the tribunal.

As an alternative to conducting a hearing in response to a patient's application for discharge, the managers could either suggest that the patient makes an application to a tribunal or, if the patient had already exercised that right during the relevant period, they could request the Secretary of State to exercise his power under either s.67 or s.71 to refer the patient's case to the tribunal if a relevant change in the patient's circumstances can be identified. The tribunal is the expert body established under this Act to consider applications made by patients for their discharge. It is the right to make an application to the tribunal, not the hospital managers, that satisfies the Government's obligation under art.5(4) of the European Convention on Human Rights to enable a patient to challenge the lawfulness of his or her detention.

Although the managers have the power to order the discharge of restricted patients, the power is exercisable only with the consent of the Secretary of State (s.41(3)(c)(iii)). Such patients are therefore entitled to request that the managers consider conducting a review of their detention.

Subject to the exceptions noted below, it is not possible for a request for a review to be made on behalf of a patient who lacks the mental capacity to make such a request. Under the Mental Capacity Act 2005, a mentally capable person (the "donor") can execute a legal document called a lasting power of attorney ("LPA") which empowers another person (the "donee") to act in his or her stead, either generally or for specific purposes. An act done by a donee can be treated as an act done by the donor. A LPA which confers on the donee (or donees) power to make decisions about the donor's personal welfare matters could cover the making of a request to the hospital managers for a review. A personal welfare LPA can only take effect after the donor has lost the mental capacity to make the decision in question. A donee could therefore make a request to the hospital managers on the patient's behalf if:

(i) the welfare LPA either gives a general power to the donee or the power to make such a request has been specified by the donor; and

(ii) the patient does not possess the mental capacity to make the request.

A deputy appointed by the Court of Protection under the 2005 Act to make personal welfare decisions on behalf of the patient can also make a request to the hospital managers on the patient's behalf if such a power has been conferred on the deputy by the court and the patient does not have the mental capacity to make the request.

As managers, when exercising their power under this section, are acting in a quasi-judicial capacity they must abide by the rules of natural justice which require decision makers to act fairly, in good faith and without bias and to afford each party the opportunity to adequately state his case. The managers are also placed under a common law duty to give reasons for their decision: see *R. (on the application of O) v West London Mental Health NHS Trust* [2005] EWHC 604 (Admin); [2005] M.H.L.R. 187 where Collins J. held that this duty arises at the time the decision is made. His Lordship further held that a legal defect which will arise if the original reasons were inadequate cannot be cured by the managers subsequently supplementing their reasons with a proper explanation.

Although the managers' power under this section is confined to either granting or not granting the patient's absolute discharge (subs.(1)), the managers could adjourn their consideration of the patient's case if, for example, an important piece of information about the patient had not been provided to them; also see the note on "Discharging him absolutely" in subs.(1).

NEAREST RELATIVE. Who does not have the power to order the discharge of a patient who is subject to a hospital order (with or without restrictions) or to a guardianship order made by a court under Pt III of this Act: see the General Note to this section. For service of the order of discharge, see reg.3(3) of the English and Welsh Regulations. Under the provisions of s.25, 72 hours' notice of the nearest relative's intention to order the patient's discharge must be given to the hospital managers. The patient's RC can nullify the discharge if a report is made to the managers during the 72-hour period specifying that in his or her opinion the patient would be dangerous if discharged (s.25(1)). A nearest relative can be displaced if he or she has exercised or is likely to exercise the power under this provision "without due regard to the welfare of the patient or the interests of the public" (s.29(3)(d)).

A doctor may visit and examine the patient for the purpose of advising a nearest relative on the exercise of his or her right of discharge (s.24(1)(2)).

Although it might be considered inappropriate for a nearest relative to be provided with a power to override professional opinion by ordering the patient's discharge, there have been occasions when the opposition of the nearest relative to the almost unanimous professional opinion about how to satisfy the patient's best interests has proved to be correct; see, for example, the report of the Local Government Ombudsman into an "Investigation into Complaint No.02/C/17068 against Bolton Metropolitan Borough Council" (November 2004). Also see the study by P. Shaw et al., noted in the General Note to s.25.

*Paragraph (b)*

**1–349**    GUARDIANSHIP.    Neither a private guardian nor a nominated medical attendant have the power to discharge the patient from guardianship. The RC has no power to prevent a nearest relative obtaining the discharge of a patient who is subject to guardianship. The nearest relative could be displaced if the discharge was either contrary to the welfare of the patient or to the interests of the public (s.29(3)(d)).

RESPONSIBLE LOCAL SOCIAL SERVICES AUTHORITY.   Is defined in s.34(3). The power of discharge can be exercised by three or more members of the local social services authority or by three or more members of a committee or sub-committee of the authority (subs.(4)). Delegation of the power of discharge to an officer is not permitted: see reg.21(2) of the English Regulations and reg.37(2) of the Welsh Regulations.

*Paragraph (c)*
In Wales, the discharge of a community patient by the RC or the hospital managers must **1–350** be in the form set out in Form CP8: see reg.21 of the Welsh Regulations.

*Subsection (3)*
This subsection does not apply to patients who are subject to guardianship (subs.(3A)). **1–351**

REGISTERED ESTABLISHMENT.   For powers relating to patients detained in such establishments, see s.24(3)(4).

SECRETARY OF STATE.   Or, in relation to Wales, the Welsh Ministers: see the General Note to this Act.

HEALTH AUTHORITY.   The functions of Health Authorities in Wales have been transferred to Local Health Boards (SI 2003/150 and SI 2003/813).

*Subsection (4)*
Neither this subsection nor subs.(5) shall apply to the exercise by the Welsh Ministers of **1–352** the powers conferred by this section (SI 2000/253 Sch.3; also see the General Note to this Act.).

THREE OR MORE MEMBERS OF THAT AUTHORITY TRUST OR BODY.   The reference to "three" is not only for the creation of a quorum: it is a requirement that each of the three members shall support the order for discharge. In the unlikely event of seven members being appointed to the panel and three being in favour of discharge there should be implied into this provision that the "three or more" should not be a minority of those appointed. (*R. (on the application of Tagoe-Thompson) v The Hospital Managers of the Park Royal Centre* [2003] EWCA Civ 330; [2003] M.H.L.R. 326). Officers (i.e. employees) cannot be members of the committee (subs.(5)).

TRUST.   The impact that the Mental Health (Amendment) Act 1994 has had on the performance by NHS Trusts of their powers under this section is explained in the following extract from NHS Management Executive letter TEL (94)2:

"The Mental Health (Amendment) Act 1994, changes the definition of 'the managers' of a Trust in section 145(1) of the Mental Health Act 1983 from 'the directors of the Trust' to 'the Trust'. The result is that NHS Trusts will, from April 14, 1994 [the commencement date of the 1994 Act], be able to delegate the managers' duties under section 23 of the 1983 Act to a committee or sub-committee made up wholly or partly of non-executive directors of the Trust, or wholly of persons who are not directors of the Trust. No executive director of the Trust or other person who is an employee of the Trust may sit on such a committee or sub-committee [see subs.(5)]. Non-executive directors of Trusts will no longer be personally liable for decisions taken about the discharge of detained patients. Liability will rest with the Trust as a body. Trusts should now appoint a committee or sub-committee to undertake the duties of the managers under section 23 of the Mental Health Act 1983. The committee or sub-committee should be made up of informed non-executive directors of the Trust and/or other appointed and informed outside persons. Any person who acts as a manager should be fully informed about the functions of managers."

The authority for NHS trusts to appoint committees of the trust "consisting wholly or partly of directors of the trust or wholly of persons who are not directors of the trust" is contained in reg.15 of the National Health Service Trusts (Membership and Procedure) Regulations 1990 (SI 1990/2024).

*Subsection (5)*

**1–353**     The payment of fees to a member of the committee (frequently referred to as an "associate hospital manager") for attending meetings of the committee does not necessarily mean that that person is disqualified from performing functions under this section by virtue of becoming an "officer" (i.e. an employee) of the trust. There are a number of factors which are taken into account by an Employment Tribunal when determining whether an employer/employee relationship exists between two parties. In essence, these are:

1. Mutuality of obligation between the parties such that the trust would be obliged to provide work to the associate managers and those managers would be obliged to accept the work.

2. The degree of control over the associate managers and the work they perform for the trust. In other words, would the trust be entitled to discipline the managers for a failure to perform their duties?

Other factors that would need be taken into consideration include tax treatment, entitlement to holiday and sick pay and any breaks in the continuity of the work provided by the trust to the managers. Similar considerations would apply to members of a committee appointed by a local authority to consider the discharge of guardianship patients. The Employment Rights Act 1996, s.230(1) defines an employee as an individual "who has entered into or works under . . . a contract of employment".

*Subsection (6)*

**1–354**     This provision enables the board of an NHS foundation trust to delegate its power of discharge to three or more people who are neither executive directors of the board or employees of the trust. The constitution of the trust cannot permit delegation of the power of discharge to executive directors (s.142B).

## Visiting and examination of patients

**1–355**     **24.**—(1) For the purpose of advising as to the exercise by the nearest relative of a patient who is liable to be detained or subject to guardianship under this Part of this Act[, or who is a community patient,] of any power to order his discharge, any registered medical practitioner [or approved clinician] authorised by or on behalf of the nearest relative of the patient may, at any reasonable time, visit the patient and examine him in private.

(2) Any registered medical practitioner [or approved clinician] authorised for the purposes of subsection (1) above to visit and examine a patient may require the production of and inspect any records relating to the detention or treatment of the patient in any hospital [or to any after-care services provided for the patient under section 117 below].

(3) Where application is made by the Secretary of State or a [[Local Health Board], Special Health Authority [, Primary Care Trust][, National Health Service trust or NHS foundation trust]] to exercise, [any power under section 23(3) above to make an order for a patient's discharge] the following persons, that is to say—

(a) any registered medical practitioner [or approved clinician] authorised by the Secretary of State or, as the case may be, that [[Local Health Board],

Special Health Authority [, Primary Care Trust][, National Health Service trust or NHS foundation trust]]; and

(b) any other person (whether a registered medical practitioner [or approved clinician] or not) authorised under [Part II of the Care Standards Act 2000] [or Part 1 of the Health and Social Care act 2008] to inspect the [the establishment in question],

may at any reasonable time visit the patient and interview him in private.

(4) Any person authorised for the purposes of subsection (3) above to visit a patient may require the production of and inspect any documents constituting or alleged to constitute the authority for the detention of the patient [, or (as the case may be) for his liability to recall,] under this Part of this Act; and any person so authorised, who is a registered medical practitioner [or approved clinician], may examine the patient in private, and may require the production of and inspect any other records relating to the treatment of the patient in the [establishment] [or to any after-care services provided for the patient under section 117 below].

AMENDMENT

In subs.(3) the words in square brackets were substituted or inserted by the Registered Homes Act 1984 s.57(1), Sch.1 para.9, the Health Authorities Act 1995 s.2(1), Sch.1 para.107(3), the Health Act 1999 (Supplementary, Consequential, etc. Provisions) Order 2000 (SI 2000/90) Sch.1 para.16(5), the Care Standards Act 2000 s.116, Sch.4 para.9(2)(3), the Health and Social Care (Community Health and Standards) Act 2003 s.34, Sch.4 para.54 and SI 2010/813, art.5(2). The words in square brackets in subss.(2) and (4) were inserted by the Mental Health (Patients in the Community) Act 1995 s.1(2), Sch.1 para.1. The remaining amendments to this section were inserted and substituted by the Mental Health Act 2007 ss.9(7), 32(4), Sch.3 para.11 and SI 2007/961 art.3, Sch. para.13(3).

DEFINITIONS

nearest relative: ss.26(3), 145(1).
patient: s.145(1).
approved clinician: s.145(1).
community patient: ss.17A(7), 145(1).
hospital: ss.34(2), 145(1).
registered establishment: ss.34(1), 145(1).

GENERAL NOTE

This section provides for the visiting and examination of patients and for the production **1–356** of documents to a doctor or approved clinician for the purpose of advising the patient's nearest relative as to the exercise of his or her power to order the discharge of a patient from detention, guardianship or supervised community treatment. Subsections (3) and (4) apply to patients who have been placed under hospital, restriction or guardianship orders by a court under ss.37 or 41 (Sch.1 Pt I para.1, Pt II para.1).

A person who fails to allow the visiting, interviewing or examination of a patient or who refuses to produce any document for inspection commits an offence under s.129.

*Subsection (1)*

There is no power to require a social work assessment to be undertaken in respect of a **1–357** patient who is subject to guardianship.

NEAREST RELATIVE. Or acting nearest relative appointed by a county court under s.29.

POWER TO ORDER HIS DISCHARGE. Under s.23(2).

**1–358**    This provision does not provide for the records of a patient who is subject to guardianship to be made available to the doctor, unless the patient is subject to s.117 after-care.

*Subsection (3)*
**1–359**    SECRETARY OF STATE.    This subsection shall have effect as if it applied to an application made by Welsh Ministers as well as to an application by the Secretary of State (SI 2000/253 Sch.3; also see the General Note to this Act.).

## Restrictions on discharge by nearest relative
**1–360**    **25.**—(1) An order for the discharge of a patient who is liable to be detained in a hospital shall not be made [under section 23 above] by his nearest relative except after giving not less than 72 hours' notice in writing to the managers of the hospital; and if, within 72 hours after such notice has been given, the [responsible clinician] furnishes to the managers a report certifying that in the opinion of [that clinician] the patient, if discharged, would be likely to act in a manner dangerous to other persons or to himself—

> (a)  any order for the discharge of the patient made by that relative in pursuance of the notice shall be of no effect; and

> (b)  no further order for the discharge of the patient shall be made by that relative during the period of six months beginning with the date of the report.

[(1A) Subsection (1) above shall apply to an order for the discharge of a community patient as it applies to an order for the discharge of a patient who is liable to be detained in a hospital, but with the reference to the managers of the hospital being read as a reference to the managers of the responsible hospital.]

(2) In any case where a report under subsection (1) above is furnished in respect of a patient who is liable to be detained in pursuance of an application for admission for treatment [, or in respect of a community patient,] the managers shall cause the nearest relative of the patient to be informed.

AMENDMENTS
The words in square brackets were substituted and inserted by the Mental Health Act 2007 ss.9(8), 32(4), Sch.3 para.12.

DEFINITIONS
**1–361**    patient: s.145(1).
hospital: ss.34(2), 145(1).
nearest relative: ss.26(3), 145(1).
the managers: s.145(1).
application for admission for treatment: ss.3, 145(1).
responsible clinician: s.34(1).
community patient: ss.17A(7), 145(1).
the responsible hospital: ss.17A(7), 145(1).

GENERAL NOTE
**1–362**    This section states that a nearest relative must give 72 hours' notice to the hospital managers of his or her intention to order the discharge of the patient from detention or from supervised community treatment (but not from guardianship) and that the order for discharge, when made, will have no effect if in the meantime the responsible clinician (RC) has reported to the managers that, in his or her opinion, the patient, if discharged, would be likely to act in a manner dangerous to other persons or to him or herself. If the RC makes such a report (a "barring report"), it will have the effect of preventing the

nearest relative from exercising the powers of discharge for the next six months. It is submitted that this prohibition would also apply to any person authorised by the nearest relative subsequent to the receipt of the barring report to perform the functions of nearest relative under reg.24 of the English Regulations or reg.33 of the Welsh Regulations as the person authorised "acts on [the nearest relative's] behalf" (para.1).

The wording of subs.(1) is ambiguous as to when the nearest relative's order of discharge is actually made. It could be argued the phrase "after giving not less than 72 hours notice" implies that there are two stages in the discharge process, namely:

(i) notification of the intention by the nearest relative to order discharge; and

(ii) the ordering of the discharge in the event of the patient's RC not issuing a report barring discharge within the 72 hour period.

However, the wording of para.(a), in particular the use of the term "made", suggests that the order for discharge can be made before the RC issues a report. In order to comply with the interpretive requirement in s.3 of the Human Rights Act 1998, it is suggested that the following interpretation is compatible with the art.8 rights of both patient and nearest relative (also see the extract from the Reference Guide, noted below, and para.29.22 of the *Code of Practice*):

(i) the notice of intention to discharge and the notice of discharge are subsumed into one event;

(ii) the implementation of the notice of discharge is postponed for 72 hours in order to provide the RC with time to consider issuing a report barring discharge; and

(iii) the nearest relative can withdraw the order of discharge within the 72 hour period in the event of the RC not issuing a barring report.

It follows that the patient's discharge takes effect at the end of the 72-hour period if the patient's RC does not issue a report barring discharge. The RC can discharge the patient under s.23 during this period.

In *Re GK (Patient: Habeas Corpus)* [1999] M.H.L.R. 128, Sedley L.J. said that the RC's power to issue a "barring order" is "there to ensure that the mere desire of, in particular, a closest relative to have a patient out does not defeat the purpose of the Act which, both in the interests of the patient and the interests of the public, has ultimate regard to the patient's mental state".

The hospital managers should consider holding a review of the patient's detention if the RC makes a report under this provision. The criteria that hospital managers must use when reviewing the detention of a patient subsequent to such a report being made were identified in *R. v Riverside Mental Health Trust Ex p. Huzzey* (1998) 43 B.M.L.R. 167, where it was held that hospital managers have a residual discretion not to order the patient's discharge even though they have overriden the RC's report certifying dangerousness. *Huzzey* is considered in the note on "the managers" in s.23(2).

Under s.29(3)(d), an application can be made to the county court to displace the patient's nearest relative on the ground that he or she "has exercised without due regard to the welfare of the patient or the interests of the public his power to discharge the patient from hospital . . . under this Part of this Act, or is likely to do so".

A study on patient discharges failed to demonstrate any significant difference in the clinical outcome of patients discharged by their nearest relative and those discharged by a psychiatrist (P. Shaw *et al.*, "In relative danger? The outcome of patients discharged by their nearest relative from sections 2 and 3 of the Mental Health Act", *Psychiatric Bulletin*, (2003), 27(2), 50–54).

*Applications to the First-tier Tribunal (Mental Health) or the Mental Health Review Tribunal for Wales*

**1–363**    In the case of a patient detained for treatment or a community patient, the patient's nearest relative has a right to apply to the tribunal within 28 days of the patient's RC issuing a report under subs.(1) (s.66(1)(g), (2)(d)).

*Code of Practice*

**1–364**    Guidance on this section can be found in Ch.29 at paras 29.18 to 29.23.

*Subsection (1)*

**1–365**    ORDER FOR THE DISCHARGE.    Under s.23(2)(a). For delivery of the notice of discharge, see reg.3(3) of the English and Welsh Regulations.

NEAREST RELATIVE.    Or acting nearest relative appointed by the county court under s.29.

72 HOURS' NOTICE.    Paragraphs 12.104 to 12.106 of the Draft Reference Guide state:

"Although in theory the order should not be served until 72 hours after the notice has been given, in practice it is appropriate for hospital managers to accept a discharge order as also being notice of intention to discharge the patient after 72 hours.

The notice (and the order for discharge itself) must be delivered at the hospital to an officer of the managers authorised by them to receive it, be sent by prepaid post to those managers at that hospital or (if the managers agree) be sent using the managers' internal mail system.

The 72-hour period starts to run from the time when the notice is received by the authorised person, when it is received by post at the hospital to which it is addressed or when it is put into the internal mail system (as the case may be)."

Paragraph 29.23 of the *Code of Practice* contains an illustrative standard letter of discharge for nearest relatives to use.

FURNISHES TO THE MANAGERS A REPORT.    The RC's report must be in the form set out in Pt 1 of Form M2: see 25 of the English Regulations (in Wales, Form NR1: see reg.34 of the Welsh Regulations).

LIKELY TO ACT.    In *Cream Holdings Ltd v Banerjee* [2004] UKHL 44; [2004] 4 All E.R.617, Lord Nicholls of Birkenhead said at para.12:

"As with most ordinary English words 'likely' has several different shades of meaning. Its meaning depends upon the context in which it is being used. Even when read in context its meaning is not always precise. It is capable of encompassing different degrees of likelihood, varying from 'more likely than not' to 'may well'."

In the context of this Act, it is submitted that the approach taken by Girvan LJ in *Boyle v SCA Packaging* [2008] NICA 48; [2009] I.R.L.R. 54 at para.19 (approved by the House of Lords at [2009] 4 All E.R. 1181) should be adopted:

"The prediction of medical outcomes is something which is frequently difficult. There are many quiescent conditions which are subject to medical treatment or drug regimes and which can give rise to serious consequences if the treatment or the drugs are stopped. These serious consequences may not inevitably happen and in any given case it may be impossible to say whether it is more probable than not that this will occur. This being so, it seems highly likely that in the context of . . . the disability legislation the word 'likely' is used in the sense of 'could well happen'."

DANGEROUS. *The Butler Committee* equated "dangerousness with a propensity to cause serious physical injury or lasting psychological harm" (para.4.10). In *Re Whitbread* [1999] C.O.D. 370, Mr David Pannick Q.C., sitting as a deputy judge of the High Court, upheld the decision of hospital managers who had concluded that the dangerousness test was satisfied in a case where there was a "very high level of probability that lasting psychological harm could be caused to others if the barring order were to be lifted"; also see para.29.21 of the *Code of Practice*. In *Rakevich v Russia* [2004] M.H.L.R. 37 para.32, the European Court of Human Rights said that "it is not necessary for the law-maker exhaustively to interpret the term 'danger', as it is hardly possible to embrace in the law the whole diversity of conditions which involve psychiatric hazards".

Some of the problems in defining dangerousness are identified by J. Atkinson and L. Patterson in *Review of Literature Relating to Mental Health Legislation* (2001) at para.2.11:

"Inherent in the problem of defining dangerousness is the difficulty of using the same word to describe harm to others and harm to self. This includes whether it is reasonable to describe 'self-neglect' as 'dangerous' as well as concerns about whether different levels of dangerousness should apply to the risk of the individual harming him/herself or others. Dangerousness is also usually situation-specific and may require complicated formulae to determine risk, for example when the likelihood of danger is high but in a rare situation".

F. Farnham and D. James have claimed that the "forecasting of dangerousness remains like that of the weather—accurate over a few days, but impotent to state longer-term outcome with any certainty" ("'Dangerousness' and dangerous law", Lancet 2001: 385: 1926). The Prins Committee reported that one of the expert witnesses it heard had argued that it was not possible to diagnose "dangerousness" and that psychiatrists and other mental health professionals were no better at judging dangerousness than the man in the street. The Committee stated that it had "some sympathy" with that view and noted that "longer term predictions of dangerousness (i.e. in order to extend a patient's committal beyond an initial observation period)" has been shown to be so inaccurate that "the official policy of the American Psychiatric Association is that psychiatrists are incapable of making them" (*Report of the Committee of Inquiry into the Death in Broadmoor Hospital of Orville Blackwood and a Review of the Death of Two Other Afro-Caribbean Patients*, S.H.S.A., 1993).

DURING THE PERIOD OF SIX MONTHS. The disqualification from ordering the patient's discharge is not affected by any change in the patient's legal status. Therefore a nearest relative who has been made the subject of a RC's report under this section subsequent to ordering the discharge of a patient who has been detained under s.2 of this Act is barred from ordering the discharge of the patient for the full six month period even though the s.2 is immediately followed by an application under s.3 (although the nearest relative could object to such an application (s.11(4))) or if the patient is discharged from the hospital and the section only to be re-admitted under a fresh application shortly thereafter.

BEGINNING WITH. Including the date of the report (*Zoan v Rouamba* [2000] 2 All E.R. 620 CA).

ORDER FOR THE DISCHARGE. For service of the order, see regs 3(1) and 25(2) of the English Regulations and regs.3(1) and 34(2) of the Welsh Regulations.

*Subsection (2)*

**1–366**    CAUSE THE NEAREST RELATIVE TO BE INFORMED.    So that the nearest relative of a patient who has been detained for treatment or who is a community patient could consider applying to a tribunal; see above. The nearest relative of a patient who has been detained for assessment does not have an equivalent right to apply.

### After-Care under supervision

**1–367**    [*Sections 25A to 25J were repealed by the Mental Health Act 2007 s.55, Sch.11 Pt 5*]

### Functions of relatives of patients

**Definition of "relative" and "nearest relative"**

**1–368**    **26.**—(1) In this Part of this Act "relative" means any of the following persons:—

(a) husband or wife [or civil partner];

(b) son or daughter;

(c) father or mother;

(d) brother or sister;

(e) grandparent;

(f) grandchild;

(g) uncle or aunt;

(h) nephew or niece.

(2) In deducing relationships for the purposes of this section, any relationship of the half-blood shall be treated as a relationship of the whole blood, and an illegitimate person shall be treated as the legitimate child of

[(a) his mother, and

(b) if his father has parental responsibility for him within the meaning of section 3 of the Children Act 1989, his father.]

(3) In this Part of this Act, subject to the provisions of this section and to the following provisions of this Part of this Act, the "nearest relative" means the person first described in subsection (1) above who is for the time being surviving, relatives of the whole blood being preferred to relatives of the same description of the half-blood and the elder or eldest of two or more relatives described in any paragraph of that subsection being preferred to the other or others of those relatives, regardless of sex.

(4) Subject to the provisions of this section and to the following provisions of this Part of this Act, where the patient ordinarily resides with or is cared for by one or more of his relatives (or, if he is for the time being an in-patient in a hospital, he last ordinarily resided with or was cared for by one or more of his relatives) his nearest relative shall be determined—

(a) by giving preference to that relative or those relatives over the other or others; and

(b) as between two or more such relatives, in accordance with subsection (3) above.

(5) Where the person who, under subsection (3) or (4) above, would be the nearest relative of a patient—

(a) in the case of a patient ordinarily resident in the United Kingdom, the Channel Islands or the Isle of Man, is not so resident; or

(b) is the husband or wife [or civil partner] of the patient, but is permanently separated from the patient, either by agreement or under an order of a court, or has deserted or has been deserted by the patient for a period which has not come to an end; or

(c) is a person other than the husband, wife, [civil partner,] father or mother of the patient, and is for the time being under 18 years of age;

(d) [ ... ]

the nearest relative of the patient shall be ascertained as if that person were dead.

(6) In this section "husband" [, "wife" and "civil partner" include a person who is living with the patient as the patient's husband or wife or as if they were civil partners], as the case may be (or, if the patient is for the time being an in-patient in a hospital, was so living until the patient was admitted), and has been or had been so living for a period of not less than six months; but a person shall not be treated by virtue of this subsection as the nearest relative of a married patient [or a patient in a civil partnership unless the husband, wife or civil partner] of the patient is disregarded by virtue of paragraph (b) of subsection (5) above.

(7) A person, other than a relative, with whom the patient ordinarily resides (or, if the patient is for the time being an in-patient in a hospital, last ordinarily resided before he was admitted), and with whom he has or had been ordinarily residing for a period of not less than five years, shall be treated for the purposes of this Part of this Act as if he were a relative but—

(a) shall be treated for the purposes of subsection (3) above as if mentioned last in subsection (1) above; and

(b) shall not be treated by virtue of this subsection as the nearest relative of a married patient [or a patient in a civil partnership unless the husband, wife or civil partner] of the patient is disregarded by virtue of paragraph (b) of subsection (5) above.

AMENDMENT

In subs.(2) the words in square brackets were substituted by the Children Act 1989 (Consequential Amendment of Enactments) Order 1991 (SI 1991/1881) art.3.

In subs.(5), para.(d) was repealed by the Children Act 1989 s.108(7), Sch.15.

The references in this section to civil partners were substituted and inserted by the Mental Health Act 2007 s.26(2)–(5).

DEFINITIONS

hospital: ss.34(2), 145(1).    **1–369**

patient: s.145(1).

GENERAL NOTE

This section defines "relative" and "nearest relative" for the purposes of Pt II of this **1–370** Act. The following patients who are subject to orders and remands under Pt III do not have nearest relatives for the purposes of this Act: restricted patients (including conditionally discharged patients), patients remanded to hospital under s.35 or s.36 and patients subject to interim hospital orders under s.38. Other patients who are detained under Pt III and who are not restricted patients and patients who have been made subject to guardianship orders by a court have nearest relatives by virtue of Sch.1 Pt.1 para.1.

The role of the nearest relative in respect of detained patients was identified by Maurice Kay J. in *R. (on the application of M) v Secretary of State for Health* [2003] EWHC 1094 (Admin); [2003] M.H.L.R. 348 at paras 4 and 5 (words in square brackets inserted by the author):

"The nearest relative plays an important part in the scheme of the Act. He may make an application for assessment (section 2), an emergency application for admission for assessment (section 4) and an application for admission for treatment (section 3). No application for admission or treatment under section 3 may be made by an [approved mental health professional (AMHP)] without first consulting with the nearest relative unless the [AMHP] considers that such consultation is not reasonably practicable or would involve unreasonable delay (section 11(4)). The manager of a psychiatric institution in which a patient is detained has to inform the nearest relative in writing about, amongst other things, the right to apply to a tribunal, the right to be discharged, the right to receive and send correspondence and the right to consent to or refuse treatment (section 132(4)). A nearest relative may order the discharge of a patient who is detained under [section 2 and] section 3 (section 23). Prior to exercising this important power the nearest relative can appoint a medical practitioner to examine the patient and the appointed practitioner can require the production of records relating to the detention or treatment of the patient (section 24). The right to order discharge under section 23 is limited when the [responsible clinician] certifies that the patient would, if released, be likely to be a danger to himself or others (section 25). Where a patient to be discharged other than by the order of the nearest relative, the detaining authority is required to notify the nearest relative of the forthcoming discharge unless the patient requests that no such information is supplied (section 133(2)).

In addition to the power to order a discharge under section 23 the nearest relative may apply to [a tribunal] for the discharge of the patient pursuant to section 66 . . . Where the nearest relative is the applicant to the Tribunal he may appoint a registered medical practitioner to visit and examine the patient and that practitioner may require production of and inspect any records relating to the detention and treatment of the patient (section 76(1))."

A person who has been identified as the patient's nearest relative is not legally obliged to act as such. He or she can authorise any person (other than the patient or a person disqualified under subs.(5)) to perform the functions of the nearest relative. The authority can be revoked at any time. Both the authority and the revocation must be in writing: see reg.24 of the English Regulations or reg.33 of the Welsh Regulations. A person who has been identified as the patient's "next of kin" has no powers under this Act unless he or she is also the patient's nearest relative.

In *R. (on the application of S) v Plymouth City Council and C* [2002] EWCA Civ 388; [2002] M.H.L.R. 118, the Court of Appeal was concerned with how the interest of a mentally incapacitated guardianship patient in preserving the confidentiality of personal information about himself is to be reconciled with his mother's interest, as his nearest relative, in having access to enough information about him to exercise her statutory functions under this Act. This case is considered in the General Note to s.8 and in the note on the Civil Procedure Rules 1998.

A nearest relative who provides a substantial amount of care on a regular and unpaid basis for the patient has a right to request the local authority that is assessing the patient's need for community care services to assess his or her ability to provide and to continue to provide such care (Carers (Recognition and Services) Act 1995, s.1).

The leave of the court is required before the nearest relative of a ward of court exercises his functions under this Act (s.33(2)).

The role of the nearest relative is comprehensively reviewed by David Hewitt in *The Nearest Relative Handbook* (2009).

*Mental Capacity Act 2005*

**1–371**    A donee of a lasting power of attorney or a deputy appointed by the Court of Protection have no power of override a decision of a nearest relative made under this Act. A donee or a deputy may only exercise the powers of the nearest relative if they are patient's nearest relative, have been nominated to perform the function of the nearest relative under reg.24, or have been appointed as acting nearest relative under s.29.

*Human Rights Act 1998*
The patient's nearest relative, as a person who has the power to exercise "functions of a  **1–372** public nature", is a "public authority" for the purposes of s.6 of the 1998 Act (s.6(3)(b)).

*Code of Practice*
Guidance on the function of the nearest relative is given in Ch.8.                          **1–373**

*Subsection (1)*
If a relative of a patient is not one of the relatives specified in this subsection, that person  **1–374** cannot be a relative for the purposes of this Part of the Act. However, such a person could be appointed by the county court to be the patient's acting nearest relative under s.29 or authorised by the nearest relative to act as such under reg.24 of the English Regulations or reg.33 of the Welsh Regulations. For the occasions when relatives will be disregarded for the purposes of ascertaining the patient's "nearest relative", see subs.(5). The remaining notes on this subsection are concerned with the definitions of relative as they affect the identification of the patient's nearest relative.

HUSBAND OR WIFE OR CIVIL PARTNER.   Even if the marital or civil partner is under the age of 18 (subs.(5)(c)). If the patient is unmarried or has not entered into a civil partnership or if the marital or civil partner can be disregarded under subs.(5)(b), a person who had been living with the patient as the patient's husband or wife or civil partner for at least six months will be treated as if he or she were the patient's husband or wife (subs.(6)).

SON OR DAUGHTER.   An adopted child is treated as the child of the adoptive parents (Adoption and Children Act 2002 s.46(2)). Once an adoption has taken place, the child's natural parents no longer have any legal connection with the child, including when the child becomes an adult. An unmarried mother's child is treated as the child of the mother (subs.(2)) and, if he has parental responsibility for the child, his father. The child must be over the age of 18 (subs.(5)(c)). A step-child is not a relative for the purposes of this provision but could become a nearest relative under the provisions of subs.(7), by being appointed as an acting nearest relative under s.29 or by being authorised to act as such under reg.24 of the English Regulations or reg.33 of the Welsh Regulations.

FATHER OR MOTHER.   Even if the parent is under the age of 18 (subs.(5)(c)). An unmarried father is to be disregarded unless he has parental responsibility (subs.(2)). In cases where a child is in the care of a local authority by virtue of a care order or where a guardian for the child has been appointed or where a residence order has been made in respect of the child, the local authority (s.27), guardian (s.28) or person named in the residence order (s.28) is deemed to be the child's nearest relative.

*Subsection (2)*
RELATIONSHIP OF THE HALF-BLOOD.   In order to determine whether a relationship exists  **1–375** for the purposes of this section, if a patient has both a full-blood relative and a half-blood relative, they are both treated as full-blood relatives. Whole blood relatives are preferred to half-blood relatives for the purposes of determining the patient's nearest relative under subs.(3).

PARENTAL RESPONSIBILITY.   An unmarried father who does not have parental responsibility for his child is not a relative for the purposes of this section. He can only become the child's nearest relative through the operation of subs.(7) or by virtue of the operation of reg.24 of the English Regulations or reg.33 of the Welsh Regulations: see the General Note to this section. An unmarried father can acquire parental responsibility for his child under the following provisions of the Children Act 1989: by obtaining a residence order (s.12(1)); by virtue of an order of the court (s.4(1)(c)); by making a parental responsibility agreement with the mother (s.4(1)(b); by being appointed the child's guardian by the court (s.5(1)); or by being appointed as the child's guardian by the mother or another guardian (s.5(3)(4)). The appointment as guardian will not take effect while the mother is alive (s.5(8)). By virtue of amendments made to s.4 of the 1989 Act by s.111 of the Adoption and Children Act 2002, unmarried fathers registered as such on the child's birth certificate under the terms of the Births and Deaths Registration Act 1953 will have parental responsibility for that child. Parental responsibility can only be acquired in this way in respect of births registered on or after December 1, 2003, which was the commencement date for s.111 (SI 2003/3079): see s.111(7) of the 2002 Act. An unmarried father's parental responsibility for his child can be ended by order of the court (s.4(2A),(3) of the 1976 Act). It will also end when the child reaches 18 (s.91(7),(8)) of the 1989 Act) or is adopted (s.46(2) of the 2002 Act).

If an unmarried father subsequently marries the mother of the child, both parents will from that date have parental responsibility for the child (Legitimacy Act 1976 s.2)

*Subsection (3)*

**1–376**     NEAREST RELATIVE.  This subsection states that the general rule for determining the patient's nearest relative is to take whoever comes first on the list of relatives set out in subs.(1), with preference being given to relatives of the whole blood, and that if there is more than one relative coming within the same category the elder or eldest is to take priority regardless of the sex of the relative, subject to preference being given to the relative who either lives with or cares for the patient (subs.(4)). The remainder of this section contains the exceptions to this rule.

If the patient has no nearest relative or if it is not reasonably practicable to ascertain whether he has such a relative, or who that relative is, an application may be made to the county court for the appointment of an acting nearest relative under s.29(3)(a).

The patient cannot choose his or her nearest relative who must be identified by applying subss.(3) to (6) to the patient's family and social situation. The fact that a relative is either mentally disordered, mentally incapable or detained under this Act does not disqualify him or her from being a nearest relative, although there could be grounds for removal under s.29(3)(b). The fact that a person has been sentenced to a period of imprisonment does not disqualify that person from being a nearest relative. Either the mental state or the imprisonment of the nearest relative could lead to an AMHP concluding that it would not be "practicable" either to consult with the relative prior to making an application for admission under s.3 (see s.11(4)) or to inform the relative that an application under s.2 is to be or has been made (see s.11(3)).

It is possible for a nearest relative to authorise another person to perform the functions of nearest relative on his behalf: see the General Note to this section.

ELDER OR ELDEST.  Thus the elder or eldest wife of a polygamous marriage would normally become her husband's nearest relative.

*Subsection (4)*

**1–377**     This subsection provides that if the patient is either living with or being cared for by a relative, that relative becomes the patient's nearest relative. If the patient is living with one relative and being cared for by another, the elder is to be preferred (subs.(3)).

ORDINARILY RESIDES.  General guidance about what is meant by this phrase has been given by Lord Scarman in *Shah v Barnet LBC* [1983] 1 All E.R. 226 235 HL:

"Unless . . . it can be shown that the statutory framework or the legal context in which the words are used requires a different meaning, I unhesitatingly subscribe to the view that 'ordinarily resident' refers to a man's abode in a particular place or country which he has adopted voluntarily and for settled purposes as part of the regular order of his life for the time being, whether short or long duration."

Buxton L.J. has said that the:

"concept of 'voluntariness' is extremely elusive. Its core meaning would seem to be that a physical movement (or a failure to move out of a particular situation when circumstances required such movement) cannot be said to have been voluntary if the subject did not (or even, probably, could not) direct his will to the movement or lack of movement in question" (*Al-Ameri v Kensington and Chelsea Royal London Borough Council* [2003] EWCA Civ 235; [2003] 2 All E.R. 1 CA para.59).

In *Mohamed v Hammersmith and Fulham LBC* [2002] UKHL 57; [2002] 1 All E.R. 176 at para.18, Lord Slynn held that the term "normally resident" in s.199(1)(a) of the Housing Act 1996 is to be given the same meaning as "ordinarily resident". Having referred to the judgment in *Shah*, his Lordship said:

"[T]he prima facie meaning of normal residence is a place where at the relevant time the person in fact resides. That therefore is the question to be asked and it is not appropriate to consider whether in a general or abstract sense such a place would be considered an ordinary or normal residence. So long as that place where he eats and sleeps is voluntarily accepted by him, the reason why he is there rather than somewhere else does not prevent that place from being his normal residence. He may not like it, he may prefer some other place, but that place is for the relevant time the place where he normally resides. If a person, having no other accommodation, takes his few belongings and moves into a barn for a period to work on a farm that is where during that period he is normally resident, however much he might prefer some more better or permanent accommodation".

A person may change his place of ordinary residence during the course of a day, e.g. a son who leaves the parental home and moves into a flat of his own with no intention of returning. But each case has to be judged on its own facts and the fact that a person has left his home does not necessarily mean that he has established an ordinary residence elsewhere. McCullough J. examined this issue in *R. v Liverpool CC Ex p. F* (CO 2744/96) April 16, 1997, a case where the patient had left the parental home in acrimonious circumstances and had gone to live with his grandmother, as well as staying at a number of other places. His Lordship said that those who were charged with the task of identifying the identity of the patient's nearest relative should have considered:

"not just the choice between whether he was ordinarily resident with his mother or with his grandmother. They should have considered also the possibility that he may not have been ordinarily resident anywhere and should have specifically asked themselves—bearing in mind his itinerant lifestyle, his lack of stability and the condition of his mental health—whether he really had settled down sufficiently at his grandmother's for her home to be regarded as his place of ordinary residence."

The issues that can be identified from the case law that are relevant to the determination of a person's ordinary residence were summarised by Charles J. in *R. (on the application of Greenwich LBC. v Secretary of State for Health* [2006] EWHC 2576 (Admin) at para.72:

"Habitual or ordinary residence is in each case a question of fact. The temptation to turn it into an abstract proposition should be resisted. Habitual or ordinary residence is not equivalent to physical presence. There can be ordinary or habitual residence without continuous presence, while physical presence is not necessarily equivalent to residence. Residence means living somewhere. The significance of ordinary or habitually is that it connotes residence adopted voluntarily and for settled purposes . . . Although ordinary residence in one place can be lost immediately acquisition of a new ordinary residence requires an appreciable period of time. The length of the appreciable period of time is not fixed since it depends on the nature and quality of the connection with the new place. However, it may only be a few weeks, perhaps, in some circumstances, even days. In order to establish ordinary residence over a period of time a person must spend more than a token part of that period in the place in question. Ordinary residence is not broken by temporary or occasional absences of long or short duration. It is possible to be ordinarily resident in more than one place at the same time.

That is, in may ways, a long winded way of saying what is encapsulated in paragraph 2 of [Department of Health Circular No. LAC (93)7], namely that the concept of ordinary residence involves questions of fact and degree and factors such as time, intention and continuity, each of which may be given different weight according to the context."

If a patient leaves home, but takes up no other place of ordinary residence and no relative is caring for him, his nearest relative can be identified by applying the general rule set out in subs.(3).

CARED FOR. A person can clearly "care about" a patient without providing "care for" that patient. In *Re D (Mental patient: habeas corpus)* [2000] 2 F.L.R. 848, the Court of Appeal held that (a) the words "ordinarily" qualifies "resided with" but not "cared for"; and (b) although the words "cared for" are not defined in this Act, they are clear and everyday words set in a context where the AMHP applicant has to act in a pragmatic and common sense manner in a situation which is fraught with emotion and difficulty. In order to justify a finding that the relative is caring for the patient, the services provided by the relative must be more than minimal and they need not have been provided over the long term. In this case the court was asked to consider the situation of a relative who assisted the patient in managing his financial affairs, checked whether he was eating appropriately and took away and cleaned his soiled clothing and bed clothes. In finding that the relative was caring for the patient the court said that there "was more than sufficient evidence to pass the 'cared for' test, wherever one sets the threshold of services amounting to 'cared for'. In other words, the services were not merely minimal. They were services which were substantial and sustained."

The patient may be "cared for" by a relative even if they do not share a residence. In *R. v Liverpool CC*, above, McCullough J. held that the quality of regularity identified by Lord Scarman in the *Shah* case, above, is equally important when considering whether there has been a change in the identity of the person who is to be regarded as caring for the patient. His Lordship said: "In such a case it will be necessary to take into account the duration, continuity and quality of the care afforded by the relative under consideration as having assumed the role . . . and also the intention of the patient himself."

If the patient either resides with more than one relative or is cared for by more than one relative, or lives with one relative and is cared for by another, the nearest relative becomes either the elder or eldest relative if both relatives come within the same category, or the relative who comes first on the list set out in subs.(1) if they do not.

*Subsection (5)*

**1–378**    This subsection, which disqualifies certain persons from acting as a patient's nearest relative, is applied to persons who have been deemed to be the patient's nearest relative by virtue of s.28 (s.28(2)).

PARAGRAPH (A); UNITED KINGDOM. "United Kingdom" means Great Britain and Northern Ireland (Interpretation Act 1978 s.5, Sch.1). It is easier for a person to lose their ordinary/habitual residence in a country than to acquire it. In *C v S (A Minor) (Abduction)* [1990] 2 F.L.R. 442 at 454 HL Lord Brandon said:

"[T]he question whether a person is or is not habitually resident in a specified country is a question of fact to be decided by reference to all the circumstances of any particular case . . . . A person may cease to be habitually resident in country A in a single day if he or she leaves it with a settled intention not to return to it but to take up long term residence in country B instead. Such a person cannot, however, become habitually resident in country B in a single day. An appreciable period of time and a settled intention will be necessary to enable him or her to become so. During that appreciable period of time the person will have ceased to be habitually resident in country A but not yet have become habitually resident in country B."

NOT SO RESIDENT.   The effect of this provision is that:

1. If the patient is ordinarily resident in the United Kingdom, the Channel Islands or the Isle of Man and the person who would normally be identified as the patient's nearest relative is not so resident, that person cannot be the patient's nearest relative. However, if that person has gone abroad temporarily, for example on business or on holiday, he or she will be the patient's nearest relative.

2. If the patient is not ordinarily resident in the United Kingdom, the Channel Islands or the Isle of Man, the nearest relative of the patient can be a person who is also not so resident.

PARAGRAPH (B); SEPARATED.   In the absence of a court order, the spouses or civil partners must have agreed that their separation is permanent; the mere fact that the couple live at different places is not sufficient to constitute separation. If one spouse or civil partner is uncertain as to whether the separation is permanent, this provision is not satisfied.

Both separation and desertion require that the couple be factually separated. It is possible for a separation to be established in a situation where both parties continue to live in the same premises, if it can be said that two separate households have been established. If there continues to be a sharing of a common life by, for example, taking meals together or sharing common living areas, the parties are not separated for the purposes of the Divorce Reform Act 1969. In *Le Brocq v Le Brocq* [1964] 1 W.L.R. 1085, the wife had excluded her husband from the matrimonial bedroom by bolting the door on the inside. There was no avoidable communication between them, but the wife continued to cook meals for her husband, although he was never allowed to take meals with her, and he paid her a weekly sum for housekeeping. The court held that the necessary factual separation had not been established: there was, as Harman L.J. put it, "separation of bedrooms, separation of hearts, separation of speaking: but one household was carried on . . ."

DESERTED.   Under matrimonial law, the main elements of desertion are the fact of separation and the intention to desert. The intention to desert involves: (a) lack of consent to the separation by the spouse who has been deserted; (b) lack of any justification for the separation; and (c) the deserting spouse having the mental capacity to form the intent; see Cretney *Principles of Family Law* (2008) paras 10–027 to 10–032. A person who has been disqualified from being a patient's nearest relative under this provision can resume that role as soon as the desertion comes to an end.

PARAGRAPH (C); UNDER 18 YEARS OF AGE.   Means before the commencement of his eighteenth birthday (Family Law Reform Act 1969 s.9(1)).

*Subsection (6)*

LIVING WITH THE PATIENT AS THE PATIENT'S HUSBAND OR WIFE OR AS IF THEY WERE CIVIL **1–379** PARTNERS.   Under this provision, an individual who has been living with the patient as the patient's husband or wife or as if they were civil partners for at least six months shall be treated as the patient's nearest relative. This rule is subject to the exception that the cohabitee of a married patient or a patient who is in a civil partnership cannot be the nearest relative of that patient unless the patient's spouse or civil partner can be disregarded under subs.(5)(b) on the ground of permanent separation or desertion.

It is not sufficient for the couple to be living together; they must be living together in a settled relationship as if they were husband or wife or civil partners. In *Mummery v Mummery* [1942] P. 107, a case on desertion, Lord Merriman P. doubted that it was possible to "give a completely exhaustive definition of cohabitation". This statement was cited in *Kimber v Kimber* [2000] 1 F.L.R. 383, where H.H. Judge Tyrer identified the following factors as being relevant to the question of determining whether a man and a woman are living together as husband and wife:

(a) are the parties living together in the same household;

(b) do they share daily tasks and duties;

(c) is there stability and a degree of permanence in the relationship;

(d) is the way in which financial matters are being handled an indication of the cohabitation;

(e) do the parties have a sexual relationship with each other;

(f) are there children of the relationship;

(g) what is the intention and motivation of the parties; and

(h) would a reasonable person of normal perceptions consider that the parties were cohabiting.

H.H. Judge Tyrer said that these factors "cannot be complete nor comprehensive".

WAS SO LIVING UNTIL THE PATIENT WAS ADMITTED. The six-month period of cohabitation must have occurred prior to the patient's admission.

PERIOD OF NOT LESS THAN SIX MONTHS. In the unreported case of *R. (on the application of Robinson) v The Hospital Managers of Park Royal Hospital*, November 26, 2007, the cohabiting partner of a detained patient purported to discharge him under s.23 on the ground that she, and not the patient's aunt, was the patient's nearest relative. The hospital argued that the partner was not the patient's nearest relative as she did not qualify under this provision and declined to discharge him. In dismissing an application for *habeas corpus* and judicial review of the hospital's decision, Stanley Burnton J. said that in calculating the six-month period, a hospital should take into account periods spent apart, including time spent abroad, and/or detention in a hospital or prison (notwithstanding that such absences are under compulsion). As such periods of detention would be recorded, it would not be impracticable for a hospital to make such calculations. Although it might be difficult to identify when a period of cohabitation began, a hospital was obliged to try, as it had a duty to investigate whether a six month cohabitation period had altered the identity of the patient's nearest relative. Whether or not a period apart would bring a cohabitation period to an end for the purposes of this provision would depend on the nature and duration of the relationship when the interruption took place (This case is considered by counsel for the claimant, Ms Laura Davidson, in "Nearest Relative Consultation and the Avoidant Approved Mental Health Professional", J.M.H.L., Spring 2009, 70–80).

With regard to the nature and duration of the relationship, the imprisonment of a patient who had been cohabiting with his partner for a number of years would be unlikely to bring the cohabitation to an end. However, if the imprisonment occurred a few days after the couple had begun to live together, it would be difficult to claim after six months that they had cohabitated.

*Subsection (7)*

This subsection provides that a person who has been living with the patient for five years **1–380** or more shall be treated as if he or she were a relative who came last on the hierarchy of relatives set out in subs.(1). By virtue of subs.(4), that person as a relative who "ordinarily resides" with the patient becomes the patient's nearest relative unless a relative who came higher in the hierarchy is either living with or caring for the patient.

There may be difficulties in identifying the patient's nearest relative in cases where the patient has been residing with a number of people who are not relatives for five years or more in a communal living situation. This could occur where, for example, the patient is a member of a religious community or if he or she lives in a group home. In this situation the provisions of subs.(3) would apply and the eldest person who had become a "relative" under this subsection would become the patient's nearest relative. However if the patient was being "cared for" by one of the "five year" people, that person would become the nearest relative: see subs.(4).

A particular difficulty has arisen with the identification of the nearest relative of an elderly patient who is the resident of a care home. Although the question of whether a person ordinarily resides with others is a question of fact and degree which must be determined in each case (see the note on "ordinarily resides" in subs.(4)), it would be difficult to argue that the residents of many such homes do not "ordinarily reside" with each other in that they will usually eat together, use common facilities and generally live a communal life. In other words, the residents share a common home. Such a finding would not be appropriate in a case where the residents lived in self-contained units within the home and only had occasional contact with each other for social purposes. If the patient is found to have ordinarily resided with a number of fellow residents for more than five years, the combined effect of subss.(3) and (4) is to identify the eldest of these residents as the patient's nearest relative. If the identified nearest relative does not wish to act in that role he or she could be asked to use the simple procedure set out in reg.24 of the English Regulations or reg.33 of the Welsh Regulations to nominate some other person to take over the responsibilities of nearest relative. If the identified nearest relative is mentally incapacitated, it will not be practicable for that person to be consulted with for the purposes of s.11(4). In this situation an application could be made to the court for an acting nearest relative to be appointed under s.29(3)(b).

A. Eldergill argues there must be some element of choice, rather than an "involuntary or institutional requirement", before a person can be said to ordinarily reside with another (*Mental Health Review Tribunals* (1997), p.103). This argument is incompatible with the decision in *R. v Waltham Forest LBC Ex p. Vale, The Times*, February 25, 1985, where Taylor J. held that a severely mentally handicapped adult who was totally dependent on her parents was ordinarily resident with her parents, which is where she was temporarily living at the relevant time, since she was in the same position as a small child who is unable to choose where to live. Alternatively his Lordship concluded that the case had to be decided in the light of all the facts, as if the young woman had capacity. It is submitted that this alternative test should be applied in cases where a mentally incapacitated adult is placed in residential care.

If a relative or a spouse of a patient who has been living in a communal situation has had a substantial and sustained contact with the patient by, for example, taking the patient out of the institution for recreational purposes, assisting with feeding the patient or entertaining the patient at his or her home, it might be possible to argue that that person was caring for the patient for the purposes of subs.(4). In these circumstances that person would take precedence over the "five year" person by virtue of subs.(3).

It is submitted that a landlord and tenant can only be considered as "ordinarily residing" with each other if they live in the same accommodation and there is a substantial sharing of household facilities and functions.

ORDINARILY RESIDES. See the note in subs.(4) under this heading. This provision does not require the patient and the person with whom he has resided for five years or more to regard each other as husband or wife, or to be lovers, or even to be friends.

FIVE YEARS. Temporary separations resulting, for example, from separate holidays being taken should be disregarded in calculating this period.

This provision covers the situation where an adult mentally disordered ex-patient has been "fostered" to carers under an adult placement scheme. It seems inappropriate that carers have to wait for five years before one of them is entitled to exercise the functions of nearest relative. It also appears to cover the situation of a child who has been placed with foster parents under either Pt III or Pt IX of the Children Act 1989. If the child remains at that home on reaching adulthood, the period when the child was fostered should be included in the calculation of the five-year period.

MARRIED PATIENT OR A PATIENT IN A CIVIL PARTNERSHIP. The "five year" person cannot be the nearest relative of a married patient or a patient in a civil partnership unless the patient's spouse or civil partner can be disregarded because of permanent separation or desertion.

## [Children and young persons in care

**1–381** **27.** Where—

(a) a patient who is a child or young person is in the care of a local authority by virtue of a care order within the meaning of the Children Act 1989; or—

(b) the rights and powers of a parent of a patient who is a child or young person are vested in a local authority by virtue of section 16 of the Social Work (Scotland) Act 1968,

the authority shall be deemed to be the nearest relative of the patient in preference to any person except the patient's husband or wife [or civil partner] (if any).]

AMENDMENT

This section was substituted by the Children Act 1989, s.108(5) Sch.13, para.48(1). The words in square brackets were inserted by the Mental Health Act 2007 s.26(6).

DEFINITIONS
**1–382** patient: s.145(1).
nearest relative: ss.26(3), 145(1).

GENERAL NOTE
**1–383** If an unmarried child or a child who is not in a civil partnership is in the care of a local authority by virtue of a care order (in England or Wales) or if parental rights and powers in respect of a child have been vested in a local authority (in Scotland), this section identifies that authority as the child's nearest relative. It would clearly be appropriate for the local authority to delegate its functions under this provision to an officer.

This section applies to children who have been placed under hospital or guardianship orders by a court under s.37 (Sch.1 Pt 1 para.1).

CHILD. Is defined in the Children Act 1989 as a person under the age of eighteen (s.105(1)).

CARE ORDER. A care order is defined in s.31(11) of the Children Act 1989 to include an interim care order made under s.38 of that Act.

**Nearest relative of minor under guardianship, etc.**

   **28.**—[(1) Where                                                              **1–384**

    (a) a guardian has been appointed for a person who has not attained the age of eighteen years; or

    (b) a residence order (as defined by section 8 of the Children Act 1989) is in force with respect to such a person,

the guardian (or guardians, where there is more than one) or the person named in the residence order shall, to the exclusion of any other person, be deemed to be his nearest relative.]

   (2) Subsection (5) of section 26 above shall apply in relation to a person who is, or who is one of the persons, deemed to be the nearest relative of a patient by virtue of this section as it applies in relation to a person who would be the nearest relative under subsection (3) of that section.

   [(3) In this section "guardian" [includes a special guardian (within the meaning of the Children Act 1989), but] does not include a guardian under this Part of this Act.]

   (4) In this section "court" includes a court in Scotland or Northern Ireland, and "enactment" includes an enactment of the Parliament of Northern Ireland, a Measure of the Northern Ireland Assembly and an Order in Council under Schedule 1 of the Northern Ireland Act 1974.

AMENDMENTS

   Subsections (1) and (3) were substituted by the Children Act 1989 s.108(5), Sch.13 para.48. The words in square brackets in subs.(3) were inserted by the Adoption and Children Act 2002 s.139, Sch.3 para.41.

DEFINITIONS

   patient: s.145(1).                                                     **1–385**
   nearest relative: ss.26(3), 145(1).

GENERAL NOTE

   This section provides for a person who has been appointed as a child's guardian (other **1–386** than under this Act), a child's special guardian or a person who is named in a residence order which has been made in respect of a child, to be that child's nearest relative. It applies to children who have been placed under hospital or guardianship orders by a court under s.37 (Sch.1 Pt 1 para.1).

*Subsection (1)*

   ATTAINED THE AGE.   At the commencement of his or her eighteenth birthday (Family **1–387** Law Reform Act 1969 s.9(1)).

   GUARDIAN.   A guardian can only be appointed under s.5 of the Children Act 1989 (*ibid.*, s.5(13)).

   GUARDIANS, WHERE THERE IS MORE THAN ONE.   Thus two persons, as co-guardians, could have equal powers as the patient's nearest relative. Compare this with s.26(3) where only a sole nearest relative is contemplated.

   RESIDENCE ORDER.   If more than one person is named in the residence order, those named will have equal powers as the patient's nearest relative.

*Subsection (2)*

**1–388**     This provides that s.26(5), which disqualifies certain persons from acting as a patient's nearest relative, applies to the person or persons deemed to be the patient's nearest relative by virtue of subs.(1).

*Subsection (3)*

**1–389**     GUARDIAN UNDER THIS PART OF THIS ACT.     Such a person could become a patient's nearest relative if, apart from guardianship responsibilities under this Act, he or she would be nearest relative by virtue of either being the person named or appointed under subs.(1) or by being identified as nearest relative under s.26.

## Appointment by court of acting nearest relative

**1–390**     **29.**—(1) The county court may, upon application made in accordance with the provisions of this section in respect of a patient, by order direct that the functions of the nearest relative of the patient under this Part of this Act and sections 66 and 69 below shall, during the continuance in force of the order, be exercisable by [the person specified in the order].

[(1A) If the court decides to make an order on an application under subsection (1) above, the following rules have effect for the purposes of specifying a person in the order—

(a) if a person is nominated in the application to act as the patient's nearest relative and that person is, in the opinion of the court, a suitable person to act as such and is willing to do so, the court shall specify that person (or, if there are two or more such persons, such one of them as the court thinks fit);

(b) otherwise, the court shall specify such person as is, in its opinion, a suitable person to act as the patient's nearest relative and is willing to do so.]

(2) An order under this section may be made on the application of—

[(za) the patient;]

(a) any relative of the patient;

(b) any other person with whom the patient is residing (or, if the patient is then an in-patient in a hospital, was last residing before he was admitted); or

(c) an [approved mental health professional];

[. . .]

(3) An application for an order under this section may be made upon any of the following grounds, that is to say—

(a) that the patient has no nearest relative within the meaning of this Act, or that it is not reasonably practicable to ascertain whether he has such a relative, or who that relative is;

(b) that the nearest relative of the patient is incapable of acting as such by reason of mental disorder or other illness;

(c) that the nearest relative of the patient unreasonably objects to the making of an application for admission for treatment or a guardianship application in respect of the patient; [. . .]

(d) that the nearest relative of the patient has exercised without due regard to the welfare of the patient or the interests of the public his power to discharge the patient [. . .] under this Part of this Act, or is likely to do so[; or

(e) that the nearest relative of the patient is otherwise not a suitable person to act as such.]

(4) If, immediately before the expiration of the period for which a patient is liable to be detained by virtue of an application for admission for assessment,

an application under this section, which is an application made on the ground specified in subsection (3)(c) or (d) above, is pending in respect of the patient, that period shall be extended—

(a) in any case, until the application under this section has been finally disposed of; and

(b) if an order is made in pursuance of the application under this section, for a further period of seven days;

and for the purposes of this subsection an application under this section shall be deemed to have been finally disposed of at the expiration of the time allowed for appealing from the decision of the court or, if notice of appeal has been given within that time, when the appeal has been heard or withdrawn, and "pending" shall be construed accordingly.

(5) An order made on the ground specified in subsection [(3)(a), (b) or (e)] above may specify a period for which it is to continue in force unless previously discharged under section 30 below.

(6) While an order made under this section is in force, the provisions of this Part of this Act (other than this section and section 30 below) and sections 66, 69, 132(4) and 133 below shall apply in relation to the patient as if for any reference to the nearest relative of the patient there were substituted a reference to the person having the functions of that relative and (without prejudice to section 30 below) shall so apply notwithstanding that the person who was the patient's nearest relative when the order was made is no longer his nearest relative; but this subsection shall not apply to section 66 below in the case mentioned in paragraph (h) of subsection (1) of that section.

AMENDMENTS

The words in square brackets were substituted and inserted by the Mental Health Act 2007 ss.21, 23, Sch.2 para.7. The words omitted were repealed by s.55, Sch.11 Pts 4 and 5.

DEFINITIONS                                                                                              **1–391**
    patient: s.145(1).
    nearest relative: ss.26(3), 145(1).
    hospital: ss.34(2), 145(1).
    approved mental health professional: s.145(1), (1AC).
    local social services authority: s.145(1).
    mental disorder: ss.1, 145(1).
    application for admission for treatment: ss.3, 145(1).
    application for admission for assessment: ss.2, 145(1).

GENERAL NOTE

The section gives the county court power to make an order directing that the functions of **1–392** the patient's nearest relative (NR) shall be exercised by another person, which can include a local social services authority (Reference Guide, para.33.39) as under the Interpretation Act 1978, Sch.1, a "person" includes a corporation. The applicant for the order can nominate a person to act as the patient's NR. Where the nominated person is, in the court's opinion, not "suitable" or there is no nomination, the court can appoint any suitable person to act as the patient's NR if he or she is willing to do so (subs.(1A)). An application to the court can be made concurrently with, or subsequent to, an application under s.3: see s.30(4) and *R. v Central London County Court Ex p. London* [1999] 3 All E.R. 991 CA. An applicant can only rely on the grounds set out in subs.(3). In order to succeed on an application the applicant must demonstrate that the statutory criteria are made out both at the date of the application and at the date of the hearing (*Lewis v Gibson* [2005] EWCA Civ 587; [2005]

M.H.L.R. 309 para.38). If the court makes an order under this section, it has no further legal role to play in respect of any subsequent application for treatment or guardianship that is made in respect of the patient. In *Barnet LBC v Robin* (1999) 2 C.C.L.R. 454, the Court of Appeal, without having heard full argument on the point, was prepared to proceed on the basis that an appeal of an order made under this section can be made to the Court of Appeal on both matters of law and of fact.

In *R. (on the application of S) v Plymouth City Council and C* [2002] EWCA Civ 388; [2002] 1 W.L.R. 2582, the Court of Appeal was concerned with how the interest of a mentally incapacitated guardianship patient in preserving the confidentiality of personal information about himself is to be reconciled with his mother's interest, as his nearest relative, in having access to enough information about him to defend a possible displacement application made under this section. This case is considered in the General Note to s.8 and in the note on the Civil Procedure Rules 1998 in Pt 3.

The provisions of s.38 of the County Court Act 1984 provide the county court with the power to make an interim order when considering an application under this section. A decision of the hospital managers to rely on such an order for the purposes of the admission and detention of a patient is lawful: see *R. v Central London County Court*, above, where Stuart-Smith L.J. said at para.24: "unless there are cogent reasons to the contrary, it is preferable that questions under s.29(3)(c) should be finally determined before an application is made under s.3, and the machinery of extension of detention under section afforded by s.29(4) should be used". This statement was considered in *R. (on the application of M) v Homerton University Hospital* [2008] EWCA Civ 197; [2008] M.H.L.R. 92, where the Court of Appeal considered the patient's claim for judicial review on the basis that, where the machinery for extended detention under subs.(4) existed, it was unlawful, in the absence of exceptional circumstances, to detain her under s.3 so that she became subject to concurrent detention regimes. In dismissing the claim, the court held that:

(i) although in might be desirable in some cases to follow the approach advocated by Stuart-Smith L.J., there was nothing in this Act or in the case law to suggest that if a hospital chooses to go down the s.29 route to try to displace the unreasonable relative, they are then bound to conclude those proceedings before taking action under s.3; and

(ii) there is no requirement that "exceptional circumstances" must exist before the s.29 and s.3 regimes may run in tandem.

In order for a s.3 application to be made in these circumstances, the court would have had to have made an interim order displacing the nearest relative. The Court of Appeal did not address the question of how a recommending doctor can certify that, given the patient is subject to an extended s.2, the requirement in s.3(2)(c) that the patient's treatment "cannot be provided unless he is detained under [s.3]" is satisfied. It is submitted that, as the powers of a patient's responsible clinician to treat the patient under s.2 and s.3 are identical, the requirement cannot be satisfied until the lapsing of the extended s.2 is imminent.

In *R. v Uxbridge County Court Ex p. Binns* [2000] M.H.L.R. 179, the court made a without notice order appointing the local authority as the acting nearest relative of the patient. Two hours' notice of the application was given to the nearest relative, who was not served with any papers. The displaced nearest relative was given permission to apply to the court, after giving notice to the local authority, to vary or discharge the order. On an application for judicial review of the order Hidden J. held that:

1. Section 38 of the 1984 Act is broad enough to encompass a temporary order which was both interlocutory and conditional and was not for a specified period.

2. There is nothing in Ord.49 r.12 of the County Court Rules (now see CPR Pt 8.1(6) and Practice Direction—Alternative Procedure for Claims, Section C, para.18.1) which is inconsistent with the general provisions of Pt 23 of the Civil Procedure

Rules which, inter alia, entitle a person against whom an order is made without notice to apply to set aside or vary it (para.23.10(1)); require the order to contain a statement of the right to make an application to set aside or vary it (para.23.9(3)); and provide a power in the court to re-list an application where an order had been made in the absence of a respondent either at the application of that person or of the court's own motion (para.23.11(2)). His Lordship said, at para.30, that the court should be slow to conclude that a practice consistent with the Civil Procedure Rules was precluded by the terms of this Act.

3. Since the Mental Health Act 1983 does not set out a complete code governing the making of orders displacing the nearest relative of a patient (for example, it does not mention interim orders), then the submission that the granting of permission to apply would necessarily be ultra vires s.30 is an incorrect one.

4. The order made by the court was proportionate.

*Binns* was applied in *R. (on the application of Holloway) v Oxfordshire County Council and others)* [2007] EWHC 776 (Admin); [2007] M.H.L.R. 225, where Beatson J. upheld an interim displacement order where the nearest relative had not been given notice of the proceedings. The conduct of the local authority in not giving notice was described, at para.33, as falling "far below what is required of a public authority in the exercise of its responsibilities to persons with mental illness and the nearest relatives of such person". His Lordship held that:

1. Order 49, r.12 did not assist the nearest relative as the words of that provision do not preclude an application being made without notice.

2. What the principles of natural justice require at the preliminary stage of a process is different from what they require where a binding decision is to be made.

3. Applications which are not determinative, such as applications for interim relief, are not subject to the guarantees set out in Art.6 of the European Convention on Human Rights unless they cause irreversible prejudice to a party's interests. An interim displacement does not fall into this category as there are sufficient safeguards in this Act for the patient and for his nearest relative.

4. An application for an interim order made without notice to the person affected should only be made where it is necessary to act urgently.

5. It is good practice for a judge hearing a without notice application to make enquiries as to whether it was practicable to have given notice to the nearest relative and to consider whether it would be possible to adjourn the hearing for such notice to be given. Those making the application should apprise the judge of all the relevant facts, including those that may be adverse to the application.

An applicant who makes a without notice application to the court has a duty to investigate the facts and to make a full and fair disclosure of all the crucial points for and against the application. It is no excuse for an applicant to say that he was not aware of the importance of matters he has omitted to state (*Marc Rich & Co v Krasner* [1999] EWCA Civ 581; also see *B Borough Council v S (By the Official Solicitor)* [2006] EWHC 2584 (Fam); [2007] 1 F.L.R. 1600 paras 37–42).

In *Surrey County Council Social Services v McMurray*, November 11, 1994, CA, Hale J., in dismissing an appeal by a nearest relative against an order that had been made under this section, said that "the displacement of a person as nearest relative in no way takes away his legitimate interest in the welfare of his daughter, which should always be paid proper respect by the authorities in making decisions about and arrangements for her care."

Section 30 gives the county court power to discharge or vary an order made under this section, and also specifies the duration of such an order, if the duration has not been established under subs.(5) of this section. An order made under this section does not expire on the transfer of the patient under s.19.

It is prima facie a contempt of court to publish information relating to proceedings brought under this section where the county court is sitting in private: see s.12 of the Administration of Justice Act 1960 and *Pickering v Liverpool Daily Post and Echo Newspapers Plc and others* [1991] 1 All E.R. 622 HL.

*Human Rights Act 1998*

**1–393**    In *R. (on the application of H) v Secretary of State for Health* [2005] UKHL 60; [2005] 4 All E.R. 1311, it was contended on behalf of the patient that this Act fails to comply with art.5(4) of the European Convention on Human Rights, which is designed to procure the speedy release of someone who should not in fact have been detained in the first place or should not be detained any longer, in that it does not provide a right of review at reasonable intervals for a patient who finds herself detained by virtue of s.29(4) and is thus deprived of the right which a patient newly detained under s.3 would have. The House of Lords held that as the system provided for by s.29(4) is *capable* of acting compatibly with art.5(4), it could not be said to be incompatible with art.5(4) although action or inaction by the authorities under it may be so. The preferable means of achieving compatibility is for the Secretary of State to use her power under s.67(1) to refer the case to the tribunal. As the Secretary of State is under a duty to act compatibly with the patient's Convention rights, she would be well advised to make such a reference as soon as the position is drawn to her attention by the patient's lawyers. Should the Secretary of State decline to exercise this power, judicial review would be swiftly available to oblige her to do so. It would also be possible for the hospital managers or the local social services authority to notify the Secretary of State whenever an application is made under s.29 so that she can consider the position. Although judicial review and/or habeas corpus may be one way of securing compliance, this would be much more satisfactorily achieved either through a speedy determination of the county court proceedings or by a Secretary of State's reference under s.67. Section 68, as substituted by the 2007 Act, requires the hospital managers to refer the case of a s.2 patient to the tribunal within six months of the patient's admission if no application or reference has been made during that period. Also see the *Code of Practice* at para.30.40.

*Applications to the First-tier Tribunal (Mental Health) or the Mental Health Review Tribunal for Wales*

**1–394**    A nearest relative who has been supplanted by an order made under subs.(3)(c) or (d) of this section can apply to a tribunal within 12 months or the order being made and during any subsequent 12 month period while the order is in force: see subs.(6) and s.66(1)(h),(2)(g). The acting nearest relative has a separate power to make an application.

*Code of Practice*

**1–395**    The displacement of the nearest relative is considered in Ch.8 at paras 8.5 to 8.23.

*Subsection (1)*

**1–396**    COUNTY COURT. For the procedure on an application to the county court, see s.31 and the Civil Procedure Rules 1998 (SI 1998/3132) Pt 8.1(6) and Practice Direction—Alternative Procedure for Claims, Section C, para.18.1 which are reproduced in Pt 3. The court has the power to make an interim order when considering an application: see the General Note to this section. Applications without notice are governed by the provisions of Pt 23.9 of the Civil Procedure Rules.

Jurisdiction under this section can only be exercised by a circuit judge (Practice Direction: Allocation of Cases to Levels of Judiciary, para.11.1).

MAY. The judge has a discretion as to whether or not to make an order displacing the nearest relative notwithstanding that one of the grounds set out in subs.(3) has been satisfied (*Barnet LBC v Robin*, above).

APPLICATION. Applications under this section "have to be dealt with quickly" (*R. (on the application of S) v Plymouth City Council*, above, per Hale L.J. at para.39). In *Derbyshire CC v Maude*, July 5, 1999, CA (unreported), Sedley L.J. described a delay of a year for an application to come to the county court as "at lowest, alarming".

PATIENT. An application cannot be made in respect of a person who is not suffering from mental disorder even if it is thought that the person would be likely to develop a mental disorder at some time in the future.

FUNCTIONS OF THE NEAREST RELATIVE. If the nearest relative has exercised the power under reg.24 of the 2004 Regulations to delegate his or her functions to another person, action under this section must be directed against the nearest relative and not the delegate. The nearest relative retains the power of discharge under s.23 during the currency of an application.

In *R. v Birmingham Mental Health Trust Ex p. Phillips* (CO/1501/95), May 25, 1995, Tucker J. refused applications for *habeas corpus* and judicial review that had been made in respect of a patient who had been detained under s.2 and whose nearest relative had been wrongly identified for the purposes of s.11(3). His Lordship held that an application that was subsequently made under this section to displace that relative was not invalildated by the mistake.

SECTIONS 66 AND 69. Which are concerned with applications to the First-tier Tribunal (Mental Health) or the Mental Health Review Tribunal for Wales.

EXERCISABLE BY THE PERSON SPECIFIED IN THE ORDER. See subs.(1A).

*Subsection (1A)*
If an order is made under this section, the patient's acting nearest will either be:  **1–397**

    (a) the person nominated in the application to perform the role if that person is willing to do so and the court considers that person to be suitable; or

    (b) otherwise, the person that the court specifies as being suitable to perform the role if that person is willing to do so.

The person appointed need not be either related to the patient or otherwise qualify as being the patient's nearest relative under s.26. With regard to (a), if the application is made by an AMHP, he or she should nominate someone who is acquainted with the patient to be the acting nearest relative if the application is successful: see para.8.18 of the *Code of Practice*. If a local social services authority is appointed as acting nearest relative, the authority must comply with its duties under s.116.

*Subsection (2)*
RELATIVE OF THE PATIENT. Is defined in s.26(1).  **1–398**

RESIDING. It is not necessary for the applicant to be ordinarily residing with the patient.

APPROVED MENTAL HEALTH PROFESSIONAL.   An AMHP applicant acts in a personal capacity and is not therefore bound to follow the advice of his or her managers. The AMHP should receive the legal advice and support that an employer would normally provide to any employee who is involved in legal proceedings by virtue of the nature of their employment.

*Subsection (3)*

**1–399**   MAY BE MADE.   There is no requirement to make an application in any of the situations specified in this provision.

THE FOLLOWING GROUNDS.   The list of grounds is exhaustive.

*Paragraph (a)*

**1–400**   AMHPs should consider acting on this ground if the patient is likely to be subject to the provisions of this Act for a lengthy period, or if a suitable person comes forward who is willing to perform the functions of the nearest relative.

*Paragraph (b)*

**1–401**   If an application is being made on the ground that the nearest relative is incapable of acting as nearest relative by reason of mental disorder, CPR Pt 21 applies and a litigation friend should be appointed if the individual lacks capacity within the terms of CPR r.21.1(2), that is a person who "lacks capacity within the meaning of the [Mental Capacity Act 2005]". Normally the Official Solicitor agrees to act as litigation friend and consents to the application on the basis of the medical evidence supplied. The Official Solicitor prefers the medical evidence to be provided by a doctor who will not be involved in the potential detention of the patient.

INCAPABLE.   This ground is only available if the person concerned is unable to perform the functions of nearest relative. It does not cover the situation of a nearest relative who exercises his or her functions in an irresponsible manner.

If an AMHP concludes that it is not practicable to consult with the patient's nearest relative under s.11(4) because of that person's mental incapacity, an application under s.3 can proceed without an application being made to the court under this provision.

*Paragraph (c)*

**1–402**   UNREASONABLY OBJECTS.   Both at the date of the application and at the date of hearing (*Lewis v Gibson*, above). In *W v L* [1974] Q.B. 711 the Court of Appeal held that the proper test for the county court to apply is an objective one: the court should ask what an objectively reasonable person would do in all the circumstances, and not ask whether the actual nearest relative involved in the case was behaving reasonably from his or her own subjective point of view. The court stated that this test is similar to the test in adoption cases in which the House of Lords have approved the following statement:

> "... in considering whether she is reasonable or unreasonable we must take into account the welfare of the child. A reasonable mother surely gives great weight to what is better for the child. Her anguish of mind is quite understandable: but still it may be unreasonable for her to withhold consent" (*Re W (An Infant)* [1971] 2 All E.R. 49 at 55 per Lord Hailsham L.C. citing Lord Denning M.R. in *Re L (An Infant)* (1962) 106 Sol. Jo. 611).

In *Re W* the court held that two reasonable parents can perfectly reasonably come to opposite conclusions on the same set of facts without forfeiting their title to be regarded as reasonable. The question before a court hearing an application under this provision is therefore whether a nearest relative's objection comes within the band of possible reasonable decisions and not whether it is right or mistaken. Lord Hailsham said in *Re W* at 56:

"Not every reasonable exercise of judgment is right, and not every mistaken exercise of judgment is unreasonable. There is a band of decisions within which no court should seek to replace the individuals judgment with his own."

In *Smirek v Williams* [2000] M.H.L.R. 38 CA Hale L.J. said that, in her view,

"it cannot possibly be outside that band of reasonable decisions for the [nearest relative] to agree with, and rely upon, a recent decision of a [tribunal] unless there has since been a change in the circumstances leading to that decision."

As the nearest relative is objecting to an application being made and as an AMHP applicant is required by s.13(1A) to consider "relevant circumstances", it would seem that a reasonable nearest relative is entitled to consider all the circumstances of the case and not just the medical evidence.

The obiter comment of Lawton L.J. in *B(A) v B(L) (Mental Health Patient)* [1980] 1 W.L.R. 116, CA, that "the judge must have some evidence that compulsory admission to hospital and detention is necessary" suggests that a court hearing an application under this paragraph should consider the merits for detaining the patient by reference to the statutory criteria before moving on to considering the reasonableness of the nearest relative's decision. The judge should not be concerned to establish whether the technical requirements of this Act relating to applications for detention or guardianship have been satisfied. In the words of Lawton L.J. at 121: "The object of an application under [this paragraph] is to enable the provisions of [s.3] to be brought into operation, and until an application has been dealt with under [this section the AMHP] is not in a position to make an application under [s.3]. It follows, so it seems to me, that if there were any defects for the purposes of [s.3] in the form of the reports tendered to the county court judge they were irrelevant for the purposes of . . . the application. The county court judge had to look at the reports for their medical content; he was not concerned with their statutory form."

*Paragraph (d)*

WITHOUT DUE REGARD. The test is an objective one (*Surrey County Council Social* **1–403** *Services v McMurray*, November 11, 1994, CA).

POWER TO DISCHARGE THE PATIENT. From detention, guardianship or supervised community treatment using the power contained in s.23. When considering an application under this paragraph the judge should consider not only the history of the matter but also the situation with which he is faced at the date of the hearing (*Lewis v Gibson*, above).

OR IS LIKELY TO DO SO. It is possible to make an application under this provision before the patient is made subject to the provisions of this Act.

*Paragraph (e)*

This paragraph, which addresses the incompatibility identified by the European **1–404** Commission of Human Rights in *JT v United Kingdom* (2000) 30 E.H.R.R. C.D. 77, provides an applicant with a right to apply to the county court for an order displacing his or her NR on the ground that the NR is unsuitable to act as such. It is considered in the *Code of Practice* at para.8.13. The Minister of State outlined what the Government had in mind in establishing this ground:

"We do not believe that a person is unsuitable to be the patient's NR simply because the patient may be upset with the NR over a trivial matter. We know that suffering with mental disorder is often a distressing and difficult time for the patient. In that environment there can be potential for disagreement between a patient who may not wish to go to hospital, for example, and the NR who reluctantly accepts that that is the best course of action. Such a disagreement should not in itself be grounds for removing important powers from the NR.

We have in mind situations where a NR's occupation of that role and its powers under the Act pose a real and present danger to the health or well-being of the patient. Where a NR has abused the patient, for instance, he should not be allowed to exercise the rights of the NR. It is not important how recently the abuse took place. If the patient or others who know or are close to the patient have a genuine fear that the abuse may be repeated – or even that a relationship with a formally abusive NR may cause the patient distress – we intend that such a person should be considered unsuitable to act as the NR of the patient. These applications will be heard, as they now are, in the county court. The court will not be asked to sit in judgment of any of the past actions or deeds of the NR. Their role will be to determine whether the NR is otherwise suitable to act as such.

The opinions and views of the patient will be very important and we fully expect that they will form part of the court's deliberations. However, we do not wish the court to feel that it is prevented from displacing a NR it deems unsuitable, even where the patient would wish that person to remain as their NR. I would instance cases where the victim of an abuser actually acts to protect the abuser, either out of fear of the abuser or through a form of identification with him. We do not wish the court to feel constrained in such circumstances in displacing a NR it finds unsuitable" (*Hansard,* HL Vol.688, col.672).

The Government also (a) confirmed that the term "suitable" is intended to "include, but not be so narrow as to be limited to, NRs who have a history of abusing or potential to abuse the patient" (*Hansard,* HL Vol.689, col.1404, per Baroness Royall), and (b) said that it "intends that a person is not suitable to be the NR where that person has no relationship with – and intends to have no further relationship with – the patient. In addition, it is intended that a person is not suitable to be the NR where the risk posed to the patient is by virtue of a third party and the NR exposes the patient to that risk" (The Government's response to the report of the Joint Committee on Human Rights, Department of Health, April 13, 2007, para.40).

The decision in *R. (on the application of E) v Bristol City Council* [2005] EWHC 74 (Admin); [2005] M.H.L.R. 83, where Bennett J. held that an applicant for the patient's detention is not placed under a duty to consult the patient's NR about the application if such consultation would be detrimental to the patient in that it would breach the patient's rights under art.8 of the European Convention on Human Rights, remains good law: see the note on s.11(4).

OTHERWISE.    An application under this ground should not be brought where the facts of the case would enable an application to be made under ground (b),(c) or (d).

*Subsection (4)*

**1–405**    This subsection provides that if the patient is detained for assessment and an application is made to the county court on ground (c) or (d) before the 28 days provided for in s.2 expire, the period for which the patient may be detained is extended until the application is finally disposed of and, if an order is made, for a further period of seven days to enable the formalities of a s.3 application to be complied with. The provisions of Pt II, including the power to grant the patient leave of absence under s.17, will continue to apply during the extended period. An authenticated copy of the application to the court should be placed with the patient's statutory documentation as this provides the hospital managers with continued authority for the patient's detention. If a patient who has had his or her detention extended by virtue of this provision has not applied to a tribunal within the first 14 days of the detention, there is no opportunity for the patient to make an application to the tribunal for the s.2 to be discharged even if the extended period is lengthy. Under s.68, the hospital managers must refer the patient to the tribunal six months after the patient's admission if no application or reference has been made during that period. For the action that should be taken in such a situation, see *R. (on the application of H) v Secretary of State for Health*, noted under "Human Rights Act 1998", above.

A fresh Mental Health Act assessment of the patient should be undertaken prior to the court hearing in order to determine whether the requirements of s.3 continue to be satisfied. It is lawful to make an application under s.3 before the proceedings under this section have been resolved (*R. (on the application of M) v Homerton University Hospital*, noted in the General Note above).

A nearest relative is not deprived of his or her power of discharge under s.23 during the period of the extended s.2. The patient's RC could prevent such a discharge taking effect if the provisions of s.25 apply. The hospital managers and the RC also retain their power of discharge during this period.

IMMEDIATELY BEFORE THE EXPIRATION OF THE PERIOD FOR WHICH A PATIENT IS LIABLE TO BE DETAINED.   Where a tribunal has ordered the discharge of the patient from s.2 and has exercised its power under s.72(3) to delay the discharge to a specified future date, the provisions of this subsection will apply if an application under this section is made to the County Court before that date (*Re W* [1999] M.H.L.R. 1).

PARAGRAPH (A); FINALLY DISPOSED OF.   The detention continues during the period for lodging an appeal, and if an appeal is lodged, the time taken to determine it.

If an application has been made under para.(c) and the nearest relative subsequently withdraws his or her objection, the application will be finally disposed of when it is formally withdrawn from the court by the applicant.

*Subsection (5)*

This subsection provides that an order made on the grounds specified in subs.(3)(a), (b) **1–406** or (e) may specify a period for which the order will remain in force, unless it is discharged. One example of a way in which a court might use this power would be to specify that the order should cease on the date when the eldest child of the patient reached 18, so that he or she could then take on the role of nearest relative. Further provision relating to the duration of orders made under these paragraphs is made in s.30(4B).

*Subsection (6)*

This subsection specifies the functions of an acting nearest relative. Apart from the **1–407** exceptions noted, the nearest relative's functions are exercisable by the acting nearest relative during the period of the appointment. It also provides that an order made under this section remains in force notwithstanding that the person who was the patient's nearest relative when the order was made is no longer his nearest relative, for example as a result of the death of that person. If the acting nearest relative dies, no-one can exercise the rights of the nearest relative unless the order is either discharged or varied under s.30.

SHALL NOT APPLY ... IN THE CASE MENTIONED IN PARAGRAPH (H).   See the note on *Applications to the First-tier Tribunal (Mental Health) or the Mental Health Review Tribunal for Wales*, above.

## Discharge and variation of orders under s.29

**30.**—(1) An order made under section 29 above in respect of a patient may be **1–408** discharged by the county court upon application made—

(a) in any case, by [the patient or] the person having the functions of the nearest relative of the patient by virtue of the order;

(b) where the order was made on the ground specified in paragraph (a) [, (b) or (e)] of section 29(3) above, or where the person who was the nearest relative of the patient when the order was made has ceased to be his nearest relative, on the application of the nearest relative of the patient.

[(1A) But, in the case of an order made on the ground specified in paragraph (e) of section 29(3) above, an application may not be made under subsection (1)(b) above by the person who was the nearest relative of the patient when the order was made except with leave of the county court.]

(2) An order made under section 29 above in respect of a patient may be varied by the county court, on the application of the person having the functions of the nearest relative by virtue of the order or on the application of [the patient or of] an [approved mental health professional], by substituting [another person for the person having those functions].

[(2A) If the court decides to vary an order on an application under subsection (2) above, the following rules have effect for the purposes of substituting another person—

    (a) if a person is nominated in the application to act as the patient's nearest relative and that person is, in the opinion of the court, a suitable person to act as such and is willing to do so, the court shall specify that person (or, if there are two or more such persons, such one of them as the court thinks fit);

    (b) otherwise, the court shall specify such person as is, in its opinion, a suitable person to act as the patient's nearest relative and is willing to do so.]

(3) If the person having the functions of the nearest relative of a patient by virtue of an order under section 29 above dies—

    (a) subsections (1) and (2) above shall apply as if for any reference to that person there were substituted a reference to any relative of the patient, and

    (b) until the order is discharged or varied under those provisions the functions of the nearest relative under this Part of this Act and sections 66 and 69 below shall not be exercisable by any person.

(4) [An order made on the ground specified in paragraph (c) or (d) of section 29(3) above shall, unless previously discharged under subsection (1) above, cease to have effect as follows]—

[(a) if—

    (i) on the date of the order the patient was liable to be detained or subject to guardianship by virtue of a relevant application, order or direction; or

    (ii) he becomes so liable or subject within the period of three months beginning with that date; or

    (iii) he was a community patient on the date of the order,

it shall cease to have effect when he is discharged under section 23 above or 72 below or the relevant application, order or direction otherwise ceases to have effect (except as a result of his being transferred in pursuance of regulations under section 19 above);

    (b) otherwise, it shall cease to have effect at the end of the period of three months beginning with the date of the order.]

[(4A) In subsection (4) above, reference to a relevant application, order or direction is to any of the following—

    (a) an application for admission for treatment;

    (b) a guardianship application;

    (c) an order or direction under Part 3 of this Act (other than under section 35, 36 or 38).]

[(4B) An order made on the ground specified in paragraph (a), (b) or (e) of section 29(3) above shall—

204

(a) if a period was specified under section 29(5) above, cease to have effect on expiry of that period, unless previously discharged under subsection (1) above;

(b) if no such period was specified, remain in force until it is discharged under subsection (1) above.]

(5) The discharge or variation under this section of an order made under section 29 above shall not affect the validity of anything previously done in pursuance of the order.

AMENDMENTS

The amendments to this section were made by the Mental Health Act 2007 ss.21, 24, 32(4), Sch.2 para.7, Sch.3 para.14.

DEFINITIONS

    patient: s.145(1).  **1–409**

    nearest relative: ss.26(3), 145(1).

    approved mental health professional: s.145(1), (1AC).

    application for admission for treatment: ss.3, 145(1).

    community patient: ss.17A(7), 145(1).

GENERAL NOTE

This section provides for the discharge or variation of an order made by a county court **1–410** under s.29 for the appointment of an acting nearest relative. It also, in subss.(4), (4A) and (4B), specifies the duration of an order.

*Subsection (1)*

PARAGRAPH (A), (B) OR (E). A nearest relative who has been displaced under s.29(3)(e) **1–411** cannot make an application for the order to be discharged without leave of the county court (subs.(1A)). A nearest relative who is displaced under s.29(3)(c) or (d) cannot apply for the order to be discharged.

*Subsection (2)*

This subsection provides for an application to be made to the county court for the vari- **1–412** ation of the order appointing the acting nearest relative.

*Subsection (3)*

If the person appointed as acting nearest relative dies, this subsection provides that (a) **1–413** any applications that could have been made by that person under subss.(1) and (2) can be made by any relative of the patient, and (b) no one can exercise the functions of nearest relative until the order that appointed the acting nearest relative is discharged or varied.

*Subsections (4), (4A)*

These subsections determine when an order appointing an acting nearest relative has **1–414** been made on the grounds specified in s.29(3)(c) or (d) ceases to have effect. Their effect is that the order will either expire: (i) after three months; or (ii) if the patient was detained or subject to guardianship at the time of the order, or within three months of it, at the time when the application, order or direction authorising the patient's detention or guardianship is either discharged or otherwise ceases to have effect. The order will not end if the patient is placed on a community treatment order or is made subject to a transfer under s.19. An application can be made under subs.(1) to discharge the order.

*Subsection (4B)*

This subsection determines when an order appointing an acting nearest relative has been **1–415** made on the grounds specified in s.29(3)(a), (b) or (e) ceases to have effect. Its effect is that the order will either last for the period stated in it (if any) or will last indefinitely. In both cases, the order will end if it is discharged under subs.(1).

*Supplemental*

**Procedure on applications to county court**

**1–416**    **31.** County court rules which relate to applications authorised by this Part of this Act to be made to a county court may make provision—

(a) for the hearing and determination of such applications otherwise than in open court;

(b) for the admission on the hearing of such applications of evidence of such descriptions as may be specified in the rules notwithstanding anything to the contrary in any enactment or rule of law relating to the admissibility of evidence:

(c) for the visiting and interviewing of patients in private by or under the directions of the court.

DEFINITION

**1–417**    patient: s.145(1).

GENERAL NOTE

**1–418**    This section is applied to patients who have been placed under hospital or guardianship orders by a court under s.37, (Sch.1 Pt I para.1).

COUNTY COURT RULES.    The reference to the "County court rules" is out of date. Now see the Civil Procedure Rules 1998 (SI 1998/3132) Pt 8.1(6) and Practice Direction— Alternative Procedure for Claims, Section C, para.18.1 which are reproduced in Pt 3.

OTHERWISE THAN IN OPEN COURT.    The publication of information relating to proceedings brought under this Act before a county court sitting in private is prima facie a contempt of court: see s.12 of the Administration of Justice Act 1960 and *Pickering v Liverpool Daily Post and Echo Newspapers Plc* [1991] 1 All E.R. 622 HL.

**Regulations for purposes of Part II**

**1–419**    **32.**—(1) The Secretary of State may make regulations for prescribing anything which, under this Part of this Act, is required or authorised to be prescribed, and otherwise for carrying this Part of this Act into full effect.

(2) Regulations under this section may in particular make provision—

(a) for prescribing the form of any application, recommendation, report, order, notice or other document to be made or given under this Part of this Act;

(b) for prescribing the manner in which any such application, recommendation, report, order, notice or other document may be proved, and for regulating the service of any such application, report, order or notice;

(c) for requiring [such bodies as may be prescribed by the regulations] to keep such registers or other records as may be [so prescribed] in respect of patients liable to be detained or subject to guardianship [. . .] under supervision] under this Part of this Act [or community patients], and to furnish or make available to those patients, and their relatives, such written statements of their rights and powers under this Act as may be so prescribed;

(d) for the determination in accordance with the regulations of the age of any person whose exact age cannot be ascertained by reference to the registers kept under the Births and Deaths Registration Act 1953; and

(e) for enabling the functions under this Part of this Act of the nearest relative of a patient to be performed, in such circumstances and subject to such conditions (if any) as may be prescribed by the regulations, by any person authorised in that behalf by that relative;

and for the purposes of this Part of this Act any application, report or notice the service of which is regulated under paragraph (b) above shall be deemed to have been received by or furnished to the authority or person to whom it is authorised or required to be furnished, addressed or given if it is duly served in accordance with the regulations.

(3) Without prejudice to subsections (1) and (2) above, but subject to section 23(4) [and (6)] above, regulations under this section may determine the manner in which functions under this Part of this Act of the managers of hospitals, local social services authorities, [[Local Health Board], Special Health Authorities[, Primary Care Trusts][, National Health Service trusts or NHS foundation trusts] are to be exercised, and such regulations may in particular specify the circumstances in which, and the conditions subject to which, any such functions may be performed by officers of or other persons acting on behalf of those managers[, boards,] and [authorities and trusts].

AMENDMENTS

The amendments to this section were made by the Health Authorities Act 1995 s.2(1), Sch.1 para.107(4), the Mental Health (Patients in the Community) Act 1995 s.2(1), Sch.1 para.2, the Health Act 1999 (Supplementary, Consequential, etc. Provisions) Order 2000 (SI 2000/90) Sch.1 para.16(6), the NHS and Community Care Act 1990 s.66(1), Sch.9 para.24(5), the Health and Social Care (Community Health and Standards) Act 2003 s.34, Sch.4 para.55, the Mental Health Act 2007 ss.32(4), 45(2), 55, Sch.3 para.15, Sch.11 Pt 5 and SI 2007/961 art.3, Sch. para.13(7).

DEFINITIONS

    community patient: ss.17A(7), 145(1).                     **1–420**
    the managers: s.145(1).
    hospital: ss.34(2), 145(1).
    local social services authority: s.145(1).
    patient: s.145(1).
    nearest relative: ss.26(3), 145(1).
    Health Authority: s.145(1).
    Special Health Authority: s.145(1).

GENERAL NOTE

This section applies to patients who have been placed under hospital, restriction or guardianship orders by a court under ss.37 or 41 (Sch.1 Pt I para.1, Pt II para.1).

*Subsection (1)*

SECRETARY OF STATE. The functions of the Minister, so far as exercisable in relation to **1–421** Wales, are exercised by the Welsh Ministers (see the General Note to this Act and (SI 1999/ 672 art.2, Sch.1).

**Special provisions as to wards of court**

1–422    **33.**—(1) An application for the admission to hospital of a minor who is a ward of court may be made under this Part of this Act with the leave of the court; and section 11(4) above shall not apply in relation to an application so made.

(2) Where a minor who is a ward of court is liable to be detained in a hospital by virtue of an application for admission under this Part of this Act [or is a community patient], any power exercisable under this Part of this Act or under section 66 below in relation to the patient by his nearest relative shall be exercisable by or with the leave of the court.

(3) Nothing in this Part of this Act shall be construed as authorising the making of a guardianship application in respect of a minor who is a ward of court, or the transfer into guardianship of any such minor.

[(4) Where a community treatment order has been made in respect of a minor who is a ward of court, the provisions of this Part of this Act relating to community treatment orders and community patients have effect in relation to the minor subject to any order which the court makes in the exercise of its wardship jurisdiction; but this does not apply as regards any period when the minor is recalled to hospital under section 17E above.]

AMENDMENT
    The words in square brackets in subs.(2) were inserted, and subs.(4) was substituted by the Mental Health Act 2007 s.32(4), Sch.3 para.16.

DEFINITIONS
1–423    hospital: ss.34(2), 145(1).
    nearest relative: ss.26(3), 145(1).
    community patient: ss.17A(7), 145(1).
    community treatment order: ss.17A(7), 145(1).

GENERAL NOTE
1–424    This section provides that the leave of the court must be obtained before a ward of court can be compulsorily detained in hospital (subs.(1)), and before the ward's nearest relative exercises his or her powers (subs.(2)). It also prohibits the reception or transfer of a ward of court into guardianship (subs.(3)) and makes any power or duty exercisable in respect of a ward who is subject to a community treatment order subject to the wardship court's jurisdiction (apart from a period when the child has been recalled to hospital) (subs.(4)).

*Subsection (1)*
1–425    SECTION 11(4) . . . SHALL NOT APPLY.    An AMHP is not required to consult the nearest relative about an application to admit a ward of court under s.3 nor may the nearest relative block the application by objecting to it.

**Interpretation of Part II**
1–426    **34.**—(1) In this Part of this Act—
    ["the appropriate practitioner" means—
        (a) in the case of a patient who is subject to the guardianship of a person other than a local social services authority, the nominated medical attendant of the patient; and
        (b) in any other case, the responsible clinician;]
    [. . .]
    "the nominated medical attendant", in relation to a patient who is subject to the guardianship of a person other than a local social services authority, means

the person appointed in pursuance of regulations made under section 9(2) above to act as the medical attendant of the patient;

["registered establishment" means an establishment which would not, apart from subsection (2) below, be a hospital for the purposes of this Part and which—

(a) in England, is a hospital as defined by section 275 of the National Health Service Act 2006 that is used for the carrying on of a regulated activity, within the meaning of Part 1 of the Health and Social Care Act 2008, which relates to the assessment or medical treatment of mental disorder and in respect of which a person is registered under Chapter 2 of that Part; and

(b) in Wales, is an establishment in respect of which a person is registered under Part 2 of the Care Standards Act 2000 as an independent hospital in which treatment or nursing (or both) are provided for persons liable to be detained under this Act;]

["the responsible clinician" means—

(a) in relation to a patient liable to be detained by virtue of an application for admission for assessment or an application for admission for treatment, or a community patient, the approved clinician with overall responsibility for the patient's case;

(b) in relation to a patient subject to guardianship, the approved clinician authorised by the responsible local social services authority to act (either generally or in any particular case or for any particular purpose) as the responsible clinician;]

[. . .]

[(1A) [. . .]

(2) Except where otherwise expressly provided, this Part of this Act applies in relation to [a registered establishment], as it applies in relation to a hospital, and references in this Part of this Act to a hospital, and any reference in this Act to a hospital to which this Part of this Act applies, shall be construed accordingly.

(3) In relation to a patient who is subject to guardianship in pursuance of a guardianship application, any reference in this Part of this Act to the responsible local social services authority is a reference—

(a) where the patient is subject to the guardianship of a local social services authority, to that authority;

(b) where the patient is subject to the guardianship of a person other than a local social services authority, to the local social services authority for the area in which that person resides.

AMENDMENT

The words in square brackets in subs.(2) were substituted, by the Care Standards Act 2000 s.116, Sch.4 para.9(4). The definition of "registered establishment was substituted by SI 2010/813, art.5(3). The definition of "appropriate practitioner" was inserted, and the definition of "responsible clinician" was substituted for the definition of responsible medical officer by the Mental Health Act 2007 s.9(9),(10). The words omitted were repealed by s.55 Sch.11 Pt 5.

DEFINITIONS

patient: s.145(1).                                                                  **1–427**

local social services authority: s.145(1).

application for admission for assessment: ss.2, 145(1).

application for admission for treatment: ss.3, 145(1).
hospital: s.145(1).

GENERAL NOTE

**1–428**     This section applies to patients who have been placed under hospital or guardianship orders made by a court under s.37, (Sch.1 Pt I para.1) and to restricted patients with the modification that in subs.(1) the definition of "the nominated medical attendant" and subs.(3) shall be omitted (Sch.1 Pt II paras 2, 8).

*Human Rights Act 1998*

**1–429**     The appropriate practitioner, the nominated medical attendant and the responsible clinician (RC) are exercising "functions of a public nature" and are therefore public authorities for the purposes of s.6 of the 1998 Act (s.6(3)(b)). Decisions made by a private hospital relating to the care or treatment of detained patients are decisions of a public nature. The hospital therefore becomes a public authority for the purposes of s.6 and its decisions are susceptible to judicial review (*R. (on the application of A) v Partnership in Care Ltd* [2002] EWHC 529; [2002] 1 W.L.R. 261).

*Subsection (1)*

**1–430**     THE NOMINATED MEDICAL ATTENDANT.     Is appointed by a private guardian under reg.22(a) of the English Regulations and reg.11(a) of the Welsh Regulations.

REGISTERED ESTABLISHMENT.     See the note on "Human Rights Act", above.

RESPONSIBLE CLINICIAN.     Who must be an approved clinician (AC). It follows that if a patient is detained in a general hospital where he or she is receiving treatment for a physical disorder, an AC from a mental health facility should be involved in the patient's case to take responsibility for the treatment of the patient's mental disorder as such treatment must be given by or under the direction of an AC (s.63). Although the responsibilities of the RC are not delegable, "the role may be occupied on a temporary basis in the absence of the usual [RC]" (Reference Guide, para.12.38). Hospitals should therefore have protocols to "ensure that cover arrangements are in place when the responsible clinician is not available (e.g. during nonworking hours, annual leave etc)" (*Code of Practice*, para.14.3). Any AC can be the temporary RC, irrespective of status. Determining the clinician who has "overall responsibility" for the patient is a question of fact. The RC should be the "available approved clinician with the most appropriate expertise to meet the patient's main assessment and treatment needs" (*Code of Practice*, para.14.3). The Reference Guide states, at para.12.37:

> "Having overall responsibility for the patient's case does not mean that the responsible clinician must personally supervise all the medical treatment provided to the patient under the Act. Indeed, because they may come from a number of different professions, responsible clinicians may not be professionally qualified to take personal responsibility for each particular type of treatment their patient is receiving".

Any dispute about the identification the RC of a detained or community patient would need to be resolved by the hospital management. Guidance on allocating a RC is contained in Ch.14 of the *Code of Practice*. Subsequent to a patient being granted leave of absence under s.17 or being made subject to a community treatment order, the responsibilities of the RC could be transferred to a community based AC. A patient has no right to determine the identity of his or her RC.

The powers given to the RC under this Act do not enable that doctor to require the Health Authority to give priority to the care of a detained patient (*R. (on the application of F) v Oxfordshire Mental Healthcare NHS Trust and Oxfordshire NHS Health Authority* [2001] EWHC Admin. 535; [2001] M.H.L.R 140). Sullivan J. said at paras 64, 66:

"Treatment is provided to all patients in the real world where the availability of facilities is constrained by resources. By way of example, the [RC] may well consider that it would be beneficial for a particular Part II or Part III patient if he/she was given better facilities whilst in hospital: more privacy, more spacious accommodation, access to particular therapy, more attention by the nursing staff, etc. There is nothing in the 1983 Act to suggest that the Health Authority must then provide those facilities. In so far as the 1983 Act confers additional powers on the [RCs], it does so *vis-à-vis* the [RC's] patient, not the Health Authority . . . In simple terms, since resources are limited, there is bound to be a queue of patients seeking treatment. I do not accept the proposition that the [RC's] position under the 1983 Act is such as to propel his or her Part II or III patients to the head of the queue".

In *R. (on the application of K) v West London Mental Health NHS Trust* [2006] EWCA Civ 118, which is noted in the General Note to s.17, the Court of Appeal held that *F* was correctly decided.

Although it will normally be the patient's RC who will decide whether a patient can be interviewed and under what conditions, he or she cannot be the final arbiter when issues arise in relation to national security. The detaining hospital can therefore impose conditions relating to security concerns which the RC may consider to be unnecessary (*R (on the application of A and others) v Home Secretary* [2003] EWCA 2846 (Admin); [2004] M.H.L.R. 98 para.26).

The RC of a guardianship patient does not have "overall responsibility for the patient's case". If a guardianship patient:

"happens to be living, or receiving medical treatment for mental disorder, in Wales, the LSSA may appoint a person who is approved by the Welsh Ministers as an approved clinician in Wales, even if that person is not also approved as an approved clinician in England. Otherwise, the responsible clinician must be approved as an approved clinician in England" (Reference Guide, para.19.75; also see the Mental Health (Mutual Recognition) Regulations 2008 which are reproduced in Part 2).

*Subsection (3)*
RESPONSIBLE LOCAL SOCIAL SERVICES AUTHORITY.   Renewal reports must be addressed **1–431** to this authority which has the power to discharge the patient from guardianship by virtue of s.23(2)(b).

RESIDES.   Temporary absences from the place where a person lives does not affect residence, as long as there is an intention to return (*R. v St Leonard's Shoreditch (Inhabitants)* (1865) L.R. 1 Q.B. 21). Also note Widgery L.J.'s statement that "A man cannot be said to reside in a particular place unless in the ordinary sense of the word one can say that for the time being he is making his home in that place" (*Fox v Stirk* [1970] 1 Q.B. 463 477).

# PART III

## PATIENTS CONCERNED IN CRIMINAL PROCEEDINGS OR UNDER SENTENCE

GENERAL NOTE
This Part deals with the circumstances in which patients may be admitted to and detained **1–432** in hospital or received into guardianship on the order of a court, or may be transferred to hospital or guardianship from penal institutions on the direction of the Secretary of State for Justice.

Home Office Circular No.66/90 (as supplemented by Home Office Circular No. 12/95) draws the attention of the courts and those services responsible for dealing with mentally disordered people who come into contact with the criminal justice system to the legal powers that exist and to the desirability of ensuring effective co-operation between agencies. Phil Fennell examines the recommendations contained in this circular and considers some of the issues involved in diverting mentally disordered offenders from the penal system in "Diversion of Mentally Disordered Offenders from Custody" [1991] Crim.L.R. 333–348.

*Secretary of State for Justice*

**1–433**    The functions of the Secretary of State with regard to the management of restricted patients are undertaken on his behalf by the:
Mental Health Casework Section
Ministry of Justice
2nd Floor
Fry Building
2 Marsham Street
London
SW1P 4DF
Tel: 020 3334 3555
In cases of emergency outside office hours: 020 7035 4848 and choose option 5. This is the switchboard of the Home Office.

Relevant guidance can be accessed at: *www.justice.gov.uk/guidance/mentally-disordered-offenders.htm*

*The functions of the Secretary of State for Justice in relation to Wales*

**1–434**    Through inadvertence, the functions of the Home Secretary (now the Secretary of State for Justice) under this Part, in so far as they are exercisable in relation to Wales, were transferred to the National Assembly for Wales under the National Assembly for Wales (Transfer of Functions) Order 1999 (SI 1999/672) art.2 Sch.1. These functions (subject to a number of exceptions that are noted in the appropriate sections) were transferred back to the Home Secretary by a means of a variation to the Order by the National Assembly of Wales (Transfer of Functions) Order 2000 (SI 2000/253) art.4 Sch.3. The period between the two transfer orders was covered by arrangements being put in place under s.41 of the Government of Wales Act 1998 enabling Home Office officials to exercise the functions on behalf of the Assembly.

*Mentally Disordered Offenders*

**1–435**    In any case where the offender is or appears to be mentally disordered, the court must obtain and consider a medical report on the offender's mental condition by a doctor approved under s.12 before passing a custodial sentence other than one fixed by law, unless the court considers this unnecessary in the circumstances. There is also a general requirement for the court to consider—

(a)    any information before it which relates to his mental condition (whether given in a medical report, a pre-sentence report or otherwise), and

(b)    the likely effect of such a sentence on that condition and on any treatment which may be available for it (Criminal Justice Act 2003, s.157).

*Defective Court Orders*

**1–436**    The concepts of voidness and voidability have no application to an order made by a superior court of record or an order made by a court of unlimited jurisdiction. The Crown Court is a superior court of record (Courts Act 1971 s.4(1)). An order made under this Act in excess of jurisdiction is irregular and can, on such ground, be set aside. Until it has been set aside it is effective and must be obeyed (*South West Yorkshire Mental Health NHS Trust v Bradford Crown Court* [2003] EWHC Admin 640; [2004]

M.H.L.R. 137). The appropriate remedy in such a case is by way of judicial review: see *R. (on the application of A) v Harrow Crown Court* [2003] EWHC 2020 (Admin), where the court held that the detention of a patient on the authority of an order mistakenly made by the Crown Court does not involve a violation of the patients rights under art.5 of the European Convention on Human Rights. If the order announced by the judge is within the court's jurisdiction but an incorrect order is subsequently signed by the court clerk, a fresh order can be signed to correct the error.

A challenge to an order made by a magistrates' court should be made by either an appeal under s.108 of the Magistrates Court Act 1980 or to the High Court by way of case stated. In the absence of special circumstances, where there is a choice between the case stated procedure and judicial review, the former is the appropriate route of challenge. After the documents have been carefully checked, s.40(1) provides hospital managers with sufficient authority to admit the patient (*R. (on the application of LS) v Brent Magistrates' Court*, unreported, July 14, 2009).

In *Mooren v Germany* (app.no.11364/03), July 9, 2009, the European Court of Human Rights held that defects in a detention order did not necessarily render the underlying detention unlawful for the purposes of art.5(1) of the European Convention on Human Rights, unless they amounted to "a gross and obvious irregularity".

### Criminal Procedure (Insanity) Act 1964

The Criminal Procedure (Insanity) Act 1964, as amended by the Criminal Procedure **1–437** (Insanity and Unfitness to Plead) Act 1991 and the Domestic Violence, Crime and Victims Act 2004, makes provision for persons who are found unfit to be tried, or not guilty by reason of insanity, in respect of criminal charges. Section 24 of the 2004 Act, which came into force on March 31, 2005, replaces s.5 of the 1964 Act with new ss.5 and 5A. New s.5 sets out new disposal options for the court to deal with such persons; s.5A sets out further provisions in respect of these options. The court now has three disposal options: to make a hospital order under s.37 of the 1983 Act, which can be accompanied by a restriction order under s.41; to make a supervision order; or to order the absolute discharge of the accused. There are also new provisions relating to appeals. Details are set out in Home Office Circular 24/2005.

### Mental Health Treatment Requirements (MHTR) under the Criminal Justice Act 2003

The MHTR, which was introduced by s.207 of the 2003 Act, is one of twelve options **1–438** available to courts when constructing a community sentence. Paragraphs 531 and 532 of the Explanatory Notes to the 2003 Act describe the effect of s.207:

"*Subsection (1)* provides for the court to direct an offender to undergo mental health treatment for certain period(s) as part of a community sentence or suspended sentence order, under the treatment of registered medical practitioner or chartered psychologist. *Subsection (2)* provides that treatment may be provided in an independent hospital or care home (within the meaning of the Care Standards Act 2000) or a hospital (within the meaning of the Mental Health Act 1983), or as a non-resident patient at a place specified in the order, or as treatment under the direction of such registered medical practitioner or chartered psychologist as specified in the order. Under *subsection (3)*, before including a mental health treatment requirement, the court must be satisfied that the mental condition of the offender requires treatment and may be helped by treatment, but is not such that it warrants making a hospital or guardianship order (within the meaning of the Mental Health Act 1983). The court must also be satisfied that arrangements can be made for the offender to receive treatment as specified in the order, and the offender's consent must be obtained before imposing the requirement.

Under *subsection (4)*, the offender's responsible officer will supervise him only to the extent necessary for revoking or amending the order. *Subsection (5)* applies section 54(2) and (3) of the Mental Health Act 1983 for the purposes of the section. *Subsection (6)* defines 'chartered psychologist'."

Section 208 of the 2003 Act allows the medical practitioner or chartered psychologist to decide that treatment would be better or more convenient in a different place from that specified in the order and make arrangements to change the place of treatment. The change cannot be made without the consent of the offender.

*DNA Profiling*

**1–439**    The Criminal Evidence (Amendment) Act 1997, which came into force on March 19, 1997, enables the police to take non-intimate samples without consent, for DNA profiling purposes, from persons who were convicted before April 10, 1995 of one of the offences listed in Sch.1 to the Act (broadly sex, violent and burglary offences) and who are serving a sentence of imprisonment, or are detained under Pt III of this Act, in respect of such an offence at the time when it is sought to take a sample. The Act also enables non-intimate samples to be taken without consent from persons detained under this Part who have been acquitted on grounds of insanity or found unfit to plead. Guidance on the Act is contained in Home Office Circular 27/1997.

*The Registration of Sex Offenders*

**1–440**    The Sex Offenders Act 1997, which came into force on September 1, 1997, imposes requirements on sex offenders, including those under 18, to notify the police of their name and address and of any subsequent changes of these. The purpose is to ensure that information on sex offenders contained within the Police National Computer is fully up to date. The Act applies to people who are subject to detention in hospital or guardianship under this Part following conviction or cautioning for a relevant offence. Guidance to hospital managers and local authority social services departments on the Act is contained in Local Authority Social Services Letter LASSL (97) 17/HSG (97) 37.

*The Multi-Agency Public Protection Arrangements*

**1–441**    The multi-agency public protection arrangements ("MAPA") grew out of the closer working relationships which developed between the police and probation (and latterly other agencies) in the late 1990s. The purpose of MAPA is to minimise the risk to the public posed by those who may reoffend, either violently or sexually. Sections 67 and 68 of the Criminal Justice and Court Services Act 2000 first placed those arrangements on a statutory footing. Sections 325 to 327 of the Criminal Justice Act 2003 re-enacted and strengthened those provisions. Essentially, the legislation requires the police, prison and probation services, acting as the "Responsible Authority" in each of the 42 administrative areas of England and Wales:

(i)    to establish arrangements for assessing and managing the risks posed by sexual and violent offenders;

(ii)    to review and monitor the arrangements; and, as part of the reviewing and monitoring arrangements; and

(iii)    to prepare and publish an annual report on their operations.

There are principally three categories of offender who fall within the MAPA, and each category could include offenders who have been made subject to a hospital or guardianship order under this Part:

(i)    sex offenders who are required to register under the Sex Offenders Act 1997;

(ii)    violent offenders and those sexual offenders who are not required to register; and

(iii)    any other offender who, because of the offences committed by them are considered to pose a risk of serious harm to the public.

Section 325 of the 2003 Act imposes a "duty to co-operate" with the MAPA Responsible Authority upon a number of bodies including councils with social services responsibilities and NHS bodies. This duty is defined in terms which require the bodies upon which it is imposed to co-operate to the extent that such co-operation is compatible with those bodies' existing statutory functions.

A summary of what the MAPA are and an outline of the nature of the "duty to co-operate" is contained in Department of Health Letter LASSL (2004)3. Guidance on the MAPA is contained in "Guidance on Part 2 of the Sexual Offences Act 2003", Home Office, 2004, at pp.63–67. The Royal College of Psychiatrists has published "Psychiatrists and Multi-Agency Public Protection Arrangements" (2005).

*Code of Practice*
Guidance on this Part is contained in Ch.33.                                        **1–442**

## Remands to hospital

### Remand to hospital for report on accused's mental condition

**35.**—(1) Subject to the provisions of this section, the Crown Court or a magis-  **1–443**
trates' court may remand an accused person to a hospital specified by the court for a report on his mental condition.

(2) For the purposes of this section an accused person is—

(a) in relation to the Crown Court, any person who is awaiting trial before the court for an offence punishable with imprisonment or who has been arraigned before the court for such an offence and has not yet been sentenced or otherwise dealt with for the offence on which he has been arraigned;

(b) in relation to a magistrates' court, any person who has been convicted by the court of an offence punishable on summary conviction with imprisonment and any person charged with such an offence if the court is satisfied that he did the act or made the omission charged or he has consented to the exercise by the court of the powers conferred by this section.

(3) Subject to subsection (4) below, the powers conferred by this section may be exercised if—

(a) the court is satisfied, on the written or oral evidence of a registered medical practitioner, that there is reason to suspect that the accused person is suffering from [mental disorder]; and

(b) the court is of the opinion that it would be impracticable for a report on his mental condition to be made if he were remanded on bail;

but those powers shall not be exercised by the Crown Court in respect of a person who has been convicted before the court if the sentence for the offence of which he has been convicted is fixed by law.

(4) The court shall not remand an accused person to a hospital under this section unless satisfied, on the written or oral evidence of the [approved clinician] who would be responsible for making the report or of some other person representing the managers of the hospital, that arrangements have been made for his admission to that hospital and for his admission to it within the period of seven days beginning with the date of the remand; and if the court is so satisfied it may, pending his admission, give directions for his conveyance to and detention in a place of safety.

(5) Where a court has remanded an accused person under this section it may further remand him if it appears to the court, on the written or oral evidence of the [approved clinician] responsible for making the report, that a further remand

is necessary for completing the assessment of the accused person's mental condition.

(6) The power of further remanding an accused person under this section may be exercised by the court without his being brought before the court if he is represented by [an authorised person who] is given an opportunity of being heard.

(7) An accused person shall not be remanded or further remanded under this section for more than 28 days at a time or for more than 12 weeks in all; and the court may at any time terminate the remand if it appears to the court that it is appropriate to do so.

(8) An accused person remanded to hospital under this section shall be entitled to obtain at his own expense an independent report on his mental condition from a registered medical practitioner [or approved clinician] chosen by him and to apply to the court on the basis of it for his remand to be terminated under subsection (7) above.

(9) Where an accused person is remanded under this section—

(a) a constable or any other person directed to do so by the court shall convey the accused person to the hospital specified by the court within the period mentioned in subsection (4) above; and

(b) the managers of the hospital shall admit him within that period and thereafter detain him in accordance with the provisions of this section.

(10) If an accused person absconds from a hospital to which he has been remanded under this section, or while being conveyed to or from that hospital, he may be arrested without warrant by any constable and shall, after being arrested, be brought as soon as practicable before the court that remanded him; and the court may thereupon terminate the remand and deal with him in any way in which it could have dealt with him if he has not been remanded under this section.

AMENDMENTS

The words in square brackets in subs.(3)(a) were substituted by the Mental Health Act 2007 s.1(4), Sch.1 para.5. The references to approved clinicians were substituted and inserted by ibid., s.10(2). The words in square brackets in subs.(6) were substituted by the Legal Services Act 2007, s.208, Sch.21, para.54.

DEFINITIONS

hospital: ss.55(5), 145(1).
mental disorder: ss.1, 145(1).
approved clinician: s.145(1).
the managers: s.145(1).
place of safety: s.55(1).
authorised person: s.55(1).

GENERAL NOTE

**1–444** This section gives effect to the recommendation of the Butler Committee that courts should have the option of remanding an accused person to hospital for the preparation of a report on his mental condition. Magistrates' courts and the Crown Court have this power if they are satisfied, on medical evidence, that there is reason to suspect that the accused person (subs.(2)) is suffering from mental disorder and that it would be impracticable for a report on his mental condition to be made if he were remanded on bail (subs.(3)). The remand, which can last for a maximum of 12 weeks (subss.(7)), cannot be made unless the court is also satisfied, on hearing evidence from an Approved Clinician, that arrangements have been made for the accused's admission to hospital (subs.(4)). If the accused person either absconds from the hospital to which he has been remanded, or absconds while being conveyed to and from that hospital, he may be arrested and brought back before the court that remanded him (subs.(10)). The court may terminate the remand at any time. A remand under this section:

"does not automatically affect any existing liability for detention for assessment or treatment on any other basis, nor bring supervised community treatment or guardianship to an end. But nor does it prevent them expiring or being discharged in the normal way" (Reference Guide, para.3.23).

In *R. v The Calder Magistrates' Court Ex p. Grant*, May 11, 1998, Richards J. expressed the following "preliminary views" on the scope of this section:

"To my mind, section 35 of the 1983 Act does not appear to be limited to a case where guilt has been established or admitted. There is, to my mind, a broader power to remand a person to the hospital provided that that person consents to the remand. The purpose for which that power may be exercised would appear on the face of it to go beyond the preparation of a report for sentencing. I am not prepared to say how much wider than that the purposes may go.

But since I have formed that view in relation to section 35(1) it does seem to me that there would be cause for concern if the magistrates were advised that the section simply has no application at all prior to or otherwise in connection with sentencing. Subject to the consent of the person charged and, of course, the other relevant conditions being fulfilled, there does appear to be a discretion to be exercised by the court. No doubt those appearing for the accused will put forward in an appropriate case reasons why they submit there would be utility in exercising that discretion and obtaining a report in advance of establishing guilt or sentencing. One of the matters suggested in the papers before me which I mention solely by way of example is that a person's mental state may effect whether he is fit to plead or indeed whether the prosecution feel it is in the public interest to proceed with the case.

Accordingly, on the face of it, the possibility of obtaining a report for purposes other than sentencing does exist and should in an appropriate case be considered."

The effect of subss.(3) and (4) of this section:

"is expected to be that the initiative for a remand to hospital will generally come either from the defendant's legal representative (who may already have taken steps to obtain the necessary evidence from an approved [clinician] before suggesting to the court that remand to hospital might be appropriate) or from the medical officer of the prison to which the defendant has been remanded in custody at an earlier court appearance. Prison medical officers are being asked to explore the possibility of a remand to hospital in appropriate cases. Prison medical officers will of course continue to comply to the best of their ability with requests from the courts for medical reports on prisoners remanded in custody for that purpose. If the court itself is considering the suitability of a remand to hospital and no prior arrangements with a hospital have been made, it will generally be necessary to adjourn the case so that the necessary medical recommendation can be sought and arrangements made for the defendant to be admitted to a hospital" (Home Office Circular No. 71/1984, Annex, paras 24, 25).

This section does not provide the remanding court with a power to either grant the patient leave of absence under s.17 (the Reference Guide states, at para.3.20, that the remanding court can agree to such leave being given, although no authority is cited to support this assertion) or to transfer the patient to another hospital under s.19 (although the court could further remand the patient to a different hospital: see the note on subs.(5)). If the patient is subsequently made subject to an application under Pt II, his or her responsible clinician (RC) cannot exercise these powers: see point (6), below. If the patient needs to leave the hospital to receive, for example, emergency medical treatment at an Accident and Emergency department, the patient should be taken there and the remanding court informed of the action that has been taken. The common law (for mentally capable consenting patients) or ss.5 and 6 of the Mental Capacity Act 2005 (for mentally incapacitated patients) would provide authority for the patient to be treated. Appropriate security arrangements should be put in place by the remanding hospital.

If the remanded person absconds, the provisions in this Act relating to patients who are absent without leave do not apply. He may be arrested without warrant by any constable and should then be brought before the court that remanded him, which may decide on some alternative approach to his case.

A person remanded under this section is not subject to the consent to treatment provisions contained in Pt IV of this Act (s.56(3)(b)). This has led to the practice of using either s.2 or s.3 of this Act to bring the patient within the scope of Pt IV. Although this practice had been regarded by legal commentators as being legally questionable, the decision in *R. v North West London Mental Health NHS Trust Ex p. Stewart* [1997] 4 All E.R. 871 CA), where the court held that the powers under Pt II and Pt III of this Act can co-exist and operate independently of each other, confirmed that either s.2 or s.3 can be used during the currency of a s.35; also see the *Code of Practice*, paras 33.28 to 33.30. This was a pragmatic decision of the Court of Appeal that does not sit easily with the scheme of this Act for the following reasons:

(i) the specific exclusion of patients remanded under this section from Pt IV of this Act is a clear indication of Parliament's intention that this section should not carry with it a power to impose treatment. In the House of Lords debate on this provision Lord Belstead, speaking for the Government, said that

> "this power is intended to be used only for diagnostic purposes . . . [T]here need be no concern that a remand for a medical report would otherwise expose a person to the risk of receiving unnecessary treatment without his consent because . . . there is no intention that a person remanded under this clause should be regarded as 'detained for treatment' for the purposes of clause 38: this is expressly excluded by subsection (9)(b) of that clause" (HL Vol.426, No.28, cols 769, 770).

Clause 38(9)(b) was subsequently enacted as section 56(1)(b) (now s.56(3)(b));

(ii) if Parliament had intended that a power to treat a patient without consent could be added to this section by the use of Pt II of this Act, why did it create two separate remand powers, one under s.36 authorising treatment without consent and exercisable only by the Crown Court and the other under this section not authorising treatment without consent and exercisable by the Crown Court or the magistrates' court;

(iii) it would be difficult to justify making an application under s.2 because the criteria set out in subs.(2)(a) and (b) of that section cannot be satisfied in that the patient is already being assessed and is subject to detention;

(iv) a patient who has been remanded under this section and subsequently made subject to an application under s.2 or s.3 could be discharged from the section by a tribunal but would continue to be liable to be detained by virtue of his remand under this section;

(v) a patient who has been remanded under this section and subsequently made subject to an application under s.2 or s.3 could have his remand terminated (see subss.(7)–(8)), yet remain liable to be detained by virtue of s.2 or s.3;

(vi) if a patient who has been remanded under this section is also made subject to an application under s.2 or s.3, it will not be possible for the patient's RC to exercise some of the key powers under Pt II of this Act (e.g. granting the patient leave of absence under s.17 or transferring the patient to another hospital or into guardianship under s.19) because the patient continues to be subject to the terms of the remand and the hospital managers have admitted him on the basis that they shall "therefore detain him in accordance with the provisions of *this* section" (subs.(9));

(vii) the scenarios identified in (4), (5) and (6) would cause difficulties for the person who is charged under s.132 with giving the patient an explanation of his legal position, as subs.(1)(a) of that section clearly envisages a patient being detained under one provision of this Act at a time; and

(viii) there is a canon of construction that Parliament is presumed not to enact legislation which interferes with the liberty of the subject without making it clear that this was its intention: see the note on Judicial Interpretation in the General Note to this Act.

The joint Home Office and Department of Health review of health and social services for mentally disordered offenders suggested that this section be amended to enable a hospital to give treatment (Final Summary Report, Cm. 2088, para.9.6ii).

If the patient has not been sectioned under s.2 or s.3 and is assessed as being mentally capable of making a decision about treatment for his mental disorder, the common law enables him to refuse to be treated. The fact of being sectioned would have no impact on a mentally capable patient's right to refuse to be treated for a physical disorder. A mentally incapable patient can be treated for both physical and mental disorder under s.5 of the Mental Capacity Act 2005 if the treatment is in his or her best interests. Restraint can be used in the provision of the treatment if it is both necessary and proportionate to prevent harm to the patient (s.6).

*Armed Services Act 2006*
For the application of this section to the 2006 Act, see *ibid.*, Sch.4, para.3.  **1–445**

*Human Right Act 1998*
It is unlikely that a claim that a patient's dual detention (see above) amounts to a dispro-  **1–446**
portionate and unjustified interference with his art.8 rights would succeed: see *R. (on the application of M) v Homerton University Hospital* [2008] Civ 197 paras 22 and 24.

*Applications to the First-tier Tribunal (Mental Health) or the Mental Health Review Tribunal for Wales*
A patient who has been remanded under this section has no right to apply to a tribunal.  **1–447**

*Orders made in other proceedings*
In certain circumstances, an order under this section can be made under the Contempt of  **1–448**
Court Act 1981 s.14(4A), the Family Law Act 1996 ss.48 and 63L, the Housing Act 1996 s.156, the Police and Justice Act 2006 s.27 and the Armed Forces Act 2006 s.169 and Sch.4 para.3.

*Subsection (1)*
This subsection "provides an alternative to remanding the accused person in custody for  **1–449**
a medical report, in circumstances where it would not be practicable to obtain the report if he were remanded on bail (for instance, if he decided to break a condition of bail that he should reside at a hospital, the hospital would be unable to prevent him from discharging himself)" (Home Office Circular No.71/1984, Annex para.1).

HOSPITAL.   For responsibility for returning the patient to court, see the General Note to s.38.

REPORT. The report can be for a purpose other than sentencing: see *R. v The Calder Magistrates' Court Ex p. Grant*, noted in the General Note to this section.

*Subsection (2)*

*Paragraph (a)*

**1–450** OFFENCE PUNISHABLE WITH IMPRISONMENT. This section applies to a person who has been accused, but not convicted, of murder (subs.(3)).

*Paragraph (b)*

**1–451** MAGISTRATES' COURT. If a person is remanded under this section by the magistrates' court and the case is subsequently committed to the Crown Court, the jurisdiction of the magistrates to make a further remand ends. Section 48 has been used to secure the person's immediate return to the hospital on a subsequent remand into custody (see A. Akinkunmi and K. Murray, "Inadequacies in the Mental Health Act 1983 in relation to Mentally Disordered Remand Prisoners", *Med. Sci. Law* (1997) 37:53–57).

OFFENCE PUNISHABLE ON SUMMARY CONVICTION WITH IMPRISONMENT. The offence could have been committed by a person under the age of 21 (s.55(2)).

SATISFIED THAT HE DID THE ACT. The power to remand for reports under this section applies to someone in respect of whom s.37(3) applies (*Bartram v Southend Magistrates' Court* [2004] EWHC 2691 (Admin); [2004] M.H.L.R. 319 para.6).

CONSENTED. The consent relates to the making of the order and not to the extension of the order under subs.(5). A withdrawal of consent is therefore not relevant to the question of renewal.

*Subsection (3)*

**1–452** PARAGRAPH (A); EVIDENCE. For general provisions as to medical evidence, see s.54. The court can call a doctor who has provided a written report to give oral evidence (s.54(2A)).

REGISTERED MEDICAL PRACTITIONER. Who must have been approved by the Secretary of State or the Welsh Ministers under s.12 (s.54(1)).

REASON TO SUSPECT. The diagnostic threshold under this section is not high.

MENTAL DISORDER. If the person has a learning disability, the disability must be associated with abnormally aggressive or seriously irresponsible conduct (s.1(2A), (2B)).

PARAGRAPH (B); IMPRACTICABLE. This presumably refers to the impracticability of preparing a sufficiently thorough report if the accused were granted bail.

FIXED BY LAW. Although the power to remand to hospital is not available in respect of a person who has been *convicted* of murder who must be sentenced to life imprisonment (Murder (Abolition of Death Penalty) Act 1965 s.1(1)), a remand under this section can be made in a murder trial before conviction. A person who charged with murder can be bailed to a hospital to enable psychiatric reports to be prepared (Bail Act 1976 s.3(6A)).

*Subsection (4)*

**1–453** An order under this section which has been made without this subsection being complied with is ultra vires. If there is doubt as to whether the hospital place would be funded, the court should adjourn for a short period to enable enquiries to be made, and if necessary, to hear evidence and/or representations from the relevant funding body (*R. (on the* *application of Bitcon) v West Allerdale Magistrates' Court* [2003] EWHC 2640 (Admin); [2003] M.H.L.R. 399).

OR OF SOME OTHER PERSON.   Who need not be an AC.

SEVEN DAYS.   The court does not have the power either to renew or extend this period.

BEGINNING WITH.   Including the date of the remand (*Zoan v Rouamba* [2000] 2 All E.R. 620 CA).

*Subsection (5)*
IT MAY.   See the note on "consented" in subs.(2).                                    **1–454**

FURTHER REMAND HIM.   Up to a maximum of 12 weeks in all (subs.(7)). It is submitted that a further remand can only be made to a different hospital if the requirements of subs.(4) are satisfied in respect of the person's admission to that hospital.

*Subsection (7)*
AT ANY TIME.   "It will be open to the [RC] in every case to inform the court if the object **1–455** of the remand is achieved before the expiry of the stipulated time, so that the adjourned hearing may be brought forward accordingly or if necessary an alternative form of remand, either in custody or on bail, may be substituted" (*Butler Committee*, para.12.9). An application could also be made to terminate the order if the patient proves to be unmanageable at the hospital.

*Subsection (8)*
This provision was successfully moved during the passage of the 1982 Act against **1–456** Government advice. The Government view was that it would be unlikely to be of great benefit to the accused person, firstly because he already has the right to commission his or her own private clinical report and, secondly, because the court is unlikely to end his remand on the basis of such a report.

APPLY TO THE COURT ON THE BASIS OF IT.   Once the accused has received the private clinical report, he or she has the right to apply to the court to seek an end to the remand even if the reports that the court has asked for are not available.

*Subsection (9)*
CONVEY.   See paras 33.25 to 33.27 of the *Code of Practice*. For general provisions **1–457** regarding conveyance, see s.137.

SHALL ADMIT HIM.   The hospital managers are placed under an obligation to admit the patient. The court should be informed immediately if, subsequent to the offer of a bed having been made, the situation at the hospital changes and it is no longer appropriate for the patient to be admitted.

*Subsection (10)*
There is no time limit on a recapture under this provision or under s.36(8).          **1–458**

### Remand of accused person to hospital for treatment
**36.**—(1) Subject to the provisions of this section, the Crown Court may, instead **1–459** of remanding an accused person in custody, remand him to a hospital specified by the court if satisfied, on the written or oral evidence of two registered medical practitioners, that,

[(a) he is suffering from mental disorder of a nature or degree which makes it appropriate for him to be detained in a hospital for medical treatment;][and

(b) the appropriate medical treatment is available for him.]

(2) For the purposes of this section an accused person is any person who is in custody awaiting trial before the Crown Court for an offence punishable with imprisonment (other than an offence the sentence for which is fixed by law) or who at any time before sentence is in custody in the course of a trial before that court for such an offence.

(3) The court shall not remand an accused person under this section to a hospital unless it is satisfied, on the written or oral evidence of the [approved clinician who would have overall responsibility for his case] or of some other person representing the managers of the hospital, that arrangements have been made for his admission to that hospital and for his admission to it within the period of seven days beginning with the date of the remand; and if the court is so satisfied it may, pending his admission, give directions for his conveyance to and detention in a place of safety.

(4) Where a court has remanded an accused person under this section it may further remand him if it appears to the court, on the written or oral evidence of the [responsible clinician], that a further remand is warranted.

(5) The power of further remanding an accused person under this section may be exercised by the court without his being brought before the court if he is represented by [an authorised person who] is given an opportunity of being heard.

(6) An accused person shall not be remanded or further remanded under this section for more than 28 days at a time or for more than 12 weeks in all; and the court may at any time terminate the remand if it appears to the court that it is appropriate to do so.

(7) An accused person remanded to hospital under this section shall be entitled to obtain at his own expense an independent report on his mental condition from a registered medical practitioner [or approved clinician] chosen by him and to apply to the court on the basis of it for his remand to be terminated under subsection (6) above.

(8) Subsections (9) and (10) of section 35 above shall have effect in relation to a remand under this section as they have effect in relation to a remand under that section.

AMENDMENTS

The words in square brackets were substituted and inserted by the Mental Health Act 2007 ss.1(4), 5(2), 10(3), Sch.1 para.6. The words in square brackets in subs.(5) were substituted by the Legal Services Act 2007, s.208, Sch.21, para.55.

DEFINITIONS

**1–460**  hospital: ss.55(5), 145(1).

mental disorder: ss.1, 145(1).

the managers: s.145(1).

responsible clinician: s.55(1).

approved clinician: s.145(1).

place of safety: s.55(1).

authorised person: s.55(1).

GENERAL NOTE

This section empowers the Crown Court to remand an accused person, who is in custody **1–461** either awaiting trial or during the course of a trial and who is suffering from mental disorder, to hospital for treatment for a maximum of 12 weeks. It provides an alternative to the Secretary of State's power under s.48 to transfer unsentenced prisoners to hospital. Where the accused person is in urgent need of treatment and is not due to appear before the Crown Court in the immediate future, the procedure under s.48 is to be preferred. Paragraph 36 of Home Office Circular No.71/1984 states:

"Section 36 provides the Crown Court with an alternative to the procedure laid down by the Criminal Procedure (Insanity) Act 1964 of finding a defendant under disability ('unfit to plead'). The power in s.36 can be used in cases in which if the defendant could receive treatment in hospital for a period it might be possible to proceed with the full trial. The Crown Court may prefer in appropriate cases to proceed in this way rather than under the Criminal Procedure (Insanity) Act, under which the defendant would thereafter have to be detained as a restricted patient (which may not be appropriate in relation to the nature of the alleged offence)."

A remand under this section "does not automatically affect any existing liability for detention for assessment or treatment on any other basis, nor bring supervised community treatment or guardianship to an end. But nor does it prevent them expiring or being discharged in the normal way" (Reference Guide para.3.23).

As this Act does not provide for the application of Pt II to a patient who has been remanded under this section, there is no power to grant the patient leave of absence under s.17 (the Reference Guide states, at para.3.20, that the remanding court can agree to such leave being given) or transfer the patient to another hospital under s.19 (although the court could further remand the patient to a different hospital: see the note on subs.(4)).

A person remanded under this section as a "patient liable to be detained under this Act" is subject to the consent to treatment provisions contained in Pt IV of this Act (s.56(3)).

If the remanded person absconds, the provisions in this Act relating to patients who are absent without leave do not apply. If the accused person either absconds from the hospital to which he has been remanded, or absconds while being conveyed to and from that hospital, he may be arrested and brought back before the court that remanded him (subs.(8)). For the conveyance of the accused person to the hospital, see subs.(8) and the notes on s.35(9).

*Armed Services Act 2006*

For the application of this section to the 2006 Act, see ibid., Sch.4, para.4.       **1–462**

*Applications to the First-tier Tribunal (Mental Health) or the Mental Health Review Tribunal for Wales*

A patient who has been remanded under this section has no right to apply to a tribunal. **1–463**

*Orders made in other proceedings*

In certain circumstances, and order under this section can be made under the Armed **1–464** Forces Act 2006 s.169 and Sch.4 para.4.

*Subsection (1)*

CROWN COURT.   But not the magistrates' court. However, such courts have the alterna- **1–465** tive, under s.37(3), of making a hospital order in respect of a defendant charged but unconvicted.

ACCUSED PERSON.   See subs.(2).

HOSPITAL.   Or a registered establishment (ss.34(2), 55(5)). For responsibility for returning the patient to court, see the General Note to s.38.

EVIDENCE. For general provisions relating to medical evidence, see s.54. The court can call a doctor who has provided a written report to give oral evidence (s.54(2A)).

TWO REGISTERED MEDICAL PRACTITIONERS. At least one of whom must have been approved by the Secretary of State or the Welsh Ministers under s.12 (s.54(1)). There is no prohibition on both of the doctors being on the staff of the same hospital.

MENTAL DISORDER. If the person has a learning disability, the disability must be associated with abnormally aggressive or seriously irresponsible conduct (s.1(2A), (2B)).

NATURE OR DEGREE. See the note on s.3(2)(a).

APPROPRIATE MEDICAL TREATMENT. See the note on s.3(2)(d).

*Subsection (2)*

**1–466**    FIXED BY LAW. Unlike s.35, this section does not apply to a person who has been charged with murder. If such a person is in need of urgent treatment, he could be removed to hospital under s.48 if he is awaiting trial having been remanded in custody by a magistrates' court. A person who charged with murder can be bailed to a hospital to enable psychiatric reports to be prepared (Bail Act 1976 s.3(6A)).

*Subsection (3)*

**1–467**    OR OF SOME OTHER PERSON. Who need not be a clinician.

BEGINNING WITH. Including the date of the remand (*Zoan v Rouamba* [2000] 2 All E.R. 620 CA).

*Subsection (4)*

**1–468**    A FURTHER REMAND IS WARRANTED. Because the criteria set out in subs.(1) still apply. It is submitted that a further remand can only be made to a different hospital if the requirements of subs.(3) are satisfied in respect of the patient's admission to that hospital.

*Subsection (7)*

**1–469**    See the notes on s.35(8).

*Subsection (8)*

**1–470**    See paras 33.25 to 33.27 of the *Code of Practice*. For general provisions regarding conveyance, see s.137.

## *Hospital and Guardianship Orders*

### Powers of courts to order hospital admission or guardianship

**1–471**    **37.**—(1) Where a person is convicted before the Crown Court of an offence punishable with imprisonment other than an offence the sentence for which is fixed by law, or is convicted by a magistrates' court of an offence punishable on summary conviction with imprisonment, and the conditions mentioned in subsection (2) below are satisfied, the court may by order authorise his admission to and detention in such hospital as may be specified in the order or, as the case may be, place him under the guardianship of a local social services authority or of such other person approved by a local social services authority as may be so specified.

[(1A) In the case of an offence the sentence for which would otherwise fall to be imposed—

(a)  under section 51A(2) of the Firearms Act 1968,

(b) under section 110(2) or 111(2) of the Powers of Criminal Courts (Sentencing) Act 2000, [...]

(c) under [section 225(2) or 226(2)] of the Criminal Justice Act 2003, [or

(d) under section 29(4) or (6) of the Violent Crime Reduction Act 2006 (minimum sentences in certain cases of using someone to mind a weapon),]

nothing in those provisions shall prevent a court from making an order under subsection (1) above for the admission of the offender to a hospital.

(1B) Reference in subsection (1A) above to a sentence falling to be imposed under any of the provisions mentioned in that subsection are to be read in accordance with section 305(4) of the Criminal Justice Act 2003.]

(2) The conditions referred to in subsection (1) above are that—

(a) the court is satisfied, on the written or oral evidence of two registered medical practitioners, that the offender is suffering from [mental disorder] and that either—

    (i) the mental disorder from which the offender is suffering is of a nature or degree which makes it appropriate for him to be detained in a hospital for medical treatment and [appropriate medical treatment is available for him]; or

    (ii) in the case of an offender who has attained the age of 16 years, the mental disorder is of a nature or degree which warrants his reception into guardianship under this Act; and

(b) the court is of the opinion, having regard to all the circumstances including the nature of the offence and the character and antecedents of the offender, and to the other available methods of dealing with him, that the most suitable method of disposing of the case is by means of an order under this section.

(3) Where a person is charged before a magistrates' court with any act or omission as an offence and the court would have power, on convicting him of that offence, to make an order under subsection (1) above in his case [...], then, if the court is satisfied that the accused did the act or made the omission charged, the court may, if it thinks fit, make such an order without convicting him.

(4) An order for the admission of an offender to a hospital (in this Act referred to as "a hospital order") shall not be made under this section unless the court is satisfied on the written or oral evidence of the [approved clinician who would have overall responsibility for his case] or of some other person representing the managers of the hospital that arrangements have been made for his admission to that hospital [ ... ], and for his admission to it within the period of 28 days beginning with the date of the making of such an order; and the court may, pending his admission within that period, give such directions as it thinks fit for his conveyance to and detention in a place of safety.

(5) If within the said period of 28 days it appears to the Secretary of State that by reason of an emergency or other special circumstances it is not practicable for the patient to be received into the hospital specified in the order, he may give directions for the admission of the patient to such other hospital as appears to be appropriate instead of the hospital so specified; and where such directions are given—

(a) the Secretary of State shall cause the person having the custody of the patient to be informed, and

(b) the hospital order shall have effect as if the hospital specified in the directions were substituted for the hospital specified in the order.

(6) An order placing an offender under the guardianship of a local social services authority or of any other person (in this Act referred to as "a guardianship order") shall not be made under this section unless the court is satisfied that that authority or person is willing to receive the offender into guardianship.

(7) [. . .]

(8) Where an order is made under this section, the court [shall not:

(a) pass sentence of imprisonment or impose a fine or make a [community order (within the meaning of Part 12 of the Criminal Justice Act 2003)] [or a youth rehabilitation order (within the meaning of Part 1 of the Criminal Justice and Immigration Act 2008] in respect of the offence,

(b) if the order under this section is a hospital order, make a referral order (within the meaning of [the Powers of Criminal Courts (Sentencing) Act 2000]) in respect of the offence, or

(c) make in respect of the offender [. . .] an order under section 105 of that Act (binding over of parent or guardian)],

but the court may make any other order which it] has power to make apart from this section; and for the purposes of this subsection "sentence of imprisonment" includes any sentence or order for detention.

AMENDMENTS

The words omitted in subs.(1) were repealed, and subss. (1A) and (1B) were substituted by the Criminal Justice Act 2003 s.304 Sch.32 para.38. The words in square brackets in subs.(1A)(c) were substituted by the Criminal Justice and Immigration Act 2008 s.148 Sch.26 para.8. The words in square brackets in subs.(2) and (4) were substituted by the Mental Health Act 2007 ss.1(4), 4(5), 10(4), Sch.1 para.7. Subs.(7) and the words omitted in subs.(3) were repealed by s.55 Sch.11 Pt 1. In subs.(1A), para. (d) was inserted, and the word at the end of para.(b) was repealed, by the Violent Crime Reduction Act 2006 ss.49,65 Sch.1 para.2, Sch.5. The words omitted in subs.(4) were repealed by the Crime (Sentences) Act 1997 s.56(2) Sch.6. In subs.(8) the words in square brackets were substituted by the Youth Justice and Criminal Evidence Act 1999 s.67 Sch.4 para.11, the Criminal Justice Act 2003 s.304 Sch.32 para.38, the Powers of Criminal Courts (Sentencing) Act 2000 s.165 Sch.9 para.90 and the Criminal Justice and Immigration Act 2008, s.6, Sch.4, para.30. The words omitted were repealed by ibid, s.149, Sch.28, Pt 1.

DEFINITIONS

**1–472**    hospital: ss.55(5), 145(1).

local social services authority: s.145(1).

mental disorder: ss.1, 145(1).

approved clinician: s.145(1).

medical treatment: s.145(1), (4).

patient: s.145(1).

the managers: s.145(1).

place of safety: s.55(1).

GENERAL NOTE

**1–473**    This section empowers a Crown Court or magistrates' court to make a hospital or guardianship order as an alternative to a penal disposal (including sentences for public protection under Pt 12 of the Criminal Justice Act 2003) for offenders who are found to be suffering from mental disorder at the time of sentencing such as to warrant their detention in hospital or reception into guardianship. No causal relationship has to be established between the offender's mental disorder and the criminal activities. The effect of hospital and guardianship orders are set out in s.40 and in the judgment of the Court of Appeal in *R. v Birch*, noted below. An offender's nearest relative has no role to play in the making by the court of a hospital or guardianship order (s.40(4)).

When a person is made subject to a hospital order or guardianship order under this section, any previous application or order made in respect of that person ceases to have effect (s.40(5)).

*Hospital orders*

The purpose and effect of a hospital order are explained in the following passage from **1–474** the judgment of the Court of Appeal in *R. v Birch* (1989) 11 Cr. App. R.(S.) 202 at 210:

"Once the offender is admitted to hospital pursuant to a hospital order or transfer order without restriction on discharge, his position is almost exactly the same as if he were a civil patient. In effect he passes out of the penal system and into the hospital regime. Neither the court nor the Secretary of State has any say in his disposal. Thus, like any other mental patient, he may be detained only for a period of six months, unless the authority to detain is renewed, an event which cannot happen unless certain conditions, which resemble those which were satisfied when he was admitted, are fulfilled. If the authority expires without being renewed, the patient may leave. Furthermore, he may be discharged at any time by the hospital managers or the 'responsible [clinician]'.'. . . .

Another feature of the regime which affects the disordered offender and the civil patient alike is the power of the responsible [clinician] to grant leave of absence from the hospital for a particular purpose, or for a specified or indefinite period of time: subject always to a power of recall . . . .

There are certain differences between the positions of the offender and of the civil patient, relating to early access to the [tribunal] and to discharge by the patient's nearest relative, but these are of comparatively modest importance. In general the offender is dealt with in a manner which appears, and is intended to be, humane by comparison with a custodial sentence. A hospital order is not a punishment. Questions of retribution and deterrence, whether personal or general, are immaterial. The offender who has become a patient is not kept on any kind of leash by the court, as he is when he consents to a probation order with a condition of in-patient treatment. The sole purpose of the order is to ensure that the offender receives the medical care and attention which he needs in the hope and expectation of course that the result will be to avoid the commission by the offender of further criminal acts."

A hospital order will cease to have effect if the offender is not admitted to the hospital named in the order within 28 days of the making of the order: see *R. (on the application of DB) v Nottinghamshire Healthcare NHS Trust*, noted under subs.(4).

Although it is lawful for a court to pass a sentence of detention on the same occasion that a hospital order is made, it is a matter of obvious impracticability for an order made under the Mental Health Act and a sentence of custody to be simultaneously carried out. A sentence of custody takes effect from the day on which it is passed, and that clearly, in practical terms, is inconsistent with the terms of the order that the defendant should be transferred to a psychiatric hospital forthwith (*R. v Rogerson* [2004] EWCA Crim 2099; [2006] M.H.L.R. 175).

The Court of Appeal has said that where a court is considering making a hospital order the defendant should, except in the rarest circumstances, be represented by counsel (*R. v Blackwood* (1974) 59 Cr. App. R. 170).

The court can make a hospital order in the case of an offender who is subject to an interim hospital order made under s.38, without his being brought before the court (s.38(2)).

A patient who has been placed under a hospital order is subject to the consent to treatment provisions in Pt IV of this Act (s.56(3)).

Where the Crown Court makes a hospital order, it may also make an order under s.41, restricting the discharge of the offender from hospital, if it considers that it is necessary for the protection of the public from serious harm so to do.

Primary Care Trusts or Local Health Boards and local social services authorities have a duty to provide after-care services for hospital order patients who cease to be liable to be detained and leave hospital (s.117).

*Applications to the First-tier Tribunal (Mental Health) or the Mental Health Review Tribunal for Wales*

**1–475**    Either the patient or the patient's nearest relative can apply to a tribunal in the period between six and 12 months after the making of the hospital order and in any subsequent period of one year (ss.66(1)(f), (2)(f), 40(4), 69(1)(a), Sch.1 Pt 1 paras 2, 6, 9). References to the tribunal are governed by s.68.

*Guardianship orders*

**1–476**    Little use has been made of guardianship orders by the courts even though, in the view of the Butler Committee, they "offer a useful form of control of some mentally disordered offenders who do not require hospital treatment [and are] particularly suited to the needs of subnormal offenders including those inadequate offenders who require help in managing their affairs" (para.15.8).

Paragraph 8(iv)(c) of Home Office Circular No. 66/90 states:

"[T]he purpose of guardianship is primarily to ensure that the offender receives care and protection rather than medical treatment, although the guardian does have powers to require the offender to attend for medical treatment. The effect of a guardianship order is to give the guardian power to require the offender to live at a specific place (this may be used to discourage the offender from sleeping rough or living with people who may exploit or mistreat him, or ensure that he resides at a particular hostel), to attend specific places at specified times for medical treatment, occupation, education, or training, and to require access to the offender to be given at the place where the offender is living to any doctor, approved social worker, or other person specified by the guardian. This power could be used, for example, to ensure the offender did not neglect himself".

The effect of a guardianship order made by a court is similar to that of civil guardianship, except that the patient's nearest relative has no power of discharge (s.40(2)(4), Sch.1, Pt I, paras 2, 8).

The provisions of s.39A of this Act apply where a court is minded to make a guardianship order.

*Applications to the First-tier Tribunal (Mental Health) or the Mental Health Review Tribunal for Wales*

**1–477**    A patient who has been made subject to a guardianship order can apply to a tribunal within the first six months of the order (s.69(1)(b)), and during each renewal period (ss.66(1)(f), 2(f), 40(4), Sch.1 Pt 1 paras 2, 6, 9). The patient's nearest relative can apply within the first 12 months of the order and in any subsequent 12-month period (s.69(1)(b)).

*Appeals*

**1–478**    A hospital order is a form of sentence and is therefore appealable to the Court of Appeal (Criminal Appeal Act 1968, ss.9(1), 50(1)). Section 11(3) of the 1968 Act provides, inter alia, that the Court of Appeal can quash a sentence if they consider that the appellant should be sentenced differently for an offence for which he was dealt with by the court below and in place of it pass such sentence or make such order as the court below had power to pass or make when dealing with him for the offence. The subsection "is sufficiently wide to permit the court to re-sentence the appellant on information placed before it which was not put before the sentencing judge . . . Such an approach clearly allows the Court of Appeal to substitute a sentence on the basis of psychiatric and other evidence coming to light after the sentence was passed" (*R. v Beatty,* below, para.51). This power has resulted in the Court of Appeal substituting a hospital order for a prison sentence: see, for example, *R. v Smith* [2001] EWCA Crim 743; [2001] M.H.L.R. 46. In *R. v Beatty* [2006] EWCA Crim 2359; [2006] M.H.L.R. 333 para.47, Scott Baker L.J., giving the judgment of the court, said:

> "There is clear authority that where the conditions for a hospital order are met at the time of sentence a hospital order rather than a discretionary life sentence should be imposed, see *Mitchell* [1997] 1 Cr App R (S) 90 and *Hutchinson* [1997] 2 Cr App R (S) 60. This is so even where the information establishing that the conditions for making a hospital order come to light after the imposition of the life sentence, see *De Silva* (1994) 15 Cr App R (S) 296. This situation is to be distinguished from that in which mental illness supervenes after the sentence has been imposed. In such a case administrative transfer by the Secretary of State under section 47 [of the Mental Health Act] is the correct course, see *Castro* (1985) 7 Cr App R (S) 68."

His Lordship said that it was obviously important, perhaps even more so now that "technical lifer status" was no longer granted, that those who should have been subject to a hospital order rather than life imprisonment should have the position rectified on appeal. That said, "the court will always scrutinise with great care cases in which an appellant seeks to rely on psychiatric evidence directed to his mental health at the date of sentence that had not been advanced at the time" (para.62).

The power of the court under s.11 must not be exercised in such a way so that an appellant is more severely dealt with on appeal than she was dealt with in the court below (*R. v Wang* [2005] EWCA Crim 3238; [2006] M.H.L.R. 109 para.17). The effect of ss.3 and 4 of the 1968 Act is to prevent the court from imposing a sentence with a direction under s.45A (*R. v Hendy* [2006] EWCA Crim 819; [2006] M.H.L.R. 244 para.53). There would appear to be no right of appeal against a decision of a judge to adjourn a case in order to facilitate the identification of a hospital bed for a patient for whom a hospital order is the appropriate disposal: see *R. v Galfetti,* which is noted under subs.(4).

If fresh medical evidence supports the contention that a hospital order should have been made in respect of an offender who was sentenced to a term of imprisonment, the nature of the Court of Appeal's powers under the this Act are statutorily circumscribed and, in particular, a hospital order cannot be made if there is no bed available for the offender or if the offender does not then suffer from a mental disorder of a nature or degree which makes it appropriate for him to be detained in hospital (*R. v Lomey* [2004] EWCA Crim 3014; [2004] M.H.L.R. 316).

It is fundamental to the trial process that a defendant must advance all aspects of his case at trial and a court will not admit fresh evidence to enable a defendant to run a different case if that case could have been run first time round (*R. v Ahluwalia* (1993) 96 Cr App R 133). The power to admit fresh evidence is conferred by s.23 of the Criminal Appeal Act 1968. Subsection (2) of that section requires the court in considering whether to receive such evidence to have regard in particular to:

(i) whether the evidence appears to the court to be capable of belief;

(ii) whether it appears to the court that the evidence may afford any ground for allowing the appeal;

(iii) whether the evidence would have been admissible in the proceedings from which the appeal lies on an issue which is the subject of the appeal; and

(iv) whether there is a reasonable explanation for a failure to adduce the evidence in those proceedings.

In *R. v Lane* [2003] EWCA Crim 382; [2003] M.H.L.R. 220 the Court of Appeal held that these factors are not exhaustive of all the potentially relevant considerations that must be taken into account and that the overriding objective in all cases are the interests of justice. Also see *R. v Gilbert* [2003] EWCA Crim 2385, para.9, where the Court of Appeal said that the fundamental question under s.23 "is whether the court thinks it necessary or expedient in the interests of justice to admit the evidence." Although it "initially had some concern", the Court of Appeal in *R. v Beatty*, above, para.38, admitted the written and oral evidence of a psychiatrist who had not seen the patient for over two years. Judicial guidance applicable to the exercise of the discretion to admit fresh psychiatric evidence is summarised in *R. v Diamond* [2008] EWCA Crim 923; [2008] M.H.L.R. 124, at paras 21 to 23.

*Sentencing options*

**1–479**     Under s.157 of the Criminal Justice Act 2003, in any case where the offender is or appears to be mentally disordered within the meaning of this Act, the court must obtain and consider a written or oral medical report from a doctor who is approved under s.12 of this Act before passing a custodial sentence (other than one fixed by law). This obligation does not apply if, in the circumstances of the case, the court is of the opinion that it is unnecessary to obtain such a report. Before passing a custodial sentence other than one fixed by law on an offender who is or appears to be mentally disordered, a court must consider:

(i)   any information before it which relates to his mental condition (whether given in a medical report, a pre-sentence report or otherwise), and

(ii)  the likely effect of such a sentence on that condition and on any treatment which may be available for it.

No custodial sentence which is passed in contravention of the above requirements is rendered invalid by virtue of that fact, but any court on an appeal against such a sentence must obtain a medical report if none was obtained by the court below, and must consider that report.

In *R. v Birch*, above, 212–213, the Court of Appeal said that in a case involving a degree of mental disorder the judge has available to him a variety of options, which he may conveniently approach in the following order:

"First, he should decide whether a period of compulsory detention is apposite. If the answer is that it is not, or may not be, the possibility of a [community order with a mental health treatment requirement] should be considered . . .

Secondly, the judge will ask himself whether the conditions contained in section 37(2)(a) for the making of a hospital order are satisfied. Here the judge acts on the evidence of the doctors. If left in doubt, he may wish to avail himself of the valuable provisions of sections 38 and 39 (which are not used as often as they might be) to make an interim hospital order, giving the court and the doctors further time to decide between hospital with or without restrictions and some other disposal, and to require the Health Authority to furnish information on arrangements for the admission of the offender. If the judge concludes that the conditions empowering him to make an order are satisfied, he will consider whether to make such an order, or whether 'the most suitable method of disposing of the case' (s.37(2)(b)) is to impose a sentence of imprisonment.

Finally, he should consider whether the further condition imposed by section 41(1) is satisfied. If it is, then he may make a restriction order; but he is not obliged to do so, and may again consider sending the offender to prison, either for life or for a fixed term (*Speake* (1957) 41 Cr. App. R. 222, a pre-1959 case which we believe to be still good law). If he does decide on a restriction order, he must then choose between an unlimited order, or one for a fixed term."

The Court of Appeal went on to say, at 215, that the choice of prison as an alternative to hospital may arise:

"in two quite different ways: (1) If the offender is dangerous and no suitable secure hospital accommodation is available. Here the judge will be driven to impose a prison sentence, see section 37(4) and *Jones* (1976) *Current Sentencing Practice*, F.2.3(b). (2) Where the sentencer considers that notwithstanding the offender's mental disorder there was an element of culpability in the offence which merits punishment. This may happen where there is no connection between the mental disorder and the offence, or where the defendant's responsibility for the offence is 'diminished' but not wholly extinguished. That the imposition of a prison sentence is capable of being a proper exercise of discretion is shown by *Morris* [1961] 2 Q.B. 237 and *Gunnell* (1966) 50 Cr. App. R. 242. Nevertheless the more recent decision in *Mbatha* (1985) 7 Cr. App. R.(S.) 373 strongly indicates that even where there is culpability, the right way to deal with a dangerous and disordered person is to make an order under sections 37 and 41.

In the absence of any question of culpability and punishment, the judge should not impose a sentence of imprisonment simply to ensure that if the [tribunal] finds that the conditions under section 73 are satisfied and is therefore constrained to order a discharge, the offender will return to prison rather than be set free: *Howell* (1985) 7 Cr. App. R.(S.) 360 and *Cockburn* (1967) Cr. App. R. 134."

Before determining that imprisonment is the preferred option for the offender, the court should consider whether, as an alternative, it would be appropriate to make a direction under ss.45A and 45B (a hospital and limitation direction) in respect of him or her.

The court's finding in *Birch* that a custodial term could be imposed on a mentally disordered defendant where a hospital order was not found to be the most suitable method of disposing of the case, was approved by the House of Lords in *R. v Drew* [2003] UKHL 25; [2003] 4 All E.R. 557 where it was held that under both national law and the jurisprudence of the European Court of Human Rights a sentence of imprisonment could be passed on a mentally disordered defendant who was criminally responsible and fit to be tried.

For a review of the developments in caselaw regarding the approach that a court should adopt when sentencing a mentally disordered offender whose offence would warrant a custodial sentence, see *R. v IA* [2005] EWCA Crim 2077; [2005] M.H.L.R. 336 which is noted in the General Note to s.41.

The court cannot defer sentence on the basis of the offender undertaking to undergo treatment at a psychiatric hospital (*R. v Skelton* [1983] Crim.L.R. 686).

### Defective Court Orders
See the General Note to this Part.                                               **1–480**

### Criminal Procedure (Insanity) Act 1964
Under s.5 of the 1964 Act, where a person is found unfit to plead, but to have done the act **1–481** or made the omission of which they are accused, the court may make an order under this section (with or without restrictions): see the General Note to this Part. It may also do so if the defendant is found not guilty by reason of insanity. Paragraphs 11.8 and 11.10 of the Reference Guide state:

"Because patients admitted to hospital when found unfit to plead have not (by definition) received a full criminal trial, they may be sent back for trial by the prosecuting authority if that authority is satisfied, after consulting their responsible clinician, that they can now properly be tried. The Secretary of State for Justice may also do this, if the patient concerned is still subject to a restriction order and still detained in hospital. This includes patients on leave of absence from hospital, but not those who have been conditionally discharged and not recalled to hospital. Before doing so, the Secretary of State must consult the patient's responsible clinician.

If sending patients back to trial, the Secretary of State may remit them either directly to the court or to prison to await trial. The patient's hospital order (and restriction order) ceases to have effect on their arrival at the court or prison."

### *Armed Services Act 2006*

**1–482**     This section is modified for the purposes of s.169(2)(a) of the 2006 Act (ibid., Sch.4, para.1).

### *Orders made in other proceedings*

**1–483**     In certain circumstances, a hospital order or a guardianship order can be made under the Contempt of Court Act 1981 s.14(4),(4A) the Family Law Act 1996 s.51 and the Armed Forces Act 2006 s.169 and Sch.4 para.1. A restriction order can also be made under the 2006 Act: see Sch.4 para.2. It is also possible for such orders to be made under the terms of the Colonial Prisoners Removal Act 1884 and the Repatriation of Prisoners Act 1984.

### *Human Rights Act 1998*

**1–484**     If an offender satisfies the criteria for a hospital order set out in subs.(2) but is not made the subject of such an order because of an inability to identify a hospital that would be willing to accept him (see subs.(4)), he could claim that his rights under art.5(1) of the European Convention on Human Rights had been breached if he was subsequently incarcerated in a non-therapeutic environment to the detriment of his mental health (*Aerts v Belgium* (2000) 29 E.H.R.R. 50).

In *Brand v Netherlands* [2001] M.H.L.R. 275, the European Court of Human Rights declared inadmissible an application that a lengthy detention of a mentally disordered person in prison pending a place being found in a secure psychiatric institution constituted a breach of art.3 of the Convention on the ground that there was no evidence that the applicant's mental health or the possibilities of treatment had suffered on account of the time spent in prison.

Determining whether the accused "did the act or made the omission charged" for the purposes of subs.(3) is not a criminal trial and the accused's rights under art.6 of the ECHR are not engaged (*Director of Public Prosecutions v P*, below, paras 55,61).

Also see note on s.3 under this heading.

### *Subsection (1)*

**1–485**     CONVICTED.   Under s.51(5)(6) the court can make a hospital order (with or without a restriction order) in respect of a mentally disordered transfer direction patient in his absence and, if he is awaiting trial, without convicting him.

FIXED BY LAW.   This section does not apply to persons who have been convicted of murder who must be sentenced to life imprisonment (Murder (Abolition of Death Penalty) Act 1965 s.1(1)).

MAGISTRATES' COURT.   If a magistrates' court believes that an order under this section should be made on a juvenile, it must remit the case to the youth court (Powers of Criminal Courts (Sentencing) Act 2000 s.8). Neither a youth court or other magistrates' court dealing with a person aged under 18 for an offence can combine a hospital order with a referral order (*ibid.*, s.16(1)(b)).

If a magistrates' court has made a hospital order under this section, it "shall send to the hospital named in the order such information in the possession of the court as it considers likely to be of assistance in dealing with the patient to whom the order relates, and in particular such information about the mental condition, character and antecedents of the patient and the nature of the offence" (Criminal Procedure Rules 2010 (SI 2010/60 (L.2), r.49.2 (1)). A similar obligation to send such information to "the local health authority" exists if the court makes a guardianship order (r.49.2 (2)). The reference to the local health authority should, if it is submitted, be a reference to the local social services authority.

Although a magistrates' court does not have the power to attach a restriction order under s.41 to a hospital order made under this section, it may, instead of making a hospital order or other disposition, commit him to the Crown Court for sentencing under s.43 with a view to a hospital order with restrictions being made.

OFFENCE PUNISHABLE ON SUMMARY CONVICTION WITH IMPRISONMENT.   For young offenders, see s.55(2).

THE COURT MAY BY ORDER.   This section confers a discretion which may be exercised where the statutory preconditions are met. The discretion can be exercised even though there is no causal connection between the mental disorder and the offending; see, for example, *R. v Eaton* [1976] Crim.L.R.390. Conversely, where there is such a connection, is not to be assumed that the discretion will be exercised [In *R v Dass* [2009] EWCA Crim 1208; [2009] M.H.L.R. 288, the Court of Appeal doubted that there is a general rule that where there is a causal link between an offence and an offender's mental illness and the illness is of a nature or degree which makes it appropriate for him to be detained in hospital for treatment, a hospital order should be imposed.]. All must depend on the facts of the case: see *R. v Nafei* [2004] EWCA Crim 3238; [2005] 2 Cr. App. R. (S.) 24, where the Court of Appeal said that it was difficult to envisage a case where the discretion will be likely to be exercised in circumstances where the offence of drug importation was committed by the offender knowingly with his eyes wide open. *Nafei* was applied in *R. v Khelifi* [2006] EWCA Crim 770; [2006] M.H.L.R. 257, where the Court of Appeal said that although a defendant's medical needs were important factors for the purposes of the discretion under this section, they were not the overriding factors as the interests of justice also had to be considered. In *R. v Smith* [2001] EWCA Crim 743; [2001] M.H.L.R. 46, the Court of Appeal said that such is the wording of this section "that it seems that a hospital order may be made even though the mental disorder suffered by the defendant has developed since the date of the offence" (per Keene L.J. at para.9). The offender's consent to the order is not required (*R. v Gunnee* [1972] Crim. L.R. 261).

The first day of the patient's detention is the date of the order (s.40(4)).

HOSPITAL.   Or a registered establishment (ss.34(2), 55(5)). A hospital order ceases to have effect if the offender is not admitted to the hospital named in the order within 28 days of the making of the order: see the note on subs.(4). The court has the power to direct who is to be responsible for conveying the defendant from the court to the receiving hospital (*Code of Practice*, 33.25). A court may request information about the availability of hospital places under s.39. The offender can be admitted to a hospital which is not situated in the locality where he is normally resident (*R. v Marsden (Practice Note)* [1968] 1 W.L.R. 785).

PLACE HIM UNDER . . . GUARDIANSHIP.   See the General Note to this section. The guardian must be willing to receive the offender into guardianship (subs.(6)). Section 39A can be used to ascertain the attitude of a potential guardian. The powers of the guardian and the effect of the guardianship order are set out in s.40. Section 18(7) provides a power to convey the offender to the place where he is required to reside. There is no provision for returning the offender to court on any subsequent failure by the offender to comply with the provisions of the guardianship order.

The first day of the patient's guardianship is the date of the order (s.40(4)).

*Subsections (1A), 1(B)*

**1–486**   These subsections, which were brought into force on April 4, 2005, do not apply to pre-commencement offences. Their effect is that the mandatory sentencing requirements contained in the provisions listed in paras (a) to (d) of subs.(1A) do not prevent the court from making a hospital order under subs.(1).

*Subsection (2)*

*Paragraph (a)*

**1–487**   EVIDENCE.   For general requirements as to medical evidence, see s.54. The court can call a doctor who has provided a written report to give oral evidence (s.54(2A)). The doctors should prepare an up-to-date assessment of a defendant so that the court may be satisfied as to his current mental condition at the time of sentencing, and as to his susceptibility to treatment at the time of sentencing (*R. v Preston* [2003] EWCA Crim 2086 para.6). When preparing their evidence from sources, doctors are not bound by the rules of evidence. They have to look at the whole picture. But they have to exercise judgment over material which is of first, second or even third hand hearsay as to the weight that can be attached to it (*Kiernan v Harrow Crown Court*, below, para.28).

In *R. v Crozier* (1990) 12 Cr. App. R.(S.) 206, the Court of Appeal applied *W v Egdell* [1990] 1 All E.R. 835 CA (noted under s.76) by holding that, given the particular circumstances of the case, a psychiatrist who had prepared a medical report for the defence had acted responsibly and reasonably when he handed a copy of his report to counsel for the prosecution. This was a case where the strong public interest in the disclosure of the psychiatrist's opinion overrode his duty of confidence to his client. The psychiatrist was "firmly of the view that the appellant suffers from psychopathic disorder, continues to be a danger to the public and should be kept in a secure hospital without limit of time. He held this opinion so strongly that he felt impelled to ensure that the court became aware of it" (per Watkins L.J. at 213).

Where there are significant differences in the evidence of the doctors giving evidence to the court, the judge should explain in his sentencing remarks why he accepted one set of evidence and rejected the other (*Kiernan v Harrow Crown Court* [2003] EWCA Crim 1052 para.19). During the course of his judgment, Scott Baker J. said, at para.25, that he could see no reason in ordinary circumstances why it would be appropriate for a doctor who was to give evidence "to begin making his own investigations by contacting the victim, or someone else in a similar situation, for his own account of events, especially if, as happened in this case, it was not possible for the applicant to give him the other side of the story".

TWO REGISTERED MEDICAL PRACTITIONERS.   One of whom must be approved under s.12 (s.54(1)). Unlike the situation that obtains when applications made under Pt II of the Act, this section does not place any constraints on the timing of the medical examinations of the offender. As the doctors are providing evidence to the court, not medical recommendations, the Mental Health (Conflict of Interest) (England) Regulations 2008 do not apply. This means, inter alia, that both doctors could be on the staff of the admitting hospital and could have a financial interest in the matter.

The Court of Appeal has advised that the trial judge should hear evidence from the doctor who will be treating the offender (*R. v Blackwood*, above).

Suffering from. The offender's mental condition at the time when the offence was committed is not at issue. The Court of Appeal has said that the condition could have developed since the date of the offence (*R. v Smith*, above).

Mental disorder. If the person has a learning disability, the disability must be associated with abnormally aggressive or seriously irresponsible conduct (s.1(2A), (2B)).

Nature or degree. The meaning of this phrase is considered in the note on s.3(2)(a).

Appropriate medical treatment. See the note on s.3(2)(d).

Attained the age. At the commencement of his or her sixteenth birthday (Family Law Reform Act 1969 s.9(1)). Also see s.55(7).

Warrants his reception into guardianship. Compare with the criteria set out in s.7(2) for guardianship applications made under Pt II of this Act.

*Paragraph (b)*
Nature of the offence. "Although hospital orders are frequently made in cases **1–488** involving grave offences of violence, the gravity of the offences is not an important consideration in making a hospital order (except in so far as it indicates a need for detention in secure conditions). Hospital orders have been upheld or imposed on appeal on offenders whose offences would not have justified a substantial term of imprisonment" (D.A. Thomas, *Principles of Sentencing* (2nd ed., 1979) p.299).

Most suitable method of disposing of the case. Note subs.(8). In *R. v Birch*, above, at 215, the Court of Appeal pointed out that prison might be chosen as an alternative to hospital either because the offender was dangerous and no suitable secure hospital accommodation was available or because there was an element of culpability in the offence which merited punishment, as might happen where there was no connection between the mental disorder and the offence or where the offender's responsibility for the offence was reduced but not wholly extinguished. As was pointed out in *R. v Drew* [2003] UKHL 25; [2003] 4 All E.R. 557 at para.17, there is no divergence in this respect between national law and Strasbourg jurisprudence. In *X v United Kingdom* (App. No. 5229/71, October 5 1972) the European Commission on Human Rights rejected as manifestly inadmissible a complaint by a mentally disordered defendant that he should be held in a psychiatric hospital and not in prison.

*Subsection (3)*
This provision, which empowers magistrates to make a hospital or guardianship order **1–489** without proceeding to conviction where the defendant is suffering from mental disorder, applies only where the court is satisfied that the defendant did the act or made the omission charged. The Butler Committee said at para.10.34: "In trivial cases the magistrates may properly have recourse to the expedient of adjourning the proceedings *sine die* or of simply not proceeding".
In *R. v Lincolnshire (Kesteven) Justices Ex p. O'Connor* [1983] 1 W.L.R. 335 DC, the accused's mental disorder was such that he was unable to understand what it meant to consent to summary trial. The magistrates decided that as they were unable to try the case, it followed that they had no power to make a hospital order under this provision. The Divisional Court held that the magistrates could have made a hospital order without holding a trial. Lord Lane C.J. said at 338:

"In our judgment the words of [s.37(3)] are clear. It gives the justices power in an appropriate case to make a hospital order without convicting the accused. No trial is therefore called for. The circumstances in which it will be appropriate to exercise this unusual power are bound to be very rare and will usually require ... the consent of those acting for the accused if he is under a disability so that he cannot be tried".

If the defendant is unrepresented, it is submitted that evidence must be heard. *O'Connor* was considered by the Divisional Court in *R. v Ramsgate Justices Ex p. Kazmarek* (1985) 80 Cr.App.R. 366 and in *R. v Chippenham Magistrates' Court Ex p. Thompson* (1996) 32 B.M.L.R. 69. In *Kazmarek* it was held that in the case of an offence triable either summarily or on indictment where the accused elects trial by jury, this subsection can apply because the magistrates "would have power, on convicting him of that offence" to make a hospital order. *Kazmarek* was distinguished in *Thompson* where the court held that this subsection cannot apply in the case of an offence triable *only* on indictment in the Crown Court because in such a case the magistrates could not convict the offender of that offence.

In *R. (on the application of Singh) v Stratford Magistrates' Court)* [2007] EWHC 1582 (Admin); [2007] 4 All E.R. 407, the Divisional Court was concerned with the meaning and ambit of this provision when an accused in the magistrates' court contends that he is insane at the time of the events charged. It was held that:

1. Insanity can be relied upon as a common law defence to a summary charge in the magistrates' court. If established by the accused in a case to which it is relevant, it prevents conviction.

2. The accused has no right to a trial on the issue of insanity. The magistrates can either:

   (a) try the issue of insanity and pronounce its conclusions upon it, without convicting or acquitting the accused, provided that the conditions for making a hospital or guardianship order under this provision are met; or
   (b) if satisfied that there is no purpose in resolving the issue of insanity, and if an order under this provision is going to be made, the court can deal with the case without trying that issue.

   If it is clear that no order under this provision is going to be possible on the medical evidence, then in the absence of some other compelling factor the case must proceed to trial, so that if the accused was insane, he is acquitted, and if he was not, he is convicted.

3. Before embarking on a case to which this provision may be applied, magistrates should make it clear that it is a possibility and should invite submissions upon the course to be adopted. In particular, careful consideration must be given to any reason advanced why the issue of insanity should be tried. Such an application should be resolved having regard to the interests of justice, which include, but are not limited, to the justice of the accused.

The procedure for determining whether a person is fit to plead in the magistrates' court is specifically provided for by this provision when read in conjunction with s.11(1) of the Powers of Criminal Courts (Sentencing) Act 2000. Section 11(1) reads as follows:

"(1) If, on the trial by a magistrates' court of an offence punishable on summary conviction with imprisonment, the court—

(a) is satisfied that the accused did the act or made the omission charged, but

(b) is of the opinion that an inquiry ought to be made into his physical or mental condition before the method of dealing with him is determined,

the court shall adjourn the case to enable a medical examination and report to be made, and shall remand him."

These two provisions provide a complete statutory framework for the determination of all issues that arise in cases of defendants who are or might be mentally disordered in the context of offences which are triable summarily only. Moreover, a youth court is a magistrates' court within the meaning of this subsection (*R. (on the application of P (a minor)) v Barking Youth Court* [2002] EWHC Admin 734; [2002] M.H.L.R. 304).

Further guidance was given by Goldring L.J. in *R. (on the application of Blouet) v Bath and Wansdyke Magistrates' Court* [2009] EWHC 759 (Admin); [2009] M.H.L.R. 71, para.9:

> "The approach which the district judge should follow is this. First, there should be up-to-date—and I emphasise the words 'up-to-date'—medical evidence before him. If there is a possibility of a s37(3) order being made, he will then try the issue in accordance with s11(1) of the Act. If thereafter there arises the obligation to adjourn for further reports then that is what must happen. It may of course be that - given the up-to-date reports which he will then have - only a very short adjournment will be needed or, if everyone agrees that in the circumstances it is not, the matter can proceed under s37(3) if that be appropriate."

*P* was applied by the Divisional Court in *Director of Public Prosecutions v P* [2007] EWHC 496 (Admin); [2007] 4 All E,R. 628, where Smith L.J. said, at para.16, that s.11(1) of the 2000 Act and this provision "do not provide the solution to all of the problems which may confront a youth court before which a young person of doubtful capacity appears". The court held that:

1. Before criminal proceedings are commenced, appropriate consideration should be given to the question of whether civil proceedings under the Children Act are more appropriate.

2. If, in criminal proceedings, the defence raises an issue relating to the capacity of the young person before any evidence is heard, the court should stay the proceedings as an abuse of process in only exceptional cases.

3. In most cases, the medical evidence concerning capacity should be considered as part of the evidence in the case and not as the sole evidence in a freestanding application.

4. The court has a duty to keep under continuing review the question of whether the criminal trial ought to continue. If at any stage the court concludes that the child is unable to participate effectively in the trial, it may decide to call a halt. If the trial is halted on this ground, the court should then consider whether to switch to a consideration of whether the young person has done the acts alleged (the fact finding process), under the procedure referred to in the *Barking* case.

5. The fact that the young person cannot take an effective part in the fact finding process does not infringe his rights under art.6 of the ECHR.

Smith L.J. said at para.56:

> "The decision as to whether or not to switch to fact finding is one for the discretion of the court. The court will wish to consider the possibility that (either on the basis of existing medical evidence or further medical evidence) it might be appropriate to make a hospital order. If that possibility exists, the court should usually find on the facts. But even if a hospital order seems unlikely, there may be other advantages in continuing to complete the fact-finding process. If the court finds that the child did the acts alleged, it may be appropriate to alert the local authority to the position with a view to consideration of care proceedings. Although the youth court's findings may not be binding in the context of care proceedings, the fact that those findings have been made might result in the

simplification of care proceedings. I consider that proceedings should be stayed as an abuse of process before fact-finding only if no useful purpose at all could be served by the finding of facts."

DID THE ACT OR MADE THE OMISSION CHARGED. In *Singh*, above, Hughes L.J. said at para.33:

"[In] all cases where an order under s.37(3) is a possibility, the court should first determine the fact-finding exercise. That may be concluded, as here, on admissions, or it may involve hearing evidence. If the court is not satisfied that the act/omission was done/made, an unqualified acquittal must follow, whatever the anxieties may be about the accused's state of health."

This fact finding exercise is not a criminal trial (*Director of Public Prosecution v P*, above). In determining the issue, the prosecution is only required to prove the ingredients which comprise the actus reus of the offence, not the mens rea (*R. v Antoine* [2000] 2 All E.R. 208 HL).

THE COURT MAY. Having heard the evidence required by subs.(4).

MAKE SUCH AN ORDER. An order under this subsection can be made even though the court has not proceeded to trial. It can therefore be made in cases where the defendant is unable by virtue of his mental disorder to give his consent as to the mode of trial (*R. v Lincolnshire (Kesteven) Justices*, above.)

WITHOUT CONVICTING HIM. The person has the same right of appeal against the order as if it had been made on his conviction (s.45). Although a person dealt with under this provision is not convicted, the order is a "conviction" for the purposes of the Rehabilitation of Offenders Act 1974 s.1(4), because it includes a finding that the person did the act or made the omission charged. A criminal records entry will therefore be made.

A person who is made subject to a hospital order under this provision is an "offender" for the purposes of s.142 of the Magistrates' Courts Act 1980. Under s.142: "A magistrates' court may vary or rescind ... [an] order ... made by it when dealing with an offender ..." There were sound practical reasons for treating a defendant, made subject to a hospital order, as an offender for the purposes of s.142. If having made a hospital order the magistrates discovered information which suggested that the defendant might not suffer from mental disorder, or might not have done the acts complained of, or, as in the present case, that arrangements could not in fact be made for his admission to hospital, it was highly desirable that there should be a procedural means by which the magistrates could rectify the error (*R. v Thames Magistrates' Court Ex p. Ramadan* 1 Cr. App. R. 386). *Ramadan* was applied in *Bartram v Southend Magistrates' Court* [2004] EWHC 2691 (Admin); [2004] M.H.L.R. 319, para.19, where Collins J. said that:

"there might be a case where it would be in the interests of the accused to have the matter reopened because whilst he was unable to give instructions and was unfit to plead, the evidence which established that he had done the act could not be challenged. When his mental state recovered sufficiently to enable him to give proper instructions, it might be that it became apparent that he did indeed have a defence to the charge which was laid against him. Thus in such a case he might want the charge to be tried because he expected that he would be acquitted of it".

*Subsection (4)*

**1–490**     In *R. (on the application of DB) v Nottinghamshire Healthcare NHS Trust* [2008] EWCA Civ 1354; [2009] 2 All E.R. 792, the Court of Appeal held that a hospital order, including a hospital order which is made subject to the restrictions contained in s.41, ceases to have effect if the offender who is the subject of the order is not admitted to the hospital named in the order within the period of 28 days from the date of the making of the order, as stipulated by it. It follows that after the 28 days have expired there is no authority either to convey the offender to the hospital or to detain him there. In this situation, "no doubt consideration can rapidly be given to the question whether the defendant can be compulsorily admitted to a hospital pursuant to Pt II of the Act rather than Pt III"; per Stanley Burnton L.J. at para.30. His Lordship said at paras 25, 26:

"It would I think be preferable for the standard form of order to specify the date when the 28 day period expires. In addition, it would be sensible for orders made under section 37 to include a direction or recommendation (for it has no statutory force) on the lines of that set out in [Circular 66/1980, noted below]. All parties should bear in mind the power of the sentencing court under section 155 of the Powers of Criminal Courts (Sentencing) Act 2000 to vary or, if necessary, to rescind an order. If an order is rescinded, a hospital order may be made subsequently; but the court should consider rescission of an order as a last resort, since the consequence will usually be to prolong a patient's detention in prison.

In the present case the orders made by the Crown Court did not make provision for the detention of the Appellant pending his transfer to hospital: the direction "that pending admission to a hospital within the 28 day period, the defendant should be conveyed to and detained in a place of safety, namely . . ." had been, in each case, deleted. The result was that there was no lawful authority for his detention during that period. The exercise by the sentencing court of the power conferred on by the last part of section 37(4) to direct conveyance to and detention in a place of safety pending admission to hospital is not automatic or mandatory. Unless the offender is to be immediately conveyed from the court to the hospital, the court must ensure that the power is expressly exercised."

This subsection applies both to orders made following conviction under subs.(1) and to orders made under subs.(3) (*R. v Thames Magistrates' Court Ex p. Ramadan*, above).

AN ORDER . . . SHALL NOT BE MADE.    A hospital order can only be made if a suitable hospital has agreed to make a bed available for the offender within 28 days. In *R. v Galfetti* [2002] EWCA Crim 1916; [2002] M.H.L.R. 418, the sentencing of a mentally disordered offender had been subject to repeated adjournments whilst attempts were made to secure a hospital bed for him. A hospital order was eventually made nine months after conviction. May L.J. giving the judgment of the court said at para.51:

"Whenever a hospital place is not available within a reasonable time for an offender for whom a hospital order is the appropriate disposal, the court is disabled from affording justice in the way which Parliament has provided".

His Lordship identified, at para.52, the following possibilities which are available to the sentencing court in these circumstances, none of which is "wholly satisfactory":

1. The judge can and should make every effort to persuade the hospital authorities to find a suitable place.

2. There may come a time in an individual case when, by reason of delay, a sentence other than a hospital order should be considered. However, it could scarcely ever be satisfactory, if a court is constrained to pass a different sentence simply because an appropriate hospital place is not available.

3. The court will take delay into account in deciding the eventual disposal. May L.J. said at para.48: "[I]n so far as it is necessary to characterise the process as providing

a remedy under Article 6(1) [of the European Convention on Human Rights], it lies in taking the delay and its consequences into account in determining the disposal".

His Lordship said, at para.53, that the court would "draw attention in appropriate quarters to our profound disquiet" at the situation that it had encountered and to "the possible lacuna which this case illustrates, that there may be no route by which a defendant convicted in the Crown Court can appeal an order adjourning his sentence".

APPROVED CLINICIAN. Who could be one of the doctors giving evidence under subs.(2)(a). "Where evidence is given that a bed will be made available within that timescale, the hospital managers must ensure that the commitment is met" ("Mental Health Act 2007: Guidance for the courts on remand and sentencing powers for mentally disordered offenders", Ministry of Justice, March 2008, para.4.20). But see subs.(5).

SOME OTHER PERSON. Who need not be a clinician.

28 DAYS. Any time that the patient is unlawfully at large is disregarded when calculating this period (s.138(5)). The Secretary of State has been given the power to reduce this period under s.54A. In Wales, this power is exercised by the Welsh Ministers (see the General Note to this Act).

BEGINNING WITH. Including the date of the making of the order (*Zoan v Rouamba* [2000] 2 All E.R. 620 CA).

CONVEYANCE ... AND DETENTION. See para.33.25 of the *Code of Practice*. General provisions relating to conveyance and detention are set out in s.137.

PLACE OF SAFETY. Is defined in s.55(1). Home Office Circular No. 66/1980 draws attention to the problem which can arise when a hospital order has been made and the defendant is committed to a place of safety under this subsection pending admission to hospital, but the hospital subsequently withdraws its undertaking to admit him. A change of procedure was introduced in 1979 in the Crown Court, which attempts to deal with this problem. The Crown Court has power, under s.155 of the Powers of Criminal Courts (Sentencing) Act 2000, to vary sentence on a defendant within 28 days, and the purpose of the new procedure is to ensure that the court is forewarned of the possible frustration of a hospital order and so has the opportunity to pass an alternative sentence. The Lord Chief Justice has directed that an additional direction be given by the court under this section, addressed to the governor of the prison which is to hold the person pending admission to hospital, which reads as follows:

"But if at any time it appears to the person in whose custody the defendant is detained in a place of safety that the defendant might not be admitted to hospital in pursuance of this order within 28 days of this date, that person shall within 21 days of this date (or at once if it becomes apparent only after 21 days that the defendant might not be admitted to hospital) report the circumstances to the Chief Clerk of the Court and unless otherwise directed by the Chief Clerk shall bring the defendant before the Court forthwith so as to enable it within 28 days of this date to make such order as may be necessary."

A patient who is detained in a place of safety is not subject to the Consent to Treatment provisions contained in Pt IV of this Act (s.56(3)(b)). However, following the decision by the Court of Appeal in *R. v North West London Mental Health NHS Trust Ex p. Stewart* [1997] 4 All E.R. 871, it seems that a patient who has been detained in a place of safety which is a hospital could be brought within the scope of Pt IV if he was made the subject of an application under s.3: see the General Note to s.35. There are no provisions for discharge or leave of absence from a place of safety.

Once the 28-day period specified in this provision has lapsed, the offender's detention in the place of safety is unauthorised and he or she has to be released. In this situation, consideration can be given to detaining the offender under Pt II (*R. (on the application of DB) v Nottinghamshire Healthcare NHS Trust,* above, para.30).

If a patient escapes from a place of safety s.138 allows for him or her to be retaken, subject to the time limits set out in s.18(4). A restriction order patient may be retaken at any time.

*Subsection (5)*

"This provision is intended to meet the case of a hospital which has agreed to accept the **1–491** patient being unavoidably unable to do so, e.g. because of a fire or an epidemic; but in practice it is generally easier for the patient to be returned to court for a further order to be made so as to give a further 28-day period in which a bed may become available. The Crown Court hospital order form 5034 is designed to facilitate this procedure" (Home Office Circular No. 69/1983 para.5).

If it proves impossible to find a bed for the offender, the Crown Court has power under s.155 of the Powers of Criminal Courts (Sentencing) Act 2000 to vary or rescind the sentence: see *R. (on the application of DB) v Nottinghamshire Healthcare NHS Trust*, above. An analogous power for magistrates' courts is contained in s.142 of the Magistrates' Courts Act 1980.

SECRETARY OF STATE. Or, in relation to Wales, the Welsh Ministers (see the General Note to this Act). In England, this function is performed by the Secretary of State for Health.

28 DAYS. See the note on subs.(4) above.

*Subsection (6)*

This subsection provides that the court cannot make a guardianship order without the **1–492** consent of the potential guardian. The consent of the offender is not required.

In *R. (on the application of Bukowicki) v Northamptonshire County Council* [2007] EWHC 310 (Admin); [2007] M.H.L.R. 121, Mole J. held that that subs.(2)(b), read with this provision, makes it clear that that the judge's judgement about the suitability of making a guardianship order must be subordinate to the willingness of the local authority to accept the guardianship. The authority has a wide discretion as to the factors that they are able to take into account in deciding if they are willing to accept an offender into guardianship. When exercising that discretion, the authority should take into account every material consideration relevant to their ability to manage him under the order. The authority should also take into account the relevant chapter of the *Code of Practice* (Ch.26) and its own policy on guardianship.

*Subsection (8)*

This provision is concerned with the powers of the court in sentencing and it has no **1–493** application to transfers ordered by the Secretary of State for Justice under s.47 (*R. (on the application of Miah) v Secretary of State for the Home Department* [2004] EWHC 2569 (Admin); [2004] M.H.L.R. 302 para.23).

ANY OTHER ORDER. For example, a compensation order or an order disqualifying the offender from driving.

## Interim hospital orders

**38.**—(1) Where a person is convicted before the Crown Court of an offence **1–494** punishable with imprisonment (other than an offence the sentence for which is fixed by law) or is convicted by a magistrates' court of an offence punishable on summary conviction with imprisonment and the court before or by which he is convicted is satisfied, on the written or oral evidence of two registered medical practitioners—

   (a)  that the offender is suffering from [mental disorder]; and

   (b)  that there is reason to suppose that the mental disorder from which the offender is suffering is such that it may be appropriate for a hospital order to be made in his case,

the court may, before making a hospital order or dealing with him in some other way, make an order (in this Act referred to as "an interim hospital order") authorising his admission to such hospital as may be specified in the order and his detention there in accordance with this section.

(2) In the case of an offender who is subject to an interim hospital order the court may make a hospital order without his being brought before the court if he is represented by [an authorised person who] is given an opportunity of being heard.

(3) At least one of the registered medical practitioners whose evidence is taken into account under subsection (1) above shall be employed at the hospital which is to be specified in the order.

(4) An interim hospital order shall not be made for admission of an offender to a hospital unless the court is satisfied, on the written or oral evidence of the [approved clinician who would have overall responsibility for his case] or of some other person representing the managers of the hospital, that arrangements have been made for his admission to that hospital and for his admission to it within the period of 28 days beginning with the date of the order; and if the court is so satisfied the court may, pending his admission, give directions for his conveyance to and detention in a place of safety.

(5) An interim hospital order—

   (a)  shall be in force for such period, not exceeding 12 weeks; as the court may specify when making the order; but

   (b)  may be renewed for further periods of not more than 28 days at a time if it appears to the court, on the written or oral evidence of the [responsible clinician], that the continuation of the order is warranted;

but no such order shall continue in force for more than [twelve months] in all and the court shall terminate the order if it makes a hospital order in respect of the offender or decides after considering the written or oral evidence of the [responsible clinician] to deal with the offender in some other way.

(6) The power of renewing an interim hospital order may be exercised without the offender being brought before the court if he is represented by counsel or a solicitor and his counsel or solicitor is given an opportunity of being heard.

(7) If an offender absconds from a hospital in which he is detained in pursuance of an interim hospital order, or while being conveyed to or from such a hospital, he may be arrested without warrant by a constable and shall, after being arrested, be brought as soon as practicable before the court that made the order; and the court may thereupon terminate the order and deal with him in any way in which it could have dealt with him if no such order had been made.

AMENDMENT

   The words in square brackets were substituted by the Mental Health Act 2007 ss.1(4), 10(5), Sch.1 para.8. The words in square brackets in subs.(2) were substituted by the

Legal Services Act 2007, s.208, Sch.21, para.56. In subs.(5) the the phrase "twelve months" was substituted by the Crime (Sentences) Act 1997 s.49(1).

DEFINITIONS
    mental disorder: ss.1, 145(1).                                        **1–495**
    hospital: ss.55(5), 145(1).
    hospital order: ss.37, 145(1).
    the managers: s.145(1).
    responsible clinician: s.55(1).
    approved clinician: s.145)(1).
    authorised person: s.55(1).

GENERAL NOTE
    The Butler Committee at para.12.5, "gained the impression that many doctors found it **1–496** difficult to decide whether to recommend that a hospital order should be made where they have been able to examine the patient only briefly in a prison hospital under the pressure of impending court proceedings, since it was often impossible to know how he would react subsequently to the psychiatric hospital regime". This section responds to this concern by empowering a Crown Court or magistrates' court to send a convicted offender to hospital for up to twelve months to enable an assessment to be made on the appropriateness of making a hospital order or direction in respect of him or her. If the court makes an order under this section "the offender's response in hospital can be evaluated without any irrevocable commitment on either side to this method of dealing with the offender if it should prove unsuitable" (Home Office Circular No.71/1984, Annex, para.15). The effect of an interim hospital order is set out in s.40(3). The purpose of an interim hospital order is "not to hold the position until a place in an appropriate hospital is available for an offender for whom a hospital order is known to be appropriate" (*R. v Galfetti* [2002] EWCA Crim 1916; [2002] M.H.L.R. 418 per May L.J. at para.7).
    An offender who is placed under an interim hospital order made under this section is subject to the consent to treatment provisions contained in Pt IV of this Act (ss.40(4), 56(3)). Otherwise, the legal position of a patient subject to such an order differs markedly from that of a patient subject to a hospital order: see the note on s.40(3). As an interim hospital order is a form of sentence, it is appealable (Criminal Appeal Act 1968 s.50(1)).
    An offender who absconds may be arrested without warrant by any constable and is then to be brought before the court that made the order, which may decide on an alternative way of dealing with him or her.
    In *R. (on the application of LS) v Brent Magistrates' Court*, unreported, July 14, 2009, the court held that an offender's presence in court is not required for the making of an order under this section by reason of the terms of subs.(2). Neither need the offender be present if the order is renewed (subs.(6)) or if the court makes a hospital order (subs.(2)).

*Armed Services Act 200*
    For the application of this section to the 2006 Act, see *ibid.*, Sch.4, para.5.        **1–497**

*Applications to the First-tier Tribunal (Mental Health) or the Mental Health Review Tribunal for Wales*
    Neither the patient nor his or her nearest relative have a right to make an application to **1–498** the tribunal: see the note on s.40(3). If, when the case returns to court for sentencing, the court makes a hospital order under s.37, the patient will be unable to make an application to a tribunal during the first six months of the order.

*Appeals*
    Under s.11(3) of the Criminal Appeal Act 1968, an interim hospital order may only be **1–499** made by the Court of Appeal if it first quashes the trial judge's sentence. The Court of

Appeal has described this state of affairs as being "obviously unsatisfactory" (*R. v Cooper* [2001] EWCA Crim 47; [2001] M.H.L.R. 2 per Hooper J. at para.18).

A court that has made an order under this section may end it and make its final sentencing decision despite the fact that an appeal against the order is outstanding: see s.11(5) of the 1968 Act.

*Orders made in other proceedings*

**1–500**    In certain circumstances, an interim hospital order may be made under the Contempt of Court Act 1981, s.14(4),(4A), the Family Law Act 1996, s.51 and the Armed Forces Act 2006 s.169 and Sch.4 para.5.

*Responsibility for returning the patient to court*

**1–501**    See paras 31 to 33 of Home Office Circular No.71/1984 which are reproduced in the note on s.35(9).

*Subsection (1)*

**1–502**    CONVICTED BY A MAGISTRATES' COURT.    Or a youth court if the offender is under 18 years of age. The court cannot make an interim hospital order in respect of an unconvicted person.

OFFENCE PUNISHABLE WITH IMPRISONMENT.    This is construed in accordance with s.47(5) (s.55(6)).

FIXED BY LAW.    This section does not apply to persons who have been convicted of murder.

OFFENCE PUNISHABLE ON SUMMARY CONVICTION WITH IMPRISONMENT.    See s.55(2).

EVIDENCE.    For general requirements as to medical evidence, see s.54. The court can call a doctor who has provided a written report to give oral evidence (s.54(2A)).

TWO REGISTERED MEDICAL PRACTITIONERS.    One of whom must be approved by the Secretary of State or the Welsh Ministers under s.12 (s.54(1)). Also note subs.(3).

IS SUFFERING FROM.    It is not sufficient that the doctors have a mere reason to suspect that the offender is suffering from mental disorder.

MENTAL DISORDER.    If the person has a learning disability, the disability must be associated with abnormally aggressive or seriously irresponsible conduct (s.1(2A), (2B)).

HOSPITAL ORDER.    Or a hospital direction and a limitation direction (s.45A(8)).

HOSPITAL.    Or an establishment registered under the Care Standards Act 2000 (ss.34(2), 55(5)). A court may request information about the availability of hospital places under s.39.

*Subsection (3)*

**1–503**    The requirement of this provision does not apply to an order made under s.37.

*Subsection (4)*

In *R. (on the application of DB) v Nottinghamshire Healthcare NHS Trust* [2008] EWCA Civ 1354; [2009] 2 All E.R. 792, noted under s.37(4), the Court of Appeal held that a hospital order ceases to have effect if the offender who is the subject of the order is not admitted to the hospital named in the order within the period of 28 days from the date of the making of the order, as stipulated by it. It is submitted that this finding applies to an order made under this section.

APPROVED CLINICIAN. Who could be the doctor referred to in subs.(3). **1–504**

SOME OTHER PERSON. Who need not be a clinician.

28 DAYS. The Secretary of State and the Welsh Ministers have been given the power to reduce this period (s.54A).

BEGINNING WITH THE DATE OF THE ORDER. Including the date of the order (*Zoan v Rouamba* [2002] 2 All E.R. 620 CA).

CONVEYANCE . . . AND DETENTION. See paras 33.25 to 33.27 of the *Code of Practice*. For general provisions relating to conveyance and detention, see s.137.

PLACE OF SAFETY. See the note on s.37(4). A significant difference between a patient who is in a place of safety under s.37(4) and a patient who is in a place of safety under this provision is that the latter is subject to the Consent to Treatment provisions contained in Pt IV (s.56(3)).

*Subsection (5)*
This provides that if doubts remain as to the appropriateness of a hospital order (or a hos- **1–505** pital direction and a limitation direction (s.45A(8)) after three months, the interim hospital order can be renewed at monthly intervals up to an overall total of 12 months.

12 WEEKS. This requirement does not apply to the remand of an accused person under s.48(1) of the Family Law Act 1996 (*Williams v Williams* [2001] EWCA Civ 197).

RENEWED. It is submitted that the order can be renewed in respect of a different hospital if the requirements of subs.(4) are satisfied in respect of the patient's admission to that hospital.

THE CONTINUATION OF THE ORDER IS WARRANTED. The continuation of the order would not be warranted in a situation where the assessment has been completed, the assessment has concluded that a hospital order would be warranted, but there is a delay in identifying a suitable hospital that would be willing to accept the patient: see *R. v Galfetti*, above.

*Subsection (7)*
There is no time limit on a recapture under this provision. **1–506**

## Information as to hospitals
**39.**—(1) Where a court is minded to make a hospital order or interim hospital **1–507** order in respect of any person it may request—
   (a) the [Primary Care Trust or] [Local Health Board] for [the area] in which that person resides or last resided; or—
   (b) [the National Assembly for Wales or any other] [Primary Care Trust or] [Local Health Board] that appears to the court to be appropriate,
to furnish the court with such information as [that [Primary Care Trust or] [Local Health Board or National Assembly for Wales] have or can reasonably obtain with respect to the hospital or hospitals (if any) in [their area] or elsewhere at which arrangements could be made for the admission of that person in pursuance of the order, and [that [Primary Care Trust or] [Local Health Board or National Assembly for Wales] shall] comply with any such request.
   [(1A) In relation to a person who has not attained the age of 18 years, subsection (1) above shall have effect as if the reference to the making of a hospital order

included a reference to a remand under section 35 or 36 above or the making of an order under section 44 below.

(1B) Where the person concerned has not attained the age of 18 years, the information which may be requested under subsection (1) above includes, in particular, information about the availability of accommodation or facilities designed so as to be specially suitable for patients who have not attained the age of 18 years.]

(2) [ ... ]

AMENDMENTS

The amendments to this section were made by the Health Authorities Act 1995 ss.2(1), 5(1), Sch.1 para.107(5), Sch.3 and the National Health Service Reform and Health Care Professions Act 2002 s.2(5), Sch.1 para.46. The amendments to subs.(1) were made by SI 2007/961 art.3 Sch. para.13(8). Subsections (1A) and (1B) were inserted by the Mental Health Act 2007 s.31(2).

DEFINITION

**1–508**   hospital order: ss.37, 145(1).
interim hospital order: ss.38, 145(1).
hospital: ss.55(5), 145(1).
Health Authority: s.145(1).

GENERAL NOTE

**1–509**   This section provides that whenever a court is considering making a hospital order, a hospital and a limitation direction (s.45A(8)) or an interim hospital order it may ask the appropriate Primary Care Trust or Local Health Board to provide information as to the availability of suitable hospital places for the person in question. It also enables the court to request information about the availability of hospital places for child offenders in respect of whom the court is considering a remand under ss.35 or 36 or, in respect of a magistrates' court, a committal to hospital under s.44. The information that may be requested includes information about the "availability of accommodation designed so as to be specially suitable" for child patients. Paragraph 105 of the Explanatory Notes states: "The purpose of this provision is to ensure that courts do not place a child in a prison setting when a suitable hospital bed would be a more appropriate option."

Paragraph 15 of Home Office Circular No.66/90, states:

"Section 39 obliges ... Health Authorities to inform the court as to the facilities they provide for detained patients, including those who may require treatment in appropriate conditions of security; and it will also enable the ... Health Authority to advise in cases where there is some room for doubt as to the patient's normal place of residence or other factor determining the appropriate hospital within whose catchment area he falls. The intention is to provide a court with all possible assistance short of removing the obligation in section 37(4) of the 1983 Act to be satisfied that the necessary arrangements have been made before making a hospital order, in cases where the necessary criteria for a hospital order are satisfied and it is minded to make one, but no hospital place has been made available. ... Health Authorities have been encouraged to make standing arrangements for meeting such requests for information from courts, and it is intended that these arrangements will reduce the number of cases in which a hospital order appears suitable but the court is frustrated in the search for a place. In cases where it is desired to make use of this provision, the clerk of the court should contact the ... Health Authority covering the area from which the offender appears to come. (There is no longer any scope for disputes between ... Health Authorities as to responsibility for dealing with the enquiry, as any Authority approached by the court is under a statutory duty to provide information about hospitals 'in [their area] or elsewhere' at which arrangements could be made for the person to be admitted. If the Authority first contacted believes it to be more appropriate for another Authority to respond, it will only be able to pass on responsibility if the second Authority agrees)."

Local Health Boards and Primary Care Trusts are required by s.140 to notify relevant social services authorities of those hospitals where patients can be treated in cases of special urgency.

*Code of Practice*
Guidance on this section is contained in Ch.33 at para.33.6.                          **1–510**

*Subsection (1)*
IT MAY REQUEST.   The Mental Health Act Commission reported that only limited use  **1–511** has been made of this power (Mental Health Act Commission, *Third Biennial Report* 1987–89, para.11.2). According to one experienced magistrate, invoking this section "can be quite effective in producing a bed" (Joy Major "What can a magistrate do", in *The Mentally Disordered Offender*, Ed. K. Herbst and J. Gunn, Butterworth-Heinemann, 1991, at p.52).

RESIDES.   Temporary absences from the place where a person lives does not affect residence, as long as there is an intention to return (*R. v St Leonard's Shoreditch (Inhabitants)* (1865) L.R. 1 Q.B. 21). Also note Widgery L.J.'s statement in *Fox v Stirk* [1970] 2 Q.B. 463 at 477 that: "A man cannot be said to reside in a particular place unless in the ordinary sense of the word one can say that for the time being he is making his home in that place."

HOSPITAL.   Or registered establishment (ss.34(2), 55(5)).

## [Information to facilitate guardianship orders

**39A.** Where a court is minded to make a guardianship order in respect of any  **1–512** offender, it may request the local social services authority for the area in which the offender resides or last resided, or any other local social services authority that appears to the court to be appropriate—

(a)  to inform the court whether it or any other person approved by it is willing to receive the offender into guardianship; and

(b)  if so, to give such information as it reasonably can about how it or the other person could be expected to exercise in relation to the offender the powers conferred by section 40(2) below;

and that authority shall comply with any such request.]

AMENDMENT
This section was inserted by the Criminal Justice Act 1991 s.27(1) and came into force on October 1, 1992 (SI 1992/333).

DEFINITIONS
local social services authority: s.145(1).                                         **1–513**
guardianship order: ss.37, 145(1).

GENERAL NOTE
This section enables the court to find out whether the relevant local social services auth-  **1–514** ority or a private guardian approved by the authority is willing to receive the offender into guardianship and, if this were to happen, how the authority or guardian might exercise their guardianship powers in relation to the offender.

*Code of Practice*
**1–515**    Guidance on this section is contained in Ch.33 at para.33.7.

## Effect of hospital orders, guardianship orders and interim hospital orders

**1–516**    **40.**—(1) A hospital order shall be sufficient authority—

(a)  for a constable, an [approved mental health professional] or any other person directed to do so by the court to convey the patient to the hospital specified in the order within a period of 28 days; and

(b)  for the managers of the hospital to admit him at any time within that period and thereafter detain him in accordance with the provisions of this Act.

(2) A guardianship order shall confer on the authority or person named in the order as guardian the same powers as a guardianship application made and accepted under Part II of this Act.

(3) Where an interim hospital order is made in respect of an offender—

(a)  a constable or any other person directed to do so by the court shall convey the offender to the hospital specified in the order within the period mentioned in section 38(4) above; and

(b)  the managers of the hospital shall admit him within that period and thereafter detain him in accordance with the provisions of section 38 above.

(4) A patient who is admitted to a hospital in pursuance of a hospital order, or placed under guardianship by a guardianship order, shall, subject to the provisions of this subsection, be treated for the purposes of the provisions of this Act mentioned in Part I of Schedule 1 to this Act as if he had been so admitted or placed on the date of the order in pursuance of an application for admission for treatment or a guardianship application, as the case may be, duly made under Part II of this Act, but subject to any modifications of those provisions specified in that Part of that Schedule.

(5) Where a patient is admitted to a hospital in pursuance of a hospital order, or placed under guardianship by a guardianship order, any previous application, hospital order or guardianship order by virtue of which he was liable to be detained in a hospital or subject to guardianship shall cease to have effect; but if the first-mentioned order, or the conviction on which it was made, is quashed on appeal, this subsection shall not apply and section 22 above shall have effect as if during any period for which the patient was liable to be detained or subject to guardianship under the order, he had been detained in custody as mentioned in that section.

[(6) Where—

(a)  a patient admitted to a hospital in pursuance of a hospital order is absent without leave;

(b)  a warrant to arrest him has been issued under section 72 of the Criminal Justice Act 1967; and

(c)  he is held pursuant to the warrant in any country or territory other than the United Kingdom, any of the Channel Islands and the Isle of Man,

he shall be treated as having been taken into custody under section 18 above on first being so held.]

AMENDMENT

The words in square brackets in subs.(1)(a) were substituted by the Mental Health Act 2007 s.21, Sch.2 para.7. Subsection (6) was inserted by the Mental Health (Patients in the Community) Act 1995 s.2(4).

DEFINITIONS
> hospital order: ss.37, 145(1). **1–517**
> approved mental health professional: s.145(1), (1AC).
> the managers: s.145(1).
> hospital: ss.55(5), 145(1).
> hospital order: s.55(4).
> guardianship order: ss.37, 55(4), 145(1).
> interim hospital order: ss.38, 145(1).
> patient: s.145(1).
> application for admission for treatment: ss.3, 145(1).

GENERAL NOTE

This section provides that, with very few exceptions, a patient who is admitted to hos- **1–518** pital under a hospital order without restrictions or placed under guardianship by a guardianship order is treated the same as a patient who has been admitted to hospital or placed under guardianship under Pt II of this Act. The necessary modifications to the provisions of Pt II are made by Pt I of Sch.I and are noted in subs.(4). The effect of hospital orders and guardianship orders was considered by the Court of Appeal in *R. v Birch* (1989) 11 Cr. App. R.(S.) 202, noted in the General Note to s.37. The effect of an interim hospital order is set out in subs.(3).

The court documents should be carefully checked by the hospital managers. The validity of an order made by a magistrates' court should not be investigated unless there are circumstances that should put the hospital managers on notice (*R. (on the application of LS) v Brent Magistrates' Court*, unreported, July 14, 2009; also see *R. v Central London County Court, ex p. London*, noted in the General Note to s.6). An order made by a superior court must be obeyed unless it has been set aside: see the note on "Defective Court Orders" in the General Note to this Part.

Any reference to hospital orders and guardianship orders in subs.(2), (4) or (5) of this section shall be construed as including a reference to any order or directions under this Part having the same effect as a hospital or guardianship order (s.55(4)).

*Subsection (1)*

CONSTABLE. Means the office of constable, and not the rank of constable (Police Act **1–519** 1996 s.29, Sch.4).

CONVEY THE PATIENT TO HOSPITAL. For general provisions relating to conveyance, see s.137. Before proceeding to convey the patient to hospital, the authorised person should confirm with the hospital that it is still willing to accept the patient because this section does not give authority to convey the patient *from* hospital if admission is refused.

WITHIN A PERIOD OF 28 DAYS. Any time that the patient is unlawfully at large is disregarded when calculating this period (s.138(5)). Once this period has expired, the hospital order ceases to provide authority for the offender's conveyance to hospital or his detention there: see *R. (on the application of DB) v Nottinghamshire Healthcare NHS Trust*, noted under s.37(4).

*Subsection (2)*

SAME POWERS. As contained in s.8(1). A patient placed under a guardianship order is **1–520** not subject to the consent to treatment provisions contained in Pt IV because he or she is not a patient who is "liable to be detained": see s.56(3).

*Subsection (3)*

This subsection sets out the effect of an interim hospital order made under s.38. Apart **1–521** from coming within the scope of Pt IV, an interim hospital, order patient is treated very differently from a hospital order patient. This is because an interim hospital order patient is not to be treated as if he had been admitted in pursuance of an application for admission for treatment: he is detained "in accordance with the provisions of s.38". The consequences of this are that neither the patient nor his nearest relative can apply to a tribunal, no-one has the right to discharge the patient and the patient may not be granted leave of absence or be transferred to another hospital. Although applications have been made to the court for authority to either grant the patient leave of absence or to transfer the patient, this Act does not provide the court with an express power to make such orders.

CONVEY THE OFFENDER TO THE HOSPITAL.   As to who is responsible for conveying the patient back to court, see the note on s.35(9).

WITHIN THE PERIOD MENTIONED IN S.38(4).   28 days beginning with the date of the order.

SHALL ADMIT HIM.   The hospital specified in an interim hospital order cannot subsequently withdraw its agreement to accept the offender.

*Subsection (4)*

**1–522**   HOSPITAL ORDER.   With three substantive exceptions, the effect of this subsection is to place a patient who has been placed under a hospital order in the same legal position as a patient who has been admitted to hospital for treatment under s.3 of this Act. The exceptions are: (1) the nearest relative of a hospital order patient cannot order his discharge under s.23 (Sch.1 paras 2, 8); (2) unlike a s.3 patient, the hospital order patient cannot apply to a tribunal within the first six months of his or her detention (Sch.1 paras 2, 9); and (3) the initial six month maximum period of detention runs from the day that the hospital order is made by the court, not the patient's admission to the hospital (Sch.1 paras 2, 6).
   If the medical conditions which justified the making of the hospital order cease to be met at any time the duty of the responsible clinician, exercising a medical judgment, is to discharge the offender from the hospital order (*R. v Drew* [2003] UKHL 25; [2003] 4 All E.R. 557 para.10).

GUARDIANSHIP ORDER.   The effect of a guardianship order made under s.37 is essentially the same as if the patient had been made the subject of a guardianship application under s.7. The major difference between the two is that with a guardianship order the power of the nearest relative to discharge the patient from guardianship does not apply (Sch.1 paras 2, 8).

*Subsection (5)*

**1–523**   CEASE TO HAVE EFFECT.   Unless a restriction order made in respect of the patient under s.41 is in force at the material time (s.41(4)). The ending of the previous order or application does not effect the continuity of the three-month period provided for in s.58(1)(b). The imposition of the subsequent order provides the patient with a fresh opportunity to make an application to a tribunal during the second six months of his or her detention under that order.
   An interim hospital order is not specified in this provision (see s.38(1)). If the patient is subject to a s.3 application when such an order is made by the court, the application should either be discharged under s.23 or allowed to continue during the currency of the interim order, in which case it will be reinstated (if it has not expired in the meantime) once the interim order is terminated. If the court proceeds to make a hospital or guardianship order in respect of the patient, this provision will terminate the s.3.

*Subsection (6)*

**1–524**   This subsection is concerned with the taking into custody of absconding patients who have gone abroad. Paragraph 31.17 of the Reference Guide states:

"The Act does not permit patients to be retaken outside the UK, the Isle of Man or the Channel Islands. However, in certain cases, under the Extradition Act 2003, patients who are convicted offenders or accused of a crime may be extradited back to England, if the necessary warrants have been issued. The effect of section 40(6) is that if a patient subject to a restricted hospital order is detained overseas under extradition arrangements, the patient is treated as having been taken into custody under section 18 when first held on the basis of the extradition warrant in the country in question, rather than when returned to the UK. If the patient's restriction order is for a fixed period, that may affect whether it is still in force when the patient returns to England or Wales."

*Restriction Orders*

**Power of higher courts to restrict discharge from hospital**

**41.**—(1) Where a hospital order is made in respect of an offender by the Crown **1–525** Court, and it appears to the court, having regard to the nature of the offence, the antecedents of the offender and the risk of his committing further offences if set at large, that it is necessary for the protection of the public from serious harm so to do, the court may, subject to the provisions of this section, further order that the offender shall be subject to the special restrictions set out in this section, [. . .] and an order under this section shall be known as "a restriction order".

(2) A restriction order shall not be made in the case of any person unless at least one of the registered medical practitioners whose evidence is taken into account by the court under section 37(2)(a) above has given evidence orally before the court.

(3) The special restrictions applicable to a patient in respect of whom a restriction order is in force are as follows—

(a) none of the provisions of Part II of this Act relating to the duration, renewal and expiration of authority for the detention of patients shall apply, and the patient shall continue to be liable to be detained by virtue of the relevant hospital order until he is duly discharged under the said Part II or absolutely discharged under section 42, 73, 74 or 75 below;

[(aa): none of the provisions of Part II of this Act relating to [community treatment orders and community patients] shall apply;]

(b) no application shall be made to [the appropriate tribunal] in respect of a patient under section 66 or 69(1) below;

(c) the following powers shall be exercisable only with the consent of the Secretary of State, namely—

(i) power to grant leave of absence to the patient under section 17 above;

(ii) power to transfer the patient in pursuance of regulations under section 19 above [or in pursuance of subsection (3) of that section]; and

(iii) power to order the discharge of the patient under section 23 above; and if leave of absence is granted under the said section 17 power to recall the patient under that section shall vest in the Secretary of State as well as the [responsible clinician]; and

(d) the power of the Secretary of State to recall the patient under the said section 17 and power to take the patient into custody and return him under section 18 above may be exercised at any time;

and in relation to any such patient section 40(4) above shall have effect as if it referred to Part II of Schedule 1 to this Act instead of Part I of that Schedule.

(4) A hospital order shall not cease to have effect under section 40(5) above if a restriction order in respect of the patient is in force at the material time.

(5) Where a restriction order in respect of a patient ceases to have effect while the relevant hospital order continues in force, the provisions of section 40 above and Part I of Schedule 1 to this Act shall apply to the patient as if he had been admitted to the hospital in pursuance of a hospital order (without a restriction order) made on the date on which the restriction order ceased to have effect.

(6) While a person is subject to a restriction order the [responsible clinician] shall at such intervals (not exceeding one year) as the Secretary of State may direct examine and report to the Secretary of State on that person; and every report shall contain such particulars as the Secretary of State may require.

AMENDMENTS

In subs.(3), para.(aa) was inserted by the Mental Health (Patients in the Community) Act 1995 s.2(1), Sch.1 para.5. The words in square brackets in subss.(3)(aa), (3)(c)) and (6) were substituted by the Mental Health Act 2007 ss.10(6), 32, Sch.3 para.17. The words in square brackets in para.(c)(ii) were inserted by the Crime (Sentences) Act 1997 s.49(2). The reference to the appropriate tribunal in subs.(3)(b) was substituted by SI 2008/2883, art.9 Sch.3 para.41. The words omitted in subs.(1) were repealed by s.55, Sch.11 Pt 8.

DEFINITIONS

**1–526**    hospital order: ss.37, 55(4), 145(1).
patient: s.145(1).
hospital: ss.55(5), 145(1).
community treatment order: ss.17A(7), 145(1).
community patient: ss.17A(7), 145(1).
responsible clinician: s.55(1).
the appropriate tribunal: ss.66(4) 145(1).

GENERAL NOTE

**1–527**    This section empowers the Crown Court, having made a hospital order under s.37, to make a further order (a "restriction order") restricting the patient's discharge, transfer or leave of absence from hospital without the consent of the Secretary of State for Justice. A restriction order, which can only be made where it is necessary to protect the public from serious harm, does not require regular renewal to prevent it from lapsing, but remains in force indefinitely until it is discharged by the responsible clinician with the agreement of the Secretary of State under s.23, by the Secretary of State under s.42, or by the tribunal under s.73. Magistrates' courts may only commit a convicted offender to the Crown Court with a view to a restriction order being made (s.43(1)).

The nature of a restriction order was considered by the Court of Appeal in *R. v Birch* (1989) 11 Cr. App. R.(S.) 202 at 211–212:

"A restriction order has no existence independently of the hospital order to which it relates; it is not a separate means of disposal. Nevertheless, it fundamentally affects the circumstances in which the patient is detained. No longer is the offender regarded simply as a patient whose interests are paramount. No longer is the control of him handed over unconditionally to the hospital authorities. Instead the interests of public safety are regarded by transferring the responsibility for discharge from the [responsible clinician] and the hospital to [ . . . ] the Secretary of State and the [tribunal]. A patient who has been subject to a restriction order is likely to be detained for much longer in hospital than one who is not, and will have fewer opportunities for leave of absence".

The court made the following observations at 213–215 on the principles to be observed in deciding whether a restriction order is appropriate:

"[The judge] is required to choose between an order without restrictions, which may enable the author of a serious act of violence to be at liberty only a matter of months after he appears in court, and a restriction order which may lead the offender to be detained for a long time: longer in some cases than the period which he would serve if sent to prison: see *Haynes* (1981) 3 Cr. App. R. (S.) 330. It is moreover a choice which depends on a prognosis, the ultimate responsibility for which is left with the judge.

This responsibility may be hard to discharge, since the judge will often have nothing on which to base his decision, if he feels reservations about the medical evidence, apart from the considerations stated by the statute, namely the nature of the offence and the antecedents of the offender: which will often consist only of a single episode of fatal violence and a blank criminal record. Where there is a trial the judge can form an impression of [the] defendant as the case unfolds which may enable him to make his own assessment of his dangerousness. But in the more usual case where a plea of guilty to manslaughter on the grounds of diminished responsibility is accepted by the prosecution and the court, this opportunity is largely absent, and did not exist at all in the present case, where the appellant was too distressed to remain for the hearing in the Crown Court . . . .

Nevertheless, section 41(1) is there and the judge must apply it. Quite plainly the addition of the words 'from serious harm' has greatly curtailed the former jurisdiction to make a restriction order: most particularly because the word 'serious' qualifies 'harm' rather than 'risk.' Thus the court is required to assess not the seriousness of the risk that the defendant will re-offend, but the risk that if he does so the public will suffer serious harm. The harm in question need not, in our view, be limited to personal injury. Nor need it relate to the public in general, for it would in our judgment suffice if a category of persons, or even a single person, were adjudged to be at risk: although the category of persons so protected would no doubt exclude the offender himself. Nevertheless the potential harm must be serious, and a high possibility of a recurrence of minor offences will no longer be sufficient.

Thus we do not consider that cases such as *Smith* (1974), *Current Sentencing Practice* F.2.4(b), *Toland* (1973) *ibid.*, F.2.4(c) (appellant was a recidivist young burglar, described as 'an anti-social person . . . a pest') and *Eaton* (1975) *ibid.*, F.2.4(d) (restriction order on appellant with behavioural difficulties, who had broken two panes in a telephone kiosk), would be decided the same way under the new legislation in the absence of special factors. This was, as it seems to us, precisely the result which the 1983 Act was intended to achieve.

*Khan* (1987) 9 Cr. App. R.(S.) 455 was, if we correctly understand the facts, a case where the offences themselves, whilst not of great gravity, included reckless driving of a very bad nature by a very disturbed young man with a megalomaniac approach to his driving prowess which, if repeated, would create a risk of serious harm to the public. We pause to note that there is nothing in the Act which requires a causal connection between the offender's mental state and what the professionals call the 'index offence'. It is sufficient for section 41 that the defendant is a convicted offender, and that the conditions of section 41 are satisfied: see *Hatt* [1962] Crim. L.R. 647.

It would however be a mistake to equate the seriousness of the offence with the probability that a restriction order will be made. This is only one of the factors which section 41(1) requires to be taken into account. A minor offence by a man who proves to be mentally disordered and dangerous may properly leave him subject to a restriction. In theory the converse is also true. *Courtney* (1987) 9 Cr. App. R.(S.) 404 shows that a serious offence committed by someone who is adjudged to have a very low risk of re-offending may lead to an unrestricted hospital order.

Nevertheless, the court will need to be very sure of its ground in such a case, and we consider that there is nothing in the 1983 Act to derogate from the following statement of principle by Lord Parker C.J., in *Gardiner* (1967) 51 Cr. App. R. 187:

> 'Thus, for example, in the case of crimes of violence, and of the more serious sexual offences, particularly if the prisoner has a record of such offences, or if there is a history of mental disorder involving violent behaviour, it is suggested that there must be compelling reasons to explain why a restriction order should not be made.'

**1–528**   Finally we would make [a further point] on section 41. [The] sentencer should not impose a restriction order simply to mark the gravity of the offence (although this is an element in the assessment of risk), nor as a means of punishment: for a restriction order merely qualifies a hospital order and a hospital order is not a mode of punishment."

In *R. v Paul Martin*, November 6, 1998, CA, Judge L.J. said:

> "There should normally be some proportionate relationship, in our judgment, between the instant offence and the history of offending, together with an assessment of risk on the basis of medical examinations before a s.41 restriction order is made."

Judge L.J.'s use of the term "normally" indicates that there can be cases where the offence leading to the conviction has no relevance to the decision to make the restriction order. This occurred in *R. v Eaton* [1976] Crim.L.R. 390, where a restriction order was made in respect of a woman with a psychopathic disorder whose offence was minor criminal damage (cited by Lord Phillips in *Gray v Thames Trains Ltd.* [2009] UKHL 33; [2009] 4 All E.R. 81, para.14).

The severity of a potential assault cannot be predicted solely on the basis of what has occurred in the past: see *R. v Kamara* [2000] M.H.L.R. 9 CA, where Scott Baker J. said:

> "Sometimes the extent of the injury that results from an assault is a matter of chance. There are cases in this court's experience where one punch has led to death and others where a grave and sustained assault has led to minimal injury. The court has to look not just at what has happened in the past but at the risk of what may happen in the future."

In *R. v IA* [2005] EWCA Crim 2077; [2005] M.H.L.R. 336, the Court of Appeal reviewed the development of caselaw regarding the approach that a court should adopt when sentencing a mentally disordered offender whose offence would warrant a custodial sentence:

1. The risk that an offender may be released prematurely by a tribunal is not a ground for passing a life sentence rather than making a restriction order: see *R. v Mitchell* [1997] 1 Cr. App. R.(S.) 90 where the Court of Appeal said that the "composition and powers of the discretionary lifer panel and the [tribunal] are closely analogous".

2. Where the medical opinion is unanimous and a bed in a secure hospital is available, a decision not to impose a restriction order should not be made because of concerns about the risk to the public should the offender be released (*R. v Howell* (1985) 2 Cr. App. R. 360). [However, where the doctors giving evidence to the court are not unanimous about the appropriateness of a hospital disposal, sentencing is a matter for the judge to resolve in the light of the evidence and all the circumstances of the case (*R. v Reid* [2005] EWCA Crim 392; [2006] M.H.L.R. 180)].

3. Prison might be chosen by a judge as an alternative to hospital either because the offender was dangerous and no suitable secure hospital accommodation was available or because there was an element of culpability in the offence which merited punishment, as might happen where there was no connection between the mental

disorder and the offence or where the offender's responsibility for the offence was reduced but not wholly extinguished (*R. v Birch*, above).

4. Save where a custodial sentence is fixed by law (as in cases of murder), the court must consider the offender's mental condition before imposing a custodial sentence. The humanity and fairness of this requirement are obvious. But it cannot, as a matter of national law, be stigmatised as wrong in principle to pass a sentence of imprisonment on a mentally disordered defendant who is criminally responsible and fit to be tried. This is made clear by the terms of section 37, for even where the conditions in subsection (2)(a)(i) or (ii) are found to be satisfied the court may make a hospital order only if it is also of opinion under subsection (2)(b) that a hospital order is "the most suitable method of disposing of the case". If it is not of that opinion, a sentence of imprisonment may be imposed even on an offender in whose case the conditions in subsection (2)(a)(i) or (ii) are satisfied (*R. v Drew* [2003] UKHL 25; [2003] 4 All E.R. 557 para.17).

*IA* was applied in *R. v Simpson* [2007] EWCA Crim 2666; [2007] M.H.L.R. 320, where the court quashed a sentence of life imprisonment imposed under s.225 of the Criminal Justice Act 2003 (see subs.(1A (c) of this section) and substituted a hospital order with restrictions. In his comment on *Simpson*, D.A. Thomas Q.C. said that the "general effect of the decision is that the new legislative framework [established by the 2003 Act] has not changed the general approach of the court, which is that a sentence of life imprisonment should not normally be imposed on an offender who is eligible for a hospital order and for whom a suitable establishment is available" ([2008] Crim.L.R. 238).

The exercise of a judge's discretion whether to impose a restriction order involves a balancing exercise of the risks of relapse resulting from a failure to continue with treatment after discharge from hospital, against the disadvantages involved in the imposition of such an order (*R. v Acharya* [2005] EWCA Crim. 772; [2005] M.H.L.R. 28 para.15).

The fact that a "very experienced psychiatrist" was of the opinion that the existence of a restriction order was "a hindrance rather than a help" to the successful rehabilitation of a very vulnerable mentally impaired patient resulted in the Court of Appeal quashing the order in *R. v Mahmood* [2002] M.H.L.R. 416.

It is the duty of a judge hearing a case who has formed a clear provisional view on the material presented to her that a restriction order should be made, to inform the parties that this is so, so that, by way of evidence and argument they will be able to deal with it (*R. v Goode* [2002] EWCA Crim 1698 at para.36). If a court is considering making an order under this section the defendant should be represented by counsel (*R. v Blackwood* (1974) 59 Cr. App. R. 170).

A restriction order remains in force even if the patient is subsequently imprisoned for an offence committed after his conditional discharge (*R. v Mersey Mental Health Review Tribunal Ex p. K* [1990] 1 All E.R. 694 CA), and the patient may be recalled to hospital on the expiry of his prison sentence (*R. v Secretary of State for the Home Department Ex p. K* [1990] 1 All E.R. 703).

In subss.(3) to (5) of this section any reference to a hospital order, a guardianship order or a restriction order are to be construed as including a reference to any order or direction under this Part having the same effect as such orders (s.55(4)).

Also see the note on "sentencing options" in the General Note to s.37 and the note on "the court may by order" in s.37(1).

*Applications to the First-tier Tribunal (Mental Health) or the Mental Health Review Tribunal for Wales*

A patient who is subject to a restriction order may apply to a tribunal in the period **1–529** between six and 12 months of the order and in any subsequent period of one year (s.70) and the Secretary of State may, and in some circumstances must, refer such patients to a tribunal (s.71). The patient's nearest relative has no power to apply to a tribunal. The powers of a tribunal when considering the case of a restricted patient are set out in s.73.

If the patient becomes subject to a "notional hospital order" by virtue of the restriction order ceasing to have effect (subs.(5)), the patient is given the same powers to apply to a tribunal as those enjoyed by a s.3 patient (s.69(2)). These powers are also enjoyed by the patient's nearest relative (s.69(1)).

*Appeals*

**1–530**     See the note on s.37 under this heading. The Court of Appeal has allowed appeals against the imposition of restriction orders because of the progress that the patient had made at the psychiatric hospital since the trial; see, for, example, *R. v Crookes* [1999] M.H.L.R. 45. However, in *R. v Griffith* [2002] EWCA Crim 1838; [2002] M.H.L.R. 427, the Court of Appeal said that a submission that a medical report made subsequent to the trial indicated that the restriction order was no longer necessary would be best directed at the tribunal who would review the appellant's case and should not be the subject of a decision by the court.

*Domestic Violence, Crime and Victims Act 2004*

**1–531**     See Ch.18 of the *Code of Practice* at paras 18.18–18.20 and Ch.30 at paras 30.29–30.31.

The Ministry of Justice has published "Duties to victims under the Domestic Violence, Crime and Victims Act 2004: Guidance for Clinicians" which is available at *www.justice.-gov.uk* (go to "guidance" and then "mentally disordered offenders") (accessed July 9, 2010).

*Armed Services Act 2006*

**1–532**     Subsection (1) of this section is modified for the purposes of s.169(2)(a) of the 2006 Act (ibid., Sch.4, para.2).

*Subsection (1)*

**1–533**     HOSPITAL ORDER IS MADE.    The offender must therefore have satisfied the conditions of s.37(2). Although this section implies that the offender will be kept in secure accommodation, this will not be necessary in all cases. The Butler Committee, at para.14.21, gave the following example of a restricted patient who might not need to be accommodated in secure accommodation:

> "the persistent molester of small children may need the continuing supervision after discharge which a restriction order allows, and should not be permitted simply to walk out of hospital whenever he wishes, but is unlikely to need the secure containment of bolts and bars".

Before it makes an order under this section the court should ensure that the receiving hospital has the facilities for keeping the offender in the degree of custody that the court considers necessary (*R. v Morris* [1961] 2 Q.B. 237).

Section 47 of the Crime (Sentences) Act 1997 provides that where a court makes an order under this section it has the power to order that the patient be admitted to and detained in a named hospital unit. A named hospital unit can be any part of a hospital which is treated as a separate unit. The effect of this power is considered in paras 5.18 to 5.20 of "Mental Health Act 2007: Guidance for the courts on remand and sentencing powers for mentally disordered offenders", Ministry of Justice, March 2008:

> "[The power under s.47] responds to the situation that the majority of hospital trusts manage accommodation ranging from medium secure to locked wards or unlocked wards. Thus a hospital order directing admission to a Primary Care Trust or an NHS Trust in Wales or a major psychiatric hospital, gives to hospital managers discretion over the level of security under which the patient is detained, from the day of his admission. The Court may wish to specify a level of security if the offender has been

found to present a risk of serious harm to others, where he presents a serious escape or abscond risk, or where his hospital admission is attached to a life, or indeterminate sentence under a hospital direction . . . .

A hospital unit can be any unit of an individual hospital which the Court chooses to name. The intention is that it should be a ward or secure unit which offers a specific level of security, so that in naming it, the Court is directing the offender's detention under that category of security. If the Court does not have adequate knowledge of the levels of security available in the hospital to which it wishes to order admission, section 39 can serve to acquire that information. Clinicians who would be responsible for the patient's care are likely to be ready to advise the Court on the naming of hospital units, but discretion lies with the Court.

The practical effect of naming a hospital unit is that the Secretary of State's authority is required to move the offender to a different level of security, whether in a different hospital or the one to which the offender was admitted. The responsible clinician for a restricted patient will otherwise have discretion to give the patient leave to the grounds of the hospital in which he is detained. That generally means allowing the patient into grounds which are not secure. Naming a hospital unit allows the Court to require that the patient be detained under the level of security it deems appropriate. For example, if a medium secure unit is named, the patient cannot be allowed into the insecure grounds of the hospital which contains the unit, without the Secretary of State's authority. The Secretary of State can agree, in due course, to remove the requirement to detain within a named unit, allowing the offender to be managed more flexibly within the hospital. This would happen after a risk assessment had concluded that the offender's management could safely be managed without the constraints of a named unit".

CROWN COURT. A Crown Court has jurisdiction to make a restriction order in respect of an offence which only became triable by that court under the provisions of s.40 of the Criminal Justice Act 1988 (*R. v Avbunudje* [1999] 2 Cr. App. R.(S.) 189 CA). Section 40 enables a summary only offence to be included in an indictment in certain specified circumstances. Although a magistrates' court cannot make a restriction order, it does have the power to commit the offender to the Crown Court with a view to such an order being made by that court (s.43(1)).

ANTECEDENTS. It has been reported that this term is:

"construed by the judges to include not just previous convictions, but also accounts of previous unprosecuted dangerous behaviour made in psychiatric reports (subject to any objection by defence counsel), and some [judges] said that evidence of failure of previous treatment might also be significant. A history of violence would cause particular concern, especially if it appeared that the violence was escalating in seriousness" (*The Restricted Hospital Order: From Court to Community*, Home Office Research Study 186, 1998, p.40).

THE PUBLIC. The public does not include an unborn child who, when born, could be protected by the provisions of the Children Act 1989 (*R. v Michelle Louise Jones* [2000] M.H.L.R. 12 CA).
In *Anderson v Scottish Ministers* [2001] UKPC D 5; [2001] M.H.L.R. 192, para.37, Lord Hope said:

"The word 'public' and the phrase 'in order to protect the public from serious harm' in each of the various amendments included in section 1 of the [Mental Health (Public Safety and Appeals) (Scotland) Act 1999] is capable of meaning either the public in general or a section of the public, as the context requires. In Doherty's case there is no question of his coming into contact with the public in general as he would be remitted to prison in the event of his discharge from hospital. But the persons with whom he would be liable to come into contact in a prison may be regarded as a section of the public. They include prison officers, other inmates and a variety of persons who visit prisons for religious, educational, social work or other purposes. Read in this way, the effect of the amendments introduced by section 1 of the 1999 Act is to require the sheriff or the Scottish Ministers, as the case may be, to be satisfied in Doherty's case that it is necessary for him to be detained in a hospital to protect that section of the public from serious harm . . ."

SERIOUS HARM.   The insertion of this phrase into the 1982 Act gave effect to recommendation of the Butler Committee which proposed that the equivalent section in the 1959 Act should be revised to make it clear that the intention of a restriction order is to protect the public from serious harm. The Committee wished to ensure that a court would not impose restrictions on "the petty recidivist because of the virtual certainty that he will persist in similar offences in the future" (para.14.24).

The court should expressly address the question whether the order is necessary for the protection of the public from serious harm (*R. v Czarnota* [2002] EWCA Crim 785; [2002] M.H.L.R. 144). In doing so, it must undertake an assessment of risk (*R. v Cooper* [2009] EWCA Crim 2646).The index offence itself need not be serious.

"Serious harm" refers to possible serious harm to the public in the future rather than to proven serious harm to the public in the past and an offender who has no history of serious violence but who, on the medical evidence, has a potentiality for causing serious harm could be made the subject of an order under this section (*R. v Kamara* [2000] M.H.L.R. 9 CA). It is not necessary that the harm should be purely physical: a risk of serious psychological harm will suffice (*R. v Melbourne* [2000] M.H.L.R. 2 CA). A risk to one person of such harm can be sufficient (*R. v Macrow* [2004] EWCA Crim 1159 para.16). The word "serious" qualifies "harm" rather than "risk". Thus the court is required "not to assess the seriousness of the risk that the defendant will re-offend, but the risk that if he does so the public will suffer serious harm": see *R. v Birch* above. In *R. v Cox* [1999] M.H.L.R. 30 the Court of Appeal said that risk of serious harm to the public must be real, rather than fanciful or remote. The imposition of a restriction order was confirmed in *R. v Golding* [2006] EWCA Crim 1965; [2006] M.H.L.R. 272, where the court found that the appellant, who had multiple convictions for burglary but had never acted violently, satisfied the "serious harm" criterion because his psychosis was not controlled and his predilection to drugs and alcohol could well lead him to behave violently if he was confronted by a householder. The court rejected counsel's submission that if "the evidence and material before the court in this case is sufficient to make a restriction order, it is difficult to consider any case where a defendant suffers from paranoid schizophrenia where he will not be susceptible to a section 41 order" on the ground that the decisions to be made as to such orders "are very much fact specific decisions" (paras 10,11). *Golding* is consistent with the decision of the Divisional Court in *R. (on the application of Jones) v Isleworth Crown Court* [2005] EWHC 662 (Admin) where the court emphasised that in deciding whether an offender posed a future risk of serious harm the judge was not bound to determine that risk by reference to the nature of past violence. Moses J. said at para.19:

"Of course the evidence as to what had happened in the past provides a guide to the future; but it does not determine the nature of the risk, particularly in the context of an escalation of violence by one who suffers from paranoid schizophrenia and hears commands to harm other people".

When making a judgment about "serious harm" the court can take into account the risk to the offender from failing to take appropriate treatment to restrain his symptoms: see *Narey v Her Majesty's Customs and Excise* [2005] EWHC 784 (Admin); [2005] M.H.L.R.194 at para.19 where the court said that the importation of kilos of cocaine inevitably leads to a risk of serious harm to those to whom it is sold for consumption. In *R. v Beaumont* (98/

02694 Y2) July 28, 1998, CA, Moses J. said that "setting fire to premises, even if it is difficult for them to ignite successfully, is likely to cause, in our judgment serious harm to others who may be affected by [the] fire".

*Subsection (2)*

ONE OF THE REGISTERED MEDICAL PRACTITIONERS. Who need not necessarily be **1–534** approved by the Secretary of State or the Welsh Ministers under s.12. In *R. v Blackwood* (1974) Cr. App. R. 170, the Court of Appeal stressed the desirability of the doctor who gives oral evidence being on the staff of the admitting hospital.

EVIDENCE. It is of the utmost importance that when medical practitioners are considering whether to recommend a restriction order, they should expressly address the question whether such an order is necessary for the protection of the public from serious harm (*R. v Chalk* [2002] EWCA Crim 2435; [2002] M.H.L.R. 430 para.34).

In *R. v Birch*, above, the Court of Appeal, at 212, gave the following answer to the question whether a Crown Court judge had jurisdiction to make a restriction order in circumstances where those doctors who expressed an opinion on the matter were unanimous that the patient was not dangerous:

"It is in our judgment quite clear that the answer is 'yes'. There is a contrast between the language of sections 37(2) and 41(1) and (2). Before a hospital order can be made, the Court must be satisfied of the stated conditions 'on the written or oral evidence of two practitioners'. But where a restriction order is in question, section 41(2) requires no more than that the Court shall hear the oral evidence of one of the medical practitioners. It need not follow the course which he recommends. Section 41(1) makes the assessment of the risk, in the light of the factors there identified, one for the court. In our judgment *R. v Blackwood* (1974) 59 Cr. App. R. 170 and *R. v Royse* (1981) 3 Cr. App. R.(S.) 58 are just as good law under the 1983 Act as they were under the earlier statute."

The finding in *Birch* was applied in *R. v Crookes* [1999] M.H.L.R. 45, where the Court of Appeal said that the judge was right to impose a restriction order in a case where the medical evidence was unanimous in recommending that such an order was not necessary. In this case the judge felt that none of the doctors was able to explain to his satisfaction why a young man with no record of violence, and not seen as in any way to be dangerous, could suddenly react with an outburst of potentially lethal ferocity. In *R. v Ristic* [2002] EWCA Crim 165; [2002] M.H.L.R. 129 at para.10, Goldring J., in giving the judgment of the court, said that the fact that none of the doctors who had prepared reports or who had given evidence had suggested a restriction order "did not mean that the judge could not impose it, after consideration of the evidence and the requirements of the section." However, the power and discretion of the judge to impose a restriction order in these circumstances should only be exercised after careful consideration and with some caution (*R. v Roberts* [2003] EWCA Crim 858, para.12). If a judge does not accept the unanimous recommendations of psychiatrists that a restriction order is not necessary, better reasons should be given in justification than the mere citing of the levels violence exhibited by the offender in the past (*R. v Haile* [2009] EWCA Crim 1996; [2009] M.H.L.R. 300; also see *R. v Hurst* [2007] EWCA Crim 3436; [2008] M.H.L.R. 43).

*Subsection (3)*

This subsection specifies the restrictions that are placed upon patients who are subject to **1–535** restriction orders. They are: (1) there is no periodic review of the authority to detain under s.20; (2) the patient cannot be discharged, transferred to another hospital (even if managed by the same hospital managers) or granted leave of absence without the consent of the Secretary of State; (3) the patient cannot be made subject to supervised community treatment; and (4) the authority to detain lasts as long as the restriction order is in force and the patient cannot obtain his discharge under the provisions of ss.17(5) or 18(4). The patient's nearest relative does not have the power to discharge the patient (s.40(4), Sch.1 Pt II paras 2,7). The Secretary of State may, at any time, discharge a restricted patient from hospital either absolutely or subject to conditions (s.42).

*Paragraph (a)*

**1–536**   PROVISIONS . . . RELATING TO THE DURATION, RENEWAL AND EXPIRATION OF AUTHORITY FOR THE DETENTION OF PATIENTS.   The effect of this provision is that no one is under any statutory obligation to consider whether the criteria for detaining the patient still apply.

*Paragraph (b)*

**1–537**   NO APPLICATION SHALL BE MADE.   This paragraph only refers to a patient in his capacity as a restricted patient detained, or liable to be detained, pursuant to the hospital order. It does not apply to the patient's detention under s.3, if such an application has been made in respect of him. A patient so detained therefore has a right to apply to a tribunal under s.66(1)(b) (*R. v North West London Mental Health NHS Trust Ex p. Stewart, The Times,* August 15, 1996, per Harrison J., whose decision on the ability of Pts II and III of this Act to coexist and operate independently of each other was affirmed by the Court of Appeal at [1997] 4 All E.R. 871).

*Paragraph (c)*

**1–538**   On a day-to-day basis, the powers of the Secretary of State for Justice under this provision are managed by the Mental Health Casework Section at the Ministry of Justice: see the General Note to this Part.

The principles that the Secretary of State should apply when exercising his functions under this provision were set out by Lightman J. in *R. v Secretary of State for the Home Department, Ex p. Harry* [1998] 3 All. E.R. 360, a case where the Secretary of State had refused to consent to the transfer of a restricted patient from Broadmoor Hospital to a regional secure unit, as recommended by a tribunal. His Lordship said at 369:

> "In short, as it seems to me, the scheme of the 1983 Act places on the [Secretary of State for Justice] the responsibility in the case of a restricted patient to balance the patient's claim to liberty against the interests of everyone else to be safeguarded against the risks to which such liberty may give rise. For his performance of these duties the [Secretary of State for Justice] is politically accountable to Parliament. His obligation is fully to satisfy himself as to the propriety of any decision before he makes it because of the serious impact of such decision, and if the finding or recommendation of the tribunal leaves him in doubt, he is not only entitled but bound to look further afield for guidance: the finding and recommendation of the tribunal may assist him to fulfil this obligation, but cannot dilute it or impede its fulfilment or obviate the need for the exercise by him of an informed judgment whether consent should be forthcoming."

LEAVE OF ABSENCE   *Harry* was applied by Silber J. in *R. (on the application of OS) v Secretary of State for the Home Department* [2006] EWHC 1903 (Admin); [2006] M.H.L.R. 275, where his Lordship said, at para.22, that it was common ground that the Secretary of State:

> "is entitled in making his assessment of risk to consider the risk that the patient will not return after being granted leave [of absence]. This is important because the [Secretary of State for Justice] will be able to take into account factors, which the [tribunal] would not or could not consider, such as the immigration status of the patient and whether this or any other factor might lead him or her not to return to their hospital after their leave has expired."

In *R. (on the application of P) v Secretary of State for Justice* [2009] EWHC 2464 (Admin); [2009] M.H.L.R. 236, para.62, Keith Lindblom QC, sitting as a Deputy Judge of the High Court, said that the Secretary of State is not bound by the opinion of professionals even if that opinion was unequivocal and unanimous, and is not required to seek a second clinical opinion to substantiate his own judgment on the question of risk. The Secretary of State "has to exercise a judgment of his own". In *R. (on the application of X) v Secretary of State for Justice* [2009] EWHC 2465 (Admin); [2009] M.H.L.R. 250, para.55, Mr Lindblom said that if the Secretary of State rejects a request for leave, he must give a rational explanation for doing so which properly bears on the protection of the public.

In *R. (on the application of OS) v Secretary of State for the Home Department* [2002] EWHC 1618; [2003] M.H.L.R. 54 at para.77, Mr. Richard Westlake, a Home Office official, "explained that shadow leave had in the past occasionally been agreed with care teams by the Secretary of State to meet the circumstances of patients for whom unescorted community leave was considered problematic. It enabled the patient to be followed by nursing staff from the hospital without him or her knowing this and that this enabled an informed decision to be taken on whether the patient could be trusted on unescorted leave in the future. Mr. Westlake explained that the practice of shadow leave was discontinued over a year ago following disquiet about the practice for a number of reasons".

In *R. (on the application of RA) v Secretary of State for the Home Department*, [2002] EWHC 1618; [2003] M.H.L.R. 54, Crane J. rejected a submission that conditions cannot be attached to the Secretary of State's consent to a grant of leave of absence under s.17. His Lordship said at para.41:

"It is true that neither section 17 nor section 41(3) provides in terms for such conditions to the consent. However, section 17 enables conditions to be imposed by the [RC] on the patient. I can see no reason why the Secretary of State cannot in law decline to give consent unless suitable conditions are imposed. He can obviously refuse consent to leave for a particular period. And since the Secretary of State has a power to recall under section 41(3)(c), there is every reason why he should be able to insist upon conditions that have the effect of providing the necessary information to him. The power of recall would then be no less effective than under section 42(2)".

His Lordship said that the operation of the provisions of ss.17 and 41(3)(c) should ensure that there is "no unreasonable delay to the implementation of a tribunal's decision" (para.58) and that the Secretary of State should "follow recommendations made by a tribunal in the absence of sound reasons or new circumstances" (para.59). His Lordship left open the question whether conditions, such as the provision of reports, can be imposed on the RC.

In *R. (on the application of Hurlock) v Dr Page and the Secretary of State for the Home Department)* [2001] EWHC Admin 380 at para.22, Ouseley J. said that s.17 and this provision cannot arguably be read as imposing an obligation to grant a patient unescorted leave of absence as an alternative to a conditional discharge granted by a tribunal where those conditions are not yet fulfilled.

The Ministry of Justice has published "Leave of absence for patients subject to restrictions—Guidance for Responsible Clinicians", March 18, 2009. This guidance, together with an application form that RCs may use to request leave for restricted patients, is available at *www.justice.gov.uk* (go to "guidance" and then "mentally disordered offenders") (accessed July 9, 2010).

Paragraph 16 of "Duties to victims under the Domestic Violence, Crime and Victims Act—Guidance for clinicians", Ministry of Justice, March 26, 2009, states:

"The DVCV Act does not change existing Ministry of Justice practice with regard to considering leave requests. When considering an application for community leave, the Ministry of Justice always takes into account any victim considerations. The Ministry of Justice may seek information from the Victim Liaison Officer (VLO) when considering an application, but it is not anticipated that this will happen in all cases or that the Ministry of Justice will always notify the VLO where leave is granted (although the VLO may be aware of this through contact with the clinical team). If the VLO is notified that a patient has been granted leave, it will be on the understanding that details of the timing and purpose of the leave should not be disclosed to the victim."

TRANSFER THE PATIENT.    A failure to consent to the transfer of a patient whose level of risk made it appropriate for him to be accommodated in medium security rather than high security could constitute a breach of his rights under art.8 of the European Convention on Human Rights.

*Subsection (4)*

**1–539**     The effect of this provision is that a hospital order coupled with a restriction order continues to have effect on the making of a subsequent hospital order and that subsequent hospital orders should be disregarded for the purposes of renewal when the restriction order ceases to have effect.

If a second restriction order is made, both orders will be in force. As the existence of parallel restriction orders could cause confusion, the Secretary of State should consider exercising his power under s.42(2) to order the absolute discharge of one of the them.

*Subsection (5)*

**1–540**     This subsection provides that when a restriction order ceases to have effect, the patient is to be treated as if he had been admitted to hospital under a hospital order without restrictions made on the date on which the restriction order ceased to have effect. If the patient has been conditionally discharged from hospital before the restrictions end, he will cease to be liable to be detained (s.42(5)).

*Subsection (6)*

**1–541**     This subsection, which was enacted in response to recommendation 114 of the Butler Committee, is aimed at preventing restricted patients being detained for unjustifiably long periods. As a patient who has been conditionally discharged from a restriction order remains subject to that order (see s.42(2)), it is submitted that this provision applies to such patients. If the Secretary of State, having considered the RC's report and having weighed all the other evidence about the patients medical condition that is available to him is satisfied that the patient is no longer suffering from mental disorder, he should discharge him: see the note to section 42(2).

## Powers of Secretary of State in respect of patients subject to restriction orders

**1–542**     **42.**—(1) If the Secretary of State is satisfied that in the case of any patient a restriction order is no longer required for the protection of the public from serious harm, he may direct that the patient shall cease to be subject to the special restrictions set out in section 41(3) above; and where the Secretary of State so directs, the restriction order shall cease to have effect, and section 41(5) above shall apply accordingly.

(2) At any time while a restriction order is in force in respect of a patient, the Secretary of State may, if he thinks fit, by warrant discharge the patient from hospital, either absolutely or subject to conditions; and where a person is absolutely discharged under this subsection, he shall thereupon cease to be liable to be detained by virtue of the relevant hospital order, and the restriction order shall cease to have effect accordingly.

(3) The Secretary of State may at any time during the continuance in force of a restriction order in respect of a patient who has been conditionally discharged

under subsection (2) above by warrant recall the patient to such hospital as may be specified in the warrant.

(4) Where a patient is recalled as mentioned in subsection (3) above—

(a) if the hospital specified in the warrant is not the hospital from which the patient was conditionally discharged, the hospital order and the restriction order shall have effect as if the hospital specified in the warrant were substituted for the hospital specified in the hospital order;

(b) in any case, the patient shall be treated for the purposes of section 18 above as if he had absented himself without leave from the hospital specified in the warrant [. . .].

(5) If a restriction order in respect of a patient ceases to have effect after the patient has been conditionally discharged under this section, the patient shall, unless previously recalled under subsection (3) above, be deemed to be absolutely discharged on the date when the order ceases to have effect, and shall cease to be liable to be detained by virtue of the relevant hospital order accordingly.

(6) The Secretary of State may, if satisfied that the attendance at any place in Great Britain of a patient who is subject to a restriction order is desirable in the interests of justice or for the purposes of any public inquiry, direct him to be taken to that place; and where a patient is directed under this subsection to be taken to any place he shall, unless the Secretary of State otherwise directs, be kept in custody while being so taken, while at that place and while being taken back to the hospital in which he is liable to be detained.

AMENDMENT

The words omitted in subs.(4)(b) were repealed by the Mental Health Act 2007 s.55, Sch.11 Pt 8.

DEFINITIONS

    patient: s.145.                                        **1–543**

    restriction order: ss.41, 55(4), 145(1).

    hospital: ss.55(5), 145(1).

    hospital order: ss.37, 55(4), 145(1).

    absent without leave: ss.18(6), 145(1).

GENERAL NOTE

This section empowers the Secretary of State to take the following action in respect of **1–544** patients who have been placed on restriction orders: (1) to direct that the order shall cease to have effect; (2) to discharge the patient from hospital absolutely; and (3) to discharge the patient from hospital subject to conditions.

A restriction order cannot cease to have effect by inference or implication (*R. v Secretary of State for the Home Department Ex p. Didlick* (1993) 16 B.M.L.R. 71 DC). Rougier J. said at 75:

"In my opinion subsection (1) and (2) [of section 42] indicate clearly that before a restriction order can be brought to an end, the Secretary of State must either make a declaration to that effect or must discharge the patient absolutely. Each of these is a positive act. There is no room, in my opinion, for the situation whereby a restriction order ceases to have effect by inference or implication. It follows, therefore, that, by merely allowing the conditions under which the applicant was discharged to lapse, the Secretary of State did not thereby bring to an end the operation of the restriction order."

Any reference in this section to a hospital order, a guardianship order or a restriction order shall be construed as including a reference to any other order or direction under this Part having the same effect as such orders (s.55(4)).

*Human Rights Act 1998*

**1–545**    A patient who is assessed as posing no risk to the public should not be denied a conditional discharge solely on the ground that the inhabitants of a particular locality feared that he might be dangerous if released (*Stojanovski v The Former Yugoslav Republic of Macedonia,* app.no.1431/03, October 22, 2009, para.35).

If a condition of a patient's discharge granted under subs.(2) interferes with the patient's right to respect for his private and family life, it must be justified under art.8(2) of the European Convention on Human Rights. In *R. (on the application of Craven) v Secretary of State for the Home Department and the Parole Board* [2001] EWHC Admin 850, Stanley Burnton J. rejected a prisoner's claim that a condition of his parole not to enter an area of Newcastle where the family of his victim lived constituted a disproportionate and therefore unlawful interference with his art.8 rights. His Lordship held that distress to the victim's family was a consideration that could lawfully be taken into account by the Parole Board and by the Secretary of State.

The exercise by the Secretary of State of his power of recall under subs.(3) will, except in emergency cases, constitute a violation of art.5(1) of the Convention in the absence of an up to date report on the patient's medical condition (see the notes on subs.(3) and art.5).

One of the consequences of the decision of the Court of Appeal in *R. v North West London Mental Health NHS Trust Ex p. Stewart,* noted under subs.(3), is that a conditionally discharged patient who is brought back to hospital under either s.2 or s.3, can be discharged from that section by a tribunal but be liable to be re-detained by the Secretary of State using his recall power under subs.(3). It is questionable whether it could be successfully claimed that the tribunal in such a case has the power to order the discharge of the patient as required by art.5(4) of the Convention, if the order can be immediately overridden by the Secretary of State.

*Applications to the First-tier Tribunal (Mental Health) or the Mental Health Review Tribunal for Wales*

**1–546**    A conditionally discharged patient has a right to apply to a tribunal between 12 months and two years after the conditional discharge and during each subsequent two-year period (s.75(2)).

The case of a conditionally discharged patient who has been recalled to hospital must be referred to a tribunal by the Secretary of State within a month of his or her return to hospital (see s.75(1)(a) and the note thereto). The patient may apply to the tribunal between six and 12 months after the recall and during each subsequent 12-month period (ss.70, 75(1)(b)). There is no duty placed on the Secretary of State to periodically refer the case of a conditionally discharged patient to the tribunal.

*Subsection (1)*

**1–547**    This subsection enables the Secretary of State to lift the restrictions from a patient who is subject to a restriction order if he considers that they are no longer necessary to protect the public from serious harm. The Secretary of State rarely exercises this power.

SECRETARY OF STATE.    The Secretary of State for Justice; in practice the Mental Health Casework Section of the Ministry of Justice: see the General Note to this Part.

PROTECTION OF THE PUBLIC.    In *R. v Parole Board Ex p. Bradley* [1990] 3 All E.R. 828 at 836, DC, Stuart-Smith L.J., on examining this provision said that "the precise level of risk is not (surely cannot be) spelt out."

THE RESTRICTION ORDER SHALL CEASE TO HAVE EFFECT.    With the patient continuing to be detained as if he or she had been admitted to hospital under a hospital order made without restrictions (s.41(5)).

*Subsection (2)*

This subsection enables the Secretary of State to order the absolute or conditional dis-   **1–548** charge of a restricted patient. The tribunal has a similar power under s.73. Notes for the guidance of clinicians who take on the role of clinical supervisors of conditionally discharged patients was published in February 2009. Guidance for the social supervisors of such patients was also published. The guidance can be accessed from the website of the Ministry of Justice *www.justice.gov.uk* (go to "guidance" and then "mentally disordered offenders").

A patient who has been conditionally discharged under this provision is not subject to the consent to treatment provisions contained in Pt IV of this Act (s.56(3)(c)). Paragraph 31 of the guidance for clinical supervisors states:

"The consent to treatment provisions in Part IV of the Mental Health Act 1983 do not apply to conditionally discharged patients. The clinical supervisor has no specific legal authority to require a conditionally discharged patient to take medication without his consent. However, where medication is prescribed to relieve mental disorder which, if untreated, would be likely to lead to the patient becoming a danger to himself or others, the patient's co-operation with such medication is likely to be fundamental to his remaining in the community. If, therefore, the patient refuses medication against the clinical supervisor's advice, he may need to be recalled to hospital as a detained patient. It is crucial that any withdrawal of co-operation with medication should be reported at once to the Mental Health [Casework Section]. Sometimes the Secretary of State will make cooperation with medication at the direction of the clinical supervisor a condition specified on the warrant of discharge. Generally this is unnecessary since it adds nothing to the powers of the supervisor or the Secretary of State, but there can be circumstances in which it is helpful in the management of a particular patient."

If the Secretary of State, after having weighed all the evidence about a patient's mental condition, is satisfied that the patient is no longer suffering from mental disorder, he should discharge the patient: see the obiter observations of Lawton L.J. in *Kynaston v Secretary of State for Home Affairs* (1981) 73 Cr. App. R. 281 CA. This course of action is required by the European Convention on Human Rights: see art.5(1) and the decision of the European Court of Human Rights in *Winterwerp v The Netherlands* (1979) 2 E.H.R.R. 387. The patient's discharge need not be absolute (*R. v Merseyside Mental Health Review Tribunal Ex p. K* [1990] 1 All E.R. 694 CA and *Johnson v United Kingdom* (1997) 27 E.H.R.R. 296).

IF HE THINKS FIT.    The Secretary of State is not bound by any statutory criteria when exercising his judgment under this provision. This contrasts with the power of the tribunal under s.73. Regular reports on the patient, prepared by his RC, will be submitted to the Secretary of State under s.41(6).

ABSOLUTELY.    An absolute discharge has the effect of extinguishing both the hospital order and the restriction order. Such action would not preclude continuing contact between the patient and his supervisors on a non-statutory basis.

The Mental Health Casework Section stated in its Newsletter of April 29, 2010:

"MHCS is responsible, on behalf of the Secretary of State, for ensuring that restricted patients are managed in such a way as to minimise the risk to the public. Our policy is that we will not grant absolute discharge (AD) unless it is clear that the restrictions are no longer required to ensure the patient's safe management. This means that we will not grant AD where the patient still has a mental disorder, and has the potential to be a risk to others if not well supervised in future, and where future supervision is not guaranteed. In forming this view we are conscious of that the Mental Health Review Tribunal is available to safeguard patient's rights."

SUBJECT TO CONDITIONS. The Secretary of State cannot impose conditions that have the effect of depriving the patient of his or her liberty: see the note on "conditional discharge" in s.73(2); also see the note on "conditions" in s.73(4). The Secretary of State has the power to vary any condition imposed by the tribunal or by him and can impose a new condition subsequent to the patient's discharge (s.73(4)(b) (5)). A condition that the patient refrains from entering a particular locality (e.g. the area where the family of the patient's victim lives) could be attached to the discharge if this was felt to be a proportionate response to the circumstances of the case: see the note on "The Human Rights Act 1998", above.

Paragraph 7 of the guidance for clinical supervisors states:

"The Secretary of State will usually make a restricted patient's discharge from hospital subject to certain conditions. The conditions usually imposed by the Secretary of State are those of residence at a stated address, supervision by a social worker and clinical supervision. The tribunal is also likely to make discharge directions conditional, and to impose similar conditions. If it does not, the Ministry of Justice, using powers under section 73(4) of the 1983 Act, will usually add conditions of social and clinical supervision. Supervisors must understand that conditions are designed to operate for the protection of the discharged patient and others and to enable the patient's safe management in the community. They are not measures for social control, nor even for crime prevention. Breach of conditions does not, in itself, justify recall to hospital, but it should act as a trigger for considering what action is necessary in response."

Paragraph 23 of the guidance states:

"A Ministry of Justice warrant for the conditional discharge of a restricted patient usually specifies that the patient 'shall comply with treatment as directed by the clinical supervisor'. This form of words allows the supervisor, in any particular case, to determine the appropriate manner and frequency of clinical supervision and treatment. The minimum frequency of contact is determined by the interval at which the Secretary of State requests reports on the patient's progress, but there will of course be many cases in which the clinical supervisor considers more frequent contact appropriate."

The *Butler Committee* agreed, at para.8.7, with the recommendation of the *Aarvold Committee* (Cmnd. 5191, para.48) that "supervision should be undertaken by the person who can bring most to the case in the way of knowledge, expertise and resources in the particular circumstances of the case. The arrangements may need to take particular account of the needs of public safety".

The Ministry of Justice has prepared a form for supervisors to use to submit their reports to the Mental Health Unit on the patient's condition and behaviour in the community. In practice, reports are normally required one month after the patient's discharge and at quarterly intervals thereafter.

*Subsection (3)*

**1–549** THE SECRETARY OF STATE MAY RECALL THE PATIENT. In *R.(on the application of MM) v The Secretary of State for the Home Department* [2007] EWCA Civ 687; [2007] M.H.L.R. 304 para.50, the Court of Appeal dismissed an appeal against the decision of Mitting J. to uphold the decision of the Secretary of State to recall the patient under this provision. Toulson L.J said at para.50:

"For the Secretary of State to recall a patient who has been conditionally discharged by [a tribunal], he has to believe on reasonable grounds that something has happened *since the decision of the tribunal*, or information has emerged *which was not available to the tribunal*, of sufficient significance to justify recalling the patient. As I have said, it is not in dispute that he must have up-to-date medical evidence about the patient's mental health. Since in the nature of things the patient will have a [RC], it is hard to imagine that (save in the most exceptional circumstances) the [Secretary of State] would recall the patient without first seeking the [AC's] clinical opinion whether it is appropriate for the patient to be detained for treatment."

[The italicised words were added to this formulation by Bean J. in *IT v Secretary of State for Justice* [2008] EWHC 1707 (Admin); [2008] M.H.L.R. 290 para.13, in order to make it consistent with *R. (on the application of von Brandenburg) v East London and the City Mental Health NHS Trust* [2003] UKHL 58. His Lordship said, at para.14, that if the Secretary of State disagreed with the decision of the tribunal the proper course was to seek judicial review.]

The test established in *MM* was considered by Burnett J in *R. (on the application of Munday) v Secretary of State for the Home Department* [2009] EWHC 3638 (Admin); [2009] M.H.L.R. 401. His Lordship said, at para.28, that the following formulation of the test, which was made by counsel for the Secretary of State at para.44 of the judgment, is correct:

". . . the [Secretary of State] should ask himself whether there had been such a material change of circumstances since the Tribunal's previous decision that he could reasonably form the view that the detention criteria were now satisfied."

In *MM* the court held that a beach of a condition imposed on the patient was not a free-standing ground for the patient's recall. The question is whether the breach has the effect of enabling the Secretary of State to form a proper judgment (i.e. one that was not unreasonable in the public law sense) on the medical evidence that the statutory criteria for detention were established.

The court further held that the language of the first statutory criterion ("of a nature or degree which makes it appropriate for him to be detained") would be unduly circumscribed if there had to be either psychotic symptoms or the certainty of psychotic symptoms in the imminent future before detention for treatment could be considered appropriate. It is therefore the case that a recall does not require any evidence of deterioration in the patient's mental state.

At first instance, Mitting J. said that in the generality of cases, it is impracticable for the Secretary of State, prior to the issue of the recall warrant, to convene an assessment at which the patient is entitled to make representations of fact ([2006] EWHC 3056 (Admin); [2006] M.H.L.R. 358 para.49). In confirming the decision of the Secretary of State to recall a patient due to concerns about deterioration of his mental health associated with illicit drug use, Mitting J. said at para.47:

"The Secretary of State is entitled to have at the forefront of his mind not just the health and safety of the patient, but also the safety of members of the public, including the patient's own family. The Secretary of State is not obliged to put the interests of people at significant risk by staying his hand in circumstances where he has medical evidence that the taking of illicit drugs would be likely to cause imminently a severe deterioration in his mental condition".

In *Munday*, above, at para.30, Burnett J. said that the second statutory criterion (the "necessity" test) is concerned with risk and that although "psychiatrists or other medical health professionals or social supervisors with their knowledge of a person might be in a position to express a view about risk, it is by its nature an exercise of evaluation which does not necessarily call for expert medical input". In this case, his Lordship held that given the patient's history of arson, a mere allegation and arrest for arson was sufficient justification for recall.

In *Kay v United Kingdom* (1998) 40 B.M.L.R. 20, it was held that, in the absence of an emergency, there had been a breach of art.5(1) of the European Convention on Human Rights when a patient had been recalled under this provision without up to date medical evidence to demonstrate that he was suffering from a true mental disorder of a kind or degree warranting compulsory confinement. Although Mitting J. accepted that the Secretary of State must have before him medical evidence which justifies the decision to recall, that medical evidence "need not be a report freshly prepared upon the precise condition recently obtaining". Where, as in *MM's* case:

"there is abundant medical evidence to the effect that [he] suffers from paranoid schizophrenia and that his condition is likely to deteriorate imminently and significantly if he takes illicit drugs, then that evidence suffices to justify recall unless there is good reason for believing that it is no longer currently valid" (para.41).

In *R. (on the application of B) v Mental Health Review Tribunal and the Home Secretary* [2002] EWHC 1553 (Admin); [2003] M.H.L.R. 19 para.31, Scott Baker J. said obiter that the medical evidence must show that the criteria for detention are met.

The Reference Guide states at para.18.11:

"In urgent cases, a direction recalling a patient may be given verbally outside office hours by a duty officer of the Ministry of Justice's Mental Health [Casework Section] on behalf of the Secretary of State. In practice, the warrant would then normally be provided on the next working day".

The policy of the Mental Health Unit (now the Mental Health Casework Section) on recalls is set out at para.5 of "The recall of conditionally discharged restricted patients", Ministry of Justice, February 4, 2009:

"Mental Health Unit's policy is that patients will be recalled where it is necessary to protect the public from the actual or potential risk posed by that patient **and** that risk is linked to the patient's mental disorder. It is not possible to specify all the circumstances when recall will be appropriate but **public safety will always be the most important factor**.

Decision on whether to recall largely turns on the degree of danger the patient might present. The gravity of any potential or actual risk will be relevant factors as will how imminent such a risk is. The more immediate the risk the more likely that recall will be indicated. Similarly, the more serious the risk or potential risk the more likely that recall is indicated.

Recall does not require any evidence of deterioration in the patient's mental state. However, except in an emergency, medical evidence is required that the patient is currently mentally disordered.

Recall will not be used to deal with anti-social or offending behaviour that is unconnected with the patient's mental disorder.

Recall decisions always give precedence to public safety considerations. This may mean that the Justice Secretary will decide to recall on public safety grounds even though the supervising psychiatrist may be of the view that recall would be counter-therapeutic for the patient.

Recall will be considered where it appears necessary for the protection of others from harm because of a combination of the patient's mental disorder and his behaviour. This includes potential behaviour where there is evidence that indicates the imminent likelihood of risk behaviours.

In an emergency the Justice Secretary will recall for assessment in the absence of an fresh evidence as regards mental disorder.

The fact that recall may not be supported by one or both the supervisors will be relevant in considering recall but not determinative. The Justice Secretary can and should recall, if his judgement is that recall is indicated on the evidence, even though the supervisors may not be recommending recall.

Where recall is supported by at least one supervisor, then the expectation is that the patient should be recalled unless there are compelling reasons not to recall."

Once a decision to recall has been made, it is the responsibility of the supervisor to identify an appropriate bed and to make the practicable arrangements for admission to hospital. However the Mental Health Unit will need to ensure that the proposed bed provides an appropriate level of security (Mental Health Unit Bulletin, Oct. 2007, p.1).

If the patient will not return to hospital willingly on being told of the recall, then the police should be asked to assist. The police should be provided with a copy of the recall warrant. Once recalled, and until they are readmitted to hospital, patients are treated as if they were absent without leave and can therefore be taken into custody and taken to the hospital specified in the warrant. There is no power of entry attached to a recall warrant. If it is not possible to gain access to a patient who has been recalled, an application may be made to a magistrate under s.135(2).

A recall is a form of legal authority which authorises the compulsory readmission and detention of the patient and the reinstatement of the regime of control under s.41: see the *Dlodlo* case, noted below. The consent to treatment provisions contained in Pt IV apply to the patient from the date of the recall (s.56(3)(c)). Revised procedures for informing restricted patients of the reasons for their recall are contained in Department of Health Circular No. HSG(93)20. The Annex to this circular identifies a three-stage procedure that should be applied when a patient is recalled:

"*Stage 1*: The person returning the patient to hospital should inform him/her in simple terms that he/she is being recalled to hospital by the Home Secretary under section 42(3) of the Mental Health Act 1983 and that, to the extent that this is possible, a further explanation will be given later. The reason(s) for recalling the patient should be explained to the nearest relative, if one is available, within 72 hours.

*Stage 2*: An explanation should be given to the patient of the reason(s) for his/her recall as soon as possible after re-admission to hospital and in any event within 72 hours. This should be done by the [RC] or deputy, an [AMHP], or an appropriate administrator representing the hospital managers. The person giving the explanation should ensure, so far as the patient's mental condition allows, that the patient understands the reason(s).

*Stage 3*: A written explanation of the reason(s) for recall should be provided for the patient within 72 hours of being re-admitted to hospital. Written information on the reason(s) should also be given to the patient's nearest relative (subject to the patient's consent)."

As "recall" must be understood as authorising not only the physical recall of the patient, **1–550** but also the reinstatement of a regime of control in respect of the patient, the Secretary of State may issue a warrant for the recall of a patient to a hospital in which the patient is already detained under ss.2 or 3 of this Act (*Dlodlo v Mental Health Review Tribunal for the South Thames Region* (1996) 36 B.M.L.R. 145 CA). Recall "will almost invariably be appropriate" in this situation ("The recall of conditionally discharged restricted patients", above, para.14). In *Dlodlo* a restriction order patient was transferred to a local hospital. The patient was subsequently given a conditional discharge by a tribunal, but, on becoming ill, he was re-admitted to the local hospital under s.3. The re-admission was followed by the issue of a warrant for the patients recall. The legality of using s.3 to detain a restriction order patient who had been conditionally discharged was confirmed by the Court of Appeal in *R. v North West London Mental Health NHS Trust Ex p. Stewart* [1997] 4 All E.R. 871, where it was held that Pts II and III of this Act are not mutually exclusive but contain powers which can coexist and operate independently of each other.

Paragraph 56 of the guidance for clinical supervisors, above, states:

"If the clinical supervisor has reason to fear for the safety of the patient or of others, he may decide to take immediate local action to admit the patient to hospital for a short period either with the patient's consent or using civil powers such as those under sections 2, 3 or 4 of the Mental Health Act 1983. Whether or not such action is taken, and even if the social supervisor does not share the clinical supervisor's s concern, the clinical supervisor should report to the Ministry of Justice at once so that consideration can be given to the patient's recall to hospital."

The policy of the Mental Health Casework Section is to consider recall where there is any admission to a psychiatric hospital ("The recall of conditionally discharged restricted patients", above, para.8).

The contact numbers of the Mental Health Casework Section at the Ministry of Justice are 020 3334 3335 and 020 7035 4848, option 5 (outside office hours).

HOSPITAL. Or registered establishment (s.34(2)). The recall can be to any hospital (or hospital unit) in England or Wales. The legality of recalling a patient to a hospital other than the hospital named in the restriction order was confirmed in the *Dlodlo* case, above.

In "The recall of conditionally discharged restricted patients", above, para.4, the Ministry of Justice states:

"There is no statutory requirement for the Justice Secretary to obtain the agreement of the hospital doctors to re-admit a recalled patient. The Justice Secretary is entitled to take a different view to that of the supervising psychiatrist, provided there are sufficient grounds/evidence to justify this and satisfy the Secretary of State that the criteria for detention under the Mental Health Act are met."

*Subsection (4)*

**1–551**  PARAGRAPH (B). This paragraph provides that a recalled patient can be taken into custody and conveyed to the specified hospital by any AMHP, officer on the staff of the hospital or any other person authorised by the hospital managers.

*Subsection (5)*

**1–552**  This subsection provides that if a restriction order ceases to have effect while the patient is on conditional discharge from hospital he will cease to be liable to be detained.

*Subsection (6)*

**1–553**  GREAT BRITAIN. England, Wales and Scotland (Union with Scotland Act 1706, preamble, art.1).

TAKEN TO THAT PLACE. See s.137 for general provisions relating to custody, conveyance and detention.

## Power of magistrates' courts to commit for restriction order

**1–554**  43.—(1) If in the case of a person of or over the age of 14 years who is convicted by a magistrates' court of an offence punishable on summary conviction with imprisonment—

(a)  the conditions which under section 37(1) above are required to be satisfied for the making of a hospital order are satisfied in respect of the offender; but

(b)  it appears to the court, having regard to the nature of the offence, the antecedents of the offender and the risk of his committing further offences if set at large, that if a hospital order is made a restriction order should also be made,

the court may, instead of making a hospital order or dealing with him in any other manner, commit him in custody to the Crown Court to be dealt with in respect of the offence.

(2) Where an offender is committed to the Crown Court under this section, the Crown Court shall inquire into the circumstances of the case and may—

(a) if that court would have power so to do under the foregoing provisions of this Part of this Act upon the conviction of the offender before that court of such an offence as is described in section 37(1) above, make a hospital order in his case, with or without a restriction order;

(b) if the court does not make such an order, deal with the offender in any other manner in which the magistrates' court might have dealt with him.

(3) The Crown Court shall have the same power to make orders under sections 35, 36 and 38 above in the case of a person committed to the court under this section as the Crown Court has under those sections in the case of an accused person within the meaning of section 35 or 36 above or of a person convicted before that court as mentioned in section 38 above.

(4) The power of a magistrates' court under [section 3 of the Powers of Criminal Courts (Sentencing) Act 2000] (which enables such a court to commit an offender to the Crown Court where the court is of the opinion that greater punishment should be inflicted for the offence than the court has power to inflict) shall also be exercisable by a magistrates' court where it is of the opinion that greater punishment should be inflicted as aforesaid on the offender unless a hospital order is made in his case with a restriction order.

(5) The power of the Crown Court to make a hospital order, with or without a restriction order, in the case of a person convicted before that court of an offence may, in the same circumstances and subject to the same conditions, be exercised by such a court in the case of a person committed to the court under section 5 of the Vagrancy Act 1824 (which provides for the committal to the Crown Court of persons who are incorrigible rogues within the meaning of that section).

AMENDMENT

The words in square brackets in subs.(4) were substituted by the Powers of Criminal Courts (Sentencing) Act 2000 s.165, Sch.9 para.91.

DEFINITIONS

hospital order: ss.37, 145(1).　　　　　　　　　　　　　　　　　　　**1–555**
restriction order: ss.41, 145(1).

GENERAL NOTE

A magistrates' court has no power to make a restriction order. If the court is satisfied that **1–556** the conditions exist in which it could make a hospital order, but also feels that a restriction order should be made in addition, it may commit an offender (if over 14 years of age) to the Crown Court under this section. The magistrates may direct that the offender be detained in a hospital, pending the hearing of the case by the Crown Court (s.44). If the Crown Court decides not to make a hospital order, it can deal with the offender in any way in which the magistrates' court could have dealt with him (subs.(2)) or it can remand him under s.35 or 36 or it can make an interim hospital order in respect of him (subs.(3)).

*Appeals*

**1–557**  In *Kiernan v Harrow Crown Court* [2003] EWCA Crim 1052; [2005] M.H.L.R. 1, the Court of Appeal, having considered ss.9 and 10 of the Criminal Appeal Act 1968, concluded that it had no jurisdiction to hear an appeal from a hospital order imposed by the Crown Court subsequent to a committal having been made under this section. In these circumstances, the court felt it appropriate to reconstitute itself as a Divisional Court of the Administrative Court and to consider the issue by way of a deemed application for judicial review of the decision of the Crown Court. Having quashed the decision of the Crown Court and having no power in judicial review proceedings to impose any separate penalty, the court remitted the case a Crown Court judge.

*Subsection (1)*

**1–558**  AGE.   See s.55(7). A person attains the age of 14 at the commencement of his or her fourteenth birthday (Family Law Reform Act 1969 s.9(1)).

CONVICTED.   The magistrates' must have convicted the offender. In *R. v Horseferry Road Magistrates' Court Ex p. K* [1996] 3 All E.R. 719 at 735 DC, Forbes J. said that this Act:

> "makes *no* provision for committal to the Crown Court by the magistrates for imposition of a restriction order under s.41 upon a person who has been acquitted of an offence by reason of insanity. The magistrates only have such a power to commit to the Crown Court for that purpose in the case of a person *convicted* of an imprisonable offence, whether indictable or summary only".

His Lordship said that this state of affairs represented an "obvious legislative lacuna."

MAGISTRATES' COURT.   Or youth court for those under the age of 18.

OFFENCE PUNISHABLE ON SUMMARY CONVICTION WITH IMPRISONMENT.   For young offenders, see s.55(2).

RISK OF HIS COMMITTING FURTHER OFFENCES.   The magistrates' court does not need to be satisfied as to the "serious harm" test set out in s.41(1).

COMMIT HIM IN CUSTODY.   Or order him to be admitted to a hospital if the conditions of s.44 are satisfied. The Secretary of State has power to transfer a mentally disordered offender from custody to hospital under s.48(2)(b).

*Subsection (2)*

**1–559**  COMMITTED TO THE CROWN COURT UNDER THIS SECTION.   Or under s.3 of the Powers of Criminal Courts (Sentencing) Act 2000 (subs.(4)).

## Committal to hospital under s.43

**1–560**  **44.**—(1) Where an offender is committed under section 43(1) above and the magistrates' court by which he is committed is satisfied on written or oral evidence that arrangements have been made for the admission of the offender to a hospital in the event of an order being made under this section, the court may, instead of committing him in custody, by order direct him to be admitted to that hospital, specifying it, and to be detained there until the case is disposed of by the Crown Court, and may give such directions as it thinks fit for his production from the hospital to attend the Crown Court by which his case is to be dealt with.

(2) The evidence required by subsection (1) above shall be given by the [approved clinician who would have overall responsibility for the offender's case] or by some other person representing the managers of the hospital in question.

(3) The power to give directions under section 37(4) above, section 37(5) above and section 40(1) above shall apply in relation to an order under this section as they apply in relation to a hospital order, but as if references to the period of 28 days mentioned in section 40(1) above were omitted; and subject as aforesaid an order under this section shall, until the offender's case is disposed of by the Crown Court, have the same effect as a hospital order together with a restriction order [. . .].

AMENDMENT
In subs.(1) the words in square brackets were substituted by the Mental Health Act 2007 s.10(7). The words omitted in subs.(3) were repealed by s.55, Sch.11 Pt 8.

DEFINITIONS
    hospital: ss.55(5), 145(1).                                     **1–561**
    hospital order: ss.37, 145(1).
    restriction order: ss.41, 145(1).
    approved clinician: s.145(1).
    the managers: s.145(1).

GENERAL NOTE
    If a magistrates' court on committing an offender to the Crown Court under s.43, is sat- **1–562** isfied that arrangements have been made for the admission of the offender to a hospital, it may direct him to be admitted to that hospital until the case is disposed of by the Crown Court. If it is impracticable or inappropriate to bring the offender before the court, the Crown Court may either adjourn the case or make a hospital order without convicting him and in his absence under s.51(5).

Rule 49.2 (3) of the Criminal Procedure Rules 2010 (SI 2010/60 (L.2) states:

"The magistrates' court by which an offender is ordered to be admitted to hospital under section 44 of the 1983 Act shall send to the hospital such information in the possession of the court as it considers likely to assist in the treatment of the offender until his case is dealt with by the Crown Court."

*Transitional provision*
    The repeal of the reference to restriction orders made for a specified period in subs.(3) **1–563** shall have no effect in respect of—

(a)  a restriction order for a specified period made before October 1, 2007, or

(b)  an order made outside England and Wales which is treated under the 1983 Act as if it were a restriction order for a specified period (Mental Health Act 2007 s.40(7) and SI 2007/2798 art.2(d)).

*Subsection (1)*
    MAGISTRATES' COURT.  Or youth court for those under the age of 18.        **1–564**

    ADMITTED TO THAT HOSPITAL.  Which will normally be the hospital which had already agreed to admit the patient in the event of the magistrates' court itself making a hospital order. Once the offender has been admitted to the hospital, subss.(5) and (6) of s.51 shall apply to him as if he were a person subject to a transfer direction made under s.47 (s.51(3)).

DIRECTIONS AS IT THINKS FIT FOR HIS PRODUCTION FROM THE HOSPITAL. It will be the hospital's duty to arrange for the offenders attendance at the court with an appropriate escort. It is not necessary to obtain the Secretary of State's consent to leave of absence from the hospital for this purpose.

*Subsection (2)*

**1–565** SOME OTHER PERSON. Who need not be a clinician.

*Subsection (3)*

**1–566** This subsection provides that the magistrates' court can direct that the offender be detained in a place of safety pending his admission to hospital. It also authorises a constable, approved mental health professional or any other person directed to do so by the court to convey the offender to hospital at any time and not within the 28-day period provided for by s.40(1). Subject to this exception, an order under this section has the same effect as a restriction order made without limit of time.

## Appeals from magistrates' courts

**1–567** **45.**—(1) Where on the trial of an information charging a person with an offence a magistrates' court makes a hospital order or guardianship order in respect of him without convicting him, he shall have the same right of appeal against the order as if it had been made on his conviction; and on any such appeal the Crown Court shall have the same powers as if the appeal had been against both conviction and sentence.

(2) An appeal by a child or young person with respect to whom any such order has been made, whether the appeal is against the order or against the finding upon which the order was made, may be brought by him or by his parent or guardian on his behalf.

DEFINITIONS

**1–568** hospital order: ss.37, 145(1).
guardianship order: ss.37, 145(1).
child: s.55(1).
young person: s.55(1).
guardian: s.55(1).

GENERAL NOTE

**1–569** This section provides a right of appeal for a person who has been made the subject of a hospital order or a guardianship order made by a magistrates' court under s.37(3).
Paragraphs 4.27 to 4.29 of the Reference Guide state:

"Under general criminal justice legislation, all patients admitted to hospital on the basis of a hospital order will have certain rights of appeal either to the Court of Appeal (Criminal Division) or to the Crown Court. This includes appeal against the conviction (or finding that the person had done the act in question) on which the order was based and against the order itself (including the restriction order, if there is one).

Section 45 of the Act itself specifically ensures that people given hospital orders by a magistrates' court under section 37(4) without being convicted have the same rights of appeal against the order as they would have if they had been convicted. Likewise, the Crown Court hearing the appeal has the same powers it would have if the appeal were against conviction and sentence. Appeals in respect of children or young people given hospital orders by magistrates' courts without being convicted may be brought on their behalf by their parents or guardians. This applies to appeals against the order itself and against the finding that the child or young person had done the act in question.

In practice, the managers of the hospital in which patients are detained are responsible for ensuring that they are taken, with an escort, to court in connection with any appeal, as necessary. If any patient who is required to appear before the court is, in the opinion of the responsible clinician, unfit to appear, the Crown Court or the Registrar of Criminal Appeals (as the case may be) will need to be notified immediately."

*[Hospital and Limitation Directions*

## Power of higher courts to direct hospital admission

**45A.**—(1) This section applies where, in the case of a person convicted before **1–570** the Crown Court of an offence the sentence for which is not fixed by law—

(a) the conditions mentioned in subsection (2) below are fulfilled; and

(b) [. . .], the court considers making a hospital order in respect of him before deciding to impose a sentence of imprisonment ("the relevant sentence") in respect of the offence.

(2) The conditions referred to in subsection (1) above are that the court is satisfied, on the written or oral evidence of two registered medical practitioners—

(a) that the offender is suffering from [mental disorder];

(b) that the mental disorder from which the offender is suffering is of a nature or degree which makes it appropriate for him to be detained in a hospital for medical treatment; and

[(c) that appropriate medical treatment is available for him.]

(3) The court may give both of the following directions, namely—

(a) a direction that, instead of being removed to and detained in a prison, the offender be removed to and detained in such hospital as may be specified in the direction (in this Act referred to as a "hospital direction"); and

(b) a direction that the offender be subject to the special restrictions set out in section 41 above (in this Act referred to as a "limitation direction").

(4) A hospital direction and a limitation direction shall not be given in relation to an offender unless at least one of the medical practitioners whose evidence is taken into account by the court under subsection (2) above has given evidence orally before the court.

(5) A hospital direction and a limitation direction shall not be given in relation to an offender unless the court is satisfied on the written or oral evidence of the [approved clinician who would have overall responsibility for his case], or of some other person representing the managers of the hospital that arrangements have been made—

(a) for his admission to that hospital; and

(b) for his admission to it within the period of 28 days beginning with the day of the giving of such directions;

and the court may, pending his admission within that period, give such directions as it thinks fit for his conveyance to and detention in a place of safety.

(6) If within the said period of 28 days it appears to the Secretary of State that by reason of an emergency or other special circumstances it is not practicable for the patient to be received into the hospital specified in the hospital direction, he may give instructions for the admission of the patient to such other hospital as appears to be appropriate instead of the hospital so specified.

(7) Where such instructions are given—

(a) the Secretary of State shall cause the person having the custody of the patient to be informed, and

(b) the hospital direction shall have effect as if the hospital specified in the instructions were substituted for the hospital specified in the hospital direction.

(8) Section 38(1) and (5) and section 39 above shall have effect as if any reference to the making of a hospital order included a reference to the giving of a hospital direction and a limitation direction.

(9) A hospital direction and a limitation direction given in relation to an offender shall have effect not only as regards the relevant sentence but also (so far as applicable) as regards any other sentence of imprisonment imposed on the same or a previous occasion.

(10) [. . .]

(11) [. . .]

AMENDMENT

This section was inserted by the Crime (Sentences) Act 1997 s.46. The words omitted in subs.(1)(b) were repealed by the Criminal Justice Act 2003 s.332, Sch.37 Pt 7. The words in square brackets in subss.(2)(a), (2)(c) and (5) were substituted by the Mental Health Act 2007 ss.1(4), 4(6), 10(8), Sch.1 para.9. Subsections (1) and (11) were repealed by s.55, Sch.11 Pt 1.

DEFINITIONS

**1–571**    mental disorder: ss.1, 145(1).
hospital: ss.55(5), 145(1).
medical treatment: s.145(1), (4).
approved clinician: s.145(1).
managers: s.145(1).
place of safety: s.55.

GENERAL NOTE

**1–572**    This section empowers the Crown Court, when imposing a prison sentence on a mentally disordered offender convicted of an offence other than one of which the sentence is fixed by law, to give a direction for immediate admission to and detention in a specified hospital (a "hospital direction"), together with a direction that they be subject to the special restrictions set out in s.41 (a "limitation direction"). The responsible clinician will have the option of seeking the patient's transfer to prison at any time before his release date if no further treatment is necessary, or is likely to be beneficial. The powers granted by this section are rarely used.

The purpose and application of the power to make a hospital direction is considered in paras 2 to 5 of Home Office Circular No.52/1997:

"It is the Government's policy that an offender needing specialist care and treatment for mental disorder should where possible receive it in hospital rather than in custodial care, wherever this is consistent with the needs of protecting the public. The hospital direction does not represent a departure from that policy. The advice given on inter-agency provision for dealing with mentally disordered offenders in Home Office Circulars 66/1990 and 12/1995 remains in force. Except where the law requires the imposition of a life sentence, courts retain the option of making a hospital order under section 37 of the 1983 Act, with or without a restriction order under section 41 of that Act.

The hospital direction is intended to give the courts greater flexibility in dealing with cases where they conclude that a prison sentence is the appropriate disposal in spite of evidence that the offender is mentally disordered. That will be either because the offender falls to be sentenced under the automatic life sentence provision in section 2 of the Crime (Sentences) Act 1997, or because the court is satisfied that a prison sentence with a hospital direction will be the most effective way to protect the public from further harm.

When sentencing mentally disordered offenders, the court is bound by the requirement in section 4 of the Criminal Justice Act 1991 to consider any information before it which relates to the defendant's mental condition. Except where the sentence is fixed by law, the court is required to consider the effect of a custodial sentence on the offender's mental disorder and on the treatment which may be available for it before passing such a sentence.

The hospital direction does not disturb this arrangement. Section 45A(1)(b) of the 1983 Act requires the court to consider making a hospital order in all cases (other than those where the sentence is fixed by law and offenders sentenced under section 2 of the Crime (Sentences) Act 1997) before attaching a hospital direction to a prison sentence. Existing procedures for giving medical evidence need not change, since the requirements for making a hospital direction are the same as those for making a restricted hospital order. The court will simply have the new option of directing to hospital when it concludes that a custodial sentence is appropriate."

The provisions of the Criminal Justice Act 1991 and the Crime (Sentences) Act 1997 which are referred to in the above circular have been superseded by the Powers of Criminal Courts (Sentencing) Act 2000 and the Criminal Justice Act 2003.

The effect of hospital and limitation directions are set out in s.45B.

In *R. v Staines* [2006] EWCA Crim 15; [2006] 2 Cr. App. R. (S.) 65, the Court of Appeal considered what the proper approach of the appellate court should be where it is alleged that evidence and developments since the trial or sentencing have brought about a situation which, had it been known or appreciated at the time of sentencing, would or might have led to the imposition of a hospital order under s.37, coupled with a restriction order under s.41, rather than the imposition of a prison sentence combined with a direction under this section. The court, at para.30, said that an order under this section "carries with it the distinct advantage that both sets of criteria can be taken into account, those which focus on medical grounds and those which focus on the safety of the public."

A hospital direction cannot be combined with a sentence of detention imposed on a young offender; it can only be combined with a sentence of imprisonment (*R. v Burridge* [2009] EWCA Crim 1693; [2009] M.H.L.R. 297).

A hospital direction and limitation direction constitute a sentence for the purpose of the Criminal Appeal Act 1968 (s.50(1)).

*Applications to the First-tier Tribunal (Mental Health) or the Mental Health Review Tribunal for Wales*

The right of a patient who is subject to directions made under this section to apply to a **1–573** tribunal is governed by s.73. The powers of a tribunal on hearing such an application are set out in s.74.

*Domestic Violence, Crime and Victims Act 2004*

See Ch.18 of the *Code of Practice* at paras 18.18 to 18.20 and Ch.30 at paras 30.29 to **1–574** 30.31. The Department of Health has published "Mental Health Act 2007: Guidance on the extension of victims' rights under the Domestic Violence, Crime and Victims Act" (2008).

*Subsection (1)*

FIXED BY LAW. This section does not apply to persons who have been convicted of mur- **1–575** der who must be sentenced to life imprisonment (Murder (Abolition of Death Penalty) Act 1965 s.1).

HOSPITAL ORDER. The court must have considered making a hospital order before imposing a sentence of imprisonment and attaching a hospital direction.

*Subsection (2)*
EVIDENCE. For general requirements as to medical evidence, see s.54. The court can call a doctor who has provided a written report to give oral evidence (s.54(2A)).

**1–576** TWO REGISTERED MEDICAL PRACTITIONERS. One of whom must be approved under s.12 of this Act (s.54(1)).

MENTAL DISORDER. If the person has a learning disability, the disability must be associated with abnormally aggressive or seriously irresponsible conduct (s.1(2A), (2B)).

NATURE OR DEGREE. See the note on s.3(2)(a).

APPROPRIATE MEDICAL TREATMENT. See the note on s.3(2)(d).

*Subsection (3)*
**1–577** BOTH OF THE . . . DIRECTIONS. The court cannot make a hospital direction without a limitation direction.

SUCH HOSPITAL AS MAY BE PRESCRIBED. By virtue of s.47 of the Crime (Sentences) Act 1997, the court has the power to order that the patient be admitted to and detained in a named hospital unit. A named hospital unit can be any part of a hospital which is treated as a separate unit. The effect of specifying a hospital unit is considered in the note on s.41(1):

*Subsection (5)*
In *R. (on the application of DB) v Nottinghamshire Healthcare NHS Trust* [2008] EWCA Civ 1354; [2009] 2 All E.R. 792, noted under s.37(4), the Court of Appeal held that a hospital order ceases to have effect if the offender who is the subject of the order is not admitted to the hospital named in the order within the period of 28 days from the date of the making of the order, as stipulated by it. It is submitted that this finding applies to directions made under this section.

**1–578** BEGINNING WITH. Including the day on which the directions were given (*Zoan v Rouamba* [2000] 2 All E.R. 620 CA).

*Subsections (6), (7)*
**1–579** SECRETARY OF STATE. These functions are exercised in England by the Secretary of State for Health. The functions of the Minister under these provisions, so far as exercisable in relation to Wales, are exercised by the Welsh Ministers: see the General Note to this Act and SI 1999/672 art.2, Sch.1, as varied by SI 2000/253 art.4, Sch.3.

*Subsection (8)*
**1–580** This provides that ss.38(1) and (5) and 39 apply in respect of the giving of a hospital and a limitation direction as they do to the making of a hospital order. Those sections enable respectively the making of an interim hospital order and the acquisition of information from health authorities on the availability of facilities.

*Subsection (9)*
**1–581** This provides that where a hospital and a limitation direction are made, they apply to all existing prison sentences passed on the offender.

## [Effect of hospital and limitation directions

**45B.**—(1) A hospital direction and a limitation direction shall be sufficient **1–582** authority—

(a) for a constable or any other person directed to do so by the court to convey the patient to the hospital specified in the hospital direction within a period of 28 days; and

(b) for the managers of the hospital to admit him at any time within that period and thereafter detain him in accordance with the provisions of this Act.

(2) With respect to any person—

(a) a hospital direction shall have effect as a transfer direction; and

(b) a limitation direction shall have effect as a restriction direction.

(3) While a person is subject to a hospital direction and a limitation direction the [responsible clinician] shall at such intervals (not exceeding one year) as the Secretary of State may direct examine and report to the Secretary of State on that person; and every report shall contain such particulars as the Secretary of State may require.]

AMENDMENT

This section was inserted by the Crime (Sentences) Act 1997 s.46. The words in square brackets in subs.(3) were inserted by the Mental Health Act 2007 s.10(9).

DEFINITIONS

hospital direction: ss.45A(3)(a), 145(1).  **1–583**

limitation direction: ss.45A(3)(b), 145(1).

hospital: ss.55(5), 145(1).

managers: s.145(1).

transfer direction: ss.47, 145(1).

restriction direction: ss.49, 145(1).

responsible clinician: s.55(1).

GENERAL NOTE

The effect of hospital and limitation directions is set out in paras 7 and 8 of the Home **1–584** Office Circular 52/1997:

"The hospital direction has the effect of ordering the offender's admission to a named hospital for treatment within 28 days, as if a hospital order had been made. Once there, the offender will be managed as if admitted under a transfer direction made under section 47 of the 1983 Act. When making a hospital direction the court must at the same time make a limitation direction. This has the same effect as a restriction direction under section 49 of the 1983 Act. The offender is made subject to the restrictions set out in section 41 of the 1983 Act.

An offender who is subject to hospital and limitation directions may serve his entire sentence in hospital if the responsible [clinician] is satisfied that he is benefiting from treatment. Alternatively he may, on the recommendation of the responsible [clinician] or [a tribunal], be transferred to prison at any time during sentence by warrant of the [Secretary of State] under section 50(1) of the 1983 Act. Transfer to prison will be considered by the [Secretary of State] on receipt of medical evidence that the patient no longer requires treatment in hospital for mental disorder, or that no other effective treatment can be given in hospital. Any subsequent transfer back to hospital would be considered under section 47 of the 1983 Act."

Although the limitation direction ends on the patient's release date, the hospital direction does not. This means that if the patient is being treated in hospital subject to the hospital direction on the release date, the patient remains in hospital as if he or she were subject to an unrestricted hospital order. If the patient is transferred to prison, both the hospital direction and the limitation direction end.

A patient who is subject to an order under s.45A comes within the after-care provisions of s.117. Paragraph 5.22 of the Reference Guide states:

"In practice, the Secretary of State for Justice expects clinical staff from the hospital and prison to meet to plan the patient's future care (a 'section 117 meeting') before directing the patient's removal to prison".

*Subsection (1)*

**1–585** CONVEY THE PATIENT. if the patient absconds, he or she may be retaken under s.138.

## *Detention during Her Majesty's pleasure*

**Persons ordered to be kept in custody during Her Majesty's pleasure**

**1–586** **46.** [*Repealed by the Armed Forces Act 1996 s.35(2), Sch.7 Pt III.*]

## *Transfers to hospital of prisoners, etc.*

**Removal to hospital of persons serving sentences of imprisonment, etc.**

**1–587** **47.**—(1) If in the case of a person serving a sentence of imprisonment the Secretary of State is satisfied, by reports from at least two registered medical practitioners—

(a) that the said person is suffering from [mental disorder]; and

(b) that the mental disorder from which that person is suffering is of a nature or degree which makes it appropriate for him to be detained in a hospital for medical treatment[; and

(c) that appropriate medical treatment is available for him.]

the Secretary of State may, if he is of the opinion having regard to the public interest and all the circumstances that it is expedient so to do, by warrant direct that that person be removed to and detained in such hospital [. . .] as may be specified in the direction; and a direction under this section shall be known as "a transfer direction".

(2) A transfer direction shall cease to have effect at the expiration of the period of 14 days beginning with the date on which it is given unless within that period the person with respect to whom it was given has been received into the hospital specified in the direction.

(3) A transfer direction with respect to any person shall have the same effect as a hospital order made in his case.

(4) [. . .]

(5) References in this Part of this Act to a person serving a sentence of imprisonment include references—

(a) to a person detained in pursuance of any sentence or order for detention made by a court in criminal proceedings [or service disciplinary proceedings] (other than an order [made in consequence of a finding of insanity or unfitness to stand trial [or a sentence of service detention within the meaning of the Armed Forces Act 2006]]);

(b) to a person committed to custody under section 115(3) of the Magistrates' Courts Act 1980 (which relates to persons who fail to comply with an order to enter into recognisances to keep the peace or be of good behaviour); and

(c) to a person committed by a court to a prison or other institution to which the Prison Act 1952 applies in default of payment of any sum adjudged to be paid on his conviction.

[(6) in subsection (5)(a) "service disciplinary proceedings" means proceedings in respect of a service offence within the meaning of the Armed Forces Act 2006.]

AMENDMENT

The words omitted from subs.(1) were repealed by the Crime (Sentences) Act 1997 s.56(2), Sch.6. The words in square brackets in subs.(1)(a) and subs.(1)(c) were substituted by the Mental Health Act 2007 ss.1(4), 4(7), Sch.1 para.10. Subsection (4) was repealed by s.55, Sch.11 Pt 1. The words in square brackets in subs.(5)(a) were substituted by the Domestic Violence, Crime and Victims Act 2004 s.58(1), Sch.10 para.18 and the Armed Forces Act 2006 s.378, Sch.16 para.97(2). Subsection (6) was added by para.97(3).

DEFINITIONS

    mental disorder: ss.1, 145(1).                                    **1–588**

    hospital: ss.55(5), 145(1).

    medical treatment: s.145(1), (4).

    hospital order: ss.37, 145(1).

GENERAL NOTE

This section enables the Secretary of State (in practice, the Mental Health Casework  **1–589** Section at the Ministry of Justice) to direct that a person serving a sentence of imprisonment or other detention be removed to and detained in a hospital. The transfer to hospital does not bring the prison sentence to an end. Such transfers can only be made on medical grounds.

In order for the Secretary of State to make a transfer direction, the following are required:

(i) agreement on the part of two medical practitioners, expressed in their reports to the Secretary of State:

    (i) that the person is mentally disordered; and

    (ii) that the requirements for detention in subs.(1)(b) and (c) are satisfied;

(ii) a hospital in which the patient may be appropriately treated; and

(iii) a place at that hospital that is available within 14 days.

In *R.(on the application of DK) v Secretary of State for the Home Department* [2010] EWHC 82 (Admin); [2010] M.H.L.R. 64, Collins J. said at para.33:

"One does not want to be over pedantic in these matters, but, as I have said, the court must bear in mind that it is dealing with liberty, and that therefore it is of the utmost importance that all the necessary preconditions for transfer leading to detention are properly seen through."

A Government document on the "Procedure for the transfer of prisoners to and from hospital under sections 47 and 48 of the 'Mental Health Act (1983)'" (2007) states at p.21:

"If a transfer is deemed necessary out of hours, it is possible for the Mental Health Unit to give verbal authority. This is sufficient to permit movement of the prisoner. The appropriate paperwork will be issued on the next working day."

**1-590**  In *R. (on the application of D) v Secretary of State for the Home Department and National Assembly for Wales* [2004] EWHC 2857 (Admin); [2005] M.H.L.R. 17 para.33, Stanley Burnton J. held that once the prison service have reasonable grounds to believe that a prisoner requires treatment in a mental hospital in which he may be detained, the Secretary of State is under a duty expeditiously to take reasonable steps to obtain appropriate medical advice, and if that advice confirms the need for transfer to a hospital, to take reasonable steps within a reasonable time to effect that transfer. In many cases, the medical advice as to the appropriateness of transfer will serve as the reports required by s.47. The steps that are reasonable will depend on the circumstances, including the apparent risk to the health of the prisoner if no transfer is effected. Inappropriate retention of a prisoner in a prison or YOI may infringe his rights under art.8 of the European Convention on Human Rights. If the consequences for the prisoner are sufficiently severe, his inappropriate retention in a prison may go so far as to bring about a breach of art.3 of the Convention, in which case the state is under an absolute duty to prevent or bring to an end his inhumane treatment.

His Lordship made the following comment, at para.45, on the position of a prisoner who has been remanded in custody:

"If there is good reason to believe that a psychiatric assessment is appropriate, it needs to be obtained before sentence, not after what is liable to be (on what on this hypothesis is the incomplete information available to the sentencing judge) an inappropriate sentence. If, before sentence, it becomes clear that detention in a hospital under the Mental Health Act 1983 is appropriate, although transfer under s.47 is not available, I do not see why arrangements cannot be made for a prisoner to be detained under that Act while being formally remanded on bail."

**1-591**  In *R. v Drew* [2003] UKHL 25; [2003] 4 All E.R. 557 HL at para.19, Lord Bingham said that if:

"it were shown that a mentally disordered defendant was held in prison, that he was there denied medical treatment, available in hospital, which his mental condition required and that he was suffering serious consequences as a result of such denial, he would have grounds for seeking judicial review of the Home Secretary's failure to direct his transfer to hospital under [this section]; (*Keenan v United Kingdom* (2001) 33 E.H.R.R. 38)".

In judicial review proceedings the High Court has jurisdiction to direct the Secretary of State to make an order under this section if the necessary medical reports had been completed (*R. (on the application of D) v Secretary of State for the Home Office* [2003] EWHC 2529 (Admin)).

A decision to transfer a prisoner to hospital at the end of his sentence heightens the scrutiny which should be applied both by the Secretary of State as to the evidence on which that decision should be taken, and heightens the scrutiny which the court must apply to the decision of the Secretary of State: see *R. (on the application of TF) v Secretary of State for Justice* [2008] EWCA Civ 1457, where Waller L.J. said at para.31:

"Where section 47 is proposed to be used at the very end of the sentence, and hopefully that will only be in very exceptional cases, the onus must be on the Secretary of State to show that the mind of the decision maker has focused on each of the criteria which it is necessary to satisfy if there is to be power to issue a warrant directing transfer to a hospital."

The Mental Health Casework Section of the Ministry of Justice (MHCS) stated in its Newsletter of April 29, 2010:

"MHCS will look at proposals for last minute transfers explicitly in terms of the prisoner's clinical needs and invite the receiving hospital to consider whether he should be admitted under Part 2 powers. If the prisoner does not qualify for admission under Part 2 powers, then it is hard to see how a s.47 direction could be justified. If he does so qualify, then his admission can be arranged on explicitly clinical grounds.

[An AMHP] may assess a prisoner in prison for the purposes of making a Part 2 proposal, and if the admission happens on the last day of sentence, prison staff may assist in conveyance to the hospital."

A direction made under this section (a "transfer direction") has the same effect as a hospital order made without restrictions under s.37 (subs.(3)), subject to the exception that the patient may apply to a tribunal within six months of his transfer (s.69(2)(b)). A patient who has been made subject to a transfer direction can therefore be discharged at any time by his responsible clinician (RC) or the hospital managers, can be transferred under the provisions of s.19, will be able to apply to a tribunal and will be subject to the consent to treatment provisions contained in Pt IV (s.56(3)). Although the patient's discharge from detention in hospital can take place before the expiration of his or her sentence, the making of a transfer direction can result in the patient remaining in hospital under compulsory powers long after the day on which he or she would have been released from prison had such a direction not been made.

When giving a transfer direction the Secretary of State may, and in most cases will, also impose the restrictions provided for under s.49 (a "restriction direction") which means the patient cannot be transferred to another hospital, sent on leave or discharged without the Secretary of State's consent. In practice, the only occasion when a restriction direction will not be made is if the prisoner is very close to his earliest date of release: see *R. (on the application of T) v Secretary of State for the Home Department*, noted in the General Note to s.49. The Secretary of State must make a restriction direction in respect of certain prisoners (s.49(1)).

Although a person who is subject to an unrestricted order under this section cannot be recalled to prison to complete his sentence, the sentence and accordingly any licence period and conditions as would normally be imposed under the Criminal Justice Act procedure, including the prospect of recall to prison on a breach of a licence condition, continue to run notwithstanding his transfer to hospital *(R. (on the application of Miah) v Secretary of State for the Home Department* [2004] EWHC 2569 (Admin); [2004] M.H.L.R. 302).

Under s.22(2)(b) of the Prison Act 1952 (as amended by the Criminal Justice Act 1982 Sch.14 para.5), the Secretary of State may, if he is satisfied that a prisoner requires "medical investigation or observation or medical or surgical treatment of any description," direct the prisoner "to be taken to a hospital or other suitable place for the purpose of the investigation, observation or treatment". A Government document on the "Procedure for transfer of prisoners to and from hospital under sections 47 and 48 of the 'Mental Health Act (1983)'", above, states at p.25:

"[The power under the 1952 Act] is generally used for people suffering from physical ailments but it can be used for persons suffering from mental disorder. Where a prisoner is transferred to hospital under this power, it is always necessary for a prison officer escort to remain with him. It is normally only used on a short-term basis. It is for the Governor of the prison to authorise any move under the Prison Act. Under the Prison Act, the prisoner is still the responsibility of the prison when in hospital.

The power is most commonly used in cases of mental disorder where the prisoner is very ill (e.g. fluid refusal) and a request for a transfer direction under section 47 (or section 48) of the Mental Health Act is under consideration but no suitable bed is available in a psychiatric unit, or a final decision has not been reached or the formalities have not been completed."

Responsibility for prison health care was fully transferred from HM Prison Service to the NHS in April 2006; see the notes to the definition of "hospital" in s.145(1).

Under s.117, Primary Care Trusts (in Wales, Local Health Boards) and local social services authorities have a duty to provide after-care services for patients who cease to be liable to be detained and leave hospital after having been transferred by the Secretary of State under this section. The responsibility for holding a "section 117 meeting" applies if the prisoner is discharged back to prison (*Code of Practice* para.33.33).

For the supervision in the community of a patient who has been transferred under this section and has been made the subject of a restriction direction under s.49, see the note on s.50(1)(b).

*Human Rights Act 1998*

**1–592**    To subject an offender requiring admission to hospital to unnecessary suffering, humiliation, distress and deterioration of his mental condition in prison could properly be regarded as inhumane or degrading treatment or punishment contrary to art.3 of the European Convention on Human Rights (*R. v Drew* [2003] UKHL 25 para.18; also see *Riviere v France* (App.No.33834/03)). It could also constitute an interference with his mental and physical integrity contrary to art.8 (*R. (on the application of D) v Secretary of State for the Home Department and National Assembly for Wales*, above).

In *Pankiewicz v Poland* (App.No.34151/04), the European Court of Human Rights held that a delay of two months and twenty five days in transferring a mentally disordered prisoner to hospital, as recommended by two psychiatrists, violated art.5(1). The Court said at paras 44, 45:

"The Court accepts the Government's arguments that it would be unrealistic and too rigid an approach to expect the authorities to ensure that a place is immediately available in a selected psychiatric hospital. However, a reasonable balance must be struck between the competing interests involved. Having regard to the balancing of interests the Court attaches weight to the fact that the applicant was held in a regular detention centre without adequate medical facilities. The delay in admission to a psychiatric hospital and thus the beginning of the treatment was obviously harmful to the applicant, in view of the expert's opinions recommending him for psychiatric treatment. In addition, the Court notes that the Government failed to advance any detailed explanation for the delay in the applicant's admission to the hospital.

The Court cannot find that, in the circumstances of the present case, a reasonable balance was struck. The Court is of the opinion that even though the delay of two months and twenty five days in the admission of the applicant to a psychiatric hospital may not at first glance seem particularly excessive, it cannot be regarded as acceptable (see *Morsink v the Netherlands,* no. 48865/99, §§ 61–70, 11 May 2004; *Brand v the Netherlands*, no. 49902/99, §§ 58–67, 11 May 2004; and *Mocarska,* cited above, § 48). To hold otherwise would entail a serious weakening of the fundamental right to liberty to the detriment of the person concerned and thus impair the very essence of the right protected by Article 5 of the Convention."

In *Morley v United Kingdom* (2005) 40 E.H.R.R. SE8, [2005] M.H.L.R. 174, the Court declared inadmissible the applicant's complaint that art.5 required the decision to transfer a prisoner to hospital to be made by the tribunal.

*Applications to the First-tier Tribunal (Mental Health) or the Mental Health Review Tribunal for Wales*

**1–593**    See the note on "Same effect of a hospital order" in subs.(3).

*Subsection (1)*

**1–594**    SENTENCE OF IMPRISONMENT.    See s.55(6), and subs.(5).

SECRETARY OF STATE.    The Secretary of State for Justice: see the General Note to this Part.

REPORTS. Although this provision does not require that the report be in writing, it is obviously important that there should be a written report (*R.(on the application of DK) v Secretary of State for the Home Department* [2010] EWHC 82 (Admin); [2010] M.H.L.R. 64, para.19). A written report using an old pro forma which related to the terms of this section before its amendment by the Mental Health Act 2007 would not invalidate the transfer as long as the doctor had by inference supported the view that there was appropriate treatment for the patient's mental disorder at the hospital. There are two questions that need to be considered: first, did the decision-maker actually apply her mind to the statutory criteria and, secondly, was the material before the decision-maker sufficient to sustain the eventual conclusion? (*R (on the application of SP) v Secretary of State for Justice* [2010] EWHC 1124 (Admin)).

There is no statutory time limit between the date of the report and the date of the decision of the Secretary of State. However, to achieve compliance with art.5(1)(e) of the European Convention on Human Rights the medical opinion cannot be seen as sufficient to justify deprivation of liberty under that provision if a significant period has elapsed since the preparation of the report (*Varbanov v Bulgaria* [2002] M.H.L.R. 263 at para.47). The practice of the Mental Health Unit of the Ministry of Justice is to require the prison to provide two medical reports (not more than two months old and dated within two weeks of the examination) one of which must be from a doctor approved under s.12 (Mental Health Unit Bulletin, March 2008).

In *R. v Secretary of State for the Home Office Ex p. Gilkes* [1999] EWHC 47 (Admin); [1999] M.H.L.R. 7 para.12, Dyson J. said:

"If the reports are manifestly unreliable, then the Secretary of State cannot reasonably be satisfied that [paragraphs (a) an (b) are satisfied] on the basis of the reports, and a decision to rely on them in such circumstances will be capable of successful challenge by judicial review. A medical report may be unreliable for a number of reasons. It may on its face not address the relevant statutory criteria. It may be based on an assessment which is so out of date that the mere fact of a lapse of time will be sufficient to render it unreliable. It may be unreliable to rely on a report based on an assessment conducted an appreciable, but not inordinate, time before the decision to transfer where the mental disorder is a fluctuating and unstable condition and/or where there has been a change of circumstances since the assessment was made. In each case, it will be for the Secretary of State to consider whether in his judgment the medical report is one on which he can safely and properly rely so as to be satisfied that the conditions set out in paragraphs (a) and (b) ... are met. One of the considerations that will be uppermost in his mind is whether the assessment on which the report is based is sufficiently recent to provide reliable evidence of the patient's current mental condition."

In this case, Dyson J. said that although it is incorrect to say that it can never be reasonable for the Secretary of State, when considering whether to make a transfer direction, to rely on a medical report made for the purposes of s.37, the Secretary of State should be slow to conclude that such a report can be safety relied on.

TWO REGISTERED MEDICAL PRACTITIONERS. One of whom must be approved by the Secretary of State or the Welsh Ministers under s.12 (s.54(1)). There is no requirement for either doctor to be an approved clinician. "In practice, the [Secretary of State] will normally want at least one of the two doctors to be practicing at the hospital named in the proposed transfer direction, so as to ensure that there is agreement as to the hospital's reception of the patient and as to his diagnosis, treatability and detention", per Stanley Burnton J. in *R. (on the application of D) v Secretary of State for the Home Department and National Assembly for Wales*, above, at para.21. The Secretary of State is not "required to shop around until he finds psychiatrists prepared to sign section 47 reports: it is his duty to obtain the reliable opinions of psychiatrists as to the transfer of a prisoner to a hospital with a vacancy that can offer appropriate care" (at para.49).

It is acceptable for the doctors not to have seen the patient for some time prior to the completion of their reports if the patient's mental disorder is an enduring rather than a fluctuating condition, and the patient has refused to see them and to be examined by them for the purposes of such reports (*R. (on the application of F) v Secretary of State for the Home Department* [2008] EWHC 2912 (Admin); [2008] M.H.L.R. 361 para.30). This was described as "appropriate advice" at the Court of Appeal (*R. (on the application of TF) v Secretary of State for Justice*, above, para.29).

*Paragraph (a)*

**1–595**  MENTAL DISORDER.  If the person has a learning disability, the disability must be associated with abnormally aggressive or seriously irresponsible conduct (s.1(2A), (2B)).

*Paragraph (b)*

**1–596**  APPROPRIATE FOR HIM TO BE DETAINED . . . FOR MEDICAL TREATMENT.  But not assessment: *South West London and St George's Mental Health NHS Trust v W*, below, para.78. In this case Crane J. said at para.80 that he did:

> "not consider that detention becomes unlawful immediately a particular form of treatment is suspended if there is a period of assessment in relation to another form of possible treatment and the process of monitoring under nursing, medical and psychological supervision continues".

In *South West London and St George's Mental Health NHS Trust v W* [2002] EWHC 1770 Admin; [2002] M.H.L.R. 392, a mentally disordered prisoner who had been convicted of a serious and unprovoked assault on a stranger was transferred to hospital under this section. The question before the judge was whether the transfer, which was aimed at securing the staged discharge of the patient from the hospital, was lawful. The plan devised for the patient was that he would be admitted to hospital for several months. He would be given increasing leave from the hospital linked to occupational and other therapy. An attempt would then be made to find a place for him in a hostel and there would be liaison between the hostel staff and the hospital team. The patient would gradually spend increasing periods out of hospital and then progress to overnight stays at the hostel. In holding that the transfer was lawful, Crane J. held, at para.64, that although s.47 cannot be used simply to postpone release, "transfer to hospital involving admission, nursing, medical, and here psychological supervision, and staged discharge under medical supervision, is capable of amounting to 'treatment' . . .".

*Paragraph (c)*

**1–597**  APPROPRIATE MEDICAL TREATMENT.  See the note on s.3(2)(d).

THE SECRETARY OF STATE MAY.  The nature of the Secretary of State's obligations under this section is considered in *D v Secretary of State for the Home Department and National Assembly for Wales*, above.

HOSPITAL.  Or registered establishment (ss.34(2), 55(5)). In *R. (on the application of D) v Secretary of State for the Home Department and National Assembly for Wales*, above, Stanley Burnton J. suggested, at para.60, that the difficulties that are sometimes encountered in finding a suitable hospital for a potential transfer direction patient could be ameliorated by the establishment of a national database that could be maintained within the Ministry of Justice, or the Department of Health, and which might be accessible (to authorised persons only) on the internet.

*Subsection (2)*

**1–598**  14 DAYS.  After which a fresh direction will be necessary if the patient has not been admitted to the hospital.

BEGINNING WITH. Including the day on which the transfer direction is given (*Zoan v Rouamba* [2000] 2 All E.R. 620 CA).

RECEIVED INTO THE HOSPITAL. Although the agreement of the hospital to which the patient is to be transferred is not a pre-condition of a transfer direction, practical considerations will normally dictate that its agreement is necessary (*R. (on the application of D) v Secretary of State for the Home Department and National Assembly for Wales*, above, para.30). In *D* the court was informed by a Home Office official that approximately six transfers take place each year without the agreement of the admitting hospital, and that about 650 transfers take place each year.

*Subsection (3)*

The only effect of this provision is to apply s.40 to a transfer direction (*R. (on the application of Miah) v Secretary of State for the Home Department* [2004] EWHC 2569 (Admin); [2004] M.H.L.R. 302 para.23).  **1–599**

SAME EFFECT AS A HOSPITAL ORDER. The patient can therefore be discharged by his RC or by the hospital managers (s.40(4)) and can continue to be detained in a hospital beyond the time set by the sentencing court for his release from prison. An application for a community treatment order can be made in respect of the patient (Sch.1 Pt.1). The patient may make an application to a tribunal within six months of the date of the direction, once during the following six months, and at yearly intervals thereafter (s.69(2)(b)). The patient's nearest relative has similar rights to make an application (s.69(1) as applied by s.55(4)). Any application, hospital order or guardianship order that was in place prior to the making of the transfer direction will cease to have effect (s.40(5)).

*Subsection (5)*

ANY SENTENCE OR ORDER FOR DETENTION MADE BY A COURT IN CRIMINAL PROCEEDINGS. These words are wide enough to cover detention during Her Majesty's pleasure (*R. v Secretary of State for the Home Department Ex p. Hickey (No.1)* [1995] 1 All E.R. 479, per Rose L.J. at 488).  **1–600**

## Removal to hospital of other prisoners

**48.**—(1) If in the case of a person to whom this section applies the Secretary of State is satisfied by the same reports as are required for the purposes of section 47 above that—  **1–601**

[(a) that person is suffering from mental disorder of a nature or degree which makes it appropriate for him to be detained in a hospital for medical treatment; and

(b) he is in urgent need of such treatment;][and

(c) appropriate medical treatment is available for him;]

the Secretary of State shall have the same power of giving a transfer direction in respect of him under that section as if he were serving a sentence of imprisonment.

(2) This section applies to the following persons, that is to say—

(a) persons detained in a prison or remand centre, not being persons serving a sentence of imprisonment or persons falling within the following paragraphs of this subsection;

(b) persons remanded in custody by a magistrates' court;

(c) civil prisoners, that is to say, persons committed by a court to prison for a limited term [. . .], who are not persons falling to be dealt with under section 47 above;

(d) persons detained under the Immigration Act 1971 [or under section 62 of the Nationality, Immigration and Asylum Act 2002 (detention by the Secretary of State)].

(3) Subsections (2) [and (3)] of section 47 above shall apply for the purposes of this section and of any transfer direction given by virtue of this section as they apply for the purposes of that section and of any transfer direction under that section.

AMENDMENT

The words omitted in subs.(2)(c) were repealed the Statute Law (Repeals) Act 2004 Sch.1 Pt 17 Group 8.

The words in square brackets in subs.(2)(d) were added by the Nationality, Immigration and Asylum Act 2002 s.62(10).

The words in square brackets in subss.(1) and (3) were substituted by the Mental Health Act 2007 ss.1(4), 5(3), Sch.1 para.11.

DEFINITIONS

**1–602**    mental disorder: ss.1, 145(1).
hospital: ss.55(5), 145(1).
medical treatment: s.145(1), (4).
transfer direction: ss.47, 145(1).
civil prisoner: s.55(1).

GENERAL NOTE

**1–603**    This section empowers the Secretary of State for Justice to direct the removal from prison to hospital of certain categories of *unsentenced* mentally disordered prisoners. A person removed to hospital under this section is placed in the same position as a person who has been made the subject of a transfer direction under s.47 which, among other things, means that he or she becomes subject to the consent to treatment provisions contained in Part IV: see the note on s.47(3). The Government has published a "Procedure for the Transfer of Prisoners to and from Hospital under Sections 47 and 48 of the 'Mental Health Act (1983)'" (2007): see the General Note to s.47.

A transfer direction made in respect of persons coming within categories (a) or (b) of subs.(2) *must* be made subject to the restrictions provided for in s.49 (s.49(1)). The Secretary of State has a discretion to direct that persons coming within categories (c) or (d) be made subject to such restrictions. In practice, the Secretary of State will always apply restrictions to a transfer under this section (Mental Health Unit Bulletin, March 2008).

In *R. (on the application of Abu-Rideh) v Mental Health Review Tribunal* [2004] EWHC 1999 (Admin); [2004] M.H.L.R. 308 at paras 19–22, Gage J. adopted the following summary, drafted by counsel, of the effect of ss.72 to 74 in the case of a patient subject to a direction made under this section and a restriction direction made under s.49 who appears before a tribunal:

1. The tribunal must, if not satisfied *either* that the patient is suffering from a mental disorder of a nature or degree which makes it appropriate for him to be liable to be detained in a hospital for medical treatment *or* that it is necessary for the health and safety of the patient or the protection of others that he continue to receive medical treatment in hospital, make a recommendation for discharge under s.74(1)(a).

2. If the tribunal is satisfied that it is not appropriate for the patient to remain liable to be recalled to hospital, they must recommend the patient's absolute discharge; if they are not so satisfied, they must recommend the patient's conditional discharge (s.73(1)(b) and 73(2)).

3. If the tribunal recommends the patient's conditional discharge then it may also make a recommendation under s.74(1)(b) that, in the event of his not being discharged under s.74, the patient should continue to be detained in hospital. If the Secretary of State accepts the recommendation the patient remains in hospital notwithstanding he no longer satisfies the criteria for detention under the Act (or under art.5(1)(e) [of the European Convention on Human Rights]).

4. By virtue of s.74(4) a patient subject to a transfer direction under s.48 *cannot* be discharged by the Secretary of State under s.74 either absolutely or conditionally. His discharge powers under s.74(2) only apply to serving prisoners transferred under s.47. The patient will automatically be remitted back to the place of his former detention if the recommendation is for absolute discharge *or* if a recommendation for conditional discharge has been made without a recommendation under s.74(1)(b). If a recommendation has been made under s.74(1)(b) the patient is not automatically remitted back to their place of detention and he will remain detained until remitted back to prison by the Secretary of State under s.53, discharged by the Secretary of State under s.42(2) or the justification for his underlying detention expires.

*Restricted Patients Detained in Special Hospitals: Information for the Special Hospitals Service Authority,* Home Office, undated, states at para.5.11: "It is important for responsible [clinicians] to bear in mind that prisoners transferred to hospital under [this section] will, in most cases, not have been tried and convicted, and consequentially they should be returned to court as soon as possible. If the responsible [clinician] believes the patient is not fit to return to court, there is provision under section 51(5) for the court to make a hospital order in the patient's absence and without convicting him".

L. Birmingham states that the:

"main disadvantage of section 48 as a diversion mechanism is that if for any reason the subject ceases to be a prisoner on remand (for example, is bailed or the case collapses) the powers conveyed under section 48 cease with immediate effect. If there is a real risk of this happening a concurrent civil order (section 3 of the MHA) can be imposed" ("Diversion from custody" (2001) *Advances in Psychiatric Treatment*, 7, 198–207).

It is submitted that it is not legally possible for an application under Pt 2 to be made during the currency of a transfer direction made under this section as the grounds for making such an application could not be satisfied. However, if the eventuality contemplated by Birmingham is anticipated, the medical recommendations to support an application under Pt 2 could be obtained and an application signed immediately after the authority to detain the patient under this section ceased.

Under s.117, Primary Care Trusts or Local Health Boards and local social services authorities have a duty to provide after-care services for patients who have ceased to be liable to be detained and leave hospital after having been transferred under this section (s.117).

*Applications to the First-tier Tribunal (Mental Health) or the Mental Health Review Tribunal for Wales*
See the notes on subs.(3) and s.47(3).                                    **1–604**

*Subsection (1)*
REPORTS. See the notes on "reports" and "two registered medical practitioners" in **1–605** s.47(1).

MENTAL DISORDER. If the person has a learning disability, the disability must be associated with abnormally aggressive or seriously irresponsible conduct (s.1(2A), 1(2B)).

APPROPRIATE FOR HIM TO BE DETAINED . . . FOR MEDICAL TREATMENT.   But not for assessment. The Reed Committee said that "it is not always feasible for thorough assessments to be undertaken in prison: a hospital can usually offer greater flexibility and specialised expertise, especially in cases where diagnosis is problematic" (*Review of Health and Social Services for Mentally Disordered Offenders and others requiring similar services*, *Final Summary Report*, Cm. 2088, para.9.6 (v)).

URGENT NEED OF SUCH TREATMENT.   The Home Office informed the Butler Committee that the procedure under this section is adopted only where a prisoner's condition is such that immediate removal to a hospital is necessary and that normally when he is well enough he is either produced at court from hospital or returned to prison to await trial (*ibid.*, para.3.38). The Reed Committee was "concerned . . . that the requirement under section 48 that the need for treatment should be 'urgent' is often interpreted narrowly". The Committee concluded that this section "should be applied where a doctor would recommend in-patient treatment if a person were seen as an out-patient in the community" (*Final Summary Report*, above, para.9.6(iv). This approach has been adopted by the Government: see the "Procedure for the transfer of prisoners to and from hospital under sections 47 and 48 of the Mental Health Act (1983)" (2007), p.8.

NATURE OR DEGREE.   See the note on s.3(2)(a).

APPROPRIATE MEDICAL TREATMENT.   See the note on s.3(2)(d).

TRANSFER DIRECTION.   Which will cease to have effect unless the prisoner is admitted to hospital within 14 days of it being given (s.47(2)).

*Subsection (2)*

**1–606**   A direction made under this section would terminate in the event of the person concerned being no longer subject to detention by, for example, being granted bail.

PARAGRAPH (A).   Persons coming within this category, who will be awaiting trial or sentence in the Crown Court, are subject to the further provisions contained in s.51.

PARAGRAPH (B).   Persons coming within this category are subject to the further provisions contained in s.52.

PARAGRAPHS (C) AND (D).   Persons coming within these categories are subject to the further provisions contained in s.53.

*Subsection (3)*

**1–607**   TRANSFER DIRECTION GIVEN BY VIRTUE OF THIS SECTION.   Has the same effect as a transfer direction made under s.47, which has the same effect as a hospital order: see the note on s.47(3).

## Restriction on discharge of prisoners removed to hospital

**1–608**   **49.**—(1) Where a transfer direction is given in respect of any person, the Secretary of State, if he thinks fit, may by warrant further direct that that person shall be subject to the special restrictions set out in section 41 above; and where the Secretary of State gives a transfer direction in respect of any such person as is described in paragraph (a) or (b) of section 48(2) above, he shall also give a direction under this section applying those restrictions to him.

(2) A direction under this section shall have the same effect as a restriction order made under section 41 above and shall be known as "a restriction direction".

(3) While a person is subject to a restriction direction the [responsible clinician] shall at such intervals (not exceeding one year) as the Secretary of State may direct examine and report to the Secretary of State on that person; and every report shall contain such particulars as the Secretary of State may require.

AMENDMENT

The words in square brackets in subs.(3) were inserted by the Mental Health Act 2007 s.10(9).

DEFINITIONS

transfer direction: ss.47, 145(1).           **1–609**
responsible clinician: s.55(1).

GENERAL NOTE

This section provides that the Secretary of State for Justice may, and in respect of certain **1–610** prisoners must, add an order restricting the patient's discharge from hospital (a "restriction direction") to a transfer direction made under s.47. The effect of a restriction direction is explained in the following passage from the judgment of the Court of Appeal in *R. v Birch* (1989) 11 Cr. App. R.(S.) 202 at 212:

"If the transfer direction under section 47 is coupled with a restriction direction by the Home Secretary under section 49 (as in practice it usually is), the offender's position is in many ways the same as if he had been sent straight to hospital with order under sections 37 and 41, but the following special provisions apply: (1) Where the offender was sentenced to a fixed term of imprisonment, the restriction will automatically lift on the expiry of his sentence (allowing for remission) [the "release date"]: section 50(2). (2) Where the responsible clinician or the [tribunal] concludes that the offender no longer requires treatment in hospital for mental disorder or that no effective treatment for his disorder can be given, the Secretary of State may: (a) release him on parole (if he is eligible), (b) return him to prison to serve out his sentence, or (c) take no action [: section 50(1)]."

If a patient is serving a life sentence, or an indeterminate sentence, the release date is the date (if any) on which the person's release is ordered by the Parole Board.

A patient who ceases to be subject to a restriction direction because his or her sentence has expired is sometimes referred to as being subject to a "notional section 37". This term, which is not found in this Act, is used to signify that on the expiry of the sentence the patient is still subject to the s.47 transfer direction which has the same legal effect as a hospital order made under s.37. A restricted patient whose restriction order has ceased to have effect is treated as if he had been admitted to hospital as an unrestricted patient on the date when the restriction order ceased to have effect (s.41(5)).

In *R. (on the application of T) v Secretary of State for the Home Department* [2003] EWHC Admin 538; [2003] M.H.L.R. 239, an official in the Mental Health Unit wrote to the patient's responsible clinician declining to lift the restriction direction that had been made in respect of the patient and referred to the policy of the Secretary of State in the following terms:

"Our normal policy is always to make a restriction direction unless it is proposed to transfer the prisoner to hospital within days of his release date and the nature of the offence suggests that restrictions are unnecessary for the protection of the public from serious harm over that short period."

The patient's challenge to this policy on the ground that a restriction order should only be imposed where there is a need for public protection was rejected by Maurice Kay J. The analogy that had been made with an order made by a court under s.37 was wrong, as when making orders under this section, the Secretary of State did not stand in the shoes of the sentencing court. Rather, the Secretary of State is concerned with a person who has already been sentenced to a term of imprisonment by a court, which has not yet been fully served. Without a restriction direction a person properly sentenced to a term of imprisonment would pass wholly into the hands of the medical authorities so far as the regaining of liberty was concerned.

Section 47 of the Crime (Sentences) Act 1997 provides that where the Secretary of State makes an order under this section he has the power to order that the patient be admitted to and detained in a named hospital unit. A named hospital unit can be any part of a hospital which is treated as a separate unit. The effect of this power is considered in the note on s.41(1).

*Applications to the First-tier Tribunal (Mental Health) or the Mental Health Review Tribunal for Wales*

**1–611**    A patient who is subject to a restriction direction may apply to a tribunal within six months of the date of the direction, once during the following six months, and at yearly intervals thereafter (s.69(2)(b)). The powers of the tribunal are set out in s.74.

*Remissions to Prison*

**1–612**    The March 2008 issue of the Mental Health Unit Bulletin contains the following statement:

> "The Secretary of State can remit to prison any patient transferred under sections 47/49 (or sections 48/49 provided he is not remanded to appear at a Magistrates' Court) to hospital if the [RC] advises that it is no longer necessary for the patient to receive treatment in hospital, or if the patient presents as untreatable. In these circumstances, the [RC] should write to the MHU recommending a return to prison. The [RC] should also source the prison to which the patient should return, most often the prison from which they came. If this is not possible, however, that prison must find an alternative establishment. Once a section 117 meeting has been held and both parties (hospital and prison) have confirmed that they are content for the remission to take place, MHU will issue a remission warrant.
>
> Further details . . . processes can be found in Prison Service Instruction 50/2007."

*Domestic Violence, Crime and Victims Act 2004*

**1–613**    See Ch.18 of the *Code of Practice* at paras 18.18 to 18.20 and Ch.30 at paras 30.29–30.31. The Department of Health has published "Mental Health Act 2007: Guidance on the extension of victims' rights under the Domestic Violence, Crime and Victims Act" (2008).

*Human Rights Act 1998*

**1–614**    See the note on "technical lifer", below.

*Technical lifer*

**1–615**    A "technical lifer" is a person who, although sentenced to life imprisonment (whether discretionary or mandatory) will in certain circumstances be treated as though he had originally been made the subject of a hospital order and a restriction order made under ss.37 and 41 of this Act. "Technical lifer" is a non-statutory status, based on an administrative process entirely within the discretion of the Home Secretary. In *R. (on the application of IR) v Dr G Shetty and the Secretary of State for the Home Department* [2003] EWHC 3152 (Admin); [2004] M.H.L.R. 130, Munby J. rejected a claim that the procedure for attaining "technical lifer" status was a "sentencing exercise" which breached art.6 of the European Convention on Human Rights. His Lordship commented, at para.10, that from the claimant's perspective "technical lifer" was "a desirable status because (a) he cannot in any circumstances be returned to prison, (b) he becomes entitled under art.5(4) of [the Convention] to periodic reviews of the lawfulness of his detention even if his tariff period has not expired (see *Van Droogenbroeck v Belgium* (1982) 4 E.H.R.R. 443 and *Benjamin and Wilson v United Kingdom* (2003) 36 E.H.R.R. 1) and (c) (see *Benjamin and Wilson v United Kingdom*, paras 28,30) he will be entitled to his liberty if [a tribunal] so recommends". In this case Government policy relating to the granting of "technical lifer" status was identified in a witness statement of the Head of Caseworking at the Mental Health Unit:

"In assessing an application for 'technical lifer' status, consideration is given to whether there is reason to believe the court's decision to impose a prison sentence rather than a hospital order has been made because the sentencing court was prevented from making an hospital order by reasons beyond its control, such as:

(a) the unavailability of a suitable hospital bed;
(b) the lack of proper clinical information to the court;
(c) medical reports which were prepared appear (in hindsight) not to have recorded accurately the patient's mental state at the time of the offence;
(d) the offender, although mentally disordered, refused to allow a diminished responsibility plea and was as a result, convicted of murder (for which a life sentence is mandatory).

Where the Secretary of State considers that there is reason to believe that, but for these reasons, the sentencing judge would have imposed a hospital order, he will refer the matter to the trial judge and the Lord Chief Justice for consultation. Following that consultation, and taking the recommendations of the trial judge and the Lord Chief Justice into account, the Secretary of State may exercise his discretion to grant a person 'technical lifer' status.

The Secretary of State does not refer every request for technical lifer status for judicial consideration. He does so only in applications where it is clear either that the Court was unable to make a hospital disposal, or there is clear subsequent evidence which might have altered the court's decision, and there are grounds to believe that the trial judge's decision would have been different had that evidence been taken into account. The Secretary of State may take the view, upon consideration of the relevant information, that there is no reason to suggest that the sentencing judge would have imposed a hospital order, in which case he does not consult the judiciary."

In *R. v Secretary of State for the Home Department Ex p. Williams*, June 21, 1994, unreported, the court said:

"The effect of being classified as a 'technical lifer' is that the patient is treated, for the purposes of discharge, as though a hospital order under section 37 and a restriction order under section 41 of the 1983 Act had been made instead of the imposition of a sentence of imprisonment. He is treated with a view to rehabilitation and eventual release direct from hospital into the community. His case will not be referred to the Parole Board and he will not be released on life licence."

In *R. v Beatty* [2006] EWCA Crim 2359, para.53, Scott Baker L.J. said that if "the decision is made that a transferred prisoner should be treated as a 'technical lifer', the Home Office [now the Ministry of Justice] guarantees:

(i) that the 'technical lifer' will not return to prison when he is well enough to leave hospital;

(ii) that his tariff date will no longer be taken into consideration in deciding whether he is entitled to be discharged into the community; and

(iii) that when he leaves hospital, [he] will go out on absolute or conditional discharge under the Mental Health Act rather than on life licence."

In *Williams*, above, the court was informed that the Home Office [now the Ministry of Justice] has an equivalent system for determinate sentence prisoners:

"... the Home Office does in fact recognise that there may be exceptional circumstances in which a determinate sentence prisoner should be rehabilitated through the hospital system and not returned to prison, even though his earliest date of release is someway ahead. This would be justifiable in cases where there was clear evidence that the sentencing Court did not dispose of the case by means of a hospital order for the kind of reason which influences the Home Office in conferring 'technical lifer' status on a transferred life sentence prisoner."

A "technical lifer" can be discharged from hospital in three possible ways. Each can be initiated only by the Secretary of State. They are:

1. A conditional or absolute discharge made under s.42(2).

2. A discharge made under s.50(1)(b).

3. Through the operation of s.74(2).

In *Benjamin and Wilson v United Kingdom* above, the European Court of Human Rights held that s.74(2) violates art.5(4) of the European Convention on Human Rights because the power of discharge rests with the Home Secretary rather than the tribunal. This decision prompted the Parliamentary Under-Secretary of State for the Home Department to make the following Written Ministerial Statement (House of Commons Hansard, January 24, 2005):

"From 2 April 2005, life sentence prisoners who have been transferred to psychiatric hospitals for treatment will no longer be considered for technical lifer status. All life sentence prisoners will have their future release determined by the Parole Board and be subject to life licence on release. This decision has been taken in the light of the judgment in the case of *Benjamin and Wilson v the United Kingdom*, which found that technical lifer policy was in breach of Art.5(4) of the European Convention on Human Rights. This will not affect those who have already been granted technical lifer status, or the consideration of any pending applications. No new applications, however, will be considered after 2 April 2005."

Those who were preparing to seek "technical lifer" status at the time when the above announcement was made had no entitlement to continue, nor had they a legitimate expectation to be consulted over the change of policy (*R. (on the application of Donaldson and Barker) v Home Secretary* [2006] EWHC 1107 (Admin); [2006] M.H.L.R. 100).

In *R. v Beatty*, above at para.59, the court said that the Criminal Cases Review Commission had pointed out that while the effect of a patient's "technical lifer" status may be identical to a hospital order there are potential benefits for the patient and the criminal justice system for a life sentence to be replaced with a hospital order. These are:

(i) the unequivocal placement of someone who is mentally disordered into a regime of expert medical care from which he can progress, if it becomes appropriate, into a less secure regime under proper supervision and safeguards; and

(ii) the substitution would reflect the change of approach signalled by the decision in *Benjamin and Wilson* and contained in the Home Office decision to make no further use of "technical lifer" status.

The court said, at paras 61, 62:

"Bearing in mind the criteria for granting 'technical lifer' status we think it very difficult to envisage circumstances where, 'technical lifer' status having been granted, the court would not substitute a hospital order with a restriction order for a life sentence. 'Technical lifer' status is only afforded if the prisoner is treatable.

It is obviously important, perhaps even more so now that 'technical lifer' status is no longer granted, that those who should have been the subject of a hospital order under sections 37/41 rather than life imprisonment should have the position rectified on appeal. That said, however, the court will always scrutinise with great care cases in which an appellant seeks to rely on psychiatric evidence directed to his mental state at the date of sentence that was not advanced at the time. Each case is likely to be decided on its own specific facts."

*Subsection (1)*
SECRETARY OF STATE.   The Secretary of State for Justice: see the General Note to this **1–616** Part.

IF HE THINKS FIT.   The Secretary of State is not bound by any statutory criteria when exercising his judgment under this provision.

*Subsection (2)*
RESTRICTION DIRECTION.   For further provisions, see s.50. The Secretary of State does **1–617** not have the power to make a time limited restriction direction.

*Subsection (3)*
REPORT.   See the note on s.41(6).                                               **1–618**

## Further provisions as to prisoners under sentence

**50.**—(1) Where a transfer direction and a restriction direction have been given **1–619** in respect of a person serving a sentence of imprisonment and before [his release date] the Secretary of State is notified by the [responsible clinician], any other [approved clinician] or [the appropriate tribunal] that that person no longer requires treatment in hospital for mental disorder or that no effective treatment for his disorder can be given in the hospital to which he has been removed, the Secretary of State may—
  (a) by warrant direct that he be remitted to any prison or other institution in which he might have been detained if he had not been removed to hospital, there to be dealt with as if he had not been so removed; or
  (b) exercise any power of releasing him on licence or discharging him under supervision which would have been exercisable if he had been remitted to such a prison or institution as aforesaid,
and on his arrival in the prison or other institution or, as the case may be, his release or discharge as aforesaid, the transfer direction and the restriction direction shall cease to have effect.

[(2) A restriction direction in the case of a person serving a sentence of imprisonment shall cease to have effect, if it has not previously done so, on his release date.

(3) In this section, references to a person's release date are to the day (if any) on which he would be entitled to be released (whether unconditionally or on licence) from any prison or other institution in which he might have been detained if the transfer direction had not been given; and in determining that day there shall be disregarded—

(a) any powers that would be exercisable by the Parole Board if he were detained in such a prison or other institution, and

(b) any practice of the Secretary of State in relation to the early release under discretionary powers of persons detained in such a prison or other institution.]

(4) For the purposes of section 49(2) of the Prison Act 1952 (which provides for discounting from the sentences of certain prisoners periods while they are unlawfully at large) a patient who, having been transferred in pursuance of a transfer direction from any such institution as is referred to in that section, is at large in circumstances in which he is liable to be taken into custody under any provision of this Act, shall be treated as unlawfully at large and absent from that institution.

[(5) The preceding provisions of this section shall have effect as if—

(a) the reference in subsection (1) to a transfer direction and a restriction direction having been given in respect of a person serving a sentence of imprisonment included a reference to a hospital direction and a limitation direction having been given in respect of a person sentenced to imprisonment;

(b) the reference in subsection (2) to a restriction direction included a reference to a limitation direction; and

(c) references in subsections (3) and (4) to a transfer direction included references to a hospital direction.]

AMENDMENT

The words in square brackets in subs.(1) and subss.(2) and (3) were substituted by the Criminal Justice Act 2003 s.294. The references to responsible clinician and approved clinician in subs.(1) were substituted by the Mental Health Act 2007 s.11(2). The reference to the appropriate tribunal in subs.(1) was substituted by SI 2008/2883 art.9, Sch.3 para.42.

Subsection (5) was inserted by the Crime (Sentences) Act 1997 s.55, Sch.4 para.12(4)(5).

DEFINITIONS

**1–620**  transfer direction: ss.47, 145(1).
restriction direction: ss.49, 145(1).
hospital: ss.55(5), 145(1).
mental disorder: ss.1, 145(1).
patient: s.145(1).
responsible clinician: s.55(1).
approved clinician: s.145(1).
the appropriate tribunal: ss.66(4), 145(1).
hospital direction: s.145(1).
limitation direction: s.145(1).

GENERAL NOTE

This section provides that if the Secretary of State for Justice is informed that a patient **1–621**
who has been placed on a restriction direction or a hospital and limitation direction no
longer requires treatment in hospital he may either direct that the patient be returned to
prison to serve the remainder of his sentence or release him from hospital on the same
terms on which he could be released from prison. It also provides for a restriction direction
or a hospital direction to cease to have effect from the date when the prisoner would have
been released from prison.

If a patient subject to a restriction direction is in hospital when the restrictions cease to
have effect, he or she will remain in hospital as a detained patient subject to a hospital order
made under s.37 (s.41(5)). Such a patient is often referred to as being the subject of a
"notional hospital order", a term that is not found in this Act.

The Secretary of State "also has the power, under s.42(2), on his own motion at any time,
and under s.74(2), to authorise the [tribunal] to arrange for the discharge of a prisoner who
has been transferred to a mental hospital"; per Rose L.J. in *R. v Secretary of State for the
Home Department Ex p. Hickey (No.1)* [1995] 1 All E.R. 479 at 483 CA.

*Human Rights Act 1998*

Any argument that there are breaches of Convention rights concerned with the operation **1–622**
of this section should be raised against the Secretary of State rather than the patient's
responsible clinician (RC), who is exercising only a clinical judgment and cannot be challenged on Convention grounds (*R. (on the application of IR) v Dr G Shetty and the Home
Secretary* [2003] EWHC 3022 (Admin); [2004] M.H.L.R. 111 para.39).

In the *Morley* case, noted under subs.(1), the applicant contended that his right to respect
for his privacy under art.8 of the European Convention on Human Rights had been
breached by virtue of his transfer from hospital to prison. The Court of Appeal dismissed
this argument on the grounds that:

> "In the absence of a breach of another article or articles, the convention does not render
> unlawful that interference with private life which inevitably follows from a lawfully
> imposed custodial sentence. Transfer from prison to hospital and hospital back to prison,
> as a part of a high-security custodial regime, cannot in present circumstances be said to
> be breach the article notwithstanding the differences in medical treatment which may
> occur" (para.49).

The patient's complaint to the European Court of Human Rights that his transfer violated
his Art.8 rights was declared inadmissible (*Morley v United Kingdom* (2005) 40 E.H.R.R.
SE8; [2005] M.H.L.R. 174). The Court said at para.47:

> "Even assuming, however, that the difference in regimes between the hospital and prison
> could be considered by itself as affecting the applicant's private life, the Court considers
> such interference may be regarded as complying with the second paragraph of Art.8
> namely as a measure 'in accordance with the law', pursuing the aims of the prevention
> of disorder and crime and protection of the rights of others, as well as being 'necessary in
> a democratic society' for those aims".

Also see the note on s.74 under this heading.

*Subsection (1)*

In *R. (on the application of Morley) v Nottinghamshire Health Care NHS Trust* [2002] **1–623**
EWCA Civ 1728; [2003] 1 All E.R. 784, the Court of Appeal held that:

1. The issue under this provision is treatability and the Secretary of State's decision
   necessarily turns upon a clinical judgment, that of the RC, and if that judgment

was fairly and rationally made, a duty in the Secretary of State to permit and consider representations from the patient does not arise.

2. There will be cases in which circumstances, including information available to the Secretary of State, either in the documents by which the notification is given, or from other sources, create a duty in the Secretary of State to make further inquiries or take further action or both.

3. The duty upon a RC before giving a notification to the Secretary of State is to make full and fair enquiries within the hospital as to whether the treatability test is satisfied and to consider views expressed, as well as his own first hand knowledge and experience, before making a recommendation. He is not placed under a duty to disclose reports on individual components of the patient's medical regime or to present to the Secretary of State contrary views which may have been expressed by some members of the inter-disciplinary team. The extent of enquiry and of disclosure of information will depend upon the circumstances of the particular case and will normally be judged as at the moment of decision.

If the Secretary of State accepts the RC's advice that the patient no longer requires treatment in hospital for a mental disorder, he has a wide and unfettered discretion as to what to do with the patient; a discretion which entitles him to take into account a wide range of facts, some no doubt referable to the patient himself but others referable to wider considerations of the public interest and in any event extending far beyond the purely clinical (*R. (on the application of IR) v Dr G Shetty and the Home Secretary*, above, para.26).

TRANSFER DIRECTION AND A RESTRICTION DIRECTION.   See subs.(5)(a).

SERVING A SENTENCE OF IMPRISONMENT.   See s.55(6).

RELEASE DATE.   See subs.(3).

SECRETARY OF STATE.   The Secretary of State for Justice: see the General Note to this Part.

NOTIFIED BY THE RESPONSIBLE CLINICIAN.   The RC should notify the Ministry of Justice at once in writing if he considers that a patient meets the criteria set out in this subsection.

ANY OTHER APPROVED CLINICIAN.   In the *Morley* case, above, Burton J., sitting at first instance, was informed by counsel for the Secretary of State that notification from this clinician is, in practice, restricted to a situation in which such a clinician "is for some reason standing in for the [RC], and if it were any other medical practitioner plainly any such recommendation would have to be looked at carefully indeed by the [Secretary of State] to see whether it was appropriate to act on it" ([2003] M.H.L.R.88 at para.29).

EFFECTIVE TREATMENT.   This probably means treatment that will benefit the patient.

MAY.   It is not possible to construe this provision so as to impose a duty on the Secretary of State (*R. (on the application of D) v Secretary of State for the Home Department* [2002] EWHC Admin 2805; [2003] 1 W.L.R. 1315 at para.29).

*Paragraph (a)*

**1–624**   Once a life sentenced patient no longer requires treatment in hospital, the normal course is for the Secretary of State to remit him to prison under this paragraph where he would be eligible for a Parole Board hearing as appropriate in the normal manner.

BY WARRANT.   There is no provision for a time limit to be attached to the warrant.

*Paragraph (b)*

In 1985, the Home Secretary made the following policy statement on life sentence pris- **1–625**
oners in response to a Parliamentary Question by Mr John Wheeler M.P.:

"When life sentence prisoners transferred to hospital under the Mental Health Act 1983
are to be released, it has hitherto been the practice to discharge such persons on a warrant
of conditional discharge under section 42(3) of the Act. I now intend to use the powers
available to me under section 50(1)(b) of the Act, which enables me to release such persons under the same arrangements as those they would have been subject to had they
remained in, or been returned to, prison. This means that, in future, such persons will
normally be released on life licences under the provisions of section 61 of the
Criminal Justice Act 1967 [now see section 28 of the Crime (Sentences) Act 1997] in
accordance with the sentencing Courts' intention, i.e. on the recommendation of the
Parole Board and after consultation with the Lord Chief Justice and, if available, the
trial judge. In exceptional cases, where the Lord Chief Justice and the trial judge so recommend, I will be prepared to consider whether it would be more appropriate to
authorise discharge under section 42(2) of the 1983 Act.

Under the new procedure, a life sentence prisoner who has been transferred to hospital, can be released on life licence without having to return to prison before release.
Persons released on life licence under these arrangements will be subject to recall to
prison under the provisions of section 62 of the 1967 Act [now see s.254 of the
Criminal Justice Act 2003]. Should their mental condition be such that they are recommended for transfer to hospital this could very quickly be effected under the
provisions of section 47 of the 1983 Act."

This policy was challenged in *R. v Secretary of State for the Home Department Ex p.
Stroud* [1993] C.O.D. 75. The applicant stated that a life prisoner released from prison
on licence remains subject to supervision for the rest of his life whereas release under
ss.42(2) or 74(2) of this Act allowed for the possibility of an eventual absolute discharge
either by the Secretary of State or by a tribunal. He contended that the normal rule of practice set out in the policy statement deprived life sentence prisoners of the potential benefit
of absolute discharge and thus the Secretary of State had fettered his discretion unlawfully.
Henry J. held, in refusing the application for judicial review, that there was no illegality in
the policy which had been adopted for legitimate reasons to ensure consistency of treatment
between all those sentenced to life imprisonment. *Stroud* is analysed by Michael Gunn at
(1993) *Journal of Forensic Psychiatry*, Vol.4, No.2, pp.330–334.

In *R. v Secretary of State for the Home Department Ex p. Hickey (No.1)* [1995] 1 All E.R.
479, the principal question before the Court of Appeal was whether a prisoner sentenced
either to a discretionary life term or to be detained during Her Majesty's pleasure, transferred subsequently to a hospital by the Secretary of State under ss.47 and 49 of this
Act, and who has served the tariff part of his sentence, can require the Secretary of State
so to act that his case is considered by the Parole Board, notwithstanding that he is still
in hospital needing, and receiving, treatment. The court held that a person who had been
made the subject of such a transfer was governed by the regime laid down in this Act
and had no right to have his case referred to the Parole Board.

In *R. (on the application of D) v Secretary of State for the Home Department*, above,
Stanley Burnton J. held that the decision of the Court of Appeal in *Hickey*, above, remains
good law, notwithstanding s.3 of the Human Rights Act 1998, but that the relevant legislation was not compatible with the European Convention on Human Rights because a
patient in respect of whom a tribunal notified the Secretary of State that he should be conditionally discharged, but that if he were not discharged he should continue to be detained
in hospital (see s.74(1)(a) and (b)), did not have a legal right to have his case considered by
the Parole Board. This incompatibility has been remedied by s.295 of the Criminal Justice
Act 2003 which amends s.74.

The question whether the Convention required that the lawfulness of the detention of a discretionary life prisoner/patient be reviewed by a single tribunal, exercising the functions of both tribunal and Parole Board was considered in *R. (on the application of P) v Secretary of State for the Home Department* [2003] EWHC 2953 (Admin); [2004] M.H.L.R. 64. Stanley Burnton J. answered the question in the negative and further held that the fact that a patient has no right to have his case considered by the Parole Board until after his discharge from detention under the Mental Health Act does not infringe his rights under art.5.4 of the Convention.

Discretionary and mandatory life prisoners who have been transferred to hospital under this Act, and whom it is not appropriate to remit to prison even though they no longer require, or can effectively be given, hospital treatment will be referred by the Secretary of State to the Parole Board, while they remain in hospital, in the same way as if they had been remitted to prison (245 HC Official Report (6th series) written answers, col.9, 20 June 1994 and *Hickey*, above, at 485, 486).

*Subsection (2)*

**1–626** RESTRICTION DIRECTION. See subs.(5)(b).

CEASE TO HAVE EFFECT. The patient is to be treated as if he had been admitted to hospital under a hospital order without restrictions on the day when the restriction direction ceased to have effect (ss.49(2), 41(5)).

Unsurprisingly, a life sentence ceases to have effect on the death of the person concerned (*D v Secretary of State for the Home Department* [2002] EWHC Admin 2805 at para.30).

*Subsection (3)*

**1–627** TRANSFER DIRECTION. Or hospital direction (subs.(5)(c)).

*Subsection (4)*

**1–628** "The effect of subsection (4), and the clear intention behind it, is that if an individual absconds from the mental hospital to which he is transferred that will be treated as him being unlawfully at large, as if the hospital were the prison from which he absconded", per Collins J. in *R. (on the application of Miah) v Secretary of State for the Home Department* [2004] EWHC 2569 (Admin); [2004] M.H.L.R. 302 at para.30.

In *R. (on the application of S) v Secretary of State for the Home Department* [2003] EWCA Civ 426; [2003] M.H.L.R. 264 at para.22, the court accepted as correct the following submission made by counsel for the Secretary of State:

"Section 50(4) of the 1983 Act places those transferred from prison to hospital under sections 47 and 48 on the same footing as those still in prison: it ensures that anyone absconding from either will be treated in the same way. But section 50(4) deals only with abscondees from hospital transferred 'from any such institution as is referred to in [section 49(2)]', that is from prisons and the like, and it dictates that they be 'treated as unlawfully at large and absent from that institution'. It says nothing about those detained in hospital otherwise than pursuant to a transfer direction (under section 47 or section 48) with the result that patients detained under other provisions of the 1983 Act, notably sections 2 and 3, are to be regarded as at large irrespective of whether they are in fact in hospital or have absconded from hospital and are liable to be taken back in custody under section 18".

The court was informed that the problem that arose in this case is unlikely to recur as the Prison Service is being instructed that when the revocation of a license is requested and the offender is already sectioned under this Act, a s.47 transfer direction (which would supersede the s.2 or s.3 (ss.40(5), 55(4)) is to be sought at the same time as the revocation request is being dealt with. This is to ensure that any revocation and transfer would operate simultaneously and so avoid the recall of an offender still subject to the s.2 or s.3 (para.32).

TRANSFER DIRECTION.  Or hospital direction (subs.(5)(c)).

## Further provisions as to detained persons

**51.**—(1) This section has effect where a transfer direction has been given in **1–629** respect of any such person as is described in paragraph (a) of section 48(2) above and that person is in this section referred to as "the detainee".

(2) The transfer direction shall cease to have effect when the detainee's case is disposed of by the court having jurisdiction to try or otherwise deal with him, but without prejudice to any power of that court to make a hospital order or other order under this Part of this Act in his case.

(3) If the Secretary of State is notified by the [responsible clinician], any other [approved clinician] or [the appropriate tribunal] at any time before the detainee's case is disposed of by that court—

(a) that the detainee no longer requires treatment in hospital for mental disorder; or

(b) that no effective treatment for his disorder can be given at the hospital to which he has been removed,

the Secretary of State may by warrant direct that he be remitted to any place where he might have been detained if he had not been removed to hospital, there to be dealt with as if he had not been so removed, and on his arrival at the place to which he is so remitted the transfer direction shall cease to have effect.

(4) If (no direction having been given under subsection (3) above) the court having jurisdiction to try or otherwise deal with the detainee is satisfied on the written or oral evidence of the [responsible clinician]—

(a) that the detainee no longer requires treatment in hospital for mental disorder; or

(b) that no effective treatment for his disorder can be given at the hospital to which he has been removed,

the court may order him to be remitted to any such place as is mentioned in subsection (3) above or[, subject to section 25 of the Criminal Justice and Public Order Act 1994,] released on bail and on his arrival at that place or, as the case may be, his release on bail the transfer direction shall cease to have effect.

(5) If (no direction or order having been given or made under subsection (3) or (4) above) it appears to the court having jurisdiction to try or otherwise deal with the detainee—

(a) that it is impracticable or inappropriate to bring the detainee before the court; and

(b) that the conditions set out in subsection (6) below are satisfied,

the court may make a hospital order (with or without a restriction order) in his case in his absence and, in the case of a person awaiting trial, without convicting him.

(6) A hospital order may be made in respect of a person under subsection (5) above if the court—

(a) is satisfied, on the written or oral evidence of at least two registered medical practitioners, that:

[(i) the detainee is suffering from mental disorder of a nature or degree which makes it appropriate for the patient to be detained in a hospital for medical treatment;][and

(ii) appropriate medical treatment is available for him; and]

(b) is of the opinion, after considering any depositions or other documents required to be sent to the proper officer of the court, that it is proper to make such an order.

(7) Where a person committed to the Crown Court to be dealt with under section 43 above is admitted to a hospital in pursuance of an order under section 44 above, subsections (5) and (6) above shall apply as if he were a person subject to a transfer direction.

AMENDMENT

The reference to the appropriate tribunal in subs.(3) was substituted by SI 2008/2883 art.9, Sch.3 para.43. In subs.(4) the words in square brackets were inserted by the Criminal Justice and Public Order Act 1994 s.168(2), Sch.10 para.51. In subs.(6) the words in square brackets were substituted by the Mental Health Act 2007 ss.1(4), 5(4), Sch.1 para.12. The references to the responsible clinician and the approved clinician were substituted by s.10(3).

DEFINITIONS

**1–630**    transfer direction: ss.47, 145(1).
hospital order: ss.37, 145(1).
responsible clinician: s.55(1).
approved clinician: s.145(1).
the appropriate tribunal: ss.66(4), 145(1).
hospital: ss.55(5), 145(1).
mental disorder: ss.1, 145(1).
restriction order: ss.41, 145(1).
medical treatment: s.145(1).

GENERAL NOTE

**1–631**    This section provides that a transfer direction made in respect of a person detained in a prison or remand centre shall cease to have effect when the case has been finally dealt with by the appropriate court (subs.(2)). The linked restriction direction will also cease to have effect at that time. In the meanwhile the Secretary of State has power to direct the patient's return to prison (subs.(3)). If the Secretary of State does not exercise this power, the court can, on receiving the requisite evidence, either order the patient to be returned to prison or released on bail (subs.(4)). The transfer direction will cease to have effect if the Secretary of State or court exercise their powers under subss.(3) and (4). If the patient has not been sent back to prison or released on bail, the court can make a hospital order in respect of a mentally disordered patient in his absence and without convicting him (subss.(5), (6)).

*Human Rights Act 1998*

**1–632**    The power of the court under subss.(5) and (6) to make a hospital order in the absence of a conviction or a finding that the person concerned "did the act or made the omission charged" (as required by, for example, s.37(3)), would appear to be a breach of art.6 of the European Convention on Human Rights in that the court has passed sentence in the absence of a trial.

*Subsection (3)*

**1–633**    SECRETARY OF STATE.    The Secretary of State for Justice: see the General Note to this Part.

NOTIFIED BY THE RESPONSIBLE CLINICIAN.    See the note on s.50(1).

NO EFFECTIVE TREATMENT.    A stronger test than the "appropriate treatment" test: see the note on s.3(2)(d).

*Subsection (4)*

WRITTEN OR ORAL EVIDENCE. For general requirements as to medical evidence, see **1–634** s.54.

*Subsection (5)*

This provision, together with subs.(6), enables the court to make a hospital order (with or **1–635** without restrictions) in respect of a mentally disordered accused person who is awaiting trial without bringing that person before the court.

In *R. (on the application of Kenneally) v Snaresbrook Crown Court* [2001] EWHC Admin. 968; [2002] M.H.L.R. 53 DC para.35, Pill L.J. said that to "pass sentence, even a sentence one of the objects of which is to assist the defendant, without first convicting him is a drastic step, one that should be taken only in exceptional circumstances". In this case the court held that it was not clear whether the power to make an order under this provision was an exercise of the Crown Court's jurisdiction in matters relating to trial on indictment within the meaning of s.29(3) of the Supreme Court Act 1981, which precludes any jurisdiction in the High Court to quash the order. The High Court did, however, have the power to quash the order if the Crown Court made a relevant jurisdictional error. Tomlinson J. said at para.52: "[I]t seems to me anomalous that the Crown Court should have and should exercise a jurisdiction affecting the liberty of the subject which apparently admits of no direct right of appeal or review". Also see the note on "without convicting him", below.

INAPPROPRIATE. In *Kenneally*, above, Pill L.J. said, at para.32, that this word,

"must be construed restrictively. [Section 51(5)] must not be used as a routine and easy way of avoiding a potentially troublesome trial. To construe it as 'sparing a defendant a trial' is superficially attractive, especially when the outcome of the trial is readily predictable, but there is a public interest as well as that of the defendant himself in the resolution of issues, and especially when the failure to resolve them . . . may have difficult and long term implications. I would not necessarily restrict the word 'inappropriate' so as to mean 'physically impossible' but a high degree of disablement or relevant disorder must be present. The section does not apply in a situation in which all that is involved is possible inconvenience for the Court and inevitable distress for the defendant and others likely to be concerned in a trial, if a trial is held".

HOSPITAL ORDER (WITH OR WITHOUT A RESTRICTION ORDER). The power of the Crown Court under this provision to make a hospital order, with a restriction order, without convicting the defendant was confirmed by Pill L.J. in *Kenneally*, above, at para.5.

A judge, prior to the imposition of a restriction order under s.41, following the making of a hospital order under this provision, is not obliged to resolve any factual dispute between the Crown case and the defence case before he makes a finding that the "serious harm" criterion in s.41(1) is satisfied (*R. v Kingston Crown Court Ex p. Mason*, July 27, 1998, CA).

PERSON AWAITING TRIAL. Once the trial has commenced, any question relating to the mental fitness of the accused to be tried must be determined under s.4 of the Criminal Procedure (Insanity) Act 1964 and not under this provision (*R. v Griffiths* [2002] EWCA Crim 1762; [2002] M.H.L.R. 407). In *Griffiths*, the court made reference to the following *obiter* comment on the meaning of this phrase made by Tomlinson J. in *Kenneally*, above, at para.48: "It seems to me likely that the word 'trial' is . . . intended to refer . . . to the more immediately recognisable features of a criminal trial, beginning, broadly, with the swearing-in of the jury".

WITHOUT CONVICTING HIM. As there has been no conviction, there is no right of appeal to the Court of Appeal (Criminal Appeal Act 1968, s.9 and *R. v Griffiths*, above).

*Subsection (6)*

**1–636**  Two registered medical practitioners.  One of whom must be approved by the Secretary of State or the Welsh Ministers under s.12 (s.54(1)).

Mental disorder.  If the person has a learning disability, the disability must be associated with abnormally aggressive or seriously irresponsible conduct (s.1(2A), (2B)).

Nature or degree.  See the note on s.3(2)(a).

Detained in a hospital for medical treatment.  But not for assessment.

Appropriate medical treatment.  See the note on s.3(2)(d).

Depositions.  The Court is entitled to have regard to the evidence in the case in deciding whether to make an order (*Kenneally*, above, at para.34).

### Further provisions as to persons remanded by magistrates' courts

**1–637**  52.—(1) This section has effect where a transfer direction has been given in respect of any such person as is described in paragraph (b) of section 48(2) above; and that person is in this section referred to as "the accused".

(2) Subject to subsection (5) below, the transfer direction shall cease to have effect on the expiration of the period of remand unless the accused is [sent] in custody to the Crown Court for trial or to be otherwise dealt with.

(3) Subject to subsection (4) below, the power of further remanding the accused under section 128 of the Magistrates' Courts Act 1980 may be exercised by the court without his being brought before the court; and if the court further remands the accused in custody (whether or not he is brought before the court) the period of remand shall, for the purposes of this section, be deemed not to have expired.

(4) The court shall not under subsection (3) above further remand the accused in his absence unless he has appeared before the court within the previous six months.

(5) If the magistrates' court is satisfied, on the written or oral evidence of the [responsible clinician]—

  (a) that the accused no longer requires treatment in hospital for mental disorder; or

  (b) that no effective treatment for his disorder can be given in the hospital to which he has been removed,

the court may direct that the transfer direction shall cease to have effect notwithstanding that the period of remand has not expired or that the accused is [sent] to the Crown Court as mentioned in subsection (2) above.

(6) If the accused is [sent] to the Crown Court as mentioned in subsection (2) above and the transfer direction has not ceased to have effect under subsection (5) above, section 51 above shall apply as if the transfer direction given in his case were a direction given in respect of a person falling within that section.

(7) The magistrates' court may, in the absence of the accused, [send him to the Crown Court for trial under section 51 or 51A of the Crime and Disorder Act 1998]

  (a) the court is satisfied, on the written or oral evidence of the [responsible clinician], that the accused is unfit to take part in the proceedings; and

  (b) [. . .], the accused is represented by [an authorised person].

AMENDMENTS

The amendments to subss.(2),(5),(6) and (7) were made by the Criminal Justice Act 2003 s.41, Sch.3 para.55(1),(3). The references to the responsible clinician were substituted by the Mental Health Act 2007 s.11(4) and the reference to an authorised person in subs.(7)(b) was substituted by the Legal Services Act 2007, s.208, Sch.21, para.57.

DEFINITIONS

transfer direction: ss.47, 145(1).                                                                   **1–638**
responsible clinician: s.55(1).
hospital: ss.55(5), 145(1).
mental disorder: ss.1, 145(1).
authorised person: s.55(1).

GENERAL NOTE

This section provides that a transfer direction made in respect of a person who has been **1–639** remanded in custody by a magistrates' court ceases to have effect at the expiration of the period of remand unless the accused is then sent in custody to the Crown Court (subs.(2)). However, if the magistrates' court further remands the accused under subs.(3) the direction will not expire. Alternatively, if the court is satisfied, on receiving the requisite evidence, that the accused no longer requires treatment in hospital it may direct that the transfer direction shall cease to have effect (subs.(5)). The court also has power to send the accused to the Crown Court for trial in his absence if it is satisfied that he is unfit to take part in the proceedings (subs.(7)).

*Subsection (4)*
MONTHS.   Means calendar months (Interpretation Act s.5, Sch.1).                      **1–640**

*Subsection (5)*
WRITTEN OR ORAL EVIDENCE.   See s.54.                                                      **1–641**

## Further provisions as to civil prisoners and persons detained under the [Immigration Acts]

**53.**—(1) Subject to subsection (2) below, a transfer direction given in respect of **1–642** any such person as is described in paragraph (c) or (d) of section 48(2) above shall cease to have effect on the expiration of the period during which he would, but for his removal to hospital, be liable to be detained in the place from which he was removed.

(2) Where a transfer direction and a restriction direction have been given in respect of any such person as is mentioned in subsection (1) above, then, if the Secretary of State is notified by the [responsible clinician], any other [approved clinician] or [the appropriate tribunal] at any time before the expiration of the period there mentioned—

(a) that that person no longer requires treatment in hospital for mental disorder; or

(b) that no effective treatment for his disorder can be given in the hospital to which he has been removed,

the Secretary of State may by warrant direct that he be remitted to any place where he might have been detained if he had not been removed to hospital, and on his arrival at the place to which he is so remitted the transfer direction and the restriction direction shall cease to have effect.

AMENDMENTS
The heading to this section was amended by the Nationality, Immigration and Asylum Act 2002 s.62(10).

In subs.(2) the words in square brackets were substituted by the Mental Health Act 2007 s.11(5). The reference to the appropriate tribunal was substituted by SI 2008/2883 art.9, Sch.3 para.44.

DEFINITIONS
**1–643**  transfer direction: ss.47, 145(1).
hospital: ss.55(5), 145(1).
restriction direction: ss.49, 145(1).
responsible clinician: s.55(1).
approved clinician: s.145(1).
mental disorder: ss.1, 145(1).
the appropriate tribunal: ss.66(4), 145(1).

GENERAL NOTE
**1–644**  This section provides that a transfer direction made in respect of a civil prisoner or a person detained under the Immigration Act 1971 ceases to have effect on the expiration of the period of detention that would have occurred had the removal to hospital not taken place (subs.(1)). Where a transfer direction *and* a restriction direction have been made the Secretary of State has power to direct that the patient be returned to prison, and on his arrival there both the transfer direction and the restriction direction shall cease to have effect (subs.(2)).

*Subsection (2)*
**1–645**  SECRETARY OF STATE.  The Secretary of State for Justice: see the General Note to this Part.

*Supplemental*

## Requirements as to medical evidence
**1–646**  **54.**—(1) The registered medical practitioner whose evidence is taken into account under section 35(3)(a) above and at least one of the registered medical practitioners whose evidence is taken into account under sections 36(1), 37(2)(a), 38(1)[, 45A(2)] and 51(6)(a) above and whose reports are taken into account under sections 47(1) and 48(1) above shall be a practitioner approved for the purposes of section 12 above by the Secretary of State as having special experience in the diagnosis or treatment of mental disorder.

[(2) For the purposes of any provision of this Part of this Act under which a court may act on the written evidence of any person, a report in writing purporting to be signed by that person may, subject to the provisions of this section, be received in evidence without proof of the following—

(a)  the signature of the person; or

(b)  his having the requisite qualifications or approval or authority or being of the requisite description to give the report.

(2A) But the court may require the signatory of any such report to be called to give oral evidence.]

(3) Where, in pursuance of a direction of the court, any such report is tendered in evidence otherwise than by or on behalf of the person who is the subject of the report, then—

(a) if that person is represented by [an authorised person], a copy of the report shall be given to [that authorised person];
(b) if that person is not so represented, the substance of the report shall be disclosed to him or, where he is a child or young person, to his parent or guardian if present in court; and
(c) except where the report relates only to arrangements for his admission to a hospital, that person may require the signatory of the report to be called to give oral evidence, and evidence to rebut the evidence contained in the report may be called by or on behalf of that person.

AMENDMENTS

In subs.(1) the figure in square brackets was inserted by the Crime (Sentences) Act 1997 s.55, Sch.4 para.12(6).

Subsections (2) and (2A) were substituted by the Mental Health Act 2007, s.11(6).

The words in square brackets in subs.(3) were substituted by the Legal Services Act 2007, s.208, Sch.21, para.58.

DEFINITIONS

    mental disorder: ss.1, 145(1).        **1–647**
    the managers: s.145(1).
    hospital: ss.55(5), 145(1).
    child: s.55(1).
    young person: s.55(1).
    guardian: s.55(1).
    authorised person: s.55(1).

GENERAL NOTE

This section specifies when medical evidence must be given by a doctor who has been **1–648** approved by the Secretary of State or the Welsh Ministers under s.12, and provides for the circumstances when written evidence by a doctor or a person representing the managers of a hospital may be accepted by a court.

A doctor who has been approved under s.12 is also approved for the purposes of s.4 of the Criminal Procedure (Insanity) Act 1964 (*R. v Ghulam* [2009] EWCA Crim 2285, para.1.19).

*Subsection (1)*

APPROVED . . . BY THE SECRETARY OF STATE. Or by the Welsh Ministers (see the General **1–649** Note to this Act and SI 2000/253, Sch.3). There is no requirement for the doctor to be an approved clinician.

*Subsection (3)*

This subsection has been enacted because medical reports "may contain facts or com- **1–650** ments which might cause distress not only to the accused but also to his relatives. If the accused wishes, however, he may insist that the medical practitioner should give oral evidence, and he may then call evidence in rebuttal" (Home Office Circular No. 69/1983, para.44).

## [Reduction of period for making hospital orders

**54A.**—(1) The Secretary of State may by order reduce the length of the periods **1–651** mentioned in sections 37(4) and (5) and 38(4) above.

(2) An order under subsection (1) above may make such consequential amendments of sections 40(1) and 44(3) above as appear to the Secretary of State to be necessary or expedient.]

AMENDMENT
This section was inserted by the Criminal Justice Act 1991 s.27(2) and came into force on October 1, 1992 (SI 1992/333).

GENERAL NOTE
**1–652**   This section enables the Secretary of State to reduce, by statutory instrument, the time periods for the admission of mentally disordered offenders to hospital.

SECRETARY OF STATE.   Or, in relation to Wales, the Welsh Ministers (see the General Note to this Act). This function is performed by the Secretary of State for Health in England.

## Interpretation of Part III
**1–653**   **55.**—(1) In this Part of this Act—
["authorised person" means a person who, for the purposes of the Legal Services Act 2007, is an authorised person in relation to an activity which constitutes the exercise of a right of audience (within the meaning of that Act);]

"child" and "young person" have the same meaning as in the Children and Young Persons Act 1933;
"civil prisoner" has the meaning given to it by section 48(2)(c) above;
"guardian", in relation to a child or young person, has the same meaning as in the Children and Young Persons Act 1933;
"place of safety", in relation to a person who is not a child or young person, means any police station, prison or remand centre, or any hospital the managers of which are willing temporarily to receive him, and in relation to a child or young person has the same meaning as in the Children and Young Persons Act 1933;
["responsible clinician", in relation to a person liable to be detained in a hospital within the meaning of Part 2 of this Act, means the approved clinician with overall responsibility for the patient's case.]

(2) Any reference in this Part of this Act to an offence punishable on summary conviction with imprisonment shall be construed without regard to any prohibition or restriction imposed by or under any enactment relating to the imprisonment of young offenders.

(3) [. . .]

(4) Any reference to a hospital order, a guardianship order or a restriction order in section 40(2), (4) or (5), section 41(3) to (5), or section 42 above or section 69(1) below shall be construed as including a reference to any order or direction under this Part of this Act having the same effect as the first-mentioned order; and the exceptions and modifications set out in Schedule 1 to this Act in respect of the provisions of this Act described in that Schedule accordingly include those which are consequential on the provisions of this subsection.

(5) Section 34(2) above shall apply for the purposes of this Part of this Act as it applies for the purposes of Part II of this Act.

(6) References in this Part of this Act to persons serving a sentence of imprisonment shall be construed in accordance with section 47(5) above.

(7) Section 99 of the Children and Young Persons Act 1933 (which relates to the presumption and determination of age) shall apply for the purposes of this Part of this Act as it applies for the purposes of that Act.

AMENDMENTS
The definition of "authorised person" was inserted by the Legal Services Act 2007, s.208, Sch.21, para.59.
The definition of "responsible clinician" was substituted by the Mental Health Act 2007 s.11(7). Subsection (3) was repealed by s.55, Sch.11 Pt 1.

DEFINITIONS
approved clinician: s.145(1). **1–654**
hospital: s.145(1).
the managers: s.145(1).
patient: s.145(1).
application for admission for treatment: ss.3, 145(1).
mental disorder: ss.1, 145(1).
hospital order: ss.37, 145(1).
guardianship order: ss.37, 145(1).
restriction order: ss.41, 145(1).

*Subsection (1)*
Under s.107(1) of the Children and Young Persons Act 1933, "child" means a person **1–655** under the age of 14 years, "young person" means a person who has attained the age of 14 years and is under the age of 18 years, "guardian," in relation to a child or young person, includes any person who, in the opinion of the relevant court, has for the time being the care of the child or young person, and "place of safety" means a community home provided by a local authority or a controlled community home, any police station, or any hospital, surgery, or any other suitable place, the occupier of which is willing temporarily to receive a child or young person.

RESPONSIBLE CLINICIAN. See the note on s.34(1).

*Subsection (4)*
HAVING THE SAME EFFECT. An interim hospital order made under s.38 does not have the **1–656** same effect as a hospital order made under s.37. See the note on s.40(3).

## PART IV

## CONSENT TO TREATMENT

GENERAL NOTE
The extent to which the 1959 Act gave authority to the responsible medical officer to **1–657** treat a detained patient without his consent was unclear. The opinion of the Department of Health and Social Security was that where the purpose of detention was treatment, the Act gave implied authority for treatment to be imposed. During the 1970s the correctness of this opinion was questioned by a number of commentators: see paras 3.57 to 3.59 of the *Butler Committee* and Ch.11 of Phil Fennell's *Treatment Without Consent: Law Psychiatry and the Treatment of Mentally Disordered People since 1895* (1996).
The purpose of this Part is to clarify the extent to which treatment for mental disorder can be imposed on detained patients in hospitals and registered establishments. It provides for three categories of treatment which have different legal consequences. They are (1): the most serious treatments which require the patient's consent *and* a second opinion (s.57); (2) treatments that can be given without consent subject to a second opinion (s.58); and (3) treatments that can be given only with the consent of a capable patient or to an incapable patient subject to a second opinion (s.58A). Treatments that do not come within these categories can be imposed on a detained patient who understands the nature and purpose of the

treatment, but expressly withholds consent (s.63). The safeguards provided for by ss.57, 58 and 58A can be overridden if the treatment is required urgently (s.62).

The Explanatory notes, at para.57, explain the frequent use of the phrase "approved clinician in charge of treatment" rather that "responsible clinician" in this Part and in Pt IVA:

> "In the majority of cases the AC in charge of the treatment will be the patient's RC, but where, for example, the RC is not qualified to make decisions about a particular treatment (e.g. medication if the RC is not a doctor or a nurse prescriber) then another appropriately qualified professional will be in charge of that treatment, with the RC continuing to retain overall responsibility for the patient's case."

Approved Clinicians owe a duty of care to the patient whenever they propose or administer treatment under this Part (*R. (on the application of Wilkinson) v Responsible Medical Officer Broadmoor Hospital* [2001] EWCA 1545; [2002] 1 W.L.R. 419 para.68).

*The Mental Capacity Act 2005*

**1–658**    With the exception of the provision of ECT under s.58A to a patient who is incapable of consenting to that treatment, an advance decision refusing medical treatment for mental disorder made by the patient under s.24 of the Mental Capacity Act 2005 is rendered ineffective if the patient comes within the scope of this Part (s.28). However, the treating psychiatrist should not ignore the existence of the advance decision. If the patient is mentally incapacitated, the advance decision should be treated as an expression of the patient's wishes and feelings about the treatment in question which should be taken into account by the psychiatrist before a decision is made on whether to provide the patient with the treatment.

Neither a donee of a lasting power of attorney nor a deputy appointed by the Court of Protection can consent to treatment coming within the scope of this Part on the patient's behalf (*ibid.*).

*Code of Practice*

**1–659**    Guidance on this Part is contained in Ch.23. The role of second opinion appointed doctors (SOADs) is considered in Ch.24 at paras 24.40 et seq.

## [Patients to whom Part 4 applies

**1–660**    **56.**—(1) Section 57 and, so far as relevant to that section, sections 59 to 62 below apply to any patient.

(2) Subject to that and to subsection (5) below, this Part of this Act applies to a patient only if he falls within subsection (3) or (4) below.

(3) A patient falls within this subsection if he is liable to be detained under this Act but not if—

(a) he is so liable by virtue of an emergency application and the second medical recommendation referred to in section 4(4)(a) above has not been given and received;

(b) he is so liable by virtue of section 5(2) or (4) or 35 above or section 135 or 136 below or by virtue of a direction for his detention in a place of safety under section 37(4) or 45A(5) above; or

(c) he has been conditionally discharged under section 42(2) above or section 73 or 74 below and he is not recalled to hospital.

(4) A patient falls within this subsection if—

(a) he is a community patient; and

(b) he is recalled to hospital under section 17E above.

(5) Section 58A and, so far as relevant to that section, sections 59 to 62 below also apply to any patient who—

    (a)  does not fall within subsection (3) above;

    (b)  is not a community patient; and

    (c)  has not attained the age of 18 years.]

AMENDMENT

This section was inserted by the Mental Health Act 2007 s.34(2).

DEFINITIONS

    patient: s.145(1).                                        **1–661**

    hospital: ss.64(1), 145(1).

    community patient: ss.17A(7), 145(1).

GENERAL NOTE

This section identifies the categories of patients to whom this Part applies. All patients **1–662** who are liable to be detained under this Act are included, with the exception of the categories set out in subs.(3). It also applies to patients who are subject to an hospital order made under s.5(2)(a) of the Criminal Procedure (Insanity) Act 1964 because such an order has the same meaning as a hospital order made under s.37 of this Act (ibid., s.5(4)). A community patient is not subject to this Part (except s.57 which applies to any patient (subs.(1)) unless he or she has been recalled to hospital under s.17E (subs.(4)), in which case the provisions of s.62A will apply. The treatment of community patients who are not subject to Pt IV is governed by Pt IVA. An informal child patient who is not subject to a community treatment order is subject to s.58A (subs.(5)).

There is an argument to support the contention that patients who are liable to be detained under s.3 and who are either sentenced, or are committed or remanded to custody, by a court for a period of less than six months continue to be subject to the provisions of this Part: see the General Note to s.22.

Patients who do not come within the scope of this Part can be treated for both mental and physical disorders under common law rules if they are mentally capable of consenting to the treatment and under the Mental Capacity Act 2005 if they are mentally incapable of making a decision relating to the treatment in question and the treatment is in their best interests.

*Subsection (1)*

This subsection extends the protection provided by s.57 to informal patients. It was orig- **1–663** inally enacted as a result on an opposition amendment to the 1982 Act which found favour with the Minister for Health who accepted the argument that "if a course of treatment is so drastic that a detained patient's consent alone should not justify it and that there should be further safeguards, it is difficult to see why the same provisions should not apply to an informal patient" (*Hansard*, HC Vol.29, col.81).

*Subsection (3)*

LIABLE TO BE DETAINED. As this provision refers to a patient who is "liable to be **1–664** detained" rather than to a patient who is actually detained, the provisions of this Part are triggered when the patient has been made subject to a duly completed application made under Pt II of this Act or to an order of the court made under Pt III. It is the existence of the application or order, rather than the acceptance of the application or order by the detaining hospital, that results in the patient being "liable to be detained".

Patients who have been granted leave of absence from hospital under s.17 continue to be **1–665** "liable to be detained" under this Act and are subject to the provisions of this Part. It is therefore important that during such leave of absence the patient's General Practitioner is informed of the content of any certificates given under this Part as he or she will be bound by them.

Patients who are subject to guardianship are not "liable to be detained" and do not, therefore, come within the scope of this Part.

*Paragraph (c)*

**1–666**     A PATIENT WHO HAS BEEN CONDITIONALLY DISCHARGED.   What is the effect of a conditional discharge on a certificate authorising medical treatment that has been issued under s.58? Does the conditional discharge constitute a break in the continuity of the patient's detention with the result that three month period provided for in s.58(1)(b) applies when the patient is recalled to hospital? Or does the discharge merely suspend the operation of this Part of the Act during the period of the discharge with the result that in the event of the patient's recall any extant certificate granted under s.58 is reactivated and the duty to review under s.61 recommences? Although the language used in this Part does not provide a clear answer to this question, the latter interpretation is to be preferred because:

1. The use of the phrase "and has not been recalled to hospital" would appear to be superfluous if the fact of the conditional discharge meant that the Part IV procedures had to be started afresh on the patient's recall.

2. In *Dlodlo v Mental Health Review Tribunal for the South Thames Region* (1996) 36 B.M.L.R. 145, the Court of Appeal held that the recall of a conditionally discharged patient authorises the reinstatement of the regime of control in respect of the patient.

3. That interpretation provides for the better protection of the patient's rights under art.8 of the European Convention on Human Rights.

The Reference Guide, at para.16.28, prefers the former interpretation.

## Treatment requiring consent and a second opinion

**1–667**     **57.**—(1) This section applies to the following forms of medical treatment for mental disorder—

(a) any surgical operation for destroying brain tissue or for destroying the functioning of brain tissue; and

(b) such other forms of treatment as may be specified for the purposes of this section by regulations made by the Secretary of State.

(2) Subject to section 62 below, a patient shall not be given any form of treatment to which this section applies unless he has consented to it and—

(a) a registered medical practitioner appointed for the purposes of this Part of this Act by [the regulatory authority] (not being the [responsible clinician (if there is one) or the person in charge of the treatment in question]) and two other persons appointed for the purposes of this paragraph by [the regulatory authority] (not being registered medical practitioners) have certified in writing that the patient is capable of understanding the nature, purpose and likely effects of the treatment in question and has consented to it; and

(b) the registered medical practitioner referred to in paragraph (a) above has certified in writing that [it is appropriate for the treatment to be given.]

(3) Before giving a certificate under subsection (2)(b) above the registered medical practitioner concerned shall consult two other persons who have been professionally concerned with the patient's medical treatment [but, of those persons—

(a) one shall be a nurse and the other shall be neither a nurse nor a registered medical practitioner; and

(b) neither shall be the responsible clinician (if there is one) or the person in charge of the treatment in question.]

(4) Before making any regulations for the purpose of this section the Secretary of State shall consult such bodies as appear to him to be concerned.

AMENDMENTS

The amendments to this section were made by the Mental Health Act 2007 ss.6(2)(a), 12(2) and the Health and Social Care Act 2008 s.52, Sch.3 para.2.

DEFINITIONS

medical treatment: s.145(1), (4).                                                    **1–668**
mental disorder: ss.1, 145(1).
patient: ss.56, 145(1).
the regulatory authority: s.145(1).
responsible clinician: s.64(1).

GENERAL NOTE

This section, which applies to all patients, whether or not detained or subject to super-  **1–669** vised community treatment (s.56(1)), provides that certain of the most serious forms of medical treatment for mental disorder can only be given if the patient consents to the treatment and three independent people appointed by the Care Quality Commission ("the Commission") or, in relation to Wales, the Welsh Ministers, one being a doctor, have certified that the patient understands the treatment and has consented to it. If the patient is not capable of consenting to the treatment, or if he or she does not consent to it, the treatment cannot proceed. The independent doctor must also certify that it is appropriate for the treatment to be given. Before issuing the certificate the doctor must consult with two persons, other than the patient's doctor, who have been professionally concerned with the patient's treatment. The certificate of consent and the certificate relating to the need for treatment together make up Form T1 of the English Regulations and Form CO1 of the Welsh Regulations.

In *X v A, B and C and the Mental Health Act Commission* (1991) 9 B.M.L.R. 91, Morland J. held that the only legal relationship between the three persons appointed under subs.(2)(a) and the Commission's predecessor, the Mental Health Act Commission (MHAC), is that of appointees and appointor. It is the Commission on behalf of the Secretary of State who appoints the panel. It then becomes the exclusive function of the panel to carry out their responsibilities and the Commission have no further responsibility or duty in relation to a person who is aggrieved by the actions of the panel. When carrying out their functions under subs.(2)(a) the panel had to discharge duties which had quasi-judicial hallmarks and which were in the field of public administrative law. Consequently no common law duty of care is owed by the panel in private law to the patient. His Lordship said at 96:

"It may very well be although I reach no definitive conclusion about it, that a doctor giving an opinion, which was negligent, that electro-convulsive therapy should be given, that that opinion, being in the certificate given under section 58(3)(b) could be in breach of a common law duty in private law. In my judgment the reason for that is that the doctor, *qua* doctor, is giving a medical opinion about a patient, albeit not his. Similar considerations would apply to a doctor's certificate ... given under section 57(2)(b)."

Paragraph 13.51 of the Code of Practice on the Mental Capacity Act 2005 states:

"The combined effect of section 57 of the Mental Health Act and section 28 of the Mental Capacity Act is, effectively, that a person who lacks the capacity to consent to [a section 57 treatment] may never be given it. Healthcare staff cannot use the Mental

Capacity Act as an alternative way of giving these kinds of treatment. Nor can an attorney [of a lasting power of attorney] or deputy [appointed by the Court of Protection] give permission for them on a person's behalf."

If a patient is given treatment under this section, the approved clinician in charge of the patient's treatment (AC) must provide the Commission with reports on the treatment and the patient's condition (s.61).

*Code of Practice*
**1–670**   Guidance on this section is given in Ch.24 at paras 24.6 to 24.9.

*Subsection (1)*
**1–671**   MEDICAL TREATMENT FOR MENTAL DISORDER.   See the note on s.58(1).

PARAGRAPH (A).   During the period 1997–2009, 55 patients were referred to the Mental Health Act Commission in relation to neurosurgery (sometimes called "psychosurgery"), with the operation being authorised in 45 cases (Mental Health Act Commission, *Twelfth Biennial Report,* 2005–2007, para.6.87; *Thirteenth Biennial Report* 2007–2009, para.3.62). It is very rare for a detained patient to be referred. The only hospital that is currently performing operations covered by this provision is the University Hospital of Wales, Cardiff. The regulatory function is therefore performed by Health Inspectorate Wales, not the Care Quality Commission.

The MHAC adopted the following procedure for neurosurgery patients referred under this section:

"When the [AC], or the unit where the operation is to take place (as in the case of patients from abroad) contacts the Commission, a doctor is appointed who will carry out the first part of the procedure within two months of the proposed date of the operation. The appointed doctor will discuss with the patient's consultant psychiatrist the proposals for psychosurgery and may visit. There may be reasons why the appointed doctor will advise against proceeding to the second stage. It sometimes happens that further treatment recommended by the specialist psychiatrist has not yet begun and the visiting doctor may advise waiting until such further treatments have been completed. Otherwise the doctor accompanied by non medical appointees will visit the patient within six weeks prior to the proposed operation and consult the relevant professionals. If all three decide to certify under sub-section 2 of section 57(2) and the appointed doctor decides to certify under sub-section (b) of the same section, then the certification will be notified immediately to those concerned and subsequently the certificate sent to the Commission office" (MHAC, *Fourth Biennial Report, 1989–1991*, para. 6.2).

PARAGRAPH (B); OTHER FORMS OF TREATMENT.   Regulation 27(1) of the English Regulations and reg.38(1) of the Welsh Regulations specify "the surgical implantation of hormones for the purposes of reducing male sex drive" as a form of treatment to which this section shall apply. The patient must be mentally disordered as well as having an abnormal sex drive for him to come within the scope of this section.

In *R. v Mental Health Act Commission Ex p. X* (1988) 9 B.M.L.R. 77 at 85 DC, the court found that the term "hormone" included synthetically produced hormones as well as the naturally occurring substance, but did not include hormone analogues, such as Goserelin, which are separate substances well known at the time the regulations were made. It was therefore held that Goserelin, even though approximately 100 times more powerful than the naturally occurring substance, is not a hormone within the meaning of reg.16. Stuart-Smith L.J. said at 83: "If Parliament passes legislation on the control of leopards, it is not to be presumed that leopards include tigers on the basis that they are larger and fiercer." On the question whether a particular procedure comes within the scope of "surgical implant" the court held that "in the end it is . . . a question of fact and degree".

The court took the view that a wide bore disposable syringe used for implanting the Goserelin was more like a conventional injection and could not be described as "surgical". It would appear that an incision must be made if an implant is to be categorised as being "surgical". The effect of this judgment is that if the administration of Goserelin is used as a treatment for mental disorder, it is governed by s.58(1)(b).

There have only been four referrals (only one of which was proceeded with) of patients for hormone implantation and there have been no referrals since 1988. "This is probably because the most widely used sexual suppressant, cyproterone acetate (Androcur), is administered by mouth" (Phil Fennell, *Treatment Without Consent: Law Psychiatry and the Treatment of Mentally Disordered People since 1845* (1996), p.188).

REGULATIONS.    See subs.(4). The *Code of Practice* can also specify treatments to which this section will apply (s.118(2)).

SECRETARY OF STATE.    The functions of the Minister under this section, so far as exercisable in relation to Wales, are exercised by the Welsh Ministers (see the General Note to this Act).

*Subsection (2)*
REGISTERED MEDICAL PRACTITIONER.    See the note on s.58(3)(a).                **1–672**

PERSON IN CHARGE OF THE TREATMENT.    Who need not be an approved clinician: see s.64(1A).

APPOINTED ... BY THE SECRETARY OF STATE.    The Commission (or, in Wales, Health Inspectorate Wales) will appoint the doctor and the two other persons referred to in this paragraph (Health and Social Care Act 2008 s.52(1)(a)). Those appointed may include members or employees of the Commission (s.52(2)). They must be allowed to interview the patient and inspect his records, and the doctor must be allowed to examine the patient: see s.119 for registered establishments and the direction of the Secretary of State, published as Annex A to DHSS Circular No.HC(83)19, for hospitals. The three appointed persons have a duty to act fairly (*R. v Mental Health Act Commission Ex p. X*, above). Having been appointed these people do not act under the Commission's direction, but are exercising their own independent judgment. Therefore their decisions cannot be appealed against to the Commission. As the appointed persons are discharging a public law function, their decisions can be challenged by way of a judicial review (*X v A, B and C and Mental Health Act Commission*, above). The appointed persons are "public authorities" for the purposes of section 6 of the Human Rights Act 1998 because they "exercise functions of a public nature" (s.6(3)(b)). Also see the note under this heading in section 58(3)(a).

CONSENTED TO IT.    Patients must consent themselves: consent cannot be provided by a donee of a lasting power of attorney or a deputy appointed by the Court of Protection (Mental Capacity Act 2005, s.28). "Consent" is not defined in this Act, although the *Code of Practice* provides a definition at para.23.31. The notion of consent is problematic when detained patients are being treated and it is important that professionals do not confuse compliance with consent: see, for example, M. Larkin et al., "Making sense of 'consent' in a constrained environment", Int. J. of Law and Psychiatry, 32, (2009), 176–183. "An apparent consent will not be a true consent if it has been obtained by fraud, misrepresentation, duress or fundamental mistake"; per Stuart-Smith L.J. in *R. v Mental Health Act Commission Ex p. X*, above, at 85. Ultimately, whether there was a true consent is always a question of fact (*Freeman v Home (No.2)* [1984] 1 QB 524). If consent is subsequently withdrawn, the treatment cannot proceed (s.60(1)). Subject to s.62, if the patient loses capacity before the completion of the treatment, the treatment cannot be given (s.60(1A), (1B)).

An explanation in "broad terms" of the nature of the procedure which is intended and its likely effects would be sufficient for the consent to be "real" (*Chatterton v Gerson* [1981] 1 Q.B. 432 at 442). This finding was followed by the House of Lords in *Sidaway v Bethlem Royal Hospital Governors* [1985] 1 All E.R. 643, where it was held that the decision on what risks should be disclosed to a patient was primarily a matter of clinical judgment and in making that judgment a doctor was required to act in accordance with a practice accepted at the time as proper by a responsible body of medical opinion. It would not matter that there may be another body of responsible medical opinion which takes a different view. However, Lords Bridge and Keith, speaking with the majority, considered the court might in certain circumstances come to the conclusion that disclosure of a particular risk was so obviously necessary to an informed choice on the part of the patient that no reasonably prudent medical man would fail to make it. This approach was confirmed by the House of Lords in *Bolitho (administratrix of the estate of Bolitho (deceased)) v City and Hackney Health Authority* [1997] 4 All E.R. 771, where it was held that in a rare case, if it could be demonstrated that the medical opinion was not capable of withstanding logical analysis, the judge would be entitled to hold that the body of opinion was not reasonable or responsible. *Bolitho* and *Sidaway* were considered by the Court of Appeal in *Pearce v United Bristol Healthcare NHS Trust* (1999) 48 B.M.L.R. 118, where Lord Woolf held that:

> "If there is a significant risk which would affect the judgment of a reasonable patient then in the normal course it is the responsibility of a doctor to inform the patient of that significant risk, if the information is needed so that the patient can determine for him or herself as to what course that he or she should adopt" (para.23).

Whether a risk is "significant" cannot be determined simply in terms of percentages. The doctor will have to:

> "take into account all the relevant considerations, which include the ability of the patient to comprehend what he has to say to him or her and the state of the patient at the particular time, both from the physical point of view and an emotional point of view" (para.24).

If a patient asks about a risk, it is the doctor's legal duty to give an honest answer (per Lord Woolf at para.5).

*Pearce* was applied in *Birch v University College London Hospital NHS Foundation Trust* [2008] EWHC 2237 (B), para.74, where Cranston J. said that "unless the patient is informed of the comparative risks of different procedures she will not be in a position to give her fully informed consent to one procedure rather than another."

In *Re R* (*A Minor*) (*Wardship: Medical Treatment*) [1991] 4 All E.R. 177 at 187, CA, a case concerning the capacity of a child to consent to treatment, Lord Donaldson M.R., said, that:

> "what is involved is not merely an ability to understand the nature of the proposed treatment—in this case compulsory medication—but a full understanding and appreciation of the consequences both of the treatment in terms of intended and possible side effects and, equally important, the anticipated consequences of a failure to treat".

Also note Stuart-Smith L.J.'s statement in *R. v Mental Health Act Commission Ex p. X*, above, at 87, that he could not "accept that a patient must understand the precise physiological process involved before he can be said to be capable of understanding the nature and likely effects of the treatment or can consent to it".

Both the patient's consent and the doctor's certificate may apply to a plan of treatment (s.59). The patient can withdraw his consent to treatment under s.60.

*Paragraph (a)*
CERTIFIED IN WRITING.   This certificate is not a substitute for a standard consent form.  **1–673**
The certificate must be in the form set out in Form T1: see s.64(2) and reg.27(1) of the
English Regulations (Form CO1 and reg.40(1) of the Welsh Regulations). The appointed
persons have to be satisfied as to the patient's capacity and to the fact of consent before
a certificate can be issued. In forming a view as to whether the patient has consented to
the treatment, the appointed persons would need to be satisfied that the patient had been
provided with sufficient information to enable a valid consent to be given. In other
words, the appointed persons must be satisfied that the patient knew what he was consenting to. It is the responsibility of the doctor proposing to treat the patient to ensure that
sufficient information has been provided.

CAPABLE OF UNDERSTANDING.   See the note on this phrase in s.58(3)(a).

NATURE, PURPOSE AND LIKELY EFFECTS OF THE TREATMENT.   See the note on this phrase
in s.58(3)(a).

*Paragraph (b)*
APPROPRIATE FOR THE TREATMENT TO BE GIVEN.   See the note to s.58(3)(b).          **1–674**

CERTIFIED.   Using Form T1 (in Wales, Form CO1). "The Commission-appointed doctors undertaking section 57 visits have been advised to set a time limit on the validity of
Form [T1], i.e. stating that the certificate 'remains valid for only eight weeks from the
date of this certificate'. It remains the view of the Commission as stated in its Fifth
Report that a new Form [T1] would be necessary if an operation was postponed for
more than eight weeks after certification. Consent of the patient to treatment is essential
for a certificate to be issued" (Mental Health Act Commission, *Sixth Biennial Report*,
1993–1995, para.5.1).
    The Commission has the power to withdraw the authority to treat provided by the cer-
tificate by issuing a notice under s.61(3).
    The appointed doctor is required to reach an independent view of the desirability and
propriety of the AC's proposal: *R. (on the application of Wilkinson) v The Responsible
Medical Officer Broadmoor Hospital* [2001] EWCA Civ 1545; [2002] 1 W.L.R. 419,
noted in s.58(3)(b) under "certified".

APPROPRIATE FOR THE TREATMENT TO BE GIVEN.   See s.64(3) and the notes on s.3(2)(d).

*Subsection (3)*
See the notes on s.58(4).                                                        **1–675**

## Treatment requiring consent or a second opinion

    **58.**—(1) This section applies to the following forms of medical treatment for  **1–676**
mental disorder—
  (a)  such forms of treatment as may be specified for the purposes of this section
       by regulations made by the Secretary of State;
  (b)  the administration of medicine to a patient by any means (not being a form
       of treatment specified under paragraph (a) above or section 57 above [or
       section 58A(1)(b) below]) at any time during a period for which he is liable
       to be detained as a patient to whom this Part of this Act applies if three
       months or more have elapsed since the first occasion in that period when
       medicine was administered to him by any means for his mental disorder.
    (2) The Secretary of State may by order vary the length of the period mentioned
in subsection (1)(b) above.

(3) Subject to section 62 below, a patient shall not be given any form of treatment to which this section applies unless—

(a) he has consented to that treatment and either the [approved clinician in charge of it] or a registered medical practitioner appointed for the purposes of this Part of this Act by [the regulatory authority] has certified in writing that the patient is capable of understanding its nature, purpose and likely effects and has consented to it; or

(b) a registered medical practitioner appointed as aforesaid (not being the [responsible clinician or the approved clinician in charge of the treatment in question]) has certified in writing that the patient is not capable of understanding the nature, purpose and likely effects of that treatment or [being so capable] has not consented to it but that [it is appropriate for the treatment to be given.]

(4) Before giving a certificate under subsection (3)(b) above the registered medical practitioner concerned shall consult two other persons who have been professionally concerned with the patient's medical treatment, [but, of those persons—

(a) one shall be a nurse and the other shall be neither a nurse nor a registered medical practitioner; and

(b) neither shall be the responsible clinician or the approved clinician in charge of the treatment in question.]

(5) Before making any regulations for the purposes of this section the Secretary of State shall consult such bodies as appear to him to be concerned.

AMENDMENTS

The amendments to this section were made by the Mental Health Act 2007 ss.6(2)(b), 12(3), 28(2) and the Health and Social Care Act 2008 s.52, Sch.3 para.3.

DEFINITIONS

**1–677**    medical treatment: s.145(1), (4).
mental disorder: ss.1, 145(1).
patient: ss.56, 145(1).
the regulatory authority: s.145(1).
responsible clinician: s.64(1).
approved clinician: s.145(1).

GENERAL NOTE

**1–678**    This section provides that certain forms of treatment shall not be given to a patient unless the patient consents *or* an independent medical practitioner appointed by the Care Quality Commission ("the Commission") or, in relation to Wales, the Welsh Ministers (s.145(1)), (a second opinion appointed doctor, usually referred to as a "SOAD") has certified that either the patient is incapable of giving consent or that the patient should receive the treatment even though he or she has not consented to it. If the patient consents to the treatment, either the approved clinician in charge of the patient's treatment (AC) or a SOAD must certify that the consent has been properly given. Treatments governed by this section may be given in emergencies prior to the involvement of a SOAD (s.62). If a patient who is subject to this Part of this Act is a child who is either not consenting to, or is incapable of consenting to the proposed treatment, the provisions of this section must be satisfied before the treatment can be given. There is no provision which enables a person with parental responsibility over such a patient to consent to the treatment on his or her behalf.

A SOAD certificate provides an authority to provide treatment; it is not a direction to do so. In the *Wilkinson* case, below, Hale L.J. said, at para.71, that although this section is not phrased in terms of permission to treat, the only sensible construction is that it does confer permission to treat in the two circumstances set out in subs.(3).

If a patient is given treatment under this section, the AC must provide the Commission with reports on the treatment and the patient's condition (s.61).

18,831 second opinions were arranged by the Commission's predecessor, the Mental Health Act Commission (MHAC) in 2005–2007. During the period 2002–2007, only two per cent of second opinion visits resulted in a "significant" change to the patient's treatment plan (MHAC, *Twelfth Biennial Report*, 2005–2007, paras 6.7, 6.20). For some unexplained reason, this figure increased significantly in the final months of the Commission's existence (MHAC, *Thirteenth Biennial Report* 2007–2009, para.3.36). The SOAD system is presumably based on the assumption that where there is a significant disagreement between the SOAD and the patient's AC about the treatment that the patient should receive, the opinion of the SOAD is to be preferred because the patient's interests would be better served by that opinion. There is no evidence to suggest that this assumption is correct, or that patients derive any benefit from the SOAD system. On the other hand, it has been said by some psychiatrists that the knowledge that their treatment decisions will be subject to outside peer review acts as a constraint on decision making. Having reviewed research on the operation of this section, Peter Bartlett and Ralph Sandland conclude that "the SOAD system has done little to protect patients from overenthusiastic treatment regimes or abuses of their legal rights" (*Mental Health Law: policy and practice*, 2007, p.332).

*Human Rights Act 1998*

This section, which enables mentally capacitated patients to be treated without their con- **1–679** sent subject to limited safeguards, does not sit easily with a principle identified by the Committee for the Prevention of Torture and Inhuman or Degrading Treatment or Punishment. In para.41 of its eighth report (1998) the Committee, which, in effect, polices art.3 of the European Convention on Human Rights (ECHR) in respect of persons deprived of their liberty on behalf of the Council of Europe, states:

"Patients should, as a matter of principle, be placed in a position to give their free and informed consent to treatment. The admission of a person to a psychiatric establishment on an involuntary basis should not be construed as authorising treatment without his consent. It follows that every competent patient, whether voluntary or involuntary, should be given the opportunity to refuse treatment or other medical intervention. Any derogation from this fundamental principle should be based upon law and only relate to clearly and strictly defined exceptional circumstances."

Article 6 of the ECHR does not entitle a patient in every case to challenge a treatment plan before an independent and impartial tribunal before being subjected to it (*R. (on the application of Wilkinson) v The Responsible Medical Officer Broadmoor Hospital* [2001] EWCA Civ 1545; [2002] 1 W.L.R. 419, *per* Simon Brown L.J. at para.34). In *R. (on the application of N) v M* [2002] EWCA Civ 1789; [2003] M.H.L.R. 157, the Court of Appeal held that:

1. Any alleged breach of a patient's art.6 rights based on the way in which the SOAD had conducted the certification process would fall away on the judge deciding the disputed facts for himself on an application for judicial review.

2. There was no requirement under art.6 for the judge to hear oral evidence on the issue.

In *Wilkinson* a patient with a heart condition was being forcibly injected in a situation where there were disputes about whether he was mentally capable and whether the treatment was in his best interests. The court held that on an application for a judicial review of the decision to treat, it would be necessary for the court to reach its own view on the disputed issues, which required them to be determined by cross-examination of the psychiatrists who had been involved with the patient's treatment. Apart from determining the issue of capacity, the court would be required to consider whether the treatment (a) would threaten the patient's life and so be impermissible under art.2, (b) would be degrading and so be impermissible under art.3, and (c) would not be justifiable as both necessary and proportionate under art.8(2) given the extent to which it would invade the appellant's right to privacy. Simon Brown L.J. said at para.29: "The precise equivalence under section 58(3)(b) between incompetent patients and competent but non-consenting patients seems to me increasingly difficult to justify". *Wilkinson* is authority for the proposition that a court, albeit exercising a judicial review function, does so, not on a *Wednesbury* basis (see *Associated Provincial Picture House Ltd v Wednesbury Corporation* [1948] 1 K.B. 223), but by deciding the matter for itself on the merits after full consideration of the evidence whether oral, or in writing. [N.B. The patient's subsequent complaint to the European Court of Human Rights that his treatment constituted a breach of arts 3, 6 and 8 of the Convention was declared inadmissible (*Wilkinson v United Kingdom* [2006] M.H.L.R. 142).]

**1–680**     *Wilkinson* was considered in *R. (on the application of N) v M*, above, where the court held that:

1. Contrary to what was said in *Wilkinson*, it should not often be necessary to adduce oral evidence with cross-examination where there are disputed issues of fact and opinion in cases where the need for forcible medical treatment of a patient is being challenged on human rights grounds. [In *R. (on the application of JB) v Dr A. Haddock* [2006] EWCA Civ 961; [2006] M.H.L.R. 306, the Court of Appeal did not see any conflict between *Wilkinson* and *N*. Auld L.J. said at para.65: "[T]he court in *Wilkinson*, could not have intended or contemplated that every case would require the hearing and testing of oral medical evidence, especially where, as here, none of the parties requested it." In *R (on the application of Taylor) v (1) Dr Haydn-Smith (2) Dr Gallimore* [2005] EWHC 1668 (Admin); [2005] M.H.L.R. 327, para.8, Collins J. said: "In my view it will only be in a rare case that [adducing oral evidence] will be appropriate. If the court has the relevant medical notes, the reasoned decisions by the doctors concerned, statements from the doctors and other professionals, and comments on any opposing views, it is difficult to see why oral evidence should be needed." Also see *M v South West Hospital and St George's Mental Health NHS Trust* [2008] EWCA Civ 1112 paras 22–24].

2. For a judge to be satisfied that it is appropriate to give permission for treatment where the patient does not consent to it he had to be satisfied that the proposed treatment was both in the patient's best interests and was "medically necessary" as that phrase should be understood and applied for the purposes of art.3 of the Convention.

3. The standard of proof required is that the court should be satisfied that medical necessity has been "convincingly" shown (*Herczegfalvy v Austria* (1992) E.H.R.R. 437 at 484, para.82).

4. The answer to the question whether the proposed treatment has been convincingly shown to be medically necessary will depend on a number of factors, including (a) how certain is it that the patient does suffer from a treatable mental disorder; (b) how serious a disorder is it; (c) how serious a risk is presented to others; (d) how likely is it that, if the patient does suffer from such a disorder, the proposed treatment will alleviate the condition; (e) how much alleviation is there likely to be; (f) how likely is it that the treatment will have adverse consequences for the patient; and (g) how severe may they be. The court rejected a submission that, in a case where there is a responsible body of opinion that a patient is not suffering from a treatable condition, that the treatment is not in the patient's best interests

and is not medically necessary, then it cannot be convincingly shown that the treatment proposed is in the patient's best interests or medically necessary.

Where there is an issue as to the patient's consent or his or her capacity to consent under subs.(3)(b), the Court of Appeal in *R. (on the application of JB) v Dr A. Haddock,* above, identified the following three-stage process:

1. The first stage is that of the AC in seeking to initiate the treatment in question.

2. The second stage is for a SOAD to issue a certificate under subs.(3)(b) authorising the treatment on the basis of medical or therapeutic necessity. Auld L.J. said at para.34(ii): "[T]he SOAD's task is a medical one, to be undertaken on the *Bolam* principle, which is likely in almost all cases to involve consideration of the best interests of the patient, and may also take into account non-clinical factors".

3. At the third stage it is for the court to determine whether the *Herczegflavy* medical or therapeutic "necessity" for the treatment has been "convincingly" established by conducting a full merits review of the lawfulness of the SOAD's certificate.

The requirement on a court to be convinced of medical necessity in the light of the medical and other evidence is not capable of being expressed in terms of a standard of evidential proof. Auld L.J. said at para.42: "It is rather a value judgment as to the future—a forecast—to be made by a court in reliance on medical evidence according to a standard of persuasion. If it is to be expressed in forensic terms at all, it is doubtful whether it amounts to more than satisfaction of medical necessity on a balance of probabilities . . .". His Lordship also said, at para.14, that courts:

"in determining whether forcible treatment of a patient has been 'convincingly shown' to be medically necessary, should, as the Court said in *R. (on the application of B) v Dr SS (RMO) and others* [2005] EWHC 86 (Admin), pay particular attention to the views of those charged with his care and well-being. And, as Simon Brown L.J. . . . observed in [*Wilkinson,* above,] at para.31, courts should not be astute to overrule a treatment plan decided upon by the [AC] and certified by a SOAD following the required consultation with two others concerned with the patient's care; see also *Herczegfalvy,* at para.86".

In *R. (on the application of B) v Dr SS (Responsible Medical Officer), Second Opinion* **1–681** *Appointed Doctor and the Secretary of State for Health* [2006] EWCA Civ 28; [2006] M.H.L.R. 131, paras 66–68, the Court of Appeal said that:

1. Where the real issue is whether the patient should be detained in a mental hospital at all, that issue is one that should be referred to a tribunal in the first instance, rather than be the subject of judicial review proceedings. In such circumstances the appropriate course may well be on the application for permission to grant an interim injunction and adjourn the application pending a hearing before the tribunal.

2. Where the challenge is not to the grounds for detention but to the treatment itself, careful consideration should be given to the procedure to ensure, in so far as is possible, that there are not protracted and expensive legal proceedings requiring oral evidence from medical witnesses where there is no prima facie case that anything untoward has occurred. It is, of course, essential that the requirements of Art.6 are satisfied but this does not mean that permission must be given for judicial review proceedings where the papers do not disclose any arguable grounds for this.

3. Section 58 imposes preconditions to compulsory treatment which ought to ensure that this is not imposed unless there is a convincing therapeutic case for it. They will only do so, however, if the SOAD satisfies himself or herself that the treatment

in question should be imposed. This requires a truly independent assessment, not merely approval of the AC's decision on the basis that it is not manifestly unsound. If s.58 is properly complied with then issues requiring cross-examination of medical witnesses should not often arise.

In *R. (on the application of B) v Dr SS, Dr G and the Secretary of State for the Department of Health*, below, Charles J. said, at para.231, that when there is no distinct and separate challenge to the certificate of the SOAD in judicial review proceedings, nonetheless (a) the SOAD should be joined to obtain a binding order in respect of his certificate and to give him the opportunity to make separate representations from the AC if he so wishes, and (b) if possible at an early directions hearing the issues of permission and the further participation of the SOAD should be addressed. In a postscript to his judgment in *R. (on the application of B) v Haddock [2005]* EWHC 921 (Admin); [2005] M.H.L.R. 317 at paras 38, 39, Collins J. said that it will be rare that it is necessary for a SOAD to be represented where he or she has granted a certificate in a case where the decision of the AC is under attack, although it will be necessary to treat the SOAD as a defendant. In this case it was confirmed that the *Herczegfalvy* test only applies to the administration of the proposed treatment; it does not apply to the determination whether the patient suffers from a mental disorder.

**1–682**   *R. (on the application of N) v Dr M*, above, was applied in *R. (on the application of PS) v G* [2003] EWHC 2335 (Admin); [2004] M.H.L.R. 1, where Silber J. held that where medical treatment is administered to a patient against his or her will, art.3 will be contravened if:

(i) the treatment reaches the minimum level of severity of ill-treatment, taking into account all the circumstances, including the positive and adverse mental and physical consequences of the treatment, the nature and context of the treatment, the manner and method of its execution, its duration and, if relevant, the sex, age and health of the patient; and

(ii) the medical or therapeutic necessity for the treatment has not been convincingly shown to exist.

With regard to (i), the European Court of Human Rights has held that the minimum level of severity threshold would only be met if the treatment involved "actual physical injury or intense physical or mental suffering" (*Pretty v United Kingdom* (2002) 35 E.H.R.R. 1 at para.52).

His Lordship said, at para.123, that where the patient has capacity, his or her lack of consent, while an important factor in determining whether treatment engages art.3, cannot be decisive and that there is no basis for concluding that the patient's objections automatically and inevitably override all other issues except where the interests of other people would be affected if the medication was not administered.

With regard to a claim made under art.8 of the Convention, his Lordship held that the phrase "in accordance with law" in that article means that the common law "best interests test" must be satisfied in that the treatment must be in accordance with responsible and competent professional opinion, a less invasive form of treatment which would be likely to achieve the same beneficial results for the patient is not available, and it is necessary that the treatment should be given to the patient with regard to (a) his resistance to treatment, (b) the degree to which treatment is likely to alleviate or prevent deterioration of his condition, (c) the risk that he presents to himself or to others, (d) the consequences of the treatment not being given and (e) any possible adverse affects of the treatment.

The decisions in *Wilkinson, N* and *PS* were considered by Silber J. in *R. (on the application of B) v Dr SS, Dr AC and the Secretary of State for Health* [2005] EWHC 86 (Admin); [2005] M.H.L.R. 96, where the claimant asserted that subs.(3)(b) of this section when considered with s.3 of the Human Rights Act authorises the compulsory treatment of a patient who has capacity to refuse to consent only where it is shown that (a) such treatment is necessary for the protection of the public from serious harm or (b) without such treatment serious harm is likely to result to his health, alternatively is incompatible with the requirements of art.3 and/or art.8 and/or art.14 of the Convention. In particular, the claimant contended that the fact that the objection to the treatment by a patient with capacity is merely an important factor in determining whether a Convention right is engaged is wrong in law. Although his Lordship found that the claim could not be pursued because of its academic nature, he held that:

1. The proposed treatment of anti-psychotic medication which was a therapeutic necessity would not amount to a breach of arts 3 or 8 merely because the patient had capacity to consent but did not consent. Treatment that was a therapeutic necessity could not be regarded as "inhuman or degrading" for the purposes of art.3. So far as art.8 was concerned, art.8(1) was engaged but treatment that was a therapeutic necessity could be justified under art.8(2) provided that it was in accordance with the law. Thus it had to satisfy both the "best interests" test at common law and the express requirements of s.58.

2. In deciding whether treatment was a therapeutic necessity, the fact that the patient did not consent to it was an important factor.

3. There was no need to "read down" s.58 and that the section was compatible with the Convention.

His Lordship also rejected the claim that the present law amounts to unlawful discrimination in breach of art.14 against a patient with capacity for reasons which included the fact that the suggested comparators were not in an analogous position and there was an objective and reasonable justification for overriding the wishes of a patient where s.58 applied.

It became clear to his Lordship during the course of the hearing that where a SOAD's certificate has been obtained difficulties arise because the certificate only lasts for three months, but under the present arrangements, the challenge in the courts to the certificate is invariably not completed in time for the treatment to be administered within the three month period. Proposals on how to resolve this problem are set out in Appendix II to the judgment. They have been endorsed by the lead judge of the Administrative Court and the Head of the Administrative Court Office. Paragraph 12 of Appendix II states:

"The best way forward would be to ensure that when any claim is brought challenging the decision of the [AC] or the SOAD to authorise medical treatment to a patient who does not consent, there should be a speedy and automatic oral case management hearing two working days after the challenge application is brought. The Mental Health Act Commission has suggested that at that case management hearing 'one of the relevant factors to take into account when making directions at such a hearing is whether the SOAD has advised on the Form [T3] that a further second opinion be obtained, and if so, at what stage'. I agree with that suggestion. Unless an application for interim relief is made very quickly, it is unlikely that an interim order would be appropriate without at least a hearing at which other parties were represented. All parties should attend that hearing and the court could then consider a timetable for steps leading up to the hearing of the substantive claim within a timetable, which would be speedy and which would enable all parties to have sufficient time in which to present their cases. In many cases, it would be appropriate at the initial hearing to order a rolled-up hearing at which the court could consider the permission application and then proceed to deal with the substantive application."

These remarks should be read subject to the comments about procedure made by the Court **1–683** of Appeal in *R. (on the application of B) v Dr SS (Responsible Medical Officer), Second Opinion Appointed Doctor and the Secretary of State for Health*, above.

The cases set out above were considered by Charles J. in *R. (on the application of B) v Dr SS, Dr G and the Secretary of State for the Department of Health* [2005] EWHC 1936 (Admin); [2005] M.H.L.R. 347. His Lordship held that:

1. The capacity of the patient is relevant to an assessment under art.3 of medical necessity, to assessments under s.58 and thus to whether what is proposed is "in accordance with the law" for the purposes of art.8(2). However, whether or not a patient has capacity does not carry significant weight. The correct approach is to take account of the wishes of the patient against a background of his understanding of and approach to the issues relating to the relevant treatment and to his appreciation of whether he is being forced to accept the treatment and the effects this could have.

2. Inhuman and degrading treatment under art.3 would not be demonstrated where it was convincingly shown to the court's satisfaction that the treatment was a therapeutic necessity. The phrase "convincingly shown" introduces a high standard of proof and that the language of the English criminal and civil standards of proof should not be imported into it.

3. Article 8 was engaged whether or not the patient had capacity. The issue was justification under art.8(2). Such justification did not require that it should be convincingly shown that the treatment was a therapeutic necessity. The conventional three-fold test fell to be applied: was the treatment: (i) in accordance with the law; (ii) for a legitimate aim; and (iii) necessary in a democratic society? Treatment would be in accordance with the law if it fell within the terms of s.58. His Lordship accepted a submission on behalf of the Secretary of State that the common law should not be considered as a separate and distinct consideration in determining whether the treatment being proposed was "in accordance with the law". His Lordship said at para.91:

   "[T]he s.58 MHA test is a distinct test set by Parliament for a particular situation and purpose and when it applies it supplants or suspends the common law. In my view when applying the statutory test the courts should remember this, whilst at the same time taking appropriate guidance from the approach at common law in applying the 'best interests test' and, I add, to the right to autonomy at common law."

This decision was upheld by the Court of Appeal ([2006] EWCA Civ 28; [2006] M.H.L.R. 131). The court held that:

1. On the findings of fact made by Charles J., the imposition of proposed anti-psychotic medication will be lawful under English law and will not infringe the Convention.

2. The judge was correct to hold that: (i) capacity is not the crucial factor in determining whether treatment can be administered without consent; and (ii) when considering the severity of treatment the fact that it is imposed by compulsion is more significant than the question of whether the patient has or has not capacity to consent to the treatment.

3. It was wrong to claim that in order to avoid infringing the Convention treatment can only be given to a competent patient against his will if the treatment is not only a "therapeutic necessity" but is also necessary for the protection of the public or to prevent the patient from suffering serious harm. The court endorsed the acceptance by Silber J. in the *PS* case of the submission that:

   "the decision to administer anti-psychotic medication has to be considered in the context that the medication is likely to lead to the claimant being rehabilitated rather than remaining subject to long-term incarceration."

The court found that it was not necessary for it to decide whether a best interests test had to **1–684** be satisfied in addition to provisions set out in s.58 in order to meet requirements of art.8(2). However, the court made a number of observations on this issue which are set out in the notes on subs.(3)(b) under the heading "Appropriate for the treatment to be given".

For the compatibility of the three-month stabilising period established by subs.(1)(b) with art.8 of the Convention, see the notes to "three months or more" in that provision.

*The Mental Capacity Act 2005*
See the General Note to this Part. **1–685**

*The Code of Practice*
Guidance on this section is given in Ch.24 at paras 24.10 to 24.17.

*Subsection (1)*
MEDICAL TREATMENT FOR MENTAL DISORDER. See the note on s.63. **1–686**

*Paragraph (a)*
SUCH FORMS OF TREATMENT. No treatments have been specified under this provision. **1–687**

REGULATIONS. See subs.(5). There is no power equivalent to that contained in s.118(2) for treatments to be specified for the purposes of this section by the *Code of Practice*.

SECRETARY OF STATE. The functions of the Minister under this section, so far as exercisable in relation to Wales, are exercised by the Welsh Ministers (see the General Note to this Act).

*Paragraph (b)*
This paragraph enables a course of medication to be imposed on a patient coming within **1–688** the scope of this Part for up to three months without the patient's consent and without the need to obtain an independent medical opinion. The protection provided by this section does not come into play until three months have elapsed since the commencement of the treatment. Authorisation for imposing treatment on the patient during the initial three months is given by s.63.

Medication that is specified in regulations made under para.(a), above, and medication that is a s.57 or s.58A treatment does not come within the scope of this paragraph.

The approach to be taken by a court when considering an application for the judicial review of decisions made by the patient's AC and a SOAD to administer medication under this section, notwithstanding the patient's refusal to consent to that treatment was considered by the Court of Appeal in *R. (on the application of N) v Doctor M*, which is considered in the note on "The Human Rights Act 1998", above.

MEDICINE. Or any combination of medicines. Drugs should be listed either by name or by the classes described in the British National Formulary (BNF) (*Code of Practice*, para.24.17). Phil Fennell reports that the "most striking aspect of the medication cases [he studied] was the surprisingly high number of occasions where BNF recommended dose limits were exceeded (12 per cent of the medicines cases), and in a small number of cases the very large margin by which they were exceeded" (*Treatment Without Consent*, 1996, p.216). In May 2006, the Royal College of Psychiatrists issued a revised "Consensus statement on high-dose antipsychotic medication" which contains recommendations in relation to the decision to treat patients in excess of BNF recommended limits.

A medicine is identified by its chemical composition and not by its method of administration. Ordinary food in liquid form, such as would be used in the tube feeding of a patient with anorexia nervosa, is therefore not a medicine within the meaning of this section. However, it is a "medical treatment" coming within the scope of s.63 (*B v Croydon*

*Health Authority* [1995] 1 All E.R. 683 CA). For the administration of placebo medication, see the note under subs.(3).

Only medicine that is prescribed as treatment for the patient's mental disorder is "medicine" for the purpose of this section. This can include medication which is aimed at relieving the symptoms of the patient's mental disorder or which is ancillary to the core treatment that the patient is receiving: see s.145(4) and *B v Croydon Health Authority*, above, which is considered in the note on s.63. Medicines do not come within the scope of this section merely because they have an effect on the patient's mental state.

THREE MONTHS OR MORE. Month means calendar month (Interpretation Act 1978, Sch.1). The first day of treatment should be included in the calculation of this period. During the debates on the Mental Health (Amendment) Bill, the Minister of State said:

"The three-month period is considered appropriate because of the time that it allows for an optimum regime of medication to be identified—or, at least, for certain options to be ruled out before a certificate is needed. Different medications need to be tried before the most suitable one is identified" (*Hansard,* HL Vol.688, cols 494,495).

The three-month period must be continuous. The period is not broken on (1) the patient being granted leave of absence or being absent without leave; (2) the patient being transferred to another hospital whilst continuing to be detained; (3) the authority to detain the patient being renewed under s.20; (4) a change of medication; (5) the medication not being administered continuously; (6) the patient being made subject to supervised community treatment or having his or her community treatment order revoked; and (7) the section under which the patient is detained being changed. As the medication must be given "at any time during a period for which [the patient] is liable to be detained", the three-month period will clearly be broken by the patient's discharge from detention. This situation could occur where the patient's detention is found to be unlawful, he is discharged from that detention, and is then immediately re-detained. The fact that medication administered to a patient within the three-month period will continue to have an effect on the patient after the period has expired is not legally relevant.

The Mental Health Act Commission expressed its "concern that the provisions of [this] Act ... allow prolonged treatment without consent or a second medical opinion in a few cases where relatively prolonged periods of detention ... , each of less than three months' duration, are interrupted by brief periods of discharge from detention" (MHAC, *Sixth Biennial Report*, 1993–1995, para.3.8).

In the Scottish case of *Petition of WM* [2002] M.H.L.R. 367, the Court of Session (Outer House) held that the three month period set out in Pt X of the Mental Health (Scotland) Act 1984 during which the consent of a mentally competent detained patient is not required for treatment of his or her mental disorder did not violate art.8 of the Convention. Although there was a closely defined departure from the principle of personal autonomy, the requirement of proportionality was not breached. The approach taken in *WM* was followed with regard to the three month period established by subs.(1)(b) in the unreported case of *R. (on the application of AM) v Central and North West London Mental Health NHS Trust*, February 1, 2007 (see Radcliffes Le Brasseur, Mental Health Law Briefing No.116).

FIRST OCCASION IN THAT PERIOD. The three-month period starts from the first occasion when medicine for mental disorder is given to a patient who is detained under a section which is not excluded by s.56(3). For example, if a patient is initially detained under s.4, which is subsequently converted to a s.2, and is then detained under s.3 the three-month period will start from the first time that medicine was administered to the patient after the second medical recommendation referred to in s.4(4) was received. The period starts irrespective of whether the patient has consented to the treatment.

*Subsection (3)*

*Concurrent use of Forms T2 and T3*

If a mentally capable patient consents to some of the treatment that is being provided for **1–689** him (for example, anti-depressant medication) but does not consent to the remainder of his treatment (for example, anti-psychotic medication), then both of the procedures set out in paras (a) and (b) should be followed. The position of the Mental Health Act Commission had been that if a patient consents to treatment A but does not consent to treatment B, a Form T3 issued under s.58(3)(b) should be completed and treatment A should be included on the form as part of the patient's plan of treatment as authorised by s.59: see Policy Briefing for Commissioners, Issue 3, Annex 2, p.4. This is to misinterpret the effect of s.59. If the patient consents to a treatment, s.58(3)(a) requires a statutory procedure involving the use of Form T2 to be followed: the treatment "shall not be given" unless the form is completed. If the patient does not consent to a treatment, s.58(3)(b) provides for a different procedure involving the use of Form T3 to be followed. Section 59 allows either Form to relate to a plan of treatment which would allow for variations in the treatment that the patient receives under the authority granted by the Form. Section 59 does not allow for the mandatory procedure set out in s.58(3)(a) to be disregarded on the ground that the treatment in question will be included in the patients plan of treatment under s.58(3)(b). The MHAC subsequently accepted the correctness of this opinion "where a patient genuinely consents to a part of a treatment plan but refuses to consent to the remainder" ("Guidance Note for Commissioners on Consent to Treatment and the Mental Health Act 1983", 2008, para.9.1; also see the Commission's *Thirteenth Biennial Report* 2007–2009, at paras 3.38 to 3.42).

*Covert administration of medication*

In para.5.8 of its *Sixth Biennial Report*, 1993–1995, the Mental Health Act Commission **1–690** made the following comments about the covert administration of medication (the references are to the 1999 edition of the *Code of Practice*):

"One of the problems associated with covert administration is that it is clearly impossible to attempt to negotiate consent to such treatment and covert administration is seemingly precluded by paragraph 16.11 in the *Code of Practice* and by section 58(3)(a) of the Act, unless it has been certified as acceptable by a Second Opinion Doctor under section 58(3)(b). In contrast, it has been argued that a doctor may be entitled to withhold information from the patient under paragraph [15.14] of the Code but must be prepared to justify that decision. However, for that to be valid, the treatment must be 'in accordance with practice accepted at the time by a responsible body of medical opinion skilled in the particular form of treatment in question' (*Code of Practice* para.[15.21]). It would seem appropriate therefore for this matter to be considered by the Royal College of Psychiatrists and the Royal College of Nursing. Meanwhile, professional judgment must be relied upon in making decisions on this important ethical issue."

That the MHAC gave such equivocal advice on this issue is to be regretted. The quotation reproduced by the MHAC is from the case of *Bolam v Friern Hospital Management Committee* [1957] 1 W.L.R. 582, which laid down the general approach to be adopted by the courts to questions of medical negligence. The argument that this common law test can override the clear statutory language of subs.(3)(a), where it is stated that "a patient shall not be given ... treatment to which this section applies unless ... he has consented to that treatment", is clearly erroneous and should not be followed. The MHAC's slightly modified final position on this issue was set out at paras 6.38 to 6.48 of its *Twelfth Biennial Report*, 2005–2007. The legal position is that the covert administration of medication can only be given to a detained patient under the powers contained in either s.63 (i.e. during the three-month period provided for in subs.(1)(b)) or para.(b) of this subsection.

Before treatment is administered covertly, the RC should consider: (a) why it is not "practicable" to seek the patient's consent (*Code of Practice* para.23.37), and (b) whether, for the purposes of art.8(2) of the ECHR, the giving of covert medication is a proportionate response to the aim of improving the patient's health or reducing the risk posed by the patient (*Code of Practice* para.23.40). The fact that the RC has considered these issues should be recorded in the patient's notes. Although it would be lawful to administer medication provided under either s.63 or para.(b) forcibly (if that is clinically possible), the RC might consider that the alternative of administering the medication covertly would be less invasive of the patient's physical integrity. Although a certificate granted under para.(b) can authorise the covert administration of medication to a patient who is mentally capable of "understanding the nature, purpose and likely effects" of the treatment but is objecting to it, the patient will obviously be aware that the treatment is likely to be given to him or her at some time in the future. It is suggested that the RC discusses the possibility of the covert administration of the medication with the SOAD, and that the SOAD be invited to agree to such action and to confirm this on Form T3. If a mentally incapable patient is informal, the treatment can be given under the authority of the Mental Capacity Act 2005 if the treatment is assessed as being in the best interests of the patient.

The Nursing and Midwifery Council has published advice on the "Covert Administration of Medicines—Disguising medicine in food and drink" which can be accessed at *http://www.nmc-uk.org* [Accessed July 7, 2010].

*Placebo medication*

1–691    In its *Eighth Biennial Report*, 1997–1999, at para.6.17, the MHAC said that "as an inert substance, a placebo does not fall within the definition of 'medicine' and, therefore, falls outside the provisions of section 58" (in its *Tenth Biennial Report* 2001–2003, para.10.52 the MHAC stated that this represented a "provisional" view). This approach fails to address the reality of the situation which is that a placebo is offered to the patient as a "medicine" which, hopefully, will lead to an improvement in his or her condition. The fact that any improvement in the patient's condition is triggered by a psychological, rather than a physiological reaction does not disqualify the substance from being categorised as a "medicine". It is instructive to note that the *Shorter Oxford English Dictionary* states that a placebo was first described, in 1811, as a "medicine given more to please than to benefit the patient". A more recent definition is "a pill, medicine, etc. prescribed more for psychological reasons than for any physiological effect" (*Oxford English Reference Dictionary* (1996)). Given that in *B v Croydon Health Authority* [1995] 1 All E.R. 683, the Court of Appeal held that "medical treatment" included "a range of acts ancillary to the core treatment that the patient is receiving", and that ancillary treatment would include treatment which is "concurrent with the core treatment", it would seem that the administration of placebo medication is the administration of a medicine for the medical treatment of the patient's mental disorder for the purposes of subs.(1)(b). However, the practical reality is that placebo medication cannot be given to either mentally capable or mentally incapable patients who come within the scope of this Part as in both instances the patient must be given an explanation of the nature, purpose and effect of the medication in order that his or her capacity to consent to the treatment can be assessed.

*Paragraph (a)*

1–692    CONSENTED.    See the note on "consented to it" in s.57(2). If the patient withdraws his or her consent or if the patient's subsequently loses mental capacity, s.60 applies. In the *Wilkinson* case, noted below, Brooke L.J. said, at para.50, that the consent "would almost invariably be in writing". Both the patient's consent and the medical practitioner's certificate may relate to a plan of treatment (s.59). Note Lord Donaldson's remark in *Re R (A Minor)* (*Wardship: Medical Treatment*) [1991] 4 All E.R. 177 at 184 CA, "that consent by itself creates no obligation to treat".

The quality of the "consent" given by a detained patient is examined by Michael Larkin et al. in "Making sense of 'consent' in a constrained environment", Int. J. of Law and Psychiatry 32 (2009) 176–183.

REGISTERED MEDICAL PRACTITIONER. A visit by a SOAD for the purposes of this paragraph should only be requested in the situation described in the *Code of Practice* at para.24.39.

APPOINTED ... BY THE SECRETARY OF STATE. The Commission (or, in Wales, Health Inspectorate Wales) makes the appointment (Health and Social Care Act 2008 s.52(1)(b)). Those appointed may include members or employees of the Commission (s.52(2)). There is no requirement for the SOAD to be an AC. Only Consultant Psychiatrists of at least five years' standing are appointed (MHAC Annual Report 2003–2004, para.27(b)). It is rare for a SOAD to issue a certificate under this paragraph. This could happen where, contrary to the prior opinion expressed by the patient's AC, the SOAD finds that the patient is both competent and consenting to the treatment. The SOAD, has a right of access to the patient and his records: see s.119 for registered establishents and the direction of the Secretary of State, published as Annex A to DHSS Circular No.HC(83)19, for hospitals. Once appointed, the SOAD will not act under the Commission's direction but will exercise his or her own independent judgment. His or her decision cannot therefore be appealed against to the Commission.

As a person who is exercising "functions of a public nature", the SOAD is a "public authority" for the purposes of s.6 of the Human Rights Act 1998; see s.6(3)(b) and *R. (on the application of Wilkinson) v The Responsible Medical Officer Broadmoor Hospital* [2001] EWCA Civ 1545; [2002] 1 W.L.R. 419, below, per Hale L.J. at para.61. He or she is "performing a statutory watchdog function on behalf of the public to protect detained persons who are in an especially vulnerable position" (para.71).

CERTIFIED. Using Form T2: see s.64(2) and reg.27(2) of the English Regulations (in Wales, Form CO2: see reg.40(2) of the Welsh Regulations). Neither this Act nor the English or Welsh Regulations provide for the renewal of the Form. The statement in para.24.79 of the *Code of Practice* that Form T2 ceases to authorise treatment where "the clinician concerned stops being the approved clinician in charge of the treatment" is, it is submitted, incorrect as para.(a) merely states that the completion of these Forms give authority for the treatment to be provided. The CQC agrees with the *Code* even though its agreement conflicts with the stance that it takes regarding the continuing validity of Form T3: see the note on "Certified" in para.(b), below. If the statement in the *Code* is correct, a new Form T2 or CO2 would have to be completed on every occasion when the patient's usual AC took annual leave or was otherwise unavailable for more than a temporary period as that clinician would not be "in charge of the treatment" during such absences. It is submitted that the authority to treat will only end if the patient's consent is withdrawn, the patient becomes mentally incapable of consenting, the patient ceases being a detained patient, or the specified treatment changes. Good practice suggests that the patient's consent be reviewed at regular intervals and when there is a change of AC.

CAPABLE OF UNDERSTANDING. In *R. (on the application of B) v Dr SS (Responsible Medical Officer)* [2006] EWCA Civ 28 paras 33, 34, Lord Phillips C.J. said that it was arguable that the words "capable of understanding the nature, purpose and likely effects of" the treatment do not go far enough to define capacity and that whatever "the precise test of capacity to consent to treatment, we think that it is plain that a patient will lack that capacity if he is not able to appreciate the likely effects of having or not having the treatment." The judgment in this case was delivered before the implementation of the Mental Capacity Act 2005. Despite the differences in the wording of the two tests, it is suggested that the test of capacity set out in ss.2 and 3 of that Act should be used to determine whether the patient is capable of understanding the treatment in question. Given the obiter remarks of Hale L.J. in

*R. (on the application of Wilkinson) v Responsible Medical Officer Broadmoor Hospital* [2001] EWCA Civ 1545; [2002] 1 W.L.R. 419 at paras 65, 66, it is likely that the courts would adopt this approach, which has been adopted by the *Code of Practice* at para.23.28. As s.1(2) of the 2005 Act states that a person must be assumed to have capacity unless it is established that he lacks capacity, a formal assessment of capacity would only be required if there is reason to believe that the presumption could be rebutted.

In *R. v Mental Health Act Commission Ex p. X* (1998) 9 B.M.L.R. 77, Stuart-Smith L.J. noted, obiter, at 85, that the words in this subsection "are 'capable of understanding' and not 'understands'. Thus the question is capacity and not actual understanding." In para.6.12 of its Fourth Biennial Report 1989–1991, the Mental Health Act Commission (MHAC) stated that the judgment in this case "appeared to suggest that consent rests not on actual understanding but simply on the patient's intellectual capacity to understand." The MHAC reported that it had "taken legal advice on this approach and advised all [Second Opinion Appointed Doctors] to continue with their approach of requiring both a capacity and adequate understanding of the treatment and its consequences." It is submitted that the MHAC's advice is correct as Stuart-Smith L.J.'s remarks do little more than distinguish the two elements of this provision, i.e. the patient's capacity and the patient's consent. In any event Stuart-Smith L.J.'s formulation, at 86, of the requirements of a valid consent—"No doubt consent has to be an informed consent in that [the patient] knows the nature and likely effect of the treatment"—is supportive of the MHAC's approach. It would also be difficult to establish whether a patient is capable of understanding particular information without, at the same time, also establishing that he actually does understand that information. However, in *R. (on the application of B) v Secretary of State for Health* [2005] EWHC 86 (Admin); [2005] M.H.L.R. 96 para.87, Silber J. said that Stuart-Smith L.J.'s comment on this phrase "might mean that a patient might be regarded as having capacity even if he does not actually understand the nature, purpose and likely effects of the treatment". This formulation is not compatible with the approach taken by the Court of Appeal in the B case, above. His Lordship endorsed the finding of Hale L.J. in *R. (on the application of Wilkinson) v The Responsible Medical Officer Broadmoor Hospital* above, that the threshold for capacity is a low one. His Lordship said at para.91:

> "The present low threshold for capacity recognises correctly the great importance to be attached to principles of autonomy, but it also means that the case for non-consensual treatment of those with capacity is increased."

NATURE, PURPOSE AND LIKELY EFFECTS OF THE TREATMENT. Prior to the passing of the Mental Capacity Act 2005, Thorpe J. held that this formulation is declaratory of the common law position relating to information that must be given to a patient before a valid consent can be obtained (*Re C (Refusal of Medical Treatment)* [1994] 1 All E.R. 819 at 824).

*Paragraph (b)*

**1–693**   This paragraph allows for the provision of medical treatments that come within the scope of this section to incapable or non-consenting patients if certain criteria are satisfied. If treatment is regulated by this section, it cannot be provided to a mentally incapable patient under the authority of the Mental Capacity Act 2005: see s.28 of that Act. This section does not place the patient's AC under an obligation to continue to provide a treatment specified in the statutory form to a patient after it has become clinically inappropriate to do so.

The decision-making process to be followed where treatment is provided under this provision was identified by the Court of Appeal in *R. (on the application of JB) v Dr A. Haddock and others*, which is noted under "Human Rights Act 1998", above.

CERTIFIED. Form T3 should be used: see s.64(2) and reg.27(2) of the English Regulations (in Wales, Form CO3 and reg.40(2) of the Welsh Regulations). Although the *Code of Practice*, at para.24.43, states that the SOAD should "interview the patient in private if possible", interviewing the patient is not a legal requirement. Therefore, a SOAD can give a certificate if the patient is either unwilling or too disturbed to be interviewed.

In its "Guidance note for Commissioners on consent to treatment and the Mental Health Act 1983", the CQC states at paras 8.2 and 8.3:

"The validity of a Form T3 is unaffected by changes in approved clinician or even detaining hospital. If a patient is transferred to another hospital under s.19 the Form T3 from their original hospital remains valid.

Whilst SOADs have the right to authorise time-limited authorisations Forms T3 are not time-limited, and the Code of Practice gives no guidance on when they should be reviewed. However, the Commission has taken the general view that Forms T3 should not normally be extant for more than two years. Commissioners who encounter Forms T3 that are more than two years old should pass the details of the form to the Commission Secretariat so that further investigation can take place."

In *R. (on the application of Wilkinson) v The Responsible Medical Officer Broadmoor Hospital*, above, the Court of Appeal said that the appointed doctor is required to reach his or her own independent view of the desirability and propriety of the AC's proposal. Simon Brown L.J. said at paras 32, 33:

"The evidence before us, however, suggests that his approach to the [AC's] proposal is perhaps more akin to that of a review than to forming his own primary judgment on the question. Indeed, in the advice issued by the Mental Health Act Commission to Second Opinion Appointed Doctors in April 1999 it is stated:

'The treatment authorised ... may not be in accord with the SOAD's personal practice but should be reasonable in the opinion of the SOAD, i.e. the SOAD is not offering an 'academic' second opinion or imposing a treatment plan on the RMO.'

Whilst, of course, it is proper for the SOAD to pay regard to the views of the AC who has, after all, the most intimate knowledge of the patient's case, that does not relieve him of the responsibility of forming his own independent judgment as to whether or not 'the treatment should be given'. And certainly, if the SOAD's certificate and evidence is to carry any real weight in cases where ... the treatment plan is challenged, it will be necessary to demonstrate a less deferential approach than appears to be the norm."

Brooke and Hale L.JJ. expressed their agreement with these obiter comments.

The question whether fairness requires a SOAD to give reasons for a decision which **1–694** sanctions the violation of the autonomy of a mentally competent adult patient was considered by the Court of Appeal in *R. (on the application of Wooder) v Feggetter and Mental Health Act Commission* [2002] EWCA Civ 554; [2003] QB 219. It was held that:

(i) a SOAD owes a duty to give in writing the reasons for his opinion when certifying under this section that a mentally competent detained patient should be given medication against his will;

(ii) there is no requirement for a SOAD to dot every "i" and cross every "t" when giving his reasons. So long as he gives his reasons clearly on what he reasonably regards as the substantive points on which he formed his clinical judgment, this will suffice;

(iii) the court will only grant a patient permission to challenge the reasons if it can be shown that there is a real prospect of establishing that a SOAD has not addressed any substantive point which he should have addressed, or that there is some material error underlying the reasons that he gave;

(iv) the reasons need not be disclosed to the patient if either the SOAD or the AC considers that such disclosure would be likely to cause serious harm to the physical or mental health of the patient or any other person;

(v) the SOAD should send a statement of his reasons to the AC or to the hospital together with any opinion he may have on the desirability of withholding them from the patient on "serious harm" grounds. The AC should then make them available to the patient to read, unless it is a case in which reliance can properly be placed on the "serious harm" exception from disclosure; and

(vi) although the reasons should be prepared and disclosed to the patient as soon as practicable, it may not always be appropriate to delay treatment once the SOAD's certificate has been given.

These findings would also apply to a mentally competent child patient. Their Lordships left open the question whether fairness also requires the AC's report to the SOAD to be disclosed to the patient in order that the patient can address its contents when interviewed by the SOAD.

The Mental Health Act Commission published Guidance Notes to SOADs and ACs on the implications of this decision. The Commission's guidance extended the duty of SOADs as identified by the Court of Appeal by requiring them to give reasons for all of their decisions, including decisions made in respect of mentally incapable patients. The correctness of this approach was implicitly endorsed by Collins J. in *R. (on the application of B) v Haddock* [2005] EWHC 921 (Admin); [2005] M.H.L.R. 317 at para.16. The SOAD's duty to give reasons is considered in the *Code of Practice* at paras 24.59 et seq.

Although the Commission has no power to attach a time limit to a Form T3, it can withdraw the power to treat provided by the Form T3 by issuing a notice under s.61(3).

NOT CAPABLE OF UNDERSTANDING.    See the note on para.(a). If the patient regains capacity, see s.60(1C), (1D). It will not be possible to assess the patient's capacity with respect to placebo medication as testing out whether the patient understands the nature, purpose and likely effects of the medication will defeat the object of the exercise: see the note on "Covert administration of medication", above.

NOT CONSENTED TO IT.    The 1978 White Paper suggested that the following principle be adopted in cases where the patient's consent is not forthcoming: "where it is not possible to agree with the patient the form the treatment is to take and the consultant feels the imposition of treatment is essential he should, wherever there is a choice, select the method of treatment the patient finds least objectionable or which would represent the minimum interference with the patient" (Cmnd. 7320 para.6.18).

APPROPRIATE FOR THE TREATMENT TO BE GIVEN.    See s.64(3) and the notes on s.3(2)(b). In *R. (on the application of B) v Dr SS (Responsible Medical Officer), Second Opinion Appointed Doctor and the Secretary of State for Health* [2006] EWCA Civ 28 at para.62, the Court of Appeal said that the phrase "likelihood of its alleviating or preventing a deterioration of his condition", which was removed by the Mental Health Act 2007:

"should not be equated with the test of whether treatment is in the best interests of a patient. That question will depend on wider considerations than the simple question of efficacy of the treatment, such as whether an alternative and less invasive treatment will achieve the same result. The distress that will be caused to the patient if the treatment has to be imposed by force will also be a relevant consideration. English common law and medical ethics both require that medical treatment shall not be imposed without the consent of the patient unless treatment is considered to be in the best interests of the patient. Thus, while the specified criteria are obviously critical to the decision of whether the treatment should be given, they are not the only considerations relevant to that question. The SOAD has to certify that the treatment should be given and we do not see how he can properly do that unless satisfied that the treatment is in the best interests of the patient."

In *R. (on the application of JB) v Dr A. Haddock*, above at para.45, Auld L.J. said that considerations such as these "underline the composite nature of the question of medical necessity. It is one to which the answer will always be one of value judgment derived from other value judgments on often difficult and complex questions of diagnosis and prognosis on which there may be some difference of medical opinion."

It is submitted that the comments made in these two cases are equally applicable to the phrase substituted by the 2007 Act.

*Subsection (4)*

SHALL CONSULT. This Act does not place an obligation on any person to act as a consultee and the SOAD is under no obligation to accept the nurse or "other person" put forward by the AC as a potential consultee. The identity and role of the consultees are considered in the *Code of Practice* at paras 24.49–24.55. Consultation could take place over the telephone.

**1–695**

If there is a significant delay in identifying an appropriate consultee, consideration could be given to treating the patient under the authority of s.62 until the completion of the consultation process.

TWO OTHER PERSONS. In *R. (on the application of B) v Haddock* [2005] EWHC 921 (Admin); [2005] M.H.L.R. 317 para.8, Collins J. said that the SOAD "should, if he thinks it desirable to do so, consult with others than the two statutory consultees, including (with the patient's consent) the patient's nearest relative, family, carers or advocate".

WHO HAVE BEEN PROFESSIONALLY CONCERNED WITH THE PATIENT'S MEDICAL TREATMENT. And will therefore have some direct knowledge of the patient's history and condition. A particular involvement with the patient is therefore required; it would not be sufficient for a potential consultee merely to have general responsibilities on the ward where the patient is being treated.

The fact that consultation must take place with two persons who have been concerned with the patient's medical treatment, rather than with persons who are so concerned, means that a consultation can take place with a person who has no current involvement with the patient. Such a consultation can only take place if identifying the person concerned was a reasonable action for the authorities to take given the non-availability of a person with a current involvement in the patient's treatment (*R. (on the application of W) v Feggetter* [2000] M.H.L.R. 200)).

NURSE. Means a qualified nurse whose name appears on the register maintained by the Nursing and Midwifery Council (Nursing and Midwifery Order 2001 (SI 2002/253) art.5).

THE OTHER. The Mental Health Act Commission in its Fifth Biennial Report 1991–1993, at para.7.16, reports that identifying the "other person" is a "major source of difficulty for Appointed Doctors when undertaking second opinion visits". While recognising that the issue has not yet been tested in the courts the MHAC "concluded that to require the statutory 'other' consultee to be invariably professionally qualified and included in a professional register would be unnecessarily restrictive". At the same time the MHAC expressed its "grave doubts about the validity of some certificates which, for example, refer to the 'ward clerk', 'Gymnasium technician' and 'Occupational Therapy Aid' ". The MHAC suggested that "the appointed doctor should endeavour to meet with somebody whose qualifications, experience and knowledge of the patient should enable them to make an effective contribution to the work of the multidisciplinary team." As Parliament has required the "other person" to be "professionally concerned" as opposed to being merely "concerned" with the patient's medical treatment, it is submitted that the other person must hold a recognised professional qualification which is directly relevant to the "medical treatment" of the patient as defined in s.145(1). Persons falling into this category could include psychologists, occupational therapists, pharmacists, psychotherapists, physiotherapists, art/music therapists and social workers. The MHAC subsequently revised its position on this issue and supported the approach advocated here: see para.9 of its Guidance Note, noted below.

In its Guidance Note People with Nursing Qualifications and Consultation with the "other" Professional in Second Opinions under the Mental Health Act" (2008), the MHAC stated that:

"it has decided to interpret the law as preventing someone who is registered as a nurse from being the 'other' consultee, whether or not s/he is acting as a nurse or even practicing in another profession (e.g. as a psychologist or social worker). We take this view on the basis that the Act requires the person not to 'be' a nurse, rather than specifying that the person's professional relationship with the patient must not involve a nursing role" (para.3).

Accordingly, the MHAC "asked SOADs to no longer accept professionals who are registered nurses as the 'other' consultee on their Second Opinion visits" (para.5).

SOADs, who must exercise their own independent judgment and do not act under the direction of the Commission's successor, the Care Quality Commission (*X v A B C and the Mental Health Act Commission*, above), should be cautious about accepting this advice for the following reasons:

1. The "other" consultee must be "professionally concerned" with the patient's medical treatment. If, for example, the other consultee is a psychologist who is providing the patient with psychological therapies and he or she also happens to have a nursing qualification, that person is professionally concerned with the patient's medical treatment in his or her capacity as a psychologist. On this interpretation, the phrase "the other shall be neither a nurse nor a registered medical practitioner" should be interpreted as meaning "the other shall be neither a nurse nor a registered medical practitioner who is treating the patient in his or her professional capacity as a nurse or a registered medical practitioner."

2. It is difficult to imagine that Parliament, when enacting this provision, understood that it was placing an obligation on SOADs to ask every "other" consultee whether he or she is also registered as a nurse.

An Independent Mental Health Advocate who is assisting the patient cannot be a consultee as he or she is representing the patient's interests and is not involved in the patient's treatment.

In the sample studied by Phil Fennell, by far the largest category of "other persons" consulted was that of social worker. He reports that "the duty to consult the other professional is becoming seen as a tiresome formality" (*Treatment Without Consent*, 1996, p.208). This attitude is partly due to the difficulties in finding another person to consult, which calls into question the extent to which multidisciplinary care is being provided to patients.

## [Electro-convulsive therapy, etc.

1–696   **58A.**—(1) This section applies to the following forms of medical treatment for mental disorder—

(a) electro-convulsive therapy; and

(b) such other forms of treatment as may be specified for the purposes of this section by regulations made by the appropriate national authority.

(2) Subject to section 62 below, a patient shall be not be given any form of treatment to which this section applies unless he falls within subsection (3), (4) or (5) below.

(3) A patient falls within this subsection if—

(a) he has attained the age of 18 years;

(b) he has consented to the treatment in question; and

(c) either the approved clinician in charge of it or a registered medical practitioner appointed as mentioned in section 58(3) above has certified in writing that the patient is capable of understanding the nature, purpose and likely effects of the treatment and has consented to it.

(4) A patient falls within this subsection if—

(a) he has not attained the age of 18 years; but

(b) he has consented to the treatment in question; and

(c) a registered medical practitioner appointed as aforesaid (not being the approved clinician in charge of the treatment) has certified in writing—

(i) that the patient is capable of understanding the nature, purpose and likely effects of the treatment and has consented to it; and

(ii) that it is appropriate for the treatment to be given.

(5) A patient falls within this subsection if a registered medical practitioner appointed as aforesaid (not being the responsible clinician (if there is one) or the approved clinician in charge of the treatment in question) has certified in writing—

(a) that the patient is not capable of understanding the nature, purpose and likely effects of the treatment; but

(b) that it is appropriate for the treatment to be given; and

(c) that giving him the treatment would not conflict with—

(i) an advance decision which the registered medical practitioner concerned is satisfied is valid and applicable; or

(ii) a decision made by a donee or deputy or by the Court of Protection.

(6) Before giving a certificate under subsection (5) above the registered medical practitioner concerned shall consult two other persons who have been professionally concerned with the patient's medical treatment but, of those persons—

(a) one shall be a nurse and the other shall be neither a nurse nor a registered medical practitioner; and

(b) neither shall be the responsible clinician (if there is one) or the approved clinician in charge of the treatment in question.

(7) This section shall not by itself confer sufficient authority for a patient who falls within section 56(5) above to be given a form of treatment to which this section applies if he is not capable of understanding the nature, purpose and likely effects of the treatment (and cannot therefore consent to it).

(8) Before making any regulations for the purposes of this section, the appropriate national authority shall consult such bodies as appear to it to be concerned.

(9) In this section—

(a) a reference to an advance decision is to an advance decision (within the meaning of the Mental Capacity Act 2005) made by the patient;

(b) "valid and applicable", in relation to such a decision, means valid and applicable to the treatment in question in accordance with section 25 of that Act;

(c) a reference to a donee is to a donee of a lasting power of attorney (within the meaning of section 9 of that Act) created by the patient, where the donee is acting within the scope of his authority and in accordance with that Act; and

(d) a reference to a deputy is to a deputy appointed for the patient by the Court of Protection under section 16 of that Act, where the deputy is acting within the scope of his authority and in accordance with that Act.

(10) In this section, "the appropriate national authority" means—

(a) in a case where the treatment in question would, if given, be given in England, the Secretary of State;

(b) in a case where the treatment in question would, if given, be given in Wales, the Welsh Ministers.]

AMENDMENT

This section was inserted by the Mental Health Act 2007, s.27.

DEFINITIONS

**1–697**     medical treatment: s.145(1), (4).
mental disorder: ss.1, 145(1).
patient: ss.56, 124(1).
responsible clinician: s.64(1).
approved clinician: ss.64(1B), 145(1).

GENERAL NOTE

**1–698**     This section provides that, except in an emergency (see below), electro-convulsive therapy (ECT) and any other treatment provided for in regulations made under this section may only be given to the patient if the patient either consents to the treatment, or a second opinion appointed doctor (SOAD) has certified that it is appropriate for the treatment to be given. It applies to adult detained patients who come within the scope of this Part, apart from those who are subject to community treatment orders (s.56(5)), and to all patients who are under the age of 18 (whether or not they are detained) (subss.(4), (7)). A certificate issued by a SOAD under Pt IVA will not provide authority for treatment under this section to be given to a community patient who has capacity or competence to consent but refuses consent when recalled to hospital or when the community treatment order is revoked (s.62A(4)).

If the patient consents to the ECT, the consent must be certified by either the approved clinician in charge of the patient's treatment (AC) or a SOAD (subs.(3)). For child patients, both detained and informal (s.56(5)), the consent must be certified by a SOAD (subs.(4)). If the child is informal, there must also be authority to treat the child (subs.(7)). Where the patient is incapable of consent, a SOAD must certify that the patient is "not capable of understanding the nature, purpose and likely effects of the treatment" and that it is appropriate for the treatment to be given (subs.(5)(a),(b)). Before issuing the certificate the SOAD must consult with two persons who have been professionally concerned with the patient's medical treatment; one must be a nurse and the other shall be neither a nurse nor a doctor nor the patient's responsible clinician (RC) or the AC (subs.(6)). The SOAD cannot complete a certificate under subs.(5) if to do so would conflict with:

(i) an advance decision of the patient not to receive the treatment in question, which the SOAD is satisfied is valid and applicable;

(ii) a decision made by the donee of a lasting power of attorney or a deputy appointed by the Court of Protection if the donee or deputy has the authority to refuse the treatment on behalf of the patient; or

(iii) an order of the Court of Protection.

Under the terms of the Mental Capacity Act 2005 a person under the age of 18 cannot make an advance decision or execute a lasting power of attorney. If a certificate is withdrawn by the appropriate national authority (see subs.(10)), the treatment can continue pending compliance with this section if the person in charge of the treatment considers that the discontinuance of the treatment would cause serious suffering to the patient (s.64H(5)–(9)).

This section is subject to the emergency provisions contained in s.62 (subs.(2)). Treatment under s.62 (as amended by the 2007 Act), including the administration of medicine as part of ECT (see reg.27(4) of the English Regulations and reg.38(2) of the Welsh Regulations), can be given to a mentally incapacitated patient even though the patient has made a valid and applicable advance decision refusing ECT. However, the treatment could not continue if the SOAD is subsequently satisfied that the patient has made such an advance decision (subs.(5)(c)(i)). Although the rationale for invoking s.62 in respect of incapacitated patients who require treatment urgently is clear, the fact that a capacious patient can be given treatment under s.62 conflicts with the underlying purpose of this section which is to respect the wishes of such patients. Baroness Murphy, a distinguished psychiatrist, said that she could not:

> "envisage a clinical situation where section 62 should ever be given to a patient who has capacity. Such treatment exists to treat profoundly depressed people who have usually stopped eating and drinking and who are seriously at risk of dehydration and death before the treatment takes effect. As the British Psychological Society has pointed out, evidence from [the] Northwick Park studies shows that if a nurse can sit with a patient day in and day out over the course of a three or four-day weekend and get liquid into him one way or another through a drip and so forth, ECT can usually be avoided. But sometimes it is necessary. Sometimes the circumstances are not right and the patient may pull out the drip and refuse treatment. But I cannot understand how such a situation could arise with a patient who had full capacity. The nature of the illness is such that it would not happen" (*Hansard,* HL Vol.689,col.978).

An informal adult incapacitated patient could be given ECT under ss.5 and 6 of the Mental Capacity Act 2005. Such treatment could not be provided if the patient had made a valid and applicable advance decision refusing ECT or if a donee or a deputy had refused such treatment on the patient's behalf.

*Code of Practice*
Guidance on this section is given in Ch.24 at paras 24.18–24.24.

*Subsection (1)*
REGULATIONS. Regulation 27(3) of the Mental Health (Hospital, Guardianship and **1–699** Treatment) Regulations 2008 specifies the administration of medicines as part of the ECT as being a form of treatment to which this section applies. Such medicines could include anaesthetics and muscle relaxants.

APPROPRIATE NATIONAL AUTHORITY. See subs.(10).

*Subsection (3)*
APPROVED CLINICIAN IN CHARGE. See s.64(1B). **1–700**

NATURE, PURPOSE AND LIKELY EFFECTS. See the note on this phrase in s.57(2).

CERTIFIED IN WRITING. Using Form T4: see reg.24(3) of the English Regulations (in Wales, Form CO4: see reg.40(3) of the Welsh Regulations).

CONSENTED TO IT.    See the note on this phrase in s.57(2). If the patient withdraws consent, the treatment must either not proceed or must be halted (s.60(1)). If the patient loses capacity before the completion of the treatment, see s.60(1A),(1B). The problems associated with obtaining a patient's informed consent to ECT are considered by the MHAC in its *Eleventh Biennial Report*, 2003–2005, at paras 4.74, 4.75.

If a mentally capable patient refuses to consent to the treatment, it cannot be given. The advice given to the patient by the AC should be recorded (*St George's Healthcare NHS Trust v S* [1998] 3 All E.R. 673 at 703).

*Subsection (4)(c)*

**1–701**    CERTIFIED IN WRITING.    Using Form T5 (in Wales, Form CO5). A fresh certificate is not required just because a young person reaches the age of 18.

APPROPRIATE FOR THE TREATMENT TO BE GIVEN.    See s.64(3) and the notes on s.3(2)(d). This criterion does not apply to adult patients.

*Subsection (5)*

**1–702**    CERTIFIED IN WRITING.    Using Form T6 (in Wales, Form CO6).

*Paragraph (c)*

**1–703**    The legal responsibility for being satisfied that an advance decision made by the patient is both "valid and applicable" is that of the SOAD. This could cause difficulties for the SOAD if there is a dispute about either the validity or the applicability of the decision. For example, the AC might dispute the existence of an advance decision in a case where the spouse of the patient claims that the patient had made an oral advance decision refusing ECT some time ago. In this situation the SOAD could not automatically rely on the judgment of the AC; the SOAD would have to form an opinion as to which view is to be preferred in order that he or she can be "satisfied" that a valid and applicable advance decision is in place. It would be difficult for the SOAD to reach such an opinion without interviewing the spouse, and possibly other relatives and the patient's GP. Such enquiries could prove to be very time consuming. In this example, such interviews would not be required if the SOAD concluded that the provision of ECT to the patient constituted a "life-sustaining treatment" for the purposes of s.25 of the Mental Capacity Act 2005, in which case the advance decision must be in writing, signed and witnessed, and must contain a statement that the decision is to take effect even if life is at risk. If, after investigation, the SOAD continued to have doubts about the validity or the applicability of an advance decision, an application would have to be made to the Court of Protection for the matter to be determined. In the meantime, the ECT could be provided if it is either life-sustaining or would prevent a serious deterioration of the patient's condition (s.26(5) of the 2005 Act).

The SOAD should also make enquiries to ascertain whether a donee or deputy has been appointed under the 2005 Act and, if so, whether the donee or deputy has the authority to make a decision to refuse ECT. The SOAD should also ascertain whether the Court of Protection has ordered that ECT should not be given to the patient. This information should be noted on the patient's medical record.

*Subsection (6)*

**1–704**    See the notes on s.58(4).

*Subsection (7)*

**1–705**    This subsection applies to mentally incapacitated patients who come within the scope of s.56(5) i.e. informal patients under 18 who cannot give consent. As this section does not "by itself confer sufficient authority" for providing treatment to such patients, authority to treat must be found elsewhere. Authority to treat is found in s.5 of the Mental Capacity Act 2005 for children over the age of 16 and by virtue of parental consent for younger children. Accordingly, s.28 of the 2005 Act, which gives preference to Pt IV of this Act in respect of treatments that come within its scope, does not apply to treatments provided under this section if the patient comes within the scope of this subsection: see s.28(1A) of the 2005 Act. The *Code of Practice,* at para.36.60, states that it would not be prudent to rely on parental consent with respect to a child under the age of 16 and that court authorisation for the treatment should be sought, unless it is an emergency.

## Plans of treatment

**59.** Any consent or certificate under section 57[, 58 or 58A] above may relate to **1–706** a plan of treatment under which the patient is to be given (whether within a specified period or otherwise) one or more of the forms of treatment to which that section applies.

AMENDMENT
The words in square brackets were substituted by the Mental Health Act 2007 s.28(3).

DEFINITION
   patient: s.145(1).                                                     **1–707**

GENERAL NOTE
   This section enables any consent or certificate obtained for the purposes of s.57, s.58 or **1–708** s.58A to relate to a plan of treatment which would involve one or more of the treatments specified under the same section. Such a plan would allow for variations in treatment within the context of the treatment objectives and enable the responsible clinician to respond rapidly to the patient's reaction to a particular drug or dosage. The plan could include a time scale for the administration of treatments. A patient may withdraw consent to a plan of treatment under s.60(2). "Treatment plans are usually described in terms of the drug categories recorded in the British National Formulary" (Mental Health Act Commission, *Fifth Biennial Report* 1991–1993, para.7.7).

## Withdrawal of consent

**60.**—(1) Where the consent of a patient to any treatment has been given for the **1–709** purpose of section 57[, 58 or 58A] above, the patient may, subject to section 62 below, at any time before the completion of the treatment withdraw his consent, and those sections shall then apply as if the remainder of the treatment were a separate form of treatment.

   [(1A) Subsection (1B) below applies where—

(a) the consent of a patient to any treatment has been given for the purposes of section 57, 58 or 58A above; but
(b) before the completion of the treatment, the patient ceases to be capable of understanding its nature, purpose and likely effects.

   (1B) The patient shall, subject to section 62 below, be treated as having withdrawn his consent, and those sections shall then apply as if the remainder of the treatment were a separate form of treatment.

   (1C) Subsection (1D) below applies where—

(a) a certificate has been given under section 58 or 58A above that a patient is not capable of understanding the nature, purpose and likely effects of the treatment to which the certificate applies; but
(b) before the completion of the treatment, the patient becomes capable of understanding its nature, purpose and likely effects.

   (1D) The certificate shall, subject to section 62 below, cease to apply to the treatment and those sections shall then apply as if the remainder of the treatment were a separate form of treatment.]

(2) Without prejudice to the application of [subsections (1) to (1D)] above to any treatment given under the plan of treatment to which a patient has consented, a patient who has consented to such a plan may, subject to section 62 below, at any time withdraw his consent to further treatment, or to further treatment of any description, under the plan.

AMENDMENT
The words in square brackets were substituted and inserted by the Mental Health Act 2007 ss.28(4), 29(2) and (3).

DEFINITION
**1–710**   patient: ss.56, 145(1).

GENERAL NOTE
**1–711**   This section provides for a patient to withdraw his or her consent to treatment under ss.57, 58 or 58A or to a plan of treatment. On the withdrawal of consent, the remainder of the treatment must be considered as a separate treatment for the purposes of those sections. It is submitted that the three-month period referred to in s.58(1)(b) is not re-activated on a patient withdrawing consent to be treated by medication. A patient cannot therefore be treated for a fresh period of three months in the absence of consent before the independent medical opinion referred to in s.58(3)(b) is obtained.

*Code of Practice*
**1–712**   Guidance on this section is given in Ch.24 at paras 24.32 to 24.37.

*Subsection (1)*
**1–713**   WITHDRAW HIS CONSENT.   The withdrawal of consent can be made in writing, orally, or through the patient's behaviour, e.g. by physically resisting the administration of the treatment.

*Subsections (1A) to (1D)*
**1–714**   The effect of these subsections is:

1. If a mentally capable patient who has consented to a s.57, s.58 or s.58A treatment loses his or her capacity to consent, the patient is to be treated as having withdrawn his or her consent to the treatment.

2. If a s.58 or s.58A treatment is being given to a mentally incapable patient but, before the treatment has been completed, the patient becomes mentally capable of consenting to the treatment, the remainder of the treatment is to be treated as a separate form of treatment for the purposes of certification under those sections.

In both instances, the treatment that the patient is receiving can continue if the approved clinician considers that stopping it would cause serious suffering to the patient (s.62(2)).

**Review of treatment**
**1–715**   **61.**—(1) Where a patient is given treatment in accordance with section 57(2)[, 58(3)(b) or 58A(4) or (5)] above[, or by virtue of section 62A below in accordance with a Part 4A certificate (within the meaning of that section),] a report on the treatment and the patient's condition shall be given [by the approved clinician in charge of the treatment] to [the regulatory authority]—
  (a) on the next occasion on which the [responsible clinician] furnishes a report [under section 20(3)[, 20A(4) or 21B(2) above in respect] of the patient]; and

(b) at any other time if so required by [the regulatory authority].

(2) In relation to a patient who is subject to a restriction order [, limitation direction] or restriction direction subsection (1) above shall have effect as if paragraph (a) required the report to be made—

(a) in the case of treatment in the period of six months beginning with the date of the order or direction, at the end of that period;

(b) in the case of treatment at any subsequent time, on the next occasion on which the [responsible clinician] makes a report in respect of the patient under section 41(6) [, 45B(3)] or 49(3) above.

(3) [the regulatory authority] may at any time give notice [. . .] directing that, subject to section 62 below, a certificate given in respect of a patient under section 57(2)[, 58(3)(b) or 58A(4) or (5)] above shall not apply to treatment given to him [whether in England or Wales] after a date specified in the notice and sections 57[, 58 and 58A] above shall then apply to any such treatment as if that certificate had not been given.

[(3A) The notice under subsection (3) above shall be given to the approved clinician in charge of the treatment.]

AMENDMENT

In subs.(1) the words in square brackets were inserted by the Mental Health (Patients in the Community) Act 1995 s.2(5).

In subs.(2) the words in square brackets were inserted by the Crime (Sentences) Act 1997 s.55, Sch.4 para.12(7).

The remaining amendments to this section were made by the Mental Health Act 2007 ss.12(4), 28(5), 34(3) and the Health and Social Care Act 2008 s.52, Sch.3 para.4.

DEFINITIONS

the regulatory authority: s.145(1).          **1–716**
limitation direction: s.145(1).
patient: ss.56, 145(1).
responsible clinician: s.64(1).
approved clinician: s.145(1).
restriction direction: s.145(1).
restriction order: s.145(1).

GENERAL NOTE

This section provides for the periodic review by the the Care Quality Commission ("the **1–717** Commission") or, in relation to Wales, the Welsh Ministers of treatment which is being given under either s.57(2) (commonly neurosurgery), s.58(3)(b) (medication after three months or treatment to be prescribed by regulations), s.58A(4) or (4) (ECT or treatment to be prescribed in regulations) or, following a recall from supervised community treatment, under s.62A in accordance with a Pt IVA certificate.

With regard to treatment provided under s.62A, the Reference Guide states at paras.17.59–17.51:

"[A] report must be given automatically to [the Commission] under section 61 if treatment is given on the basis of a Part 4A certificate to an SCT patient who has been recalled to hospital (including one whose CTO is then revoked), in lieu of a SOAD certificate under section 58 or 58A . . . . This will only apply to treatment to which the patient either did not, or could not, consent.

In such cases, a report must be submitted by the approved clinician in charge of the treatment at the same time it would have to be given if the treatment had, in fact, been given on the basis of a section 58 or 58A SOAD certificate . . . . This means the approved clinician must make a report to [the Commission] on the next occasion that the responsible clinician submits a report under section 20 to renew the patient's detention, under section 20A to extend the patient's SCT, or under section 21B to confirm the patient's detention or SCT after absence without leave for more than 28 days."

A review is not required where a patient has consented to treatment being given to him under s.58(3)(a) or s.58A(3) (which does not apply to child patients).

A letter from the Chairman of the Mental Health Act Commission (MHAC) dated September 1984 notified health authorities of the arrangements for reports to be given under this section and set out the form (now Form "Section 61—Review of Treatment Form", previously Form MHAC 1) to be used for this purpose. This letter states that when a report has been given to the MHAC, as required by this section, consent to continue treatment may be assumed unless the MHAC gives notice of the withdrawal of consent. In its *Fourth Biennial Report*, 1989–1991, para.6.4, the MHAC stated that there:

"is still some misunderstanding about the Commission's requirements of hospitals under s.61. Whereas some hospitals have been submitting reports regularly every few months, other hospitals have forwarded very few reports on forms MHAC 1. Hospital Managers should ensure that MHAC 1 forms are completed and returned to the Commission at the beginning of every period of renewable detention and to furnish additional reports if requested by the Second Opinion Appointed Doctor. Patients under restriction order must have a review of treatment reported on MHAC 1 annually when a report is sent to the [Ministry of Justice]. In addition hospitals are asked to inform the Commission when a detained patient receiving treatment on the authority of a Form [T3] is discharged or consents to treatment. Hospitals are advised to institute a system at ward level for monitoring the cancellation or changes of Form [T2] and Form [T3] since at present ward records are often found to be unclear as to the current consenting status of the patient."

*Code of Practice*

**1–718**    This section is considered in Ch.24 at paras 24.72 et seq.

*Subsection (1)*

**1–719**    REPORT ON THE TREATMENT AND THE PATIENT'S CONDITION. The approved clinician (AC) in charge of the patient's treatment should report on the treatment and the patient's response to it. There is no requirement under paragraph (a) for the AC to report on an *informal* patient who has been treated under s.57. However, the Commission can require such a report to be made under para.(b).

ON THE NEXT OCCASION.    And on each subsequent occasion when the authority to detain the patient or the keep the patient subject to a community treatment order is renewed.

*Subsection (2)*

**1–720**    This subsection specifies the timing of the treatment review in respect of patients who are subject to a restriction order, limitation direction or restriction direction.

*Subsection (3)*

**1–721**    This subsection provides that the Commission may at any time give notice to the AC that a certificate given under ss.57(2), 58(3)(b) or s.58A(4) or (5) shall cease to apply after the date it specifies. If the AC wished to continue with the treatment specified in the notice he or she would need to start afresh with the procedures laid down in ss.57, 58 or s.58A, unless the criteria for urgent treatment set out in s.62(2) were satisfied.

The MHAC has published "Advice on the timescales for treatment authorised on Forms 39". This is reproduced in "Policy Briefing for Commissioners", Issue 7, which can be accessed on the Commission's website.

**Urgent treatment**

**62.**—(1) Sections 57 and 58 above shall not apply to any treatment—  **1–722**

(a)  which is immediately necessary to save the patient's life; or

(b)  which (not being irreversible) is immediately necessary to prevent a serious deterioration of his condition; or

(c)  which (not being irreversible or hazardous) is immediately necessary to alleviate serious suffering by the patient; or

(d)  which (not being irreversible or hazardous) is immediately necessary and represents the minimum interference necessary to prevent the patient from behaving violently or being a danger to himself or to others.

[(1A) Section 58A above, in so far as it relates to electro-convulsive therapy by virtue of subsection (1)(a) of that section, shall not apply to any treatment which falls within paragraph (a) or (b) of subsection (1) above.

(1B) Section 58A above, in so far as it relates to a form of treatment specified by virtue of subsection (1)(b) of that section, shall not apply to any treatment which falls within such of paragraphs (a) to (d) of subsection (1) above as may be specified in regulations under that section.

(1C) For the purposes of subsection (1B) above, the regulations—

(a)  may make different provision for different cases (and may, in particular, make different provision for different forms of treatment);

(b)  may make provision which applies subject to specified exceptions; and

(c)  may include transitional, consequential, incidental or supplemental provision.]

(2) Sections 60 and 61(3) above shall not preclude the continuation of any treatment or of treatment under any plan pending compliance with section 57[, 58 or 58A] above if the [approved clinician in charge of the treatment] considers that the discontinuance of the treatment or of treatment under the plan would cause serious suffering to the patient.

(3) For the purposes of this section treatment is irreversible if it has unfavourable irreversible physical or psychological consequences and hazardous if it entails significant physical hazard.

AMENDMENTS

The amendments to this section were made by the Mental Health Act 2007 ss.12(5), 28(6) and (7).

DEFINITIONS

patient: ss.56, 145(1).  **1–723**

approved clinician: s.145(1).

GENERAL NOTE

This section states that the procedural safeguards provided for in ss.57 and 58 shall not  **1–724** apply to the categories of urgent treatment set out in paras (a) to (d) of subs.(1). Where the treatment is ECT provided under s.58A, urgent treatment can only be given if either if the grounds set out in para.(a) or (b) are satisfied (subs.(1A)). Where the treatment is another form of s.58A treatment (to be determined by regulations made under s.58A), the Secretary of State (for England) or the Welsh Ministers (for Wales) may make regulations regarding which of the criteria in subs.(1) are to apply to that treatment (subss.(1B), (1C)). Existing treatments can continue if the "serious suffering" criterion set out in subs.(2) is satisfied.

This section is not applicable to any treatment that does not come within the remit of either ss.57, 58 or s.58A. As neither ss.57, 58 nor 58A applies to treatments given under this section, there is no legal requirement to certify whether the patient is capable of consenting to the treatment in question. A consequence of this is that treatment under this section can be given to a mentally incapacitated patient even though the patient has made an advance decision refusing the treatment in question. As a matter of good practice, issues relating to the patient's mental capacity and attitude to receiving the treatment should be noted on the patient's file. This section applies irrespective of whether to patient is capable of consenting to the treatment in question.

In its *Third Biennial Report* 1987–1989, the Mental Health Act Commission (MHAC) stated at para.7.6(j):

> "When second opinion consultations are requested for medication it is unusual for emergency drugs to be given in the interval between the request for a consultation and the [SOAD's] visit. When ECT is requested it is more common for one or two administrations of ECT to be required urgently before the consultation is undertaken. This usually happens with a very sick patient, where one treatment may be given within the two days taken to arrange the consultation, or perhaps a few more over an extended bank holiday weekend."

The MHAC expressed its concern:

> "about treatment given in emergency situations which fall outside the Consent to Treatment provisions of the Act. Some treatment is described as being given under the provisions of section 62 when in fact the patient is either not detained or is held under the short-term holding powers of the Act to which section 62 does not apply" (*Fifth Biennial Report* 1991–1993, para.7.12).

If treatment is to be given in these circumstances, it must be justified under either the common law or the Mental Capacity Act 2005.

Although there is no statutory form to be completed when this section is invoked, the *Code of Practice*, at para.24.37, recommends that hospital managers should devise a form (or other method) to ensure compliance with this section.

*Subsection (1)*

**1–725**    The test in this provision is not one of mere necessity; the treatment must be *immediately* necessary. The immediacy refers to the need for treatment and not to the consequences that would flow if the treatment was not provided. It follows that depot medication can be given under this provision even though the effect of the treatment is not immediate, i.e. the treatment is immediately required to ensure that the patient's medication level does not drop below the therapeutic dose. As treatment under this section is provided under the authority of s.63, it is for the approved clinician (AC) in charge of the patient's treatment to determine whether the criteria set out in this subsection are satisfied.

SECTIONS 57 AND 58.    As the treatments covered by s.57 are not emergency treatments, it is difficult to envisage the circumstances that would lead a doctor to consider invoking this section in respect of such treatments.

SHALL NOT APPLY.    Which means that the treatment can be given to a detained patient without consent by virtue of the power given to the patient's AC by s.63. As s.63 does not apply to informal patients, the AC must find a justification under the Mental Capacity Act 2005 for proceeding without the patient's consent if he or she plans to give a s.57 treatment to a mentally incapable informal patient in any of the circumstances set out in paras (a) to (d).

TREATMENT. This section provides authorisation for treatment to be given as a response to an immediate crisis. If it is proposed to continue with the treatment thereafter, the procedures set out under ss.57, 58 or s.58A should be observed. "Our view, expressed in the First Biennial Report, remains that where this section is invoked a request should generally simultaneously be made for a second opinion, so that repeated use does not arise" (MHAC, *Second Biennial Report*, 1985–87, para.7.6).

*Subsection (1A)*

See the General Note to s.58A.                                                 **1–726**

*Subsection (2)*

This subsection provides that an existing course of treatment or a plan of treatment can **1–727** continue notwithstanding that the patient has withdrawn his or her consent if the AC considers that discontinuing the treatment or plan of treatment would cause the patient *serious* suffering. It also applies to patients who lose capacity to consent before the completion of the treatment (s.60(1A)) and where the Commission has given a notice under s.61(3). Paragraph 11.4 of the Commission's "Guidance Note for Commissioners on Consent to Treatment and the Mental Health Act 1983" states:

"This power might be used, for example, to provide authority for a plan of treatment to be continued whilst a Second Opinion visit is pending, following the patient's withdrawal of consent or loss of capacity. The reference in this subsection to 'treatment under any plan' allows in these circumstances that the approved clinician may make a single record in the patient's notes evoking the powers of this section, without having to record the use of Section 62 powers at every administration of medication."

SERIOUS SUFFERING. Treatment must cease as soon as its cessation would no longer cause the patient serious suffering.

*Subsection (3)*

Paragraph 6.25 of the White Paper Cmnd. 7320 contains the following definitions of **1–728** "irreversible" and "hazardous" treatments: "irreversible treatments" are "treatments which necessitate the removal or destruction of brain tissue or are designed to effect irreversible change in cerebral or bodily functions"; "hazardous treatments" are "treatments where the risk of adverse reaction or the severity of such reaction would be disproportionate to the degree of benefit the treatment is likely to confer or the prospect of success."

ECT is not regarded as an irreversible treatment.

UNFAVOURABLE. At the Special Standing Committee the Under-Secretary of State cited the removal of a brain tumour and the removal of a diseased thyroid as examples of treatments which are irreversible and which can be reasonably expected to have favourable consequences. (Sitting of June 29, 1982.)

## [Treatment on recall of community patient or revocation of order

**62A.**—(1) This section applies where—                                       **1–729**

(a) a community patient is recalled to hospital under section 17E above; or

(b) a patient is liable to be detained under this Act following the revocation of a community treatment order under section 17F above in respect of him.

(2) For the purposes of section 58(1)(b) above, the patient is to be treated as if he had remained liable to be detained since the making of the community treatment order.

(3) But section 58 above does not apply to treatment given to the patient if—

(a) the certificate requirement is met for the purposes of section 64C or 64E below; or

(b) as a result of section 64B(4) or 64E(4) below, the certificate requirement would not apply (were the patient a community patient not recalled to hospital under section 17E above).

(4) Section 58A above does not apply to treatment given to the patient if there is authority to give the treatment, and the certificate requirement is met, for the purposes of section 64C or 64E below.

(5) In a case where this section applies, the certificate requirement is met only in so far as—

(a) the Part 4A certificate expressly provides that it is appropriate for one or more specified forms of treatment to be given to the patient in that case (subject to such conditions as may be specified); or

(b) a notice having been given under subsection (5) of section 64H below, treatment is authorised by virtue of subsection (8) of that section.

(6) Subsection (5) above shall not preclude the continuation of any treatment, or of treatment under any plan, pending compliance with section 58 or 58A above if the approved clinician in charge of the treatment considers that the discontinuance of the treatment, or of the treatment under the plan, would cause serious suffering to the patient.

(7) In a case where subsection (1)(b) above applies, subsection (3) above only applies pending compliance with section 58 above.

(8) In subsection (5) above—

"Part 4A certificate" has the meaning given in section 64H below; and

"specified", in relation to a Part 4A certificate, means specified in the certificate.]

AMENDMENT

This section was inserted by the Mental Health Act 2007, s.34(4).

DEFINITIONS

1–730     community patient: ss.17A(7), 145(1).
hospital: s.145(1).
patient: ss.56, 145(1).
community treatment order: ss.17A(7), 145(1).
approved clinician: s.145(1).

GENERAL NOTE

1–731     This complex section regulates the treatment of the mental disorders of community patients who have either been recalled to hospital under s.17E, or who have had their community treatment order (CTO) revoked under s.17F (subs.(1)). Subject to the exceptions set out in subs.(3), the treatment of such patients cannot proceed unless it is permitted by this Part. This means that if a certificate under Pt IV was in place before the CTO was made and the certificate covers the patient's current treatment needs and consent status, the certificate remains valid and a fresh certificate will not be required. Note, however, that the *Code of Practice*, at para.24.81, states, without explanation, that it is "not good practice" to rely on such certificates even though they are "technically valid". In the case of administration of medicine, a certificate is not required if "the patient is still within the period before which a certificate is required i.e. either one month has elapsed from the time when the CTO was made [see s.64B(4) and s.64E(4)] or the three month period from when medication was first given to the patient, as provided for in s.58(1)(b) has not elapsed" (Explanatory Notes, para.127). The patient can be treated with medication for his or her mental disorder without formality during this period. For the purpose of calculating the three-month period, patients are to be treated as if they had remained liable to be detained since the making of the CTO (subs.(2)); in other words, the three-month period does not start afresh on the patient's recall.

Under subs.(3), patients who come within the scope of this section will *not* be subject to this Part if the Pt IVA certificate requirement set out in s.64C or 64E is met (subs.(3)(a)). The certificate requirement is met only in so far as:

(i) the certificate expressly provides that it is appropriate for the specified treatment to be given on recall, and giving the treatment would not be contrary to any condition attached to the certificate, or

(ii) although the regulatory body has given notice under s.64H(5) that the treatment must stop, the treatment can continue under s.64H(8) because its discontinuance would cause serious suffering to the patient (subs.(5)).

Unless the Part IVA certificate specifies otherwise, it will authorise the treatment even if the patient has capacity to refuse it. However, the certificate will not provide authority for treatment under s.58A to be given to a patient who has capacity or competence to consent but refuses consent when recalled to hospital or when the CTO is revoked (subs.(4)).

Existing treatment which does not satisfy the certification requirement can be continued, pending compliance with s.58 or s.58A, if the approved clinician in charge of the patient's treatment considers that its discontinuance would cause serious suffering to the patient (subs.(6)). In addition, in cases of urgency the provisions of s.62 or 64G will apply.

If the patient's CTO is revoked, with the patient being once again detained in hospital for treatment, treatment can be given on the authority of a Pt IVA certificate only until a s.58 or s.58A certificate can be arranged (subs.(7)).

The medical treatment of a CTO patient who is admitted to hospital informally is governed by Pt IVA.

*Code of Practice*
The treatment of SCT patients who have been recalled to hospital is considered in Ch.24 at paras 24.28 to 24.31.  **1–732**

*Subsection (6)*
"Subsection (5)" should read "subsection 5(a)".  **1–733**

## Treatment not requiring consent
**63.** The consent of a patient shall not be required for any medical treatment given to him for the mental disorder from which he is suffering[, not being a form of treatment to which section 57, 58 or 58A above applies,] if the treatment is given by or under the direction of the [approved clinician in charge of the treatment].  **1–734**

AMENDMENT
The words in square brackets were substituted by the Mental Health Act 2007 ss.12(6), 28(8).

DEFINITIONS
    patient: ss.56, 145(1).  **1–735**
    medical treatment: s.145(1), (4).
    mental disorder: ss.1, 145(1).
    approved clinician: s.145(1).

GENERAL NOTE

**1–736** This section provides that the consent of a patient to whom this Part applies (see s.56) is not required for treatment which does not fall within ss.57, 58 or s.58A if it is given by or under the direction of the approved clinician in charge of the treatment. It should be noted that this section "does not absolve the doctor of his ordinary duties of care towards his patient, judged on the usual *Bolam/Bolitho* principles" (*R. (on the application of Wilkinson) v The Responsible Medical Officer Broadmoor Hospital* [2001] EWCA Civ 1545; [2002] 1 W.L.R. 419 per Hale L.J. at para.68).

The Minister for Health's response to the argument that detained patients should not be forced to receive treatment is contained in the following passage from his speech to the Special Standing Committee:

"[That argument would] lead us to conclude that those who were forcibly detained and had lost their liberty against their will ... should be kept in custody in places in which they received no treatment despite the fact that those who looked after them would have to gaze on them knowing perfectly well that some treatment could be given to alleviate their suffering and distress and enable them eventually to recover their liberty. Hospitals are places of treatment and we cannot have hospitals in which people are locked up and left to wander about without receiving treatment" (sitting of June 29, 1982).

The Government's response to the criticism that this provision might authorise a disturbingly wide range of interventions was given by Lord Elton, who emphasised that it was not intended to apply to "borderline" or "experimental" treatments, but to "things which a person in hospital for treatment ought to undergo for his own good and for the good of the running of the hospital and for the good of other patients ... perfectly routine, sensible treatment"(*Hansard* H.L. Vol.426, col.107).

There is no statutory form for treatments given under the authority of this section.

*Human Rights Act 1998*

**1–737** In *B v Croydon Health Authority*, below, counsel for the patient submitted that if the meaning of "medical treatment for ... mental disorder" was wide enough to include ancillary forms of treatment, this section would involve a breach of art.8 of the European Convention on Human Rights. He referred to *Herczegfalvy v Austria* (1993) 15 E.H.R.R. 437 at 485 where the European Court of Human Rights said that a measure constituting an interference with private life and therefore prima facie contrary to art.8(1) (like involuntary tube feeding) can only be justified under art.8(2) if, among the other requirements of that article, its terms are sufficiently precise to enable the individual "to foresee its consequences for him". The Court confirmed that this requirement is necessary to prevent such measures from being a source of arbitrary power, contrary to the rule of law. In rejecting counsel's submission, Hoffmann L.J. said at 688: "In my judgment section 63 amply satisfies this test. There is no conceptual vagueness about the notion of treating the symptoms or consequences of a mental disorder, although naturally there will be borderline cases. But there is no question of exercise of arbitrary power".

In the Scottish case of *Petition of WM*, Outer House, Court of Session [2002] M.H.L.R. 367, Lord Eassie rejected the petitioner's contention that s.103 of the Mental Health (Scotland) Act 1984 (which in all material respects replicates this section) contravenes art.8. The grounds for the contention were (a) the scope of the section was broader than necessary in a democratic society and incorporated apparently arbitrary limits, and (b) the section lacked appropriate procedural safeguards.

Neither art.3 nor art.8 of the Convention would be breached if forcible treatment is given to a mentally incompetent detained patient in a situation where, "according to the psychiatric principles generally accepted at the time, medical necessity justified the treatment in issue" (*Herczegfalvy v Austria*, above, paras 83, 86). The approach that the domestic courts adopt when determining whether such treatment breaches either article is considered in the note on s.58 under this heading.

*Mental Capacity Act 2005*
See the General Note to this Part.                                                    **1–738**

CONSENT ... SHALL NOT BE REQUIRED.   Although treatments which do not come within ss.57, 58 or 58A may be given to a patient without his consent, "in practice it is impossible to undertake many of the therapies concerned without a patient's co-operation" (Cmnd. 8405, para.37).

MEDICAL TREATMENT ... FOR THE MENTAL DISORDER.   Also see the definition of "medical treatment" in s.145(1). The leading case on the meaning of this phrase is *B v Croydon Health Authority* [1995] 1 All E.R. 683, where the Court of Appeal held that:

(i)  a range of acts ancillary to the core treatment that the patient is receiving fall within the term "medical treatment" as defined in s.145(1);

(ii)  treatment is capable of being ancillary to the core treatment if it is nursing and care "concurrent with the core treatment or as a necessary prerequisite to such treatment or to prevent the patient from causing harm to himself or to alleviate the consequences of the disorder ... " (*per* Hoffmann L.J. at 687);

(iii)  relieving the symptoms of the mental disorder is just as much a part of treatment as relieving its underlying cause. (NB This finding is reflected in s.145(4) which was inserted by the 2007 Act.); and

(iv)  treatment for a physical disorder will not amount to a treatment for a mental disorder where the treatment for the physical disorder is entirely unconnected with the pre-existing mental disorder.

Applying these findings to the case before it, the Court of Appeal held that the feeding by nasogastric tube of a patient who was suffering from borderline personality disorder was treatment which fell within the scope of this section because such treatment was aimed at treating a symptom of the disorder which was a refusal to eat in order to inflict self harm. The nasogastric feeding of a patient suffering from anorexia nervosa also comes within the scope of this section (*Re KB* [1997] 2 F.L.R. 180). Although Douglas Brown J. suggested in *Re VS (Adult: Mental Disorder)* (1995) 3 Med.L.Rev. 292 that cases involving force-feeding under this section should routinely be brought before the court for consideration, it is submitted that such action should only be taken if there is uncertainty about the application of this section to a particular case or if the case is controversial. In *R. v Collins and Ashworth Hospital Authority Ex p. Brady* [2000] M.H.L.R. 17, Kay J., held that as the patient's hunger strike was a manifestation or symptom of his personality disorder, the force feeding of the patient came within this section because it constituted a form of treatment for his disorder. David Pannick Q.C., in his comment on this case, said that "it is a considerable expansion of the s.63 principle to bring within its scope a person who would prefer to die rather than submit to control by those detaining him" ("State should not go out of its way to keep Brady alive", *The Times*, March 14, 2000). A similar finding in a case where the patient's refusal to eat was a form of self-harm and the consequence of malnourishment had a deleterious effect on her mental health was made by the High Court, Northern Ireland, in *Application by JR18 for Judicial Review* [2007] NIQB 104; [2008] M.H.L.R. 50.

The decision in the *Croydon* case brings the monitoring of the blood of a patient who is being treated with Clozapine within the definition of treatment for mental disorder for the purposes of this section because such monitoring is clearly ancillary to the core treatment which is the administration of Clozapine. Treatment under this section also includes medical and surgical treatment for the physical consequences of self-poisoning or self-injury if the self-poisoning or self-injury can be categorised as either the consequence of or a symptom of the patient's mental disorder. In the *Croydon* case, Hoffmann L.J. said at 687,688:

> "It would seem strange to me if a hospital could, without the patient's consent, give him treatment directed to alleviating a psychopathic disorder showing itself in suicidal tendencies, but not without such consent be able to treat the consequences of the suicide attempt".

The *Croydon* ruling would also include treatment that was required to prevent a patient with assessed suicidal tendencies from attempting to commit suicide and treatments, such as nursing care, to respond to self neglect where such neglect is a manifestation of the patient's mental disorder. Treatments which are given to respond to the side effects of the patient's core treatment for his or her mental disorder also come within the scope of this section, e.g. antiparkinsonian agents used to alleviate the motor side effects of anti-psychotic medication. When coming to a judgment as to which treatments fall into this category, the Mental Health Act Commission (MHAC) sought "to distinguish between ancillary treatments that are an essential adjunct to the core treatment, without which the latter could not reasonably be given, and treatments of more widespread physical complaints that may or may not be related to the core treatment" (Psychiatric Bulletin (2008) 32:358).

In *R. (on the application of Munjaz) v Mersey Care National Health Service Trust* [2005] UKHL 58; [2005] M.H.L.R. 276 at para.67, Lord Hope said that the seclusion of a patient "falls within the scope of the phrase 'the medical treatment of patients suffering from mental disorder' set out in s.118(1)(b)". This statement confirms the finding of the Court of Appeal in this case that seclusion is "medical treatment" for the purposes of this section: see [2003] EWCA Civ 1036; [2003] M.H.L.R. 362. In the House of Lords, Lord Bingham said, at para.19, that the definition of "medical treatment" in s.145(1) is "wide enough to cover the nursing and caring of a patient in seclusion, even though seclusion cannot properly form part of a treatment programme." This finding is not affected by the amendment made to s.145(1) by the 2007 Act.

Deep-brain stimulation (i.e. the implantation of electrodes in the brain that are activated by the patient through an external stimulator) comes within the scope of this section if the procedure is used to treat the patient's mental disorder and it does not involves an operation for the destruction of brain tissue or function, in which case it will come within the scope of s.57; see further, the *Tenth Biennial Report* 2001–2003 of the Mental Health Act Commission at paras 10.65–10.69 and the MHAC's *Eleventh Biennial Report 2003–2005* at paras 4.83–4.86.

The fact that a remedy can be bought in the High Street does not prevent it from being a medical treatment for the purposes of this section. Such treatments would include St John's Wort prescribed for mild to moderate depression and fish oils prescribed to enhance the efficacy of anti-psychotic drugs; see further, MHAC, *Twelfth Biennial Report* 2005–2005 paras 6.49–6.54.

If a patient's refusal to pay attention to his or her personal hygiene or to be treated for a physical condition is assessed as being a manifestation or symptom of the patient's mental disorder, the patient can be washed or treated under the authority of the *Croydon* case. If a non-detained patient is mentally incapable of making decisions about such matters, intervention must be justified under the Mental Capacity Act 2005.

Enquiries made to a third party about either the patient's diagnosis or treatment are enquiries made with a view to treatment and do not themselves constitute treatment: see *R. (on the application of O'Reilly) v Blenheim Healthcare Ltd* [2005] EWHC 241 (Admin) where Stanley Burnton J. said, at para.14, that it "does not follow from [the judgment in *Croydon*] that acts carried out for the purposes of treatment, or with a view to deciding on treatment, are themselves treatment."

The *Croydon* case was applied by Wall J. in *Tameside and Glossop Acute Services Trust v CH* [1996] 1 F.L.R. 762, where a pregnant patient who was suffering from schizophrenia had been detained under s.3 of this Act. She had the delusional belief that the doctors who were caring for her wished to harm her baby. The baby was not developing well and the obstetrician took the view that if the pregnancy was allowed to continue the baby might die in the womb. For that reason the obstetrician wished to induce labour and, if necessary, perform a caesarean section. The trust sought a declaration that it would be lawful to carry out such treatment without the patient's consent and to use any necessary force to restrain her in order to facilitate the treatment. Wall J. held, at 773, that there were "several strands in the evidence" which brought the proposed treatment within the scope of this section:

"First, there is the proposition that an ancillary reason for the induction and, if necessary, the birth by caesarean section is to prevent a deterioration in the [patient's] mental state. Secondly, there is the clear evidence of [the patient's psychiatrist] that in order for the treatment of her schizophrenia to be effective, it is necessary for her to give birth to a live baby. Thirdly, the overall structure of her treatment requires her to receive strong anti-psychotic medication. The administration of that treatment has been necessarily interrupted by her pregnancy and cannot be resumed until her child is born. It is not, therefore, I think stretching language unduly to say that achievement of a successful outcome of her pregnancy is a necessary part of the overall treatment of her mental disorder."

His Lordship granted the declaration sought, distinguishing *Re C (Adult: Refusal of* **1–739** *Medical Treatment)* [1994] 1 All E.R. 819 where a schizophrenic patient was held to have the mental capacity to refuse treatment for gangrene which was considered to be life threatening, on the ground that "C's gangrene was not likely to affect his mental condition: the manner in which the delivery of the [patient's] child is treated is likely to have a direct effect on her mental state". As the patient's pregnancy was neither a symptom nor a consequence of her mental disorder, this finding appears to allow a doctor to claim that the treatment of a condition which has no apparent connection with the patient's mental disorder comes within the scope of this section if such treatment will either enhance, or prevent a deterioration of, the patient's mental condition. Although it has been said that the decision of the Court of Appeal in *St George's Healthcare NHS Trust v S* [1998] 3 All E.R. 673 (where it was held that a patient's need for treatment for an unrelated physical disorder does not provide the necessary warrant for detention) would result in the *Tameside* case not being followed in future (see L. Jewell, "Treatment Without Consent" [1998] Fam. Law 774), this case did not overrule *Tameside* or subject the notion of "ancillary treatment" to analysis. In the *St George's* case, *B v Croydon Health Authority* was cited as authority for the proposition that this section "may apply to the treatment of any condition which is integral to the mental disorder" (per Judge L.J. at 693). As the treatment of a condition that is "a necessary part of the overall treatment of [the] mental disorder" (see Wall J., above) is treatment which is "integral to the mental disorder", the judgments in the *St George's* and *Tameside* cases would appear to be compatible.

The reason why a declaration was sought in the *Tameside* case was the fact that the obstetrician might have had to use force on the patient. Wall J. held that it was permissible, should the doctor deem it to be clinically necessary, to use restraint to the extent to which it may be reasonably required in order to achieve the delivery by the patient of a healthy baby. It is therefore lawful for doctors and nurses to use restraint, so far as reasonably required and clinically necessary, to administer treatment under this section. His Lordship agreed, at 774, with counsel's proposition that "in cases in which the question of restraint arose or was likely to arise, and the doctor was doubtful about the lawfulness of the application of restraint or the use of force, an application should be made to the court for a declaration that the treatment would be lawful". In *R. (on the application of Wilkinson) v The Responsible Medical Officer Broadmoor Hospital*, above, Hale L.J.

said, at para.64, that where a mentally incapacitated patient is "actively opposed to a course of action, the benefits which it holds for him will have to be carefully weighed against the disadvantages of going against his wishes, especially if force is required to do this". It is submitted that these remarks, which were concerned with the application of the "best interests" test under common law, are equally applicable to the situation of a detained patient, irrespective of patient's mental capacity.

Treatment for a physical disorder that is not related to the patient's mental disorder in that it would not impact on that disorder does not come within the scope of this section even if the refusal of treatment is caused by the mental disorder (*GJ v Foundation Trust* [2009] EWHC 2972 (Fam)). Such treatment can be provided if the patient is deprived of her capacity to decide for herself, in which case the treatment would be authorised under ss.5 and 6 of the Mental Capacity Act 2005 (*St George's Healthcare NHS Trust v S*, above). It would be unlawful to treat a person under this Act in a situation where the patient's physical disorder was giving rise to symptoms that effected the patient's mental state unless those symptoms could be categorised as constituting a mental disorder.

## Supplementary provisions for Part IV

1–740    **64.**—(1) In this Part of this Act ["the responsible clinician" means the approved clinician with overall responsibility for the case] of the patient in question and "hospital" includes a [registered establishment].

[(1A) References in this Part of this Act to the approved clinician in charge of a patient's treatment shall, where the treatment in question is a form of treatment to which section 57 above applies, be construed as references to the person in charge of the treatment.]

[(1B) References in this Part of this Act to the approved clinician in charge of a patient's treatment shall, where the treatment in question is a form of treatment to which section 58A above applies and the patient falls within section 56(5) above, be construed as references to the person in charge of the treatment.

(1C) Regulations made by virtue of section 32(2)(d) above apply for the purposes of this Part as they apply for the purposes of Part 2 of this Act.]

(2) Any certificate for the purposes of this Part of this Act shall be in such form as may be prescribed by regulations made by the Secretary of State.

[(3) For the purposes of this Part of this Act, it is appropriate for treatment to be given to a patient if the treatment is appropriate in his case, taking into account the nature and degree of the mental disorder from which he is suffering and all other circumstances of his case.]

AMENDMENT

The words in square brackets in subs.(1) were substituted by the Care Standards Act 2000 s.116, Sch.4 para.9(2). The other amendments to this section were made by the Mental Health Act 2007 ss.6(3), 12(7), 28(9).

DEFINITIONS

1–741    approved clinician: s.145(1).
patient: s.145(1).
hospital: s.145(1).
registered establishment: ss.34(1), 145(1).

GENERAL NOTE

*Subsection (1)*

1–742    RESPONSIBLE CLINICIAN.   See the note on s.34(1).

APPROVED CLINICIAN IN CHARGE OF A PATIENT'S TREATMENT. This clinician will not be subject to the supervision of another clinician in respect of the provision of the treatment in question. The Reference Guide states at para.16.10:

"Where a patient has a responsible clinician in overall charge of their case, the responsible clinician need not be in charge of any particular form of treatment. There may be different clinicians in charge of different forms of treatment."

Any dispute between the RC and the AC concerning, the medical treatment of the patient that cannot be resolved through discussion would have to be referred to the hospital management for resolution.

*Subsection (2)*
SECRETARY OF STATE. Or, in relation to Wales, the Welsh Ministers (see the General **1–743** Note to this Act and SI 1999/672 art.2, Sch.1).

SUBSECTION (3)
Note the circularity of this definition. Also the notes on s.3(2)(d).                    **1–744**

## [PART 4A

## TREATMENT OF COMMUNITY PATIENTS NOT RECALLED TO HOSPITAL]

GENERAL NOTE
This Part authorises the provision of "relevant treatment" to either a mentally capable or **1–745** mentally incapable community patient who has not been recalled to hospital. Such patients can only be given treatment if they consent or, if they lack the capacity to consent, do not actively object. The medical treatment of community patients who have been recalled to hospital is governed by s.62A.
There is no requirement for the treatment provided under this Part to be given in a clinical setting.

*Code of Practice*
Guidance on this Part is contained in Ch.23 and in Ch.24 at paras 24.25–24.27. The role **1–746** of second opinion appointed doctors (SOADs) is considered in Ch.24 at paras 24.38 et seq.

## [Meaning of "relevant treatment"
**64A.**—In this Part of this Act "relevant treatment", in relation to a patient, **1–747** means medical treatment which—
   (a) is for the mental disorder from which the patient is suffering; and
   (b) is not a form of treatment to which section 57 above applies.]

AMENDMENT
This section was inserted by the Mental Health Act 2007 s.35(1).

DEFINITIONS
   medical treatment; s.145(1), (4).                                                     **1–748**
   mental disorder: ss.1, 145(1).
   patient: s.145(1).

GENERAL NOTE

1–749    The meaning of the phrase "medical treatment . . . for the mental disorder" was explained by the Court of Appeal in *B v Croydon Health Authority* [1995] 1 All E.R. 683 which is considered in the note on s.63.

Section 57 treatments are regulated by the requirements of that section which apply to "any patient" receiving such treatment (s.56(1)).

## [Adult community patients

1–750    **64B.**—(1) This section applies to the giving of relevant treatment to a community patient who—

(a)  is not recalled to hospital under section 17E above; and

(b)  has attained the age of 16 years.

(2) The treatment may not be given to the patient unless—

(a)  there is authority to give it to him; and

(b)  if it is section 58 type treatment or section 58A type treatment, the certificate requirement is met.

(3) But the certificate requirement does not apply if—

(a)  giving the treatment to the patient is authorised in accordance with section 64G below; or

(b)  the treatment is immediately necessary and—

(i)  the patient has capacity to consent to it and does consent to it; or

(ii)  a donee or deputy or the Court of Protection consents to the treatment on the patient's behalf.

(4) Nor does the certificate requirement apply in so far as the administration of medicine to the patient at any time during the period of one month beginning with the day on which the community treatment order is made is section 58 type treatment.

(5) The reference in subsection (4) above to the administration of medicine does not include any form of treatment specified under section 58(1)(a) above.]

AMENDMENT

This section was inserted by the Mental Health Act 2007 s.35(1).

DEFINITION

1–751    community patient: ss.17A(7), 145(1).

GENERAL NOTE

1–752    This section and s.64C provide authority to treat a community patient who is over the age of 16 if there is authority to give it to him or her because either the patient has capacity and consents to the treatment (even the emergency treatment of such patients requires their consent), or a donee or a deputy or the Court of Protection consents to it on his or her behalf, or it is authorised under s.64D (treatment for patients who lack capacity) or 64G (emergency treatment for patients who lack capacity) (subs.(2)(a) and s.64C(2)) and, if it is a treatment coming within the scope of s.58 or 58A, the certificate requirement is met in that a SOAD has certified that the treatment (or a plan of treatment (s.64H(1)) should be given to the patient (subs.(2)(b) and s.64C(4)). The certificate requirement does *not* apply if the treatment:

(i)  is emergency treatment given to a mentally incapacitated patient which is authorised under s.64G (subs.(3)(a)), or

(ii) is immediately necessary (see s.64C(5)–(7)) and either the patient has the capacity to consent to it and does consent to it or a donee or a deputy of a mentally incapacitated patient consents to the treatment on his or her behalf (subs.(3)(b)), or

(iii) is medication coming within the scope of s.58(1)(b) and the medication is being given to the patient within a month of the CTO being made (subss.(4), (5)) or three months from when the medication was first given to the patient (whether in the community or in hospital), whichever is later.

The situations set out in paras.(i) and (ii) allow for treatment to continue pending a SOAD visit after the one or three-month period set out in para.(iii) has elapsed, as long as the relevant criteria are satisfied.

If a certificate is withdrawn by the regulatory authority, the treatment can continue pending compliance with the this section if the person in charge of the treatment considers that the discontinuance of the treatment would cause serious suffering to the patient (s.64H(5)–(9)).

Where treatment has been given on the basis of a Pt IVA certificate, the person in charge of the treatment must send the regulatory authority a report on the treatment and the patient's condition if required by that authority (s.64H(4)).

*Subsection (1)*
RELEVANT TREATMENT.   See s.64C(3).                                                     **1–753**

HOSPITAL.   See s.64K(7).

*Subsection (2)(a)*
See s.64C(2).                                                                           **1–754**

*Subsection (2)(b)*
The meaning of a "section 58 type treatment or section 58A type treatment" is explained **1–755** in s.64C(3).

CERTIFICATE REQUIREMENT.   See s.64C(4).                                                **1–756**

*Subsection (3)(b)*
IMMEDIATELY NECESSARY.   See s.64C(5) to (9) and reg.28(2) of the English Regulations and reg.39(a) of the Welsh Regulations.

CAPACITY TO CONSENT.   See s.64K(2). The emergency treatment of patients who lack capacity or competence is governed by s.64G.

DONEE; DEPUTY.   The decision must be within the scope of the authority of the donee or deputy: see s.64K(4), (5).

*Subsection (4)*
PERIOD OF ONE MONTH.   The certificate requirement also does not apply during the **1–757** period of three months from the date when the medication was first given to the patient: see the note on s.64C(4). The SOAD certificate is required from the later of the two periods.

## [Section 64B: supplemental

**64C.**—(1) This section has effect for the purposes of section 64B above.         **1–758**

(2) There is authority to give treatment to a patient if—

(a) he has capacity to consent to it and does consent to it;

(b) a donee or deputy or the Court of Protection consents to it on his behalf; or

(c) giving it to him is authorised in accordance with section 64D or 64G below.

(3) Relevant treatment is section 58 type treatment or section 58A type treatment if, at the time when it is given to the patient, section 58 or 58A above (respectively) would have applied to it, had the patient remained liable to be detained at that time (rather than being a community patient).

(4) The certificate requirement is met in respect of treatment to be given to a patient if—

(a) a registered medical practitioner appointed for the purposes of Part 4 of this Act (not being the responsible clinician or the person in charge of the treatment) has certified in writing that it is appropriate for the treatment to be given or for the treatment to be given subject to such conditions as may be specified in the certificate; and

(b) if conditions are so specified, the conditions are satisfied.

(5) In a case where the treatment is section 58 type treatment, treatment is immediately necessary if—

(a) it is immediately necessary to save the patient's life; or

(b) it is immediately necessary to prevent a serious deterioration of the patient's condition and is not irreversible; or

(c) it is immediately necessary to alleviate serious suffering by the patient and is not irreversible or hazardous; or

(d) it is immediately necessary, represents the minimum interference necessary to prevent the patient from behaving violently or being a danger to himself or others and is not irreversible or hazardous.

(6) In a case where the treatment is section 58A type treatment by virtue of subsection (1)(a) of that section, treatment is immediately necessary if it falls within paragraph (a) or (b) of subsection (5) above.

(7) In a case where the treatment is section 58A type treatment by virtue of subsection (1)(b) of that section, treatment is immediately necessary if it falls within such of paragraphs (a) to (d) of subsection (5) above as may be specified in regulations under that section.

(8) For the purposes of subsection (7) above, the regulations—

(a) may make different provision for different cases (and may, in particular, make different provision for different forms of treatment);

(b) may make provision which applies subject to specified exceptions; and

(c) may include transitional, consequential, incidental or supplemental provision.

(9) Subsection (3) of section 62 above applies for the purposes of this section as it applies for the purposes of that section.]

AMENDMENT
This section was inserted by the Mental Health Act 2007 s.35(1).

DEFINITIONS
**1–759**    patient: s.145(1).
responsible clinician: ss.34(1), 64K(6).

*Subsection (2)(a)*
**1–760**    If the patient has fluctuating capacity, capacity should be regularly re-assessed. With the exception of s.58A treatments, a mentally capable patient may only be treated without consent on being recalled to hospital (s.62A).

*Subsection (2)(b)*

If a valid consent has been given by a donee or deputy or the Court of Protection (i.e. the consent is valid in that the donee or deputy have the authority to make such a decision (s.64(4),(5))) the treatment may be given despite the objections of the incapacitated patient. The donee, deputy and the court have an obligation to act in the best interests of the patient: see ss.4 and 16(3) of the 2005 Act. **1–761**

*Subsection (4)*

The Explanatory Notes state at para.133: **1–762**

"All community patients receiving the type of treatment which falls under s.58 or 58A of the 1983 Act must have that treatment certified by a SOAD in accordance with the provisions of Part IVA. For treatment specified in s.58(1)(b), i.e. medication, a certificate is not required immediately, but must be in place after a certain period. This period is one month from when a patient leaves hospital or three months from when the medication was first given to the patient (whether that medication was given in the community or in hospital), whichever is later. The SOAD must certify in writing that it is appropriate for the treatment to be given".

The one month period is specified in s.64B(4). The legal rationale for the alternative period of three months from when the medication was first given is that during that period the provision of medication is not a "section 58 type treatment" (see subs.(3)) as that section would not have applied to it during that period.

A certificate for a s.58A type treatment is required immediately before the treatment is started.

CERTIFIED IN WRITING. Although the *Code of Practice*, at para.24.43, states that the SOAD should "interview the patient in private if possible", interviewing the patient is not a legal requirement. Therefore, a SOAD can give a certificate if the patient is unwilling to be interviewed. Before giving a certificate, the SOAD must undertake the consultation exercise provided for in s.64H(3). Form CTO11: see reg.28(1) of the English Regulations (in Wales, Form CO7: see reg.40(4) of the Welsh Regulations) must be used. The SOAD's role when completing the Form is confined to considering whether it would be appropriate for the treatment to be given to the patient. In other words, the SOAD is not required to confirm the patient's consent to the treatment as the two conditions set out in s.64B(2) are not dependent on each other. This interpretation is supported by the following advice that the Mental Health Act Commission (MHAC) received from the Department of Health which is reproduced in the Commission's *Thirteenth Biennial Report* 2007-2009, at para.3.73:

"'Appropriateness' does not include [legal] authority. The Act itself provides that treatment cannot lawfully be given unless there is authority to do so, and sets out when such authority will exist. So it is not necessary . . . for SOADs to concern themselves with the question of whether there would be authority to give the treatment. So, in effect, the SOAD is required to consider whether it would be appropriate for the treatment to be given, assuming there were legal authority to give it."

The MHAC, having considered relevant extracts from the *Code of Practice,* took the view that:

"making a clinical judgment about the appropriateness of treatment cannot be undertaken without at least talking to the patient about their consent and taking that information into account as appropriate. . . . If a SOAD certifies that treatment with medication for mental disorder 'is appropriate' at the point when an SCT patient refuses consent to it, that SOAD is in effect stating that the treatment will be appropriate at some future date when the patient's consent or capacity circumstances have changed" ("Second Opinions for Supervised Community Treatment patients who are refusing medication for mental disorder", Jan. 2009, p.4; also see the Commission's *Thirteenth Biennial Report* 2007–2009, at paras 3.76 to 3.83.).

The fact that a patient who is subject to a community treatment order does not consent to treatment that is deemed to be appropriate for him or her suggests that long term s.17 leave would be the more appropriate option: see the *Code of Practice* at para.28.6.

CONDITIONS.    See para.24.27 of the *Code of Practice*. The Explanatory Notes state at para.134:

"The SOAD may specify within the certificate that certain treatment can be given to the patient only if certain conditions are satisfied: so, for example, the SOAD could specify that a particular antipsychotic and dosage can only be given in the community if the patient retains capacity to consent to it. The SOAD can also specify whether and if so what treatments can be given to the patient on recall to hospital and the circumstances in which the treatment can be given. For example, the SOAD can specify, if appropriate, that an antipsychotic can be given to the patient on recall without the patient's consent."

The MHAC urged "SOADs to take particular care when considering the exercise of this power, and to be mindful that an SCT patient's recall to hospital may take place long after the certificate is issued under quite different circumstances than the SOAD encounters during the second opinion visit" ("Guidance for SOADs", 2008, p.8). Also see the *Code of Practice* at para.24.30.

If the certificate specifies conditions, the treatment may only be given in accordance with those conditions.

*Subsection (4)(a)*

**1–763**    APPROPRIATE FOR THE TREATMENT TO BE GIVEN.    See ss.64K(8) and 64(3).

*Subsection (5)*

**1–764**    In this provision, the immediacy refers to the need for treatment and not to the consequences that would flow if the treatment was not provided.

*Subsection (6)*

**1–765**    Treatment under this provision can be given to a mentally incapacitated patient even though the patient has made an advance decision refusing ECT.

*Subsection (9)*

**1–766**    Section 62(3) defines "irreversible" and "hazardous".

## [Adult community patients lacking capacity

**1–767**    **64D.**—(1) A person is authorised to give relevant treatment to a patient as mentioned in section 64C(2)(c) above if the conditions in subsections (2) to (6) below are met.

(2) The first condition is that, before giving the treatment, the person takes reasonable steps to establish whether the patient lacks capacity to consent to the treatment.

(3) The second condition is that, when giving the treatment, he reasonably believes that the patient lacks capacity to consent to it.

(4) The third condition is that—

(a) he has no reason to believe that the patient objects to being given the treatment; or

(b) he does have reason to believe that the patient so objects, but it is not necessary to use force against the patient in order to give the treatment.

(5) The fourth condition is that—

(a) he is the person in charge of the treatment and an approved clinician; or

(b) the treatment is given under the direction of that clinician.

(6) The fifth condition is that giving the treatment does not conflict with—

(a) an advance decision which he is satisfied is valid and applicable; or

(b) a decision made by a donee or deputy or the Court of Protection.

(7) In this section—

(a) reference to an advance decision is to an advance decision (within the meaning of the Mental Capacity Act 2005) made by the patient; and

(b) "valid and applicable", in relation to such a decision, means valid and applicable to the treatment in question in accordance with section 25 of that Act.]

AMENDMENT
This section was inserted by the Mental Health Act 2007 s.35(1).

DEFINITIONS
relevant treatment: s.64A.  **1–768**
patient: s.145(1).

GENERAL NOTE
This section sets out the conditions that must be satisfied before relevant treatment (see **1–769** s.64A) can be provided to a community patient who lacks the capacity to consent to the treatment. It provides authority to give treatment to the patient for the purposes of ss.64B(2)(a): see 64C(2)(c). The treatment cannot be given if force would have to be used to ensure that an objecting patient received the treatment (subs.(4); but force can be used in an emergency (s.64G)), or if it conflicts with a valid and applicable advance decision made under the Mental Capacity Act or a decision made by a donee, a deputy or the Court of Protection (subs.(6)).

Nothing in this section excludes a person's liabilities resulting from his or her negligence in undertaking anything authorised to be done under it (s.64I).

*Subsection (2)*
The capacity of the patient to consent to the treatment should be assessed using the tests **1–770** set out in ss.2 and 3 of the Mental Capacity Act 2005 (s.64K(2)).

*Subsection (4)*
The factors to be considered in determining whether a patient objects to the treatment are **1–771** set out in s.64J. If the patient does not object to the treatment, the use of force, which is not defined, is permitted under this section "in cases where, for example, the patient is suffering from tremor and physical force is needed as a practical measure to administer the treatment" (Explanatory Notes, para.130).

Force. The Mental Capacity Act 2005, s.6, uses the term "restraint".

*Subsection (5)(b)*
The patient's GP can only prescribe medication for the patient's mental disorder if it is **1–772** covered by the SOAD certificate or if a donee or deputy has consented to the medication on the patient's behalf.

*Subsection (6)*

**1–773**     Under the terms of the Mental Capacity Act 2005 a person who is under the age of 18 cannot make an advance decision or execute a lasting power of attorney.

ADVANCE DECISION.     See subs.(7).

DONEE OR DEPUTY.     The decision must be within the scope of the authority of the donee or deputy: See s.64K(4), (5).

## [Child community patients

**1–774**     **64E.**—(1) This section applies to the giving of relevant treatment to a community patient who—

  (a)  is not recalled to hospital under section 17E above; and

  (b)  has not attained the age of 16 years.

  (2) The treatment may not be given to the patient unless—

  (a)  there is authority to give it to him; and

  (b)  if it is section 58 type treatment or section 58A type treatment, the certificate requirement is met.

  (3) But the certificate requirement does not apply if—

  (a)  giving the treatment to the patient is authorised in accordance with section 64G below; or

  (b)  in a case where the patient is competent to consent to the treatment and does consent to it, the treatment is immediately necessary.

  (4) Nor does the certificate requirement apply in so far as the administration of medicine to the patient at any time during the period of one month beginning with the day on which the community treatment order is made is section 58 type treatment.

  (5) The reference in subsection (4) above to the administration of medicine does not include any form of treatment specified under section 58(1)(a) above.

  (6) For the purposes of subsection (2)(a) above, there is authority to give treatment to a patient if—

  (a)  he is competent to consent to it and he does consent to it; or

  (b)  giving it to him is authorised in accordance with section 64F or 64G below.

  (7) Subsections (3) to (9) of section 64C above have effect for the purposes of this section as they have effect for the purposes of section 64B above.

  (8) Regulations made by virtue of section 32(2)(d) above apply for the purposes of this section as they apply for the purposes of Part 2 of this Act.]

AMENDMENT
This section was inserted by the Mental Health Act 2007 s.35(1).

DEFINITIONS
**1–775**     relevant treatment: s.64A.
community patient: ss.17A(7), 145(1).
hospital: s.64K(7).

GENERAL NOTE
**1–776**     This section identifies when relevant treatment (see s.64A) can be provided to a community patient who is under the age of 16 and who has not been recalled to hospital under s.17E. Such treatment cannot be provided to the patient unless he or she is competent to consent to it and does consent to it, or the giving of the treatment is authorised by s.64F (treatment for child patients lacking competence) or s.64G (emergency treatment for child

patients lacking competence) (subss.(2)(a),(6)) and, if it is a treatment coming within the scope of s.58 or s.58A, the certificate requirement is met in that a SOAD has certified that the treatment (or plan of treatment (s.64H(1)) should be given (subss.(2)(b), (7) and s.64C(4)). The certificate requirement does not apply if the treatment:

(i)  is emergency treatment which is authorised under s.64G (subs.(3)(a)), or

(ii)  is immediately necessary (subss.(3)(b), (7), s.64C(5), (6)), or

(iii)  is medication coming within the scope of s.58(1)(b) and the medication is being given to the patient within a month of the CTO being made (subss.(4), (5)) or three months from when the medication was first given to the patient (whether in the community or in hospital), whichever is later.

A certificate for a s.58A type treatment is required immediately before the treatment is started.

If a certificate is withdrawn by the regulatory authority, the treatment can continue pending compliance with the this section if the person in charge of the treatment considers that the discontinuance of the treatment would cause serious suffering to the patient (s.64H(5)–(9)).

A parent (or another person with parental responsibility) cannot either consent to or refuse treatment for mental disorder on behalf of a child who is subject to a CTO.

*Subsection (2)*
The meaning of "section 58 type treatment or section 58A type treatment" is explained **1–777** in s.64C(3) (subs.(7)).

*Subsection (3)(b)*
IMMEDIATELY NECESSARY.   See reg.28(2) of the English Regulations and reg.39(a) of **1–778** the Welsh Regulations.

## [Child community patients lacking competence

**64F.**—(1) A person is authorised to give relevant treatment to a patient as men- **1–779** tioned in section 64E(6)(b) above if the conditions in subsections (2) to (5) below are met.

(2) The first condition is that, before giving the treatment, the person takes reasonable steps to establish whether the patient is competent to consent to the treatment.

(3) The second condition is that, when giving the treatment, he reasonably believes that the patient is not competent to consent to it.

(4) The third condition is that—
(a) he has no reason to believe that the patient objects to being given the treatment; or
(b) he does have reason to believe that the patient so objects, but it is not necessary to use force against the patient in order to give the treatment.

(5) The fourth condition is that—
(a) he is the person in charge of the treatment and an approved clinician; or
(b) the treatment is given under the direction of that clinician.]

AMENDMENT
This section was inserted by the Mental Health Act 2007 s.35(1).

DEFINITION
    patient: s.145(1).                                                      **1–780**

GENERAL NOTE

**1–781**   This section sets out the conditions that must be satisfied before relevant treatment (see s.64A) can be provided to a community patient who is under the age of 16 and who lacks the competence to consent to the treatment. Children lack competence (the equivalent of "capacity" for adults) if they do not have sufficient understanding and intelligence to enable them fully to understand what is involved in a proposed treatment. The treatment cannot be given if force would have to be used to ensure that an objecting patient received the treatment (subs.(4); but force can be used in an emergency (s.64G)). As is the case with capacious adults, treatment cannot be given to a child in the community who is competent to consent and does not consent to it.

A person with parental responsibility for a child patient may not consent on the child's behalf to treatment for mental disorder (or refuse it) while the child is a community patient.

Nothing in this section excludes a person's liabilities resulting from his or her negligence in undertaking anything authorised to be done under it (s.64I).

*Subsection (4)*

**1–782**   The factors to be considered in determining whether a patient objects to the treatment are set out in s.64J.

## [Emergency treatment for patients lacking capacity or competence

**1–783**   **64G.**—(1) A person is also authorised to give relevant treatment to a patient as mentioned in section 64C(2)(c) or 64E(6)(b) above if the conditions in subsections (2) to (4) below are met.

(2) The first condition is that, when giving the treatment, the person reasonably believes that the patient lacks capacity to consent to it or, as the case may be, is not competent to consent to it.

(3) The second condition is that the treatment is immediately necessary.

(4) The third condition is that if it is necessary to use force against the patient in order to give the treatment—

(a)  the treatment needs to be given in order to prevent harm to the patient; and

(b)  the use of such force is a proportionate response to the likelihood of the patient's suffering harm, and to the seriousness of that harm.

(5) Subject to subsections (6) to (8) below, treatment is immediately necessary if—

(a)  it is immediately necessary to save the patient's life; or

(b)  it is immediately necessary to prevent a serious deterioration of the patient's condition and is not irreversible; or

(c)  it is immediately necessary to alleviate serious suffering by the patient and is not irreversible or hazardous; or

(d)  it is immediately necessary, represents the minimum interference necessary to prevent the patient from behaving violently or being a danger to himself or others and is not irreversible or hazardous.

(6) Where the treatment is section 58A type treatment by virtue of subsection (1)(a) of that section, treatment is immediately necessary if it falls within paragraph (a) or (b) of subsection (5) above.

(7) Where the treatment is section 58A type treatment by virtue of subsection (1)(b) of that section, treatment is immediately necessary if it falls within such of paragraphs (a) to (d) of subsection (5) above as may be specified in regulations under section 58A above.

(8) For the purposes of subsection (7) above, the regulations—

(a) may make different provision for different cases (and may, in particular, make different provision for different forms of treatment);

(b) may make provision which applies subject to specified exceptions; and

(c) may include transitional, consequential, incidental or supplemental provision.

(9) Subsection (3) of section 62 above applies for the purposes of this section as it applies for the purposes of that section.]

AMENDMENT

This section was inserted by the Mental Health Act 2007 s.35(1).

DEFINITION

patient: s.145(1).                                                                                    **1–784**

GENERAL NOTE

This section sets out the criteria that must be satisfied before relevant treatment (see **1–785** s.64A) can be given in an emergency to adult community patients who lacks capacity or child community patients who lacks competence, and identifies when force can be used in order to provide such treatment. The requirement to obtain a certificate from a SOAD does not apply to such treatment (s.64B(3)(a)). The person providing the treatment need not be acting under the direction of an approved clinician (*Code of Practice*, para.23.21). Emergency treatment should be provided in those rare situations where it is the best interests of the patient to be immediately treated with force in the community rather than be transported to hospital under the recall power contained in s.17E for the treatment to be provided there. Such treatment can be given even if it conflicts with an advance decision to refuse the treatment or a decision of a donee or a deputy. The provisions of subs.(5) are virtually identical to the criteria that must be satisfied before urgent treatment can be given under s.62.

The emergency circumstances in which s.58A type treatment can be given are more limited than the circumstances in which other treatments can be given in an emergency: see subss.(6) to (8).

Nothing in this section excludes a person's liabilities resulting from his or her negligence in undertaking anything authorised to be done under it (s.64I).

*Code of Practice*

This section is considered at paras 23.21–23.25 and 24.32–24.37.                        **1–786**

*Subsection (1)*

TREATMENT.    Including the treatment specified in reg.28(3) of the English Regulations **1–787** and reg.39(b) of the Welsh Regulations.

*Subsection (2)*

LACKS CAPACITY.    See s.64K(2).                                                           **1–788**

*Subsection (3)*

IMMEDIATELY NECESSARY.    See subss.(5) to (8) and the note on the meaning of this **1–789** phrase in s.62(1).

*Subsection (4)*

Although physical force (*Code of Practice,* para.23.17) cannot be used to provide treat- **1–790** ment in order to prevent harm to others, treatment which is aimed at preventing harm to the patient could also have that effect. For example, treatment which is aimed at preventing the patient being aggressive to others could have the effect of preventing harm to the patient through possible retaliation.

*Subsection (9)*

**1–791**    Section 62(3) defines "irreversible" and "hazardous".

## [Certificates: supplementary provisions

**1–792**    **64H.**—(1) A certificate under section 64B(2)(b) or 64E(2)(b) above (a "Part 4A certificate") may relate to a plan of treatment under which the patient is to be given (whether within a specified period or otherwise) one or more forms of section 58 type treatment or section 58A type treatment.

(2) A Part 4A certificate shall be in such form as may be prescribed by regulations made by the appropriate national authority.

(3) Before giving a Part 4A certificate, the registered medical practitioner concerned shall consult two other persons who have been professionally concerned with the patient's medical treatment but, of those persons—

(a) at least one shall be a person who is not a registered medical practitioner; and

(b) neither shall be the patient's responsible clinician or the person in charge of the treatment in question.

(4) Where a patient is given treatment in accordance with a Part 4A certificate, a report on the treatment and the patient's condition shall be given by the person in charge of the treatment to the [regulatory authority] if required by that authority.

(5) The [regulatory authority] may at any time give notice directing that a Part 4A certificate shall not apply to treatment given to a patient after a date specified in the notice, and the relevant section shall then apply to any such treatment as if that certificate had not been given.

(6) The relevant section is—

(a) if the patient is not recalled to hospital in accordance with section 17E above, section 64B or 64E above;

(b) if the patient is so recalled or is liable to be detained under this Act following revocation of the community treatment order under section 17F above—

(i) section 58 above, in the case of section 58 type treatment;

(ii) section 58A above, in the case of section 58A type treatment; (subject to section 62A(2) above).

(7) The notice under subsection (5) above shall be given to the person in charge of the treatment in question.

(8) Subsection (5) above shall not preclude the continuation of any treatment or of treatment under any plan pending compliance with the relevant section if the person in charge of the treatment considers that the discontinuance of the treatment or of treatment under the plan would cause serious suffering to the patient.

(9) In this section, "the appropriate national authority" means—

(a) in relation to community patients in respect of whom the responsible hospital is in England, the Secretary of State;

(b) in relation to community patients in respect of whom the responsible hospital is in Wales, the Welsh Ministers.]

AMENDMENT

This section was inserted by the Mental Health Act 2007 s.35(1). In subss.(4) and (5), the words in square brackets were substituted by the Health and Social Care Act 2008 s.52, Sch.3 para.5.

 patient: s.145(1).              **1–793**
 the regulatory authority: s.145(1).

GENERAL NOTE

*Subsection (2)*                 **1–794**
 APPROPRIATE NATIONAL AUTHORITY. See subs.(9).

*Subsection (3)*
 Paragraph 3.84 of the Mental Health Act Commission's *Thirteenth Biennial Report* **1–795**
2007–2009 states:

"Section 64H(3) of the Act requires that any SOAD certifying that treatment is appropriate in the case of an SCT patient must first have consulted with two persons who have been professionally concerned with the patient's treatment, at least one of whom shall not be a doctor, and neither of whom may be the responsible clinician or approved clinician in charge of the treatment in question. As such, there is no positive requirement to consult with a specific type of professional, in contrast to the arrangements for SOAD visits to detained patients, where one of the statutory consultees must be a nurse. Regrettably, both the Codes of Practice for England and Wales misrepresent the law in this area, implying that a nurse must be one consultee for all second opinions. We have raised this matter with the Department of Health, who have accepted that this is not the intention of the Code. As such, we have advised SOADs that they should disregard the apparent implication of the Code and are free to choose or not choose to consult with a nurse for SCT visits, as they wish."

*Subsections (4), (5)*
 THE REGULATORY BODY. Is the Care Quality Commission or, in relation to Wales, the **1–796**
Welsh Ministers (s.145(1)).

*Subsection (5)*
 RELEVANT SECTION. See subs.(6).           **1–797**

## [Liability for negligence

 **64I.**—Nothing in section 64D, 64F or 64G above excludes a person's civil liab- **1–798**
ility for loss or damage, or his criminal liability, resulting from his negligence in
doing anything authorised to be done by that section.]

AMENDMENT
 This section was inserted by the Mental Health Act 2007 s.35(1).

## [Factors to be considered in determining whether patient objects to treatment

 **64J.**—(1) In assessing for the purposes of this Part whether he has reason to **1–799**
believe that a patient objects to treatment, a person shall consider all the circumstances so far as they are reasonably ascertainable, including the patient's behaviour, wishes, feelings, views, beliefs and values.
 (2) But circumstances from the past shall be considered only so far as it is still
appropriate to consider them.]

AMENDMENT
 This section was inserted by the Mental Health Act 2007 s.35(1).

**1–800**    patient: s.145(1).

GENERAL NOTE
**1–801**    An objection is not rendered invalid because a view is taken that it is unreasonable. Guidance on the identification of a patient's objection is contained in paras.23.18 and 23.19 of the *Code of Practice*.

### [Interpretation of Part 4A
**1–802**    **64K.**—(1) This Part of this Act is to be construed as follows.

(2) References to a patient who lacks capacity are to a patient who lacks capacity within the meaning of the Mental Capacity Act 2005.

(3) References to a patient who has capacity are to be read accordingly.

(4) References to a donee are to a donee of a lasting power of attorney (within the meaning of section 9 of the Mental Capacity Act 2005) created by the patient, where the donee is acting within the scope of his authority and in accordance with that Act.

(5) References to a deputy are to a deputy appointed for the patient by the Court of Protection under section 16 of the Mental Capacity Act 2005, where the deputy is acting within the scope of his authority and in accordance with that Act.

(6) Reference to the responsible clinician shall be construed as a reference to the responsible clinician within the meaning of Part 2 of this Act.

(7) References to a hospital include a registered establishment.

(8) Section 64(3) above applies for the purposes of this Part of this Act as it applies for the purposes of Part 4 of this Act.]

AMENDMENT
This section was inserted by the Mental Health Act 2007 s.35(1).

DEFINITION
**1–803**    patient: s.145(1).

GENERAL NOTE

*Subsection (6)*
**1–804**    RESPONSIBLE CLINICIAN. See s.34(1) and the notes thereto.

## PART V

## MENTAL HEALTH REVIEW TRIBUNALS

### *Constitution, etc.*

### Mental Health Review [Tribunal for Wales]
**1–805**    **65.**—[(1) There shall [be a Mental Health Review Tribunal for Wales.]

(1A) The purpose of [that tribunal] is to deal with applications and references by and in respect of patients under the provisions of this Act.]

(2) The provisions of Schedule 2 to this Act shall have effect with respect to the constitution of [the Mental Health Review Tribunal for Wales].

(3) Subject to the provisions of Schedule 2 to this Act, and to rules made by the Lord Chancellor under this Act, the jurisdiction of [the Mental Health Review

Tribunal for Wales] may be exercised by any three or more of its members, and references in this Act to [the Mental Health Review Tribunal for Wales] shall be construed accordingly.

[(4) The Welsh Ministers may pay to the members of the Mental Health Review Tribunal for Wales such remuneration and allowances as they may determine, and defray the expenses of that tribunal to such amount as they may determine, and may provide for that tribunal such officers and servants, and such accommodation, as that tribunal may require.]

AMENDMENT

Subsections (1) and (1)(A) were substituted by the Mental Health Act 2007 s.38(2). The other amendments to this section were made by SI 2008/2883 art.9, Sch.3 para.45.

DEFINITION

patient: s.145(1).                                                                    **1–806**

GENERAL NOTE

This section, together with Sch.2, provides for the establishment of a Mental Health **1–807** Review Tribunal for Wales. This Tribunal, which covers the whole of Wales, has its office within the National Assembly for Wales administrative building in Cardiff and a Chairman for Wales. The equivalent tribunal in England, the First-tier Tribunal (Mental Health), was established under the Tribunals, Courts and Enforcement Act 2007 (the 2007 Act). The two tribunals have identical powers and duties to discharge patients and to make recommendations.

*The First-tier Tribunal (Mental Health)*

In the report of his Review of Tribunals, *Tribunals for Users—One System, One Service,* **1–808** published in August 2001, Sir Andrew Leggatt recommended extensive reform to the tribunals system. He recommended that tribunals should be brought together in a single system, that they should become separate from their current sponsoring departments, and that such a system be administered instead by a single Tribunals Service. The Government agreed and its response is to be found in the 2007 Act. The Act creates two new, generic tribunals, the First-tier Tribunal and the Upper Tribunal, into which existing tribunal jurisdictions have been transferred: see SI 2008/2833 art.3, Sch.1. The Upper Tribunal is primarily, but not exclusively, an appellate tribunal from the First-tier Tribunal. The new system is administered by the Tribunals Service (*www.tribunals.gov.uk*) which is an executive agency of the Ministry of Justice.

The Act also provides for the establishment of "chambers" within the two tribunals which enable tribunals to be grouped appropriately. A Health, Education and Social Care Chamber has been created which, inter alia, has functions relating to "applications and references by and in respect of patients under the provisions of the Mental Health Act 1983 or paragraph 5(2) of the Schedule to the Repatriation of Prisoners Act 1984" (SI 2008/2684 art.5(h)). The tribunal within the Health, Education and Social Care Chamber that deals with mental health cases is known as the First-tier Tribunal (Mental Health) (referred to here as the "tribunal") which has a website at *www.mhrt.org.uk*. Each Chamber is headed by a Chamber President and the tribunals judiciary is headed by a Senior President of Tribunals. The First-tier Tribunal (Mental Health) only has jurisdiction in England.

A decision of the First-tier Tribunal (and the Mental Health Review Tribunal for Wales: see s.78A) apart from an "excluded decision" may be appealed to the Administrative Appeals Chamber of the Upper Tribunal (s.11 of the 2007 Act and SI 2008/2684, arts.6, 7(a)(i) and (iv)), and a decision of the Upper Tribunal may be appealed to the Court of Appeal. The Administrative Appeals Chamber of the Upper Tribunal hears appeals from the tribunal. The grounds of appeal must relate to a point of law. The rights of appeal may only be exercised with permission of the First-tier Tribunal or the Upper Tribunal itself. If the Upper Tribunal exercises its discretion to set aside the decision of the First-tier Tribunal it must either remit the case to the tribunal with directions for its reconsideration, or remake the decision: see s.12(2) of the 2007 Act. The procedure of the Upper Tribunal, which is a superior court of record (2007 Act, s.3(5)) and can therefore lay down authoritative precedents, is governed by the Tribunal Procedure (Upper Tribunal) Rules 2008 (SI 2008/2698) (as amended). The Upper Tribunal has published a leaflet on "Appealing to the Administrative Appeals Chamber of the Upper Tribunal from the First-tier Tribunal Mental Health Decisions", a form for applying for permission to appeal (Form UT3) and a guidance note to accompany the form. These can be downloaded from the website of the Upper Tribunal (*www.osscsc.gov.uk*) (accessed July 22, 2010). The Upper Tribunal will also deal with most judicial review cases which would otherwise have been dealt with by the High Court. Applications to the Upper Tribunal for judicial review may be made by virtue of ss.15 to 18 of the 2007 Act where the application does not seek a declaration of incompatibility under the Human Rights Act 1998 and it is within the scope of *Practice Direction (Upper Tribunal: Judicial Review Jurisdiction)* [2009] 1 W.L.R. 327 made by the Lord Chief Justice under s.18(6) of the 2007 Act. The fact that the Upper Tribunal is a superior court of record does not mean that it can avoid judicial review of its decisions (*R.(Cart, U and XC) v Upper Tribunal and Special Immigration Appeals Commission* [2009] EWHC 3052; [2010] M.H.L.R. 35).

Sections 9 of the 2007 Act provides the First-tier Tribunal with powers to review its decision, and to correct accidental errors, amend reasons given for the decision, or to set aside the decision. This power is aimed at preventing an appeal being made if a decision is clearly wrong. If the decision is set aside, the tribunal must either re-decide the matter, or refer the case to the Upper Tribunal which will re-decide the matter. Section 10 of the 2007 Act provides the Upper Tribunal with similar review powers. The 2007 Act also provides for the membership of the tribunals and the making of Tribunal Procedure Rules, which can be supplemented by means of practice directions. The First-tier Tribunal (Health, Education and Social Care Chamber) Rules 2008 (SI 2008/2699) (the "Tribunal Rules") and Practice Direction—First-Tier Tribunal, Health Education and Social Care Chamber, Mental Health Cases are reproduced in Part 3.

As it is a creature of statute, a tribunal has no inherent jurisdiction. It is obliged to follow the procedure laid down in the Tribunal Rules and where the Rules are silent on a point of procedure the tribunal must follow the rules of natural justice, i.e. it should act in a fair and unbiased way and should provide an opportunity for each party to adequately state his case (*Secretary of State for the Home Department v Oxford Regional Mental Health Review Tribunal* [1987] 3 All E.R. 8 HL). In *W v Egdell* [1989] 1 All E.R. 1089 at 1095, Scott J. described the nature of a hearing before a tribunal as inquisitorial, not adversarial. However, tribunal procedure was said by Stanley Burnton J. to be "to a significant extent inquisitorial" in *R. (on the application of Ashworth Hospital Authority) v Mental Health Review Tribunal for the West Midlands and North West Regions* [2001] EWHC Admin 901; [2002] M.H.L.R. 13 at para.16.

A tribunal "should apply its mind to the matters before it in each case. It should not feel itself fettered by a previous decision but of course it should pay due regard to it" (*R. v South West Thames Mental Health Review Tribunal Ex p. Demetri* [1997] C.O.D. 44 CA per Aldous L.J.).

Although a tribunal has no powers itself to deal with the contempt of its proceedings, the ruling of the House of Lords in *Pickering v Liverpool Daily Post and Echo Newspapers Plc* [1991] 1 All E.R. 622 that Mental Health Review Tribunals were courts for the purposes of the law of contempt means that it is open to a party of the proceedings to apply to the High Court for the committal of any party who is in contempt of the tribunal. It is submitted that the finding in *Pickering* also applies to the First-tier Tribunal (Mental Health).

The function of a tribunal is to review the justification for the patient's continued detention, guardianship or supervised community treatment at the time of the hearing. It has no power to consider the validity of the admission which gave rise to the liability to be detained (*R. v East London and The City Mental Health Trust Ex p. Brandenburg* [2003] UKHL 58; [2004] 1 All E.R. 400 at para.9(3)), to consider whether a patient who had been detained for assessment under s.2 should have been detained for treatment under s.3, or to investigate the circumstances that led to the powers of this Act being invoked in respect of the patient. However, such circumstances would need to be taken account of when the tribunal considers the patient's condition at the time of the hearing. Although the tribunal will receive a significant amount of evidence on the medical and other treatment that the patient is receiving, the tribunal's task is confined to considering such evidence only in so far as it relates to the statutory grounds.

The question whether the tribunal was biased because the consultant psychiatrist who sat as a member of the tribunal was a consultant who was employed by the detaining NHS Trust was considered in *R. (on the application of PD) v West Midlands and North West Mental Health Review Tribunal* [2004] EWCA Civ 311; [2004] M.H.L.R 174, which is considered in the General Note to r.34 of the Tribunal Rules. *PD* was applied in *R. (on the application of M) v Mental Health Review Tribunal* [2005] EWHC 2791 (Admin) where Bennett J. confirmed that cases involving a consideration of bias are fact-sensitive and that an examination of case precedent was of limited value. In this case his Lordship found that the fair-minded and informed observer, having taken account of the facts of the case, would not say that there was a real possibility of bias on the part of a judge when sitting as a legal member of the tribunal in November 2004 on the ground that he had imposed a hospital order and a restriction order on the patient in September 2003.

There is nothing to prevent the chairman of a tribunal from presiding over more than one hearing involving the same patient (*R. v Oxford Regional Mental Health Review Tribunal Ex p. Mackman, The Times*, June 2, 1986). This ruling would undoubtedly apply to other members of the tribunal.

The legality of a decision to make an application to detain a patient immediately after a decision of a tribunal to discharge him is considered in the General Note to s.3.

By virtue of ss.132(1)(b) and 132A of this Act, hospital managers have a duty to inform patients of their right to make an application to a tribunal.

*Rules of Precedence in the Upper Tribunal*
The following guidelines were identified by the Upper Tribunal in *Dorset Healthcare* **1–809**
*NHS Foundation Trust v MH* [2009] UKUT 4 (AAC); [2009] MHLR 102, para.37:

(i) Judges of the Upper Tribunal in the AAC speak with equal authority. All their decisions may be cited to the Upper Tribunal, First-tier Tribunals and other tribunals from which appeals to the AAC come and the appropriate decision-making authorities. Where they decide questions of legal principle they must be followed by the appropriate decision-making authorities and the tribunals below in cases involving the application of that principle, unless they can be distinguished. It should be borne in mind that similarity in underlying facts does not automatically give rise to similarity in the principle to be applied and questions of fact should not be elevated into questions of legal principle.

(ii) If confronted with decisions which conflict, the appropriate decision-making authority and tribunals below must prefer the decision of a Three-Judge Panel of the AAC to that of a single judge.

(iii) In so far as the AAC is concerned, on questions of legal principle, a single judge shall follow a decision of a Three-Judge Panel of the AAC . . . unless there are compelling reasons why he should not, as, for instance, a decision of a superior court affecting the legal principles involved. A single judge in the interests of comity and to avoid confusion on questions of legal principle normally follows the decisions of other single judges. It is recognised however that a slavish adherence to this could lead to the perpetuation of error and he is not bound to do so.

*Habeas Corpus and Judicial Review*

**1–810**   If a patient considers that the initial admission was unlawful he or she can attempt to secure release by making an application to the High Court for a writ of habeas corpus. The writ of habeas corpus runs to the party having the applicant in his custody (the hospital managers) and not the doctor who made medical recommendation in support of an application under Pt II of this Act (*R. v South Western Hospital, Managers Ex p. M* [1994] 1 All E.R. 161). An alternative course of action would be to make an application for judicial review. Most cases that would in the past have resulted in applications to the High Court for the judicial review of a tribunal decision will now be dealt with as appeals on points of law to the Upper Tribunal, which also has a judicial review jurisdiction (see above). The Upper Tribunal has no jurisdiction over the decisions of hospital managers taken under s.23.

The distinction between the habeas corpus and judicial review procedures was explained by Lord Donaldson M.R. in the following extract from his judgment in *R. v Secretary of State for the Home Department Ex p. Cheblak* [1991] 2 All E.R. 319 at 322, 323, a case where the applicant was seeking to challenge his arrest and the decision to deport him:

> "Although, as I have said, the two forms of relief which Mr. Cheblak seeks are interrelated on the facts of his case, they are essentially different. A writ of *habeas corpus* will issue where someone is detained without any authority or the purported authority is beyond the powers of the person authorising the detention and so is unlawful. *The remedy of judicial review* is available where the decision or action sought to be impugned is within the powers of the person taking it but, due to procedural error, a misappreciation of the law, a failure to take account of relevant matters, a taking account of irrelevant matters or the fundamental unreasonableness of the decision or action, it should never have been taken. In such a case the decision or action is lawful, unless and until it is set aside by a court of competent jurisdiction. In the case of detention, if the warrant, or the underlying decision to deport, were set aside but the detention continued, a writ of *habeas corpus* would issue."

The distinction between the two forms of proceedings was applied to this Act in *Re S-C (Mental Patient: Habeas Corpus)* [1996] 1 All E.R. 532, CA, where the patient was challenging the lawfulness of his detention on the ground that the application signed by the approved [mental health professional] was not "duly completed" as required by s.6(1) because a condition precedent relating to the s.3 application was not present in that the patient's nearest relative had not been consulted as required by s.11(4). The Court held that as the patient's challenge was not directed to an administrative decision but to the jurisdiction of the hospital managers to detain him, an application for habeas corpus was the appropriate remedy rather than proceedings for judicial review.

In *B v Barking Havering and Brentwood Community Healthcare NHS Trust* [1999] 1 F.L.R. 106, CA, Lord Woolf M.R. referred to a passage in the judgment of Sir Thomas Bingham M.R. in *Re S-C*, above, where his Lordship said that on the facts of that case "an application for habeas corpus is *an* appropriate, and possibly even *the* appropriate course to pursue". Lord Woolf expressed his disagreement with the suggestion that "possibly" an application for habeas corpus was the only procedure that was appropriate. While accepting that in *Re S-C* habeas corpus was an appropriate procedure, his Lordship suggested that judicial review was equally appropriate and would even have advantages over habeas corpus. His Lordship would discourage applications for habeas corpus unless it was clear that no other form of relief would be required. Where applications were made for both judicial review and habeas corpus, the proceedings should be harmonised if at all possible.

**1–811**   In *Re Doreen Trew* [2000] M.H.L.R. 53, the applicant submitted that the court considering the remedy of habeas corpus is not limited to considering whether the procedural requisites for detention are met, but can also take action where there is inadequate evidence to justify the detention. Owen J., in refusing the application, held that although there was authority to support the contention that habeas corpus is available when there is no evidence to justify the decision to detain (see *R. v Board of Control Ex p. Rutty* [1956] 2 QB 109), this does not support an argument that when a case before a tribunal is strong, but no decision has been given because the tribunal adjourned the hearing, the court hearing the application can consider the evidence, sideline the tribunal, and find that the tribunal should discharge. His Lordship said that in these circumstances "it is evident that the tribunal should make the decision."

The court considering an application for judicial review is exercising a public law jurisdiction and is not required to grant the application even if unlawfulness is established. The courts have shown a reluctance to grant an application if a tribunal hearing is imminent. In order to succeed in an application one of the established grounds must be made out, namely that the decision maker has acted illegally, has behaved irrationally, has abused power, or has failed to act with procedural fairness toward one of the parties. The court will also consider whether there has been a breech of the applicant's rights under the European Convention on Human Rights (*R. v Secretary of State for the Home Department, ex p. Daly* [2001] 2 AC 532, HL).

If, on an application for judicial review, an order quashing the decision of the tribunal to discharge the patient is made, this has the effect of treating the decision to discharge as never having been made and restoring the patient to the status of a detained patient (*R. (on the application of Wirral Health Authority and Wirral Borough Council) v Mental Health Review Tribunal and DE* [2001] EWCA Civ 1901; [2002] M.H.L.R. 34). However, the remedies afforded on judicial review are as flexible as justice requires and the need for a fresh tribunal decision does not automatically require a quashing order. In *R. (on the application of the Secretary of State for the Home Department) v Mental Health Review Tribunal and BR* [2005] EWCA Civ 1616; [2006] M.H.L.R. 172, the patient appealed against the effect of a quashing order made following a successful appeal by the Home Secretary against a decision by a tribunal that the patient be unconditionally discharged from hospital. The issue before the tribunal was whether discharge should be absolute or conditional, not whether he was entitled to be discharged at all. The effect of the quashing order was to allow the patient to be detained again, which is what happened. On allowing the appeal, the Court of Appeal made orders quashing as much of the tribunal's decision as granted the patient an absolute discharge, and declaring that pending a rehearing the patient is entitled to be treated as having been conditionally discharged. Sedley L.J. said at para.16:

"Modern public law is quite capable enough to do this if necessary, and here it was called for by the requirements both of the common law and the European Convention on Human Rights that nobody is to be deprived of his liberty except according to law."

### Administrative Justice and Tribunals Council
The AJTC is required "keep under review, and report on, the constitution and working" **1–812** of the First-tier Tribunal (Mental Health) (Tribunals, Courts and Enforcement Act 2007 s.44(2), Sch.7 paras 14, 25), and the Mental Health Review Tribunal for Wales (SI 2007/ 2591) art.2). The AJTC's predecessor, the Council on Tribunals, published a Special Report on Mental Health Review Tribunals in 2000 (Cm. 4740).

### Legal Aid
Legal aid is available through the Community Legal Services (CLS) Fund to fund **1–813** legal advice and representation for patients before the tribunal, without requiring any assessment of the patient's means. The Reference Guide, at para.20.21 states: "Legal aid for appeals to the Upper Tribunal is means-tested and subject to a merits test". The CLS Fund is the responsibility of the Legal Services Commission.

### Human Rights Act 1998
The tribunal is a "public authority" for the purposes of the 1998 Act (*ibid.*, s.6(3)(a)). **1–814**

In *MD v Nottinghamshire Health Care NHS Trust* [2010] UKUT 59 (AAC), para.47, Judge Jacobs said:

> "[T]he tribunal, like all judicial bodies, is under a duty to comply with the Convention right to a hearing. As part of that duty, it must ensure an equality of arms as that is understood in the Strasbourg jurisprudence. It is relevant that the tribunal is not merely a body that hears evidence, finds facts and decides on arguments. It is, as I have said, a body with its own expertise. Its use of that expertise is an important contribution to ensuring an equality of arms. The psychiatrist on the panel makes an examination of the patient and the panel uses its collective knowledge, experience and expertise to assess the evidence. Both those tasks are performed independently. They reduce the need, which may exist in the court system, for the parties to have their own expert evidence. Patients are, of course, entitled to produce evidence on their own behalf. My point is simply that greater access to experts is not a necessary, or the only, way to ensure the equality of arms that the law requires."

Article 5 of the European Convention on Human Rights does not enable a patient who has failed before a tribunal and who had a favourable medical opinion which had not been accepted by the tribunal, to be bound to be granted leave to bring judicial review proceedings to challenge the tribunal's decision (*R. (on the application of MacDonald) v Mental Health Review Tribunal* [2001] EWHC Admin 1032, at para.18).

*Code of Practice*
**1–815**    Guidance on the role of the tribunal is given in Ch.32.

*Applications and references concerning Part II patients*

**Applications to tribunals**
**1–816**    **66.**—(1) Where—

(a) a patient is admitted to a hospital in pursuance of an application for admission for assessment; or

(b) a patient is admitted to a hospital in pursuance of an application for admission for treatment; or

(c) a patient is received into guardianship in pursuance of a guardianship application; or

[(ca) a community treatment order is made in respect of a patient; or

(cb) a community treatment order is revoked under section 17F above in respect of a patient; or]

[. . .]

(e) a patient is transferred from guardianship to a hospital in pursuance of regulations made under section 19 above; or

(f) a report is furnished under section 20 above in respect of a patient and the patient is not discharged [under section 23 above]; or

[(fza) a report is furnished under section 20A above in respect of a patient and the patient is not discharged under section 23 above; or]

[(fa) a report is furnished under subsection (2) of section 21B above in respect of a patient and subsection (5) of that section applies (or subsections (5) and (6)(b) of that section apply) in the case of the report; or

[(faa) a report is furnished under subsection (2) of section 21B above in respect of a community patient and subsection (6A) of that section applies (or subsections (6A) and (6B)(b) of that section apply) in the case of the report; or]

[. . .]

(g) a report is furnished under section 25 above in respect of a patient who is detained in pursuance of an application for admission for treatment [or a community patient]; or

[. . .]

(h) an order is made under section 29 above [on the ground specified in paragraph (c) or (d) of subsection (3) of that section] in respect of a patient who is or subsequently becomes liable to be detained or subject to guardianship under Part II of this Act [or who is a community patient],

an application may be made to [the appropriate tribunal] within the relevant period—

(i) by the patient (except in the cases mentioned in paragraphs (g) and (h) above) [. . .] and

(ii) in the cases mentioned in paragraphs (g) and (h) above, by his nearest relative.

(2) In subsection (1) above "the relevant period" means—

(a) in the case mentioned in paragraph (a) of that subsection, 14 days beginning with the day on which the patient is admitted as so mentioned;

(b) in the case mentioned in paragraph (b) of that subsection, six months beginning with the day on which the patient is admitted as so mentioned;

(c) in the [case mentioned in paragraph (c)] of that subsection, six months beginning with the day on which the application is accepted;

[(ca) in the case mentioned in paragraph (ca) of that subsection, six months beginning with the day on which the community treatment order is made;

(cb) in the case mentioned in paragraph (cb) of that subsection, six months beginning with the day on which the community treatment order is revoked;]

(d) [in the case mentioned in paragraph (g)] of that subsection, 28 days beginning with the day on which the applicant is informed that the report has been furnished;

(e) in the case mentioned in paragraph (e) of that subsection, six months beginning with the day on which the patient is transferred;

(f) in the case mentioned in paragraph (f) [or (fa) of that subsection, the period or periods] for which authority for the patient's detention or guardianship is renewed by virtue of the report;

[(fza) in the cases mentioned in paragraphs (fza) and (faa) of that subsection, the period or periods for which the community treatment period is extended by virtue of the report;]

[. . .]

(g) in the case mentioned in paragraph (h) of that subsection, 12 months beginning with the date of the order, and in any subsequent period of 12 months during which the order continues in force.

[(2A) Nothing in subsection (1)(b) above entitles a community patient to make an application by virtue of that provision even if he is admitted to a hospital on being recalled there under section 17E above.]

(3) Section 32 above shall apply for the purposes of this section as it applies for the purposes of Pt II of this Act.

[(4) In this Act "the appropriate tribunal" means the First-tier Tribunal or the Mental Health Review Tribunal for Wales.

(5) For provision determining to which of those tribunals applications by or in respect of a patient under this Act shall be made, see section 77(3) and (4) below.]

AMENDMENTS

The amendments to this section were made by the Mental Health Act 2007 ss.1(4), 25, 36(3), 55, Sch.1 para.13, Sch.11 Pts 1 and 5 and SI 2008/2883 art.9, Sch.3 para.46.

DEFINITIONS

**1–817**

patient: s.145(1).

hospital: ss.79(6), 145(1).

application for admission for assessment: ss.2, 145(1).

application for admission for treatment: ss.3, 145(1).

nearest relative: ss.26(3), 145(1).

community treatment order: ss.17A(7), 145(1).

community patient: ss.17A(7), 145(1).

the appropriate tribunal: subs.(4).

GENERAL NOTE

**1–818**

This section identifies the occasions on which a patient or his or her nearest relative may make an application to a tribunal. If either the patient or the nearest relative changes his or her mind subsequent to making an application, the application must proceed unless it is formally withdrawn with the consent of the tribunal under r.17 the Tribunal Rules.

Donees of lasting powers of attorneys and deputies appointed by the Court of Protection are able to exercise a patient's rights to apply to the tribunal for discharge from detention, guardianship or SCT if they have the relevant authority under the LPA or the order of the court appointing them and the patient concerned lacks the capacity to do so themselves. Such an application would be made "in respect of" the patient for the purposes of s.77(1); also see para.9.6 of the *Code of Practice*.

In *R. v South Thames Mental Health Review Tribunal Ex p. M* [1998] C.O.D. 38, Collins J. held that the right of a patient to make an application to a tribunal is founded on the patient's admission, which is something that happens in a moment of time, and not on his detention. Applying this ruling to the situation of a patient who is admitted and detained under s.2 and who is subsequently detained under s.3 during the currency of the s.2, his Lordship held that the following passage from para.5.3 of the *Code of Practice* (1993 edition) is correct:

> "Changing a patient's status from section 2 to section 3 will not deprive him of a Mental Health Review Tribunal hearing if the change takes place after a valid application has been made to the Tribunal but before it has been heard. The patient's right to apply for a Tribunal under section 66(1)(b) in the first period of detention after his change of status are unaffected."

His Lordship said that in these circumstances the tribunal must consider the patient's case by using the s.3 criteria set out in s.72(1)(b). The determination of the tribunal on the s.2 application cannot prevent the patient from making a subsequent s.3 application during the first six months of detention if the s.2 application is unsuccessful.

Does an application to the tribunal by a s.3 patient lapse on the patient being made subject to community treatment order (CTO)? This question was answered by Judge Rowland in *AA v Cheshire and Wirral Partnership NHS Foundation Trust* [2009] UKUT 195 (AAC); [2009] M.H.L.R. 308. His Honour, in distinguishing *Ex p.M*, held that a tribunal has the power—or, if the conditions of s.72(1)(c) are satisfied, a duty—to direct that a person subject to a CTO order be discharged notwithstanding that that person made the application to the tribunal while liable to be detained under s.2 or 3. Therefore, an application to the First-tier Tribunal made by or on behalf of a person detained under s.2 or 3 does not lapse if a CTO is made in respect of that person before the application is determined. His Honour said at para.61:

" . . . parties need to co-operate sensibly with each other and the First-tier Tribunal if a patient is made the subject of a CTO while an application to the tribunal is pending. In particular, it will clearly be incumbent on any representative of the applicant to inform the tribunal as soon as possible whether or not the application is being withdrawn and it is also clearly incumbent on all parties to inform the tribunal whether or not a postponement of any hearing that has already been fixed will be required in the light of the change of circumstances."

In *KF v Birmingham and Solihull Mental Health NHS Foundation Trust* [2010] UKUT 185 (AAC), a three judge panel of the Upper Tribunal was satisfied that *AA* was correctly decided. The issue of principle that was considered in this case was: what should happen where an appeal from a First-tier Tribunal's substantive decision on a s.2 application is overtaken by events. Having undertaken a comprehensive analysis, the tribunal concluded that:

" . . . any movement from s.2 to s.3 or to community patient status does not affect the continuing validity of an extant and undetermined application or reference to the First-tier Tribunal. The application or reference still falls to be determined by the tribunal in accordance with the patient's status at the time of the actual hearing and subject to the relevant criteria under section 72(1)(a)–(c)" (para.59).

The use of the tribunal's case management powers to deal with the practical consequences of this finding was considered at para.60:

"The effective use of the First-tier Tribunal's case management powers should enable outstanding proceedings to be consolidated, heard and determined together. . . . [T]he position may be more complicated where there is a change in the patient's status from s.3 to a CTO. Different clinicians and other mental health professionals may become involved in the patient's care and reports provided by the professionals who were involved in the patient's care whilst he or she was an in-patient may not address the criteria which the First-tier Tribunal will have to consider at the hearing in accordance with the patient's status at that time. This is an important factor which judges dealing with case management will need to keep firmly in mind when using case management powers, to ensure that cases are dealt with in a timely fashion and that, when appropriate and possible, hearing dates already fixed are retained for the hearing of the new application or reference. Appropriate and imaginative use of the case management powers should be encouraged to ensure that the relevant professionals are able to provide the required reports in time, notwithstanding the presence of a sometimes rapidly changing landscape in respect of the patient's status".

It is not always appropriate for the tribunal to refuse permission to appeal a s.2 application on the ground that the appeal was academic because the patient had in the meantime been detained under s.3. The UT said at para.30 (also see the note to r.17 of the Tribunal Rules):

"In general, unless there is good reason why not, if the First-tier Tribunal is asked to review a tribunal decision on a s.2 application, and concludes that it involves an error of law, then the appropriate way forward is for the First-tier Tribunal to set aside the substantive decision and to re-list the case for hearing together with any existing s.3 application."

For patients who have been placed under hospital or guardianship orders by a court under s.37, subss.(1) and (2) of this section read as follows:

"(1) Where—

(e) a patient is transferred from guardianship to a hospital in pursuance of regulations made under section 19 above; or

(f) a report is furnished under section 20 above in respect of a patient and the patient is not discharged; or

(fza) a report is furnished under section 20A above in respect of a patient and the patient is not discharged under section 23 above; or

(fa) a report is furnished under subsection (2) of section 21B above in respect of a patient and subsection (5) of that section applies (or subsections (5) and (6)(b) of that section apply) in the case of the report; or

(faa) a report is furnished under subsection (2) of section 21B above in respect of a community patient and subsection (6A) of that section applies (or subsections (6A) and (6B)(b) of that section apply) in the case of the report;

an application may be made to the appropriate tribunal within the relevant period by the patient.

(2) In subsection (1) above 'the relevant period' means—

(ca) in the case mentioned in paragraph (ca) of that subsection, six months beginning with the day on which the community treatment order is made;

(cb) in the case mentioned in paragraph (cb) of that subsection, six months beginning with the day on which the community treatment order is revoked;

(d) in the case mentioned in paragraph (gb) of that subsection, 28 days beginning with the day on which the applicant is informed that the report has been furnished;

(e) in the case mentioned in paragraph (e) of that subsection, six months beginning with the day on which the patient is transferred;

(f) in the case mentioned in paragraph (f) [or (fa) of that subsection, the period or periods] for which authority for the patient's detention or guardianship is renewed by virtue of the report; or

(fza) in the cases mentioned in paragraphs (fza) and (faa) of that subsection, the period or periods for which the community treatment period is extended by virtue of the report (Sch.1, Pt 1, paras 2,9).

The effect of subss.(1)(f), (2)(f), as amended by Sch.1, is to enable a hospital order patient to make his first application to a tribunal during the *second* six months of his detention. The rationale for this is explained in the note to s.69(1). Thereafter the patient's entitlement to make applications corresponds to the entitlements accruing on renewal of the authority to detain Pt II patients.

Applications by or on behalf of hospital and guardianship order patients can also be made under s.69. Applications by restricted patients are governed by ss.70 and 79.

*Human Rights Act 1998*

**1–819**  Article 5(4) of the European Convention on Human Rights does not require there to be an automatic review of the lawfulness of a patient's detention under s.2, even if the patient lacks the mental capacity to make an application to a tribunal: see *R. (on the application of H) v Secretary of State for Health* [2005] UKHL 60; [2005] 4 All E.R. 1311, which is noted in s.2 under this heading.

*Subsection (1)*

**1–820**  PARAGRAPH (A); APPLICATION FOR ADMISSION FOR ASSESSMENT.  See the note on "The Human Rights Act 1998", above. If the patient's status changes to a s.3 patient, see *R. v South Thames Mental Health Review Tribunal Ex p. M*, which is considered in the General Note to this section. Patients admitted under s.4 are not excluded as an application under that section is "an application for admission for assessment" (s.4(1)) which is founded on one medical recommendation. An application which was made immediately after admission would automatically lapse if the second medical recommendation required by s.4(4) was not forthcoming.

PARAGRAPH (B); APPLICATION FOR ADMISSION FOR TREATMENT. If the patient does not make an application within six months of his admission, including any period of detention under s.2 (s.68(5)(b)), the hospital managers will automatically refer the case to the tribunal (s.68(1)(b), (2)). A patient who is subject to a hospital order can make his first application to a tribunal during the *second* six months of his detention: see the General Note, above.

A conditionally discharged patient who has been made subject to an application under s.3 has a right to make an application under this paragraph (*R. v North West London Mental Health NHS Trust Ex p. Stewart* [1997] C.O.D. 42).

PARAGRAPH (E). A patient who does not exercise his or her right to apply to a tribunal within six months of the transfer (subs.(2)(e)) will have his or her case automatically referred to a tribunal by the hospital managers (s.68(1)(e), (2)).

PARAGRAPH (H). Applications under this paragraph can only be made by nearest relatives who have been displaced by the court on the grounds that they have unreasonably objected to an application being made or have used (or were likely to use) their powers of discharge without due regard to the welfare of the patient or the interests of the public.

AN APPLICATION. This refers to the process for beginning the proceedings before the tribunal (*R. (on the application of SR) v Mental Health Review Tribunal*, above, para.20). The statutory restriction contained in s.77(2) is not on more than one application being made to a tribunal in any specified period because more than one application can be made in any period, if it is of a different kind from that made in that period (*SR*, para.26).

NEAREST RELATIVE. Or, except in relation to para.(h), an acting nearest relative. Where **1–821** an acting nearest relative has been appointed under s.29 that person exercises the right of the nearest relative to make applications to a tribunal under this section and under s.69 (s.29(1)). However, the supplanted nearest relative can make one application to a tribunal for the patient's discharge within the periods specified in subs.(2)(g) (s.29(6)).

If the patient is a ward of court the nearest relative cannot make an application to a tribunal without the leave of the High Court (s.33(2)).

The nearest relative could consider using his or her powers of discharge under s.23(2)(a) as an alternative to making an application to a tribunal.

*Subsection (2)*

14 DAYS. The application must be *received* by the tribunal within the 14-day period: see **1–822** r.31(1)(c) of the Tribunal Rules. For the calculation of time, see r.12.

A patient who has been detained under s.2, who has had their period of detention extended by virtue of s.29(4) will have his or her case referred to the tribunal six months after admission if the application to the county court has not been determined (s.68(1)(a), (2)).

BEGINNING WITH. Means "including" (*Zoan v Rouamba* [2000] 2 All E.R. 620, CA).

## References to tribunals by Secretary of State concerning Part II patients

**67.**—(1) The Secretary of State may, if he thinks fit, at any time refer to [the **1–823** appropriate tribunal] the case of any patient who is liable to be detained or subject to guardianship [. . .] under Part II of this Act [or of any community patient].

(2) For the purpose of furnishing information for the purposes of a reference under subsection (1) above any registered medical practitioner [or approved

clinician] authorised by or on behalf of the patient may, at any reasonable time, visit the patient and examine him in private and require the production of and inspect any records relating to the detention or treatment of the patient in any hospital [or to any after-care services provided for the patient under section 117 below].

(3) Section 32 above shall apply for the purposes of this section as it applies for the purposes of Part II of this Act.

AMENDMENTS

The reference to the appropriate tribunal in subs.(1) was substituted by SI 2008/2883 art.9, Sch.3 para.47. The reference to after-care services in subs.(2) was inserted by the Mental Health (Patients in the Community) Act 1995 s.2(1), Sch.1 para.8. The other amendments to this section were inserted by the Mental Health Act 2007 ss.13(2)(a), 32(4), Sch.3 para.19. The words omitted in subs.(1) were repealed by s.55, Sch.11 Pt 5.

DEFINITIONS

**1–824**    the appropriate tribunal: ss.66(4), 145(1).
community patient: ss.17A(7), 145(1).
approved clinician: s.145(1).
hospital: ss.79(6), 145(1).
patient: s.145(1).

GENERAL NOTE

**1–825**    This section enables the Secretary of State (or, in relation to Wales, the Welsh Ministers) to refer a patient who is liable to be detained, or subject to guardianship or to a community treatment order to a tribunal at any time. It applies to patients who have been placed under hospital or guardianship orders by a court under s.37 (Sch.1, Pt 1, para.1). The Secretary of State for Justice has a similar power to refer the case of a restricted patient to a tribunal under s.71(1).

Anyone may request a referral. Requests for referrals with respect to patients detained in England should be sent to:

Department of Health
Mental Health Legislation
Area 224 Wellington House
133-155 Wellington Road
London SE1 8UG
Fax: 020 7972 4147
E-mail:mentalhealthact2007@dh.gsi.gov.uk

The address for patients detained in Wales is:

Head of Mental Health, Vulnerable Groups & Offenders Branch
Welsh Assembly Government
Cathays Park
Cardiff CF10 3NQ

The following guidance has been published by the Department of Health (2010):

**"Information required to support the request**

Your letter will need to set out clearly why a Secretary of State's reference under s.67 is being sought. You will need to fill in the relevant tribunal application form on the Tribunal website *http://www.mhrt.org.uk/FormsGuidance/forms.htm* when requesting a s.67 reference and attach it to your letter. Please do not sign or date the form. In addition to the information to be given in the form, please indicate in your letter the length of time the patient has been on the section of the Act.

**The issues that the Secretary of State for Health will take into account when considering making a reference under section 67**

The issues that the Secretary of State for Health will take into account include but are not limited to:

the reason for the request;

the length of time since the case was last considered by a Tribunal (if ever);

the length of time it may be before an application may (or a reference must) be made under other sections of the Act; and

whether any decision being sought falls within the remit of a Tribunal.

These are not, however, the only factors. Each case will be considered on its merits. The Secretary of State will not refer cases where the patient has already been discharged from their section.

If the Secretary of State makes a reference under s.67, he will ask the Tribunal Secretariat to make the necessary arrangements, and the person who made the request will be informed."

Hospital managers should normally request a referral by the Secretary of State when a patient's detention is extended pending a displacement decision under s.29 and the patient lacks the capacity to make a request (*Code of Practice*, para.30.41).

*Subsection (1)*

SECRETARY OF STATE.    In practice, the Secretary of State for Health. The functions of **1–826** the Minister, so far as exercisable in relation to Wales, are exercised by the Welsh Ministers (see the General Note to this Act).

IF HE THINKS FIT.    A reference could be made if the Secretary of State considered that there were good reasons for a tribunal hearing to take place before the date when the patient would be next eligible to make an application under s.66.

*Subsection (2)*

This subsection provides for a patient whose case has been referred to a tribunal under **1–827** this section to call for an independent clinical opinion. A failure to allow the clinician to examine the patient could amount to an offence under s.129.

**[Duty of managers of hospitals to refer cases to tribunal**

**68.**—(1) This section applies in respect of the following patients—    **1–828**
- (a) a patient who is admitted to a hospital in pursuance of an application for admission for assessment;
- (b) a patient who is admitted to a hospital in pursuance of an application for admission for treatment;
- (c) a community patient;
- (d) a patient whose community treatment order is revoked under section 17F above;
- (e) a patient who is transferred from guardianship to a hospital in pursuance of regulations made under section 19 above.

(2) On expiry of the period of six months beginning with the applicable day, the managers of the hospital shall refer the patient's case to [the appropriate tribunal].

(3) But they shall not do so if during that period—
- (a) any right has been exercised by or in respect of the patient by virtue of any of paragraphs (b), (ca), (cb), (e), (g) and (h) of section 66(1) above;

(b) a reference has been made in respect of the patient under section 67(1) above, not being a reference made while the patient is or was liable to be detained in pursuance of an application for admission for assessment; or

(c) a reference has been made in respect of the patient under subsection (7) below.

(4) A person who applies to a tribunal but subsequently withdraws his application shall be treated for these purposes as not having exercised his right to apply, and if he withdraws his application on a date after expiry of the period mentioned in subsection (2) above, the managers shall refer the patient's case as soon as possible after that date.

(5) In subsection (2) above, "the applicable day" means—

(a) in the case of a patient who is admitted to a hospital in pursuance of an application for admission for assessment, the day on which the patient was so admitted;

(b) in the case of a patient who is admitted to a hospital in pursuance of an application for admission for treatment—

    (i) the day on which the patient was so admitted; or

    (ii) if, when he was so admitted, he was already liable to be detained in pursuance of an application for admission for assessment, the day on which he was originally admitted in pursuance of the application for admission for assessment;

(c) in the case of a community patient or a patient whose community treatment order is revoked under section 17F above, the day mentioned in subparagraph (i) or (ii), as the case may be, of paragraph (b) above;

(d) in the case of a patient who is transferred from guardianship to a hospital, the day on which he was so transferred.

(6) The managers of the hospital shall also refer the patient's case to [the appropriate tribunal] if a period of more than three years (or, if the patient has not attained the age of 18 years, one year) has elapsed since his case was last considered by such a tribunal, whether on his own application or otherwise.

(7) If, in the case of a community patient, the community treatment order is revoked under section 17F above, the managers of the hospital shall also refer the patient's case to [the appropriate tribunal] as soon as possible after the order is revoked.

(8) For the purposes of furnishing information for the purposes of a reference under this section, a registered medical practitioner or approved clinician authorised by or on behalf of the patient may at any reasonable time—

(a) visit and examine the patient in private; and

(b) require the production of and inspect any records relating to the detention or treatment of the patient in any hospital or any after-care services provided for him under section 117 below.

(9) Reference in this section to the managers of the hospital—

(a) in relation to a community patient, is to the managers of the responsible hospital;

(b) in relation to any other patient, is to the managers of the hospital in which he is liable to be detained.]

AMENDMENT
This section was inserted by the Mental Health Act 2007 s.37(3). The references to the appropriate tribunal in subss.(2), (6) and (7) were substituted by SI 2008/2883 art.9, Sch.3 para.48.

DEFINITIONS

application for admission for assessment: ss.2, 145(1).　　　　　　　　　**1–829**
application for admission for treatment: ss.3, 145(1).
the appropriate tribunal: ss.66(4), 145(1).
approved clinician: s.145(1).
community patient: ss.17A(7), 145(1).
community treatment order: ss.17A(7), 145(1).
the managers: s.145(1).
responsible hospital: ss.17A(7), 145(1).
patient: s.145(1).

GENERAL NOTE
This section requires the hospital managers to refer a patient to a tribunal in specified **1–830** circumstances. The purpose of the referral system is to "ensure that patients who lack the ability or initiative to make an application to a Tribunal . . . have the safeguard of an independent review of their case" (Cmnd.8405, para.24). The key provisions are:

1. A requirement to make a referral six months from the day on which the patient was first detained, whether under s.2 for assessment or s.3 for treatment, or the day on which he or she was detained in hospital following a transfer from guardianship. The day in question is defined as "the applicable day" (subs.(5)). The applicable day for a patient who was detained under either s.2 or 3 is not affected by the patient being subsequently place on a community treatment order (subs.(5)(c)). Under s.68A, the six-month period can be reduced by order of the Secretary of State, in relation to hospitals in England, or the Welsh Ministers, in relation to hospitals in Wales.

2. The removal by the 2007 Act of the previous link that existed between renewals and referrals. This means that the only requirement for referrals under this section, apart from referrals under subs.(2), is that the tribunal has not considered the patient's case in three years (or one year if the patient is under 18) (subs.(6)). The order making power under s.68A can be used to reduce the three-year and one-year periods. Under s.71(2), the Secretary of State for Justice must refer the case of a restricted patient whose case has not been considered by the tribunal for three years.

3. The requirement to make referrals applies to community patients (subs.(1)(c)).

4. The hospital managers of the detaining hospital must refer the case of a community patient to the tribunal as soon as possible after the community treatment order (CTO) is revoked: see subs.(7) and the note thereto.

5. Either a registered medical practitioner or an approved clinician may visit and examine the patient, including a community patient, for the purposes of gathering information in preparation for the tribunal hearing (subs.(8)). A failure to allow such a person to undertake this function could amount to an offence under s.129.

Any change in the patient's legal status, for example from a s.3 to a community patient, does not affect the continuing validity of an extant and undetermined reference to the First-tier Tribunal (*KF v Birmingham and Solihull Mental Health NHS Foundation Trust* [2010] UKUT 185 (AAC))

The fact that a reference has been made under this section does not prevent the patient the patient making an application under s.66(1)(f) during the period of detention when the reference takes place. Although s.77(2) prohibits the making of more than one application during a specific period of detention, a reference is not an application.

Patients who are absent without leave at the point at which they should be referred to the tribunal must be referred on their return to hospital (s.21(2)).

For the application of this section to Part III patients who have been made subject to hospital orders without restrictions or to guardianship orders, see Sch.1 Pt1, paras 2, 10. Paragraph 157 of the Explanatory Notes states:

> "Only those Part III patients who are transferred from a guardianship order to a hospital qualify for a referral by the hospital managers after the first six months. Part III patients placed on a hospital order will not be entitled to a referral in the first six months of their detention, as their initial detention has been subject to judicial consideration by the sentencing court and they cannot themselves apply to the tribunal in that period. The referral at three years (or one year) will extend to all Part III patients detained in hospital or on SCT and not subject to restrictions."

*Subsection (2)*

**1–831**     This provision requires a reference to be made if a s.2 patient is still detained under that section by virtue of the effect of s.29(4).

BEGINNING WITH.   Means "including" (*Zoan v Rouamba* [2000] 2 All.E.R. 620, CA).

MANAGERS OF THE HOSPITAL.   See subs.(9).

*Subsection (6)*

**1–832**     ATTAINED THE AGE.   At the commencement of his or her 18th birthday (Family Law Reform Act 1969 s.9(1)).

CONSIDERED.   At a hearing.

*Subsection (7)*

**1–833**     The Deputy Chamber President of the First-tier Tribunal (Mental Health) has decided that if following a reference under this provision, the patient is subsequently placed on a CTO, "the 68(7) reference will be treated as having lapsed, and no further action will be taken by the tribunal in relation to it. . . . Accordingly, if a CTO patient is recalled and the CTO is revoked under section 17F, Hospital Managers must continue to refer cases to the tribunal pursuant to section 68(7)—but *must then notify the tribunal immediately if the patient is placed on a new CTO.* Following such notification the referral will be treated as having lapsed, the parties should be notified, and the file will be closed unless there are other outstanding references or applications, in which case consideration will be given to the management or consolidation of any continuing proceedings, under case management powers." Ignoring the reference means that it is treated for the purposes of subs.(3)(c) as if it had never been made, so that the duty under subs.(2) to make a reference after six months will apply. The statement of the Deputy Chamber President, "References made under section 68(7) Mental Health Act 1983 (as amended)", can be found on the website of the First-tier Tribunal (Mental Health) (*www.mhrt.org.uk*—accessed July 23, 2010).

## [Power to reduce periods under section 68

**1–834**     **68A.**—(1) The appropriate national authority may from time to time by order amend subsection (2) or (6) of section 68 above so as to substitute for a period mentioned there such shorter period as is specified in the order.

(2) The order may include such transitional, consequential, incidental or supplemental provision as the appropriate national authority thinks fit.

(3) The order may, in particular, make provision for a case where—

(a) a patient in respect of whom subsection (1) of section 68 above applies is, or is about to be, transferred from England to Wales or from Wales to England; and

(b) the period by reference to which subsection (2) or (6) of that section operates for the purposes of the patient's case is not the same in one territory as it is in the other.

(4) A patient is transferred from one territory to the other if—

(a) he is transferred from a hospital, or from guardianship, in one territory to a hospital in the other in pursuance of regulations made under section 19 above;

(b) he is removed under subsection (3) of that section from a hospital or accommodation in one territory to a hospital or accommodation in the other;

(c) he is a community patient responsibility for whom is assigned from a hospital in one territory to a hospital in the other in pursuance of regulations made under section 19A above;

(d) on the revocation of a community treatment order in respect of him under section 17F above he is detained in a hospital in the territory other than the one in which the responsible hospital was situated; or

(e) he is transferred or removed under section 123 below from a hospital in one territory to a hospital in the other.

(5) Provision made by virtue of subsection (3) above may require or authorise the managers of a hospital determined in accordance with the order to refer the patient's case to [the appropriate tribunal].

(6) In so far as making provision by virtue of subsection (3) above, the order—

(a) may make different provision for different cases;

(b) may make provision which applies subject to specified exceptions.

(7) Where the appropriate national authority for one territory makes an order under subsection (1) above, the appropriate national authority for the other territory may by order make such provision in consequence of the order as it thinks fit.

(8) An order made under subsection (7) above may, in particular, make provision for a case within subsection (3) above (and subsections (4) to (6) above shall apply accordingly).

(9) In this section, "the appropriate national authority" means—

(a) in relation to a hospital in England, the Secretary of State;

(b) in relation to a hospital in Wales, the Welsh Ministers.]

AMENDMENT

This section was inserted by the Mental Health Act 2007 s.37(3). The reference to the appropriate tribunal in subs.(5) was substituted by SI 2008/2883 art.9, Sch.3 para.49.

DEFINITIONS

    patient: s.145(1).                                                               **1–835**

    hospital: s.145(1)

    community patient: ss.17A(7), 145(1).

    community treatment order: ss.17A(7), 145(1).

    responsible hospital: ss.17A(7), 145(1).

    the appropriate tribunal: ss.66(4), 145(1).

GENERAL NOTE

**1–836**    This section enables the Secretary of State and the Welsh Ministers to make an order reducing the referral periods specified in s.68. It "enables the order to include any consequential provisions that may be required to ensure that patients who are transferred from England to Wales or vice versa between the period of referral in one territory and the other do not miss out on a referral to the tribunal by virtue of the transfer" (Explanatory Notes, para.154).

*Subsection (1)*
APPROPRIATE NATIONAL AUTHORITY.    See subs.(9).

BY ORDER.    See s.143(1).

SHORTER PERIOD.    There is no power to lengthen the periods.

*Applications and references concerning Part III patients*

**Applications to tribunals concerning patients subject to hospital and guardianship orders**

**1–837**    **69.**—(1) Without prejudice to any provision of section 66(1) above as applied by section 40(4) above, an application to [the appropriate tribunal] may also be made—

[(a)  in respect of a patient liable to be detained in pursuance of a hospital order or a community patient who was so liable immediately before he became a community patient, by the nearest relative of the patient in any period in which an application may be made by the patient under any such provision as so applied;] and

(b)  in respect of a patient placed under guardianship by a guardianship order—
  (i)  by the patient, within the period of six months beginning with the date of the order;
  (ii)  by the nearest relative of the patient, within the period of 12 months beginning with the date of the order and in any subsequent period of 12 months.

(2)  Where a person detained in a hospital—

(a)  is treated as subject to a hospital order [, hospital direction] or transfer direction by virtue of section 41(5) above, [or section 80B(2), 82(2) or 85(2) below.] [. . .]; or

(b)  is subject to a direction having the same effect as a hospital order by virtue of section [. . .] 47(3) or 48(3) above,

then, without prejudice to any provision of Part II of this Act as applied by section 40 above, that person may make an application to [the appropriate tribunal] in the period of six months beginning with the date of the order or direction mentioned in paragraph (a) above or, as the case may be, the date of the direction mentioned in paragraph (b) above.

[(3)  The provisions of section 66 above as applied by section 40(4) above are subject to subsection (4) below.

(4)  If the initial detention period has not elapsed when the relevant application period begins, the right of a hospital order patient to make an application by virtue of paragraph (ca) or (cb) of section 66(1) above shall be exercisable only during whatever remains of the relevant application period after the initial detention period has elapsed.

(5) In subsection (4) above—

(a) "hospital order patient" means a patient who is subject to a hospital order, excluding a patient of a kind mentioned in paragraph (a) or (b) of subsection (2) above;

(b) "the initial detention period", in relation to a hospital order patient, means the period of six months beginning with the date of the hospital order; and

(c) "the relevant application period" means the relevant period mentioned in paragraph (ca) or (cb), as the case may be, of section 66(2) above.]

AMENDMENTS

In this section the words in square brackets were substituted and inserted by the Mental Health Act 2007 ss.32(4), 39(2), Sch.3 para.20, Sch.5 Pt 2 para.18. The words omitted in subs.(2)(b) were repealed by s.55, Sch.11 Pt 5 and the Domestic Violence, Crime and Victims Act 2004 s.58(2), Sch.11. The references to the appropriate tribunal in subs.(1) and (2) were substituted by SI 2008/2883 art.9, Sch.3 para.50.

DEFINITIONS

the appropriate tribunal: ss.66(4), 145(1).          **1–838**
patient: s.145(1).
hospital: ss.79(6), 145(1).
hospital order: ss.37, 55(4), 145(1).
guardianship order: s.55(4).
transfer direction: ss.47, 145(1).
nearest relative: ss.26(3), 145(1).
community patient: ss.17A(7), 145(1).

GENERAL NOTE

This section specifies when a tribunal application can be made by the nearest relative of a **1–839** patient who has been placed under a hospital order made by a court under s.37 or who is a community patient. It also enables tribunal applications to be made in respect of guardianship order patients and provides an opportunity for certain other patients who have been admitted to hospital after having committed offences to have their cases reviewed by a tribunal. Applications by restricted patients are governed by s.70.

*Subsection (1)*
PERIOD IN WHICH AN APPLICATION MAY BE MADE BY THE PATIENT.   See subss.(3) to (5).   **1–840**

NEAREST RELATIVE.   Or acting nearest relative appointed by the county court (s.29(6)).

*Subsection (2)*
This subsection affects:          **1–841**

"certain categories of patient whose cases have not recently been looked at by a court but who are, simply by reason of the way [this Act is] put together, deemed to be detained as though subject to a fresh hospital order. [. . .] As a result of [Schedule 1, Part 1, paragraphs 2, 9], such patients, who may already have been in hospital for a substantial period, would have a six months' gap during which they were not entitled to apply to a Tribunal and had not just had their cases looked at by a court ... [This subsection removes] that gap. In addition, [it] seeks to meet the concern which has been expressed ... about the position of patients immediately after they have been transferred from prison. Again, the grounds for their detention in hospital will not previously have been considered by a court. The Government now accept that such people should have an immediate right to a Tribunal hearing"; per Lord Belstead, *Hansard* HL, Vol.427, col.868.

### Applications to tribunals concerning restricted patients

1–842    **70.** A patient who is a restricted patient within the meaning of section 79 below and is detained in a hospital may apply to [the appropriate tribunal]—

(a)  in the period between the expiration of six months and the expiration of 12 months beginning with the date of the relevant hospital order [, hospital direction] or transfer direction; and

(b)  in any subsequent period of 12 months.

AMENDMENT

The reference to the appropriate tribunal was substituted by SI 2008/2883 art.9, Sch.3 para.51. In para.(b) the words in square brackets were inserted by the Crime (Sentences) Act 1997 s.55, Sch.4 para.12(9).

DEFINITIONS

1–843    patient: s.145(1).
restricted patient: s.79(1).
hospital: ss.79(6), 145(1).
the appropriate tribunal: ss.66(4), 145(1).
hospital direction: s.145(1).

GENERAL NOTE

1–844    This section provides for a tribunal application to be made by a restricted patient during the second six months of the duration of the hospital order or transfer direction, and at yearly intervals thereafter. Tribunals hearing applications by restricted patients will be chaired by a lawyer who has had substantial experience in the criminal courts: see the note on s.78(4).

A tribunal considering an application made by a restricted patient under this section has no power to adjourn the proceedings so as to monitor the patient's progress in the hope that a projected course of treatment would eventually permit it to discharge the patient (*R. v Nottingham Mental Health Review Tribunal Ex p. Secretary of State for the Home Department, The Times*, March 25, 1987).

An application made under this section ceases to have effect if the patient ceases to be a restricted patient. However, it is the practice of the tribunal to treat such an application as converted into one made under s.69(2)(a) so as to avoid the patient being placed under a disadvantage to which he would have otherwise have been placed of having to wait six months before he could make an application (*R. (on the application of MN) v Mental Health Review Tribunal*) [2008] EWHC 3383 (Admin); [2009] M.H.L.R. 98). A restricted patient whose restriction order has ceased to have effect is treated as if he had been admitted to hospital as an unrestricted patient on the date when the restriction order ceased to have effect: see s.41(5).

A PATIENT.    The nearest relative of a restricted patient does not have a right to make an application to a tribunal.

BEGINNING WITH.    Including the date of the hospital order or transfer direction (*Zoan v Rouamba* [2001] 2 All E.R. 620 CA).

### References by Secretary of State concerning restricted patients

1–845    **71.**—(1) The Secretary of State may at any time refer the case of a restricted patient to [the appropriate tribunal].

(2) The Secretary of State shall refer to [the appropriate tribunal] the case of any restricted patient detained in a hospital whose case has not been considered by

such a tribunal, whether on his own application or otherwise, within the last three years.

(3) The Secretary of State may by order vary the length of the period mentioned in subsection (2) above.

[(3A) An order under subsection (3) above may include such transitional, consequential, incidental or supplemental provision as the Secretary of State thinks fit.]

(4) Any reference under subsection (1) above in respect of a patient who has been conditionally discharged and not recalled to hospital shall be made to the tribunal for the area in which the patient resides.

(5), (6) [*Repealed by the Domestic Violence, Crime and Victims Act 2004 s.58(2), Sch.11*].

AMENDMENT

Subs.(3A) was inserted by the Mental Health Act 2007 s.37(4). The references to the appropriate tribunal in subss.(1) and (2) were substituted by SI 2008/2883 art.9, Sch.3 para.52.

DEFINITIONS

    restricted patient: s.79(1). **1–846**
    the appropriate tribunal: ss.66(4), 145(1).
    hospital: ss.79(6), 145(1).
    hospital order: ss.37, 145(1).
    restriction order: ss.41, 145(1).
    patient: s.145(1).

GENERAL NOTE

This section provides that the Secretary of State for Justice may, and in certain circum- **1–847** stances must refer the case of a restricted patient to a tribunal. It not apply to a conditionally discharged patient. The meaning of "restricted patient" is set out in s.79(1).

*Subsection (1)*

The nature of the Secretary of State's discretion under this provision was examined in *R.* **1–848** *(on the application of C) v The Secretary of State for the Home Department* [2001] EWHC Admin 501; [2001] M.H.L.R. 100, where Collins J. held that:

(i) the discretion of the Secretary of State to refer a case in a situation where the tribunal has reached a decision is not untrammelled, in that the Secretary of State must pay proper respect to the decision of the tribunal. He should not use his power merely because he disagreed with the decision reached by the tribunal; and

(ii) a reference can be made: (a) where the decision of the tribunal has been ruled unlawful or stayed by the court on judicial review; (b) where the tribunal has imposed a condition that has proved impossible to put into effect; and (c) where there has been a material change of circumstances. With regard to (c), to be consistent with the patient's rights under art.5 of the European Convention on Human Rights, a reference should only be made if the Secretary of State has formed the view that it is probable that the material in question would have affected the decision of the tribunal in that it would have decided either that a more onerous condition be imposed or that a conditional discharge would not have been ordered.

This case went to appeal and point (ii)(b) of Collins J.'s judgment must be read subject to the following finding of the Court of Appeal. If a change in the patient's circumstances is brought to the Secretary of State's attention after a tribunal has made a deferred conditional discharge but before discharge has been directed, he should utilise the procedure set out in *R. (on the application of IH) v The Secretary of State for the Home Department and the Secretary of State for Health* [2002] EWCA Civ 646, by inviting the tribunal to reconsider its decision. He should not make a referral to a fresh tribunal under this provision (*R. (on the application of C) v Secretary of State for the Home Department* [2002] EWCA Civ 647; [2002] M.H.L.R. 105). The decision of the Court of Appeal in *IH* in so far as it relates to the ability of the tribunal to reconsider its decision was affirmed by the House of Lords in *R. v Secretary of State for the Home Department Ex p. IH* [2003] UKHL 59; [2004] 1 All E.R. 412, which is noted under s.73(7).

SECRETARY OF STATE.   Functions under this provision have not been transferred to Welsh Ministers (see the General Note to this Act and SI 1999/672 art.2, Sch.1).

*Subsection (2)*

**1–849**     This provision applies to a patient who has received a deferred conditional discharge but three years have elapsed without the conditions being met or the tribunal reconvening to consider the case.

## Discharge of patients

### Powers of tribunals

**1–850**     **72.**—[(1) Where application is made to [the appropriate tribunal] by or in respect of a patient who is liable to be detained under this Act [or is a community patient], the tribunal may in any case direct that the patient be discharged, and—

  (a)  the tribunal shall direct the discharge of a patient liable to be detained under section 2 above if [it is] not satisfied—

    (i)  that he is then suffering from mental disorder or from mental disorder of a nature or degree which warrants his detention in a hospital for assessment (or for assessment followed by medical treatment) for at least a limited period; or

    (ii)  that his detention as aforesaid is justified in the interests of his own health or safety or with a view to the protection of other persons;

  (b)  the tribunal shall direct the discharge of a patient liable to be detained otherwise than under section 2 above if [it is] not satisfied—

    (i)  that he is then suffering from [mental disorder or from mental disorder] of a nature or degree which makes it appropriate for him to be liable to be detained in a hospital for medical treatment; or

    (ii)  that it is necessary for the health or safety of the patient or for the protection of other persons that he should receive such treatment; or

    [(iia)  that appropriate medical treatment is available for him; or]

    (iii)  in the case of an application by virtue of paragraph (g) of section 66(1) above, that the patient, if released, would be likely to act in a manner dangerous to other persons or to himself.]

  [(c)  the tribunal shall direct the discharge of a community patient if [it is] not satisfied—

    (i)  that he is then suffering from mental disorder or mental disorder of a nature or degree which makes it appropriate for him to receive medical treatment; or

    (ii)  that it is necessary for his health or safety or for the protection of other persons that he should receive such treatment; or

    (iii) that it is necessary that the responsible clinician should be able to exercise the power under section 17E(1) above to recall the patient to hospital; or

    (iv) that appropriate medical treatment is available for him; or

    (v) in the case of an application by virtue of paragraph (g) of section 66(1) above, that the patient, if discharged, would be likely to act in a manner dangerous to other persons or to himself.]

[(1A) In determining whether the criterion in subsection (1)(c)(iii) above is met, the tribunal shall, in particular, consider, having regard to the patient's history of mental disorder and any other relevant factors, what risk there would be of a deterioration of the patient's condition if he were to continue not to be detained in a hospital (as a result, for example, of his refusing or neglecting to receive the medical treatment he requires for his mental disorder).]

    (2) [. . .]

    (3) A tribunal may under subsection (1) above direct the discharge of a patient on a future date specified in the direction; and where a tribunal [does not] direct the discharge of a patient under that subsection the tribunal may—

    (a) with a view to facilitating his discharge on a future date, recommend that he be granted leave of absence or transferred to another hospital or into guardianship; and

    (b) further consider his case in the event of any such recommendation not being complied with.

[(3A) Subsection (1) above does not require a tribunal to direct the discharge of a patient just because [it thinks] it might be appropriate for the patient to be discharged (subject to the possibility of recall) under a community treatment order; and a tribunal—

    (a) may recommend that the responsible clinician consider whether to make a community treatment order; and

    (b) may (but need not) further consider the patient's case if the responsible clinician does not make an order.]

    (4) Where application is made to [the appropriate tribunal] by or in respect of a patient who is subject to guardianship under this Act, the tribunal may in any case direct that the patient be discharged, and shall so direct if [it is] satisfied—

    (a) that he is not then suffering from [mental disorder]; or

    (b) that it is not necessary in the interests of the welfare of the patient, or for the protection of other persons, that the patient should remain under such guardianship.

    [(4A) [. . .]

    (5) [. . .]

    (6) Subsections (1) to [(4)] above apply in relation to references to [the appropriate tribunal] as they apply in relation to applications made to [the appropriate tribunal] by or in respect of a patient.

    (7) Subsection (1) above shall not apply in the case of a restricted patient except as provided in sections 73 and 74 below.

AMENDMENTS

Subsection (1) was substituted from November 26, 2001, by the Mental Health Act 1983 (Remedial Order) Order 2001 (SI 2001/3712) art.3.

The words and figure in square brackets were substituted and inserted by the Mental Health Act 2007 ss.1(4), 2(8), 32(4), Sch.1 para.14, Sch.3 para.21. Subsections (2), (4A) and (5) were repealed by s.55, Sch.11 Pts 1, 2 and 5.

The other amendments to this section were made by SI 2008/2883 art.9, Sch.3 para.53.

DEFINITIONS

**1–851**    the appropriate tribunal: ss.66(4), 145(1).
patient: s.145(1).
community patient: ss.17A(7), 145(1).
mental disorder: ss.1, 145(1).
hospital: ss.79(6), 145(1).
medical treatment: s.145(1).
responsible clinician: ss.34(1), 79(6).
community treatment order: ss.17A(7), 145(1).

GENERAL NOTE

**1–852**    This section empowers tribunals to discharge patients from hospital, guardianship or supervised community treatment and directs tribunals to discharge such patients if specified criteria are satisfied. For detained patients, the actual discharge can take place at a specified future date (subs.(3)).

The tribunal's powers under this section are confined to granting or refusing relief in respect of persons who are liable to be detained or liable to be recalled; it has no power to consider the validity of the admission which gave rise to the liability to be detained (*R. v East London and The City Mental Health trust Ex p. Brandenburg* [2003] UKHL 58; [2004] 1 All E.R. 400 para.9(3); also see the note on "then suffering" in subs.(1)(a)).

The legality of a decision to make an application to detain a patient immediately after a decision of a tribunal to discharge him is considered in the General Note to s.3 under the heading "The re-sectioning of a patient subsequent to a discharge by the First-tier Tribunal (Mental Health) or the Mental Health Review Tribunal for Wales".

*Human Rights Act 1998*

**1–853**    In *R. (on the application of H) v Mental Health Review Tribunal, North and East London Region* [2001] EWCA Civ 415; [2001] M.H.L.R. 48, the Court of Appeal made a declaration under s.4 of the Human Rights Act that:

> "Sections 72(1) and 73(1) Mental Health Act 1983 are incompatible with Articles 5(1) and 5(4) of the European Convention on Human Rights in that, for the Mental Health Review Tribunal to be obliged to order a patient's discharge, the burden is placed upon the patient to prove that the criteria justifying his detention in hospital for treatment no longer exist; and that Articles 5(1) and 5(4) require the Tribunal to be positively satisfied that all the criteria justifying the patient's detention in hospital for treatment continue to exist before refusing to order a patient's discharge."

In order to remove the incompatibility, the Mental Heath Act 1983 (Remedial) Order 2001 (SI 2001/3712) amended subs.(1) of this section and subss.(1) and (2) of s.73 from November 26, 2001, to provide that a tribunal shall direct the discharge of a patient if they are not satisfied that the criteria justifying his detention in hospital continue to exist. The Remedial Order was considered in the Sixth Report of the Joint Committee on Human Rights. The Committee believed that:

> "the failure to include in the remedial order a provision allowing a person detained in breach of Art.5 by virtue of the previously incompatible legislation to claim compensation as of right would automatically give rise to a violation of Art.5(5) if it proved that the person had been affected by the incompatibility" (para.28).

The Government decided to adopt an ex gratia scheme which provides for compensation to be paid where a "patient is able to demonstrate that were it not for the double negative part of the test he would have been discharged" (letter to the Chairman of the Joint Committee from the Minister of State, Department of Health, dated October 15, 2001).

In *R. (on the application of H) v Mental Health Review Tribunal and the Secretary of State for Health* [2002] EWHC Admin 1522; [2002] M.H.L.R. 362, a declaration of incompatibility was sought on the basis that this section does not authorise a tribunal to consider and to determine questions such as whether a hospital is a particularly suitable hospital in terms of the degree of security or in terms of geographical proximity to the family of a patient. With regard to the latter point, it was claimed that as this section does not empower a tribunal to consider or to determine the rights of a patient or the members of his family under art.8 it is incompatible with the Convention. The application was rejected on the authority of *Re S (Care Plan)* [2002] UKHL 10; [2002] 2 All E.R. 192, where the House of Lords held that a lacuna in an Act, or a failure to provide an effective remedy for a violation of a Convention right, does not lead to the conclusion that the Act is incompatible with that Convention right or the provisions of the Convention in question.

Although, when making a determination under this section the tribunal must consider the proportionality which the patient's mental state and needs bear to the steps proposed by the responsible clinician (RC), there is no requirement under art.5 that detention must be proportionate. Article 5 protects against arbitrary detention; it does not incorporate any additional requirement of proportionality. There was therefore no need for the court to consider whether this section, which sets out a test to prevent arbitrary detention, is itself a proportional response to art.5(1)(e) (*R. (on the application of CS) v Mental Health Review Tribunal* [2004] EWHC 2958 (Admin); [2004] M.H.L.R. 355).

The question whether a decision not to discharge a patient who had been granted a conditional discharge by a tribunal due to a failure to put in place appropriate after-care facilities in the community constitutes a violation of art.5 is considered in the notes on s.117 under this heading.

*Subsection (1)*

This provision requires a tribunal to discharge an unrestricted patient if they are not sat-  **1–854** isfied as to any one of the criteria set out in (a)(i)(ii) or (b)(i)(ii)(iii). A community patient must be discharged if the tribunal are not satisfied as to any one of the criteria set out in (c)(i), (ii), (iii), (iv) or (v). When determining whether criterion (c)(iii) is met, the tribunal must consider the matters set out in subs.(1A). A tribunal is not required to discharge a patient because they think it might be appropriate for the patient to be made subject to a community treatment order (CTO) (subs.3A).

In *Devon Partnership NHS Trust v Secretary of State for Justice* [2010] UKUT 102 (AAC), Judge Jacobs rejected a submission that the tribunal had to apply a test of proportionality to the patient's detention:

"The tribunal must discharge the patient unless detention for treatment is necessary for the patient's health or safety or for the protection of others. The legislation authorises detention by reference to the twin requirements of treatment and protection, moderated by the word 'necessary'. That is a demanding test and provides ample protection for the patient without the need for any additional consideration of proportionality." (para.27)

As essentially the same criteria have to be applied in relation to admission and discharge (*Reid v Secretary of State for Scotland*, below, per Lord Clyde at 503 and *R. v East London and City Mental Health NHS Trust Ex p. Brandenburg* [2001] EWCA Civ 239; [2001] M.H.L.R. 36, per Lord Phillips at para.18), reference should be made to the notes on the admission criteria under ss.2(2) and 3(2). As the tribunal is also required to apply the caselaw on renewals (*R. (on the application of CS) v Mental Health Review Tribunal* [2004] EWHC 2958 (Admin); [2004] M.H.L.R. 355), reference should also be made to the notes on s.20(4). It is not fatal to a decision of a tribunal if it does not expressly consider whether the patient meets the admission criteria, so long as it considers the discharge criteria and provided that in the process it has effectively considered all the criteria that would be relevant to admission (*R. (on the application of H) v Mental Health Review Tribunal, North and East London Region* [2000] M.H.L.R. 242). Crane J. said at para.52:

"Moreover, if the question is asked, namely would the admission criteria be fulfilled if this patient presented today, that question undoubtedly requires amplification in the case of a patient detained in hospital. If a doctor is considering admission criteria, he must ask himself whether there is a risk of failure to take medication in the future and of a consequent deterioration. So, similarly, if the patient is already in hospital, a similar question must be asked. If he is no longer in hospital, to what extent is there a risk of a failure to take medication and of consequent deterioration? It would plainly be too simplistic a question simply to ask, if he were as he is today, would he qualify for admission?"

A similar approach was adopted by Latham J. in *R. v London South West Region Mental Health Review Tribunal Ex p. Moyle* [1999] M.H.L.R. 195, para.34, where his Lordship said that although the discharge criteria mirror the admission criteria:

"the patient applying for discharge is *ex hypothesi* in a different situation from the person who is in the community. As a patient, he or she is receiving care and medication in the controlled environment of the hospital and not ... free to exercise his or her own wishes. In a case like the present, the assessment of risk must involve a judgment as to the extent to which release into the community will give rise to the likelihood that he or she will not comply with medication, with the consequences described by the psychiatrist".

It is therefore submitted that the patient's RC should not be asked: "Would the patient's current mental state justify making an application for detention?" Rather, he or she should be asked to identify the consequences for the patient and/or the public if the tribunal decided to discharge the patient from detention.

The question of what after-care services will be available in the community is relevant to the issue of whether the criteria in this provision are met: see *R. (on the application of Ashworth Hospital Authority) v Mental Health Review Tribunal for the West Midlands and North West Regions*, noted under para.(b). A tribunal should not assume that after-care services will be provided to a discharged patient: evidence of the services that could be provided to the patient should be placed before the tribunal.

This subsection only applies to restricted patients to the extent provided for in ss.73 and 74 (subs.(7)).

APPLICATION. Or a reference made by the Secretary of State (subs.(6)).

IN RESPECT OF A PATIENT WHO IS LIABLE TO BE DETAINED UNDER THIS ACT OR IS A COMMUNITY PATIENT. In *KF v Birmingham and Solihull Mental Health NHS Foundation Trust* [2010] UKUT 185 (AAC), para.57, the Upper Tribunal said:

(i) in the context of references, these words refer to the patient's status both at the date the reference is made and at the subsequent hearing of that reference;

(ii) a patient may therefore fall within this provision by being liable to be detained under the Act when the reference is made and by being a community patient at the time of the hearing; and

(iii) sub-paragraphs (a) to (c) of subs.(1) refer *only* to the patient's status as at the time of the hearing (not the date of the reference), and set out the legal tests to be applied depending on the patient's particular status at that time (see *AA v Cheshire and Wirral Partnership NHS Trust* [2009] UKUT 195 (AAC) at para. 45).

MAY IN ANY CASE DIRECT THAT THE PATIENT BE DISCHARGED. The tribunal has power to discharge the patient even though the legal grounds for compulsory detention still subsist. This discretion is rarely invoked. The discharge could take place some time after the tribunal's decision (subs.(3)).

*Paragraph (a)*

Where the discharge of a patient who has been detained under s.2 has been barred by the **1–855** RC issuing a report under s.25, a tribunal is not obliged to consider the dangerousness criterion in that section when exercising its discretion to discharge even if the patient's detention under s.2 has been extended by the operation of s.29(4). Whether it does so will depend on its assessment of the facts of an individual case (*R. (on the application of MH (acting by the Official Solicitor as Litigation Friend)) v Secretary of State for Health and the Mental Health Review Tribunal* [2004] EWHC 56 (Admin); [2004] M.H.L.R. 155).

SHALL DIRECT. The tribunal *must* discharge the patient if they are not satisfied as to either of the criteria set out in paras (i) and (ii).

DISCHARGE. Since the coming into force of the Human Rights Act 1998, the term "discharge" has to be read in a way that is compatible with art.5(1) of the European Convention on Human Rights. Consequently a person is discharged from detention if he is no longer deprived of his liberty: see *Secretary of State for the Home Department v Mental Health Review Tribunal* [2002] EWCA Civ 1868; [2002] M.H.L.R. 241 which is noted under s.73(2).

SATISFIED. The burden of proof is placed on the detaining authority to satisfy the tribunal as to the matters set out in this provision: see the note on "The Human Rights Act 1998", above. In *R. (on the application of N) v Mental Health Review Tribunal (Northern Region)* [2005] EWCA Civ 1605; [2006] 4 All E.R. 194, the Court of Appeal held that:

1. The correct standard of proof to be applied by the tribunal under this section and s.73 is the civil standard of proof on the balance of probabilities (or preponderance of probability). Richards L.J. said at para.62:

   "Although there is a single *standard* of proof, it is flexible in its *application*. In particular, the more serious the allegation or the more serious the consequences if the allegation is proved, the stronger must be the evidence before a court will find the allegation proved on the balance of probabilities. Thus the flexibility of the standard lies not in any adjustment to the degree of probability required for an allegation to be proved (such that a more serious allegation has to be proved to a higher degree of probability), but in the strength or quality of the evidence that will in practice be required for an allegation to be proved on the balance of probabilities."

2. In relation to this section and s.73, no more than cogent evidence that was accepted as correct will be required in order to satisfy the tribunal, on the balance of probabilities, that the conditions for continuing detention are met. Demanding an especially high evidential requirement would subvert the obvious purpose of the 1983 Act which sought both to protect the interests of the individual whose ability to act in his own best interests was impaired and at the same time enable a proportionate balance to be struck between individual and public interests.

3. The findings in 1 and 2 are in full conformity with the requirements of the European Convention on Human Rights.

4. The standard of proof has a potential part to play in the decision-making process even in relation to issues that are the subject of judgment and evaluation. Richards L.J said at para.103:

> "We . . . think it likely that the tribunal's task will be made easier if, instead of dividing up the issues into matters that are susceptible to proof to a defined standard and those that are not, it approaches the entire range of issues by reference to the standard of proof on the balance of probabilities, whilst recognising that in practice the standard of proof will have a much more important part to play in the determination of disputed issues of fact that it will generally have in matters of judgment as to appropriateness and necessity."

The finding made by Richards L.J. in point 1 was endorsed by the House of Lords in *Re D* [2008] UKHL 33 para.27, where Lord Carswell said that it "effectively states in concise terms the proper state of the law on this topic". Lord Carswell stated that he would add one small qualification to the statement made by Richard's L.J. concerning the seriousness of the anticipated consequences. His view was that this should be considered as no more than a facet of the seriousness of the allegation. The following example was given, at para.28, to illustrate the point:

> "if it is alleged that a bank manager has committed a minor peculation, that could entail very serious consequences for his career, so making it less likely that he would risk doing such a thing."

THEN SUFFERING. The term "then" refers to the time of the tribunal's review and the tribunal has no power to consider the validity of the admission which gave rise to the liability to detain. The tribunal will doubtless endeavour to assess a patient's condition in the round, and in considering issues of health, safety and public protection under this provision and under sub-para.(b)(ii) it cannot ignore the foreseeable future consequences of discharge, but the temporal reference of "then" is clear and the tribunal is not called upon to make an assessment which will remain accurate indefinitely or for any given period of time (*R. v East London and The City Mental Health Trust Ex p. Brandenburg* [2003] UKHL 58 para.9(3)).

NATURE OR DEGREE.    See the note on para.(b)(i), below.

DETENTION.    Or the patient's liability to be detained during a period of leave of absence granted under s.17: see the note on "liable to be detained", below, and the judgment of Lord Woolf in *B v Barking Havering and Brentford Community Healthcare NHS Trust* [1999] 1 F.L.R. 106.

PROTECTION OF OTHER PERSONS.    See the note on para.(b)(ii), below.

*Paragraph (b)*

**1–856**    "[S]atisfaction of the criteria for the discharge of a patient under [this provision] may depend on the availability of suitable after-care. If no such after-care is available, it may follow that it is appropriate for the patient to be liable to be detained, or that it is necessary for him to receive treatment in a hospital"; per Stanley Burnton J. in *R. (on the application of Ashworth Hospital Authority) v Mental Health Review Tribunal for West Midlands and North West Regions* [2001] EWHC Admin 901; [2002] M.H.L.R. 13 at para.64.

This case was appealed and the following observations of Stanley Burnton J. were endorsed by the Court of Appeal:

> "If there is uncertainty as to the putting in place of the after-care arrangements on which satisfaction of the discharge criteria depends, the tribunal should adjourn . . . to enable

them to be put in place, indicating their views and giving appropriate directions" ([2002] EWCA Civ 923; [2002] M.H.L.R. 314).

SHALL DIRECT. The tribunal *must* discharge the patient if they are not satisfied as to any one of the criteria set out in paras (i), (ii) and (iii). Where a tribunal is considering the matters specified in paras (i) or (ii) they must bear in mind the distinction between the two matters and "one must somehow be able to read from the reasons the issue to which the reasons are directed" (*R. v Mental Health Review Tribunal Ex p. Pickering* [1986] 1 All E.R. 99 at 104, per Forbes J).

DISCHARGE. See the note on para.(a).

*Sub-paragraph (i)*
THEN SUFFERING. See the note on para.(a).

**1–857**

MENTAL DISORDER. If the person has a learning disability, the disability must be associated with abnormally aggressive or seriously irresponsible conduct (s.1(2A), (2B)).

NATURE OR DEGREE. The meaning of this phrase is considered in the note on s.3(2)(a). In *R. v The Mental Health Review Tribunal or the South Thames Region Ex p. Smith* [1999] C.O.D. 148, the tribunal refused to discharge the patient who was suffering from paranoid schizophrenia, the symptoms of which were well controlled by medication. On refusing the patient's application to judicially review this decision, Popplewell J. said:

"[At the time of the tribunal hearing the patient] was in a stable condition and it is quite clear that the illness was not of a degree which of itself made it appropriate for him to be liable to be detained. The reason for that was because he had a chronic condition which was static. However, the nature of the condition was that it might cease to be static so that the interpretation that nature is in some way unchanging in one view may be right, but the effect of the condition is that because of its very nature it may not remain static. It seems to me that if the facts upon which the tribunal rely have shown that it may not be static, that goes to the nature of the condition. The degree in the instant case, in relation to his condition, was not relevant because it was static and stable."

His Lordship continued:

"If one had simply to look at the degree it would have been right for the discharge to take place, but the nature of the condition was such that it was clear that he should not be discharged. It may well be in a great number of cases that nature and degree involve much the same questions ... and it maybe that tribunals will be wise, if they have any doubts about it, to include them both [in their conclusions]."

*Smith* was followed by Latham J. in *R. v London and South West Region Mental Health Review Tribunal Ex p. Moyle* [1999] M.H.L.R. 195 where his Lordship, when considering the position of a patient with a history of relapsing, said:

"The correct analysis, in my judgment, is that the nature of the illness of a patient such as the applicant is that it is an illness which will relapse in the absence of medication. The question that then has to be asked is whether the nature of that illness is such as to make it appropriate for him to be liable to be detained in hospital for medical treatment. Whether it is appropriate or not will depend upon an assessment of the probability that he will relapse in the near future if he were free in the community."

A finding by a tribunal that the patient's "illness is of a nature to justify detention in hospital but not at present of a degree" constituted a misdirection of law because it erroneously treated "nature or degree" as conjunctive rather than disjunctive. Separate consideration of nature and degree is needed (*R. (on the application of the Home Secretary) v Mental Health Review Tribunal* [2003] EWHC 2864 (Admin); [2004] M.H.L.R. 91 para.57). In *R. (on the application of the Secretary of State for the Home Department) v Mental Health Review Tribunal and CH* [2005] EWHC 746 (Admin); [2005] M.H.L.R. 199, Stanley Burnton J. said, at para.33, that he had "some sympathy" with the difficulties faced by tribunals in addressing the statutory criteria and the distinction between "nature" and "degree", and that in many cases "the distinction is elusive, and it may not matter under which head the question is addressed."

The question whether the continued detention of an asymptomatic patient contravenes art.5 of the European Convention on Human Rights was considered by the Court of Appeal in *R. (on the application of H) v Mental Health Review Tribunal, North and North East London Region* [2001] EWCA Civ 415; [2001] M.H.L.R. 48, where Lord Phillips M.R. said at para.33:

"The circumstances of the present case, which are similar to those considered by Latham J. in [*Moyle*], are not uncommon. A patient is detained who is unquestionably suffering from schizophrenia. While in the controlled environment of the hospital he is taking medication, and as a result of the medication is in remission. So long as he continues to take the medication he will pose no danger to himself or to others. The nature of the illness is such, however, that if he ceases to take the medication he will relapse and pose a danger to himself or to others. The professionals may be uncertain whether, if he is discharged into the community, he will continue to take the medication. We do not believe that Article 5 requires that the patient must always be discharged in such circumstances. The appropriate response should depend upon the result of weighing the interests of the patient against those of the public having regard to the particular facts. Continued detention can be justified if, but only if, it is a proportionate response having regard to the risks that would be involved in discharge."

APPROPRIATE FOR HIM TO BE LIABLE TO BE DETAINED IN A HOSPITAL FOR MEDICAL TREATMENT. In *R. (on the application of the Secretary of State for the Home Department) v Mental Health Review Tribunal)* [2002] EWHC Admin 1128; [2002] M.H.L.R. 241 para.24, Elias J. cited the observations of Lord Phillips above and said:

"In determining whether it is appropriate to detain a patient in hospital, the interests of the patient have to be weighed against those of the public, and the tribunal has to determine whether the detention is proportional to the risks involved. If it is not satisfied that it is a proportional response to those risks to detain the patient, then he must be discharged."

**1–858**     His Lordship said, at para.26, that, with regard to a restricted patient, the proportionate response to the risk may be achieved by the imposition of suitable conditions on a conditional discharge rather than by continuing the patient's detention.

A judgment on proportionality also has to be made with respect to the risk to the patient's health should he or she be discharged from detention even if there is no risk to the public. In *Smirek v Williams* [2000] M.H.L.R. 38, the Court of Appeal held that it can be appropriate for a patient to be liable to be detained in a hospital if the evidence is that, without being detained in hospital, the patient will not take the medication that is required to prevent the deterioration of a chronic mental illness.

In *R. (on the application of Epsom and St Helier NHS Trust) v Mental Health Review Tribunal* [2001] EWHC Admin 101; [2001] M.H.L.R. 8, the Trust challenged the decision of the tribunal to discharge the patient. The tribunal's decision was made on the ground that as the patient, who had been granted leave of absence under s.17 to reside in a nursing home, was not receiving in-patient treatment it was not "appropriate for her to be liable to be detained in hospital for medical treatment" for the purposes of this provision. Sullivan J. held that:

1. The decision of the Court of Appeal in *R. v Barking Havering and Brentwood Community Healthcare NHS Trust* [1999] 1 F.L.R. 106 is authority for the proposition that one has to look at the whole course of the patient's treatment. To do so, one has to look at the past, present and future. His Lordship said at para.47:

   "It is not enough to say that the patient is not receiving treatment at a particular time. If, for example, it was proposed that the patient should be admitted to hospital for in-patient treatment in the week following the expiration of a six-month period of liability to detention, it would be absurd if the tribunal could not take that fact into account. The timing of in-patient treatment, whether it falls within or outside a particular period of liability to detention might be dictated by factors other than the patient's own state of health, for example, resource availability or the availability of specialised staff, and so forth."

2. It would be inconsistent with the scheme of the Act if the mere prospect, that at some unspecified future time in-patient treatment would or might be required, compelled a tribunal to reject a patient's application for discharge. His Lordship said at para.52:

   "The matter has to be looked at in the round, including the prospect of future in-patient treatment, but there will come a time when, even though it is certain that treatment will be required at some stage in the future, the timing of that treatment is so uncertain that it is no longer 'appropriate' for the patient to continue to be liable to detention. It is the tribunal's function to use its expertise to decide whether the certainty, or the possibility, of the need for in-patient treatment at some future date makes it 'appropriate' that the patient's liability to detention shall continue."

His Lordship's references to "in-patient treatment" should now be read as if they were references to "hospital treatment": see *DR*, noted below.

The phrase "liable to be detained" includes patients who have been granted leave of absence from hospital (*R. v Hallstrom Ex p. W; R. v Gardner Ex p. L* [1986] 2 All E.R. 306 at 312). A patient is therefore not entitled to be discharged on satisfying the tribunal that he or she no longer needs actual *detention* in order to receive the treatment that they need if the tribunal considers that he or she needs to be liable to be detained (and therefore liable to be recalled) in order to receive it. The correctness of this interpretation was confirmed by Sullivan J. in *R. (on the application of Epsom and St Helier NHS Trust) v Mental Health Review Tribunal)*, above, where his Lordship concluded, at para.46, that the tribunal was right to reject an argument that the patient was "... automatically entitled to be discharged under s.72 purely by virtue of the fact that she is not receiving any element of in-patient treatment whilst on [s.17] leave". The decision in *R. (on the application of DR) v Mersey Care NHS Trust* [2002] EWHC 1810 (Admin); [2002] M.H.L.R. 386, is authority for the proposition that a patient can be said to be receiving treatment *in* a hospital if he or she is being treated *at* that hospital as an out-patient. *DR* was applied in *R. (on the application of CS) v Mental Health Review Tribunal* [2004] EWHC 2958 (Admin); [2004] M.H.L.R. 355, where Pitchford J. said, at para.40, that the lawfulness of a patient's detention does not depend on the degree of control exercised over the patient's movements, since the degree of control may be infinitely variable depending upon the patient's precise needs without undermining the concept of treatment in a hospital. *DR* and *CS* are considered in the note on s.20(4)(c).

*Sub-paragraph (ii)*
NECESSARY. The standard "is one of necessity, not desirability" (*Reid v Secretary of* **1–859** *State for Scotland* [1999] 1 All E.R. 481 per Lord Clyde at 504).

PROTECTION OF OTHER PERSONS. See the notes on this phrase in s.2(2). In *R. v Parole Board Ex p. Bradley* [1990] 3 All E.R. 828 at 836 DC, Stuart-Smith L.J., on examining this provision, said that "the precise level of risk is not (surely cannot be) spelt out". In *R. (on the application of N) v Mental Health Review Tribunal* [2001] EWHC 1133 (Admin); [2002] M.H.L.R. 70, Gibbs J., having referred to *Bradley*, made the following comments on risk assessment at paras 53–54:

> "It is submitted that there was a requirement on the Tribunal itself to quantify the risk in the face of Dr Gravett's expressed inability at this stage, to do so. I accept ... that there may arise a stage at which a Tribunal must reasonably be required to quantify a risk. It depends on the context. If it was clear that all available evidence was there for it to consider but that the tribunal simply walked away from its responsibility and sat on the fence, then there would be justice in the criticism. I acknowledge also that even where the medical evidence before it does not enable it to quantify the risk there must come, or may come, a point in where continuous deferment of quantification is unreasonable ... Here the context is one in which Dr Gravett is, in my judgment, clearly expressing the view that there is a substantial and unacceptable, in unquantifiable, risk. There is a project for the treatment of the [patient], partially completed, one of the purposes of which is to define that risk more closely. There is, in my judgment, nothing wrong in principle in the psychiatrist, pending the outcome of that process, defining the possible range of risk widely. Nor, in my judgment, is there anything wrong in principle with the Tribunal accepting the psychiatrist's view. It is, in my judgment, unreasonable in that context to say that the Tribunal should attempt the impossible and reach some kind of assessment of risk which would be in danger of amounting to purely arbitrary speculation."

In *R. (on the application of Munday) v Secretary of State for the Home Department* [2009] EWHC 3638 (Admin), para.30, Burnett J. said:

> "Although psychiatrists or other medical health professionals or social supervisors with their knowledge of a person might be in a position to express a view about risk, it is by its nature an exercise of evaluation which does not necessarily call for expert medical input."

The fact that a patient could pose a risk to the public for reasons unconnected with his mental illness is not relevant to the tribunal's decision (*R. (on the Application of LI) v Mental Health Review Tribunal* [2004] EWHC 51 (Admin)).

THAT HE SHOULD RECEIVE SUCH TREATMENT. Compare with the criterion set out in para.(a)(ii).

*Sub-paragraph (iia)*

**1–860**    APPROPRIATE MEDICAL TREATMENT. It will be difficult for a patient to successfully challenge an RC's assertion that this test is satisfied: see the notes on s.3(2)(d).

*Sub-paragraph (iii)*

**1–861**    PARAGRAPH (G) OF SECTION 66(1). Which provides for an application to a tribunal to be made by a nearest relative on the issue by the RC of a report under s.25, barring the nearest relative's discharge powers. Although the tribunal is under a duty to consider the "dangerousness" criterion where an application has been made by a nearest relative under s.66(1)(g), there is no such duty in the case of an application by the patient, although the tribunal is entitled to take it into account when deciding whether to exercise its discretionary power to discharge (*R. (on the application of W) v Mental Health Review Tribunal* [2004] EWHC 3266 (Admin); [2005] M.H.L.R. 134).

Section 66(1)(g) does not apply to patients who are detained under Pt III of this Act: applications made by or in respect of such patients are governed by s.69(1)(a) (*R. (on the application of Central and North West London Mental Health NHS Trust) v Mental Health Review Tribunal (Southern Region)* [2005] EWHC 337 (Admin); [2005] M.H.L.R. 183).

The test in para.(iii) is much narrower than that in para.(ii). It implies a likely serious psychological or physical injury to the patient or to some other person. A mere suspicion that the patient might be dangerous is not sufficient: see the notes on "likely to act" and "dangerous" in s.25(1). If they are not satisfied as to the criterion set out in this paragraph, the tribunal must discharge the patient, even if detention is still justified under paras (i) and (ii).

IF RELEASED. This phrase does not necessarily refer to immediate release; the tribunal could make an order for the deferred discharge of the patient (*R. (on the application of B) v Mental Health Review Tribunal* [2003] EWHC 815 (Admin); [2003] M.H.L.R. 218 para.8).

*Paragraph (c)*
This paragraph states that if the tribunal is not satisfied as to any of the matters set out in **1–862** (i) to (v) in relation to a community patient, the patient must be discharged. Sub-paragraphs (i) to (iv) replicate the criteria set out in s.17A(5)(a), (b), (d) and (e) and reference should be made to the notes thereto. The tribunal also has a general discretion to discharge the patient.

*Sub-paragraph (i)*
MENTAL DISORDER. If the person has a learning disability, the disability must be associ- **1–863** ated with abnormally aggressive or seriously irresponsible conduct (s.1(2A), (2B)).

*Sub-paragraph (iii)*
See subs.(1A).                                                                                    **1–864**

*Sub-paragraph (v)*
See *R. (on the application of W) v Mental Health Review Tribunal*, noted under **1–865** para.(b)(iii), above.

*Subsection (1A)*
See the notes on s.17A(6).                                                                        **1–866**

*Subsection (3)*
If a patient's discharge is deferred under this provision, there is no power for the tribunal **1–867** to reconsider the deferment if circumstances show that what is required to provide after-care services to the patient cannot be put in place; see further the decision of the Court of Appeal in *R. (on the application of H) v Ashworth Hospital Authority,* below.

The discharge on a future date of a patient who is found by the tribunal not to be suffering from a mental disorder would be in danger of violating art.5(1)(e) of the European Convention on Human Rights if the delay between the decision to discharge and the date of discharge was excessive: see *Johnson v United Kingdom* (1999) 27 E.H.R.R. 296, noted in art.5(1)(e) under "persons of unsound mind". Also see the note on "The Human Rights Act 1998" in s.73.

In *R. (on the application of H) v Mental Health Review Tribunal and the Secretary of State for Health* [2002] EWHC Admin 1522; [2002] M.H.L.R. 362, Stanley Burnton J. held that a recommendation made outside the scope of this provision could not be distinguished from an extra statutory recommendation made by an adjudicator in immigration cases as was the subject of consideration by the Court of Appeal in *Khatib-Shahidi v Immigration Appeal Tribunal* [2001] I.A.R. 124, in which the court held that a decision not to make such a recommendation was not susceptible to judicial review because it had no legal force. His Lordship expressed no view on whether a failure to make a recommendation within the scope of this provision would be susceptible to judicial review in circumstances where the contentions and material before the tribunal justified its consideration of such a recommendation.

A TRIBUNAL MAY.   The power to defer discharge applies to situations where the tribunal has exercised either its mandatory or its discretionary duty to discharge (*R. v Mental Health Review Tribunal for the North Thames Region Ex p. Pierce* [1996] C.O.D. 467).

This provision can be used enable preparations to be made to receive a patient back into the community. However, in *R. (on the application of H) v Ashworth Hospital Authority*; *R. (on the application of Ashworth Hospital Authority) v Mental Health Review Tribunal for West Midlands and North West Region* [2002] EWCA Civ 923; [2002] M.H.L.R. 362, Dyson L.J. said at para.68:

> "If the tribunal had any doubt as to whether [after-care] services would be available, they should have adjourned to obtain any necessary information. I regard the alternative of a deferral under [this provision] as less satisfactory ... [I]f the tribunal is in doubt as to whether suitable after-care arrangements will be available, it is difficult to see how they can specify a particular date for discharge. In cases of doubt, the safer course is to adjourn."

The power to defer discharge may also be used in a case of an application made by a nearest relative under s.66(1)(g) (*R. (on the application of B) v Mental Health Review Tribunal*, above). Stanley Burnton J. said at para.8:

> "If a tribunal, on the evidence before it, comes to the conclusion that a patient, if released immediately, would be likely to act in a manner dangerous to other persons, or to himself or herself, but that if proper after-care arrangements are put in place that will not be the position, in my judgement, it is clear that the tribunal may make an order for a deferred discharge under section 72(3) deferring discharge to a date when it is reasonably assured that the appropriate aftercare arrangements will be in place."

**1–868**    As a patient who is subject to a deferred discharge continues to be "liable to be detained", the RC retains the power to grant leave of absence during the period of deferment.

In *Perkins v Bath District Health Authority; R. v Wessex Health Review Tribunal Ex p. Wiltshire CC*, 4 B.M.L.R. 145, the tribunal directed the patient's discharge from a s.2 order but directed that the patient's discharge be deferred "to give an adequate opportunity to those responsible to consider whether an application for treatment might be appropriate". Although counsel for the tribunal was prepared to accept that a tribunal cannot defer discharge under this provision to enable the authorities to decide whether there is some other basis for lawful detention, the Court of Appeal was not required to resolve the point. It is likely that counsel's concession would be upheld if the point was required to be resolved. The tribunal could defer discharge if it was felt that the patient would be fit for discharge at the expiration of a further short period of treatment.

DIRECT THE DISCHARGE OF A PATIENT UNDER THAT SUBSECTION.   i.e. under subs.(1) which is concerned with the powers of tribunals to discharge unrestricted patients. This subsection does not therefore apply to patients who are subject to restriction orders (*R. v Oxford Mental Health Authority Review Tribunal Ex p. Smith*, January 25, 1995 CA). A submission that art.5(4) of the European Convention on Human Rights requires that this subsection be construed to apply to restricted patients was rejected by Collins J. in *R. (on the application of the Secretary of State for the Home Department) v Mental Health Review Tribunal* [2001] A.C.D. 62).

The power to defer does not apply to patients who are subject to guardianship because applications under subs.(1) can only be made in respect of patients who are "liable to be detained".

SPECIFIED IN THE DIRECTION.    It is submitted that Gostin and Fennell are correct in arguing at p.91 that a tribunal "could not specify a date for discharge after that on which the authority for a patient's detention expires" (*Mental Health: Tribunal Procedure*, 1992, p.91). The date specified in the direction cannot be changed by the tribunal subsequent to the communication to the patient of the decision to defer discharge: see *Secretary of State for the Home Department v Oxford Regional Mental Health Review Tribunal* [1987] 3 All E.R. 8, noted under s.73(7).

WITH A VIEW TO FACILITATING HIS DISCHARGE ON A FUTURE DATE.    There is no power under this provision to make a recommendation with a view to doing something other than facilitating the discharge of the patient on a future date. For example, there is no power to make a recommendation for the transfer the patient to another hospital more convenient for him or his family (*R. (on the application of H) v Mental Health Review Tribunal and the Secretary of State for Health*, above).

RECOMMEND.    A failure to make a recommendation is not amenable to judicial review because it is not a final decision (*R. (on the application of LH) v Mental Health Review Tribunal and the Secretary of State for Health* [2002] EWHC 170 (Admin); [2002] M.H.L.R. 130), although a failure to give reasons for not making a recommendation might be susceptible to judicial review in circumstances where the contentions and material before the tribunal justified its consideration of such a recommendation (*R. (on the application of H) v Mental Health Review Tribunal and the Secretary of State for Health* [2002] EWHC 1522 (Admin); [2002] M.H.L.R. 362 para.24). The appropriate procedure now would be for an application to be made to the tribunal under r.49 of the Tribunal Rules for it to review its decision.

The tribunal does not have the power to make a recommendation which is contingent upon an event occurring, such as the patient's mental disorder being stabilised.

TRANSFERRED TO ANOTHER HOSPITAL.    The lack of a power to secure the transfer of a patient to another hospital does not breech art.5 of the European Convention on Human Rights (*MP v Nottinghamshire Healthcare NHS Trust* [2003] EWHC 1782 (Admin); [2003] M.H.L.R. 381).

FURTHER CONSIDER HIS CASE.    The tribunal will set a time limit at the expiration of which it will reconsider the case. It may then decide to reconvene the hearing. At such a hearing the tribunal has all the powers available that it enjoyed at the original hearing: see *Mental Health Review Tribunal v Hempstock* (1998) 39 B.M.L.R. 123 where Kay J. said:

"[T]he tribunal [has] all the powers at the time of further consideration that it had originally. It can, if it considers appropriate, order immediate discharge or future discharge. Clearly, the tribunal will only take either of those courses if it deems such a course right, applying the usual principles. Bearing in mind its earlier decision, it will no doubt be a rarity that it will reach such a conclusion after a short period particularly so far as immediate discharge is concerned."

*Hemstock* was applied in *R. (on the application of O) v Mental Health Review Tribunal* [2006] EWHC 2659 (Admin); [2006] M.H.L.R. 326, where Collins J. held that the phrase "his case" meant the patient's application to the tribunal. Accordingly, that application and the tribunal's powers in respect of it, including the power to agree to the patient's request

for his application to be withdrawn, remain extant after the tribunal has made a recommendation under this provision.

*Subsection (3A)*

**1–869**     This subsection states that a tribunal is not required to discharge a patient because they
think it might be appropriate for the patient to be made subject to a CTO. If the tribunal has
formed such a view, they can recommend to the RC that he or she considers applying for a
CTO and can reconvene in the event of the recommendation not being followed. The
tribunal could discharge the patient at the re-convened hearing: see *Hemstock* and *O*, above.

     If the tribunal is concerned about the availability of after-care arrangements on which
satisfaction of the discharge criteria depends, they should adjourn to enable them to be
put in place, indicating there views and giving appropriate directions (*R. (on the application of H) v Ashworth Hospital Authority*, above, para.69).

*Subsection (4)*

**1–870**     This subsection enables the tribunal to discharge a patient under guardianship and directs
the tribunal to discharge the patient if either of the criteria set out in paras (a) or (b) is satisfied. The tribunal does not have the power either to defer the patient's discharge or to
make recommendations with a view to facilitating discharge at a later date.

     When Parliament responded to the declaration of incompatibility made by the Court of
Appeal in *R. (on the application of H) v Mental Health Review Tribunal, North and East
London Region*, noted under "Human Rights Act 1998", above, by approving the
Mental Health Act 1983 (Remedial Order) 2001 (SI 2001/3712), it did not act to amend
this subsection by requiring the tribunal to be positively satisfied that the criteria justifying
guardianship continue to exist before refusing to order a patient's discharge. This failure
could raise a compatibility issue with art.5 of the European Convention on Human
Rights if the use of the powers contained in s.18(7) constitute a deprivation of the patient's
liberty.

     Note the failure in this provision to reproduce the "nature or degree" requirement which
is found in s.7(2)(a).

*Paragraph (a)*

**1–871**     MENTAL DISORDER.   If the person has a learning disability, the disability must be associated with abnormally aggressive or seriously irresponsible conduct (s.1(2A), (2B)).

*Paragraph (b)*

**1–872**     WELFARE.   See the note on s.7(2).

## Power to discharge restricted patients

**1–873**     **73.**—[(1) Where an application to [the appropriate tribunal] is made by a
restricted patient who is subject to a restriction order, or where the case of such
a patient is referred to [the appropriate tribunal], the tribunal shall direct the absolute discharge of the patient if—

     (a)  [the tribunal is] not satisfied as to the matters mentioned in paragraph (b)(i)
          [, (ii) or (iia)] of section 72(1) above; and
     (b)  [the tribunal is] satisfied that it is not appropriate for the patient to remain
          liable to be recalled to hospital for further treatment.

     (2) Where in the case of any such patient as is mentioned in subsection (1)
above—

     (a)  paragraph (a) of that subsection applies; but
     (b)  paragraph (b) of that subsection does not apply,
the tribunal shall direct the conditional discharge of the patient.]

(3) Where a patient is absolutely discharged under this section he shall there-upon cease to be liable to be detained by virtue of the relevant hospital order, and the restriction order shall cease to have effect accordingly.

(4) Where a patient is conditionally discharged under this section—

(a) he may be recalled by the Secretary of State under subsection (3) of section 42 above as if he had been conditionally discharged under subsection (2) of that section; and

(b) the patient shall comply with such conditions (if any) as may be imposed at the time of discharge by the Tribunal or at any subsequent time by the Secretary of State.

(5) The Secretary of State may from time to time vary any condition imposed (whether by the Tribunal or by him) under subsection (4) above.

(6) Where a restriction order in respect of a patient ceases to have effect after he has been conditionally discharged under this section the patient shall, unless previously recalled, be deemed to be absolutely discharged on the date when the order ceases to have effect and shall cease to be liable to be detained by virtue of the relevant hospital order.

(7) A Tribunal may defer a direction for the conditional discharge of a patient until such arrangements as appear to the Tribunal to be necessary for that purpose have been made to [its satisfaction]; and where by virtue of any such deferment no direction has been given on an application or reference before the time when the patient's case comes before the Tribunal on a subsequent application or reference, the previous application or reference shall be treated as one on which no direction under this section can be given.

(8) This section is without prejudice to section 42 above.

AMENDMENT

Subsections (1) and (2) were substituted from November 26, 2001, by the Mental Health Act 1983 (Remedial) Order 2001 (SI 2001/3712) art.4.

In subs.(1)(a) the words in square brackets were substituted by the Mental Health Act 2007 s.4(9).

The other amendments to this section were made by SI 2008/2883 art.9, Sch.3 para.54.

DEFINITIONS 1–874
the appropriate tribunal: ss.66(4), 145(1).
restricted patient: s.79(1).
restriction order: ss.41, 145(1).
hospital: ss.79(6), 145(1).
relevant hospital order: s.79(2).

GENERAL NOTE

Under the 1959 Act, a patient subject to a restriction order had no right to apply for his or 1–875 her discharge to a tribunal. The patient could only require that his or her case be referred to the tribunal by the Secretary of State in order that the advice of the tribunal be obtained. The decision whether or not he should be discharged rested with the Secretary of State. In *X v United Kingdom* (1981) 4 E.H.R.R. 181, this state of the law was held by the European Court of Human Rights not to be in conformity with art.5(4) of the European Convention on Human Rights which entitles those detained on grounds of unsoundness of mind to a review of the lawfulness of their detention at periodic intervals before a court which must be empowered to order their discharge. This section, which specifies when a tribunal must direct either the absolute or conditional discharge of restricted patients, was enacted as a direct consequence of the ruling in *X v United Kingdom*.

The tribunal has no general discretion to order the discharge of a restricted patient where the statutory criteria are not met and has no power to adjourn the patient's application to give an opportunity for the patient's condition to improve or to see if an improvement already made is sustained (*R. v Nottingham Mental Health Review Tribunal Ex p. Secretary of State for the Home Department*; *R. v Trent Mental Health Review Tribunal Ex p. Secretary of State for the Home Department, The Times*, October 12, 1988 CA).

Although the tribunal has no power under this section equivalent to that under s.72(3) to make recommendations in relation to unrestricted patients (*Grant v Mental Health Review Tribunal, The Times*, April 26, 1986; *R. v Oxford Mental Health Authority Review Tribunal Ex p. Smith*, January 25, 1995 CA), the following Written Answer was given by a Home Office Minister to a question on what would happen if a tribunal which had considered the case of a restricted patient included in its decision a recommendation that the patient be granted leave of absence or be transferred to another hospital or be transferred to guardianship:

"Any such recommendation received in the Home Office [now the Ministry of Justice] is acknowledged, and any comments are offered which can usefully be made at that stage. Correspondence with the tribunal is copied to the patient's [responsible clinician] since it is for this officer to consider the recommendation in the first instance. If the [responsible clinician] submits a proposal based on a tribunal's recommendation, full account is taken of the tribunal's views. At any subsequent hearing of the case, the statement which the Home Office provides will explain the outcome of any recommendation which the tribunal had made" (*Hansard* HC Vol.121, cols 261, 262, October 28, 1987).

If such a recommendation is made, the question of risk has ultimately to be determined by the Secretary of State who is the statutory decision-maker, and not by the court or the tribunal. The court could not substitute its own decision, and would afford the decision-maker a margin of discretion, though it would scrutinise the decision and ensure that all relevant material has been taken into account. The recommendation is an important input, but it is not determinative. Article 8 of the European Convention of Human Rights did not alter the legal framework (*R. (on the application of P) v Mersey Care NHS Trust and others* [2003] EWHC 994 (Admin); [2004] M.H.L.R. 107) In *MP v Nottinghamshire Healthcare NHS Trust* [2003] EWHC 1782 (Admin); [2003] M.H.L.R. 381, Silber J. held that art.5 of the Convention does not require the tribunal to be able to secure the transfer of a restricted patient to less secure accommodation. The relationship between the Secretary of State and the tribunal has been described as being one of "constructive tension" ; per the Parliamentary Under-Secretary of State, Department for Constitutional Affairs (*Hansard*, HL Vol.688, col.740).

A tribunal cannot use its power to adjourn an application to enable it to decide whether an extra-statutory recommendation should be made (*R. (on the application of the Secretary of State for the Home Department) v Mental Health Review Tribunal* [2000] M.H.L.R. 209).

The legality of a decision to make an application to detain a patient immediately after a decision of a tribunal to discharge him is considered in the General Note to s.3.

Guidance for the clinical supervisors of conditionally discharged patients was published by the Mental Health Unit of the Ministry of Justice in February 2009. It can be accessed at the website of the Ministry of Justice (*www.justice.gov.uk*). Go to "guidance" and then "mentally disordered offenders".

*Human Rights Act 1998*

**1–876**    There have been a number of cases on whether the power to defer a patient's discharge under subs. (7) is compatible with art.5 of the European Convention on Human Rights: see the notes on subs.(7).

In *Johnson v United Kingdom* (1997) 27 E.H.R.R. 296, the Court held that the absence of a power to ensure that the deferred conditional discharge of a patient who is found not to be suffering from mental disorder is not unreasonably delayed, is a violation of art.5; also see

*Kolanis v United Kingdom* (2006) 42 E.H.R.R. 12. In *R. v Camden and Islington Health Authority Ex p. K* [2001] EWCA Civ 240; [2001] 3 W.L.R. 553, the Court of Appeal said that the decision of the House of Lords in *Secretary of State for the Home Department v Oxford Regional Mental Health Review Tribunal* [1987] 3 All E.R. 8, to the effect that should it prove to be impossible to implement the conditions specified by a tribunal on a deferred conditional discharge, that tribunal could not consider whether to impose alternative conditions, may not be consistent with art.5 as interpreted by the Court in *Johnson*. The Oxford case was subsequently found to be incompatible with the Convention and was overruled by the House of Lords in *R. (on the application of H) v Secretary of State for the Home Department* [2003] UKHL 59; [2004] 1 All E.R. 412.

In *R. (on the application of Hurlock) v Dr Page and the Secretary of State for the Home Department* [2001] EWHC Admin 380, Ouseley J. said that conditional discharge:

"cannot be regarded as a wholly autonomous and separate remedy, the operation of which is incapable of being affected by other provisions in the Act. This means that it is very difficult to see that there can be a breach of Art.5 where the discharge conditions are not met, because of the views formed by the relevant psychiatrists, provided that those views are reasonable ... and provided that they are not formed with a view to frustrating the decision of the tribunal."

The question whether a decision not to discharge a patient because of a failure to put in place appropriate after-care facilities in the community would constitute a violation of art.5 is considered in the General Note to s.117 under this heading.

The granting of a discharge with a condition that the patient continues to accept medication will not contravene the Convention if one of the grounds in art.8(2) is satisfied (*L v Sweden*, noted under art.8(2) under "protection of health").

*Subsections (1), (2)*

These subsections were substituted to remove an incompatibility with art.5(1) and (4) of **1–877** the European Convention on Human Rights which had been declared by the Court of Appeal in *R. (on the application of H) v Mental Health Review Tribunal, North and East London Region*, which is noted under s.72 under "The Human Rights Act 1998".

*Subsection (1)*

The effect of this subsection is that a tribunal must order the *absolute* discharge of a **1–878** restricted patient if:

  (i) they are not satisfied that he is then suffering from mental disorder of a nature or degree which makes it appropriate for him to be liable to be detained in a hospital for medical treatment; *or*

  (ii) they are not satisfied that it is necessary for the health and safety of the patient or for the protection of other persons that he should receive such treatment; *or*

  (iii) they are not satisfied that appropriate medical treatment is available for him; *and*

  (iv) they are satisfied that it is not appropriate for the patient to remain liable to be recalled to hospital for further treatment.

RESTRICTED PATIENT.   A restricted patient who is no longer suffering from a mental disorder remains a "patient" for the purposes of this section until he or she is discharged absolutely (*R. v Merseyside Mental Health Review Tribunal Ex p. K* [1990] 1 All E.R. 694 CA). The relevant extract from the judgment of Butler-Sloss L.J. is reproduced in the note on "patient" in s.145(1); also see *Johnson v United Kingdom*, noted under subs.(2).

REFERRED TO SUCH A TRIBUNAL. See the note on s.75(1).

DISCHARGE. Means discharge from the patient's liability to be detained (see the note on "may in any case direct that the patient be discharged" in s.72(1)). There is no power in the tribunal to defer an absolute discharge (*R. (on the application of Secretary of State for Home Department) v Mental Health Review Tribunal* [2004] EWHC 1029 (Admin) [2004] M.H.L.R. 184).

If the High Court quashes an order of the tribunal granting a conditionally discharged patient an absolute discharge, the court can declare that pending a rehearing the patient is to be treated as if he had been conditionally discharged: see *R. (on the application of the Secretary of State for the Home Department) v Mental Health Review Tribunal and BR* [2005] EWCA Civ 1616, noted in the General Note to s.65 under the heading "Habeas Corpus and Judicial Review".

SATISFIED. See the note on s.72(1)(a).

MATTERS MENTIONED IN PARAGRAPH (B)(I), (II) OR (IIA) OF SECTION 72(1). Reference should be made to the notes thereto.

RECALLED TO HOSPITAL FOR FURTHER TREATMENT. This paragraph is relevant only to the question of whether any discharge should be conditional or absolute. The tribunal would have to be satisfied at the time of the hearing that it would not be appropriate for the patient to remain liable to be recalled to hospital to receive treatment that might be required at some time in the future. In *R. (on the application of the Secretary of State) v Mental Health Tribunal* [2001] EWHC Admin 849; [2002] M.H.L.R. 260, the Administrative Court quashed the decision of the tribunal to grant the patient an absolute discharge on the ground that the tribunal ignored this provision when giving the reasons for its decision. Pill L.J. said at para.25: "The possible consequences for the safety of member of the public and the patient, when an order of absolute discharge is made are such that the question of liability to be recalled must be dealt with expressly". This case was cited in *R. (on the application of Secretary of State for Home Department) v Mental Health Review Tribunal*, above, para.21, where Moses J. said that even where the tribunal conclude that the patient is not mentally disordered, "it is incumbent upon the tribunal in cases of restricted patients to go on to consider whether it is satisfied that it is not appropriate for the patient to remain liable to be recalled to hospital for further treatment."

*Subsection (2)*

**1–879**    The effect of this subsection is that a tribunal must order the *conditional* discharge of a restricted patient if:

(i)   they are not satisfied that he is then suffering from mental disorder of a nature or degree which makes it appropriate for him to be liable to be detained in a hospital for medical treatment; *or*

(ii)  they are not satisfied that it is necessary for the health and safety of the patient or for the protection of other persons that he should receive such treatment *or*

(iii) they are not satisfied that appropriate medical treatment is available to him.

This provision:

"gives to the tribunal power to impose a conditional discharge and retain residual control over patients not then suffering from mental disorder or not to a degree requiring continued detention in hospital. This would appear to be a provision designed both for the support of the patient in the community and the protection of the public, and is an important discretionary power vested in an independent tribunal, one not lightly to be set aside in the absence of clear words"; per Butler-Sloss L.J. in *R. v Merseyside Mental Health Review Tribunal Ex p. K*, above, at 699, 700.

In *Johnson v United Kingdom* (1997) 27 E.H.R.R. 296, the European Court of Human Rights, having considered the case law on art.5(1)(e) of the European Convention on Human Rights, held that a finding that a detained patient was no longer suffering from the mental disorder which led to his confinement need not inevitably lead to his immediate discharge. A tribunal is entitled to retain some measure of supervision over the progress of such a patient once he is released into the community and to that end make his discharge subject to conditions, such as residence in a hostel. The court further held that it is of paramount importance that the patient's discharge is not unreasonably delayed if such a condition is imposed and that safeguards should exist to prevent this.

PARAGRAPH (B) OF THAT SUBSECTION DOES NOT APPLY. In *R. v Mental Health Review Tribunal Ex p. Cooper*, unreported, February 14, 1990, Rose J. held that the tribunal could direct a conditional discharge, rather than an absolute discharge, solely for therapeutic reasons and that it was not the case that the maintenance of liability to recall under para.(b) of subs.(1) of this section can only be proper if the applicant poses some danger to others.

CONDITIONAL DISCHARGE. For the nature of the conditions that can be imposed, see **1–880** subs.(4). A conditional discharge can be deferred under subs.(7). In order for a patient to be discharged he must no longer be deprived of his liberty for the purposes of Art.5(1) of the European Convention on Human Rights. The principles established in the Strasbourg jurisprudence as applicable to the interpretation of art.5(1) were identified by the Court of Appeal in *Secretary of State for the Home Department v Mental Health Review Tribunal* and *PH* [2002] EWCA Civ 1868; [2003] M.H.L.R. 2002. They are:

(i) a distinction is to be drawn between mere restrictions on liberty of movement and the deprivation of liberty;

(ii) the distinction is one merely of degree or intensity of restrictions, not of nature or substance. In *Guzzardi v Italy* (1980) 3 E.H.R.R. 33 the court observed at para.93:

"The difference between deprivation of and restriction upon liberty is . . . merely one of degree and intensity, and not one of nature or substance. Although the process of classification into one or other of these categories sometimes proves to be no easy task in that some borderline cases are a matter of pure opinion, the Court cannot avoid making the selection upon which the applicability or inapplicability of Article 5 depends";

(iii) the court must start with the concrete or actual situation of the individual concerned and take account of a range of criteria, such as type, duration, effects and manner of implementation of the measure in question;

(iv) account must be taken of the cumulative effect of the various restrictions;

(v) the purpose of any measures of restriction is a relevant consideration; and

(vi) if the measures are taken principally in the interests of the individual who is being restricted, they may well be regarded as not amounting to a deprivation of liberty. [NB For subsequent judicial comment on principles (v) and (vi), see Part 6.]

On applying these principles, the court held that there could be an effective discharge of a patient even though the patient may be required to reside at another hospital. The court found that conditions which required that the patient (a) should "reside at suitable specialist accommodation which provides 24-hour trained nursing care and daytime trained psychiatric nursing care and appropriate security" and (b) "shall not leave the accommodation without an escort", did not inevitably mean that he would be in a regime so restrictive that he would be deprived of his liberty. Keene L.J. said at para.24:

"Condition [(a)] is sufficiently broadly phrased as to allow for measures which would fall short of such a deprivation, and both it (where it deals with security) and condition [(b)] have as their purpose the protection of [the patient] himself and would therefore be in his interests."

In *R. (on the application of G) v Mental Health Review Tribunal* [2004] EWHC 2193 (Admin); [2004] M.H.L.R. 265, Collins J. said, at para.13:

"Any detention of a mentally ill person for treatment may be regarded as in his best interests, but that cannot prevent such detention being a deprivation of liberty within the meaning of art.5. It seems to me that the court in the *PH* case was very much influenced by the evidence that the restrictions proposed by the tribunal were in the patient's interests and for his benefit to enable him to be discharged and were not primarily imposed because otherwise there would be a risk of danger to the public."

His Lordship also said that it "is important to bear in mind that the purpose of any measure of restriction, while a relevant consideration, must not be given too much weight" (para.12). In this case it was held that while it is possible for a patient to cease to be detained if discharged with a condition that he receives and is subject to supervision at the same hospital in which he is detained, it is difficult to see that that could occur when the regime and the purposes of the restrictions were the same. It was further held that the fact that a patient might consent to the deprivation of his liberty did not enable a tribunal to order a conditional discharge that had such an effect.

In *R. (on the application of the Secretary of State for the Home Department) v Mental Health Review Tribunal* [2004] EWHC 2194 (Admin); [2004] M.H.L.R. 273 Collins J. found that there would be a deprivation of the patient's liberty and therefore no discharge where the purpose of the conditions was to ensure that the patient, who was a paedophile with a high risk of re-offending, could not get out into the community unsupervised or unescorted. There was a need for security because, if the patient left the accommodation where he was required to reside unescorted, he would be a danger to young boys. His Lordship said, at para.13, that where it was contended that there would inevitably be a deprivation of liberty, it was sensible and desirable that a challenge be brought as soon as possible, if only to avoid unnecessary actions by those who would be responsible for drawing up the patient's care plan.

The cases noted above were reviewed in *RB v First-tier Tribunal (Review)* [2010] UKUT 160 (AAC) where the Upper Tribunal said, at para.47, that it was arguable that what is incompatible with conditional discharge is the patient's continued detention in a hospital, rather than a care home.

In *IT v Secretary of State for Justice* [2008] EWHC 1707 (Admin); [2008] M.H.L.R. 290, it was held that a condition that the patient was to have one-to-one escorted leave did not amount to a deprivation of liberty as it was only a temporary measure, with unescorted leave being introduced within a few weeks.

*Subsection (3)*

**1–881**    THEREUPON. The absolute discharge of a restricted patient cannot be deferred under subs.(7).

*Subsection (4)*

**1–882**    MAY BE RECALLED. And have his case referred to a tribunal under s.75(1)(a). Only the Secretary of State can recall the patient to hospital: see the note on s.42(3).

CONDITIONS. This section does not empower the attachment of any sanction for failure to comply with a condition, but provides for a general power of recall which, except in an emergency situation, cannot be exercised without up to date medical evidence being obtained by the Secretary of State: see the notes to s.42(3).

A tribunal cannot impose conditions that have the effect of depriving the patient of his liberty by, for example, continuing the patient's detention at another hospital: see the note on "conditional discharge" in subs.(2). A tribunal has a duty to impose such conditions of discharge of a restricted patient as it considers necessary, even if was in no position to enforce those conditions and it was apparent that it would be difficult to put in place arrangements to enable the conditions to be satisfied (*R. v Mental Health Review Tribunal, Ex p. Hall* [2000] 1 W.L.R. 1323 CA). When imposing conditions the tribunal may have regard not only to considerations relating to treatment itself, but also to the question of risk, both to the patient and to the public (*R. (on the application of the Secretary of State for the Home Department v Mental Health Review Tribunal)*, above, at para.27). Only reasonable conditions can be imposed and a condition that the tribunal positively knows will be impossible or highly unlikely to be put into effect is not reasonable. If necessary, the tribunal should use its power of adjournment to ascertain whether conditions which appear attractive are achievable: see the *H* case noted under subs.(7). The tribunal should give reasons for its decision to impose conditions. It would be helpful in a situation where the patient continues to suffer from an underlying mental illness which can only be managed in the community provided the conditions imposed are implemented if the tribunal says so when it orders the patient's conditional discharge: see *W v Doncaster MBC*, which is noted under subs.(7).

In *R (on the application of SH) v Mental Health Review Tribunal* [2007] EWHC 884 (Admin); [2007] M.H.L.R. 234 paras 18–20, Holman J. said that a condition: (a) could not lawfully be capricious; (b) must be relevant and for a proper purpose within the scope of this Act; and (c) is subject to the principle of legality as described by Lord Hoffmann in *R. v Secretary of State for the Home Department, Ex p. Simms* [2000] 2 A.C. 115, i.e. the courts presume that even the most general words were intended to be subject to the basic rights of the individual.

The tribunal cannot lawfully impose a condition which effectively makes the conditional discharge subject to the agreement of some other body, such as the Ministry of Justice, as such a requirement is not a condition of discharge, but a pre-condition to discharge (*R (on the application of Secretary of State for the Home Department) v Mental Health Review Tribunal* [2007] EWHC 2224 (Admin); [2008] M.H.L.R. 212). The Secretary of State for Justice is the sole decision maker on whether a restricted patient should be granted leave of absence.

The usual conditions relate to supervision, residence and medical treatment; see further, the notes on s.42(2) under the heading "Subject to conditions". In his "Review of Homicides by Patients with Severe Mental Illness" (March 2006), Professor Tony Maden made the following recommendation at p.63: "In patients subject to a restriction order there should always be consideration of setting conditions relating to abstinence from drugs or alcohol and the standard procedure should be immediate recall if that condition is breached."

Although a condition may require that the patient attends for treatment, treatment cannot be forced upon him or her in the absence of his consent because conditionally discharged patients are not subject to the consent to treatment provisions contained in Pt IV of this Act (s.56(3)(c)). In *R. (on the application of SH) v Mental Health Review Tribunal*, above, Holman J. held that:

(i) a condition that the patient "shall comply" with medication prescribed by his responsible [clinician] was lawfully imposed as it did not interfere with the patient's absolute right to choose whether to accept treatment, nor did it interfere with his rights under art.8(1) the European Convention on Human Rights;

(ii) the condition must be read as respecting and being subject to the patient's own final choice, which must be his real or true choice; and

(iii) a tribunal should not impose such a condition unless it has a proper basis for anticipating that the patient does and will consent to the treatment in question.

His Lordship said, at para.42, that it would be preferable for a tribunal, when imposing a similar condition to add words such as the following: "subject always to his right to give or withhold consent to treatment on any given occasion."

The finding by Mann J. in *Secretary of State for the Home Department v Mental Health Review Tribunal for the Mersey Regional Health Authority* [1986] 3 All E.R. 233 that a condition requiring a patient to remain in hospital is inconsistent with the duty to discharge albeit conditionally was doubted by Elias J. in *R. (on the application of the Secretary of State for the Home Department v Mental Health Review Tribunal* [2002] EWHC 1128 (Admin); [2002] M.H.L.R. 241. His Lordship said at para.30:

"In my view, the fallacy is to treat release from discharge as meaning release from hospital. It seems to me that it means release from detention in hospital or sometimes . . . from liability to be detained. Release from hospital is neither a sufficient nor a necessary condition for constituting the discharge. If there is such a release but it is to another institution where the patient is detained in the sense that he is deprived of his liberty, then that would not . . . constitute a proper and lawful discharge. By the same token . . . if the patient is discharged from detention in a hospital such that he is no longer deprived of his liberty, then there is still an effective discharge notwithstanding that the conditions are such that he is required to reside in another hospital pending further consideration of his absolute discharge. The central issue, it seems to me, is whether or not the conditions constitute a continued detention. If they do not, it is irrelevant where the patient resides thereafter."

**1–883**     In applying his ruling, his Lordship found that conditions which required the patient to (1) continue to take and receive medication as prescribed; (2) accept and comply with regular supervision by a consultant psychiatrist and social supervisor; (3) reside at suitable specialist accommodation which provides 24-hour trained nursing care and daytime psychiatric nursing care and appropriate security; and (4) not leave the accommodation without an escort, did not constitute a continuing deprivation of liberty within the meaning of art.5 the European Convention on Human Rights and the English legislation. Elias J.'s decision was affirmed by the Court of Appeal at [2002] EWCA Civ 1868; [2003] M.H.L.R. 202. The court described the judge's reasoning at para.30 of his judgment as being "compelling" (at para.25). The Court of Appeal's decision, which effectively overrules the finding of Mann J., is considered in the note on "conditional discharge" in subs.(2). An after-care body is not placed under an absolute obligation to satisfy the conditions imposed by the tribunal: see *R. v Camden and Islington Health Authority Ex p. K* [2001] EWCA Civ 240 CA, noted in the General Note to s.117.

After a conditional discharge the patient's progress in the community will be monitored by the Ministry of Justice in the same way as that of a patient conditionally discharged by the Secretary of State, and the Secretary of State may vary conditions imposed by the tribunal (subs.(5)).

A conditionally discharged patient can apply to a tribunal for his absolute discharge under s.75.

IF ANY.    The tribunal is not obliged to impose conditions on a conditionally discharged patient. In practice, it is unlikely that a patient will be conditionally discharged without conditions being imposed either by the tribunal or the Secretary of State.

Secretary of State. Functions under this provision have not been transferred to Welsh Ministers (see the General Note to this Act and SI 1999/672 art.2, Sch.1). The Secretary of State can impose conditions even though the tribunal has not.

*Subsection (7)*

A tribunal may defer. There is no power in the tribunal to defer an absolute dis- **1–884** charge (*R. (on the application of the Secretary of State for the Home Department) v Mental Health Review Tribunal* [2004] EWHC 1029 (Admin)). The purpose of the defer- ment is to enable arrangements to be made to satisfy the conditions which the tribunal has attached to the patient's conditional discharge. The tribunal has no power equivalent to that contained in s.72(3) for unrestricted patients to make recommendations. A deferred con- ditional discharge is only available to the tribunal if it is satisfied that the patient meets the test for release from detention (*MP v Nottinghamshire Healthcare NHS Trust* [2003] EWHC 1782 (Admin); [2003] M.H.L.R. 381, para.29). It is unlawful for a tribunal to make a "wait and see" decision to defer discharge for the purpose of seeing whether any change in the patient's circumstances might arise and thus provide material which will point to the correct decision in the application: see *R. (on the application of the Secretary of State for the Home Department) v Mental Health Review Tribunal; PG as Interested Party* [2002] EWHC Admin 2043; [2002] M.H.L.R. 381, where the tribunal used its power under this provision to await the results of a therapeutic assessment of the patient. The Ministry of Justice has no role to play in either satisfying the conditions or in determining whether the conditions are met.

In *R. (on the application of H) v Secretary of State for the Home Department and the Secretary of State for Health* [2002] EWCA Civ 646; [2002] M.H.L.R. 87, the Court of Appeal considered the problem that can develop where a tribunal determines that a restric- ted patient is entitled to release on condition that he or she receives psychiatric supervision, but no psychiatrist can be found who is prepared to provide that supervision. In *Secretary of State for the Home Department v Oxford Regional Mental Health Review Tribunal*, above, the House of Lords had held that in this situation a tribunal cannot subsequently reconvene to reconsider its original decision that the patient be discharged. The Court of Appeal held that:

1. The decision of the House of Lords could lead to the patient finding himself "in limbo" should it prove impossible to make the necessary arrangements for him to comply with the proposed condition.

2. The period spent "in limbo" may last too long to be compatible with art.5(4) of the European Convention on Human Rights and may result in the patient being detained in violation of art.5(1) of the Convention: see *Johnson v United Kingdom*, noted, above.

3. Tribunals should no longer proceed on the basis that they cannot reconsider a decision to direct a conditional discharge on specified conditions where, after defer- ral and before directing discharge, there is a material change of circumstances. Such a change may be demonstrated by fresh material placed before or obtained by a tri- bunal. Such material may, for instance, show that the patient's condition has relapsed. It may show that the patient's condition has improved. It may demonstrate that it is not possible to put in place arrangements necessary to enable the conditions that the tribunal proposed to impose on the patient to be satisfied. The original decision should be treated as a provisional decision, and the tribunal should monitor progress towards implementing it so as to ensure that the patient is not left "in limbo" for an unreasonable length of time.

4. Accordingly, where a tribunal decides (i) that a restricted patient is suffering from mental disorder for which psychiatric treatment is necessary for the health or safety of the patient or for the protection of other persons and (ii) that detention in hospital

is not necessary if, but only if, psychiatric treatment is provided in the community, the tribunal can properly make a provisional decision to direct a conditional discharge, but defer giving that direction to enable arrangements to be made for providing psychiatric treatment in the community. The Health Authority (and the local authority: see *W v Doncaster MBC*, below) subject to the s.117 duty will then be bound to use its best endeavours to put in place the necessary aftercare. If it fails to use its best endeavours it will be subject to judicial review. If, despite its best endeavours, the Health Authority is unable to provide the necessary services, the tribunal must think again. If, as is likely in those circumstances, it concludes that it is necessary for the patient to remain detained in hospital in order to receive the treatment, it should record that decision.

**1–885** The court summarised the position where a tribunal considers a conditional discharge at para.98:

1. The tribunal can, at the outset, adjourn the hearing to investigate the possibility of imposing conditions.

2. The tribunal can make a provisional decision to make a conditional discharge on specified conditions, including submitting to psychiatric supervision, but defer directing a conditional discharge while the authorities responsible for after-care under s.117 of this Act make the necessary arrangements to enable the patient to meet those conditions.

3. The tribunal should meet after an appropriate interval to monitor progress in making these arrangements if they have not been put in place.

4. Once the arrangements have been made, the tribunal can direct a conditional discharge without holding a further hearing.

5. If problems arise with making arrangements to meet the conditions, the tribunal has a number of options, depending on the circumstances.

   (a) It can defer for a further period, perhaps with suggestions as to how any problems can be overcome.
   (b) It can amend or vary the proposed conditions to seek to overcome the difficulties that have been encountered.
   (c) It can order a conditional discharge without specific conditions, thereby making the patient subject to recall.
   (d) It can decide that the patient must remain detained in hospital for treatment.

6. It will not normally be appropriate for a tribunal to direct a conditional discharge on conditions with which the patient will be unable to comply because it has not proved possible to make the necessary arrangements.

The decision of the Court of Appeal was affirmed by the House of Lords in *R. (on the application of H) v Secretary of State for the Home Department* [2003] UKHL 59; [2004] 1 All E.R. 412 where their Lordships overruled *Secretary of State for the Home Department v Oxford Regional Mental Health Review Tribunal*, above, and held that it was not the case that, because the tribunal lacked the power to secure compliance with its conditions, it lacked the coercive power which is one of the essential attributes of a court for the purposes of art.5 of the European Convention on Human Rights. Lord Bingham said at para.26:

"What Article 5(1)(e) and (4) require is that a person of unsound mind compulsorily detained in hospital should have access to a court with power to decide whether the detention is lawful and, if not, to order his release. This power the tribunal had. Nothing in Article 5 suggests that discharge subject to conditions is impermissible in principle, and nothing in the Convention jurisprudence suggests that the power to discharge conditionally (whether there are specific conditions or a mere liability to recall), properly used, should be viewed with disfavour."

The conditional discharge regime set out in this section is therefore not incompatible with art.5. This was implicitly confirmed by the European Court of Human Rights in *Kolanis v United Kingdom* (2006) 42 E.H.R.R. 12; [2005] M.H.L.R. 238.

In *H*, their Lordships identified a "categorical difference" between the case of a patient who had been found by the tribunal not to be mentally disordered and who did not therefore satisfy the criteria identified in *Winterwerp v Netherlands* (1979) 2 E.H.R.R. 387 (as was the case in *Johnson v United Kingdom* (1997) 27 E.H.R.R. 296), and the case of a patient who did satisfy the *Winterwerp* criteria and the tribunal considered that he or she could be satisfactorily treated and supervised in the community. In the former case, if the conditions of discharge were not met the alternative was not continued detention but discharge, either absolutely or subject only to a condition of recall. In this situation the conditional discharge must not be deferred beyond a reasonable limited period if a violation of art.5(4) is to be avoided. In the latter case, if the tribunal's conditions proved impossible to meet the alternative was continued detention.

The implications of this aspect of the decision in *H* were explained by Mance L.J. in *W v Doncaster MBC* [2004] EWCA Civ 378; [2004] M.H.L.R. 201 at paras 72, 73:

"The central question is whether the *Winterwerp* criteria for detention are satisfied. If a person is no longer suffering from any mental illness, these criteria are clearly not met. If someone is still suffering from mental illness, they may or may not be met. It may still be possible to release the person in question into the community, either unconditionally or in the expectation that he or she will receive treatment there under appropriate conditions. In the latter case, there are two alterative possibilities. Upon true analysis, the provision of the expected treatment either may or may not be regarded by the tribunal as an essential pre-requisite of discharge from detention: contrast paragraphs 91 and 96 of the Master of the Rolls judgment in [the Court of Appeal], quoted with approval in the House of Lords at ... paragraphs 24 and 28.

If such treatment is an essential pre-requisite of discharge (as it was in *H*), but it proves impossible to provide, then continuing detention is lawful, although the impossibility of providing the treatment envisaged by the tribunal means that the matter will have to return to the tribunal for reconsideration: [2003] UKHL 59, paragraph 27. If such treatment is not an essential pre-requisite to discharge, then, although discharge may be delayed for a period while efforts are made to arrange the expected treatment, discharge cannot be unreasonably delayed, even if it proves impossible to arrange it: see *Johnson v United Kingdom* (1997) 27 E.H.R.R. 296."

Scott Baker L.J. said, at 70, that it would be helpful if in cases where the patient continues to suffer from an underlying mental illness which can only be managed in the community provided the conditions imposed are implemented, the tribunal says so when it makes the conditional discharge order.

The *Winterwerp* case, above, determined that detention on the ground of mental disorder is only lawful under art.5 of the Convention if (1) there is objective medical evidence that the patient suffers from mental disorder; (2) the mental disorder is of a kind or degree warranting compulsory confinement; and (3) the mental disorder persists.

In *Kolanis v United Kingdom*, above, the court observed, at paras 68–70, that in *Johnson* **1–886** the tribunal had found that the applicant was no longer suffering from a mental disorder, no longer had the symptoms and did not require any further medication or treatment. In the case before it, the applicant continued to suffer from mental illness and continued to require treatment and medical supervision in order to control her illness. The court was therefore unable to accept the applicant's contention that the tribunal's decision that she could be discharged subject to conditions was tantamount to a finding that the second criterion in *Winterwerp* was no longer fulfilled, i.e. that her disorder was not of a kind or degree requiring compulsory confinement. The discharge of the applicant had only been regarded as appropriate if the continued treatment or supervision necessary to protect her own health and the safety of the community was available. In the absence of that treatment, her detention continued to be necessary in line with the purposes of art.5(1)(e).

The decision of the Court of Appeal that a Health Authority was not under an absolute obligation to procure compliance with the tribunal's conditions was also affirmed by the House of Lords in *H*; the obligation is for the authority is to use its best endeavours to secure compliance. The tribunal has "no power to require any psychiatrist to act in a way which conflicted with the conscientious professional judgment of that psychiatrist" (para.29). Their Lordships found it unnecessary to determine whether in this context psychiatrists were or could be a hybrid public authority within the meaning of s.6 of the Human Rights Act 1998. If such a finding were made it would have the effect of requiring a psychiatrist to supervise a patient who had been conditionally discharged by a tribunal even though the psychiatrist was professionally opposed to conditions attached to the discharge. It is unlikely that the courts would countenance such an outcome.

If a change in the patient's circumstances or the availability of additional material relating to the patient is brought to the Secretary of State's attention after deferral but before discharge has been directed, he should utilise the procedure set out in *H*, above, by inviting the tribunal to reconsider its decision. He should not make a referral to a fresh tribunal using his power under s.71(1) (*R. (on the application of C) v Secretary of State for the Home Department* [2002] EWCA Civ 647; [2002] M.H.L.R. 105).

The deferment cannot be to a fixed date (*Secretary of State for the Home Department v Oxford Regional Mental Health Review Tribunal*, above, at 13).

**1–887**    When a deferred conditional discharge has been granted by a tribunal, leave of absence, with the consent of the Secretary of State (see s.41(3)(c)), is the normal method designed by this Act to facilitate the patient's discharge from hospital by, for example, providing for overnight stays in a hostel. The Secretary of State should only use his power under s.42(2) to grant such a patient a conditional discharge if there is some development that the tribunal is unable to deal with (*R. (on the application of RA) v Secretary of State for the Home Department* [2002] EWHC Admin 1618; [2003] M.H.L.R. 54).

A deferment should not result in the patient's discharge being unreasonably delayed: see the decision of the European Court of Human Rights in *Johnson v United Kingdom*, noted under subs.(2). Subsequent to this decision the Department of Health wrote to health and social services authorities asking the authorities "to give priority to ensuring that all cases of deferred conditional discharge are implemented within six months of the [tribunal's] decision". In *Kolanis v United Kingdom* above, the court, at para.80, confirmed that where a tribunal finds that a patient may be conditionally discharged,

> "new issues of lawfulness may arise where the detention nonetheless continues due, for example, to difficulties in fulfilling the conditions. It follows that such patients are entitled under Art.5(4) to have the lawfulness of that continued detention determined by a court with requisite promptness".

However, where the treatment considered to be necessary as a condition of discharge was not available, there could be no question of interpreting art.5(1)(e) as requiring discharge without the stipulated conditions for the protection of the applicant and the public being fulfilled, or as imposing an absolute obligation on the authorities to ensure that those conditions were fulfilled (para.71). In *R. (on the application of RA) v Secretary of State for the Home Department*, above, Crane J. said at para.59:

> "[T]he Secretary of State has a duty to respond with reasonable promptness to recommendations by a tribunal and to requests by a [responsible clinician]; not to obstruct or cause unreasonable delay to the implementation of a tribunal's decision;

and to follow recommendations made by a tribunal in the absence of sound reasons or new circumstances."

It is desirable for there to be, as far as practicable, a continuation of the membership of a tribunal which is to monitor and continue to consider a deferred conditional discharge (*R. (on the application of A) v Secretary of State for the Home Department and the Mental Health Review Tribunal* [2003] EWHC 270 (Admin); [2005] M.H.L.R. 144)). Stanley Burnton J. said at para.16:

"Where a relatively short time has passed between the original decision and its reconsideration, the advantages and the fairness involved in requiring the original constitution to reconsider the matter must be greater than when a considerable time has passed."

SUCH ARRANGEMENTS AS APPEAR TO THE TRIBUNAL TO BE NECESSARY. A deferment to secure a patient's admission to another hospital would be lawful as long as the patient was not deprived of his liberty in that hospital: see the note on "conditional discharge" in subs.(2).

HAVE BEEN MADE TO THEIR SATISFACTION. The wording of this provision clearly implies that the tribunal is required to formally indicate whether the arrangements that have been put in place to enable the patient to be discharged are satisfactory.

THE PREVIOUS APPLICATION OR REFERENCE. The patient cannot be discharged on the basis of the earlier deferred direction: the matter must be considered afresh.

*Subsection (8)*
SECTION 42. Which, inter alia, empowers the Secretary of State to discharge the patient  **1–888**
from hospital either absolutely or subject to conditions.

## Restricted patients subject to restriction directions

**74.**—(1) Where an application to [the appropriate tribunal] is made by a restric-  **1–889**
ted patient who is subject to [a limitation direction or] a restriction direction, or where the case of such a patient is referred to [the appropriate tribunal], the Tribunal—

(a) shall notify the Secretary of State whether, in [its] opinion, the patient would, if subject to a restriction order, be entitled to be absolutely or conditionally discharged under section 73 above; and

(b) if [the tribunal notifies] him that the patient would be entitled to be conditionally discharged, may recommend that in the event of his not being discharged under this section he should continue to be detained in hospital.

(2) If in the case of a patient not falling within subsection (4) below—

(a) the Tribunal [notifies] the Secretary of State that the patient would be entitled to be absolutely or conditionally discharged; and

(b) within the period of 90 days beginning with the date of that notification the Secretary of State gives notice to the Tribunal that the patient may be so discharged,

the Tribunal shall direct the absolute or, as the case may be, the conditional discharge of the patient.

(3) Where a patient continues to be liable to be detained in a hospital at the end of the period referred to in subsection (2)(b) above because the Secretary of State has not given the notice there mentioned, the managers of the hospital shall, unless

[the tribunal has] made a recommendation under subsection (1)(b) above, transfer the patient to a prison or other institution in which he might have been detained if he had not been removed to hospital, there to be dealt with as if he had not been so removed.

(4) If, in the case of a patient who is subject to a transfer direction under section 48 above, the Tribunal [notifies] the Secretary of State that the patient would be entitled to be absolutely or conditionally discharged, the Secretary of State shall, unless [the tribunal has] made a recommendation under subsection (1)(b) above, by warrant direct that the patient be remitted to a prison or other institution in which he might have been detained if he had not been removed to hospital, there to be dealt with as if he had not been so removed.

(5) Where a patient is transferred or remitted under subsection (3) or (4) above [the relevant hospital direction and the limitation direction or, as the case may be,] the relevant transfer direction and the restriction direction shall cease to have effect on his arrival in the prison or other institution.

[(5A) Where [the tribunal has] made a recommendation under subsection (1)(b) above in the case of a patient who is subject to a restriction direction or a limitation direction—

  (a) the fact that the restriction direction or limitation direction remains in force does not prevent the making of any application or reference to the Parole Board by or in respect of him or the exercise by him of any power to require the Secretary of State to refer his case to the Parole Board, and

  (b) if the Parole Board make a direction or recommendation by virtue of which the patient would become entitled to be released (whether unconditionally or on licence) from any prison or other institution in which he might have been detained if he had not been removed to hospital, the restriction direction or limitation direction shall cease to have effect at the time when he would become entitled to be so released.]

(6) Subsections (3) to (8) of section 73 above shall have effect in relation to this section as they have effect in relation to that section, taking references to the relevant hospital order and the restriction order as references to [the hospital direction and the limitation direction or, as the case may be, to] the transfer direction and the restriction direction.

(7) This section is without prejudice to subsections 50 to 53 above in their application to patients who are not discharged under this section.

AMENDMENTS

In subss.(1), (5) and (6) the words in square brackets were inserted by the Crime (Sentences) Act 1997 s.55, Sch.4 para.12.

Subsection (5A) was inserted by the Criminal Justice Act 2003 s.295.

The other amendments to this section were made by SI 2008/2883 art.9, Sch.3 para.55.

DEFINITIONS

**1–890**   the appropriate tribunal: ss.66(4), 145(1).

restricted patient: s.79(1).

restriction direction: ss.49, 145(1).

restriction order: ss.41, 145(1).

hospital: ss.79(6), 145(1).

hospital direction: s.145(1).

limitation direction: s.145(1).

the managers: s.145(1).

transfer direction: ss.47, 145(1).

GENERAL NOTE

This section provides for the procedure to be adopted on an application to a tribunal by a **1–891**
patient who has been transferred from prison to hospital under either s.47 or 48, subject to
the special restrictions set out in s.49, or has been made the subject of hospital and limitation directions under s.45A. It also applies to references to tribunals made in respect of
such patients by the Secretary of State. A patient who has been transferred subject to a
restriction direction ceases to be subject to restrictions on reaching his release date had
he remained in prison (s.50(2)(3)).

The Reference Guide, at paras 21.25 to 21.34, describes the effect of this section:

"As with other restricted patients, the Tribunal has no general discretion to discharge
patients subject to hospital and limitation directions or restricted transfer directions.

In addition, because these patients are liable to resume serving their sentence of imprisonment (or its equivalent) if they no longer require treatment in hospital, special
arrangements apply where the Tribunal believes that the criteria for discharge from
detention are met.

The criteria for the discharge of patients subject to these directions are the same as those
for patients subject to restricted hospital orders . . . .

Where the Tribunal decides that such a patient would be entitled to be discharged absolutely or conditionally if the patient were subject to a restriction order . . . , it must inform
the Secretary of State for Justice.

If the patient would be entitled to conditional discharge, the Tribunal may recommend
that the patient continue to be detained in hospital (rather than going to prison or
other custodial institution) if the patient is not, in fact, discharged.

In the case of patients who are remand prisoners or other unsentenced prisoners subject
to restricted transfer directions under section 48, the Secretary of State has no discretion.
If the Tribunal has decided that such a patient would be entitled to be conditionally discharged and has made a recommendation for the patient's continued detention in
hospital, the patient remains detained and subject to the restriction direction or limitation
direction. Otherwise, the Secretary of State must issue a warrant directing the person's
return to prison (or any other place of detention in which the patient could have been
detained but for being in hospital).

In the case of a sentenced prisoner subject to hospital and limitation directions or a
restricted transfer direction under section 47, the Secretary of State has the discretion
to agree to the patient's discharge.

In these cases, the Secretary of State has 90 days from being informed of the Tribunal's
findings in which to give notice that the patient may be discharged. If the Secretary of
State does so, the Tribunal must discharge the patient. Otherwise, the patient must be
returned to prison (or its equivalent) by the hospital managers, unless the Tribunal has
recommended that the patient remain in hospital if not conditionally discharged.

Where sentenced prisoners subject to hospital and limitation directions or transfer directions remain in hospital only as a result of a recommendation by the Tribunal, they have
the right to apply to the Parole Board for release once they have served the minimum
period set by the court (the 'tariff' period), in the same way as other prisoners. If that
point has already been reached when the Tribunal recommendation is first acted on,
the Secretary of State will refer the case automatically to the Parole Board.

The fact that a patient remains in hospital as a result of a recommendation by the Tribunal
does not alter the Secretary of State's discretionary powers to remit or return them to

prison if they no longer need treatment for mental disorder or cannot be treated effectively in the relevant hospital . . ."

The policy of the Secretary of State on receiving a notification under paras (a) and (b) of subs.(1) is set out in the note on s.50(1)(b).

*Human Rights Act 1998*

**1–892**     In *Benjamin and Wilson v United Kingdom* (2003) 36 E.H.R.R. 1, the European Court of Human Rights held that s.74(2) violates art.5(4) of the European Convention on Human Rights because the power of discharge rests with the Secretary of State rather than the tribunal. The court said, at para.36, that the violation "is not a matter of form but impinges on the fundamental principle of separation of powers and detracts from a necessary guarantee against the possibility of abuse". In *R. (on the application of D) v Secretary of State for the Home Department* [2002] EWHC Admin 2805; [2003] M.H.L.R. 193, Stanley Burnton J. said that *Benjamin and Wilson* is authority for the proposition that art.5(4) requires the court to which it refers to have the legal power to direct the release of a prisoner. His Lordship found that under the current statutory regime, a discretionary life prisoner who had served the minimum period of his detention but who remains compulsory detained under a transfer direction under s.47/49 has no statutory right to apply to the Parole Board, or to require the Secretary of State to refer his case to the Board (see the *Hickey* case, noted under s.50(1)(b)). Given that this section did not provide the tribunal with a power to order the patient's discharge, the absence of such a right was found to be incompatible with art.5(4). The incompatibility was cured by the insertion of subs.(5A) by the Criminal Justice Act 2003.

*Subsection (1)*

**1–893**     PATIENT.   See the note on "any such patient" in s.73(2).

SECRETARY OF STATE.   Functions under this provision have not been transferred to Welsh Ministers (see the General Note to this Act and SI 1999/672 art.2, Sch.1).

DISCHARGE.   See the note on "discharge" in s.73(1). In the context of para.(a) this term means only discharge from hospital; it does not exclude consideration of discharge back to prison (*R. (on the application of Abu-Rideh) v Mental Health Review Tribunal* [2004] EWHC 1999 (Admin); [2004] M.H.L.R. 308 para.45).

*Subsection (2)*

**1–894**     BEGINNING WITH.   Including the date of the notification (*Zoan v Rouamba* [2000] 2 All E.R. 620 CA).

CONDITIONAL DISCHARGE.   A patient who has been conditionally discharged under this provision is not subject to the consent to treatment provisions contained in Pt IV of this Act (s.56(3)(c)).

*Subsection (5)*

**1–895**     RELEVANT HOSPITAL DIRECTION . . . RELEVANT TRANSFER DIRECTION.   See s.79(2).

*Subsection (5A)*

**1–896**     This subsection relates to transferred prisoners detained in hospital beyond their release date whose detention in hospital has been found by the tribunal to be no longer justified by their mental disorder, but who the tribunal has recommended should remain in hospital, rather than return to prison, in the event that the Secretary of State does not agree to discharge them from hospital. It provides that the fact that restrictions under this Act remain in force does not prevent an application or reference to the Parole Board for release. It further provides that if the Parole Board directs or recommends release, the restrictions cease to have effect at the time he is entitled to release. The effect of this is that the transferred prisoner is assured access to the Parole Board, and the possibility of release on licence, once he has reached his release date and the tribunal find he is no longer appropriately detained in hospital for medical treatment.

*Subsection (6)*
RELEVANT HOSPITAL ORDER.   See s.79(2).                                                **1–897**

## Applications and references concerning conditionally discharged restricted patients

75.—(1) Where a restricted patient has been conditionally discharged under  **1–898**
section 42(2), 73 or 74 above and is subsequently recalled to hospital—
  (a) the Secretary of State shall, within one month of the day on which the patient returns or is returned to hospital, refer his case to [the appropriate tribunal]; and
  (b) section 70 above shall apply to the patient as if the relevant hospital order [, hospital direction] or transfer direction had been made on that day.
  (2) Where a restricted patient has been conditionally discharged as aforesaid but has not been recalled to hospital he may apply to [the appropriate tribunal]—
  (a) in the period between the expiration of 12 months and the expiration of two years beginning with the date on which he was conditionally discharged; and
  (b) in any subsequent period of two years.
  (3) Sections 73 and 74 above shall not apply to an application under subsection (2) above but on any such application the Tribunal may—
  (a) vary any condition to which the patient is subject in connection with his discharge or impose any condition which might have been imposed in connection therewith; or
  (b) direct that the restriction order [, limitation direction] or restriction direction to which he is subject shall cease to have effect;
and if the tribunal [gives] a direction under paragraph (b) above the patient shall cease to be liable to be detained by virtue of the relevant hospital order [, hospital direction] or transfer direction.

AMENDMENT
  In subs.(1)(b) the words in square brackets were inserted by the Crime (Sentences) Act 1997 s.55, Sch.4 para.12(13).
  In subs.(3) the references to limitation and hospital directions were inserted by the Mental Health Act 2007 s.41.
  The other amendments to this section were made by SI 2008/2883 art.9, Sch.3 para.56.

DEFINITIONS                                                                              **1–899**
  restricted patient: s.79(1).
  hospital: ss.79(6), 145(1).
  the appropriate tribunal: ss.66(4), 145(1).
  limitation direction: s.145(1).
  hospital direction: s.145(1).
  relevant hospital order: s.79(2).
  relevant transfer direction: s.79(2).
  restriction order: ss.41, 145(1).
  restriction direction: ss.49, 145(1).

GENERAL NOTE

**1–900**    This section directs the Secretary of State to refer the case of a conditionally discharged restricted patient who has been recalled to hospital to a tribunal (subs.(1)). It also provides for a tribunal application to be made by a conditionally discharged restricted patient who has not been recalled to hospital. On hearing such an application the tribunal has the power to vary the conditions of the discharge, to impose new conditions, or to direct that the restriction order, restriction direction or hospital direction shall cease to have effect (subs.(3)).

A restricted patient who is no longer suffering from a mental disorder remains a "patient" for the purposes of this section until discharged absolutely (*R. v Merseyside Mental Health Review Tribunal Ex p. K* [1990] 1 All E.R. 694 CA).

*Human Rights Act 1998*

**1–901**    In *Secretary of State for Justice v Rayner* [2008] EWCA Civ 176; [2008] M.H.L.R. 115, the Court of Appeal held that this section was capable of satisfying the requirement of art.5(4) of the European Convention on Human Rights for the lawfulness of the patient's detention to be decided "speedily" if the Secretary of State referred the patient's case to the tribunal with reasonable dispatch, having regard to all the material circumstances. Keene L.J., who gave the only judgment of substance, said, at para.25, that one would normally expect a reference to be made within days, not weeks, of the return of the patient to hospital, and normally with a few days. The Court also considered whether subs.(1)(b) of this section, which has the effect of enabling a recalled patient to make an application to a tribunal only after six months has elapsed since his return to hospital, violates the entitlement in art.5(4) for the patient to "take proceedings" to challenge the lawfulness of the detention. In concluding that it did not, Keene L.J. said at para.46:

> "I conclude that while s.75 . . ., if it stood alone, might now not be regarded as sufficient to achieve the protection of Art.5(4) rights required by the ECHR and the Strasbourg jurisprudence, the combination of that statutory mechanism, the right of the patient to enforce the Secretary of State's statutory duty (as interpreted in the light of the Convention) by way of judicial review, and the right of the patient to challenge the lawfulness of his detention directly in the courts on its substantive merits by judicial review and/or *habeas corpus* does suffice to comply with Art.5(4). The patient has direct access as of right to the courts and can obtain swift redress if he is being unlawfully detained. I would only add that, as a matter of procedure, if judicial review has to be resorted to by a patient, he or she would normally find it quicker and more effective to apply for an order enforcing the Secretary of State's statutory duty rather than embark on a direct challenge in the courts to the lawfulness of the detention."

In *R. (on the application of SC) v Mental Health Review Tribunal and the Secretary of State for Health* [2005] EWHC 17 (Admin); [2005] M.H.L.R. 31, Munby J. held that subs.(3) is not incompatible with arts 6 and 8 of the Convention as the relevant law is both sufficiently foreseeable and adequate to protect the patient from all risk of arbitrariness.

*Subsection (1)*

**1–902**  *Paragraph (a)*

If, before a reference made under this provision is determined, the patient is conditionally discharged again, then the reference lapses: see footnote 1 of the statement of the Deputy Chamber President of the First-tier Tribunal (Mental Health) on "References made under section 68(7) Mental Health Act 1983 (as amended)" which can be found on the website of the First-tier Tribunal (Mental Health) (*www.mhrt.org.uk*—accessed July 23, 2010).

WITHIN ONE MONTH. Disregarding the day of the patient's return to hospital (*Stewart v Chapman* [1951] 2 K.B. 792). The referral should normally be made within a few days of the patient's return to hospital (*Secretary of State for Justice v Rayner,* above). If the patient is already in the hospital as an informal patient when he or she is recalled, the one-month period runs from the date of the recall (*R (on the application of Rayner) v Secretary of State for the Home Department* [2007] EWHC 1028 (Admin); [2007] 1 W.L.R. 2239 para.7). In *R. v Secretary of State for the Home Department Ex p. K* [1990] 1 All E.R. 703 at 712, McCullough J. said:

"In requiring the Secretary of State to refer the case to a [tribunal] within one month of the patient's recall, rather than sooner or later, Parliament was striking a balance between the need to have the question considered by a court at the earliest opportunity and the need to provide the tribunal with evidence of appropriate quality; such evidence would obviously include assessments made in hospital after recall."

REFER HIS CASE TO THE APPROPRIATE TRIBUNAL. The tribunal will exercise its powers under s.73. In *R. v Mental Health Review Tribunal for Merseyside Ex p. Kelly* [1998] 39 B.M.L.R. 114, Keene J. said that he could:

"see that in general terms the events leading up to a recall of a patient may not be relevant to the issues arising under s.72(1)(b)(i) and (ii) [see s.73(1)(a)] ... However, it is also true that such events prior to a patient's recall may be relevant. Diagnosis of and opinions as to such matters as are referred to in the relevant statutory paragraphs are not arrived at by ignoring events which have happened. The behaviour of the patient may well be material to such diagnosis and opinions. It will depend at least partly on how the expert witness or witnesses have arrived at their conclusions."

In this case, his Lordship declared that the decision of the tribunal was ultra vires in that it was contrary to the rules of natural justice because of a refusal by the tribunal to allow the cross-examination of the patient's responsible clinician on statements that he had made in his report to the tribunal concerning allegations that had been made about the patient's conduct prior to his recall to hospital.

Although the tribunal may consider events leading up to the recall, there is no jurisdiction to examine "the underlying circumstances of the mechanics of the recall and particularly the extent to which there had been discussion between [the patient's Responsible Clinician and the Mental Health Casework Section]" (*R. (on the application of Munday) v Secretary of State for the Home Department* [2009] EWHC 3638 (Admin), para.23, per Burnett J.).

*Paragraph (b)*
The effect of this provision is that a recalled patient may not make an application to a **1–903** tribunal until six months after his return to hospital.

*Subsection (2)*
CONDITIONALLY DISCHARGED. A patient is conditionally discharged for the purposes of **1–904** calculating time under this provision, not on the date when the tribunal decided that he be discharged subject to conditions being met, but on the date when he actually leaves hospital once those conditions had been met: see *R. v Canons Park Mental Health Review Tribunal Ex p. Martins* (1995) 26 B.M.L.R. 134 where Ognall J. followed Mann J.'s finding in *Secretary of State for the Home Department v Mental Health Review Tribunal for the Mersey Regional Health Authority* [1986] 3 All E.R. 233 at 237 that:

"The word 'discharge' as employed in sections 72 to 75 of the Act of 1983 means, and in my judgment can only mean, release from hospital. The release may be absolute or it may be conditional."

NOT BEEN RECALLED TO HOSPITAL. A conditionally discharged restricted patient who has been brought back to hospital under either s.2 or s.3 has not been "recalled to hospital" as such a recall can only be made by the Secretary of State under s.42(3).

MAY APPLY. To the tribunal for the area in which he resides (s.77(4)).

BEGINNING WITH. Including the date of his conditional discharge (*Zoan v Rouamba* [2000] 2 All E.R. 620 CA) which is day when he leaves hospital: see the note on "conditionally discharged" above.

*Subsection (3)*

**1–905**    In *R. (on the application of SC) v Mental Health Review Tribunal and the Secretary of State for Health*, above, paras 56, 57, Munby J. said that a patient who makes an application under subs.(2) will have been convicted of an offence grave enough to merit a possible sentence of imprisonment, found to have been suffering from a mental disorder meriting detention in hospital for treatment, and to have presented a risk of re-offending such that a restriction order was necessary for the protection of the public from serious harm; and found by a tribunal to be someone who, although not requiring detention for treatment for the time being, nonetheless required to remain liable to recall. Accordingly, when exercising its powers under this provision, the tribunal

"will need to consider such matters as the nature, gravity and circumstances of the patient's offence, the nature and gravity of his mental disorder, past present and future, the risk and likelihood of the patient re-offending, the degree of harm to which the public may be exposed if he re-offends, the risk and likelihood of a recurrence or exacerbation of any mental disorder, and the risk and likelihood of his needing to be recalled in the future for further treatment in hospital. The tribunal will also need to consider the nature of any conditions previously imposed, whether by the tribunal or by the Secretary of State, under ss.42(2), 73(4)(b) or 73(5), the reasons why they were imposed and the extent to which it is desirable to continue, vary or add to them."

His Lordship said, at para.60, that the effect of this provision:

"is not to *preclude* the tribunal from considering the kind of factors which fall for consideration under s.73. Rather . . . the effect is that the tribunal, when exercising its discretion under s.75(3), is not constrained by the mandatory terms of s.73 which bind the approach of the tribunal when considering the exercise of its powers under s.73".

His Lordship further stated, at para.59, that:

"in effect, one of the key questions that the tribunal will wish to ask is whether it is—as s.73(1)(b) puts it—'satisfied that it is not appropriate for the patient to remain liable to be recalled to hospital for further treatment.' If the tribunal is not so satisfied, then it is difficult to see that it could be appropriate for it to make an order under s.75(3)(b)".

MAY. The tribunal is not bound by any criteria in the exercise of its discretion.

*General*

## Visiting and examination of patients

**1–906**    **76.**—(1) For the purpose of advising whether an application to [the appropriate tribunal] should be made by or in respect of a patient who is liable to be detained or subject to guardianship [. . .] under Part II of this Act [or a community patient,] or of furnishing information as to the condition of a patient for the purposes of such an application, any registered medical practitioner [or approved clinician] authorised by or on behalf of the patient or other person who is entitled to make or has made the application—

    (a)  may at any reasonable time visit the patient and examine him in private, and

    (b)  may require the production of and inspect any records relating to the detention or treatment of the patient in any hospital [or to any after-care services provided for the patient under section 117 below].

(2) Section 32 above shall apply for the purposes of this section as it applies for the purposes of Part II of this Act.

### AMENDMENTS

The words in square brackets in subs. (1) were inserted by the Mental Health Act 2007 ss.13(2)(b), 32(4), Sch.3 para.22. The words omitted were repealed by s.55, Sch.11 Pt 5. The reference to the appropriate tribunal in subs.(1) was substituted by SI 2008/2883 art.9, Sch.3 para.57.

### DEFINITIONS

the appropriate tribunal: ss.66(4), 145(1).                                   **1–907**

patient: s.145(1).

hospital: ss.79(6), 145(1).

### GENERAL NOTE

This section, which is applied to patients who have been placed under hospital, restric- **1–908** tion or guardianship orders by a court under s.37 or 41 of this Act (Sch.1, Pt 1, para.1; Pt 2, para.1), provides for a doctor or approved clinician to be authorised by or on behalf of the patient, or anyone else entitled to make an application to a tribunal, to advise on whether an application should be made, or to provide information on the patient's condition for the purposes of an application. The authorised person may visit and examine the patient, and inspect relevant records.

A failure to allow authorised persons to carry out their functions under this section could amount to an obstruction under s.129.

*Subsection (1)*

FURNISHING INFORMATION. In *W v Egdell* [1990] 1 All E.R. 835, the Court of Appeal **1–909** held that where a doctor is called on to examine a patient with a view to providing an independent psychiatric report to support the patient's application to a tribunal, he owes a duty not only to his patient but also a duty to the public. His duty to the public would enable him to place before the proper authorities the results of his examination if, in his opinion, the public interest so required. This would be so whether or not the patient instructed him not to do so. Bingham L.J. said at 852 853:

"There is one consideration [in this case] which in my judgment . . . weighs the balance of public interest decisively in favour of disclosure. It may be shortly put. Where a man has committed multiple killings under the disability of serious mental illness, decisions which may lead directly or indirectly to his release from hospital should not be made unless a responsible authority is properly able to make an informed judgment that the risk of repetition is so small as to be acceptable. A consultant psychiatrist who becomes aware, even in the course of a confidential relationship, of information which leads him, in the exercise of what the court considers a sound professional judgment, to fear that such decisions may be made on the basis of inadequate information and with a real risk of consequent danger to the public is entitled to take such steps as are reasonable in all the circumstances to communicate the grounds of his concern to the responsible authorities."

### General provisions concerning tribunal applications

1–910    77.—(1) No application shall be made to [the appropriate tribunal by or in respect of a patient under this Act] except in such cases and at such times as are expressly provided by this Act.

(2) Where under this Act any person is authorised to make an application to [the appropriate tribunal] within a specified period, not more than one such application shall be made by that person within that period but for that purpose there shall be disregarded any application which is withdrawn in accordance with [Tribunal Procedure Rules or] rules made under section 78 below.

(3) Subject to subsection (4) below an application to [a tribunal] authorised to be made by or in respect of a patient under this Act shall be made by notice in writing addressed

[(a)  in the case of a patient who is liable to be detained in a hospital, [to the First-tier Tribunal where that hospital is in England and to the Mental Health Review Tribunal for Wales where that hospital is in Wales];

(b)  in the case of a community patient, [to the First-tier Tribunal where the responsible hospital is in England and to the Mental Health Review Tribunal for Wales where that hospital is in Wales];

(c)  in the case of a patient subject to guardianship, [to the First-tier Tribunal where the patient resides in England and to the Mental Health Review Tribunal for Wales where the patient resides in Wales].]

(4) Any application under section 75(2) above shall be made [to the First-tier Tribunal where the patient resides in England and to the Mental Health Review Tribunal for Wales where the patient resides in Wales].

AMENDMENTS

The amendments to this section were made by the Mental Health Act 2007 s.32(4), Sch.3 para.23; SI 2008/2883 art.9, Sch.3 para.58 and SI 2009/1307 art.5, Sch.1 para.161.

DEFINITIONS

1–911    patient: s.145(1).

the appropriate tribunal: ss.66(4), 145(1).

hospital: ss.79(6), 145(1).

GENERAL NOTE

1–912    This section provides, in subss.(1) and (2), that there is no right to apply to a tribunal apart from those situations expressly provided for in this Act, that where the Act gives rise to a right to make an application within a specified period only one such application may be made within that period, and that where the tribunal authorises the withdrawal of an application the applicant can re-apply during the relevant period. Where a patient is transferred between England and Wales, a tribunal application made in one country counts as an application to a tribunal in the other.

Subsections (3) and (4) determine whether an application should be made to the First-tier Tribunal (Mental Health) or the Mental Health Review Tribunal for Wales.

*Subsection (2)*

1–913    See the note on "an application" in s.66(1).

WITHDRAWN IN ACCORDANCE WITH THE RULES.    References cannot be withdrawn.

*Subsection (4)*
APPLICATION UNDER SECTION 75(2). By a restricted patient who has been conditionally **1–914** discharged from hospital.

RESIDES. Temporary absences from the place where a person resides does not affect residence, as long as there is an intention to return to it (*R. v St Leonard's Shoreditch (Inhabitants)* (1865) L.R. 1 Q.B. 21). Also note Widgery L.J.'s statement in *Fox v Stirk* [1970] 2 Q.B. 463 at 477 that: "A man cannot be said to reside in a particular place unless in the ordinary sense of the word one can say that for the time being he is making his home in that place."

### Procedure of [Mental Health Review Tribunal for Wales]

**78.**—(1) The Lord Chancellor may make rules with respect to the making of **1–915** applications to [the Mental Health Review Tribunal for Wales] and with respect to the proceedings of [that tribunal] and matters incidental to or consequential on such proceedings.

(2) Rules made under this section may in particular make provision—

(a) for enabling [the tribunal], or the chairman of [the tribunal], to postpone the consideration of any application by or in respect of a patient, or of any such application of any specified class, until the expiration of such period (not exceeding 12 months) as may be specified in the rules from the date on which an application by or in respect of the same patient was last considered and determined [under this Act by the tribunal or the First-tier Tribunal];

[(b) for the transfer of proceedings to or from the Mental Health Review Tribunal for Wales in any case where, after the making of the application, the patient is moved into or out of Wales;]

(c) for restricting the persons qualified to serve as members of [the tribunal] for the consideration of any application, or of an application of any specified class;

(d) for enabling [the tribunal] to dispose of an application without a formal hearing where such a hearing is not requested by the applicant or it appears to the tribunal that such a hearing would be detrimental to the health of the patient;

(e) for enabling [the tribunal] to exclude members of the public, or any specified class of members of the public, from any proceedings of the tribunal, or to prohibit the publication of reports of any such proceedings or the names of any persons concerned in such proceedings;

(f) for regulating the circumstances in which, and the persons by whom, applicants and patients in respect of whom applications are made to [the tribunal] may, if not desiring to conduct their own case, be represented for the purposes of those applications;

(g) for regulating the methods by which information relevant to an application may be obtained by or furnished to the tribunal, and in particular for authorising the members of [the tribunal], or any one or more of them, to visit and interview in private any patient by or in respect of whom an application has been made;

(h) for making available to any applicant, and to any patient in respect of whom an application is made to [the tribunal], copies of any documents obtained by or furnished to the tribunal in connection with the application, and a statement of the substance of any oral information so obtained or furnished except where the Tribunal considers it undesirable in the interests of the patient or for other special reasons;

(i) for requiring [the tribunal], if so requested in accordance with the rules, to furnish such statements of the reasons for any decision given by the tribunal as may be prescribed by the rules, subject to any provision made by the rules for withholding such a statement from a patient or any other person in cases where the tribunal considers that furnishing it would be undesirable in the interests of the patient or for other special reasons;

(j) for conferring on the [tribunal] such ancillary powers as the Lord Chancellor thinks necessary for the purposes of the exercise of [its] functions under this Act;

(k) for enabling any functions of [the tribunal] which relate to matters preliminary or incidental to an application to be performed by the chairman of the tribunal.

(3) Subsections (1) and (2) above apply in relation to references to [the Mental Health Review Tribunal for Wales] as they apply in relation to applications to [that tribunal] by or in respect of patients.

(4) Rules under this section may make provision as to the procedure to be adopted in cases concerning restricted patients and, in particular—

(a) for restricting the persons qualified to serve as president of [the tribunal] for the consideration of an application or reference relating to a restricted patient;

[(b) for the transfer of proceedings to or from the tribunal in any case where, after the making of a reference or application in accordance with section 71(4) or 77(4) above, the patient begins or ceases to reside in Wales.]

(5) Rules under this section may be so framed as to apply to all applications or references or to applications or references of any specified class and may make different provision in relation to different cases.

(6) Any functions conferred on the chairman of [the Mental Health Review Tribunal for Wales] by rules under this section may [. . .], be exercised by another member of that tribunal appointed by him for the purpose.

(7) [The Mental Health Review Tribunal for Wales] may pay allowances in respect of travelling expenses, subsistence and loss of earnings to any person attending the Tribunal as an applicant or witness, to the patient who is the subject of the proceedings if he attends otherwise than as the applicant or a witness and to any person (other than [an authorised person (within the meaning of Part 3)]) who attends as the representative of an applicant.

(8) [. . .]

(9) [Part I of the Arbitration Act 1996] shall not apply to any proceedings before [the Mental Health Review Tribunal for Wales] except so far as any provisions of that Act may be applied, with or without modifications, by rules made under this section.

AMENDMENTS

The amendments to this section were made by the Arbitration Act 1996 s.107(1), Sch.3 para.40, the Mental Health Act 2007 ss.38(3)(e), 55, Sch.11 Pt.6, SI 2008/2883 art.9, Sch.3 para.59 and the Legal Services Act 2007, s.208, Sch.21, para.60.

DEFINITION

**1–916**   patient: s.145(1).

The Mental Health Review Tribunal for Wales Rules 2008 (S.I. 2008/2705 (L.17)) gov- **1–917** ern the practice and procedure to be followed in proceedings before the Mental Health Review Tribunal for Wales.

*Subsection (1)*
THE LORD CHANCELLOR.   Who cannot transfer his functions under this section to another **1–918** person (Constitutional Reform Act 2005 s.19, Sch.7).

*Subsection (2)*
PARAGRAPH (A); PRESIDENT OF A TRIBUNAL.   See Sch.2 para.2.   **1–919**

PARAGRAPH (B); AREA OF THE TRIBUNAL.   See s.65(1).

*Subsection (4)*
QUALIFIED TO SERVE AS CHAIRMAN OF A TRIBUNAL.   Provision for restricting those who **1–920** can act as president in cases relating to restricted patients is made in r.11(2) of the Welsh Rules. There is no equivalent provision in the Tribunal Rules.

*Subsection (7)*
LOSS OF EARNINGS.   This would not cover the payment of a fee for representing the **1–921** client or acting as an expert witness.

ATTENDING.   Expenses cannot be paid for preparatory work.

AUTHORISED PERSON.   Is defined in s.55(1).

## [Appeal from the Mental Health Review Tribunal for Wales to the Upper Tribunal

**78A.**—(1) A party to any proceedings before the Mental Health Review **1–922** Tribunal for Wales may appeal to the Upper Tribunal on any point of law arising from a decision made by the Mental Health Review Tribunal for Wales in those proceedings.

(2) An appeal may be brought under subsection (1) above only if, on an application made by the party concerned, the Mental Health Review Tribunal for Wales or the Upper Tribunal has given its permission for the appeal to be brought.

(3) Section 12 of the Tribunals, Courts and Enforcement Act 2007 (proceedings on appeal to the Upper Tribunal) applies in relation to appeals to the Upper Tribunal under this section as it applies in relation to appeals to it under section 11 of that Act, but as if references to the First-tier Tribunal were references to the Mental Health Review Tribunal for Wales.]

This section was inserted by SI 2008/2883 art.9, Sch.3 para.60.

As the Mental Health Review Tribunal for Wales is not administered through the **1–923** Tribunal Service, this section ensures that the onward appeal right to the Upper Tribunal which is enjoyed by the First-tier Tribunal (Mental Health) is also available in Wales.

## Interpretation of Part V

**79.**—(1) In this Part of this Act "restricted patient" means a patient who is sub- **1–924** ject to a restriction order [, limitation direction] or restriction direction and this

Part of this Act shall, subject to the provisions of this section, have effect in relation to any person who

[(a) is treated by virtue of any enactment as subject to a hospital order and a restriction order; or]

(b) [. . .]

[(c) is treated as subject to a hospital order and a restriction order, or to a hospital direction and a limitation direction, or to a transfer direction and a restriction direction, by virtue of any provision of Part 6 of this Act (except section 80D(3), 82A(2) or 85A(2) below),]

as it has effect in relation to a restricted patient.

(2) Subject to the following provisions of this section, in this Part of this Act "the relevant hospital order" [, "the relevant hospital direction"] and "the relevant transfer direction," in relation to a restricted patient, mean the hospital order [, the hospital direction] or transfer direction by virtue of which he is liable to be detained in a hospital.

(3) In the case of a person within paragraph (a) of subsection (1) above, references in this Part of this Act to the relevant hospital order or restriction order shall be construed as references to the direction referred to in that paragraph.

(4) In the case of a person within paragraph (b) of subsection (1) above, references in this Part of this Act to the relevant hospital order or restriction order shall be construed as references to the order under the provisions mentioned in that paragraph.

(5) In the case of a person within paragraph (c) of subsection (1) above, references in this Part of this Act to the relevant hospital order, [the relevant hospital direction,] the relevant transfer direction, the restriction order [, the limitation direction] or the restriction direction or to a transfer direction under section 48 above shall be construed as references to the hospital order, [hospital direction,] transfer direction, restriction order, [limitation direction,] restriction direction or transfer direction under that section to which that person is treated as subject by virtue of the provisions mentioned in that paragraph.

[(5A) Section 75 above shall, subject to the modifications in subsection (5C) below, have effect in relation to a qualifying patient as it has effect in relation to a restricted patient who is conditionally discharged under section 42(2), 73 or 74 above.

(5B) A patient is a qualifying patient if he is treated by virtue of section 80D(3), 82A(2) or 85A(2) below as if he had been conditionally discharged and were subject to a hospital order and a restriction order, or to a hospital direction and a limitation direction, or to a transfer direction and a restriction direction.

(5C) The modifications mentioned in subsection (5A) above are—

(a) references to the relevant hospital order, hospital direction or transfer direction, or to the restriction order, limitation direction or restriction direction to which the patient is subject, shall be construed as references to the hospital order, hospital direction or transfer direction, or restriction order, limitation direction or restriction direction, to which the patient is treated as subject by virtue of section 80D(3), 82A(2) or 85A(2) below; and

(b) the reference to the date on which the patient was conditionally discharged shall be construed as a reference to the date on which he was treated as conditionally discharged by virtue of a provision mentioned in paragraph (a) above.]

(6) In this Part of this Act, unless the context otherwise requires, "hospital" means a hospital [, and "the responsible clinician" means the responsible clinician,] within the meaning of Part II of this Act.

(7) [*Repealed by SI 2008/2883 art.9, Sch.3 para.61*]

AMENDMENTS

Subsection (1)(a) was substituted by the Domestic Violence, Crime and Victims Act 2004 s.58(1), Sch.10 para.21(a), subs.(1)(b) was repealed by s.58(2), Sch.11 of that Act, and the words in square brackets in para.(c) were substituted by SI 2005/2078 Sch.1 para.2(3). The references to limitation directions and hospital directions in subss.(1) and (2) were inserted by the Crime (Sentences) Act 1997 s.55, Sch.4 para.12(14)(15). The other amendments to this section were made by the Mental Health Act 2007 ss.13(3), 38(4), 39(2), Sch.5 Pt 2 para.19.

DEFINITIONS

    patient: s.145(1).                                                    **1–925**

    restriction order: ss.41, 145(1).

    restriction direction: ss.49, 145(1).

    hospital order: ss.37, 145(1).

    transfer direction: ss.47, 145(1).

    hospital direction: s.145(1).

    limitation direction: s.145(1).

GENERAL NOTE

*Subsection (6)*

HOSPITAL.   See section 34(2).                                      **1–926**

## PART VI

## REMOVAL AND RETURN OF PATIENTS WITHIN UNITED KINGDOM, ETC.

GENERAL NOTE

This Part deals with the transfer between the United Kingdom jurisdictions and the **1–927** Channel Islands or the Isle of Man of patients who are subject to certain compulsory powers. It ensures that the patients remain in legal custody whilst in transit and that they are liable to equivalent compulsory powers on their arrival in the receiving jurisdiction. It also provides, in s.86, powers for moving mentally disordered patients who are neither British citizens nor Commonwealth citizens with the right of abode in the United Kingdom from hospitals in England and Wales to countries abroad.

The procedure to be followed on the removal of a patient to England under this Part is set out in regs 15 and 16 of the English Regulations and reg.29 of the Welsh Regulations.

*[Removal to and from Scotland*

## Removal of patients to Scotland

**80.**—(1) If it appears to the Secretary of State, in the case of a patient who is for **1–928** the time being liable to be detained [. . .] under this Act (otherwise than by virtue of section 35, 36 or 38 above), that it is in the interests of the patient to remove him to Scotland, and that arrangements have been made for admitting him to a hospital [. . .] there [or, where he is not to be admitted to a hospital, for his detention in hospital to be authorised by virtue of the Mental Health (Care and Treatment)

(Scotland) Act 2003 or the Criminal Procedure (Scotland) Act 1995], the Secretary of State may authorise his removal to Scotland and may give any necessary directions for his conveyance to his destination.

(2)—(6) [*Repealed by SI 2005/2078 art.16, Sch.3*]

(7) In this section "hospital" has the same meaning as in the [Mental Health (Care and Treatment) (Scotland) Act 2003].

[(8) Reference in this section to a patient's detention in hospital being authorised by virtue of the Mental Health (Care and Treatment) (Scotland) Act 2003 or the Criminal Procedure (Scotland) Act 1995 shall be read as including references to a patient in respect of whom a certificate under one of the provisions listed in section 290(7)(a) of the Act of 2003 is in operation.]

AMENDMENTS

The amendments to this section were made by SI 2003/2078 Sch.1 para.2(4) and the Mental Health Act 2007 s.55, Sch.11 Pt 7. The cross-heading immediately above this section was substituted by s.39(2), Sch.5 Pt 1 para.2.

DEFINITIONS

**1–929**    patient: s.145(1).
hospital: subs. (7).
restriction order: ss.41, 145(1).
restriction direction: ss.49, 145(1).
application for admission for assessment: ss.2, 145(1).
transfer direction: ss.47, 145(1).

GENERAL NOTE

**1–930**    This section enables the Secretary of State (or, for certain categories of patient, noted below, in relation to Wales, the Welsh Ministers) to transfer a patient who is detained (otherwise than under s.35, 36 or 38) in England or Wales to Scotland without a break in the powers of detention. The Secretary of State (or the Welsh Ministers) must be satisfied that such a move is in the interests of the patient. Transfer to Scotland requires the approval of Scottish Ministers in accordance with the Mental Health (Cross Border transfers: patients subject to detention requirements or otherwise in hospital) (Scotland) Regulations 2005 (SSI 2005/467) which regulate both the removal of patients from Scotland as well as the reception of patients into Scotland. In terms of the reception of patients into Scotland, reg.24 sets out that the consent of Scottish Ministers is required for any patients coming into Scotland and lists the information that needs to be made available to Scottish Ministers to allow them to consider a request for transfer; this includes details of the relevant measures to which the patient is currently subject. Scottish Ministers are then required, under reg.24(5) to consider the request and give notice to the relevant hospital managers whether their consent has been given. Regulation 30(5) provides that, following reception into Scotland, the order to which a patient is now subject will be treated as if that measure was made or given on the date which the order the patient was subject to immediately preceding transfer was made or given. Given this, difficulties have arisen where a patient is received into a Scottish hospital with only a few days left to run on their order. In such cases, there is often insufficient time for the Scottish Responsible Medical Officer to adequately discharge their responsibilities in relation to the appropriate assessment and possible re-detention of a patient. In view of this "it will now be our practice in considering requests for the consent of Scottish Ministers to the transfer of patients into Scotland to request that, where an application is made under the 2005 Regulations for a patient to transfer into Scotland, there must be a minimum of 10 days and, where possible, at least 14 days left before the expiry of their existing detention order" (Letter from the Mental Health Division of the Primary and Community Directorate, January 29, 2010).

The Department of Health or the Welsh Ministers (or the Ministry of Justice for restricted patients) will seek approval directly from the Scottish Executive. When the transfer is completed, the application, order or direction on the basis of which the patient was detained in England, ceases to have effect and cannot be revived. For the patient to return to England a further transfer would be necessary, in accordance with Scottish legislation, which will require the agreement of the Scottish Ministers.

Once the transfer of a detained patient has been agreed in principle between the sending and receiving hospitals, the sending hospital should write to:

Department of Health
Wellington House
133–155 Waterloo Road
London SE1 8UG
Tel: 020 7972 2000

The Department of Health has devised a pro-forma (Gateway ref. 14651) for completion by responsible hospitals in England to request transfer of on-restricted patients to a hospital outside England and Wales. The pro-forma should be completed by or on behalf of the managers of the responsible hospital in England. The Department's e-mail address for this purpose is: *mentalhealthact2007@dh.gsi.gov.uk.*

For patients who are detained in Wales, the information should be sent to:

The National Assembly for Wales
Cathays Park
Cardiff CF10 3NQ
Tel: 029 20825111

Full details of the proposed transfer of a restricted patient should be sent to:

Mental Health Casework Section
Ministry of Justice
2nd Floor
Fry Building
2 Marsham Street
London
SW1P 4DF
Tel: 020 3334 3555

For the effect of a transfer under this section on the existing application, see s.91.

*Subsection (1)*

SECRETARY OF STATE.  The functions of the Secretary of State, so far as exercisable in **1–931** relation to Wales, are exercised by the Welsh Ministers (see the General Note to this Act and SI 1999/672 art.2, Sch.1, as varied by SI 2000/253 art.4, Sch.3) except in relation to a patient who is subject to one or more of the following, namely:

(a)  a restriction order;

(b)  a hospital direction;

(c)  a limitation direction; or

(d)  a restriction direction,

made under ss.41, 45A or, as the case may be, 49.

CONVEYANCE TO HIS DESTINATION. General provisions relating to the custody, conveyance and detention of patients are contained in s.137.

"The Scottish Ministers may also give directions about the patient's conveyance once in Scotland under Scottish regulations (or authorise the patient's intended responsible medical officer in Scotland to do so)" (Reference Guide, para.26.12).

## [Transfer of responsibility for community patients to Scotland

**1–932**    **80ZA.**—(1) If it appears to the appropriate national authority, in the case of a community patient, that the conditions mentioned in subsection (2) below are met, the authority may authorise the transfer of responsibility for him to Scotland.

(2) The conditions are—

(a) a transfer under this section is in the patient's interests; and

(b) arrangements have been made for dealing with him under enactments in force in Scotland corresponding or similar to those relating to community patients in this Act.

(3) The appropriate national authority may not act under subsection (1) above while the patient is recalled to hospital under section 17E above.

(4) In this section, "the appropriate national authority" means—

(a) in relation to a community patient in respect of whom the responsible hospital is in England, the Secretary of State;

(b) in relation to a community patient in respect of whom the responsible hospital is in Wales, the Welsh Ministers.]

AMENDMENT
This section was inserted by the Mental Health Act 2007 s.39(2), Sch.5 Pt 1 para.3(1).

DEFINITIONS
**1–933**    community patient: ss.17A(7), 145(1).
responsible hospital: ss.17A(7), 145(1).

GENERAL NOTE
**1–934**    This section enables a community patient who has not been recalled to hospital to be transferred to Scotland and long as the transfer is in the patient's best interests and arrangements have been made for dealing with him or her under the corresponding legislation in Scotland. In practice, this means "a compulsory treatment order under the Mental Health (Care and Treatment) (Scotland) Act 2003 (or a compulsion order under the Criminal Procedure (Scotland) Act 1995), which does not authorise the patient's detention in hospital" (Reference Guide, para.26.21). The Mental Health (England and Wales Cross-border transfer: patients subject to requirements other than detention) (Scotland) Regulations 2008 (SSI 2008/356) enable the cross-border transfer of Scottish patients on community-based orders to England and Wales and allow patients on community-treatment orders in England and Wales to transfer to Scotland. The arrangements for the transfer will be made by either the Secretary of State or the Welsh Ministers depending on the location of the responsible hospital. A transfer of responsibility for a community patient does not give anyone the power to convey the patient to Scotland against the patient's will.

The Department of Health has devised a pro-forma (Gateway ref. 14651) for completion by responsible hospitals in England to request transfer of community patients to Scotland. The pro-forma should be completed by or on behalf of the managers of the responsible hospital in England. The Department's e-mail address for this purpose is: *mentalhealthact2007@dh.gsi.gov.uk.*

There is no power to transfer a guardianship patient to guardianship in Scotland.
For the effect of a transfer under this section on the existing order, see s.91.

**[Transfer of responsibility for conditionally discharged patients to Scotland]**

**80A.**—(1) If it appears to the Secretary of State, in the case of a patient who— **1–935**

(a)  is subject to a restriction order under section 41 above; and

(b)  has been conditionally discharged under section 42 or 73 above,

that a transfer under this section would be in the interests of the patient, the Secretary of State may, with the consent of the Minister exercising corresponding functions in Scotland, transfer responsibility for the patient to that Minister.]

(2)—(3) *[Repealed by SI 2005/2078, art.16, Sch.3]*

AMENDMENT

This section was inserted by the Crime (Sentences) Act 1997 s.48, Sch.3 para.1. The heading was substituted by the Mental Health Act 2007 s.39(2), Sch.5 Pt 1 para.4.

DEFINITIONS

patient: s.145(1).   **1–936**

restriction order: ss.41, 145(1).

GENERAL NOTE

This section makes provision for the transfer of responsibility for conditionally dis- **1–937** charged restricted patients from England and Wales to Scotland. It enables the Secretary of State for Justice to authorise such a transfer where it appears to be in the interests of the patient, and where the relevant Scottish Minister has consented to the transfer.

For the effect of a transfer under this section on the existing order, see s.91.

SERETARY OF STATE.   Functions under this provision have not been transferred to Welsh Ministers (see the General Note to this Act and SI 1999/672 art.2, Sch.1).

**[Removal of detained patients from Scotland**

**80B.**—(1) This section applies to a patient if—   **1–938**

(a)  he is removed to England and Wales under regulations made under section 290(1)(a) of the Mental Health (Care and Treatment) (Scotland) Act 2003 ("the 2003 Act");

(b)  immediately before his removal, his detention in hospital was authorised by virtue of that Act or the Criminal Procedure (Scotland) Act 1995; and

(c)  on his removal, he is admitted to a hospital in England or Wales.

(2) He shall be treated as if, on the date of his admission to the hospital, he had been so admitted in pursuance of an application made, or an order or direction made or given, on that date under the enactment in force in England and Wales which most closely corresponds to the enactment by virtue of which his detention in hospital was authorised immediately before his removal.

(3) If, immediately before his removal, he was subject to a measure under any enactment in force in Scotland restricting his discharge, he shall be treated as if he were subject to an order or direction under the enactment in force in England and Wales which most closely corresponds to that enactment.

(4) If, immediately before his removal, the patient was liable to be detained under the 2003 Act by virtue of a transfer for treatment direction, given while he was serving a sentence of imprisonment (within the meaning of section 136(9) of that Act) imposed by a court in Scotland, he shall be treated as if the sentence had been imposed by a court in England and Wales.

(5) If, immediately before his removal, the patient was subject to a hospital direction or transfer for treatment direction, the restriction direction to which

he is subject by virtue of subsection (3) above shall expire on the date on which that hospital direction or transfer for treatment direction (as the case may be) would have expired if he had not been so removed.

(6) If, immediately before his removal, the patient was liable to be detained under the 2003 Act by virtue of a hospital direction, he shall be treated as if any sentence of imprisonment passed at the time when that hospital direction was made had been imposed by a court in England and Wales.

(7) Any directions given by the Scottish Ministers under regulations made under section 290 of the 2003 Act as to the removal of a patient to which this section applies shall have effect as if they were given under this Act.

(8) Subsection (8) of section 80 above applies to a reference in this section as it applies to one in that section.

(9) In this section—

"hospital direction" means a direction made under section 59A of the Criminal Procedure (Scotland) Act 1995; and

"transfer for treatment direction" has the meaning given by section 136 of the 2003 Act.]

AMENDMENT
This section was inserted by the Mental Health Act 2007 s.39(2), Sch.5 Pt 1 para.4(1).

DEFINITIONS
**1–939**    patient: s.145(1).
hospital:ss.92(1), 145(1).

GENERAL NOTE
**1–940**    This section applies to a detained patient who is transferred from Scotland to England or Wales. The date of his hospital admission will be the date of his arrival at the hospital in England or Wales under the provision in force which most closely corresponds to the legislation that the patient was detained under in Scotland. For example, if a patient who is detained in Scotland under the equivalent of s.3 is transferred to England on August 1, he will be treated as if he had been admitted to the hospital in England on August 1 under s.3. Such a patient is therefore given the same powers to apply to a tribunal as those enjoyed by a s.3 patient (s.69(2)). These powers are also enjoyed by the patient's nearest relative (s.69(1), as applied by s.55(4)).

Paragraph 25.28 of the Reference Guide states:

"In practice, the Scottish Executive will generally ask the Department of Health (or the Ministry of Justice for restricted patients) to confirm that arrangements have been made for the transfer. The Secretary of State for Justice will not, in practice, agree to the transfer of a restricted patient to England unless satisfied that the proposed arrangements will enable the patient's safe management in England."

The Mental Health (Care and Treatment) (Scotland) Act 2003 provides for the transfer of patients subject to a detention requirement or otherwise in hospital from Scotland and for patients subject to corresponding measures in England and Wales to be received in Scotland. The Mental Health (Cross-border transfer: patients subject to detention requirement or otherwise in hospital) (Scotland) Regulations 2005 (SSI 2005/467) make provision for those transfers to take place.

*Subsection (3)*

MOST CLOSELY CORRESPONDS. See the table set out at p.231 of the Reference Guide. **1–941**

**[Removal of patients subject to compulsion in the community from Scotland**

**80C.**—(1) This section applies to a patient if— **1–942**

(a) he is subject to an enactment in force in Scotland by virtue of which regulations under section 289(1) of the Mental Health (Care and Treatment) (Scotland) Act 2003 apply to him; and

(b) he is removed to England and Wales under those regulations.

(2) He shall be treated as if on the date of his arrival at the place where he is to reside in England or Wales—

(a) he had been admitted to a hospital in England or Wales in pursuance of an application or order made on that date under the corresponding enactment; and

(b) a community treatment order had then been made discharging him from the hospital.

(3) For these purposes—

(a) if the enactment to which the patient was subject in Scotland was an enactment contained in the Mental Health (Care and Treatment) (Scotland) Act 2003, the corresponding enactment is section 3 of this Act;

(b) if the enactment to which he was subject in Scotland was an enactment contained in the Criminal Procedure (Scotland) Act 1995, the corresponding enactment is section 37 of this Act.

(4) "The responsible hospital", in the case of a patient in respect of whom a community treatment order is in force by virtue of subsection (2) above, means the hospital to which he is treated as having been admitted by virtue of that subsection, subject to section 19A above.

(5) As soon as practicable after the patient's arrival at the place where he is to reside in England or Wales, the responsible clinician shall specify the conditions to which he is to be subject for the purposes of section 17B(1) above, and the conditions shall be deemed to be specified in the community treatment order.

(6) But the responsible clinician may only specify conditions under subsection (5) above which an approved mental health professional agrees should be specified.]

AMENDMENT

This section was inserted by the Mental Health Act 2007, s.39(2), Sch.5 Pt 1 para.4(1).

DEFINITIONS **1–943**

  patient: s.145(1).
  community treatment order: ss.17A(7), 145(1).
  responsible clinician: ss.34(1), 145(1).
  approved mental health professional: s.145(1).

GENERAL NOTE

This section applies to a patient who is subject to compulsion in the community in **1–944** Scotland who is transferred to England or Wales. On arrival at the place where he is required to reside in England or Wales, the patient will be treated as if he had been admitted to a hospital in England or Wales on that date under s.3 or s.37 and a CTO had been made discharging him from that hospital. As soon as practicable after the patient's arrival, "a CTO should be made" (Explanatory Notes, para.164).

The Mental Health (England and Wales Cross-border transfer: patients subject to requirements other than detention) (Scotland) Regulations 2008 (SSI 2008/356) allow for patients who are subject to community-based orders to be transferred from Scotland.

*Subsection (5)*

**1–945**    SHALL SPECIFY THE CONDITIONS. On form CTO 9; see reg.16(4) of the English Regulations.

## [Transfer of conditionally discharged patients from Scotland

**1–946**    **80D.**—(1) This section applies to a patient who is subject to—

(a) a restriction order under section 59 of the Criminal Procedure (Scotland) Act 1995; and

(b) a conditional discharge under section 193(7) of the Mental Health (Care and Treatment) (Scotland) Act 2003 ("the 2003 Act").

(2) A transfer of the patient to England and Wales under regulations made under section 290 of the 2003 Act shall have effect only if the Secretary of State has consented to the transfer.

(3) If a transfer under those regulations has effect, the patient shall be treated as if—

(a) on the date of the transfer he had been conditionally discharged under section 42 or 73 above; and

(b) he were subject to a hospital order under section 37 above and a restriction order under section 41 above.

(4) If the restriction order to which the patient was subject immediately before the transfer was of limited duration, the restriction order to which he is subject by virtue of subsection (3) above shall expire on the date on which the first-mentioned order would have expired if the transfer had not been made.]

AMENDMENT

This section was inserted by the Mental Health Act 2007 s.39(2), Sch.5 Pt 1 para.4(1).

DEFINITIONS

**1–947**    patient: s.145(1).
hospital order: ss.37, 145(1).
restriction order: ss.41, 145(1).

GENERAL NOTE

**1–948**    This section makes provision for the transfer of a conditionally discharged patient from Scotland to England or Wales. On his arrival in England or Wales the patient will be treated as if he was a restricted patient who had been granted a conditional discharge under either ss.42 or 73. The transfer can only take place if the Secretary of State (subs.(2)) and the Scottish Ministers (Mental Health (Cross-border transfer: patients subject to detention requirement or otherwise in hospital) (Scotland) Regulations 2005 (SSI 2005/467)) have consented to it.

*Removal to and from Northern Ireland*

## Removal of patients to Northern Ireland

**1–949**    **81.**—(1) If it appears to the Secretary of State, in the case of a patient who is for the time being liable to be detained or subject to guardianship under this Act (otherwise than by virtue of section 35, 36 or 38 above), that it is in the interests of the patient to remove him to Northern Ireland, and that arrangements have been made for admitting him to a hospital or, as the case may be, for receiving him into guardianship there, the Secretary of State may authorise his removal to Northern Ireland and may give any necessary directions for his conveyance to his destination.

(2) Subject to the provisions of subsections (4) and (5) below, where a patient liable to be detained under this Act by virtue of an application, order or direction under any enactment in force in England and Wales is removed under this section and admitted to a hospital in Northern Ireland, he shall be treated as if on the date of his admission he had been so admitted in pursuance of an application made, or [a restriction order or a restriction direction] made or given, on that date under the corresponding enactment in force in Northern Ireland, and, [where he is subject to a hospital order and a restriction order or a transfer direction and a restriction direction under any enactment in this Act, as if he were subject to a hospital order and a restriction order or a transfer direction and a restriction direction under the corresponding enactment] in force in Northern Ireland.]

(3) Where a patient subject to guardianship under this Act by virtue of an application, order or direction under any enactment in force in England and Wales is removed under this section and received into guardianship in Northern Ireland, he shall be treated as if on the date on which he arrives at the place where he is to reside he had been so received in pursuance of an application, order or direction under the corresponding enactment in force in Northern Ireland, and as if the application had been accepted or, as the case may be, the order or direction had been made or given on that date.

(4) Where a person removed under this section was immediately before his removal liable to be detained by virtue of an application for admission for assessment under this Act, he shall, on his admission to a hospital in Northern Ireland, be treated as if he had been admitted to the hospital in pursuance of an application [for assessment under Article 4 of the Mental Health (Northern Ireland) Order 1986] made on the date of his admission.

(5) Where a person removed under this section was immediately before his removal liable to be detained by virtue of an application for admission for treatment under this Act, he shall, on his admission to a hospital in Northern Ireland, be treated as if [he were detained for treatment under Part II of the Mental Health (Northern Ireland) Order 1986 by virtue of a report under Article 12(1) of that Order made on the date of his admission.]

(6) Where a person removed under this section was immediately before his removal liable to be detained under this Act by virtue of a transfer direction given while he was serving a sentence of imprisonment (within the meaning of section 47(5) above) imposed by a court in England and Wales, he shall be treated as if the sentence had been imposed by a court in Northern Ireland.

(7) Where a person removed under this section was immediately before his removal subject to a [. . .] restriction direction of limited duration, [the [. . .] restriction direction] to which he is subject by virtue of subsection (2) above shall expire on the date on which [the first mentioned [. .] restriction direction would have expired if he had not been so removed.

(8) In this section "hospital" has the same meaning as in the Mental Health [(Northern Ireland) Order 1986].

AMENDMENT

In this section the words in square brackets were substituted by the Mental Health (Northern Ireland Consequential Amendments) Order 1986 (SI 1986/596) art.2 and the Mental Health Act 2007 s.39(2), Sch.5 Pt 1 para.5. The words omitted in subs.(7) were repealed by s.55, Sch.11 Pt 8.

DEFINITIONS

**1–950**   patient: s.145(1).
hospital order: ss.37, 145(1).
restriction order: ss.41, 145(1).
restriction direction: ss.49, 145(1).
application for admission for assessment: ss.2, 145(1).
application for admission for treatment: ss.3, 145(1).
transfer direction: ss.47, 145(1).

GENERAL NOTE

**1–951**   This section enables the Secretary of State (or, for certain categories of patient in relation to Wales, the Welsh Ministers) to transfer a patient who is detained (otherwise than under ss.35, 36 or 38) or subject to guardianship in England or Wales to Northern Ireland without a break in the powers of detention or guardianship. The Secretary of State (or the Welsh Ministers) must be satisfied that such a move is in the interests of the patient and that suitable arrangements have been made for admitting him to hospital or receiving him into guardianship in Northern Ireland. On arrival in Northern Ireland the patient will become subject to the equivalent Northern Irish legislation, and the application or direction made in England or Wales will cease to have effect.

Once the transfer of a detained patient has been agreed in principle between the sending and receiving hospitals, the sending hospital should contact either the Department of Health or the National Assembly for Wales. The Department of Health has devised a pro-forma to be used by hospitals in England for non-restricted patients: see the General Note to s.80. Details of the proposed transfer of a restricted patient should be sent to the Ministry of Justice: see the General Note to s.80.

For the effect of a transfer under this section on the existing application, see s.91.

It is not possible to grant a patient escorted leave of absence under s.17 to Northern Ireland because the escort would have no jurisdiction there.

*Transitional provision*

**1–952**   The repeal of the reference to restriction orders made in subs.(7) shall have no effect in respect of:

(a) a restriction order for a specified period made before October 1, 2007, or

(b) an order made outside England and Wales which is treated under the 1983 Act as if it were a restriction order for a specified period (Mental Health Act 2007 s.40(7) and SI 2007/2798 art.2(d)).

*Subsection (1)*

**1–953**   SECRETARY OF STATE.   See the note on s.80(1).

GUARDIANSHIP.   "In practice, a request for a transfer warrant should be made by, or on behalf of, the patient's responsible local social services authority in England to the Department of Health. The request should explain why the transfer would be in the patient's interests, the arrangements that have been agreed for the patient to be received into guardianship in Northern Ireland, and whether (and if so why) the patient needs to be kept in custody while being taken there" (Reference Guide, para.27.23).

ARRANGEMENTS. For the transmission of information about these arrangements, see the general note to s.80.

*Subsection (6)*
TRANSFER DIRECTION. See s.92(5). **1–954**

*Subsection (8)*
HOSPITAL. Is defined in art.2 of the 1986 Order. **1–955**

## [Removal of community patients to Northern Ireland

**81ZA.**—(1) Section 81 above shall apply in the case of a community patient as **1–956** it applies in the case of a patient who is for the time being liable to be detained under this Act, as if the community patient were so liable.

(2) Any reference in that section to the application, order or direction by virtue of which a patient is liable to be detained under this Act shall be construed, for these purposes, as a reference to the application, order or direction under this Act in respect of the patient.]

AMENDMENT
This section was inserted by the Mental Health Act 2007 s.39(2), Sch.5 Pt 1 para.6.

GENERAL NOTE
Paragraphs 27.19-27.21 of the Reference Guide state: **1–957**

"At the time of publication, there is no equivalent of SCT under Northern Ireland legislation, so responsibility for SCT patients may not be transferred to a hospital in Northern Ireland.

However, if it is in their interests, SCT patients may instead be transferred to detention in Northern Ireland under a transfer warrant [made under s.81], as if (in effect) they had never become an SCT patient.

In practice, a request for the transfer of an SCT patient should be made to the Department of Health by, or on behalf of, the managers of the patient's responsible hospital."

## [Transfer of responsibility for patients to Northern Ireland

**81A.**—(1) If it appears to the Secretary of State, in the case of a patient who— **1–958**
[(a) is subject to a hospital order under section 37 above and a restriction order under section 41 above or to a transfer direction under section 47 above and a restriction direction under section 49 above;] and
(b) has been conditionally discharged under section 42 or 73 above,
that a transfer under this section would be in the interests of the patient, the Secretary of State may, with the consent of the Minister exercising corresponding functions in Northern Ireland, transfer responsibility for the patient to that Minister.

(2) Where responsibility for such a patient is transferred under this section, the patient shall be treated—
(a) as if on the date of the transfer he had been conditionally discharged under the corresponding enactment in force in Northern Ireland; and
(b) as if he were subject to [a hospital order and a restriction order, or to a transfer direction and a restriction direction,] under the corresponding enactment in force in Northern Ireland.

(3) Where a patient responsibility for whom is transferred under this section was immediately before the transfer subject to a [. . .] or restriction direction of limited duration, the [. . ] or restriction direction to which he is subject by virtue of subsection (2) above shall expire on the date on which the first-mentioned [. . .] direction would have expired if the transfer had not been made.]

AMENDMENTS

This section was inserted by the Crime (Sentences) Act 1997 s.48, Sch.3 para.2. The words in square brackets in subss.(1) and (2) were substituted by the Mental Health Act 2007 s.39(2), Sch.5 Pt 1 para.7. The words omitted in subs.(3) were repealed by s.55, Sch.11 Pt 8.

DEFINITIONS

**1–959**    patient: s.145(1).
hospital order: ss.37, 145(1).
restriction order: ss.41, 145(1).
restriction direction: ss.49, 145(1).

GENERAL NOTE

**1–960**    This section makes provision for the transfer of responsibility for conditionally discharged restricted patients from England and Wales to Northern Ireland. It is an equivalent provision to s.80A and reference should be made to the notes on that section.

*Transitional provision*

**1–961**    The repeal of the reference to restriction orders in subs.(3) shall have no effect in respect of:

(a)  a restriction order for a specified period made before October 1, 2007, or

(b)  an order made outside England and Wales which is treated under the 1983 Act as if it were a restriction order for a specified period (Mental Health Act 2007 s.40(7) and SI 2007/2798 art.2(d)).

*Subsection (1)*

**1–962**    SECRETARY OF STATE.  Functions under this provision have not been transferred to Welsh Ministers (see the General Note to this Act and SI 1999/672, art.2, Sch.1).

## Removal to England and Wales of patients from Northern Ireland

**1–963**    **82.**—(1) If it appears to the responsible authority, in the case of a patient who is for the time being liable to be detained or subject to guardianship under the Mental Health [(Northern Ireland) Order 1986 (otherwise than by virtue of Article 42, 43 or 45 of that Order)], that it is in the interests of the patient to remove him to England and Wales, and that arrangements have been made for admitting him to a hospital or, as the case may be, for receiving him into guardianship there, the responsible authority may authorise his removal to England and Wales and may give any necessary directions for his conveyance to his destination.

(2) Subject to the provisions of [subsections (4) and (4A)] below, where a patient who is liable to be detained under the [Mental Health (Northern Ireland) Order 1986] by virtue of an application, order or direction under any enactment in force in Northern Ireland is removed under this section and admitted to a hospital in England and Wales, he shall be treated as if on the date of his admission he had been so admitted in pursuance of an application made, or an order or direction made or given, on that date under the corresponding enactment

in force in England and Wales and, [where he is subject to a hospital order and a restriction order or a transfer direction and a restriction direction under any enactment in that Order, as if he were subject to a hospital order and a restriction order or a transfer direction and a restriction direction under the corresponding enactment] in force in England and Wales].

(3) Where a patient subject to guardianship under the [Mental Health (Northern Ireland) Order 1986] by virtue of an application, order or direction under any enactment in force in Northern Ireland is removed under this section and received into guardianship in England and Wales, he shall be treated as if on the date on which he arrives at the place where he is to reside he had been so received in pursuance of an application, order or direction under the corresponding enactment in force in England and Wales and as if the application had been accepted or, as the case may be, the order or direction had been made or given on that date.

[(4) Where a person removed under this section was immediately before his removal liable to be detained for treatment by virtue of a report under Article 12(1) or 13 of the Mental Health (Northern Ireland) Order 1986, he shall be treated, on his admission to a hospital in England and Wales, as if he had been admitted to the hospital in pursuance of an application for admission for treatment made on the date of his admission.

(4A) Where a person removed under this section was immediately before his removal liable to be detained by virtue of an application for assessment under Article 4 of the Mental Health (Northern Ireland) Order 1986, he shall be treated, on his admission to a hospital in England and Wales, as if he had been admitted to the hospital in pursuance of an application for admission for assessment made on the date of his admission.]

(5) Where a patient removed under this section was immediately before his removal liable to be detained under the [Mental Health (Northern Ireland) Order 1986] by virtue of a transfer direction given while he was serving a sentence of imprisonment (within the meaning of [Article 53(5) of that Order)] imposed by a court in Northern Ireland, he shall be treated as if the sentence had been imposed by a court in England and Wales.

(6) Where a person removed under this section was immediately before his removal subject to [a restriction order or restriction direction] of limited duration, the restriction order or restriction direction to which he is subject by virtue of subsection (2) above shall expire on the date on which the [first-mentioned restriction order or restriction direction] would have expired if he had not been so removed.

(7) In this section "the responsibility authority" means the Department of Health and Social Services for Northern Ireland or, in relation to a patient who is subject to [a restriction order or restriction direction], the Secretary of State.

AMENDMENTS

In this section the words in square brackets were substituted or inserted by the Mental Health (Northern Ireland Consequential Amendments) Order 1986 (SI 1986/596) art.2 and the Mental Health Act 2007 s.39(2), Sch.5 Pt 1 para.8.

DEFINITIONS

   patient: s.145(1).

   hospital: ss.92(1), 145(1).

   application for admission for assessment: ss.2, 145(1).

   application for admission for treatment: ss.3, 145(1).

   hospital order: ss.37, 145(1).

**1–964**

transfer direction: ss.47, 145(1).
restriction order: ss.41, 145(1).
restriction direction: ss.49, 145(1).

GENERAL NOTE

**1–965**    This section provides that a patient who is detained or subject to guardianship in Northern Ireland may be transferred to England or Wales without a break in the powers of detention or guardianship. On arrival in England or Wales the patient will become subject to detention or guardianship under this Act.

Paragraph 25.33 of the Reference Guide states:

"In practice, the Northern Ireland authorities will generally ask the Department of Health (or the Ministry of Justice for restricted patients) to confirm that arrangements have been made for the transfer. The Secretary of State for Justice will not, in practice, agree to the transfer of a restricted patient to England unless satisfied that the proposed arrangements will enable the patient's safe management in England."

*Applications to the First-tier Tribunal (Mental Health) or the Mental Health Review Tribunal for Wales*

**1–966**    A patient who has been transferred under this section has a right to apply to a tribunal within six months of his transfer (ss.66(1), 69(2)(a)). The patient's nearest relative has similar rights to make an application (s.69(1), as applied by s.55(4)).

*Subsection (1)*

**1–967**    CORRESPONDING ENACTMENT.    See the table set out at p.233 of the Reference Guide.

*Subsection (2)*

**1–968**    DATE OF HIS ADMISSION.    Which must be recorded on Form M1: see reg.15 of the English Regulations (in Wales, Form TC7: see reg.29 of the Welsh Regulations).

## [Transfer of responsibility for [conditionally discharged] patients to England and Wales from Northern Ireland

**1–969**    **82A.**—(1) If it appears to the relevant Minister, in the case of a patient who—

(a) is subject to a restriction order or restriction direction under Article 47(1) or 55(1) of the Mental Health (Northern Ireland) Order 1986; and

(b) has been conditionally discharged under Article 48(2) or 78(2) of that Order,

that a transfer under this section would be in the interests of the patient, that Minister may, with the consent of the Secretary of State, transfer responsibility for the patient to the Secretary of State.

(2) Where responsibility for such a patient is transferred under this section, the patient shall be treated—

(a) as if on the date of the transfer he had been conditionally discharged under section 42 or 73 above; and

[(b) as if he were subject to a hospital order under section 37 above and a restriction order under section 41 above or to a transfer direction under section 47 above and a restriction direction under section 49 above.]

(3) Where a patient responsibility for whom is transferred under this section was immediately before the transfer subject to a restriction order or restriction direction of limited duration, the restriction order or restriction direction to which he is subject by virtue of subsection (2) above shall expire on the date

on which the first-mentioned order or direction would have expired if the transfer had not been made.

(4) In this section "the relevant Minister" means the Minister exercising in Northern Ireland functions corresponding to those of the Secretary of State.]

AMENDMENTS

This section was inserted by the Crime (Sentences) Act 1997 s.48, Sch.3 para.3. In subs.(2) the words in square brackets were substituted by the Mental Health Act 2007 s.39(2), Sch.5 Pt 1 para.9. The heading to this section was amended by the 2007 Act.

DEFINITIONS                                                                                                    **1–970**
    patient: s.145(1).
    hospital order: ss.37, 145(1).
    restriction order: ss.41, 145(1).
    restriction direction: ss.41, 145(1).

GENERAL NOTE

This section enables the Secretary of State to authorise the transfer of a conditionally dis-  **1–971** charged restricted patient from Northern Ireland to England and Wales. The expiry date of the original order or direction is not effected by the transfer.

*Subsection (1)*

SECRETARY OF STATE. Functions under this provision have not been transferred to  **1–972** Welsh Ministers (see the General Note to this Act and SI 1999/672 art.2, Sch.1).

*Removal to and from Channel Islands and Isle of Man*

## Removal of patients to Channel Islands or Isle of Man

**83.** If it appears to the Secretary of State, in the case of a patient who is for the  **1–973** time being liable to be detained or subject to guardianship under this Act (otherwise than by virtue of section 35, 36 or 38 above), that it is in the interests of the patient to remove him to any of the Channel Islands or to the Isle of Man, and that arrangements have been made for admitting him to a hospital or, as the case may be, for receiving him into guardianship there, the Secretary of State may authorise his removal to the island in question and may give any necessary directions for his conveyance to his destination.

DEFINITIONS                                                                                                    **1–974**
    patient: s.145(1).
    hospital: ss.92(1), 145(1).

GENERAL NOTE

This section provides for patients who are detained or subject to guardianship in England  **1–975** or Wales to be transferred to the Channel Islands or the Isle of Man by the Secretary of State (or, for certain categories of patient in relation to Wales, the Welsh Ministers) without a break in the powers of detention or guardianship. Transfers may require the approval of the relevant island authorities in accordance with the local legislation. The Department of Health (or the Ministry of Justice) will seek this as necessary. The Department of Health has devised a pro-forma to be used by hospitals in England for non-restricted patients: see the General Note to s.80.

For the effect of a transfer under this section on the existing application, see s.91.

If a patient is granted escorted leave of absence under s.17 to travel to the Isle of Man or any of the Channel Islands, the escort would have no jurisdiction on arrival there.

SECRETARY OF STATE.  See the note on s.80(1).

GUARDIANSHIP.  "In practice, a request for a transfer warrant should be made by, or on behalf of, the patient's responsible local social services authority in England to the Department of Health. The request should explain why the transfer would be in the patient's interests, the arrangements that have been agreed for the patient to be received into guardianship in the island in question, and whether (and if so why) the patient needs to be kept in custody while being taken there. The transfer may also have to be agreed with the relevant island authorities in accordance with local legislation" (Reference Guide, para.28.24).

ARRANGEMENTS.  For the transmission of information about these arrangements, see the General Note to s.80.

CONVEYANCE.  General provisions relating to the custody, conveyance and detention of patients are contained in s.137.

## [Removal or transfer of community patients to Channel Islands or Isle of Man

**1–976**  **83ZA.**—(1) Section 83 above shall apply in the case of a community patient as it applies in the case of a patient who is for the time being liable to be detained under this Act, as if the community patient were so liable.

(2) But if there are in force in any of the Channel Islands or the Isle of Man enactments ("relevant enactments") corresponding or similar to those relating to community patients in this Act—

(a) subsection (1) above shall not apply as regards that island; and

(b) subsections (3) to (6) below shall apply instead.

(3) If it appears to the appropriate national authority, in the case of a community patient, that the conditions mentioned in subsection (4) below are met, the authority may authorise the transfer of responsibility for him to the island in question.

(4) The conditions are—

(a) a transfer under subsection (3) above is in the patient's interests; and

(b) arrangements have been made for dealing with him under the relevant enactments.

(5) But the authority may not act under subsection (3) above while the patient is recalled to hospital under section 17E above.

(6) In this section, "the appropriate national authority" means—

(a) in relation to a community patient in respect of whom the responsible hospital is in England, the Secretary of State;

(b) in relation to a community patient in respect of whom the responsible hospital is in Wales, the Welsh Ministers.]

AMENDMENT
This section was inserted by the Mental Health Act 2007 s.39(2), Sch.5 Pt 1 para.10.

DEFINITION
**1–977**  community patient: ss.17A(7), 145(1).

GENERAL NOTE
**1–978**  This section and s.85ZA provide for community patients to be transferred from England and Wales to the Channel Islands and the Isle of Man and vice versa. The Explanatory Notes state at para.166:

"At present the Channel Islands and the Isle of Man do not have legislation enabling patients to be treated in the community under arrangements similar to Supervised Community Treatment so [these sections] would not, as things stand, have any effect in relation to the Channel Islands or the Isle of Man".

Paragraphs 28.21 to 28.22 of the Reference Guide states:

"If there is no equivalent of SCT in the island in question, an SCT patient may instead be transferred to detention in the island under a transfer warrant [made under s.83], as if (in effect) they had never become an SCT patient.

In practice, a request for the transfer of an SCT patient should be made to the Department of Health by, or on behalf of, the managers of the patient's responsible hospital. The Department will seek any necessary approval from the relevant island authorities."

## [Transfer of responsibility for conditionally discharged patients to Channel Islands or Isle of Man

**83A.** If it appears to the Secretary of State, in the case of a patient who—  **1–979**
  (a)  is subject to a restriction order or restriction direction under section 41 or 49 above; and
  (b)  has been conditionally discharged under section 42 or 73 above,
that a transfer under this section would be in the interests of the patient, the Secretary of State may, with the consent of the authority exercising corresponding functions in any of the Channel Islands or in the Isle of Man, transfer responsibility for the patient to that authority.]

AMENDMENT
  This section was inserted by the Crime (Sentences) Act 1997 s.48, Sch.3 para.4. The heading was substituted by the Mental Health Act 2007 s.39(2), Sch.5 Pt 1 para.10.

DEFINITIONS
  patient: s.145(1).  **1–980**
  restriction order: ss.41, 145(1).
  restriction direction: ss.49, 145(1).

GENERAL NOTE
  This section provides for the Secretary of State to authorise the transfer of a conditionally **1–981** discharged restricted patient from England and Wales to the Channel Island or the Isle of Man.
  For the effect of a transfer under this section on the existing order or direction, see s.91.

  SECRETARY OF STATE.  Functions under this provision have not been transferred to Welsh Ministers (see the General Note to this Act and SI 1999/672, art.2, Sch.1).

## Removal to England and Wales of offenders found insane in Channel Islands and Isle of Man

**84.**—(1) The Secretary of State may by warrant direct that any offender found **1–982** by a court in any of the Channel Islands or in the Isle of Man to be insane or to have been insane at the time of the alleged offence, and ordered to be detained during Her Majesty's pleasure, be removed to a hospital in England and Wales.

(2) A patient removed under subsection (1) above shall, on his reception into the hospital in England and Wales, be treated as if he [were subject to a hospital order together with a restriction order [. . .]

(3) The Secretary of State may by warrant direct that any patient removed under this section from any of the Channel Islands or from the Isle of Man be returned to the island from which he was so removed, there to be dealt with according to law in all respects as if he had not been removed under this section.

AMENDMENT

The words in square brackets in subs.(2) were substituted by the Domestic Violence, Crime and Victims Act 2004 s.58(1), Sch.10 para.22. The words omitted in subs.(2) were repealed by the Mental Health Act 2007 s.55, Sch.11 Pt 8.

DEFINITIONS

**1–983**    hospital: ss.92(1), 145(1).
patient: s.145(1).

GENERAL NOTE

**1–984**    This section enables the Secretary of State to transfer to a hospital in England or Wales an offender who has been found to be insane by a court in the Channel Islands or Isle of Man. For procedure and tribunal rights, see the General Note to s.82.

*Transitional provision*

**1–985**    The repeal of the reference to restriction orders made for a specified period in subs.(2) shall have no effect in respect of—

    (a)  a restriction order for a specified period made before October 1, 2007, or

    (b)  an order made outside England and Wales which is treated under the 1983 Act as if it were a restriction order for a specified period (Mental Health Act 2007 s.40(7) and SI 2007/2798 art.2(d)).

*Subsection (1)*

**1–986**    SECRETARY OF STATE. Functions under this provision have not been transferred to Welsh Ministers (see the General Note to this Act and SI 1999/672 art.2, Sch.1).

## Patients removed from Channel Islands or Isle of Man

**1–987**    **85.**—(1) This section applies to any patient who is removed to England and Wales from any of the Channel Islands or the Isle of Man under a provision corresponding to section 83 above and who immediately before his removal was liable to be detained or subject to guardianship in the island in question under a provision corresponding to an enactment contained in this Act (other than section 35, 36 or 38 above).

(2) Where the patient is admitted to a hospital in England and Wales he shall be treated as if on the date of his admission he had been so admitted in pursuance of an application made, or an order or direction made or given, on that date under the corresponding enactment contained in this Act and, where he is subject to an order or direction restricting his discharge, as if he were subject [to a hospital order and a restriction order or to a hospital direction and a limitation direction or to a transfer direction and a restriction direction].

(3) Where a patient is received into guardianship in England and Wales, he shall be treated as if on the date on which he arrives at the place where he is to reside he had been so received in pursuance of an application, order or direction under the

corresponding enactment contained in this Act and as if the application had been accepted or, as the case may be, the order or direction had been made or given on that date.

(4) Where the patient was immediately before his removal liable to be detained by virtue of a transfer direction given while he was serving a sentence of imprisonment imposed by a court in the island in question, he shall be treated as if the sentence had been imposed by a court in England and Wales.

(5) Where the patient was immediately before his removal subject to an order or direction restricting his discharge, being an order or direction of limited duration, the restriction order or restriction direction to which he is subject by virtue of subsection (2) above shall expire on the date on which the first-mentioned order or direction would have expired if he had not been removed.

(6) While being conveyed to the hospital referred to in subsection (2) or, as the case may be, the place referred to in subsection (3) above, the patient shall be deemed to be in legal custody, and section 138 below shall apply to him as if he were in legal custody by virtue of section 137 below.

(7) In the case of a patient removed from the Isle of Man the reference in subsection (4) above to a person serving a sentence of imprisonment includes a reference to a person detained as mentioned in section 60(6)(a) of the Mental Health Act 1974 (an Act of Tynwald).

AMENDMENT

In subs.(2) the words in square brackets were substituted by the Mental Health Act 2007 s.39(2), Sch.5 Pt 1 para.11.

DEFINITIONS
    patient: s.145(1).                                                        **1–988**
    hospital: ss.92(1), 145(1).
    hospital order: ss.37, 145(1).
    hospital direction: ss.45A(3), 145(1).
    limitation direction: ss.45A(3), 145(1).
    restriction order: ss.41, 145(1).
    restriction direction: ss.49, 145(1).
    transfer direction: ss.47, 145(1).

GENERAL NOTE

This section provides for a patient who is detained or subject to guardianship in the **1–989** Channel Islands or the Isle of Man to be transferred to England or Wales without a break in the powers of detention or guardianship.

Paragraphs 25.38–25.39 of the Reference Guide state:

"Patients transferred from the Isle of Man or the Channel Islands are treated on their arrival in England or Wales as if subject to the application, order or direction which corresponds to the provisions to which they were subject in the island in question. Advice should be sought from the island authorities or from the Department of Health or the Ministry of Justice (as applicable) if there is doubt about what the relevant corresponding provision is. Patients subject to the equivalent of remand to hospital under sections 35 or 36, or an interim hospital order under section 38, cannot be transferred.

For patients transferred from the Isle of Man who become subject to the equivalent of hospital directions or restriction directions in England, detention under section 60(6)(a) of the Mental Health Act 1974 (an Act of Tynwald) is treated (where relevant) as if it were a sentence of imprisonment which has been given by a court in England or Wales."

For the procedure to be followed when a patient is transferred to England or Wales, see reg.15 of the English Regulations and reg.29 of the Welsh Regulations.

*Applications to the First-tier Tribunal (Mental Health) or the Mental Health Review Tribunal for Wales*

**1–990**     A patient who has been transferred under this section has a right of appeal to a tribunal within six months of his transfer (ss.66(1), 69(2)(a)). The patient's nearest relative has similar rights to make an application (s.69(1), as applied by s.55(4)).

*Subsection (1)*

**1–991**     ISLE OF MAN.   Where mentally disordered patients are detained under the Mental Health Act 1998 (as amended).

## [Responsibility for community patients transferred from Channel Islands or Isle of Man

**1–992**     **85ZA.**—(1) This section shall have effect if there are in force in any of the Channel Islands or the Isle of Man enactments ("relevant enactments") corresponding or similar to those relating to community patients in this Act.

(2) If responsibility for a patient is transferred to England and Wales under a provision corresponding to section 83ZA(3) above, he shall be treated as if on the date of his arrival at the place where he is to reside in England or Wales—

(a) he had been admitted to the hospital in pursuance of an application made, or an order or direction made or given, on that date under the enactment in force in England and Wales which most closely corresponds to the relevant enactments;
and

(b) a community treatment order had then been made discharging him from the hospital.

(3) "The responsible hospital", in his case, means the hospital to which he is treated as having been admitted by virtue of subsection (2) above, subject to section 19A above.

(4) As soon as practicable after the patient's arrival at the place where he is to reside in England or Wales, the responsible clinician shall specify the conditions to which he is to be subject for the purposes of section 17B(1) above, and the conditions shall be deemed to be specified in the community treatment order.

(5) But the responsible clinician may only specify conditions under subsection (4) above which an approved mental health professional agrees should be specified.]

AMENDMENT

This section was inserted by the Mental Health Act 2007 s.39(2), Sch.5 Pt 1 para.12.

DEFINITIONS

**1–993**     patient: s.145(1).
community treatment order: ss.17A(7), 145(1).
responsible clinician: ss.34(1), 145(1).
approved mental health professional: s.145(1).

GENERAL NOTE

**1–994**     See the General Notes to ss.83ZA and 85.

*Subsection (4)*

SHALL SPECIFY THE CONDITIONS. On form CTO 9: see reg.16(4) of the English **1–995** Regulations.

## [Responsibility for conditionally discharged patients transferred from Channel Islands or Isle of Man

**85A.**—(1) This section applies to any patient responsibility for whom is trans- **1–996** ferred to the Secretary of State by the authority exercising corresponding functions in any of the Channel Islands or the Isle of Man under a provision corresponding to section 83A above.

(2) The patient shall be treated—

(a) as if on the date of the transfer he had been conditionally discharged under section 42 or 73 above; and

[(b) as if he were subject to a hospital order under section 37 above and a restriction order under section 41 above, or to a hospital direction and a limitation direction under section 45A above, or to a transfer direction under section 47 above and a restriction direction under section 49 above.]

(3) Where the patient was immediately before the transfer subject to an order or direction restricting his discharge, being an order or direction of limited duration, the restriction order[, limitation direction] or restriction direction to which he is subject by virtue of subsection (2) above shall expire on the date on which the first-mentioned order or direction would have expired if the transfer had not been made.]

AMENDMENTS

This section was inserted by the Crime (Sentences) Act 1997 s.48, Sch.3 para.4. The amendments to it were made by the Mental Health Act 2007 s.39(2), Sch.5 Pt 1 paras 12, 13.

DEFINITIONS

    patient: s.145(1).                                                        **1–997**

    hospital order: ss.37, 145(1).

    hospital direction: ss.45A(3), 145(1).

    limitation direction: ss.45A(3), 145(1).

    restriction order: ss.41, 145(1).

    restriction direction: ss.49, 145(1).

GENERAL NOTE

This section states that a patient who has been transferred from the Channel Islands or the **1–998** Isle of Man under a provision that corresponds to section 83A, above, shall be treated as if on the date of the transfer he was a conditionally discharged restricted patient. Also see the General Note to s.85.

*Subsection (1)*

SECRETARY OF STATE. Functions under this provision have not been transferred to **1–999** Welsh Ministers (see the General Note to this Act and SI 1999/672 art.2, Sch.1).

*Removal of Aliens*

## Removal of alien patients

**86.**—(1) This section applies to any patient who is neither a British citizen nor a **1–1000** Commonwealth citizen having the right of abode in the United Kingdom by virtue of section 2(1)(b) of the Immigration Act 1971, being a patient who is receiving treatment for [mental disorder] as an in-patient in a hospital in England and Wales or a hospital within the meaning of the Mental Health Act [(Northern Ireland) Order 1986] and is detained pursuant to—

(a) an application for admission for treatment or [a report under Article 12(1) or 13 of that Order];

(b) a hospital order under section 37 above or [Article 44 of that Order]; or

(c) an order or direction under this Act (other than under section 35, 36 or 38 above) or [under that Order (other than under Article 42, 43 or 45 of that Order] having the same effect as such a hospital order.

(2) If it appears to the Secretary of State that proper arrangements have been made for the removal of a patient to whom this section applies to a country or territory outside the United Kingdom, the Isle of Man and the Channel Islands and for his care or treatment there and that it is in the interests of the patient to remove him, the Secretary of State may, subject to subsection (3) below—

(a) by warrant authorise the removal of the patient from the place where he is receiving treatment as mentioned in subsection (1) above, and

(b) give such directions as the Secretary of State thinks fit for the conveyance of the patient to his destination in that country or territory and for his detention in any place or on board any ship or aircraft until his arrival at any specified port or place in any such country or territory.

(3) The Secretary of State shall not exercise his powers under subsection (2) above in the case of any patient except with the approval of [the appropriate tribunal] or, as the case may be, of the Mental Health Review Tribunal for Northern Ireland.

[(4) In relation to a patient receiving treatment in a hospital within the meaning of the Mental Health (Northern Ireland) Order 1986, the reference in subsection (1) above to mental disorder shall be construed in accordance with that Order.]

AMENDMENTS

In subs.(1) the words in square brackets were substituted by the Mental Health (Northern Ireland Consequential Amendments) Order 1986 (SI 1986/596) art.2. The reference to mental disorder in subs.(1) was substituted, and subs.(4) was inserted by the Mental Health Act 2007 s.1(4), Sch.1 para.15. The reference to the appropriate tribunal in subs.(3) was substituted by SI 2008/2883 art.9, Sch.3 para.62.

DEFINITIONS

1–1001    patient: s.145(1).
hospital: ss.92(2), 145(1).
application for admission for treatment: ss.3, 145(1).
hospital order: ss.37, 145(1).
the appropriate tribunal: ss.66(4), 145(1).

GENERAL NOTE

1–1002    This section empowers the Secretary of State (or the Welsh Ministers: see subs.(2)) to authorise the removal to any country abroad of certain detained patients (see subs.(1)) who do not have a right of abode in this country and who are receiving in-patient treatment for mental disorder. Before they exercise their powers the Secretaries of State or the Welsh Ministers must have obtained the approval of the appropriate tribunal.

The main purpose of this section is to "enable patients who are either irrationally opposed to their removal, or are unable to express a view, to be compulsorily removed to another country when this is judged to be in their best interests. It is also used to enable patients to be kept under escort on their journey home if this is necessary" (Cmnd. 7320, para.8.26).

If the patient is not a restricted patient, the patient will be granted leave of absence under s.17 to travel to the port of embarkation. The Secretary of State for Justice will use his power under s.42 to conditionally discharge a restricted patient, subject to the condition that he or she is taken directly to the port of embarkation. In *MJ (Angola) v Secretary of State for the Home Department* [2010] EWCA Civ 557, the Court of Appeal held that it was lawful for the Secretary of State to (a) use s.42 for this purpose and (b) make a decision to deport a person who is a restricted patient.

There is nothing to prevent a patient who has been removed under this section from applying for re-admission to the UK. If the patient was subject to a hospital order with restrictions when he or she was removed, both the hospital order and the restriction order will remain in force (s.91(2)). Otherwise the application, order or direction will cease to have effect (s.91(1)).

Proposals for the removal of Pt II patients should be made to the Secretary of State for Health (Wellington House, 133–155 Waterloo Road, London SE1 8UG). Proposals for the removal of Pt III patients should be made to the Secretary of State for Justice (Mental Health Unit, 2nd Floor, Fry Building, 2 Marsham Street, London SW1P 4DF). Functions under this section, so far as exercisable in relation to Wales, are transferred to the Welsh Ministers except in relation to a patient who is subject to a restriction order made under s.41, a hospital direction made under s.45A(3)(a), a limitation direction made under s.45A(3)(b), or a restriction direction made under s.49 (SI 2008/1786 art.2).

The Reference Guide states at para.29.7:

"Before deciding whether to seek the agreement of the tribunal, the Department of Health or the Ministry of Justice will need to have details of the reasons for the proposed transfer and the arrangements that have or could be made for the patient's transport (in the UK and abroad) and for the patient's subsequent care and treatment. In practice, the Departments will expect the managers of the hospital in which the patient is detained to provide this information and (if the case is referred to the tribunal) to provide any further information which the tribunal requires."

In *R. (on the application of X) v Secretary of State for the Home Department* [2001] W.L.R. 740; [2000] M.H.L.R. 67, the Court of Appeal held that where a person detained under this Act had no basis for remaining in the UK under the Immigration Act 1971, the Secretary of State was entitled to remove him or her under the provisions of that Act, and was not obliged to do so only in accordance with his power of removal under this section. Schiemann L.J. said at para.28:

"There appears to us no reason why the two regimes should not run in parallel in the case of a person who is both an immigrant and mentally ill. Clearly if the [Secretary of State] proposes to use his Immigration Act powers in relation to a mentally ill person that illness will be a factor which he must take into account."

In *MJ (Angola) v Secretary of State for the Home Department*, above, para.28, the Court of Appeal said that the reasoning that led to the Court of Appeal to reach its conclusion in *X* should be applied in cases involving the deportation of the mentally ill where no issue under this section arises as that decision "shows the extent to which the [Secretary of State] can exercise his 1971 Act powers without regard to careful and detailed provisions of the MHA."

As an alternative to the use of this section, the voluntary repatriation of restricted patients can be considered. This process is described in "Foreign national restricted patients: Guidance on repatriation", Ministry of Justice, March 25, 2009, p.3:

"Voluntary repatriation is an arrangement whereby the Ministry of Justice conditionally discharges the patient, subject to the condition that the patient is taken directly to a port of embarkation and from there to their home country The process is largely in the hands of the RC, and allows the RC the opportunity to contact and liaise with psychiatric services abroad to ensure that suitable care would be available for the patient on his or her return home. In order for a patient to be repatriated in this way the RC needs to be satisfied that:

- The patient is willing to return;

- The authorities in his home country are prepared to accept him;

- There are acceptable arrangements for continued treatment, including detention if appropriate;

- There are suitable transport arrangements.

If all of these provisions were met, a request for repatriation should be made to the [Mental Health Casework Section]. Once he is satisfied that the conditions are met, the Justice Secretary can issue a conditional discharge under section 42 of the Mental Health Act. The patient can then be conveyed, in accordance with the conditions of the discharge, to their destination country."

A similar approach, which would not involve either the Mental Health Casework Section or the Secretary of State, can be adopted for the voluntary repatriation of consenting non-restricted patients.

It is possible for a patient who has been made subject to a hospital order or restriction order by a court to be transferred out of the UK by a warrant issued by the Secretary of State under the Repatriation of Prisoners Act 1984. Advice should be sought from the Ministry of Justice.

Section 32 of the UK Borders Act 2007 makes provision for the deportation of certain categories of foreign criminals where this is conducive to the public good. Section 33 of that Act provides that if the criminal is made the subject of a hospital order, a guardianship order, a hospital direction or a transfer direction, there is not an automatic assumption that deportation is conducive to the public good.

*Travel Restriction Orders*

**1–1003**     Section 33 of the Criminal Justice and Police Act 2001 gives power in some circumstances to the Crown Court to make travel restriction orders in relation to offenders convicted of drug trafficking offences. Such orders prohibit the offender from leaving the UK for a specified period after release from custody. Section 37 of the Act provides that a travel restriction order made in relation to any person shall not prevent that person being removed from the UK under a prescribed removal power. The Travel Restrictions Order (Prescribed Removal Powers) Order 2002 (SI 2002/313), Sch.1, designates subs.2(a) and (b) of this section as a prescribed removal power for the purposes of s.37.

*Human Rights Act 1998*

**1–1004**     The removal of a patient under this section could involve a breach of art.3 of the European Convention on Human Rights if there is a real risk of the patient being the subject of inhuman or degrading treatment in the country to which he is sent. In *D v United Kingdom* (1997) 24 E.H.R.R. 423 para.54, the European Court of Human Rights said:

"... [T]he court emphasises that aliens who have served their prison sentences and are subject to expulsion cannot in principle claim any entitlement to remain in the territory of a Contracting State in order to continue to benefit from the medical, social or other forms of assistance provided by the expelling State during their stay in prison".

The same principle would apply to persons who are detained under this Act; also see *N v United Kingdom* (2008) 47 E.H.R.R. 39 and the notes to art.3 in Part 5.

Article 8 of the Convention is also engaged in deportation cases. In *Maslov v Austria* (2008) E.H.R.R. 20, para.75, the ECtHR held that "for a settled migrant who has lawfully spent all or the major part of his or her childhood and youth in the host country very serious reasons are required to justify expulsion. This is all the more so where the person concerned committed the offences underlying the expulsion measure as a juvenile."

*Subsection (1)*

UNITED KINGDOM.   Means Great Britain and Northern Ireland (Interpretation Act 1978 **1–1005** s.5, Sch.1).

IN-PATIENT.   This section does not apply to detained patients who have been granted leave of absence under s.17.

DETAINED.   The use of this section is not appropriate where the patient is likely to be discharged within six months ("Foreign national restricted patients: Guidance on repatriation", above, p.4).

*Subsection (2)*

BY WARRANT AUTHORISE.   Paragraph 29.8 of the Reference Guide states: **1–1006**

"If the Secretary of State obtains the Tribunal's approval and decides to authorise the patient's transfer, the Secretary of State will issue a warrant which will include any appropriate directions to allow the patient to be conveyed (while remaining in legal custody) out of the UK. This includes being kept in custody while en route to another country, e.g. on a plane or ship. But the Secretary of State cannot authorise the patient being kept in custody or detained once the patient has arrived in another country. Any escort arrangements for the rest of the journey would have to be made under the law of that country (if that is allowed)."

CONVEYANCE ... AND FOR HIS DETENTION.   General provisions relating to the custody, **1–1007** conveyance and detention of patients are contained in s.137.

*Subsection (3)*

THE APPROVAL OF THE APPROPRIATE TRIBUNAL.   The Secretary of State or the Welsh **1–1008** Ministers will exercise their discretionary powers to refer the patient to a tribunal.

### Return of patients absent without leave

GENERAL NOTE

**Scotland**

Authority for the retaking of patients who have absconded from hospitals or other places **1–1009** in Scotland is contained in art.8 of the Mental Health (Care and Treatment) (Scotland) Act 2003 (Consequential Provisions) Order 2005 (SI 2005/2078) which is reproduced in Part 2.

## Patients absent from hospitals in Northern Ireland

    **87.**—(1) Any person who— **1–1010**
    (a) under [Article 29 or 132 of the Mental Health (Northern Ireland) Order 1986] (which provide, respectively, for the retaking of patients absent without leave and for the retaking of patients escaping from custody); or
    (b) under the said [Article 29 as applied by Article 31 of the said Order] (which makes special provision as to persons sentenced to imprisonment),

may be taken into custody in Northern Ireland, may be taken into custody in, and returned to Northern Ireland from, England and Wales by an [approved mental health professional], by any constable or by any person authorised by or by virtue of the [said Order] to take him into custody.

(2) This section does not apply to any person who is subject to guardianship.

AMENDMENTS

In subs.(1) the words in square brackets were substituted by the Mental Health (Northern Ireland Consequential Amendments) Order 1986 (SI 1986/596) art.2 and the Mental Health Act 2007 s.21, Sch.2 para.7.

DEFINITIONS

1–1011    patient: s.145(1).
absent without leave: ss.18(6), 145(1).
approved mental health professional: s.145(1), (1AC).

GENERAL NOTE

1–1012    This section permits a patient from Northern Ireland who has either escaped from custody or who is absent without leave from a hospital, to be taken into custody in England or Wales and returned to Northern Ireland. It does not apply to patients subject to guardianship.

*Subsection (1)*

1–1013    RETURNED.  For the powers of a constable or approved mental health professional on taking the patient into custody and returning him to Northern Ireland, see s.137. The period during which the patient may be returned may not be the same as it is for patients subject to similar forms of detention in England. Advice should be sought from the Northern Ireland authorities on this point.

## Patients absent from hospitals in England and Wales

1–1014    **88.**—(1) Subject to the provisions of this section, any person who, under section 18 above or section 138 below or under the said section 18 as applied by section 22 above, may be taken into custody in England and Wales may be taken into custody in, and returned to England and Wales from, [Northern Ireland].

[(2) For the purposes of the enactments referred to in subsection (1) above in their application by virtue of this section, the expression "constable" includes an officer or constable of the Police Service of Northern Ireland.]

(3) For the purposes of the said enactments in their application by virtue of this section [. . .], any reference to an [approved mental health professional] shall be construed as including a reference—

(a) [. . .];

(b) [. . .] to any [approved social worker within the meaning of the Mental Health (Northern Ireland) Order 1986.]

(4) This section does not apply to any person who is subject to guardianship.

AMENDMENTS

In this section (apart from subs.(3)(b)) the words in square brackets were substituted by the Mental Health Act 2007 ss.21, 39(2), Sch.2 para.7, Sch.5 Pt 1 para.14. The words omitted in subs.(3) were repealed by s.55, Sch.11 Pt 7. In subs.(3)(b) the words in square brackets were substituted by the Mental Health (Northern Ireland Consequential Amendments) Order 1986 (SI 1986/596) art.2.

DEFINITION
approved mental health professional s.145(1).                                     **1–1015**

GENERAL NOTE
This section permits patients from England or Wales who are absent without leave from **1–1016**
hospital or who have escaped from custody, to be taken into custody in, and returned to
England and Wales from Northern Ireland. It does not apply to patients who are subject
to guardianship.
For patients who have absconded to Scotland, see the General Note to s.18.
The Explanatory Notes state at para.167:

"The Channel Islands and the Isle of Man have powers of their own, which they can use
to return patients from England and Wales."

*Subsection (1)*
TAKEN INTO CUSTODY.   Within the time limits specified in ss.18 and 22.          **1–1017**

## Patients absent from hospitals in the Channel Islands or Isle of Man

**89.**—(1) Any person who under any provision corresponding to section 18 **1–1018**
above or 138 below may be taken into custody in any of the Channel Islands or
the Isle of Man may be taken into custody in, and returned to the island in question
from, England and Wales by an [approved mental health professional] or a
constable.
(2) This section does not apply to any person who is subject to guardianship.

AMENDMENT
The words in square brackets in subs.(1) were substituted by the Mental Health Act 2007
s.21, Sch.2 para.7.

DEFINITION
approved mental health professional: s.145(1).                                   **1–1019**

GENERAL NOTE
The purpose of this section is to ensure that a detained patient who absconds to England **1–1020**
or Wales from the Channel Islands or the Isle of Man can be apprehended and returned to
the island in question. It does not apply to patients who are subject to guardianship.

RETURNED.   For the powers of a constable or approved mental health professional, see
s.137. The period during which the patient may be returned may not be the same as it is for
patients subject to similar forms of detention in England. Advice should be sought from the
relevant authority on this point.

### *General*

## Regulations for purposes of Part VI

**90.** Section 32 above shall have effect as if references in that section to Part II of **1–1021**
this Act included references to this Part of this Act[, so far as this Part of this Act
applies to patients removed to England and Wales or for whom responsibility is
transferred to England and Wales.]

AMENDMENT
In this section the words in square brackets were substituted by the Mental Health Act
2007, s.39(2), Sch.5, Pt 1, para.15.

**1–1022**    patient: s.145(1).

## General provisions as to patients removed from England and Wales
**1–1023**    **91.**—(1) Subject to subsection (2) below, where a patient liable to be detained or subject to guardianship by virtue of an application, order or direction under Part II or III of this Act (other than section 35, 36 or 38 above) is removed from England and Wales in pursuance of arrangements under this Part of this Act, the application, order or direction shall cease to have effect when he is duly received into a hospital or other institution, or placed under guardianship [or, where he is not received into a hospital but his detention in hospital is authorised by virtue of the Mental Health (Care and Treatment) (Scotland) Act 2003 or the Criminal Procedure (Scotland) Act 1995], in pursuance of those arrangements.

(2) Where the Secretary of State exercises his powers under section 86(2) above in respect of a patient who is detained pursuant to a hospital order under section 37 above and in respect of whom a restriction order is in force, those orders shall continue in force so as to apply to the patient if he returns to England and Wales [. . .].

[(2A) Where responsibility for a community patient is transferred to a jurisdiction outside England and Wales (or such a patient is removed outside England and Wales) in pursuance of arrangements under this Part of this Act, the application, order or direction mentioned in subsection (1) above in force in respect of him shall cease to have effect on the date on which responsibility is so transferred (or he is so removed) in pursuance of those arrangements.]

[(3) Reference in this section to a patient's detention in hospital being authorised by virtue of the Mental Health (Care and Treatment) (Scotland) Act 2003 or the Criminal Procedure (Scotland) Act 1995 shall be read as including references to a patient in respect of whom a certificate under one of the provisions listed in section 290(7)(a) of the Act of 2003 is in operation.]

AMENDMENTS
The amendments to this section were made by SI 2005/2078 Sch.1 para.2(7) and the Mental Health Act 2007 s.39(2), Sch.5 Pt 1 para.16. The words omitted in subs.(2) were repealed by s.55, Sch.11 Pt 8.

DEFINITIONS
**1–1024**    patient: s.145(1).
hospital: ss.92(2), 145(1).
hospital order: ss.37, 145(1).
restriction order: ss.41, 145(1).
community patient: ss.17A(7), 145(1).

GENERAL NOTE
**1–1025**    This section provides that, with one exception, when a patient is removed from England or Wales under a provision in this Part, any application, order or direction made in respect of him (other than s.35, 36 or 38) will cease to have effect on arrival at his or her destination (subs.(1)) or, in the case of a community patient, the date on which responsibility for the patient is transferred (subs.(2A)). The exception is that if a patient who is subject to a hospital order with restrictions is removed, both the hospital order and the restriction order will remain in force (subs.(2)).

*Transitional provision*

The repeal of the reference to restriction orders made for a specified period in subs.(2) **1–1026** shall have no effect in respect of—

(a) a restriction order for a specified period made before October 1, 2007, or

(b) an order made outside England and Wales which is treated under the 1983 Act as if it were a restriction order for a specified period (Mental Health Act 2007 s.40(7) and SI 2007/2798 art.2(d)).

## Interpretation of Part VI

**92.**—(1) References in this Part of this Act to a hospital, being a hospital in **1–1027** England and Wales, shall be construed as references to a hospital within the meaning of Part II of this Act.

[(1A) References in this Part of this Act to the responsible clinician shall be construed as references to the responsible clinician within the meaning of Part 2 of this Act.]

(2) Where a patient is treated by virtue of this Part of this Act as if he had been removed to a hospital in England and Wales in pursuance of a direction under Part III of this Act, that direction shall be deemed to have been given on the date of his reception into the hospital.

(3) [. . .]

[(4) Sections 80 to 85A above shall have effect as if—

(a) any hospital direction under section 45A above were a transfer direction under section 47 above; and

(b) any limitation direction under section 45A above were a restriction direction under section 49 above.

(5) Sections 80(5), 81(6) and 85(4) above shall have effect as if any reference to a transfer direction given while a patient was serving a sentence of imprisonment imposed by a court included a reference to a hospital direction given by a court after imposing a sentence of imprisonment on a patient.]

AMENDMENTS

Subsection (1A) was inserted by the Mental Health Act 2007 s.39(2), Sch.5 Pt 1 para.17. **1–1028** Subsection (3) was repealed by s.55, Sch.11 Pt 1.

Subsection (4) and (5) were inserted by the Crime (Sentences) Act 1997 s.55, Sch.4 para.16.

DEFINITIONS

responsible clinician: ss.34(1), 145(1).   **1–1029**
patient: s.145(1).
mental disorder: ss.1, 145(1).
hospital direction: s.145(1).
transfer direction: s.145(1).
limitation direction: s.145(1).
restriction direction: s.145(1).

*Subsection (1)*

HOSPITAL.   See section 34(2).   **1–1030**

PART VII

**1–1031**        *[Repealed by the Mental Capacity Act 2005 s.67(2), Sch.7.]*

PART VIII

MISCELLANEOUS FUNCTIONS OF LOCAL AUTHORITIES AND THE
SECRETARY OF STATE

*[Approved mental health professionals*

**Approval by local social services authority**
**1–1032**        **114.**—(1) A local social services authority may approve a person to act as an
approved mental health professional for the purposes of this Act.

(2) But a local social services authority may not approve a registered medical
practitioner to act as an approved mental health professional.

(3) Before approving a person under subsection (1) above, a local social services authority shall be satisfied that he has appropriate competence in dealing
with persons who are suffering from mental disorder.

(4) The appropriate national authority may by regulations make provision in
connection with the giving of approvals under subsection (1) above.

(5) The provision which may be made by regulations under subsection (4)
above includes, in particular, provision as to—

(a)  the period for which approvals under subsection (1) above have effect;

(b)  the courses to be undertaken by persons before such approvals are to be
     given and during the period for which such approvals have effect;

(c)  the conditions subject to which such approvals are to be given; and

(d)  the factors to be taken into account in determining whether persons have
     appropriate competence as mentioned in subsection (3) above.

(6) Provision made by virtue of subsection (5)(b) above may relate to courses
approved or provided by such person as may be specified in the regulations (as
well as to courses approved under section 114A below).

(7) An approval by virtue of subsection (6) above may be in respect of a course
in general or in respect of a course in relation to a particular person.

(8) The power to make regulations under subsection (4) above includes power
to make different provision for different cases or areas.

(9) In this section "the appropriate national authority" means—

(a)  in relation to persons who are or wish to become approved to act as
     approved mental health professionals by a local social services authority
     whose area is in England, the Secretary of State;

(b)  in relation to persons who are or wish to become approved to act as
     approved mental health professionals by a local social services authority
     whose area is in Wales, the Welsh Ministers.

(10) In this Act "approved mental health professional" means—

(a)  in relation to acting on behalf of a local social services authority whose area
     is in England, a person approved under subsection (1) above by any local
     social services authority whose area is in England, and

(b)  in relation to acting on behalf of a local social services authority whose area
     is in Wales, a person approved under that subsection by any local social ser-
     vices authority whose area is in Wales.]

AMENDMENT

This section was substituted by the Mental Health Act 2007 s.18.

DEFINITIONS                                                                              **1–1033**

local social services authority: s.145(1).

mental disorders. ss.1, 145(1).

approved mental health professional: subs.(10), s.145(1C).

GENERAL NOTE

This section replaces the role of Approved Social Worker (ASW) with that of the **1–1034** Approved Mental Health Professional (AMHP) which means that a wider group of mental health professionals, including the employees of the detaining authority, will be able to carry out the functions that ASWs performed under the Act. AMHPs will be drawn from social workers; first level nurses, whose field of practice is mental health or learning disability nursing; occupational therapists; and chartered psychologists: see the Mental Health (Approved Mental Health Professionals) (Approval) (England) Regulations (SI 2008/ 1206), which are reproduced in Pt 2. The equivalent regulations for Wales are SI 2008/ 2436 (W.209). A registered medical practitioner is specifically prohibited from being approved to act as an AMHP (subs.(2)).

The *Code of Practice*, at para.4.33, states that local authorities should ensure that sufficient AMHPs are available to carry out their functions under this Act and that arrangements must be in place to provide a 24-hour service that can respond to patient's needs. The Association of Directors of Adult Social Services issued an advice note to its members in July 2008 on "Local Social Services Authorities (LSSAs) and the Approved Mental Health Professional Role". In order to meet its obligations under this section, the Association recommends that LSSAs "enter into a contractual arrangement with the individual AMHP to cover remuneration, training requirements, disciplinary procedures, access to legal advice and legal indemnity whilst carrying out duties on behalf of the LSSA" (para.5.1). LASSAs are prevented from entering into agreements under s.75 of the National Health Service Act 2006 for NHS Trusts to provide exercise functions under this section on their behalf: see NHS Bodies and Local Authorities Partnership Arrangements Regulations 2000 (SI 2000/617) reg.6(a)(iv). SI 2000/617 has effect as if made under s.75, by virtue of the National Health Service (Consequential Provisions) Act 2006 s.4, Sch.2 Pt 1 para.1.

Although all of the professionals involved in an assessment of the patient for detention may be employed by the NHS, "the skills and training required of AMHPs aim to ensure that they provide an independent social perspective" (Explanatory Notes, para.64). An AMHP acts in a personal capacity when performing functions under this Act (see the notes on subs.(10) and on "that professional" in s.13(1A)).

The approval of an AMHP is made by the LSSA (subs.(1)) and the AMHP acts on behalf of the authority (s.145(1AC)). As an AMHP acts on behalf of the local authority, that authority will be vicariously liable for any lack of care or bad faith on behalf of the AMHP (*TMM v London Borough of Hackney* [2010] EWHC 1349 (Admin), para.35). Approval will only be granted if the authority is satisfied that the applicant has appropriate competence in dealing with mentally disordered people (subs.(3)) and complies with any regulations issued by the Secretary of State if the authority is located in England, or the Welsh Ministers if the authority is located in Wales (subss.(4)–(8)).

Although an AMHP can only be approved by one LSSA, he or she can perform AMHP functions in the area of another LSSA (or LSSAs) if that authority has authorised the AMHP to perform such functions on its behalf. On such an authorisation being made, the AMHP must notify the approving LSSA (SI 2008/1206, reg.5(b)). The Reference Guide states, at para.32.5:

"Being approved by an LSSA to be an AMHP is not the same thing as being permitted by an LSSA to act on its behalf. It is for each LSSA to establish its own arrangements for determining which AMHPs may act as such on its behalf and when they may do so. A LSSA may arrange for AMHPs to act on its behalf, even though they are approved by a different LSSA".

To act as an AMHP on behalf of a Welsh LSSA would require approval by a Welsh LSSA under the Mental Health (Approval of Persons to be Approved Mental Health Professionals (Wales) Regulations 2008 (SI 2008/2436 (W.209). However, there is nothing to prevent an AMHP acting on behalf of an English LSSA in Wales where necessary. Paragraph 32.32 of the Reference Guide states:

"So, for example, an AMHP acting on behalf of an English LSSA can make applications for admission to hospitals in Wales, or apply for a warrant under section 135 of the Act to a magistrates' court in Wales. Similarly, an AMHP acting on behalf of a Welsh LSSA can make applications to hospitals in England or to English magistrates' courts."

In this situation, the AMHP acting on behalf of the English LSSA would have to use the statutory forms that are applicable in Wales, and vice versa.

Schedule 1 to SI 2008/2561 requires LSSAs to treat as an AMHP a person who had been approved as an ASW by an LSSA in Wales immediately before November 3, 2008.

Courses for the training of English and Welsh AMHPs will be approved by the General Social Care Council and the Care Council for Wales under s.114A.

*Human Rights Act 1998*

**1–1035**     An AMHP who is performing functions under this Act is exercising "functions of a public nature" and is therefore a "public authority" for the purposes of the 1998 Act: see s.6(3)(b) of that Act and *R. (on the application of Wilkinson) v Responsible Medical Officer Broadmoor Hospital* [2001] EWCA Civ 1545; [2002] 1 W.L.R. 419, per Hale L.J. at para.61). The effect of this is that it is unlawful for an AMHP to act in a way which is incompatible with a patient's rights under the European Convention on Human Rights (s.6(1)).

*Subsection (1)*

**1–1036**     LOCAL SOCIAL SERVICES AUTHORITY.     Who have the sole right to approve AMHPs. A person may be approved as an AMHP by only one LSSA in England at any time.

APPROVE.     An AMHP should be provided with documentary evidence of his or her approval as some sections of this Act require the production of such a document (see, for example, s.115). There is no statutory form that can be used for this purpose. The document, which should be authenticated by a senior officer of the approving authority, could read as follows: "[Name] has been approved under s.114 of the Mental Health Act 1983 to perform the functions of an Approved Mental Health Professional under that Act". It would be advisable to reproduce s.115, which provides AMHPs with a power of entry and inspection, on the document.

FOR THE PURPOSES OF THIS ACT.     AMHPs perform functions under the following sections of this Act: ss.4, 6, 8, 10, 11, 13, 14, 17A, 17B, 17F, 20A, 18, 21B, 29, 30, 40, 47, 87, 88, 89, 115, 130B, 145, 135, 136 and 138.

*Subsection (2)*

**1–1037**     Doctors cannot be appointed as AMHPs, even if they also have a qualification listed in the approval regulations.

*Subsection (3)*
APPROPRIATE COMPETENCE.   See the competencies set out in Sch.2 to SI 2008/1206. The **1–1038** approving LSSA should have a mechanism in place to enable it to be satisfied that AMHPs continue to possess "appropriate competence" after approval.

*Subsection (4)*
APPROPRIATE NATIONAL AUTHORITY.   See subs.(9).                                          **1–1039**

REGULATIONS.   See SIs 2008/1206 and SI 2008/2436 (W.209), noted above.

*Subsection (10)*
ACTING ON BEHALF OF A LOCAL SOCIAL SERVICES AUTHORITY.   Concern was expressed in **1–1040** Parliament that if an AMHP is said to be acting on behalf of a LSSA, the authority could in some way direct the decisions of the AMHP. The Government denied that this was the case. Baroness Royall, speaking for the Government, said:

"An AMHP is required to make an independent decision about whether to make an application. I can assure your Lordships that nothing changes this. Paragraph 5(2) of Schedule 2 [which amends s.13 of the Act] makes it clear that AMHPs must make an application only if they are personally satisfied that it is necessary and proper to do so. The decision cannot be overturned by the local social services authority for which they are acting. The AMHP acts independently and will continue to do so in their decision making.

The [Act] makes it clear [in s.145(1AC)] that an AMHP carries out their functions on behalf of the LSSA. This underlines the independence of the AMHP from the trust that may employ the doctors who also examine a patient's case for admission. It also ensures that the responsibility for providing that an AMHP service is in place clearly lies with the LSSA, whether or not it chooses to enter into arrangements with another body, such as a trust, to provide the service" (*Hansard*, HL Vol.688, cols.681,682).

As AMHPs act on behalf of the appointing LSSA, that authority should provide legal advice on AMHP responsibilities to AMHPs, including those who are not employees of the authority. It might not always be easy to determine when an AMHP is performing the functions of an AMHP and, therefore, acting on behalf of the LSSA, and when the AMHP is performing his or her normal professional role and being accountable to his or her employer, which might not be the LSSA.

## Approval of courses etc for approved mental health professionals

[**114A.**—(1) The relevant Council may, in accordance with rules made by it, **1–1041** approve courses for persons who are or wish to become approved mental health professionals.

(2) For that purpose—

(a) subsections (2) to (4)(a) and (7) of section 63 of the Care Standards Act 2000 apply as they apply to approvals given, rules made and courses approved under that section; and

(b) sections 66 and 71 of that Act apply accordingly.

(3) In subsection (1), "the relevant Council" means—

(a) in relation to persons who are or wish to become approved to act as approved mental health professionals by a local social services authority whose area is in England, the General Social Care Council;

(b) in relation to persons who are or wish to become approved to act as approved mental health professionals by a local social services authority whose area is in Wales, the Care Council for Wales.

(4) The functions of an approved mental health professional shall not be considered to be relevant social work for the purposes of Part 4 of the Care Standards Act 2000.

(5) The General Social Care Council and the Care Council for Wales may also carry out, or assist other persons in carrying out, research into matters relevant to training for approved mental health professionals.]

AMENDMENT
This section was inserted by the Mental Health Act 2007 s.19.

DEFINITION
**1–1042**  approved mental health professional: s.145(1), (1AC).

GENERAL NOTE
**1–1043**  The statutory bodies which regulate the social work profession are the General Social Care Council (GSCC) and the Care Council for Wales (CCW). This section enables the GSCC and the CCW to approve course for the training of English and Welsh AMHPs respectively, regardless of the trainees' profession.

*Subsection (4)*
**1–1044**  By making it clear that AMHP functions are not "relevant social work" for the purposes of Pt 4 of the Care Standards Act, this provision ensures that the GSCC's and CCW's codes of practice do not apply to AHHPs who are not social workers. AMHPs who are not social workers will continue to be regulated by their own professional bodies. The GSCC and the CCW have the power under s.62(1A) of the Care Standards Act 2000 to establish standards of conduct and practice that will be expected of social workers when carrying out the functions of AMHPs.

## Powers of entry and inspection
**1–1045**  [**115.**—(1) An approved mental health professional may at all reasonable times enter and inspect any premises (other than a hospital) in which a mentally disordered patient is living, if he has reasonable cause to believe that the patient is not under proper care.

(2) The power under subsection (1) above shall be exercisable only after the professional has produced, if asked to do so, some duly authenticated document showing that he is an approved mental health professional.]

AMENDMENT
This section was substituted by the Mental Health Act 2007 s.21, Sch.2 para.8.

DEFINITIONS
**1–1046**  approved mental health professional: s.145(1), (1AC).
hospital: s.145(1).
mental disorder: ss.1, 145(1).
patient: s.145(1).

GENERAL NOTE
**1–1047**  This section provides approved mental health professionals (AMHPs) with a power to enter and inspect premises where a mentally disordered patient is believed to be living. It does not provide the AMHP with authority to remove the patient. The power, which is

not limited to premises within the area of the approving authority, does not apply to hospitals.

A visiting headquarters, as defined by art.3 of the Visiting Forces and International Headquarters (Application of Law) Order 1999 (SI 1999/1736), is exempted from the operation of this section (art.12, Sch.5).

*Subsection (1)*

ALL REASONABLE TIMES.    The reasonableness of the time will presumably depend upon **1–1048** the urgency of the situation.

ENTER AND INSPECT.    This section does not empower the AMHP to force entry on to the premises, or to override the owner's refusal to give permission to enter. The Court of Appeal has held that a wife who is the co-owner of a house may give permission for a person to enter the house, and that person shall not be a trespasser, notwithstanding that the husband purports to refuse permission: see *Slade v Guscott*, July 28, 1981, 78/0656, (unreported), noted in L. Gostin, *Mental Health Services—Law and Practice*, 1986, at para.21.13.5. There is also authority for the proposition that a co-occupier of premises can allow entry to another person: see the cases cited by Gostin. Permission to enter premises may also be given by a landlord in a situation where the tenant does not enjoy an exclusive right of occupation. Also see *R. v Rosso* [2003] EWCA Crim 3242, noted in the General Note to s.135.

If entry is refused, the AMHP could point out to the person concerned that a refusal to allow the inspection to take place would constitute an offence under s.129. If this information fails to impress the obstructor and entry is still denied, the AMHP should consider whether the facts of the case would justify making an application to a justice of the peace under s.135 for a warrant authorising a policeman to enter the premises by force. The police have a power under s.17(1)(e) of the Police and Criminal Evidence Act 1984 to enter premises without a warrant if such action is required to save "life or limb" or to prevent "serious damage to property". Section 17(1)(e) is considered in the General Note to s.135.

Whether the common law doctrine of necessity would provide a defence if force is used to gain entry to private property to apprehend a dangerous mentally disordered person in cases where there is an imminent threat of serious harm either to that person or to others and action is required before the arrival of the police is undecided; see Brenda Hale, *Mental Health Law* (2010), p.114. Also see the discussion of the doctrine in *R. v Bournewood Community and Mental Health NHS Trust, ex p. L* [1998] 3 All E.R. 289 and the statement by Hale L.J. on the use of the common law in *R. (on the application of Munjaz) v Mersey Care NHS Trust* which is reproduced at point 1 in Appendix A.

MENTALLY DISORDERED PATIENT.    The use of this phrase rather than the term "patient" (see s.145(1)), suggests that this section can only be invoked in respect of persons who have been diagnosed as being mentally disordered. If the patient is living in a registered establishment and there is some doubt as to whether he or she is mentally disordered, the registration authority could be asked to exercise its powers of inspection under the Care Standards Act 2000.

*Subsection (2)*

PRODUCED, IF ASKED TO DO SO.    The right of entry is not dependent upon someone being **1–1049** available to whom the document can be produced (*Grove v Eastern Gas Board* [1952] 1 K.B. 77).

DULY AUTHENTICATED DOCUMENT.    See the note on "approve" in s.114(1).

*Visiting Patients*

**Welfare of certain hospital patients**

1–1050    **116.**—(1) Where a patient to whom this section applies is admitted to a hospital [, independent hospital or care home] in England and Wales (whether for treatment for mental disorder or for any other reason) then, without prejudice to their duties in relation to the patient apart from the provisions of this section, the authority shall arrange for visits to be made to him on behalf of the authority, and shall take such other steps in relation to the patient while in the hospital [, independent hospital or care home] as would be expected to be taken by his parents.

(2) This section applies to—

[(a)  a child or young person—

    (i) who is in the care of a local authority by virtue of a care order within the meaning of the Children Act 1989, or

    (ii) in respect of whom the rights and powers of a parent are vested in a local authority by virtue of section 16 of the Social Work (Scotland) Act 1968;]

(b)  a person who is subject to the guardianship of a local social services authority under the provisions of this Act [. . .]; or

(c)  a person the functions of whose nearest relative under this Act [. . .] are for the time being transferred to a local social services authority.

AMENDMENTS

The words in square brackets in subs.(1) were substituted by the Care Standards Act 2000 s.116, Sch.4 para.9(5).

In subs.(2) the words in square brackets were substituted by the Courts and Legal Services Act 1990 s.116, Sch.16 para.42. The words omitted were repealed by SI 2005/2078 art.16, Sch.3.

DEFINITIONS

1–1051    patient: s.145(1).
hospital: s.145(1).
care home; s.145(1).
independent hospital: s.145(1).
mental disorder: ss.1, 145(1).
local social services authority: s.145(1).
nearest relative: ss.26(3), 145(1).

GENERAL NOTE

1–1052    This section obliges local authorities to arrange for visits to be made to certain categories of patients who have been admitted to hospitals, independent hospitals and care homes. It also requires local authorities to take other steps in relation to the patients as would be expected to be taken by patients' parents. There is no requirement that the patients concerned need to be receiving treatment for mental disorder.

Where a child is provided with accommodation by any Local Health Board, Primary Care Trust, Special Health Authority, NHS Trust, NHS Foundation Trust or local education authority for a period of three months, s.85 of the Children Act 1989 requires that body to notify the appropriate local authority which shall take steps to ensure that the child's welfare is safeguarded. Similar responsibilities are placed on the proprietors of care homes and independent hospitals by s.86 of the 1989 Act.

Section 131A places a duty on hospital managers to place mentally disordered children who are admitted to hospital, whether informally or under compulsion, in a child friendly environment.

Section 11 of the Children Act 2004 places an obligation on children's services authorities and NHS bodies in England to carry out their functions having regard to the need to safeguard and promote the welfare of children, and to guidance provided by the Secretary of State. This duty continues to apply where services are contracted out. An equivalent provision in respect of Wales is contained in s.28 of that Act. Also note the duties placed on local authorities by paras 10, 15 and 17 of Sch.2 to the Children Act 1989 which are noted in the *Code of Practice* at para.36.81.

The Secretary of State and, in relation to Wales, the Welsh Ministers (see the General Note to this Act and SI 1999/672 art.2, Sch.1) have the power to conduct, or assist other persons in conducting, research into this section so far as it relates to children looked after by local authorities (Children Act 1989 s.83).

*Subsection (1)*

SUCH OTHER STEPS.   Which could include discussing the patient's condition with the **1–1053** hospital doctors and providing a child patient with toys and reading matter.

*Subsection (2)*

PARAGRAPH (A) CHILD.   This section does not apply to children who are wards of court. **1–1054**

PARAGRAPH (C) FOR THE TIME BEING TRANSFERRED TO A LOCAL SOCIAL SERVICES AUTHORITY. By virtue of s.29.

## *After-Care*

## After-care

**117.**—(1) This section applies to persons who are detained under section 3 **1–1055** above, or admitted to a hospital in pursuance of a hospital order made under section 37 above, or transferred to a hospital in pursuance of [a hospital direction made under section 45A above or] a transfer direction made under section 47 or 48 above, and then cease to be detained and [(whether or not immediately after so ceasing)] leave hospital.

(2) It shall be the duty of the [Primary Care Trust or] [Local Health Board] and of the local social services authority to provide, in co-operation with relevant voluntary agencies, after-care services for any person to whom this section applies until such time as the [Primary Care Trust or] [Local Health Board] and the local social services authority are satisfied that the person concerned is no longer in need of such services [; but they shall not be so satisfied in the case of a [community patient while he remains such a patient.]]

[ . . . ]

[(2B) Section 32 above shall apply for the purposes of this section as it applies for the purposes of Part II of this Act.]

[(2C) References in this Act to after-care services provided for a patient under this section include references to services provided for the patient—

(a) in respect of which direct payments are made under regulations under section 57 of the Health and Social Care Act 2001 or section 12A(4) of the National Health Service Act 2006, and

(b) which would be provided under this section apart from the regulations.]

(3) In this [section "the [Primary Care Trust or] [Local Health Board]" means the [Primary Care Trust or] [Local Health Board], and "the local social services

authority" means the local social services authority, for the area] in which the person concerned is resident or to which he is sent on discharge by the hospital in which he was detained.

AMENDMENTS

The amendments to this section were made by the Health Authorities Act 1995 s.2(1), Sch.1 para.107(8), the Mental Health (Patients in the Community) Act 1995 s.2(1), Sch.1 para.15, Crime (Sentences) Act 1997 s.55, Sch.4 para.12(17), the National Health Service Reform and Health Care Professions Act 2000 s.2(5), Sch.1 para.47, SI 2007/961 art.3, Sch. para.13(9), the Mental Health Act 2007 s.32(4), Sch.3 para.24 and the Health Act 2009, s.13, Sch.1, para.3. Subsection (2A) was repealed by 1997 Act s.55, Sch.11 Pt 5.

DEFINITIONS

**1–1056**     hospital: s.145(1).
hospital order: ss.37, 145(1).
transfer direction: ss.47, 145(1).
local social services authority: s.145(1), subs.(3).
Health Authority: s.145(1).

GENERAL NOTE

**1–1057**     This section, imposes an enforceable duty to provide after-care services for certain categories of mentally disordered patients who have ceased to be detained and leave hospital (or prison, having spent part of their sentence detained in hospital). The duty stands by itself; this section does not place a duty on the "responsible after-care bodies" to prove services under other legislation such as the National Assistance Act 1948 or the National Health Service Act 2006: see the note on "Charging for local authority services provided under section 117", below. A consequence of this is that the normal rules about commissioning responsibility (in the NHS) or ordinary residence (for social services) do not apply. Social services and health bodies should establish jointly agreed policies on providing services under this section (HSC 2000/003 : LAC(2000)3, para.3). Functions under this section are NHS functions for the purposes of the NHS Bodies and Local Authorities Partnership Arrangements Regulations 2000 (SI 2000/617) (as amended): see "Partnership arrangements", below.

The duty to provide after-care services applies to patients irrespective of their country of origin. This section does not appear in the list of provisions set out in Sch.3 to the Nationality, Immigration and Asylum Act 2002. Section 54 and Sch.3 to the 2002 Act have the effect of preventing local authorities from providing support under the provisions listed in the Schedule to certain categories of refugees and asylum seekers.

The nature of the obligation placed on authorities by this section was considered in *R. v Ealing District Health Authority Ex p. Fox* [1993] 3 All E.R. 170. Otton J. held that (1) a "proper interpretation of this section to be that it is a continuing duty in respect of any patient who may be discharged and falls within s.117, although the duty to any particular patient is only triggered at the moment of discharge"; and (2) a Health Authority "acts unlawfully in failing to seek to make practical arrangements for after-care prior to [a] patient's discharge from hospital where such arrangements are required by a [tribunal] in order to enable the patient to be conditionally discharged from hospital".

In *R. v Mental Health Review Tribunal Ex p. Hall* [1999] 3 All E.R. 132, Scott Baker J. said, at 143:

"In my judgment *Ex p. Fox* supports the following propositions which I accept to be the law: (i) an authority's duty to provide after-care services includes a duty to set up the arrangements that will be required on discharge. It is not a duty that arises for the first time at the moment of discharge; (ii) an authority with a duty to provide after-care arrangements acts unlawfully by failing to seek to make arrangements for the fulfilling of conditions imposed by a [tribunal] under section 73(2); (iii) if such an authority is unable to make the necessary arrangements it must try to obtain them from another authority; (iv) if arrangements still cannot be made an impasse should not be allowed to continue; the case must be referred back to a [tribunal] through the Secretary of State."

*Fox* and *Hall* were considered by Stanley Burnton J. in *R. (on the application of W) v Doncaster MBC* [2003] EWHC Admin 192; [2004] M.H.L.R. 189. His Lordship held that:

1. Neither *Fox* nor *Hall* is authority for the proposition that in a contested case the after-care bodies are placed under a duty to put in place after-care arrangements before the decision of a tribunal because the duty under this section only arises if (i) the patient has been in hospital under one of the provisions specified in subs.(1); (ii) the patient ceases to be detained; and (iii) the patient leaves hospital. His Lordship said at para.34:

   "It would be wasteful of the limited resources of (in this case) a local social services authority for it to have to plan and make arrangements for the after-care of all patients whose applications come before [tribunals]. Most applications are contested, and a relatively small proportion of contested applications succeed".

   His Lordship noted that in *R. v Mental Health Review Tribunal Ex p. Hall* (1999) 2 C.C.L.R. 383, 390, Kennedy L.J. said that the terms of para.27.7 of the 1999 edition of the *Code of Practice* suggest that a care plan "at least in embryo" should be available before a tribunal hearing takes place.

2. In the case of a restricted patient the bodies are normally bound before actual discharge to endeavour to put in place the arrangements required by the tribunal as conditions of a conditional discharge, or which the tribunal requires before a deferred discharge takes effect, or which the tribunal provisionally decides should be put in place.

3. With both restricted and non-restricted patients where the discharge is not contested, the bodies should if practicable plan after-care before a tribunal hearing in order for it to be able to comply with its duty under this section on the patient's discharge.

With regard to the first proposition set out by Scott Baker J. in *Hall*, above, his Lordship **1–1058** said, at para.39, that it is "confined to cases in which the tribunal has decided on the discharge of the patient, and the arrangements ... were those specified by the tribunal". In *W v Doncaster MBC* [2004] EWCA Civ 378; [2004] M.H.L.R. 201. Scott Baker L.J. said, at para.49, that Stanley Burnton J. was correct in his analysis and that the observations that had been made by Otton J. in *Fox* and by himself in *Hall* to the effect that there is a duty under this section to set up after-care arrangements prior to the patient's discharge should not be followed. His Lordship said at para.51:

"Although the section 117 duty does not bite on local authorities or health authorities until after the tribunal decision, they do not at that point start entirely from scratch. Most such authorities will be faced fairly frequently with circumstances in which they are expected to exercise their section 117 duty to help to rehabilitate mental patients within the community. It is reasonable to suppose therefore that they have procedures in place for coping with situations of this kind. Also, they certainly have the *power*, in appropriate cases, to start making plans before the tribunal sits. Kennedy L.J. in *Hall* referred to them as plans in embryo. Once the tribunal has made its decision it will be a case of tailoring their procedures to meet the needs of the particular case."

The nature of the duty imposed by this section was also considered in *R. v Camden and Islington Health Authority Ex p. K* [2001] EWCA Civ 240; [2001] M.H.L.R. 24, where the

Court of Appeal confirmed that this section does not impose on Health Authorities an absolute obligation to satisfy any conditions that a tribunal may specify as prerequisites to the discharge of a patient. Lord Phillips M.R. said at para.29:

"[This section] imposes on Health Authorities a duty to provide after care facilities for the benefit of patients who are discharged from mental hospitals. The nature and extent of those facilities must, to a degree, fall within the discretion of the Health Authority which must have regard to other demands on its budget".

The issue of resources was also highlighted by Scott Baker L.J. in *W v Doncaster MBC*, above, at para.59:

"Unfortunately there is neither a bottomless pit of funds nor an adequate supply of suitable accommodation and support to cope with these difficult cases. Stretched local authorities and healthcare providers have to make do as best they can with the facilities and resources that are available."

In *K*, Lord Phillips endorsed a concession that had been made by the Health Authority that a failure to use reasonable endeavours to fulfil conditions imposed by a tribunal, in the absence of strong reasons, would be likely to be an unlawful exercise of discretion. If, despite the exercise of all reasonable endeavours, it proves impossible for the after-care bodies to fulfil the tribunal's conditions, the continued detention of the patient would not violate art.5 of the European Convention on Human rights: also see the note on "The Human Rights Act 1998", below. In *R. v Secretary of State for the Home Department Ex p. IH* [2003] UKHL 59; [2004] 1 All E.R. 412, para.29, the House of Lords confirmed that the "best endeavours" principle (which is the same as the "reasonable endeavours" principle (*W v Doncaster MBC*, above, para.50)) applies whether under this section or in response to the conditions attached to a patients discharge by the tribunal.

**1–1059**   In *R. (on the application of B) v Camden LBC and Camden and Islington Mental Health and Social Care Trust* [2005] EWHC 1366 (Admin); [2005] M.H.L.R. 258, B, a patient who had been made subject to a deferred conditional discharge, claimed that the defendants, in breach of their duties under this section and, in respect of the local authority, s.47 of the National Health Service and Community Care Act 1990, had caused his discharge to be delayed so as to give rise to a claim for damages for violating his rights under arts 5 and 8 of the European Convention on Human Rights. Section 47 of the 1990 Act requires local authorities to provide community care services, which include services provided under this section, to people who are assessed as having a need for such services.

The issue between the parties as to the effect of this section was whether the duty imposed by subs.(2) arose before B's discharge. Stanley Burnton J. held that:

1. As the duty under subs.(2) is only owed to a person who ceases to be detained and leaves hospital, the duty could not have arisen until after the decision of the tribunal that the preconditions for B's discharge had been satisfied. However, there is a power to make preparatory after-care plans prior to the patient leaving hospital: see the *obiter* remarks of Scott Baker L.J. in the *Doncaster* case, above.

2. The practical effect of the concession endorsed by Lord Phillips in *K*, above, is that a s.117 authority is under a duty to use reasonable endeavours to fulfil the conditions attached by the tribunal to the conditional discharge before the discharge has taken place.

3. It is unrealistic and wrong to require s.117 authorities to act to provide residential accommodation without exploring funding issues. Resources are limited, and any authority is entitled to consider, without dragging its feet, whether a suggested placement would involve an efficient use of its resources, and therefore whether there is a

possibility of that placement being funded by central government or by another authority.

4. A s.117 authority is not placed under a duty to monitor the condition of a detained patient with a view to deciding whether there is occasion to exercise their discretion to arrange for the provision of after-care services in case he is discharged. Where a patient is represented before the tribunal, the patient's solicitor should inform the s.117 authorities of the decision; and the hospital should do so too. His Lordship said, at para.72, that consideration should be given to sending the written tribunal decision to the s.117 authorities in any case where a deferred conditional discharge is ordered.

On the s.47 point, his Lordship held that:

1. The words "a person . . . may be in need of [community care] services" in s.47(1) refer to a person who may be in need at that time, or who may be about to be in need. A detained patient who is the subject of a deferred conditional discharge decision of a tribunal, which envisages his conditional discharge once s.117 after-care services are in place, is a person who "may be in need of such services", since if such services are available to him he will be discharged and immediately need them.

2. However, the duty under s.47 does not arise until it "appears" to the local authority that a person may be in need, and it cannot appear to it that he may be in need unless it knows of his possible need. It follows that s.47 does not impose an obligation on a local authority to monitor a patient detained in hospital in case he should at some later time be in need. The decision of the local authority under s.47(1)(b) (see below) whether his needs call for the provision of services falls to be made by reference to the result of the assessment it has carried out. It follows that s.47 cannot require the local authority to monitor the situation of a patient to consider providing for his changed needs.

His Lordship said obiter, following the comments made by Scott Baker L.J. in *W v Doncaster MBC*, above, that even if the after-care bodies had been in breach of their duties to B under this section or s.47, and that breach had prolonged his detention, they would not have been liable for damages under ss.6 and 8 of the Human Rights Act 1998 for breaches of B's rights under arts 5 or 8 of the Convention as it was only the detaining authority that could potentially be liable for such breaches. Permission to appeal this case was refused by Wall L.J. at an oral hearing held on February 21, 2006 ([2006] EWCA Civ 256). **1–1060**

If there is uncertainty as to the putting in place of the after-care arrangements in respect of a patient, a tribunal should adjourn to enable them to be put in place, indicating their views and giving appropriate directions (*R. (on the application of H) v Ashworth Hospital Authority; R. (on the application of Ashworth Hospital Authority) v Mental Health Review Tribunal for West Midlands and North West Region* [2002] EWCA Civ 923; [2002] M.H.L.R. 314, per Dyson L.J. at para.68).

Services provided under this section are "community care" services for the purposes of the National Health Service and Community Care Act 1990. (s.46(3)).The meaning of the words "a person . . . may be in need of [community care] services" in s.47(1) of the 1990 Act was explained by Stanley Burnton J. in *R. (on the application of B) v Camden LBC and Camden and Islington Mental Health and Social Care Trust*, above. If it appears to the local authority that a person comes within this category, his or her need for community care services must be assessed (s.47(1)(a)). Under s.47(1)(b) of the 1990 Act the local authority "having regard to the results of that assessment, shall then decide whether his needs call for the provision by them of any such services". As s.117 places a *duty* on a local authority to provide after-care services, it is submitted that the correct interpretation of s.47(1)(b) is that when the assessment identifies a need for after-care services, then the authority must determine that such need calls for the provision of those services. Although the authority is placed under an obligation to provide a service that it has determined will meet an assessed need, it has a discretion in identifying the level and precise nature of the service to be provided given resource constraints (*R. v Gloucestershire CC Ex p. Barry* [1997] 2 All E.R. 1). A failure by a local authority to provide a care plan which complies with statutory guidance and to make a service delivery decision under s.47(1)(b) in respect of a patient who had been assessed as being fit for discharge from NHS premises, resulted in successful judicial review proceedings in *R. v Sutton LBC Ex p. Tucker* [1997] C.O.D. 144.

Mentally disordered patients who have been detained under this Act and who are discharged from hospital, including patients who are subject to community treatment orders and guardianship, are subject to the Care Programme Approach. Revised guidance on the Care Programme Approach, *Reforming the Care Programme Approach: Policy and Positive Practice Guidance*, was published in March 2008. Guidance on the implementation of the Care Programme Approach in Wales was published by the Welsh Assembly Government in February 2003.

The *Report of the Inquiry into the Care and Treatment of Christopher Clunis*, HMSO, 1994, identified, at para.44.0.3, 14 recommendations as a "guide to aftercare". A further recommendation that a "new form should be designed for use in all section 117 after care cases" (para.45.1.2(i)) has been acted on by the Government which has published an after-care form which is designed to be used for *all* patients discharged from psychiatric in-patient treatment. The *Clunis Report* recommended that these forms should be reviewed regularly by the hospital managers (para.45.6.2(x)).

*Human Rights Act 1998*

**1–1061**     Section 145 of the Health and Social Care Act 2008 was enacted to give effect to the Government's commitment to reverse the decision of the House of Lords in *YL v Birmingham City Council* [2007] UKHL 27; [2007] 3 All E.R. 957, where it was held that an independent sector care home providing care and accommodation for a publicly funded resident was not exercising functions of a public nature within s.6(3)(b) of the Human Rights Act. It followed that the care home was not a "public authority" obliged to act compatibly with the European Convention on Human Rights under s.6 of the Act. However, s.145 only applies to accommodation provided in an independent sector care home by a local authority pursuant to ss.21(1)(a) and 26 of the National Assistance Act 1948; it does not apply to accommodation provided under this section. The decision in *R. (on the application of A) v Partnership in Care Ltd* [2002] EWHC 529; [2002] 1 W.L.R. 261, which is noted under s.34, suggests that a court would find that independent sector homes providing accommodation under this section are acting as public authorities for the purposes of the 1998 Act.

Whether a decision not to discharge a patient who had been granted a conditional discharge by a tribunal due to a failure to put in place appropriate after-care facilities in the community would constitute a violation of art.5 of the Convention was considered by the House of Lords in *R. (on the application of H) v Secretary of State for the Home Department*, and by the European Court of Human Rights in *Johnson* and *Kolanis*. These cases are analysed in the notes to s.73(7), above. In *Brand v The Netherlands*, App. No. 49902/99, paras 64, 65, the court accepted that funding is a relevant consideration in the determination of the issue whether there has been a breach of art.5.

The question whether the Convention places a general duty on states to provide community based services to respond to the needs of mentally disordered patients was considered by the Court of Appeal in *R. (on the application of H) v The Secretary of State for the Home Department and the Secretary of State for Health* [2002] EWCA Civ 646; [2002] M.H.L.R. 87, where Lord Phillips M.R. said at para.87:

"We are not aware of any Strasbourg jurisprudence that indicates that a Member State owes a duty under the Convention to put in place facilities for the treatment in the community of those suffering from mental disorder so as to render it unnecessary to detain them in hospital. In these circumstances we think that it must be a matter for the individual Member State to decide what resources to devote to the provision of mental care in the community. Available resources may make it possible for essential treatment to be provided to a mental patient in the community in circumstances which will not place in jeopardy either his own health or safety or the safety of others. In that event it will be a breach of Article 5(1) to detain the patient in hospital. If the law of a Member State requires the authorities of that state to provide facilities in the community so as to obviate the need to detain in hospital those with mental disorders, a breach of that domestic law, which results in the detention of a mental patient in hospital, is likely also to constitute a violation of Article 5(1). This is because under Article 5(1)(e) detention of a person of unsound mind can only be justified if it is lawful according to the law of the Member State concerned."

In *Clunis v United Kingdom* [2001] M.H.L.R. 162, ECtHR, the applicant maintained that the failure of the authorities to implement their duties under this section amounted to a breach of the Government's positive obligations under art.8 of the Convention, having regard to the harm which he had suffered. In declaring the complaint inadmissible, the Court said at paras 82, 83:

"[T]he Court considers that in the instant case there is no direct link between the measures which, in the applicant's view, should have been taken by Camden and the prejudice caused to his psychiatric well-being attendant on the realisation of the gravity of his act, his conviction and subsequent placement in a hospital placement without limit of time. The Court acknowledges that the assumption of responsibilities by the authorities of a Contracting State for the health of an individual may in certain defined contexts engage their liability under the Convention with respect to that individual as well as respect to third parties.

However, in the Court's opinion it cannot be said that Camden's failure to discharge its statutory duty under section 117 . . . led inevitably to the fatal stabbing of Jonathan Zito. It is a matter of speculation as to whether the applicant would have consented to become an in-patient on a voluntary basis or followed a prescribed course of medication or co-operated in any other way with the authorities. In these circumstances, and without prejudice to the question as to whether Article 8 is applicable in the circumstances of this case, the Court finds that the applicant's complaint does not disclose an appearance of a violation of that Article."

In *W v Doncaster MBC* [2004] EWCA Civ 378 para.67, Scott Baker L.J. said that the European Convention on Human Rights places no greater obligation upon a s.117 after-care authority than domestic legislation.

*Charging for local authority services provided under section 117*

In *R. v Manchester City Council Ex p. Stennett* [2002] UKHL 34; [2002] 4 All E.R. 124, **1–1062** the House of Lords dismissed an appeal from the Court of Appeal ([2001] 1 All E.R. 436) by holding that as this section imposes a freestanding duty to provide after-care services, as opposed to being a "gateway" section which imposes a duty to ensure that after-care services are provided under such other enactments as may be appropriate, and, as there is no express power to charge for services provided under it, such services must be provided free of charge.

At the first instance hearing ((1999) 2 C.C.L.R. 402), Sullivan J. held that:

(i) if a charged for service is being provided to the patient prior to the patient's admission under one of the provisions set out in subs.(1), that service would have to be provided free of charge on the patient's discharge from hospital if the provision of the service was a component of the patient's after-care plan; and

(ii) the fact that a patient has either been granted leave of absence under s.17 or transferred from detention under s.3 into guardianship under the provisions of s.19, does not affect his entitlement to receive services under this section.

These findings, which are considered in Department of Health Circular LAC (2000) 3, are unaffected by the decision of the House of Lords.

The following points arise from the decision in *Stennett*: (1) this section does not provide the Government with a power to regulate its use; and (2) the National Assistance Act 1948 (Choice of Accommodation) Directions 1992 do not apply to accommodation provided under this section. Although issues under of the Human Rights Act 1998 were not considered in the House of Lords, it could be argued that a patient who has been discharged from a psychiatric hospital and is being charged for residential accommodation that is being provided for his mental health needs would have a claim under art.14 of the European Convention on Human Rights in that his art.8 rights are invoked and he is suffering discrimination as a result of his non-detained status.

The finding of the House of Lords leads to the following consequences with regard to charging:

Case 1. A 50-year-old man with pre-senile dementia is admitted informally to hospital as a compliant mentally incompetent patient. He is assessed as requiring residential care on his discharge from hospital. He will almost certainly require such accommodation for the rest of his life. He will be charged for the accommodation by virtue of s.22 of the National Assistance Act 1948.

Case 2. A 50-year-old man with pre-senile dementia and with identical needs to the man in Case 1 is admitted to hospital under s.3 of this Act because he happened not to be compliant when the crisis in his mental health occurred. He is assessed as requiring residential care on his discharge from hospital. He will almost certainly require such accommodation for the rest of his life. He will be provided with the accommodation without charge because he comes within the scope of s.117.

In *Stennett*, counsel for the local authority described this scenario as the anomaly of the compliant and non-compliant patients in adjacent beds. Lord Steyn rejected this view as being "too simplistic". His Lordship said, at para.13, that there:

"may well be a reasonable view that generally patients compulsorily admitted under ss.3 and 37 pose greater risks upon discharge to themselves and others than compliant patients. Moreover, Parliament necessarily legislates for the generality of cases".

Nicolette Priaulx comments that the anomaly is far from "simplistic" in that it highlights "the manifest unfairness which can arise from differential treatment in circumstances where the 'need' of the patients are objectively no different at all" ("Charging for After-care services under Section 117 of the Mental Health Act 1983—The Final Word?", *Journal of Mental Health Law* (2002), 8, 313–322, at 317; see also Phil Fennell, All E.R. Rev. 2002, paras 18.57, 18.58). In *R. v Bournewood Community and Mental Health NHS Trust Ex p. L* [1998] 3 All E.R. 298 at 309, Lord Steyn described mentally incapable compliant patients as being "diagnostically indistinguishable from compulsory patients."

For many patients who are provided with after-care under this section, the administration of medication for their mental disorder will be a key component of their after-care plan. "Psychiatric treatment" was identified as an after-care service by Lord Steyn in *Stennett* (at para.7). By virtue of the principle established in *Stennett*, medication provided by the Health Authority as an after-care service is provided under this section and the National Health Service (Charges for Drugs and Appliances) Regulations 2000 (SI 2000/620) do not apply. The medication should therefore be provided free of charge. Regulation 2, as amended by SI 2008/2593, provide that patients who are subject to a community treatment order must be provided with medicines for the treatment of their mental disorder free of charge.

The three Local Government Ombudsmen, pursuant to their power under s.23(12A) of the Local Government Act 1974, have produced a "Special Report" providing "advice and guidance on the funding of aftercare under s.117 of the Mental Health Act 1983" (2003). The report considers the extent to which authorities are liable for financial restitution to those who have been charged for s.117 services.

If a local authority refunds charges that were wrongly made for residential care provided under this section, the refund is to be taken into account as capital by the Department of Work and Pensions in determining a claimant's entitlement to income support after the date of the repayment (Decision of the Social Security Commissioner (CIS/3760/2006), October 2007).

*NHS Continuing Healthcare*

Paragraphs 114 to 116 of the *National Framework for NHS Continuing Healthcare and* **1–1063**
*NHS-funded Nursing Care* (July 2009) state:

"Responsibility for the provision of section 117 services lies jointly with LAs and the NHS. The specific arrangements for how responsibilities are shared are determined locally. The absence of a local policy agreed between PCTs and LAs on section 117 responsibilities is not a reason for awarding eligibility for NHS continuing healthcare as a substitute for the use of section 117 powers. Some PCTs may use a common budget to fund both section 117 and NHS continuing healthcare, but this does not mean that those in receipt of section 117 support are eligible for NHS continuing healthcare. It is important for PCTs to be clear in each case whether the individual is being funded under section 117, NHS continuing healthcare or any other powers.

There are no powers to charge for services provided under section 117, regardless of whether they are provided by the NHS or LAs. Accordingly, the question of whether services should be 'free' NHS services (rather than potentially charged-for social services) does not arise. It is not, therefore, necessary to assess eligibility for NHS continuing healthcare if all the services in question are to be provided as after-care services under section 117.

However, a person in receipt of after-care services under section 117 may also have needs for continuing care that are not related to their mental disorder and that may, therefore, not fall within the scope of section 117. An obvious example would be a person who was already receiving continuing care for physical health problems before they were detained under the 1983 Act and whose physical health problems remain on discharge. Where such needs exist, it may be necessary to carry out an assessment for NHS continuing healthcare that looks at whether the individual has a primary health need on the basis of the needs arising from their physical problems. Any mental health after-care needs that fall within section 117 responsibilities would not be taken into account in considering NHS continuing healthcare eligibility in such circumstances."

*Top-up payments*

The National Assistance (Residential Accommodation) (Additional Payments and **1–1064**
Assessment of Resources) (Amendment) (England) Regulations 2001 (SI 2001/3441) make provision for additional payments to be made so that a person who has been assessed as needing residential accommodation under the National Assistance Act 1948 can choose to live in accommodation which is more expensive than the local authority would usually pay for someone with that person's assessed needs. Top-up payments are usually made by a third party, such as a family member, and, subject to specified exceptions, cannot be made by the resident. As, by virtue of the decision of the House of Lords in *Stennett*, above, the 2001 Regulations do not apply to accommodation that is provided under this section, can either the patient or a member of the patient's family make top-up payments with regard to such accommodation? It would seem that as long as the authority commits itself to providing a level of funding that will adequately meet the assessed needs of the patient for

accommodation, there is nothing to prevent top-up payments being made by the patient or another person to fund accommodation that provides for a higher level of either service or accommodation.

*Independent Mental Capacity Advocates*

**1–1065**    Section 39 of the Mental Capacity Act 2005 applies if a local authority intends to arrange for a patient to be provided with long-stay residential accommodation under this section, or for the accommodation to be changed, if:

(i) there is no-one apart from a professional or paid carer for the authority to consult in determining whether the placement would be in the patient's best interests; and

(ii) the patient lacks the mental capacity to make a decision about the arrangements.

In this situation, the authority is required to instruct an independent mental capacity advocate (IMCA) to represent the patient and any information given, or submissions made, by the IMCA must be taken into account when a decision is made about the placement. Such consultation need not take place if the patient is likely to stay in the accommodation for less than eight weeks or if the need for the accommodation is urgent. However, the consultation must take place after the placement has been effected if the authority subsequently believes that the accommodation will be provided for the patient for at least eight weeks. Section 39 does not apply if the accommodation is provided as a result of an obligation imposed on the patient under this Act; see further, paras 1–319 to 1–326 of the author's *Mental Capacity Act Manual* (2008).

*Partnership arrangements*

**1–1066**    This section is prescribed as a NHS function which may be the subject of a partnership arrangement with local authorities under s.75 of the National Health Service Act 2006 (NHS Bodies and Local Authority Partnership Arrangements Regulations 2000 (SI 2000/617) reg.5. Section 75 enables NHS bodies and local authorities to pool resources, delegate functions and transfer resources from one body to another so that there can be a single provider of services. This section is a health-related function of a local authority that may be the subject of a partnership arrangement by virtue of reg.6 of SI 2000/617 SI 2000/617 has effect as if made under s.75, by virtue of the National Health Service (Consequential Provisions) Act 2006 s.4, Sch.2 Pt 1 para.1.

Local authorities are allowed to make payments to NHS bodies toward expenditure incurred by them in connection with their performance under this section (National Health Service (Payments by Local Authorities to NHS Bodies) (Prescribed Functions) Regulations (SI 2000/618), reg.2).

*Code of Practice*

**1–1067**    Guidance on this section is contained in Ch.27.

*Subsection (1)*

**1–1068**    HOSPITAL ORDER MADE UNDER SECTION 37.    This section also applies to hospital order patients who have been made subject to restriction orders under s.41. A person who is admitted to a hospital in pursuance of an admission order made otherwise than under s.14A of the Criminal Appeal Act 1968 shall be treated for the purposes of this Act as if he had been admitted in pursuance of a hospital order or, if the court so directs, a restriction order (Criminal Procedure (Insanity and Unfitness to Plead) Act 1991 Sch.1 para.2(1)).

TRANSFER DIRECTION MADE UNDER SECTION 47.    This section also applies to transfer direction patients who have been made subject of restriction directions under s.49.

A Government document on the "Procedures for the transfer of prisoners to and from hospital under sections 47 and 48 of the Mental Health Act 1983" (2007) states at p.11:

"It is expected, in keeping with best practice protocols and the Mental Health Act 1983, that prisoners returning from hospital to prison will be accompanied by a CPA Care Plan that incorporates the requirements of section 117 of the Mental Health Act 1983 (i.e. indicating whether the individual requires on-going mental health services or not at the time of transfer) . . . Mental health service providers working in the prison receiving the transferred patient must be invited to attend the pre-discharge planning meeting and make best efforts to attend. Where representation from the receiving prison is not possible in a timely manner this should not delay the prisoner returning to prison. This meeting needs to include thought and planning for both return to custody and future release from prison including transportation arrangements.

Only in exceptional, emergency circumstances (i.e. where the patient poses a severe, non-containable risk) can a patient be returned to prison before a section 117 plan has been agreed. In such a case a section 117 meeting needs to be organised as soon as possible after his/her return to prison. This will be reinforced by the Mental Health Unit which will not issue a remission warrant unless such a meeting has been arranged, except in exceptional circumstances. The MHU must be advised to which prison the patient is to be returned before the remission warrant can be issued."

CEASE TO BE DETAINED. The duty to provide after-care services under this section extends to patients who, having been detained under s.3, are granted leave of absence under s.17. In *R. v Richmond LBC Ex p. W* [1999] M.H.L.R. 149, Sullivan J. said at para.99:

"In my view, this section is dealing with a practical problem: what after-care is to be provided for a patient who has suffered from mental illness requiring inpatient treatment when he actually leaves hospital? A person on leave under section 17 is in just as much, if not more, need of care after he leaves hospital as a person who leaves hospital subject to guardianship or supervision. For the purposes of section 17, he has ceased to be detained, and left hospital. It would be remarkable if, in such circumstances there was no duty to provide him with after-care under section 117, even though it would almost certainly have been a condition of his being given leave that he should reside in particular accommodation."

His Lordship's reasoning on this point would also apply to a restricted patient who had been conditionally discharged from hospital. His Lordship further held that the duty under this section extends to s.3 patients who are transferred into guardianship under the provisions of s.19.

Whether patients who have been granted s.17 leave will require after-care services during such leave will "depend on the specific circumstances of the case" (Reference Guide, para.24.13).

WHETHER OR NOT IMMEDIATELY AFTER SO CEASING. This section applies to a patient who has been detained under one of the sections mentioned in this subsection and who subsequently acquires informal status prior to leaving hospital. It also applies to a patient who having been discharged from the s.3, is re-detained under another provision of this Act (e.g. under s.5(2)) prior to his discharge from hospital.

*Subsection (2)*

DUTY. The nature of this duty is considered in the General Note to this section. In *R.* **1–1069** *(on the application of W) v Doncaster MBC*, above, Stanley Burnton J. held that although a breach of the duty imposed by this section does not of itself give rise to a cause of action for damages for breach of statutory duty (*Clunis v Camden and Islington Health Authority* [1998] 3 All E.R. 180 CA), an authority whose breach of its duty causes the detention (or prolongs the detention) of a patient who would otherwise be discharged will normally cause an infringement of his rights under art.5(1) of the European Convention on Human Rights.

The duty to provide after-care services is not broken by the patient's subsequent readmission to hospital for assessment under s.2. The duty would end on the patient's readmission under s.3: see the note under "Primary Care Trust . . . local social services authority" below.

A person who is aggrieved by a failure by either a health body or the local authority to meet its obligations under this section could consider the following options:

(i) making a complaint to the relevant health body or local authority under the Local Social Services and National Health Service Complaints (England) Regulations 2009 (SI 2009/309 (as amended)). If the complainant remains dissatisfied with the result of the investigation, there is a right to refer the complaint to the Commissioner for Local Administration or the Parliamentary Health and Services Commissioner;

(ii) making a complaint to the Care Quality Commission or the Welsh Ministers under s.120(4);

(iii) requesting the Secretary of State to exercise his discretion under s.7D of the Local Authority Social Services Act 1970 to declare the local authority to be in default. This option is only available where it is alleged that the authority has not complied with its duty: it cannot be used to regulate the exercise of the authority's discretion under this section. The default power for NHS bodies contained in s.68 of the National Health Service Act 2006 only applies to functions conferred or imposed on such bodies by that Act;

(iv) instituting judicial review proceedings if it is alleged that an after-care body has acted illegally, irrationally or with procedural impropriety. If a failure to comply with the requirements of this section results in a significant threat to the patient's mental health on his or her discharge from hospital, an urgent application for judicial review to obtain appropriate services can be made. An example of this occurred in *R. v Wrexham Social Services and Housing Department Ex p. Edwards*, August 18, 2000 (noted by M. Mullins at Legal Action, Dec. 2000, 15) where Newman J. granted permission and an interim injunction requiring the provision of emergency interim accommodation and emergency support for the applicant; and

(v) instituting an action claiming damages for a breach of the claimant's rights under the European Convention on Human Rights (Human Right Act 1998, s.8).

When considering these alternatives the court will prefer the avenue of redress which is the most convenient, expeditious and effective (*R. v London Borough of Sutton Ex p. Tucker* [1997] C.O.D. 144).

In *Clunis v Camden and Islington Health Authority*, above, the Court of Appeal held that (1) the duty under this section to provide after-care services does not give rise to a private law claim for damages if it is not fulfilled; and (2) the primary method of enforcement of the duty is by complaint to the Secretary of State. The patient's complaint under art.6(1) of the European Convention on Human Rights that he was denied a right of access to a court to argue his case against the defendant after-care body was declared inadmissible by the European Court of Human Rights on September 11, 2001. In *K v Central and North West London Mental Health Trust* [2008] EWHC 1217 (Q.B.); [2008] M.H.L.R. 168, King J., in allowing an appeal in a striking out action, said that: (1) the proposition expounded in *Clunis* was confined to the facts of that case; and (2), in any event, subsequent legal developments, particularly arising under the European Convention on Human Rights, meant that *Clunis* could no longer be regarded as a definitive ruling on the question of a common law duty of care in the context of functions being performed under this section.

LOCAL SOCIAL SERVICES AUTHORITY.   There is no requirement for the authority's duty **1–1070**
to be carried out by approved mental health practitioners (*Nottingham City Council v Unison* [2004] EWHC 893, para.24).

AFTER-CARE SERVICES.   This section imposes a free-standing duty to provide after-care
services: it is not a "gateway" section, which imposes a duty to ensure that services are
provided under other relevant Acts, such as the National Assistance Act 1948 or the
Chronically Sick and Disabled Person's Act 1970 (*R. v Manchester City Ex p. Stennett*,
noted under "Charging for local authority services provided under section 117", above).

As after-care services are not defined, this section gives a considerable discretion to the
after-care bodies as to the nature and extent of the services that can be provided (*R. v
Camden and Islington Health Authority, ex p. K*, above, para.29). In *Clunis v Camden
and Islington Health Authority*, above, at 191, 225, Beldam L.J. noted that:

"They would normally include social work, support in helping the ex-patient with problems of employment, accommodation or family relationships, the provision of
domiciliary services and the use of day centre and residential facilities."

In *Stennett*, at para.9, it was common ground that this is a correct description of after-care
services, although "psychiatric treatment" was also identified as such a service at para.7.
The *Code of Practice*, at paras 27.5 and 27.13, gives further consideration to the identification of possible after-care services.

It is suggested that an after-care service is a service which is (1) provided in order to meet **1–1071**
an assessed need that arises from a person's mental disorder; and (2) aimed at reducing that
person's chance of being re-admitted to hospital for treatment for that disorder. This formulation was endorsed by Hickinbottom J. in *R. (on the application of Mwanza) v Greenwich
L.B.C. and another* [2010] EWHC 1462 (Admin), paras 64 and 79. The person's need for
such services will usually change over time. The fact that the services that are currently
being provided differ from those which were provided at the time of the person's discharge
does not have the effect of extinguishing the duty to provide after-care services under this
section.

In *R. (on the application of B) v London Borough of Lambeth* [2006] EWHC 2362
(Admin), Judge Gilbart QC held that the provision of ordinary accommodation to an individual constituted an after-care service for the purposes of this section. The correctness of
this finding must be doubted. The provision of accommodation meets a basic human need
that relates to all individuals, irrespective of their mental health. Ordinary accommodation
cannot therefore be said to constitute a service that is provided to meet a need that arises
from the person's mental disorder. In *Mwanza*, above, Hickinbottom J. said that he did
not agree with this statement insofar as it "suggests that, as a matter of law, ordinary
accommodation can never fall within the scope of s.117". However, his Lordship conceded
that "it is difficult readily to envisage in practice circumstances in which a mere roof over
the head would, on the facts of a particular case, be necessary to meet a need arising from a
person's mental disorder" (para.67) and said that s.21 of the National Assistance Act 1948
is "a far more appropriate vehicle for requiring authorities to provide mere housing, than
the provisions relating to mental health" (para.78). His Lordship doubted the finding of
Judge Gilbart "on the basis of a proper construction of s.117" (para.74). In *Stennett*,
above, it was agreed that "*caring* residential accommodation", such as a care home that
meets an individuals mental health needs, is within the scope of this section: see Lord
Steyn at para.8 (emphasis added). Undertaking repairs to a patient's home to enable the
patient to be discharged there is not an after-care service for the purpose of this section
as the need does not arise from the patient's mental disorder. If an individual needs to be
supported with domiciliary care whilst living at his or her home and such care meets a
need that arises from the individual's mental disorder, such care would come within the
scope of this section.

The fact that a patient was receiving a service, such as residential care, for his or her mental health needs prior to the admission to hospital does not mean that that service cannot be an "after-care" service for the purposes of this section. The residential care would have been provided under the National Assistance Act 1948 prior to the admission (apart from self-funders), and under this section on discharge as long as the patient still required the accommodation to meet his or her mental health needs. The patient could therefore not be charged for the accommodation on returning to it from hospital even if he or she was a self-funder prior to the admission. This interpretation is supported by the decision of Sullivan J. in the *Stennett* case which is noted under "Charging for local authority services under section 117", above.

The search for necessary after-care services should not be confined to those services and facilities provided directly by the health and social services authorities.

The fact that after-care services are being provided under this section does not of itself mean that the person receiving the services is in need of "care and attention" for the purposes of s.21(1)(a) of the National Assistance Act 1948 (*R. (on the application of Wahid) v Tower Hamlets LBC* [2002] EWCA Civ 287 per Pill L.J. at para.24).

ANY PERSON. No person is legally obliged to accept the after-care services that are offered. If the person is a child, the local authority should ensure that it complies with its responsibilities under Pt III of the Children Act 1989.

**1–1072** SATISFIED. That the person concerned is no longer in need of such services. The after-care bodies cannot be so satisfied if the patient is a community patient. A decision that a patient no longer qualifies under this section can only be made if the after-care bodies have monitored the patient's progress in the community since discharge. It "is for the authority responsible for providing particular services to take the lead in deciding whether those services are no longer required. The patient, his/her carer and other agencies should always be consulted" (Local Authority Circular LAC (2000) 3, para.4). The duty to provide after care services continues until *both* authorities have come to a decision that the patient no longer needs *any* after-care service. Given the nature of after-care services, many patients will require such services for substantial periods. A patient should not be discharged from care under this section solely on the ground that: (1) he or she has been discharged from the care of a responsible clinician or specialist mental health services (2) an arbitrary period has elapsed since the care was first provided; (3) the provision of care is successful in that the patient is well settled in the community or in residential care; (4) he or she is no longer subject to supervised community treatment or s.17 leave; (5) he or she returns to hospital as an informal patient or under s.2; or (6) the patient has had the deprivation of his or her liberty authorised under the Mental Capacity Act 2005. See further, the *Code of Practice* at para.27.20. With regard to (3), B. Murray and R. Jacoby state that a person can be "discharged" from s.117 "by the responsible clinician once the situation seems stable (e.g. once a patient with dementia seems settled in a new nursing home)" ("The interface between old age psychiatry and the law", *Advances in Psychiatric Treatment* (2002), 8, 271–280). This ignores the fact that the trigger for after-care services is that of need and that a need can continue to exist even though it is being successfully met. In his investigation into Complaint No. 06/B/16774, the Local Government Ombudsman said at para.18:

"Whether or not a person is 'settled in a [care home]' is an irrelevant consideration [to the question of discharge from this section]. The key question must be, would removal of this person (settled or not) from this [care home] mean that she is at risk of readmission to hospital. If the answer is yes then the person cannot be discharged from aftercare."

Responsibility under this section could end in such a situation if the needs that were being addressed after the patient became settled in the home related to the patient's age and mental frailty rather than to the patient's mental disorder. The fact that a patient's needs may change with the passage of time was recognised by Sullivan J. in *R. v Richmond LBC Ex p. Watson* (1999) 2 C.C.L.R. 402 at 416:

"There may be cases where, in due course, there will be no need for after care services for the person's mental condition, but he or she will still need social service provision for other needs, for example physical disability. Such cases will have to be examined individually on their facts, through the assessment process provided for by section 47 [of the NHS and Community Care Act 1990]."

An unwillingness to receive after-care services; should not be equated with an absence of a need for such services. A patient's continued refusal to receive after-care services should be confirmed by professional inquiry at appropriate intervals.

A patient's expressed wish to be "discharged" from this section has no legal effect if she continues to have a need for after-care services; see further, the report of the Local Government Ombudsman on an investigation into complaint no. 04/B/01280 against York City Council.

COMMUNITY PATIENT WHILE HE REMAINS SUCH A PATIENT.    The fact that the patient is no longer a community patient does not necessarily mean that he or she is no longer in need of after-care services under this section.

*Subsection (2C)*

This provision brings within the scope of this section relevant services provided for the **1–1073** patient under regulations made under the direct payments scheme. Paragraphs 19 to 21 of the Explanatory Notes to the Health Act 2009 state:

"Direct payments have been used in lieu of social care services for some time. Social care direct payments are payments for individuals to purchase services from various providers directly, to meet their social care needs. The Act allows for a similar model of direct payments to be used for health care.

Section 11 in Chapter 3 of Part 1 of the [2009 Act] amends the National Health Service Act 2006 to allow the Secretary of State to make monetary payments to patients in lieu of providing them with health care services. In practice the intention is to delegate this power to local NHS organisations, generally Primary Care Trusts, though some Strategic Health Authorities or Special Health Authorities may also wish to use direct payments. Initially, the power will be available under regulations in pilot schemes only.

Direct payments for health care will allow patients to purchase health care services directly from a variety of providers, including private organisations and the voluntary sector."

The National Health Service (Direct Payments) Regulations 2010 (SI 2010/1000) enable the Secretary of State to make pilot schemes in accordance with which direct payments may be made to secure the provision of services under this section.

*Subsection (3)*

In *R. v Mental Health Review Tribunal Ex p. Hall,* above, Scott Baker J. held that for the **1–1074** purposes of this provision, the relevant after-care bodies were those for the area in which the patient was resident at the time he was detained and that this was the case notwithstanding that he may be discharged to a different area and is unlikely to return to their area. His Lordship further held that if the patient had no place of residence at the time of his detention, the relevant bodies would be those for the area where he was sent on discharge. Scott Baker J.'s judgment is considered in Department of Health Circular LAC (2000) 3. Paragraph 9 of this circular states:

"Where a patient is discharged to an area different from that where he/she was resident at the time of admission, the 'responsible authorities' may need to purchase services in that area. They should inform the health and social services authorities in the receiving area of the arrangements made for the patient's after-care."

*Hall* was cited in *R. (on the application of M) v Hammersmith and Fulham L.B.C.* [2010] EWHC 562 (Admin); [2010] M.H.L.R. 110 where Mitting J. held that:

1. There is no perceptible difference between the terms "resident", ordinarily resident" and "normally resident" in that all three connote settled presence in a particular place other than under compulsion (see further the note on s.26(4) under "ordinarily resides").

2. As a patient who is being accommodated in a care home under this section is not being accommodated under s.21 of the National Assistance Act 1948, the deeming provisions contained in s.24(5) of that Act do not apply to this section. It followed that if a patient:

   (i) had been placed by local authority A, the authority for the area where the patient resided, in a care home in the area of local authority B, and
   (ii) he was subsequently admitted to hospital under s.3, and
   (iii) if he had nowhere to live in the area of local authority A, then
   (iv) he was resident in the area of authority B for the purposes of this section.
   [NB this finding was anticipated in *Ordinary Residence: Guidance on the identification of the ordinary residence of people in need of community care services, England*, Department of Health March 2010, para.183. Disputes about a patient's residence cannot be referred to the Secretary of State or the Welsh Ministers for determination under s.32(3) of the 1948 Act (ibid., para.189)].

3. There was no material before the court to show that the agreement reached by the Association of County Councils and the Association of Metropolitan Authorities in 1998 relating to responsibility for costs of accommodation had been universally and consistently fulfilled over the years and could therefore give rise to a legitimate expectation that authority A was responsible for the funding of services under s.117.

The responsibility for providing after-care services under this section will last until the after care bodies are satisfied that the patient no longer needs any after-care service for his or her mental health needs. Apart from a situation where authorities agree to a transfer of responsibility for providing s.117 services, the only occasion when such responsibility would change is where the patient who is subject to s.117 moves to a new area, becomes a resident of that area and is subsequently detained under one of the provisions set out in subs.(1). Such an admission would trigger the duty under this section and the rulings in *Hall* and *M* mean that the relevant after-care bodies would be the health and social services authorities for the area where the patient resided at the time of the subsequent admission. This interpretation is given support by the following obiter comment by Levenson J. in *Tinsley (by his Receiver and Litigation Friend Conroy) v Sarkar* [2005] EWHC 192 Q.B., a case involving a person who was in receipt of services provide under this section:

"Here it is common ground that Mr. Tinsley may require to be compulsorily detained in the future whereupon any support which he has under section 117 will go; on discharge, his position falls to be considered afresh".

*Functions of the Secretary of State*

## Code of practice

**118.**—(1) The Secretary of State shall prepare, and from time to time revise, a **1–1075**
code of practice—

    (a) for the guidance of registered medical practitioners[, approved clinicians],
managers and staff of hospitals[, independent hospitals and care homes] and
[approved mental health professionals] in relation to the admission of
patients to hospitals [and registered establishments] under this Act [and
to guardianship and [community patients] under this Act]; and

    (b) for the guidance of registered medical practitioners and members of other
professions in relation to the medical treatment of patients suffering from
mental disorder.

(2) The code shall, in particular, specify forms of medical treatment in addition
to any specified by regulations made for the purposes of section 57 above which in
the opinion of the Secretary of State give rise to special concern and which should
accordingly not be given by a registered medical practitioner unless the patient
has consented to the treatment (or to a plan of treatment including that treatment)
and a certificate in writing as to the matters mentioned in subsection (2)(a) and (b)
of that section has been given by another registered medical practitioner, being a
practitioner [appointed for the purposes of this section by the regulatory
authority].

[(2A) The code shall include a statement of the principles which the Secretary
of State thinks should inform decisions under this Act.

(2B) In preparing the statement of principles the Secretary of State shall, in particular, ensure that each of the following matters is addressed—

    (a) respect for patients' past and present wishes and feelings,

    (b) respect for diversity generally including, in particular, diversity of religion,
culture and sexual orientation (within the meaning of section 35 of the
Equality Act 2006),

    (c) minimising restrictions on liberty,

    (d) involvement of patients in planning, developing and delivering care and
treatment appropriate to them,

    (e) avoidance of unlawful discrimination,

    (f) effectiveness of treatment,

    (g) views of carers and other interested parties,

    (h) patient wellbeing and safety, and

    (i) public safety.

(2C) The Secretary of State shall also have regard to the desirability of
ensuring—

    (a) the efficient use of resources, and

    (b) the equitable distribution of services.

(2D) In performing functions under this Act persons mentioned in subsection
(1)(a) or (b) shall have regard to the code.]

(3) Before preparing the code or making any alteration in it the Secretary of
State shall consult such bodies as appear to him to be concerned.

(4) The Secretary of State shall lay copies of the code and of any alteration in
the code before Parliament; and if either House of Parliament passes a resolution
requiring the code or any alteration in it to be withdrawn the Secretary of State

shall withdraw the code or alteration and, where he withdraws the code, shall prepare a code in substitution for the one which is withdrawn.

(5) No resolution shall be passed by either House of Parliament under subsection (4) above in respect of a code or alteration after the expiration of the period of 40 days beginning with the day on which a copy of the code or alteration was laid before that House; but for the purposes of this subsection no account shall be taken of any time during which Parliament is dissolved or prorogued or during which both Houses are adjourned for more than four days.

(6) The Secretary of State shall publish the code as for the time being in force.

[(7) The Care Quality Commission may at any time make proposals to the Secretary of State as to the content of the code of practice which the Secretary of State must prepare, and from time to time revise, under this section in relation to England.]

AMENDMENTS

In subs.(1) the words in square brackets were inserted and substituted by the Mental Health (Patients in the Community) Act 1995 s.2(1), Sch.1 para.16, the Care Standards Act 2000 s.116, Sch.4 para.9(6) and the Mental Health Act 2007 ss.14(2), 21, 32(4), Sch.2 para.9, Sch.3 para.25. Subsections (2A) to (2D) were inserted by s.8.

The words in square brackets in subs.(2) were substituted, and subs.(7) was inserted by the Health and Social Care Act 2008 s.52, Sch.3 para.6.

DEFINITIONS

**1–1076**   the managers: s.145(1).
hospital: s.145(1).
registered establishment: ss.34(1), 145(1).
care home: s.145(1).
independent hospital: s.145(1).
approved mental health professional: s.145(1), (1AC).
patient: s.145(1).
community patient: ss.17A(7), 145(1).
medical treatment: s.145(1), (4).
mental disorder: ss.1, 145(1).
the regulatory body: s.145(1).

GENERAL NOTE

**1–1077**   This section imposes a duty on the Secretary of State (and, in relation to Wales, the Welsh Ministers) to prepare, publish and from time to time revise, a *Code of Practice* for the guidance of those concerned with the admission, treatment, guardianship and supervised community treatment of mentally disordered patients. A failure to have regard to the *Code* could be used in legal or disciplinary proceedings as prima facie evidence of either bad practice or unlawful behaviour, although the effect of non-compliance will largely depend upon the nature of the provision in the *Code* that has not been followed. The *Code* states that, in reviewing any departures from its guidance, the court will "scrutinise the reasons for the departure to ensure that there is sufficiently convincing justification in the circumstances" (Introduction, para.iv).

The legal status of the *Code* was considered by the House of Lords in *R. (on the application of Munjaz) v Mersey Care National Health Service Trust* [2005] UKHL 58; [2006] 4 All E.R. 736, where it was contended that the policy of Ashworth Hospital relating to the seclusion of patients was unlawful because it provided for less frequent medical reviews, particularly after the first week of seclusion, than that laid down in the *Code*. Ashworth had also adopted a definition of seclusion that differed from that set out in the 1999 edition of the *Code*. It was held that:

1. The *Code* does not have the binding effect which a statutory provision or a statutory instrument would have. It is what it purports to be, guidance and not instruction.

2. The guidance in the *Code* should be given great weight. Although it is not instruction, the *Code* is much more than mere advice which an addressee is free to follow or not as it chooses. In other words, it is more than something to which those to whom it is addressed must "have regard to".

3. The *Code* contains guidance which should be considered with great care, and should be followed unless there are cogent reasons for not doing so. The reason need not be confined to the facts of an individual case; it can relate to a matter of policy. The requirement that cogent reasons must be shown for any departure sets a high standard which is not easily satisfied. With regard to subsection (2) of this section, Lord Bingham said, at para.69, that "any departure would call for even stronger reasons".

4. In reviewing any departures from the *Code*, the court should scrutinise the reasons given for departure with the intensity which the importance and sensitivity of the subject matters requires.

5. There were cogent reasons for Ashworth's decision not to follow the guidance in the Code, even though there were many eminent professional experts who took a different view. The reasons were:

    (a) The *Code* was directed at the generality of mental hospitals and did not address the special problems of high security hospitals;

    (b) The *Code* did not recognise the special position of patients whom it was necessary to seclude for longer than a very few days.

    (c) The statutory scheme, while providing for the Secretary of State to give guidance, deliberately left the power and responsibility of final decision to those who bear the legal and practicable responsibility for detaining, treating, nursing and caring for patients.

6. For the purpose of determining whether Ashworth's policy on seclusion was compatible with the European Convention on Human Rights, the *Code* is irrelevant: if the policy is incompatible, consistency with the *Code* will not save it; if it is compatible, it requires no support from the *Code*. The policy on seclusion was compatible with the Convention because it did not expose patients to a significant risk of treatment prohibited by art.3, did not amount to a separate deprivation of liberty which engages art.5, and any possible breach of art.8(1) was proportionate, in accordance with the law and had a purpose that fell within art.8(2). Lord Bingham said at para.34:

    "The procedure adopted by the Trust does not permit arbitrary or random decision-making. The rules are accessible, foreseeable and predictable. It cannot be said, in my opinion, that they are not in accordance with or prescribed by law."

It is suggested that the following circumstances could provide cogent reasons for not following the guidance contained in the *Code*:

1. A determination by the High Court a particular aspect of the *Code* is not legally accurate (see, for example, *AR (by her litigation friend JT) v Bronglais Hospital and Pembrokeshire and Derwen NHS Trust* [2001] EWHC 792 (Admin); [2001] M.H.L.R. 175, which is noted under s.12(2)).

2. A requirement of the *Code* has been made redundant by subsequent caselaw or legislation.

3. Legal advice has been received which casts a significant doubt on the legal correctness of an aspect of the guidance.

4. Following the guidance would involve breaching the patient's Convention rights.

5. A judgment is made that a particular aspect of the guidance should not be followed for safety or another cogent reason relating to the care or treatment of patients (see, for example, para.2.20.59 of the *Committee of Inquiry into the Personality Disorder Unit, Ashworth Special Hospital* (1999) where para.26.3 of the 1999 edition of the *Code* was described as being "untenable" in the context of a high security hospital).

Reasons for departing from the guidance in the *Code* "must be spelled out clearly, logically and consistently" (*Munjaz*, above, per Lord Hope at para.69).

In *R. v Secretary for State for Health Ex p. Pfizer Ltd* (1999) 2 C.C.L.R. 270, Collins J. held that Government guidance which is expressed in unqualified and mandatory language and which appeared to override the clinical judgment which a doctor was entitled to exercise in an individual case, was unlawful.

The *Code* can specify forms of treatment which give rise to special concern and which should not be given without the patient's consent and an independent second medical opinion (subs.(2)).

The latest edition of the *Code* for England is reproduced in Pt 4. A separate Code of Practice has been published for Wales.

*Subsection (1)*

**1–1078**    PARAGRAPH (A): ADMISSION OF PATIENTS TO HOSPITALS.    This term is not limited to the actual admission process; it covers what happens to the patient after he or she has been detained (*R. v Mersey Care National Health Service Trust Ex p. Munjaz*, above, para.19).

PARAGRAPH (B).    This provision is not limited to the hospital care of patients; it also covers care in the community.

The term "medical treatment", as defined in s.145(1), is wide enough to cover nursing and caring for a patient in seclusion, even though seclusion cannot properly form part of a treatment programme (*Munjaz*, above, para.19).

*Subsection (2)*

**1–1079**    SPECIFY FORMS OF MEDICAL TREATMENT.    The *Code* has not added to the forms of treatment covered by s.57.

*Subsections (2A) to (2C)*

**1–1080**    Speaking at the third reading of the Mental Health Bill, the Minister of State said that "the question of how the Government should express principles to inform practitioners making decisions under the Act as amended by the Bill has dominated our discussions and caused a great deal of interest" (*Hansard,* HL Vol.690, col.118). A considerable amount of Parliamentary time was spent debating whether the principles should be contained in this Act or, as the Government preferred, in the Code of Practice. A compromise was eventually reached by the Government proposing an amendment to the Bill which is given legislative effect in these provisions. The purpose of the amendment was described by the Minister of State:

"Our amendment places in statute a new requirement that the Secretary of State and Welsh Ministers include a statement of principles in the respective codes of practice for England and Wales, which should inform decision-making under the 1983 Act. The amendment legally obliges the Secretary of State and the Welsh Ministers to address certain fundamental issues in preparing this statement of principles." (*ibid.*, col.119).

Guidance of the statement of principles is given in Ch.1 of the *Code*.

*Subsection (2A)*

The principles should be considered by the decision maker if a decision is made under **1–1081** this Act. In this context, it should be noted that s.6 of the Human Rights Act 1998 requires all public authorities to act compatibly with the European Convention on Human Rights.

Whether the requirement for the principles to "inform decisions" differs from the general duty of practitioners to "have regard" to the *Code* (subs.(2D)) is not clear.

*Subsection (2C)*

In her response to concern that had been expressed about this provision, the Minister of **1–1082** State said:

"I can also reassure hon. Members that there is nothing sinister about the wording of proposed subsection (2C). [It] was drafted to include the fundamental matters considered most important in England and Wales. The Welsh national service framework for mental health has four underpinning principles: the so-called four Es of equality, equity, efficiency and effectiveness. When drafting the clause, we wanted to ensure that the Welsh principles were incorporated, given that the legislation covers England and Wales" (Public Bill Committee, col.208).

*Subsection (2D)*

Although the purpose of this provision was said to be the giving of legislative effect to **1–1083** the decision of the House of Lords in *R. (on the application of Munjaz) v Mersey Care NHS Trust (Hansard*, HL Vol.690, col.118; also see the Explanatory Notes, para.45), it could be argued that it diminishes the effect of that decision in that Lord Hope, speaking with the majority, said that the Code is less than a direction but is "more than something to which those to whom it is addressed must 'have regard to'" (para.68). However, it is clear that this was not the intention of Parliament and it is therefore submitted that this provision should be interpreted in accordance with the principles set out in *Munjaz,* above.

## Practitioners approved for Part IV and section 118

**119.**—(1) [The regulatory authority] may make such provision as [it] may with **1–1084** the approval of the Treasury determine for the payment of remuneration, allowances, pensions or gratuities to or in respect of registered medical practitioners appointed [by the authority] for the purposes of Part IV of this Act and section 118 above and to or in respect of other persons appointed for the purposes of section 57(2)(a) above.

(2) A registered medical practitioner or other person appointed [. . .] for the purposes of the provisions mentioned in subsection (1) above may, for the purpose of exercising his functions under those provisions [or under Part 4A of this Act], at any reasonable time—

(a) visit and interview and, in the case of a registered medical practitioner, examine in private any patient detained [in a hospital or registered establishment or any community patient in a hospital or [regulated establishment (other than a hospital)] or (if access is granted) other place]; and

(b) require the production of and inspect any records relating to the treatment of the patient [there].

[(3) In this section, "regulated establishment" means—

(a) an establishment in respect of which a person is registered under Part 2 of the Care Standards Act 2000; or

(b) premises used for the carrying on of a regulated activity, within the meaning of Part 1 of the Health and Social Care Act 2008, in respect of which a person is registered under Chapter 2 of that Part.]

AMENDMENTS
In this section the words in square brackets were substituted and inserted by the Mental Health Act 2007 s.35(2) and the Health, Social Care Act 2008 s.52, Sch.3 para.7 and SI 2010/813, art.5(4). The words omitted in subs.(2) were repealed by s.166, Sch.15 Pt.1 of the 2008 Act.

DEFINITIONS

**1–1085**   the regulatory authority: s.145(1).

patient: s.145(1).

residential establishment: ss.34(1), 145(1).

GENERAL NOTE

**1–1086**   This section provides for the payment of medical practitioners appointed by the Care Quality Commission or, in relation to Wales, the Welsh Ministers to carry out certain functions under this Act, and for them to have access to detained and community patients and their records.

*Subsection (2)*

**1–1087**   Anyone who obstructs a person in the exercise of his functions under this section commits an offence under s.129.

## [General protection of relevant patients

**1–1088**   **120.**—(1) The regulatory authority must keep under review and, where appropriate, investigate the exercise of the powers and the discharge of the duties conferred or imposed by this Act so far as relating to the detention of patients or their reception into guardianship or to relevant patients.

(2) Relevant patients are—

(a)  patients liable to be detained under this Act,

(b)  community patients, and

(c)  patients subject to guardianship.

(3) The regulatory authority must make arrangements for persons authorised by it to visit and interview relevant patients in private—

(a)  in the case of relevant patients detained under this Act, in the place where they are detained, and

(b)  in the case of other relevant patients, in hospitals and regulated establishments and, if access is granted, other places.

(4) The regulatory authority must also make arrangements for persons authorised by it to investigate any complaint as to the exercise of the powers or the discharge of the duties conferred or imposed by this Act in respect of a patient who is or has been detained under this Act or who is or has been a relevant patient.

(5) The arrangements made under subsection (4)—

(a)  may exclude matters from investigation in specified circumstances, and

(b)  do not require any person exercising functions under the arrangements to undertake or continue with any investigation where the person does not consider it appropriate to do so.

(6) Where any such complaint as is mentioned in subsection (4) is made by a Member of Parliament or a member of the National Assembly for Wales, the results of the investigation must be reported to the Member of Parliament or member of the Assembly.

(7) For the purposes of a review or investigation under subsection (1) or the exercise of functions under arrangements made under this section, a person authorised by the regulatory authority may at any reasonable time—

(a) visit and interview in private any patient in a hospital or regulated establishment,

(b) if the authorised person is a registered medical practitioner or approved clinician, examine the patient in private there, and

(c) require the production of and inspect any records relating to the detention or treatment of any person who is or has been detained under this Act or who is or has been a community patient or a patient subject to guardianship.

(8) The regulatory authority may make provision for the payment of remuneration, allowances, pensions or gratuities to or in respect of persons exercising functions in relation to any review or investigation for which it is responsible under subsection (1) or functions under arrangements made by it under this section.

(9) In this section "regulated establishment" means—

(a) an establishment in respect of which a person is registered under Part 2 of the Care Standards Act 2000, or

(b) premises used for the carrying on of a regulated activity (within the meaning of Part 1 of the Health and Social Care Act 2008) in respect of which a person is registered under Chapter 2 of that Part.]

AMENDMENT
This section was substituted by the Health and Social Care Act 2008 s.52, Sch.3 para.8.

DEFINITIONS
the regulatory authority: s.145(1).                                           **1–1089**
patients: s.145(1)
relevant patients: subs.(2).
community patient: s.145(1).
hospital: s.145(1).
regulated establishment: subs.(9).
approved clinician: s.145(1).

GENERAL NOTE
This section places a duty on the regulatory authority to review and, where appropriate, **1–1090** investigate the exercise of powers and the discharge of duties in relation to detention, supervised community treatment and guardianship under this Act. For the purposes of such reviews and investigations, the regulatory body can authorise persons to visit and examine patients in hospitals and regulated establishments, and to inspect relevant records (subs.(7)). There is no right to enter private premises. Reports of reviews and investigations may be published (s.120A). Under subs.(3), the regulatory body must make arrangements for authorised persons to visit and interview "relevant patients" as defined in subs.(2). The regulatory body must also make arrangements for authorised persons to investigate complaints concerning the exercise of relevant powers under the Act in respect of detained or relevant patients. Such an investigation need not be either instigated or continued if this is considered not to be appropriate (subss.(4),(5)).

The Care Quality Commission requires all service providers to notify it when a patient dies while detained or liable to be detained under this Act. A form that must be used for this purpose may be downloaded from the Commission's website (*www.cqc.org.uk*).

One curious aspect of the duty imposed by this section is that the regulatory authority, as the sole provider of the second opinion appointed doctor service which operates in Pts IV and IVA, is required to review its own service provision.

The Optional Protocol to the United Nations Convention Against Torture, which the UK ratified in December 2003, requires states to establish a "national preventative mechanism" (NPM) to carry out a system of regular visits to places of detention in order to prevent torture and other cruel, inhuman or degrading treatment or punishment. The Government has designated a number of bodies to form the United Kingdom NPM, including the Care Quality Commission and the Healthcare Inspectorate of Wales (*Hansard,* March 31, 2009, col.55WS).

*Subsection (1)*

**1–1091**    REGULATORY AUTHORITY.    Is the Care Quality Commission or, in relation to Wales, the Welsh Ministers (s.145(1)). The functions of the Welsh Ministers under this section are exercised by the Health Inspectorate Wales (HIW). Persons authorised by the Commission may include members or employees of the Commission (Health and Social Care Act 2008 s.52(2)). When performing its functions, the Commission must have regard to:

"the need to protect and promote the rights of people who use health and social care services (including, in particular, the rights of children, of persons detained under the Mental Health Act 1983, of persons who are deprived of their liberty in accordance with the Mental Capacity Act 2005, and of other vulnerable adults)" (2008 Act, s.4(1)(d)).

The contact details of the Commission and HIW for issues relating to the Mental Health Act are:

Care Quality Commission
The Belgrave Centre
Stanley Place
Talbot Street
Nottingham
NG1 5GG

tel no: 0115 873 6250

Healthcare Inspectorate Wales
Bevan House
Caerphilly Business Park
Van Road
Caerphilly
CF83 3ED

tel no: 029 2092 8850

POWERS AND . . . DUTIES.    Including the powers and duties which flow necessarily and by implication from detention (*R. v Mental Health Act Commission Ex p. Smith,* below).

*Subsection (4)*

**1–1092**    EXERCISE OF THE POWERS OR THE DISCHARGE OF THE DUTIES.    In *R. v Mental Health Act Commission Ex p. Smith* (1998) 43 B.M.L.R. 174, complaints were made to the Mental Health Act Commission (MHAC) is respect of a hospital patient who had committed suicide during a period when he was subject to detention under s.3 of the Act. There were four essential complaints:

(i)  it was said that the patient's original detention was neither appropriate nor legal;

(ii)  it was said that he was inappropriately detained in a secure unit for a period;

(iii)  it was alleged that the patient was given drugs in such quantities that it was unlikely that he could have given consent, and the level of dosage was inappropriate; and

(iv)  it was said that the patient was inadequately cared for during his detention, and his condition was not adequately assessed for the purposes of determining whether there was any risk of self harm.

The MHAC had always been prepared to accept jurisdiction to entertain complaint (i), was persuaded that it had jurisdiction to accept complaint (iii), but only to a limited extent, but considered that it did not have jurisdiction to entertain complaints (ii) and (iv). On a judicial review of the MHAC's decision, Latham J. held that it is too restrictive to construe this provision as referring only to the express powers and duties set down in the Act. Rights and duties which flow necessarily and by necessary implication from the patient's detention also come within its scope. It followed that any complaints arising out of the exercise of the power to detain, manage and control, and the duty to treat detained patients could be investigated by the MHAC. Accordingly, the MHAC had jurisdiction to consider complaints (ii) and (iv), and had an unrestricted jurisdiction to consider complaint (iii).

## [Investigation reports

**120A.**—(1) The regulatory authority may publish a report of a review or investigation carried out by it under section 120(1).  **1–1093**

(2) The Secretary of State may by regulations make provision as to the procedure to be followed in respect of the making of representations to the Care Quality Commission before the publication of a report by the Commission under subsection (1).

(3) The Secretary of State must consult the Care Quality Commission before making any such regulations.

(4) The Welsh Ministers may by regulations make provision as to the procedure to be followed in respect of the making of representations to them before the publication of a report by them under subsection (1).]

AMENDMENT
This section was inserted by the Health and Social Care Act 2008 s.52, Sch.3 para.9.

DEFINITION
the regulatory authority: s.145(1).  **1–1094**

GENERAL NOTE
Under s.84 of the Health and Social Care Act 2008, the Care Quality Commission must  **1–1095** make copies of any reports published under this Act available for inspection at its offices by any person at any reasonable time and any person who requests a copy of the report is entitled to have one on payment of such reasonable fee (if any) as the Commission considers appropriate.

## [Action statements

**120B.**—(1) The regulatory authority may direct a person mentioned in subsection (2) to publish a statement as to the action the person proposes to take as a result of a review or investigation under section 120(1).  **1–1096**

(2) The persons are—
(a)  the managers of a hospital within the meaning of Part 2 of this Act;
(b)  a local social services authority;
(c)  persons of any other description prescribed in regulations.

(3) Regulations may make further provision about the content and publication of statements under this section.

(4) "Regulations" means regulations made—

(a) by the Secretary of State, in relation to England;

(b) by the Welsh Ministers, in relation to Wales.]

AMENDMENT

This section was inserted by the Health and Social Care Act 2008 s.52, Sch.3 para.9.

DEFINITIONS

**1–1097**    the regulatory authority: s.145(1).

the managers: s.145(1).

hospital: s.145(1).

local social services authority: s.145(1).

GENERAL NOTE

**1–1098**    This section enables the regulatory authority to require hospital managers, social services departments and other prescribed people to publish a statement of the action they propose to take in response to any recommendations following a review or investigation undertaken under s.120(1). Paragraph 223 of the Explanatory Notes on the Health and Social Care Act 2008 states:

> "[It] is not only hospital managers and social services authorities and their staff who exercise relevant functions under the Mental Health Act and contribute to its operation. There may, therefore, be circumstances in which reviews or investigations make recommendations that are addressed (in whole or in part) to other people. In these cases, it would make sense for the people concerned to be asked directly to publish a report of the action they propose to take as a result. This might include, for example, other NHS bodies that are responsible for providing or commissioning services for patients subject to the Mental Health Act."

**[Provision of information**

**1–1099**    **120C.**—(1) This section applies to the following persons—

(a) the managers of a hospital within the meaning of Part 2 of this Act;

(b) a local social services authority;

(c) persons of any other description prescribed in regulations.

(2) A person to whom this section applies must provide the regulatory authority with such information as the authority may reasonably request for or in connection with the exercise of its functions under section 120.

(3) A person to whom this section applies must provide a person authorised under section 120 with such information as the person so authorised may reasonably request for or in connection with the exercise of functions under arrangements made under that section.

(4) This section is in addition to the requirements of section 120(7)(c).

(5) "Information" includes documents and records.

(6) "Regulations" means regulations made—

(a) by the Secretary of State, in relation to England;

(b) by the Welsh Ministers, in relation to Wales.]

AMENDMENT

This section was inserted by the Health and Social Care Act 2008 s.52, Sch.3 para.9.

the managers: s.145(1).
hospital: s.145(1).
local social services authority: s.145(1).
the regulatory authority: s.145(1).
information: subs.(5).

**1–1100**

GENERAL NOTE
This section obliges hospital managers, local social services authorities and other pre- **1–1101**
scribed people to provide the regulatory authority with information, including records
and documents, that the authority may require in relation to its functions under s.120.

Paragraph 224 of the Explanatory Notes on the Health and Social Care Act 2008 states
that examples "of the kind of information which might be requested are:

- statistical information on people subject to the formal powers under the Mental
  Health Act, including data relating to particular groups of patients such as children,
  adolescents, women, and black and ethnic minority patients;

- information on the use of particular powers, such as the granting of leave of absence;

- the number of deaths and other serious incidents;

- information on the use of seclusion in respect of patients."

## [**Annual reports**

**120C.**—(1) The regulatory authority must publish an annual report on its **1–1102**
activities in the exercise of its functions under this Act.

(2) The report must be published as soon as possible after the end of each financial year.

(3) The Care Quality Commission must send a copy of its annual report to the
Secretary of State who must lay the copy before Parliament.

(4) The Welsh Ministers must lay a copy of their annual report before the
National Assembly for Wales.

(5) In this section "financial year" means—

(a) the period beginning with the date on which section 52 of the Health and
Social Care Act 2008 comes into force and ending with the next 31
March following that date, and

(b) each successive period of 12 months ending with 31 March.]

AMENDMENT
This section was inserted by the Health and Social Care Act 2008 s.52, Sch.3 para.9.

DEFINITIONS
the regulatory authority: s.145(1). **1–1103**
financial year: subs.(5).

## **Mental Health Act Commission**
**121.** [*Repealed by the Health and Social Care Act 2008 s.166, Sch.15 Pt.1*] **1–1104**

## **Provision of pocket money for in-patients in hospital**
**122.**—(1) The Secretary of State may pay to persons who are receiving treat- **1–1105**
ment as in-patients (whether liable to be detained or not) in [ ... ] hospitals
wholly or mainly used for the treatment of persons suffering from mental disorder,
such amounts as he thinks fit in respect of their occasional personal expenses

where it appears to him that they would otherwise be without resources to meet those expenses.

(2) For the purposes of the [National Health Service Act 2006 and the National Health Service (Wales) Act 2006], the making of payments under this section to persons for whom hospital services are provided under [either of those Acts] shall be treated as included among those services.

AMENDMENTS

The words omitted in subs.(1) were repealed by the Health Act 1999 s.65, Sch.5. The words in square brackets in subs.(2) were substituted by the National Health Service (Consequential Provisions) Act 2006 s.2, Sch.1 para.67.

DEFINITIONS

**1–1106**    patient: s.145(1).
        special hospital: s.145(1).
        hospital: s.145(1).
        mental disorder: ss.1, 145(1).

GENERAL NOTE

**1–1107**    This section enables a patient in a psychiatric hospital to receive "pocket money" from the Secretary of State to cover personal expenses, if he or she is without other resources. In practice, payments under this section are limited to patients who were admitted to hospital before November 17, 1975. Patients admitted after that date will be supported by the Department for Work and Pensions if they come within the appropriate eligibility criteria. Paragraph 12.139 of the Reference Guide states:

"This power has been delegated to primary care trusts, who may (if they wish) include arrangements for the payment of such expenses in the contracts they make with relevant hospitals from which they commission mental health in-patient services *(The National Health Service (Functions of Strategic Health Authorities and Primary Care Trusts and Administration Arrangements) (England) Regulations 2002*, SI 2002/2375, as amended*)*."

*Subsection (1)*

**1–1108**    SECRETARY OF STATE.    The functions of the Minister, so far as exercisable in relation to Wales, are exercised by the Welsh Ministers (see the General Note to this Act).

## Transfers to and from special hospitals

**1–1109**    **123.**—(1) Without prejudice to any other provisions of this Act with respect to the transfer of patients, any patient who is for the time being liable to be detained ['. . . ] under this Act (other than under sections 35, 36 or 38 above) [in a hospital at which high security psychiatric services are provided] may, upon the directions of the Secretary of State, at any time be removed into any [other hospital at which those services are provided].

(2) Without prejudice to any such provision, the Secretary of State may give directions for the transfer of any patient who is for the time being liable to be so detained into a hospital [at which those services are not provided].

(3) Subsections (2) and (4) of section 19 above shall apply in relation to the transfer or removal of a patient under this section as they apply in relation to the transfer or removal of a patient from one hospital to another under that section.

AMENDMENTS
The amendments to subss.(1) and (2) were made by the Health Act 1999 Sch.4, para.67 Sch.5.

DEFINITIONS                                                                    **1–1110**
    patient: s.145(1).
    special hospital: s.145(1).
    hospital: s.145(1).

GENERAL NOTE
This section enables the Secretary of State to direct the transfer of a patient from one high **1–1111** security psychiatric hospital to another (subs.(1)) and to direct the transfer of a patient from a high security psychiatric hospital to a hospital which is not a high security psychiatric hospital (subs.(2)). A patient who has been transferred under this section will be detained in the hospital to which he has been transferred as if the application for his or her compulsory admission had been made to that hospital (s.19(2)).

A patient has no right to be consulted prior to a decision to transfer him or her under this section. (*R. v Secretary of State for the Home Department Ex p. Pickering* [1990] C.O.D. 455, CA). In *R. (on the application of DB) v Secretary of State for the Home Department* [2006] EWHC 659 (Admin); [2006] M.H.L.R. 158 at para.36, Davis J. said that practical considerations would "normally dictate" that the power under this section would not be exercised without the agreement of the receiving hospital.

For the responsibility to inform the patient's nearest relative of a transfer under this section, see reg. r.26(1)(a) of the English Regulations.

*Subsection (1)*                                                               **1–1112**
    OTHER PROVISIONS.   See s.19.

    SECRETARY OF STATE.   The functions of the Minister, so far as exercisable in relation to Wales, are exercised by the Welsh Ministers (see the General Note to this Act).

    REMOVED.   For general provisions relating to the conveyance of patients, see s.137.

### Default powers of Secretary of State
**124.** [*Repealed by the National Health Service and Community Care Act 1990* **1–1113** *s.66(2), Sch.10.*]

### Inquiries
**125.** [*Repealed by the Inquiries Act 2005 s.49, Sch.3.*]                    **1–1114**

## PART IX

## OFFENCES

GENERAL NOTE
Part I of the Sexual Offences Act 2003 creates a number of offences "against persons **1–1115** with a mental disorder impeding choice". They are:

- Sexual activity with a person with a mental disorder impeding choice (s.30).

- Causing or inciting a person, with a mental disorder impeding choice, to engage in sexual activity (s.31).

- Engaging in sexual activity in the presence of a person with a mental disorder impeding choice (s.32).

- Causing a person, with a mental disorder impeding choice, to watch a sexual act (s.33).

- Inducement, threat or deception to procure sexual activity with a person with a mental disorder (s.34).

- Causing a person with a mental disorder to engage in or agree to engage in sexual activity by inducement, threat or deception (s.35).

- Engaging in sexual activity in the presence, procured for inducement, threat or deception, of a person with a mental disorder (s.36).

- Causing a person with a mental disorder to watch a sexual act by inducement, threat or deception (s.37).

The 2003 Act also introduces a number of specific offences that relate to care workers. They elevate the position of trust and responsibility enjoyed by a care worker from a simple aggravating feature of an offence to an offence in its own right. The definition of care worker in s.42 is extremely broad and includes informal carers who provide services to the mentally disordered. The offences are:

- Care workers: sexual activity with a person with a mental disorder (s.38).

- Care workers: causing or inciting sexual activity (s.39).

- Care workers: sexual activity in the presence of a person with a mental disorder (s.40).

- Care workers: causing a person with a mental disorder to watch a sexual act (s.41).

"Guidance on Part I of the Sexual Offences Act 2003", which considers the offences set out above, is attached to Home Office Circular 21/2004.

### Forgery, false statements, etc.

**1–1116**　**126.**—(1) Any person who without lawful authority or excuse has in his custody or under his control any document to which this subsection applies, which is, and which he knows or believes to be, false within the meaning of Part I of the Forgery and Counterfeiting Act 1981, shall be guilty of an offence.

(2) Any person who without lawful authority or excuse makes or has in his custody or under his control, any document so closely resembling a document to which subsection (1) above applies as to be calculated to deceive shall be guilty of an offence.

(3) The documents to which subsection (1) above applies are any documents purporting to be—
(a)　an application under Part II of this Act;
(b)　a medical [or other] recommendation or report under this Act; and
(c)　any other document required or authorised to be made for any of the purposes of this Act.

(4) Any person who—
(a)　wilfully makes a false entry or statement in any application, recommendation, report, record or other document required or authorised to be made for any of the purposes of this Act; or

(b) with intent to deceive, makes use of any such entry or statement which he knows to be false,

shall be guilty of an offence.

(5) Any person guilty of an offence under this section shall be liable—

(a) on summary conviction, to imprisonment for a term not exceeding six months or to a fine not exceeding the statutory maximum, or to both;

(b) on conviction on indictment, to imprisonment for a term not exceeding two years or to a fine of any amount, or to both.

AMENDMENT

In subs.(3)(b) the words in square brackets were inserted by the Mental Health (Patients **1–1117** in the Community) Act 1995 s.2(1), Sch.1 para.17.

DEFINITION

statutory maximum: s.145(2). **1–1118**

GENERAL NOTE

Under this section, it is an offence either to forge or make false statements in applica- **1–1119** tions, recommendations or other documents made under this Act.

*Subsection (1)*

ANY PERSON. Or corporation (Interpretation Act s.5, Sch.1). **1–1120**

FALSE. This term is defined for the purposes of the Forgery and Counterfeiting Act 1981 in s.9 of that Act. An entry or statement may be false on account of what it omits, even though the statement or entry itself is literally true (*R. v Lord Kylsant* [1932] 1 K.B. 442).

OFFENCE. Proceedings can be instituted by a local social services authority (s.130).

*Subsection (2)*

TO DECEIVE. "To deceive is . . . to induce a man to believe a thing to be true which is **1–1121** false, and which the person practising the deceit knows or believes to be false," per Buckley J. in *Re London and Globe Finance Corporation Ltd* [1903] 1 Ch.728 at 732. In *Weltham v DPP* [1961] A.C. 103 Lord Radcliffe extended the scope of Buckley J.'s obiter remarks to include the inducing of a man to believe a thing to be false which is true.

## Ill-treatment of patients

**127.**—(1) It shall be an offence for any person who is an officer on the staff of or **1–1122** otherwise employed in, or who is one of the managers of, a hospital [, independent hospital or care home]—

(a) to ill-treat or wilfully to neglect a patient for the time being receiving treatment for mental disorder as an in-patient in that hospital or home; or

(b) to ill-treat or wilfully to neglect, on the premises of which the hospital or home forms part, a patient for the time being receiving such treatment there as an out-patient.

(2) It shall be an offence for any individual to ill-treat or wilfully to neglect a mentally disordered patient who is for the time being subject to his guardianship under this Act or otherwise in his custody or care (whether by virtue of any legal or moral obligation or otherwise).

[ . . . ]

(3) Any person guilty of an offence under this section shall be liable—

    (a) on summary conviction, to imprisonment for a term not exceeding six months or to a fine not exceeding the statutory maximum, or to both;

    (b) on conviction on indictment, to imprisonment for a term not exceeding [five years] or to a fine of any amount, or to both.

    (4) No proceedings shall be instituted for an offence under this section except by or with the consent of the Director of Public Prosecutions.

AMENDMENT

**1–1123**    In subs.(1) the words in square brackets were substituted by the Care Standards Act 2000 s.116, Sch.4 para.9(8).

    Subs.(2A) was repealed by the Mental Health Act 2007 s.55, Sch.11 Pt 5.

    The words in square brackets in subs.(3)(b) were substituted by s.42.

DEFINITIONS

**1–1124**    the managers: s.145(1).

    hospital: s.145(1).

    independent hospital: s.145(1).

    care home: ss.34(1), 145(1).

    patient: s.145(1).

    mental disorder: ss.1, 145(1).

    statutory maximum: s.145(2).

GENERAL NOTE

**1–1125**    This section, which fortifies the common law duty of care owed by those who have custody of or treat or look after patients (*R. v Mersey Care National Health Service Trust Ex p. Munjaz* [2005] UKHL 58; [2006] 4 All E.R. 736 para.4), creates two separate offences. Under subs.(1) it is an offence for an employee or a manager of a hospital, independent hospital or care home to ill-treat or wilfully to neglect an in-patient or out-patient of that hospital or home. Under subs.(2) it is an offence for a guardian or some other person who has the custody or care of a mentally disordered person who is living in the community to ill-treat or wilfully to neglect that person. It is an essential pre-requisite for each offence that the victim is a mentally disordered person within the meaning of s.1 at the time when the offence is committed.

    In *R. v Newington* (1990) 91 Cr. App. R. 247, the Court of Appeal said that "ill-treatment" could not be equated with "wilfully to neglect". Their Lordships therefore advised the Crown Prosecution Service that, when proceedings were brought under this section, charges of "ill-treatment" and of "wilfully to neglect" should be put in separate counts in the indictment.

    Proceedings under this section can either be instituted by the Director of Public Prosecutions, or by a local social services authority with the Director's consent (s.130 and subs.(4)). As s.139 of this Act does not apply to proceedings brought under this section (s.139(3)), prosecutions may be commenced without proof of bad faith or lack of reasonable care.

    In *R. v Spencer* [1986] 2 All E.R. 928, the House of Lords held that a trial judge should warn the jury of the dangers of convicting on the uncorroborated evidence of witnesses each of whom had a criminal record and suffered from a mental disorder. This case, which was concerned with the alleged ill-treatment of Rampton Hospital patients contrary to s.126 of the Mental Health Act 1959, has limited applicability to cases involving mentally disordered people who have not committed any criminal offence. Lord Ackner described the Rampton patients as "men of bad character . . . mentally unbalanced . . . anti authoritarian, prone to lie or exaggerate . . . [and who] could well have old scores which they were seeking to pay off" (at 937).

    Under s.44 of the Mental Capacity Act 2005, it is an offence for either a lay or professional carer, a donee of a lasting power of attorney (or of an enduring power of attorney) or a deputy appointed by the Court of Protection to ill-treat or wilfully neglect a person who lacks, or is believed to lack, mental capacity.

The English "No Secrets" and the Welsh "In Safe Hands" guidance set out the multiagency procedures to be followed when a vulnerable adult is believed to be suffering abuse. Abuse is defined as "a violation of an individual's human and civil rights by any other person or persons" (No Secrets, para.2.5). The guidance was issued under s.7 of the Local Authority Social Services Act 1970.

*Subsection (1)*

OFFICER ON THE STAFF OF THE HOSPITAL. "Officer" is not defined in this Act. The term **1–1126** could include a person who is neither a nurse nor a doctor.

CARE HOME. Registration of such a home under the Care Standards Act 2000 is not the test of whether an establishment is a care home. The fact of being a care home triggers the obligation to register, not the reverse (*R. v Davies and Poolton* [2000] Crim.L.R. 297, CA).

ILL-TREAT. It is not necessary to establish a course of conduct as a single act, such as slapping the patient's face on one occasion, could constitute ill-treatment under this section (*R. v Holmes* [1979] Crim.L.R. 52, Bodmin Crown Court).

In *R. v Newington*, above, the Court of Appeal held that for there to be a conviction of illtreatment under this section (the case in question was brought under subs.(2)), the Crown would have to prove: (1) deliberate conduct by the accused which could properly be described as ill-treatment irrespective of whether it damaged or threatened to damage the victim's health; (2) a guilty mind involving either an appreciation by the accused that she was inexcusably ill-treating a patient, or that she was reckless as to whether she was inexcusably acting in that way; and (3) that the victim was a mentally disordered person within the meaning of s.1. The court disapproved of a direction given by the trial judge "that violence would inevitably amount to ill-treatment" on the ground that violence necessarily used for the reasonable control of a patient would not amount to ill-treatment. As the court found that for the offence to have been committed there is no need for the prosecution to show that the treatment caused actual injury to the victim, it is clear that "illtreatment" encompasses a wide range of conduct. M. J. Gunn has stated that the decision in *R. v Newington* suggests that an offence of ill-treatment "might deal with matters such as inadequate feeding, heating, etc., or the use of harsh words and gratuitous bullying as well as what would be ordinarily understood to be ill-treatment" (*Journal of Forensic Psychiatry* (1990) 1(3), at p. 361; also see Gunn's commentary on this case at [1990] Crim. L.R. 595–597).

In *R. v Davies and Poolton*, above, the Court of Appeal held that it was not a requirement of an offence under this section that the accused should be aware that the establishment where she worked was a mental nursing home (now an independent hospital or a care home) and that the victim of ill-treatment or wilful neglect was receiving treatment for mental disorder. The relevant mens rea is found in the element of ill-treatment or wilful neglect that is the gist of the offence.

WILFULLY. The leading case on this term is *R. v Sheppard* [1981] A.C. 394 HL, a case **1–1127** brought under s.1(1) of the Children and Young Persons Act 1933 where it was held that the primary meaning of "wilful" is "deliberate", but it may also include recklessness. (In *R. v Salisu* [2009] EWCA Crim 2702; [2010] 58), a case involving appeals against convictions under this section, Hughes L.J. said, at para.11, that in *R. v G* [2003] UKHL 50; [2003] 4 All E.R. 765, the House of Lords had "made clear that recklessness involves subjective fault and actual foresight of risk".) Lord Keith said at 418:

"It is used here to describe the mental element, which, in addition to the fact of neglect, must be proved . . . The primary meaning of 'wilful' is 'deliberate'. So a parent who knows that his child needs medical care and deliberately, that is by conscious decision, refrains from calling a doctor, is guilty under the subsection. As a matter of general principle, recklessness is to be equiparated with deliberation. A parent who fails to provide medical care which his child needs because he does not care whether it is needed or not is reckless of his child's welfare. He too is guilty of an offence. But a parent who has genuinely failed to appreciate that his child needs medical care, through personal inadequacy or stupidity or both, is not guilty."

A direction of the kind suggested by Lord Keith's reasoning, suitably tailored to the facts of the case, should be given by the trail judge hearing a case under this section: see *R. v Morrell* [2002] EWCA Crim 2547, where Poole J. said at para.45:

"We do recognise the force of Crown counsel's argument that in the [appellant's] case, that of an experienced professional, unlike the feckless parent being considered by Lord Keith, questions of inadequacy or stupidity scarcely arose. Nonetheless there is or can be room for genuine mistake, even in an experienced practitioner, and we are quite satisfied that a suitably tailored direction should have been given".

In *De Maroussem v Commissioner of Income Tax* [2004] UKPC 43 at para.41, the Privy Council held that the meaning to be attributed to the expression "wilful neglect" may vary according to the context but generally the expression should be taken to mean that there has been an intentional or purposive omission to do something that the person in question knows he or she has a duty to do.

NEGLECT. Is an objective state which is not defined in this Act. In the context of a verdict of neglect made at a Coroner's inquest, Sir Thomas Bingham MR said the neglect

"means a gross failure to provide adequate nourishment or liquid, or provide or procure basic medical attention or shelter or warmth for someone in a dependent position (because of youth, age, illness or incarceration) who cannot provide it for himself. Failure to provide medical attention for a dependent person whose physical condition is such as to show that he obviously needs it may amount to neglect. So it may be if it is the dependent person's mental condition which obviously calls for medical attention (as it would, for example, if a mental nurse observed that a patient had a propensity to swallow razor blades and failed to report this propensity to a doctor, in a case where the patient had no intention to cause himself injury but did thereafter swallow razor blades with fatal results). In both cases the crucial consideration will be what the dependent person's condition, whether physical or mental, appeared to be" (*R. v Humberside and Scunthorpe Coroner Ex p. Jamieson* [1994] 3 All E.R. 972 at 990, 991).

PATIENT. There is no requirement under this subsection for the victim to have been detained under the provisions of this Act. The ill-treatment or wilful neglect of an *in-patient* need not have taken place on the hospital premises.

*Subsection (2)*

**1-1128**  MENTALLY DISORDERED PATIENT. Is a person who is either suffering or appearing to be suffering from mental disorder (*R. v Newington*, above). There is no need for the victim to be receiving treatment for his or her mental disorder, to have had a history of in-patient treatment in a hospital, or to have been a detained patient or a detained patient on leave of absence from a hospital. At the time of the offence the victim could, for example, be living in his own home, with relatives or friends, or in accommodation registered under the Care Standards Act 2000.

OTHERWISE IN HIS CUSTODY OR CARE. The custodians or carers could include social workers, residential care workers, teachers, relatives or friends. It is submitted that the use of the term "moral obligation" extends the scope of this section to include a family member, friend or volunteer who is caring for the mentally disordered person. As to legal custody, see s.137.

## Assisting patients to absent themselves without leave, etc.

**128.**—(1) Where any person induces or knowingly assists another person who **1–1129** is liable to be detained in a hospital within the meaning of Part II of this Act or is subject to guardianship under this Act [or is a community patient] to absent himself without leave he shall be guilty of an offence.

(2) Where any person induces or knowingly assists another person who is in legal custody by virtue of section 137 below to escape from such custody he shall be guilty of an offence.

(3) Where any person knowingly harbours a patient who is absent without leave or is otherwise at large and liable to be retaken under this Act or gives him any assistance with intent to prevent, hinder or interfere with his being taken into custody or returned to the hospital or other place where he ought to be he shall be guilty of an offence.

(4) Any person guilty of an offence under this section shall be liable—

(a) on summary conviction, to imprisonment for a term not exceeding six months or to a fine not exceeding the statutory maximum, or to both;

(b) on conviction on indictment, to imprisonment for a term not exceeding two years or to a fine of any amount, or to both.

AMENDMENT

In subs.(1) the words in square brackets were inserted by the Mental Health Act 2007 **1–1130** s.32(4), Sch.3 para.28.

DEFINITIONS
    hospital: s.145(1).     **1–1131**
    absent without leave: ss.18(6), 145(1).
    patient: s.145(1).
    community patient: ss.17A(7), 145(1).
    hospital: ss.34(2), 145(1).

GENERAL NOTE

Under this section it is an offence to induce or to help a patient escape from custody or to **1–1132** absent himself from hospital or place where he or she is required to be without leave, or to harbour or prevent the recapture or return of such patients. The patient does not commit an offence by absenting himself without leave. Proceedings under this section can be instituted by local social services authorities (s.130).

*Subsection (1)*

KNOWINGLY. The use of this term emphasises the requirement of mens rea (*R. v Dunne*, **1–1133** *The Times*, March 16, 1998 CA).

*Subsection (3)*

OTHER PLACE WHERE HE OUGHT TO BE. Such as a specified place of residence under **1–1134** guardianship or a community treatment order.

**Obstruction**

1–1135 **129.**—(1) Any person who without reasonable cause—

    (a) refuses to allow the inspection of any premises; or

    (b) refuses to allow the visiting, interviewing or examination of any person by a person authorised in that behalf by or under this Act [or to give access to any person to a person so authorised]; or

    (c) refuses to produce for the inspection of any person so authorised any document or record the production of which is duly required by him; or

    [(ca) fails to comply with a request under section 120C; or]

    (d) otherwise obstructs any such person in the exercise of his functions,

shall be guilty of an offence.

(2) Without prejudice to the generality of subsection (1) above, any person who insists on being present when required to withdraw by a person authorised by or under this Act to interview or examine a person in private shall be guilty of an offence.

(3) Any person guilty of an offence under this section shall be liable on summary conviction to imprisonment for a term not exceeding three months or to a fine not exceeding level 4 on the standard scale or to both.

AMENDMENT

In subs.(1)(b) the words in square brackets were inserted by the Mental Health (Patients in the Community) Act 1995 s.2(1), Sch.1 para.19. Subs.(1)(ca) was inserted by the Health and Social Care Act 2008 s.52, Sch.3 para.10.

GENERAL NOTE

1–1136    This section specifies when a person commits the offence of obstruction under this Act. The Committee of Inquiry into Complaints about Ashworth Hospital stated that they were "inclined to the view that the right of silence is abrogated by [this section] which makes it an offence for anyone, without reasonable excuse, to obstruct an authorised investigation" (Cm. 2028, Vol.1, Ch. XIII, p.126). This opinion runs counter to the decision of the Divisional Court in *Rice v Connolly*, see below.

*Subsection (1)*

1–1137    ANY PERSON.   Or corporation (Interpretation Act 1978 s.5, Sch.1).

OBSTRUCTS.   Cases on the offence of obstructing a policeman in the execution of his duty suggest that an offence under this section: (1) need not involve physical violence (*Hinchcliffe v Sheldon* [1955] 1 W.L.R. 1207); (2) is not committed on a mere refusal to answer questions or otherwise assist with enquiries (*Rice v Connolly* [1966] 2 Q.B. 414) or on advising a person not to answer questions (*Green v DPP* [1991] Crim. L.R. 782 DC); (3) will be committed if a person exercising powers under this Act approaches a person who he or she is entitled to approach and that person runs away (*Sekfali v DPP* [2006] EWHC 894 (Admin)); and (4) might be committed if a verbal warning of an impending inspection was given (*Green v Moore* [1982] 2 W.L.R. 671). There is also authority to support the contention that an offence is committed if the defendant's conduct makes it more difficult for an authorised person to carry out his duties; see the dictum of Lord Goddard C.J. in *Hinchcliffe v Sheldon*, above, at 1210 which was followed by the Divisional Court in *Lewis v Cox* [1984] 3 W.L.R. 875. In *Barge v British Gas Corporation* (1982) 81 L.G.R. 53, a case heard under the Trade Descriptions Act 1968, it was held that a refusal to co-operate will be an offence only in relation to a valid requirement which the enforcement officer is entitled to make.

During the debates on the Mental Health Bill, a Government Minister said that behaviour intended to stop a professional from making an independent decision that they are required to make under this Act could constitute the offence of obstruction (*Hansard,* HL Vol.688, col.749).

OFFENCE.    Proceedings can be instituted by a local social services authority (s.130).

*Subsection (2)*
IN PRIVATE.    Although an approved mental health professional (AMHP) is required to interview a patient "in a suitable manner" before making an application under Pt II of this Act (s.13(2)), there is no express provision authorising him to interview the patient *in private.* A person who disrupts an AMHP's interview with a patient would be guilty of an offence under subs.(1)(d) of this section.    **1–1138**

## Prosecutions by local authorities
**130.** A local social services authority may institute proceedings for any offence under this Part of this Act, but without prejudice to any provision of this Part of this Act requiring the consent of the Director of Public Prosecutions for the institution of such proceedings.    **1–1139**

DEFINITION
local social services authority: s.145(1).    **1–1140**

GENERAL NOTE
This section empowers a local social services authority to institute proceedings for an offence alleged to have been committed under this Part.    **1–1141**

Local authority staff who are charged with the duty of investigating offences under this Part must have regard to relevant provisions of the Codes of Practice issued under the Police and Criminal Evidence Act 1984 (s.67(9)). In particular, the following caution must be administered to a suspect before any questions about the offence are put to him or her: "You do not have to say anything. But it may harm your defence if you do not mention when questioned something which you later rely on in court. Anything you do say may be given in evidence" (*Code of Practice C* (2008 revision), para.10.5).

CONSENT OF THE DIRECTOR OF DIRECTOR PROSECUTIONS.    Is required by s.127.

# PART X

## MISCELLANEOUS AND SUPPLEMENTARY

### *Miscellaneous Provisions*

## Independent mental health advocates
**[130A.**—(1) The appropriate national authority shall make such arrangements as it considers reasonable to enable persons ("independent mental health advocates") to be available to help qualifying patients.    **1–1142**

(2) The appropriate national authority may by regulations make provision as to the appointment of persons as independent mental health advocates.

(3) The regulations may, in particular, provide—

(a)    that a person may act as an independent mental health advocate only in such circumstances, or only subject to such conditions, as may be specified in the regulations;

(b)    for the appointment of a person as an independent mental health advocate to be subject to approval in accordance with the regulations.

(4) In making arrangements under this section, the appropriate national authority shall have regard to the principle that any help available to a patient under the arrangements should, so far as practicable, be provided by a person who is independent of any person who is professionally concerned with the patient's medical treatment.

(5) For the purposes of subsection (4) above, a person is not to be regarded as professionally concerned with a patient's medical treatment merely because he is representing him in accordance with arrangements—

(a) under section 35 of the Mental Capacity Act 2005; or

(b) of a description specified in regulations under this section.

(6) Arrangements under this section may include provision for payments to be made to, or in relation to, persons carrying out functions in accordance with the arrangements.

(7) Regulations under this section—

(a) may make different provision for different cases;

(b) may make provision which applies subject to specified exceptions;

(c) may include transitional, consequential, incidental or supplemental provision.]

AMENDMENT

This section was inserted by the Mental Health Act 2007 s.30(2).

GENERAL NOTE

**1–1143** This section places a duty on the Secretary of State and the Welsh Ministers to make arrangements for independent mental health advocates (IMHAs) to be available to help "qualifying patients". In making arrangements under this section the Secretary of State and the Welsh Ministers must have regard to the principle that any help provided under the arrangements to a qualifying patient should, as far as practicable, be provided by a person who is independent of anyone who is professionally concerned with the patient's treatment (subs.(4)). Qualifying patients are defined in s.130C(2), (3), (4). Much of the detail of the new scheme are set out in the Mental Health Act 1983 (Independent Mental Health Advocates) (England) Regulations 2008 (SI 2008/3166) which are reproduced in Part 2. (subss.(2), (3)). The IMHA must help the patient to obtain information about and to understand the matters set out in s.130B(1) and (2).

Paragraph 34.11 of the Reference Guide states:

"The help which independent mental health advocacy services must provide also includes helping patients to exercise their rights, which can include representing them and speaking on their behalf. But independent mental health advocacy services are not designed to take the place of advice from, or representation by, qualified legal professionals".

However, there is nothing to prevent IMHAs from accompanying patients to tribunals and hospital managers hearings and speaking on their behalf.

The powers available to the IMHA are identified in s.130B(3). A "responsible person", as defined in s.130D(2), has a duty to provide a qualifying patient with oral and written information about the IMHA service (s.130D(1), (4)). A qualifying patient can decline the services of an IMHA (s.130B(6)). It has been reported that a Mental Health Act Commissioner advised a hospital that it should be routinely providing the IMHA service with a list of current detained patients. Hospitals do not have the power to provide such information. In any event, acceding to such a request would clearly involve a breach of patient confidentiality.

Hospital managers cannot withhold correspondence between patients and their IMHAs (s.134(3)(eb), (3A)).

Functions under this section are NHS functions for the purposes of the NHS Bodies and Local Authorities Partnership Arrangements Regulations 2000 (SI 2000/617) (as amended). Partnership arrangements are considered in the General Note to s.117.

"Independent Mental Health Advocacy: Guidance for Commissioners" can be downloaded from the website of the National Mental Health Development Unit (*www.nmhdu.org.uk*).

*Code of Practice*
Guidance on IMHAs is contained in Ch.20.                                      **1–1144**

*Subsection(1)*
APPROPRIATE NATIONAL AUTHORITY.    See s.130C(5), (6).                        **1–1145**

QUALIFYING PATIENTS.    See s.130C(2)–(4).

*Subsection (2)*
REGULATIONS.    See SI 2008/3166, noted above. The Welsh Ministers have made separ-   **1–1146**
ate Regulations in relation to Wales: see SI 2008/2437 (W.210).

*Subsection (4)*
PROFESSIONALLY CONCERNED.    See subs.(5).                                    **1–1147**

*Subsection (5)*
SECTION 35 OF THE MENTAL CAPACITY ACT 2005.    Which provides for the appointment of IMHAs.

SPECIFIED IN REGULATIONS.    See reg.7 of SI 2008/3166, noted above.

## Arrangements under section 130A

[**130B.**—(1) The help available to a qualifying patient under arrangements  **1–1148**
under section 130A above shall include help in obtaining information about and understanding—
  (a)  the provisions of this Act by virtue of which he is a qualifying patient;
  (b)  any conditions or restrictions to which he is subject by virtue of this Act;
  (c)  what (if any) medical treatment is given to him or is proposed or discussed in his case;
  (d)  why it is given, proposed or discussed;
  (e)  the authority under which it is, or would be, given; and
  (f)  the requirements of this Act which apply, or would apply, in connection with the giving of the treatment to him.
  (2) The help available under the arrangements to a qualifying patient shall also include—
  (a)  help in obtaining information about and understanding any rights which may be exercised under this Act by or in relation to him; and
  (b)  help (by way of representation or otherwise) in exercising those rights.
  (3) For the purpose of providing help to a patient in accordance with the arrangements, an independent mental health advocate may—
  (a)  visit and interview the patient in private;
  (b)  visit and interview any person who is professionally concerned with his medical treatment;

(c) require the production of and inspect any records relating to his detention or treatment in any hospital or registered establishment or to any after-care services provided for him under section 117 above;

(d) require the production of and inspect any records of, or held by, a local social services authority which relate to him.

(4) But an independent mental health advocate is not entitled to the production of, or to inspect, records in reliance on subsection (3)(c) or (d) above unless—

(a) in a case where the patient has capacity or is competent to consent, he does consent; or

(b) in any other case, the production or inspection would not conflict with a decision made by a donee or deputy or the Court of Protection and the person holding the records, having regard to such matters as may be prescribed in regulations under section 130A above, considers that—

(i) the records may be relevant to the help to be provided by the advocate; and

(ii) the production or inspection is appropriate.

(5) For the purpose of providing help to a patient in accordance with the arrangements, an independent mental health advocate shall comply with any reasonable request made to him by any of the following for him to visit and interview the patient—

(a) the person (if any) appearing to the advocate to be the patient's nearest relative;

(b) the responsible clinician for the purposes of this Act;

(c) an approved mental health professional.

(6) But nothing in this Act prevents the patient from declining to be provided with help under the arrangements.

(7) In subsection (4) above—

(a) the reference to a patient who has capacity is to be read in accordance with the Mental Capacity Act 2005;

(b) the reference to a donee is to a donee of a lasting power of attorney (within the meaning of section 9 of that Act) created by the patient, where the donee is acting within the scope of his authority and in accordance with that Act;

(c) the reference to a deputy is to a deputy appointed for the patient by the Court of Protection under section 16 of that Act, where the deputy is acting within the scope of his authority and in accordance with that Act.]

AMENDMENT

This section was inserted by the Mental Capacity Act 2007 s.30(2).

DEFINITIONS

**1–1149**    medical treatment: s.145(1), (4).

hospital: s.145(1).

registered establishment: s.145(1).

local social services authority: s.145(1).

nearest relative: s.145(1).

responsible clinician. ss.34(1), 145(1).

approved mental health professional: s.145(1), (1C).

GENERAL NOTE

**1–1150**    This section identifies the help that an IMHA should provide to the patient (subss.(1), (2)) and the powers of the IMHA (subss.(3), (4), (7)), requires the IMHA to comply with the reasonable requests of specified persons to visit and interview the patient (subs.(5)) and provides the patient with the power to decline the assistance of an IMHA (subs.(6)).

*Subsections (1),(2)*
Note that the IMHA is not entitled to adopt either a befriending or campaigning role.   **1–1151**

*Subsection (2)(b)*
Help under this provision could include providing assistance to the patient in bringing **1–1152** legal proceedings relating to his or her detention. The IMHA has no independent right to take such action.

*Subsection (3)*
The normal rules of confidentiality apply to conversations between professionals and **1–1153** IMHAs: see para.20.24 of the *Code of Practice*.

*Paragraph (d)*
Anyone who refuses, without reasonable cause, to produce records that an IMHA has a **1–1154** right to inspect may be guilty of the offence of obstruction under s.129.

*Subsection (4)*
An IMHA's access to patients' records is considered in the *Code of Practice* at **1–1155** paras.20.25–20.33. In "Supplementary guidance on access to patient records under s.130B of the Mental Health Act 1983", April 2009, the Department of Health provides advice on whether this section allows IMHAs to see information in records which the patient would have no right to see and, if so, whether IMHAs may share that information with patients. The following key points arising from the advice are set out on p.4:

"● record holders may not withhold information from IMHAs simply because it would not be disclosed to the patient under the Data Protection Act, either because it is provided by or relates to a third party, or because it would risk serious harm to the patient or anyone else. But, exceptionally, there may be special circumstances in which confidential third party information should not be disclosed.

● IMHAs should make clear to record holders whether or not they wish to see information in records which would not be disclosed to the patient under the Data Protection Act.

● record holders must tell IMHAs if they provide any information which would not have been disclosed to the patient because of a risk of serious harm. They are strongly recommended to tell IMHAs if any third party information they are providing would not have been disclosed to the patient.

● generally speaking, where a duty of confidentiality arises, IMHAs should not pass on information about or relating to third parties without their consent. But this will depend on the individual case.

● IMHAs must not pass on information which would not have been disclosed to the patient because of a risk of serious harm."

*Paragraph (b)*
CAPACITY; DONEE; DEPUTY.   See subs.(7).   **1–1156**

PERSON HOLDING THE RECORD.   It is for this person, and not the IMHA, to determine whether to record is relevant and its production or inspection is appropriate.

*Subsection (7)*
CAPACITY.   Is to be determined by using the tests set out in ss.2 and 3 of the 2005 Act. **1–1157**

**Section 130A: supplemental**

**1–1158**    [**130C.**—(1) This section applies for the purposes of section 130A above.

(2) A patient is a qualifying patient if he is—

(a) liable to be detained under this Act (otherwise than by virtue of section 4 or 5(2) or (4) above or section 135 or 136 below);

(b) subject to guardianship under this Act; or

(c) a community patient.

(3) A patient is also a qualifying patient if—

(a) not being a qualifying patient falling within subsection (2) above, he discusses with a registered medical practitioner or approved clinician the possibility of being given a form of treatment to which section 57 above applies; or

(b) not having attained the age of 18 years and not being a qualifying patient falling within subsection (2) above, he discusses with a registered medical practitioner or approved clinician the possibility of being given a form of treatment to which section 58A above applies.

(4) Where a patient who is a qualifying patient falling within subsection (3) above is informed that the treatment concerned is proposed in his case, he remains a qualifying patient falling within that subsection until—

(a) the proposal is withdrawn; or

(b) the treatment is completed or discontinued.

(5) References to the appropriate national authority are—

(a) in relation to a qualifying patient in England, to the Secretary of State;

(b) in relation to a qualifying patient in Wales, to the Welsh Ministers.

(6) For the purposes of subsection (5) above—

(a) a qualifying patient falling within subsection (2)(a) above is to be regarded as being in the territory in which the hospital or registered establishment in which he is liable to be detained is situated;

(b) a qualifying patient falling within subsection (2)(b) above is to be regarded as being in the territory in which the area of the responsible local social services authority within the meaning of section 34(3) above is situated;

(c) a qualifying patient falling within subsection (2)(c) above is to be regarded as being in the territory in which the responsible hospital is situated;

(d) a qualifying patient falling within subsection (3) above is to be regarded as being in the territory determined in accordance with arrangements made for the purposes of this paragraph, and published, by the Secretary of State and the Welsh Ministers.]

AMENDMENT

This section was inserted by the Mental Health Act 2007 s.30(2).

DEFINITIONS

**1–1159**    community patient: ss.17A(7), 145(1).

local social services authority: s.145(1).

GENERAL NOTE

**1–1160**    This section defines a "qualifying patient" (subss.(2) to (4)) and "the appropriate national authority" (subss.(5), (6)) for the purposes of s.130A.

A patient who lacks the capacity to decline the assistance of an IMHA (see s.130B(6)) is a qualifying patient for the purposes of this provision. Paragraph 5.3 of "Independent Mental Health Advocacy—Guidance for Commissioners", NIMH for England,

Dec.2008, which is headed "Instructed and non-instructed advocacy", offers the following guidance on patients who lack the capacity to instruct an advocate:

"Wherever possible IMHAs will take instruction from the person they are supporting. An IMHA may support a person to obtain information, explore options and carry out actions, but throughout this process the IMHA will be directed by the person and act only on their behalf. IMHAs may also provide non-instructed advocacy when helping patients who are unable to express their wishes clearly, or at all, because they lack the mental capacity to instruct or have difficulties communicating. When providing non-instructed advocacy, the IMHA will represent the patient's wishes (as far as those wishes are known) and ensure the patient's rights are respected. Where a patient qualifies for both an IMHA and an Independent Mental Capacity Advocate (IMCA), the IMCA will represent the patient in line with the IMCA's statutory role. An example is a qualifying patient who lacks capacity and it is being considered for cancer treatment: in this case, the IMCA would represent the patient in the decision making process for this treatment."

*Subsection (2)(a)*
The exclusions reflect the fact that the IMHA service is not intended to be an emergency **1–1161** response service.

*Subsections (3), (4)*
The Reference Guide states, at para.34.5, that informal patients who qualify because they **1–1162** are being considered for one of the treatments specified in this provision, "remain eligible until the treatment is finished (or stopped) or it is decided that they will not be given the treatment for the time being".

*Subsection (6)(d)*
Appendix 5 of the NIMH document, above (which has been published by the Department **1–1163** of Health under Gateway reference 11061) states:

"For the purposes of 130C(6)(d) of the Mental Health Act 1983, a qualifying patient falling within subsection 130C(3)(a) or 130C(3)(b) of that Act is to be regarded as being in the territory where they are resident, unless that person is receiving treatment for a mental disorder as an in-patient in an NHS hospital or an independent hospital, in which case they are regarded as being in the territory where that hospital or independent hospital is situated.
Where there is doubt as to where a person is resident:

(1) They shall be treated as resident at the address which they give to the registered medical practitioner or approved clinician discussing the treatment with them;
(2) If they give no such address, then they shall be treated as resident at the address they give as their most recent address;
(3) Where their residence cannot be determined in accordance with (1) and (2) above, or they are not resident in England or Wales, then they shall be treated as resident in the territory in which they are present.

*Explanation of these arrangements*

As a result of the Mental Health Act 2007, the Mental Health Act 1983 (the 1983 Act) requires the "appropriate national authority" to arrange for independent mental health advocates to be available to "qualifying patients". For England, the appropriate national authority means the Secretary of State and for Wales it means the Welsh Ministers. (In practice, both the Secretary of State and the Welsh Ministers can arrange for other people–like the NHS locally–to commission IMHA services on their behalf.)

In most cases, the 1983 Act itself says whether a particular qualifying patient is to be treated as "English" or "Welsh" for these purposes.

- **For qualifying patients who are liable to be detained under the 1983 Act (even if they are currently on leave of absence from the hospital or conditionally discharged)**: responsibility for making an IMHA available falls to the national authority for the country in which the hospital or registered establishment where they are liable to be detained is situated.

- **For qualifying patients under Guardianship**: responsibility for making an IMHA available falls to the national authority for the country where the area of the responsible local social services authority is situated.

- **For patients on supervised community treatment**: responsibility for making an IMHA available falls to the national authority for the country in which the responsible hospital is situated.

However, for patients who qualify under 130C(3) (a) or 130C(3)(b) of the 1983 Act, the Act leaves it to the Secretary of State and the Welsh Ministers to publish a statement setting out the rules as to which of them will be responsible.

Patients qualifying under 130C(3)(a) are informal patients of any age being considered for section 57 treatment (psychosurgery or the surgical implantation of hormones to reduce the male sex drive). Patients qualifying under 130C (3)(b) are informal patients aged under 18 being considered for section 58A treatment (electroconvulsive therapy). "Informal patient" in this context means a patient who is not otherwise a qualifying patient (e.g. as a result of being detained, or on SCT, Guardianship or conditional discharge).

The effect of the statement above is that if a patient qualifies for an IMHA under 130C(3)(a) or 130C(3)(b) of the 1983 Act, responsibility for making an IMHA available falls to the national authority for the country in which the patient lives or, if they are in hospital or subsequently go into hospital for treatment for a mental disorder, to the authority for the country where that hospital is. If it is not clear where a person lives, then they shall be treated as living at the address which they give to the registered medical practitioner or approved clinician discussing the treatment with them, or if they give no such address, then they shall be treated as living at the address they give as their most recent address. If where they live cannot be determined in either of these ways, or if they do not live in England or Wales, then they shall be treated as living where they are present.

*Examples of how these arrangements may work in practice:*

If a patient who is being considered for section 57 treatment lives in England, the English authority is responsible for providing them with an IMHA. If that patient subsequently becomes an informal in-patient in a hospital in Wales while still being considering for section 57 treatment, the Welsh authority is responsible for providing them with an IMHA.

If a patient aged under 18 who is being considered for section 58A treatment is an informal in-patient in a hospital in England, the English authority is responsible for providing them with an IMHA. If that patient is subsequently discharged from hospital and goes to live in Wales, while still being considered for section 58A treatment, the Welsh authority is responsible for providing them with an IMHA."

## Duty to give information about independent mental health advocates

**1–1164** **[130D.**—(1) The responsible person in relation to a qualifying patient (within the meaning given by section 130C above) shall take such steps as are practicable to ensure that the patient understands—

(a) that help is available to him from an independent mental health advocate; and

(b)  how he can obtain that help.

(2) In subsection (1) above, "the responsible person" means—

(a)  in relation to a qualifying patient falling within section 130C(2)(a) above (other than one also falling within paragraph (b) below), the managers of the hospital or registered establishment in which he is liable to be detained;

(b)  in relation to a qualifying patient falling within section 130C(2)(a) above and conditionally discharged by virtue of section 42(2), 73 or 74 above, the responsible clinician;

(c)  in relation to a qualifying patient falling within section 130C(2)(b) above, the responsible local social services authority within the meaning of section 34(3) above;

(d)  in relation to a qualifying patient falling within section 130C(2)(c) above, the managers of the responsible hospital;

(e)  in relation to a qualifying patient falling within section 130C(3) above, the registered medical practitioner or approved clinician with whom the patient first discusses the possibility of being given the treatment concerned.

(3) The steps to be taken under subsection (1) above shall be taken—

(a)  where the responsible person falls within subsection (2)(a) above, as soon as practicable after the patient becomes liable to be detained;

(b)  where the responsible person falls within subsection (2)(b) above, as soon as practicable after the conditional discharge;

(c)  where the responsible person falls within subsection (2)(c) above, as soon as practicable after the patient becomes subject to guardianship;

(d)  where the responsible person falls within subsection (2)(d) above, as soon as practicable after the patient becomes a community patient;

(e)  where the responsible person falls within subsection (2)(e) above, while the discussion with the patient is taking place or as soon as practicable thereafter.

(4) The steps to be taken under subsection (1) above shall include giving the requisite information both orally and in writing.

(5) The responsible person in relation to a qualifying patient falling within section 130C(2) above (other than a patient liable to be detained by virtue of Part 3 of this Act) shall, except where the patient otherwise requests, take such steps as are practicable to furnish the person (if any) appearing to the responsible person to be the patient's nearest relative with a copy of any information given to the patient in writing under subsection (1) above.

(6) The steps to be taken under subsection (5) above shall be taken when the information concerned is given to the patient or within a reasonable time thereafter.]

AMENDMENT
This section was inserted by the Mental Health Act 2007 s.30(2).

DEFINITIONS
the managers: s.145(1).                                                                          **1–1165**
hospital: s.145(1).
registered establishment: s.145(1).
responsible hospital: ss.17A(7), 145(1).
local social services authority: s.145(1).
responsible clinician: ss.34(1), 145(1).
community patient: ss.17A(7), 145(1).

nearest relative: s.145(1).

GENERAL NOTE
**1–1166** This section places a duty on the "responsible person", as defined in subs.(2), to take practicable steps to ensure that a qualifying patient understands the help that an IMHA can provide and how to obtain such help (subs.(1)). The information, which has to be given both orally and in writing (subs.(4)), must be given to the patient as soon as practicable after the patient becomes a qualifying patient (subs.(3)). The nearest relative of a patient who comes within s.130C(2) (but not a Pt III patient) must be given a written copy of the information that the patient receives unless the patient objects (subss.(5), (6)).

## Informal admission of patients

**1–1167** **131.**—(1) Nothing in this Act shall be construed as preventing a patient who requires treatment for mental disorder from being admitted to any hospital or [registered establishment] in pursuance of arrangements made in that behalf and without any application, order or direction rendering him liable to be detained under this Act, or from remaining in any hospital or [registered establishment] in pursuance of such arrangements after he has ceased to be so liable to be detained.

[(2) Subsections (3) and (4) below apply in the case of a patient aged 16 or 17 years who has capacity to consent to the making of such arrangements as are mentioned in subsection (1) above.

(3) If the patient consents to the making of the arrangements, they may be made, carried out and determined on the basis of that consent even though there are one or more persons who have parental responsibility for him.

(4) If the patient does not consent to the making of the arrangements, they may not be made, carried out or determined on the basis of the consent of a person who has parental responsibility for him.

(5) In this section—

(a)  the reference to a patient who has capacity is to be read in accordance with the Mental Capacity Act 2005; and

(b)  "parental responsibility" has the same meaning as in the Children Act 1989.]

AMENDMENTS
In subs.(1) the words in square brackets were substituted by the Care Standards Act 2000 s.116, Sch.4 para.9(2).
In subs.(2) the words in square brackets were substituted by the Children Act 1989 s.108(5), Sch.13 para.48(5).
Subs.(2)–(5) were substituted by the Mental Health Act 2007 s.43.

DEFINITIONS
**1–1168** patient: s.145(1).
mental disorder: ss.1, 145(1).
hospital: s.145(1).
registered establishment: ss.34(1), 145(1).

GENERAL NOTE
**1–1169** This section provides that a patient can either enter hospital for treatment for mental disorder on an informal basis, or remain in hospital on an informal basis once the authority for his or her original detention has come to an end. It also provides that in the case of patients aged 16 or 17 years who have the capacity to consent to their informal admission to hospital for treatment for their mental disorder, they may consent (or may not consent) to the

admission and their decision cannot be overridden by a person with parental responsibility for them. If such a child does not consent to the admission, he or she could be admitted for compulsory treatment under Pt II if the relevant criteria are satisfied.

This section applies to (a) mentally capable patients who consent to their admission to hospital (voluntary patients) and (b) patients lacking such capacity who do not object to their admission (informal patients) (*R. v Bournewood NHS Trust, ex p.L* [1998] 3 All E.R. 389).

A mentally incapacitated patient cannot be admitted informally if the admission constitutes a deprivation of the patient's liberty: see Part 6. If a deprivation of liberty is not involved in the admission, ss.5 and 6 of the Mental Capacity Act 2005 (MCA) enable both lay and professional carers to restrain a patient who is over the age of 16 if the restraint is necessary to prevent harm to the patient and its use is proportionate both to the likelihood and seriousness of the harm. The patient can be restrained even if the patient is resisting the admission and the restraint involves using force which restricts the patient's liberty of movement (s.6(4) of the 2005 Act). The admission must be in the patient's best interests: see s.4 of the 2005 Act.

With the exception of treatments provided under s.57 and s.58A (for child patients only), informal patients are not subject to the consent to treatment provisions contained in Pt IV of this Act and are therefore free to refuse treatment if they possess the required mental capacity. If a mentally capable patient who has been admitted informally fails to accept necessary treatment for mental disorder or refuses to co-operate with the hospital authorities, consideration should be given to either discharging the patient from the hospital or assessing him or her for possible detention under Pt II.

In *R. v Kirklees Metropolitan Borough Council Ex p. C* [1992] 2 F.L.R. 117, Kennedy J., on an application for the judicial review of a decision by the local authority to consent to the admission of an adolescent girl (the applicant) to a psychiatric hospital, held that an admission to a psychiatric hospital can be lawful even though it does not take place within the framework of this Act, which did not cover all eventualities. His Lordship found that there is no reason to conclude that the right to arrange an informal admission is limited to the terms of this section. If that were the case it would produce the surprising result that no one, adult or child, who had not been diagnosed as being mentally disordered, could ever be admitted to a psychiatric hospital for assessment. This section did not apply to the applicant because there was no evidence that she required "treatment for mental disorder" (see subs.(1)). The local authority was entitled to consent on the applicants behalf because a care order had been made in respect of her and at the material time she was not "Gillick competent" (see subs.(2)). On affirming this decision at [1993] 2 F.L.R. 187, the Court of Appeal confirmed that although the informal admission of a patient for assessment is not covered by this section, there is nothing to prohibit such an admission taking place under common law. The effect of this decision is merely to fill a gap in the statutory scheme, a gap which was described by Lloyd L.J., at 190, as being "odd".

J. Bindman and his colleagues found that a third of patients who had been admitted informally to a psychiatric hospital felt highly coerced at admission, and the majority were uncertain that they were free to leave the hospital ("Perceived coercion at admission to psychiatric hospital and engagement with follow up", Soc. Psychiatry Psychiatr Epidemiol (2005) 40: 160–166). Informal patients should therefore be "made aware of their legal position and rights" (Code of Practice, para.2.45).

*Human Rights Act 1998*
The decisions of the European Court on Human Rights on the meaning of a "deprivation **1–1170** of liberty" are considered in Part 6. Also see the notes on Art.5 of the European Convention on Human Rights in Part 5.

Article 5 applies to children. In *Nielsen v Denmark* (1989) 11 E.H.R.R. 175, the court found that no deprivation of liberty had occurred when the mother of a 12-year-old boy consented to his admission to a psychiatric hospital against his wishes and that of his father.

Among the factors that were cited in support of this decision, the court emphasised, at para.72:

(i) the fact that the mother was the sole holder of parental responsibility in respect of the child. The court said that the "care and upbringing of children normally and necess- arily require that the parents or an only parent decide where the child must reside and also impose, or authorise others to impose, various restrictions on the child's lib- erty". However, it accepted that "the rights of the holder of parental authority cannot be unlimited and that it is incumbent on the State to provide safeguard's against abuse";

(ii) that the "restrictions to which the [child] was subject were no more than the normal requirements for the care of a child of 12 years of age receiving treatment in hospi- tal"; and

(iii) its view that the child "was still of an age at which it would be normal for a decision to be made by the parent against the wishes of the child".

The court concluded by stating that it "must be possible for a child like the applicant to be admitted to hospital at the request of the holder of parental rights, a case which is clearly not covered by paragraph 1 of Article 5". This statement was made because the child, not having been diagnosed as being mentally ill, was not detained as a person of unsound mind so as to bring the case with this sub-paragraph.

It has been said that although Nielsen is a recent decision, "there must be doubt how far, if at all, [it] will be followed in future. In considering any similar issue today, account should be taken of the Convention of the Rights of the Child 1989" (S. Grosz, J. Beatson, P. Duffy, Human Rights: The 1998 Act and the European Convention, (2000), p.199.) In *Storck v Germany* (2006) 43 E.H.R.R. 6, the court found that a child who had admitted to hospital by parental consent was being deprived of her liberty.

*Code of Practice*

**1–1171**    The informal admission of patients is consider in Ch.4. Guidance on working with men- tally disordered children and young people is contained in Ch.36.

*Subsection (1)*

**1–1172**    TREATMENT.   But not assessment (*R. v Kirklees Metropolitan Borough Council Ex p. C*, above). The treatment and care of mentally incapable informal patients is authorised under ss.5 and 6 of the Mental Capacity Act 2005 if such treatment and care is in the patient's best interests.

WITHOUT ANY APPLICATION.   Although informal admission should be the preferred mode of admission, there is nothing in this Act which expressly prevents an application being made in respect of a mentally capable patient who is willing to enter hospital as an informal patient. While it is true that s.5 of this Act can be invoked to prevent an infor- mal patient from leaving hospital, circumstances can arise which justify the use of compulsion on a "willing" patient. The *Code of Practice*, at para.4.9 suggests that compul- sion should be considered where such a patient presents a "clear danger to themselves or others" because of their mental disorder.

*Subsection (2)–(5)*

*Children aged 16 or 17*

**1–1173**    These subsections provide that patients aged 16 or 17 who have the capacity to consent to their admission to a hospital or registered establishment for treatment for mental disorder can consent or not consent to such arrangements on their own behalf. If the patient consents to the making of arrangements, he or she can be informally admitted to hospital, and the consent cannot be over-ridden by a person with parental responsibility for him or her. If the patient does not consent to the making of the arrangements, he or she cannot be informally admitted on the basis of consent from a person with parental responsibility. Parental responsibility is defined in s.3(1) of the Children Act 1989 as "all the rights, duties powers, responsibility and authority which by law a parent of a child has in relation to the child and his property".

The Minister of State said:

"Practitioners must, of course, satisfy themselves that, where the patient appears to be consenting, he understands what he is consenting to and the consequences of that consent. Where the practitioner is not content that the consent is sound, they may not use the consent of a person with parental responsibility. The patient can be admitted to hospital for treatment under the Mental Health Act 1983 if they meet the relevant criteria. There is also, of course, the possibility of applying to the court for authority, but we would not expect that route to be used often where there is the statutory alternative of the Mental Health Act" (*Hansard*, HL Vol.689, col.1463).

The capacity of the patient to consent to the arrangements should be assessed according to the test set out in ss.2 and 3 of the MCA 2005 (MCA). The person undertaking the assessment would be the person who is offering the patient the opportunity to be admitted to the hospital or registered establishment.

Once admitted, a capable 16 or 17 year old can consent to treatment on the authority of s.8(1) of the Family Law Reform Act 1969 which provides the consent of such a child:

"to any surgical, medical or dental treatment which, in the absence of consent, would constitute a trespass to the person, shall be as effective as it would be if he were of full age; and where a minor has by virtue of this section given an effective consent to any treatment, it shall not be necessary to obtain any consent for it from his parent or guardian."

Although the current state of the law is that a mentally capable child's refusal of medical treatment can be overridden by a person with parental responsibility for that child (*Re W (A Minor) (Medical Treatment)*, below), it would be advisable to seek a declaration of the court before proceeding to treat on this basis; see the *Axon*, case below. If the child is mentally incapable of consenting to the treatment, the provisions of the MCA will apply.

The authority for the informal admission of a mentally incapable child aged 16 or 17 in a situation where the child is not subject to a deprivation of liberty is found in ss.5 and 6 of the MCA. Such a child can be treated for both physical and mental disorders if the treatment is in the child's best interests (s.4 of the MCA). However, if the treatment is ECT it may only be given if the requirements of s.58A are satisfied. If a deprivation of liberty is involved, a person with parental responsibility for the child could consent to the admission if the matter is within the zone of parental control: see below. If it is outside the zone, detention under this Act should be considered. The deprivation of the liberty of a person who is under the age of 18 cannot be authorised under the MCA.

*Children under the age of 16*

The legal position of patients aged under 16 was explained by the Minister:   **1–1174**

"Where the child is Gillick-competent [see *Gillick v West Norfolk and Wisbech AHA* [1986] A.C. 112]—that is, it is deemed that they understand what they are consenting to and the consequences of that consent—and the child consents, the draft [Code of Practice] plainly says that he can be admitted informally on that basis. . . . Where a Gillick-competent child refuses, our guidance will state that it would be unwise to rely on the consent of a person with parental responsibility, and to detain a Gillick-competent child against his wishes might be in breach of Art.5 of the European Convention on Human Rights. The Code will suggest that detention under the Mental Health Act should be considered, although again there is the possibility of an application to the court. . . . [W]here the child is not Gillick-competent to make such a decision, if the decision falls within the zone of parental [control], a person with parental responsibility will be able to give consent and the child can be admitted informally on the basis of that consent. Guidance as to what is within what is known as the zone of parental [control] will be given in the [Code of Practice.]. . . . Where the child is not Gillick-competent and either it is not considered that the child could be admitted informally on the basis of the consent of a person with parental responsibility, or no person with parental responsibility is prepared to consent, consideration should be given to the use of compulsion or, occasionally, an application to the court" (*Hansard*, HL Vol.689, cols 1465,1466).

The notion of the zone of parental control, which is considered in the Code of Practice at paras.36.9 to 36.15, and by Ralph Sandland in *Principles of Mental Health Law and Policy* (2010) at 18.97 to 18.106, has been criticised as being too vague to be helpful and so confused that it might cause actual harm (David Hewitt, "Too young to decide" (2008) 152 S.J. 37).

The *Gillick* case was considered in *Re W* (*A Minor*) (*Medical Treatment*) [1992] 4 All E.R. 627 CA, where Lord Donaldson M.R. held, at 639, 640, that:

"[N]o minor of whatever age has power by refusing consent to treatment to override a consent to treatment by someone who has parental responsibility for the minor and *a fortiori* a consent by the court. Nevertheless such a refusal is a very important consideration in making clinical judgments and for parents and the court in deciding whether themselves to give consent. Its importance increases with the age and maturity of the minor".

Although this finding may be regarded as the authoritative statement of the law on this issue, the child's refusal would clearly influence the doctor's decision. The decision in *Re W*, which was made before the Human Rights Act was passed, must be read in the light of subsequent case law, in particular *R. (on the application of Axon) v Secretary of State for Health and the Family Planning Association* [2006] EWHC 37 (Admin) where Silber J. made the following obiter remarks:

"As a matter of principle, it is difficult to see why a parent should still retain an Article 8 right to parental authority relating to a medical decision where the young person concerned *understands* the advice provided by the medical professional and its implications."

It is submitted that if the issue returned to the High Court, the court would be likely to find that the refusal of a *Gillick* competent child either to be admitted to hospital informally or to be treated cannot be overridden by a person with parental responsibility for that child because such action would contravene art.5 (for the admission) and art.8 (for the admission and the treatment) of the European Convention on Human Rights. Such an "informal" admission would also contravene art.37(d) of the United Nations *Convention on the Rights of the Child* which states:

"Every child deprived of his or her liberty shall have the right to prompt access to legal and other appropriate assistance, as well as the right to challenge the legality of the deprivation of his or her liberty before a court or other competent, independent and impartial authority, and to a prompt decision on any such action."

If it is felt that admission to hospital for treatment for mental disorder is necessary despite the refusal of a *Gillick* competent child to be admitted, an assessment for compulsory admission under Pt II of this Act should take place.

When assessing the capacity of a child under the age of 16, the test set out in ss.2 and 3 of the MCA should be applied even though, generally speaking, that Act does not apply to a person under the age of 16. Such an approach should be adopted because the test provides a practical dimension to the determination of capacity: see *Re C (Detention: Medical Treatment)* [1997] 2 F.L.R. 180 where Wall J. applied the common law test of capacity for adults established by the Court of Appeal in *Re MB (Medical Treatment)* [1997] 2 F.L.R. 426 to assessing the capacity of children under the age of 16.

It should be noted that in *Re R (A Minor) (Wardship: Medical treatment)* [1992] 1 F.L.R. 190, 200, Lord Donaldson M.R. said:

"'*Gillick* competence' is a developmental concept and will not be lost on a day-to-day or week-to-week basis. In the case of mental disability, that disability must also be taken into account, particularly where it is fluctuating in its effect."

The assessing clinician would need to consider whether the decision to agree to informal admission is really that of the child. In *Re T (Adult: Refusal of Medical Treatment)* [1992] 4 All E.R. 649,662, Lord Donaldson M.R. said:

"The real question in each case is, 'Does the patient really mean what he says or is he merely saying it for a quiet life, to satisfy someone else or because the advice and persuasion to which he has been subjected is such that he can no longer think and decide for himself?' In other words, 'Is it a decision in form only, not in reality?'".

His Lordship said that when considering the effect of outside influences, two aspects can be of crucial importance. They are the strength of will of the patient and the relationship of the "persuader" to the patient. With regard to the latter, the "influence of parents on their children . . . can be, but is by no means necessarily, much stronger than would be the case in other relationships". If the clinician concludes that the child has been subjected to the undue influence of the persuader when making the decision, the decision is invalid.

The medical treatment of a mentally incapable child who is under the age of 16 is governed by the common law. Although the MCA 2005 does not apply to the treatment of such children, it is submitted that clinicians should apply the checklist set out in s.4 of that Act when determining whether a proposed treatment is in the child's best interests.

If there is an irreconcilable conflict between clinicians and the parents of an incapacitated child of any age as to the treatment that the child should receive, the following advice contained in the Department of Health's *Reference guide to consent for examination or treatment* (2nd edn) at p.36, para.21 should be followed:

"The European Court of Human Rights judgment in a case where doctors treated a child contrary to his mother's wishes, without a court order (*Glass v United Kingdom*), made clear that the failure to refer such cases to the court is not only a breach of professional guidance but also potentially a breach of the European Convention on Human Rights. In situations where there is continuing disagreement or conflict between those with parental responsibility and doctors, and where the child is not competent to provide consent, the court should be involved to clarify whether a proposed treatment, or withholding of treatment, is in the child's best interests. Parental refusal can only be overridden in an emergency."

In a case where the primary purpose of the detention of a child of any age is not that of providing medical treatment for the child's mental disorder, consideration should be given to making an application under s.25 of the Children Act 1989 to authorise the detention: see the note on "Hospitals as 'secure accommodation'", below. Such an application might be appropriate if, for example, a learning disabled child is "likely to injure himself or other persons" (s.25(1)(b)).

Under ss.85 and 86 of the Children Act 1989, where a child is to be accommodated by a Primary Care Trust, Local Health Board or NHS trust for a consecutive period of at least three months, or where a child is to be accommodated in a care home or independent hospital for a similar period, the accommodating authority or the person carrying on the home must notify the local authority for the area where the child is ordinarily resident. The local authority is then placed under a duty to determine whether the child's welfare is being adequately safeguarded and to consider whether it should exercise any of its functions under the 1989 Act in respect of the child.

*Hospitals as "secure accommodation"*

**1–1175**    If the main objective is to detain the child because of the child's behavioural disturbance rather than to hospitalise the child to provide medical treatment for the child's mental disorder, it might be appropriate to invoke s.25 of the Children Act 1989 which sets out the criteria that must be satisfied before a child can be placed in secure accommodation; see further the *Code of Practice* at paras 36.17 and 36.18. Regulation 5 of the Children (Secure Accommodation) Regulations 1991 (SI 1991/1505) provides that s.25 does not apply to a child who is detained under any provision of this Act, although it will apply if the child is granted leave of absence under s.17 (*Hereford and Worcester County Council v S* [1993] 2 F.L.R. 360). Section 25 will also apply if the child is either admitted informally under this section or is admitted under the common law powers identified in *R. v Kirklees Metropolitan Borough Council Ex p. C*, above, if the unit of the hospital where the child is being accommodated is "secure accommodation". Secure accommodation is defined as "accommodation which is provided for the purpose of restricting the liberty of children to whom section 25 [of the 1989 Act] applies" (reg.2(1)). Paragraph 8.10 of the *Children Act 1989: Guidance and Regulations, Vol.4, Residential Care*, HMSO, 1991, states that "it is important to recognise that any practice or measure which prevents a child from leaving a room or building of his own free will may be deemed by the court to constitute restriction of liberty." In *R. v Northampton Juvenile Court Ex p. London Borough of Hammersmith and Fulham* [1985] F.L.R. 193 an adolescent "behaviour modification unit" of a private hospital where "the locking of the unit is part of the planned treatment regime which enables the medical staff to control, modify and eliminate aggressive and dangerous behaviour" was held to be "accommodation provided for the purpose of restricting liberty". Ewbank J. found that the purpose of the unit was to restrict the liberty of the children with a view to modifying their behaviour. A psychiatric unit which Douglas Brown J. held in *South Glamorgan County Council v W and B* [1993] 1 F.L.R. 574, to be "just short" of a secure unit was described in the following terms:

> "Although Merrifield is not a secure unit, we would endeavour to prevent [the child] from leaving the premises unaccompanied and it will be important that we have clear permission from the court to do this, otherwise it would not be possible to admit [the child] to our unit without her consent."

These cases were referred to by Wall J. in *Re C (Detention: Medical Treatment)* [1997] 2 F.L.R. 180, where his Lordship held that a psychiatric unit for the treatment of eating disorders did not constitute secure accommodation. The primary purpose of the placement of a child in the unit:

> "is to achieve treatment: the accommodation provides a structure for that treatment. The fact that such a structure includes a degree of restriction on the patient's liberty is ... an incident of the treatment programme, and the fact that steps can be taken to prevent [a child] leaving the premises does not, of itself, render the clinic secure accommodation" (at 192, 193).

In doubting the finding of Cazalet J. in *A Metropolitan Borough Council v DB* [1997] 1 F.L.R. 767, that a maternity ward to which entry and exit could only be effected by the use of a key out pass was secure accommodation, Wall J. said that the natural meaning of the words "provided for the purpose of restricting liberty" is "designed for, or having as its primary purpose" the restriction of liberty.

*The power of the High Court to make declarations regarding the detention of child patients*
In *Re C (Detention: Medical Treatment)*, above, a 16-year-old child needed treatment for **1–1176** anorexia nervosa in a private psychiatric unit in circumstances where the unit would not accept patients who were detained under this Act and where there were sound reasons for not instituting care proceedings. Wall J. held that:

(i) the High Court has the power under the inherent jurisdiction to order the detention of a child in a specified institution for the purpose of medical treatment being administered to the child without her agreement (see *Re W (A Minor) (Medical Treatment)*, above);

(ii) the court has power to authorise the use of reasonable force (if necessary) to detain the child in the institution and to ensure that any necessary treatment is received (see *Norfolk and Norwich Healthcare (NHS) Trust v W* [1996] 2 F.L.R. 613);

(iii) as the clinic was not "secure accommodation" for the purposes of s.25 of the Children Act 1989 and the attendant regulations (see above), the inherent jurisdiction was not ousted. An application under s.25 for a secure accommodation order would have had to have been made if the clinic did constitute secure accommodation;

(iv) although s.25 did not apply, the court should pay careful attention to the scheme laid down by Parliament under that section, and an order should not be made under the inherent jurisdiction unless the s.25 criteria are, by analogy to the facts of the case, met. The rights given to a child who is the subject of a s.25 application should be made available, and equivalent safeguards to those provided for in s.25 should be built into the order; and

(v) although consideration should always be given to alternative avenues (for example, under s.31 of the Children Act or the Mental Health Act) a refusal to exercise the inherent jurisdiction on the basis that an alternative avenue was available could lead to the child falling between several statutory stools, and not receiving the treatment that he or she needs. A primary purpose of the inherent jurisdiction is to fill lacunae in the statutory schemes; if the court is satisfied that in the particular circumstances of the case no statutory scheme is available, it should not hesitate to use its powers under the inherent jurisdiction.

## Accommodation, etc. for children
[**131A.**—(1) This section applies in respect of any patient who has not attained **1–1177** the age of 18 years and who—
(a) is liable to be detained in a hospital under this Act; or
(b) is admitted to, or remains in, a hospital in pursuance of such arrangements as are mentioned in section 131(1) above.
(2) The managers of the hospital shall ensure that the patient's environment in the hospital is suitable having regard to his age (subject to his needs).
(3) For the purpose of deciding how to fulfil the duty under subsection (2) above, the managers shall consult a person who appears to them to have knowledge or experience of cases involving patients who have not attained the age of 18 years which makes him suitable to be consulted.

(4) In this section, "hospital" includes a registered establishment.]

AMENDMENT

**1–1178**    This section was inserted by the Mental Health Act 2007 s.31(3).

DEFINITIONS

**1–1179**    patient: s.145(1).
hospital: s.145(1).
the managers: s.145(1).
registered establishment: ss.34(1), 145(1).

GENERAL NOTE

**1–1180**    This section places a duty on hospital managers to ensure that the hospital environment of a detained or informal mentally disordered patient who is under the age of 18 is "suitable having regard to his age (subject to his needs)" (subs.(2)). If such a child is placed in adult accommodation because his or her needs could not be met in an age appropriate environment, every effort should be made to tailor the environment to meet the child's needs.

A mentally disordered child is a child in need for the purposes of Pt III of the Children Act 1989 which is concerned with local authority support for children and families: see ibid., s.17(11). Under s.11 of the Children Act 2004, all NHS bodies have a duty to ensure that their functions (including contracted out functions) are discharged having regard to the need to safeguard and promote the welfare of children.

Prior to making a decision about how to fulfil the duty contained in this section with regard to an individual patient, the managers must consult with a suitable person as defined in subs.(3). This person is likely to be a child and adolescent mental health services professional.

The Minister of State said:

"We have used the word 'environment' because what matters to a child or young person goes well beyond mere physical segregation from older people. . . . By using the word 'environment' we can ensure not only that children and young people have separate facilities, but that they are appropriate physical facilities, with staff who have the right training to understand and address their specific needs as children, and a hospital routine that will allow their personal, social and educational development to continue as normally as possible" (*Hansard*, HC, Vol.461, col.1144).

As from December 1, 2008, Government policy is that no child under 16 should be placed in an adult psychiatric ward. Any such admissions are treated as Serious Untoward Incidents The notification to the Strategic Health Authority should include information on how the child will be moved to appropriate accommodation within 48 hours and in the intervening time, how the ward and staffing have been made appropriate to the child's needs (Department of Health, letter to SHA Chief Executives, June 29, 2007).

See s.140 for the duty of Primary Care Trusts and Local Health Boards to notify local authorities of the arrangements that are in force for the provision of accommodation or facilities designed to be specially suitable for mentally disorder child patients.

Article 37(c) of the United Nations *Convention on the Rights of the Child* states that "every child deprived of liberty shall be separated from adults unless it is considered in the child's best interest not to do so". The United Kingdom entered the following reservation to this aspect of the Convention:

"Where at any time there is a lack of suitable accommodation or adequate facilities for a particular individual in any institution in which young offenders are detained, or where the mixing of adults and children is deemed to be mutually beneficial, the United

Kingdom reserves the right not to apply Article 37(c) in so far as those provisions require children who are to be detained to be accommodated separately from adults."

The National Mental Health Development Unit (*www.nmhdu.org.uk*) has published the following briefing for commissioners of adult mental health services and child and adolescent mental health services: "Working together to provide age-appropriate environments and services for mental health patients aged under 18" (June 2009). The Royal College of Psychiatrists has developed a set of standards to identify safe and appropriate care for young people on adult wards: see "Safe and Appropriate Care for Young People on Adult Mental Health Wards", July, 2009.

The risks that children face when placed in adult psychiatric wards was highlighted by the Children's Commissioner for England in his report "Pushed into the Shadows: Young People's Experience of Adult Mental Health Facilities" (2007).

*Human Rights Act 1998*
Article 3 of the ECHR could be engaged if a child who has a history of being abused is **1–1181** placed on an adult ward which contains adults of the same sex as the child's abuser.

*Code of Practice*
This section is considered in Ch.36 at paras 36.67–36.74. **1–1182**

## Duty of managers of hospitals to give information to detained patients

**132.**—(1) The managers of a hospital or [registered establishment] in which a **1–1183** patient is detained under this Act shall take such steps as are practicable to ensure that the patient understands—

(a) under which of the provisions of this Act he is for the time being detained and the effect of that provision; and

(b) what rights of applying to a [tribunal] are available to him in respect of his detention under that provision;

and those steps shall be taken as soon as practicable after the commencement of the patient's detention under the provision in question.

(2) The managers of a hospital or [registered establishment] in which a patient is detained as aforesaid shall also take such steps as are practicable to ensure that the patient understands the effect, so far as relevant in his case, of sections 23, 25, 56 to 64, 66(1)(g), 118 and 120 above and section 134 below; and those steps shall be taken as soon as practicable after the commencement of the patient's detention in the hospital or [establishment].

(3) The steps to be taken under subsections (1) and (2) above shall include giving the requisite information both orally and in writing.

(4) The managers of a hospital or [registered establishment] in which a patient is detained as aforesaid shall, except where the patient otherwise requests, take such steps as are practicable to furnish the person (if any) appearing to them to be his nearest relative with a copy of any information given to him in writing under subsections (1) and (2) above; and those steps shall be taken when the information is given to the patient or within a reasonable time thereafter.

AMENDMENTS
The amendments to subss.(1), (2) and (3) were made by the Care Standards Act 2000 s.116, Sch.4 para.9(2). The reference to "establishment" in subs.(2) was substituted by the Mental Health Act 2007 s.32 (4), Sch.3 para.29. The reference to the tribunal in subs.(1)(b) was substituted by SI 2008/2883 art.9, Sch.3 para.63.

**1–1184**     the managers: s.145(1).
hospital: s.145(1).
registered establishment: ss.34(1), 145(1).
nearest relative: ss.26(3), 145(1).

GENERAL NOTE
**1–1185**     This section, requires the managers of a hospital or registered establishment to inform a detained patient of his or her legal position and rights. It does not apply to a community patient who has been recalled to hospital unless the patient's community treatment order is revoked and the patient becomes a detained patient. Unless the patient requests otherwise, the information must also be given to the patient's nearest relative. Section 132A places a similar duty on hospital managers with respect to community patients. There is also a duty placed on hospital managers to inform a patient when his or her detention is renewed (s.20(3); also see reg.26(1)(d) of the English Regulations and reg.8 of the Welsh Regulations).

In addition to the information provided for in this section, the patient should also be provided with relevant information about welfare benefits and the availability of legal representation at tribunals. As a result of the decision in *R. (on the application of Wooder) v Feggetter and Mental Health Act Commission*, noted under s.58(3)(b), a patient should be informed of the reasons for the imposition of treatment given without consent under s.58. The patient should also be informed when he or she is discharged from detention or if the authority for detention expires.

Regulation 26 of the English Regulations and regs.8, 22, 39 and 32 of the Welsh Regulations provides that the nearest relative of the patient must be informed of various statutory events concerning the patient unless the patient objects to the information being provided or providing the information would not be practicable.

*Human Rights Act 1998*
**1–1186**     Although this section does not place an obligation on the managers to inform the patient of the facts that gave rise to his or her detention, the European Court of Human Rights has held that the provisions of art.5(4) of the European Convention on Human Rights, which provides a detained person with a right to challenge the lawfulness of his detention speedily, would be breached if the person concerned is not "promptly and adequately informed of the facts and legal authority relied on to deprive him of his liberty" (*X v United Kingdom* (1981) 1 B.M.L.R. 98, at 119; see also *Van der Leer v Netherlands* (1990) 12 E.H.R.R. 567, at paras 27, 28). In *Fox, Campbell and Hartley v United Kingdom* (1991) 2 E.H.R.R. 287, the court said that a detained person has a right to be provided with the reasons for his detention in "simple, non-technical language that he can understand" and that the reasons must contain "the essential legal and factual grounds for his [detention]." Also of relevance in this context is the requirement in art.5(2) that anyone arrested or detained should be "informed promptly, in a language which he understands, of the reasons for his arrest . . .". The detention of a mentally disordered person is an "arrest" in Convention terms. In *Saadi v United Kingdom* (2007) 44 E.H.R.R. 50, para.55, the court held that a delay of 76 hours in providing the applicant with reasons for his detention is not compatible with the requirement in art.5(2) that such reasons should be given "promptly". It is likely that the ourt would support the contention that the provision of reasons to a mentally disordered person can be delayed until the person has the mental capacity to understand the reasons. In order to comply with art.5(2), a detained patient should be provided with information about the facts that gave rise to his or her detention as well as the legal information set out in subss.(1) and (2): see para. 2.13 of the *Code of Practice*. Although an approved mental health professional (AMHP) applicant might well have confirmed the facts that gave rise to the patient's detention during the interview required by s.13(2), it would be prudent for hospital staff to reinforce this information for such patients, and to provide such information to patients who were either admitted pursuant to a nearest relative application

or were too unwell to absorb the information during the interview with the AMHP. Also see finding (3) in *R. v East London and the City Mental Health Trust Ex p. Brandenburg*, which is considered in the General Note to s.3 under the heading "The re-sectioning of a patient subsequent to a discharge by the First-tier Tribunal (Mental Health) or the Mental Health Review Tribunal for Wales".

*Code of Practice*
Guidance this section and on providing information to patients and their nearest relatives **1–1187** is given in Ch.2.

*Leaflets*
Model leaflets on patients' rights that have been designed to assist hospitals and local **1–1188** social services authorities to meet their legal obligations under this section have been produced by the Department of Health. They can be accessed at: *www.dh.gov.uk/en/ Publicationsandstatistics/Publications/PublicationsPolicyAndGuidance/DH_089275* (accessed July 23, 2010).

*Subsection (1)*
DETAINED UNDER THIS ACT.   There is no requirement to give information under this sec- **1–1189** tion to patients who are detained under this Act in places other than a hospital or registered establishment, e.g. a patient who is detained in a police station under s.136.

SUCH STEPS AS ARE PRACTICABLE.   The steps must include giving the requisite information both orally and in writing (subs.(3)).

ENSURE THAT THE PATIENT UNDERSTANDS.   If the patient initially fails to understand the information provided, the managers must persist with their efforts in an attempt to achieve the required level of understanding. In appropriate cases, the managers should use an interpreter.

FOR THE TIME BEING DETAINED.   This provision requires the patient to be provided with the relevant information when the section under which he or she is detained changes.

RIGHTS OF APPLYING TO A TRIBUNAL.   If the patient (or his or her nearest relative) has missed an opportunity to apply to a tribunal because of a failure to provide the information set out in this provision, the patient (or his or her representative) should request that the Secretary of State refers the case to the tribunal under s.67 or s.71.

AS SOON AS PRACTICABLE.   Having regard to the patient's state of mind and his or her ability to understand the information.

*Subsection (2)*
Sections 23, 25 and 66(1)(a) are concerned with the powers of the responsible clinician, **1–1190** the hospital managers and the nearest relative to discharge the patient, ss.56 to 64 contain the consent to treatment provisions, s.118 provides for the publishing of the *Code of Practice*, s.120 is concerned with the Care Quality Commission and the Welsh Ministers' functions relating to the general protection of patients who are subject to this Act and s.134 deals with the withholding of detained patient's correspondence.

*Subsection (4)*
If the patient is mentally incapable of requesting that the information be not copied to his **1–1191** or her nearest relative, the information should be sent unless the patient, when mentally capable, had indicated that the nearest relative should not be contacted by the hospital. This opinion is subject to the note on "such steps as are practicable", below.

PATIENT OTHERWISE REQUESTS.    It is submitted that the patient should be informed of the provisions of this subsection at the same time as he or she is given the information required by subs.(1) and (2). A nearest relative will usually be informed about an admission under s.2 (s.11(3)) and consulted about an admission under s.3 (s.11(4)).

SUCH STEPS AS ARE PRACTICABLE.    It is submitted that it would not be practicable to copy the information to the nearest relative of a mentally incapacitated patient if to do so would be likely to harm the patient and therefore breach the patient's rights under art.8 of the European Convention on Human Rights: see *(R. (on the application of E) v Bristol City Council*, noted under "not reasonably practicable" in s.11(4).

APPEARING TO THEM.    The hospital managers must take reasonable steps to ascertain the identity of the patient's nearest relative.

NEAREST RELATIVE.    Or acting nearest relative (s.29(6)). If the nearest relative is mentally incapable, an AMHP should be asked to consider making an application to the court under s.29(3)(b) for an acting nearest relative to be appointed.

## [Duty of managers of hospitals to give information to community patients

**1–1192**    **132A.**—(1) The managers of the responsible hospital shall take such steps as are practicable to ensure that a community patient understands—
(a)  the effect of the provisions of this Act applying to community patients; and
(b)  what rights of applying to a [tribunal] are available to him in that capacity; and those steps shall be taken as soon as practicable after the patient becomes a community patient.
(2) The steps to be taken under subsection (1) above shall include giving the requisite information both orally and in writing.
(3) The managers of the responsible hospital shall, except where the community patient otherwise requests, take such steps as are practicable to furnish the person (if any) appearing to them to be his nearest relative with a copy of any information given to him in writing under subsection (1) above; and those steps shall be taken when the information is given to the patient or within a reasonable time thereafter.]

AMENDMENTS
This section was inserted by the Mental Health Act 2007 s.32(4), Sch.3 para.30. The reference to the tribunal in subs.(1)(b) was substituted by SI 2008/2883 art.9, Sch.3 para.64.

DEFINITIONS
**1–1193**    the managers: s.145(1).
responsible hospital: ss.17A(7), 135(1).
community patient: ss.17A(7), 145(1).
nearest relative: s.145(1).

GENERAL NOTE
**1–1194**    This section places a duty on the managers of the responsible hospital to inform a community patient, both orally and in writing, of the legal effect of being a community patient and of his or her rights to make an application to a tribunal. Unless the patient otherwise requests, the written information must also be sent to the patient's nearest relative. This section mirrors the duty contained in s.132 and reference should be made to the notes on that section. There is also a duty placed on hospital managers to inform a patient when his or her CTO renewed (s.20A(5); also see reg.26(1)(g) of the English Regulations and reg.22(2) of the Welsh Regulations).

**1–1195**

*Code of Practice*
Guidance on this section this section and on providing information to patients and their **1–1195**
nearest relatives is contained in Ch.2.

## Duty of managers of hospitals to inform nearest relatives of discharge

**133.**—(1) Where a patient liable to be detained under this Act in a hospital or **1–1196**
[registered establishment] is to be discharged otherwise than by virtue of an order
for discharge made by his nearest relative, the managers of the hospital or [registered establishment] shall, subject to subsection (2) below, take such steps as are
practicable to inform the person (if any) appearing to them to be the nearest relative of the patient; and that information shall, if practicable, be given at least seven
days before the date of discharge.

[(1A) The reference in subsection (1) above to a patient who is to be discharged
includes a patient who is to be discharged from hospital under section 17A above.

(1B) Subsection (1) above shall also apply in a case where a community patient
is discharged under section 23 or 72 above (otherwise than by virtue of an order
for discharge made by his nearest relative), but with the reference in that subsection to the managers of the hospital or registered establishment being read as a
reference to the managers of the responsible hospital.]

(2) Subsection (1) above shall not apply if the patient or his nearest relative has
requested that information about the patient's discharge should not be given under
this section.

AMENDMENTS
In subs.(1) the words in square brackets were substituted by the Care Standards Act 2000
s.116, Sch.4 para.9(2). Subsections (1A) and (1B) were inserted by the Mental Health Act
2007 s.32(4), Sch.3 para.31.

DEFINITIONS
    patient: s.145(1).                                                           **1–1197**
    hospital: s.145(1).
    registered establishment: ss.34(1), 145(1).
    nearest relative: ss.26(3), 145(1).
    the managers: s.145(1).
    community patient: ss.17A(7), 145(1).

GENERAL NOTE
This section places a duty on the managers of hospitals or registered establishments to **1–1198**
inform the nearest relative of a detained patient that the patient is about to be discharged
from detention (including being discharged subject to a community treatment order) or discharged from a community treatment order (other than a discharge ordered by the patient's
nearest relative). The information should be given at least seven days before the date of discharge if this is practicable. The duty does not arise if either the patient or his or her nearest
relative has requested that this information should not be given.
Restricted patients, patients remanded to hospital under s.35 or s.36 and patients subject
to interim hospital orders under s.38 do not have nearest relatives for the purposes of this
Act.

*Subsection (1)*
SUCH STEPS AS ARE PRACTICABLE. See the note on s.132(4).            **1–1199**

**Correspondence of patients**

**1–1200**   **134.**—(1) A postal packet addressed to any person by a patient detained in a hospital under this Act and delivered by the patient for dispatch may be withheld from [the postal operator concerned]—

    (a) if that person has requested that communications addressed to him by the patient should be withheld; or

    (b) subject to subsection (3) below, if the hospital is [one at which high security psychiatric services are provided] and the managers of the hospital consider that the postal packet is likely—

        (i) to cause distress to the person to whom it is addressed or to any other person (not being a person on the staff of the hospital); or

        (ii) to cause danger to any person;

and any request for the purposes of paragraph (a) above shall be made by a notice in writing given to the managers of the hospital, the [approved clinician with overall responsibility for the patient's case] or the Secretary of State.

(2) Subject to subsection (3) below, a postal packet addressed to a patient detained [under this Act in a hospital at which high security psychiatric services are provided] may be withheld from the patient if, in the opinion of the managers of the hospital, it is necessary to do so in the interests of the safety of the patient or for the protection of other persons.

(3) Subsections (1)(b) and (2) above do not apply to any postal packet addressed by a patient to, or sent to a patient by or on behalf of—

    (a) any Minister of the Crown [or the Scottish Ministers] or Member of either House of Parliament [or a Member of the Scottish Parliament] [or of the Northern Ireland Assembly];

  [(aa) any of the Welsh Ministers, the Counsel General of the Welsh Assembly Government or a member of the National Assembly for Wales;]

  [(b) any judge or officer of the Court of Protection, any of the Court of Protection Visitors or any person asked by that Court for a report under section 49 of the Mental Capacity Act 2005 concerning the patient;]

    (c) the Parliamentary Commissioner for Administration, [the Scottish Public Services Ombudsman] [the Public Services Ombudsman for Wales] the Health Service Commissioner for England, [. . .] or a Local Commissioner within the meaning of Part III of the Local Government Act 1974;

  [(ca) the Care Quality Commission;]

    (d) [the First-tier Tribunal or the Mental Health Review Tribunal for Wales];

    (e) a [Strategic Health Authority,] [Local Health Board][, Special Health Authority or Primary Care Trust]], a local social services authority, a Community Health Council [. . .]] or a [local probation board established under section 4 of the Criminal Justice and Court Services Act 2000] [or a provider of probation services];

  [(ea) a provider of a patient advocacy and liaison service for the assistance of patients at the hospital and their families and carers;

  (eb) a provider of independent advocacy services for the patient;]

    (f) the managers of the hospital in which the patient is detained;

    (g) any legally qualified person instructed by the patient to act as his legal adviser; or

    (h) the European Commission of Human Rights or the European Court of Human Rights [and for the purposes of paragraph (d) above the reference to the First-tier Tribunal is a reference to that tribunal so far as it is acting for the purposes of any proceedings under this Act or paragraph 5(2) of the Schedule to the Repatriation of Prisoners Act 1984.]

   [(3A) In subs.(3) above—

   (a) "a patient advocacy and liaison service" means a service of a description prescribed by regulations made by the Secretary of State, and

  [(b) "independent advocacy services" means services provided under—

      (i) arrangements under section 130A above;

      (ii) arrangements under section 248 of the National Health Service Act 2006 or section 187 of the National Health Service (Wales) Act 2006; or

      (iii) arrangements of a description prescribed as mentioned in paragraph (a) above.]

   (4) The managers of a hospital may inspect and open any postal packet for the purposes of determining—

   (a) whether it is one to which subsection (1) or (2) applies, and

   (b) in the case of a postal packet to which subsection (1) or (2) above applies, whether or not it should be withheld under that subsection;

and the power to withhold a postal packet under either of those subsections includes power to withhold anything contained in it.

   (5) Where a postal packet or anything contained in it is withheld under subsection (1) or (2) above the managers of the hospital shall record that fact in writing.

   (6) Where a postal packet or anything contained in it is withheld under subsection (1)(b) or (2) above the managers of the hospital shall within seven days give notice of that fact to the patient and, in the case of a packet withheld under subsection (2) above, to the person (if known) by whom the postal packet was sent; and any such notice shall be given in writing and shall contain a statement of the effect of [section 134A(1) to (4)].

   (7) The functions of the managers of a hospital under this section shall be discharged on their behalf by a person on the staff of the hospital appointed by them for that purpose and different persons may be appointed to discharge different functions.

   (8) The Secretary of State may make regulations with respect to the exercise of the powers conferred by this section.

   (9) In this section [and section 134A] "hospital" has the same meaning as in Part II of this Act, [and "postal operator" and] "postal packet" [have] the same meaning as in [the Postal Services Act 2000].

AMENDMENTS

   In subss.(1) and (2) the words in square brackets were substituted by the Health Act 1999 s.65, Sch.4 para.68. The words in the second set of square brackets in subs.(1) were substituted by the Mental Health Act 2007 s.14(4).

   The words in square brackets in subs.(3)(a) were inserted by the Scotland Act 1998 (Consequential Modifications) (No.2) Order 1999 (SI 1999/1820) art.4, Sch.2 para.71 and the Northern Ireland Act 1998 s.99, Sch.13 para.5(2). Subs.(3)(aa) was substituted by SI 2007/1388 art.3, Sch.1 para.18. Subs.(3)(b) was substituted by the Mental Capacity Act 2005 s.67(1), Sch.6 para.29(2). In subs.(3)(c) the words in square brackets were inserted by the Government of Wales Act 1998 s.125, Sch.12 para.22. and SI 2004/ 1823 and substituted by the Public Services Ombudsman (Wales) Act 2005 s.39(1),

Sch.6 para.21. The words omitted were repealed by s.39(2), Sch.7. Subs.(3)(ca) was inserted by the Health and Social Care Act 2008 s.52, Sch.3 para.11.

In subs.(3)(e) the words in square brackets were substituted by the Health Authorities Act 1995 s.2(1), Sch.1 para.107(10), the Health Act 1999 (Supplementary, Consequential, etc., Provisions) Order 2000 (SI 2000/90) Sch.1 para.16(7), the Criminal Justice and Court Services Act 2000 s.74, Sch.7 para.74, the NHS Reform and Health Care Professions Act 2002 s.19(6), the National Health Service Reform and Health Care Professions Act 2002 (Supplementary, Consequential, etc. Provisions) Regulations 2002 (SI 2002/2469) reg.4, Sch.1 SI 2007/961 art.3, Sch. para.13(10) and SI 2008/912 art.3, Sch.1 Pt 1 para.7. The words omitted were repealed by the Local Government and Public Involvement in Health Act 2007 s.241, Sch.18 Pt 18.

Paras (ea) and (eb) of subs.(3) and subs.(3A) were inserted by the Health and Social Care Act 2001 s.67, Sch.5 para.6. Subs.(3A) was substituted by the Mental Health Act 2007 s.30(3).

Subs.(3)(d) and the words in square brackets at the end of that subsection were substituted and inserted by SI 2008/2883 art.9, Sch.3 para.65.

The amendments to subs.(6) were made by the Health and Social Care Act 2008 s.52, Sch.3 para.11.

The amendments to subs.(9) were made by the Postal Services Act 2000 Sch.8 para.19, and Sch.9. and the Health and Social Care Act 2008 s.52, Sch.3 para.11.

DEFINITIONS

**1–1201**    patient: s.145(1).
 hospital: ss.34(2), 145(1).
 approved clinician: s.145(1).
 high security psychiatric services: s.145(1).
 special managers: s.145(1).
 the managers: s.145(1).
 local social services authority: s.145(1).
 Health Authority: s.145(1).
 Special Health Authority: s.145(1).

GENERAL NOTE

**1–1202**    This section provides authority for the inspection and withholding of a detained patient's outgoing and incoming mail. There is no power to take such action under common law or under the Mental Capacity Act 2005, or to interfere with the mail of an informal patient.

If either a detained or an informal patient is sent articles of potential danger, such as weapons, explosives or matches, through the mail, s.3(1) of the Criminal Law Act 1967 and the common law provide authority for hospital staff to take reasonable measures to prevent the patient from receiving or keeping the article in his possession (see, further, *Consultative Document*, para.10.28 and Appendix A.). The Malicious Communications Act 1988 makes provision for the prosecution of persons who send or deliver letters or other articles for the purpose of causing distress or anxiety.

Further provisions relating to items brought to hospital premises for patients, patients' access to computer equipment and mobile phones, patients' post and patients' telephone calls for patients at Ashworth, Broadmoor and Rampton Hospitals can be found in the Safety and Security in Ashworth, Broadmoor and Rampton Hospitals Directions 2000 (as amended) which are reproduced at Appendix C. In *R. v Franey Ex p. Warren* [1998] EWHC 5, Turner J., in refusing leave to bring judicial review proceedings, held that the decision of the Chief Executive of Broadmoor Hospital to remove, inter alia, personal computers from patients' rooms was a lawful decision which did not prevent patients from communicating with the authorities or the courts. Arrangements had been made for patients to have access to their computers in the hospital's day areas.

The Reference Guide, at paras 14.16 to 14.20, describes the procedure for reviewing decisions to withhold a patient's mail:

"MHAC must review any decision to withhold post (except at the request of the addressee) if an application to review such a decision is made by the relevant person within six months of when they receive written notice of the decision.

In the case of outgoing post, it is only the patient who may apply, but in the case of incoming mail, both the patient and the sender may apply.

The application need not be made in writing, but must be made in accordance with guidance provided by MHAC. The applicant must provide MHAC with the written notice of the withholding or a copy of it.

When reviewing a withholding decision, MHAC may require the relevant people to produce any documents, information and evidence (including what was withheld) which it reasonably requires.

MHAC can direct that what was withheld should no longer be withheld. The managers must comply with any such direction."

The functions of the Mental Health Act Commission (MHAC) are now performed by the Care Quality Commission ("the Commission") or, in relation to Wales, the Welsh Ministers.

For the procedure to be adopted when mail is opened and inspected, see reg.29 of the English Regulations and reg.41 of the Welsh Regulations.

*Human Rights Act 1998*

A restriction on a patient's freedom to communicate with others constitutes an inter- **1–1203** ference with the patient's right to respect for his private life under art.8(1) of the European Convention on Human Rights. Such an interference will contravene art.8 unless it is "in accordance with the law", pursues one or more of the legitimate aims referred to in art.8(2) and is "necessary in a democratic society" in order to achieve them. It is likely that the power contained in this section does not contravene art.8, given the interpretation that the Court has given to art.8(2) in *Herczegfalvy v Austria* (1993) 15 E.H.R.R. 437, at paras 85 to 92; also see the note on art.10(2) of the Convention.

*Subsection (1)*

This subsection authorises a person appointed by the hospital managers (subss.(4), (7)) to **1–1204** withhold a detained patient's outgoing mail if the addressee has requested that the communications addressed to him by the patient should be withheld. The outgoing mail of patients detained in a high security psychiatric hospital can also be withheld if it is felt that the communication is likely to cause distress or danger to any person. It is intended that this power should be used to withhold, for example, threatening letters, letters to victims of crime, or dangerous objects. There is no provision equivalent to that which was contained in s.36 of the Mental Health Act 1959 which authorised the withholding of outgoing mail which would "be likely to prejudice the interests of the patient". A patient whose mail is withheld under subs.(1)(b) or (2) can have the decision reviewed by the Commission or, in relation to Wales, the Welsh Ministers (s.134A).

Paragraph 1.135 of the MHAC's , *Thirteenth Biennial Report* 2007–2009, states:

"Some medium secure hospital policies stipulate that, whilst it is unlawful to withhold incoming mail from a patient, or to open mail addressed to a patient without that patient's permission, if a staff member has concerns about the possible contents of a particular package or letter, it is acceptable for the patient to be advised that he or she may only open it in a controlled environment (i.e. the nurses' office) in the presence of staff. Once open, the contents may be treated like any other item of patient property and confiscated if necessary. The MHAC accepts the need for such arrangements as a last resort, but they should be carefully monitored and reviewed to ensure that they are and continue to be a justified interference with the patient's rights to privacy, and must never [be] used as a blanket measure irrespective of individual risk assessment."

POSTAL PACKET. Is defined in subs.(9).

WITHHELD. There is no authority for the hospital managers to censor correspondence, i.e. to strike out certain passages in a letter. However, there is power to withhold something contained in a postal packet (subs.(4)).

Paragraph 14.15 of the Reference Guide states:

"In practice, because of MHAC's power to review decisions to withhold post, anything addressed to a patient which is withheld should be retained for at least six months, unless it is necessary to give it to the police or other similar body. After that—assuming that MHAC is not in the process of reviewing the decision—it may be returned to the sender, if that can be done safely."

This section does not confer on a hospital a power to require the return of a patient's mail once it has reached its destination. In *Broadmoor Hospital Authority v R* [2000] 2 All E.R. 727, the Court of Appeal refused the hospital's application for an injunction requiring the return of a draft manuscript of a book which had been sent by a patient to his agent. The hospital considered that the contents of the book, if published, would be prejudicial to the interests of the sender and would cause distress to the family of his victim. The court held that it could, if appropriate, grant an injunction to restrain an activity outside the hospital if it could be shown that it was having a sufficiently significant impact on the security of the hospital or the treatment of a patient; see further the General Note to this Act under the heading "Injunctions to support an authority's performance of its duties under this Act".

PARAGRAPH (A). The review procedure set out in s.121(7)(8) does not apply to outgoing mail which is withheld under the provisions of this paragraph.

REQUESTED. The Hospital Managers are not placed under a statutory obligation to inform the patient that such a request has been made. It is suggested that the withheld post be retained by the hospital managers until the patient ceases to be detained when it should be returned to him or her.

PARAGRAPH (B): MANAGERS OF THE HOSPITAL. Their functions shall be discharged by a member of the hospital staff (subs.(7)).

*Subsection (2)*

**1–1205** This subsection authorises the withholding of the incoming mail of a patient detained in a high security hospital if it is considered that such action is necessary in the interests of the safety of the patient or for the protection of other persons. Either the patient or the sender can have the decision reviewed by the Commission or, in relation to Wales, the Welsh Ministers (s.134A). There is no power to withhold incoming mail on the ground that it would cause distress to the patient.

Paragraph 1.127 of the MHAC's *Thirteenth Biennial Report* 2007–2009, states:

"Legal advice received by the MHAC in 1997 suggested that the first ground under s.134(2) for withholding mail addressed to High Security Hospital patients ('necessary in the interests of the safety of the patient') should not be deemed to extend to include the patient's health or welfare. However, the second ground ('protection of others') might apply individually in these cases to the authors of the letters, or indeed to classes of persons, such as women or children, provided that the actual risk posed by the patient should he receive such material is clearly expressed. Such a risk could, in our view, be related to the patient's pathology and the treatment he is receiving for it, but a decision must be taken on the facts of any individual case."

HIGH SECURITY.   There is no power to withhold the incoming mail of a patient who is detained in a hospital which is not a high security hospital.

THE MANAGERS.   See subs.(7).

*Subsection (3)*

This subsection excludes the provisions of subss.(1)(b) and (2) in respect of certain **1–1206** bodies and individuals. Any person listed in this subsection can request that communications addressed to him or her by the patient be withheld (subs.(1)(a)).

Although the Criminal Cases Review Commission is not a body that is listed in this provision, it is suggested that, given the function of the Commission, letters addressed to it should not be opened unless the Commission has requested otherwise.

The Mental Health Act Commission held the view that:

"patient telephone calls to the same organisations [listed in this subsection] should attract a similar degree of privacy and that whilst any supervision of phone calls should not generally include listening into the contents of the calls (in certain circumstances this may be necessary) such listening in should never take place when the patient's phone call is with one of the specific organisations referred to above" (MHAC, *Sixth Biennial Report* 1993–1995, para.9.8).

Any policy that restricts a patient's access to a telephone must be consistent with the patient's rights under art.8 of the European Convention on Human Rights (*Valle v Finland* [2000] M.H.L.R. 255).

PATIENT ADVOCACY AND LIAISON SERVICE.   See the note of "Regulations" in subs.(3A).

*Subsection (3A)*

REGULATIONS.   For the purposes of subs.(3)(ea), above, "patient advocacy and liaison **1–1207** service" is defined in reg.31(1) of the English Regulations.

For the purposes of para.(b)(iii), the prescribed arrangements are arrangements in respect of independent mental capacity advocates: see *ibid.*, reg.31(2) and reg.42 of the Welsh Regulations.

*Subsection (4)*

THE MANAGERS.   See subs.(7).                                                                **1–1208**

OPEN.   It will not usually be necessary to open the mail of patients who are not detained in high security hospitals, as the requirements of subs.(1)(a) can be met by looking at the addresses on patients' outgoing mail. However, it would be permissible for such mail to be opened if staff had a reasonable suspicion that a postal packet contained letters which the patient wanted the addressee to forward to people who had requested that mail be withheld. In high security psychiatric hospitals it will be necessary to open both outgoing and incoming mail if there is a reasonable suspicion that either subs.(1) or (2) applies. If, as a result of the inspection, nothing is withheld from the patient, the procedure set out in reg.29(1) of the English Regulations should be followed.

Although the issue has not been tested in the courts, it is likely that the inspection of the contents of a postal packet can include viewing the contents of a computer disc.

*Subsection (5)*

**1–1209**    RECORD. See reg.29(2) of the English Regulations and reg.41(a) of the Welsh Regulations.

WITHHELD. The obligation to record does not apply to the opening of mail under subs.(4).

*Subsection (6)*

**1–1210**    NOTICE. See reg.29(3) of the 2008.

*Subsection (7)*

**1–1211**    SHALL BE DISCHARGED. The hospital managers must appoint a member of staff to discharge their functions under this section. This person will need to consult with the patient's responsible clinician when a decision is made to withhold post.

*Subsection (8)*

**1–1212**    SECRETARY OF STATE. The functions of the Minister, so far as exercisable in relation to Wales, are exercised by the Welsh Ministers (see the General Note to this Act and SI 1999/ 672, art.2, Sch.1).

*Subsection (9)*

**1–1213**    POSTAL OPERATOR. Means "a person who provides the service of conveying postal packets from one place to another by post or any of the incidental services of receiving, collecting, sorting and delivering such packets" (Postal Services Act 2000 s.125(1)).

POSTAL PACKET. Means "a letter, parcel, packet or other article transmitted by post": 2000 Act s.125(1).

## [Review of decisions to withhold correspondence

**1–1214**    **134A.**—(1) The regulatory authority must review any decision to withhold a postal packet (or anything contained in it) under subsection (1)(b) or (2) of section 134 if an application for a review of the decision is made—

   (a) in a case under subsection (1)(b) of that section, by the patient; or

   (b) in a case under subsection (2) of that section, either by the patient or by the person by whom the postal packet was sent.

(2) An application under subsection (1) must be made within 6 months of receipt by the applicant of the notice referred to in section 134(6).

(3) On an application under subsection (1), the regulatory authority may direct that the postal packet (or anything contained in it) is not to be withheld.

(4) The managers of the hospital concerned must comply with any such direction.

(5) The Secretary of State may by regulations make provision in connection with the making to and determination by the Care Quality Commission of applications under subsection (1), including provision for the production to the Commission of any postal packet which is the subject of such an application.

(6) The Welsh Ministers may by regulations make provision in connection with the making to them of applications under subsection (1), including provision for the production to them of any postal packet which is the subject of such an application.]

AMENDMENT

This section was inserted by the Health and Social Care Act 2008 s.52, Sch.3 para.12.

DEFINITIONS
    the regulatory authority: s.145(1).                              **1–1215**
    postal packet: s.134(9).
    patient: s.145(1).
    the managers: s.145(1).
    hospital:ss.134(9), 24(2), 145(1).

GENERAL NOTE
    This section provides that the regulatory authority must review any decision made under **1–1216**
s.134 to withhold a postal packet or anything contained within it if an application is made
by a person specified in subs.(1)(a) or (b) within the timescale set out in subs.(2).
Subsection (3) provides that such a review could result in the regulatory authority directing
that the postal packet is not withheld.

*Subsection (1)*
    REGULATORY AUTHORITY.   Is the Care Quality Commission or, in relation to Wales, the **1–1217**
Welsh Ministers (s.145(1)).

## Warrant to search for and remove patients

    **135.**—(1) If it appears to a justice of the peace, on information on oath laid by **1–1218**
an [approved mental health professional], that there is reasonable cause to suspect
that a person believed to be suffering from mental disorder—
    (a)  has been, or is being, ill-treated, neglected or kept otherwise than under
          proper control, in any place within the jurisdiction of the justice, or
    (b)  being unable to care for himself, is living alone in any such place,
the justice may issue a warrant authorising any constable [. . .] to enter, if need be
by force, any premises specified in the warrant in which that person is believed to
be, and, if thought fit, to remove him to a place of safety with a view to the making
of an application in respect of him under Part II of this Act, or of other arrangements for his treatment or care.

    (2) If it appears to a justice of the peace, on information on oath laid by any
constable or other person who is authorised by or under this Act or under [article
8 of the Mental Health (Care and Treatment) (Scotland) Act 2003 (Consequential
Provisions) Order 2005] to take a patient to any place, or to take into custody or
retake a patient who is liable under this Act or under the said [article 8] to be so
taken or retaken—
    (a)  that there is reasonable cause to believe that the patient is to be found on
          premises within the jurisdiction of the justice; and
    (b)  that admission to the premises has been refused or that a refusal of such
          admission is apprehended,
the justice may issue a warrant authorising any constable [. . .] to enter the premises, if need be by force, and remove the patient.

    (3) A patient who is removed to a place of safety in the execution of a warrant
issued under this section may be detained there for a period not exceeding 72
hours.

    [(3A) A constable, an approved mental health professional or a person author-
ised by either of them for the purposes of this subsection may, before the end of the
period of 72 hours mentioned in subsection (3) above, take a person detained in a
place of safety under that subsection to one or more other places of safety.

(3B) A person taken to a place of safety under subsection (3A) above may be detained there for a period ending no later than the end of the period of 72 hours mentioned in subsection (3) above.]

(4) In the execution of a warrant issued under subsection (1) above, [a constable] shall be accompanied by an [approved mental health professional] and by a registered medical practitioner, and in the execution of a warrant issued under subsection (2) above [a constable] may be accompanied—

(a) by a registered medical practitioner;

(b) by any person authorised by or under this Act or under [article 8 of the Mental Health (Care and Treatment) (Scotland) Act 2003 (Consequential Provisions) Order 2005] section 83 of the [Mental Health (Scotland) Act 1984] to take or retake the patient.

(5) It shall not be necessary in any information or warrant under subsection (1) above to name the patient concerned.

(6) In this section "place of safety" means residential accommodation provided by a local social services authority under Part III of the National Assistance Act 1948 [. . .], a hospital as defined by this Act, a police station, [an independent hospital or care home] for mentally disordered persons or any other suitable place the occupier of which is willing temporarily to receive the patient.

AMENDMENTS

In subss.(2) and (4) the words in square brackets which refer to the Mental Health (Care and Treatment) (Scotland) Act 2003 were substituted by SI 2005/2078 Sch.1 para.2(9). In subss.(1) and (2) the words omitted were repealed by the Police and Criminal Evidence Act 1984 s.119, Sch.7. In subs.(4) the words in square brackets were substituted by s.119, Sch.6 para.26. In subs.(6) the words omitted were repealed by the National Health Service and Community Care Act 1990 s.66(2), Sch.10 and the words in square brackets were substituted by the Care Standards Act 2000 s.116, Sch.4 para.9(9). The references to approved mental health professional in subss.(1) and (4) were made by the Mental Health Act 2007 s.21, Sch.2 para.10. Subss.(3A) and (3B) were inserted by s.44(2).

DEFINITIONS

**1–1219**
approved mental health professional: s.145(1), (1AC).
mental disorder: ss.1, 145(1).
patient: s.145(1).
local social services authority: s.145(1).
hospital: ss.34(2), 145(1).
independent hospital: s.145(1).
care home: s.145(1).

GENERAL NOTE

**1–1220**
This section provides for a magistrate to issue a warrant authorising a policeman to enter premises, using force if necessary, for the purpose of removing a mentally disordered person to a place of safety for a period not exceeding 72 hours. It provides a means by which an entry which would otherwise be a trespass, becomes a lawful act. The warrant is executed once entry to the premises has been effected by the constable, either by force or by invitation. However, if the occupier of the premises allows entry without knowledge of the existence of the warrant and without the constable producing the warrant to him, it is submitted that the warrant has not been executed. Note the distinction between warrants issued under subss.(1) and (2). Subsection (1) is used where there is concern about the well being of a person who is not liable to be detained under this Act. Subsection (2) is used where the person concerned is either liable to be detained or is required to reside at a particular place

under the terms of guardianship, a community treatment order (CTO) or under the Scottish legislation. In both instances, the person can be transferred to another place of safety during the 72-hour period (subss.(3)(A), (3)(B)) and reasonable force may be used in the transfer if this proves to be necessary (s.137).

A person who is detained under this section can be restrained in order to prevent risk to others. In *R. (on the application of Munjaz) v Mersey Care NHS Trust* [[2003] EWCA Civ 1036; [2003] M.H.L.R. 362, Hale L.J. said at para.46:

"There is a general power to take such steps as are reasonably necessary and proportionate to protect others from the immediate risk of significant harm. This applies whether or not the patient lacks the capacity to make decisions for himself."

"Guidance on Responding to People with Mental Ill Health or Learning Disabilities", National Police Improvement Agency (2010), para.6.8.7, states that a warrant will also "permit a degree of control of others within the premises to ensure the safety of everyone present . . . "

Part IV of this Act does not apply to a patient who is detained under this section (s.56(3)(b)). If the person is mentally capable of making a decision about treatment, the common law enables him or her to refuse to be treated for either a physical or mental disorder. However, if the person is assessed as being mentally incapable of making a decision about treatment, the treatment can be provided under s.5 of the Mental Capacity Act 2005 if it is deemed to be in his or her best interests. Restraint can be used in the provision of the treatment if its use is both necessary and proportionate to prevent harm to the person (2005 Act s.6).

By virtue of para.16.1 of Sch.1 to the Magistrates Courts Fees Order 2008 (SI 2008/1052) a fee of £18 shall be charged for the issuing of a warrant under this section.

A warrant under this section would not be required if a co-owner or, possibly, a co-occupier of the premises gives permission for the mental health professionals to enter: see the note on "enter and inspect" in s.115. If permission is granted to enter premises, such as a hotel, where members of the public can reside, a warrant under this section is not required to enter a room in the premises that the mentally disordered person is occupying if that person has no right of exclusive occupation of the room (*R. v Rosso* [2003] EWCA Crim 3242; [2003] M.H.L.R. 404). The Court of Appeal, at para.19, determined whether a warrant was required by asking the following questions:

1. Does the occupant have a right of exclusive occupation of the room?

2. Does the occupant have a right to exclude others from the room?

3. Does the occupant have the right to deny anybody access to the room?

In *Ward v Commissioner of Police for the Metropolis* [2005] UKHL 32; [2005] 3 All E.R. 1013, the House of Lords held that when issuing a warrant under subs.(1) a magistrate has no power to impose a condition that the constable executing it should be accompanied by a *named* approved mental health professional (AMHP) and/or medical practitioner. The reasoning adopted by the House of Lords would also apply to warrants issued under subs.(2).

Section 15(1) of the Police and Criminal Evidence Act 1984 (PACE) states:

"This section and section 16 . . . have effect in relation to the issue to constables under any enactment, including an enactment contained in an Act passed after this Act, of warrants to enter and search premises, and an entry on or search of premises under a warrant is unlawful unless it complies with this section and section 16 . . ."

Although it would appear from the heading of this section that a warrant issued to a con- **1–221** stable under either subs.(1) or (2) comes within the scope of ss.15 and 16 of PACE, the wording of s.15(4), which states that the "constable shall answer on oath any question that the justice of the peace ... hearing the application asks him", suggests that the two sections only relate to warrants issued on the application of a constable. However, in *Ward v Commissioner of Police for the Metropolis*, above, Baroness Hale said, at para.27, that she was "inclined to the view" that ss.15 and 16 do apply to warrants issued under this section. It is submitted that the view expressed by Baroness Hale should be followed and that the following requirements of PACE be satisfied:

1. The application for the warrant shall be made without notice and the information laid before the magistrate must be in writing (s.15(3)).

2. The warrant shall authorise an entry on one occasion only unless it specifies that it authorises multiple entries (either unlimited or limited to a specified maximum) (s.15(5), (5A)).

3. The warrant shall specify the name of the person who applies for it, the date on which it is issued, and the fact that it was issued under the Mental Health Act (s.15(6)).

4. The warrant shall identify, so far as is practicable, the person to be sought (s.15(6)).

5. Apart from a warrant that authorises multiple entries where as many copies as are reasonably required may be made, two copies shall be made of the warrant and the copies shall be clearly certified as copies (s.15(7),(8)). One copy is retained by the police and the other is handed to the occupier of the premises. It is suggested that a third copy be taken for retention by the person in charge of the place of safety to which the patient is removed.

6. Entry and search under the warrant must be within three months from the date of its issue (s.16(3)).

7. Entry and search under the warrant must be at a reasonable hour unless it appears to the constable executing it that the purpose of the search may be frustrated on an entry at a reasonable hour (s.16(4)).

8. If the occupier of the premises is present at the time when the constable seeks to execute the warrant, the constable shall (a) identify himself; (b) produce the warrant to him; and (c) supply him with a copy of it. If the occupier of the premises is not present but some other person who appears to the constable to be in charge of the premises is present, the above procedure will be followed in respect of that other person. If there is no person present who appears to the constable to be in charge of the premises, he shall leave a copy of the warrant in a prominent place on the premises (s.16(5), (6), (7)).

9. A search under the warrant may only be a search to the extent required for the purpose for which the warrant was issued (s.16(8)).

10. The constable executing the warrant shall make an endorsement on it stating whether the person sought was found (s.16(9)).

11. A warrant which has been executed, or which has not been executed within the time authorised for its execution, shall be returned to the designated officer for the local justice area in which the justice was acting who shall retain it for a period of 12 months. During this period the occupier of the premises to which the warrant relates shall be allowed to inspect the warrant (s.16(10), (10A), (11), (12)).

**1–1222** The constable may use reasonable force, if necessary, when executing the warrant (PACE, s.117), which can include restricting the movement of those in occupation of the premises while the premises are being searched (*DPP v Meaden* [2003] EWHC 3005 (Admin); [2004] 1 W.L.R. 945 at para.32).

*Code of Practice C* on the "Detention, Treatment and Questioning of Persons by Police Officers", which is issued under PACE, applies to a person who has been removed to a police station as a place of safety under this section (para.1.10). The implications of this requirement are set out in the General Note to s.136.

In *D'Souza v Director of Public Prosecutions* [1992] 4 All E.R. 545, the House of Lords held that the power to obtain a warrant under subs.(2) of this section is not the exclusive method of gaining access to premises in order to retake a detained patient who has absconded from hospital and that an alternative is provided for in s.17(1)(d) of PACE. Section 17(1)(d) states that a policeman "may enter and search any premises for the purpose ... of recapturing a person who is unlawfully at large and whom he is pursuing". The leading speech in the House of Lords was given by Lord Lowry who held, at 556, that the

> "verb in the clause 'whom he is pursuing' is in the *present continuous* tense and therefore, give or take a few seconds or minutes—this is a question of degree—the pursuit must be almost contemporaneous with the entry into the premises. There must, I consider, be an act of pursuit, that is a chase, however short in time or distance. It is not enough for the police to form an intention to arrest, which they put into practice by resorting to the premises where they believe that the person whom they seek may be found".

His Lordship further held, at 553, 554, that if a person who is lawfully detained in hospital under s.6(2) of this Act goes absent without leave, he is by virtue of s.18(1) liable to be taken into custody and returned to the hospital, and is therefore "unlawfully at large" for the purposes of s.17(1)(d) of PACE.

Section 17(1)(e) of PACE provides the police with the power to enter and search any premises without a warrant if such action is required to save "life or limb" or to prevent "serious damage to property". In *Baker v Crown Prosecution Service* [2009] EWHC 299 (Admin), the Divisional Court held that:

1.  The power enables the police to enter premises where permission has not been given if there is a reasonable belief that the requirements of s.17(1)(e) are satisfied. The requirements will not be satisfied if the police merely have a concern for the welfare of someone within the premises (*Syed v Director of Public Prosecutions,* January 13, 2010, DC).

2.  The words "saving life or limb" (a) refer to a degree of apprehended *serious* bodily injury and (b) are wide enough to cover saving a person from seriously harming himself or herself, as well as seriously harming third parties.

3.  The power to search in s.17(4) is only a power to search to the extent that is reasonably required for the purpose for which the power of entry is exercised; it is not a general power to search.

Although s.17(1)(e) does not provide the police with authority to remove any person from the premises the police could arrest the person for any offence that might have been committed.

The Police and Criminal Evidence Act has not removed the common law power of the police to enter private premises without a warrant to prevent a breach of the peace occurring if they reasonably believe that an imminent breach of the peace, usually an assault, is likely to occur on the premises (*McLeod v Commissioner of Police of the Metropolis* [1994] 4 All E.R. 553 CA). The nature of a breach of the peace is considered in Appendix A.

*Human Rights Act 1998*

Use of this section involves an interference with the mentally disordered person's home **1–1223** and private life that must be justified under art.8(2) of the European Convention on Human Rights. Entry to the person's home must be a proportionate measure in all the circumstances and the reasons adduced to justify the search must be relevant and sufficient (*McLeod v United Kingdom* (1999) 27 E.H.R.R. 493). In *Camenzind v Switzerland* (1999) 28

E.H.R.R. 458 at para.45, the European Court of Human Rights held that the State's governing legislation and practice must afford adequate and effective safeguards against abuse if the test of proportionality is to be satisfied. Although it has been argued that the failure to give formal notification to the mentally disordered person of an impending application might breach art.8, it is likely that a court would find that the adjudication of the application by a magistrate provides the "adequate and effective" safeguard required.

*Code of Practice*

**1–1224**   The issuing of warrants under this section is considered in Ch.10. Guidance on the conveyance of patients is to be found in Ch.11.

*Subsection (1)*

**1–1225**   This subsection enables an AMHP, when acting on behalf of a local social services authority, to make an application to a magistrate for a warrant authorising a policeman to enter premises where a mentally disordered person is believed to be living for the purpose of removing that person to a place of safety if an initial assessment indicates that removal is required. If the patient is removed to a place of safety, a further assessment will be undertaken there. The power is confined to assessing whether the person should be removed to a place of safety; there is no power while in the premises to subject the person to an assessment for sectioning under Pt II. As the wording of this provision makes clear, this should take place at the place of safety. The power to remove the person only applies if such action is thought to be necessary: see the note on "if thought fit", below.

This procedure can be invoked even though the name of the mentally disordered person is not known (subs.(5)). The relevant premises must be specified in the warrant.

During the debates on the Mental Health Bill, a Government Minister said: "Under [this] provision, the ill-treatment, neglect, lack of proper control or inability to care for oneself need not be linked to the existence of the mental disorder from which the person is suffering" (*Hansard,* HL Vol.688, col.663).

INFORMATION.   There is no requirement for the person who is the subject of the application to be informed of the fact that it is being made: see the note on "The Human Rights Act 1998", above.

APPROVED MENTAL HEALTH PROFESSIONAL.   Only an AMHP can apply for a warrant to be issued under this subsection. If the person has a care co-ordinator who is not an AMHP, he or she can accompany the AMHP applicant and provide evidence to the magistrate.

BELIEVED TO BE SUFFERING FROM MENTAL DISORDER.   But has not yet reliably been shown to be so (*Ward v Commissioner of Police for the Metropolis*, above, para.13).

KEPT OTHERWISE THAN UNDER PROPER CONTROL.   This phrase encompasses not only the situation where a person is being subjected to a degree of improper control, but also the situation where a person is suffering from the absence of control.

UNABLE TO CARE FOR HIMSELF.   This paragraph is aimed at a mentally disordered person who is unable to look after himself appropriately. As "care" is a broad term which encompasses matters that relate to a person's daily needs, a warrant could be applied for where the main cause of concern is the apparent failure of the person to take essential prescribed medication.

LIVING ALONE.   The suggestion by the Royal College of Psychiatrists that this section should also provide for a situation where two mentally disordered people were living together and were unable to care for themselves was not adopted (Cmnd. 7320, para.2.21).

AUTHORISING.   The warrant does not require the constable to enter the premises. The arrival of the constable at the premises could have the effect of persuading the person concerned to admit the AMHP and the doctor.

CONSTABLE.   Any police officer can execute the warrant: see the note on "constable" in s.136(1). The constable must be accompanied by an AMHP and a doctor (subs.(4)). The AMHP need not necessarily be the person who applied for the warrant.

ENTER.   The power to enter the premises also includes to power to search those premises in order to find the person believed to be suffering from mental disorder (*Ward v Commissioner of Police for the Metropolis*, above, para.23).

IF NEED BE BY FORCE.   Where a person is admitted to accommodation provided under Pt III of the National Assistance Act 1948 or to any hospital, and it appears to the local social services authority that there is a danger of loss or damage to the person's moveable property by reason of his temporary or permanent inability to protect or deal with the property and no other suitable arrangements have been made, s.48 of the 1948 Act places the authority under a duty to take reasonable steps to prevent or mitigate the loss or damage. The authority has the power to enter the person's home in order to carry out this duty, and to recover its reasonable expenses.

PREMISES.   It is submitted that this term includes the land on which the building in question is situated. The constable would therefore have power to remove the person from the garden of the premises specified in the warrant. In *Ward v Commissioner of Police for the Metropolis*, above, the person concerned had locked herself in her car. The policeman executing the warrant gained access to the car and the person was taken to the place of safety by ambulance.

IF THOUGHT FIT.   This section does not specify whose decision this is. It is suggested that the policeman's role is to gain entry to the premises and to ensure the safety of the doctor and the AMHP, whose joint role is to assess whether the patient should be removed to a place of safety for further assessment there. In *Ward v Commissioner of Police for the Metropolis*, above, Baroness Hale said that "professionals should be able to help the police officer to decide whether or not it is 'fit' to take the person concerned to a place of safety" (para.12), and that it may be "that the police officer can authorise others, such as the ambulance service or an [AMHP], to transport the person to the place of safety rather than doing it himself" (para.23).

PLACE OF SAFETY.   See the note on subs.(3).

MAKING AN APPLICATION IN RESPECT OF HIM ... OR ... OTHER ARRANGEMENTS FOR HIS TREATMENT OR CARE.   The authority to detain the patient ceases once it has been decided to take no action in respect of him or her.

*Subsection (2)*
This subsection provides for the issue of a warrant to a policeman to enter premises, **1–1226** using force if necessary, for the purposes of taking or retaking a patient who is *already* liable to be detained into custody. It also applies to a patient under guardianship, a CTO or the Scottish legislation who has absconded from a place where he or she is required to reside. Also note the power of the police under s.17(1)(d) of the Police and Criminal Evidence Act 1984 which is considered in the General Note to this section.

ANY CONSTABLE.   Who *may* be accompanied by a doctor or any other person, such as an AMHP, who is authorised to take or retake the patient (subs.(4); also see para.10.6 of the *Code of Practice*).

PERSON AUTHORISED. The persons authorised to retake patients under s.18 of this Act (and who can therefore be applicants under this provision) are, in addition to a constable, any officer on the staff of the hospital, any AMHP or any person authorised by the hospital managers, or, in the case of a patient subject to guardianship, any officer on the staff of a local social services authority, or any person authorised by the guardian or a local social services authority. For community patients, see s.18(2A). It is unusual for a policeman to be the applicant. Mental Health Act Administrators, care co-ordinators and nurses have made applications under this provision.

REMOVE THE PATIENT. To the place where the patient is required to be.

*Subsection (3)*

**1–1227**   REMOVED. For general provisions relating to the conveyance of patients from one place to another, see s.137.

PLACE OF SAFETY. Is defined in subs.(6). The place of safety is not obliged to accept the person. If entry to the preferred place of safety is refused, it is lawful to take the person to another place of safety. The patient can be transferred to another place of safety during the 72 hour period (subss.(3A), (3B)):

   If a person escapes while being taken to or detained in a place of safety, he or she can only be retaken within the 72-hour period specified in s.138(3).

72 HOURS. This is the maximum period of detention. It starts from the time when the person arrives at the place of safety. If the place of safety is a hospital, this period cannot be continued under s.5(2) or (4) as it is Parliament's intention that the assessment be completed within the 72 hours: see *R. v Wilson Ex p. Williamson* [1996] C.O.D. 42, noted in the General Note to s.2.

*Subsections (3A), (3B)*

**1–1228**   These provisions, which respond to concern that was expressed during debates on the 2007 Act about mentally disordered people being detained in a police cell (see for e.g. *Hansard,* HL Vol. 689, col.1467), enable a person who has been detained in a place of safety under this section to be transferred to another one before the time limit of 72 hours for detention has expired. Such a transfer does not have the effect of increasing the 72-hour limit. Guidance on transfers between places of safety is reproduced in the notes on s.136(3), (4).

*Subsection (4)*

**1–1229**   APPROVED MENTAL HEALTH PROFESSIONAL. Who need not be the AMHP who made the application.

REGISTERED MEDICAL PRACTITIONER. This section does not provide the doctor with a power to override the objection of a mentally capable person to being medically examined.

*Subsection (6)*

**1–1230**   ANY OTHER SUITABLE PLACE. Which could be the home of a relative or friend of the patient.

## Mentally disordered persons found in public places

**1–1231**   **136.**—(1) If a constable finds in a place to which the public have access a person who appears to him to be suffering from mental disorder and to be in immediate need of care or control, the constable may, if he thinks it necessary to do so in the interests of that person or for the protection of other persons, remove that person to a place of safety within the meaning of section 135 above.

(2) A person removed to a place of safety under this section may be detained there for a period not exceeding 72 hours for the purpose of enabling him to be examined by a registered medical practitioner and to be interviewed by an [approved mental health professional] and of making any necessary arrangements for his treatment or care.

[(3) A constable, an approved mental health professional or a person authorised by either of them for the purposes of this subsection may, before the end of the period of 72 hours mentioned in subsection (2) above, take a person detained in a place of safety under that subsection to one or more other places of safety.

(4) A person taken to a place of a safety under subsection (3) above may be detained there for a purpose mentioned in subsection (2) above for a period ending no later than the end of the period of 72 hours mentioned in that subsection.]

AMENDMENT

In subs.(2) the words in square brackets were substituted by the Mental Health Act 2007 s.21, Sch.2 para.10. Subss.(3) and (4) were inserted by s.44(3).

DEFINITIONS

    mental disorder: ss.1, 145(1).                                         **1–1232**

    approved mental health professional: s.145(1), (1AC).

GENERAL NOTE

    This section empowers a policeman to remove a person from a public place to a place of  **1–1233** safety if he considers that the person is suffering from mental disorder and is in immediate need of care or control. The power is available whether or not the person has, or is suspected of having committed a criminal offence. The person can be detained in a place of safety for up to 72 hours so that he or she can be examined by a doctor and interviewed by an approved mental health professional (AMHP) in order that suitable arrangements can be made for his or her treatment or care. The detained person can be transferred to another place of safety as long as the 72-hour period has not expired (subss.(3), (4)). This section, which is not supported by any statutory forms, is usually invoked "where a person's abnormal behaviour is causing nuisance or offence" (Cmnd. 7320, para.2.2.2). There is nothing to prevent a patient who is already liable to be detained under this Act, for example, a patient on s.17 leave, from being detained under this section. The powers contained in this section:

    "inevitably require that the person concerned can be kept safe in the sense that harm to himself or others is prevented until he can be seen by a doctor and, if necessary, given some form of sedation . . . A police officer in exercising his powers under s.136 is entitled to use reasonable force. If someone is violent, he can be restrained" (*R. on the application of Anderson) v HM Coroner for Inner North Greater London* [2004] EWHC 2729 (Admin); [2004] M.H.L.R. 324 paras 8, 9).

If a person escapes while being taken to or detained in a place of safety, he or she can only be retaken within the period specified in s.138(3).

A person who is detained under this section is not subject to the consent to treatment provision contained in Pt IV (s.56(3)(b)). If the person is mentally capable of making a decision about treatment, the common law enables him or her to refuse to be treated for either a physical or mental disorder. However, if the person is assessed as being mentally incapable of making a decision about treatment, the treatment can be provided under ss.5 and 6 of the Mental Capacity Act 2005 if it is deemed to be in his or her best interests.

It is submitted that it is lawful for the police to take a person who has been detained under this section to a hospital Accident and Emergency department as an out-patient to enable emergency treatment to be given for a physical injury prior to transporting the person to the place of safety. In this situation the Accident and Emergency department would not become the place of safety under this provision.

As the purpose of the section "is to allow for assessment within the shortest possible period, up to a maximum of 72 hours ... it should *not* therefore be treated, as in the case of some hospitals, as an admission section authorising 72 hours' detention" (Mental Health Act Commission, *Second Biennial Report* 1985–87, para.11.1(e)).

If a person (who may or may not appear to be mentally disordered) either is, or is about to commit an offence, s.24 of the Police and Criminal Evidence Act 1984 (PACE) enables a constable to arrest the person without a warrant if the constable has reasonable cause to believe that it is necessary to use the power of arrest in order to prevent the person in question:

(a)  causing physical injury to himself or any other person;

(b)  suffering physical injury;

(c)  causing loss or damage to property;

(d)  committing an offence against public decency where a member of the public cannot reasonably expected to avoid the person in question; or

(e)  causing an unlawful obstruction of the highway.

A citizen has a similar power of arrest under s.24A in respect of (a), (b) and (c), above, and has an additional power of arrest to prevent the person in question from making off before a constable can assume responsibility for him. However, the citizen's power of arrest only applies if the person is, or is about to commit an indictable offence, i.e. those that are triable only on indictment, or triable "either way".

The power to arrest under this section was specifically preserved by s.26 and Sch.2 of PACE (the references below are to sections of PACE). Apart from providing the arresting policeman with a power to search the person concerned (see s.32 and para.10.45 of the *Code of Practice*), this means that a person who has been removed to a place of safety under this section is given the following rights: to be told that they have been arrested and the grounds for the arrest as soon as practicable (s.28), to have another person of his choice informed of his removal (s.56) and to consult a solicitor privately at any time (s.58). Although s.58 relates to a patient who is being "held in custody in a police station *or other premises*", the wording of the section suggests that it is not intended to apply where a patient is detained under this section in a hospital. Section 58 states that where a patient makes a request to consult privately with a solicitor, the time when the request was made "shall be recorded in the custody record" (s.58(2)). Under para.2.1 of *Code of Practice C* (2008 revision), a custody record is only opened in respect of "each person brought to a police station under arrest or arrested at the station having gone there voluntarily". As the mandatory requirement in s.58(2) cannot be satisfied in respect of a patient who is detained in a hospital, it would appear that s.58 does not apply in such circumstances.

**1–1234**     *Code of Practice C*, which is concerned with the "Detention, Treatment and Questioning of Persons by Police Officers", applies to persons who have been removed to a police station under this section (para.1.10). Paragraph 3.15 of *Code C* requires the police to secure the attendance of an "appropriate adult" if the person being detained appears to be mentally disordered. As the principle function of the appropriate adult is to protect the interests of a mentally disordered suspect during police questioning, it is difficult to see what role this person has to play under this section where the mentally disordered person is being detained for assessment by mental health professionals and not for questioning by the police and it is instructive to note that the relevant chapter of the *Code of Practice* (Ch.10) makes no reference to the appropriate adult. However, it has been argued that the early appearance of an appropriate adult could help to ensure that the detained person is aware of the effect of this section, is given information about what is to happen to him and has been informed of his rights under PACE. There can be no doubt that the attendance of an appropriate adult is necessary if a person who, having been detained under this section, is also going to be involved in a procedure under the criminal law. This happened in *Francis v Director of Public Prosecutions, The Times*, May 2, 1996, where the Divisional Court held that detention under this section does not give rise to any legal bar to any subsequent use of the breath specimen procedure under s.7 of the Road Traffic Act 1988. The court held that the fact of detention under this Act, while giving rise to obligations on the police, was not determinative of the issue of whether the procedure could be used, and that the propriety or fairness of using the procedure in such circumstances fell to be decided on the facts. If a person who has been detained under this section does become involved in a procedure under the criminal law, the appropriate adult should not be the AMHP who has been involved with that person's assessment. "Guidance on Responding to People with Mental Ill Health or Learning Disabilities", National Police Improvement Agency (2010), para.6.4.4.1, states that "there is nothing in law to prevent police officers from using s.136 and the power of arrest for a criminal offence in the same case at the same time".

Paragraph 3.16 of *Code C* states:

"It is imperative a mentally disordered or otherwise mentally vulnerable person, detained under the Mental Health Act 1983, s.136, be assessed as soon as possible. If that assessment is to take place at the police station, an AMHP and a registered medical practitioner shall be called to the station as soon as possible in order to interview and examine the detainee. Once the detainee has been interviewed, examined and suitable arrangements made for their treatment or care, they can no longer be detained under s.136. A detainee must be immediately discharged from detention under s.136 if a registered medical practitioner, having examined them, concludes they are not mentally disordered within the meaning of the Act."

This paragraph does not sit easily with the statement in para.10.32 of the *Code of Practice* that a patient may not be detained in a police station under this section once the custody officer "deems that detention is no longer appropriate". It is suggested that this statement should read:

"detention is no longer appropriate because there is no legal authority to detain the patient further because, for example, the patient has been assessed as not being mentally disordered, the objectives of the detention have been achieved, or the 72 hour period has expired".

There is no statutory form that can be used to record an admission of a person to a hospital which is acting as a place of safety under this section. If such an admission takes place, the hospital should not record it on Form H3 (in Wales, Form HO14) as no application has been made in respect of that person: see reg.4(4) of the English Regulations and reg.4(3) of the Welsh Regulations.

If a person is removed to a hospital or registered establishment home under this section, the managers of the hospital or establishment are obliged to give him information under s.132.

A person who has been arrested and detained in a police station other than under the provisions of this section can be subjected to a mental health assessment (Home Office Circular No. 66/90, paras 4(iii) and 7).

The Royal College of Psychiatrists has published "Standards on the use of Section 136 of the Mental Health Act 1983" (College Report CR149) which considers all aspects of the process of detaining and assessing a person under this section.

The literature on this section has been reviewed by R.D. Borchmann et al. in "Section 136 of the Mental Health Act: a new literature review" Medicine, Science and the Law 2010; 50: 34–39.

*Human Rights Act 1998*

**1–1235**    In *Winterwerp v Netherlands* (1979) 2 E.H.R.R. 387 at para.39, the European Court of Human Rights held that "except in emergency cases", an individual "should not be deprived of his liberty unless he has been reliably shown to be of 'unsound mind' ". The court has subsequently said that it cannot "be inferred from the *Winterwerp* judgment that [a medical report on the patient] must in all conceivable cases be obtained before rather than after the confinement of a person on the ground of unsoundness of mind" (*X v United Kingdom* (1981) 4 E.H.R.R. 188 at para.41; also see *Varbanov v Bulgaria* [2000] M.H.L.R. 263, para.47). As the power under this section applies to a person who appears to be in *immediate* need of care or control and lasts for a relatively brief period, it is clearly an emergency measure which complies with art.5(1)(e) of the Convention. A medical assessment should take place promptly after the person's arrival at the place of safety. The continued detention of a person under this section subsequent to a finding by the assessing doctor that the person was not mentally disordered would contravene the Convention as there would be no ground under art.5(1)(e) to detain him or her.

Although it could be argued that using a police station as a place of safety contravenes art.5(1)(e) of the Convention because it does not provide a therapeutic environment for the medical assessment (*Aerts v Belgium* (2000) 29 E.H.R.R. 50), it is likely that the court would hold that the emergency nature of this provision would justify the use of such an environment for a limited period.

The common law and statutory powers of the police to enter private premises to prevent a breach of the peace (which is preserved by s.17(6) of the Police and Criminal Evidence Act 1984) do not beach the Convention as such action can be said to be both "in accordance with law" and pursued for the legitimate aim of "the prevention of disorder or crime" for the purposes of art.8(2). However, the action of the police must be a proportionate measure in all the circumstances (*McLeod v United Kingom* (1999) 27 E.H.R.R. 493). The nature of a breach of the peace is considered in Appendix A

*Code of Practice*

**1–1236**    The issuing of warrants under this section is considered in Ch.10. Guidance on the conveyance of patients is to be found in Ch.11.

*Subsection (1)*

**1–1237**    CONSTABLE.   Means the office of constable, and not the rank of constable (Police Act 1964, s.18, Sch.2). Therefore, any police officer can exercise this power. In *Clunis v Camden and Islington Health Authority* [1998] 3 All E.R. 180, the Court of Appeal doubted whether the wording of this section places on the constable a duty to take care which gives rise to a claim for damages at the suit of the disordered person.

It is for the constable to determine whether he is detaining a person under this section; he cannot make a determination which is conditional on a subsequent confirmation by a superior officer.

FINDS.   It is submitted that if a constable arrests a person inside their home for a breach of the peace and then takes that person outside, this section cannot be invoked there because the constable has not "found" that person in a place to which the public have access. In *Seal v Chief Constable of South Wales Police* [2007] UKHL 31; [2007] 4 All E.R. 177 at para.60, Baroness Hale said obiter:

"If [Mr Seal] was 'removed' under s.136 of the 1983 Act from his mother's home, he cannot have been 'found in a place to which the public have access'. If he was arrested in her home for a breach of the peace, and then 'removed' under s.136 after they had taken him outside, can it be said that they 'found' him there?"

In *McMillan v CPS* [2008] EWHC 1457 (Admin), a police constable was held to have acted lawfully when he physically escorted a woman from a private garden to a public footpath and then arrested her for the criminal offence of being drunk and disorderly in a public place. The court noted, at para.12, that at the Magistrates' Court the Justices had "rejected any suggestion that [Ms McMillan] was being moved from a private place to a public place simply so as to justify an arrest outside the garden for an offence which had a public place requirement." It follows that although a police constable has the right to escort a person from a private place to a public place if, for example, that is necessary to diffuse an emotionally fraught situation, it would not be lawful to remove the person solely for the purpose of bringing him or her within the scope of this section.

PLACE TO WHICH THE PUBLIC HAVE ACCESS. This phrase is not defined. It probably includes (1) places to which members of the public have open access, e.g. the public highway; (2) places to which members of the public have access if a payment is made, e.g. a cinema; and (3) places to which members of the public have access at certain times of day, e.g. a public house. It does not cover areas such as a private garden where members of the public have access by virtue of being visitors to private premises: see *R. v Edwards* (1978) 67 Cr. App. R. 228, where the Court of Appeal held that the fact that the public can obtain access to a private house as visitors through the front garden does not make the garden a public place for the purposes of the Public Order Act 1936. A garden is not a place to which the public have access even if a person standing in the garden could injure a passing pedestrian with a knife (*R v Roberts* [2003] EWCA Crim 2753). In *Knox v Anderton* (1983) 76 Cr. App. R. 156, a case under s.1(4) of the Prevention of Crime Act 1953, the Divisional Court held that a "public place" to which the public have access could include premises where there are no barriers or notices restricting access, such as the upper landing of a block of flats which could be entered by members of the public without hindrance. *Roberts* and *Anderton* were applied in *Harriot v Director of Public Prosecutions* [2005] EWHC 965 (Admin) where the Divisional Court held that the forecourt of a bail hostel to which access from the street was unimpeded, whether physically or by displayed notices, was not a "public place" within the meaning of s.139 of the Criminal Justice Act 1988. A case on the Road Traffic Act 1988 suggests that the phrase would also cover a private car park which was attached to premises and which did not restrict access to members of the public, even though the car park was intended for the use of customers of the premises (*May v DPP* [2005] EWHC 1280 (Admin)). In the only reported case on this section, *Carter v Metropolitan Police Commissioner* [1975] 1 W.L.R. 507, the Court of Appeal proceeded on the basis that a communal balcony in a block of flats was a "place to which the public have access." The Reference Guide states, at para.30.17, that "a 'public place' can be taken to mean any place (whether indoors or outdoors) to which the public have access, whether by right, by explicit or implicit permission, on payment, or otherwise".

The Mental Health Act Commission reported that there "have been occasions when police, called to a disturbed individual in an Accident and Emergency Department, have declined to use s.136 on grounds that it is not a public place" (*Fifth Biennial Report* 1991–1993, para.10.7(a)). As a hospital Accident and Emergency Department waiting area is a place at which members of the public can attend without hindrance for a particular purpose, it is submitted that such a place comes within the scope of this provision. However, a hospital ward is excluded as it is a place to which only particular members of the public can attend at the request (actual or implied) of the patient and with the permission of the hospital managers.

If there is serious concern about the safety of a person who is on private premises and the police are refused access to the premises, the police could use their power under s.17(1)(e) of PACE to gain access without a warrant. Section 17(1)(e) is considered in the General Note to s.135.

A Person.    Of any age. As an alternative to invoking this section where he has reasonable cause to believe that a person under 18 would otherwise be likely to suffer significant harm, a constable may remove that person to "suitable accommodation and keep him there" (Children Act 1989, s.46).

Appears to him.    No medical evidence is needed. All that is required is that the constable has a reasonable belief that the person is mentally disordered within the meaning of s.1. The studies examined by Borchmann et al., see above, reported a very high correlation between the assessments made by police officers regarding the existence of a mental disorder and those conducted by psychiatrists at a later date.

Necessary to do so.    There is nothing to prevent the person from being escorted to hospital without this section being invoked if the person is willing to be admitted as an informal patient, is thought not likely to abscond and the hospital is prepared to accept him or her.

Remove.    A person who is being conveyed to a place of safety is deemed to be in legal custody (s.137) and, as the person has been arrested, reasonable force may be used to facilitate the removal.

This section does not specify who, other than the constable, might have the power to convey the patient to the place of safety. The Butler Committee, at para.9.2, had "no doubt" that the constable's power "extends to persons acting under his direction, such as the ambulance staff who are taking the disordered person to hospital."

*Subsection (2)*

**1–1238**    Place of safety.    Is defined in s.135(6). The choice of place of safety is for the police, bearing in mind that a hospital is not legally obliged to act as a place of safety under this section. Although para.10.21 of the *Code of Practice* states that a "police station should be used as a place of safety only on an exceptional basis", research by the Independent Police Complaints Commission found that twice as many people are detained in police cells for assessment under this section as those taken to hospital for the same purpose ("Police Custody as a 'Place of Safety': a National Study Examining the Use of Section 136 of the Mental Health Act 1983" (2008)).

If the person is taken to a hospital as the place of safety, the police officer is only legally obliged to remain there if his presence is required to prevent crime caused by violent behaviour. College Report CR149 of the Royal College of Psychiatrists, noted above, states that it "may be necessary for the police to remain at the place of safety for a short period to ensure the safety of the individual or staff" (p.32). "Guidance on Responding to People with Mental Ill Health or Learning Disabilities", National Police Improvement Agency (2010) states, at para.6.4.7.3, that in general, "the police should only need to stay where, in their professional judgement, there is a medium to high risk of violence or breach of the peace".

**1–1239**    May be detained.    "The powers of detention given by section 136(2) are not conferred expressly on the police, but are given to any person who is a party to the detention of the disordered person once he has been brought to a place of safety" (Butler Committee, para.9.2). As the purpose of this section is to provide the individual with a mental health assessment, assessment by both doctor and AMHP should begin as soon as possible after the arrival at the place of safety. If an admission to a hospital acting as a place of safety takes place late at night, it would seem reasonable to delay summoning the AMHP until the following morning.

72 hours.    The power to detain under this section will lapse as soon as the person has been examined and interviewed and it is considered that no further arrangements need be made for his or her treatment or care. As the 72 hour period starts from the time when the

person arrives at the place of safety, a record of the time of arrival there should be made immediately. If the place of safety is a hospital, this period cannot be continued under s.5(2) or (4) as it is Parliament's intention that the assessment be completed within the 72 hours; see *R. v Wilson Ex p. Williamson* [1996] C.O.D. 42, noted in the General Note to s.2 and the *Code of Practice* at para.10.53. If a person escapes from the place of safety he or she cannot be retaken after the 72 hours have expired (s.138(3)).

REGISTERED MEDICAL PRACTITIONER.   The authority to detain under this section ends **1–1240** immediately if the doctor's assessment leads him or her to conclude that the person is not mentally disordered. The further detention of the patient in these circumstances would be unlawful: see the note on "The Human Rights Act 1998", above. Wherever possible, the examining doctor should be approved under s.12 (*Code of Practice*, para.10.27).

In its *Second Biennial Report*, 1985–87, the Mental Health Act Commission reported at para.11.1(e) that it had:

"found that doubt exists when the person brought to the hospital [under this section] has been examined by the doctor but no [AMHP] is available to conduct the interview. The legal consequences of failure to provide an [AMHP] interview are open to debate. Has the person to remain in detention even though the doctor does not consider that compulsory admission is necessary, until the [AMHP] is available? Good practice would suggest that if the delay is going to be considerable (say more than four hours) then the requirements of the section shall be deemed to have been fulfilled so that detention may end. The case where the doctor decides that compulsory admission is appropriate is more controversial, since Parliament clearly intended that the [AMHP's] opinion would be of great importance both in providing a safeguard for the rights of the individual and in deciding what arrangements are most appropriate to provide the care which the person needs".

It is submitted that the wording of subs.(2) clearly envisages the person being both examined by a doctor and interviewed by an AMHP and that in both of the situations identified by the MHAC the patient will remain subject to detention under this section until the interview by the AMHP takes place or the 72-hour period expires. In the passage quoted the MHAC appears to assume that the sole purpose of being removed to a place of safety is to assess the patient for possible compulsory admission. Such an outcome is, in fact, only one of a number of options that would be considered on an assessment. Although the authority to detain the patient would not end on a finding by the doctor that the person was suffering from mental disorder but did not satisfy the grounds for compulsory admission, it would end if the doctor found that the person was not suffering from a mental disorder. The MHAC adopted a more orthodox approach to this section in its *Ninth Biennial Report* 1999–2001 at paras 4.7–4.9.

NECESSARY ARRANGEMENTS.   If it is established that the patient is absent without leave from the detaining hospital, he or she can be immediately returned to that hospital under the authority of s.18. If the patient is either on leave of absence under s.17 or is subject to a community treatment order, the assessment of the patient should be completed. The patient's responsible clinician should be contacted to establish whether the patient is going to be recalled to hospital.

*Subsections (3),(4)*

These provisions, which respond to concern that was expressed during debates on the **1–1241** 2007 Act about mentally disordered people being detained in a police cell (see, for e.g., *Hansard,* HL Vol. 689, col.1467), enable a person who has been detained in a place of safety under this section to be transferred to another one before the time limit of 72 hours for detention has expired. Such a transfer does not have the effect of increasing the 72 hour limit. The transfer can take place before the assessment has begun, while it is in progress, or after it has been completed while arrangements are being put in place for the person's treatment or care.

The Minister of State responded to criticism that the 72-hour period is too long for someone to be detained in a police station which is being used as the place of safety as follows:

"I . . . accept that 72 hours may seem to some people to be a long time. It should be borne in mind that that is an upper limit. Recently published emerging evidence from a study being undertaken by the Independent Police Complaints Commission suggests that the average amount of time [spent] in police custody under s.136 is 10 hours and that the majority of detainees leave police custody within 18 hours. That is reassuring, although from this evidence it is clear that some people need to be detained for longer than 24 hours" (*Hansard,* HL Vol.689, cols 1468, 1469).

Before a transfer takes place, the agreement of a person in control of the new place of safety to accept the patient must be obtained. On arrival at the new place of safety, the person in control should be informed, preferably in writing, of the time when the original detention under this section started.

The transfer of a person between places of safety is considered in the *Code of Practice* at paras 10.34 to 10.39. Also see Home Office Circular No.007/2008.

## Provisions as to custody, conveyance and detention

1–1242     **137.**—(1) Any person required or authorised by or by virtue of this Act to be conveyed to any place or to be kept in custody or detained in a place of safety or at any place to which he is taken under section 42(6) above shall, while being so conveyed, detained or kept, as the case may be, be deemed to be in legal custody.

(2) A constable or any other person required or authorised by or by virtue of this Act to take any person into custody, or to convey or detain any person shall, for the purposes of taking him into custody or conveying or detaining him, have all the powers, authorities, protection and privileges which a constable has within the area for which he acts as constable.

(3) In this section "convey" includes any other expression denoting removal from one place to another.

GENERAL NOTE

1–1243     This section specifies the circumstances whereby a person is deemed to be in legal custody for the purposes of this Act. It also provides that a person who is required or authorised to detain or convey a person who is in legal custody shall have the powers of a constable when so acting. These powers include the power to use reasonable force to secure the conveyance of the person. A person who escapes from legal custody can be retaken under s.138.

The powers contained in this section do not include the power to use force to enter premises to remove a person simply because he or she was believed to be suffering from a mental disorder or was a person liable to be taken into custody under this Act (*R. v Rosso* [2003] EWCA Crim 3242; [2003] M.H.L.R. 404 para.17). Section 135 should be used in such circumstances.

*Subsection (2)*

1–1244     In *R. v Broadmoor Special Hospital Authority and The Secetary of State for the Department of Health Ex p. SH and D*, February 5, 1998, Potts J. held that this subsection was concerned with the limited function of detention for the purpose of conveyance to hospital, not with detention once there. This finding was referred to without comment when this case reached the Court of Appeal: see [1998] C.O.D. 199.

POWERS . . . WHICH A CONSTABLE HAS. Which include the power to arrest a person who is wilfully obstructing him in the execution of his duties, the power to use reasonable force in effecting an arrest or to prevent a person escaping, and the power to require other persons to assist him in the execution of his duties.

## Retaking of patients escaping from custody

**138.**—(1) If any person who is in legal custody by virtue of section 137 above **1–1245** escapes, he may, subject to the provisions of this section, be retaken—

(a) in any case, by the person who had his custody immediately before the escape, or by any constable or [approved mental health professional];

(b) if at the time of the escape he was liable to be detained in a hospital within the meaning of Part II of this Act, or subject to guardianship under this Act, [or a community patient who was recalled to hospital under section 17E above,] by any other person who could take him into custody under section 18 above if he had absented himself without leave.

(2) A person to whom paragraph (b) of subsection (1) above applies shall not be retaken under this section after the expiration of the period within which he could be retaken under section 18 above if he had absented himself without leave on the day of the escape unless he is subject to a restriction order under Part III of this Act or an order or direction having the same effect as such an order; and subsection (4) of the said section 18 shall apply with the necessary modifications accordingly.

(3) A person who escapes while being taken to or detained in a place of safety under section 135 or 136 above shall not be retaken under this section after the expiration of the period of 72 hours beginning with the time when he escapes or the period during which he is liable to be so detained, whichever expires first.

(4) This section, so far as it relates to the escape of a person liable to be detained in a hospital within the meaning of Part II of this Act, shall apply in relation to a person who escapes—

(a) while being taken to or from such a hospital in pursuance of regulations under section 19 above, or of any order, direction or authorisation under Part III or VI of this Act (other than under section 35, 36, 38, 53, 83 or 85) or under section 123 above; or

(b) while being taken to or detained in a place of safety in pursuance of an order under Part III of this Act (other than under section 35, 36 or 38 above) pending his admission to such a hospital,

as if he were liable to be detained in that hospital and, if he had not previously been received in that hospital, as if he had been so received.

(5) In computing for the purposes of the power to give directions under section 37(4) above and for the purposes of sections 37(5) and 40(1) above the period of 28 days mentioned in those sections, no account shall be taken of any time during which the patient is at large and liable to be retaken by virtue of this section.

(6) Section 21 above shall, with any necessary modifications, apply in relation to a patient who is at large and liable to be retaken by virtue of this section as it applies in relation to a patient who is absent without leave and references in that section to section 18 above shall be construed accordingly.

AMENDMENT

In subs.(1) the words in square brackets were substituted and inserted by the Mental Health Act 2007 ss.21, 32(4), Sch.2 para.10, Sch.3 para.32.

DEFINITIONS
**1–1246**    approved mental health professional: s.145(1).
absent without leave: ss.18(6), 145(1).
restriction order: ss.41, 145(1).
patient: s.145(1).
community patient: ss.17A(7), 145(1).

GENERAL NOTE
**1–1247**    This section provides for the retaking of persons who have escaped from legal custody. A patient who has been made subject to an application under Pt II of this Act and who escapes whilst on the way to hospital, can only be retaken if he or she can be apprehended within the relevant period set out in either para.(a) or para.(b) of s.6(1). A person who assists another person who is in legal custody to escape commits an offence under s.128(2).

*Subsection (1)*
**1–1248**    RETAKEN.   This section does not provide authority for force to be used to enter premises where the patient is believed to be. An application to a magistrate under s.135 should be made if such action is deemed to be necessary.

HOSPITAL WITHIN THE MEANING OF PART II.   See s.34(2).

*Subsection (6)*
**1–1249**    The effect of this subsection is that if the patient is retaken within the last week of the period during which he or she can be retaken, the authority to detain will end a week after the day he or she is retaken.

**Protection for acts done in pursuance of this Act**
**1–1250**    **139.**—(1) No person shall be liable, whether on the ground of want of jurisdiction or on any other ground, to any civil or criminal proceedings to which he would have been liable apart from this section in respect of any act purporting to be done in pursuance of this Act or any regulations or rules made under this Act, [. . .] unless the act was done in bad faith or without reasonable care.

(2) No civil proceedings shall be brought against any person in any court in respect of any such act without the leave of the High Court; and no criminal proceedings shall be brought against any person in any court in respect of any such act except by or with the consent of the Director of Public Prosecutions.

(3) This section does not apply to proceedings for an offence under this Act, being proceedings which, under any other provision of this Act, can be instituted only by or with the consent of the Director of Public Prosecutions.

(4) This section does not apply to proceedings against the Secretary of State or against a [Strategic Health Authority,] [Local Health Board][, Special Health Authority or Primary Care Trust]] [or against a National Health Service trust established under [the National Health Service Act 2006 or the National Health Service (Wales) Act 2006]] [or NHS foundation trust.]

(5) In relation to Northern Ireland the reference in this section to the Director of Public Prosecutions shall be construed as a reference to the Director of Public Prosecutions for Northern Ireland.

AMENDMENTS
**1–1251**    The words omitted in subs.(1) were repealed by the Mental Capacity Act 2005 s.67(2), Sch.7. In subs.(4) the words in square brackets were added by the National Health Service and Community Care Act 1990 s.66(1), Sch.9 para.24(7) and the Health Authorities Act

1995, s.2(1), Sch.1 para.107(11). The reference to Primary Care Trusts was inserted by the Health Act 1999 (Supplementary, Consequential, etc. Provisions) Order 2000 (SI 2000/90) Sch.1 para.16(8) and the reference to a Strategic Health Authority was inserted by the National Health Service Reform and Health Care Professions Act 2002 (Supplementary, Consequential, etc. Provisions) Regulations 2002 (SI 2002/2469), reg.4, Sch.1. The reference to an NHS foundation trust was inserted by the Health and Social Care (Community Health and Standards) Act 2003 s.34, Sch.4 para.56, the reference to Local Health Board was substituted by SI 2007/961 art.3, Sch. para.13(11) and the references to the National Health Service Act 2006 and the National Health Service (Wales) Act 2006 were made by the National Health Service (Consequential Provisions) Act 2006 s.2, Sch.1 para.6.

DEFINITIONS

Health Authority: s.145(1). **1–1252**

Special Health Authority: s.145(1).

GENERAL NOTE

This section, which has its origins in s.330 of the Lunacy Act 1890, provides that: (1) **1–1253** apart from proceedings against a Strategic Health Authority, a Local Health Board, a National Health Service trust, a Primary Care Trust, a National Health Service foundation trust, the Secretary of State or the Welsh Ministers and proceedings under s.127, no civil or criminal proceedings can be brought against any person in any court in respect of an act purporting to be done under this Act without the leave of the High Court or the Director of Public Prosecutions; and (2) for such proceedings to succeed the court must be satisfied that the person proceeded against acted in bad faith or without reasonable care. In *TMM v London Borough of Hackney* [2010] EWHC 1349 (Admin), para.5, Colins J. said that it seemed "slightly anomalous" that the protection given by this section "is in effect removed in the case of public but not in the case of private hospitals".

This section does not affect the right of a patient to apply to the High Court for his discharge by means of a writ of habeas corpus: "If Parliament is to suspend habeas corpus, it must do so expressly or by clear implication"; per Lord Denning M.R. in *R. v Governor of Pentonville Prison Ex p. Azam* [1974] A.C. 18 at 31. *Azam* was referred to by Ackner L.J. in *R. v Hallstrom and another Ex p. W* [1985] 3 All E.R. 775 where the Court of Appeal held that leave under this section is also not required for applications for judicial review: see the note on civil proceedings, below.

In *Winch v Jones*, [1985] 3 All E.R. 97, the Court of Appeal held that the test to be applied by the court when considering to grant leave under this section was whether, on the materials immediately available to the court, the applicant's complaint appeared to deserve the fuller investigation which will be possible if the intended applicant is allowed to proceed. Sir John Donaldson M.R. said, at 102, that this section:

"is intended to strike a balance between the legitimate interests of the applicant to be allowed, at his own risk as to costs, to seek the adjudication of the courts on any claim which is not frivolous, vexatious or an abuse of the process and the equally legitimate interests of the respondent to such an application not to be subjected to the undoubted exceptional risk of being harassed by baseless claims by those who have been treated under the Mental Health Acts".

In *Seal v Chief Constable of South Wales Police*, below, para.20, Lord Bingham said that the judgment in *Winch v Jones* set the threshold for obtaining leave "at a very unexacting level . . . an applicant with an arguable case will be granted leave". Lord Brown said, at para.70, that "the test is now simply whether the case deserves further investigation by the court". Both remarks were made obiter. In *Johnston v Chief Constable of Merseyside Police* [2009] EWHC 2969 (QB); [2009] M.H.L.R. 343, Coulson J. considered whether the test identified by Sir John Donaldson in *Which v Jones* should be modified to take account of CPR Part 24 which introduced a new emphasis on allowing claims to go to trial only where they have a real prospect of success. His Lordship concluded, at para.15, "that a court faced with an application for permission under section 139 (2) of the Act must strive to apply the test set out by Sir John Donaldson MR in *Winch v Jones* . . ., with the proviso that the court should also consider whether, in all the circumstances, the proposed claim has a real prospect of success." *Winch v Jones* was cited in *James v Mayor and Burgesses of the London Borough of Havering*, (1992) 15 B.M.L.R. 1 CA, where Farquharson L.J. said, in a leave application, that the effect of this section goes further than that identified by Sir John Donaldson M.R. in that "it is not only protection against frivolous claims; it is also a protection from error in the circumstances set out in [subs.(1)]." His Lordship described the point of this section as providing a protection for mental health professionals "from the consequences of a wrong decision made in purported compliance with this Act" and said that "what one has to look at in deciding whether they are entitled to the protection of [this section] is what appeared to the social worker and the doctor at the time and how they reacted to it". Insofar as the decisions in *Winch* and *James* are inconsistent, it is submitted that *Winch* is to be preferred because it received the approval of the House of Lords in *Seal*.

The following remarks made by Lord Simon of Glaisdale in *Pountney v Griffiths*, below, on the precursor of this section in the 1959 Act are worthy of note:

> "Patients under the Mental Health Act may generally be inherently likely to harass those concerned with them by groundless charges and litigation, and may therefore have to suffer modification of the general right of free access to the courts. But they are, on the other hand, a class of citizen which experience has shown to be peculiarly vulnerable. I therefore presume to suggest that the operation of section 141 should be kept under close scrutiny by Parliament and the Department of Health and Social Security."

A successful application under subs.(2) of this section does not inhibit a judge on an application to strike out reaching a conclusion following fuller investigation that a statement of claim should be struck out as disclosing no reasonable cause of action (*X v A, B and C and the Mental Health Act Commission* (1991) 9 B.M.L.R. 91).

Article 12 of the Mental Health (Care and Treatment) (Scotland) Act 2003 (Consequential Provisions) Order 2005 (SI 2005/2078), which is reproduced in Pt 2, extends the protection afforded by this section to acts done in pursuance of that Order.

*Human Rights Act 1998*

**1–1254**    The provisions of this section do not transgress a patient's right to a fair trial under art.6(1) of the European Convention on Human Rights (*Seal v Chief Constable of South Wales Police* [2007] UKHL 31; [2007] 4 All E.R. 177 at para.20, applying *Ashingdane v United Kingdom* (1979) 2 E.H.R.R. 387).

In the *Wilkinson* case, below, Brooke L.J. said that in his opinion a claim under s.7 of the Human Rights Act 1998 would be caught by the language of this subsection and would require the leave of the High Court pursuant to subs.(2). His Lordship said: "Although the matter was not argued, I do not see why section 139 protection would fall foul of E.C.H.R. Article 6(1) so long as a full merits review is available in judicial review proceedings" (para.54). Hale L.J. said that she "was inclined to agree" with Brooke L.J. on this point (at para.61). In *R. (on the application of W) v Doncaster MBC* [2003] EWHC 192 Admin; 2003 6 C.C.L.R. 301 at para.56 Stanley Burnton J. said that if he had to decide the point he "would have been disposed to read [this section] down so as not to apply to breaches of Convention Rights".

*Subsection (1)*

**1–1255**    This "subsection does not create any cause of action and only relates to pre-existing possible liability. It creates a hurdle for a plaintiff to surmount"; per Morland J. in *X v A, B and C and the Mental Health Act Commission*, above, at 96.

PERSON. Or corporation (Interpretation Act 1978, s.5, Sch.1).

SHALL BE LIABLE. The question whether the protection of this section can be claimed by a health body in a situation where that body is vicariously liable for any shortcomings of a doctor employee in the performance of duties vested in him or her personally by this Act is undecided: see the conflicting opinions of Brooke and Hale L.JJ. in *R. (on the application of Wilkinson) v The Responsible Medical Officer Broadmoor Hospital, the Mental Health Act Commission Second Opinion Appointed Doctor and the Secretary of State for Health* [2001] EWCA Civ 1545; [2002] 1 W.L.R. 419, at paras 42 and 58.

CIVIL OR CRIMINAL PROCEEDINGS. The proceedings need not necessarily involve a patient.

ACT PURPORTING TO BE DONE IN PURSUANCE OF THIS ACT. This section applies to patients who are subject to guardianship and supervised community treatment. It would seem that the protection afforded by this section does not apply to omissions, such as a failure to detain a person under this Act. Nearly all acts done "in pursuance of this Act" will relate to detained patients. During the passage of the 1982 Act the Government resisted an amendment to exclude the provisions of this section for informal patients on the ground that this would remove the protection given to someone who purports to do something under the Act when he *believes* that the patient is a detained patient. The Minister for Health gave the following illustration in support of this argument:

"An ambulance man . . . has a patient in his charge whom he believes is a detained patient because he is told so. Therefore, he is told that he should prevent the patient escaping. If the patient attempts to go off and he takes steps to stop him escaping, he might be liable to an action thereafter, but he would be protected if we retain [this section] with its present wording" (*Hansard* HC, Vol.29, Col.173).

This interpretation is consistent with the use of the term "purporting " in this provision. Although there is Crown Court authority for the contention that this section does not cover acts done in respect of informal patients (*R. v Runighian* [1977] Crim. L.R. 361), Cox J. in *Labrooy v Hammersmith and Fulham LBC*, below, at para.15, rejected a submission that this section "only applies to those who have been detained under [the 1983] Act". It is submitted that the Government's approach is correct, and that although this section does not apply to every act done in respect of informal patients, it does apply to an informal patient if the individual undertaking the act genuinely believes at the relevant time that he or she is acting under a provision of this Act.

In *Pountney v Griffiths* [1976] A.C. 314, the House of Lords quashed the conviction of a nurse who had been charged with assaulting a patient when ushering the patient to his ward after a visit from the patient's family, on the ground that leave to prosecute had not been obtained under subs.(2) of this section. Their Lordships approved the finding of Lord Widgery C.J. in the Court of Appeal that "when a male nurse is on duty and exercising his functions of controlling the patients in the hospital, acts done in pursuance of such control are acts within the scope of [s.139] and are thus protected by the section." Although this Act provides for the detention and treatment of patients, it nowhere explicitly refers to the control of patients. The House of Lords held that : (1) this subsection extends to any act, provided that it had been carried out in purported pursuance of this Act, and that its scope is not limited to acts done or purported to be done in pursuance of functions specifically provided for in the terms of this Act; and (2) treating patients necessarily involves the exercise of discipline and control, and that suitable arrangements for visits to patients by family and friends was an obvious part of the patient's treatment. *Pountney v Griffiths* was cited by Auld L.J. in *R. v Broadmoor Special Hospital and the Secretary of State for the Department of Health Ex p. S, H, and D* [1998] C.O.D. 199, where the Court of Appeal held that the exercise of discipline and control in respect of a detained patient includes, where necessary, a power to search patients with or without cause and despite individual medical objections. To be lawful, a hospital's search policy must: (1) be proportionate to the level of risk posed by the patient population to the maintenance of a safe and therapeutic environment; and (2) take account of a patient's right to respect for private life under art.8 of the ECHR. The application of art.8 to the searching of patients is considered in the notes on that article in Pt 5 under the heading "Private life". A strip and intimate body search could engage art.3: see *Wainwright v United Kingdom* (2007) 44 E.H.R.R. 40, paras 42,43, noted in the General Note to art.3. Guidance on the searching of patients is given in the *Code of Practice* in Ch.16. In *S, H, and D,* Auld L.J. said that both this Act and the 1959 Act:

> "leave unspoken many of the necessary incidents of control flowing from a power of detention for treatment, including: the power to restrain patients, to keep them in seclusion . . ., to deprive them of their personal possessions for their own safety and to regulate the frequency and manner of visits to them'. . .".

Observations to similar effect, drawing on this judgment, were made by Lord Woolf M.R. in *Broadmoor Hospital Authority v R.* [2000] 2 All E.R. 727 at para.26. In *R. v Mersey Care National Health Service Trust Ex p. Munjaz* [2005] UKHL 58; [2006] 4 All E.R. 736, Lord Bingham said at para.34:

> "[T]he power to seclude a patient within a hospital is implied from the power to detain as a 'necessary ingredient flowing from a power of detention for treatment': see Auld L.J. in *R. v Broadmoor Special Hospital Authority Ex p. S,H and D* (February 5, 1998, unreported) and the Court of Appeal judgment in the present case".

In *Munjaz*, the House of Lords held that art.5 of the ECHR is not engaged in relation to the seclusion of a detained patient.

In *R. (on the application of E.) v Ashworth Hospital Authority* [2001] EWHC Admin. 1089; [2002] M.H.L.R. 150, Richards J., in holding that the power to control what patients wear is a necessary incident of the power to detain, said that to be lawful the implied power must be exercised:

   (i)   for the purpose of detention and/or treatment rather than for some ulterior purpose;

   (ii)  in accordance with *Wednesbury* principles of reasonableness; and

   (iii) compatibly with the European Convention on Human Rights and in particular with art.8.

**1–1256**    In the unreported case of *Ashingdane v Secretary of State for Social Services*, February 18, 1980, the Court of Appeal held that the immunity conferred by this section is confined to an act done by a person to whom authority to do an act of that type is expressly or impliedly conferred by this Act or by regulations made under it. Applying this test the Court held that the decision of a nurses' union not to allow patients who were subject to restriction orders to be transferred to a particular hospital was a policy decision which fell outside their express or implied authority and was not, therefore, covered by this section. Bridge L.J. said:

> "[Subs.(1)] clearly propound[s] a subjective and not an objective test. If a person is acting honestly with the intention of performing, in the best way he knows how, the statutory functions or duties which are cast upon him, then it seems to me he is acting in purported pursuance of the statute."

This section was engaged in a case where it was alleged that the defendants had made maliciously false, defamatory allegations in medical notes made by them in conection with the management and care of the claimant when he had suffered from mental illness. The information disclosed in the reports consisted of observations made in the course of formal records which formed part of the assessments and inquiries carried out for the purpose of determining whether the claimant should be admitted to hospital as a detained patient, or for investigating his mental health generally with a view to determining appropriate treatment or social care: see *Labrooy v Hammersmith and Fulham LBC* [2006] EWHC 1976 (QB); [2006] M.H.L.R. 253.

ACTED IN BAD FAITH OR WITHOUT REASONABLE CARE. In *Richardson v London County Council* [1957] 1 W.L.R. 751 it was held that: (1) whether a person has acted in bad faith or without reasonable care is a question of fact with the burden of proof lying with the applicant; and (2) this section offers protection even though the person proceeded against acted either without jurisdiction or misconstrued this Act, as long as the misconstruction was one which this Act was reasonably capable of bearing. In *R. (on the application of Wilkinson) v The Responsible Medical Officer Broadmoor Hospital, the Mental Health Act Commission Second Opinion Appointed Doctor and the Secretary of State for Health*, above, at para.57, Hale L.J., citing *Richardson*, said that it may well be that the immunity provided by this section does not relieve against "a negligent mistake of law as to the extent of the legal authority conferred by [this] Act".

If bad faith were established, there could be a private law claim based on misfeasance in public office (*TMM v London Borough of Hackney* [2010] EWHC 1349 (Admin), para.36).

*Subsection (2)*

Failure to obtain the necessary leave or consent required by this provision before the pro- **1–1257** ceedings are begun renders the proceedings a nullity (*Seal v Chief Constable of South Wales Police* [2007] UKHL 31; [2007] 4 All E.R. 177).

CIVIL PROCEEDINGS. This phrase does not include proceedings for judicial review. Acts purportedly done in pursuance of this Act can therefore be reviewed even if bad faith or lack of reasonable care are not alleged (*R. v Hallstrom and another Ex p. W*, above).

LEAVE. The leave of a High Court judge is required even if the case would normally be heard in the county court. An appeal lies to the Court of Appeal against a judge's decision but either the leave of the judge or of the Court of Appeal is required before the appeal can be made (*Moore v Commissioner of Metropolitan Police* [1968] 1 Q.B. 26). No appeal lies to the House of Lords from a refusal of the Court of Appeal of leave to appeal to the House (*Whitehouse v Board of Control* [1960] 1 W.L.R. 1093 HL).

The onus is on the applicant to satisfy the court or the D.P.P. that the proceedings should be commenced (*Carter v Commissioner of Police for the Metropolis* [1975] 1 W.L.R. 507 CA). The "overriding objective" set out in Pt 1 of the Civil Procedure Rules 1998 has no application to an application for leave under this section (*C v South London and Maudsley Hospital National Health Service Trust and the London Borough of Lambeth* [2001] M.H.L.R. 269.).

*Subsection (3)*

CONSENT OF THE DIRECTOR OF PUBLIC PROSECUTIONS. Is required for proceedings under **1–1258** s.127.

*Subsection (4)*

DOES NOT APPLY. The acts of a local social services authority performed in pursuance **1–1259** of this Act are protected by this section.

An approved mental health professional (AMHP) who is employed by a health body is acting on behalf of a local social services authority when performing the functions of an AMHP and is therefore protected by this section: see s.145(1AC).

SECRETARY OF STATE.    Or the Welsh Ministers (see the General Note to this Act and SI 2000/253, Sch.3).

HEALTH AUTHORITY    See the note on "shall be liable" in subs.(1) for the vicarious liability of health bodies.

### Notification of hospitals having arrangements for reception of urgent cases

1–1260    **140.** It shall be the duty of [every Primary Care Trust and of] every [Local Health Board] to give notice to every local social services authority for an area wholly or partly comprised within the [area of the Primary Care Trust or [Local Health Board]] specifying the hospital or hospitals administered by [or otherwise available] [to the [Primary Care Trust or] [Local Health Board]] in which arrangements are from time to time in force [—
   (a)  for the reception of patients in cases of special urgency;
   (b)  for the provision of accommodation or facilities designed so as to be specially suitable for patients who have not attained the age of 18 years.]

AMENDMENT
   The amendment to this section was made by the National Health Service and Community Care Act 1990 s.66(1), Sch.9 para.24(8), the Health Authorities Act 1995 s.2(1), Sch.1 para.107(12), the National Heath Service Reform and Health Care Professions Act 2002 s.2(5), Sch.2 para.48, the Mental Health Act 2007 s.31(4) and SI 2007/961 art.3, Sch. para.13(12).

DEFINITIONS
1–1261    Health Authority: s.145(1).
   local social services authority: s.145(1).
   hospital: s.145(1).
   patient: s.145(1).

GENERAL NOTE
1–1262    This section requires relevant health bodies to notify local social services authorities within their area of the arrangements that are in force for the reception of mentally disordered patients to hospital in cases of special urgency and the provision of accommodation or facilities designed to be specially suitable for child patients who are mentally disordered. For the duty to provide suitable accommodation and facilities for children, see s.131A, above. Also note the duty placed on Local Health Boards and Primary Care Trusts by s.39 to provide the courts with information as to the availability of hospital places.
   The Mental Health Act Commission suggested that if a patient cannot be admitted to hospital in an emergency for want of a bed the approved mental health professional should complete an application, making it out to the hospital which has been the subject of a notification under this provision, and convey the patient to that hospital. For a comment on this suggestion, see the note on "to hospital" in s.6(1).

RECEPTION.    This section does not oblige the specified hospitals to admit patients.

PATIENTS.    Are people who are suffering or appear to be suffering from mental disorder (s.145(1)). The patient may be either detained or informal.

### Members of Parliament suffering from mental illness

1–1263    **141.**—(1) Where a member of the House of Commons is authorised to be detained [under a relevant enactment] on the ground (however formulated) that he is suffering from [mental disorder], it shall be the duty of the court, authority or person on whose order or application, and of any registered medical practitioner upon whose recommendation or certificate, the detention was authorised, and of the person in charge of the hospital or other place in which the member is authorised to be detained, to notify the Speaker of the House of Commons that the detention has been authorised.

(2) Where the Speaker receives a notification under subsection (1) above, or is notified by two members of the House of Commons that they are credibly informed that such an authorisation has been given, the Speaker shall cause the member to whom the notification relates to be visited and examined by two registered medical practitioners appointed in accordance with subsection (3) below.

(3) The registered medical practitioners to be appointed for the purposes of subsection (2) above shall be appointed by the President of the Royal College of Psychiatrists and shall be practitioners appearing to the President to have special experience in the diagnosis or treatment of mental disorders.

(4) The registered medical practitioners appointed in accordance with subsection (3) above shall report to the Speaker whether the member is suffering from [mental disorder] and is authorised to be detained [under a relevant enactment] as such.

(5) If the report is to the effect that the member is suffering from [mental disorder] and authorised to be detained as aforesaid, the Speaker shall at the expiration of six months from the date of the report, if the House is then sitting, and otherwise as soon as may be after the House next sits, again cause the member to be visited and examined by two such registered medical practitioners as aforesaid, and the registered medical practitioners shall report as aforesaid.

(6) If the second report is that the member is suffering from [mental disorder] and authorised to be detained as mentioned in subsection (4) above, the Speaker shall forthwith lay both reports before the House of Commons, and thereupon the seat of the member shall become vacant.

[(6A) For the purposes of this section, the following are relevant enactments—
(a) this Act;
(b) the Criminal Procedure (Scotland) Act 1995 and the Mental Health (Care and Treatment) Scotland Act 2003 ("the Scottish enactments"); and
(c) the Mental Health (Northern Ireland) Order 1986 ("the 1986 Order").

(6B) In relation to an authorisation for detention under the Scottish enactments or the 1986 Order, the references in this section to mental disorder shall be construed in accordance with those enactments or that Order (as the case may be).]

[(6C) References in this section to a member who is authorised to be detained shall not include a member who is a community patient (whether or not he is recalled to hospital under section 17E above).]

(7) Any sums required for the payment of fees and expenses to registered medical practitioners acting in relation to a member of the House of Commons under this section shall be defrayed out of moneys provided by Parliament.

[(8) This section also has effect in relation to members of the Scottish Parliament but as it—
(a) any references to the House of Commons or the Speaker were references to the Scottish Parliament or (as the case may be) the Presiding Officer, and
(b) subsection (7) were omitted.]

[(9) This section also has effect in relation to members of the National Assembly for Wales but as if—

(a) references to the House of Commons were to the Assembly and references to the Speaker were to the presiding officer, and

(b) in subsection (7), for "defrayed out of moneys provided by Parliament" there were substituted "paid by the National Assembly for Wales [Commission]".]

[(10) This section also has effect in relation to members of the Northern Ireland Assembly but as if—

(a) references to the House of commons were to the Assembly and references to the Speaker were to the Presiding Officer; and

(b) in subsection (7), for "provided by Parliament" there were substituted "appropriated by Act of the Assembly".]

AMENDMENTS

The words in square brackets in subss.(1), (4), (5) and (6) were substituted, and subss.(6A) to (6C) were inserted by the Mental Health Act 2007 ss.1(4), 32(4), Sch.1 para.16, Sch.3 para.33.

Subsection (8) was added by the Scotland Act 1998 s.125, Sch.8 para.19, subs.(9) was inserted by the Government of Wales Act 1998 s.125, Sch.12 para.23 and subs.(10) was inserted by the Northern Ireland Act 1998 s.99, Sch.13 para.5. The word in square brackets in subs.(9)(b) was inserted by the Government of Wales Act 2006 s.160, Sch.10 para.13.

DEFINITIONS

**1–1264**  hospital: s.145(1).

mental disorder: ss.1, 145(1).

GENERAL NOTE

**1–1265**  This section sets out the procedure for vacating the seat of a member of the House of Commons, the Scottish Parliament (subs.(8)), the National Assembly for Wales (subs.(9)) and the Northern Ireland Assembly (subs.(10)) who has been detained under a relevant enactment (see subs.(6A)) on the ground that he or she is suffering from mental disorder. As this section is concerned with members who are unable to attend the legislature because they have been detained, it does not apply to a member who is a community patient (subs.6(C)).

During the debates on the Mental Health Bill, the Minister of State said that this provision has not been used since this Act became law (*Hansard,* HL Vol.688, col.760). It has been reported that the only occasion when an MP has been removed from the House of Commons on the ground of unsoundness of mind was in August 1916 when the Speaker invoked the Lunacy (Vacating Seats) Act 1886 in respect of a liberal MP, Dr Charles Leach (David McKie, "Bedlam on the benches", *The Guardian*, July 12, 2007).

*Human Rights Act 1998*

**1–1266**  This section engages art.3 of Protocol 1 of the European Convention on Human Rights which has been interpreted to include the right to stand for electoral office. It is likely that a court would hold that the power to vacate a seat pursues a legitimate aim, namely the removal of a member when he or she is unable to fulfil the representative function due to the fact of prolonged detention, and is proportionate.

## Pay, pensions, etc. of mentally disordered persons

**1–1267**  **142.**—(1) Where a periodic payment falls to be made to any person by way of pay or pension or otherwise in connection with the service or employment of that or any other person, and the payment falls to be made directly out of moneys provided by Parliament or the Consolidated Fund [or the Scottish Consolidated Fund], or other moneys administered by or under the control or supervision of a government department, the authority by whom the sum in question is payable, if satisfied after considering medical evidence that the person to whom it is payable (referred to in this section as "the patient") is incapable by reason of mental disorder of managing and administering his property and affairs, may, instead of paying the sum to the patient, apply it in accordance with subsection (2) below.

(2) The authority may pay the sum or such part of it as they think fit to the institution or person having the care of the patient, to be applied for his benefit and may pay the remainder (if any) or such part of the remainder as they think fit—

(a) to or for the benefit of persons who appear to the authority to be members of the patient's family or other persons for whom the patient might be expected to provide if he were not mentally disordered, or

(b) in reimbursement, with or without interest, of money applied by any person either in payment of the patient's debts (whether legally enforceable or not) or for the maintenance or other benefit of the patient or such persons as are mentioned in paragraph (a) above.

(3) In this section "government department" does not include a Northern Ireland department.

AMENDMENT

The words in square brackets in subsection (1) were inserted by the Scotland Act 1998 (Consequential Modifications) (No.2) Order 1999 (SI 1999/1820) art.4, Sch.2 para.71.

DEFINITION

mental disorder: ss.1, 145(1).                                                    **1–1268**

REPEAL

Although this section has been repealed by the Mental Capacity Act 2005 s.67(2), Sch.7   **1–1269**
it is reproduced because of the terms of s.67(1), Sch.6 para.29(5) and (6) of that Act which state:

"(5) Sub-paragraph (6) applies where, before the [repeal of s.142 on October 1, 2007], an authority has, in respect of a person referred to in that section as 'the patient', made payments under that section—

(a) to an institution or person having the care of the patient, or
(b) in accordance with subsection (2)(a) or (b) of that section.

(6) The authority may, in respect of the patient, continue to make payments under that section to that institution or person, or in accordance with subsection (2)(a) or (b) of that section, despite the [repeal of s.142]".

GENERAL NOTE

Under this section provision is made in the case of any pay, pension or similar payment   **1–1270**
payable by Parliament or the Government, for direct payment to the institution or person having the care of the patient. Any sums which remain can be paid to members of the patient's family, or to other persons for whom the patient might be expected to provide were he not mentally disordered, or to reimburse people who have paid his debts or helped to maintain him or his family. This section applies to any person who "is incapable by reason of mental disorder of managing and administering his property and affairs" and is not limited to either detained or hospital patients.

## [Regulations as to approvals in relation to England and Wales

1–1271    **142A.**—The Secretary of State jointly with the Welsh Ministers may by regulations make provision as to the circumstances in which—

(a) a practitioner approved for the purposes of section 12 above, or

(b) a person approved to act as an approved clinician for the purposes of this Act, approved in relation to England is to be treated, by virtue of his approval, as approved in relation to Wales too, and vice versa.]

AMENDMENT
This section was inserted by the Mental Health Act 2007 s.17.

GENERAL NOTE
1–1272    This section gives the Secretary of State, jointly with Welsh Ministers, the power to set out in regulations the circumstances in which approval in England under s.12, and approval as an approved clinician should be considered to mean approval in Wales, and vice versa.
The Mental Health (Mutual Recognition) Regulations 2008 (SI 2008/1204), which are reproduced in Pt 2, have been made under this section.

## [Delegation of powers of managers of NHS foundation trusts

1–1738    **142B.**—(1) The constitution of an NHS foundation trust may not provide for a function under this Act to be delegated otherwise than in accordance with provisions made by or under this Act.

(2) Paragraph 15(3) of Schedule 7 to the National Health Service Act 2006 (which provides that the powers of a public benefit corporation may be delegated to a committee of directors or to an executive director) shall have effect subject to this section.]

AMENDMENT
This section was inserted by the Mental Health Act 2007 s.45(3).

GENERAL NOTE
1–1274    Schedule 7 of the National Health Service Act 2006 sets out mandatory requirements for the contents of the constitution of a NHS foundation trust. The effect of this section is that the constitution may not permit the trust's functions under this Act to be delegated to executive directors or committees of directors unless that is permitted by this Act.

*Supplemental*

## General provisions as to regulations, orders and rules

1–1275    **143.**—(1) Any power of the Secretary of State or the Lord Chancellor to make regulations, orders or rules under this Act shall be exercisable by statutory instrument.

(2) Any Order in Council under this Act [or any order made [by the Secretary of State] under section 54A [or 68A(7)][. . .] above] and any statutory instrument containing regulations [made by the Secretary of State, or rules made,] under this Act shall be subject to annulment in pursuance of a resolution of either House of Parliament.

(3) No order shall be made [by the Secretary of State] under section [45A(10)] [68A(1)]) or 71(3) above unless a draft of it has been approved by a resolution of each House of Parliament.

[(3A) Subsections (3B) to (3D) apply where power to make regulations or an order under this Act is conferred on the Welsh Ministers (other than by or by virtue of the Government of Wales Act 2006).

(3B) Any power of the Welsh Ministers to make regulations or an order shall be exercisable by statutory instrument.

(3C) Any statutory instrument containing regulations, or an order under section 68A(7) above, made by the Welsh Ministers shall be subject to annulment in pursuance of a resolution of the National Assembly for Wales.

(3D) No order shall be made under section 68A(1) above by the Welsh Ministers unless a draft of it has been approved by a resolution of the National Assembly for Wales.

(3E) In this section—
(a) references to the Secretary of State include the Secretary of State and the Welsh Ministers acting jointly; and
(b) references to the Welsh Ministers include the Welsh Ministers and the Secretary of State acting jointly.]

[(4) This section does not apply to rules which are, by virtue of section 108 of this Act, to be made in accordance with Part 1 of Schedule 1 to the Constitutional Reform Act 2005.]

AMENDMENTS
In subs.(2) the words in square brackets were inserted by the Criminal Justice Act 1991 s.27(3). The words in square brackets were substituted and inserted by the Mental Health Act 2007 ss.37(5), 47(2),(3). The words omitted were repealed by s.55, Sch.11 Pt 6.

In subs.(3) the figure in square brackets was inserted by the Crime (Sentences) Act 1997 s.55, Sch.4 para.12(18).

Subs.(4) was inserted by the Constitutional Reform Act 2005, s.12, Sch.1, para.16.

GENERAL NOTE

*Subsection (1)*
SECRETARY OF STATE. Or, in relation to Wales, the Welsh Ministers (see the General **1–1276** Note to this Act and SI 1999/672 art.2, Sch.1).

THE LORD CHANCELLOR. Who cannot transfer his functions under this provision to another person (Constitutional Reform Act 2005 s.19, Sch.7).

## Power to amend local Acts
**144.** Her Majesty may by Order in Council repeal or amend any local enact- **1–1277** ment so far as appears to Her Majesty to be necessary in consequence of this Act.

## Interpretation
**145.**—(1) In this Act, unless the context otherwise requires— **1–1278**
"absent without leave" has the meaning given to it by section 18 above and related expressions [(including expressions relating to a patient's liability to be returned to a hospital or other place)] shall be construed accordingly;
"application for admission for assessment" has the meaning given in section 2 above;
"application for admission for treatment" has the meaning given in section 3 above;
["the appropriate tribunal" has the meaning given by section 66(4) above;]

["approved clinician" means a person approved by the Secretary of State (in relation to England) or by the Welsh Ministers (in relation to Wales) to act as an approved clinician for the purposes of this Act;]

["approved mental health professional" has the meaning given by section 114, above;]

["care home" has the same meaning as in the Care Standards Act 2000;]

["community patient" has the meaning given in section 17A above;]

["community treatment order" and "the community treatment order" have the meanings given in section 17A above;]

["the community treatment period" has the meaning given in section 20A above;]

[. . .]

["high security psychiatric services" has the same meaning as in [section 4 of the National Health Service Act 2006 or section 4 of the National Health Service (Wales) Act 2006]

"hospital" means—

(a) any health service hospital within the meaning of [National Health Service Act 2006 or the National Health Service (Wales) Act 2006]; and

(b) any accommodation provided by a local authority and used as a hospital or on behalf of the Secretary of State under [the National Health Service Act 2006, or of the Welsh Ministers under the National Health Service (Wales) Act 2006][; and

(c) any hospital as defined by section 206 of the National Health Service (Wales) Act 2006 which is vested in a Local Health Board;]

and "hospital within the meaning of Part II of this Act" has the meaning given in section 34 above;

["hospital direction" has the meaning given in section 45A(3)(a) above;]

"hospital order" and "guardianship order" have the meanings respectively given in section 37 above;

["independent hospital"—

(a) in relation to England, means a hospital as defined by section 275 of the National Health Service Act 2006 that is not a health service hospital as defined by that section, and

(b) in relation to Wales, has the same meaning as in the Care Standards Act 2000;]

"interim hospital order" has the meaning given in section 38 above;

["limitation direction" has the meaning given in section 45A(3)(b) above;]

["Local Health Board" means a Local Health Board established under section 11 of the National Health Services (Wales) Act 2006;]

"local social services authority" means a council which is a local authority for the purpose of the Local Authority Social Services Act 1970;

"the managers" means—

(a) in relation to a hospital vested in the Secretary of State for the purposes of his functions under [the National Health Service Act 2006, or in the Welsh Ministers for the purposes of their functions under the National Health Service (Wales) Act 2006], and in relation to any accommodation provided by a local authority and used as a hospital by or on behalf of the Secretary of State under [the National Health Service

Act 2006, or of the Welsh Ministers under the National Health Service (Wales) Act 2006,] the [Primary Care Trust,] [Strategic Health Authority,] [[Local Health Board] or Special Health Authority] responsible for the administration of the hospital;

(b) [ . . . ];

[(bb) in relation to a hospital vested in [a Primary Care Trust or] a National Health Service trust, [ . . . ] the trust;]

[(bc) in relation to a hospital vested in an NHS foundation trust, the trust;]

[(bd) in relation to a hospital vested in a Local Health Board, the Board;]

[(c) in relation to a registered establishment—

(i) if the establishment is in England, the person or persons registered as a service provider under Chapter 2 of Part 1 of the Health and Social Care Act 2008 in respect of the regulated activity (within the meaning of that Part) relating to the assessment or medical treatment of mental disorder that is carried out in the establishment, and

(ii) if the establishment is in Wales, the person or persons registered in respect of the establishment under Part 2 of the Care Standards Act 2000;]

and in this definition "hospital" means a hospital within the meaning of Part II of this Act;

"medical treatment" includes nursing, [psychological intervention and specialist mental health habilitation, rehabilitation and care (but see also subsection (4) below);]

["mental disorder" has the meaning given in section 1 above (subject to sections 86(4) and 141(6B));]

[ . . . ];

"nearest relative," in relation to a patient, has the meaning given in Part II of this Act;

"patient" [ . . .] means a person suffering or appearing to be suffering from mental disorder;

["Primary Care Trust" means a Primary Care Trust established under [section 18 of the National Health Service Act 2006];]

["registered establishment" has the meaning given in section 34 above;]

["the regulatory authority" means—

(a) in relation to England, the Care Quality Commission;

(b) in relation to Wales, the Welsh Ministers;]

[ . . .]

["the responsible hospital" has the meaning given in section 17A above;]

"restriction direction" has the meaning given to it by section 49 above;

"restriction order" has the meaning given to it by section 41 above;

["Special Health Authority" means a Special Health Authority established under [section 28 of the National Health Service Act 2006, or section 22 of the National Health Service (Wales) Act 2006];]

[ . . . ]

[ . . . ]

["Strategic Health Authority" means a Strategic Health Authority established under [section 13 of the National Health Service Act 2006];]

[ . . .]

"transfer direction" has the meaning given to it by section 47 above.

[(1AA) Where high security psychiatric services and other services are provided at a hospital, the part of the hospital at which high security psychiatric services are provided and the other part shall be treated as separate hospitals for the purposes of this Act.]

[(1AB) References in this Act to appropriate medical treatment shall be construed in accordance with section 3(4) above.]

[(1AC) References in this Act to an approved mental health professional shall be construed as references to an approved mental health professional acting on behalf of a local social services authority, unless the context otherwise requires.]

[. . .]

(2) [ . . . ]

(3) In relation to a person who is liable to be detained or subject to guardianship [or a community patient] by virtue of an order or direction under Part III of this Act (other than under section 35, 36, or 38), any reference in this Act to any enactment contained in Part II of this Act or in section 66 or 67 above shall be construed as a reference to that enactment as it applies to that person by virtue of Part III of this Act.

[(4) Any reference in this Act to medical treatment, in relation to mental disorder, shall be construed as a reference to medical treatment the purpose of which is to alleviate, or prevent a worsening of, the disorder or one or more of its symptoms or manifestations.]

AMENDMENTS

**1–1279**    In subs.(1) the words in square brackets were substituted or inserted by the Registered Homes Act 1984 s.57(1), Sch.1 para.11, the National Health Service and Community Care Act 1990 s.66(1), Sch.9 para.24(9), the Health Authorities Act 1995 s.2(1), Sch.1 para.107(14), the Mental Health (Patients in the Community) Act 1995 s.1(2), Sch.1 para.20, the Health Act 1999 s.65, Sch.4 para.69, the Crime (Sentences) Act 1997 s.55, Sch.4 para.12(19), the Health Act 1999 (Supplementary, Consequential, etc. Provisions) Order 2000 (SI 2000/90) Sch.1 para.16(9), the Care Standards Act 2000 s.116, Sch.4 para.9(10), the National Health Service and Health Care Professions Act 2002 s.2(5), Sch.2 para.49, the National Health Service Reform and Health Care Professions Act 2002 (Supplementary, Consequential, etc. Provisions) Regulations 2002 (SI 2002/2469) reg.4, Sch.1. the Mental Health Act 2007 ss.1(4), 7(2), 14(5), 21, 32(4), 46, Sch.1 para.17, Sch.2 para.11(2), Sch.3 para.34, SI 2007/961 art.3, Sch. para.13(13), SI 2008/2883 art.9, Sch.3 para.66, the Health and Social Care Act 2008 s.52, Sch.3 para.13 and SI 2010/813, art.5(5). Subsection (1A) and the definitions of "responsible after-care bodies" and "supervision application" in subs.(1) were repealed by the Mental Health Act 2007 s.55, Sch.11 Pt 5. The definition of "standard scale" and subs.(2) were repealed by the Statute Law (Repeals) Act 1993 s.1(1), Sch.1 Pt XIV, Group 2. The words omitted from para.(bb) of the definition of "the managers" were repealed by the Mental Health (Amendment) Act 1994 s.1. In the definition of "patient", the words omitted were repealed by the Mental Capacity Act 2005 s.67(2), Sch.7. In the definition of "the managers", paragraph (bc) was inserted by the Health and Social Care (Community Health and Standards) Act 2003 s.34, Sch.4 para.57. The definition of "special hospital" and para.(b) of the definition of "the managers" were repealed and subs.(1AA) was inserted by the Health Act 1999 s.65, Sch.4 para.69, Sch.5. Subsection (1AB) was inserted by the Mental Health Act 2007 s.4(1) and subs.(1AC) was inserted by s.21, Sch.2 para.11(3). The definition of "mental nursing home" was repealed by the Care Standards Act 2000 s.117(2), Sch.6. The references to the National Health Service Act 2006 and the National Health Service

(Wales) Act were substituted by the National Health Service (Consequential Provisions) Act 2006 s.2, Sch.1 para.70.

The words in square brackets in subs.(3) were inserted by Mental Health Act 2007 s.32(4), Sch.3 para.34(4). Subsection (4) was inserted by s.7(3).

GENERAL NOTE

*Subsection (1)*

APPROVED CLINICIAN. The Mental Health Act 1983 Approved Clinician (General) **1–1280** Directions 2008 are reproduced at Appendix D. In England, responsibility to approve a person as an approved clinician (AC) is given to Strategic Health Authorities who may delegate this function to a PCT : see paras 2 and 3 of the Directions. Approval is for the whole of England. Doctors who are approved as ACs are automatically approved as doctors who are approved under s.12(2) (s.12(2A)). See s.142A for the mutual recognition of approval as an AC in England and Wales.

CARE HOME. Under s.3 of the Care Standards Act 2000, an establishment is a care home **1–1281** if it provides accommodation together with nursing or personal care for any of the following persons:

(a) persons who are or have been ill;

(b) persons who have or have had a mental disorder;

(c) persons who are disabled or infirm;

(d) persons who are or have been dependent on alcohol or drugs.

HIGH SECURITY PSYCHIATRIC SERVICES. These comprise:

"hospital accommodation and services for persons who are—(a) liable to be detained under the Mental Health Act 1983, and (b) in the opinion of the Secretary of State require treatment under conditions of high security on account of their dangerous, violent or criminal propensities" (National Health Service Act 2006, s.4(1)).

HOSPITAL. The definition of hospital in s.275(1) of the 2006 Act is very broad:

"'hospital' means—

(a) any institution for the reception and treatment of persons suffering from illness,

(b) any maternity home, and

(c) any institution for the reception and treatment of persons during convalescence or persons requiring medical rehabilitation,

and includes clinics, dispensaries and out-patient departments maintained in connection with any such home or institution, and 'hospital accommodation' must be construed accordingly".

In *Re Couchman's Will Trusts* [1952] Ch. 391, Danckwerts J. considered a similar definition in s.79(1) of the National Health Service Act 1946 and held that:

1. "Reception" means taking people into a building and keeping them there. An institution that confines itself to treating patients as out-patients does not qualify.

2. The phrase "maintained in connection with" means maintained in connection with a particular hospital. It does not cover a clinic which was "maintained for the purpose of dealing with people who needed subsequent treatment, and it would have dealt

with persons coming from any hospital—a hospital, perhaps in another country—or with persons who were not connected with any hospital".

The definition does not include an independent hospital, which is brought within the scope of this Act by s.34(2).

Patients may be admitted under this Act to any hospital which is willing to admit them.

Prison "hospitals" are excluded from the definition as such facilities are provided under prison legislation. In *Knight v Home Office* [1990] 3 All E.R. 237, Pill J. held that the standard of care provided for a mentally ill prisoner in a prison hospital was not required to be as high as the standard of care provided in a psychiatric hospital outside prison. His Lordship refused, at 243, to "speculate on what an appropriate standard might be". Responsibility for prison health care was fully transferred from HM Prison Service to the NHS in April 2006. The Government has stated that "prisoners should have access to the same range and quality of services appropriate to their needs as are available to the general population through the NHS" (*Changing the Outlook*, DH and MHPS, 2001, p.5). This policy was considered in *Roberts v Secretary of State for Justice* [2009] EWHC 2321, where Michael Supperstone QC said at para.20:

"In my view, if there is any restriction on the access that prisoners have to health services so that prisoners are not provided with access to the same range and quality of healthcare services as the general public receives, it is in the public interest that such restriction be published and made generally known."

In *Riviere v France* (app.no.33834/03) the European Court of Human Rights observed that Recommendation No. R (98) 7 of the Committee of Ministers of the Council of Europe concerning the ethical and organisational aspects of health care in prison provides that prisoners suffering from serious mental disturbance should be kept and cared for in a hospital facility that was adequately equipped and possessed appropriately trained staff.

INDEPENDENT HOSPITAL.   Under s.2(2) of the Care Standards Act 2000, an independent hospital is a hospital which is not a health service hospital.

LOCAL SOCIAL SERVICES AUTHORITY.   In England is a non-metropolitan county council, a metropolitan district council, a London borough council or the Common Council of the City of London. In Wales is a county council or a county borough council (Local Authority Social Services Act 1970, s.1). As far as the Isles of Scilly are concerned, this expression shall, in relation to the Isles, mean the Council of the Isles constituted under the Isles of Scilly Order 1978: see the note on "Extent" in the General Note to this Act.

THE MANAGERS.   General guidance on the functions of the hospital managers is given in Ch.30 of the *Code of Practice*. Managers are accountable for the lawfulness of each patient's detention under this Act (ss.6(2), 40(1)(b)). The hospital managers "are primarily the people who 'detain' and therefore at common law are legally liable for any deprivation of liberty which is not justified by the Act," (Mental Health Act Commission, *First Biennial Report*, 1983–1985, para.8.13).

"Hospitals vested in the Secretary of State" include hospitals vested in the Welsh Ministers for the purposes of their functions under the National Health Service (Wales) Act 2006 (see the General Note to this Act and SI 2000/253, Sch.3).

The managers of a registered establishment act as a "public authority" within s.6 of the Human Rights Act 1998 when making decisions relating to the staffing and/or facilities to be provided to a detained patient (*R. (on the application of A) v Partnerships in Care* [2002] EWHC Admin 529; [2002] 1 W.L.R. 2610).

MEDICAL TREATMENT.    This definition, which should be considered along with subs.(4),  **1–1282**
is inclusive, not exhaustive. Medical treatment for the purposes of this Act also includes the
specific treatments mentioned in Pt IV. The treatments in the definition includes interventions that are not ordinarily considered to be "medical". Cases on the definition prior to its
amendment by the 2007 Act confirmed that the mere fact of being cared for or nursed is
sufficient to constitute medical treatment; see, for example *R. v South East Thames
Mental Health Review Tribunal Ex p. Ryan*, DC, June 30, 1987, where Watkins L.J. adopted
Denning L.J.'s definition of care in *Minister of Health v Royal Midland Counties Home for
Incurables at Leamington Spa* [1954] Ch.530 as being "the homely art of making people
comfortable and providing for their well being" so far as their condition allows, and *R. v
Mersey Mental Health Review Tribunal Ex p. D, DC, The Times,* April 13, 1987, where
the continued detention of the patient was upheld even though there was nothing other
than nursing care that could be provided for him. In *R. (on the application of Epsom and
St Helier NHS Trust) v Mental Health Review Tribunal* [2001] EWHC 101; [2001]
M.H.L.R. 8, Sullivan J. said at para.47:

"[O]ne has to look at the whole course of treatment. To do so, one has to look at the past,
present and future. It is not enough to say that a patient is not receiving treatment at a
particular time."

As the definition of mental disorder in s.1(2) includes "paraphilias like fetishism or paedophilia" (Explanatory Notes, para.24), medication which acts as a sexual suppressant could
be medical treatment for the purposes of this provision.

Practical examples of psychological interventions include "cognitive therapy, behaviour
therapy and counselling" (ibid., para.39).

A decision to transfer a patient to another hospital can, in certain circumstances, be
regarded as part of the patient's medical treatment: see *R. (on the application of F) v
Oxfordshire Mental Healthcare NHS Trust* [2001] EWHC 535 (Admin); [2002]
M.H.L.R. 140 where Sullivan J. said at para.68:

"Treatment includes rehabilitation, and I can envisage cases where transfer to a particular institution because of the particular form of therapy available there would be a
necessary step in the patient's rehabilitation."

An illustration of the distinction between habilitation and rehabilitation was given by Mr
Terry Davis MP at the Special Standing Committee on the Mental Health (Amendment)
Act 1982:

"'Habilitation' would cover those cases in which someone, probably a child, was so
severely mentally impaired that he had never learnt certain social skills such as being
able to eat or communicate in some way. The remedying of that impairment cannot
be called 'rehabilitation' because that person never had those skills, so one has to use
the word 'habilitation' in its technical sense" (Sitting of June 22, 1982).

PATIENT.    In *R. v Davies and Poolton,* December 16, 1999, the Court of Appeal considered a similar definition of patient found in s.22 of the Registered Homes Act 1984.
The court said:

"It is obvious that a person may be receiving treatment for mental disorder, without actually suffering from it, if he or she *appears* to be suffering from it. Much medical
diagnosis and treatment is based on probability, not certainty or therefore, in some
cases, actuality."

In *R. v Merseyside Mental Health Review Tribunal Ex p. K* [1990] 1 All E.R. 694 CA, the
appellant, a restricted patient, sought judicial review of the tribunal's decision on the

ground that once it had found as a fact that he was not suffering from mental disorder he was no longer a "patient" as defined in this section and he was therefore entitled to an absolute discharge. The Court of Appeal affirmed the tribunal's decision to grant the patient a conditional discharge and held that a restricted patient remains a "patient" until he is discharged absolutely. Butler-Sloss L.J. said at 699:

"At the time the offender is detained under a hospital order he is a patient within the interpretation of section 145. By section 41(3)(a) a restricted patient continues to be liable to be detained until discharged under section 73 and, in my judgment, remains a patient until he is discharged absolutely, if at all, by the tribunal. Any other interpretation of the word 'patient' makes nonsense of the framework of the 1983 Act and the hoped-for progression to discharge of the treatable patient, treatable being a prerequisite of his original admission."

REGULATORY AUTHORITY. The regulatory functions of the Welsh Ministers under this Act are performed by Health Inspectorate Wales.

*Subsection (1AA)*

**1–1283**    If a hospital contains a unit where high security services are provided, that unit is treated as a separate hospital for the purposes of this Act.

*Subsection (1AC)*

**1–1284**    The fact that the AMHP acts on behalf of the local authority does not provide the authority with a power to direct the AMHP to make a particular decision while performing a function under this Act: see the note on s.114(10).

*Subsection (3)*

**1–1285**    I gratefully adopt Phil Fennell's interpretation of this obscurely drafted provision:

"For certain purposes, such as the renewal of detention, and entitlement to [tribunals hearings], parties liable to be detained under Part III are treated as if liable to be detained under section 3. What section 145(3) does is to ensure that this happens subject to the modifications specified in sections 40(4), 41(3) and (5), 55(4) and Schedule 1, Part 1. . . . The modifications relate to the powers to remand and to sentence to interim hospital orders. People who are on remand remain under the jurisdiction of the courts. They are liable to be detained, but they remain under the jurisdiction of the courts rather than the mental health system. The reason that they are expressly mentioned in section 145(3) is that they have no rights to seek discharge from a [tribunal]" ("Double Detention under the Mental Health Act 1984—A Case of Extra Parliamentary Legislation?" [1991] J.S.W.F.L. 200).

*Subsection (4)*

**1–1286**    This provision, which is considered in the *Code of Practice* at paras 6.3 to 6.5, was tabled as an amendment to the Mental Health Bill by Mr Chris Bryant MP. It received cross party support and was accepted by the Government because of the concerns that had been expressed about the absence of any reference to therapeutic benefit in the appropriate treatment test: see the notes on s.3(2)(d). The test set out here is one of an intention to bring about therapeutic benefit, rather than the likelihood of achieving such benefit; also see para.6.4 of the *Code of Practice*. In *MD v Nottinghamshire Health Care NHS Trust* [2010] UKUT 59 (AAC), para.34, Judge Jacobs said that this provision did not require the treatment to reduce risk.

Baroness Royall, speaking for the Government, explained the distinction between symptoms and manifestations:

"[S]ymptoms and manifestations are intended to cover all the ways that the disorder affects the patient's functioning, in terms of how the patient thinks, feels or believes. While there is almost certainly some overlap between the two, broadly speaking we think that 'symptoms' covers the consequences of which patients themselves complain while 'manifestations' more obviously covers the evidence of the disorder as seen by other people. In the end, the important point is not the distinction between the two words but the certainty that between them they cover the whole gamut of what can be addressed by medical treatment" (*Hansard*, HL Vol.693, col.835).

Mr Bryant gave the following example of the need for the manifestation to have a direct relationship with the mental disorder:

"Someone who is schizophrenic might suffer and be extremely angry because he has just split up with his partner. He might be furious with her. However, we should not be allowed to detain somebody solely to treat that anger unless the perhaps violent anger is a direct manifestation of the mental disorder from which he suffers" (*Hansard*, HC Vol.461, col.1280).

## Application to Scotland
**146.** Sections 42(6), 80, [. . .], 116, 122, [. . .], 137, 139(1), 141, 142, 143 (so **1–1287** far as applicable to any Order in Council extending to Scotland) and 144 above shall extend to Scotland together with any amendment or repeal by this Act or any provision of Schedule 5 to this Act relating to any enactment which so extends; but, except as aforesaid and except so far as it relates to the interpretation or commencement of the said provisions, this Act shall not extend to Scotland.

AMENDMENT
The words omitted were repealed by the Mental Capacity Act 2005 s.67(2), Sch.7 and the Mental Health Act 2007 s.55, Sch.11 Pts 5 and 7.

DEFINITION
    patient: s.145(1).     **1–1288**

GENERAL NOTE
    This section provides for a limited application to this Act to Scotland.     **1–1289**

## Application to Northern Ireland
**147.** Sections 81, 82, 86, 87, 88 (and so far as applied by that section sections **1–1290** 18, 22, and 138), [. . .], section 128 (except so far as it relates to patients subject to guardianship), 137, 139, 141, 142, 143 (so far as applicable to any Order in Council extending to Northern Ireland) and 144 above shall extend to Northern Ireland together with any amendment or repeal by this Act of or any provision of Schedule 5 to this Act relating to any enactment which so extends; but except as aforesaid and except so far as it relates to the interpretation or commencement of the said provisions, this Act shall not extend to Northern Ireland.

AMENDMENT
The words omitted were repealed by the Mental Capacity Act 2005, s.67(2), Sch.7.

DEFINITION
    patient: s.145(1).     **1–1291**

GENERAL NOTE

**1–1292**    This section provides for a limited application of this Act to Northern Ireland.

## Consequential and transitional provisions and repeals

**1–1293**    **148.**—(1) Schedule 4 (consequential amendments) and Schedule 5 (transitional and saving provisions) to this Act shall have effect but without prejudice to the operation of sections 15 to 17 of the Interpretation Act 1978 (which relate to the effect of repeals).

(2) Where any amendment in Schedule 4 to this Act affects an enactment amended by the Mental Health (Amendment) Act 1982 the amendment in Schedule 4 shall come into force immediately after the provision of the Act of 1982 amending that enactment.

(3) The enactments specified in Schedule 6 to this Act are hereby repealed to the extent mentioned in the third column of that Schedule.

## Short title, commencement and application to Scilly Isles

**1–1294**    **149.**—(1) This Act may be cited as the Mental Health Act 1983.

(2) Subject to subsection (3) below and Schedule 5 to this Act, this Act shall come into force on September 30, 1983.

(3) [*Repealed by the Statute Law (Repeals) Act 2004, Sch.1, Pt 17, Group 8.*]

(4) Section 130(4) of the National Health Service Act 1977 (which provides for the extension of that Act to the Isles of Scilly) shall have effect as if the references to that Act included references to this Act.

GENERAL NOTE

*Subsection (4)*

**1–1295**    The Isles of Scilly (Mental Health) Order 1985 (SI 1985/149) extends this Act to the Isles of Scilly from March 12, 1985, with the modification that the expression "local social services authority" in this Act shall, in relation to the Isles, mean the Council of the Isles of Scilly.

## SCHEDULES

**1–1296**    Sections 40(4),                    SCHEDULE 1
41(3) and (5),
and 55(4)

### APPLICATION OF CERTAIN PROVISIONS TO PATIENTS SUBJECT TO HOSPITAL AND GUARDIANSHIP ORDERS

### PART I

### PATIENTS NOT SUBJECT TO SPECIAL RESTRICTIONS

**1–1297**    1. Sections 9, 10, 17 [to 17C, 17E, 17F, 20A], [21 to 21B], 24(3) and (4), [26] to 28, 31, 32, 34, 67 and 76 shall apply in relation to the patient without modification.

2. Sections [. . .], [17D, 17G, 18 to 20, 20B], 22, 23[, 66 and 68] shall apply in relation to the patient with the modifications specified in [paragraphs 2A][to 10] below.

[2A In section 17D(2)(a) for the reference to section 6(2) above there shall be substituted a reference to section 40(1)(b) below.

2B In section 17G—

(a) in subsection (2) for the reference to section 6(2) above there shall be substituted a reference to section 40(1)(b) below;

(b) in subsection (4) for paragraphs (a) and (b) there shall be substituted the words "the order or direction under Part 3 of this Act in respect of him were an order or direction for his admission or removal to that other hospital"; and

(c) in subsection (5) for the words from "the patient" to the end there shall be substituted the words "the date of the relevant order or direction under Part 3 of this Act were the date on which the community treatment order is revoked".]

3. [. . .]
4. In section 18 subsection (5) shall be omitted.
5. In section 19(2) for the words from "as follows" to the end of the subsection there shall be substituted the words "as if the order or direction under Part III of this Act by virtue of which he was liable to be detained or subject to guardianship before being transferred were an order or direction for his admission or removal to the hospital to which he is transferred, or placing him under the guardianship of the authority or person into whose guardianship he is transferred, as the case may be".

[5A In section 19A(2), paragraph (b) shall be omitted.]
6. In section 20—

(a) in subsection (1) for the words from "day on which he was" to "as the case may be" there shall be substituted the words "date of the relevant order or direction under Part III of this Act;" [. . .]

[6A In section 20B(1), for the reference to the application for admission for treatment there shall be substituted a reference to the order or direction under Part 3 of this Act by virtue of which the patient is liable to be detained.]

7. In section 22 for references to an application for admission or a guardianship application there shall be substituted references to the order or direction under Part III of this Act by virtue of which the patient is liable to be detained or subject to guardianship.

8. In section 23(2)—

(a) in paragraph (a) the words "for assessment or" shall be omitted; and

(b) in paragraphs (a) [to (c)] the references to the nearest relative shall be omitted.

[. . .]
9. In section 66—

(a) in subsection (1), paragraphs (a), (b), (c), (g) and (h), the words in parenthesis in paragraph (i) and paragraph (ii) shall be omitted; and

(b) in subsection (2), paragraphs (a), (b), (c) and (g) [, and in paragraph (d), "(g)", shall be omitted.]

[10. In section 68—

(a) in subsection (1) paragraph (a) shall be omitted; and

(b) subsections (2) to (5) shall apply if the patient falls within paragraph (e) of subsection (1), but not otherwise.]

AMENDMENTS
The amendments to this Part were made by the Mental Health (Patients in the Community) Act 1995 s.2(1), Sch.1 and the Mental Health Act 2007 ss.32(4), 36(4), 37(6), 55, Sch.3 para.36, Sch.11 Pts 1 and 5.

PART II

PATIENTS SUBJECT TO SPECIAL RESTRICTIONS

1. Sections 24(3) and (4), 32 and 76 shall apply in relation to the patient without modification. **1–1298**

2. Sections [17, 18, 19], 22, 23 and 34 shall apply in relation to the patient with the modifications specified in paragraphs 3 to 8 below.

3. In section 17—

(a) in subsection (1) after the word "may" there shall be inserted the words "with the consent of the Secretary of State";

[(aa) subsections (2A) and (2B) shall be omitted;]

(b) in subsection (4) after the words ["the responsible clinician"] and after the words ["that clinician"] there shall be inserted the words "or the Secretary of State"; and

(c) in subsection (5) after the word "recalled" there shall be inserted the words ["by the responsible clinician"], and for the words from "he has ceased" to the end of the subsection there shall be substituted the words "the expiration of the period of [twelve] months beginning with the first day of his absence on leave".

4. In section 18 there shall be omitted—

(a) in subsection (1) the words "subject to the provisions of this section"; and

(b) subsections (3), (4) and (5).

5. In section 19—

(a) in subsection (1) after the word "may" in paragraph (a) there shall be inserted the words "with the consent of the Secretary of State", and the words from "or into" to the end of the subsection shall be omitted; [...]

(b) in subsection (2) for the words from "as follows" to the end of the subsection there shall be substituted the words "as if the order or direction under Part III of this Act by virtue of which he was liable to be detained before being transferred were an order or direction for his admission or removal to the hospital to which he is transferred" [and

(c) in subsection (3) after the words "may at any time" there shall be inserted the words ", with the consent of the Secretary of State",]

[6. In section 22, subsections (1) and (5) shall not apply.]

7. In section 23—

(a) in subsection (1) references to guardianship shall be omitted and after the word "made" there shall be inserted the words "with the consent of the Secretary of State and"

(b) in subsection (2)—

(i) in paragraph (a) the words "for assessment or" and "or by the nearest relative of the patient" shall be omitted; and

(ii) paragraph (b) shall be omitted.

8. In section 34, in subsection (1) the definition of "the nominated medical attendant" and subsection (3) shall be omitted.

AMENDMENT

In paras 2 and 3 the figures and words in square brackets were substituted, and para.6 was substituted by the Mental Health Act 2007 ss.11(8), 33(4), 33(3), Sch.3 para.37. The substitution of "twelve" in para.3(c) was made by the Mental Health (Patients in the Community) Act 1995 s.3(3).

The word omitted in para.5 was repealed by the Crime (Sentences) Act 1997 s.56(2), Sch.6. Paragraph 5(c) was inserted by s.49(3).

DEFINITIONS

**1–1299**    hospital order: ss.37, 145(1).
patient: s.145(1).

**SCHEDULE 2**

MENTAL HEALTH REVIEW [TRIBUNAL FOR WALES]

1. [The Mental Health Review Tribunal for Wales] shall consist of— **1–1300**

(a) a number of persons (referred to in this Schedule as "the legal members") appointed by the Lord Chancellor and having such legal experience as the Lord Chancellor considers suitable;

(b) a number of persons (referred to in this Schedule as "the medical members") being registered medical practitioners appointed by the Lord Chancellor [. . .]; and

(c) a number of persons appointed by the Lord Chancellor [. . .] and having such experience in administration, such knowledge of social services or such other qualifications or experience as the Lord Chancellor considers suitable.

[1A. As part of the selection process for an appointment under paragraph 1(b) or (c) the Judicial Appointments Commission shall consult the Secretary of State.]

2. [Subject to paragraph 2A below,] the members of [the Mental Health Review Tribunal for Wales] shall hold and vacate office under the terms of the instrument under which they are appointed, but may resign office by notice in writing to the Lord Chancellor; and any such member who ceases to hold office shall be eligible for re-appointment.

[2A. A member of [the Mental Health Review Tribunal for Wales] shall vacate office on the day on which he attains the age of 70 years; but this paragraph is subject to section 26(4) to (6) of the Judicial Pensions and Retirement Act 1993 (power to authorise continuance in office up to the age of 75 years).]

[3. (1) [. . .]

(2) The Lord Chancellor shall appoint one of the legal members of the Mental Health Review Tribunal for Wales to be the President of that tribunal.]

4. Subject to rules made by the Lord Chancellor under section 78(2)(c) above, the members who are to constitute [the Mental Health Review Tribunal for Wales] for the purposes of any proceedings or class or group of proceedings under this Act shall be appointed by the chairman of the tribunal or [. . .], by another member of the tribunal appointed for the purpose by the chairman; and of the members so appointed—

(a) one or more shall be appointed from the legal members;

(b) one or more shall be appointed from the medical members; and

(c) one or more shall be appointed from the members who are neither legal nor medical members.

[5.—(1) A member of the First-tier Tribunal who is eligible to decide any matter in a case under this Act may, at the request of the President of the Mental Health Review Tribunal for Wales and with the approval of the Senior President of Tribunals, act as a member of the Mental Health Review Tribunal for Wales.

(2) Every person while acting under this paragraph may perform any of the functions of a member of the Mental Health Review Tribunal for Wales.

(3) Until section 38(7) of the Mental Health Act 2007 comes into force, the reference in sub-paragraph (1) to the President of the Mental Health Review Tribunal for Wales is to be read as a reference to the chairman of the tribunal.]

6. Subject to any rules made by the Lord Chancellor under section 78(4)(a) above, where the chairman of the tribunal is included among the persons appointed under para.4 above, he shall be President of the tribunal; and in any other case the chairman of the tribunal shall be such one of the members so appointed (being one of the legal members) as the chairman may nominate.

AMENDMENTS

The amendments to this Schedule were made by the Judicial Pensions and Retirement Act 1993 s.26, Sch.6 para.40, the Constitutional Reform Act 2005 ss.15, 146, Sch.4 para.158(3), Sch.18 Pt.2; the Mental Health Act 2007 s.38(7)(b); SI 2008/2833 art.9, Sch.3 para.67; and SI 2009/1307 art.5, Sch.1 para.162.

GENERAL NOTE

**1–1301**    The President and members of the MHRT for Wales are subject to the selection process set out in ss.86 to 93 of the Constitutional Reform Act 2005 (s.85, Sch.14 Pt 3).

*Paragraph 1*

**1–1302**    THE LORD CHANCELLOR.   Who, in the exercise of his functions under this provision in relation to Wales, is required to consult with the Welsh Ministers with regard to appointments made under paragraphs (b) and (c) (see the General Note to this Act and SI 1999/ 672 art.5, Sch.2). The Lord Chancellor cannot transfer his functions under this paragraph, or under paras 2 or 3, to another person (Constitutional Reform Act 2005 s.19, Sch.7).

*Paragraph 5*

**1–1303**    This allows members of the First-tier Tribunal who may hear mental health cases to sit in the Mental Health Review Tribunal for Wales. There is no reciprocal arrangement.

| Section 113 | **SCHEDULE 3** |
|---|---|

**1–1304**    *[Repealed by the Mental Capacity Act 2005 s.67(2), Sch.7.]*

| Section 148 | **SCHEDULE 4** |
|---|---|

CONSEQUENTIAL AMENDMENTS

**1–1305**    *[Not reproduced.]*

| Section 148 | **SCHEDULE 5** |
|---|---|

TRANSITIONAL AND SAVING PROVISIONS

**1–1306**    1. Where any period of time specified in an enactment repealed by this Act is current at the commencement of this Act, this Act shall have effect as if the corresponding provision of this Act had been in force when that period began to run.

2. Nothing in this Act shall affect the interpretation of any provision of the Mental Health Act 1959 which is not repealed by this Act and accordingly sections 1 and 145(1) of this Act shall apply to any such provision as if it were contained in this Act.

3. Where, apart from this paragraph, anything done under or for the purposes of any enactment which is repealed by this Act would cease to have effect by virtue of that repeal it shall have effect as if it had been done under or for the purposes of the corresponding provisions of this Act.

4. [. . .]

**1–1307**    5. [. . .]

6. This Act shall apply in relation to any authority for the detention or guardianship of a person who was liable to be detained or subject to guardianship under the Mental Health Act 1959 immediately before September 30, 1983 as if the provisions of this Act which derive from provisions amended by section 1 or 2 of the Mental Health (Amendment) Act 1982 and the amendments in Sch.3 to that Act which are consequential on those sections were included in this Act in the form the provisions from which they derive would take if those amendments were disregarded but this provision shall not apply to any renewal of that authority on or after that date.

7. [. . .]

8. [. . .]

9.—(1) [. . .]

(2) Section 20(2) of this Act shall have effect in relation to any authority renewed before October 1, 1983 with the substitution for the words "six months" of the words "one year" and for the words "one year" in both places they occur of the words "two years".

(3) [. . .]

10. [. . .]

11. [. . .]

12. [. . .]

13. [. . .]

14. [. . .]

15. The provisions of this Act which derive from sections 24 to 27 of the Mental Health (Amendment) Act 1982 shall have effect in relation to a transfer direction given before September 30, 1983 as well as in relation to one given later, but where, apart from this paragraph, a transfer direction given before September 30, 1983 would by virtue of the words in section 50(3) of this Act which are derived from section 24(3) of the Mental Health (Amendment) Act 1982 have ceased to have effect before that date it shall cease to have effect on that date.

16. The words in section 42(1) of this Act which derive from the amendment of section 66(1) of the Mental Health Act 1959 by section 28(1) of the Mental Health (Amendment) Act 1982 and the provisions of this Act which derive from section 28(3) of and Sch.1 to that Act have in relation to a restriction order or, as the case may be, a restriction direction made or given before September 30, 1983 as well as in relation to one made or given later, but—

    (a)  any reference to a tribunal under section 66(6) of the said Act of 1959 in respect of a patient shall be treated for the purposes of subsections (1) and (2) of section 77 of this Act in their application to sections 70 and 75(2) of this Act as an application made by him; and

    (b)  sections 71(5) and 75(1)(*a*) of this Act do not apply where the period in question has expired before September 30, 1983.

17. Section 91(2) of this Act shall not apply in relation to a patient removed from England and Wales before September 30, 1983.

18.[. . .]

19. [. . .]

20. The repeal by the Mental Health (Amendment) Act 1982 of section 77 of the Mental Health Act 1959 does not affect subsection (4) of that section in its application to a transfer direction given before September 30, 1983, but after the coming into force of this Act that subsection shall effect for that purpose as if for the references to subsection (6) of section 60, Part IV of that Act and the provisions of that Act there were substituted respectively references to section 37(8), Part III and the provisions of this Act.

[21. Any direction to which section 71(4) of the Mental Health Act 1959 applied immediately before the commencement of this Act shall have the same effect as a hospital order together with a restriction order, made without limitation of time.]

22. [. . .]

23. For any reference in any enactment, instrument, deed or other document to a receiver under Part VIII of the Mental Health Act 1959 there shall be substituted a reference to a receiver under Part VII of this Act.

24. Nothing in this Act shall affect the operation of the proviso to section 107(5) of the Mental Health Act 1959 in relation to a charge created before the commencement of this Act under that section.

25. Nothing in this Act shall affect the operation of subsection (6) of section 112 of the Mental Health Act 1959 in relation to a charge created before the commencement of this Act by virtue of subsection (5) of that section.

26. [. . .]

27. Nothing in this Act shall affect the operation of section 116 of the Mental Health Act 1959 in relation to orders made, directions or authorities given or other instruments issued before the commencement of this Act.

28. References to applications, recommendations, reports and other documents in section 126 of this Act shall include those to which sections 125 of the Mental Health Act 1959 applied immediately before the commencement of this Act and references in section 139 of this Act to the acts to which that section applies shall include those to which section 141 of the said Act of 1959 applied at that time.

29. The repeal by the Mental Health Act 1959 of the Mental Treatment Act 1930 shall not affect any amendment effected by section 20 of that Act in any enactment not repealed by the said Act of 1959.

30. The repeal by the Mental Health Act 1959 of the provisions of the Lunacy Act 1890 and of the Mental Deficiency Act 1913 relating to the superannuation of officers or employees shall not affect any arrangements for the payment of allowances or other benefits made in accordance with those provisions and in force on November 1, 1960.

31.—(1) Any patient who immediately before the commencement of this Act was liable to be detained in a hospital or subject to guardianship by virtue of para.9 of Sch.6 to the Mental Health Act 1959 shall unless previously discharged continue to be so liable for the remainder of the period of his treatment current on November 1, 1960.

(2) The patient may before the expiration of the period of treatment referred to in sub-paragraph (1) above apply to a Mental Health Review Tribunal.

32. Any patient who immediately before the commencement of this Act was liable to be detained or subject to guardianship by virtue of an authority which had been renewed under para.11 of Sch.6 to the Mental Health Act 1959 shall unless previously discharged continue to be so liable during the period for which that authority was so renewed.

33.—(1) This paragraph applies to patients who at the commencement of this Act are liable to be detained or subject to guardianship by virtue of para.31 or 32 above.

(2) Authority for the detention or guardianship of the patient may on the expiration of the relevant period, unless the patient has previously been discharged, be renewed for a further period of two years.

(3) Sections 20(3) to (10) and 66(1)(*f*) of this Act shall apply in relation to the renewal of authority for the detenton or guardianship of a patient under this paragraph as they apply in relation to the renewal of authority for the detention or guardianship of the patient under section 20(2).

**1–1308**   (4) In this paragraph "the relevant period" means—

(a) in relation to a patient liable to be detained or subject to guardianship by virtue of the said paragraph 31, the period of his treatment referred to in that paragraph;

(b) in relation to a patient detained by virtue of the said paragraph 32, the period for which authority for the detention or guardianship of the patient has been renewed under paragraph 11 of Schedule 6 to the 1959 Act;

(c) in relation to a patient the authority for whose detention or guardianship has previously been renewed under this paragraph, the latest period for which it has been so renewed.

34.—(1) Any patient who is liable to be detained in a hospital or subject to guardianship by virtue of para.31 above shall (subject to the exceptions and modifications specified in the following provisions of this paragraph) be treated as if he has been admitted to the hospital in pursuance of an application for admission for treatment under Part II of this Act or had been received into guardianship in pursuance of a guardianship application under the said Part II and had been so admitted or received as a patient suffering from the form or forms of mental disorder recorded under para.7 of Sch.6 to the Mental Health Act 1959 or, if a different form or forms have been specified in a report under section 38 of the Act as applied by that paragraph, the form or forms so specified.

(2) Section 20 of this Act shall not apply in relation to the patient, but the provisions of para.33 above shall apply instead.

(3) Any patient to whom para.9(3) of Sch.6 to the Mental Health Act 1959 applied at the commencement of this Act who fell within paragraph (*b*) of that paragraph shall cease to be liable to be detained on attaining the age of 25 years unless, during the period of two months ending on the date when he attains that age, the responsible medical officers records his opinion under the following provisions of this Schedule that the patient is unfit for discharge.

(4) If the patient was immediately before November 1, 1960 liable to be detained by virtue of section 6, 8(1) or 9 of the Mental Deficiency Act 1913, the power of discharging him under section 23 of this Act shall not be exercisable by his nearest relative, but his nearest relative may make one application in respect of him to [the appropriate tribunal] in any period of 12 months.

35.—(1) The responsible medical officer may record for the purposes of para.34(3) above his opinion that a patient detained in a hospital is unfit for discharge if it appears to the responsible medical officer—

(a) that if that patient were released from the hospital he would be likely to act in a manner dangerous to other persons or to himself, or would be likely to resort to criminal activities; or

(b) that that patient is incapable of caring for himself and that there is no suitable hospital or other establishment into which he can be admitted and where he would be likely to remain voluntarily;

and where the responsible medical officer records his opinion as aforesaid he shall also record the grounds for his opinion.

(2) Where the responsible medical officer records his opinion under this paragraph in respect of a patient, the managers of the hospital or other persons in charge of the establishment where he is for the time being detained or liable to be detained shall cause the patient to be informed, and the patient may, at any time before the expiration of the period of 28 days beginning with the date on which he is so informed, apply to a Mental Health Review Tribunal.

(3) On any application under sub-paragraph (2) above the tribunal shall, if satisfied that none of the conditions set out in paragraphs (*a*) and (*b*) of sub-paragraph (1) above are fulfilled, direct that the patient be discharged, and subsection (1) of section 72 of this Act shall have effect in relation to the application as if paragraph (*b*) of that subsection were omitted.

36. Any person who immediately before the commencement of this Act was deemed to have been named as the guardian of any patient under para.14 of Sch.6 to the Mental Health Act 1959 shall be deemed for the purposes of this Act to have been named as the guardian of the patient in an application for his reception into guardianship under Part II of this Act accepted on that person's behalf by the relevant local authority.

37.—(1) This paragraph applies to patients who immediately before the commencement of this Act **1–1309** were transferred patients within the meaning of para.15 of Sch.6 to the Mental Health Act 1959.

(2) A transferred patient who immediately before the commencement of this Act was by virtue of sub-paragraph (2) of that paragraph treated for the purposes of that Act as if he were liable to be detained in a hospital in pursuance of a direction under section 71 of that Act shall be treated as if he were so liable in pursuance of a [hospital order together with a restriction order, made without limitation of time].

(3) A transferred patient who immediately before the commencement of this Act was by virtue of sub-paragraph (3) of that paragraph treated for the purposes of the Act as if he were liable to be detained in a hospital by virtue of a transfer direction under section 72 of that Act and as if a direction restricting his discharge had been given under section 74 of that Act shall be treated as if he were liable by virtue of a transfer direction under section 47 of this Act and as if a restriction direction had been given under section 49 of this Act.

(4) Section 84 of this Act shall apply to a transferred patient who was treated by virtue of sub-paragraph (5) of that paragraph immediately before the commencement of this Act as if he had been removed to a hospital under section 89 of that Act as if he had been so removed under the said section 84.

(5) Any person to whom sub-paragraph (6) of that paragraph applied immediately before the commencement of this Act shall be treated for the purposes of this Act as if he were liable to be detained in a hospital in pursuance of a transfer direction given under section 48 of this Act and as if a restriction direction had been given under section 49 of this Act [. . .].

38. Any patient who immediately before the commencement of this Act was treated by virtue of sub-paragraph (1) of para.16 of Sch.6 to the Mental Health Act 1959 as if he had been conditionally discharged under section 66 of that Act shall be treated as if he had been conditionally discharged under section 42 of this Act and any such direction as is mentioned in paragraph (*b*) of that sub-paragraph shall be treated as if it had been given under the said section 42.

39. [. . .]

40. A person who immediately before the commencement of this Act was detained by virtue of para.19 of Sch.6 to the Mental Health Act 1959 may continue to be detained until the expiration of the period of his treatment current on November 1, 1960 or until he becomes liable to be detained or subject to guardianship under this Act, whichever occurs first, and may be so detained in any place in which he might have been detained under that paragraph.

41. Any opinion recorded by the responsible medical officer under the foregoing provisions of this Schedule shall be recorded in which form as may be prescribed by regulations made by the Secretary of State.

42.—(1) In the foregoing provisions of this Schedule—

(a) references to the period of treatment of a patient that was current on November 1, 1960 are to the period for which he would have been liable to be detained or subject to guardianship by virtue of any enactment repealed or excluded by the Mental Health Act 1959, or any enactment repealed or replaced by any such enactment as aforesaid, being a period which began but did not expire before that date; and

(b) "the responsible medical officer" means—

    (i) in relation to a patient subject to guardianship, the medical officer authorised by the local social services authority to act (either generally or in any particular case or for any particular purpose) as the responsible medical officer;

    (ii) in relation to any other class of patient, the registered medical practitioner in charge of the treatment of the patient.

(2) Subsection (2) of section 34 of this Act shall apply for the purposes of the foregoing provisions of this Schedule as it applies for the purposes of Part II of this Act.

(3) The sentence or other period of detention of a person who was liable to be detained or subject to guardianship immediately before November 1, 1960 by virtue of an order under section 9 of the Mental Deficiency Act 1913 shall be treated for the purposes of the foregoing provisions of this Schedule as expiring at the end of the period for which that person would have been liable to be detained in a prison or other institution if the order had not been made.

(4) For the purposes of the foregoing provisions of this Schedule, an order sending a person to an institution or placing a person under guardianship made before March 9, 1956 on a petition presented under the Mental Deficiency Act 1913 shall be deemed to be valid if it was so deemed immediately before the commencement of this Act by virtue of section 148(2) of the Mental Health Act 1959.

43. [. . .]
44. [. . .]
45. [. . .]
46. [. . .]

AMENDMENT

The repeals to this Schedule were made by the Health Authorities Act 1995 s.5(1), Sch.3 the Statute Law (Repeals) Act 2004 Sch.1 Pt 17, the Mental Capacity Act 2005 s.67(2), Sch.7 and the Mental Health Act 2007 s.55, Sch.11 Pt 1.

Paragraph 21 and the words in square brackets in para.37(2) were substituted by the Domestic Violence, Crime and Victims Act 2004 s.58(1), Sch.10 para.23.

The words in square brackets in para.34(4) were substituted by SI 2008/2833 art.9, Sch.3 para.68.

DEFINITIONS

**1–1310**   local social services authority: s.145(1).
approved mental health professional: s.145(1).
application for admission for treatment: ss.3, 145(1).
patient: s.145(1).
nearest relative: ss.26(3), 145(1).
hospital order: ss.37, 145(1).
transfer direction: ss.47, 145(1).
restriction order: ss.41, 145(1).
restriction direction: ss.49, 145(1).
mental disorder: ss.2, 145(1).
hospital: s.145(1).
the managers: s.145(1).
appropriate tribunal: ss.66(4), 135(1).

GENERAL NOTE

**1–1311**   This Schedule makes provision to cover the transition from the Mental Health Act 1959, as amended by the Mental Health (Amendment) Act 1982, to this Act. It therefore affects patients detained on or before the commencement date of this Act (September 30, 1983) and anything which was in the process of being done at that date.

*Paragraph 1*

**1–1312**   This paragraph states the general rule that any period of time specified in legislation which was in force on September 30, 1983 will be replaced by the corresponding provision in this Act, calculated from the time when the original order or application was made. This rule is subject to the important exceptions set out in para.9.

*Paragraph 6*

**1–1313**   This paragraph ensures that the changes in the definitions of mental disorder will not affect the authority to detain somebody who was detained prior to September 30, 1983. This paragraph does not apply to the renewal of authority.

*Paragraph 9*

When an authority to detain a patient admitted for treatment or to subject a patient to **1–1314** guardianship is renewed before October 1, 1983 the duration of the authority applicable under the 1959 Act (of one or two years) will continue to apply. However, where the authority has been renewed for two years and less than 16 months has passed since the renewal by September 30, 1983, that period of detention will expire after 18 months rather than two years. If that detention is subsequently renewed the period of one year will apply.

*Paragraphs 31 to 42*

Inter alia, provide authority for the continued detention or guardianship of patents whose **1–1315** detention or guardianship commenced before the Mental Health Act 1959 came into force.

**Section 134**                                    **SCHEDULE 6**

*[Not reproduced.]*                                                               **1–1316**

## DELEGATED LEGISLATION

## THE MENTAL HEALTH (CARE AND TREATMENT) (SCOTLAND) ACT 2003 (CONSEQUENTIAL PROVISIONS) ORDER 2005

### (SI 2005/2078)

*Dated July 21, 2005 and made by the Secretary of State for Constitutional* **2–001**
*Affairs under the Scotland Act 1998 (c.46) sections 104, 11291) and 113*

GENERAL NOTE

This Order makes provision consequential on the Mental Health (Care and Treatment) **2–002**
(Scotland) Act 2003 ("the 2003 Act"). Only those articles that extend to England and
Wales are reproduced.

Article 8 provides that any person who may be taken into custody in Scotland under the
2003 Act or regulations made under the 2003 Act may be taken into custody in any other
part of the UK and returned to Scotland. Article 10 makes it an offence in England and
Wales and in Northern Ireland to do anything in relation to a person subject to the 2003
Act that would be an offence under s.316 of the 2003 Act if done in Scotland. Section
316 makes it an offence to induce or assist patients to abscond. Article 11 provides that
where patients are being conveyed to any place in England, Wales or Northern Ireland
by virtue of the 2003 Act or this Order they will be in legal custody while being conveyed
through those territories and that persons taking patients into custody or conveying or
detaining them by virtue of the 2003 Act or this Order will have all the powers and privileges of a constable. Article 12 extends the protection afforded by s.139 of the Mental
Health Act 1983 to acts done in pursuance of this Order.

### Citation, commencement, interpretation and extent

**1.**—(1) This Order may be cited as the Mental Health (Care and Treatment) **2–003**
(Scotland) Act 2003 (Consequential Provisions) Order 2005 and, subject to paragraph (2), shall come into force on 5th October 2005.

(2) The entry in Schedule 3 to this Order in respect of the Mental Health
(Scotland) Act 1984 shall come into force immediately after the coming into
force of the entry in Schedule 5 to the 2003 Act in respect of the Mental Health
(Scotland) Act 1984.

(3) In this Order, unless the context otherwise requires—

"the 1995 Act" means the Criminal Procedure (Scotland) Act 1995;

"the 2003 Act" means the Mental Health (Care and Treatment) (Scotland) Act
2003;

"hospital", except as provided in articles 2(7) and 4(8), has the meaning given
in section 329(1) of the 2003 Act;

"hospital direction" means a direction made under section 59A of the 1995
Act;

"patient" has the meaning given in section 329(1) of the 2003 Act;

"restriction order" means an order made under section 59 of the 1995 Act; and "transfer for treatment direction" has the meaning given by section 136 of the 2003 Act.

(4) A reference in this Order to "a patient whose detention in hospital was authorised by virtue of the 2003 Act or the 1995 Act" shall be read as including references to a patient in respect of whom a certificate under one of the provisions listed in section 290(7)(a) of the 2003 Act is in operation.

(5) [. . .]

(6) Articles 4, 5, 6, 7 and 9 extend to Northern Ireland only.

(7) Articles 8, 10, 11 and 12(2) extend to England and Wales and Northern Ireland only.

(8) Articles 12(1), 13 and 14 extend to Scotland only.

(9) Subject to paragraph (10), the modifications in Schedules 1 and 2 and the repeals in Schedule 3 have the same extent as the provisions being modified or repealed.

(10) Those modifications and repeals do not extend to Scotland other than the modifications in paragraphs 1(4)(b), 5 and 6 of Schedule 1 and paragraph 20 of Schedule 2 and the repeal in Schedule 3 of the Mental Health (Scotland) Act 1984.

AMENDMENT
Paragraph (5) was repealed by the Mental Health Act 2007 s.55, Sch.11 Pt 7.

### Removal to England and Wales of hospital patients from Scotland
2–004    **2.** *[Repealed by the Mental Health Act 2007 s.55, Sch.11 Pt 7]*

### Transfer of patients to England and Wales from Scotland: conditional discharge
2–005    **3.** *[Repealed by the Mental Health Act 2007 s.55, Sch.11 Pt 7]*

\*     \*     \*     \*

### [Patients absent from hospitals or other places in Scotland]
2–006    **8.**—(1) Subject to the provisions of this article, any person who may be taken into custody in Scotland under—

(a) sections 301 to 303 of the 2003 Act; or

(b) regulations made under section [289, 290, 309, 309A] or 310 of that Act, may be taken into custody in, and returned to Scotland from, any other part of the United Kingdom.

(2) For the purposes of the enactments referred to in paragraph (1), in their application by virtue of this article to England and Wales or Northern Ireland

(a) "constable" includes a constable in England or Wales or a constable of the Police Service of Northern Ireland, as the case may be; and

(b) "mental health officer" includes—
    (i) in England and Wales, any approved [mental health professional] within the meaning of the Mental Health Act 1983; and
    (ii) in Northern Ireland, any approved social worker within the meaning of the Mental Health (Northern Ireland) Order 1986.

AMENDMENTS
The amendments to this article were made by the Mental Health Act 2007 s.39(2), Sch.5 Pt 2 para.21(3); and SI 2008/2828 art.20.

\*     \*     \*     \*

## Assisting patients to absent themselves without leave etc.

**10.**—(1) Any person who in England and Wales or Northern Ireland does any- **2–007** thing in relation to a person whose detention in hospital is authorised by the 2003 Act which, if done in Scotland, would make him guilty of an offence under section 316 of the 2003 Act shall be guilty of an offence.

(2) Where a person is charged with an offence under paragraph (1) as it applies to section 316(1)(b) of the 2003 Act, it shall be a defence for such person to prove that the doing of that with which the person is charged—

(a) did not obstruct the discharge by any person of a function conferred or imposed on that person by virtue of the 2003 Act or this Order; and

(b) was intended to protect the interests of the patient.

(3) Any person guilty of an offence under this article shall be liable—

(a) on summary conviction, to imprisonment for a term not exceeding 3 months or to a fine not exceeding level 5 on the standard scale;

(b) on conviction on indictment, to imprisonment for a term not exceeding 2 years or to a fine, or both.

## Provisions as to custody, removal and detention

**11.**—(1) Any person required or authorised by or by virtue of the 2003 Act or by **2–008** virtue of this Order to be moved to any place or to be kept in custody or detained in a place of safety shall, while being so moved, kept or detained, as the case may be, be deemed to be in legal custody.

(2) A constable or any other person required or authorised by or by virtue of that Act or by virtue of this Order to take any person into custody, or to move or detain any person shall, for the purposes of taking him into custody or moving or detaining him, have all the powers, authorities, protection and privileges which a constable has—

(a) in the case of a constable, within the area for which he acts as constable; and

(b) in the case of any other person, in the area where he has taken any person into custody or is moving or detaining him.

## Protection for acts done under this Order

**12.**—(1) [*Applies to Scotland*]. **2–009**

(2) Section 139 of the Mental Health Act 1983 (which relates to protection for acts done in pursuance of that Act) shall apply in respect of any act purporting to be done in pursuance of articles [4 to 11] of this Order.

AMENDMENT

The amendment to para.(2) was made by the Mental Health Act 2007 s.39(2), Sch.5 Pt 2 para.21(4).

\*     \*     \*     \*

# THE MENTAL HEALTH (MUTUAL RECOGNITION) REGULATIONS 2008

## (SI 2008/1204)

*Dated April 28, 2008 and made by the Secretary of State and the Welsh Ministers acting jointly under the Mental Health Act 1983, section 142A*

GENERAL NOTE

2–010    These Regulations set out the circumstances in which a practitioner approved in England for the purposes of s.12 of the Mental Health Act 1983 ("the Act") or a person approved in relation to England to act as an approved clinician for the purposes of the Act may be treated as approved in relation to Wales by virtue of that approval, and vice versa. They apply where a patient is liable to be detained, subject to a community treatment order or subject to guardianship under the Act. This flexibility is likely to be particularly important in areas near the border between England and Wales, where services are accessed for patients across that border.

### Citation, commencement and interpretation

2–011    **1.**—(1) These Regulations may be cited as the Mental Health (Mutual Recognition) Regulations 2008 and shall come into force on 3rd November 2008.

(2) In these Regulations, "the Act" means the Mental Health Act 1983.

### Approval under section 12(2) of the Act

2–012    **2.**—(1) Any person who is approved in relation to England for the purposes of section 12(2) of the Act, or treated as approved by virtue of section 12(2A) of the Act, shall in all circumstances relevant to the purposes of section 12(2) be treated as approved in relation to Wales.

(2) Any person who is approved in relation to Wales for the purposes of section 12(2) of the Act, or treated as approved by virtue of section 12(2A) of the Act, shall in all circumstances relevant to the purposes of section 12(2) be treated as approved in relation to England.

### Person approved to act as an approved clinician

2–013    **3.**—(1) The circumstances in which a person who is approved to act as an approved clinician in relation to England shall be treated, by virtue of his approval, as approved in relation to Wales too are where—

(a) the approved clinician is acting in respect of a patient who is liable to be detained in accordance with the provisions of the Act or is subject to a community treatment order,

(b) the patient is in Wales, and

(c) the patient's relevant hospital is in England.

(2) The circumstances in which a person who is approved to act as an approved clinician in relation to Wales shall be treated, by virtue of his approval, as approved in relation to England too are where—

(a) the approved clinician is acting in respect of a patient who is liable to be detained in accordance with the provisions of the Act or is subject to a community treatment order,

(b) the patient is in England, and

(c) the patient's relevant hospital is in Wales.

(3) In this regulation, "relevant hospital"—

(a) in respect of a patient liable to be detained, means the hospital in which the patient is liable to be detained in accordance with the provisions of the Act;

(b) in respect of a patient subject to a community treatment order, has the same meaning as "the responsible hospital".

## Guardianship

**4.**—(1) In relation to a patient subject to guardianship, the circumstances in **2–014** which a responsible local social services authority in England may treat a person who is approved to act as an approved clinician in relation to Wales as approved in relation to England in order to authorise that person to be the patient's responsible clinician are where—

(a) the patient is in Wales, or

(b) the patient receives medical treatment for mental disorder in Wales.

(2) In relation to a patient subject to guardianship, the circumstances in which a responsible local social services authority in Wales may treat a person who is approved to act as an approved clinician in relation to England as approved in relation to Wales in order to authorise that person to be the patient's responsible clinician are where—

(a) the patient is in England, or

(b) the patient receives medical treatment for mental disorder in England.

(3) In relation to a patient subject to guardianship, the circumstances in which a person approved to act as an approved clinician in England shall be treated as approved to act as an approved clinician in relation to Wales are where—

(a) that approved clinician has been authorised to act as the patient's responsible clinician by the patient's responsible local social services authority in England, and

(b) that approved clinician is acting in respect of a patient who is in Wales.

(4) In relation to a patient subject to guardianship, the circumstances in which a person approved to act as an approved clinician in Wales shall be treated as approved to act as an approved clinician in relation to England are where—

(a) that approved clinician has been authorised to act as the patient's responsible clinician by the patient's responsible local social services authority in Wales, and

(b) that approved clinician is acting in respect of a patient who is in England.

(5) In this regulation, "responsible local social services authority" has the same meaning as in section 34(3) of the Act.

# THE MENTAL HEALTH (CONFLICTS OF INTEREST) (ENGLAND) REGULATIONS 2008

## (SI 2008/1205)

*Dated April 28, 2008 and made by the Secretary of State under the Mental Health Act 1983, section 12A*

GENERAL NOTE

**2–015**  These Regulations, which are considered in Ch.7 of the *Code of Practice,* set out the circumstances in which there is a potential conflict of interest such that an approved mental health professional (AMHP) cannot make an application mentioned in s.11(1) of the Mental Health Act 1983, or a registered medical practitioner cannot make a medical recommendation for the purposes of such an application. Irrespective of the terms of these Regulations, professionals should always decline to act if a factor leads them to believe that their ability to act, or to be seen to act, independently has been compromised.

An AMHP considering making such an application, or a registered medical practitioner considering giving a medical recommendation for the purposes of such an application, will have a potential conflict of interest if the reasons set out in the Regulations apply. These may be financial reasons (reg.4), business reasons (reg.5), professional reasons (reg.6) or because of a personal relationship existing between the assessor and another assessor, or between the assessor and the patient or, where the application is to be made by the patient's nearest relative, the nearest relative (reg.7).

There is provision for an AMHP or a registered medical practitioner to make an application or a medical recommendation despite a potential conflict of interest for professional reasons in specified circumstances in cases of urgent necessity where there would otherwise be a delay with a serious risk to the health or safety of the patient or to others (reg.6).

The Welsh Ministers have made separate Regulations in relation to Wales: see the Mental Health (Conflicts of Interest) (Wales) Regulations 2008 (SI 2008/2440) (W.213).

## Citation, commencement and application

**2–016**  **1.**—(1) These Regulations may be cited as the Mental Health (Conflicts of Interest) (England) Regulations 2008 and shall come into force on 3rd November 2008.

(2) These Regulations apply to England only.

## Interpretation

**2–017**  **2.** In these Regulations—

"the Act" means the Mental Health Act 1983;

"AMHP" means an approved mental health professional;

"application" means an application mentioned in section 11(1) of the Act;

"assessor" means—

(a) an AMHP, or

(b) a registered medical practitioner.

## General

**2–018**  **3.** Regulations 4 to 7 set out the circumstances in which there would be a potential conflict of interest within the meaning of section 12A(1) of the Act such that an AMHP shall not make an application or a registered medical practitioner shall not give a medical recommendation.

**Potential conflict for financial reasons**

**4.**—(1) A assessor shall have a potential conflict of interest for financial 2–019 reasons if the assessor has a financial interest in the outcome of a decision whether or not to make an application or give a medical recommendation.

(2) Where an application for the admission of the patient to a hospital which is a registered establishment is being considered, a registered medical practitioner who is on the staff of that hospital shall have a potential conflict of interest for financial reasons where the other medical recommendation is given by a registered medical practitioner who is also on the staff of that hospital.

**Potential conflict of interest for business reasons**

**5.**—(1) When considering making an application or considering giving a medi- 2–020 cal recommendation in respect of a patient, an assessor shall have a potential conflict of interest for business reasons if both the assessor and the patient or another assessor are closely involved in the same business venture, including being a partner, director, other office-holder or major shareholder of that venture.

(2) Where the patient's nearest relative is making an application, a registered medical practitioner who is considering giving a medical recommendation in respect of that patient shall have a potential conflict of interest for business reasons if that registered medical practitioner and the nearest relative are both closely involved in the same business venture, including being a partner, director, other office-holder or major shareholder of that venture.

**Potential conflict of interest for professional reasons**

**6.**—(1) When considering making an application or considering giving a medi- 2–021 cal recommendation in respect of a patient, an assessor shall have a potential conflict of interest for professional reasons if the assessor—

(a) directs the work of, or employs, the patient or one of the other assessors making that consideration;

(b) except where paragraph (3) applies, is a member of a team organised to work together for clinical purposes on a routine basis and—

(i) the patient is a member of the same team, or

(ii) the other two assessors are members of the same team.

(2) Where the patient's nearest relative is making an application, a registered medical practitioner who is considering giving a medical recommendation in respect of that patient shall have a potential conflict of interest for professional reasons if that registered medical practitioner—

(a) directs the work of, or employs, the nearest relative, or

(b) works under the direction of, or is employed by, the patient's nearest relative.

(3) Paragraph (1)(b) shall not prevent a registered medical practitioner giving a medical recommendation or an AMHP making an application if, in their opinion, it is of urgent necessity for an application to be made and a delay would involve serious risk to the health or safety of the patient or others.

GENERAL NOTE
*Paragraph (3)*
IN THEIR OPINION. This criterion is to be judged by adopting a subjective test.          **2–022**

**Potential conflict of interest on the basis of a personal relationship**

2–023     7.—(1) A assessor who is considering making an application or considering giving a medical recommendation in respect of a patient, shall have a potential conflict of interest on the basis of a personal relationship if that assessor is—

    (a) related to a relevant person in the first degree;

    (b) related to a relevant person in the second degree;

    (c) related to a relevant person as a half-sister or half-brother;

    (d) the spouse, ex-spouse, civil partner or ex-civil partner of a relevant person, or

    (e) living with a relevant person as if they were a spouse or a civil partner.

    (2) For the purposes of this regulation—

    (a) "relevant person" means another assessor, the patient, or, if the nearest relative is making the application, the nearest relative;

    (b) "related in the first degree" means as a parent, sister, brother, son or daughter and includes step relationships;

    (c) "related in the second degree" means as an uncle, aunt, grandparent, grandchild, first cousin, nephew, niece, parent-in-law, grandparent-in-law, grandchild-in-law, sister-in-law, brother-in-law, son-in-law, daughter-in-law and includes step relationships;

    (d) references to step relationships and in-laws in sub-paragraph (b) and (c) are to be read in accordance with section 246 of the Civil Partnership Act 2004.

# THE MENTAL HEALTH (APPROVED MENTAL HEALTH PROFESSIONALS) (APPROVAL) (ENGLAND) REGULATIONS 2008

## (SI 2008/1206)

*Dated April 28, 2008 and made by the Secretary of State under the Mental Health Act 1983, section 114*

GENERAL NOTE

These Regulations set out a number of matters in connection with the giving by local **2–024** social services authorities (LSSAs) in England of approvals to persons to act as approved mental health professional (AMHPs) for the purposes of the Mental Health Act 1983.

Before a person can be approved (or re-approved) in England to act as an AMHP by a LSSA, the person must have appropriate competence. In deciding whether it is satisfied that the person has appropriate competence to act as an AMHP, the LSSA must take into account that the person has at least one of the professional requirements set out in Sch.1 and the matters set out in Sch.2 (reg.3).

Before a person can be approved to act as an AMHP if he or she has not been approved before, that person must have completed a course within the last five years that was approved by the General Social Care Council or the Care Council for Wales. The period for which an AMHP is approved (or re-approved) is five years (reg.4). Approval (or re-approval) is subject to specified conditions (reg.5).

The approval shall be suspended for any period that the AMHP is suspended from the register or list relevant to the AMHP's professional requirements (reg.6).

The approval or re-approval of an AMHP will end when the period of approval expires or before that in specified circumstances. When the approval ends, the LSSA must inform the AMHP and any other LSSA for which it knows that AMHP has agreed to act. If one LSSA approves a person to act as an AMHP who is already approved by another, it must inform that other LSSA (reg.7).

Each LSSA is required to keep records with specified details of AMHPs for whom it is the approving local social services authority (reg.8).

The Welsh Ministers have made separate regulations relating to the approval of persons to act as AMHPs in relation to Wales: see the Mental Health (Approval of Persons to be Approved Mental Health Professionals) (Wales) Regulations 2008 (SI 2008/2436) (W.209). The Schedule to Mental Health Act 2007 (Commencement No. 8 and Transitional Provisions) Order 2008 (SI 2008/2561) requires LSSAs to treat as AMHPs a person who has been approved as an approved social worker by an LSSA in Wales immediately before November 3, 2008.

*Transitional Provisions*

Paragraphs 4 and 5 of the Schedule to the Mental Health Act 2007 (Commencement **2–025** No.7 and Transitional Provisions) Order 2008 (SI 2008/1900) require LSSAs to treat as an AMHP a person who had been approved as an approved social worker by an LSSA in England immediately before November 3, 2008. Paragraphs 6 to 11 of the Schedule, which are set out below, apply parts of these Regulations to persons treated in England as AMHPs with specified modifications:

"6. Subject to regulation 7 of the Approval Regulations, an English approval shall be for the unexpired period of that person's approval as an ASW.

7. Regulation 7 of the Approval Regulations shall apply to an English approval as if paragraph 2(b) of that regulation read—

'(b) if it is not satisfied that the AMHP has appropriate competence taking into account the matters set out in Schedule 2;'.

8. An English approval shall be subject to the conditions set out in regulation 5 of the Approval Regulations.

9. Any ASW whose registration as a social worker is suspended on the commencement day shall be treated as an AMHP whose approval is suspended in accordance with regulation 6 of the Approval Regulations for so long as that registration is suspended.

10. An English approval may be suspended in accordance with regulation 6 of the Approval Regulations.

11. An LSSA in England shall record details of an English approval in accordance with regulation 8 of the Approval Regulations, as if paragraph (1)(c) of that regulation read—

'(c) the date that the person was approved as an ASW, and the date on which that approval expires;'"

### Citation, commencement and application

2–026   **1.**—(1) These Regulations may be cited as the Mental Health (Approved Mental Health Professionals) (Approval) (England) Regulations 2008 and shall come into force on 3rd November 2008.

(2) These Regulations apply to England only.

### Interpretation

2–027   **2.** In these Regulations—

"the Act" means the Mental Health Act 1983;

"AMHP" means an approved mental health professional;

"approve" and "approval" include "re-approve" and "re-approval";

"approving LSSA" means the local social services authority in England that has approved the person to act as an AMHP;

"Care Council for Wales" has the meaning given by section 54(1) of the Care Standards Act 2000;

"General Social Care Council" has the meaning given by section 54(1) of the Care Standards Act 2000;

"LSSA" means a local social services authority in England;

"professional requirements" means the requirements set out in Schedule 1.

### Granting approval

2–028   **3.**—(1) An LSSA may only approve a person to act as an AMHP if it is satisfied that the person has appropriate competence in dealing with persons who are suffering from mental disorder.

(2) In determining whether it is satisfied a person has appropriate competence, the LSSA must take into account the following factors—

(a) that the person fulfils at least one of the professional requirements, and

(b) the matters set out in Schedule 2.

(3) Before an LSSA may approve a person to act as an AMHP who has not been approved, or been treated as approved, before in England and Wales, the person must have completed within the last five years a course approved by the General Social Care Council or the Care Council for Wales.

### Period of approval

2–029   **4.** An LSSA may approve a person to act as an AMHP for a period of five years.

**Conditions**

**5.** When any approval is granted under these Regulations, it shall be subject to **2–030** the following conditions—

(a) in each year that the AMHP is approved, the AMHP shall complete at least 18 hours of training agreed with the approving LSSA as being relevant to their role as an AMHP;

(b) the AMHP shall undertake to notify the approving LSSA in writing as soon as reasonably practicable if they agree to act as an AMHP on behalf of another LSSA, and when such agreement ends;

(c) the AMHP shall undertake to cease to act as an AMHP and to notify the approving LSSA immediately if they are suspended from any of the registers or listings referred to in the professional competencies, or if any such suspension ends, and

(d) the AMHP shall undertake to cease to act as an AMHP and to notify the approving LSSA immediately if they no longer meet at least one of the professional requirements.

**Suspension of approval**

**6.**—(1) If at any time after being approved, the registration or listing required **2–031** by the professional requirements of a person approved to act as an AMHP is suspended, the approving LSSA shall suspend that AMHP's approval for as long as the AMHP's registration or listing is suspended.

(2) Where an AMHP's approval is suspended, that person may not act as an AMHP unless and until the suspension of approval is ended by the approving LSSA in accordance with subsection (3).

(3) Where the approving LSSA is notified that the suspension of the AMHP's registration or listing has ended, the approving LSSA shall, unless it is not satisfied the AMHP has appropriate competence in dealing with persons suffering from mental disorder, end the suspension of approval.

(4) Where the suspension of approval has ended, the approval shall continue to run for any unexpired period of approval, unless the approving LSSA ends it earlier in accordance with regulation 7.

**End of approval**

**7.**—(1) Except where paragraph (2) applies, a person shall cease to be approved **2–032** to act as an AMHP at the end of the day on which their period of approval expires.

(2) Except where regulation 6 applies, the approving LSSA shall end the approval of a person it has approved to act as an AMHP before their period of approval expires—

(a) in accordance with a request in writing to do so from that AMHP;

(b) if it is no longer satisfied that the AMHP has appropriate competence taking into account the matters set out in Schedule 2;

(c) immediately upon becoming aware that the AMHP—

(i) is no longer a person who meets at least one of the professional requirements;

(ii) is in breach of any of the conditions set out in regulation 5, or

(iii) has been approved to act as an AMHP by another LSSA.

(3) When an approval ends, the approving LSSA shall notify the AMHP immediately that the approval has ended and give reasons for ending the approval.

(4) When an approval ends, the approving LSSA shall notify that fact to any other LSSA for whom it knows the AMHP has agreed to act as an AMHP.

(5) If an LSSA approves a person as an AMHP knowing that that AMHP is already approved by another LSSA, it shall notify the previous approving LSSA.

GENERAL NOTE
*Paragraph (2)(b),(c)(i)(ii)*

**2–033**

The AMHP has no right of appeal against the decision of the local authority.

**Records**

**2–034**    8.—(1) The approving LSSA shall keep a record of each AMHP it approves which shall include—

(a)  the name of the AMHP;

(b)  the AMHP's profession;

(c)  the AMHP's date of approval;

(d)  details of any period of suspension under regulation 6;

(e)  details of the completion of training to comply with regulation 5(a);

(f)  details of any previous approvals as an AMHP within the previous five years;

(g)  the names of other LSSAs for whom the AMHP has agreed to act as an AMHP, and

(h)  the date of and reason for the end of approval, if applicable.

(2) The record referred to in paragraph (1) shall be retained by the approving LSSA for a period of five years commencing with the day on which the AMHP's approval ended.

**SCHEDULE 1**   Regulation 2

**PROFESSIONAL REQUIREMENTS**

The professional requirements are as follows—   **2–035**
(a) a social worker registered with the General Social Care Council;
(b) a first level nurse, registered in Sub-Part 1 of the Nurses' Part of the Register maintained under article 5 of the Nursing and Midwifery Order 2001, with the inclusion of an entry indicating their field of practice is mental health or learning disabilities nursing;
(c) an occupational therapist registered in Part 6 of the Register maintained under article 5 of the Health Professions Order 2001; or
(d) a chartered psychologist who is listed in the British Psychological Society's Register of Chartered Psychologists and who holds a relevant practising certificate issued by that Society.

GENERAL NOTE
*Paragraph (d)*
Until the end of 30 June 2012, the reference to a chartered psychologist is to be treated as a reference to a chartered psychologist or a psychologist registered in Part 14 of the register maintained by the Health Professions Council (Health Care and Associated Professions (Miscellaneous Amendments and Practitioner Psychologists) Order 2009 (Commencement No 1 and Transitional Provisions) Order of Council 2009, SI 2009/ 1357, art 3(a)).

Regulation 3(2)   **SCHEDULE 2**

MATTERS TO BE TAKEN INTO ACCOUNT TO DETERMINE COMPETENCE

**1. Key Competence Area 1: Application of Values to the AMHP Role**   **2–036**
Whether the applicant has—
(a) the ability to identify, challenge and, where possible, redress discrimination and inequality in all its forms in relation to AMHP practice;
(b) an understanding of and respect for individuals' qualities, abilities and diverse backgrounds, and is able to identify and counter any decision which may be based on unlawful discrimination;
(c) the ability to promote the rights, dignity and self determination of patients consistent with their own needs and wishes, to enable them to contribute to the decisions made affecting their quality of life and liberty, and
(d) a sensitivity to individuals' needs for personal respect, confidentiality, choice, dignity and privacy while exercising the AMHP role.

**2. Key Competence Area 2: Application of Knowledge: The Legal and Policy Framework**
(1) Whether the applicant has—
(a) appropriate knowledge of and ability to apply in practice—
  (i) mental health legislation, related codes of practice and national and local policy guidance, and
  (ii) relevant parts of other legislation, codes of practice, national and local policy guidance, in particular the Children Act 1989, the Children Act 2004, the Human Rights Act 1998 and the Mental Capacity Act 2005;

(b) a knowledge and understanding of the particular needs of children and young people and their families, and an ability to apply AMHP practice in the context of those particular needs;

(c) an understanding of, and sensitivity to, race and culture in the application of knowledge of mental health legislation;

(d) an explicit awareness of the legal position and accountability of AMHPs in relation to the Act, any employing organisation and the authority on whose behalf they are acting;

(e) the ability to—

    (i) evaluate critically local and national policy to inform AMHP practice, and

    (ii) base AMHP practice on a critical evaluation of a range of research relevant to evidence-based practice, including that on the impact on persons who experience discrimination because of mental health.

(2) In paragraph (1), "relevant" means relevant to the decisions that an AMHP is likely to take when acting as an AMHP.

### 3. Key Competence Area 3: Application of Knowledge: Mental Disorder

Whether the applicant has a critical understanding of, and is able to apply in practice—

(a) a range of models of mental disorder, including the contribution of social, physical and development factors;

(b) the social perspective on mental disorder and mental health needs, in working with patients, their relatives, carers and other professionals;

(c) the implications of mental disorder for patients, their relatives and carers, and

(d) the implications of a range of treatments and interventions for patients, their relatives and carers.

### 4. Key Competence Area 4: Application of Skills: Working in Partnership

Whether the applicant has the ability to—

(a) articulate, and demonstrate in practice, the social perspective on mental disorder and mental health needs;

(b) communicate appropriately with and establish effective relationships with patients, relatives, and carers in undertaking the AMHP role;

(c) articulate the role of the AMHP in the course of contributing to effective inter-agency and inter-professional working;

(d) use networks and community groups to influence collaborative working with a range of individuals, agencies and advocates;

(e) consider the feasibility of and contribute effectively to planning and implementing options for care such as alternatives to compulsory admission, discharge and aftercare;

(f) recognise, assess and manage risk effectively in the context of the AMHP role;

(g) effectively manage difficult situations of anxiety, risk and conflict, and an understanding of how this affects the AMHP and other people concerned with the patient's care;

(h) discharge the AMHP role in such a way as to empower the patient as much as practicable;

(h) plan, negotiate and manage compulsory admission to hospital or arrangements for supervised community treatment;

(j) manage and co-ordinate effectively the relevant legal and practical processes including the involvement of other professionals as well as patients, relatives and carers, and

(k) balance and manage the competing requirements of confidentiality and effective information sharing to the benefit of the patient and other persons concerned with the patient's care.

**5. Key Competence Area 5: Application of Skills: Making and Communicating Informed Decisions**

Whether the applicant has the ability to—

(a) assert a social perspective and to make properly informed independent decisions;

(b) obtain, analyse and share appropriate information having due regard to confidentiality in order to manage the decision-making process including decisions about supervised community treatment;

(c) compile and complete statutory documentation, including an application for admission;

(d) provide reasoned and clear verbal and written reports to promote effective, accountable and independent AMHP decision making;

(e) present a case at a legal hearing;

(f) exercise the appropriate use of independence, authority and autonomy and use it to inform their future practice as an AMHP, together with consultation and supervision;

(g) evaluate the outcomes of interventions with patients, carers and others, including the identification of where a need has not been met;

(h) make and communicate decisions that are sensitive to the needs of the individual patient, and

(i) keep appropriate records with an awareness of legal requirements with respect to record keeping and the use and transfer of information.

## THE MENTAL HEALTH (HOSPITAL, GUARDIANSHIP AND TREATMENT) (ENGLAND) REGULATIONS 2008

### (SI 2008/1184)

*Dated April 28, 2008 and made by the Secretary of State under the Mental Health Act 1983, sections 9, 17F(2), 19(1) and (4), 31(1), (2) and 3, 57(1)(b), 58A(1)(b), 64(2), 64H(2), 134(3A)(a) and 134(8)*

GENERAL NOTE

**2–037**  These regulations, which replace the revoked Mental Health (Hospital, Guardianship and Consent to Treatment) Regulations 1983 and the Mental Health (Correspondence of Patients, Advocacy and Liaison Services) Regulations 2003, are the principal regulations dealing with the exercise of powers in respect of persons who are liable to be detained, or subject to supervised community treatment or guardianship under the Mental Health Act 1983. They provide for certain applications, recommendations and records under the Act to be in the form set in the Forms in Sch.1.

The Welsh Ministers have made separate Regulations in relation to Wales (the "Welsh Regulations"): see the Mental Health (Hospital, Guardianship, Community Treatment and Consent to Treatment) (Wales) Regulations 2008 (SI 2008/2439) (W.212).

*Code of Practice*

**2–038**  The receipt and scrutiny of documents is considered in Ch.13.

### PART 1

### GENERAL

**Citation and commencement**

**2–039**  **1.**—(1) These Regulations may be cited as the Mental Health (Hospital, Guardianship and Treatment) (England) Regulations 2008 and shall come into force on 3rd November 2008.

(2) These Regulations apply to England only.

**Interpretation**

**2–040**  **2.**—(1) In these Regulations—

"the Act" means the Mental Health Act 1983;

"bank holiday" includes New Year's Day, Good Friday, Easter Monday, Christmas Day and Boxing Day;

"business day" means any day except Saturday, Sunday or a bank holiday;

"the Commission" means the [Care Quality Commission] referred to in section 121;

"document" means any application, recommendation, record, report, order, notice or other document;

"electronic communication" has the same meaning as in section 15(1) of the Electronic Communications Act 2000;

"guardianship patient" means a person who is subject to guardianship under the Act;

"private guardian", in relation to a patient, means a person, other than a local social services authority, who acts as guardian under the Act;

"responsible registered establishment" is a registered establishment which is a responsible hospital;

"served", in relation to a document, includes addressed, delivered, given, forwarded, furnished or sent.

(2) Unless otherwise stated, any reference in these Regulations to—

(a) a numbered section is to the section of the Act bearing that number;

(b) an alphanumeric form is a reference to the form in Schedule 1 bearing that designation.

AMENDMENT

The amendment to the definition of "the Commission" was made by SI 2009/462 art.12, Sch.5 para.25(a).

## Documents

**3.**—(1) Except in a case to which paragraph (2), (3), (4) or (5) applies, or in a  **2–041** case to which regulation 6(3) (recall notices in respect of community patients) applies, any document required or authorised to be served upon any authority, body or person by or under Part 2 of the Act (compulsory admission to hospital, guardianship or community treatment orders) or these Regulations may be served by delivering it to—

(a) the authority, body or person upon whom it is to be served;

(b) any person authorised by that authority, body or person to receive it;

(c) by sending it by pre-paid post addressed to—

    (i) the authority or body at their registered or principal office; or

    (ii) the person upon whom it is to be served at that person's usual or last known residence, or

(d) by delivering it using an internal mail system operated by the authority, body or person upon whom it is to be served, if that authority, body or person agrees.

(2) Any application for the admission of a patient to a hospital under Part 2 of the Act shall be served by delivering the application to an officer of the managers of the hospital to which it is proposed that the patient shall be admitted, who is authorised by them to receive it.

(3) Where a patient is liable to be detained in a hospital under Part 2 of the Act—

(a) any order by the nearest relative of the patient under section 23 for the patient's discharge, and

(b) the notice of such order given under section 25(1), shall be served either by—

    (i) delivery of the order or notice at that hospital to an officer of the managers authorised by the managers to receive it, or

    (ii) sending it by pre-paid post to those managers at that hospital, or

    (iii) delivering it using an internal mail system operated by the managers upon whom it is to be served, if those managers agree.

(4) Where a patient is a community patient—

(a) any order by the nearest relative of the patient under section 23 for the patient's discharge, and

(b) the notice of such order given under section 25( 1A), shall be served by—

    (i) delivery of the order or notice at the patient's responsible hospital to an officer of the managers authorised by the managers to receive it,

(ii) sending it by pre-paid post to those managers at that hospital, or

(iii) delivering it using an internal mail system operated by the managers upon whom it is to be served, if those managers agree.

(5) Any report made under subsection (2) of section 5 (detention of patient already in hospital for 72 hours) shall be served by—

(a) delivery of the report to an officer of the managers of the hospital authorised by those managers to receive it, or

(b) delivering it using an internal mail system operated by the managers upon whom it is to be served, if those managers agree.

(6) Where a document referred to in this regulation is sent by pre-paid—

(a) first class post, service is deemed to have taken place on the second business day following the day of posting;

(b) second class post, service is deemed to have taken place on the fourth business day following posting,

unless the contrary is shown.

(7) Where a document under this regulation is delivered using an internal mail system, service is considered to have taken place immediately it is delivered into the internal mail system.

(8) Subject to sections 6(3) and 8(3) (proof of applications), any document—

(a) required or authorised by or under Part 2 of the Act or these Regulations, and

(b) purporting to be signed by a person required or authorised by or under that Part or these Regulations to do so,

shall be received in evidence and be deemed to be such a document without further proof.

(9) Where under Part 2 of the Act or these Regulations the managers of a hospital are required to make any record or report, that function may be performed by an officer authorised by those managers in that behalf.

(10) Where under these Regulations the decision to accept service by a particular method requires the agreement of the managers of a hospital, that agreement may be given by an officer authorised by those managers in that behalf.

DEFINITIONS

**2–042**   document: reg.2(1).
served: reg.2(1).
the Act: reg.2(1).

GENERAL NOTE

**2–043**   The regulation sets out rules on how documents required under the Act are to be served.

*Paragraph (1)*

**2–044**   PERSON AUTHORISED.   The authorisation should be formally recorded. Hospitals should ensure that there is a 24-hour cover from staff with good knowledge of the Act.

PREPAID POST.   See para.(6). If a notice of recall to hospital is sent to the patient's last known residence, he or she becomes absent without leave if there is a failure to respond to the notice.

INTERNAL MAIL SYSTEM.   See para.(7).

*Paragraph (2)*
SERVED.  The application documents cannot be served by post.  **2–045**

OFFICER.  In *R. (on the application of PD) v West Midlands and North West Mental Health Review Tribunal* [2004] EWCA Civ 311; [2004] M.H.L.R. 174, the Court of Appeal held that the meaning of "officer" will depend upon the context in which it is used, and that in the context of a tribunal hearing an "officer" means a person holding office and taking part in the management of the authority that is detaining the patient. It is submitted that in the context of these regulations, which are largely concerned with process issues rather than decision making, the meaning of "officer" should be extended to embrace an "employee".

*Paragraph (3)(b)*
SERVED.  In *Re GK (Patient: Habeas Corpus)* [1999] M.H.L.R. 128, the nearest relative  **2–046**
of a patient who had been admitted to hospital under s.3 handed a letter to the ward receptionist requesting the patient's discharge. This took place on May 27. The nearest relative was told that the letter would be handed to the appropriate person, namely the Mental Health Act administrator. The letter was received by the administrator on June 3. On that day, as no barring report under s.25 had been issued, the nearest relative arrived on the ward, seeking the discharge of the patient. A barring report was then made. In rejecting an application for *habeas corpus,* the court held that the purpose of this provision was to ensure that an order for discharge came to the notice of the proper authorised person without delay. That being the case, the handing of the letter to the ward receptionist did not satisfy that requirement and was not good delivery. The notice was served when the letter was received by the administrator on June 3.

*Paragraph 3(8)*
WITHOUT FURTHER PROOF.  The officer checking the document may therefore take cer-  **2–047**
tain statements at face value. For example, there is no need to check that the doctor who states that he or she is a registered medical practitioner is so registered, or that the mental health professional who states that he or she is an approved mental health practitioner has been approved under s.114.

*Paragraphs (9), (10)*
OFFICER AUTHORISED.  See the note on "officer" in para.2, above.  **2–048**

PART 2

PROCEDURES AND RECORDS RELATING TO HOSPITAL ADMISSIONS, GUARDIANSHIP
AND COMMUNITY TREATMENT ORDERS

**Procedure for and record of hospital admissions**
  **4.**—(1) Subject to paragraph (2), for the purposes of admission to hospital  **2–049**
under Part 2 of the Act—
  (a) any application for admission for assessment under section 2 shall be in the
      form set out—
      (i) where made by the nearest relative, in Form A1,
      (ii) where made by an approved mental health professional, in Form A2;
  (b) any medical recommendation for the purposes of section 2 shall be in the
      form set out—
      (i) in the case of joint recommendations, in Form A3,
      (ii) in any other case, in Form A4;

(c) any application for admission for treatment under section 3 shall be in the form set out—
    (i) where made by the nearest relative, in Form A5,
    (ii) where made by an approved mental health professional, in Form A6;

(d) any medical recommendation for the purposes of section 3 shall be in the form set out—
    (i) in the case of joint recommendations, in Form A7,
    (ii) in any other case, in Form A8;

(e) any emergency application under section 4 shall be in the form set out—
    (i) where made by the nearest relative, in Form A9,
    (ii) where made by an approved mental health professional, in Form A10;

(f) any medical recommendation for the purposes of section 4 shall be in the form set out in Form A11;

(g) any report made under subsection (2) of section 5 (detention of in-patient already in hospital for a maximum 72 hours) by—
    (i) the registered medical practitioner or approved clinician in charge of the treatment of the patient, or
    (ii) any person nominated by the registered medical practitioner or approved clinician to act for them,
    shall be in the form set out in Part 1 of Form H1 and the hospital managers shall record receipt of that report in Part 2 of that Form;

(h) any record made under subsection (4) of section 5 (power to detain an in-patient for a maximum of 6 hours) by a nurse of the class for the time being prescribed for the purposes of that subsection shall be in the form set out in Form H2.

(2) For the purposes of any medical recommendation under sections 2, 3, 4 and 7 (admission for assessment, admission for treatment, admission for assessment in cases of emergency and application for guardianship respectively) in the case of—

(a) a single recommendation made in respect of a patient whom a doctor has examined in Wales, the medical recommendation shall be in the form required by Regulations made by the Welsh Ministers to similar effect for Wales;

(b) joint recommendations made in respect of a patient whom both doctors have examined in Wales, the medical recommendation shall be in the form required by Regulations made by the Welsh Ministers to similar effect for Wales;

(c) joint recommendations made in respect of a patient whom one doctor has examined in Wales and one doctor has examined in England, the medical recommendation shall either be in the form required by these Regulations or in the form required by Regulations made by the Welsh Ministers to similar effect for Wales.

(3) For the purposes of section 15 (rectification of applications and recommendations), the managers of the hospital to which a patient has been admitted in pursuance of an application for assessment or for treatment may authorise an officer on their behalf—

(a) to consent under subsection (1) of that section to the amendment of the application or any medical recommendation given for the purposes of the application;

(b) to consider the sufficiency of a medical recommendation and, if the recommendation is considered insufficient, to give written notice as required by subsection (2) of that section.

(4) Where a patient has been admitted to a hospital pursuant to an application under section 2, 3 or 4 (admission for assessment, admission for treatment and admission for assessment in cases of emergency respectively), a record of admission shall be made by the managers of that hospital in the form set out in Part 1 of Form H3 and shall be attached to the application.

(5) Where a patient has been admitted to a hospital pursuant to an application under section 4 (admission for assessment in cases of emergency), a record of receipt of a second medical recommendation in support of the application for admission of the patient shall be made by the managers in the form set out in Part 2 of Form H3 and shall be attached to the application.

DEFINITION
the Act: reg.2(1).                                                                          **2–050**

GENERAL NOTE
*Paragraph (1)*
SHALL BE IN THE FORM SET OUT.   See the General Note to Sch.1.                **2–051**

*Paragraph (2)*
This paragraph sets out when the equivalent Welsh forms are to be used for medical rec- **2–052**
ommendations for patients who have been examined by doctors in Wales. If patients who
are admitted to hospitals in Wales are medically examined in England, the forms set out in
these Regulations must be used: see reg.(4)(4) of the Welsh Regulations.

*Paragraph (3)*
AN OFFICER.   See the note on reg.3(2). This officer is unlikely to be the person who **2–053**
records the patient's admission for the purposes of reg.4(4). The scrutiny of documents
for the purposes of possible rectification need not take place on the day of the patient's
admission. Also see the notes to s.6(3).

*Paragraph (4)*
FORM H3.   If an application has been "duly completed" for the purposes of s.6(1), a **2–054**
failure to comply with the requirement to complete this form would not invalidate the
detention of a patient made pursuant to an application because the application is "sufficient
authority" to detain the patient (s.6(2)). The form should be completed retrospectively on
the omission being discovered.

## Procedure for and acceptance of guardianship applications
5.—(1) For the purposes of section 7 (application for guardianship)—            **2–055**
(a) an application for guardianship shall be in the form set out—
    (i) where made by the nearest relative, in Part 1 of Form G1,
    (ii) where made by an approved mental health professional, in Part 1 of
    Form G2;
(b) where a person other than a local social services authority is named as
guardian, the statement of willingness of that person to act as guardian
shall be in the form set out in Part 2 of Form G1 or, as the case may be, G2;
(c) any medical recommendation shall be in the form set out—
    (i) in the case of joint recommendations, in Form G3,
    (ii) in any other case, in Form G4.

(2) Where an application for guardianship is accepted by the responsible local social services authority, it shall record its acceptance of the application in the form set out in Form G5 (which shall be attached to the application).

**Procedure for and records relating to community treatment orders**

**2–056**     **6.**—(1) For the purposes of section 17A (community treatment orders)—

(a)  an order made by the responsible clinician shall be in the form set out in Parts 1 and 3 of Form CTO1;

(b)  the agreement of the approved mental health professional shall be in the form set out in Part 2 of Form CTO1;

(c)  as soon as reasonably practicable, the responsible clinician shall furnish the managers of the responsible hospital with that order.

(2) For the purposes of section 17B (conditions in community treatment orders)—

(a)  the conditions to which the patient is subject whilst the order remains in force shall be in the form set out in Form CTO1;

(b)  a variation of any of those conditions by the responsible clinician shall be in the form set out in Form CTO2;

(c)  as soon as reasonably practicable, the responsible clinician shall furnish the managers of the responsible hospital with Form CTO2.

(3) For the purposes of section 17E (power to recall a community patient to hospital)—

(a)  a responsible clinician's notice recalling a patient to hospital shall be in the form set out in Form CTO3;

(b)  as soon as reasonably practicable, the responsible clinician shall furnish the managers of the hospital to which the patient is recalled with a copy of the notice recalling the patient to hospital;

(c)  where the patient is recalled to a hospital which is not the responsible hospital, the responsible clinician shall notify the managers of the hospital to which the patient is recalled in writing of the name and address of the responsible hospital;

(d)  the managers of the hospital to which the patient is recalled shall record the time and date of the patient's detention pursuant to that notice in the form set out in Form CTO4.

(4) Where the patient's responsible hospital is in Wales, the patient's recall shall be effected in accordance with Regulations made by the Welsh Ministers to similar effect for Wales.

(5) A responsible clinician's notice recalling a patient to hospital for the purposes of section 17E (power to recall a community patient to hospital) in Form CTO3 shall be served by—

(a)  delivering it by hand to the patient,

(b)  delivering it by hand to the patient's usual or last known address, or

(c)  sending it by pre-paid first class post addressed to the patient at the patient's usual or last known address.

(6) Notice of recall in Form CTO3 is considered served—

(a)  in the case of sub-paragraph 5(a), immediately on delivery of the notice to the patient;

(b)  in the case of sub-paragraph 5(b), on the day (which does not have to be a business day) after it is delivered;

(c)  in the case of sub-paragraph 5(c), on the second business day after it was posted.

(7) As soon as practicable following the patient's recall, the managers of the responsible hospital shall take such steps as are reasonably practicable to—

(a)  cause the patient to be informed, both orally and in writing, of the provisions of the Act under which the patient is for the time being detained and the effect of those provisions, and

(b)  ensure that the patient understands the effect, so far as is relevant to the patient's case, of sections 56 to 64 (consent to treatment).

(8) For the purposes of section 17F (powers in respect of recalled patients)—

(a)  an order referred to in subsection (4) (responsible clinician's order revoking a community treatment order) shall be in the form set out in Parts 1 and 3 of Form CTO5;

(b)  a statement of an approved mental health professional referred to in that subsection (signifying agreement with the responsible clinician's opinion and that it is appropriate to revoke the order) shall be in the form set out in Part 2 of Form CTO5;

(c)  as soon as practicable, the responsible clinician shall furnish the managers of the hospital to which the patient is recalled with that Form;

(d)  where the patient is recalled to a hospital which is not the responsible hospital, the managers of that hospital shall (as soon as reasonably practicable) furnish the managers of the hospital which was the patient's responsible hospital prior to the revocation of the patient's community treatment order, with a copy of Form CTO5.

DEFINITION

    the Act: reg.2(1).          **2–057**
    served: reg.2(1).

GENERAL NOTE

*Paragraph (4)*

    Where a patient's responsible hospital is in Wales, the patient's recall to hospital is be **2–058** effected in accordance with the Welsh Regulations and the appropriate Welsh forms should be used (even if the patient is to be recalled to a hospital in England).

*Paragraph (7)*

    This is similar to the duty that hospital managers have under s.132 of the Act in respect of **2–059** detained patients as recalled SCT patients do not count as detained patients for the purposes of s.132.

## Transfer from hospital to hospital or guardianship

7.—(1) This regulation shall apply in respect of any patient ("a hospital **2–060** patient") to whom section 19(1)(a) applies and who is not a patient transferred under—

(a)  section 19(3) (transfer between hospitals under the same managers), or

(b)  section 123(1) and (2) (transfers between and from special hospitals).

(2) A hospital patient may be transferred to another hospital where—

(a)  an authority for transfer is given by the managers of the hospital in which the patient is liable to be detained in the form set out in Part 1 of Form H4, and

(b) those managers are satisfied that arrangements have been made for the admission of the patient to the hospital to which the patient is being transferred within a period of 28 days beginning with the date of the authority for transfer.

(3) Upon completion of the transfer of the patient, the managers of the hospital to which the patient is transferred shall record the patient's admission in the form set out in Part 2 of Form H4.

(4) A hospital patient may be transferred into the guardianship of a local social services authority, or a person approved by a local social services authority, where—

(a) an authority for transfer is given by the managers of the hospital in which the patient is detained in the form set out in Part 1 of Form G6;

(b) the transfer has been agreed by the local social services authority, which will be the responsible local social services authority if the proposed transfer takes effect;

(c) that local social services authority has specified the date on which the transfer shall take place;

(d) the managers of the transferring hospital have recorded the agreement of the local social services authority referred to in paragraph (b) and the date for transfer referred to in paragraph (c), in the form set out in Part 1 of that Form;

(e) in the case of a person other than a local social services authority being named as guardian, the agreement of that person to act as guardian is recorded in the form set out in Part 2 of that Form.

(5) A hospital patient who is detained in a registered establishment—

(a) may be transferred from that registered establishment to another registered establishment where both are under the same management, and paragraph (2) shall not apply, and

(b) where such a patient is maintained under a contract with a Strategic Health Authority, Local Health Board, Primary Care Trust, National Health Service trust, National Health Service foundation trust, a Special Health Authority or the Welsh Ministers, any authority for transfer required under paragraph (2)(a) or, as the case may be, (4)(a), and the record (where relevant) required under paragraph (4)(d), may be made or given by an officer of that authority, board or trust authorised by that authority, board or trust in that behalf, or by those Ministers, instead of by the managers.

(6) The functions of the managers referred to in this regulation may be performed by an officer authorised by them in that behalf.

GENERAL NOTE

**2–061**  See reg.10 for transfers between Wales and England.

*Paragraph 5(b)*

**2–062**  The effect of this provision is explained in paras.13.13 and 13.14 of the Reference Guide:

"If an NHS patient is detained in an independent hospital, an authorisation to transfer the patient to a hospital under different managers (but not to a hospital under the same managers) may also be given by an officer of the relevant NHS body who has been authorised by that body to do so.

In other words, the relevant NHS body can authorise the patient's transfer without the agreement of the managers of the independent hospital. But for restricted patients, the agreement of the Secretary of State for Justice is still required."

*Paragraph (2)*

The conveyance of a patient who is transferred to another hospital is governed by reg.11.  **2–063**

TRANSFERRED TO ANOTHER HOSPITAL.   There must be a physical transfer of the patient within the 28 day period allowed for in para.(b).

*Paragraph (4)*

DATE ON WHICH THE TRANSFER TAKES.   The patient could be granted leave of absence  **2–064** under s.17 to take up residence in the place where he or she will be required to reside before that date.

*Paragraph (6)*

OFFICER.   See the note on reg.3(2).                                                   **2–065**

## Transfer from guardianship to guardianship or hospital

**8.**—(1) A guardianship patient may be transferred into the guardianship of  **2–066** another local social services authority or person where—

(a)  an authority for transfer is given by the guardian in the form set out in Part 1 of Form G7;

(b)  that transfer has been agreed by the receiving local social services authority, which will be the responsible local social services authority if the proposed transfer takes effect;

(c)  that local social services authority has specified the date on which the transfer shall take place;

(d)  the guardian has recorded the agreement of the receiving local social services authority mentioned in paragraph (b) and the date for transfer mentioned in paragraph (c) in Part 1 of that Form;

(e)  a person other than a local social services authority is named in the authority for transfer as proposed guardian, the statement of willingness of that person to act as guardian is recorded in the form set out in Part 2 of that Form.

(2) An authority for transfer to hospital of a guardianship patient may be given by the responsible local social services authority in the form set out in Part 1 of Form G8 where—

(a)  an application for admission for treatment has been made by an approved mental health professional in the form set out in Form A6;

(b)  that application is founded on medical recommendations given by two registered medical practitioners in accordance with section 12 in the form set out—

(i)  in the case of joint recommendations, in Form A7;

(ii)  in any other case, in Form A8;

(c)  the responsible local social services authority is satisfied that arrangements have been made for the admission of the patient to that hospital within the period of 14 days beginning with the date on which the patient was last examined by a registered medical practitioner for the purposes of paragraph (b).

(3) Where paragraph (2)(a) applies, for the purposes of the application referred to in that paragraph, sections 11(4) (consultation with nearest relative) and 13

(duty of approved mental health professional) shall apply as if the proposed transfer were an application for admission for treatment.

(4) On the transfer of a guardianship patient referred to in paragraph (2), a record of admission shall be made by the managers of the hospital to which the patient is transferred in the form set out in Part 2 of Form G8 and shall be attached to the application referred to in paragraph (2)(a).

(5) Where the conditions of paragraph (2) are satisfied, the transfer of the patient must be effected within 14 days of the date on which the patient was last examined, failing which the patient will remain subject to guardianship.

(6) The functions of the managers referred to in this regulation may be performed by an officer authorised by them in that behalf.

DEFINITION

2–067    guardianship patient: reg.2(1).

GENERAL NOTE

2–068    A patient who has been transferred from guardianship to hospital has a right to apply to a tribunal within six months of the day of the transfer (s.66(1)(e), (2)(e)). If the patient does not exercise this right, the hospital managers must automatically refer the case to the tribunal (s.68(1)).

*Paragraph (1)(e)*

2–069    PERSON OTHER THAN A LOCAL SOCIAL SERVICES AUTHORITY.    Who, after the transfer has been completed, must appoint a doctor to act as the nominated medical attendant of the patient and send relevant details to the local social security authority (reg.22).

*Paragraph (2)*

2–070    The provisions of s.15 of the Act concerning the rectification of applications and medical recommendations do not apply to documents given in support of a transfer. The application and recommendations should therefore be scrutinised carefully to ensure that they comply with legislative requirements before the authority for transfer is signed.

The patient must be admitted to the hospital within 14 days beginning with the date of the latter of the two medical examinations on which the medical recommendations are based (reg.11(1)(b)).

*Paragraph (3)*

2–071    OFFICER.    See the note on reg.3(2).

## Transfer of community patients recalled to hospital

2–072    **9.**—(1) The managers of a hospital in which a community patient is detained, having been recalled to hospital, may authorise the transfer of that patient to another hospital.

(2) Where the hospital to which the patient has been recalled and the hospital to which the patient is being transferred are not under the same management, a transfer may only take place if the requirements of paragraphs (3) to (5) are satisfied.

(3) Those requirements are that the managers of the hospital to which the patient was recalled—

(a)  authorise the transfer of the patient in the form set out in Part 1 of Form CTO6, and

(b)  are satisfied that arrangements have been made for the admission of the patient to the hospital to which the patient is being transferred.

604

(4) The managers of the hospital from which the patient is being transferred shall furnish the managers of the hospital to which the patient is being transferred with a copy of Form CTO4 (record of patient's detention in hospital after recall) before, or at the time of, the patient's transfer.

(5) On the transfer of the patient, the managers of the hospital to which the patient is transferred shall record the patient's admission in the form set out in Part 2 of Form CTO6.

(6) Where—

(a) a patient has been recalled to a registered establishment, and

(b) that patient is maintained under a contract with a Strategic Health Authority, Local Health Board, Primary Care Trust, National Health Service trust, National Health Service foundation trust, a Special Health Authority or the Welsh Ministers,

any authority for transfer required under paragraph (3)(a) may be given by an officer of that authority, board or trust authorised by that authority, board or trust in that behalf, or by those Ministers, instead of the managers.

(7) The functions of the managers referred to in this regulation may be performed by an officer authorised by them in that behalf.

GENERAL NOTE

This regulation allows community patients who have been recalled to one hospital to be **2–073** transferred to another, provided this is done within the 72-hour maximum period allowed for a patient to be detained following recall. The requirements are similar to those for the transfer of detained patients between hospitals under reg.7. In particular, no statutory form is required when managers authorise the transfer of a patient between hospitals which are both under their own management. The conveyance of a patient who is transferred under this provision is governed by reg.12. Assignment of responsibility for SCT patients between one hospital and another is dealt with in reg.17.

If a recalled patient is to be transferred from a hospital in Wales to one in England, the transfer must be authorised and recorded in accordance with the Welsh Regulations. Transfers from England to Wales are to be made in accordance with these regulations.

*Paragraph (7)*
OFFICER. See the note on reg.3(2). **2–074**

## Transfers from England to Wales and from Wales to England

**10.**—(1) Where a patient who is liable to be detained or is subject to guardian- **2–075** ship under the Act is transferred from a hospital or guardianship in England to a hospital or guardianship in Wales, that transfer shall be subject to the conditions in these Regulations.

(2) Where a patient who is liable to be detained or is subject to guardianship under the Act is transferred from a hospital or guardianship in Wales to a hospital or guardianship in England, that transfer and the duty to record the admission of a patient so transferred shall be subject to such conditions as may be prescribed in Regulations made by the Welsh Ministers to similar effect for Wales.

(3) Where paragraph (2) applies and any Regulations made by the Welsh Ministers to similar effect for Wales provide for authority to convey a patient in Wales, those Regulations shall provide authority to convey the patient whilst in England.

2–076    This regulation deals with transfers of detained and guardianship patients between England and Wales. Its main effect is that, if a patient is to be transferred from Wales to England, the procedure in the Welsh Regulations is to be followed.

## Conveyance to hospital on transfer from hospital or guardianship

2–077    **11.**—(1) Where the conditions of regulation 7(2) or 8(2) are satisfied, the authority for transfer given in accordance with those regulations shall be sufficient authority for the following persons to take the patient and convey the patient to the hospital to which the patient is being transferred within the periods specified—

(a) in a case to which regulation 7(2) applies—
   (i) an officer of the managers of either hospital, or
   (ii) any person authorised by the managers of the hospital to which the patient is being transferred,
   within the period of 28 days beginning with the date of the authority for transfer;

(b) in a case to which regulation 8(2) applies—
   (i) an officer of, or
   (ii) any person authorised by,
   the responsible local social services authority, within the period of 14 days beginning with the date on which the patient was last examined by a medical practitioner for the purposes of regulation 8(2)(b).

(2) Paragraph (1) shall apply to a patient who—

(a) is liable to be detained under the Act and is removed to another hospital in circumstances to which section 19(3) applies, as if the authority given by the managers for that transfer were an authority for transfer given in accordance with regulation 7(2);

(b) is liable to be detained in a hospital at which high security psychiatric services are provided and who, pursuant to a direction given by the Secretary of State under section 123(1) or (2) (transfers to and from special hospitals), is removed or transferred to another hospital, as if that direction were an authority for transfer given in accordance with regulation 7(2).

(3) In a case to which regulation 7(5)(a) applies, an officer of or any other person authorised by the managers of the registered establishment may take and convey the patient to the registered establishment to which the patient is being transferred.

2–078    Paragraph 13.20 of the Reference Guide states:

"In all cases [of patients being conveyed to hospital], patients are deemed to be in legal custody while being conveyed, which means (among other things) that the person conveying them can take steps to stop them absconding, and retake them if they do . . . . If they abscond while being transferred, they are also treated as if they were absent without leave (AWOL) from both hospitals—which affects who may take them into custody and allows them to be returned to either hospital . . . ."

## Conveyance from hospital to hospital following recall of community patients

2–079    **12.** Where the conditions of regulation 9(1) or (3) are satisfied, the authority for transfer given in accordance with that regulation shall be sufficient authority for the following persons to take the patient and convey him to the hospital to which he is being transferred—

(a) an officer of the managers of either hospital, or

(b) any person authorised by the managers of the hospital to which the patient is being transferred,

within the period of 72 hours beginning with the time of the patient's detention pursuant to the patient's recall under section 17E (power to recall to hospital).

### Renewal of authority for detention or guardianship and extension of community treatment period

**13.**—(1) Any report for the purposes of section 20(3) (medical recommen- **2–080** dation for renewal of authority to detain) shall be in the form set out in Parts 1 and 3 of Form H5.

(2) The statement for the purposes of section 20(5A) (agreement with medical recommendation for renewal of authority to detain) shall be in the form set out in Part 2 of Form H5.

(3) The receipt of Form H5 shall be recorded by the managers of the hospital in which the patient is liable to be detained in the form set out in Part 4 of that Form.

(4) Any report for the purposes of section 20(8) (medical recommendation for renewal of guardianship) shall be in the form set out in Part 1 of Form G9.

(5) The responsible social services authority shall record receipt of Form G9 in the form set out in Part 2 of that Form.

(6) For the purposes of section 20A (community treatment period)—

(a) a report for the purposes of subsection (4) of that section (responsible clinician's report extending the community treatment period) shall be in the form set out in Parts 1 and 3 of Form CTO7;

(b) a statement for the purposes of subsection (8) of that section (approved mental health professional's statement that it is appropriate to extend the order) shall be in the form set out in Part 2 of Form CTO7.

(7) The managers of the responsible hospital shall record the receipt of Form CTO7 in the form set out in Part 4 of that Form.

### Detention, guardianship or community treatment after absence without leave for more than 28 days

**14.**—(1) In relation to a patient who is liable to be detained— **2–081**

(a) any report for the purposes of section 21B(2) (authority for detention or guardianship of patients who are taken into custody or return after more than 28 days) shall be in the form set out in Part 1 of Form H6, and

(b) the receipt of that report shall be recorded by the managers of the hospital in which the patient is liable to be detained in the form set out in Part 2 of that Form.

(2) In relation to a patient who is subject to guardianship—

(a) any report for the purposes of section 21B(2) shall be in the form set out in Part 1 of Form G10, and

(b) the receipt of that report shall be recorded by the responsible local social services authority in the form set out in Part 2 of that Form.

(3) In relation to a community patient—

(a) any report for the purposes of section 21B(2) shall be in the form set out in Part 1 of Form CTO8, and

(b) the receipt of that report shall be recorded by the managers of the responsible hospital in the form set out in Part 2 of that Form.

**Removal to England**

2–082    **15.**—(1) This regulation shall apply to a patient who is removed from Scotland, Northern Ireland, any of the Channel Islands or the Isle of Man to England ("a removed patient") under—

(a) section 82, 84 or 85 (as the case may be), or

(b) regulations made under section 290 of the Mental Health (Care and Treatment) (Scotland) Act 2003 (removal and return of patients within United Kingdom).

(2) Where a removed patient is liable to be detained in a hospital, the managers of the hospital shall record the date on which the patient is admitted to the hospital in the form set out in Form M1.

(3) The managers of the hospital shall take such steps as are reasonably practicable to inform the person (if any) appearing to them to be the patient's nearest relative as soon as practicable of the patient's admission to hospital.

(4) Where a removed patient is received into guardianship—

(a) the guardian shall record the date on which the patient arrives at the place at which the patient is to reside on the patient's reception into guardianship under the Act in the form set out in Form M 1;

(b) the guardian shall take such steps as are reasonably practicable to inform the person (if any) appearing to them to be the patient's nearest relative as soon as practicable that the patient has been received into guardianship under the Act;

(c) a private guardian shall notify the responsible local social services authority of the—

(i) date mentioned in sub-paragraph (a), and

(ii) particulars mentioned in regulation 22(1)(b) and (e).

DEFINITION

2–083    private guardian: reg.2(1).

GENERAL NOTE

2–084    This regulation deals with the statutory forms to be used to record the arrival in England of detained and guardianship patients from Scotland, Northern Ireland, and any of the Channel Islands or the Isle of Man.

*Paragraphs (3),(4)(b)*

2–085    SUCH STEPS AS ARE REASONABLY PRACTICABLE. See Ch.2 of the *Code of Practice* for guidance on when steps may not be reasonably practicable because they would breach patients' rights under the European Convention on Human Rights.

**Removal to England of patients subject to compulsion in the community**

2–086    **16.**—(1) This regulation shall apply to a patient who is removed from Scotland, any of the Channel Islands or the Isle of Man to England under—

(a) section 289(1) of the Mental Health (Care and Treatment) (Scotland) Act 2003 (crossborder transfer: patients subject to requirement other than detention) in the case of Scotland; or

(b) section 85ZA (responsibility for community patients transferred from any of the Channel Islands or the Isle of Man) in the case of any of the Channel Islands or the Isle of Man.

(2) The managers of the responsible hospital shall record the date on which the patient arrived at the place where the patient is to reside in the form set out in Form M1.

(3) The managers of the hospital shall take such steps as are reasonably practicable to inform the person (if any) appearing to them to be the patient's nearest relative as soon as practicable that the patient is a community patient.

(4) The conditions specified by the responsible clinician under section 80C(5) (removal of patients subject to compulsion in the community from Scotland) or section 85ZA(4), shall be recorded by that responsible clinician in Part 1 of Form CTO9.

(5) The approved mental health professional's agreement to the conditions referred to in paragraph (4) shall be recorded by that approved mental health professional in Part 2 of Form CTO9.

GENERAL NOTE

This regulation deals with the reception of patients into SCT on their transfer from **2–087** Scotland, any of the Channel Islands or the Isle of Man.

*Paragraph (3)*

SUCH STEPS AS ARE REASONABLY PRACTICABLE. See Ch.2 of the *Code of Practice* for **2–088** guidance on when steps may not be reasonably practicable because they would breach patients' rights under the European Convention on Human Rights.

## Assignment of responsibility for community patients

**17.**—(1) This regulation applies to a community patient whether or not the **2–089** patient has been recalled to hospital in accordance with section 17E (power to recall to hospital).

(2) Responsibility for a patient referred to in paragraph (1) may be assigned by the managers of the responsible hospital to any other hospital whether or not that other hospital is under the same management as the responsible hospital.

(3) Responsibility for a patient shall not be assigned to a hospital which is not under the same management as the responsible hospital unless—

(a) an authority for the assignment is given by the managers of the assigning responsible hospital in the form set out in [assignment] Form CTO10;

(b) that [. . .] has been agreed by the managers of the hospital which will be the responsible hospital if the proposed [assignment] takes effect;

(c) the managers of the hospital referred to in (b) have specified the date on which the [assignment] shall take place;

(d) the managers of the assigning responsible hospital record—
   (i) the agreement of the managers of the new responsible hospital to the assignment, and
   (ii) the date on which the assignment is to take place,
   in the form set out in that Form.

(4) The managers of the receiving hospital must notify the patient in writing of—

(a) the assignment, either before it takes place or as soon as reasonably practicable thereafter; and

(b) their name and address (irrespective of whether or not there are any changes in the managers).

(5) Where responsibility for a patient is assigned from a responsible registered establishment to another hospital which is not under the same management and the patient is maintained under a contract with a Strategic Health Authority, Local Health Board, Primary Care Trust, National Health Service trust, National Health Service foundation trust, a Special Health Authority or the Welsh Ministers, any authority for [assignment] required under paragraph (3)(a), and the record required under paragraph (3)(b), may be given by an officer of that authority, board or trust authorised by it in that behalf, or by those Ministers, instead of by the managers.

(6) Any hospital to which a patient has been assigned may, in accordance with the provisions of this regulation, assign the patient to another hospital.

(7) The functions of the managers referred to in this regulation may be performed by an officer authorised by them in that behalf.

AMENDMENTS

The amendments to this regulation were made by SI 2008/2560 reg.2(2).

GENERAL NOTE

**2–090** This regulation sets out the procedure to be followed to authorise the reassignment of responsibility for a SCT patient from one hospital to another. No statutory form is required when managers authorise the transfer of responsibility for the patient between hospitals which are both under their management.

If responsibility is to be assigned from a hospital in Wales to one in England, the assignment must be made in accordance with the Welsh Regulations. This regulation should be followed for assignments from England to Wales.

*Paragraph (7)*

**2–091** OFFICER. See the note on reg.3(2).

## Discharge of patients

**2–092** **18.** For the purposes of section 23 (discharge of patients) a responsible clinician's order for the discharge of—

(a) a patient liable to be detained under the Act, or a community patient, shall be sent to the managers of the hospital in which the patient is liable to be detained or the responsible hospital (as applicable) as soon as practicable after it is made;

(b) a guardianship patient, shall be sent to the guardian as soon as practicable after it is made.

DEFINITION

**2–093** guardianship patient: reg.2(1).

GENERAL NOTE

**2–094** This regulation deals with the discharge of a patient under s.23 by the responsible clinician. There is no statutory form to be used for this purpose in England; a letter to the appropriate body would suffice. In Wales, if an RC discharges a patient from detention Form HO17 must be used. This Form must also be used in Wales if the hospital managers order discharge: see reg.7 of the Welsh Regulations.

## Delegation of hospital managers' functions under the Act

**19.** The functions of the managers of a hospital in respect of the following—  **2–095**

(a) notifying local social services authorities under section 14 (social reports) of patients detained on the basis of applications by their nearest relatives;

(b) authorising persons under section 17(3) (leave of absence from hospital) to keep in custody patients who are on leave of absence who are subject to a condition that they remain in custody;

(c) authorising persons under sections 18(1) and (2A) (return and readmission of patients absent without leave) to take and return detained and community patients respectively who are absent without leave,

may be performed by any person authorised by them in that behalf.

GENERAL NOTE

For the avoidance of doubt, this regulation expressly allows hospital managers to auth-  **2–096**
orise a person to exercise on their behalf the functions set out in paras (a), (b) and (c).

## Delegation of managers' functions under the Domestic Violence, Crime and Victims Act 2004

**20.** The functions of the managers of a hospital under sections 35 to 44B of the  **2–097**
Domestic Violence, Crime and Victims Act 2004 (provision of information to victims of patients under the Act etc.) may be performed by any person authorised by them in that behalf.

GENERAL NOTE

The Explanatory Memorandum to these regulations states:  **2–098**

"The Committee's attention is drawn to section 45(4) of the Domestic Violence, Crime and Victims Act 2004 which provides that a function conferred on the managers of a hospital under sections 35 to 44B of that Act is to be treated as a function of those managers under Part 3 of the 1983 Act for the purposes of section 32(3) of the 1983 Act (regulations as to delegation of managers' functions, etc). Section 32(3) of the 1983 Act, in turn, allows for the delegation of the functions of hospital managers under the 1983 Act."

## Delegation by local social services authorities

**21.**—(1) Except as provided by paragraph (2), a local social services authority  **2–099**
may delegate its functions under Parts 2 and 3 of the Act and these Regulations in the same way and to the same persons as its functions referred to in the Local Government Act 1972 may be delegated in accordance with section 101 of that Act.

(2) The function of the local social services authority under section 23 (discharge of patients) may not be delegated otherwise than in accordance with that section.

GENERAL NOTE

This regulation confirms that local social services authorities to whom s.101 of the Local  **2–100**
Government applies (those authorities who do not operate executive arrangements) may delegate their functions under Pts II and III of this Act (apart from decisions made under s.23), and under these regulations, in any way and to any person to whom they could delegate them under that section. Authorities which operate executive arrangements have separate and extensive powers of delegation under the Local Government Act 2000.

PART 3

FUNCTIONS OF GUARDIANS AND NEAREST RELATIVES

**Duties of private guardians**

2–101    22.—(1) It shall be the duty of a private guardian—

(a) to appoint a registered medical practitioner to act as the nominated medical attendant of the patient;

(b) to notify the responsible local social services authority of the name and address of the nominated medical attendant;

(c) in exercising the powers and duties of a private guardian conferred or imposed by the Act and these Regulations, to comply with such directions as that authority may give;

(d) to furnish that authority with all such reports or other information with regard to the patient as the authority may from time to time require;

(e) to notify that authority—

(i) on the reception of the patient into guardianship, of the private guardian's address and the address of the patient,

(ii) except in a case to which paragraph (f) applies, of any permanent change of either address, before or not later than 7 days after the change takes place;

(f) on any permanent change of the private guardian's address, where the new address is in the area of a different local social services authority, to notify that authority—

(i) of that address and that of the patient,

(ii) of the particulars mentioned in paragraph (b),

and to notify the authority which was formerly responsible of the permanent change in the private guardian's address;

(g) in the event of the death of the patient, or the termination of the guardianship by discharge, transfer or otherwise, to notify the responsible local social services authority as soon as reasonably practicable.

(2) Any notice, reports or other information under this regulation may be given or furnished in any other way (in addition to the methods of serving documents provided for by regulation 3(1)) to which the relevant local social services authority agrees, including orally or by electronic communication.

DEFINITION

2–102    private guardian: reg.2(1).

GENERAL NOTE

*Paragraph (1)(a)*

2–103    The nominated medical attendant is responsible for examining the patient for the purposes of renewing guardianship (ss.20(6), 34(1)). This doctor could be the patient's general practitioner.

**Visits to patients subject to guardianship**

2–104    **23.** The responsible local social services authority shall arrange for every patient received into guardianship under the Act to be visited at such intervals as the authority may decide, but—

(a) in any case at intervals of not more than 3 months, and

(b)  at least one such visit in any year shall be made by an approved clinician or a practitioner approved by the Secretary of State for the purposes of section 12 (general provisions as to medical recommendations).

GENERAL NOTE

The approved clinician need not be a medical practitioner.                    **2–105**

## Performance of functions of nearest relative

**24.**—(1) Subject to the conditions of paragraph (7), any person other than—    **2–106**
(a)  the patient;
(b)  a person mentioned in section 26(5) (persons deemed not to be the nearest relative), or
(c)  a person in respect of whom the court has made an order on the grounds set out in section 29(3)(b) to (e) (which sets out the grounds on which an application to the court for the appointment of a person to exercise the functions of a nearest relative may be made) for so long as an order under that section is in effect, may be authorised in accordance with paragraph (2) to act on behalf of the nearest relative in respect of the matters mentioned in paragraph (3).

(2) Subject to paragraph (8), the authorisation mentioned in paragraph (1) must be given in writing by the nearest relative.

(3) The matters referred to in paragraph (1) are the performance in respect of the patient of the functions conferred upon the nearest relative under—
(a)  Part 2 of the Act (as modified by Schedule 1 to the Act as the case may be), and
(b)  section 66 (applications to tribunals).

(4) An authorisation given under paragraph (1) shall take effect upon its receipt by the person authorised.

(5) Subject to the conditions of paragraph (7), the nearest relative of a patient may give notice in writing revoking that authorisation.

(6) Any revocation of such authorisation shall take effect upon the receipt of the notice by the person authorised.

(7) The conditions mentioned in paragraphs (1) and (5) are that the nearest relative shall immediately notify—
(a)  the patient;
(b)  in the case of a patient liable to be detained in a hospital, the managers of that hospital;
(c)  in the case of a patient subject to guardianship, the responsible local social services authority and the private guardian, if any;
(d)  in the case of a community patient, the managers of the responsible hospital, of the authorisation or, as the case may be, its revocation.

(8) An authorisation or notification referred to in this regulation may be transmitted by means of electronic communication if the recipient agrees.

DEFINITIONS
    private guardian: reg,2(1).                                              **2–107**
    electronic communication: reg.2(1).

GENERAL NOTE
    This regulation enables the patient's nearest relative to delegate the functions specified **2–108** in para.(3) to another person. It follows that the delegate does not have the power to further

delegate such functions to another. A delegation cannot be made to the persons identified in para.(1)(a),(b) or (c). The patient, who cannot prevent the nearest relative from making a delegation, does not need to be subject to the Act's provisions at the time when the delegation is made. If this is the case, the only formality that is required is for the nearest relative to give written notice of the authorisation to the authorised person and for the patient to be notified of the authorisation. The authorisation or notification may be given by electronic means if the recipient agrees (para.(8)). Notification to one of the bodies mentioned in para.(7) is required if the patient is subject to the Act's provisions at the time of the authorisation. If a delegation is made, the nearest relative may revoke it at any time by notifying the authorised person in writing (para.(5)) or electronically (para.(8)).

A delegation made under this provision would end on the nearest relative ceasing to have that status by virtue of the operation of either s.26 or s.29.

An acting nearest relative appointed by the court under s.29 of the Act cannot use this power but must apply to the county court under s.30 for the s.29 order to be varied if he or she no longer wishes to perform the functions of acting nearest relative.

*Paragraph (1)*

**2–109**     ANY PERSON.   The person authorised need not be a relative of the patient. Although there is no requirement for the person concerned to have consented to the delegation, it must be assumed that such consent is a pre-condition of delegation.

## Discharge by nearest relative

**2–110**     **25.**—(1) Any report given by the responsible clinician for the purposes of section 25 (restrictions on discharge by nearest relative)—

(a)  shall be in the form set out in Part 1 of Form M2, and

(b)  the receipt of that report by—

    (i) the managers of the hospital in which the patient is liable to be detained, or

    (ii) the managers of the responsible hospital in the case of a community patient, shall be in the form set out in Part 2 of that Form.

(2) In addition to the methods of serving documents provided for by regulation 3(1), reports under this regulation may be furnished by—

(a)  transmission by facsimile, or

(b)  the transmission in electronic form of a reproduction of the report, if the managers of the hospital agree.

GENERAL NOTE

**2–111**     Paragraph 29.23 of the *Code of Practice* contains an illustrative letter for discharge from detention and SCT.

PART 4

PROVISION OF INFORMATION

**2–112**     **26.**—(1) Unless the patient requests otherwise, where —

(a)  a patient is to be or has been transferred from hospital to hospital pursuant to section 19 or section 123 (regulations as to transfer of patients and transfer to and from special hospitals respectively), the managers of the hospital to which the patient is to be or has been transferred shall take such steps as are reasonably practicable to cause the person (if any) appearing to them to be the patient's nearest relative to be informed of that transfer before it takes place or as soon as practicable thereafter;

(b) a patient's detention is renewed pursuant to a report furnished under section 20 (duration of authority), the managers of the responsible hospital shall take such steps as are reasonably practicable to cause the person (if any) appearing to them to be the patient's nearest relative to be informed of that renewal as soon as practicable following their decision not to discharge the patient;

(c) by virtue of section 21B(7) (patients who are taken into custody or return after more than 28 days) a patient's detention is renewed pursuant to a report furnished under section 21B(2), the managers of the responsible hospital in which the patient is liable to be detained shall take such steps as are reasonably practicable to cause the person (if any) appearing to them to be the patient's nearest relative to be informed of that renewal as soon as practicable following their decision not to discharge the patient;

(d) by virtue of section 21B(5) and (6) (patients who are taken into custody or return after more than 28 days), a patient's detention is renewed retrospectively pursuant to a report furnished under section 21B(2), the managers of the hospital in which the patient is liable to be detained shall take such steps as are reasonably practicable to cause the patient and the person (if any) appearing to them to be the patient's nearest relative to be informed of that renewal as soon as practicable following their receipt of that report;

(e) a patient's period of community treatment is extended pursuant to a report furnished under section 20A (community treatment period), the managers of the responsible hospital shall take such steps as are reasonably practicable to cause the person (if any) appearing to them to be the patient's nearest relative to be informed of that extension as soon as practicable following their decision not to discharge the patient;

(f) by virtue of section 21B(7A) (patients who are taken into custody or return after more than 28 days) a patient's period of community treatment is extended pursuant to a report furnished under section 21B(2), the managers of the responsible hospital shall take such steps as are reasonably practicable to cause the person (if any) appearing to them to be the patient's nearest relative to be informed of that extension as soon as practicable following their decision not to discharge the patient;

(g) by virtue of section 21B(6A) and (6B) (patients who are taken into custody or return after more than 28 days) a patient's period of community treatment is extended retrospectively pursuant to a report furnished under section 21B(2), the managers of the responsible hospital shall take such steps as are reasonably practicable to cause the patient and the person (if any) appearing to them to be the patient's nearest relative to be informed of that extension as soon as practicable following their receipt of that report;

(h) a patient is to be or has been assigned to another hospital which assumes responsibility for that patient as a community patient, the managers of the hospital to which the patient is to be or has been assigned shall take such steps as are reasonably practicable to cause the person (if any) appearing to them to be the patient's nearest relative to be informed of that assignment before or as soon as practicable following it taking place;

(i) a patient is to be or has been transferred from hospital to guardianship pursuant to section 19 (regulations as to transfer of patients), the responsible local social services authority shall take such steps as are reasonably practicable to cause the person appearing to it to be the patient's nearest relative to be informed of that transfer before it takes place or as soon as practicable thereafter;

(j) a patient is to be or has been transferred from the guardianship of one person to the guardianship of another person pursuant to section 19 (regulations as to transfer of patients), the new responsible local social services authority shall take such steps as are reasonably practicable to cause the person (if any) appearing to it to be the patient's nearest relative to be informed of that transfer before it takes place or as soon as practicable thereafter;

(k) a patient's guardianship becomes vested in the local social services authority or the functions of a guardian are, during the guardian's incapacity, transferred to the authority or a person approved by it under section 10 (transfer of guardianship in case of death, incapacity, etc of guardian), the responsible local social services authority shall take such steps as are reasonably practicable to cause the person (if any) appearing to it to be the patient's nearest relative to be informed of that vesting, or as the case may be, transfer before it takes place or as soon as practicable thereafter;

(l) a patient's guardianship is renewed pursuant to a report furnished under section 20 (duration of authority), the responsible local social services authority shall take such steps as are reasonably practicable to cause the person (if any) appearing to it to be the patient's nearest relative to be informed of that renewal as soon as practicable following the decision of the responsible local social services authority [not] to discharge the patient;

(m) by virtue of section 21B(7) (patients who are taken into custody or return after more than 28 days) a patient's guardianship is renewed pursuant to a report furnished under section 21B(7), the responsible local social services authority shall take such steps as are reasonably practicable to cause the person (if any) appearing to it to be the patient's nearest relative to be informed of that renewal as soon as practicable following the decision of the responsible local social services authority not to discharge the patient;

(n) by virtue of section 21B(5) and (6) (patients who are taken into custody or return after more than 28 days) a patient's guardianship is renewed retrospectively pursuant to a report furnished under section 21B(2), the responsible local social services authority shall take such steps as are reasonably practicable to cause the patient and person (if any) appearing to it to be the patient's nearest relative to be informed of that renewal as soon as practicable following the receipt by the responsible local social services authority of that report.

(2) Where paragraph (1)(m) or (n) applies, the responsible local social services authority shall, as soon as practicable inform the private guardian (if any) of its receipt of a report furnished under section 21B (patients who are taken into custody or return after more than 28 days).

(3) Upon a patient becoming subject to guardianship under the Act, the responsible local social services authority shall take such steps as are reasonably practicable to cause to be informed both the patient and the person (if any) appearing to the authority to be the patient's nearest relative of the rights referred to in paragraph (4).

(4) Those rights are—

(a) the patient's rights under section 66 (applications to tribunals),

(b) the nearest relative's right, as the case may be, to—

(i) discharge the patient under section 23 (discharge of patients), or

    (ii) make an application under section 69 (application to tribunals concerning patients subject to hospital and guardianship orders where the patient is, or is treated as being, subject to guardianship under section 37).

(5) Where information referred to in paragraph (1)(d), (g) or (n), or in paragraph (3) is to be given to the patient, it shall be given both orally and in writing.

(6) Where information referred to in paragraph (1) [or (3)] is to be given to the person appearing to be the patient's nearest relative, it shall be given in writing.

(7) Where information referred to in paragraph (2) is to be given to the private guardian, it shall be given in writing.

(8) Information that is to be given in writing under paragraphs (6) and (7) may be transmitted by means of electronic communication if the recipient agrees.

(9) The functions of the managers referred to in this regulation may be performed by an officer authorised by them in that behalf.

AMENDMENTS
The amendments to this regulation were made by SI 2008/2560 reg.2(3).

GENERAL NOTE
This regulation sets out when hospital managers and local authorities are required to give **2–113** information about various statutory events to the patient's nearest relative (and sometimes patients themselves and, where applicable, private guardians). This requirement is in addition to the duties placed on hospital managers by ss.132, 132A and 133 of the 1983 Act to give information to patients and their nearest relatives. The information must not be given to the nearest relative if this is the patient's wish (para.(1)) or it is not "reasonably practicable" to provide the information. Chapter 2 of the *Code of Practice* provides guidance on what steps may not be reasonably practicable because they would breach the patient's rights under the European Convention on Human Rights. The regulation, in paras (3) and (4), also places duties on local social services authorities to give information to guardianship patients and their nearest relatives.

PART 5

CONSENT TO TREATMENT

**Consent to treatment**
    **27.**—(1) For the purposes of section 57 (treatment requiring consent and a **2–114** second opinion)—
    (a) the form of treatment to which that section shall apply, in addition to the treatment mentioned in subsection (1)(a) of that section (any surgical operation for destroying brain tissue or for destroying the functioning of brain tissue), shall be the surgical implantation of hormones for the purpose of reducing male sexual drive, and
    (b) the certificates required for the purposes of subsection (2)(a) and (b) of that section shall be in the form set out in Form T 1.

(2) For the purposes of section 58 (treatment requiring consent or a second opinion) the certificates required for the purposes of subsection (3)(a) and (b) of that section shall be in the form set out in Forms T2 and T3 respectively.

(3) For the purposes of section 58A (electro-convulsive therapy, etc.)—
    (a) the form of treatment to which that section shall apply, in addition to the administration of electro-convulsive therapy mentioned in subsection

(1)(a) of that section, shall be the administration of medicine as part of that therapy; and

(b) the certificates required for the purposes of subsections (3), (4) and (5) of that section shall be in the form set out in Forms T4, T5 and T6 respectively.

(4) Section 58A does not apply to treatment by way of the administration of medicine as part of electro-convulsive therapy where that treatment falls within section 62(1)(a) or (b) (treatment immediately necessary to save the patient's life or to prevent a serious deterioration in the patient's condition).

GENERAL NOTE
*Paragraph (1)(a)*

**2–115**   The oral administration of hormones for the purpose of reducing the male sex drive does not come within the scope of s.57.

*Paragraph (4)*

**2–116**   This provides that administration of medicine as part of ECT (like ECT itself: see para.(3)(a)) does not require a certificate from a SOAD if it is immediately necessary to save the patient's life or to prevent a serious deterioration of his or her condition.

PART 6

TREATMENT OF COMMUNITY PATIENTS NOT RECALLED TO HOSPITAL

**2–117**   **28.**—(1) For the purposes of Part 4A of the Act (treatment of community patients not recalled to hospital), the certificates required for the purposes of sections 64B(2)(b) and 64E(2)(b) (which set out when treatment under Part 4A of the Act may be given to adult and child community patients respectively) shall be in the form set out in Form CTO11.

(2) Treatment of a patient to whom section 64B(3)(b) or section 64E(3)(b) applies (adult and child patients for whom treatment is immediately necessary), may include treatment by way of administration of medicine as part of electro-convulsive therapy but only where that treatment falls within section 64C(5)(a) or (b) (treatment immediately necessary to save the patient's life or to prevent a serious deterioration in the patient's condition).

(3) Treatment of a patient to whom section 64G (emergency treatment for patients lacking capacity or competence) applies may include treatment by way of the administration of medicine as part of electro-convulsive therapy but only where that treatment falls within section 64G(5)(a) or (b) (treatment immediately necessary to save the patient's life or to prevent a serious deterioration in the patient's condition).

GENERAL NOTE

**2–118**   This regulation makes similar provision to reg.27(2) to (4) in respect of SCT patients who have not been recalled to hospital.

PART 7

CORRESPONDENCE OF PATIENTS

**Inspection and opening of postal packets**
**29.**—(1) Where under section 134(4) (inspection and opening of postal packets **2–119** addressed to or by patients in hospital) any postal packet is inspected and opened, but neither the packet nor anything contained in it is withheld under section 134(1) or (2) the person appointed who inspected and opened it, shall record in writing—
  (a) that the packet had been so inspected and opened,
  (b) that nothing in the packet has been withheld, and
  (c) the name of the person appointed and the name of the hospital, and shall, before resealing the packet, place the record in that packet.
  (2) Where under section 134(1) or (2) any postal packet or anything contained in it is withheld by the person appointed—
  (a) that person shall record in a register kept for the purpose—
    (i) that the packet or anything contained in it has been withheld,
    (ii) the date on which it was so withheld,
    (iii) the grounds on which it was so withheld,
    (iv) a description of the contents of the packet withheld or of any item withheld, and
    (v) the name of the person appointed; and
  (b) if anything contained in the packet is withheld, the person appointed shall record in writing—
    (i) that the packet has been inspected and opened,
    (ii) that an item or items contained in the packet have been withheld,
    (iii) a description of any such item,
    (iv) the name of the person appointed and the name of the hospital, and
    (v) in any case to which section 134(1)(b) or (2) applies, the further particulars required for the purposes of section 134(6),
    and shall, before resealing the packet, place the record in that packet.
  (3) In a case to which section 134(1)(b) or (2) applies—
  (a) the notice required for the purposes of section 134(6) shall include—
    (i) a statement of the grounds on which the packet in question or anything contained in it was withheld, and
    (ii) the name of the person appointed who so decided to withhold that packet or anything contained in it and the name of the hospital; and
  (b) where anything contained in a packet is withheld the record required by paragraph (2)(b) shall, if the provisions of section 134(6) are otherwise satisfied, be sufficient notice to the person to whom the packet is addressed for the purposes of section 134(6).
  (4) For the purposes of this regulation "the person appointed" means a person appointed under section 134(7) to perform the functions of the managers of the hospital under that section.

GENERAL NOTE
Paragraph 14.15 of the *Reference Guide to the Mental Health Act 1983* states:     **2–120**

"In practice, because of [CQC's] power to review decisions to withhold post, anything addressed to a patient which is withheld should be retained for at least six months, unless it is necessary to give it to the police or other similar body. After that—assuming that [CQC] is not in the process of reviewing the decision—it may be returned to the sender, if that can be done safely."

### Review of decisions to withhold postal packets

**2–121**    **30.**—(1) Every application for review by the Commission under [section 134A(1) (review of decisions to withhold correspondence)] shall be—

    (a)  made in such manner as the Commission may accept as sufficient in the circumstances of any particular case or class of case and may be made otherwise than in writing, and

    (b)  made, delivered or sent to an office of the Commission.

(2) Any person making such an application shall furnish to the Commission the notice of the withholding of the postal packet or anything contained in it, given under section 134(6), or a copy of that notice.

(3) For the purpose of determining any such application the Commission may direct the production of such documents, information and evidence as it may reasonably require.

AMENDMENT

In para.(1), the words in square brackets were substituted by SI 2009/462 art.12, Sch.5 para.25(b).

DEFINITION

**2–122**    the Commission: reg.2(1).

### Patient advocacy and liaison services and independent mental capacity advocate services

**2–123**    **31.**—(1) In section 134 (correspondence of patients), for the purposes of subsection (3)(ea) "patient advocacy and liaison service" means a service affording assistance in the form of advice and liaison for patients, their families and carers provided by—

    (a)  an NHS trust,

    (b)  an NHS foundation trust, or

    (c)  a Primary Care Trust.

(2) For the purposes of section 134(3A)(b)(iii), the prescribed arrangements are arrangements in respect of independent mental capacity advocates made under section 35 to 41 of the Mental Capacity Act 2005 (independent advocacy service).

PART 8

REVOCATIONS

### Revocations

**2–124**    **32.** The Regulations specified in column 1 of Schedule 2 are hereby revoked to the extent mentioned in column 3 of that Schedule.

**Regulations 4–9,13–17, 25, 27 and 28**                    **SCHEDULE 1**

AMENDMENTS

The amendments to Forms A7, A9, H2, CTO8 and CTO 11 were made by SI 2008/2560 reg.2(4).

GENERAL NOTE

Health bodies and local authorities can produce their own forms as long as the wording **2–125** set out in this Schedule is reproduced. A handwritten form would suffice in an emergency if printed forms were not available. An alternative course of action would be to remove the appropriate pages from this Manual.

The use of a form which failed to produce the exact wording set out in these regulations would not necessarily invalidate the application or recommendation because minor departures would be regarded by the courts as being de minimis, i.e. too trivial to be of any consequence. In *Re E (Mental Health: Habeas Corpus)*, December 10, 1966, the court held that the detention of a patient was lawful in a situation where obsolete forms had been used because the differences between the two sets of forms was de minimis and were not intended by this Act to be taken account of. It is likely that a court would find a patient's detention to be unlawful if the statutory criteria set out in the form failed to reproduce the correct wording in some material respect.

Although only reg.25 provides specific authority for a form to be served by fax, it is submitted that a faxed reproduction of a completed form can be acted upon if (a) the recipient confers with the signatory by telephone to confirm that that the form was completed by the signatory; and (b) the original is delivered to the recipient at the earliest opportunity. The Mental Health Act Commission endorsed the use of faxed forms (MHAC, *Sixth Biennial Report*, 1993-1995, para.3.13).

*Lost forms*

If the forms that were used to provide authority for the patient's detention or guardian- **2–126** ship are lost, the authority for the detention or guardianship no longer exists and a fresh assessment under this Act must be undertaken if it is considered that the patient has a continuing need for either detention or guardianship. However, if copies of the original forms were made there would be no need for a fresh assessment if the signatories endorsed the relevant copy as a true copy of the original form.

**FORMS FOR USE IN CONNECTION WITH COMPULSORY
ADMISSION TO HOSPITAL, GUARDIANSHIP AND
TREATMENT**

*Form A1*                                      *Regulation 4(1)(a)(i)*

**2–127  Mental Health Act 1983 section 2—application by nearest relative for admission for assessment**

To the managers of [name and address of hospital]

I [PRINT your full name and address] apply for the admission of [PRINT full name and address of patient] for assessment in accordance with Part 2 of the Mental Health Act 1983.

*Complete (a) or (b) as applicable and delete the other.*

(a)  To the best of my knowledge and belief I am the patient's nearest relative within the meaning of the Act

I am the patient's [state your relationship with the patient].

(b)  I have been authorised to exercise the functions under the Act of the patient's nearest relative by a county court/the patient's nearest relative *<delete the phrase which does not apply>*, and a copy of the authority is attached to this application.

I last saw the patient on [date], which was within the period of 14 days ending on the day this application is completed.

This application is founded on two medical recommendations in the prescribed form.

If neither of the medical practitioners had previous acquaintance with the patient before making their recommendations, please explain why you could not get a recommendation from a medical practitioner who did have previous acquaintance with the patient:—

. . . . . . . . . . . . . . . . . . . . . . . . . . . . . . . . . . . . . . . . . . . . . . . . . . . . . . . . . . . . . . . . . . . . . . . . . . . . . . .
. . . . . . . . . . . . . . . . . . . . . . . . . . . . . . . . . . . . . . . . . . . . . . . . . . . . . . . . . . . . . . . . . . . . . . . . . . . . . . .
. . . . . . . . . . . . . . . . . . . . . . . . . . . . . . . . . . . . . . . . . . . . . . . . . . . . . . . . . . . . . . . . . . . . . . . . . . . . . . .

If you need to continue on a separate sheet please indicate here [ ] and attach that sheet to this form]

Signed  . . . . . . . . . . . . . . . . . . . . . . . . . . .

Date  . . . . . . . . . . . . . . . . . . . . . . . . . . .

Form A2                                    *Regulation 4(1)(a)(ii)*

**Mental Health Act 1983 section 2—application by an approved mental health professional for admission for assessment**  **2–128**

To the Managers of [name and address of hospital]

I [PRINT your full name and address] apply for the admission of [PRINT full name and address of patient] for assessment in accordance with Part 2 of the Mental Health Act 1983.

I am acting on behalf of [PRINT name of local social services authority] and am approved to act as an approved mental health professional for the purposes of the Act by *<delete as appropriate>*

that authority
[name of local social services authority that approved you, if different]

*Complete the following if you know who the nearest relative is.*

*Complete (a) or (b) as applicable and delete the other.*

(a) To the best of my knowledge and belief [PRINT full name and address] is the patient's nearest relative within the meaning of the Act.

(b) I understand that [PRINT full name and address] has been authorised by a county court/the patient's nearest relative* to exercise the functions under the Act of the patient's nearest relative.
*<\*Delete the phrase which does not apply>*

I have/have not yet* informed that person that this application is to be made and of the nearest relative's power to order the discharge of the patient. *<\*Delete the phrase which does not apply>*

*Complete the following if you do not know who the nearest relative is.*

*Delete (a) or (b).*

(a) I have been unable to ascertain who is the patient's nearest relative within the meaning of the Act.

(b) To the best of my knowledge and belief this patient has no nearest relative within the meaning of the Act.

*The remainder of the form must be completed in all cases.*

I last saw the patient on [date], which was within the period of 14 days ending on the day this application is completed.

I have interviewed the patient and I am satisfied that detention in a hospital is in all the circumstances of the case the most appropriate way of providing the care and medical treatment of which the patient stands in need.

This application is founded on two medical recommendations in the prescribed form.

If neither of the medical practitioners had previous acquaintance with the patient before making their recommendations, please explain why you could not get a recommendation from a medical practitioner who did have previous acquaintance with the patient—

. . . . . . . . . . . . . . . . . . . . . . . . . . . . . . . . . . . . . . . . . . . . . . . . . . . . . . . . . . . . . . . . . . . . . . .
. . . . . . . . . . . . . . . . . . . . . . . . . . . . . . . . . . . . . . . . . . . . . . . . . . . . . . . . . . . . . . . . . . . . . . .
. . . . . . . . . . . . . . . . . . . . . . . . . . . . . . . . . . . . . . . . . . . . . . . . . . . . . . . . . . . . . . . . . . . . . . .

[If you need to continue on a separate sheet please indicate here [ ] and attach that sheet to this form]

Signed . . . . . . . . . . . . . . . . . . . . . . . . . . .

Date . . . . . . . . . . . . . . . . . . . . . . . . . . . .

**2–129**  **Mental Health Act 1983 section 2—joint medical recommendation for admission for assessment**

We, registered medical practitioners, recommend that [PRINT full name and address of patient] be admitted to a hospital for assessment in accordance with Part 2 of the Mental Health Act 1983.

I [PRINT full name and address of first practitioner] last examined this patient on [date].

*I had previous acquaintance with the patient before I conducted that examination.

*I am approved under section 12 of the Act as having special experience in the diagnosis or treatment of mental disorder.

<*Delete if not applicable>

I [PRINT full name and address of second practitioner] last examined this patient on [date].

*I had previous acquaintance with the patient before I conducted that examination.

*I am approved under section 12 of the Act as having special experience in the diagnosis or treatment of mental disorder.

<*Delete if not applicable>

In our opinion

    (a)  this patient is suffering from mental disorder of a nature or degree which warrants the detention of the patient in hospital for assessment (or for assessment followed by medical treatment) for at least a limited period,

AND

    (b)  ought to be so detained
       (i)  in the interests of the patient's own health
      (ii)  in the interests of the patient's own safety
     (iii)  with a view to the protection of other persons
      <*Delete the indents not applicable>

Our reasons for these opinions are:

[Your reasons should cover both (a) and (b) above. As part of them: describe the patient's symptoms and behaviour and explain how those symptoms and behaviour lead you to your opinion; explain why the patient ought to be admitted to hospital and why informal admission is not appropriate.]

. . . . . . . . . . . . . . . . . . . . . . . . . . . . . . . . . . . . . . . . . . . . . . . . . . . . . . . . . . . . . . . . . . . . . . . . . . .
. . . . . . . . . . . . . . . . . . . . . . . . . . . . . . . . . . . . . . . . . . . . . . . . . . . . . . . . . . . . . . . . . . . . . . . . . . .
. . . . . . . . . . . . . . . . . . . . . . . . . . . . . . . . . . . . . . . . . . . . . . . . . . . . . . . . . . . . . . . . . . . . . . . . . . .

[If you need to continue on a separate sheet please indicate here [ ] and attach that sheet to this form]

                           Signed . . . . . . . . . . . . . . . . . . . . . . . . . . .

                           Date . . . . . . . . . . . . . . . . . . . . . . . . . . . . .

                           Signed . . . . . . . . . . . . . . . . . . . . . . . . . . .

                           Date . . . . . . . . . . . . . . . . . . . . . . . . . . . . .

**NOTE: AT LEAST ONE OF THE PRACTITIONERS SIGNING THIS FORM MUST BE APPROVED UNDER SECTION 12 OF THE ACT.**

*Form A4*　　　　　　*Regulation 4(1)(b)(ii)*

**Mental Health Act 1983 section 2—medical recommendation for admission for assessment**　　**2–130**

I [PRINT full name and address of medical practitioner], a registered medical practitioner, recommend that [PRINT full name and address of patient] be admitted to a hospital for assessment in accordance with Part 2 of the Mental Health Act 1983.

I last examined this patient on [date].

*I had previous acquaintance with the patient before I conducted that examination.

*I am approved under section 12 of the Act as having special experience in the diagnosis or treatment of mental disorder.

<*Delete if not applicable>

In my opinion,

    (a) this patient is suffering from mental disorder of a nature or degree which warrants the detention of the patient in hospital for assessment (or for assessment followed by medical treatment) for at least a limited period,

AND

    (b) ought to be so detained
       (i) in the interests of the patient's own health
      (ii) in the interests of the patient's own safety
     (iii) with a view to the protection of other persons
     <*Delete the indents not applicable>

My reasons for these opinions are:

[Your reasons should cover both (a) and (b) above. As part of them: describe the patient's symptoms and behaviour and explain how those symptoms and behaviour lead you to your opinion; explain why the patient ought to be admitted to hospital and why informal admission is not appropriate.]

. . . . . . . . . . . . . . . . . . . . . . . . . . . . . . . . . . . . . . . . . . . . . . . . . . . . . . . . . . . . . . . . . . . . . . . . . . . . . .
. . . . . . . . . . . . . . . . . . . . . . . . . . . . . . . . . . . . . . . . . . . . . . . . . . . . . . . . . . . . . . . . . . . . . . . . . . . . . .
. . . . . . . . . . . . . . . . . . . . . . . . . . . . . . . . . . . . . . . . . . . . . . . . . . . . . . . . . . . . . . . . . . . . . . . . . . . . . .

[If you need to continue on a separate sheet please indicate here [ ] and attach that sheet to this form]

Signed . . . . . . . . . . . . . . . . . . . . . . . . . .

Date . . . . . . . . . . . . . . . . . . . . . . . . . .

**2–131** **Mental Health Act 1983 section 3—application by nearest relative for admission for treatment**

To the Managers of [name and address of hospital]

I [PRINT your full name and address] apply for the admission of [PRINT full name and address of patient] for treatment in accordance with Part 2 of the Mental Health Act 1983.

*Complete either (a) or (b) as applicable and delete the other*

(a) To the best of my knowledge and belief I am the patient's nearest relative within the meaning of the Act.

I am the patient's [state relationship with the patient].

(b) I have been authorised to exercise the functions under the Act of the patient's nearest relative by a county court/the patient's nearest relative <*delete the phrase which does not apply*>, and a copy of the authority is attached to this application.

I last saw the patient on [date], which was within the period of 14 days ending on the day this application is completed.

This application is founded on two medical recommendations in the prescribed form.

If neither of the medical practitioners had previous acquaintance with the patient before making the recommendations, please explain why you could not get a recommendation from a medical practitioner who did have previous acquaintance with the patient—

. . . . . . . . . . . . . . . . . . . . . . . . . . . . . . . . . . . . . . . . . . . . . . . . . . . . . . . . . . . . . . . . . . . . . . . . . . . . . . . . .
. . . . . . . . . . . . . . . . . . . . . . . . . . . . . . . . . . . . . . . . . . . . . . . . . . . . . . . . . . . . . . . . . . . . . . . . . . . . . . . . .
. . . . . . . . . . . . . . . . . . . . . . . . . . . . . . . . . . . . . . . . . . . . . . . . . . . . . . . . . . . . . . . . . . . . . . . . . . . . . . . . .
. . . . . . . . . . . . . . . . . . . . . . . . . . . . . . . . . . . . . . . . . . . . . . . . . . . . . . . . . . . . . . . . . . . . . . . . . . . . . . . . .
. . . . . . . . . . . . . . . . . . . . . . . . . . . . . . . . . . . . . . . . . . . . . . . . . . . . . . . . . . . . . . . . . . . . . . . . . . . . . . . . .

[If you need to continue on a separate sheet please indicate here [ ] and attach that sheet to this form]

Signed  . . . . . . . . . . . . . . . . . . . . . . . . . . .

Date  . . . . . . . . . . . . . . . . . . . . . . . . . . . .

**Mental Health Act 1983 section 3—application by an approved mental health professional for    2–132 admission for treatment**

To the managers of [name and address of hospital]

I [PRINT your full name and address] apply for the admission of [PRINT full name and address of patient] for treatment in accordance with Part 2 of the Mental Health Act 1983.

I am acting on behalf of [name of local social services authority] and am approved to act as an approved mental health professional for the purposes of the Act by <*delete as appropriate*>

　　that authority
　　[name of local social services authority that approved you, if different]

*Complete the following where consultation with the nearest relative has taken place.*

*Complete (a) or (b) and delete the other.*

  (a)　I have consulted [PRINT full name and address] who to the best of my knowledge and belief is the patient's nearest relative within the meaning of the Act.

  (b)　I have consulted [PRINT full name and address] who I understand has been authorised by a county court/the patient's nearest relative* to exercise the functions under the Act of the patient's nearest relative.
　<**Delete the phrase which does not apply*>

That person has not notified me or the local social services authority on whose behalf I am acting that he or she objects to this application being made

*Complete the following where the nearest relative has not been consulted.*

*Delete whichever two of (a), (b) and (c) do not apply.*

  (a)　I have been unable to ascertain who is this patient's nearest relative within the meaning of the Act.

  (b)　To the best of my knowledge and belief this patient has no nearest relative within the meaning the Act.

  (c)　I understand that [PRINT full name and address] is

     (i)　this patient's nearest relative within the meaning of the Act,

    (ii)　authorised to exercise the functions of this patient's nearest relative under the Act,
　　　　<*Delete either (i) or (ii)*>

but in my opinion it is not reasonably practicable/would involve unreasonable delay <*delete as appropriate*> to consult that person before making this application, because—

. . . . . . . . . . . . . . . . . . . . . . . . . . . . . . . . . . . . . . . . . . . . . . . . . . . . . . . . . . . . . . . . . . . . . . . . . .
. . . . . . . . . . . . . . . . . . . . . . . . . . . . . . . . . . . . . . . . . . . . . . . . . . . . . . . . . . . . . . . . . . . . . . . . . .
. . . . . . . . . . . . . . . . . . . . . . . . . . . . . . . . . . . . . . . . . . . . . . . . . . . . . . . . . . . . . . . . . . . . . . . . . .

[If you need to continue on a separate sheet please indicate here [ ] and attach that sheet to this form]

*The remainder of this form must be completed in all cases.*

I saw the patient on [date], which was within the period of 14 days ending on the day this application is completed.

I have interviewed the patient and I am satisfied that detention in a hospital is in all the circumstances of the case the most appropriate way of providing the care and medical treatment of which the patient stands in need.

This application is founded on two medical recommendations in the prescribed form.

If neither of the medical practitioners had previous acquaintance with the patient before making their recommendations, please explain why you could not get a recommendation from a medical practitioner who did have previous acquaintance with the patient—

.........................................................................................
.........................................................................................
.........................................................................................

[If you need to continue on a separate sheet please indicate here [ ] and attach that sheet to this form]

Signed ...........................

Date ...........................

*Form A7*                    *Regulation 4(1)(d)(i)*

**Mental Health Act 1983 section 3—joint medical recommendation for admission for treatment** **2–133**

We, registered medical practitioners, recommend that [PRINT full name and address of patient] be admitted to a hospital for treatment in accordance with Part 2 of the Mental Health Act 1983.

I [PRINT full name and address of first practitioner] last examined this patient on [date].

*I had previous acquaintance with the patient before I conducted that examination.

*I am approved under section 12 of the Act as having special experience in the diagnosis or treatment of mental disorder.

<*Delete if not applicable>

I [PRINT name and address of second practitioner] [last examined this patient on [date].]

*I had previous acquaintance with the patient before I conducted that examination.

*I am approved under section 12 of the Act as having special experience in the diagnosis or treatment of mental disorder.

<*Delete if not applicable>

In our opinion,

(a)  this patient is suffering from mental disorder of a nature or degree which makes it appropriate for the patient to receive medical treatment in a hospital,

AND

(b)  it is necessary
 (i)  for the patient's own health
 (ii)  for the patient's own safety
 (iii)  for the protection of other persons
  <delete the indents not applicable>

that this patient should receive treatment in hospital, AND

(c)  such treatment cannot be provided unless the patient is detained under section 3 of the Act,

because—[Your reasons should cover (a), (b) and (c) above. As part of them: describe the patient's symptoms and behaviour and explain how those symptoms and behaviour lead you to your opinion; say whether other methods of treatment or care (eg out-patient treatment or social services) are available and, if so, why they are not appropriate; indicate why informal admission is not appropriate.]

. . . . . . . . . . . . . . . . . . . . . . . . . . . . . . . . . . . . . . . . . . . . . . . . . . . . . . . . . . . . . . . . . . . . . . . . . .
. . . . . . . . . . . . . . . . . . . . . . . . . . . . . . . . . . . . . . . . . . . . . . . . . . . . . . . . . . . . . . . . . . . . . . . . . .
. . . . . . . . . . . . . . . . . . . . . . . . . . . . . . . . . . . . . . . . . . . . . . . . . . . . . . . . . . . . . . . . . . . . . . . . . .

[If you need to continue on a separate sheet please indicate here [ ] and attach that sheet to this form]

. . . . . . . . . . . . . . . . . . . . . . . . . . . . . . . . . . . . . . . . . . . . . . . . . . . . . . . . . . . . . . . . . . . . . . . . . .

We are also of the opinion that, taking into account the nature and degree of the mental disorder from which the patient is suffering and all the other circumstances of the case, appropriate medical treatment is available to the patient at the following hospital (or one of the following hospitals):—

[Enter name of hospital(s). If appropriate treatment is available only in a particular part of the hospital, say which part.]

..............................................................................
..............................................................................
..............................................................................

Signed ..........................

Date ..........................

Signed ..........................

Date ..........................

**NOTE: AT LEAST ONE OF THE PRACTITIONERS SIGNING THIS FORM MUST BE APPROVED UNDER SECTION 12 OF THE ACT.**

*Form A8*                    *Regulation 4(1)(d)(ii)*

**Mental Health Act 1983 section 3—medical recommendation for admission for treatment**                    **2–134**

I [PRINT full name and address of practitioner], a registered medical practitioner, recommend that [PRINT full name and address of patient] be admitted to a hospital for treatment in accordance with Part 2 of the Mental Health Act 1983.

I last examined this patient on [date].

*l had previous acquaintance with the patient before I conducted that examination.

*I am approved under section 12 of the Act as having special experience in the diagnosis or treatment of mental disorder.

<*Delete if not applicable>

In my opinion,

(a) this patient is suffering from mental disorder of a nature or degree which makes it appropriate for the patient to receive medical treatment in a hospital,

AND

(b) it is necessary
    (i) for the patient's own health
    (ii) for the patient's own safety
    (iii) for the protection of other persons
        <delete the indents not applicable>

that this patient should receive treatment in hospital,

AND

(c) such treatment cannot be provided unless the patient is detained under section 3 of the Act,

because — [Your reasons should cover (a), (b) and (c) above. As part of them: describe the patient's symptoms and behaviour and explain how those symptoms and behaviour lead you to your opinion; say whether other methods of treatment or care (eg out-patient treatment or social services) are available and, if so, why they are not appropriate; indicate why informal admission is not appropriate.]

. . . . . . . . . . . . . . . . . . . . . . . . . . . . . . . . . . . . . . . . . . . . . . . . . . . . . . . . . . . . . . . . . . . . . . . . . . . .
. . . . . . . . . . . . . . . . . . . . . . . . . . . . . . . . . . . . . . . . . . . . . . . . . . . . . . . . . . . . . . . . . . . . . . . . . . . .
. . . . . . . . . . . . . . . . . . . . . . . . . . . . . . . . . . . . . . . . . . . . . . . . . . . . . . . . . . . . . . . . . . . . . . . . . . . .

[If you need to continue on a separate sheet please indicate here [ ] and attach that sheet to this form]

I am also of the opinion that, taking into account the nature and degree of the mental disorder from which the patient is suffering and all the other circumstances of the case, appropriate medical treatment is available to the patient at the following hospital (or one of the following hospitals):—

. . . . . . . . . . . . . . . . . . . . . . . . . . . . . . . . . . . . . . . . . . . . . . . . . . . . . . . . . . . . . . . . . . . . . . . . . . . .
. . . . . . . . . . . . . . . . . . . . . . . . . . . . . . . . . . . . . . . . . . . . . . . . . . . . . . . . . . . . . . . . . . . . . . . . . . . .

[Enter name of hospital(s). If appropriate treatment is available only in a particular part of the hospital, say which part.]

Signed . . . . . . . . . . . . . . . . . . . . . . . . . . . .

Date . . . . . . . . . . . . . . . . . . . . . . . . . . . . .

**2–135** **Mental Health Act 1983 section 4—emergency application by nearest relative for admission for assessment**

THIS FORM IS TO BE USED ONLY FOR AN EMERGENCY APPLICATION

To the managers of [name and address of hospital]

I [PRINT your full name and address] apply for the admission of [PRINT full name and address of patient] for assessment in accordance with Part 2 of the Mental Health Act 1983.

*Complete (a) or (b) as applicable and delete the other.*

    (a)  To the best of my knowledge and belief I am the patient's nearest relative within the meaning of the Act.

        I am the patient's [state your relationship with the patient].

    (b)  I have been authorised to exercise the functions under the Act of the patient's nearest relative by a county court/the patient's nearest relative *<delete the phrase which does not apply>*, and a copy of the authority is attached to this application.

I last saw the patient on [date] [at time]], which was within the last 24 hours.

In my opinion it is of urgent necessity for the patient to be admitted and detained under section 2 of the Act and compliance with the provisions of Part 2 of the Act relating to applications under that section would involve undesirable delay.

This application is founded on a medical recommendation in the prescribed form.

If the medical practitioner did not have previous acquaintance with the patient before making the recommendation, please explain why you could not get a recommendation from a medical practitioner who did have previous acquaintance with the patient—

. . . . . . . . . . . . . . . . . . . . . . . . . . . . . . . . . . . . . . . . . . . . . . . . . . . . . . . . . . . . . . . . . . . . . . . . . . . . . . . . . . . . .
. . . . . . . . . . . . . . . . . . . . . . . . . . . . . . . . . . . . . . . . . . . . . . . . . . . . . . . . . . . . . . . . . . . . . . . . . . . . . . . . . . . . .
. . . . . . . . . . . . . . . . . . . . . . . . . . . . . . . . . . . . . . . . . . . . . . . . . . . . . . . . . . . . . . . . . . . . . . . . . . . . . . . . . . . . .

[If you need to continue on a separate sheet please indicate here [ ] and attach that sheet to this form]

                                    Signed . . . . . . . . . . . . . . . . . . . . . . . . . . .

                                      Date . . . . . . . . . . . . . . . . . . . . . . . . . . . . .

                                      Time . . . . . . . . . . . . . . . . . . . . . . . . . . . . .

*Form A10*        *Regulation 4(1)(e)(ii)*

**Mental Health Act 1983 section 4—emergency application by an approved mental health pro-**    **2–136**
**fessional for admission for assessment**

THIS FORM IS TO BE USED ONLY FOR AN EMERGENCY APPLICATION

To the managers of [name and address of hospital]

I [PRINT your full name and address] apply for the admission of [PRINT full name and address of patient] for assessment in accordance with Part 2 of the Mental Health Act 1983.

I am acting on behalf of [name of local social services authority] and am approved to act as an approved mental health professional for the purposes of the Act by *<delete as appropriate>*

     that authority
     [name of local social services authority that approved you, if different].

I last saw the patient on [date] at [time], which was within the last 24 hours.

I have interviewed the patient and I am satisfied that detention in a hospital is in all the circumstances of the case the most appropriate way of providing the care and medical treatment of which the patient stands in need.

In my opinion it is of urgent necessity for the patient to be admitted and detained under section 2 of the Act and compliance with the provisions of Part 2 of the Act relating to applications under that section would involve undesirable delay.

This application is founded on a medical recommendation in the prescribed form.

If the medical practitioner did not have previous acquaintance with the patient before making the recommendation, please explain why you could not get a recommendation from a medical practitioner who did have previous acquaintance with the patient—

. . . . . . . . . . . . . . . . . . . . . . . . . . . . . . . . . . . . . . . . . . . . . . . . . . . . . . . . . . . . . . . . . . . . . . . . . . .
. . . . . . . . . . . . . . . . . . . . . . . . . . . . . . . . . . . . . . . . . . . . . . . . . . . . . . . . . . . . . . . . . . . . . . . . . . .
. . . . . . . . . . . . . . . . . . . . . . . . . . . . . . . . . . . . . . . . . . . . . . . . . . . . . . . . . . . . . . . . . . . . . . . . . . .

[If you need to continue on a separate sheet please indicate here [ ] and attach that sheet to this form]

                   Signed . . . . . . . . . . . . . . . . . . . . . . . . . .

                   Date . . . . . . . . . . . . . . . . . . . . . . . . . . .

                   Time . . . . . . . . . . . . . . . . . . . . . . . . . . .

**2–137** **Mental Health Act 1983 section 4—medical recommendation for emergency admission for assessment**

THIS FORM IS TO BE USED ONLY FOR AN EMERGENCY APPLICATION

I [PRINT name and address of medical practitioner], a registered medical practitioner, recommend that [PRINT full name and address of patient] be admitted to a hospital for assessment in accordance with Part 2 of the Mental Health Act 1983.

I last examined this patient on [date] at [time].

*I had previous acquaintance with the patient before I conducted that examination.

*I am approved under section 12 of the Act as having special experience in the diagnosis or treatment of mental disorder.

<*Delete if not applicable>

I am of the opinion,

    (a)  this patient is suffering from mental disorder of a nature or degree which warrants the detention of the patient in hospital for assessment (or for assessment followed by medical treatment) for at least a limited period,

AND

    (b)  this patient ought to be so detained
        (i)  in the interests of the patient's own health
       (ii)  in the interests of the patient's own safety
      (iii)  with a view to the protection of other persons,
       <delete the indents not applicable>
AND

    (c)  it is of urgent necessity for the patient to be admitted and detained under section 2 of the Act.

My reasons for these opinions are: [Your reasons should cover (a), (b) and (c) above. As part of them: describe the patient's symptoms and behaviour and explain how those symptoms and behaviour lead you to your opinion; and explain why the patient ought to be admitted to hospital urgently and why informal admission is not appropriate.]

. . . . . . . . . . . . . . . . . . . . . . . . . . . . . . . . . . . . . . . . . . . . . . . . . . . . . . . . . . . . . . . . . . . .
. . . . . . . . . . . . . . . . . . . . . . . . . . . . . . . . . . . . . . . . . . . . . . . . . . . . . . . . . . . . . . . . . . . .
. . . . . . . . . . . . . . . . . . . . . . . . . . . . . . . . . . . . . . . . . . . . . . . . . . . . . . . . . . . . . . . . . . . .

[If you need to continue on a separate sheet please indicate here [ ] and attach that sheet to this form]

Compliance with the provisions of Part 2 of the Act relating to applications under section 2 would involve undesirable delay, because— [Say approximately how long you think it would take to obtain a second medical recommendation and what risk such a delay would pose to the patient or to other people.]

. . . . . . . . . . . . . . . . . . . . . . . . . . . . . . . . . . . . . . . . . . . . . . . . . . . . . . . . . . . . . . . . . . . .
. . . . . . . . . . . . . . . . . . . . . . . . . . . . . . . . . . . . . . . . . . . . . . . . . . . . . . . . . . . . . . . . . . . .

[If you need to continue on a separate sheet please indicate here [ ] and attach that sheet to this

                               Signed . . . . . . . . . . . . . . . . . . . . . . . . .

                               Date . . . . . . . . . . . . . . . . . . . . . . . . . . .

                               Time . . . . . . . . . . . . . . . . . . . . . . . . . . .

**Mental Health Act 1983 section 5(2)—report on hospital in-patient**     **2–138**

PART 1

*(To be completed by a medical practitioner or an approved clinician qualified to do so under section 5(2) of the Act)*

To the managers of [name and address of hospital]

I am [PRINT full name]

and I am *<Delete (a) or (b) as appropriate>*

  (a)  the registered medical practitioner/the approved clinician (who is not a registered medical practitioner)*<delete the phrase which does not apply>*

  (b)  a registered medical practitioner/an approved clinician (who is not a registered medical practitioner)* who is the nominee of the registered medical practitioner or approved clinician (who is not a registered medical practitioner) *<*delete the phrase which does not apply>*

in charge of the treatment of [PRINT full name of patient], who is an in-patient in this hospital and not at present liable to be detained under the Mental Health Act 1983.

It appears to me that an application ought to be made under Part 2 of the Act for this patient's admission to hospital for the following reasons—

. . . . . . . . . . . . . . . . . . . . . . . . . . . . . . . . . . . . . . . . . . . . . . . . . . . . . . . . . . . . . . . . . . . . . . . . . . . . . . . . . .
. . . . . . . . . . . . . . . . . . . . . . . . . . . . . . . . . . . . . . . . . . . . . . . . . . . . . . . . . . . . . . . . . . . . . . . . . . . . . . . . . .
. . . . . . . . . . . . . . . . . . . . . . . . . . . . . . . . . . . . . . . . . . . . . . . . . . . . . . . . . . . . . . . . . . . . . . . . . . . . . . . . . .

[The full reasons why informal treatment is no longer appropriate must be given. If you need to continue on a separate sheet please indicate here [ ] and attach that sheet to this form.]

I am furnishing this report by: *<Delete the phrase which does not apply>*

    consigning it to the hospital managers' internal mail system today at [time]

    delivering it (or having it delivered) by hand to a person authorised by the hospital managers to receive it.

                  Signed . . . . . . . . . . . . . . . . . . . . . . . . . . . .

                  Date . . . . . . . . . . . . . . . . . . . . . . . . . . . . .

## Delegated Legislation

*(To be completed on behalf of the hospital managers)*

This report was *<Delete the phrase which does not apply>*

furnished to the hospital managers through their internal mail system

delivered to me in person as someone authorised by the hospital managers to receive this report at [time] on [date]

Signed .........................
on behalf of the hospital managers

PRINT NAME ....................
Date ..........................

**Mental Health Act 1983 section 5(4)—record of hospital in-patient**                **2–139**

To the managers of [name and address of hospital]

[PRINT full name of the patient]

It appears to me that—

(a) this patient, who is receiving treatment for mental disorder as an in-patient of this hospital, is suffering from mental disorder to such a degree that it is necessary for the patient's health or safety or for the protection of others for this patient to be immediately restrained from leaving the hospital;

AND

(b) it is not practicable to secure the immediate attendance of a registered medical practitioner or an approved clinician [(who is not a registered medical practitioner)] for the purpose of furnishing a report under section 5(2) of the Mental Health Act 1983.

I am [PRINT full name], a nurse registered—
<Delete whichever do not apply>

(a) in Sub-Part 1 of the register, whose entry includes an entry to indicate the nurse's field of practice is mental health nursing;

(b) in Sub-Part 2 of the register, whose entry includes an entry to indicate the nurse's field of practice is mental health nursing;

(c) in Sub-Part 1 of the register, whose entry includes an entry to indicate the nurse's field of practice is learning disabilities nursing;

(d) in Sub-Part 2 of the register, whose entry includes an entry to indicate the nurse's field of practice is [learning disabilities nursing].

Signed . . . . . . . . . . . . . . . . . . . . . . . . . . .

Date . . . . . . . . . . . . . . . . . . . . . . . . . . . .

Time . . . . . . . . . . . . . . . . . . . . . . . . . . . .

*Form H3*                                    *Regulation 4(4) and (5)*

**2–140** **Mental Health Act 1983 sections 2, 3 and 4—record of detention in hospital**

(*To be attached to the application for admission*)

PART 1

[Name and address of hospital]

[PRINT full name of patient]

*Complete (a) if the patient is not already an in -patient in the hospital.*
*Complete (b) if the patient is already an in-patient.*

*Delete the one which does not apply.*

(a)  The above named patient was admitted to this hospital on [date of admission to hospital] at [time] in pursuance of an application for admission under section [state section] of the Mental Health Act 1983.

(b)  An application for the admission of the above named patient (who had already been admitted to this hospital) under section [state section] of the Mental Health Act 1983 was received by me on behalf of the hospital managers on [date] at [time] and the patient was accordingly treated as admitted for the purposes of the Act from that time.

Signed  . . . . . . . . . . . . . . . . . . . . . . . . . . . .
on behalf of the hospital managers

PRINT NAME  . . . . . . . . . . . . . . . . . . . . . .
Date  . . . . . . . . . . . . . . . . . . . . . . . . . . . .

PART 2

(*To be completed only if the patient was admitted in pursuance of an emergency application under section 4 of the Act*)

On [date] at [time] I received, on behalf of the hospital managers, the second medical recommendation in support of the application for the admission of the above named patient.

Signed  . . . . . . . . . . . . . . . . . . . . . . . . . . . .
on behalf of the hospital managers

PRINT NAME  . . . . . . . . . . . . . . . . . . . . .
Date  . . . . . . . . . . . . . . . . . . . . . . . . . . . .

**NOTE: IF THE PATIENT IS BEING DETAINED AS A RESULT OF A TRANSFER FROM GUARDIANSHIP, THE PATIENT's ADMISSION SHOULD BE RECORDED IN PART 2 OF THE FORM G8 WHICH AUTHORISED THE TRANSFER.**

Form H4                    *Regulation 7(2)(a) and 7(3)*

**Mental Health Act 1983 section 19—authority for transfer from one hospital to another under 2–141 different managers**

PART 1

*(To be completed on behalf of the managers of the hospital where the patient is detained)*

Authority is given for the transfer of [PRINT full name of patient] from [name and address of hospital in which the patient is liable to be detained] to [name and address of hospital to which patient is to be transferred] in accordance with the Mental Health (Hospital, Guardianship and Treatment) (England) Regulations 2008 within 28 days beginning with the date of this authority.

Signed ...........................
on behalf of the managers of the first named hospital

PRINT NAME ....................
Date ............................

PART 2

RECORD OF ADMISSION

*(This is not part of the authority for transfer but is to be completed at the hospital to which the patient is transferred)*

This patient was transferred to [name of hospital] in pursuance of this authority for transfer and admitted to that hospital on [date of admission to receiving hospital] at [time].

Signed ...........................
on behalf of the managers of the receiving hospital

PRINT NAME ....................
Date ............................

**2–142**  **Mental Health Act 1983 section 20—renewal of authority for detention**

PART 1

*(To be completed by the responsible clinician)*

To the managers of [name and address of hospital in which the patient is liable to be detained]

I examined [PRINT full name of patient] on [date of examination].

The patient is liable to be detained for a period ending on [date authority for detention is due to expire].

I have consulted [PRINT full name and profession of person consulted] who has been professionally concerned with the patient's treatment.

In my opinion,

    (a)  this patient is suffering from mental disorder of a nature or degree which makes it appropriate for the patient to receive medical treatment in a hospital,

AND

    (b)  it is necessary
        (i)  for the patient's own health
        (ii)  for the patient's own safety
        (iii)  for the protection of other persons
        *<delete the indents not applicable>*

that this patient should receive treatment in hospital,

because— [Your reasons should cover both (a) and (b) above. As part of them: describe the patient's symptoms and behaviour and explain how those symptoms and behaviour lead you to your opinion; say whether other methods of treatment or care (eg out-patient treatment or social services) are available and, if so, why they are not appropriate.]

. . . . . . . . . . . . . . . . . . . . . . . . . . . . . . . . . . . . . . . . . . . . . . . . . . . . . . . . . . . . . . . . . . .
. . . . . . . . . . . . . . . . . . . . . . . . . . . . . . . . . . . . . . . . . . . . . . . . . . . . . . . . . . . . . . . . . . .
. . . . . . . . . . . . . . . . . . . . . . . . . . . . . . . . . . . . . . . . . . . . . . . . . . . . . . . . . . . . . . . . . . .

[If you need to continue on a separate sheet please indicate here [ ] and attach that sheet to this form]

Such treatment cannot be provided unless the patient continues to be detained under the Act, for the following reasons — [Reasons should indicate why informal admission is not appropriate.]

. . . . . . . . . . . . . . . . . . . . . . . . . . . . . . . . . . . . . . . . . . . . . . . . . . . . . . . . . . . . . . . . . . .
. . . . . . . . . . . . . . . . . . . . . . . . . . . . . . . . . . . . . . . . . . . . . . . . . . . . . . . . . . . . . . . . . . .
. . . . . . . . . . . . . . . . . . . . . . . . . . . . . . . . . . . . . . . . . . . . . . . . . . . . . . . . . . . . . . . . . . .

[If you need to continue on a separate sheet please indicate here [ ] and attach that sheet to this form.]

I am also of the opinion that, taking into account the nature and degree of the mental disorder from which the patient is suffering and all the other circumstances of the case, appropriate medical treatment is available to the patient.

Signed  . . . . . . . . . . . . . . . . . . . . . . . . . . .

PRINT NAME  . . . . . . . . . . . . . . . . . . . .

Profession . . . . . . . . . . . . . . . . . . . . . . . .

Date  . . . . . . . . . . . . . . . . . . . . . . . . . . . .

## Mental Health Regulations 1983, Form H5

## PART 2

*(To be completed by a professional who has been professionally concerned with the patient's medical treatment and who is of a different profession from the responsible clinician)*

I agree with the responsible clinician that: this patient is suffering from mental disorder of a nature or degree which makes it appropriate for the patient to receive medical treatment in a hospital; it is necessary for the patient's own health or safety or for the protection of other persons that the patient should receive treatment and it cannot be provided unless the patient continues to be detained under the Act; and that, taking into account the nature and degree of the mental disorder from which the patient is suffering and all other circumstances of the case, appropriate medical treatment is available to the patient.

Signed . . . . . . . . . . . . . . . . . . . . . . . . . .

PRINT NAME . . . . . . . . . . . . . . . . . . . .

Profession . . . . . . . . . . . . . . . . . . . . . . . .

Date . . . . . . . . . . . . . . . . . . . . . . . . . . . .

PART 3

*(To be completed by the responsible clinician)*

I am furnishing this report by: *<Delete the phrase which does not apply>*

today consigning it to the hospital managers' internal mail system.

sending or delivering it without using the hospital managers' internal mail system.

Signed . . . . . . . . . . . . . . . . . . . . . . . . . .

PRINT NAME . . . . . . . . . . . . . . . . . . . .

Date . . . . . . . . . . . . . . . . . . . . . . . . . . . .

PART 4

*(To be completed on behalf of the hospital managers)*

This report was *<Delete the phrase which does not apply>*

furnished to the hospital managers through their internal mail system.

received by me on behalf of the hospital managers on [date].

Signed . . . . . . . . . . . . . . . . . . . . . . . . . .
on behalf of the hospital managers

PRINT NAME . . . . . . . . . . . . . . . . . . . .
Date . . . . . . . . . . . . . . . . . . . . . . . . . . . .

**2–143  Mental Health Act 1983 section 21B—authority for detention after absence without leave for more than 28 days**

PART 1

*(To be completed by the responsible clinician)*

To the managers of [name and address of hospital in which the patient is liable to be detained]

I examined [PRINT full name of patient] on [date of examination] who:

(a)  was absent without leave from hospital or the place where the patient ought to have been beginning on [date absence without leave began];

(b)  was/is* liable to be detained for a period ending on [date authority for detention would have expired, apart from any extension under section 21, or date on which it will expire]; <*delete the phrase which does not apply*> and

(c)  returned to the hospital or place on [date].

I have consulted [PRINT full name of approved mental health professional] who is an approved mental health professional.

I have also consulted [PRINT full name and profession of person consulted] who has been professionally concerned with the patient's treatment.

In my opinion,

(a)  this patient is suffering from mental disorder of a nature or degree which makes it appropriate for the patient to receive medical treatment in a hospital,

AND

(b)  it is necessary
    (i)  for the patient's own health
    (ii)  for the patient's own safety
    (iii)  for the protection of other persons
    <*delete the indents not applicable*>

that this patient should receive treatment in hospital,

because— [Your reasons should cover both (a) and (b) above. As part of them: describe the patient's symptoms and behaviour and explain how those symptoms and behaviour lead you to your opinion; say whether other methods of treatment or care (eg out-patient treatment or social services) are available and, if so, why they are not appropriate.]

. . . . . . . . . . . . . . . . . . . . . . . . . . . . . . . . . . . . . . . . . . . . . . . . . . . . . . . . . . . . . . . . . . . . . . . .
. . . . . . . . . . . . . . . . . . . . . . . . . . . . . . . . . . . . . . . . . . . . . . . . . . . . . . . . . . . . . . . . . . . . . . . .
. . . . . . . . . . . . . . . . . . . . . . . . . . . . . . . . . . . . . . . . . . . . . . . . . . . . . . . . . . . . . . . . . . . . . . . .

[If you need to continue on a separate sheet please indicate here [ ] and attach that sheet to this form]

Such treatment cannot be provided unless the patient continues to be detained under the Act, for the following reasons— [Reasons should indicate why informal admission is not appropriate.]

. . . . . . . . . . . . . . . . . . . . . . . . . . . . . . . . . . . . . . . . . . . . . . . . . . . . . . . . . . . . . . . . . . . . . . . .
. . . . . . . . . . . . . . . . . . . . . . . . . . . . . . . . . . . . . . . . . . . . . . . . . . . . . . . . . . . . . . . . . . . . . . . .
. . . . . . . . . . . . . . . . . . . . . . . . . . . . . . . . . . . . . . . . . . . . . . . . . . . . . . . . . . . . . . . . . . . . . . . .

[If you need to continue on a separate sheet please indicate here [ ] and attach that sheet to this form]

## Mental Health Regulations 1983, Form H6

I am also of the opinion that, taking into account the nature and degree of the mental disorder from which the patient is suffering and all other circumstances of the case, appropriate medical treatment is available to the patient.

The authority for the detention of the patient is/is not* due to expire within a period of two months beginning with the date on which this report is to be furnished to the hospital managers. <*Delete the phrase which does not apply>

Complete the following only if the authority for detention is due to expire within that period of two months.

This report shall/shall not* have effect as a report duly furnished under section 20(3) for the renewal of the authority for the detention of the patient. <*Delete the phrase which does not apply>

Complete the following in all cases.

I am furnishing this report by: <Delete the phrase which does not apply>

today consigning it to the hospital managers' internal mail system.

sending or delivering it without using the hospital managers' internal mail system.

Signed . . . . . . . . . . . . . . . . . . . . . . . . . .

PRINT NAME . . . . . . . . . . . . . . . . . . . .

Date . . . . . . . . . . . . . . . . . . . . . . . . . . . .

PART 2

(To be completed on behalf of the hospital managers)

This report was <Delete the phrase which does not apply>

furnished to the hospital managers through their internal mail system

received by me on behalf of the hospital managers on [date]

Signed . . . . . . . . . . . . . . . . . . . . . . . . . .
on behalf of the hospital managers

PRINT NAME . . . . . . . . . . . . . . . . . . . .
Date . . . . . . . . . . . . . . . . . . . . . . . . . . . .

Form G1     *Regulation 5(1)(a)(i) and (1)(b)*

**Mental Health Act 1983 section 7—guardianship application by nearest relative**

PART 1

*(To be completed by the nearest relative)*

**2–144** To the [name of local social services authority]

I [PRINT your full name and address] apply for the reception of [PRINT full name and address of patient] into the guardianship of [PRINT full name and address of proposed guardian] in accordance with Part 2 of the Mental Health Act 1983.

*Complete (a) or (b) as applicable and delete the other.*

(a) To the best of my knowledge and belief I am the patient's nearest relative within the meaning of the Act.

I am the patient's [state your relationship with the patient].

(b) I have been authorised to exercise the functions under the Act of the patient's nearest relative by a county court/the patient's nearest relative <*delete the phrase which does not apply*>, and a copy of the authority is attached to this application.

*The patient's date of birth is [date]

OR

*I believe the patient is aged 16 years or over.
<*Delete the phrase which does not apply.*>

I last saw the patient on [date], which was within the period of 14 days ending on the day this application is completed.

This application is founded on two medical recommendations in the prescribed form.

If neither of the medical practitioners had previous acquaintance with the patient before making their recommendations, please explain why you could not get a recommendation from a medical practitioner who did have previous acquaintance with the patient—

. . . . . . . . . . . . . . . . . . . . . . . . . . . . . . . . . . . . . . . . . . . . . . . . . . . . . . . . . . . . . . . . . . . . . . . . .
. . . . . . . . . . . . . . . . . . . . . . . . . . . . . . . . . . . . . . . . . . . . . . . . . . . . . . . . . . . . . . . . . . . . . . . . .

[If you need to continue on a separate sheet please indicate here [ ] and attach that sheet to this form]

Signed . . . . . . . . . . . . . . . . . . . . . . . . . . .

Date . . . . . . . . . . . . . . . . . . . . . . . . . . .

PART 2*

<*Complete only if proposed guardian is not a local social services authority>
*(To be completed by the proposed guardian)*

My full name and address is as entered in Part 1 of this form and I am willing to act as the guardian of the above named patient in accordance with Part 2 of the Mental Health Act 1983.

Signed . . . . . . . . . . . . . . . . . . . . . . . . . . .

Date . . . . . . . . . . . . . . . . . . . . . . . . . . .

Form G2          Regulation 5(1)(a)(ii) and 5(1)(b

**Mental Health Act 1983 section 7—guardianship application by an approved mental health professional**

PART 1

*(To be completed by the approved mental health professional)*

To the [name of local social services authority]                                    **2–145**

I [PRINT your full name and address] apply for the reception of [PRINT full name and address of patient] into the guardianship of [PRINT full name and address of proposed guardian] in accordance with Part 2 of the Mental Health Act 1983.

I am acting on behalf of [name of local social services authority] and am approved to act as an approved mental health professional for the purposes of the Act by *<delete as appropriate>*

that authority
[name of local social services authority that approved you, if different.]

*Complete the following where consultation with the nearest relative has taken place.*

*Complete (a) or (b) as applicable and delete the other.*

(a)  I have consulted [PRINT full name and address] who to the best of my knowledge and belief is the patient's nearest relative within the meaning of the Act;

(b)  I have consulted [PRINT full name and address] who I understand has been authorised by a county court/ the patient's nearest relative to exercise the functions under the Act of the patient's nearest relative. *<Delete the phrase which does not apply>*

That person has not notified me or the local social services authority on whose behalf I am acting that he or she objects to this application being made.

*Complete the following where the nearest relative has not been consulted. Delete whichever two of (a), (b) and (c) do not apply.*

(a)  I have been unable to ascertain who is this patient's nearest relative within the meaning of the Act,

OR

(b)  to the best of my knowledge and belief this patient has no nearest relative within the meaning of the Act,

OR

(c)  [PRINT full name and address] is
    (i)  this patient's nearest relative within the meaning of the Act,
    (ii)  authorised to exercise the functions of this patient's nearest relative under the Act,

*<Delete either (i) or (ii)>*

but in my opinion it is not reasonably practicable/would involve unreasonable delay *<delete as appropriate>* to consult that person before making this application, because—

. . . . . . . . . . . . . . . . . . . . . . . . . . . . . . . . . . . . . . . . . . . . . . . . . . . . . . . . . . . . . . . . . . . . . . . . . . .
. . . . . . . . . . . . . . . . . . . . . . . . . . . . . . . . . . . . . . . . . . . . . . . . . . . . . . . . . . . . . . . . . .

[If you need to continue on a separate sheet please indicate here [ ] and attach that sheet to this form]

*The remainder of Part 1 of this form must be completed in all cases.*

645

I last saw the patient on [date], which was within the period of 14 days ending on the day this application is completed.

*The patient's date of birth is [date]

OR

*I believe the patient is aged 16 years or over.
<*Delete the phrase which does not apply.>

This application is founded on two medical recommendations in the prescribed form.

If neither of the medical practitioners had previous acquaintance with the patient before making their recommendations, please explain why you could not get a recommendation from a medical practitioner who did have previous acquaintance with the patient—

. . . . . . . . . . . . . . . . . . . . . . . . . . . . . . . . . . . . . . . . . . . . . . . . . . . . . . . . . . . . . . . . . . . . . . . . . . . . .
. . . . . . . . . . . . . . . . . . . . . . . . . . . . . . . . . . . . . . . . . . . . . . . . . . . . . . . . . . . . . . . . . . . . . . . . . . . . .

[If you need to continue on a separate sheet please indicate here [ ] and attach that sheet to this form]

Signed . . . . . . . . . . . . . . . . . . . . . . . . . . .

Date . . . . . . . . . . . . . . . . . . . . . . . . . . .

PART 2*

<*Complete only if proposed guardian is not a local social services authority>

*(To be completed by the proposed guardian)*

My full name and address is as entered in Part 1 of this form and I am willing to act as the guardian of the above named patient in accordance with Part 2 of the Mental Health Act 1983.

Signed . . . . . . . . . . . . . . . . . . . . . . . . . . .

Date . . . . . . . . . . . . . . . . . . . . . . . . . . .

Form G3                                    *Regulation 5(1)(c)(i)*

**Mental Health Act 1983 section 7—joint medical recommendation for reception into guardianship**

We, registered medical practitioners, recommend that [PRINT full name and address of patient] be **2–146** received into guardianship in accordance with Part 2 of the Mental Health Act 1983.

I [PRINT full name and address of first practitioner] last examined this patient on [date], and

< *\*delete if not applicable>*

\* I had previous acquaintance with the patient before I conducted that examination.

\* I am approved under section 12 of the Act as having special experience in the diagnosis or treatment of mental disorder.

I [PRINT full name and address of second practitioner] last examined this patient on [date], and

< *\*delete if not applicable>*

\* I had previous acquaintance with the patient before I conducted that examination.

\* I am approved under section 12 of the Act as having special experience in the diagnosis or treatment of mental disorder.

In our opinion,

(a)  this patient is suffering from mental disorder of a nature or degree which warrants the patient's reception into guardianship under the Act,

AND

(b)  it is necessary
   (i)  in the interests of the welfare of the patient
   (ii)  for the protection of other persons
   *<delete (i) or (ii) unless both apply>*

that the patient should be so received.

Our reasons for these opinions are:

[Your reasons should cover both (a) and (b) above. As part of them: describe the patient's symptoms and behaviour and explain how those symptoms and behaviour lead you to your opinion; and explain why the patient cannot appropriately be cared for without powers of guardianship.]

. . . . . . . . . . . . . . . . . . . . . . . . . . . . . . . . . . . . . . . . . . . . . . . . . . . . . . . . . . . . . . . . . . . . . . .
. . . . . . . . . . . . . . . . . . . . . . . . . . . . . . . . . . . . . . . . . . . . . . . . . . . . . . . . . . . . . . . . . . . . . . .
. . . . . . . . . . . . . . . . . . . . . . . . . . . . . . . . . . . . . . . . . . . . . . . . . . . . . . . . . . . . . . . . . . . . . . .

[If you need to continue on a separate sheet please indicate here [ ] and attach that sheet to this form]

Signed  . . . . . . . . . . . . . . . . . . . . . . . . . . .
Date  . . . . . . . . . . . . . . . . . . . . . . . . . . . .

Signed  . . . . . . . . . . . . . . . . . . . . . . . . . . .
Date  . . . . . . . . . . . . . . . . . . . . . . . . . . . .

**NOTE: AT LEAST ONE OF THE PRACTITIONERS SIGNING THIS FORM MUST BE APPROVED UNDER SECTION 12 OF THE ACT.**

**Mental Health Act 1983 section 7—medical recommendation for reception into guardianship**

**2–147** [PRINT full name and address of practitioner], a registered medical practitioner recommend that [PRINT full name and address of patient] be received into guardianship in accordance with Part 2 of the Mental Health Act 1983.

I last examined this patient on [date].

*I had previous acquaintance with the patient before I conducted that examination.

*I am approved under section 12 of the Act as having special experience in the diagnosis or treatment of mental disorder. <*Delete if not applicable>

In my opinion,

    (a) this patient is suffering from mental disorder of a nature or degree which warrants the patient's reception into guardianship under the Act,

AND

    (b) it is necessary
       (i) in the interests of the welfare of the patient
      (ii) for the protection of other persons
      *<delete (i) or (ii) unless both apply>*

that the patient should be so received.

My reasons for these opinions are:

[Your reasons should cover both (a) and (b) above. As part of them: describe the patient's symptoms and behaviour and explain how those symptoms and behaviour lead you to your opinion; and explain why the patient cannot appropriately be cared for without powers of guardianship.]

. . . . . . . . . . . . . . . . . . . . . . . . . . . . . . . . . . . . . . . . . . . . . . . . . . . . . . . . . . . . . . . . . . . .
. . . . . . . . . . . . . . . . . . . . . . . . . . . . . . . . . . . . . . . . . . . . . . . . . . . . . . . . . . . . . . . . . . . .
. . . . . . . . . . . . . . . . . . . . . . . . . . . . . . . . . . . . . . . . . . . . . . . . . . . . . . . . . . . . . . . . . . . .

[If you need to continue on a separate sheet please indicate here [ ] and attach that sheet to this form]

                                Signed . . . . . . . . . . . . . . . . . . . . . . . . . . .
                                  Date . . . . . . . . . . . . . . . . . . . . . . . . . . .

**Mental Health Act 1983 section 7—record of acceptance of guardianship application**

*(To be attached to the guardianship application)*

[PRINT full name and address of patient]                                    **2–148**

This application was accepted by/on behalf* of the local social services authority on [date].
<*Delete the phrase that does not apply>

        Signed .......................................
         on behalf of the responsible local social services authority
        PRINT NAME .................................
        Date .......................................

*Form G6*        *Regulation 7(4)(a),(d) and (e)*

**Mental Health Act 1983 section 19—authority for transfer from hospital to guardianship**

PART 1

*(To be completed on behalf of the managers of the hospital where the patient is detained)*

**2–149**   Authority is given for the transfer of [PRINT full name of patient] who is at present liable to be detained in [name and address of hospital] to the guardianship of [PRINT full name and address of proposed guardian] in accordance with the Mental Health (Hospital, Guardianship and Treatment) (England) Regulations 2008.

This transfer was agreed by the [name of local social services authority] on [date of confirmation].

The transfer is to take place on [date].

Signed  . . . . . . . . . . . . . . . . . . . . . . . .
on behalf of the hospital managers
PRINT NAME  . . . . . . . . . . . . . . . . . . .
Date  . . . . . . . . . . . . . . . . . . . . . . . . . .

PART 2*

<*Complete only if proposed guardian is not a local social services authority>

*(To be completed by the proposed private guardian)*

My full name and address is as entered in Part 1 of this form and I am willing to act as the guardian of the above named patient in accordance with Part 2 of the Mental Health Act 1983.

Signed  . . . . . . . . . . . . . . . . . . . . . . . .
Date  . . . . . . . . . . . . . . . . . . . . . . . . . .

**IF THE GUARDIAN IS TO BE A PRIVATE GUARDIAN, THE TRANSFER MAY NOT TAKE PLACE UNTIL BOTH PARTS OF THIS FORM ARE COMPLETED**

Form G7         *Regulation 8(1)(a), (d) and (e)*

**Mental Health Act 1983 section 19— authority for transfer of a patient from the guardianship of one guardian to another**

PART 1

*(To be completed by the present guardian)*

Authority is given for the transfer of [PRINT full name and address of patient] from the guardianship of **2–150** [PRINT full name and address of the present guardian] to the guardianship of [PRINT full name and address of the proposed guardian] in accordance with the Mental Health (Hospital, Guardianship and Treatment) (England) Regulations 2008.

This transfer was agreed by the [name of local social services authority] on [date of confirmation].

The transfer is to take place on [date].

Signed . . . . . . . . . . . . . . . . . . . . . . . . . . . . . . . . . . . .
the guardian/on behalf of the local social services
authority which is the guardian
*<Delete whichever does not apply>*
PRINT NAME . . . . . . . . . . . . . . . . . . . .
Date . . . . . . . . . . . . . . . . . . . . . . . . . . .

PART 2*
<*Complete only if proposed guardian is not a local social services authority>

*(To be completed by the proposed private guardian)*

My full name and address is as entered in Part 1 of this form and I am willing to act as the guardian of the above named patient in accordance with Part 2 of the Mental Health Act 1983.

Signed . . . . . . . . . . . . . . . . . . . . . . . . . . .
Date . . . . . . . . . . . . . . . . . . . . . . . . . . . .

**IF THE NEW GUARDIAN IS TO BE A PRIVATE GUARDIAN, THE TRANSFER MAY NOT TAKE PLACE UNTIL BOTH PARTS OF THIS FORM ARE COMPLETED**

*Form G8*                    *Regulation 8(2) and (4)*

**Mental Health Act 1983 section 19— authority for transfer from guardianship to hospital**

PART 1

*(To be completed on behalf of the local social services authority)*

2–151   Authority is given for the transfer of [PRINT full name and address of patient] who is at present under the guardianship of [name and address of guardian] to [name and address of hospital] in accordance with the Mental Health (Hospital, Guardianship and Treatment) (England) Regulations 2008.

Signed . . . . . . . . . . . . . . . . . . . . . . . . . . . . . . . . . . . . . . .
on behalf of the local social services authority
PRINT NAME  . . . . . . . . . . . . . . . . . . . . . . . . . . . . . .
Date  . . . . . . . . . . . . . . . . . . . . . . . . . . . . . . . . . . . . . .

PART 2
RECORD OF ADMISSION

*(This is not part of the authority for transfer but is to be completed at the hospital to which the patient is transferred)*

This patient was admitted to the above named hospital in pursuance of this authority for transfer on [date of admission to receiving hospital] at [time].

Signed . . . . . . . . . . . . . . . . . . . . . . . . . . . . . . . . . . . . .
on behalf of the managers of the receiving hospital
PRINT NAME  . . . . . . . . . . . . . . . . . . . . . . . . . . . . . .
Date  . . . . . . . . . . . . . . . . . . . . . . . . . . . . . . . . . . . . . .

**Mental Health Act 1983 section 20 — renewal of authority for guardianship**

PART 1

*(To be completed by the responsible clinician or nominated medical attendant)*     **2–152**

To    [name of guardian]
      [name of responsible local social services authority if it is not the guardian]

I examined [PRINT full name and address of patient] on [date].

The patient is subject to guardianship for a period ending on [date authority for guardianship is due to expire].

In my opinion,

(a) this patient is suffering from mental disorder of a nature or degree which warrants the patient's reception into guardianship under the Act,

AND

(b) it is necessary

      (i) in the interests of the welfare of the patient
      (ii) for the protection of other persons

      *<delete (i) or (ii) unless both apply>*

that the patient should remain under guardianship under the Act.

My reasons for these opinions are:

[Your reasons should cover both (a) and (b) above. As part of them: describe the patient's symptoms and behaviour and explain how those symptoms and behaviour lead you to your opinion; and explain why the patient cannot appropriately be cared for without powers of guardianship.]
. . . . . . . . . . . . . . . . . . . . . . . . . . . . . . . . . . . . . . . . . . . . . . . . . . . . . . . . . . . . . . . . . . . . . . . . . . . . . . . . . .
. . . . . . . . . . . . . . . . . . . . . . . . . . . . . . . . . . . . . . . . . . . . . . . . . . . . . . . . . . . . . . . . . . . . . . . . . . . . . . . . . .
. . . . . . . . . . . . . . . . . . . . . . . . . . . . . . . . . . . . . . . . . . . . . . . . . . . . . . . . . . . . . . . . . . . . . . . . . . . . . . . . . .

[If you need to continue on a separate sheet please indicate here [ ] and attach that sheet to this form]

Signed . . . . . . . . . . . . . . . . . . . . . . . . . . . . .
*Responsible clinician
*Nominated medical attendant
*<Delete whichever does not apply>*
PRINT NAME . . . . . . . . . . . . . . . . . . . . . . .
Date . . . . . . . . . . . . . . . . . . . . . . . . . . . . . .

## Delegated Legislation

*(To be completed on behalf of the responsible local social services authority)*

This report was received by me on behalf of the local social services authority on [date].

Signed .......................................
on behalf of the local social services authority
PRINT NAME ...............................
Date .......................................

**Mental Health Act 1983 section 21B — authority for guardianship after absence without leave for more than 28 days**

PART 1

*(To be completed by the responsible clinician or nominated medical attendant)*          **2–153**

To    [name of guardian]
      [name of responsible local social services authority if it is not the guardian]

I examined [PRINT full name and address of patient] on [date of examination] who:

(a)  was absent without leave from the place where the patient is required to reside beginning on [date absence without leave began];

(b)  was/is* subject to guardianship for a period ending on [date authority for guardianship would have expired, apart from any extension under section 21, or date on which it will expire]; <*delete phrase which does not apply>* and

(c)  returned to that place on [date].

In my opinion,

(a)  this patient is suffering from mental disorder of a nature or degree which warrants the patient's reception into guardianship under the Act,

AND

(b)  it is necessary

   (i)  in the interests of the welfare of the patient
   (ii)  for the protection of other persons

   *<delete (i) or (ii) unless both apply>*

that the patient should remain under guardianship under the Act.

My reasons for these opinions are:

[Your reasons should cover both (a) and (b) above. As part of them: describe the patient's symptoms and behaviour and explain how those symptoms and behaviour lead you to your opinion; and explain why the patient cannot appropriately be cared for without powers of guardianship.]
. . . . . . . . . . . . . . . . . . . . . . . . . . . . . . . . . . . . . . . . . . . . . . . . . . . . . . . . . . . . . . . . . . . . . . . .
. . . . . . . . . . . . . . . . . . . . . . . . . . . . . . . . . . . . . . . . . . . . . . . . . . . . . . . . . . . . . . . . . . . . . . . .
. . . . . . . . . . . . . . . . . . . . . . . . . . . . . . . . . . . . . . . . . . . . . . . . . . . . . . . . . . . . . . . . . . . . . . . .

[If you need to continue on a separate sheet please indicate here [ ] and attach that sheet to this form]

The authority for the guardianship of the patient is/is not* due to expire within a period of two months beginning with the date on which this report is to be furnished. <*Delete the phrase which does not apply>

*Complete the following only if the authority for guardianship is due to expire within that period of two months.*

This report shall/shall not* have effect as a report duly furnished under section 20(6) for the renewal of the authority for the guardianship of the patient. <*Delete the phrase which does not apply>

Signed ............................
*Responsible clinician
*Nominated medical attendant
<*Delete whichever does not apply>
PRINT NAME ......................
Date ...............................

## PART 2

*(To be completed on behalf of the responsible local social services authority)*

This report was received by me on behalf of the local social services authority on [date].

Signed .......................................
on behalf of the local social services authority
PRINT NAME ...............................
Date .......................................

*Form M1*        *Regulation 15(2), (4)(a) and 16(2)*

**Mental Health Act 1983 Part 6—date of reception of a patient in England**

[PRINT full name of patient]

**2–154**

*was admitted to [name and address of hospital] at [time] on [date]

*was received into the guardianship of [name and address of guardian] on [date]

*became a community patient as if discharged from [name and address of responsible hospital], on [date].

<*Complete as appropriate and delete the others>

Signed ........................

on behalf of the hospital managers/

on behalf of the local social services authority/

the private guardian

<Delete whichever do not apply>

PRINT NAME ...................

Date ...........................

**Mental Health Act 1983 section 25—report barring discharge by nearest relative**

PART 1

*(To be completed by the responsible clinician)*

**2–155**  To the managers of [name and address of hospital]

[Name of nearest relative] gave notice at [time] on [date] of an intention to discharge [PRINT full name of patient].

I am of the opinion that the patient, if discharged, would be likely to act in a manner dangerous to other persons or to himself or herself.

The reasons for my opinion are—

. . . . . . . . . . . . . . . . . . . . . . . . . . . . . . . . . . . . . . . . . . . . . . . . . . . . . . . . . . . . . . . . . . . . . . . . . . . . . . . . . . . . . . . . .

. . . . . . . . . . . . . . . . . . . . . . . . . . . . . . . . . . . . . . . . . . . . . . . . . . . . . . . . . . . . . . . . . . . . . . . . . . . . . . . . . . . . . . . . .

. . . . . . . . . . . . . . . . . . . . . . . . . . . . . . . . . . . . . . . . . . . . . . . . . . . . . . . . . . . . . . . . . . . . . . . . . . . . . . . . . . . . . . . . .

[If you need to continue on a separate sheet please indicate here [ ] and attach that sheet to this form]

I am furnishing this report by: *<Delete the phrase which does not apply>*

consigning it to the hospital managers' internal mail system today at [time].

sending or delivering it without using the hospital managers' internal mail system.

Signed  . . . . . . . . . . . . . . . . . . . . . . . . . .
Responsible clinician

PRINT NAME  . . . . . . . . . . . . . . . . . . . .
Date  . . . . . . . . . . . . . . . . . . . . . . . . . . . .
Time . . . . . . . . . . . . . . . . . . . . . . . . . . . .

PART 2

*(To be completed on behalf of the hospital managers)*

This report was: *<Delete the phrase which does not apply>*

furnished to the hospital managers through their internal mail system.

received by me on behalf of the hospital managers at [time] on [date].

Signed  . . . . . . . . . . . . . . . . . . . . . . . . . .
on behalf of the hospital managers

PRINT NAME  . . . . . . . . . . . . . . . . . . . .
Date  . . . . . . . . . . . . . . . . . . . . . . . . . . . .

658

*Form T1*                                    *Regulation 27(1)(b)*

**Mental Health Act 1983 section 57—certificate of consent to treatment and second opinion**

*(Both parts of this certificate must be completed)*

PART 1

I [PRINT full name and address], a registered medical practitioner appointed for the purposes of Part 4 **2–156** of the Act (a SOAD), and we [PRINT full name, address and profession], being two persons appointed for the purposes of section 57(2)(a) of the Act, certify that [PRINT full name and address of patient]

   (a)  is capable of understanding the nature, purpose and likely effects of: [Give description of treat-
        ment or plan of treatment. Indicate clearly if the certificate is only to apply to any or all of the
        treatment for a specific period.]

. . . . . . . . . . . . . . . . . . . . . . . . . . . . . . . . . . . . . . . . . . . . . . . . . . . . . . . . . . . . . . . . . . . . . . . . . . . .
. . . . . . . . . . . . . . . . . . . . . . . . . . . . . . . . . . . . . . . . . . . . . . . . . . . . . . . . . . . . . . . . . . . . . . . . . . . .
. . . . . . . . . . . . . . . . . . . . . . . . . . . . . . . . . . . . . . . . . . . . . . . . . . . . . . . . . . . . . . . . . . . . . . . . . . . .

[If you need to continue on a separate sheet please indicate here [ ] and attach that sheet to this form]

AND

   (b)  has consented to that treatment.

                              Signed  . . . . . . . . . . . . . . . . . . . . . . . . . .
                              Date  . . . . . . . . . . . . . . . . . . . . . . . . . . . .

                              Signed  . . . . . . . . . . . . . . . . . . . . . . . . . .
                              Date  . . . . . . . . . . . . . . . . . . . . . . . . . . . .

                              Signed  . . . . . . . . . . . . . . . . . . . . . . . . . .
                              Date  . . . . . . . . . . . . . . . . . . . . . . . . . . . .

PART 2

*(To be completed by SOAD only)*

I, the above named registered medical practitioner appointed for the purposes of Part 4 of the Act have consulted [PRINT full name of nurse] a nurse and [PRINT full name and profession] who have been professionally concerned with the medical treatment of the patient named above and certify that it is appropriate for the treatment to be given.

My reasons are as below/I will provide a statement of my reasons separately. *<Delete as appropriate>* [When giving reasons please indicate if, in your opinion, disclosure of the reasons to the patient would be likely to cause serious harm to the physical or mental health of the patient or to that of any other person.]

. . . . . . . . . . . . . . . . . . . . . . . . . . . . . . . . . . . . . . . . . . . . . . . . . . . . . . . . . . . . . . . . . . . . . . . . . . . .
. . . . . . . . . . . . . . . . . . . . . . . . . . . . . . . . . . . . . . . . . . . . . . . . . . . . . . . . . . . . . . . . . . . . . . . . . . . .
. . . . . . . . . . . . . . . . . . . . . . . . . . . . . . . . . . . . . . . . . . . . . . . . . . . . . . . . . . . . . . . . . . . . . . . . . . . .

## Delegated Legislation

If you need to continue on a separate sheet please indicate here [ ] and attach that sheet to this form.]

Signed .........................

Date ...........................

*Form T2*                                        *Regulation 27(2)*

**Mental Health Act 1983 section 58(3)(a)—certificate of consent to treatment**

I [PRINT full name and address], the approved clinician in charge of the treatment described below/a **2–157**
registered medical practitioner appointed for the purposes of Part 4 of the Act (a SOAD) <*delete the
phrase which does not apply*> certify that [PRINT full name and address of patient]

  (a)  is capable of understanding the nature, purpose and likely effects of: [Give description of treat-
       ment or plan of treatment. Indicate clearly if the certificate is only to apply to any or all of the
       treatment for a specific period.]

. . . . . . . . . . . . . . . . . . . . . . . . . . . . . . . . . . . . . . . . . . . . . . . . . . . . . . . . . . . . . . . . . . . . . . . . . . . .
. . . . . . . . . . . . . . . . . . . . . . . . . . . . . . . . . . . . . . . . . . . . . . . . . . . . . . . . . . . . . . . . . . . . . . . . . . . .
. . . . . . . . . . . . . . . . . . . . . . . . . . . . . . . . . . . . . . . . . . . . . . . . . . . . . . . . . . . . . . . . . . . . . . . . . . . .

[If you need to continue on a separate sheet please indicate here [ ] and attach that sheet to this form.]

AND

  (b)  has consented to that treatment.

                                   Signed  . . . . . . . . . . . . . . . . . . . . . . . . . .
                                   Date  . . . . . . . . . . . . . . . . . . . . . . . . . .

**Mental Health Act 1983 section 58(3)(b)—certificate of second opinion**

**2–158**  I [PRINT full name and address], a registered medical practitioner appointed for the purposes of Part 4 of the Act (a SOAD), have consulted [PRINT full name of nurse], a nurse and [PRINT full name and profession] who have been professionally concerned with the medical treatment of [PRINT full name and address of patient].

I certify that the patient— *<Delete the phrase which does not apply>*

    (a)  is not capable of understanding the nature, purpose and likely effects of

    (b)  has not consented to

the following treatment: [Give description of treatment or plan of treatment. Indicate clearly if the certificate is only to apply to any or all of the treatment for a specific period.]
. . . . . . . . . . . . . . . . . . . . . . . . . . . . . . . . . . . . . . . . . . . . . . . . . . . . . . . . . . . . . . . . . . . . . . . . . . . . . . . .
. . . . . . . . . . . . . . . . . . . . . . . . . . . . . . . . . . . . . . . . . . . . . . . . . . . . . . . . . . . . . . . . . . . . . . . . . . . . . . . .
. . . . . . . . . . . . . . . . . . . . . . . . . . . . . . . . . . . . . . . . . . . . . . . . . . . . . . . . . . . . . . . . . . . . . . . . . . . . . . . .

[If you need to continue on a separate sheet please indicate here [ ] and attach that sheet to this form]

but that it is appropriate for the treatment to be given.

My reasons are as below/I will provide a statement of my reasons separately. *<Delete as appropriate>* [When giving reasons please indicate if, in your opinion, disclosure of the reasons to the patient would be likely to cause serious harm to the physical or mental health of the patient, or to that of any other person.]

. . . . . . . . . . . . . . . . . . . . . . . . . . . . . . . . . . . . . . . . . . . . . . . . . . . . . . . . . . . . . . . . . . . . . . . . . . . . . . . .
. . . . . . . . . . . . . . . . . . . . . . . . . . . . . . . . . . . . . . . . . . . . . . . . . . . . . . . . . . . . . . . . . . . . . . . . . . . . . . . .
. . . . . . . . . . . . . . . . . . . . . . . . . . . . . . . . . . . . . . . . . . . . . . . . . . . . . . . . . . . . . . . . . . . . . . . . . . . . . . . .

[If you need to continue on a separate sheet please indicate here [ ] and attach that sheet to this form.]

Signed  . . . . . . . . . . . . . . . . . . . . . . . . . .
Date  . . . . . . . . . . . . . . . . . . . . . . . . . .

Form T4                                    Regulation 27(3)(b)

**Mental Health Act 1983 section 58A(3)—certificate of consent to treatment (patients at least 18 years old)**

**THIS FORM IS NOT TO BE USED FOR PATIENTS UNDER 18 YEARS OF AGE**

I [PRINT full name and address], the approved clinician in charge of the treatment described below/a **2–159** registered medical practitioner appointed for the purposes of Part 4 of the Act (a SOAD) <*delete as appropriate*> certify that [PRINT full name and address of patient] who has attained the age of 18 years,

(a)  is capable of understanding the nature, purpose and likely effects of: [Give description of treatment or plan of treatment. Indicate clearly if the certificate is only to apply to any or all of the treatment for a specific period.]

. . . . . . . . . . . . . . . . . . . . . . . . . . . . . . . . . . . . . . . . . . . . . . . . . . . . . . . . . . . . . . . . . . . . . . . .
. . . . . . . . . . . . . . . . . . . . . . . . . . . . . . . . . . . . . . . . . . . . . . . . . . . . . . . . . . . . . . . . . . . . . . . .
. . . . . . . . . . . . . . . . . . . . . . . . . . . . . . . . . . . . . . . . . . . . . . . . . . . . . . . . . . . . . . . . . . . . . . . .

[If you need to continue on a separate sheet please indicate here [ ] and attach that sheet to this form]

AND

(b)  has consented to that treatment.

Signed  . . . . . . . . . . . . . . . . . . . . . . . . . .
Date  . . . . . . . . . . . . . . . . . . . . . . . . . . . .

**Mental Health Act 1983 section 58A(4)—certificate of consent to treatment and second opinion (patients under 18)**

**THIS FORM IS ONLY TO BE USED FOR PATIENTS UNDER 18 YEARS OF AGE**

**2–160**   I [PRINT full name and address], a registered medical practitioner appointed for the purposes of Part 4 of the Act (a SOAD) certify that [PRINT full name and address of patient] who has not yet attained the age of 18 years,

    (a)   is capable of understanding the nature, purpose and likely effects of: [Give description of treatment or plan of treatment. Indicate clearly if the certificate is only to apply to any or all of the treatment for a specific period.]

.................................................................................................
.................................................................................................
.................................................................................................

[If you need to continue on a separate sheet please indicate here [ ] and attach that sheet to this form]

AND

    (b)   has consented to that treatment.

In my opinion it is appropriate for that treatment to be given.

My reasons are as below/I will provide a statement of my reasons separately. *<Delete as appropriate>* [When giving reasons please indicate if, in your opinion, disclosure of the reasons to the patient would be likely to cause serious harm to the physical or mental health of the patient, or to that of any other person.]

.................................................................................................
.................................................................................................
.................................................................................................

[If you need to continue on a separate sheet please indicate here [ ] and attach that sheet to this form.]

                            Signed  .........................
                            Date  ...........................

**Mental Health Act 1983 section 58A(5)—certificate of second opinion (patients who are not capable of understanding the nature, purpose and likely effects of the treatment)**

I [PRINT full name and address], a registered medical practitioner appointed for the purposes of Part 4 **2–161** of the Act (a SOAD), have consulted [PRINT full name of nurse] a nurse and [PRINT full name and profession] who have been professionally concerned with the medical treatment of [PRINT full name and address of patient].

I certify that the patient is not capable of understanding the nature, purpose and likely effects of: [Give description of treatment or plan of treatment. Indicate clearly if the certificate is only to apply to any or all of the treatment for a specific period.]

......................................................................................
......................................................................................
......................................................................................

[If you need to continue on a separate sheet please indicate here [ ] and attach that sheet to this form]

but that it is appropriate for the treatment to be given.

My reasons are as below/I will provide a statement of my reasons separately. *<Delete as appropriate>* [When giving reasons please indicate if, in your opinion, disclosure of the reasons to the patient would be likely to cause serious harm to the physical or mental health of the patient or to that of any other person.]

......................................................................................
......................................................................................
......................................................................................

[If you need to continue on a separate sheet please indicate here [ ] and attach that sheet to this form.]

I further certify that giving the treatment described above to the patient would not conflict with—

    (i) any decision of an attorney appointed under a Lasting Power of Attorney or deputy (appointed by the Court of Protection) of the patient as provided for by the Mental Capacity Act 2005

    (ii) any decision of the Court of Protection, or

    (iii) any advance decision to refuse treatment that is valid and applicable under the Mental Capacity Act 2005.

Signed .............................
Date .............................

**2–162** **Mental Health Act 1983 section 17A—community treatment order**

*(Parts 1 and 3 of this form are to be completed by the responsible clinician and Part 2 by an approved mental health professional)*

PART 1

I [PRINT full name and address of the responsible clinician] am the responsible clinician for [PRINT full name and address of patient].

In my opinion,

(a) this patient is suffering from mental disorder of a nature or degree which makes it appropriate for the patient to receive medical treatment,

(b) it is necessary for
　　(i) the patient's health
　　(ii) the patient's safety
　　(iii) the protection of other persons
　　*<delete any phrase which is not applicable>*

　　that the patient should receive such treatment;

(c) such treatment can be provided without the patient continuing to be detained in a hospital provided the patient is liable to being recalled to hospital for medical treatment;

(d) it is necessary that the responsible clinician should be able to exercise the power under section 17E(1) to recall the patient to hospital;

(e) taking into account the nature and degree of the mental disorder from which the patient is suffering and all other circumstances of the case, appropriate medical treatment is available to the patient.

My opinion is founded on the following grounds—

. . . . . . . . . . . . . . . . . . . . . . . . . . . . . . . . . . . . . . . . . . . . . . . . . . . . . . . . . . . . . . . . . . . . . . . . . . . . .
. . . . . . . . . . . . . . . . . . . . . . . . . . . . . . . . . . . . . . . . . . . . . . . . . . . . . . . . . . . . . . . . . . . . . . . . . . . . .
. . . . . . . . . . . . . . . . . . . . . . . . . . . . . . . . . . . . . . . . . . . . . . . . . . . . . . . . . . . . . . . . . . . . . . . . . . . . .

[If you need to continue on a separate sheet please indicate here [ ] and attach that sheet to this form]

I confirm that in determining whether the criterion at (d) above is met, I have considered what risk there would be of deterioration of the patient's condition if the patient were not detained in hospital, with regard to the patient's history of mental disorder and any other relevant factors.

### *Conditions to which the patient is to be subject by virtue of this community treatment order*

The patient is to make himself or herself available for examination under section 20A, as requested.

If it is proposed to give a certificate under Part 4A of the Act in the patient's case, the patient is to make himself or herself available for examination to enable the certificate to be given, as requested.

The patient is also to be subject to the following conditions (if any) under section 17B(2) of the Act:

. . . . . . . . . . . . . . . . . . . . . . . . . . . . . . . . . . . . . . . . . . . . . . . . . . . . . . . . . . . . . . . . . . . . . . . . . . . . .
. . . . . . . . . . . . . . . . . . . . . . . . . . . . . . . . . . . . . . . . . . . . . . . . . . . . . . . . . . . . . . . . . . . . . . . . . . . . .
. . . . . . . . . . . . . . . . . . . . . . . . . . . . . . . . . . . . . . . . . . . . . . . . . . . . . . . . . . . . . . . . . . . . . . . . . . . . .

[If you need to continue on a separate sheet please indicate here [ ] and attach that sheet to this form]

I confirm that I consider the above conditions to be made under section 17B(2) of the Act are necessary or appropriate for one or more of the following purposes:

- to ensure that the patient receives medical treatment
- to prevent risk of harm to the patient's health or safety
- to protect other persons.

Signed ............................

Date ............................

### PART 2

I [PRINT full name and address] am acting on behalf of [name of local social services authority] and am approved to act as an approved mental health professional for the purposes of the Act by *<delete as appropriate>*

that authority
[name of local social services authority that approved you, if different].

I agree that:

    (i) the above patient meets the criteria for a community treatment order to be made
    (ii) it is appropriate to make a community treatment order, and
    (iii) the conditions made above under section 17B(2) are necessary or appropriate for one or more of the purposes specified.

Signed ........................
Approved mental health professional

Date ............................

### PART 3

I exercise my power under section 17A of the Mental Health Act 1983 to make a community treatment order in respect of the patient named in Part 1 of this Form.

This community treatment order is to be effective from [date] at [time].

Signed ........................
Responsible clinician

Date ............................

**THIS COMMUNITY TREATMENT ORDER IS NOT VALID UNLESS ALL THREE PARTS ARE COMPLETED AND SIGNED**

**IT MUST BE FURNISHED AS SOON AS PRACTICABLE TO THE MANAGERS OF THE HOSPITAL IN WHICH THE PATIENT WAS LIABLE TO BE DETAINED BEFORE THE ORDER WAS MADE**

**2–163**  **Mental Health Act 1983 section 17B—variation of conditions of a community treatment order**

I [PRINT full name and address of the responsible clinician] am the responsible clinician for [PRINT full name and address of the community patient].

I am varying the conditions attaching to the community treatment order for the above named patient.

The conditions made under section 17B(2), as varied, are: [List the conditions as varied in full (including any which are not being varied) or state that there are no longer to be any such conditions.]

. . . . . . . . . . . . . . . . . . . . . . . . . . . . . . . . . . . . . . . . . . . . . . . . . . . . . . . . . . . . . . . . . . . . . . . . . .
. . . . . . . . . . . . . . . . . . . . . . . . . . . . . . . . . . . . . . . . . . . . . . . . . . . . . . . . . . . . . . . . . . . . . . . . . .
. . . . . . . . . . . . . . . . . . . . . . . . . . . . . . . . . . . . . . . . . . . . . . . . . . . . . . . . . . . . . . . . . . . . . . . . . .

[If you need to continue on a separate sheet please indicate here [ ] and attach that sheet to this form]

The variation is to take effect from [date].

I confirm that I consider the above conditions to be necessary or appropriate for one or more of the following purposes:

- to ensure that the patient receives medical treatment
- to prevent risk of harm to the patient's health or safety
- to protect other persons.

Signed  . . . . . . . . . . . . . . . . . . . . . . . . . . . .
Responsible clinician

Date  . . . . . . . . . . . . . . . . . . . . . . . . . . . .

**THIS FORM MUST BE FURNISHED AS SOON AS PRACTICABLE TO THE MANAGERS OF THE RESPONSIBLE HOSPITAL**

*Form CTO3*                                        *Regulation 6(3)(a)*

**Mental Health Act 1983 section 17E—community treatment order: notice of recall to hospital**    **2–164**

*(To be completed by the responsible clinician)*

I notify you, [PRINT name of community patient], that you are recalled to [PRINT full name and address of the hospital] under section 17E of the Mental Health Act 1983.

*Complete either (a) or (b) below and delete the one which does not apply.*

   (a)  In my opinion,
      (i)  you require treatment in hospital for mental disorder, AND
      (ii)  there would be a risk of harm to your health or safety or to other persons if you were not recalled to hospital for that purpose.

This opinion is founded on the following grounds—

. . . . . . . . . . . . . . . . . . . . . . . . . . . . . . . . . . . . . . . . . . . . . . . . . . . . . . . . . . . . . . . . . . . . . . . . . . .
. . . . . . . . . . . . . . . . . . . . . . . . . . . . . . . . . . . . . . . . . . . . . . . . . . . . . . . . . . . . . . . . . . . . . . . . . . .
. . . . . . . . . . . . . . . . . . . . . . . . . . . . . . . . . . . . . . . . . . . . . . . . . . . . . . . . . . . . . . . . . . . . . . . . . . .

[If you need to continue on a separate sheet please indicate here [ ] and attach that sheet to this form]

   (b)  You have failed to comply with the condition imposed under section 17B of the Mental Health Act 1983 that you make yourself available for examination for the purpose of: *<delete as appropriate>*
      (i)  consideration of extension of the community treatment period under section 20A
      (ii)  enabling a Part 4A certificate to be given.

Signed  . . . . . . . . . . . . . . . . . . . . . . . . . .
                                       Responsible clinician

PRINT NAME  . . . . . . . . . . . . . . . . . . . .
Date  . . . . . . . . . . . . . . . . . . . . . . . . . . . .
Time . . . . . . . . . . . . . . . . . . . . . . . . . . . . .

**A COPY OF THIS NOTICE IS TO BE FORWARDED TO THE MANAGERS OF THE HOSPITAL TO WHICH THE PATIENT IS RECALLED AS SOON AS POSSIBLE AFTER IT IS SERVED ON THE PATIENT. IF THAT HOSPITAL IS NOT THE RESPONSIBLE HOSPITAL, YOU SHOULD INFORM THE HOSPITAL MANAGERS THE NAME AND ADDRESS OF THE RESPONSIBLE HOSPITAL.**

*This notice is sufficient authority for the managers of the named hospital to detain the patient there in accordance with the provisions of section 17E of the Mental Health Act 1983.*

**2–165** **Mental Health Act 1983 section 17E — community treatment order: record of patient's detention in hospital after recall**

[PRINT full name and address of patient] ('the patient') is currently a community patient.

In pursuance of a notice recalling the patient to hospital under section 17E of the Act, the patient was detained in [full name and address of hospital] on [enter date and time at which the patient's detention in the hospital as a result of the recall notice began].

Signed .........................
on behalf of the hospital managers

PRINT NAME ...................
Date .........................
Time .........................

*Form CTO5*　　　　　　　　*Regulation 6(8)(a) and (b)*

**Mental Health Act 1983 section 17F(4)—revocation of community treatment order**　　　**2–166**

*(Parts 1 and 3 of this form are to be completed by the responsible clinician and Part 2 by an approved mental health professional)*

PART 1

I [PRINT full name and address of the responsible clinician] am the responsible clinician for [PRINT full name and address of community patient] who is detained in [name and address of hospital] having been recalled to hospital under section 17E(1) of the Act.

In my opinion,

(a) this patient is suffering from mental disorder of a nature or degree which makes it appropriate for the patient to receive medical treatment in a hospital,

AND

(b) it is necessary for
　　(i) the patient's own health
　　(ii) the patient's own safety
　　(iii) the protection of other persons
　　*<delete the indents not applicable>*

that this patient should receive treatment in hospital,

AND

(c) such treatment cannot be provided unless the patient is detained for medical treatment under the Act,

because— [Your reasons should cover (a), (b) and (c) above. As part of them: describe the patient's symptoms and behaviour and explain how those symptoms and behaviour lead you to your opinion; say whether other methods of treatment or care (eg out-patient treatment or social services) are available and, if so, why they are not appropriate; indicate why informal admission is not appropriate.]

. . . . . . . . . . . . . . . . . . . . . . . . . . . . . . . . . . . . . . . . . . . . . . . . . . . . . . . . . . . . . . . . . . . . . . . . . . . .
. . . . . . . . . . . . . . . . . . . . . . . . . . . . . . . . . . . . . . . . . . . . . . . . . . . . . . . . . . . . . . . . . . . . . . . . . . . .
. . . . . . . . . . . . . . . . . . . . . . . . . . . . . . . . . . . . . . . . . . . . . . . . . . . . . . . . . . . . . . . . . . . . . . . . . . . .

[If you need to continue on a separate sheet please indicate here [ ] and attach that sheet to this form]

I am also of the opinion that taking into account the nature and degree of the mental disorder from which the patient is suffering and all other circumstances of the case, appropriate medical treatment is available to the patient at the hospital named above.

Signed . . . . . . . . . . . . . . . . . . . . . . . . . . . .<br>Responsible clinician

Date . . . . . . . . . . . . . . . . . . . . . . . . . . . .

PART 2

I [PRINT full name and address] am acting on behalf of [name of local social services authority] and am approved to act as an approved mental health professional for the purposes of the Act by *<delete as appropriate>*

671

that authority
[name of local social services authority that approved you, if different].

I agree that:

    (i) the patient meets the criteria for detention in hospital set out above and
    (ii) it is appropriate to revoke the community treatment order.

Signed ...........................
Approved mental health professional

Date ...........................

PART 3

I exercise my power under section 17F(4) to revoke the community treatment order in respect of the patient named in Part 1 who has been detained in hospital since [time] on [date], having been recalled under section 17E(1).

Signed ...........................
Responsible clinician

Date ...........................

**THIS REVOCATION ORDER IS NOT VALID UNLESS ALL THREE PARTS ARE COMPLETED AND SIGNED**

**IT MUST BE SENT AS SOON AS PRACTICABLE TO THE MANAGERS OF THE HOSPITAL IN WHICH THE PATIENT IS DETAINED**

*Form CTO6*                         *Regulation 9(3)(a) and (5)*

**Mental Health Act 1983 section 17F(2)—authority for transfer of recalled community patient to** **2–167**
**a hospital under different managers**

*(To be completed on behalf of the managers of the hospital in which the patient is detained by virtue of recall)*

### PART 1

This form authorises the transfer of [PRINT full name of patient] from [name and address of hospital in which the patient is detained] to [name and address of hospital to which patient is to be transferred] in accordance with the Mental Health (Hospital, Guardianship and Treatment) (England) Regulations 2008.

I attach a copy of Form CTO4 recording the patient's detention in hospital after recall.

*The hospital in which the patient is currently detained is the patient's responsible hospital.

*The hospital to which the patient is to be transferred is the patient's responsible hospital.

*The patient's responsible hospital is [name and address of responsible hospital].
<*Delete the phrases which do not apply>

Signed .........................
on behalf of managers of the first named hospital

PRINT NAME ...................
Date ...........................

### PART 2

### RECORD OF ADMISSION

*(This is not part of the authority for transfer but is to be completed at the hospital to which the patient is transferred)*

This patient was admitted to [name of hospital] in pursuance of this authority for transfer on [date of admission to receiving hospital] at [time].

Signed .........................
on behalf of managers of the receiving hospital

PRINT NAME ...................
Date ...........................

**Mental Health Act 1983 section 20A — community treatment order: report extending the community treatment period**

**2–168**  *Parts 1 and 3 of this form are to be completed by the responsible clinician and Part 2 by an approved mental health professional. Part 4 is to be completed by or on behalf of the managers of the responsible hospital.*

PART 1

To the managers of [name and address of the responsible hospital]

I am [PRINT full name and address of the responsible clinician] the responsible clinician for [PRINT full name and address of patient].

The patient is currently subject to a community treatment order made on [enter date].

I examined the patient on [date].

In my opinion,

    (a)  this patient is suffering from mental disorder of a nature or degree which makes it appropriate for the patient to receive medical treatment;

    (b)  it is necessary for
        (i)  the patient's health
        (ii)  the patient's safety
        (iii)  the protection of other persons
        *<delete any indent which is not applicable>*

that the patient should receive such treatment;

    (c)  such treatment can be provided without the patient continuing to be detained in a hospital provided the patient is liable to being recalled to hospital for medical treatment;

    (d)  it is necessary that the responsible clinician should continue to be able to exercise the power under section 17E(1) to recall the patient to hospital;

    (e)  taking into account the nature and degree of the mental disorder from which the patient is suffering and all other circumstances of the case, appropriate medical treatment is available to the patient.

My opinion is founded on the following grounds—

. . . . . . . . . . . . . . . . . . . . . . . . . . . . . . . . . . . . . . . . . . . . . . . . . . . . . . . . . . . . . . . . . . . . . . . . . . . . . . . . . . . . . . . . . .
. . . . . . . . . . . . . . . . . . . . . . . . . . . . . . . . . . . . . . . . . . . . . . . . . . . . . . . . . . . . . . . . . . . . . . . . . . . . . . . . . . . . . . . . . .

[If you need to continue on a separate sheet please indicate here [ ] and attach that sheet to this form]

I confirm that in determining whether the criterion at (d) above is met, I have considered what risk there would be of deterioration of the patient's condition if the patient were to continue not to be detained in hospital, with regard to the patient's history of mental disorder and any other relevant factors.

Signed . . . . . . . . . . . . . . . . . . . . . . . . . . . .
Responsible clinician
Date . . . . . . . . . . . . . . . . . . . . . . . . . . . .

## *Mental Health Regulations 1983, Form CTO7*

I [PRINT full name and address] am acting on behalf of [name of local social services authority] and am approved to act as an approved mental health professional for the purposes of the Act by *<delete as appropriate>*

that authority

[name of local social services authority that approved you, if different].

I agree that:

(i) the patient meets the criteria for the extension of the community treatment period and

(ii) it is appropriate to extend the community treatment period.

Signed ...........................
Approved mental health professional
Date ............................

PART 3

Before furnishing this report, I consulted [PRINT full name and profession of person consulted] who has been professionally concerned with the patient's treatment.

I am furnishing this report by: *<Delete the phrase which does not apply>*

today consigning it to the hospital managers' internal mail system.

sending or delivering it without using the hospital managers' internal mail system.

Signed .........................
Responsible clinician
Date ...........................

**THIS REPORT IS NOT VALID UNLESS PARTS 1, 2 & 3 ARE COMPLETED AND SIGNED**

PART 4

This report was *<Delete the phrase which does not apply>*

furnished to the hospital managers through their internal mail system.

received by me on behalf of the hospital managers on [date].

Signed .........................
on behalf of the managers of the
responsible hospital
PRINT NAME ...................
Date ...........................

675

**Mental Health Act 1983 section 21B—authority for extension of community treatment period after absence without leave for more than 28 days**

PART 1

*(To be completed by the responsible clinician)*

**2–169**  To the managers of [enter name and address of responsible hospital]

I am [PRINT full name and address of the responsible clinician] the responsible clinician for [PRINT full name and address of patient].

I examined the patient on [date of examination] who:

(a) was recalled to hospital on [date] under section 17E of the Mental Health Act 1983;

(b) was absent without leave from hospital beginning on [date absence without leave began];

(c) was/is *<delete as appropriate>* subject to a community treatment order for a period ending on [date community treatment order would have expired, apart from any extension under section 21, or date on which it will expire]; and

(d) returned to the hospital on [date].

I have consulted [PRINT full name of approved mental health professional] who is an approved mental health professional.

I have also consulted [PRINT full name and profession of person consulted] who has been professionally concerned with the patient's treatment.

In my opinion,

(a) this patient is suffering from mental disorder of a nature or degree which makes it appropriate for the patient to receive medical treatment;

(b) it is necessary for

    (i) the patient's health
    (ii) the patient's safety
    (iii) the protection of other persons
    *<delete any indent which is not applicable>*

that the patient should receive such treatment;

(c) such treatment can be provided without the patient continuing to be detained in a hospital provided the patient is liable to being recalled to hospital for medical treatment;

(d) it is necessary that the responsible clinician should continue to be able to exercise the power under section 17E(1) to recall the patient to hospital;

(e) taking into account the nature and degree of the mental disorder from which the patient is suffering and all other circumstances of the case, appropriate medical treatment is available to the patient.

I confirm that in determining whether the criterion at (d) above is met, I have considered what risk there would be of deterioration of the patient's condition if the patient were to continue not to be detained in hospital, with regard to the patient's history of mental disorder and any other relevant factors.

My opinion is founded on the following grounds—

. . . . . . . . . . . . . . . . . . . . . . . . . . . . . . . . . . . . . . . . . . . . . . . . . . . . . . . . . . . . . . . . . . . . . . . . .
. . . . . . . . . . . . . . . . . . . . . . . . . . . . . . . . . . . . . . . . . . . . . . . . . . . . . . . . . . . . . . . . . . . . . . . . .

## *Mental Health Regulations 1983, Form CTO8*

[If you need to continue on a separate sheet please indicate here [ ] and attach that sheet to this form]

The community treatment order is/is not* due to expire within a period of two months beginning with the date on which this report is to be furnished to the managers of the responsible hospital. *<\*Delete the phrase which does not apply>*

[*Complete the following only if the community treatment order is due to expire within that period of two months*]

This report shall/shall not* have effect as a report duly furnished under section 20A(4) for the extension of the community treatment period for this patient. *<\*Delete the phrase which does not apply>*

*Complete the following in all cases.*

I am furnishing this report by: *<Delete the phrase which does not apply>*

today consigning it to the hospital managers' internal mail system.

sending or delivering it without using the hospital managers' internal mail system.

Signed  . . . . . . . . . . . . . . . . . . . . . . . . . . .
Date  . . . . . . . . . . . . . . . . . . . . . . . . . . .

PART 2

*(To be completed on behalf of the managers of the responsible hospital)*

This report was *<Delete the phrase which does not apply>*

furnished to the hospital managers through their internal mail system. received by me on behalf of the hospital managers on [date].

Signed  . . . . . . . . . . . . . . . . . . . . . . . . . . .
on behalf of the hospital managers
PRINT NAME. . . . . . . . . . . . . . . . . . . . .
Date  . . . . . . . . . . . . . . . . . . . . . . . . . . .

**Mental Health Act 1983 Part 6—community patients transferred to England**

PART 1

*(To be completed by the responsible clinician)*

**2–170** I [PRINT full name and address of the responsible clinician] am the responsible clinician for [PRINT full name and address of patient] who is treated as if subject to a community treatment order having been transferred to England.

The patient is to be subject to the following conditions by virtue of that community treatment order:

The patient is to make himself or herself available for examination under section 20A, as requested.

If it is proposed to give a certificate under Part 4A of the Act in the patient's case, the patient is to make himself or herself available for examination to enable the certificate to be given, as requested.

The patient is also to be subject to the following conditions (if any) under section 17B(2) of the Act:

. . . . . . . . . . . . . . . . . . . . . . . . . . . . . . . . . . . . . . . . . . . . . . . . . . . . . . . . . . . . . . . . . . . . . . . .
. . . . . . . . . . . . . . . . . . . . . . . . . . . . . . . . . . . . . . . . . . . . . . . . . . . . . . . . . . . . . . . . . . . . . . . .

[If you need to continue on a separate sheet please indicate here [ ] and attach that sheet to this form]

I confirm that I consider the above conditions to be made under section 17B(2) of the Act are necessary or appropriate for one or more of the following purposes:

- to ensure that the patient receives medical treatment
- to prevent risk of harm to the patient's health or safety
- to protect other persons.

Signed  . . . . . . . . . . . . . . . . . . . . . . . . . . . . . .
Responsible clinician
Date  . . . . . . . . . . . . . . . . . . . . . . . . . . . . . .

PART 2

*(To be completed by the approved mental health professional)*

I [PRINT full name and address] am acting on behalf of [name of local social services authority] and am approved to act as an approved mental health professional for the purposes of the Act by *<Delete as appropriate>*

that authority
[name of local social services authority that approved you, if different].

## *Mental Health Regulations 1983, Form CTO9*

I agree that the conditions made above under section 17B(2) are necessary or appropriate for one or more of the purposes specified.

Signed  . . . . . . . . . . . . . . . . . . . . . . . .
Approved mental health professional
Date  . . . . . . . . . . . . . . . . . . . . . . . . . .

**THE PATIENT IS NOT SUBJECT TO THE CONDITIONS SET OUT IN THIS FORM UNLESS BOTH PARTS OF THE FORM ARE COMPLETED.**

**Mental Health Act 1983 section 19A—authority for assignment of responsibility for community patient to hospital under different managers**

*(To be completed on behalf of the responsible hospital)*

**2–171**  This form gives authority for the assignment of responsibility for [PRINT full name and address of patient] from [name and address of responsible hospital] to [name and address of hospital to which responsibility is to be assigned in accordance with the Mental Health (Hospital, Guardianship and Treatment) (England) Regulations 2008.

This assignment was agreed by the managers of the hospital to which the responsibility is to be assigned on [date of confirmation]

The assignment is to take place on [date].

Signed  . . . . . . . . . . . . . . . . . . . . . . . . .
on behalf of managers of first named hospital
PRINT NAME. . . . . . . . . . . . . . . . . . . .
Date  . . . . . . . . . . . . . . . . . . . . . . . . . .

*Form CTO11*                                             *Regulation 28(1)*

**Mental Health Act 1983 section 64C(4) — certificate of appropriateness of treatment to be given to community patient (Part 4A certificate)**

[. . .]

I [PRINT full name and address] am a registered medical practitioner appointed for the purposes of **2–172** Part 4 of the Act (a SOAD).

I have consulted [PRINT full name and profession] and [full name and profession] who have been professionally concerned with the medical treatment of [PRINT full name and address of patient] who is subject to a community treatment order.

I certify that it is appropriate for the following treatment to be given to this patient while the patient is not recalled to hospital, subject to any conditions specified below. The treatment is: [Give description of treatment or plan of treatment.]

. . . . . . . . . . . . . . . . . . . . . . . . . . . . . . . . . . . . . . . . . . . . . . . . . . . . . . . . . . . . . . . . . . . . . . . .
. . . . . . . . . . . . . . . . . . . . . . . . . . . . . . . . . . . . . . . . . . . . . . . . . . . . . . . . . . . . . . . . . . . . . . . .
. . . . . . . . . . . . . . . . . . . . . . . . . . . . . . . . . . . . . . . . . . . . . . . . . . . . . . . . . . . . . . . . . . . . . . . .

I specify the following conditions (if any) to apply: [Conditions may include time-limits on the approval of any or all of the treatment.]

. . . . . . . . . . . . . . . . . . . . . . . . . . . . . . . . . . . . . . . . . . . . . . . . . . . . . . . . . . . . . . . . . . . . . . . .
. . . . . . . . . . . . . . . . . . . . . . . . . . . . . . . . . . . . . . . . . . . . . . . . . . . . . . . . . . . . . . . . . . . . . . . .
. . . . . . . . . . . . . . . . . . . . . . . . . . . . . . . . . . . . . . . . . . . . . . . . . . . . . . . . . . . . . . . . . . . . . . . .

I certify that it is appropriate for the following treatment (if any) to be given to this patient following any recall to hospital under section 17E of the Act, subject to any conditions specified below. The treatment is: [Give description of treatment or plan of treatment].

. . . . . . . . . . . . . . . . . . . . . . . . . . . . . . . . . . . . . . . . . . . . . . . . . . . . . . . . . . . . . . . . . . . . . . . .
. . . . . . . . . . . . . . . . . . . . . . . . . . . . . . . . . . . . . . . . . . . . . . . . . . . . . . . . . . . . . . . . . . . . . . . .
. . . . . . . . . . . . . . . . . . . . . . . . . . . . . . . . . . . . . . . . . . . . . . . . . . . . . . . . . . . . . . . . . . . . . . . .

I specify the following conditions (if any) to apply to the treatment which may be given to the patient following any recall to hospital under section 17E: [Conditions may include time-limits on the approval of any or all of the treatment.]

. . . . . . . . . . . . . . . . . . . . . . . . . . . . . . . . . . . . . . . . . . . . . . . . . . . . . . . . . . . . . . . . . . . . . . . .
. . . . . . . . . . . . . . . . . . . . . . . . . . . . . . . . . . . . . . . . . . . . . . . . . . . . . . . . . . . . . . . . . . . . . . . .
. . . . . . . . . . . . . . . . . . . . . . . . . . . . . . . . . . . . . . . . . . . . . . . . . . . . . . . . . . . . . . . . . . . . . . . .

My reasons are as below/I will provide a statement of my reasons separately. *<Delete as appropriate>* [When giving reasons please indicate if, in your opinion, disclosure of the reasons to the patient would be likely to cause serious harm to the physical or mental health of the patient, or to that of any other person.]

. . . . . . . . . . . . . . . . . . . . . . . . . . . . . . . . . . . . . . . . . . . . . . . . . . . . . . . . . . . . . . . . . . . . . . . .
. . . . . . . . . . . . . . . . . . . . . . . . . . . . . . . . . . . . . . . . . . . . . . . . . . . . . . . . . . . . . . . . . . . . . . . .
. . . . . . . . . . . . . . . . . . . . . . . . . . . . . . . . . . . . . . . . . . . . . . . . . . . . . . . . . . . . . . . . . . . . . . . .

[If you need to continue on a separate sheet for any of the above please indicate here [ ] and attach that sheet to this form.]

Signed  . . . . . . . . . . . . . . . . . . . . . . . . . . . . .
Date  . . . . . . . . . . . . . . . . . . . . . . . . . . . . . . .

2–173 **Regulations 32**

**SCHEDULE 2**

**REVOCATIONS**

[Not reproduced]

# THE MENTAL HEALTH ACT 1983 (INDEPENDENT MENTAL HEALTH ADVOCATES) (ENGLAND) REGULATIONS 2008

## (SI 2008/3166)

*Dated December 9, 2008, and made by the Secretary of State under the Mental* **2–174**
*Health Act 1983, section 130A, and the National Health Service Act 2006,*
*sections 7, 8, 14, 19, 75, 272(7) and (8) and 233(4).*

GENERAL NOTE

Section 130A of the Mental Health Act 1983 ("the Act") provides that the Secretary of **2–175**
State shall make arrangements to enable Independent Mental Health Advocates (IMHAs)
to be available to help qualifying patients. These Regulations contain provisions about the
arrangements for the appointment of IMHAs and as to who can be appointed to act as an
IMHA.

Regulation 3 directs that where relevant a commissioning body or provider of advocacy
services must ensure that an individual who is appointed to act as an IMHA satisfies the
conditions in reg.6. Commissioning bodies are also directed to take reasonable steps to
ensure that the different needs and circumstances of qualifying patients, in respect of
whom they may exercise the functions under s.130A of the Act ("section 130A functions")
are taken into consideration.

Regulation 4 amends reg.5(b) of the NHS Bodies and Local Authorities Partnership
Arrangements Regulations 2000 (S.I. 2000/617) to include s.130A functions in the definition of "Functions of NHS bodies". This enables the commissioning of IMHAC to be
exercised within the scope of partnership arrangements, with local social services author-
ties under s.75 of the National Health Service Act 2006. Paragraph 6.1 of "Independent
Mental Health Advocacy—Guidance for Commissioners", NIMH for England,
December 2008, states:

"Reasons why partnership arrangements might be considered are that:

● Local authorities already commission some mental health advocacy services;

● Many qualifying patients will be receiving both health and social services;

● The configuration of mental health services, for example community mental health
teams, include staff both from health and social care; and

● There are successful examples of partnership arrangements for IMCA commissioning across England that could be replicated for IMHA commissioning mental health
service provider.

PCTs should notify the Department of Health of all intended use of partnership
arrangements."

Regulation 5 amends the National Health Service (Functions of Strategic Health
Authorities and Primary Care Trusts and Administration Arrangements) (England)
Regulations 2002 (S.I. 2002/2375) so that s.130A functions are exercisable by a commissioning body i.e. (1) Strategic Health Authorities, for performance management purposes,
and (2) by Primary Care Trusts. Regulation 3 of those Regulations is amended to provide
for circumstances where a Primary Care Trust must exercise s.130A functions for the benefit of qualifying patients who are not otherwise within their area or the area of another
Primary Care Trust and who are (1) resident in Scotland, Wales or Northern Ireland but
are present in its area, and (2) present in Wales, but liable to be detained under the Act
in a hospital or registered establishment in its area. A further amendment is made to
reg.10 of those Regulations preventing Primary Care Trusts exercising s.130A functions
jointly with NHS trusts.

Regulation 6 provides that a person can only act as an IMHA if he has satisfied certain requirements as to experience, training, good character and independence. That regulation also provides that in deciding whether to appoint a person to act has an IMHA, regard is to be had to guidance issued from time to time by the Secretary of State.

Regulation 7 specifies those who are not to be treated as concerned in the patient's treatment (a status that would otherwise prevent them from acting an IMHA).

### Citation, commencement and extent
**2–176**  **1.**—(1) These Regulations may be cited as the Mental Health Act 1983 (Independent Mental Health Advocates) (England) Regulations 2008.

(2) These Regulations shall come into force on 1st April 2009.

(3) These Regulations apply in relation to England only.

### Interpretation
**2–177**  **2.** In these Regulations—

"the Act" means the Mental Health Act 1983;

"commissioning body" means a body, individual or group of individuals (or any combination of these) authorised under regulations 3 and 10 of the National Health Service (Functions of Strategic Health Authorities and Primary Care Trusts and Administration Arrangements) (England) Regulations 2002 or regulation 4 of the NHS Bodies and Local Authorities Partnership Arrangements Regulations 2000 to exercise section 130A functions;

"IMHA" means an independent mental health advocate;

"provider of advocacy services" means a person (including a voluntary organisation) that employs or engages individuals who may be made available to act as an IMHA but does not include a commissioning body;

"section 130A functions" means the Secretary of State's functions under section 130A of the Act.

### Directions in respect of section 130A functions
**2–178**  **3.**—(1) Where a commissioning body, in exercising section 130A functions, enters into arrangements with an individual who may be made available to act as an IMHA the Secretary of State directs that the commissioning body must be satisfied that the conditions set out in regulation 6 are satisfied.

(2) Where a commissioning body, in exercising section 130A functions, enters into arrangements with a provider of advocacy services the Secretary of State directs that such arrangements must include a term that the provider of advocacy services is satisfied that the conditions set out in regulation 6 are satisfied.

(3) The Secretary of State directs that a commissioning body, in exercising section 130A functions must, as far as reasonably practicable, have regard to the diverse circumstances (including but not limited to the ethnic, cultural and demographic needs) of qualifying patients in respect of whom that commissioning body may exercise those functions.

### Amendment of the NHS Bodies and Local Authorities Partnership Arrangements Regulations 2000
**2–179**  **4.** *[not reproduced]*

## Amendment of the National Health Service (Functions of Strategic Health Authorities and Primary Care Trusts and Administration Arrangements) (England) Regulations 2002

**5.** *[not reproduced]*                                                                                  **2–180**

## Independent Mental Health Advocates: conditions

**6.**— (1) A person may not act as an IMHA unless the conditions specified in **2–181** paragraph (2) are satisfied.

(2) Those conditions are that the person referred to in paragraph (1)—

(a) has appropriate experience or training or an appropriate combination of experience and training;

(b) is a person of integrity and good character;

(c) is able to act independently of any person who is professionally concerned with the qualifying patient's medical treatment; and

(d) is able to act independently of any person who requests that person to visit or interview the qualifying patient.

(3) For the purposes of the condition referred to in paragraph (2)(a) regard must be had to standards in guidance that may be issued from time to time by the Secretary of State.

(4) The standards referred to in paragraph (3) may include any qualification that the Secretary of State may determine as appropriate.

[(5) For the purposes of the condition referred to in paragraph (2)(b) there must be obtained, in respect of that person, an enhanced criminal record certificate issued pursuant to section 113B of the Police Act 1997 which includes—

(a) where the qualifying patient has not attained the age of 18, suitability information relating to children (within the meaning of section 113BA of the Police Act 1997);

(b) where the qualifying patient has attained the age of 18, suitability information relating to vulnerable adults (within the meaning of section 113BB of that Act).]

AMENDMENT
Paragraph (5) was substituted by SI 2009/2376, reg.3.

GENERAL NOTE
The Department of Health has published the following guidance under Gateway refer- **2–182** ence: 10593:

"This is guidance on what constitutes appropriate experience and training for Independent Mental Health Advocates (IMHAs), including an appropriate qualification, referred to in regulation 6 of the Mental Health Act 1983 (Independent Mental Health Advocates) (England) Regulations 2008.

In deciding whether a person has appropriate experience and training, the person or organisation appointing the IMHA should in particular consider:

– Previous experience working in advocacy, particularly mental health advocacy
– Previous experience working with people with mental health needs
– Successful completion of an advocacy qualification, in particular the IMHA module of the National Advocacy Qualification (see below).

**National Advocacy Qualification**

To achieve national consistency in the way IMHA services are delivered by multiple independent advocacy providers, a national advocacy qualification is being developed. The qualification is to be modular in structure, consisting of four core modules on generic advocacy, and several specialist modules, including an IMHA module. Learners will be able to take any unit in any order, and there will be no requirement to complete the core units before completing a specialist unit.

As it is a competency-based qualification and reliant on practical experience, not all potential IMHAs will be able to complete the IMHA module before starting to practise. However, to ensure that IMHAs are appropriately trained to meet the needs of patients, IMHAs should be expected to have successfully completed the IMHA module by the end of their first year of practice (making necessary adjustments for any maternity leave, long term sickness or other similar absences)."

**Persons not professionally concerned with a patient's medical treatment**

2–183     **7.** For the purposes of section 130A(5) of the Act a person is not to be regarded as professionally concerned with a qualifying patient's medical treatment if that person—

    (a)  is representing the patient in accordance with—

        (i)  arrangements made for the purposes of section 130A functions;

        (ii)  arrangements made other than for the purposes of that section;

    (b)  has in the past represented the qualifying patient in accordance with arrangements referred to in sub-paragraph (a) and in doing so was not otherwise professionally concerned in that patient's treatment.

## PART 3

## PRACTICE AND PROCEDURE

## CIVIL PROCEDURE RULES 1998

### (S.I. 1998/3132)

### PART 8

#### ALTERNATIVE PROCEDURE FOR CLAIMS

Types of claims in which Part 8 procedure may be followed                    **3–001**

. . .

**8.1(6)** A rule or practice direction may, in relation to a specified type of proceedings—

(a) require or permit the use of the Part 8 procedure; and

(b) disapply or modify any of the rules set out in this Part as they apply to those proceedings.

(Rule 8.9 provides for other modifications to the general rules where the Part 8 procedure is being used)

. . .

**Practice Direction – Alternative Procedure for Claims**

. . .

**Section C**

**Special Provisions**

**10.1** The following special provisions apply to the applications indicated.

. . .

**Applications under Mental Health Act 1983**

**18.1**   In this paragraph—                                                **3–002**

(1) a section referred to by a number refers to the section so numbered in the Mental Health Act 1983 and 'Part II' means Part II of that Act;

(2) 'hospital manager' means the manager of a hospital as defined in section 145(1) of the Act; and

(3) 'place of residence' means, in relation to a patient who is receiving treatment as an in-patient in a hospital or other institution, that hospital or institution.

**18.2** The claim form must be filed—

(1) in the court for the district in which the patient's place of residence is situated; or

(2) in the case of an application under section 30, in the court that made the order under section 29 which the application seeks to discharge or vary.

**18.3** Where an application is made under section 29 for an order that the functions of the nearest relative of the patient are to be exercisable by some other person—

(1) the nearest relative must be made a respondent, unless—

(a) the application is made on the grounds that the patient has no nearest relative or that it is not reasonably practicable to ascertain whether he has a nearest relative; or

(b) the court orders otherwise; and

(2) the court may order that any other person shall be made a respondent.

**18.4** Subject to paragraph 18.5, the court may accept as evidence of the facts relied upon in support of the application, any report made—

(1) by a medical practitioner; or

(a)  a probation officer;

(b)  an officer of a local authority;

(c)  an officer of a voluntary body exercising statutory functions on behalf of a local authority; or

(d)  an officer of a hospital manager.

**18.5** The respondent must be informed of the substance of any part of the report dealing with his fitness or conduct that the court considers to be material to the determination of the claim.

**18.6** An application under Part II shall be heard in private unless the court orders otherwise.

**18.7** The judge may, for the purpose of determining the application, interview the patient. The interview may take place in the presence of, or separately from, the parties. The interview may be conducted elsewhere than at the court. Alternatively, the judge may direct the district judge to interview the patient and report to the judge in writing.

GENERAL NOTE

**3–003**     This provision is concerned with applications to the County Court under ss.29 and 30 of the Mental Health Act 1983. The court, on hearing an application under s.29, has the power to make an interim order: see the General Note to s.29.

A district judge does not have jurisdiction to hear a case under this provision (Practice Direction: Allocation of Cases to Levels of Judiciary, para.11.1(a)(vii)).

*Paragraph 18.3*

**3–004**     Neither the wording of this paragraph nor the judgment of the Court of Appeal in *Lewis v Gibson*, below, preclude an application for an interim displacement being made without notice being given to the nearest relative: see *R. (on the application of Holloway) v Oxfordshire County Council* [2007] EWHC 776 (Admin) which is considered in the General Note to s.29. In *Lewis v Gibson* EWCA Civ 587; [2005] M.H.L.R. 309, the Court of Appeal endorsed the Official Solicitor's proposal for the implementation of this paragraph, as it appeared in CCR, Ord.49 r.12, in such a way as to ensure compliance with the patient's Convention rights. Thorpe L.J. said at para.40:

"Although [this paragraph] does not require it, I support the Official Solicitor's conclusion that the patient must be served with the proceedings and notified of the right to be joined. Second the County Court Judge must at the earliest stage enquire whether the patient has been so served and ensure that appropriate steps are taken to secure the patient's Article 6 and 8 rights. Third he should extend his enquiry into the patient's capacity in order to ensure that a person willing to act as litigation friend has been identified and served. These precautions must be taken even in cases where urgent relief is sought. I accept the Official Solicitor's submission that it is difficult to conceive of circumstances in which a patient could lawfully be deprived of any opportunity to participate in proceedings. Any justification would have to address the patient's Article 6 and 8 rights."

*Paragraph 18.5*

**3–005**     To comply with the requirement of this paragraph, it is sufficient if a report is handed to the respondent's legal adviser in circumstances where the legal adviser can give advice and take instructions (*B(A) v B(L) (Mental Health: Patient)* [1980] 1 W.L.R. 116). This case was considered by Hale L.J. in *R. (on the application of S) v Plymouth City Council and C* [2002] EWCA Civ 388, paras 36 to 38, where her Ladyship held that:

(i)  this paragraph, as it appeared in CCR Ord.49, r.12, imposes a minimum obligation;

(ii) the court has to comply with the rules of natural justice, which normally require that anything relevant to the court's decision be seen by both parties to the dispute;

(iii) the right to see all the documents in a case may be outweighed by other considerations, but there must be a clear and proper public objective and the limitation must be proportionate to that objective;

(iv) in general one would expect disclosure of all the information put before the court in proceedings under s.29 for the purposes of establishing that the nearest relative has "exercised without due regard to the welfare of the patient or the interests of the public his power to discharge the patient from guardianship, or is likely to do so", unless there was a demonstrable risk of harm to the patient or others in so doing; and

(v) in principle, the approach of a court in a s.29 application should be no less open than that of a Mental Health Review Tribunal.

*Paragraph (18.6)*
The publication of information relating to proceedings before any court sitting in private **3–006** shall be a contempt of a court where the proceedings are brought under the 1983 Act authorising an application or reference to be made to the First-tier Tribunal, the Mental Health Review Tribunal for Wales or to a county court (Administration of Justice Act 1960, s.12(1)(b)).

*Paragraph (18.7)*
In using this power, the judge will act in accordance with s.6(1) of the Human Rights Act **3–007** 1998 and will not act in a way which is incompatible with the patient's rights under Art.5 of the European Convention on Human Rights (*R. (on the application of MH (acting by the Official Solicitor as Litigation Friend)) v Secretary of State for Health and the Mental Health Review Tribunal* [2004] EWHC 56 (Admin); [2004] M.H.L.R. 155 at para.45).

# TRIBUNAL PROCEDURE (FIRST-TIER TRIBUNAL) (HEALTH, EDUCATION AND SOCIAL CARE CHAMBER) RULES 2008

## SI 2008/2699

*Made* - - - - - - - - - *9th October 2008*
*Laid before Parliament* - - *15th October 2008*
*Coming into force* - - - - *3rd November 2008*

## CONTENTS

### PART 1

#### INTRODUCTION

### PART 2

#### GENERAL POWERS AND PROVISIONS

### PART 3

#### PROCEEDINGS BEFORE THE TRIBUNAL OTHER THAN IN MENTAL HEALTH CASES

*[Not reproduced]*

PART 4

PROCEEDINGS BEFORE THE TRIBUNAL IN MENTAL HEALTH CASES

CHAPTER 1

BEFORE THE HEARING

31. Application of Part 4
32 Procedure in mental health cases
33. Notice of proceedings to interested persons
34. Medical examination of the patient

CHAPTER 2

HEARINGS

35. No disposal of proceedings without a hearing
36. Entitlement to attend a hearing
37. Time and place of hearings
38. Public and private hearings
39. Hearings in a party's absence
40. Power to pay allowances

CHAPTER 3

DECISIONS

41. Decisions
42. Provisional decisions

PART 5

CORRECTING, SETTING ASIDE, REVIEWING AND APPEAL TRIBUNAL DECISIONS

43. Interpretation
44. Clerical mistakes and accidental slips or omissions
45. Setting aside a decision which disposes of proceedings
46. Application for permission to appeal
47. Tribunal's consideration of application for permission to appeal
48. Application for review in special educational needs cases
49. Review of a decision
50. Power to treat an application as a different type of application

SCHEDULE—[*Not reproduced*]

After consulting in accordance with paragraph 28(1) of the Tribunals, Courts and Enforcement Act 2007, the Tribunal Procedure Committee has made the following Rules in exercise of the power conferred by sections 9(3), 22 and 29(3) and (4) of, and Schedule 5 to, that Act.

The Lord Chancellor has allowed the Rules in accordance with paragraph 28(3) of Schedule 5 to the Tribunals, Courts and Enforcement Act 2007.

GENERAL NOTE

Under para.3 of the Practice Statement "Composition of Tribunals in relation to matters **3–010** that fall to be decided by the Health, Education and Social Care Chamber on or after 3 November 2008", issued by the Senior President of Tribunals on December 15, 2008, a "decision that disposes of proceedings or determines a preliminary issue made at, or following, a hearing [in respect of a mental health case] must be made by:

One judge; and
One other member who is a registered medical practitioner; and
One other member who has substantial experience of health or social care matters".

An account of the genesis and functions of the First-tier Tribunal (Mental Health) and of rights of appeal from decisions of the tribunal can be found in the General Note to s.65 of the 1983 Act.

Separate rules have been made to govern the practice and procedure to be followed in proceedings before the Mental Health Review Tribunal for Wales: see the Mental Health Review Tribunal for Wales Rules 2008 (SI 2008/2705 (L.17) (the "Welsh Rules")).

*Victims*

The Tribunal Service (Mental Health) has published a paper on "Procedures concerning **3–011** the rights of access to MHT hearings of victims of certain criminal offences committed by patients" (April 2010) which can be accessed at www.mhrt.org.uk/Documents/TSMH_VictimsPolicy_April2010.pdf (accessed July 6, 2010).

*Human Rights Act 1998*

As a "public authority" for the purposes of the 1998 Act, the tribunal is required to act in **3–012** a way which is compatible with the rights contained in the European Convention on Human Rights (the "ECHR")(s.6) and these Rules must be read and given effect in a way which is compatible with such rights (s.3). Articles 5(4) and 6(1) of the ECHR are particularly relevant to the operation of the tribunal: see Pt 5.

## PART 1

### Introduction

### Citation, commencement, application and interpretation

**1.**—(1) These Rules may be cited as the Tribunal Procedure (First-tier **3–013** Tribunal) (Health, Education and Social Care Chamber) Rules 2008 and come into force on 3rd November 2008.

(2) These Rules apply to proceedings before the Tribunal which have been assigned to the Health, Education and Social Care Chamber by the First-tier Tribunal and Upper Tribunal (Chambers) Order 2008.

(3) In these Rules—

"the 2007 Act" means the Tribunals, Courts and Enforcement Act 2007;

"applicant" means a person who—

    (a) starts Tribunal proceedings, whether by making an application, an appeal, a claim or a reference;

    (b) makes an application to the Tribunal for leave to start such proceedings; or

    (c) is substituted as an applicant under rule 9(1) (substitution and addition of parties);

"childcare provider" means a person who is a childminder or provides day care as defined in section 79A of the Children Act 1989, or a person who provides childcare as defined in section 18 of the Childcare Act 2006;

"disability discrimination in schools case" means proceedings concerning disability discrimination in the education of a child or related matters;

"dispose of proceedings" includes, unless indicated otherwise, disposing of a part of the proceedings;

"document" means anything in which information is recorded in any form, and an obligation under these Rules or any practice direction or direction to provide or allow access to a document or a copy of a document for any purpose means, unless the Tribunal directs otherwise, an obligation to provide or allow access to such document or copy in a legible form or in a form which can be readily made into a legible form;

"Health, Education and Social Care Chamber" means the Health, Education and Social Care Chamber of the First-tier Tribunal established by the First-tier Tribunal and Upper Tribunal (Chambers) Order 2008;

"hearing" means an oral hearing and includes a hearing conducted in whole or in part by

video link, telephone or other means of instantaneous two-way electronic communication;

"legal representative" means [a person who, for the purposes of the Legal Services Act 2007, is an authorised person in relation to an activity which constitutes the exercise of a right of audience or the conduct of litigation within the meaning of that Act]

"mental health case" means proceedings brought under the Mental Health Act 1983 or paragraph 5(2) of the Schedule to the Repatriation of Prisoners Act 1984;

"nearest relative" has the meaning set out in section 26 of the Mental Health Act 1983;

"party" means—

    (a) in a mental health case, the patient, the responsible authority, the Secretary of State (if the patient is a restricted patient or in a reference under rule 32(8) (seeking approval under section 86 of the Mental Health Act 1983)), and any other person who starts a mental health case by making an application;

    (b) in any other case, a person who is an applicant or respondent in proceedings before the Tribunal or, if the proceedings have been concluded, a person who was an applicant or respondent when the Tribunal finally disposed of all issues in the proceedings;

"patient" means the person who is the subject of a mental health case;

"practice direction" means a direction given under section 23 of the 2007 Act;

"respondent" means—

    (a) in an appeal against an order made by a justice of the peace under section 79K of the Children Act 19892 , section 20 of the Care Standards Act 2000 or section 72 of the Childcare Act 2006, the person who applied to the justice of the peace for the order;

    (b) in an appeal against any other decision, the person who made the decision;

    (c) in proceedings on a claim under section 28I of the Disability Discrimination Act 1995, the body responsible for the school as determined in accordance with paragraph 1 of Schedule 4A to that Act or, if the claim concerns the residual duties of a local education authority under section 28F of that Act, that local education authority;

(d) in proceedings on an application under section 4(2) of the Protection of Children Act 1999 or section 86(2) of the Care Standards Act 2000, the Secretary of State; or

(e) a person substituted or added as a respondent under rule 9 (substitution and addition of parties);

"responsible authority" means—

(a) in relation to a patient detained under the Mental Health Act 1983 in a hospital within the meaning of Part 2 of that Act, the managers (as defined in section 145 of that Act);

(b) in relation to a patient subject to guardianship, the responsible local social services authority (as defined in section 34(3) of the Mental Health Act 1983);

(c) in relation to a community patient, the managers of the responsible hospital (as defined in section 145 of the Mental Health Act 1983);

(d) in relation to a patient subject to after-care under supervision, the Primary Care Trust or Local Health Board which has the duty to provide after-care for the patient.

"restricted patient" has the meaning set out in section 79(1) of the Mental Health Act 1983;

"special educational needs case" means proceedings concerning the education of a child who has or may have special educational needs;

"Suspension Regulations" means regulations which provide for a right of appeal against a decision to suspend, or not to lift the suspension of, a person's registration as a childcare provider;

"Tribunal" means the First-tier Tribunal;

"working day" means any day except a Saturday or Sunday, Christmas Day, Good Friday or a bank holiday under section 1 of the Banking and Financial Dealings Act 1971.

AMENDMENT

In the definition of "legal representative" in para.(3), the words in square brackets were **3–014** substituted by SI 2010/15, r.15.

GENERAL NOTE

*Paragraph (3)*

"PARTY". The identity of the responsible authority in para.(a) can change if the patient **3–015** is subject to a transfer under s.19 of the 1983 Act after the decision under challenge has been made.

"RESPONDENT". The tribunal can give a direction adding a person to the proceedings as a respondent (r.9(2)). It is not clear who might be added as a respondent in a mental health case.

## Overriding objective and parties' obligation to co-operate with the Tribunal

**2.**—(1) The overriding objective of these Rules is to enable the Tribunal to deal **3–016** with cases fairly and justly.

(2) Dealing with a case fairly and justly includes—

(a) dealing with the case in ways which are proportionate to the importance of the case, the complexity of the issues, the anticipated costs and the resources of the parties;

(b) avoiding unnecessary formality and seeking flexibility in the proceedings;

(c) ensuring, so far as practicable, that the parties are able to participate fully in the proceedings;

(d) using any special expertise of the Tribunal effectively; and

(e) avoiding delay, so far as compatible with proper consideration of the issues.

(3) The Tribunal must seek to give effect to the overriding objective when it—

(a) exercises any power under these Rules; or

(b) interprets any rule or practice direction.

(4) Parties must—

(a) help the Tribunal to further the overriding objective; and

(b) co-operate with the Tribunal generally.

DEFINITIONS

**3–017**    Tribunal: r.1(3).
party: r.1(3).
practice direction: r.1(3).

GENERAL NOTE

**3–018**    This rule establishes that the tribunal's overriding objective when performing functions under these Rules is to deal with cases fairly and justly. It also requires parties to help the tribunal to further this objective and to co-operate with the tribunal.

The objective of dealing with cases fairly and justly:

> "includes the avoidance of unnecessary applications and unnecessary delay. That requires parties to cooperate and liaise with each other concerning procedural matters, with a view to agreeing a procedural course promptly where they are able to do so, before making any application to the tribunal. This is particularly to be expected where parties have legal representation. Parties should endeavour to agree disclosure issues without the need for the tribunal to make a ruling. However, even where a direction from the tribunal may be required (for example, where a responsible authority holding medical records requires an order for the disclosure of medical records to overcome issues of confidentiality or arising from the Data Protection Act, or where there are genuine issues as to how most appropriately to proceed), it will assist the tribunal to further the overriding objective if the parties can identify any directions they are able to agree, subject to the approval of the tribunal. Where they are unable to agree every aspect, this liaison will at least have the advantage of crystallising their positions, and more clearly identifying the issue(s) upon which the tribunal will have to rule. We stress that, in the context of an urgent application in the mental health jurisdiction, this liaison between the parties must not lead to any unavoidable delay" (*Dorset Healthcare NHS Foundation Trust v MH* [2009] UKUT 4 (AAC); [2009] M.H.L.R. 102 at para.13).

A failure to comply with these Rules does not render the tribunal proceedings void (r.7).

*Paragraph (2).*

**3–019**    INCLUDES.    The list is not exclusive.

*Paragraph (4)*

**3–020**    This paragraph was not included in the Welsh Rules because it was felt that placing an obligation on the patient to co-operate with the tribunal was undesirable.

In *MD v Nottinghamshire Health Care NHS Trust* [2010] UKUT 59 (AAC); [2010] M.H.L.R. 93, para.46, Judge Jacobs said that the duties paced on the parties under this provision "must include making their experts available to comply with any directions that are given by the tribunal."

## Alternative dispute resolution and arbitration

**3.**—(1) The Tribunal should seek, where appropriate—                    **3–021**
 (a) to bring to the attention of the parties the availability of any appropriate alternative procedure for the resolution of the dispute; and
 (b) if the parties wish and provided that it is compatible with the overriding objective, to facilitate the use of the procedure.

(2) Part 1 of the Arbitration Act 1996 does not apply to proceedings before the Tribunal.

DEFINITIONS                                                               **3–022**
  Tribunal: r.1(3).
  party: r.1(3).

GENERAL NOTE
  Although this rule is not applicable to mental health cases, the tribunal could draw the **3–023** attention of a patient to the availability of relevant complaint procedures.

## PART 2

### GENERAL POWERS AND PROVISIONS

## Delegation to staff

**4.**—(1) Staff appointed under section 40(1) of the 2007 Act (tribunal staff and **3–024** services) may, with the approval of the Senior President of Tribunals, carry out functions of a judicial nature permitted or required to be done by the Tribunal.

(2) The approval referred to at paragraph (1) may apply generally to the carrying out of specified functions by members of staff of a specified description in specified circumstances.

(3) Within 14 days after the date on which the Tribunal sends notice of a decision made by a member of staff under paragraph (1) to a party, that party may apply in writing to the Tribunal for that decision to be considered afresh by a judge.

DEFINITIONS
  the 2007 Act: r.1(3).                                                   **3–025**
  Tribunal: r.1(3).
  party: r.1(3).

GENERAL NOTE
  This rule enables judicial functions, such as case management, to be undertaken by tri- **3–026** bunal staff if this is authorised by the Senior President of Tribunals.

## Case management powers

**5.**—(1) Subject to the provisions of the 2007 Act and any other enactment, the **3–027** Tribunal may regulate its own procedure.

(2) The Tribunal may give a direction in relation to the conduct or disposal of proceedings at any time, including a direction amending, suspending or setting aside an earlier direction.

(3) In particular, and without restricting the general powers in paragraphs (1) and (2), the Tribunal may—

(a) extend or shorten the time for complying with any rule, practice direction or direction, unless such extension or shortening would conflict with a provision of another enactment containing a time limit;

(b) consolidate or hear together two or more sets of proceedings or parts of proceedings raising common issues, or treat a case as a lead case;

(c) permit or require a party to amend a document;

(d) permit or require a party or another person to provide documents, information or submissions to the Tribunal or a party;

(e) deal with an issue in the proceedings as a preliminary issue;

(f) hold a hearing to consider any matter, including a case management issue;

(g) decide the form of any hearing;

(h) adjourn or postpone a hearing;

(i) require a party to produce a bundle for a hearing;

(j) stay proceedings;

(k) transfer proceedings to another court or tribunal if that other court or tribunal has jurisdiction in relation to the proceedings and—

(i) because of a change of circumstances since the proceedings were started, the Tribunal no longer has jurisdiction in relation to the proceedings; or

(ii) the Tribunal considers that the other court or tribunal is a more appropriate forum for the determination of the case; or

(l) suspend the effect of its own decision pending the determination by the Tribunal or the Upper Tribunal of an application for permission to appeal against, and any appeal or review of, that decision.

DEFINITIONS

**3–028**  the 2007 Act: r.1(3).
Tribunal: r.1(3).
practice direction: r.1(3).
party: r.1(3).
document: r.1(3).
hearing: r.1(3).

GENERAL NOTE

**3–029**  This rule, which should be read with r.6, enables the tribunal to give case management directions so as to facilitate: (1) the speedy determination of the case in compliance with the art.5(4) of the European Convention on Human Rights; and (2) the overriding objective of dealing with cases fairly and justly under r.2. In *B v Mental Health Review Tribunal and the Secretary of State for the Home Department* [2002] EWHC Admin 1553; [2003] M.H.L.R. 19, Scott Baker J. said at para.49:

"At each stage the tribunal should have had in mind the delay that has occurred until then and given directions against that background. The longer the delay that has occurred the more aggressive the directions will need to be to ensure early disposal of the case. There comes a time when the convenience of expert witnesses must cede to the need for the tribunal to conclude a substantive hearing".

Rule 6(5) provides a mechanism to enable a party to challenge a direction made by the tribunal.

Under paras.8 and 9 of the Practice Statement "Composition of Tribunals in relation to matters that fall to be decided by the Health, Education and Social Care Chamber on or after 3 November 2008", issued by the Senior President of Tribunals on December 15, 2008, where the tribunal:

"has given a decision that disposes of proceedings ("the substantive decision"), any matter decided under, or in accordance with, Rule 5(3)(l)  must be decided by one judge, unless the Chamber President considers it appropriate that it is decided either by:—

(a) the same members of the Tribunal as gave the substantive decision; or
(b) a Tribunal . . . comprised of different members of the Tribunal to that which gave the substantive decision.

Any other decision, including striking out a case under Rule 8 . . . (except at, or following, a hearing) or giving directions under Rule 5 . . . (whether or not at a hearing) must be made by:—

One judge."

The Senior President of Tribunals has issued a Practice Direction on "Child, Vulnerable Adult and Sensitive Witnesses" which is reproduced below.

*Paragraph (3)(a)*
The following provisions of the 1983 Act contain time limits which relate to tribunal **3–030** applications or references which cannot be altered by the tribunal under this provision: ss.66(1),(2), 68(2), 69(1),(2),(4), 70, 71(2), and 75(1).

*Paragraph (3) (d)*
This provision enables tribunals to direct those who are late in producing reports to do so **3–031** forthwith. It also enables the tribunal to direct a party or other person to produce a document that the party or person had no intention of submitting to the tribunal. A failure to comply with such a requirement could result in the tribunal using its power under r.16.

A patient's victim could be invited to make written submissions to the tribunal under this provision.

*Paragraph (3) (h)*
ADJOURN.   In considering a request for an adjournment, the tribunal should bear in mind **3–032** its obligation to avoid delay (r.2(2)(e)) and the requirement in art.5(4) of the European Convention on Human Rights for a speedy decision. In *B v Mental Health Review Tribunal and the Secretary of State for the Home Department* [2002] EWHC Admin 1533, Scott Baker J. held that:

1. It is not good practice to adjourn a hearing without any indication of when it will be resumed. If for some reason it is impossible to identify a specific date at the moment of adjournment, it is perfectly in order to say that the adjourned hearing will take place no later than a certain date.

2. What is required is not only a return date when the case could be heard but also some clear directions to ensure that all the expert evidence was available for the adjourned hearing. To provide for expert evidence to be obtained sequentially is a recipe for delay.

3. There is no reason why experts should not meet at an early stage to try and identify, and if possible narrow, any differences of opinion.

4. An adjournment should not be granted without giving the patient's representatives an opportunity to be heard.

5. Brief reasons should be given for a decision to adjourn.

B was applied *in R. (on the application of X) v Mental Health Review Tribunal* [2003] EWHC 1272 (Admin); [2003] M.H.L.R. 299, where Collins J. held that:

1. Although the tribunal will normally rely upon the material that is put before it by the parties, the tribunal has power of its own motion to adjourn for the purposes of obtaining information, even though the parties have decided not to put that information before it.

2. The tribunal should not adjourn a case unless it regards it as necessary for the purpose of doing justice and of reaching the right result in a given case, and in deciding whether it is necessary, it will have to balance the need which it perceives for the extra information against any delay that that will occasion to the determination of the application before it.

A tribunal should give serious consideration to an adjournment if the tribunal considers that the absence of a doctor from a hearing "is likely to affect materially the weight they feel able to give to the opinions expressed in their written reports, and if that is likely to be critical to their ultimate decision" or if it has concerns about the availability of the after-care services that will be available for the patient (*R. (on the application of H) v Ashworth Hospital Authority* [2000] EWCA Civ 923; [2002] M.H.L.R. 314 at paras 68, 85).

The power to adjourn can only be exercised in relation to a function which the Mental Health Act either permits or requires the tribunal to do. In the case of a restricted patient, the tribunal cannot therefore adjourn for the sole purpose of assisting its determination of whether to exercise its non-statutory discretion to recommend the patient's transfer to another hospital; it can only adjourn for the purpose of assisting it in determining whether the patient should be discharged or not and, if a discharge is being considered, what conditions should be attached to it (*R. (on the application of the Secretary of State for the Home Department v Mental Health Review Tribunal* [2000] M.H.L.R. 209).

It is unlawful to adjourn the proceedings so as to monitor the patient's progress in the hope that a projected course of treatment would eventually permit the tribunal to discharge the patient (*R. v Nottinghamshire Mental Health Review Tribunal Ex p. Secretary of State for the Home Department, The Times,* October 12, 1988 CA). It is submitted that any adjournment that purports to exercise a general supervisory function over the patient's progress would be unlawful.

In *R. v Mental Health Review Tribunal Ex p.Cleveland* (1989) CO/819/88, unreported, Popplewell J. upheld the decision of a tribunal not to adjourn the proceedings to enable the applicant to submit further evidence on the ground that even if the evidence sought had been available it would not have effected the tribunal's decision.

As the tribunal has no power to consider the validity of the admission which gave rise to the patient's liability to be detained (*R. v East London and The City Mental Health Trust Ex p. Brandenburg* [2003] UKHL 58; [2004] 1 All E.R. 400), it is submitted that the tribunal has no power to adjourn an application to enable the parties to consider an alleged defect in the admission papers. Any concerns that the patient's legal representative might have about the contents of the statutory documentation should be raised with the hospital prior to the hearing.

**3–033** HEARING. This term embraces the proceedings before the tribunal until it reaches its formal decision (*R. (on the application of X) v Mental Health Review Tribunal,* above at para.20).

*Paragraph (3) (k)*

The provision enables a case to be transferred to the Mental Health Review Tribunal for **3–034** Wales if a patient is transferred to a Welsh hospital. Rule 23(2) of the Welsh Rules provides the MHRT for Wales with an equivalent power.

## Procedure for applying for and giving directions

**6.**—(1) The Tribunal may give a direction on the application of one or more of **3–035** the parties or on its own initiative.

(2) An application for a direction may be made—

(a) by sending or delivering a written application to the Tribunal; or

(b) orally during the course of a hearing.

(3) An application for a direction must include the reason for making that application.

(4) Unless the Tribunal considers that there is good reason not to do so, the Tribunal must send written notice of any direction to every party and to any other person affected by the direction.

(5) If a party, or any other person given notice of the direction under paragraph (4), wishes to challenge a direction which the Tribunal has given, they may do so by applying for another direction which amends, suspends or sets aside the first direction.

DEFINITIONS

    Tribunal: r.1(3). **3–036**

    party: r.1(3).

    hearing: r.1(3).

GENERAL NOTE

A tribunal does not have the power to make a direction after it has determined an appli- **3–037** cation. It is therefore not possible for a tribunal to incorporate a direction into the reasons that it gives for a decision not to discharge the patient, unless the case has not been fully determined because the tribunal has reserved to itself the possibility of reconvening by virtue of s.72(3)(b) or s.72(3A)(b).

The tribunal cannot use its power under this provision either to circumvent its obligations under the 1983 Act or to direct a party to do something which it is prevented from doing by legislation. Neither can it require a party to undertake a task which it is not legally obliged to perform under the 1983 Act, e.g. to direct the after-care bodies to provide the tribunal with a fully developed after-care plan prior to the hearing (*W v Doncaster MBC* [2004] EWCA Civ.378; [2004] M.H.L.R. 201, noted under s.117).

It is advisable for a without notice direction to include a reference to the right to make an application under para.(5) if there is an objection to the direction (*Dorset Healthcare NHS Foundation Trust v MH* [2009] UKUT 4 (AAC); [2009] M.H.L.R. 102 at para.35).

## Failure to comply with rules etc.

**7.**—(1) An irregularity resulting from a failure to comply with any requirement **3–038** in these Rules, a practice direction or a direction, does not of itself render void the proceedings or any step taken in the proceedings.

(2) If a party has failed to comply with a requirement in these Rules, a practice direction or a direction, the Tribunal may take such action as it considers just, which may include—

(a) waiving the requirement;

(b) requiring the failure to be remedied;

(c) exercising its power under rule 8 (striking out a party's case);

(d) exercising its power under paragraph (3); or

(e) except in mental health cases, restricting a party's participation in the proceedings.

(3) The Tribunal may refer to the Upper Tribunal, and ask the Upper Tribunal to exercise its power under section 25 of the 2007 Act in relation to, any failure by a person to comply with a requirement imposed by the Tribunal—

(a) to attend at any place for the purpose of giving evidence;

(b) otherwise to make themselves available to give evidence;

(c) to swear an oath in connection with the giving of evidence;

(d) to give evidence as a witness;

(e) to produce a document; or

(f) to facilitate the inspection of a document or any other thing (including any premises).

DEFINITIONS

**3–039**     practice direction: r.1(3).
party: r.1(3).
Tribunal: r.1(3).
mental health case: r.1(3).
document: r.1(3).

GENERAL NOTE

**3–040**     This rule identifies the options open to the tribunal should a party fail to comply with these Rules, a practice direction or a direction. The tribunal also has the option of using its power under r.16 to summons witnesses and to order the production of documents.

*Paragraph (3)*

**3–041**     Section 25 of the 2007 Act vests the Upper Tribunal with the powers of the High Court to require the attendance and examination of witnesses and the production and inspection of documents, together with such other matters as are incidental to its functions.

**Striking out a party's case**

**3–042**     **8.**—(1) With the exception of paragraph (3), this rule does not apply to mental health cases.

(2) [*Not reproduced*].

(3) The Tribunal must strike out the whole or a part of the proceedings if the Tribunal—

(a) does not have jurisdiction in relation to the proceedings or that part of them; and

(b) does not exercise its power under rule 5(3)(k)(i) (transfer to another court or tribunal) in relation to the proceedings or that part of them.

(4)–(9) [*Not reproduced*]

DEFINITIONS

**3–043**     mental health case: r.1(3).
Tribunal: r.1(3)

GENERAL NOTE

**3–044**     A decision made under this rule must be made by a judge: see the General Note to r.5.

**Substitution and addition of parties**

**3–045**     **9.**—(1) The Tribunal may give a direction substituting a party if—

    (a)  the wrong person has been named as a party; or

    (b)  the substitution has become necessary because of a change in circumstances since the start of proceedings.

(2) The Tribunal may give a direction adding a person to the proceedings as a respondent.

(3) If the Tribunal gives a direction under paragraph (1) or (2) it may give such consequential directions as it considers appropriate.

DEFINITIONS
    Tribunal: r.1(3).                                              **3–046**
    party: r.1(3).
    respondent: r.1(3).

GENERAL NOTE
*Paragraph (1)*
    Where the responsible hospital for a patient made subject to a community treatment **3–047** order is not the same as the hospital where the patient was formerly detained, this provision can be used to substitute the managers of the responsible hospital as a party in place of the managers of the other hospital.

## Orders for costs

    **10.**—(1) Subject to paragraph (2), the Tribunal may make an order in respect of **3–048** costs only—

    (a)  under section 29(4) of the 2007 Act (wasted costs); or

    (b)  if the Tribunal considers that a party or its representative has acted unreasonably in bringing, defending or conducting the proceedings.

(2) The Tribunal may not make an order under paragraph (1)(b) in mental health cases.

(3) The Tribunal may make an order in respect of costs on an application or on its own initiative.

(4) A person making an application for an order under this rule must—

    (a)  send or deliver a written application to the Tribunal and to the person against whom it is proposed that the order be made; and

    (b)  send or deliver a schedule of the costs claimed with the application.

(5) An application for an order under paragraph (1) may be made at any time during the proceedings but may not be made later than 14 days after the date on which the Tribunal sends the decision notice recording the decision which finally disposes of all issues in the proceedings.

(6) The Tribunal may not make an order under paragraph (1) against a person (the "paying person") without first—

    (a)  giving that person an opportunity to make representations; and

    (b)  if the paying person is an individual, considering that person's financial means.

(7) The amount of costs to be paid under an order under paragraph (1) may be ascertained by—

    (a)  summary assessment by the Tribunal;

    (b)  agreement of a specified sum by the paying person and the person entitled to receive the costs ("the receiving person"); or

    (c)  assessment of the whole or a specified part of the costs incurred by the receiving person, if not agreed.

(8) Following an order for assessment under paragraph (7)(c), the paying person or the receiving person may apply to a county court for a detailed assessment of costs in accordance with the Civil Procedure Rules 1998 on the standard basis or, if specified in the order, on the indemnity basis.

DEFINITIONS
**3–049**   Tribunal: r.1(3).
party: r.1(3).
mental health case: r.1(3).

GENERAL NOTE
*Paragraph (1)(a)*
**3–050**   Section 29(4) of the 2007 Act enables the tribunal to disallow wasted costs incurred by "the legal or other representative" of a party. It follows that a wasted costs order cannot be made against a hospital that is not represented at a tribunal hearing.

*Paragraph (1)(b)*
**3–051**   This paragraph does not apply to mental health cases (para.(2)).

## Representatives
**3–052**   **11.**—(1) A party may appoint a representative (whether a legal representative or not) to represent that party in the proceedings.

(2) If a party appoints a representative, that party (or the representative if the representative is a legal representative) must send or deliver to the Tribunal and to each other party written notice of the representative's name and address.

(3) Anything permitted or required to be done by a party under these Rules, a practice direction or a direction may be done by the representative of that party, except—
(a)  signing a witness statement; or
(b)  signing an application notice under rule 20 (the application notice) if the representative is not a legal representative.

(4) A person who receives due notice of the appointment of a representative—
(a)  must provide to the representative any document which is required to be provided to the represented party, and need not provide that document to the represented party; and
(b)  may assume that the representative is and remains authorised as such until they receive written notification that this is not so from the representative or the represented party.

(5) At a hearing a party may be accompanied by another person whose name and address has not been notified under paragraph (2) but who, subject to paragraph (8) and with the permission of the Tribunal, may act as a representative or otherwise assist in presenting the party's case at the hearing.

(6) Paragraphs (2) to (4) do not apply to a person who accompanies a party under paragraph (5).

(7) In a mental health case, if the patient has not appointed a representative, the Tribunal may appoint a legal representative for the patient where—
(a)  the patient has stated that they do not wish to conduct their own case or that they wish to be represented; or
(b)  the patient lacks the capacity to appoint a representative but the Tribunal believes that it is in the patient's best interests for the patient to be represented.

(8) In a mental health case a party may not appoint as a representative, or be represented or assisted at a hearing by—

(a) a person liable to be detained or subject to guardianship or after-care under supervision, or who is a community patient, under the Mental Health Act 1983; or

(b) a person receiving treatment for mental disorder at the same hospital as the patient.

DEFINITIONS

    party: r.1(3).                                               **3–053**

    legal representative: r.1(3).

    Tribunal: r.1(3).

    practice direction: r.1(3).

    document: r.1(3).

    patient: r.1(3).

GENERAL NOTE

    This rule enables a party to appoint a representative to represent that party in the proceed- **3–054** ings. The representative need not be legally qualified (para.(1)). Subject to para.(8), a patient is entitled to have anyone to act as a representative. A representative is entitled to question witnesses and to make submissions to the tribunal (*R. (on the application of Mersey Care NHS Trust) v Mental Health Review Tribunal* [2003] EWHC 1182 (Admin); [2003] M.H.L.R. 354). Apart from the exceptions noted in para.(3), the representative can act on behalf of the party. Written notice of the appointment must be given to the tribunal and to other parties (para.(2)). Documents which are provided to the representative need not be provided to the represented party (para.(4)(a)). Provision is made in para.(5) for a party to be represented or otherwise assisted by a person who has not given prior notice to the tribunal. Paragraph (7), which enables the tribunal to appoint a legal representative for the patient, applies in mental health cases where the patient has said that he or she either does not wish to conduct the case or does not wish to be represented, or the patient lacks the capacity to appoint a representative. The tribunal does not have the power to compel representation for an unwilling mentally capable patient. Paragraph (8) disqualifies certain persons from acting as a representative.

    Although the patient's responsible clinician is usually seen as the appropriate person to represent the detaining authority, there is nothing to prevent another member of staff, such as a nurse or a Mental Health Act Administrator, from performing this role.

*Skeleton Arguments*

    The website of the First-tier Tribunal (Mental Health) (*www.mhrt.org.uk*) provides the **3–055** following guidance to legal representatives on skeleton arguments (accessed July 6, 2010):

    "The Tribunal regards it as good practice to submit a skeleton argument for cases of complexity and/or involving points of law. Skeleton arguments should contain a numbered list of points, stated in no more than a few sentences. Each point should have references to documentation that is relied on later. In the case of points of law, authorities relied on should be cited with reference to the particular pages where the principle concerned is set out.

    Where a Human Rights Act issue is raised, the 1st Practice Direction to Civil Procedure Rules, Part 39 (Hearings) shall apply as follows:

    If it is necessary for a party to give evidence of an authority at a hearing referred to in section 2 of the HRA 1998:

    • the authority to be cited should be an authoritative and complete report;

- the party must give to the Tribunal and any other party a list of the authorities they intend to cite, and copies of the reports not less than 3 days before the hearing;

- copies of the complete original texts issued by the European Court or Commission, either paper based upon, or from the Court's judgement database (HUDOC), which is available on the Internet, may be used."

*Paragraph (1)*

**3–056**   MAY.   A party is not required to appoint a representative.

*Paragraph (7)*

**3–057**   This provision was considered in *AA v Cheshire and Wirral Partnership NHS Foundation Trust* [2009] UKUT 195 (AAC); [2009] M.H.L.R. 308 where Judge Rowland made the following findings:

1. The tribunal is a creature of statute and has no statutory power to appoint a person to represent a patient's interests other than the power contained in this provision.

2. There is nothing in this provision that specifically says that a solicitor necessarily acts without instructions if appointed by the tribunal, particularly if the appointment is under paragraph (a). A patient may be capable of giving valid instructions and, where valid instructions are given, a solicitor must act in accordance with them. Where a patient lacks the capacity to give valid instructions, wishes that are expressed cannot bind the solicitor in the same way as instructions.

3. Paragraph (b) is necessarily concerned with an appointment in respect of a patient who lacks the capacity to appoint his or her own representative. For the purposes of the case before him, Judge Rowland was prepared to accept a submission that such a patient may, in some cases, still be able to give valid instructions in respect of aspects of his or her case. Nonetheless, paragraph (b) plainly contemplates the possibility of a solicitor being appointed to represent a patient who does not have the capacity to give any instructions at all. In such a case, the rule must anticipate that the solicitor will ascertain any relevant wishes that the patient may be able to express, will inform the tribunal of such wishes, make such points in support of them as can properly be made and generally ensure that the tribunal has all the relevant material before it and does not overlook any statutory provision. However, in the absence of the patient's capacity to give valid instructions, the rule must also anticipate that the solicitor will exercise his or her judgment and advance any argument that he or she considers to be in the patient's "best interests", which will not necessarily involve arguing for the patient's discharge. In those circumstances the solicitor has the same freedom of action as a litigation friend in the courts.

4. However, even where a patient has full capacity, a solicitor may be entitled, and in some circumstances may be under a duty, to draw a tribunal's attention to significant matters—particularly points of law—that appear to be in the patient's best interests despite his or her instructions and which it appears the tribunal might otherwise overlook. A solicitor has a duty not just to his or her client but also to the tribunal or, perhaps more accurately, to the administration of justice. A distinction is to be drawn between merely drawing a matter to a tribunal's attention and fully arguing it.

The finding at point 4, which is found at para.20 of the judgment, appears to be inconsistent with Judge Rowland's statement, at para.15, that where valid instructions are given by a capacious patient, "a solicitor must act in accordance with them."

REPRESENTATIVE.   Only a legal representative may be appointed by the tribunal.

LACKS THE CAPACITY. Using the test set out in ss.2 and 3 of the Mental Capacity Act 2005.

### Calculating time

**12.**—(1) An act required by these Rules, a practice direction or a direction to be **3–058** done on or by a particular day must be done by 5pm on that day.

(2) If the time specified by these Rules, a practice direction or a direction for doing any act ends on a day other than a working day, the act is done in time if it is done on the next working day.

(3)–(4) [*These paragraphs do not apply to mental health cases*]

DEFINITIONS
   practice direction: r.1(3).                                   **3–059**
   working day: r.1(3).
   Tribunal: r.1(3).

### Sending and delivery of documents

**13.**—(1) Any document to be provided to the Tribunal under these Rules, a **3–060** practice direction or a direction must be—
  (a) sent by pre-paid post or delivered by hand to the address specified for the proceedings;
  (b) sent by fax to the number specified for the proceedings; or
  (c) sent or delivered by such other method as the Tribunal may permit or direct.

(2) Subject to paragraph (3), if a party provides a fax number, email address or other details for the electronic transmission of documents to them, that party must accept delivery of documents by that method.

(3) If a party informs the Tribunal and all other parties that a particular form of communication, other than pre-paid post or delivery by hand, should not be used to provide documents to that party, that form of communication must not be so used.

(4) If the Tribunal or a party sends a document to a party or the Tribunal by email or any other electronic means of communication, the recipient may request that the sender provide a hard copy of the document to the recipient. The recipient must make such a request as soon as reasonably practicable after receiving the document electronically.

(5) The Tribunal and each party may assume that the address provided by a party or its representative is and remains the address to which documents should be sent or delivered until receiving written notification to the contrary.

DEFINITIONS
   document: r.1(3).                                         **3–061**
   Tribunal: r.1(3).
   practice direction: r.1(3).
   party: r.1(4).

### Use of documents and information

**14.**—(1) The Tribunal may make an order prohibiting the disclosure or publi- **3–062** cation of—
  (a) specified documents or information relating to the proceedings; or
  (b) any matter likely to lead members of the public to identify any person whom the Tribunal considers should not be identified.

(2) The Tribunal may give a direction prohibiting the disclosure of a document or information to a person if—

(a) the Tribunal is satisfied that such disclosure would be likely to cause that person or some other person serious harm; and

(b) the Tribunal is satisfied, having regard to the interests of justice, that it is proportionate to give such a direction.

(3) If a party ("the first party") considers that the Tribunal should give a direction under paragraph (2) prohibiting the disclosure of a document or information to another party ("the second party"), the first party must—

(a) exclude the relevant document or information from any documents that will be provided to the second party; and

(b) provide to the Tribunal the excluded document or information, and the reason for its exclusion, so that the Tribunal may decide whether the document or information should be disclosed to the second party or should be the subject of a direction under paragraph (2).

(4) The Tribunal must conduct proceedings as appropriate in order to give effect to a direction given under paragraph (2).

(5) If the Tribunal gives a direction under paragraph (2) which prevents disclosure to a party who has appointed a representative, the Tribunal may give a direction that the documents or information be disclosed to that representative if the Tribunal is satisfied that—

(a) disclosure to the representative would be in the interests of the party; and

(b) the representative will act in accordance with paragraph (6).

(6) Documents or information disclosed to a representative in accordance with a direction under paragraph (5) must not be disclosed either directly or indirectly to any other person without the Tribunal's consent.

(7) Unless the Tribunal gives a direction to the contrary, information about mental health cases and the names of any persons concerned in such cases must not be made public.

DEFINITIONS

**3–063**    Tribunal: r.1(3).
document: r.1(3).
party: r.1(3).
mental health case: r.1(3).

GENERAL NOTE

**3–064**    This rule enables the tribunal to make an order prohibiting the disclosure or publication of material relating to the proceedings to a person (para.(1)). Such an order can only be made if the tribunal is satisfied that the disclosure would be likely to cause serious harm to that person or another, and that it is proportionate, having regard to the interests of justice, to make such an order (para.(2)). Reasons for requesting the tribunal to exclude a document or information must be provided (para.(3)). An excluded document or information can be disclosed to the patient's representative (not necessarily a legal representative) as long as the representative does not disclose it further without the tribunal's consent (paras (5), (6)). Unless the tribunal directs otherwise, information about mental health cases must not be made public (para.(7)).

Although the tribunal is not explicitly required to give reasons for its decision on non-disclosure, a brief statement of reasons which avoids identifying the nature of the material under consideration should be given because the time limit for appealing the decision on a point of law is determined by the date when the person was sent "written reasons for the decision" (r.46(2)(a)).

The tribunal can decide to exclude the patient while the issue of non-disclosure is discussed (r.38(4)(b) and can direct that a person be excluded from the hearing in order to give effect to a direction made under para.(2) (r.38(4)(c)).

In *Dorset Healthcare NHS Foundation Trust v MH* [2009] UKUT 4 (AAC); [2009] M.H.L.R. 102 at paras 23–34, the Upper Tribunal, after stating that the "starting point is that full disclosure of all relevant material should generally be given" (para.20), provided the following obiter guidance to assist parties who seek the disclosure of the patient's medical records (note that the published transcript has two paragraphs numbered 29):

"23. However, rule 14 does not provide the only procedure by which disclosure of documents can be withheld. The medical records of many patients contain documents from third parties which, irrespective of any harm to the patient that may ensure from their disclosure, may be sensitive. For example, a relative of a patient may provide details of his/her own medical condition which may be relevant to that person's ability to look after the patient if the patient were returned home: or simply set out reasons why, if the patient were returned home, relatives or potential carers would be unable to cope. Sometimes such documents are submitted to the responsible authority holding the medical records with an express requirement that they be kept confidential from the patient (and sometimes also from even the patient's solicitors). In any event, that authority often considers, rightly, that it owes a duty of confidence to the relevant third-parties and is unwilling to disclose documents to the patient (and occasionally even to the patient's solicitors) without an order. If the documents are relevant to the issues in an application made by the patient (as they usually will be), leaving aside the various common law and statutory obligations that fall on the responsible authority holding the medical records, there is an obvious potential tension between the Article 6 rights of the patient and the Article 8 rights of the third parties, and it is important that all of these rights are properly considered and maintained (see *R (B) v Crown Court at Stafford* [2007] 1 WLR 1524, especially at [23]). What is the correct approach in these circumstances?

24. As we have already observed, in dealing with such a situation the parties should first do all they can to agree the approach to be adopted and avoid applying to the tribunal unless it is essential. Disclosure does not and should not present a problem in the vast majority of cases.

25. Given the general rule in favour of full disclosure the burden will be on the responsible authority to demonstrate that it is appropriate to withhold disclosure of any particular documents.

26. Where there are third-party documents which the responsible authority considers may be confidential to the third-party, then, where this is practical, the authority may seek the relevant third parties' consent to disclosure. However, this may not be practical because of the delay that would be involved in identifying and locating the third parties.

27. In most cases where there are confidential third-party documents, it should be possible for the responsible authority to disclose all such documents to the patient's solicitors subject to an undertaking from the solicitors not to disclose to the patient third-party documents specifically identified by the authority. The solicitors can then take a view as to whether the third-party rights override the rights of the patient, or vice versa. Where they consider the documents ought to be disclosed to the patient, then they must make an application to the tribunal for disclosure.

28. In other circumstances, the responsible authority may take the view that the documents are so sensitive that they should not be disclosed even to the solicitors or they are unable to rely on an undertaking that the representative will not disclose to the patient documents received. However, an undertaking from a solicitor (who owes a duty to the tribunal) will only not be acceptable in quite exceptional circumstances.

29. Where a responsible authority seeks to avoid disclosure of documents even to the patient's representative, then it should submit a skeleton argument setting out the reasons

709

for resisting disclosure and should identify the documents in question. The skeleton argument, but not the documents, should be served on the patient's solicitors who will be given an opportunity to respond in writing.

29. In circumstances in which the responsible authority has served all of the documents on the solicitors subject to an undertaking, and the solicitor then wishes to disclose the documents (or some of them) to the patient, the procedure will be reversed; and the patient's solicitor should submit a skeleton argument setting out why it is considered appropriate to disclose the documents to the patient and the authority will be given the opportunity to respond in writing.

30. Where the exchange of skeleton arguments does not resolve the issue, then an application to the tribunal will be necessary. Where a patient's solicitor is seeking permission to disclose documents to a patient, then the application should be made by that solicitor: if a responsible authority is seeking to deny disclosure to even the patient's solicitor then the application should be made by the authority.

31. In most cases, any application should be capable of being determined by the tribunal on the day of the substantive hearing. However, there may be circumstances where the issue is more complicated, when it would be appropriate for the matter to be considered and determined by a single judge in advance of the substantive hearing. Depending on the circumstances and complexity this could be either on written submissions or by holding an oral hearing.

32. We can also envisage circumstances in which the tribunal will need to obtain information as to the third-party's views on the issue of disclosure. Where this occurs, the tribunal should notify the responsible authority which should then obtain this information and submit it to the tribunal, thus avoiding where possible any direct involvement by the third-party in the tribunal's procedures.

33. All of these steps can be taken under the general case management powers of the tribunal, particularly under rule 5(3)(d). The steps are all consistent with the specific provisions set out in rule 14, to which we have already made reference: and the parties should adopt a similar procedure in circumstances in which rule 14 might apply. Again in most instances those applications should be dealt with on the day of the substantive hearing and only exceptionally should it be necessary for a single judge to determine the issue on written submissions or by a separate hearing prior to the substantive hearing.

34. This guidance is intended to assist all parties who seek disclosure of medical records, and face requests for disclosure of medical records; and hopefully there will be few cases where the procedures suggested above will not suffice. However, this is only guidance and is not prescriptive for all cases. In cases where there are idiosyncratic features or complexities, it is always open to either party to make an application to the tribunal for specific directions or for a tribunal of its own motion to give appropriate directions."

The Data Protection Act 1998 provides patients with a right of access to their medical records. The patient's representative should obtain the written authority of the patient to apply for such access.

The following guidance is provided by the Tribunal Service in *Reports for Mental Health Tribunals* (2010) at p.9:

"If the Responsible Authority, or the source or author of the information, statement, report or document considers that the tribunal should give a direction prohibiting the disclosure of the material to the patient, they must:

a. separate and exclude the relevant information, statement, report or document from any other material submitted;

b. separately provide to the tribunal copies of the excluded information, statement, report or document, ensuring that the excluded material is clearly marked:

## NOT TO BE DISCLOSED TO THE PATIENT WITHOUT

## THE EXPRESS PERMISSION OF THE TRIBUNAL

c. provide the tribunal with full written reasons for the proposed exclusion, so that the tribunal may decide for itself whether the grounds for exclusion have been made out and whether the information, statement, report or document should be disclosed to the patient, or whether it should be excluded."

*Human Rights Act 1998*

A decision by the tribunal not to disclose a document or information to the patient under **3–065** para.(1) would constitute an interference with the patient's right to respect for his private and family life under art.8(1) of the European Convention on Human Rights. Article 8(2) provides a justification for such an interference on the ground of either protecting the patient's "health or morals" or the prevention of "disorder or crime". An interference on the general ground of protecting the "welfare of the patient" is not allowed for in art.8(2). In *Winterwerp v Netherlands* (App. No. 6301/73), the European Commission of Human Rights said that the patient's lawyer had the right to examine the patient's file, but that it was not necessary for the patient to be informed of all the evidence or that he be allowed access to all of the information in his medical file. This approach was confirmed by the court in *Nikolova v Bulgaria* (2001) E.H.R.R. 3 at para.58, where it was said that "[e]quality of arms is not ensured if counsel is denied access to those documents in the investigation file which are essential in order effectively to challenge the lawfulness of his client's detention".

In *Roberts v Nottinghamshire Healthcare NHS Trust*, below at para.25, Cranston J. said that although a party has a right to a fair trial under art.6 "that does not mean that he or she has an absolute or unqualified right to see every document."

Although there have been no reported case which has considered the compatibility of this rule with art.5(4) of the Convention, in *McGrady's application for Judicial Review* [2003] NIQB 15, Kerr J. considered a similar provision in r.12(2) of the Mental Health Review Tribunal Rules (Northern Ireland) 1986 (SI 1986/1298). His Lordship said at paras 20 to 22:

"20. Where . . . disclosure may cause harm to the applicant or to the informant, the tribunal must balance the right of the applicant under Art.5(4) with the interests that may be adversely affected if the material is disclosed. In this context the tribunal will want to consider carefully whether the convention rights of the informant would be infringed if the material that that person has provided in confidence is revealed to the applicant.

21. It appears to me that the tribunal will also take into account that the applicant's legal representatives have seen the material in question. While they may not disclose that material to the applicant, they may nevertheless take his instructions on the themes with which the material is concerned. There is no reason that the applicant should not be at liberty to present material to the tribunal on the matters raised in the addendum even if he remains unaware of its contents.

22. If the tribunal concludes that the addendum's contents should not be disclosed to the applicant it should approach the assessment with care. It must keep in mind that details of the information have not been revealed to the applicant. Its duty is to ensure that the proceedings are conducted fairly. This duty arises under pre-incorporation law as well as under the convention. But the applicant is not denied fairness simply because the material is withheld from him. As I have said, a balance must be struck between, on the one hand, the requirement that an applicant applying for discharge should generally have the opportunity to see and comment on all material adverse to him and, on the other, that the safety of the informant should not be imperilled. Unfairness would arise if the tribunal failed to acknowledge that the applicant has not been able to see and answer specifically the details of the allegations made against him. Provided they are conscious of this and cater for it in their approach to the assessment of the addendum, the proceedings will not be unfair to the applicant"

*Victims*

**3–066** Paragraphs 12 and 13 of "Procedures concerning the rights of access to MHT hearings of victims of certain criminal offences committed by patients" (see the General Note to these Rules) state:

"It is a decision for the Tribunal whether or not any document should be withheld under Rule 14. Where the victim wishes for this to be considered this should be clearly indicated on the victim's representations. The Tribunal will consider whether or not to disclose the document to the patient. This may be done at the hearing or by the Tribunal Judge at a preliminary hearing. A victim may request to attend in person to argue that a document be withheld, but whether or not this is allowed will be a matter for the discretion of the Tribunal. The decision on whether to order disclosure involves consideration of general ECHR principles as well as rule 14 . . ..

Any application by a victim to attend the Tribunal hearing and give oral evidence must be considered under Rule 38. In particular, the Tribunal has power under Rule 38(5) to exclude a victim from a hearing until the victim gives their evidence."

*Paragraph (2)*

**3–067** The criterion of "serious harm" is not the exclusive rationale for non-disclosure, as issues of third party confidentiality may arise: see *Dorset Healthcare NHS Foundation Trust v MH*, above, and Kris Gledhill, "The First Flight of the Fledgling: the Upper Tribunal's Substantive Debut", J.M.H.L., Spring 2009, 81 at 89–91.

When considering the "interests of justice" criterion in para.(b), the test to be applied is: does the non-disclosure allow the patient to make an effective challenge to the decision to detain him? (*RM v St Andrew's Healthcare* [2010] UKUT 119 (AAC), para.23). Judge Jacobs said at para.31:

"The Convention right under Article 6 guarantees a fair hearing. [*Secretary of State for the Home Department v AF (No.3)* [2009] UKHL 28; [2009] 3 All E.R. 643] shows how highly a fair hearing is rated in the balance with non-disclosure. . . . The overriding objective in r.2 requires that the rules of procedure be applied so that cases are dealt with fairly and justly. This includes ensuring full participation, so far as is practicable. Rule 14(2) requires the tribunal to have regard to the interests of justice. Justice and fairness generally require openness. Sometimes, they are not compatible and a compromise is possible. It may, for example, be possible and necessary to conduct proceedings while concealing that the true prognosis is worse than the patient realises. In this case, I have set out the full implications of the tribunal's order. They involve more than a compromise between justice and openness. They involve the sacrifice of the patient's right to challenge his detention effectively."

In this case, the non-disclosure order made by the First-tier tribunal referred to documents relating to the fact that the patient was being covertly medicated. Prior to being covertly medicated, the patient had been refusing medication and, as a consequence, had become very ill to the point where he was at risk of sudden, unexpected death (para.3). The question that had to be answered was: can the patient effectively challenge his detention without knowing that he was being covertly medicated? (para.26). The non-disclosure order was set aside on the ground that it would "exclude [the patient] completely from knowing the real process that was being followed and allow him to participate only in a pretence of a process" and "would severely hamper his legal team in participating effectively in that process" (para.32). The finding in this case is troubling in that the consequence of enabling the patient to fully participate in the tribunal hearing could be his death.

His Honour said that a tribunal should draft non-disclosure orders in terms of information rather that documents. Although the terms of such an order would depend upon the facts of the individual case, the following was offered, at para.36, as "a useful starting point":

"'The Tribunal prohibits disclosure to the patient of:

> (a) information relating to . . .;
> (b) any document containing or referring to that information, in particular—
>> (i) the reports of . . .;
>> (ii) any other report prepared in connection with these proceedings; and
>> (iii) this order.'

Paragraph (a) deals with the key issue of the information that must not be disclosed. It needs to be precise, clear and exhaustive. Paragraph (b) deals with the means by which disclosure might be made, directly or indirectly. It is supportive of paragraph (a) and need not be exhaustive.

The tribunal also needs to consider the patient's access to medical records. The order did not prohibit disclosure of the patient's medical records that, no doubt, contain details of his medication. A patient is entitled to access to medical records under section 7 of the Data Protection Act 1998. This is subject to the Data Protection (Subject Access Modification) (Health) Order 2000 (SI No 413). Article 5(1) contains an exemption from section 7 'to the extent to which the application of that section would be likely to cause serious harm to the physical or mental health or condition of the data subject or any other person.' That condition is effectively the same as rule 14(2)(a). The decision whether the exemption applies is made by the data controller."

In *AF (No.3)* above, para.105, Baroness Hale said obiter:

"These days, a . . . Tribunal would be unlikely to uphold a non-disclosure claim on the general ground that disclosure would be damaging to the doctor patient relationship. They would want to know precisely what it was in this doctor's evidence that might cause serious harm to this patient or to some other person and to weigh that damage against the interests of fairness . It will be an individualised balancing act carried out after discussion with the patient's own advocate and in the light of the opinions of the patient's own independent medical adviser."

DOCUMENT. The natural limit of this provision is on documents that are relevant to the proceedings (*RM v St Andrew's Healthcare*, above, para.15).

WOULD BE LIKELY TO CAUSE . . . SERIOUS HARM. A similar phrase is found in the Data Protection (Subject Access Modification) (Health) Order 2000 (SI 2000/413) para.5. In *Roberts v Nottinghamshire Healthcare NHS Trust* [2008] EWHC 1934 (QB); [2008] M.H.L.R. 294 at para.9, Cranston J. interpreted the phrase contained in the 2000 Order as follows:

"The question is whether there may very well be a risk of harm to health even if the risk falls short of being more probable that not. Harm to health could arise in various ways. In the context of mental health, it could be self harm or harm to others. The issue demands a factual enquiry: taking all matters into account such as the personality of the applicant, his past history, the care regime to which he is subject and so on, might there very well be a risk of harm to health on release of the data?"

His Lordship applied the judgment of Munby J. in *R (on the application of Lord) v Secretary of State for the Home Department* [2004] Prison Law Reports 65, where it was said that the term "likely . . . connotes a degree of probability where there would be a significant and weighty chance of prejudice to the identified public interest. The degree of risk must be such that there 'may very well' be prejudice to those interests, even if the risk falls short of being more probable than not."

### Evidence and submissions

**3–068**  **15.**—(1) Without restriction on the general powers in rule 5(1) and (2) (case management powers), the Tribunal may give directions as to—

(a) issues on which it requires evidence or submissions;

(b) the nature of the evidence or submissions it requires;

(c) whether the parties are permitted or required to provide expert evidence, and if so whether the parties must jointly appoint a single expert to provide such evidence;

(d) any limit on the number of witnesses whose evidence a party may put forward, whether in relation to a particular issue or generally;

(e) the manner in which any evidence or submissions are to be provided, which may include a direction for them to be given—

  (i) orally at a hearing; or

  (ii) by written submissions or witness statement; and

(f) the time at which any evidence or submissions are to be provided.

(2) The Tribunal may—

(a) admit evidence whether or not—

  (i) the evidence would be admissible in a civil trial in England and Wales; or

  (ii) the evidence was available to a previous decision maker; or

(b) exclude evidence that would otherwise be admissible where—

  (i) the evidence was not provided within the time allowed by a direction or a practice direction;

  (ii) the evidence was otherwise provided in a manner that did not comply with a direction or a practice direction; or

  (iii) it would otherwise be unfair to admit the evidence.

(3) The Tribunal may consent to a witness giving, or require any witness to give, evidence on oath, and may administer an oath for that purpose.

(4)–(5) [*These paragraphs do not apply to mental health cases*]

DEFINITIONS

**3–069**  Tribunal: r.1(3).

party: r.1(3).

practice direction: r.1(3).

GENERAL NOTE

**3–070**  The evidence of the patient's responsible clinician (RC) is likely to be of "particular centrality" in any hearing before the tribunal (*R. (on the application of Nottingham Healthcare NHS Trust) v Mental Health Review Tribunal (GK Interested Party)* [2008] EWHC 2445 (Admin); [2008] M.H.L.R. 326 para.19). The importance of such evidence, and the way in which a tribunal should approach it, was touched upon in a different context by Dyson L.J in *R. (on the application of K) v West London Mental Health NHS Trust* [2006] EWCA Civ 118; [2006] M.H.L.R. 89 at para.70:

"The weight to be given to opinion of [RCs] must be a matter for the decision-maker having regard to all relevant circumstances. It is not appropriate to attempt an exhaustive definition of what these might be. But they will include how long the [RC] has been in charge of the treatment of the patient, the strength of conviction with which the [RC's] clinical judgment has been expressed, the weight of other clinical opinion and the reasons given by other medical practitioners for their disagreement with the opinion expressed by the [RC]."

The medical evidence that is given on behalf of the responsible authority need not come from the patient's RC. However, the medical evidence must be up to date (*R. v Mental Health Review Tribunal, London and North East Ex p. Manns* [1999] M.H.L.R. 101 at para.28). If the tribunal concludes that it should hear evidence from the RC and the RC is not available, it could consider using its power to adjourn the hearing under r.5(3)(h).

Oral evidence given by the authors of clinical reports can only address the position as it is at the time of the hearing (*BB v South London & Maudsley NHS Trust* [2009] UKUT 157 (AAC); [2009] M.H.L.R. 302, para.10).

*Paragraph (2)*

With regard to the use of hearsay evidence, Munby J. said in *R. (on the application of DJ)* **3–071** *v Mental Health Review Tribunal; R. (on the application of AN) v Mental Health Review Tribunal* [2005] EWHC 587 (Admin); [2005] M.H.L.R. 56 at para.129:

"If the tribunal is relying on hearsay evidence it must take into account the fact that it is hearsay and must have regard to the particular dangers involved in relying upon second, third or fourth hand hearsay. The tribunal must be appropriately cautious of relying upon assertions as to past events which are not securely recorded in contemporaneous notes, particularly if the only evidence is hearsay. The tribunal must be alert to the well-known problem that constant repetition in 'official' reports or statements may, in the 'official' mind, turn into established fact something which rigorous forensic investigation shows is in truth nothing more than 'institutional folklore' with no secure foundation in either recorded or provable fact. The tribunal must guard against too quickly jumping to conclusions adverse to the patient in relation to past events where the only direct evidence is that of the patient himself, particularly where there is no clear account in contemporaneous notes of what is alleged to have happened. In relation to past incidents which are centrally important to the decision it has to take the tribunal must bear in mind the need for proof to the civil standard of proof; it must bear in mind the potential difficulties of relying upon second or third hand hearsay; and, if the incident is really fundamental to its decision, it must bear in mind fairness may require the patient to be given the opportunity to cross-examine the relevant witness(es) if their evidence is to be relied on at all."

On appeal, the Court of Appeal said that it saw "no reason to disagree" with this guidance [2005] EWCA Civ 1605; [2006] 4 All E.R. 194 at para.77.

## Summoning of witnesses and orders to answer questions or produce documents

**16.**—(1) On the application of a party or on its own initiative, the Tribunal **3–072** may—

(a) by summons require any person to attend as a witness at a hearing at the time and place specified in the summons; or

(b) order any person to answer any questions or produce any documents in that person's possession or control which relate to any issue in the proceedings.

(2) A summons under paragraph (1)(a) must—

(a) give the person required to attend 14 days' notice of the hearing, or such shorter period as the Tribunal may direct; and

(b) where the person is not a party, make provision for the person's necessary expenses of attendance to be paid, and state who is to pay them.

(3) No person may be compelled to give any evidence or produce any document that the person could not be compelled to give or produce on a trial of an action in a court of law.

(4) A summons or order under this rule must—

(a) state that the person on whom the requirement is imposed may apply to the Tribunal to vary or set aside the summons or order, if they have not had an opportunity to object to it; and

(b) state the consequences of failure to comply with the summons or order.

DEFINITIONS

**3–073**   party: r.1(3).
Tribunal: r.1(3).
hearing: r.1(3).

GENERAL NOTE

**3–074**   The Senior President of Tribunals has issued a Practice Direction on "Child, Vulnerable Adult and Sensitive Witnesses" which is reproduced below.

The tribunal can refer a person's failure to comply with a requirement imposed by it to the Upper Tribunal (r.7(3)).

*Paragraph (1)*

**3–075**   Although the summonsed person can be required to attend the hearing, he or she cannot be compelled to give evidence or to produce a document if para.(3) applies.

## Withdrawal

**3–076**   **17.**—(1) Subject to paragraphs (2) and (3), a party may give notice of the withdrawal of its case, or any part of it—

(a) at any time before a hearing to consider the disposal of the proceedings (or, if the Tribunal disposes of the proceedings without a hearing, before that disposal), by sending or delivering to the Tribunal a written notice of withdrawal; or

(b) orally at a hearing.

(2) Notice of withdrawal will not take effect unless the Tribunal consents to the withdrawal except—

(a) in proceedings concerning the suitability of a person to work with children or vulnerable adults; or

(b) in proceedings started by a reference under section 67 or 71(1) of the Mental Health Act 1983.

(3) A party which started a mental health case by making a reference to the Tribunal under section 68, 71(2) or 75(1) of the Mental Health Act 1983 may not withdraw its case.

(4) A party which has withdrawn its case may apply to the Tribunal for the case to be reinstated.

(5) An application under paragraph (4) must be made in writing and be received by the Tribunal within 28 days after—

(a) the date on which the Tribunal received the notice under paragraph (1)(a); or

(b) the date of the hearing at which the case was withdrawn orally under paragraph (1)(b).

(6) The Tribunal must notify each party in writing of a withdrawal under this rule.

DEFINITIONS

**3–077**   party: r.1(3).
Tribunal: r.1(3).

hearing: r.1(3).

GENERAL NOTE

This rule, which enables an applicant to apply to the tribunal in writing to withdraw a **3–078** case, does not apply to references (para.(3)). A withdrawal cannot take effect without the consent of the tribunal (para.(2)). If an application is withdrawn, the applicant can make a further application during the relevant period (s.77(2)). Provision is made for the reinstatement of a withdrawn case in paras.(4) and (5).

*Paragraph (1)*

BEFORE A HEARING TO CONSIDER THE DISPOSAL OF THE PROCEEDINGS. An application to **3–079** withdraw the case can be made after a recommendation has been made by the tribunal but before it reconvened to consider the case when the recommendation was not followed (*R. (on the application of O) v Mental Health Review Tribunal* [2006] EWHC 2659 (Admin); [2006] M.H.L.R. 326).

*Paragraph (2)*

UNLESS THE TRIBUNAL CONSENTS. The tribunal should not consent "if it takes the view **3–080** that [the application for withdrawal] is merely a tactical ploy and is not in the interests of the patient" (*R. (on the application of O) v Mental Health Review Tribunal*, above at para.41, Collins J.). An example of a tactical ploy was encountered by the author in a case where the tribunal agreed to a withdrawal where the application was made after all of the evidence has been heard, but before the tribunal has reached its decision.

*O* was considered by the Upper Tribunal in *KF v Birmingham and Solihull Mental Health NHS Foundation Trust* [2010] UKUT 185 (AAC) at paras 37–38:

"In our view a First-tier Tribunal would certainly be justified in refusing consent to a withdrawal where it is no more than such a tactical ploy. However, that should not be taken as meaning that a tribunal should *only* refuse its agreement in such a scenario. There is plainly no automatic right to withdraw, and we agree with both counsel that the case for accepting a withdrawal will depend very much on the particular circumstances of the case (or cases). The 1983 rules did not contain either the overriding objective or the extensive case management powers to which we have already made reference and the First-tier Tribunal should always have regard to those provisions when considering whether or not it is appropriate to consent to a withdrawal.

Mr Pezzani submitted that a patient's desire to make an application whenever legitimately possible within the terms of the Act can hardly amount to a 'tactical ploy'. In most cases we doubt whether it is helpful to use the terminology of 'tactical ploy'. The question is whether a patient who has both an outstanding s.2 application and a subsequent s.3 application in hand near the start of a six month period may be justified in seeking to withdraw the latter application in order to preserve the possibility of making such an application later in that period of treatment. There may be a number of relevant factors, for example the initial s.3 application may have been taken without the benefit of legal advice, and an individual's mental health may well change considerably over time. The danger of an unduly broad approach to the notion of a 'tactical ploy' is that a patient might be denied what would otherwise be a legitimate opportunity to question their continued detention."

# PART 3

PROCEEDINGS BEFORE THE TRIBUNAL OTHER THAN IN MENTAL HEALTH CASES

*[Not reproduced]*

## PART 4

PROCEEDINGS BEFORE THE TRIBUNAL IN MENTAL HEALTH CASES

CHAPTER 1

Before the hearing

**Application of Part 4**

**3–081**     **31.**This Part applies only to mental health cases.

DEFINITION

**3–082**     mental health case: r.1(3).

**Procedure in mental health cases**

**3–083**     **32.**—(1) An application or reference must be—

(a)  made in writing;

(b)  signed (in the case of an application, by the applicant or any person author-ised by the applicant to do so); and

(c)  sent or delivered to the Tribunal so that it is received within the time speci-fied in the Mental Health Act 1983 or the Repatriation of Prisoners Act 1984.

(2) An application must, if possible, include—

(a)  the name and address of the patient;

(b)  if the application is made by the patient's nearest relative, the name, address and relationship to the patient of the patient's nearest relative;

(c)  the provision under which the patient is detained, liable to be detained, sub-ject to guardianship, a community patient or subject to after-care under supervision;

(d)  whether the person making the application has appointed a representative or intends to do so, and the name and address of any representative appointed;

(e)  the name and address of the responsible authority in relation to the patient.

(3) Subject to rule 14(2) (withholding evidence likely to cause harm), when the Tribunal receives a document from any party it must send a copy of that document to each other party.

(4) If the patient is a conditionally discharged patient (as defined in the Mental Health Act 1983) the Secretary of State must send or deliver a statement contain-ing the information and documents required by the relevant practice direction to the Tribunal so that it is received by the Tribunal as soon as practicable and in any event within 6 weeks after the Secretary of State received a copy of the application or a request from the Tribunal.

(5) In proceedings under section 66(1)(a) of the Mental Health Act 1983 (appli-cation for admission for assessment), on the earlier of receipt of the copy of the application or a request from the Tribunal, the responsible authority must send or deliver to the Tribunal—

(a)  the application for admission;

(b)  the medical recommendations on which the application is founded;

(c)  such of the information specified in the relevant practice direction as is within the knowledge of the responsible authority and can reasonably be provided in the time available; and

718

(d) such of the documents specified in the relevant practice direction as can reasonably be provided in the time available.

(6) If paragraph (4) or (5) does not apply, the responsible authority must send or deliver a statement containing the information and documents required by the relevant practice direction to the Tribunal so that it is received by the Tribunal as soon as practicable and in any event within 3 weeks after the responsible authority received a copy of the application or reference.

(7) If the patient is a restricted patient the responsible authority must also send the statement under paragraph (6) to the Secretary of State, and the Secretary of State must send a statement of any further relevant information to the Tribunal as soon as practicable and in any event—

(a) in proceedings under section 75(1) of the Mental Health Act 1983, within 2 weeks after the Secretary of State received the relevant authority's statement; or

(b) otherwise, within 3 weeks after the Secretary of State received the relevant authority's statement.

(8) If the Secretary of State wishes to seek the approval of the Tribunal under section 86(3) of the Mental Health Act 1983, the Secretary of State must refer the patient's case to the Tribunal and the provisions of these Rules applicable to references under that Act apply to the proceedings.

DEFINITIONS
    applicant: r.1(3).                                                 **3–084**
    Tribunal: r.1(3).
    patient: r.1(3).
    nearest relative: r.1(3).
    party: r.1(3).
    responsible authority: r.1(3).
    practice direction: r.1(3).

GENERAL NOTE
    This Rule deals with applications to tribunals in mental health cases (paras (1), (2)) and **3–085** the submission of information to the tribunal by the responsible authority and the Secretary of State (paras (4)–(8)). Subject to r.14(2), a copy of every document received by the tribunal must be sent to each other party (para.(3)). An application may be withdrawn under r.17.

    With s.2 cases, the information set out in para.(5) must be sent to the tribunal prior to the hearing date. In other cases, the responsible authority must ensure that the tribunal receives the information required by the practice direction on mental health cases within three weeks of the authority receiving a copy of the application or reference (para.(6)). If the patient is a restricted patient, the authority must also send the statement to the Secretary of State (para.(7)), and the Secretary of State must send a statement of "further relevant information" to the tribunal within the time limits set out in para.(7). If the patient is a conditionally discharged patient, the Secretary of State must send a statement containing the information required by the practice direction so that it is received by the tribunal within six weeks of the Secretary of State receiving a copy of the application or a request by the tribunal (para.(4)).

    Where the tribunal receives the information required by paras (4), (5) or (6) it must give notice of the proceedings to the persons and/or bodies specified in r.33.

    There is provision for the time limits in this rule to be extended (r.5(3)(a)). See rr.12 and 13 for the calculation of time and methods of service.

The references in this rule to "the relevant practice direction" are to "Practice Direction—First-Tier Tribunal, Health Education and Social Care Chamber, Mental Health Cases", which is reproduced below.

*Paragraph (1)(b)*

**3–086**    An application can only be made if the applicant either has the mental capacity to sign the application or to authorise a person to sign the application on his or her behalf. Only a "very limited capacity" is required for either purpose (*R. (on the application of H) v Secretary of State for Health* [2005] UKHL 60; [2005] 4 All E.R. 1311 at para.4 per Baroness Hale).

Under the Mental Capacity Act 2005, a mentally capable person (the "donor") can execute a legal document called a lasting power of attorney ("LPA") which empowers another person (the "donee") to act in his or her stead, either generally or for specific purposes. An act done by a donee can be treated as an act done by the donor. A LPA which confers on the donee (or donees) power to make decisions about the donor's personal welfare matters could cover the making of an application to a tribunal. A personal welfare LPA can only take effect after the donor has lost the mental capacity to make the decision in question. A donee could therefore make an application to a tribunal on the patient's behalf if:

(i)   the welfare LPA either gives a general power to the donee or the power to make such an application has been specified by the donor; and

(ii)   the patient does not possess the mental capacity to make the application.

A deputy appointed by the Court of Protection under the 2005 Act to make personal welfare decisions on behalf of the patient can also make an application to the tribunal on the patient's behalf if such a power has been conferred on the deputy by the court and the patient does not have the mental capacity to make the application.

*Paragraph (2)*

**3–087**    There are no statutory forms. Application and referral forms provided by the Tribunal Service can be downloaded at: *www.mhrt.org.uk/FormsGuidance/forms.htm* (accessed July 6, 2010)

*Paragraph (3)*

**3–088**    A failure to comply with this provision could give rise to a right to challenge the tribunal's decision under r.45. A failure to give notice to the Secretary of State in the case of a restricted patient would inevitably lead to the tribunal setting aside its decision under that rule in that there would have been a breach of the most fundamental rule of natural justice, in that the Secretary of State, as a vitally interested party whose role was to safeguard the public interest, was denied a hearing (*Secretary of State for the Home Department v Oxford Regional Mental Health Review Tribunal* [1987] 3 All E.R. 8, HL and *R. (on the application of the Secretary of State for the Home Department) v Mental Health Review Tribunal* [2004] EWHC 650 (Admin)).

*Paragraph (8)*

**3–089**    Section 86(3).    Which states that the Secretary of State or the Welsh Ministers must not exercise their power to remove a patient from the UK under that section without the approval of the tribunal.

## Notice of proceedings to interested persons

**3–090**    **33.** When the Tribunal receives the information required by rule 32(4), (5) or (6) (procedure in mental health cases) the Tribunal must give notice of the proceedings—

(a) where the patient is subject to the guardianship of a private guardian, to the guardian;

(b) where there is an extant order of the Court of Protection, to that court;

(c) subject to a patient with capacity to do so requesting otherwise, where any person other than the applicant is named by the authority as exercising the functions of the nearest relative, to that person;

(d) where a health authority, Primary Care Trust, National Health Service trust or NHS foundation trust has a right to discharge the patient under the provisions of section 23(3) of the Mental Health Act 1983, to that authority or trust; and

(e) to any other person who, in the opinion of the Tribunal, should have an opportunity of being heard.

DEFINITIONS

Tribunal: r.1(3).                                                                                      **3–091**
mental health case: r.1(3).
patient: r.1(3).
nearest relative: r.1(3).

GENERAL NOTE

A person who is notified under this rule may either attend and take part in the proceed- **3–092** ings to such extent as the tribunal considers proper, or provide written submissions to the tribunal (r.36).

*Paragraph (e)*

ANY OTHER PERSON.    Including the victim of the patient. Victims need to be advised that **3–093** any written representations that are made under r.36(2)(b) will be disclosed to the patient unless r.14(2) applies.

## Medical examination of the patient

**34.**—(1) Before a hearing to consider the disposal of a mental health case, an **3–094** appropriate member of the Tribunal must, so far as practicable—

(a) examine the patient; and

(b) take such other steps as that member considers necessary to form an opinion of the patient's mental condition.

(2) For the purposes of paragraph (1) that member may—

(a) examine the patient in private;

(b) examine records relating to the detention or treatment of the patient and any after-care services;

(c) take notes and copies of records for use in connection with the proceedings.

DEFINITIONS

hearing: r.1(3).                                                                                      **3–095**
mental health case: r.1(3).
Tribunal: r.1(3).
patient: r.1(3).

GENERAL NOTE

This rule, which is based on r.11 of the Mental Health Review Tribunal Rules 1983, **3–096** requires "an appropriate member" of the tribunal to examine the patient in order to form an opinion of the patient's mental condition. Under para.4 of the Practice Statement "Composition of Tribunals in relation to matters that fall to be decided by the

Health, Education and Social Care Chamber on or after 3 November 2008", issued by the Senior President of Tribunals on December 15, 2008, this person is the member of the tribunal who is a registered medical practitioner. Although the tribunal will doubtless be guided by the member on this issue, it is the tribunal as a whole which determines issues relating to the patient's mental condition in the light of their own experience and examination of the patient (*R. v Trent Mental Health Review Tribunal Ex p. Ryan* [1992] C.O.D. 15 DC). The tribunal may not proceed with a hearing in the absence of the patient unless the requirements of this rule have been satisfied (r.39(2)(a)).

The question whether the tribunal was biased because the consultant psychiatrist who sat as a member of the tribunal was a consultant who was employed by the detaining NHS Trust was considered in *R. (on the application of PD) v West Midlands and North West Mental Health Review Tribunal* [2004] EWCA Civ 311; [2004] M.H.L.R 174, where the patient challenged the legality of the decision of the Mental Health Review Tribunal not to discharge him on the ground that the tribunal was biased in that the consultant psychiatrist who sat as a member of the tribunal was a consultant who was employed by the detaining NHS Trust. It was alleged that the involvement of the psychiatrist in the decision was incompatible with art.6 of the European Convention on Human Rights (ECHR) and with natural justice and, in particular, the common law test of bias. The Court of Appeal held that the test of apparent bias under the Convention and under public law is the same and that the court had to consider the case by applying the following test which had been established by the House of Lords in *Lawal v Northern Spirit Ltd* [2003] UKHL 35: would a fair minded and informed observer who is neither complacent nor unduly sensitive or suspicious conclude that there was a real possibility that the tribunal was biased when it made the decision under challenge. Applying this test to the facts of this case, the question was whether the reasonable and informed member of the public might suspect that someone in the position of the psychiatrist would be so concerned at the potential reaction of the managers of the trust if the patient were to be discharged, and the implications of such reaction for his own position, that this might consciously or unconsciously affect his decision. The court answered this question by rejecting the contention that an appearance of bias arises simply from the fact that the psychiatrist was employed by the detaining trust. The court said that an appearance of bias could have arisen if the psychiatrist had been employed at the hospital where the patient was detained.

In *R. (on the application of S) v Mental Health Review Tribunal* [2002] EWHC Admin 2522; [2003] M.H.L.R. 118 at para.34, Stanley Burnton J. said that:

"if during the course of the hearing, it appears that there is a factual conflict between the medical member and the patient, for example, as to what was said by the patient to the medical member, and that conflict may be material to the decision of the tribunal, the tribunal must consider whether it can properly continue to hear the patient's application".

The patient can commission a medical report on his or her condition that can be presented to the tribunal as evidence (see ss.67(2), 69(3) and 76).

*Human Rights Act 1998*

**3–097**   In *DN v Switzerland* (2003) 37 E.H.R.R. 21; [2001] M.H.L.R. 117 the European Court of Human Rights held that the fact that a psychiatrist member of a court who, in his role as judge rapporteur, had previously prepared an expert opinion on the patient and had communicated his opinion on whether the patient's application should succeed to the court, constituted a violation of art.5(4) of the ECHR. The court said, at para.54, that the psychiatrist's position in the proceedings gave rise to legitimate fears in the applicant that "he had a preconceived opinion as to her request for release from detention and that he was not, therefore, approaching her case with due impartiality". *DN* was applied in *R. (on the application of S) v Mental Health Review Tribunal*, above, where Stanley Burnton J. held that:

1. This rule does not expressly require the medical member to form an opinion of the patient's mental condition: it requires him to take the steps necessary to form an opinion.

2. The medical member must not form a concluded opinion on the patient's mental condition until the conclusion of the hearing, since otherwise the outcome of the hearing would be prejudiced.

3. The forming and expression of a provisional opinion by the medical member does not give rise to unfairness.

4. As a matter of domestic law, there can be no objection to the expression of a provisional opinion by a medical member to his tribunal colleagues prior to the hearing, provided the other members are aware that is only a provisional opinion and treat it as such, and provided that they understand that they are free to disagree with it if the evidence and submissions before them lead them to a different conclusion.

5. The phrase "due impartiality" used by the court in *DN* requires a member of a tribunal not to have a preconceived concluded opinion on the merits of the patient's case. The court did not suggest that a provisional view formed before the commencement of the hearing is objectionable. If an otherwise impartial and independent member of a tribunal has a preconceived concluded opinion, or if he expresses himself in such a way as to give rise to reasonable apprehension that he has a preconceived concluded opinion, he lacks the necessary impartiality, but not otherwise.

6. It follows that this rule [as it appeared in the MHRT Rules 1983] is not inconsistent with the requirements of art.5(4) as interpreted in *DN*.

*S* was applied in *R. (on the application of RD) v Mental Health Review Tribunal* [2007] EWHC 781 (Admin) where Munby J. held that the power to express preliminary views was not confined to the medical member and that such views could relate to all aspects of the case. His Lordship said at para.19:

"The communication by the medical member of her 'very preliminary view' was manifestly lawful, notwithstanding that it went to the ultimate issue and not merely to the question of [the patient's] mental condition. There is nothing in r.11 [of the MHRT Rules 1983] to disable the medical member from doing what she (like other members of the tribunal) would otherwise plainly be entitled to do, namely to discuss all aspects of the case with the other members of the tribunal before the hearing and to express to them her preliminary views either on the case as a whole or on any particular aspect of the case, just as there is nothing in r.11 to disable the medical member (like other members of the tribunal) from expressing to the parties at the outset of the hearing her preliminary views either on the case as a whole or on any particular aspect of the case. The contrary, in my judgment, is simply unarguable."

*Paragraph (1)*
AN APPROPRIATE MEMBER OF THE TRIBUNAL. See the General Note, above.

**3–098**

MUST, SO FAR AS PRACTICABLE. This covers the situation where the patient refuses to see the member.

EXAMINE THE PATIENT. The member will be protected by s.139 of the Act when acting under this rule.

AN OPINION OF THE PATIENT'S MENTAL CONDITION. The opinion must be provisional: see the note on "Human Rights Act 1998", above. The tribunal is entitled to rely on the evidence of the member even if the evidence of the patient's responsible clinician (RC) and the patient's independent psychiatrist asserts that the patient is not suffering from a detainable mental disorder. However, any evidence or information which has only been made available to the member must be shown at least to the patient's representative so that he or she can have the opportunity to present countervailing arguments (*R. v Mental Health Review Tribunal Ex p. Clatworthy* [1985] 3 All E.R. 699 DC). In *R. (on the application of H) v Ashworth Hospital Authority; R. (on the application of Ashworth Hospital Authority) v Mental Health Review Tribunal for West Midlands and North West Region* [2002] EWCA Civ 923; [2002] M.H.L.R. 314 at para.84 Dyson L.J. said:

> "It seems to me both fair and sensible that, if the medical member of the tribunal has formed any views on the basis of his or her interview with the patient, the substance of those views should be communicated to the patient and/or those who are representing him. I cannot think of any good reason why this should not be a requirement, although I would not wish to rule out the possibility of exceptional cases where such a course may not be practicable."

This passage was cited by Stanley Burnton J. in *R. (on the application of S) v Mental Health Review Tribunal*, above, where his Lordship said, at para.34, that the following guidance taken from para.7 of "The Members' Handbook of the Mental Health Review Tribunals in England and Wales" must be followed:

> "[The medical member] must appreciate that he performs a dual role at the tribunal as a fact finder and as a decision-maker and it is therefore essential that his opinion of the patient's mental condition, if it differs significantly from that of the [RC], should have been disclosed to the patient and the representative at the outset of the hearing. Thus, a situation will be avoided where the members of the tribunal are acting on the basis of evidence known only to themselves which would, of course, be a breach both of fundamental principle, and likely to invalidate the decision."

Further guidance on this point was provided in *R. (on the application of KW) v Avon and Wiltshire Mental Health Partnership NHS Trust and Bristol City Council* [2003] EWHC 919 (Admin); [2003] M.H.L.R. 315 (Admin) at para.25, where it was held that if the medical member makes a finding relevant to the existence of the patient's mental disorder, or forms a provisional opinion as to the existence or otherwise of a mental disorder, that view should be shared with the patient's RC in the course of the hearing.

*Paragraph (2)*

**3–099**  RECORDS.  The tribunal may use its powers under r.16 if there is a refusal to provide them.

CHAPTER 2

Hearings

**No disposal of proceedings without a hearing**

**3–100**  **35.**—(1) The Tribunal must not dispose of proceedings without a hearing.
(2) This rule does not apply to a decision under Part 5.

DEFINITIONS

**3–101**  Tribunal: r.1(3).
dispose of proceedings: r.1(3).

hearing: r.1(3).

*Accommodation for hearings*
In March 2010, the Tribunal issued guidance to Responsible Authorities on "Room **3–102** specification requirements for tribunal hearings". Also see paras 32.33 and 32.34 of the *Code of Practice.*

## Entitlement to attend a hearing

**36.**—(1) Subject to rule 38(4) (exclusion of a person from a hearing), each party **3–103** to proceedings is entitled to attend a hearing.

(2) Any person notified of the proceedings under rule 33 (notice of proceedings to interested persons) may—
(a) attend and take part in a hearing to such extent as the Tribunal considers proper; or
(b) provide written submissions to the Tribunal.

DEFINITIONS
    party: r.1(3).                                                 **3–104**
    hearing: r.1(3).
    Tribunal: r.1(3).

GENERAL NOTE
    A hearing can take place in the absence of a party if r.39 applies.         **3–105**

*Paragraph (1)*
    PARTY.   Note r.11(5).                                          **3–106**

## Time and place of hearings

**37.**—(1) In proceedings under section 66(1)(a) of the Mental Health Act 1983 **3–107** the hearing of the case must start within 7 days after the date on which the Tribunal received the application notice.

(2) In proceedings under section 75(1) of that Act, the hearing of the case must start at least 5 weeks but no more than 8 weeks after the date on which the Tribunal received the reference.

(3) The Tribunal must give reasonable notice of the time and place of the hearing (including any adjourned or postponed hearing), and any changes to the time and place of the hearing, to—
(a) each party entitled to attend a hearing; and
(b) any person who has been notified of the proceedings under rule 33 (notice of proceedings to interested persons).

(4) The period of notice under paragraph (3) must be at least 14 days, except that—
(a) in proceedings under section 66(1)(a) of the Mental Health Act 1983 the period must be at least 3 working days; and
(b) the Tribunal may give shorter notice—
    (i) with the parties' consent; or
    (ii) in urgent or exceptional circumstances.

DEFINITIONS
    Tribunal: r.1(3).                                               **3–108**
    party: r.1(3).
    hearing: r.1(3).

working day: r.1(3).

GENERAL NOTE

**3–109**    In *R. (on the application of C) v Mental Health Review Tribunal London South and South West Region* [2001] EWCA Civ 1110; [2001] M.H.L.R. 110, the Court of Appeal held that:

1. A uniform policy that tribunal hearings requested by patients who had been detained under s.3 of the Act would be fixed eight weeks after the date of the application did not comply with art.5(4) of the European Convention on Human Rights, which requires the lawfulness of the patient's detention to be decided speedily. Each application had to be heard as soon as reasonably practicable.

2. However urgent the patient's demand for a hearing, such time could properly be allowed for preparation as was reasonably necessary to ensure that the tribunal was in a position adequately and fairly to adjudicate on the issues before it.

3. There was nothing inconsistent with art.5(4) in having a target date of eight weeks maximum for the listing of hearings. In cases requiring eight weeks' preparation, that period would not conflict with the requirement that a decision on the application had to be reached speedily.

Lord Phillips M.R. said at para.60:

"It seems to me that the [appropriate] stage at which to fix a [hearing] date would be after receipt of the statement required by rule 6 [now see r.32], when the scope of the remaining activities that would need to take place before the hearing would be clear".

*C* was applied by Stanley Burnton J. in *R. (on the application of KB) v The Mental Health Review Tribunal and the Secretary of State for Health* [2002] EWHC 639 (Admin); [2003] M.H.L.R. 1 at para.31, where his Lordship said:

"What is a speedy decision in any case will depend on a number of factors, including the nature and importance of the subject matter of the case, the complexity of the issues, the preparation required before the hearing, and the evidence to be considered. Factors extraneous to the particular case may also be relevant, such as a sudden increase in similar applications, or the intervention of a holiday period. However, in my judgment the fact that a patient's case is perceived to be unmeritorious does not deprive him of his right to a speedy hearing; and similarly, if there is unjustified delay before the hearing, the fact that his case is belatedly held to be unmeritorious does not excuse the infringement of that right."

Having considered the causes of the delays involved in the cases before him, his Lordship said that:

1. In the ordinary way it should be practicable for tribunal hearings in s.3 cases to take place within eight weeks of the application.

2. Central government should ensure that tribunals are provided with the resources and administrative systems that would enable them to satisfy this expectation.

3. In any sensibly managed judicial system there are bound to be adjournments and cancelled hearings for a number of reasons: the illness of a judge or the unavailability of a necessary witness, the over-running of an earlier hearing, or the need to accommodate an urgent case. The postponement of a hearing for such reasons does not necessarily involve any infringement of a Convention right. The correct approach to adopt in a case where there has been a delay in arranging a tribunal hearing is to consider whether the delay in question is, on the face of it, inconsistent with

726

the requirement for a speedy hearing. If it is, the onus is on the state to excuse the delay. It may do so by establishing, for example, that the delay has been caused by a sudden and unpredictable increase in the workload of the tribunal, and it has taken effective and sufficient measures to remedy the problem. But if the state fails to satisfy that onus, the claimant will have established a breach of his right under art.5(4).

In this case his Lordship identified the approach that a court should take when assessing damages under art.5(5) for a breech of art.5(4).

*Accommodation for hearings*
In March 2010, the Tribunal issued guidance to Responsible Authorities on "Room specification requirements for tribunal hearings". Also see paras 32.33 and 32.34 of the *Code of Practice*.

## Public and private hearings
**38.**—(1) All hearings must be held in private unless the Tribunal considers that **3–110** it is in the interests of justice for the hearing to be held in public.

(2) If a hearing is held in public, the Tribunal may give a direction that part of the hearing is to be held in private.

(3) Where a hearing, or part of it, is to be held in private, the Tribunal may determine who is permitted to attend the hearing or part of it.

(4) The Tribunal may give a direction excluding from any hearing, or part of it—
  (a) any person whose conduct the Tribunal considers is disrupting or is likely to disrupt the hearing;
  (b) any person whose presence the Tribunal considers is likely to prevent another person from giving evidence or making submissions freely;
  (c) any person who the Tribunal considers should be excluded in order to give effect to a direction under rule 14(2) (withholding information likely to cause harm); or
  (d) any person where the purpose of the hearing would be defeated by the attendance of that person.

(5) The Tribunal may give a direction excluding a witness from a hearing until that witness gives evidence.

DEFINITIONS
  hearing: r.1(3).                                                          **3–111**
  Tribunal: r.1(3).

GENERAL NOTE
Tribunal hearings are to be held in private unless the tribunal considers that the interests **3–112** of justice require a public hearing (para.(1)). The hearing can be part public and part private (para.(2)). The overwhelming majority of hearings are held in private. The tribunal has the power to give directions excluding various categories of persons from both public and private hearings (paras.(4), (5)).

In *AH v West London Mental Health Trust*, [2010] UKUT 264AAC, para.44, the Upper Tribunal considered that the relevant factors in deciding whether to direct a hearing in public are:

- Is it consistent with the subjective and informed wishes of the applicant (assuming he is competent to make an informed choice)?

- Will it have an adverse effect on his mental health in the short or long term, taking account of the views of those treating him and any other expert views?

- Are there any other special factors for or against a public hearing?

- Can practical arrangements be made for an open hearing without disproportionate burden on the authority?

The Upper Tribunal said, at para.25, that although the underlying assumption in this rule is that the interests of justice will normally require a hearing in private, having regard to the reasons for the exception to the right to a public hearing under art.6 of the European Convention of Human Rights (ECHR) the principal consideration remains the protection of the interests of the patient.

In *R. (on the application of Mersey Care NHS Trust) v Mental Health Review Tribunal* [2004] EWHC 1749 (Admin); [2005] 2 All E.R. 820, Beatson J. held that:

1. Rule 21 of the Mental Health Review Tribunal Rules 1983, which dealt with the privacy of proceedings, created a presumption that hearings before tribunals are private [A similar presumption is made by para.(1) of this rule]. Such a presumption can be justified under art.6 of the ECHR where it is considered necessary in the interests of morals, public order or national security or where required by the interests of juveniles or the protection of the private life of the parties (*B and P v United Kingdom* (2002) 34 E.H.R.R. 529 at para.39). In *AH v West London Mental Health Trust*, above, para.20, the Upper Tribunal said mental health cases can be added to this list.

2. The High Court has jurisdiction to commit for the contempt of an order of a tribunal: see *Pickering v Liverpool Daily Post and Echo Newspapers plc* [1991] 1 All E.R. 622, where the House of Lords held that a tribunal is, by virtue of s.19 of the Contempt of Court Act 1981 and s.12 of the Administration of Justice Act 1960, a "court" whose proceedings are subject to the law of contempt.

3. Although the general rule in s.12 of the 1960 Act is that the publication of information relating to proceedings before any court sitting in private shall not of itself be a contempt of court, proceedings in mental health tribunals are one of the exceptions so that publication of such information is itself a contempt: s.12(1)(b) of the 1960 Act.

4. Where a tribunal holds a public hearing, the control over publicity is by means of the "strict liability" rule in s.2 of the Contempt of Court Act 1981. The fact that the protection afforded by the strict liability rule would be only for a limited period coupled with the difficulty of determining in advance what kind of public comment about proceedings will create "a substantial risk that the course of justice . . . will be seriously impeded or prejudiced" (s.2(2)) of the 1981 Act) mean that the tribunal's powers if the hearing is in public are significantly more limited than they are if it is in private.

5. Any restrictions on the right to "impart information and ideas" gained by attendance at a public hearing held by a mental health tribunal would prima facie require justification under art.10(2) of the ECHR.

*Human Rights Act 1998*

**3–113** Article 6 of the European Convention on Human Rights is engaged when a tribunal reviews the detention of a patient: see *Aerts v Belgium* (1998) 29 E.H.R.R. 50, para.59 and the notes to art.6 in Part 5.

*Observers*

**3–114** The following "Guidance for the observation of tribunal hearings" was issued by the Chamber President, Deputy President and Judge Wright on November 5, 2009:

"The purpose of this guidance is to set down the terms and conditions for the observation of tribunal hearings, which are usually held in private, and for the appropriate handling of confidential reports and other documentary evidence.

### The Tribunal Procedure Rules 2008
1. Rule 38(1) provides that all hearings must be held in private unless the tribunal considers that it is in the interests of justice for the hearing to be held in public.

   Rule 14(7) also provides that, unless the tribunal gives a direction to the contrary, information about mental health cases and the names of any persons concerned in such cases must not be made public. Where a hearing, or part of it, is to be held in private, the tribunal may determine who is permitted to attend the hearing or part of it (Rule 38(3)).

2. Except in relation to judge or member induction or training, appraisals, or observations by the Administrative Justice and Tribunals Council (AJTC), the strong presumption in all cases is in favour of privacy and confidentiality, and individual tribunals should not exercise powers to hold proceedings in public, or disclose any information about mental health cases to others outside the jurisdiction *(including to judges in other jurisdictions)*, without first consulting the Deputy Chamber President or, in his absence, the Principal Salaried Judge. Additionally, save as above, the views of the patient and/or the patient's representative must be sought before any disclosure of relevant confidential information takes place, and any objections from the patient and/or the patient's representative must be respected.

### Categories of observers

### Judge or Member Induction or Training
3. Following appointment as a judge or member of the tribunal, it is a term and condition of a person's appointment that, unless they have adequate relevant previous experience, they should observe a number of tribunal hearings as part of their induction or training before they are entitled to sit. These observations have to be facilitated and, subject to the tribunal judge and the booking and listing team being made aware in advance, the following guidelines apply:—

3.1 The presence of the observer at the hearing is not subject to the consent of the patient, witnesses, individual tribunal members, or any other party. However, if the presence of the observer causes a patient to feel particular discomfort or distress, the observer and the tribunal judge (having consulted colleagues) may agree that the observation should not take place, or should be abandoned.

3.2 The observer is entitled to receive copies of the reports or other documents before the tribunal, either in advance of, or at, the hearing, on the strict understanding that the contents must not be made public under any circumstances.

3.3 The tribunal judge should agree with the observer as to how the observer will be introduced to the parties.

3.4 The observer should sit where the tribunal judge (having consulted colleagues) feels it is appropriate, and should adopt as passive a role as is possible having regard to the lay-out of the hearing room and the proximity of the parties.

3.5 The observer must not intervene in any way during the hearing.

3.6 The observer is entitled to make such notes as are appropriate for the purposes of the observation. Such notes must be maintained as strictly confidential and (except in general terms for the purposes of a report to the AJTC, such that the patient cannot be identified) must not be made public under any circumstances.

3.7 The observer is entitled to be present during the tribunal's deliberations, but shall take no part whatsoever in the deliberations.

**Appraisers**

4. Appraisals have to be facilitated although the tribunal judge and the booking and listing team must be made aware in advance. In the sense that an appraiser is an observer, the role and functions of an appraiser attending the hearing to appraise one of the members are set out in the Appraisal Guide for Members—1 October 2008, at paragraph 16.2 onwards. The guidance set out at paragraphs 3.1 to 3.7 above also applies, as appropriate.

**Members of the Administrative Justice & Tribunals Council**

5. A member of the Council has the right to attend and observe the proceedings of a tribunal in such capacity although the tribunal judge must be made aware in advance. The guidance set out at paragraphs 3.1 to 3.7 above also applies, as appropriate.

**Other persons seeking to observe a tribunal hearing**

6. It is impossible to attempt to list all the categories of persons wishing to observe a tribunal hearing. Examples may include persons selected by the Ministry of Justice to participate in a judicial work-shadowing scheme, or a solicitor or barrister wishing to undertake mental health work and needing to gain experience. All observation requests not covered by paragraphs 3, 4, and 5 above should be, in the first instance, forwarded, in advance, to the Deputy Chamber President or, in his absence, the Principal Salaried Judge for a preliminary decision. If a representative, hospital staff member or other involved professional appears at a hearing with a student or observer without having sought advance permission, the tribunal must deal with any application under Rules 14 and 38 on its merits. However, in all such cases, it must be recognised that such observers are unlikely to be members of the jurisdiction and, therefore, the rules referred to in paragraph 1, and the guidance in paragraph 2 above, will apply.

7. If asked in advance, the Deputy Chamber President or, in his absence, the Principal Salaried Judge, may indicate that he has no objection to the presence of the particular observer for the reasons given in support of the request, but, even so, the patient, witnesses, tribunal members and other parties must be asked for their views before the tribunal hearing the case makes a direction under Rule 38(3) permitting the presence of the observer.

8. In the event that permission for observation is granted, the following guidance shall apply:-

8.1. The reports and any other documents before the Tribunal must not be disclosed at any time to the observer.

8.2. The tribunal judge shall advise the observer in private that the proceedings before the tribunal are confidential and that information about the proceedings and the names of any persons concerned in the proceedings must not, under any circumstances, be made public by the observer.

8.3. The tribunal judge should agree with the observer as to how the observer will be introduced to the parties.

8.4. The observer should sit where the tribunal judge (having consulted with colleagues) feels it is appropriate and should adopt as passive a role as is possible having regard to the lay-out of the hearing room and the proximity of the parties.

8.5. The observer shall not intervene in any way during the hearing.

8.6. The observer should not take any notes during the hearing.

8.7. The observer is not entitled to be present during the tribunal's deliberations and should withdraw, along with the parties, from the hearing room at such times when the tribunal is deliberating."

*Paragraph (1)*
INTERESTS OF JUSTICE. See *B and P v United Kingdom,* above, and the overriding objec- **3–116** tive set out in r.2.

*Paragraph (3)*
The tribunal can authorise a member of the clinical team to be present to hear the evi- **3–117** dence of the patient contrary to the wishes of the patient (*R. (on the application of B) v South Region Mental Health Review Tribunal* [2008] EWHC 2356 (Admin); [2008] M.H.L.R. 312).

## Hearings in a party's absence
**39.**—(1) Subject to paragraph (2), if a party fails to attend a hearing the **3–118** Tribunal may proceed with the hearing if the Tribunal—
  (a)  is satisfied that the party has been notified of the hearing or that reasonable steps have been taken to notify the party of the hearing; and
  (b)  considers that it is in the interests of justice to proceed with the hearing.
  (2) The Tribunal may not proceed with a hearing in the absence of the patient unless—
  (a)  the requirements of rule 34 (medical examination of the patient) have been satisfied; and
  (b)  the Tribunal is satisfied that—
      (i) the patient has decided not to attend the hearing; or
      (ii) the patient is unable to attend the hearing for reasons of ill health.

DEFINITIONS
  party: r.1(3).                                                              **3–119**
  hearing: r.1(3).
  Tribunal: r.1(3).
  patient: r.1(3).

GENERAL NOTE
This rule could be invoked if a patient does not wish to attend a reference hearing.      **3–120**

*Paragraph (2)(a)*
Note that the requirements of r.34 can be satisfied if medically examining the patient **3–121** proves not to be "practicable".

## Power to pay allowances
**40.** The Tribunal may pay allowances in respect of travelling expenses, subsist- **3–122** ence and loss of earnings to—
  (a)  any person who attends a hearing as an applicant or a witness;
  (b)  a patient who attends a hearing otherwise than as the applicant or a witness; and
  (c)  any person (other than a legal representative) who attends as the represen- tative of an applicant.

DEFINITIONS
  Tribunal: r.1(3).                                                          **3–123**

hearing: r.1(3).
applicant: r.1(3).
legal representative: r.1(3).

CHAPTER 3

Decisions

**Decisions**
**3–124**    **41.**—(1) The Tribunal may give a decision orally at a hearing.
(2) Subject to rule 14(2) (withholding information likely to cause harm), the Tribunal must provide to each party as soon as reasonably practicable after making a decision which finally disposes of all issues in the proceedings (except a decision under Part 5)—
(a) a decision notice stating the Tribunal's decision;
(b) written reasons for the decision; and
(c) notification of any right of appeal against the decision and the time within which, and the manner in which, such right of appeal may be exercised.
(3) The documents and information referred to in paragraph (2) must—
(a) in proceedings under section 66(1)(a) of the Mental Health Act 1983, be provided at the hearing or sent within 3 working days after the hearing; and
(b) in other cases, be provided at the hearing or sent within 7 days after the hearing.
(4) The Tribunal may provide written reasons for any decision to which paragraph (2) does not apply.

DEFINITIONS
**3–125**    Tribunal: r.1(3).
hearing: r.1(3).
respondent: r.1(4).

GENERAL NOTE
**3–126**    A tribunal has its statutory duty to perform and could not avoid that by accepting a submission that it is bound to follow another tribunal's decision, even though there had been no change of circumstances. It must come to its own decision, no doubt taking into account a previous decision. There could be no res judicata (the legal principle that a matter which has been settled by a court cannot be reopened or challenged as to the matter decided) (*R. v South-West Thames Mental Health Review Tribunal Ex p. Demitri* [1997] C.O.D. 44 CA).
There is nothing to prevent the tribunal from forming a provisional view about the evidence as it unfolds as long as it considers all the evidence with an open mind and provided it is ready to amend or change its view in the light of all the evidence when necessary (*R. (on the application of B) v South Region Mental Health Review Tribunal* [2008] EWHC 2356 (Admin); [2008] M.H.L.R. 312).
An error made by a tribunal in its decision as to the legal status of the patient does not justify the High Court remitting the issue to the tribunal in judicial review proceedings if the error is not material to the decision not to discharge him (*R. (on the application of Warren) v Mental Health Review Tribunal London North and East Region* [2002] EWHC Admin 811; [2002] M.H.L.R. 146).
If a decision of a tribunal which appears to have been made without jurisdiction has not been quashed by proceedings which were properly commenced within time, the decision

must be treated as being a valid decision *(Bath and North East Somerset Council v AJC* [1999] M.H.L.R. 184).

*Paragraph (2)*
FINALLY DISPOSES.   See r.42.                                                                       **3–127**

WRITTEN REASONS FOR THE DECISION.   Excluding reasons which would be likely to cause serious harm to the patient or another (r.14(2)). The reasons must contain numbered paragraphs (Practice Statement on Form of Decisions and Neutral Citation, issued by the Senior President on October 31, 2008).

The importance of the requirement for a decision-maker to give reasons was emphasised by Sedley J. in *R. v Solihull Metropolitan Borough Council Housing Benefits Review Board Ex p. Simpson* (1993) 26 H.L.R. 370 at 377:

> "A statutory duty imposed on a named decision maker to give reasons . . . is not simply a bureaucratic chore or an opportunity for lawyers to find fault. It is, and is increasingly recognised as being, a fundamental aspect of good public administration (underpinned increasingly by law) because it focuses the decision maker's mind on exactly what it is that has to be decided, within what legal framework, and according to what relevant evidence and material. Experience shows that it will sometimes produce an opposite conclusion to that which was initially in the decision-makers mind before the rigour of formulating acceptable reasons was applied."

The following notes of caution need to be made when considering the adequacy of reasons given to justify the decision of a tribunal: (1) the decision of a tribunal "is not required to be an elaborate formalistic product of refined legal draftsmanship" *(Meek v Birmingham City Council* [1987] I.R.L.R. 250, para.8, per Sir Thomas Bingham M.R.); (2) tribunal reasons "are not intended to include a comprehensive and detailed analysis of the case, either in terms of fact or in law . . . their purpose remains what it has always been, which is to tell the parties in broad terms why they lose or, as the case may be, win. I think it would be a thousand pities if these reasons began to be subjected to a detailed analysis and appeals were to be brought based upon any such analysis. This, to my mind, is to misuse the purpose for which the reasons are given" *(UCATT v Brain* [1981] I.R.L.R. 225, 227 per Donaldson L.J.); (3); "it is probable that in understanding and applying the law in their specialised field the tribunal will have got it right . . . Their decisions should be respected unless it is quite clear that they have misdirected themselves in law" *(Secretary of State for the Home Department v AH (Sudan)* [2007] UKHL 49; [2008] 4 All E.R. 190, para.30, Baroness Hale); and (4) there is a danger of "elevating into general principles what are statements by judges made by reference to the facts and circumstances of particular cases but taken out of context" *(H v East Sussex County Council* [2009] EWCA Civ 249, para.15, per Waller L.J.).

The duty to give reasons under this provision (as it appeared in r.23 of the MHRT Rules 1983) was considered by the Court of Appeal in *R. (on the application of H) v Ashworth Hospital Authority; R. (on the application of Ashworth Hospital Authority) v Mental Health Review Tribunal for West Midlands and North West Region* [2002] EWCA Civ 923; [2002] M.H.L.R. 314. The leading judgment was given by Dyson L.J. who adopted the approach taken by the Court of Appeal in *English v Emery Reimbold & Strick Ltd* [2002] EWCA Civ 605; [2002] 3 All E.R. 385 where Lord Phillips M.R. summarised the present state of the law regarding appeals from lower to higher courts. Lord Phillips said that, putting the matter at its simplest, "justice will not be done if it is not apparent to the parties why one has won and the other lost" (para.16). A judge should:

> "provide an explanation as to why he has accepted the evidence of one expert and rejected that of another. It may be that the evidence of one or the other accorded more satisfactorily with facts found by the Judge. It may be that the explanation of one was

more inherently credible than that of the other. It may simply be that one was better qualified, or manifestly more objective, than the other. Whatever the explanation may be, it
should be apparent from the judgment" (para.20).

Dyson L.J. rejected a submission that inadequate reasons may be treated as adequate on the
ground that inadequate resources were made available to the tribunal (para.76). His
Lordship said that "it is at least arguable" that the "informed audience point" (see *R. v
Mental Health Review Tribunal Ex p. Booth,* noted below) "has less force in relation to
a tribunal decision than to a decision by a lower court in the civil justice system." This
is because, in the light of *R. v East London and City Mental Health NHS Trust Ex p.
Brandenburg* [2001] EWCA Civ 239; [2001] M.H.L.R. 36, it is essential that an approved
mental health professional who is contemplating re-sectioning a patient subsequent to a tribunal discharge "should know the facts and circumstances which a tribunal took into
account when deciding to discharge a patient, and the reasons for its decision".

In *H*, the Court of Appeal found the tribunal's reasons to be inadequate for two principal
reasons:

1. The tribunal had failed to indicate the reasoning process by which they decided to
   accept the minority medical evidence and reject the majority medical evidence.
   Dyson L.J. said, at para.80, that the following passage from the judgment of
   Henry L.J. in *Flannery v Halifax Estate Agencies Ltd* [2001] 1 W.L.R. 277 at
   381–382, is "as apt in relation to the decisions of tribunals as it is to lower courts
   generally":
   "Where there is a straightforward factual dispute whose resolution depends simply on which witness is telling the truth about events which he claims to recall, it is
   likely to be enough for the judge (having no doubt, summarised the evidence) to
   indicate simply that he believes X rather than Y; indeed there may be nothing else
   to say. But where the dispute involves something in the nature of an intellectual
   exchange, with reasons and analysis advanced on either side, the judge must
   enter into issues canvassed before him and explain why he prefers one case
   over another. This is likely to apply particularly in litigation where as here
   there is disputed expert evidence; but it is not necessarily limited to such cases."

2. The tribunal failed to give any reasons for not adjourning in order to see whether
   suitable after-care would be made available for the patient, or whether an order
   for deferred discharge would be appropriate. In this case the question of what
   after-care arrangements would be available in the community was relevant to the
   issue of whether the statutory criteria were met.

With regard to point 1, if the tribunal has accepted the evidence of the patient as to the risk
or lack of risk of her accepting medication, if discharged into the community, and implicitly
rejected the views of her responsible clinician and nurse, it is particularly important for the
tribunal to explain the basis of its decision and the reasons for its preferring one witness to
another (*R. (on the application of the Secretary of State for the Home Department) v Mental
Health Review Tribunal and CH* [2005] EWHC 746 (Admin); [2005] M.H.L.R. 199 per
Stanley Burton J. at para.35). The reasons "must be read as a whole, in a common sense
way, not as a legal treatise"; per Sullivan J. in *R. (on the application of Epsom & St
Helier NHS Trust v The Mental Health Review Tribunal* [2001] M.H.L.R. 8 at para.49.
They must be "adequate and intelligible . . . and must grapple with the important issues
raised" (*R. v Mental Health Review Tribunal Ex p. Pickering* [1986] 1 All E.R. 99 at
102 per Forbes J.). It is therefore not sufficient for the tribunal's reasons merely to (1) recite
the evidence or submissions (*L v Devon County Council* [2001] EWHC 958 (Admin)); or
(2) recite the statutory criteria for discharge (*Bone v Mental Health Review Tribunal* [1985]
3 All E.R. 330).

*Bone* was referred to in the judgment of Mann J. in *R. v Mental Health Review Tribunal Ex p. Clatworthy* [1985] 3 All E.R. 699 at 704, where his Lordship quashed the decision of a tribunal because the reasons given by it did not enable the applicant to know why the case advanced in detail on his behalf by his responsible [clinician] and an independent psychiatrist had not been accepted. His Lordship said that:

> "where a tribunal desires to proceed on the basis of some point which has not been put before it and which on the face of the matter is not in dispute, it is in my view in the highest degree desirable that the person whose case is being considered by the tribunal should be alerted to the possibility. . . . Were it to be the case . . . that this tribunal proceeded on some basis unknown to others but known to themselves, then I would have regarded that decision as flawed by reference to [the principle of natural justice which requires that a party should know the case against him.]"

The approach that the tribunal should adopt with regard to expert evidence was considered by the Upper Tribunal in *Hampshire County Council v JP* [2009] UKUT 239 (AAC), para.37:

> "The fact that an expert has given an opinion is not in itself an adequate reason for a tribunal to adopt that opinion unless the opinion is unchallenged. In the event of a conflict of opinions, it is necessary for a tribunal to give a reason for preferring one opinion rather than the other. Where an opinion is fully reasoned, a tribunal accepting the opinion may be taken to have adopted the reasoning and in those cases merely referring to the opinion may be sufficient provided that the expert has given adequate reasons for disagreeing with any opposing view."

In *RH v South London and Maudsley NHS Foundation Trust* [2010] UKHT 32 (AAC), para.17, Judge Rowland said that where the tribunal merely disagreed with the conclusion to be drawn from the professional assessments when it came to considering whether a restriction order should cease to have effect, it was difficult to "give reasons beyond those required to show that the tribunal has directed itself correctly as to the law and to show to what matters the tribunal has had regard".

Where a tribunal gives reasons for its decision "one must somehow be able to read from the reasons the issue to which the reasons are directed": see *R. v Mental Health Review Tribunal Ex p. Pickering,* above where Forbes J. said, that it is "essential" for the tribunal to distinguish between "the diagnostic question" of whether the patient is still suffering from a mental disorder and "the policy question" of whether it is safe to discharge him. There is no need for the tribunal to state why alternatives to rejecting a patient's application for discharge were rejected when it gives reasons for its decision (*R. v Mental Health Review Tribunal for the South Thames Region Ex p. Smith* [1999] C.O.D. 148, paras 104 and 101).

In *R. v Mental Health Review Tribunal Ex p. Booth* [1998] C.O.D. 203, Laws J. said:

> "It has to be remembered . . . that the quality of reasons required of a Mental Health Review Tribunal has to be looked at in light of the fact that the decision is addressed to an informed audience. Those who receive it and who are concerned with it will be familiar with the essential documents in the case . . . They will be familiar with what has been said at the tribunal by way of oral evidence and what the issues there were which had been argued. Given that necessary familiarity, if there was a case in which it could still be said that the parties simply were not told why the tribunal arrived at the decision it did, then no doubt there would be a sound basis for a legal challenge."

This passage must be read subject to the caveat expressed by Dyson L.J. in *R. (on the Application of H) v Ashworth Hospital Authority; R. (on the application of Ashworth*

*Hospital Authority) v Mental Health Review Tribunal for West Midlands and North West Region,* above.

A "court is entitled to proceed on the basis that specialist Tribunals know and understand the law which governs their particular jurisdiction and that this court is entitled to assume that they have correctly understood and applied the relevant law and the facts they have found, unless of course there is something to be found in the decision of the tribunal to demonstrate that it would be inappropriate or unsafe to make that assumption" (*R. (on the application of W) v Mental Health Review* [2004] EWHC 3266 (Admin); [2005] M.H.L.R. 134 at para.18 per Munby J.).

If the tribunal provides reasons that are considered to be inadequate, the review procedure should be invoked: see rr.45, 47(1) and 49.

*Paragraph (3)(b)*
3–128   7 DAYS.   Not 7 working days.

*Paragraph (4)*
3–129   It is submitted that the overriding objective (r.2) requires the tribunal to provide reasons for all disputed decisions.

### Provisional decisions
3–130   **42.** For the purposes of this Part and Parts 1, 2 and 5, a decision with recommendations under section 72(3)(a) or (3A)(a) of the Mental Health Act 1983 or a deferred direction for conditional discharge under section 73(7) of that Act is a decision which disposes of the proceedings.

DEFINITION
3–131   dispose of proceedings: r.1(3).

## PART 5

CORRECTING, SETTING ASIDE, REVIEWING AND APPEALING TRIBUNAL DECISIONS

### Interpretation
3–132   **43.** In this Part—
"appeal" means the exercise of a right of appeal on a point of law under section 11 of the 2007 Act; and
"review" means the review of a decision by the Tribunal under section 9 of the 2007 Act.

DEFINITION
3–133   Tribunal: r.1(3).

### Clerical mistakes and accidental slips or omissions
3–134   **44.** The Tribunal may at any time correct any clerical mistake or other accidental slip or omission in a decision, direction or any document produced by it, by—
(a) sending notification of the amended decision or direction, or a copy of the amended document, to all parties; and
(b) making any necessary amendment to any information published in relation to the decision, direction or document.

DEFINITIONS
3–135   Tribunal: r.1(3).

document: r.1(3).
party: r.1(3).

## Setting aside a decision which disposes of proceedings

**45.**—(1) The Tribunal may set aside a decision which disposes of proceedings, **3–136**
or part of such a decision, and re-make the decision or the relevant part of it, if—

(a) the Tribunal considers that it is in the interests of justice to do so; and
(b) one or more of the conditions in paragraph (2) are satisfied.

(2) The conditions are—

(a) a document relating to the proceedings was not sent to, or was not received
at an appropriate time by, a party or a party's representative;
(b) a document relating to the proceedings was not sent to the Tribunal at an
appropriate time;
(c) a party, or a party's representative, was not present at a hearing related to the
proceedings; or
(d) there has been some other procedural irregularity in the proceedings.

(3) A party applying for a decision, or part of a decision, to be set aside under paragraph (1) must make a written application to the Tribunal so that it is received no
later than 28 days after the date on which the Tribunal sent notice of the decision
to the party.

DEFINITIONS
Tribunal: r.1(3). **3–137**
dispose of proceedings: r.1(3).
document: r.1(3).
party: r.1(3).
hearing: r.1(3).

GENERAL NOTE
This rule enables the tribunal to set aside a decision, or part of a decision, which disposes **3–138**
of proceedings (see r.42) and to remake the decision or the relevant part of it on the ground
of procedural irregularity if such action is in the interests of justice. An application form for
this purpose (Form P9), together with a guidance note, can be downloaded form the tribunal's website (*www.mhrt.org.uk*) under "Forms and Guidance" (accessed July 6, 2010).

A decision by the tribunal to set aside a decision cannot be appealed to the Upper
Tribunal (Tribunals, Courts and Enforcement Act 2007, s.11(1),(5)(d)(iii)).

*Paragraph (3)*
28 Days. See rr.12 and 13 for the calculation of time and methods of service. There is **3–139**
provision for this time limit to be extended (r.5(3)(a)).

## Application for permission to appeal

**46.**—(1) A person seeking permission to appeal must make a written appli- **3–140**
cation to the Tribunal for permission to appeal.

(2) An application under paragraph (1) must be sent or delivered to the Tribunal
so that it is received no later than 28 days after the latest of the dates that the
Tribunal sends to the person making the application—

(a) written reasons for the decision;
(b) notification of amended reasons for, or correction of, the decision following
a review; or
(c) notification that an application for the decision to be set aside has been
unsuccessful.

(3) The date in paragraph (2)(c) applies only if the application for the decision to be set aside was made within the time stipulated in rule 45 (setting aside a decision which disposes of proceedings) or any extension of that time granted by the Tribunal.

(4) If the person seeking permission to appeal sends or delivers the application to the Tribunal later than the time required by paragraph (2) or by any extension of time under rule 5(3)(a) (power to extend time)—

    (a)  the application must include a request for an extension of time and the reason why the application was not provided in time; and

    (b)  unless the Tribunal extends time for the application under rule 5(3)(a) (power to extend time) the Tribunal must not admit the application.

(5) An application under paragraph (1) must—

    (a)  identify the decision of the Tribunal to which it relates;

    (b)  identify the alleged error or errors of law in the decision; and

    (c)  state the result the party making the application is seeking.

DEFINITIONS

**3–141**    appeal: r.43.
Tribunal: r.1(3).
review: r.43.
dispose of proceedings: r.43.
party: r.1(3).

GENERAL NOTE

**3–142**    Under s.11 of the 2007 Act, an appeal lies to the Upper Tribunal "on any point of law arising from a decision made by the First-tier Tribunal". The scope of this rule is not confined to appeals against the tribunal's decision which disposes of proceedings.

An application form for permission to appeal (Form P10), together with a guidance note, can be downloaded form the tribunal's website (*www.mhrt.org.uk*) under "Forms and Guidance" (accessed July 6, 2010). On receiving the application, the tribunal must first consider whether to review the decision in accordance with r.49 (r.47(1)). If permission to appeal is refused, reasons must be given (r.47(4)).

There is nothing unfair in an initial application for permission to appeal being made to the judge who made the decision being challenged: see *AA v Cheshire and Wirral Partnership NHS Foundation Trust* [2009] UKUT 195 (AAC); [2009] M.H.L.R. 308, where Judge Rowland said at para.27:

"The advantage to a superior court or tribunal of having this kind of procedure is that it gives the judge whose decision is being challenged, who will have the relevant issues in mind, an opportunity to comment on the grounds of appeal and indicate whether he or she thinks there is anything in them."

An example of how a combination of this rule and r.49 can provide a party with speedy redress is given in the Annual Report of the Senior President of Tribunals, *Tribunals Transformed*, February 2010, para.52:

"Application by restricted patient, convicted of arson with intent, heard by the Restricted Patient Panel on 18 November 2008 when the patient was conditionally discharged into the community. The discharge was deferred. On 22 December, the Secretary of State for Justice applied under rule 46 for permission to appeal on the grounds that the condition as to residence in the community amounted to a continuation of deprivation of liberty and was, therefore, unlawful. It was also claimed that the Tribunal had failed to give adequate and intelligible reasons. On 13 January 2009, the Tribunal's decision was set aside on the grounds as claimed and remitted for hearing before a freshly constituted Tribunal. Case reheard on 4 March 2009 following updated hospital reports and further comments from the Secretary of State. Patient not discharged."

Encouragement to respondents, especially public authority respondents, to take part in proceedings before the Upper Tribunal was given by Judge Rowland in *RH v South London and Maudsley NHS Foundation Trust* [2010] UKHT 32 (AAC) at para.29 et seq.

*Paragraph (2)*
28 DAYS.  See rr.2 and 13 for the calculation of time and methods of service. There is **3–143** provision for this time limit to be extended (r.5(3)(a)).

## Tribunal's consideration of application for permission to appeal
**47.**—(1) On receiving an application for permission to appeal the Tribunal **3–144** must first consider, taking into account the overriding objective in rule 2, whether to review the decision in accordance with rule 49 (review of a decision).

(2) If the Tribunal decides not to review the decision, or reviews the decision and decides to take no action in relation to the decision, or part of it, the Tribunal must consider whether to give permission to appeal in relation to the decision or that part of it.

(3) The Tribunal must send a record of its decision to the parties as soon as practicable.

(4) If the Tribunal refuses permission to appeal it must send with the record of its decision—

(a) a statement of its reasons for such refusal; and

(b) notification of the right to make an application to the Upper Tribunal for permission to appeal and the time within which, and the method by which, such application must be made.

(5) The Tribunal may give permission to appeal on limited grounds, but must comply with paragraph (4) in relation to any grounds on which it has refused permission.

DEFINITIONS
    appeal: r.43.                                      **3–145**
    Tribunal: r.1(3).
    party: r.1(3).

GENERAL NOTE
In *KF v Birmingham and Solihull Mental Health NHS Foundation Trust* [2010] UKUT **3–146** 185 (AAC), para.19, the Upper Tribunal accepted the following analysis of the relevant legislative provisions that had been prepared by counsel:

"On receipt of an application for permission to appeal, the First-tier Tribunal has a *discretion* as to whether to undertake a review (r.47(1)). If there is no review, the First-tier Tribunal has a *duty* to consider whether to give permission to appeal but a *discretion* as to whether or not to grant permission (r.47(2)). If permission is refused and the application is renewed before the Upper Tribunal, the Upper Tribunal also has a *discretion* as to whether to give permission (Tribunal Procedure (Upper Tribunal) Rules 2008, SI 2008/2698, r.21(2)). If permission is granted and the Upper Tribunal finds an error of law, it has a *discretion* as to whether to set aside the First-tier Tribunal decision (s.12(2)(a) of the 2007 Act), but if that tribunal decision is set aside, then the Upper Tribunal has a *duty* either to re-make the decision or to remit it to the First-tier Tribunal for a re-hearing (s.12(2)(b) of the 2007 Act)."

In this case, the UT said, at para.41, that there may be circumstances in which it is appropriate to grant either a review or permission to appeal notwithstanding the fact that the patient has been discharged:

"In many cases where the patient has since been released, there will be no individual or wider public interest in continuing proceedings, even where the decision of the First-tier Tribunal under challenge may well be suspect. To that extent we would agree that there may well be a presumption in practice against granting either a review or permission to appeal or against setting aside on appeal in such cases. However, we do not accept that it will never be appropriate to exercise such a procedural discretion in the patient's favour where he or she has already been released. We recognise that these are cases involving fundamental issues about the liberty of the subject. There may well be circumstances in which it remains appropriate for there to be further scrutiny of the initial tribunal decision, notwithstanding the individual's subsequent discharge. There may be a danger that a future decision-maker may give inappropriate weight to a flawed decision. Moreover, there may be an urgent need for the legal principles at stake to be clarified."

## Application for review in special educational needs cases

3–147    **48.** [*Applies to special educational needs cases*]

## Review of a decision

3–148    **49.**—(1) The Tribunal may only undertake a review of a decision—

    (a)  pursuant to rule 47(1) (review on an application for permission to appeal) if it is satisfied that there was an error of law in the decision; or

    (b)  pursuant to rule 48 (application for review in special educational needs cases).

(2) The Tribunal must notify the parties in writing of the outcome of any review, and of any right of appeal in relation to the outcome.

(3) If the Tribunal takes any action in relation to a decision following a review without first giving every party an opportunity to make representations, the notice under paragraph (2) must state that any party that did not have an opportunity to make representations may apply for such action to be set aside and for the decision to be reviewed again.

DEFINITIONS

3–149    Tribunal: r.1(3).
review: r.43.
appeal: r.43.
party: r.1(3).

GENERAL NOTE

3–150    This power is intended to capture decisions that are clearly wrong in that there is an error of law in the decision, so avoiding the need for an appeal. The tribunal also has the power to review a decision on its own initiative under s.9(2)(a) of the 2007 Act. The power of the tribunal on undertaking a review are set out in s.9(4) to (6) of the Tribunals, Courts and Enforcement Act 2007:

"(4) Where the First-tier Tribunal has under subsection (1) reviewed a decision, the First-tier Tribunal may in the light of the review do any of the following—

(a) correct accidental errors in the decision or in a record of the decision;

(b) amend reasons given for the decision;

(c) set the decision aside.

(5) Where under subsection (4)(c) the First-tier Tribunal sets a decision aside, the First-tier Tribunal must either—

(a) re-decide the matter concerned, or
(b) refer that matter to the Upper Tribunal.
(6) Where a matter is referred to the Upper Tribunal under subsection (5)(b), the Upper Tribunal must re-decide the matter."

A decision by the tribunal either to review, or not to review a decision cannot be appealed to the Upper Tribunal (s.11(1),(5)(d)(i) of the 2007 Act).

In *R (RB) v First-tier Tribunal (Review)* [2010] UKUT 160 (AAC), the Upper Tribunal held that:

1. This Rule cannot be used to usurp the Upper Tribunal's function of determining appeals on contentious points of law. The power to set aside a decision should only be done in clear cases (para.24). It should be possible to give brief reasons for the decision; it will be seldom be necessary to set out the facts or the background legislation or to cite at length from authorities (para.32).

2. Even if there is a clear error of law, the tribunal may decide to give permission to appeal if it would be helpful to have an authoritative decision of the Upper Tribunal on the point (para.27).

3. Paragraph (3) of this Rule enables the First-tier Tribunal to take a robust approach when it first receives an application for permission to appeal because it enables it to take a decision without calling for representations by the other side, on the basis that if the other side objects there can be an application to set aside. However, in many cases it will be preferable to invite representations before concluding that an original decision should be set aside (para.26).

4. There may be occasions when it is desirable for a case to be reconsidered by the First-tier Tribunal so that further findings may be made even if it is likely to go to the Upper Tribunal eventually (para.28).

In general, unless there is good reason why not, if the tribunal is asked to review a tribunal decision on a s.2 application where the patient has been subsequently detained under s.3, and concludes that it involves an error of law, then the appropriate way forward is for the tribunal to set aside the substantive decision and to re-list the case for hearing together with any existing s.3 application. The patient has the right to apply to withdraw that application under r.17. This approach has a number of practical ramifications. Some of the issues that may arise in this regard are as follows: (i) time limits; (ii) case management and consolidation; (iii) withdrawal; and (iv) provision of reports (*KF v Birmingham and Solihull Mental Health NHS Foundation Trust* [2010] UKUT 185 (AAC), para.30).

When deciding whether to set aside a decision, it is relevant to consider whether such action could be of practical benefit to any of the parties. This is unlikely to be this case where a further hearing was due to take place which would consider the up-to-date position and would proceed on the basis that the previous decision would be erroneous in law (*BB v South London and Maudsley NHS Trust* [2009] UKUT 157 (AAC); [2009] M.H.L.R. 302).

There is nothing unfair in a review being undertaken by the judge who made the decision being challenged (*AA v Cheshire and Wirral Partnership NHS Foundation Trust* [2009] UKUT 195 (AAC); [2009] M.H.L.R. 308).

A review decision cannot be used to criticise a decision that is under appeal (*RM v St Andrew's Healthcare* [2010] UKUT 119 (AAC), para.5).

**Power to treat an application as a different type of application**

3–151    **50.** The Tribunal may treat an application for a decision to be corrected, set aside or reviewed, or for permission to appeal against a decision, as an application for any other one of those things.

DEFINITIONS
3–152    Tribunal: r.1(3).
review: r.43.
appeal: r.43.

3–153                    SCHEDULE        Rules 20(1)(a) and 21(1)(a)

[*The Schedule does not apply to mental health cases*]

3–154                    **PRACTICE DIRECTION**
**FIRST-TIER TRIBUNAL**
**HEALTH EDUCATION AND SOCIAL CARE CHAMBER**
**MENTAL HEALTH CASES**

GENERAL NOTE
    The Tribunal Service has published *Reports for Mental Health Tribunals* (2010) which provides guidance, based on this Practice Direction, for those who have to prepare reports for the tribunal. It can be accessed on the website of the Tribunal Service (*www.mhrt.org*).
    1. This Practice Direction applies to a "mental health case" as defined in Rule 1(3) the Tribunal Procedure (First-tier Tribunal) (Health, Education and Social Care Chamber) Rules 2008 ("the 2008 Rules").
    2. For the purposes of this Practice Direction, a patient is an "in-patient" if at the time of the application or referral he is receiving in-patient treatment for mental disorder, even if it is being given informally or under an application, order or direction other than that to which the Tribunal application or reference relates.

**CONTENTS OF STATEMENTS FROM THE RESPONSIBLE AUTHORITY AND SECRETARY OF STATE**
3–155    3. The responsible authority must send a statement to the Tribunal and, in the case of a restricted patient other than a conditionally discharged patient, to the Secretary of State, so that it is received by the Tribunal as soon as is practicable and in any event within three weeks after the responsible authority received a copy of the application or reference.
    4. If the patient is a conditionally discharged patient, the Secretary of State must send or deliver a statement to the Tribunal so that it is received by the Tribunal as soon as practicable, and in any event within 6 weeks after the Secretary of State received a copy of the application or a request from the Tribunal.
    5. If the patient is neither a conditionally discharged patient, nor a community patient subject to supervised community treatment, nor a patient subject (or to be subject) to after-care under supervision, the statement to the Tribunal must contain the information, documents and reports specified in paragraphs 8(a) to (e) below.
    6. If the patient is a conditionally discharged patient, the statement to the Tribunal must, where possible, contain the reports specified in paragraphs 8(c) and (d) below.
    7. If the patient is a community patient subject to supervised community treatment the statement to the Tribunal must contain the reports specified in paragraph 8(f) below.
    8. The information, documents and reports referred to above are:

a.  the information about the patient set out at Section B below;

b.  the documents concerning the patient set out at Section C below;

   c.  the clinician's report set out at Section D below;

   d.  the social circumstances report set out at Section E below;

   e.  if the patient is an in-patient, the nursing report set out at Section F below;

   f.  the reports set out in Section H below.

9. Where the patient is a restricted patient, the Secretary of State must send to the Tribunal as soon as practicable and in any event within 3 weeks after the Secretary of State received the responsible authority's statement (within 2 weeks in proceedings under section 75(1) of the Mental Health Act 1983), a statement containing the information set out at Section G below.

10. If the patient is subject (or to be subject) to after-care under supervision, the statement must include the information, documents and reports specified in the Annex to this Practice Direction.

## SECTION B. INFORMATION ABOUT THE PATIENT

11. The statement provided to the Tribunal must, in so far as it is within the knowledge of **3–156** the responsible authority, include the following information:

   a.  the patient's full name (and any alternative names used in his patient records);

   b.  the patient's date of birth, age and usual place of residence;

   c.  the patient's first language and, if it is not English, whether an interpreter is required, and if so in which language;

   d.  if the patient is deaf whether the patient will require the services of a British Sign Language interpreter, or a Relay Interpreter;

   e.  the date of admission or transfer of the patient to the hospital in which the patient is detained or liable to be detained, or of the reception of the patient into guardianship, together with details of the application, order or direction that constitutes the original authority for the detention or guardianship of the patient, including the Act of Parliament and the section of that Act by reference to which detention was authorised and details of any subsequent renewal of or change in the authority for detention;

   f.  details as applicable of the hospital at which the patient is detained or liable to be detained, or the place where the patient is living if received into guardianship;

   g.  details of any transfers under section 19 or section 123 of the Mental Health Act 1983 since the application, order or direction was made;

   h.  where the patient is detained or liable to be detained in an independent hospital, details of any NHS body that funds or will fund the placement;

   i.  where relevant, the name and address of the local social services authority and NHS body having the duty under section 117 of the Mental Health Act 1983 to provide after-care services for the patient (or which would have it were the patient to leave hospital);

   j.  the name of the patient's responsible clinician and the period which the patient has spent under the care of that clinician;

   k.  the name of any care co-ordinator appointed for the patient;

   l.  except in the case of a restricted patient, the name and address of the patient's nearest relative or of the person exercising that function, and whether the patient has requested that this person is not consulted or kept informed about their care or treatment;

m. the name and address of any person who plays a significant part in the care of the patient but who is not professionally concerned with it;

n. where the patient is subject to the guardianship of a private guardian, the name and address of that guardian;

o. the name and address of any deputy or attorney appointed under the Mental Capacity Act 2005;

p. details of any registered lasting power of attorney made by the patient that confers authority to make decisions about his personal welfare, and the donee(s) appointed by him;

q. details of any registered lasting or enduring power of attorney made by the patient that confers authority to make decisions about his property and affairs, and the donee(s) appointed by him; and

r. details of any existing advance decisions to refuse treatment for mental disorder made by the patient.

## SECTION C. DOCUMENTS CONCERNING THE PATIENT

**3–157** 12. If the Tribunal so directs, copies of the following documents must be included in the statement provided to the Tribunal if they are within the possession of the responsible authority (otherwise they must be made available to the Tribunal if requested at any other time by the Tribunal):

a. the application, order or direction that constitutes the original authority for the patient's detention or guardianship under the Mental Health Act 1983, together with all supporting recommendations, reports and records made in relation to it under the Mental Health (Hospital, Guardianship and Treatment) Regulations 2008;

b. a copy of every Tribunal decision, and the reasons given, since the application, order or direction being reviewed was made or accepted; and

c. where the patient is liable to be detained for treatment under section 3 of the Mental Health Act 1983, a copy of any application for admission for assessment that was in force immediately prior to the making of the section 3 application.

## SECTION D. CLINICIAN's REPORT

**3–158** 13. The statement provided to the Tribunal must include an up-to-date clinical report prepared for the Tribunal.

14. Unless it is not reasonably practicable, the report must be written or countersigned by the patient's responsible clinician;

15. This report must describe the patient's relevant medical history, to include:

a. full details of the patient's mental state, behaviour and treatment for mental disorder;

b. in so far as it is within the knowledge of the person writing the report a statement as to whether the patient has ever neglected or harmed himself, or has ever harmed other persons or threatened them with harm, at a time when he was mentally disordered, together with details of any neglect, harm or threats of harm;

c. an assessment of the extent to which the patient or other persons would be likely to be at risk if the patient is discharged by the Tribunal, and how any such risks could best be managed;

d. an assessment of the patient's strengths and any other positive factors that the Tribunal should be aware of in coming to a view on whether he should be discharged; and

e. if appropriate, the reasons why the patient might be treated in the community without continued detention in hospital, but should remain subject to recall on supervised community treatment.

## SECTION E. SOCIAL CIRCUMSTANCES REPORT

16. The statement provided to the Tribunal must, include an up-to-date social circum- **3–159** stances report prepared for the Tribunal.

17. This report must include the following information:

a. the patient's home and family circumstances;

b. in so far as it is practicable, and except in restricted cases, a summary of the views of the patient's nearest relative, unless (having consulted the patient) the person compiling the report thinks it would be inappropriate to consult the nearest relative;

c. in so far as it is practicable, the views of any person who plays a substantial part in the care of the patient but is not professionally concerned with it;

d. the views of the patient, including his concerns, hopes and beliefs in relation to the Tribunal proceedings and their outcome;

e. the opportunities for employment and the housing facilities available to the patient;

f. what (if any) community support is or will be made available to the patient and its effectiveness, if the patient is discharged from hospital;

g. the patient's financial circumstances (including his entitlement to benefits);

h. an assessment of the patient's strengths and any other positive factors that the Tribunal should be aware of in coming to a view on whether he should be discharged; and

i. an assessment of the extent to which the patient or other persons would be likely to be at risk if the patient is discharged by the Tribunal, and how any such risks could best be managed.

GENERAL NOTE

Guidance on completing a social circumstances report which complies with section E of **3–160** this Practice Direction is provided by C. Curran et al in "Social Circumstances Reports for Mental Health Tribunals", Legal Action, June 2010, 30–32 and July 2010, 30–32.

## SECTION F. IN-PATIENT NURSING REPORT

18. This report must include in relation to the patient's current in-patient episode, full **3–161** details of the following:

a. the patient's understanding of and willingness to accept the current treatment for mental disorder provided or offered;

b. the level of observation to which the patient is subject;

c. any occasions on which the patient has been secluded or restrained, including the reasons why seclusion or restraint was considered to be necessary;

d. any occasions on which the patient has been absent without leave whilst liable to be detained, or occasions when he has failed to return when required, after being granted leave of absence; and

e. any incidents where the patient has harmed himself or others, or has threatened other persons with violence.

19. A copy of the patient's current nursing plan must be appended to the report.

GENERAL NOTE

**3–162**    The following advice to Panels from Regional Tribunal Judges was published on February 29, 2009:

**"1. Does the actual author of the nursing report have to attend the hearing or is another health professional acceptable?**
Yes if at all possible, though we must recognize that the shift patterns of nurses may at times render this impractical. Where for a good reason it is not possible for the report author to attend, to avoid delay another nurse should attend, and speak to the report.

**2. What questions should normally be posed to nurses, and what questions normally should not?**
As a general rule, questions should be confined to the issues contained in the report i.e. patient's attitude to treatment, current observation levels, details of any seclusion or restraint imposed upon patient, any abuse of leave, and any violent incidents. The nurse should also be encouraged to relate the positive as well as any negative feature of patient's progress on the ward. Although at times it might be helpful and necessary to move outside the confines of the issues in the report, questions should always be confined to the nursing aspects of the patient's treatment. It is not appropriate normally for nurses to be involved in diagnostic matters."

### SECTION G. THE SECRETARY OF STATE's STATEMENT (RESTRICTED PATIENTS ONLY)

**3–163**    20. In cases involving a restricted patient, the Secretary of State must provide a statement to the Tribunal containing any written comments he wishes to make upon the statement he has received from the responsible authority, together with any further information relevant to the application as may be available to him.

21. In addition, the Secretary of State must provide to the Tribunal the following further information:

   a. a summary of the offence or alleged offence that resulted in the patient being detained in hospital subject to a restriction order or, in the case of a patient subject to a restriction or limitation direction, that resulted in him being remanded in custody, kept in custody or sentenced to imprisonment;

   b. a record of any other criminal convictions or findings recorded against the patient;

   c. full details of the history of the patient's liability to detention under the Mental Health Act 1983 since the restrictions were imposed.

### SECTION H. PATIENTS RECEIVING SUPERVISED COMMUNITY TREATMENT (SCT)

**Clinical Reports**

**3–164**    22. The statement provided to the Tribunal must include an up-to-date clinical report prepared for the Tribunal.

23. Unless it is not reasonably practicable to do so, the report must be written or countersigned by the patient's responsible clinician.

24. This report must include:

   a. details of the original authority for the patient's supervised community treatment under the Mental Health Act 1983;

   b. the name of the patient's responsible clinician and the length of time the patient has been under their care;

   c. full details of the patient's mental state, behaviour and treatment for mental disorder, and relevant medical history;

d. in so far as it is within the knowledge of the person writing the report, a statement as to whether the patient has ever neglected or harmed himself, or has ever harmed other persons or threatened them with harm, at a time when he was mentally disordered, together with details of any neglect, harm or threats of harm;

e. an assessment of the extent to which the patient or other persons would be likely to be at risk if the patient is discharged by the Tribunal, and how any such risks could best be managed;

f. an assessment of the patient's strengths and any other positive factors that the Tribunal should be aware of in coming to a view on whether he should be discharged;

g. the reasons why the patient can be treated as a community patient without continued detention in hospital, and why it is necessary that the responsible clinician should be able to exercise the power under section 17E(1) of the Mental Health Act 1983 to recall the patient to hospital; and

h. details of any specific conditions in force regarding the patient under section 17B of the Mental Health Act 1983.

**Social Circumstances Report**

25. The statement provided to the Tribunal must include an up-to-date social circum- **3–165** stances report prepared for the Tribunal.

26. This report must include the following information:

a. the patient's home and family circumstances;

b. in so far as it is practicable a summary of the views of the patient's nearest relative, unless (having consulted the patient) the person compiling the report thinks it would be inappropriate to consult the nearest relative;

c. the views of any person who plays a significant part in the care of the patient but is not professionally concerned with it;

d. the views of the patient, including his concerns, hopes and beliefs in relation to the Tribunal;

e. the opportunities for employment, or for occupation and the housing facilities available to the patient;

f. the effectiveness of the community support available to the patient; or the likely effectiveness of the community support which would be available to the patient if discharged from supervised community treatment;

g. details of the patient's financial circumstances (including his entitlement to benefits);

h. an assessment of the patient's strengths and any other positive factors that the Tribunal should be aware of in coming to a view on whether he should be discharged;

i. an account of the patient's progress while a community patient, and any conditions or requirements to which he is subject under the community treatment order, and details of any behaviour that has put him or others at risk of harm; and

j. an assessment of the extent to which the patient or other persons would be likely to be at risk if the patient remains a community patient.

**ANNEX**

**PATIENTS WHO ARE, OR WILL BE, SUBJECT TO AFTER-CARE UNDER SUPERVISION**

**3–166** 27. The statement provided to the Tribunal must include;

  a. the details of the after-care services being (or to be) provided under section 117 of the Mental Health Act 1983;

  b. details of any requirements imposed (or to be imposed) on the patient under section 25D of the Mental Health Act 1983;

  c. the information about the patient specified in Section I below;

  d. the documents concerning the patient specified in Section J below;

  e. the reports specified in Section K below.

**SECTION I. INFORMATION ABOUT THE PATIENT**

**3–167** 28. The statement provided to the Tribunal must include, in so far as it is within the knowledge of the responsible authority, the following information;

  a. the patient's full name, date of birth, age and address;

  b. the date of the acceptance of the supervision application in respect of the patient;

  c. any reclassification of the form of mental disorder from which the patient is recorded as suffering in the supervision application reported in accordance with section 25F(1) of the Mental Health Act 1983;

  d. the name and address of the person who is (or is to be) the patient's responsible clinician and the period (if any) during which he has been in charge of the patient's medical treatment;

  e. the name and address of the person who is (or is to be) the patient's supervisor;

  f. where a registered medical practitioner other than the patient's responsible clinician is or has recently been largely concerned in the treatment of the patient, details of the name and address of that practitioner and the period which the patient has spent under his care;

  g. the name and address of any place where the patient (if he has been discharged) is receiving medical treatment;

  h. the name and address of the hospital where the patient was detained or liable to be detained when the supervision application was made;

  i. the dates of any previous tribunal hearings in relation to the patient since he became subject to after-care under supervision, the decisions reached at such hearings and the reasons given;

  j. details of any proceedings in the Court of Protection and of any receivership order made in respect of the patient;

  k. the name and address of the patient's nearest relative or of any other person who is exercising that function;

  l. the name and address of any other person who takes a close interest in the patient.

**SECTION J. DOCUMENTS CONCERNING THE PATIENT**

**3–168** 29. Copies of the following documents must be made available to the Tribunal if they are within the possession of the responsible authority;

a. the original supervision application;

b. any report furnished under section 25G(3)(b) of the Mental Health Act 1983 in relation to renewal of the supervision application;

c. any record of modification of the after-care services provided.

## SECTION K. REPORTS

### Clinical report

30. The statement provided to the Tribunal must include an up-to-date clinician report **3–169** prepared for the Tribunal.

31. Unless it is not reasonable practicable, the report must be written or countersigned by the patients responsible clinician.

32. This report must describe the patient's relevant medical history and contain a full report on the patient's mental condition.

### Supervisor's Report

33. Where the patient is subject to after-care under supervision the statement provided to **3–170** the Tribunal must include an up-to-date report prepared for the Tribunal by the patient's supervisor.

34. This report must include the following information:

a. the patient's home and family circumstances, including the attitude of the patient's nearest relative or the person so acting and the attitude of any person who plays a substantial part in the care of the patient but is not professionally concerned with any of the after-care services provided to the patient;

b. his progress in the community whilst subject to after-care under supervision including an assessment of the effectiveness of that supervision.

### Social Circumstances Report

35. Where the patient has not yet left hospital the statement provided to the Tribunal must **3–171** include an up-to-date social circumstances report prepared for the Tribunal.

36. This report must include the following information: **3–172**

a. the patient's home and family circumstances, including the attitude of the patient's nearest relative or the person so acting;

b. the opportunities for employment or occupation and the housing facilities which would be available to the patient upon his discharge from hospital;

c. the availability of community support and relevant medical facilities;

d. the financial circumstances of the patient.

37. This Practice Direction is made by the Senior President of tribunals with the agreement of the Lord Chancellor. It is made in the exercise of powers conferred by the Tribunals, Courts and Enforcement Act 2007.

**LORD JUSTICE CARNWATH**
**SENIOR PRESIDENT OF TRIBUNALS**
**30 October 2008**

**3–173**

# PRACTICE DIRECTION
## FIRST TIER AND UPPER TRIBUNAL
### CHILD, VULNERABLE ADULT AND SENSITIVE WITNESSES

1. In this Practice Direction:

 a. "child" means a person who has not attained the age of 18;

 b. "vulnerable adult" has the same meaning as in the Safeguarding Vulnerable Groups Act 2006;

 c. "sensitive witness" means an adult witness where the quality of evidence given by the witness is likely to be diminished by reason of fear or distress on the part of the witness in connection with giving evidence in the case.

## CIRCUMSTANCES UNDER WHICH A CHILD, VULNERABLE ADULT OR SENSITVE WITNESS MAY GIVE EVIDENCE

**3–174** 2. A child, vulnerable adult or sensitive witness will only be required to attend as a witness and give evidence at a hearing where the Tribunal determines that the evidence is necessary to enable the fair hearing of the case and their welfare would not be prejudiced by doing so.

3. In determining whether it is necessary for a child, vulnerable adult or sensitive witness to give evidence to enable the fair hearing of a case the Tribunal should have regard to all the available evidence and any representations made by the parties.

4. In determining whether the welfare of the child, vulnerable adult or sensitive witness would be prejudiced it may be appropriate for the Tribunal to invite submissions from interested persons, such as a child's parents.

5. The Tribunal may decline to issue a witness summons under the Tribunal Procedure Rules or to permit a child, vulnerable adult or sensitive witness to give evidence where it is satisfied that the evidence is not necessary to enable the fair hearing of the case and must decline to do so where the witness's welfare would be prejudiced by them giving evidence.

## MANNER IN WHICH EVIDENCE IS GIVEN

**3–175** 6. The Tribunal must consider how to facilitate the giving of any evidence by a child, vulnerable adult or sensitive witness.

7. It may be appropriate for the Tribunal to direct that the evidence should be given by telephone, video link or other means directed by the Tribunal, or to direct that a person be appointed for the purpose of the hearing who has the appropriate skills or experience in facilitating the giving of evidence by a child, vulnerable adult or sensitive witness.

8. This Practice Direction is made by the Senior President of Tribunals with the agreement of the Lord Chancellor. It is made in the exercise of powers conferred by the Tribunals, Courts and Enforcement Act 2007.

**LORD JUSTICE CARNWATH**
**SENIOR PRESIDENT OF TRIBUNALS**
**30 October 2008**

# PART 4

## GOVERNMENT GUIDANCE

## CODE OF PRACTICE MENTAL HEALTH ACT 1983

### PUBLISHED 2008, PURSUANT TO SECTION 118 OF THE ACT

### DEPARTMENT OF HEALTH

ARRANGEMENT OF SECTIONS

GENERAL NOTE

**4–002**   References set out in bold to "sections" are to sections of the Mental Health Act 1983 itself. References to chapters and paragraphs of the "Reference Guide" are to the Mental Health Act Reference Guide produced by the Department of Health. They do not form part of the Code itself.

## INTRODUCTION

**4–003**   i. This revised Code of Practice ("the Code") has been prepared in accordance with section 118 of the Mental Health Act 1983 ("the Act") by the Secretary of State for Health after consulting such bodies as appeared to him to be concerned, and laid before Parliament. The Code will come into force on 3 November 2008.

### Purpose and legal status of the Code of Practice
**4–004**   ii  The Code provides guidance to registered medical practitioners ("doctors"), approved clinicians, managers and staff of hospitals, and approved mental health professionals on how they should proceed when undertaking duties under the Act.

iii It also gives guidance to doctors and other professionals about certain aspects of medical treatment for mental disorder more generally.

iv While the Act does not impose a legal duty to comply with the Code, the people listed above to whom the Code is addressed must have regard to the Code. The reasons for any departure should be recorded. Departures from the Code could give rise to legal challenge, and a court, in reviewing any departure from the Code, will scrutinise the reasons for the departure to'ensure that there is sufficiently convincing justification in the circumstances.

v  The Code should also be beneficial to the police and ambulance services and others in health and social services (including the independent and voluntary sectors) involved in providing services to people who are, or may become, subject to compulsory measures under the Act.

vi It is intended that the Code will also be helpful to patients, their representatives, carers, families and friends, and others who support them.

### Presentation of this Code
**4–005**   vii Throughout this Code, the Mental Health 1983 is referred to as "the Act". Where there is reference to sections of others acts, the relevant act is clearly indicated. Where the Code refers to "the regulations", it means regulations made under the Act.

viii The Code is intended to offer guidance on the operation of the Act, and does not set out to explain each and every aspect of the Act and the regulations, orders and directions which go with it.

ix To guide readers to more detailed information and explanation, references are given in the margins of the Code to relevant legislation and to other reference material.

x A list of relevant matrial is also provided at the end of each chapter, where appropriate. These references do not form part of the Code and do not attract the same legal status. The information is provided for assistance only.

### Scenarios—applying the principles

xi In a number of the chapters of the Code, scenarios have been included which **4–006** are intended to illustrate the way in which the guiding principles set out in **chapter 1** might be applied to decisions which people have to take under the Act. The scenarios are not intended to provide a template for decisions in applying the principles in similar situations. The scenarios themselves are only illustrative and do not form part of the Code.

### References to patients, children and young people

xii The Code refers throughout to "patients" when it means people who are, or **4–007** appear to be, suffering from a mental disorder. This use of the term is not a recommendation that the term "patient" should be used in practice in preference to other terms such as "services users", "clients" or similar. It is simply a reflection of the terminology used in the Act itself.

xiii When the Code refers to "children" it means people under the age of 16. When it refers to "young people" it means people aged 16 or 17.

### References to the Commission and Tribunal

xiv The Code refers in a number of places to the Commission which is respon- **4–008** sible for monitoring the operation of the Act. At the time of publication, this is the Mental Health Act Commission (MHAC). However, legislation is currently before Parliament which will abolish the MHAC and transfer its functions to the Care Quality Commission, a new integrated health and adult social care regulator, bringing together existing health and social care regulators into one body. Subject to Parliament, it is expected that the new Commission will be established in April 2009.

xv Similarly, the Code refers frequently to the Tribunal which has the power to discharge patients from detention and other compulsory measures under the Act. At the time of publication, this means the Mental Health Review Tribunal (MHRT). However, subject to Parliament, the MHRT is intended to be replaced in England by a new First Tier Tribunal established under the Tribunals, Courts and Enforcement Act 2007.

### Mental Capacity Act 2005

xvi There are many references throughout this Code to the Mental Capacity Act **4–009** 2005 (MCA). The Code assumes that its readers are familiar with the main provisions of the MCA as it relates to the care and treatment of people with mental disorders who lack the capacity to take particular decisions for themselves, and does not attempt to explain them.

xvii It will be difficult for professionals involved in providing care for people with mental health problems to carry out their work (including their responsibilities under the Act) without an understanding of key concepts in the MCA.

xviii In particular, they will need to be familiar with the principles of the MCA to understand what it means to lack capacity and to know when decisions can be taken in the best interests of people who lack capacity to take those decisions themselves, the steps to be taken before doing so, and the principles to be applied. They will also need to be familiar with the concepts of advance decisions to refuse treatment, lasting powers of attorney and donees of such powers ("attorneys"), court-appointed deputies and independent mental capacity advocates.

xix Although patients' capacity to consent to treatment does not by itself determine whether they can or ought to be detained under the Act, people involved in deciding whether patients should be detained under the Act will also need to understand the circumstances in which deprivation of liberty in hospitals and care homes may be authorised under the deprivation of liberty safeguards added to the MCA by the Mental Health Act 2007, and the procedures for so doing.

## 1. STATEMENT OF GUIDING PRINCIPLES

**4–010**   1.1 This chapter provides a set of guiding principles which should be considered when making decisions about a course of action under the Act.

### Guiding principles

*Purpose principle*

**4–011**   1.2 Decisions under the Act must be taken with a view to minimising the undesirable effects of mental disorder, by maximising the safety and wellbeing (mental and physical) of patients, promoting their recovery and protecting other people from harm.

*Least restriction principle*

**4–012**   1.3 People taking action without a patient's consent must attempt to keep to a minimum the restrictions they impose on the patient's liberty, having regard to the purpose for which the restrictions are imposed.

*Respect principle*

**4–013**   1.4 People taking decisions under the Act must recognise and respect the diverse needs, values and circumstances of each patient, including their race, religion, culture, gender, age sexual orientation and any disability. They must consider the patient's views, wishes and feelings (whether expressed at the time or in advance), so far as they are reasonably ascertainable, and follow those wishes wherever practicable and consistent with the purpose of the decision. There must be no unlawful discrimination.

*Participation principle*

**4–014**   1.5 Patients must be given the opportunity to be involved, as far as is practicable in the circumstances, in planning, developing and reviewing their own treatment and care to help ensure that it is delivered in a way that is as appropriate and effective for them as possible. The involvement of carers, family members and other people who have an interest in the patient's welfare should be encouraged (unless there are particular reasons to the contrary) and their views taken seriously.

*Effectiveness, efficiency and equity principle*

1.6 People taking decisions under the Act must seek to use the resources available to them and to patients in the most effective, efficient and equitable way, to meet the needs of patients and achieve the purpose for which the decision was taken. **4–015**

**Using the principles**
1.7 All decisions must, of course, be lawful and informed by good professional **4–016** practice. Lawfulness necessarily includes compliance with the Human Rights Act 1998.

1.8 The principles inform decisions, they do not determine them. Although all the principles must inform every decision made under the Act, the weight given to each principle in reaching a particular decision will depend on the context.

1.9 That is not to say that in making a decision any of the principles should be disregarded. It is rather that the principles as a whole need to be balanced in different ways according to the particular circumstances of each individual decision.

---

**Related material**

• Human Rights Act 1998

This material does not form part of the Code. It is provided for assistance only.

---

## 2. INFORMATION FOR PATIENTS, NEAREST RELATIVES AND OTHERS

2.1 This chapter gives guidance on the information that must be given to **4–017** patients and their nearest relatives. It also gives guidance on communication with patients and others generally.

**Communication with patients**
2.2 Effective communication is essential in ensuring appropriate care and **4–018** respect for patients' rights. It is important that the language used is clear and unambiguous and that people giving information check that the information that has been communicated has been understood.

2.3 Everything possible should be done to overcome barriers to effective communication, which may be caused by any of a number of reasons—for example, if the patient's first language is not English. Patients may have difficulty in understanding technical terms and jargon or in maintaining attention for extended periods. They may have a hearing or visual impairment or have difficulty in reading or writing. A patient's cultural background may also be very different from that of the person speaking to them.

2.4 Those with responsibility for the care of patients need to identify how communication difficulties affect each patient individually, so that they can assess the needs of each patient and address them in the most appropriate way. Hospitals and other organisations should make people with specialist expertise (eg in sign language or Makaton) available as required.

2.5 Where an interpreter is needed, every effort should be made to identify who is appropriate to the patient, given the patient's gender, religion, language, dialect, cultural background and age. The patient's relatives and friends should only exceptionally be used as intermediaries or interpreters. Interpreters (both professional and nonprofessional) must respect the confidentiality of any personal information they learn about the patient through their involvement.

2.6 Independent advocates engaged by patients can be invaluable in helping patients to understand the questions and information being presented to them and in helping them to communicate their views to staff. (See **chapter 20.**)

2.7 Wherever possible, patients should be engaged in the process of reaching decisions which affect their care and treatment under the Act. Consultation with patients involves assisting them in understanding the issue, their role and the roles of others who are involved in taking the decision. Ideally decisions should be agreed with the patient. Where a decision is made that is contrary to the patient's wishes, that decision and the authority for it should be explained to the patient using a form of communication that the patient understands.

**Information for detained patients and patients on supervised community treatment (Sections 132 and 132A; Reference Guide Chapters 12 (detention) and 15 (SCT))**

**4–019**    2.8 The Act requires hospital managers to take steps to ensure that patients who are detained in hospital under the Act, or who are on supervised community treatment (SCT), understand important information about how the Act applies to them. This must be done as soon as practicable after the start of the patient's detention or SCT. This information must also be given to SCT patients who are recalled to hospital.

2.9 Information must be given to the patient both orally and in writing. These are not alternatives. Those providing information to patients should ensure that all relevant information is conveyed in a way that the patient understands.

2.10 It would not be sufficient to repeat what is already written on an information leaflet as a way of providing information orally.

*Information about detention and SCT*

**4–020**    2.11 Patients must be informed:

- of the provisions of the Act under which they are detained or on SCT, and the effect of those provisions;

- of the rights (if any) of their nearest relative to discharge them (and what can happen if their responsible clinician does not agree with that decision); and

- for SCT patients, of the effect of the community treatment order, including the conditions which they are required to keep to and the circumstances in which their responsible clinician may recall them to hospital.

2.12 As part of this, they should be told:

- the reasons for their detention or SCT;

- the maximum length of the current period of detention or SCT;

- that their detention or SCT may be ended at any time if it is no longer required or the criteria for it are no longer met;

- that they will not automatically be discharged when the current period of detention or SCT ends; and

- that their detention or SCT will not automatically be renewed or extended when the current period of detention or SCT ends.

2.13 Patients should also be told the essential legal and factual grounds for their detention or SCT. For the patient to be able to effectively challenge the grounds for their detention or SCT, should they wish, they should be given the full facts rather than simply the broad reasons. This should be done promptly and clearly.

2.14 In addition, a copy of the detention or SCT documentation should be made available to the patient, unless the hospital managers are of the opinion (based on the advice of the authors of the documents) that the information disclosed would adversely affect the health or wellbeing of the patient or others. It may be necessary to remove any personal information about third parties.

2.15 Where the section of the Act under which the patient is being detained changes, they must be provided with the above information to reflect the new situation. This also applies where a detained patient becomes an SCT patient, where an SCT patient's community treatment order is revoked, or where a conditionally discharged patient is recalled to hospital.

*Information about consent to treatment*

2.16 Patients must be told what the Act says about treatment for their mental **4–021** disorder. In particular they must be told:

- the circumstances (if any) in which they can be treated without their consent – and the circumstances in which they have the right to refuse treatment;

- the role of second opinion appointed doctors (SOADs) and the circumstances in which they may be involved; and

- (where relevant) the rules on electro-convulsive therapy (ECT).

*Information about seeking a review of detention or SCT*

2.17 Patients must be informed: **4–022**

- of the right of the responsible clinician and the hospital managers to discharge them (and, for restricted patients, that this is subject to the agreement of the Secretary of State for Justice);

- of their right to ask the hospital managers to discharge them;

- that the hospital managers must consider discharging them when their detention is renewed or their SCT extended;

- (for NHS patients in independent hospitals) of the power of the relevant NHS body to discharge them;

- of their rights to apply to the Tribunal;

- of the rights (if any) of their nearest relative to apply to the Tribunal on their behalf;

- about the role of the Tribunal; and

- how to apply to the Tribunal.

2.18 Hospital managers should ensure that patients are offered assistance to request a hospital managers' hearing or make an application to the Tribunal. They should also be told:

- how to contact a suitably qualified legal representative (and should be given assistance to do so if required);

- that free legal aid may be available; and

- how to contact any other organisation which may be able to help them make an application to the Tribunal.

2.19 It is particularly important that patients on SCT who may not have daily contact with people who could help them make an application to the Tribunal are informed and supported in this process.

2.20 SCT patients whose community treatment orders are revoked, and conditionally discharged patients recalled to hospital, should be told that their cases will be referred automatically to the Tribunal.

*Information about the Commission*

**4–023**  2.21 Patients must be informed about the role of the Commission and of their right to meet visitors appointed by the Commission in private. Patients should be told when the Commission is to visit their hospital and be reminded of the Commission's role.

2.22 Patients may also make a complaint to the Commission, and they should be informed of the process for this. Support should be made available to patients to do this, if required. Patients should also be given information about the hospital's own complaints system and how to use it.

**Information about withholding of correspondence**

**4–024**  2.23 Detained patients must be told that post sent by them may be withheld if the person to whom it is addressed asks the hospital managers to do so. Patients in high security psychiatric hospitals must be told about the other circumstances in which their correspondence may be withheld, the procedures that will be followed and their right to ask the Commission to review the decisions taken.

**Keeping patients informed of their rights**

2.24 Those with responsibility for patient care should ensure that patients are **4–025** reminded from time to time of their rights and the effects of the Act. It may be necessary to convey the same information on a number of different occasions or in different formats and to check regularly that the patient has fully understood it. Information given to a patient who is unwell may need to be repeated when their condition has improved.

2.25 A fresh explanation of the patient's rights should be considered in particular where:

- the patient is considering applying to the Tribunal, or when the patient becomes eligible again to apply to the Tribunal;

- the patient requests the hospital managers to consider discharging them;

- the rules in the Act about their treatment change (for example, because three months have passed since they were first given medication, or because they have regained capacity to consent to treatment—see **chapters 23** and **24**);

- any significant change in their treatment is being considered;

- there is to be a Care Programme Approach review (or its equivalent);

- renewal of their detention or extension of their SCT is being considered; or

- a decision is taken to renew their detention or to extend their SCT.

2.26 When a patient is discharged from detention or SCT, or the authority for their detention or SCT expires, this fact should be made clear to them. The patient should also be given an explanation of what happens next, including any section 117 after-care or other services which are to be provided.

**Information for nearest relatives (Section 133)**

2.27 The Act also requires hospital managers to take such steps as are practi- **4–026** cable to give the patient's nearest relative a copy of any information given to the patient in writing, unless the patient requests otherwise. The information should be given to the nearest relative when the information is given to the patient, or within a reasonable time afterwards.

2.28 When a patient detained under the Act or on SCT is given information, they should be told that the written information will also be supplied to their nearest relative, so that they have a chance to object.

2.29 The nearest relative should also be told of the patient's discharge from detention or SCT (where practicable), unless either the patient or the nearest relative has requested that information about discharge should not be given. This includes discharge from detention onto SCT. If practicable, the information should be given at least seven days in advance of the discharge.

2.30 In addition, regulations require nearest relatives to be informed of various other events, including the renewal of a patient's detention, extension of SCT and transfer from one hospital to another.

2.31 These duties to inform nearest relatives are not absolute. In almost all cases, information is not to be shared if the patient objects.

2.32 In addition, there will occasionally be cases where these duties do not apply because disclosing information about the patient to the nearest relative cannot be considered practicable, on the grounds that it would have a detrimental impact on the patient that is disproportionate to any advantage to be gained from informing the nearest relative. This would therefore be a breach of the patient's right to privacy under the European Convention on Human Rights. The risk of this is greatest where the nearest relative is someone whom the patient would not have chosen themselves.

2.33 Before disclosing information to nearest relatives without a patient's consent, the person concerned must consider whether the disclosure would be likely to:

- put the patient at risk of physical harm or financial or other exploitation;

- cause the patient emotional distress or lead to a deterioration in their mental health; or

- have any other detrimental effect on their health or wellbeing, and if so whether the advantages to the patient and the public interest of the disclosure outweigh the disadvantages to the patient, in the light of all the circumstances of the case.

### Communication with other people nominated by the patient

**4–027**  2.34 Patients may want to nominate one or more people who they would wish to be involved in, or notified of, decisions related to their care and treatment.

2.35 Patients may nominate an independent mental health advocate, another independent advocate or a legal professional. But they may also nominate a relative, friend or other informal supporter.

2.36 The involvement of such friends, relatives or other supporters can have significant benefits for the care and treatment of the patient. It can provide reassurance to the patient, who may feel distrustful of professionals who are able to impose compulsory measures on them, or are relatively unfamiliar and unknown to the patient. People who know the patient well can provide knowledge of the patient and perspectives that come from long-standing and intimate involvement with the patient prior to (and during) their involvement with mental health services. They can provide practical assistance in helping the patient to convey information and views and may have knowledge of advance decisions or statements made by the patient (see **chapter 17**).

2.37 Professionals should normally agree to a patient's request to involve relatives, friends or other informal supporters. They should tell the patient whenever such a request will not be, or has not been, granted. Where a patient's request is refused, it is good practice to record this in the patient's notes, giving reasons for the refusal. It may not always be appropriate to involve another person as requested by the patient, for example where:

- contacting and involving the person would result in a delay to the decision in question that would not be in the patient's best interests;

- the involvement of the person is contrary to the best interests of the patient; or

- that person has requested that they should not be involved.

2.38 Professionals should also take steps to find out whether patients who lack capacity to take particular decisions for themselves have an attorney or deputy with authority to take the decision on their behalf. Where there is such a person, they act as the agent of the patient, and should be informed in the same way as the patient themselves about matters within the scope of their authority.

### Involvement of carers

2.39 Carers frequently play a vital role in helping to look after relatives and **4–028** friends who have mental disorders. It is important to identify all individuals who provide regular and substantial care for patients, to ensure that health and social services assess those carers' needs and, where relevant, provide services to meet them.

2.40 Unless there are reasons to the contrary, patients should be encouraged to agree to their carers being involved in decisions under the Act and to them being kept informed. If patients lack capacity to consent to this, it may be appropriate to involve and inform carers if it is in the patient's best interests—although that decision must always be made in the light of the specific circumstances of the case.

2.41 In order to ensure that carers can, where appropriate, participate fully in decision-making, it is important that they have access to:

- practical and emotional help and support to help them to participate; and

- timely access to comprehensive, up-to-date and accurate information.

2.42 Even if carers cannot be given detailed information about the patient's case, where appropriate they should be offered general information which may help them understand the nature of mental disorder, the way it is treated, and the operation of the Act.

### Information for patients' children

2.43 In considering the kind and amount of information which children and **4–029** young people (especially young carers) should receive about a parent's condition or treatment, the people giving the information will need to balance the interests of the child or young person against the patient's right to privacy and their wishes and feelings. Any such information should be appropriate to the age and under-standing of the child or young person.

### Hospital managers' information policy

2.44 The formal duty to ensure that detained and SCT patients and their nearest **4–030** relatives have been informed about their legal situation and rights falls to the hos-pital managers. In practice, it would usually be more appropriate for professionals working with the patient to provide them with the information. In order to fulfil their statutory duties hospital managers should have policies in place to ensure that:

- the correct information is given to patients and their nearest relatives;

- information is given in accordance with the requirements of the legislation, at a suitable time and in an accessible format, where appropriate with the aid of assistive technologies and interpretative and advocacy services;

- people who give the information have received sufficient training and guidance;

- a record is kept of the information given, including how, when, where and by whom it was given, and an assessment made of how well the information was understood by the recipient; and

- a regular check is made that information has been properly given to each patient and understood by them.

### Information for informal hospital in-patients

**4–031**    2.45 Although the Act does not impose any duties to give information to informal patients, these patients should be made aware of their legal position and rights. Local policies and arrangements about movement around the hospital and its grounds must be clearly explained to the patients concerned. Failure to do so could lead to a patient mistakenly believing that they are not allowed freedom of movement, which could result in an unlawful deprivation of their liberty.

### Information for those subject to guardianship (Reference Guide chapter 19)

**4–032**    2.46 Responsible local social service authorities (LSSAs) are required to take steps to ensure that guardianship patients understand their rights to apply to the Tribunal and the rights of their nearest relatives. The same information must also normally be given to nearest relatives. More generally, LSSAs (and private guardians) should do what they can to ensure that patients understand why they have been made subject to guardianship and what it means for them.

## 3. MENTAL DISORDER

**4–033**    3.1 This chapter gives guidance on the definition of mental disorder for the purposes of the Act.

### Definition of mental disorder (Section 1(2))

**4–034**    3.2 Mental disorder is defined for the purposes of the Act as "any disorder or disability of the mind". Relevant professionals should determine whether a patient has a disorder or disability of the mind in accordance with good clinical practice and accepted standards of what constitutes such a disorder or disability.

3.3 Examples of clinically recognised conditions which could fall within this definition are given in the following box:

---

*Clincially recognised conditions which could fall within the Act's definition of mental disorder*

- affective disorders, such as depression and bipolar disorder

- schizophrenia and delusional disorders

- neurotic, stress-related and somatoform disorders, such as anxiety, phobic disorders, obsessive compulsive disorders, post-traumatic stress disorder and hypochondriacal disorders

- organic mental disorders such as dementia and delirium (however caused)

---

- personality and behavioural changes caused by brain injury or damage (however acquired)

- personality disorders

- mental and behavioural disorders caused by psychoactive substance use (but see **paragraphs 3.8–3.12**)

- eating disorders, non-organic sleep disorders and non-organic sexual disorders

- learning disabilities (but see **paragraphs 3.13–3.15**)

- autistic spectrum disorders (including Asperger's syndrome) (but see **paragraphs 3.16–3.17**)

- behavioural and emotional disorders of children and adolescents

(Note: this list is not exhaustive.)

3.4 The fact that someone has a mental disorder is never sufficient grounds for any compulsory measure to be taken under the Act. Compulsory measures are permitted only where specific criteria about the potential consequences of a person's mental disorder are met. There are many forms of mental disorder which are unlikely ever to call for compulsory measures.

3.5 Care must always be taken to avoid diagnosing, or failing to diagnose, mental disorder on the basis of preconceptions about people or failure to appreciate cultural and social differences. What may be indicative of mental disorder in one person, given their background and individual circumstances, may be nothing of the sort in another person.

3.6 Difference should not be confused with disorder. No-one may be considered to be mentally disordered solely because of their political, religious or cultural beliefs, values or opinions, unless there are proper clinical grounds to believe that they are the symptoms or manifestations of a disability or disorder of the mind. The same is true of a person's involvement, or likely involvement, in illegal, anti-social or "immoral" behaviour. Beliefs, behaviours or actions which do not result from a disorder or disability of the mind are not a basis for compulsory measures under the Act, even if they appear unusual or cause other people alarm, distress or danger.

3.7 A person's sexual orientation towards people of the same gender (or both the same and the other gender) is not a mental disorder for any purpose.

**Dependence on alcohol or drugs**

3.8 Section 1(3) of the Act states that dependence on alcohol or drugs is not **4–035** considered to be a disorder or disability of the mind for the purposes of the definition of mental disorder in the Act.

3.9 This means that there are no grounds under the Act for detaining a person in hospital (or using other compulsory measures) on the basis of alcohol or drug dependence alone. Drugs for these purposes may be taken to include solvents and similar substances with a psychoactive effect.

3.10 Alcohol or drug dependence may be accompanied by, or associated with, a mental disorder which does fall within the Act's definition. If the relevant criteria are met, it is therefore possible (for example) to detain people who are suffering from mental disorder, even though they are also dependent on alcohol or drugs. This is true even if the mental disorder in question results from the person's alcohol or drug dependence.

3.11 The Act does not exclude other disorders or disabilities of the mind related to the use of alcohol or drugs. These disorders—for example, withdrawal state with delirium or associated psychotic disorder, acute intoxication and organic mental disorders associated with prolonged abuse of drugs or alcohol—remain mental disorders for the purposes of the Act.

3.12 Medical treatment for mental disorder under the Act (including treatment with consent) can include measures to address alcohol or drug dependence if that is an appropriate part of treating the mental disorder which is the primary focus of the treatment.

### Learning disabilities and autistic spectrum disorders (Reference Guide 1.12–1.15)

**4–036**    3.13 Learning disabilities and autistic spectrum disorders are forms of mental disorder as defined in the Act.

3.14 However, someone with a learning disability and no other form of mental disorder may not be detained for treatment or made subject to guardianship or supervised community treatment unless their learning disability is accompanied by abnormally aggressive or seriously irresponsible conduct on their part.

3.15 This "learning disability qualification" applies only to specific sections of the Act. In particular, it does not apply to detention for assessment under section 2 of the Act (**Section 1(2A) and (2B)**).

3.16 The learning disability qualification does not apply to autistic spectrum disorders (including Asperger's syndrome). It is possible for someone with an autistic spectrum disorder to meet the criteria for compulsory measures under the Act without having any other form of mental disorder, even if their autistic spectrum disorder is not associated with abnormally aggressive or seriously irresponsible behaviour. While experience suggests that this is likely to be necessary only very rarely, the possibility should never automatically be discounted.

3.17 For further guidance on particular issues relating to people with learning disabilities or autistic spectrum disorders (including further guidance on the learning disability qualification), see **chapter 34**.

### Personality disorders

**4–037**    3.18 Apart from the learning disability qualification described above, the Act does not distinguish between different forms of mental disorder. The Act therefore applies to personality disorders (of all types) in exactly the same way as it applies to mental illness and other mental disorders.

3.19 No assumptions should be made about the suitability of using the Act—or indeed providing services without using the Act—in respect of personality disorders or the people who have them. The factors which should inform decisions are the needs of the individual patient, the risks posed by their disorder and what can be done to address those needs and risks, in both the short and longer term (see **chapter 35** for further guidance on personality disorders).

## 4. APPLICATIONS FOR DETENTION IN HOSPITAL

4.1 This chapter gives guidance on the making of applications for detention in **4–038** hospital under Part 2 of the Act (**Reference Guide chapter 2**).

### Grounds for making an application for detention

4.2 An application for detention may only be made where the grounds in either **4–039** section 2 or section 3 of the Act are met (see box below).

---

*Criteria for applications*

A person can be detained for assessment under section 2 only if both the following criteria apply:

- the person is suffering from a mental disorder of a nature or degree which warrants their detention in hospital for assessment (or for assessment followed by treatment) for at least a limited period; and

- the person ought to be so detained in the interests of their own health or safety or with a view to the protection of others.

A person can be detained for treatment under section 3 only if all the following criteria apply:

- the person is suffering from a mental disorder of a nature or degree which makes it appropriate for them to receive medical treatment in hospital;

- it is necessary for the health or safety of the person or for the protection of other persons that they should receive such treatment and it cannot be provided unless the patient is detained under this section; and

- appropriate medical treatment is available.

---

4.3 The criteria require consideration of both the nature and degree of a patient's mental disorder. Nature refers to the particular mental disorder from which the patient is suffering, its chronicity, its prognosis, and the patient's previous response to receiving treatment for the disorder. Degree refers to the current manifestation of the patient's disorder.

4.4 Before it is decided that admission to hospital is necessary, consideration must be given to whether there are alternative means of providing the care and treatment which the patient requires. This includes consideration of whether there might be other effective forms of care or treatment which the patient would be willing to accept, and of whether guardianship would be appropriate instead.

4.5 In all cases, consideration must be given to:

- the patient's wishes and view of their own needs;

- the patient's age and physical health;

- any past wishes or feelings expressed by the patient;

- the patient's cultural background;

- the patient's social and family circumstances;

- the impact that any future deterioration or lack of improvement in the patient's condition would have on their children, other relatives or carers, especially those living with the patient, including an assessment of these people's ability and willingness to cope; and

- the effect on the patient, and those close to the patient, of a decision to admit or not to admit under the Act.

### Factors to consider—the health or safety of the patient

**4–040**    4.6 Factors to be considered in deciding whether patients should be detained for their own health or safety include:

- the evidence suggesting that patients are at risk of:
  - suicide;
  - self-harm;
  - self-neglect or being unable to look after their own health or safety; or
  - jeopardising their own health or safety accidentally, recklessly or unintentionally;

  or that their mental disorder is otherwise putting their health or safety at risk;

- any evidence suggesting that the patient's mental health will deteriorate if they do not receive treatment;

- the reliability of such evidence, including what is known of the history of the patient's mental disorder;

- the views of the patient and of any carers, relatives or close friends, especially those living with the patient, about the likely course of the disorder and the possibility of it improving;

- the patient's own skills and experience in managing their condition;

- the potential benefits of treatment, which should be weighed against any adverse effects that being detained might have on the patient's wellbeing; and

- whether other methods of managing the risk are available.

### Factors to consider—protection of others

**4–041**    4.7 In considering whether detention is necessary for the protection of other people, the factors to consider are the nature of the risk to other people arising from the patient's mental disorder, the likelihood that harm will result and the severity of any potential harm, taking into account:

- that it is not always possible to differentiate risk of harm to the patient from the risk of harm to others;

- the reliability of the available evidence, including any relevant details of the patient's clinical history and past behaviour, such as contact with other agencies and (where relevant) criminal convictions and cautions;

- the willingness and ability of those who live with the patient and those who provide care and support to the patient to cope with and manage the risk; and

- whether other methods of managing the risk are available.

4.8 Harm to other people includes psychological as well as physical harm.

### Alternatives to detention—patients with capacity to consent to admission

4.9 When a patient needs to be in hospital, informal admission is usually appro- **4-042** priate when a patient who has the capacity to do so consents to admission. (See **chapter 36** for guidance on when parents might consent to admission on behalf of children and young people.)

4.10 However, this should not be regarded as an absolute rule, especially if the reason for considering admission is that the patient presents a clear danger to themselves or others because of their mental disorder.

4.11 Compulsory admission should, in particular, be considered where a patient's current mental state, together with reliable evidence of past experience, indicates a strong likelihood that they will have a change of mind about informal admission, either before or after they are admitted, with a resulting risk to their health or safety or to the safety of other people.

4.12 The threat of detention must not be used to induce a patient to consent to admission to hospital or to treatment (and is likely to invalidate any apparent consent).

### Alternatives to detention—patients who lack capacity to consent to admission or treatment

4.13 In deciding whether it is necessary to detain-patients, doctors and **4-043** approved mental health professionals (AMHPs) must always consider the alternative ways of providing the treatment or care they need.

4.14 The fact that patients cannot consent to the treatment they need, or to being admitted to hospital, does not automatically mean that the Act must be used. It may be possible to rely instead on the provisions of the Mental Capacity Act 2005 (MCA) to provide treatment in the best interests of patients who are aged 16 or over and who lack capacity to consent to treatment.

4.15 This may be possible even if the provision of treatment unavoidably involves depriving patients of their liberty. Deprivation of liberty for the purposes of care or treatment in a hospital or care home can be authorised in a person's best interests under the deprivation of liberty safeguards in the MCA if the person is aged 18 or over.[1]

4.16 If admission to hospital for assessment or treatment for mental disorder is necessary for a patient who lacks capacity to consent to it, an application under the Mental Health Act should be made if:

---

[1] The deprivation of liberty safeguards are expected to be in force from April 2009. It is also possible for the Court of Protection to authorise deprivation of liberty under the MCA, but doctors and AMHPs are not required to apply to the court before considering whether the use of the Mental Health Act is necessary.

- providing appropriate care or treatment for the patient will unavoidably involve depriving them of their liberty and the MCA deprivation of liberty safeguards cannot be used; or[2]

- for any other reason, the assessment or treatment the patient needs cannot be safely or effectively delivered by relying on the MCA alone.

4.17 The MCA deprivation of liberty safeguards can be used only if the six qualifying requirements summarised in the table below are met.

*Summary of qualifying requirements in the MCA's deprivation of liberty safeguards*

|  |  |  |
|---|---|---|
| **4–044** | Age requirement | The person is at least 18 years old. |
| | Mental health requirement | The person has a mental disorder. |
| | Mental capacity requirement | The person lacks capacity to decide whether to be in a hospital or care home for the proposed treatment or care. |
| | Best interests requirement | The proposed deprivation of liberty is in the person's best interests and it is a necessary and proportionate response to the risk of them suffering harm. |
| | Eligibility requirement | The person is not subject, or potentially subject, to specified provisions of the Mental Health Act in a way that makes them ineligible. |
| | No refusals requirement | There is no advance decision, or decision of an attorney or deputy which makes the proposed deprivation of liberty impossible. |

4.18 The key points when considering whether an application for detention should be made under the Mental Health Act instead of relying on the MCA's deprivation of liberty safeguards are that those safeguards cannot be used if:

- the patient is aged under 18;

- the patient has made a valid and applicable advance decision refusing a necessary element of the treatment for which they are to be admitted to hospital (see **chapter 17**);

- the use of the safeguards would conflict with a decision of the person's attorney or deputy or of the Court of Protection; or

---

[2] The version of the Code presented to Parliament also included the words "there is no attorney or deputy willing to consent to admission and treatment on their behalf"—but, in fact, those words are redundant because attorneys or deputies may not consent to deprivation of liberty.

- the patient meets the criteria in section 2 or section 3 of the Mental Health Act and is objecting to being admitted to (or remaining in) hospital for mental health treatment (unless an attorney or deputy consents on their behalf).[3]

4.19 In that last case, whether a patient is objecting has to be considered in the round, taking into account all the circumstances, so far as they are reasonably ascertainable. The decision to be made is whether the patient objects to treatment—the reasonableness of that objection is not the issue. In many cases the patient will be perfectly able to state their objection. But in other cases doctors and AMHPs will need to consider the patient's behaviour, wishes, feelings, views, beliefs and values, both present and past, so far as they can be ascertained. If there is reason to think that a patient would object, if able to do so, then the patient should be taken to be objecting.

4.20 Even if providing appropriate care or treatment will not unavoidably involve a deprivation of liberty, it may be necessary to detain a patient under the Mental Health Act rather than relying on the MCA because:

- the patient has, by means of a valid and applicable advance decision, refused a necessary element of the treatment required; or

- the patient lacks capacity to make decisions on some elements of the care and treatment they need, but has capacity to decide about a vital element—eg admission to hospital—and either has already refused it or is likely to do so.

4.21 Whether or not the deprivation of liberty safeguards could be used, other reasons why it may not be possible to rely on the MCA alone include the following:

- the patient's lack of capacity to consent is fluctuating or temporary and the patient is not expected to consent when they regain capacity. This may be particularly relevant to patients having acute psychotic, manic or depressive episodes;

- a degree of restraint needs to be used which is justified by the risk to other people but which is not permissible under the MCA because, exceptionally, it cannot be said to be proportionate to the risk to the patient personally; and

- there is some other specific identifiable risk that the person might not receive the treatment they need if the MCA is relied on and that either the person or others might potentially suffer harm as a result.

4.22 Otherwise, if the MCA can be used safely and effectively to assess or treat a patient, it is likely to be difficult to demonstrate that the criteria for detaining the patient under the Mental Health Act are met.

4.23 For further information on the MCA deprivation of liberty safeguards, see the addendum to the MCA Code of Practice.

---

[3] The final words in brackets were omitted by mistake from the version of the Code presented to Parliament.

4.24 For the different considerations which apply to children and young people, see **chapter 36**.

**Section 2 or section 3**

**4–045**     4.25 An application for detention can be made under either section 2 or section 3 of the Mental Health Act.

4.26 Section 2 should be used if:

- the full extent of the nature and degree of a patient's condition is unclear;

- there is a need to carry out an initial in-patient assessment in order to formulate a treatment plan, or to reach a judgement about whether the patient will accept treatment on a voluntary basis following admission; or

- there is a need to carry out a new in-patient assessment in order to re-formulate a treatment plan, or to reach a judgement about whether the patient will accept treatment on a voluntary basis.

4.27 Section 3 should be used if:

- the patient is already detained under section 2 (detention under section 2 cannot be renewed by a new section 2 application); or

- the nature and current degree of the patient's mental disorder, the essential elements of the treatment plan to be followed and the likelihood of the patient accepting treatment on a voluntary basis are already established.

**The assessment process**

**4–046**     4.28 An application for detention may be made by an AMHP or the patient's nearest relative. An AMHP is usually a more appropriate applicant than a patient's nearest relative, given an AMHP's professional training and knowledge of the legislation and local resources, together with the potential adverse effect that an application by the nearest relative might have on their relationship with the patient.

4.29 An application must be supported by two medical recommendations given in accordance with the Act.

4.30 Doctors who are approached directly by a nearest relative about making an application should advise the nearest relative that it is preferable for an AMHP to consider the need for a patient to be admitted under the Act and for the AMHP to make any consequent application. Doctors should also advise the nearest relative of their right to require a local social services authority (LSSA) to arrange for an AMHP to consider the patient's case. Doctors should never advise a nearest relative to make an application themselves in order to avoid involving an AMHP in an assessment.

**Objective of the assessment**

**4–047**     4.31 The objective of the assessment is to determine whether the criteria for detention are met and, if so, whether an application for detention should be made.

4.32 Because a proper assessment cannot be carried out without considering alternative means of providing care and treatment, AMHPs and doctors should, as far as possible in the circumstances, identify and liaise with services which may potentially be able to provide alternatives to admission to hospital. That could include crisis and home treatment teams.

**Responsibilities of local social services authorities**

4.33 LSSAs are responsible for ensuring that sufficient AMHPs are available to **4–048** carry out their roles under the Act, including assessing patients to decide whether an application for detention should be made. To fulfil their statutory duty, LSSAs must have arrangements in place in their area to provide a 24-hour service that can respond to patients' needs.

4.34 Section 13 of the Act places a specific duty on LSSAs to arrange for an AMHP to consider the case of any patient who is within their area if they have reason to believe that an application for detention in hospital may need to be made in respect of the patient. LSSAs must make such arrangements if asked to do so by (or on behalf of) the nearest relative.

4.35 If a patient is already detained under section 2 as the result of an application made by an AMHP, the LSSA on whose behalf that AMHP was acting is responsible for arranging for an AMHP to consider the patient's case again if the LSSA has reason to believe that an application under section 3 may be necessary. This applies even if the patient has been detained outside that LSSA's area.

4.36 These duties do not prevent any other LSSA from arranging for an AMHP to consider a patient's case if that is more appropriate.

**Setting up the assessment**

4.37 Local arrangements should, as far as possible, ensure that assessments are **4–049** carried out by the most appropriate AMHP and doctors in the particular circumstances.

4.38 Where a patient is known to belong to a group for which particular expertise is desirable (eg they are aged under 18 or have a learning disability), at least one of the professionals involved in their assessment should have expertise in working with people from that group, wherever possible.

4.39 If this is not possible, at least one of the professionals involved in the person's assessment should, if at all possible, consult with one or more professionals who do have relevant expertise and involve them as closely as the circumstances of the case allow.

4.40 Unless different arrangements have been agreed locally between the relevant authorities, AMHPs who assess patients for possible detention under the Act have overall responsibility for co-ordinating the process of assessment. In doing so, they should be sensitive to the patient's age, gender (and gender identity), social, cultural, racial and religious background and sexual orientation. They should also consider how any disability the patient has may affect the way the assessment needs to be carried out.

4.41 Given the importance of good communication, it is essential that those professionals who assess patients are able to communicate with the patient effectively and reliably to prevent potential misunderstandings. AMHPs should establish, as far as possible, whether patients have particular communication needs or difficulties and take steps to meet them, for example by arranging a signer or a professional interpreter. AMHPs should also be in a position, where appropriate, to supply suitable equipment to make communication easier with patients who have impaired hearing, but who do not have their own hearing aid.

4.42 See **paragraphs 4.106–4.110** for specific guidance in relation to the assessment of people who are deaf. For further guidance on specific issues that may arise when assessing people who have a learning disability or an autistic spectrum disorder, or who have a personality disorder, see **chapter 34** and **chapter 35** respectively.

4.43 Doctors and AMHPs undertaking assessments need to apply professional judgement and reach decisions independently of each other, but in a framework of co-operation and mutual support.

4.44 Unless there is good reason for undertaking separate assessments, patients should, where possible, be seen jointly by the AMHP and at least one of the two doctors involved in the assessment.

4.45 While it may not always be feasible for the patient to be examined by both doctors at the same time, they should both discuss the patient's case with the person considering making an application for the patient's detention.

4.46 Everyone involved in an assessment should be alert to the need to provide support for colleagues, especially where there is a risk of the patient causing physical harm. People carrying out assessments should be aware of circumstances in which the police should be asked to provide assistance, in accordance with arrangements agreed locally with the police, and of how to use that assistance to maximise the safety of everyone involved in the assessment.

4.47 Locally agreed arrangements on the involvement of the police should include a joint risk assessment tool to help determine the level of risk, what (if any) police assistance may be required and how quickly it is needed. In cases where no warrant for the police to enter premises under section 135 of the Act is being applied for (see **chapter 10**), the risk assessment should indicate the reasons for this and explain why police assistance is nonetheless necessary.

**The role of approved mental health professionals (Section 13(1A) and (2))**

**4–050** 4.48 AMHPs may make an application for detention only if they:

- have interviewed the patient in a suitable manner;
- are satisfied that the statutory criteria for detention are met; and
- are satisfied that, in all the circumstances of the case, detention in hospital is the most appropriate way of providing the care and medical treatment the patient needs.

4.49 Once AMHPs have decided that an application should be made, they must then decide whether it is necessary or proper for them to make the application themselves. If they decide it is, having considered any views expressed by the patient's relatives and all the other relevant circumstances, AMHPs must make the application.

4.50 At the start of an assessment, AMHPs should identify themselves to the person being assessed, members of the person's family, carers or friends and the other professionals present. AMHPs should ensure that the purpose of the visit, their role and that of the other professionals are explained. They should carry documents with them at all times which identify them as AMHPs and which specify both the LSSA which approved them and the LSSA on whose behalf they are acting.

4.51 Although AMHPs act on behalf of a LSSA, they cannot be told by the LSSA or anyone else whether or not to make an application. They must exercise their own judgement, based on social and medical evidence, when deciding whether to apply for a patient to be detained under the Act. The role of AMHPs is to provide an independent decision about whether or not there are alternatives to detention under the Act, bringing a social perspective to bear on their decision.

4.52 If patients want someone else (eg a familiar person or an advocate) to be present during the assessment and any subsequent action that may be taken, then ordinarily AMHPs should assist in securing that person's attendance, unless the urgency of the case makes it inappropriate to do so. Patients may feel safer or more confident with a friend or other person they know well in attendance. Equally, an advocate can help to reassure patients. Some patients may already be receiving help from an advocate.

4.53 Patients should usually be given the opportunity of speaking to the AMHP alone. However, if AMHPs have reason to fear physical harm, they should insist that another professional is present.

4.54 It is not desirable for patients to be interviewed through a closed door or window, and this should be considered only where other people are at serious risk. Where direct access to the patient is not possible, but there is no immediate risk of physical danger to the patient or to anyone else, AMHPs should consider applying for a warrant under section 135 of the Act, allowing the police to enter the premises (see **chapter 10**).

4.55 Where patients are subject to the short-term effects of alcohol or drugs (whether prescribed or self-administered) which make interviewing them difficult, the AMHP should either wait until the effects have abated before interviewing the patient or arrange to return later. If it is not realistic to wait, because of the patient's disturbed behaviour and the urgency of the case, the assessment will have to be based on whatever information the AMHP can obtain from reliable sources. This should be made clear in the AMHP's record of the assessment.

### The AMHP and the nearest relative

4.56 AMHPs are required by the Act to attempt to identify the patient's nearest **4–051** relative as defined in section 26 of the Act.

4.57 When AMHPs make an application for detention under section 2, they must take such steps as are practicable to inform the nearest relative that the application is to be (or has been) made and of the nearest relative's power to discharge the patient (**Section 11(3)**).

4.58 Before making an application for detention under section 3, AMHPs must consult the nearest relative, unless it is not reasonably practicable or would involve unreasonable delay (**Section 11(4)**).

4.59 Circumstances in which the nearest relative need not be informed or consulted include those where:

- it is not practicable for the AMHP to obtain sufficient information to establish the identity or location of the nearest relative, or where to do so would require an excessive amount of investigation involving unreasonable delay; and

- consultation is not possible because of the nearest relative's own health or mental incapacity.

4.60 There may also be cases where, although physically possible, it would not be reasonably practicable to inform or consult the nearest relative because there would be a detrimental impact on the patient which would result in infringement of the patient's right to respect for their privacy and family life under article 8 of the European Convention on Human Rights and which could not be justified by the benefit of the involvement of the nearest relative.[4] Detrimental impact may include cases where patients are likely to suffer emotional distress, deterioration in their mental health, physical harm, or financial or other exploitation as a result of the consultation.

4.61 Consulting and notifying the nearest relative is a significant safeguard for patients. Therefore decisions not to do so on these grounds should not be taken lightly. AMHPs should consider all the circumstances of the case, including:

- the benefit to the patient of the involvement of their nearest relative;

- the patient's wishes (taking into account whether they have the capacity to decide whether they would want their nearest relative involved and any statement of their wishes they have made in advance);

- any detrimental effect that involving the nearest relative would have on the patient's health and wellbeing; and

- whether there is any good reason to think that the patient's objection may be intended to prevent information relevant to the assessment being discovered.

4.62 AMHPs may also consider the degree to which the nearest relative has been willing to be involved on previous occasions, but unwillingness to act previously should not automatically be taken to imply current unwillingness.

4.63 If they do not consult or inform the nearest relative, AMHPs should record their reasons. Consultation must not be avoided purely because it is thought that the nearest relative might object to the application.

4.64 When consulting nearest relatives AMHPs should, where possible:

- ascertain the nearest relative's views about both the patient's needs and the nearest relative's own needs in relation to the patient;

- inform the nearest relative of the reasons for considering an application for detention and what the effects of such an application would be; and

- inform the nearest relative of their role and rights under the Act.

4.65 If the nearest relative objects to an application being made for admission for treatment under section 3, the application cannot be made. If it is thought necessary to proceed with the application to ensure the patient's safety and the nearest relative cannot be persuaded to agree, the AMHP will need to consider

---

[4] See in particular R. (on the application of E) v Bristol City Council [2005] EWHC 74 (Admin).

applying to the county court for the nearest relative's displacement under section 29 of the Act (see **chapter 8**).

## Consultation with other people

4.66 Although there are specific requirements to consult the nearest relative, it **4–052** is important to recognise the value of involving other people, particularly the patient's carers and family, in the decision-making process as well. Carers and family members are often able to provide a particular perspective on the patient's circumstances. Insofar as the urgency of the case allows, AMHPs should consider consulting with other relevant relatives, carers or friends and should take their views into account.

4.67 Where patients are under 18, AMHPs should in particular consider consulting with the patient's parents (or other people who have parental responsibility for the patient), assuming they are not the patient's nearest relative anyway.

4.68 In deciding whether it is appropriate to consult carers and other family members, AMHPs should consider:

- the patient's wishes;

- the nature of the relationship between the patient and the person in question, including how long the relationship has existed; and

- whether the patient has referred to any hostility between them and the person in question, or there is other evidence of hostility, abuse or exploitation.

4.69 AMHPs should also consult wherever possible with other people who have been involved with the patient's care. These could include people working for statutory, voluntary or independent mental health services and other service providers who do not specialise in mental health services but have contact with the patient. For example, the patient may be known to services for older people or substance misuse services.

4.70 Some patients may have an attorney or deputy appointed under the MCA who has authority to make decisions about their personal welfare. Where such a person is known to exist, AMHPs should take reasonable steps to contact them and seek their opinion. Where attorneys or deputies have the power to consent or refuse treatment for mental disorder on the patient's behalf, they should also be given the opportunity to talk directly to the doctors assessing the patient, where practicable.

## Medical examination by doctors as part of the assessment

4.71 A medical examination must involve:                                        **4–053**

- direct personal examination of the patient and their mental state; and

- consideration of all available relevant clinical information, including that in the possession of others, professional or non-professional.

4.72 If direct physical access to the patient is not immediately possible and it is not desirable to postpone the examination in order to negotiate access, consideration should be given to requesting that an AMHP apply for a warrant under section 135 of the Act (see **paragraph 4.54**).

4.73 Where practicable, at least one of the medical recommendations must be provided by a doctor with previous acquaintance with the patient. Preferably, this should be a doctor who has personally treated the patient. But it is sufficient for the doctor to have had some previous knowledge of the patient's case.

4.74 It is preferable that a doctor who does not have previous acquaintance with the patient be approved under section 12 of the Act. The Act requires that at least one of the doctors must be so approved.

4.75 If the doctors reach the opinion that the patient needs to be admitted to hospital, it is their responsibility to take the necessary steps to secure a suitable hospital bed. It is not the responsibility of the applicant, unless it has been agreed locally between the LSSA and the relevant NHS bodies that this will be done by any AMHP involved in the assessment. Primary care trusts are responsible for commissioning mental health services to meet the needs of their areas. They should ensure that procedures are in place through which beds can be identified where required.

4.76 Doctors must give reasons for the opinions stated in their recommendations. When giving a clinical description of the patient's mental disorder as part of these reasons, doctors should include a description of the patient's symptoms and behaviour, not merely a diagnostic classification.

4.77 When making recommendations for detention under section 3, doctors are required to state that appropriate medical treatment is available for the patient (see **chapter 6**). Preferably, they should know in advance of making the recommendation the name of the hospital to which the patient is to be admitted. But, if that is not possible, their recommendation may state that appropriate medical treatment will be available if the patient is admitted to one or more specific hospitals (or units within a hospital).

### Communicating the outcome of the assessment

**4–054**    4.78 Having decided whether or not to make an application for detention, AMHPs should inform the patient, giving their reasons. Subject to the normal considerations of patient confidentiality, AMHPs should also give their decision and the reasons for it to:

- the patient's nearest relative;
- the doctors involved in the assessment;
- the patient's care co-ordinator (if they have one); and
- the patient's GP, if they were not one of the doctors involved in the assessment.

4.79 An AMHP should, when informing the nearest relative that they not do intend to make an application, advise the nearest relative of their right to do so instead. If the nearest relative wishes to pursue this, the AMHP should suggest that they consult with the doctors involved in the assessment to see if they would be prepared to provide recommendations anyway.

4.80 Where the AMHP has considered a patient's case at the request of the nearest relative, the reasons for not applying for the patient's detention must be given to the nearest relative in writing. Such a letter should contain, as far as possible, sufficient details to enable the nearest relative to understand the decision while at the same time preserving the patient's right to confidentiality **(Section 13(4))**.

### Action when it is decided not to apply for detention

4.81 There is no obligation on an AMHP or nearest relative to make an appli- **4–055** cation for detention just because the statutory criteria are met.

4.82 Where AMHPs decide not to apply for a patient's detention they should record the reasons for their decision. The decision should be supported, where necessary, by an alternative framework of care and treatment. AMHPs must decide how to pursue any actions which their assessment indicates are necessary to meet the needs of the patient. That might include, for example, referring the patient to social, health or other services.

4.83 The steps to be taken to put in place any new arrangements for the patient's care and treatment, and any plans for reviewing them, should be recorded in writing and copies made available to all those who need them (subject to the normal considerations of patient confidentiality).

4.84 It is particularly important that the patient's care coordinator (if they have one) is fully involved in decisions about meeting the patient's needs.

4.85 Arrangements should be made to ensure that information about assessments and their outcome is passed to professional colleagues where appropriate, for example where an application for detention is not immediately necessary but might be in the future. This information will need to be available at short notice at any time of day or night.

4.86 More generally, making out-of-hours services aware of situations that are ongoing—such as when there is concern over an individual but no assessment has begun, or when a person has absconded before an assessment could start or be completed—assists out-of-hours services in responding accordingly.

### Action when it is decided to make an application

4.87 Most compulsory admissions require prompt action. However, applicants **4–056** have up to 14 days (depending on when the patient was last examined by a doctor as part of the assessment) in which to decide whether to make the application, starting with the day they personally last saw the patient. There may be cases where AMHPs conclude that they should delay taking a final decision, in order to see whether the patient's condition changes, or whether successful alternatives to detention can be put in place in the interim **(Sections 6(1) and 11(5))**.

4.88 Before making an application, AMHPs should ensure that appropriate arrangements are in place for the immediate care of any dependent children the patient may have and any adults who rely on the patient for care. Their needs should already have been considered as part of the assessment.

4.89 Where relevant, AMHPs should also ensure that practical arrangements are made for the care of any pets and for the LSSA to carry out its other duties under the National Assistance Act 1948 to secure the patient's home and protect their property.

4.90 Applications for detention must be addressed to the managers of the hospital where the patient is to be detained. An application must state a specific hospital. An application cannot, for example, be made to an NHS trust without specifying which of the trust's hospitals the patient is to be admitted to.

4.91 Where units under the management of different bodies exist on the same site (or even in the same building), they will be separate hospitals for the purposes of the Act, because one hospital cannot be under the control of two sets of managers. Where there is potential for confusion, the respective hospital managers should ensure that there are distinct names for the units. In collaboration with LSSAs, they should take steps to ensure that information is available to AMHPs who are likely to be making relevant applications to enable them effectively to distinguish the different hospitals on the site and to describe them correctly in applications.

4.92 Once an application has been completed, the patient should be conveyed to the hospital as soon as possible, if they are not already in the hospital. But patients should not be moved until it is known that the hospital is willing to accept them.

4.93 A properly completed application supported by the necessary medical recommendations provides the applicant with the authority to convey the patient to hospital even if the patient does not wish to go. That authority lasts for 14 days from the date when the patient was last examined by one of the doctors with a view to making a recommendation to support the application. See **chapter 11** for further guidance on conveyance **(Section 6(1))**.

4.94 The AMHP should provide an outline report for the hospital at the time the patient is first admitted or detained, giving reasons for the application and details of any practical matters about the patient's circumstances which the hospital should know. Where possible, the report should include the name and telephone number of the AMHP or a care co-ordinator who can give further information. LSSAs should consider the use of a standard form on which AMHPs can make this outline report.

4.95 Where it is not realistic for the AMHP to accompany the patient to the hospital—for example, where the admitting hospital is some distance from the area in which the AMHP operates—it is acceptable for them to provide the information outlined above by telephone or fax or other means compatible with transferring confidential information. If providing the information by telephone, the AMHP should ensure that a written report is sent to the admitting hospital as soon as possible.

4.96 An outline report does not take the place of the full report which AMHPs are expected to complete for their employer or the LSSA on whose behalf they are acting (if different).

4.97 If the patient is a restricted patient, the AMHP should ensure that the Mental Health Unit of the Ministry of Justice is notified of the detention as soon as possible. A duty officer is available at all times to receive this information, which should not be left until office hours.[5]

4.98 An application cannot be used to admit a patient to any hospital other than the one stated in the application (although once admitted a patient may be transferred to another hospital—see **chapter 30**).

4.99 In exceptional circumstances, if patients are conveyed to a hospital which has agreed to accept them, but there is no longer a bed available, the managers and staff of that hospital should assist in finding a suitable alternative for the patient. This may involve making a new application to a different hospital. If the application is under section 3, new medical recommendations will be required, unless the original recommendations already state that appropriate medical treatment is available in the proposed new hospital. The hospital to which the original

---

[5] At the time of publication the telephone number is 020 7035 4848.

application was made should assist in securing new medical recommendations if they are needed. A situation of this sort should be considered a serious failure and should be recorded and investigated accordingly.

**Resolving disagreements**

4.100 Sometimes there will be differences of opinion between professionals **4–057** involved in the assessment. There is nothing wrong with disagreements: handled properly they offer an opportunity to safeguard the interests of the patient by widening the discussion on the best way of meeting their needs. Doctors and AMHPs should be ready to consult other professionals (especially care co-ordinators and others involved with the patient's current care), while themselves retaining the final responsibility for their decision. Where disagreements do occur, professionals should ensure that they discuss these with each other.

4.101 Where there is an unresolved dispute about an application for detention, it is essential that the professionals do not abandon the patient. Instead, they should explore and agree an alternative plan—if necessary on a temporary basis. Such a plan should include a risk assessment and identification of the arrangements for managing the risks. The alternative plan should be recorded in writing, as should the arrangements for reviewing it. Copies should be made available to all those who need them (subject to the normal considerations of patient confidentiality).

**Responsibilities of strategic health authorities for doctors approved under section 12 (Reference Guide chapter 32)**

4.102 The Secretary of State has delegated to strategic health authorities **4–058** (SHAs) the task of approving medical practitioners under section 12(2) of the Act. Medical practitioners who are approved clinicians under the Act are automatically treated as being approved under section 12 as well.

4.103 SHAs should:

- take active steps to encourage sufficient doctors, including GPs and those working in prison health services and the police service, to apply for approval;

- ensure that arrangements are in place for 24-hour on-call rotas of approved doctors (or an equivalent arrangement) sufficient to cover each area for which they are responsible;

- ensure that regularly updated lists of approved doctors are maintained which indicate how they can be contacted and the hours that each is available; and

- ensure that the up-to-date list of approved doctors and details of 24-hour on-call rotas (or the equivalent arrangement) are available to all those who may need them, including GPs, providers of hospital and community mental health services and social services.

**Co-operation between local agencies**

4.104 NHS bodies and LSSAs should co-operate in ensuring that there are **4–059** opportunities for regular communication between professionals involved in mental health assessments, in order to promote understanding and to provide a forum for clarification of their respective roles and responsibilities. NHS bodies and

LSSAs should also keep in mind the interface with the criminal justice agencies, including the probation service and the police.

4.105 Opportunities should also be sought to involve and learn directly from people with experience of being assessed.

**Patients who are deaf**

**4–060**  4.106 AMHPs and doctors assessing a deaf person should, wherever possible, have had deaf awareness training, including basic training in issues relating to mental health and deafness. Where required, they should also seek assistance from specialists with appropriate expertise in mental health and deafness. This may be available from one of the specialist hospital units for deafness and mental health. Contact with such units may, in particular, help to prevent deaf people being wrongly assessed as having a learning disability or another mental disorder.

4.107 Unless different arrangements have been agreed locally, the AMHP involved in the assessment should be responsible for booking and using registered qualified interpreters with expertise in mental health interpreting, bearing in mind that the interpretation of thoughtdisordered language requires particular expertise. Relay interpreters (interpreters who relay British Sign Language (BSL) to hands-on BSL or visual frame signing or close signing) may be necessary, such as when the deaf person has a visual impairment, does not use BSL to sign or has minimal language skills or a learning disability.

4.108 Reliance on unqualified interpreters or health professionals with only limited signing skills should be avoided. Family members may (subject to the normal considerations about patient confidentiality) occasionally be able to assist a professional interpreter in understanding a patient's idiosyncratic use of language. However, family members should not be relied upon in place of a professional interpreter, even if the patient is willing for them to be involved.

4.109 Pre-lingual deafness may cause delayed language acquisition, which may in turn influence social behaviour. People carrying out assessments of deaf people under the Act should have an awareness and knowledge of how mental health problems present in pre-lingually deaf people.

4.110 Cultural issues need to be taken into account, for instance in people who are pre-lingually deaf, as they have a visual perspective of the world and may consider themselves to be part of a cultural and linguistic minority. This means that they may behave in ways which are misperceived as evidence of mental disorder. For example, animated signing may be misunderstood as aggression, while touching a hearing person to talk to them may be misunderstood as an assault. Deaf people's spoken or written English may be poor, giving rise to a false assumption of thought disorder.

---

- Mental Capacity Act 2005
- *Mental Capacity Act 2005 Code of Practice*, TSO, 2007
- *Deprivation of Liberty Safeguards*, Addendum to the *Mental Capacity Act 2005 Code of Practice*
- National Assistance Act 1948

  This material does not form part of the Code. It is provided for assistance only.

---

## 5. EMERGENCY APPLICATIONS FOR DETENTION

5.1 This chapter gives guidance on the making of emergency applications for **4–061** detention in hospital under section 4 of the Act **(Reference Guide 2.46–2.54)**.

### Applications for detention for assessment in an emergency

5.2 The Act permits an application for detention for assessment to be made **4–062** under section 4 on the basis of a single medical recommendation, but only in very limited circumstances. An application for detention under section 4 may be made only when:

- the criteria for detention for assessment under section 2 are met;

- the patient's detention is required as a matter of urgent necessity; and

- obtaining a second medical recommendation would cause undesirable delay.

5.3 An application under section 4 may be made only if the applicant has seen the patient personally within the previous 24 hours. Otherwise, the duties of approved mental health professionals (AMHPs) in respect of applications are the same as for applications under section 2. The guidance given in **chapter 4** about the way in which assessments should be carried out applies equally to applications under section 4 (except, of course, that there will be only one doctor involved).

### Urgent necessity

5.4 Section 4 should be used only in a genuine emergency, where the patient's **4–063** need for urgent assessment outweighs the desirability of waiting for a second doctor.

5.5 Section 4 should never be used for administrative convenience. So, for example, patients should not be detained under section 4 merely because it is more convenient for the second doctor to examine the patient in, rather than outside, hospital.

5.6 An emergency may arise where the patient's mental state or behaviour presents problems which those involved cannot reasonably be expected to manage while waiting for a second doctor. To be satisfied that an emergency has arisen, the person making the application and the doctor making the supporting recommendation should have evidence of:

- an immediate and significant risk of mental or physical harm to the patient or to others;

- danger of serious harm to property; or

- a need for physical restraint of the patient.

### Availability of second medical recommendation

5.7 It is the responsibility of primary care trusts (and other NHS com- **4–064** missioners) to ensure that doctors are available in a timely manner to examine patients under the Act when requested to do so by AMHPs and in other cases where such an examination is necessary.

5.8 If AMHPs find themselves having to consider making emergency applications because of difficulties in securing a second doctor, they should report that fact to the local social services authority (LSSA) on whose behalf they are acting (or in accordance with locally agreed arrangements, if they are different).

5.9 Hospital managers and LSSAs should monitor the use of section 4 to ensure that it is not misused and to allow action to be taken to rectify any problems with the availability of doctors.

**Detention under section 4**

**4–065**    5.10 The authority to convey a patient to hospital and to start their detention there on the basis of an emergency application lasts only for 24 hours from the last time at which the doctor examined the patient for the purposes of the application, or from the time the application is made, whichever is the earlier. A patient may then be detained only for a maximum of 72 hours unless a second medical recommendation is provided to the hospital managers in accordance with the Act (**Section 6(1)**).

5.11 Patients detained under section 4 should be examined by an appropriate second doctor as soon as possible, to decide whether they should continue to be detained. If the doctor who made the recommendation for the section 4 application was not a doctor approved under section 12, the Act requires the doctor making the second recommendation to be so approved.

5.12 Patients detained on the basis of emergency applications may not be treated without their consent under Part 4 of the Act unless or until the second medical recommendation is received. Until then they are in exactly the same position in respect of consent to treatment as patients who are not detained under the Act (**Section 56**).

5.13 An application for detention for treatment under section 3 of the Act may be made while a patient is detained under section 4—but two fresh medical recommendations would be required.

## 6. THE APPROPRIATE MEDICAL TREATMENT TEST

**4–066**    6.1 This chapter gives guidance on the application of the appropriate medical treatment test in the criteria for detention and supervised community treatment (SCT) under the Act.

**Purpose of medical treatment for mental disorder**

**4–067**    6.2 For the purposes of the Act, medical treatment also includes nursing, psychological intervention and specialist mental health habilitation, rehabilitation and care. Habilitation means equipping someone with skills and abilities they have never had, whereas rehabilitation means helping them recover skills and abilities they have lost (**Section 145(1)**).

6.3 In the Act, medical treatment for mental disorder means medical treatment which is for the purpose of alleviating, or preventing a worsening of, a mental disorder or one or more of its symptoms or manifestations (**Section 145(4)**).

6.4 Purpose is not the same as likelihood. Medical treatment may be for the purpose of alleviating, or preventing a worsening of, a mental disorder even though it cannot be shown in advance that any particular effect is likely to be achieved.

6.5 Symptoms and manifestations include the way a disorder is experienced by the individual concerned and the way in which the disorder manifests itself in the person's thoughts, emotions, communication, behaviour and actions. But it should be remembered that not every thought or emotion, or every aspect of the behaviour, of a patient suffering from a mental disorder will be a manifestation of that disorder.

6.6 Even if particular mental disorders are likely to persist or get worse despite treatment, there may well be a range of interventions which would represent appropriate medical treatment. It should never be assumed that any disorders, or any patients, are inherently or inevitably untreatable. Nor should it be assumed that likely difficulties in achieving long-term and sustainable change in a person's underlying disorder make medical treatment to help manage their condition and the behaviours arising from it either inappropriate or unnecessary.

**Appropriate medical treatment test**

6.7 The purpose of the appropriate medical treatment test is to ensure that no-**4–068** one is detained (or remains detained) for treatment, or is an SCT patient, unless they are actually to be offered medical treatment for their mental disorder.

6.8 This medical treatment must be appropriate, taking into account the nature and degree of the person's mental disorder and all their particular circumstances, including cultural, ethnic and religious considerations. By definition, it must be treatment which is for the purpose of alleviating or preventing a worsening of the patient's mental disorder or its symptoms or manifestations.

6.9 The appropriate medical treatment test requires a judgement about whether an appropriate package of treatment for mental disorder is available for the individual in question. Where the appropriate medical treatment test forms part of the criteria for detention, the medical treatment in question is treatment for mental disorder in the hospital in which the patient is to be detained. Where it is part of the criteria for SCT it refers to the treatment for mental disorder that the person will be offered while on SCT.

**Applying the appropriate medical treatment test**

6.10 The test requires a judgement about whether, when looked at in the round, **4–069** appropriate medical treatment is available to the patient, given:

- the nature and degree of the patient's mental disorder; and
- all the other circumstances of the patient's case.

In other words, both the clinical appropriateness of the treatment and its appropriateness more generally must be considered.

6.11 The other circumstances of a patient's case might include factors such as:

- the patient's physical health—how this might impact on the effectiveness of the available medical treatment for the patient's mental disorder and the impact that the treatment might have in return;
- any physical disabilities the patient has;
- the patient's culture and ethnicity;
- the patient's age;
- the patient's gender, gender identity and sexual orientation;

- the location of the available treatment;
- the implications of the treatment for the patient's family and social relationships, including their role as a parent;
- its implications for the patient's education or work; and
- the consequences for the patient, and other people, if the patient does not receive the treatment available. (For mentally disordered offenders about to be sentenced for an offence, the consequence will sometimes be a prison sentence.)

6.12 Medical treatment need not be the most appropriate treatment that could ideally be made available. Nor does it need to address every aspect of the person's disorder. But the medical treatment available at any time must be an appropriate response to the patient's condition and situation.

6.13 Medical treatment must actually be available to the patient. It is not sufficient that appropriate treatment could theoretically be provided.

6.14 What is appropriate will vary greatly between patients. It will depend, in part, on what might reasonably be expected to be achieved given the nature and degree of the patient's disorder.

6.15 Medical treatment which aims merely to prevent a disorder worsening is unlikely, in general, to be appropriate in cases where normal treatment approaches would aim (and be expected) to alleviate the patient's condition significantly. For some patients with persistent mental disorders, however, management of the undesirable effects of their disorder may be all that can realistically be hoped for.

6.16 Appropriate medical treatment does not have to involve medication or individual or group psychological therapy—although it very often will. There may be patients whose particular circumstances mean that treatment may be appropriate even though it consists only of nursing and specialist day-to-day care under the clinical supervision of an approved clinician, in a safe and secure therapeutic environment with a structured regime.

6.17 Simply detaining someone—even in a hospital—does not constitute medical treatment.

6.18 A patient's attitude towards the proposed treatment may be relevant in determining whether the appropriate medical treatment test is met. But an indication of unwillingness to co-operate with treatment generally, or with a specific aspect of treatment, does not make such treatment inappropriate.

6.19 In particular, psychological therapies and other forms of medical treatments which, to be effective, require the patient's co-operation are not automatically inappropriate simply because a patient does not currently wish to engage with them. Such treatments can potentially remain appropriate and available as long as it continues to be clinically suitable to offer them and they would be provided if the patient agreed to engage.

6.20 People called on to make a judgement about whether the appropriate medical treatment test is met do not have to be satisfied that appropriate treatment will be available for the whole course of the patient's detention or SCT. What is appropriate may change over time, as the patient's condition changes or clinicians obtain a greater understanding of the patient's case. But they must satisfy themselves that appropriate medical treatment is available for the time being, given the patient's condition and circumstances as they are currently understood.

## 7. CONFLICTS OF INTEREST

7.1 This chapter is concerned with the circumstances in which applications by **4–070** approved mental health professionals (AMHPs) for a person to be admitted under the Act to hospital or guardianship, or provision of medical recommendations by doctors for the purpose of such applications, must not be made because of potential conflicts of interest. It also discusses some other potential conflicts.

### Conflict of Interest Regulations

7.2 The Mental Health (Conflict of Interest) (England) Regulations 2008 set out **4–071** the circumstances in which a potential conflict of interest prevents an AMHP making an application for a patient's detention or guardianship and a doctor making a recommendation supporting the application. AMHPs and these doctors are collectively referred to as "assessors" in this chapter **(Reference Guide 2.55– 2.59 (detention) and 19.42–19.46 (guardianship))**.

7.3 These potential conflicts of interest may concern the relationship of AMHPs and doctors to each other, to the patient, to the nearest relative or to the hospital where the patient is to be admitted. They concern potential conflicts of interest for financial, business, professional and personal reasons.

*Financial conflict*

7.4 Where the patient is to be admitted to an independent hospital and the doc- **4–072** tor providing one of the medical recommendations is on the staff of that hospital, the other medical recommendation must be given by a doctor who is not on the staff of that hospital. That is, there will be a potential conflict if both doctors giving recommendations are on the staff of the independent hospital.

7.5 There will be no potential conflict of interest for financial reasons just because both doctors are on the staff of an NHS hospital to which the patient will be admitted.

7.6 An assessor will have a conflict of interest for financial reasons if the assessor stands to make a financial benefit (or loss) from their decision. There will not be a potential conflict of interest for financial reasons where an assessor is paid a fee for making an application or giving a medical recommendation if it is paid regardless of the outcome of the assessment.

*Business conflict*

7.7 An assessor will have a potential conflict of interest if both that assessor and **4–073** one of the other assessors, the patient or the nearest relative (if the nearest relative is the applicant) are closely involved in the same business venture. Being closely involved is not defined in the regulations, but examples could include being a partner in a partnership, being a director or other office-holder of a company, or being a major shareholder in it. This will apply even if the business venture is not associated with the provision of services for the care and treatment of persons with a mental disorder.

7.8 Business ventures include any form of commercial enterprise from which the person concerned stands to profit. Such people include: directors and major investors in a company (of any size) which provides goods or services for profit; partners in a GP practice; partners in a business established as a limited liability partnership. Involvement in a business venture does not include involvement in societies and similar organisations which are essentially non-commercial, and from which the people concerned do not stand to profit.

*Professional conflict*

**4–074**    7.9 Regulations set out that a conflict of interest for professional reasons will occur where:

- the assessor is in a line management or employment relationship with one of the other assessors or the patient or the nearest relative (where the nearest relative is the applicant);
- the assessor is a member of the same team as the patient; or
- where there are three assessors, all of them are members of the same team.

7.10 A line management relationship will exist whether an assessor manages, or is managed by, one of the other assessors, the patient or the nearest relative (where the nearest relative is the applicant). Similarly an employment relationship will exist whether the assessor employs, or is employed by, one of the other assessors, the patient or the nearest relative (where the nearest relative is the applicant).

7.11 For the purposes of the regulations a team is defined as a group of professionals who work together for clinical purposes on a routine basis. That might include a community mental health team, a crisis resolution or home treatment team, or staff on an in-patient unit (but not necessarily the staff of an entire hospital).

**Urgent necessity**
**4–075**    7.12 If there is a case of urgent necessity all three assessors may be from the same team. However, this should happen only in a genuine emergency, where the patient's need for urgent assessment outweighs the desirability of waiting for another assessor who has no potential conflict of interest. Any decisions made to proceed despite a potential conflict of interest should be recorded, with reasons, in case notes.

7.13 In a case of urgent necessity it is preferable to proceed with three assessors, despite a potential conflict of interest, rather than make the application under section 4 of the Act with only two assessors (one doctor and one AMHP). (See **paragraphs 5.4–5.6**.)

7.14 There are no other circumstances in which potential conflicts of interest can be set aside because of urgent necessity.

**Other potential conflicts**
**4–076**    7.15 There may be circumstances not covered by these regulations where the assessor feels, nonetheless, that there is (or could be seen to be) a potential conflict of interest. Assessors should work on the principle that in any situation where they believe that the objectivity or independence of their decision is (or could be seen to be) undermined, they should not become involved or should withdraw.

7.16 These regulations do not cover potential conflicts of interest relating to supervised community treatment (SCT). However, the responsible clinician and the AMHP responsible for making the decision as to whether to place a patient on SCT, or any decision to revoke a community treatment order, should not have any financial interest in the outcome of the decision. Similarly, neither the responsible clinician nor the AMHP should be a relative of the patient or of each other.

7.17 The Act requires an AMHP to take an independent decision about whether or not to make an application under the Act. If an AMHP believes that they are being placed under undue pressure to make, or not make, an application, they should raise this through the appropriate channels. Local arrangements should be in place to deal with such circumstances.

## 8. THE NEAREST RELATIVE

8.1 This chapter gives guidance on the identification, appointment and dis- **4–077** placement of nearest relatives under the Act **(Reference Guide chapter 33)**.

### Identification of the nearest relative

8.2 Section 26 of the Act defines "relative" and "nearest relative" for the pur- **4–078** poses of the Act. It is important to remember that the nearest relative for the purposes of the Act may not be the same person as the patient's next of kin. The identity of the nearest relative may also change with the passage of time (eg if the patient enters into a marriage or civil partnership). (See **paragraphs 4.56–4.65.**)

8.3 Patients remanded to hospital under sections 35 and 36 of the Act and people subject to interim hospital orders under section 38 do not have nearest relatives (as defined by the Act). Nor do patients subject to special restrictions under Part 3 of the Act (restricted patients).

### Delegation of nearest relative functions

8.4 A nearest relative is not obliged to act as such. They can authorise, in writ- **4–079** ing, another person to perform the functions of the nearest relative on their behalf. The procedure for doing this is set out in the Mental Health (Hospital, Guardianship and Treatment) (England) Regulations 2008.

### Where there is no nearest relative

8.5 Where an approved mental health professional (AMHP) discovers, when **4–080** assessing a patient for possible detention or guardianship under the Act (or at any other time), that the patient appears to have no nearest relative, the AMHP should advise the patient of their right to apply to the county court for the appointment of a person to act as their nearest relative.

### Displacement of nearest relatives and appointment of acting nearest relatives by the county court (Sections 29 and 30)

*Grounds for displacement and appointment*

8.6 An acting nearest relative can be appointed by the county court on the **4–081** grounds that:

- the nearest relative is incapable of acting as such because of illness or mental disorder;

- the nearest relative has objected unreasonably to an application for admission for treatment or a guardianship application;

- the nearest relative has exercised the power to discharge a patient without due regard to the patient's health or wellbeing or the safety of the public;

- the nearest relative is otherwise not a suitable person to act as such; or

- the patient has no nearest relative within the meaning of the Act, or it is not reasonably practicable to ascertain whether the patient has a nearest relative or who that nearest relative is.

8.7 The effect of a court order appointing an acting nearest relative is to displace the person who would otherwise be the patient's nearest relative.

8.8 However, as an alternative to an order by the court, it may sometimes be enough for the actual nearest relative to delegate their role to someone else (see **paragraph 8.4**).

*Who can make an application to the court?*

**4–082**    An application to displace the nearest relative may be made by any of the following people:

- the patient;

- any relative of the patient;

- anyone with whom the patient is residing (or was residing prior to admission); or

- an AMHP.

*Applications to the court by AMHPs*

**4–083**    8.10 AMHPs will need to consider making an application for displacement or appointment if:

- they believe that a patient should be detained in hospital under section 3 of the Act, or should become a guardianship patient, but the nearest relative objects; or

- they believe that the nearest relative is likely to discharge a patient from detention or guardianship unwisely.

8.11 They should also consider doing so if they think that:

- a patient has no identifiable nearest relative or their nearest relative is incapable of acting as such; or

- they have good reasons to think that a patient considers their nearest relative unsuitable and would like them to be replaced;

and it would not be reasonable in the circumstances to expect the patient, or anyone else, to make an application.

8.12 AMHPs should bear in mind that some patients may wish to apply to displace their nearest relative but may be deterred from doing so by the need to apply to the county court.

8.13 It is entirely a matter for the court to decide what constitutes "suitability" of a person to be a nearest relative. But factors which an AMHP might wish to consider when deciding whether to make an application to displace a nearest relative on grounds of unsuitability, and when providing evidence in connection with an application, could include:

- any reason to think that the patient has suffered, or is suspected to have suffered, abuse at the hands of the nearest relative (or someone with whom the nearest relative is in a relationship), or is at risk of suffering such abuse;

- any evidence that the patient is afraid of the nearest relative or seriously distressed by the possibility of the nearest relative being involved in their life or their care; and

- a situation where the patient and nearest relative are unknown to each other, there is only a distant relationship between them, or their relationship has broken down irretrievably.

This is not an exhaustive list.

8.14 In all cases, the decision to make an application lies with the AMHP personally.

8.15 Before making an application for displacement, AMHPs should consider other ways of achieving the same end, including:

- whether the nearest relative will agree to delegate their role as the patient's nearest relative to someone else; or

- providing or arranging support for the patient (or someone else) to make an application themselves. This could include support from an independent mental health advocate.[6]

8.16 Local social services authorities (LSSAs) should provide clear practical guidance to help AMHPs decide whether to make an application and how to proceed. Before producing such guidance, LSSAs should consult with the county court. LSSAs should ensure that they have access to the necessary legal advice and support.

*Making an application*

8.17 People making an application to the county court will need to provide the **4–084** court with the facts that will help it make a decision on the application. Exactly what will be required will depend on the type of application and the specific circumstances of the case.

8.18 When applying to displace a nearest relative, AMHPs should nominate someone to become the acting nearest relative in the event that the application

---

[6] Independent mental health advocacy services under the Act are expected to be introduced in April 2009.

is successful. Wherever practicable, they should first consult the patient about the patient's own preferences and any concerns they have about the person the AMHP proposes to nominate. AMHPs should also seek the agreement of the proposed nominee prior to an application being made, although this is not a legal requirement.

8.19 LSSAs should provide clear practical guidance to help the AMHP decide who it is appropriate to nominate when making an application to displace a nearest relative.

8.20 If the patient has any concerns that any information given to the court on their views on the suitability of the nearest relative may have implications for their own safety, an application can be made to the court seeking its permission not to make the current nearest relative a party to the proceedings. The reasons for the patient's concerns should be set out clearly in the application.

8.21 Hospital managers should provide support to detained patients to enable them to attend the court, if they wish, subject to the patient being granted leave under section 17 for this purpose.

8.22 If, exceptionally, the court decides to interview the patient (as the applicant), the court has the discretion to decide where and how this interview may take place and whether it should take place in the presence of, or separate from, other parties.

8.23 If the court decides that the nearest relative should be displaced and finds the proposed replacement to be suitable, and that person is willing to act as nearest relative, then the court will appoint them.

## 9. ATTORNEYS AND DEPUTIES

**4–085**     9.1 This chapter gives guidance on the effect of the Mental Health Act on the powers of donees of lasting power of attorney (attorneys) and deputies appointed under the Mental Capacity Act 2005 (MCA).

### Powers of attorneys and deputies
**4–086**     9.2 In general, the fact that a person is subject to the Mental Health Act does not affect the validity of any lasting power of attorney (LPA), nor the scope of the authority of an attorney or deputy (or the Court of Protection) to make decisions on their behalf.

9.3 Attorneys and deputies can take any decisions in relation to the welfare, property or affairs of a person subject to the Act that they are otherwise authorised to take, with two exceptions:

- they will not be able to consent on the patient's behalf to treatment which is regulated by Part 4 of the Mental Health Act, including neurosurgery for mental disorder and other treatments under section 57 (see **chapter 23,**); and

- they will not be able to take decisions about where a patient subject to guardianship is to live, nor take other decisions which conflict with decisions that a guardian has a legal right to make (see **chapter 26**).

9.4 Being subject to compulsory measures under the Mental Health Act does not prevent people creating new LPAs under the MCA if they have the capacity to do so. Nor does it prevent the Court of Protection from appointing a deputy to take decisions for them which they lack the capacity to make themselves.

9.5 In certain cases, conditions can be imposed on patients subject to the Mental Health Act in relation to leave of absence from hospital, supervised community treatment (SCT) or conditional discharge. If an attorney or deputy takes a decision on the patient's behalf which goes against one of these conditions, the patient will be taken to have gone against the condition. In SCT and conditional discharge cases, this might result in the patient's recall to hospital being considered.

9.6 Attorneys and deputies are able to exercise a patient's rights under the Mental Health Act on their behalf, if they have the relevant authority under the LPA or the order of the court appointing them and the patient concerned lacks the capacity to do so themselves. In particular, personal welfare attorneys and deputies may be able to exercise the patient's various rights to apply to the Tribunal for discharge from detention, guardianship or SCT.

9.7 It is good practice, where practicable, for clinicians and others involved in the assessment or treatment of patients under the Act to try to find out whether the person has an attorney or deputy and to establish effective means of communication to ensure that the attorney or deputy is informed and, where relevant, consulted about the patient's care.

### Relationship between the powers of attorneys and deputies and the role of nearest relatives

9.8 The rights of the nearest relative are not affected just because a patient has **4–087** an attorney or deputy.

9.9 Attorneys and deputies may not exercise the rights of the nearest relative, unless they are themselves the nearest relative (because the rights belong to the nearest relative, not the patient).

9.10 There may sometimes be a disagreement between a nearest relative and an attorney or deputy (eg over whether the attorney or deputy should exercise the patient's right to apply to the Tribunal, or whether the nearest relative should make a discharge order). If so, it may be helpful for the two to discuss the issue, perhaps with the assistance of one of the professionals involved in the patient's case. But ultimately they have different roles, and each must act as they think best. Specifically, an attorney or deputy must act in accordance with their authority and in the patient's best interests.

---

**Related material**

- Mental Capacity Act 2005
- *Mental Capacity Act 2005 Code of Practice*, TSO, 2007

  This material does not form part of the Code. It is provided for assistance only.

---

## 10. POLICE POWERS AND PLACES OF SAFETY

**4–088**     10.1 This chapter deals with entry to premises under the Act and powers temporarily to remove people who appear to be suffering from a mental disorder to a place of safety (**Reference Guide chapter 30**).

### Section 135: warrant to search for and remove patients
**4–089**     10.2 A police officer may use powers of entry under section 135(1) of the Act when it is necessary to gain access to premises to remove a person who is believed to have a mental disorder and is not receiving proper care. This requires a magistrate's warrant. A magistrate may issue a warrant under section 135(1) in response to an application from an approved mental health professional (AMHP).

10.3 The warrant gives any police officer the right to enter the premises, by force if necessary. When acting on the warrant, the officer must be accompanied by an AMHP and a doctor. It may be helpful if the doctor who accompanies the police officer is approved for the purposes of section 12(2) of the Act. The police officer may then remove the person to a place of safety, where they can be detained for up to 72 hours from the time of their arrival.

10.4 Following entry under section 135(1), the AMHP and doctor between them should, if feasible, carry out a preliminary assessment of the person to determine whether they need to be assessed further for an application under the Act or for other arrangements for care or treatment. It may be possible to carry out any such further assessment in the premises themselves.

10.5 Section 135(2) provides for the issue of a warrant by a magistrate authorising entry by the police to remove a patient who is liable to be taken or returned to hospital or any other place or into custody under the Act. It enables a police officer to enter the premises and remove the patient so that they can be taken or returned to where they ought to be. Such a warrant may be used, for example, to help return a patient who has absconded, or who needs to be conveyed to hospital, if access to the premises where they are staying has been refused or is likely to be refused. (See **chapter 22** for detailed guidance on patients who are absent from hospital without leave.)

10.6 When a warrant issued under section 135(2) is being used, it is good practice for the police officer to be accompanied by a person with authority from the managers of the relevant hospital (or local social services authority (LSSA), if applicable) to take the patient into custody and to take or return them to where they ought to be. For patients on supervised community treatment (SCT) it is good practice for this person to be, if possible, a member of the multi-disciplinary team responsible for the patient's care.

10.7 LSSAs should ensure that guidance is available to AMHPs on how and when to apply for a warrant.

10.8 LSSAs and hospital managers should ensure that there are procedures in place for obtaining warrants, both during and outside court hours. These should describe the necessary processes, the evidence which individuals may be reasonably expected to produce, and the documents that should be prepared to help the process run smoothly.

10.9 Where a section 135 warrant is used, the AMHP, the hospital managers or the LSSA (as appropriate) should ensure that an ambulance or other transport is available to take the person to the place of safety or to the place where they ought to be, in accordance with a locally agreed policy on the transport of patients under the Act (see **chapter 11**).

10.10 Magistrates have to be satisfied that it is appropriate to issue a warrant. They are likely to ask applicants why they are applying for a warrant, whether reasonable attempts to enter without a warrant have been made and, if not, why not. Applicants should provide documented reasons for seeking a warrant if they have not already tried to gain access.

10.11 Thought should be given to the choice of the place of safety before a warrant is applied for under section 135(1). Proper planning should mean that it is almost never necessary to use a police station as a place of safety for people removed under section 135(1).

### Section 136: mentally disordered people found in public places

10.12 Section 136 allows for the removal to a place of safety of any person **4–090** found in a place to which the public have access (by payment or otherwise) who appears to a police officer to be suffering from mental disorder and to be in immediate need of care or control.

10.13 Removal to a place of safety may take place if the police officer believes it necessary in the interests of that person, or for the protection of others.

10.14 The purpose of removing a person to a place of safety in these circumstances is only to enable the person to be examined by a doctor and interviewed by an AMHP, so that the necessary arrangements can be made for the person's care and treatment. It is not a substitute for an application for detention under the Act, even if it is thought that the person will need to be detained in hospital only for a short time. It is also not intended to substitute for or affect the use of other police powers.

10.15 The maximum period a person may be detained under section 136 is 72 hours. The imposition of consecutive periods of detention under section 136 is unlawful.

### Local policies on the use of police powers and places of safety

10.16 It is important to ensure that a jointly agreed local policy is in place **4–091** governing all aspects of the use of sections 135 and 136. Good practice depends on a number of factors. For example:

- LSSAs, hospitals, NHS commissioners, police forces and ambulance services should ensure that they have a clear and jointly agreed policy for use of the powers under sections 135 and 136, as well as the operation of agreed places of safety within their localities;

- all professionals involved in implementation of the powers should understand them and their purpose, and the roles and responsibilities of other people involved, and should follow the local policy;

- professionals involved in implementation of the powers should receive the necessary training; and

- the parties to the local policy should meet regularly to discuss its effectiveness in the light of experience.

10.17 The policy should define responsibilities for:

- commissioning and providing secure places of safety in healthcare settings;
- identifying and agreeing the most appropriate place of safety in individual cases;
- providing prompt assessment and, where appropriate, admission to hospital for further assessment or treatment;
- securing the attendance of police officers, where appropriate for the patient's health or safety or the protection of others;
- the safe, timely and appropriate conveyance of the person to and between places of safety (bearing in mind that hospital or ambulance transport will generally be preferable to police transport, which should be used exceptionally, such as in cases of extreme urgency or where there is a risk of violence);
- deciding whether it is appropriate to transfer the person from the place of safety to which they have been taken to another place of safety (see **paragraphs 10.34–10.39);**
- dealing with people who are also under the effects of alcohol or drugs;
- dealing with people who are behaving, or have behaved, violently;
- arranging access to a hospital accident and emergency department for assessment, where necessary;
- record keeping (see **paragraphs 10.40–10.41)** and monitoring (see **paragraphs 10.42–10.44)** and audit of practice against policy; and
- the release, transport and follow-up of people assessed under section 135 or 136 who are not then admitted to hospital or immediately accommodated elsewhere.

10.18 Responsibilities should be allocated to those who are best placed to discharge them, bearing in mind the different purposes for which health and social services and the police service exist. Local policies should ensure that police officers know whom to contact prior to the removal of a person to a place of safety under section 136.

10.19 Such policies may be best maintained by the establishment of a liaison committee, which might also take responsibility for examining the processes in place for other multi-agency tasks, such as conveyance of persons under the Act and policies in respect of patients who go absent without leave.

**Places of safety**

**4–092** 10.20 The process for identifying the most appropriate place of safety to which a particular person is to be removed should be clearly outlined in the local policy.

10.21 A police station should be used as a place of safety only on an exceptional basis. It may be necessary to do so because the person's behaviour would pose an unmanageably high risk to other patients, staff or users of a healthcare setting. It is preferable for a person thought to be suffering from a mental disorder to be detained in a hospital or other healthcare setting where mental health services are provided (subject, of course, to any urgent physical healthcare needs they may have).

10.22 A police station should not be assumed to be the automatic second choice if the first choice place of safety is not immediately available. Other available options, such as a residential care home or the home of a relative or friend of the person who is willing to accept them temporarily, should also be considered.

10.23 If a police station is used, health and social care agencies should work with the police in arranging, where appropriate, the transfer of the person to a more suitable place of safety. In defining responsibility for providing a prompt assessment, the locally agreed policy should set out the time within which it would be reasonable to expect the appropriate health and social care professionals to attend the police station to assess the person or to assist in arranging to transfer them.

10.24 In identifying the most appropriate place of safety for an individual, consideration should be given to the impact that the proposed place of safety (and the journey to it) may have on the person and on their examination and interview. It should always be borne in mind that the use of a police station can give the impression that the person detained is suspected of having committed a crime. This may cause distress and anxiety to the person concerned and may affect their co-operation with, and therefore the effectiveness of, the assessment process.

10.25 Where an individual is removed to a place of safety by the police, the following recommendations apply:

- where the place of safety is a hospital, the police should make immediate contact with both the hospital and the LSSA (or the people arranging AMHP services on its behalf), and this contact should take place prior to the person's arrival at the place of safety. This will allow arrangements to be made for the person to be interviewed and examined as soon as possible. Where a warrant has been issued under section 135, these arrangements should, wherever possible, have been made in advance by the AMHP, the hospital or any other organisation responsible for the person;

- where a hospital is used as a place of safety, it is a local decision whether the person is admitted to a bed on arrival or whether that happens only after they have been interviewed and examined; and

- where a police station is to be used as the place of safety, contact should be quickly made with the LSSA (or its AMHP service) and with an appropriate doctor. This will enable the examination and interview to be conducted as quickly as possible, thus ensuring that the person spends no longer than necessary in police custody before being released or taken to hospital. Early assessment will also allow consideration to be given to the possibility of a transfer to an alternative place of safety as soon as this is considered to be safe and appropriate in all the circumstances.

**Assessment at a place of safety**

10.26 The same care should be taken in examining and interviewing people in **4–093** places of safety as in any other assessment. No assumptions should be made about them simply because the police have been involved, nor should they be assumed to be in any less need of support and assistance during the assessment. The guidance on assessment in **chapter 4** applies in these circumstances as in any others.

10.27 Doctors examining patients should, wherever possible, be approved under section 12 of the Act. Where the examination has to be conducted by a doctor who is not approved under section 12, the doctor concerned should record the reasons for that.

10.28 Assessment by the doctor and AMHP should begin as soon as possible after the arrival of the individual at the place of safety. Where possible, the assessment should be undertaken jointly by the doctor and the AMHP.

10.29 It is desirable for either a consultant psychiatrist in learning disabilities or an AMHP with knowledge and experience of working with people with learning disabilities to be available to make the assessment where it appears that the detained person has a learning disability.

10.30 Similarly, where the person detained is under the age of 18, or is known to have moved recently to adult mental health services, either a child and adolescent mental health services (CAMHS) consultant or an AMHP with knowledge and experience of caring for this age group should undertake the assessment, if possible.

10.31 The authority to detain a person under section 135(1) or 136 ends as soon as it has been decided to make no application in respect of them under Part 2 of the Act or other arrangements for their treatment or care. This means that where a doctor has completed an examination of such a person prior to the arrival of the AMHP and concludes that the person is not mentally disordered, the person can no longer be detained and must immediately be released.

10.32 In no case may a patient continue to be detained in a police station under section 136 once a custody officer deems that detention is no longer appropriate.

10.33 If the doctor sees the person first and concludes that they have a mental disorder and that, while compulsory admission to hospital is not necessary, they may still need treatment or care (whether in or out of hospital), the person should still be seen by an AMHP. The AMHP should consult the doctor about any arrangements that might need to be made for the person's treatment or care.

### Transfer between places of safety

**4–094** 10.34 A person removed to a place of safety under section 135 or section 136 may be moved to a different place of safety before the end of the maximum 72-hour period for which they may be detained. The maximum period of detention begins from the time of the person's arrival at the first place of safety to which they are taken and cannot be extended if the person is transferred to another place of safety.

10.35 The person may be taken to the second or subsequent place of safety by a police officer, an AMHP or a person authorised by either a police officer or an AMHP.

10.36 A person may be transferred before their assessment has begun, while it is in progress or after it is completed and they are waiting for any necessary arrangements for their care or treatment to be put in place. If it is unavoidable, or it is in the person's interests, an assessment begun by one AMHP or doctor may be taken over and completed by another, either in the same location or at another place to which the person is transferred.

10.37 Although it may be helpful for local policies to outline circumstances in which a person is usually to be transferred between places of safety, the decision in each case should reflect the individual circumstances, including the person's needs and the level of risk. For example, where the purpose of the transfer would be to move a person from a police station to a more appropriate healthcare setting, the benefit of that move needs to be weighed against any delay it might cause in the person's assessment and any distress that the journey might cause them.

10.38 Someone with the authority to effect a transfer should proceed by agreement wherever possible. Unless it is an emergency, a person should not be transferred without the agreement of an AMHP, a doctor or another healthcare professional who is competent to assess whether the transfer would put the person's health or safety (or that of other people) at risk. It is for those professionals to decide whether they first need to see the person themselves.

10.39 Unless it is unavoidable, a person should never be moved from one place of safety to another unless it has been confirmed that the new place of safety is willing and able to accept them.

### Record keeping

10.40 A record of the person's time of arrival must be made immediately when **4–095** they reach the place of safety. As soon as detention in a place of safety under section 135 or 136 ends, the individual must be told that they are free to leave by those who are detaining them. The organisation responsible for the place of safety (where there is one) should ensure that proper records are kept of the end of the person's detention under these sections.

10.41 Given that the maximum period of detention at a place of safety is not affected by any subsequent transfer to a different place of safety (see **paragraph 10.34**), it is very important to ensure that the time of detention at the first place of safety is recorded clearly. This information should be shared between the transferring and receiving place of safety in the event of a transfer.

### Monitoring the use of the Act to remove people

10.42 The locally agreed policy should include arrangements for the use of sec- **4–096** tion 136 (in particular) to be monitored effectively so that:

- a check can be made of how, in what circumstances and with what outcome it is being used, including its use in relation to people from black and minority ethnic communities and children and young people; and

- the parties to the policy can consider any changes to the mental health services or police operations or any other matters that might result in a reduction in its use.

10.43 The local policy should address who is responsible for collecting, analysing and disseminating the information required for monitoring purposes. It should also set target times for the commencement of assessment at a place of safety, and the relevant NHS bodies and LSSAs should review local practice against these targets.

10.44 Although information systems (and definitions) may differ between organisations, efforts should be made to ensure that the most important data for monitoring purposes is collected in a way that allows it to be analysed so that is of use to all the parties to the policy.

**Rights of persons detained in places of safety**

**4–097**   10.45 A person removed under section 136 is deemed to be "arrested" for the purposes of the Police and Criminal Evidence Act 1984 (PACE). This means that police officers have the power to search a person they detain under section 136, as they would in the case of a person arrested for an offence. Under section 54 of PACE, the custody officer at the police station has the power to ascertain what items the person has on them, to remove items (where permitted) and to search the person as necessary for those purposes.

10.46 Where a hospital is used as a place of safety, the managers must ensure that the provisions of section 132 (giving of information) are complied with. In addition, access to legal advice should be facilitated whenever it is requested.

10.47 If a person is detained in a police station as a place of safety, they have a right of access to legal advice under PACE. The conditions of detention and treatment of the person must be in accordance with PACE Code of Practice C. Among other things, this requires that the person must be notified of their rights and entitlements, both orally and in writing. This will be achieved by handing the person a copy of the Notice of Rights and Entitlements.

10.48 In all cases, the person detained should be told that the 82 maximum period of detention is 72 hours.

**Places of safety and consent to treatment (Section 56)**

**4–098**   10.49 Detaining a patient in a place of safety under section 135 or 136 does not confer any power under the Act to treat them without their consent. In other words, they are in exactly the same position in respect of consent to treatment as patients who are not detained under the Act.

**Making necessary arrangements following assessment**

**4–099**   10.50 Once the assessment has been concluded, it is the responsibility of the doctors and AMHPs involved to make any necessary further arrangements for the person's treatment and care.

10.51 Where compulsory admission is indicated, the AMHP should arrange for a second doctor to examine the patient in accordance with the Act (unless it has been agreed locally that someone else should make such arrangements).

10.52 It is unlikely that an emergency application will be justified in these circumstances. If there is an urgent need to secure the transfer of the patient to hospital, the power of transfer between places of safety can be used.

10.53 A person who is detained in hospital under section 135 or 136 pending completion of their assessment should not have their detention extended by use of section 5(2) or section 5(4).

10.54 It should also be borne in mind that a person who is removed to a place of safety may already be on SCT or conditional discharge or may be on leave of absence from detention in hospital and that their recall to hospital may need to be considered. If it becomes apparent that this is the case, the professionals assessing the patient should make an effort to contact the patient's responsible clinician as soon as possible.

10.55 Where the person is known to be on SCT and compulsory admission is indicated, the recall power should be used. An application for detention cannot be made in respect of a person who is known to be on SCT.

---

**Related material**

● *Police and Criminal Evidence Act 1984 (PACE) Code C: Code of Practice for the Detention, Treatment and Questioning of Persons by Police Officers*, Home Office, 2008

This material does not form part of the Code. It is provided for assistance only.

---

**Applying the Principles**

This scenario is not intended to provide a template for decisions in applying the principles in similar situations. The scenario itself is only illustrative and does not form part of the Code itself. **4–100**

---

**Transfer between places of safety**

Following an incident in the street, Fred has been detained under section 136 and taken to a police station as a place of safety. The police have contacted the local mental health services to make arrangements for a mental health assessment.

Fred is in an agitated state, but settles slightly after arriving at the police station. He advises that he is 17 years old and lives some distance away with his mother. The local mental health service confirms that he is known to CAMHS in his local area and that there is a place of safety in the local hospital where he could be assessed.

Neither the AMHP nor the doctor are specialists working with young people, and with the police they need to consider whether they should move Fred to the place of safety in his home area. In making this determination, the guiding principles of this Code should be considered. This could include thinking about the following questions.

**Purpose principle**

● Would transferring Fred be to his benefit?
● Would transferring Fred create a risk to the public?
● Would assessing him where he is help him or protect other people?

**Least restriction principle**

● Is there anything to choose between the police station and the local place of safety in terms of Fred's freedom of action, or how he might feel about being detained?
● If the local place of safety would be less restrictive, what about the restrictions that would have to be placed on him to get him there?

**Respect principle**

● Does Fred have any views about whether he would rather see the clinical team that knows him?
● If he cannot focus on the question of where he would rather be, is he expressing any concerns about seeing the assessing AMHP or doctors, or about being seen by people he does not know?

---

- Has this situation arisen before (as far as anyone can easily discover)? If so, how was it handled previously? Was it successfully managed?
- Fred is strong and young—are we sure we are not making any unwarranted assumptions about the risk his behaviour poses, or about his ability to know and say what he wants?

**Participation principle**

- Can we explain the options to Fred and ask him for his views?
- If he were to be transferred, would he want to go before or after he had eaten or slept?
- Can his family be contacted? Does Fred want his family to be contacted? What do they want—and what do they think he would want?

**Effectiveness, efficiency and equity principle**

- If the assessment is carried out in the police station by people who do not know him, is it effectively going to have to be carried out again very shortly anyway by the team that does?
- Could someone from that team come and see him in the police station?
- Which option would serve Fred's best interests, balancing these against any risk to the public?
- What would the implications be for that team's ability to serve its other patients?
- Does the custody officer at the police station have any view about what should happen?

## 11. CONVEYANCE OF PATIENTS

**4–101**　　11.1 This chapter provides guidance on the conveyance of patients under the Act.

### General considerations

**4–102**　　11.2 Patients should always be conveyed in the manner which is most likely to preserve their dignity and privacy consistent with managing any risk to their health and safety or to other people.

11.3 This applies in all cases where patients are compulsorily conveyed under the Act, including:

- taking patients to hospital to be detained for assessment or treatment;
- transferring patients between hospitals;
- returning patients to hospital if they are absent without leave;
- taking supervised community treatment (SCT) patients or patients who have been conditionally discharged to hospital on recall;
- taking and returning patients who are subject to guardianship to the place their guardian requires them to live;
- taking patients to and between places of safety; and

- taking patients to and from court.

11.4 When deciding on the most appropriate method for conveying a patient, factors to be taken into account include:

- the availability of different transport options;
- the distance to be travelled;
- the wishes and views of the patient, including any relevant statement of those views or wishes made in advance;
- the patient's age;
- any physical disability the patient has;
- any risks to the health and safety of the patient and any need for support, supervision and clinical care or monitoring during the journey. This is particularly important where sedation has been, or may be, used;
- the nature of the patient's mental disorder and their current state of mind;
- the likelihood of the patient behaving in a violent or dangerous manner;
- the health and safety of the people conveying the patient and anyone else accompanying them;
- the likelihood that the patient may attempt to abscond and the risk of harm to the patient or other people were that to happen;
- the impact that any particular method of conveying the patient will have on the patient's relationship with the community to which they will return;
- the effect on the patient of who accompanies them, for example, whether the presence of the approved mental health professional (AMHP) or one of the doctors involved in the decision to detain them may have a detrimental effect; and
- the availability of transport to return those who accompany the patient.

11.5 Patients who have been sedated before being conveyed should always be accompanied by a health professional who is knowledgeable in the care of such patients, is able to identify and respond to any physical distress which may occur and has access to the necessary emergency equipment to do so.

## Local protocols

11.6 It is for primary care trusts (PCTs) to commission ambulance and patient **4–103** transport services to meet the needs of their areas. This includes services for transporting patients to and from hospital (and other places) under the Act.

11.7 PCTs should ensure, through their contracts, that appropriate transport will be made available in a timely manner where it is needed to convey patients under the Act. It is for service providers, whoever they are, to provide those services in accordance with their contracts.

11.8 However, if the patient is a private patient in an independent hospital, it is for the managers of that hospital to make arrangements for any necessary transport.

11.9 The respective responsibilities of different agencies and service providers for conveying patients in different circumstances should be clearly established locally and communicated to the professionals who need to know.

11.10 In particular, it is essential to have clear agreements in place so that people who need assistance in conveying patients under the Act can secure it without delay. Authorities, including NHS bodies responsible for hospitals, ambulance services and the police, should agree joint local policies and procedures. These should include, in particular:

- a clear statement of the respective roles and obligations of each agency and service provider (and their staff);

- the form of any authorisation to be given by AMHPs (and others) when authorising people to convey patients on their behalf;

- the assistance that managers and staff of hospitals will provide to AMHPs to make necessary arrangements for the conveyance of patients who are to be admitted to their hospital;

- guidance and training on legal powers in relation to conveying patients;

- a clear statement of how risk assessment and management should be conducted and how the outcomes will influence decisions in relation to the conveyance of patients;

- agreement on the appropriate use of different methods of restraint in conveying patients and how decisions on their use will be made in any given case;

- any special arrangements where patients need to be conveyed outside the local area; and

- processes for reviewing and monitoring the involvement of the different agencies, including standards against which delivery will be monitored.

11.11 Policies should ensure that AMHPs (in particular) are not left to negotiate arrangements with providers of transport services on an ad hoc basis, in the absence of clear expectations about the responsibilities of all those involved.

11.12 Policies should also be consistent with those agreed in relation to the use of the police powers in sections 135 and 136 of the Act (see **chapter 10**).

**Conveying patients to hospital on the basis of an application for detention (Section 6; Reference Guide 2.66–2.69)**

**4–104**    11.13 A properly completed application for detention under the Act, together with the required medical recommendations, gives the applicant (the AMHP or nearest relative) the authority to convey the patient to the hospital named in the application.

11.14 Where AMHPs are the applicant, they have a professional responsibility to ensure that all the necessary arrangements are made for the patient to be conveyed to hospital.

11.15 If the nearest relative is the applicant, any AMHP and other professionals involved in the assessment of the patient should give advice and assistance. But they should not assist in a patient's detention unless they believe it is justified and lawful.

11.16 AMHPs should make decisions on which method of transport to use in consultation with the other professionals involved, the patient and (as appropriate) their carer, family or other supporters. The decision should be made following a risk assessment carried out on the basis of the best available information.

11.17 If the patient is likely to be unwilling to be moved, the applicant should provide the people who are to convey the patient (including any ambulance staff or police officers involved) with authority to convey the patient. It is that authorisation which confers on them the legal power to transport the patient against their will, using reasonable force if necessary, and to prevent them absconding en route.

11.18 If the patient's behaviour is likely to be violent or dangerous, the police should be asked to assist in accordance with locally agreed arrangements. Where practicable, given the risk involved, an ambulance service (or similar) vehicle should be used even where the police are assisting.

11.19 The locally agreed arrangements should set out what assistance the police will provide to AMHPs and health services in transporting patients safely, and what support ambulance or other health services will be expected to provide where patients are, exceptionally, transported in police vehicles.

11.20 Where it is necessary to use a police vehicle because of the risk involved, it may be necessary for the highest qualified member of an ambulance crew to ride in the same vehicle with the patient, with the appropriate equipment to deal with immediate problems. In such cases, the ambulance should follow directly behind to provide any further support that is required.

11.21 AMHPs should not normally agree to a patient being conveyed by car unless satisfied that it would not put the patient or other people at risk of harm and that it is the most appropriate way of transporting the patient. In these circumstances there should be an escort for the patient other than the driver.

11.22 People authorised by the applicant to convey patients act in their own right and not as the agent of the applicant. They may act on their own initiative to restrain patients and prevent them absconding, if necessary. However, when they are the applicant, AMHPs retain a professional responsibility to ensure that the patient is conveyed in a lawful and humane manner and should give guidance to those asked to assist.

11.23 Patients may be accompanied by another person, provided that the AMHP and the person in charge of the vehicle are satisfied that this will not increase the risk of harm to the patient or others.

11.24 Before patients are moved, the applicant should ensure that the receiving hospital is expecting the patient and has been told the likely time of arrival. If possible, the name of the person who will be formally receiving the patient and their admission documents should be obtained in advance.

11.25 Where the applicant is not travelling in the same vehicle as the patient, the application form and medical recommendations should be given to the person authorised to convey the patient, with instructions for them to be presented to the member of hospital staff receiving the patient.

**Conveying patients between hospitals and returning patients who abscond**

11.26 Where a patient requires transport between hospitals, it is for the man- **4–105** agers of the hospitals concerned to make sure that appropriate arrangements are put in place. The managers of the hospital from which the patient is being transferred remain responsible for the patient until the patient is admitted to the new hospital.

11.27 Where a patient who is absent without leave from a hospital is taken into custody by someone working for another organisation, the managers of the hospital from which the patient is absent are responsible for making sure that any necessary transport arrangements at put in place for the patient's return.

11.28 However, the organisation which temporarily has custody of the patient is responsible for them in the interim and should therefore assist in ensuring that the patient is returned in a timely and safe manner.

11.29 When making arrangements for the return of patients temporarily held in police custody, hospital managers should bear in mind that police transport to return them to hospital will not normally be appropriate. Decisions about the kind of transport to be used should be taken in the same way as for patients being detained in hospital for the first time.

**Conveying SCT patients who are recalled to hospital (Reference Guide 15.66)**

**4–106**     11.30 A notice of recall, properly completed by the responsible clinician and served on the patient in accordance with regulations, provides the authority to convey an SCT patient to hospital compulsorily, if necessary (see **paragraphs 25.47–25.64**).

11.31 Unless it has been agreed otherwise locally, the responsible clinician has responsibility for co-ordinating the recall process. The factors outlined above at **paragraph 11.4,** and the urgency of the situation, will need to be considered in deciding the best way to transport the patient to hospital. The guidance in **paragraphs 11.13–11.25** about taking patients to hospital when they are first to be detained applies here as well, except that an AMHP will not necessarily be involved.

11.32 An SCT patient who has been recalled can be conveyed by any officer on the staff of the hospital to which the patient is recalled, any police officer, any AMHP or any other person authorised in writing by the responsible clinician or the managers of that hospital. Who the most appropriate person to convey the patient is will depend on the individual circumstances.

## 12. HOLDING POWERS

**4–107**     12.1 This chapter provides guidance on the use of holding powers available to doctors and approved clinicians under section 5(2) of the Act and to certain nurses under section 5(4) **(Reference Guide 2.71–2.85)**.

**Holding power of doctors and approved clinicians under section 5(2)**

*Nature of the power*

**4–108**     12.2 The power can be used where the doctor or approved clinician in charge of the treatment of a hospital in-patient (or their nominated deputy) concludes that an application for detention under the Act should be made. It authorises the detention of the patient in the hospital for a maximum of 72 hours so that the patient can be assessed with a view to such an application being made.

12.3 The identity of the person in charge of a patient's medical treatment at any time will depend on the particular circumstances. But a professional who is treating the patient under the direction of another professional should not be considered to be in charge.

12.4 There may be more than one person who could reasonably be said to be in charge of a patient's treatment, for example where a patient is already receiving treatment for both a physical and a mental disorder. In a case of that kind, the psychiatrist or approved clinician in charge of the patient's treatment for the mental disorder is the preferred person to use the holding power, if necessary.

12.5 The period of detention starts at the moment the doctor's or approved clinician's report is furnished to the hospital managers (eg when it is handed to an officer who is authorised by the managers to receive it, or when it is put in the hospital's internal mail system).

12.6 In this context, a hospital in-patient means any person who is receiving in-patient treatment in a hospital, except a patient who is already liable to be detained under section 2, 3 or 4 of the Act, or who is a supervised community treatment patient. It includes patients who are in hospital by virtue of a deprivation of liberty authorisation under the Mental Capacity Act 2005[7] (see **chapter 4**). It does not matter whether or not the patient was originally admitted for treatment primarily for a mental disorder.

12.7 The power cannot be used for an out-patient attending a hospital's accident and emergency department, or any other out-patient. Patients should not be admitted informally with the sole intention of then using the holding power.

12.8 Section 5(2) should only be used if, at the time, it is not practicable or safe to take the steps necessary to make an application for detention without detaining the patient in the interim. Section 5(2) should not be used as an alternative to making an application, even if it is thought that the patient will only need to be detained for 72 hours or less.

12.9 Doctors and approved clinicians should use the power only after having personally examined the patient.

12.10 Sometimes a report under section 5(2) may be made in relation to a patient who is not at the time under the care of a psychiatrist or an approved clinician. In such cases, the doctor invoking the power should make immediate contact with a psychiatrist or an approved clinician to obtain confirmation of their opinion that the patient needs to be detained. If possible, the doctor should seek such advice before using the power.

## Nomination of deputies

12.11 Section 5(3) allows the doctor or approved clinician in charge of an in- **4–109** patient's treatment to nominate a deputy to exercise the holding power in their absence. The deputy will then act on their own responsibility.

12.12 Only a doctor or approved clinician on the staff of the same hospital may be a nominated deputy (although the deputy does not have to be a member of the same profession as the person nominating them). Only one deputy may be authorised at any time for any patient, and it is unlawful for a nominated deputy to nominate another.

12.13 Doctors should not be nominated as a deputy unless they are competent to perform the role. If nominated deputies are not approved clinicians (or doctors approved under section 12 of the Act), they should wherever possible seek advice from the person for whom they are deputising, or from someone else who is an

---

[7] The deprivation of liberty safeguards are expected to be in force from April 2009.

approved clinician or section 12 approved doctor, before using section 5(2). Hospital managers should see that arrangements are in place to allow nominated deputies to do this.

12.14 Nominated deputies should report the use of section 5(2) to the person for whom they are deputising as soon as practicable.

12.15 It is permissible for deputies to be nominated by title, rather than by name—for example, the junior doctor on call for particular wards—provided that there is only one nominated deputy for any patient at any time and it can be determined with certainty who that nominated deputy is.

12.16 Hospital managers should ensure that ward staff know who the nominated deputy for a particular patient is at any given time.

12.17 Doctors and approved clinicians may leave instructions with ward staff to contact them (or their nominated deputy) if a particular patient wants or tries to leave. But they may not leave instructions for their nominated deputy to use section 5, nor may they complete a section 5 report in advance to be used in their absence.

*Assessment for admission while a patient is detained under section 5(2)*

**4–110**    12.18 Arrangements for an assessment to consider an application under section 2 or section 3 of the Act should be put in place as soon as the section 5(2) report is furnished to the hospital managers.

*Ending section 5(2)*

**4–111**    12.19 Although the holding power lasts for a maximum of 72 hours, it should not be used to continue to detain patients after:

- the doctor or approved clinician decides that, in fact, no assessment for a possible application needs to be carried out; or

- a decision is taken not to make an application for the patient's detention.

12.20 Patients should be informed immediately that they are no longer detained under the holding power and are free to leave the hospital, unless the patient is to be detained under some other authority, such as an authorisation under the deprivation of liberty safeguards in the Mental Capacity Act 2005 (see **chapter 4**).

**Holding power of nurses under section 5(4)**

*Nature of the power*

**4–112**    12.21 Nurses of the "prescribed class" may invoke section 5(4) of the Act in respect of a hospital in-patient who is already receiving treatment for mental disorder.[8]

12.22 This power may be used only where the nurse considers that:

- the patient is suffering from mental disorder to such a degree that it is necessary for the patient to be immediately prevented from leaving the

---

[8] The prescribed classes at the time of publication are nurses registered in sub-parts 1 or 2 of the register maintained by the Nursing and Midwifery Council whose entry in the register indicates that their field of practice is either mental health nursing or learning disability nursing.

hospital either for the patient's health or safety or for the protection of other people; and

- it is not practicable to secure the attendance of a doctor or approved clinician who can submit a report under section 5(2).

It can be used only when the patient is still on the hospital premises.

12.23 The use of the holding power permits the patient's detention for up to six hours or until a doctor or approved clinician with the power to use section 5(2) arrives, whichever is the earlier. It cannot be renewed.

12.24 The patient may be detained from the moment the nurse makes the necessary record. The record must then be sent to the hospital managers.

12.25 The decision to invoke the power is the personal decision of the nurse, who cannot be instructed to exercise the power by anyone else.

12.26 Hospital managers should ensure that suitably qualified, experienced and competent nurses are available to all wards where there is a possibility of section 5(4) being invoked, particularly acute psychiatric admission wards and wards where there are patients who are acutely unwell or who require intensive nursing care. Where nurses may have to apply the power to patients from outside their specialist field, it is good practice for hospital managers to arrange suitable training in the use of the power in such situations.

*Assessment before invoking section 5(4)*

12.27 Before using the power, nurses should assess:                                    **4–113**

- the likely arrival time of the doctor or approved clinician, as against the likely intention of the patient to leave. It may be possible to persuade the patient to wait until a doctor or approved clinician arrives to discuss the matter further; and
- the consequences of a patient leaving the hospital before the doctor or approved clinician arrives—in other words, the harm that might occur to the patient or others.

12.28 In doing so, nurses should consider:

- the patient's expressed intentions;
- the likelihood of the patient harming themselves or others;
- the likelihood of the patient behaving violently;
- any evidence of disordered thinking;
- the patient's current behaviour and, in particular, any changes in their usual behaviour;
- whether the patient has recently received messages from relatives or friends;
- whether the date is one of special significance for the patient (eg the anniversary of a bereavement);

- any recent disturbances on the ward;

- any relevant involvement of other patients;

- any history of unpredictability or impulsiveness;

- any formal risk assessments which have been undertaken (specifically looking at previous behaviour); and

- any other relevant information from other members of the multi-disciplinary team.

12.29 Nurses should be particularly alert to cases where patients suddenly decide to leave or become determined to do so urgently.

12.30 Nurses should make as full an assessment as possible in the circumstances before using the power, but sometimes it may be necessary to invoke the power on the basis of only a brief assessment.

*Action once section 5(4) is used*

**4–114**  12.31 The reasons for invoking the power should be entered in the patient's notes. Details of any patients who remain subject to the power at the time of a shift change should be given to staff coming on duty.

12.32 The use of section 5(4) is an emergency measure, and the doctor or approved clinician with the power to use section 5(2) in respect of the patient should treat it as such and arrive as soon as possible. The doctor or approved clinician should not wait six hours before attending simply because this is the maximum time allowed.

12.33 If the doctor or approved clinician arrives before the end of the six hour maximum period, the holding power lapses on their arrival. But if the doctor or approved clinician then uses their own holding power, the maximum period of 72 hours runs from when the nurse first made the record detaining the patient under section 5(4).

12.34 If no doctor or approved clinician able to make a report under section 5(2) has attended within six hours, the patient is no longer detained and may leave if not prepared to stay voluntarily. This should be considered as a serious failing, and should be reported and investigated locally as such.

**General points about using section 5**

*Recording the end of detention*

**4–115**  12.35 The time at which a patient ceases to be detained under section 5(2) or 5(4) should be recorded, preferably using a standardised system established by the hospital managers for the purpose. The reason why the patient is no longer detained under the power should also be recorded, as well as what then happened to the patient (eg the patient remained in hospital voluntarily, was discharged, or was detained under a different power).

12.36 Detention under section 5(2) or 5(4) cannot be renewed, but that does not prevent it being used again on a future occasion if necessary.

*Monitoring use*

12.37 Hospital managers should monitor the use of section 5, including:     **4–116**

- how quickly patients are assessed for detention and discharged from the holding power;
- the attendance times of doctors and approved clinicians following the use of section 5(4); and
- the proportion of cases in which applications for detention are, in fact, made following use of section 5.

*Information*

12.38 Hospital managers must ensure that patients detained under section 5 are **4–117** given information about their position and their rights, as required by section 132 of the Act.

*Medical treatment of patients* **(Section 56)**

12.39 Detaining patients under section 5 does not confer any power under the **4–118** Act to treat them without their consent. In other words, they are in exactly the same position in respect of consent to treatment as patients who are not detained under the Act.

*Transfer to other hospitals*

12.40 It is not possible for patients detained under section 5 to be transferred to **4–119** another hospital under section 19 (because they are not detained by virtue of an application made under Part 2 of the Act).

---

**Related material**

- Mental Capacity Act 2005
- *Mental Capacity Act 2005 Code of Practice,* TSO, 2007
- *Deprivation of Liberty Safeguards,* Addendum to the *Mental Capacity Act 2005 Code of Practice*

This material does not form part of the Code. It is provided for assistance only.

---

## 13. RECEIPT AND SCRUTINY OF DOCUMENTS

13.1 This chapter provides guidance on the receipt and scrutiny of documents **4–120** under the Act.

**Statutory forms**

13.2 Regulations require specific statutory forms to be used for certain applica- **4–121** tions, recommendations, decisions, reports and records under the Act. The forms are set out in the regulations themselves.

13.3 If no hard copies of the statutory forms are available, photocopies of the original blank forms can be completed instead, as can computer-generated versions. However, the wording of the forms must correspond to the current statutory versions of the forms set out in the regulations.

**Applications for detention in hospital and supporting medical recommendations (Reference Guide 2.86–2.110)**

**4–122**    13.4 Regulations say that applications for detention under the Act must be delivered to a person who is authorised by the hospital managers to receive them.

13.5 People who sign applications and make the supporting medical recommendations must take care to comply with the requirements of the Act. People who act on the authority of these documents should also make sure that they are in the proper form, as an incorrectly completed or indecipherable form may not constitute authority for a patient's detention.

13.6 This chapter distinguishes between receiving admission documents and scrutinising them. For these purposes, receipt involves physically receiving documents and checking that they appear to amount to an application that has been duly made (since that is sufficient to give the managers the power to detain the patient). Scrutiny involves more detailed checking for omissions, errors and other defects and, where permitted, taking action to have the documents rectified after they have already been acted on.

13.7 Hospital managers should formally delegate their duties to receive and scrutinise admission documents to a limited number of officers, who may include clinical staff on wards. Someone with the authority to receive admission documents should be available at all times at which patients may be admitted to the hospital. A manager of appropriate seniority should take overall responsibility on behalf of the hospital managers for the proper receipt and scrutiny of documents.

13.8 Hospitals should have a checklist for the guidance of people delegated to receive documents ("receiving officers"), to help them detect those errors which fundamentally invalidate an application and which cannot be corrected at a later stage in the procedure.

13.9 When a patient is being admitted on the application of an approved mental health professional (AMHP), the receiving officer should go through the documents and check their accuracy with the AMHP.

13.10 Receiving officers should have access to a manager for advice outside office hours, especially at night.

13.11 Where the receiving officer is not also authorised by the hospital managers to agree to the rectification of a defective admission document, the documents must be scrutinised by a person who is authorised to do so. This scrutiny should happen at the same time as the documents are received or as soon as possible afterwards (and certainly no later than the next working day).

13.12 Documents should be scrutinised for accuracy and completeness and to check that they do not reveal any failure to comply with the procedural requirements of the Act in respect of applications for detention. Medical recommendations should also be scrutinised by someone with appropriate clinical expertise to check that the reasons given appear sufficient to support the conclusions stated in them.

13.13 If admission documents reveal a defect which fundamentally invalidates the application and which cannot, therefore, be rectified under section 15 of the

Act, the patient can no longer be detained on the basis of the application. Authority for the patient's detention can be obtained only through a new application (or, in the interim, by the use of the holding powers under section 5 if the patient has already been admitted to the hospital).

### Guardianship applications and supporting medical recommendations (Reference Guide 19.56–19.59)

13.14 Where a guardianship application is made, the person receiving the docu- **4–123** ments on behalf of the local social services authority (LSSA) should check them for inaccuracies and defects with the AMHP or nearest relative making the application.

13.15 LSSAs should prepare a checklist for the guidance of those delegated to receive guardianship applications on their behalf. That checklist should identify those errors which can be rectified and those which cannot.

### Supervised community treatment documentation

13.16 There are no provisions in the Act for community treatment orders and **4–124** related documents to be rectified once made. Hospital managers should nonetheless ensure that arrangements are in place to check that documents have been properly completed. Significant errors or inadequacies in community treatment orders themselves may render patients' supervised community treatment (SCT) invalid, and errors in recall notices or revocations may invalidate hospital managers' authority to detain.

13.17 To avoid errors being made, hospital managers should ensure that responsible clinicians have access to advice about how the relevant forms should be completed and the opportunity (where practicable) to have them checked in advance by someone else familiar with what the Act requires.

### Audit

13.18 Hospital managers are responsible for ensuring that patients are lawfully **4–125** detained or on SCT. LSSAs are responsible for ensuring that guardianship is lawful.

13.19 Hospital managers and LSSAs should ensure that the people they authorise to receive and scrutinise statutory documents on their behalf are competent to perform these duties, understand the requirements of the Act and receive suitable training.

13.20 Hospital managers and LSSAs should also ensure that arrangements are in place to audit the effectiveness of receipt and scrutiny of documents on a regular basis.

## 14. ALLOCATING OR CHANGING A RESPONSIBLE CLINICIAN

14.1 This chapter deals with the identification of responsible clinicians for **4–126** patients being assessed and treated under the Act.

### Allocating a responsible clinician

14.2 The responsible clinician is the approved clinician who will have overall **4–127** responsibility for the patient's case **(Reference Guide 12.36–12.38 and 15.5)**.

14.3 Hospital managers should have local protocols in place for allocating responsible clinicians to patients. This is particularly important when patients move between hospitals or from the hospital to the community and vice versa. The protocols should:

- ensure that the patient's responsible clinician is the available approved clinician with the most appropriate expertise to meet the patient's main assessment and treatment needs;

- ensure that it can be easily determined who a particular patient's responsible clinician is;

- ensure that cover arrangements are in place when the responsible clinician is not available (eg during nonworking hours, annual leave etc);

- include a system for keeping the appropriateness of the responsible clinician under review.

14.4 To ensure that the most appropriate available clinician is allocated as the patient's responsible clinician, hospital managers should keep a register of approved clinicians to treat patients for whom they are responsible.

14.5 The selection of the appropriate responsible clinician should be based on the individual needs of the patient concerned. For example, where psychological therapies are central to the patient's treatment, it may be appropriate for a professional with particular expertise in this area to act as the responsible clinician. There are special considerations for patients aged under 18. (See **chapter 36**.)

14.6 Even if the patient's main treatment needs are not immediately clear, it will be necessary to allocate a responsible clinician promptly upon the patient's detention in hospital.

### Change of responsible clinician

**4–128**    14.7 As the needs of the patient may change over time, it is important that the appropriateness of the responsible clinician is kept under review through the care planning process. It may be appropriate for the patient's responsible clinician to change during a period of care and treatment, if such a change enables the needs of the patient to be met more effectively. However, in considering such a change it is also important to take account of the need for continuity and continuing engagement with, and knowledge of, the patient.

14.8 Where a patient's treatment and rehabilitation require movement between different hospitals or to the community, successive responsible clinicians need to be identified in good time to enable movement to take place The existing responsible clinician is responsible for overseeing the patient's progress through the system.

If movement to another hospital is indicated, responsible clinicians should take the lead in identifying their successors, and hospital managers should respond promptly to requests to assist in this process.

14.9 There may be circumstances where the responsible clinician is qualified with respect to the patient's main assessment and treatment needs but is not appropriately qualified to be in charge of a subsidiary treatment needed by the patient (eg medication which the responsible clinician is not qualified to prescribe). In such situations, the responsible clinician will maintain their overarching responsibility for the patient's case, but another appropriately qualified professional will take responsibility for a specific treatment or intervention.

14.10 Where the person in charge of a particular treatment is not the patient's responsible clinician, the person in charge of the treatment should ensure that the responsible clinician is kept informed about the treatment and that treatment decisions are discussed with the responsible clinician in the context of the patient's overall case. Guidance should be available locally on the procedures to follow, including when to seek a second opinion, if there are unresolved differences of opinion.

### Applying the principles

This scenario is not intended to provide a template for decisions in applying the **4–129** principles in similar situations. The scenario itself is only illustrative and does not form part of the Code itself.

---

### ALLOCATING THE RESPONSIBLE CLINICIAN

Frank is a 24 year old man; he was admitted to hospital having presented himself at A&E. He was seen by the crisis team and was admitted under section 2; this is his first admission to hospital under the Act. On admission, the duty team saw him and a psychiatrist was allocated as responsible clinician for his case.

Frank was subsequently placed on section 3 and has been in hospital for four months. Over this time, his needs have changed and the multi-disciplinary team arranges a review to determine the most appropriate available approved clinician to be the responsible clinician in charge of his care. In making this determination, the guiding principles should be considered. This could include thinking about the following questions.

#### Purpose principle

- What are Frank's main assessment treatment needs?
  Which approved clinician has the expertise to best meet these needs, in order to maximise Frank's wellbeing and minimise risk of harm to Frank and others?

- Is the choice of responsible clinician likely to affect Frank's wellbeing in any other way?

- Which professional may be best suited to acting as Frank's responsible clinician?

#### Least restriction principle

- Are there any reasons to think that the choice of responsible clinician will affect Frank's freedom within the hospital? (Eg might having a responsible clinician who is only available at specific times interrupt Frank's routine on the ward in a way he would find distressing?)

#### Respect principle

- Does Frank have any views about who should be his responsible clinician?

- Is there any reason to think that Frank would prefer a male rather than a female clinician (or vice versa)?

---

**Participation principle**

- What is the best way of explaining the options to Frank and asking for his view?

- Are there any paid, or unpaid, carers, family members or friends whose views ought to be sought? Does Frank have any view about whether to involve these people?

- Has Frank been reminded of his right to an independent mental health advocate (IMHA) to assist him?[9]

**Effectiveness, efficiency and equity principle**

- If Frank does have views about a particular professional being allocated as his responsible clinician, and such a clinician is appropriate, is the particular clinician available?

- Could Frank's wishes be accommodated without there being a disproportionate effect on resources available to other patients?

## 15. SAFE AND THERAPEUTIC RESPONSES TO DISTURBED BEHAVIOUR

**4–130**     15.1 The guidance in this chapter covers a range of interventions which may be considered for the safe and therapeutic management of hospital patients whose behaviour may present a particular risk to themselves or to others, including those charged with their care. Except where otherwise stated, this guidance applies to all patients presenting such behaviour, whether or not they are detained under the Act.

15.2 Nationally recognised guidelines, such as those of the National Institute for Health and Clinical Excellence (NICE), complement the guidance provided in this chapter.

**Assessment and management of disturbed behaviour**
**4–131**     15.3 On admission, all patients should be assessed for immediate and potential risks of going missing, suicide, self-harm and possible harm to others, and individual care plans should be developed including actions to be taken should any of these occur.

15.4 Individuals in need of care and treatment for mental disorder may, as a consequence of their disorder, present particular risks to themselves or others. These might include hyperactivity, leaving the ward without permission, self-harming, aggressive and threatening behaviour towards others, physical violence and drug or alcohol abuse. Staff should also be aware of other risks that may not be so apparent, such as self-neglect.

15.5 Factors which may contribute to disturbed behaviour include:

- boredom and lack of environmental stimulation;

---

[9] Independent mental health advocacy services under the Act are expected to be introduced in April 2009.

- too much stimulation, noise and general disruption;

- excessive heating, overcrowding and lack of access to external space;

- personal frustrations associated with being in a restricted environment;

- difficulties in communication;

- emotional distress, eg following bereavement;

- antagonism, aggression or provocation on the part of others;

- the influence of alcohol or drugs;

- physical illness; and

- an unsuitable mix of patients.

15.6 All hospitals should have a policy on the recognition and prevention of disturbed, or violent behaviour, as well as risk assessment and management, including the use of de-escalation techniques, enhanced observation, physical intervention, rapid tranquilisation and seclusion. Local policies should suit the needs of the particular groups of patients who may be treated in the hospital.

15.7 The primary focus of any policy for managing patients who may present with disturbed or violent behaviour (or both) should be the establishment of a culture which focuses on early recognition, prevention and de-escalation of potential aggression, using techniques that minimise the risk of its occurrence.

15.8 Interventions such as physical restraint, rapid tranquilisation, seclusion and observation should be used only where de-escalation alone proves insufficient, and should always be used in conjunction with further efforts at de-escalation; they must never be used as punishment or in a punitive manner.

15.9 Any such intervention must be used in a way that minimises any risk to the patient's health and safety and that causes the minimum interference to their privacy and dignity, while being consistent with the need to protect the patient and other people.

15.10 Staff must try to gain the confidence of patients so that they can learn to recognise potential danger signs. Staff should understand when to intervene to prevent harm from occurring. Continuity of staffing is an important factor in both the development of professional skills and consistency in managing patients.

15.11 Patients who are identified as being at risk of disturbed or violent behaviour should be given the opportunity to have their views and wishes recorded, in the form of an advance statement. They should be encouraged to identify as clearly as possible what interventions they would and would not wish to be used. Patients should be encouraged to review their wishes with staff from time to time, and any changes should be recorded. Guidance on advance statements of wishes and feelings can be found in **chapter 17**.

15.12 Services and their staff should demonstrate and encourage respect for racial and cultural diversity and recognise the need for privacy and dignity. These are essential values that must be engendered and asserted in all policy, educational material, training, and practice initiatives related to the safe and therapeutic management of patients.

15.13 Patients' behaviour should be seen in context. Professionals should not categorise behaviour as disturbed without taking account of the circumstances under which it occurs. While it is an important factor in assessing current risk, they should not assume that a previous history of disturbance means that a patient will necessarily behave in the same way in the immediate future.

15.14 Particular care needs to be taken to ensure that negative and stigmatising judgements about certain diagnoses, behaviours or personal characteristics do not obscure a rigorous assessment of the degree of risk which may be presented—or the potential benefits of appropriate treatment to people in severe distress.

15.15 Wherever practicable, the circumstances (if any) in which medication is to be used as a response to episodes of particularly disturbed behaviour should be established in advance in each patient's treatment plan. The use of medication as an unplanned response to disturbed behaviour should be exceptional. Medication should never be used to manage patients as a substitute for adequate staffing.

15.16 Individual care plans are fundamental to the appropriate management of disturbed behaviour. In addition, problems may be minimised by promoting the therapeutic culture of the ward or other environment and by identifying and managing problem areas. Among such general measures are:

- engaging patients and keeping them fully informed, in a way they can understand, of what is happening and why;

- developing a therapeutic relationship between each patient and a key worker or nurse;

- seeking patients' co-operation, and encouraging their participation in the general running of the ward;

- ensuring an appropriate mix of patients;

- ensuring an appropriate mix of staff to meet patients' needs;

- identifying those patients most at risk and implementing appropriate risk management plans;

- involving patients in identification of their own trigger factors and early warning signs of disturbed or violent behaviour and in how to respond to them;

- organising the ward to provide, for example, quiet rooms, recreation rooms, single-sex areas, separate visitors' rooms and access to fresh air;

- giving each patient a defined personal space and a secure locker for the safe keeping of possessions;

- ensuring access to open space;

- ensuring that patients are able to make telephone calls in private, wherever possible;

- providing appropriate activities for all patients, including exercise, and encouraging patients to take part in activities appropriate to them;

- providing training for staff in the management of disturbed behaviour, including prevention and de-escalation; and

- ensuring that patients' complaints are dealt with quickly and fairly.

**Interventions where de-escalation is insufficient**

15.17 Interventions such as physical restraint, seclusion or rapid tranquillisa-  **4–132**
tion should be considered only if de-escalation and other strategies have failed
to calm the patient.

15.18 The most common reasons for needing to consider such interventions
are:

- physical assault;

- dangerous, threatening or destructive behaviour;

- self-harm or risk of physical injury by accident;

- extreme and prolonged over-activity that is likely to lead to physical
  exhaustion; and

- attempts to abscond (where the patient is detained under the Act).

15.19 The method chosen must balance the risk to others with the risk to the
patient's own health and safety and must be a reasonable, proportionate and justifiable response to the risk posed by the patient.

15.20 The purposes of interventions where de-escalation has failed are to:

- take immediate control of a dangerous situation;

- end or reduce significantly the danger to the patient or others around them;
  and

- contain or limit the patient's freedom for no longer than is necessary.

**Policy on physical restraint**

15.21 Hospitals' policies on the management of disturbed behaviour should  **4–133**
include clear written policies on the use of restraint and physical interventions,
and all relevant staff should be aware of the policies. The policies should include
provisions for post-incident reviews.

15.22 Any physical restraint used should:

- be reasonable, justifiable and proportionate to the risk posed by the patient;

- be used for only as long as is absolutely necessary;

- involve a recognised technique that does not depend on the deliberate application of pain (the application of pain should be used only for the immediate
  relief or rescue of staff where nothing else will suffice); and

- be carried out by those who have received appropriate training in the use of
  restraint techniques.

15.23 Managing aggressive behaviour by using physical restraint should be
done only as a last resort and never as a matter of course. It should be used in
an emergency when there seems to be a real possibility that harm would occur
if no intervention is made.

15.24 Any initial attempt to restrain aggressive behaviour should, as far as the
situation allows, be non-physical—for example, assistance should be sought by

the call system or by verbally summoning help. A single member of staff should assume control of the incident. The patient should be approached, where possible, and agreement sought to stop the behaviour. The special needs of patients with sensory impairments should be taken into consideration—approaches to deaf or hearing-impaired patients should be made within their visual field. Where possible, an explanation should be given to the patient of the consequences of refusing the request from staff to desist.

15.25 Verbal de-escalation should continue throughout the intervention, and negotiations with the patient to comply with requests to stop the behaviour should continue, where appropriate.

15.26 A member of staff should take the lead in caring for other patients and moving them away from the area of disturbance. Staff not involved in the use of physical restraint should leave the area quietly.

15.27 Throughout the period when physical restraint is being used:

- a doctor should be quickly available to attend an alert by staff members;

- staff should continue to employ de-escalation;

- staff should be alert to the risk of any respiratory or cardiac distress;

- emergency resuscitation devices should be readily available in the area where the restraint is taking place; and

- the patient's physical and psychological wellbeing should be monitored.

15.28 Where physical restraint is used staff should:

- record the decision and the reasons for it; and

- document and review every episode of physical restraint, which should include a detailed account of the restraint.

15.29 Hospitals should have in place a system of post-incident support and review which allows the organisation to learn from experience of using physical restraint and which caters for the needs of the patient who has been restrained, any other patients in the area where the restraint occurred, the staff involved in the incident, the restrained patient's carers and family (where appropriate) and any visitors who witnessed the incident.

15.30 After physical restraint has been used, staff should reassess the patient's care plan and help them reintegrate into the ward environment. They should also give the patient an opportunity to write their account of the episode, which will be filed in their notes.

### Use of mechanical restraint

**4–134**    15.31 Mechanical restraint is not a first-line response or standard means of managing disturbed or violent behaviour in acute mental health settings. Its use should be exceptional. If any forms of mechanical restraint are to be employed a clear policy should be in place governing their use. Restraint which involves tying (whether by means of tape or by using a part of the patient's garments) to some part of a building or its fixtures should never be used.

## Restraint in order to administer medication

15.32 Restraint is also used in order to administer medication (or other forms of **4–135** treatment) to an unwilling patient, where there is legal authority to treat the patient without consent. It should not be used unless there is such legal authority (whether under the Mental Health Act, the Mental Capacity Act 2005 (MCA) or otherwise). In particular, restraint may not be used to treat an informal patient who has the capacity to refuse treatment and who has done so.

15.33 The use of restraint to administer treatment in non-emergency circumstances should be avoided wherever possible, but may sometimes be necessary, especially if not administering the treatment would increase the likelihood of an emergency situation occurring. The decision to use restraint should first be discussed with the clinical team and should be properly documented in the patient's notes, along with the justification for it.

## Restraint as an indicator of the need for detention under the Act

15.34 If a patient is not detained, but restraint in any form has been deemed **4–136** necessary (whether as an emergency or as part of the patient's treatment plan), consideration should be given to whether formal detention under the Act is appropriate (subject to the criteria being met).

15.35 Where a patient is deprived of liberty in a hospital for mental health treatment under the deprivation of liberty safeguards in the MCA,[10] the use of restraint may well indicate that the patient objects to treatment or to being in hospital and is therefore no longer eligible to be held under those safeguards. If so, consideration will need to be given to whether the patient can and should be detained under the Mental Health Act instead.

## Training

15.36 All hospitals should have a policy on training of staff who work in areas **4–137** where they may be exposed to aggression or violence, or who may need to become involved in the restraint of patients. The policy should specify who will receive what level of training (based on training needs analysis), how often they will be trained and the techniques in which they will be trained. The training should be delivered during the induction period of new staff members or as soon as is practicably possible thereafter.

15.37 All staff who practise physical intervention in the management of disturbed behaviour should also be competent in physical monitoring and emergency resuscitation techniques to ensure the safety of patients following administration of rapid tranquillisation and during periods of restraint or seclusion.

15.38 All clinical staff who undertake training in the recognition, prevention and management of violence and aggression and associated physical skills training (formerly known as control and restraint training) should attend periodic refresher or update education and training programmes.

15.39 Training should be specifically designed for healthcare settings.

## Observation

15.40 Increased levels of observation may be used both for the short-term man- **4–138** agement of disturbed behaviour and to prevent suicide or serious self-harm.

---

[10] The deprivation of liberty safeguards are expected to be in force from April 2009.

15.41 Staff must balance the potentially distressing effects on the patient of increased levels of observation, particularly if these levels of observation are proposed for many hours or days, against the identified risk of self-injury. Levels of observation and risk should be regularly reviewed and a record made of agreed decisions in relation to increasing or decreasing the observation.

15.42 All hospitals should have clear written policies on the use of observation.

## Seclusion

**4–139**    15.43 Seclusion is the supervised confinement of a patient in a room, which may be locked. Its sole aim is to contain severely disturbed behaviour which is likely to cause harm to others.

15.44 Alternative terminology such as "therapeutic isolation", "single-person wards" and "enforced segregation" should not be used to deprive patients of the safeguards established for the use of seclusion. All episodes which meet the definition in the previous paragraph must be treated as seclusion, regardless of the terminology used.

15.45 Seclusion should be used only as a last resort and for the shortest possible time. Seclusion should not be used as a punishment or a threat, or because of a shortage of staff. It should not form part of a treatment programme. Seclusion should never be used solely as a means of managing self-harming behaviour. Where the patient poses a risk of self-harm as well as harm to others, seclusion should be used only when the professionals involved are satisfied that the need to protect other people outweighs any increased risk to the patient's health or safety and that any such risk can be properly managed.

15.46 Seclusion of an informal patient should be taken as an indication of the need to consider formal detention.

15.47 Hospital policies should include clear written guidelines on the use of seclusion. Guidelines should:

- ensure the safety and wellbeing of the patient;

- ensure that the patient receives the care and support rendered necessary by their seclusion both during and after it has taken place;

- distinguish between seclusion and psychological behaviour therapy interventions (such as "time out");

- specify a suitable environment that takes account of the patient's dignity and physical wellbeing;

- set out the roles and responsibilities of staff; and

- set requirements for recording, monitoring and reviewing the use of seclusion and any follow-up action.

## Procedure for seclusion

**4–140**    15.48 Local policies should set out the procedures for starting and reviewing seclusion.

15.49 The decision to use seclusion can be made in the first instance by a doctor, a suitably qualified approved clinician or the professional in charge of the ward. Where the professional in charge of the ward takes the decision, the patient's responsible clinician or the duty doctor (or equivalent) should be notified at once and should attend immediately unless the seclusion is only for a very brief period. It is for hospitals to determine which of their non-medical approved clinicians are suitably qualified to fulfil functions in relation to seclusion.

15.50 An initial multi-disciplinary review of the need for seclusion should be carried out as soon as practicable after the seclusion begins. If it is concluded that seclusion needs to continue, the review should establish the individual care needs of the patient while they are in seclusion and the steps that should be taken in order to bring the need for seclusion to an end as quickly as possible.

15.51 Unless the initial multi-disciplinary review concludes that different arrangements are appropriate, the need to continue seclusion should be reviewed:

- every two hours by two nurses or other suitably skilled professionals (one of whom was not involved directly in the decision to seclude); and

- every four hours by a doctor or a suitably qualified approved clinician.

15.52 However, local policies may allow different review arrangements to be applied during the night when patients in seclusion are asleep.

15.53 If the review concludes that seclusion is no longer necessary, it should be ended.

15.54 If the patient is secluded for more than:

- 8 hours consecutively; or

- 12 hours over a period of 48 hours,

a multi-disciplinary review should be completed by a senior doctor or suitably qualified approved clinician, and nurses and other professionals who were not involved in the incident which led to the seclusion. Where an independent multi-disciplinary review takes place it is good practice for those involved in the original decision to be consulted in the review.

15.55 A suitably skilled professional should be readily available within sight and sound of the seclusion room at all times throughout the period of the patient's seclusion.

15.56 The aim of this observation is to monitor the condition and behaviour of the patient and to identify the time at which seclusion can be ended. The level of observation should be decided on an individual basis. A documented report must be made at least every 15 minutes.

15.57 For patients who have received sedation a skilled professional will need to be outside the door at all times with adequate call facilities available to them.

15.58 Any professional taking over responsibility for observing a patient in seclusion should have a full handover, including details of the incident that resulted in the need for seclusion and subsequent reviews.

15.59 If the need for seclusion is disputed by any member of the multi-disciplinary team, the local policy should set out arrangements for the matter to be referred to a senior manager or clinician.

*Conditions of seclusion*

15.60 The room used for seclusion should:  **4–141**

- provide privacy from other patients, but enable staff to observe the patient at all times;

- be safe and secure and should not contain anything which could cause harm to the patient or others;

- be adequately furnished, heated, lit and ventilated; and

- be quiet but not soundproofed and should have some means of calling for attention (operation of which should be explained to the patient).

15.61 Staff may decide what a patient may take into the seclusion room, but the patient should always be clothed.

### Record keeping
**4–142**  15.62 Detailed and contemporaneous records should be kept in the patient's case notes of any use of seclusion, the reasons for its use, and subsequent activity. Records should also be kept in a special seclusion recording system which should contain a step-by-step account of the seclusion procedure in every instance. Responsibility for the accuracy and completeness of these records should lie with the professional in charge of the ward. Local policies should require the records of each episode of seclusion to be reviewed by a more senior professional.

### Longer-term segregation
**4–143**  15.63 There is a very small number of patients who are not responsive to short-term management of their aggression and violence and who could be described as "long-term dangerous". By this it is meant that they present a risk to others which is a constant feature of their presentation and is not subject to amelioration by a short period of seclusion combined with any other form of treatment. The clinical judgement in these cases is that, if the patient were allowed to mix freely in the general ward environment, other patients or staff would continuously be open to the potential of serious injury or harm.

15.64 It is permissible to manage this small number of patients by ensuring that their contact with the general ward population is strictly limited. When not locked in a room on their own (which can be their own bedroom rather than a seclusion room), they may be accompanied by staff at all times.

15.65 In these cases, the way that the patient's situation is reviewed needs to reflect the specific nature of their management plan. The purpose of a review is to determine whether the patient has settled sufficiently to return to the ward community and to check on their general health and welfare. The decision to return the patient to the general community will be taken by their multi-disciplinary team, following a thorough risk assessment and observations from staff of the patient's presentation during close monitoring of the patient in the company of others.

15.66 Hospitals proposing to allow longer-term segregation should have a policy in place that sets out when it is to be used and how it is to be kept under review. Policies should provide for the use of long-term segregation to be subject to periodic review by a senior clinician who is not involved with the case. The outcome of each review (whether internal or external) and the reasons for continued segregation should be recorded.

**Deprivation of daytime clothing**

15.67 Patients should never be deprived of appropriate daytime clothing during **4–144** the day with the intention of restricting their freedom of movement. They should not be deprived of other aids necessary for their daily living.

---

**Related material**

- *Violence: The Short-term Management of Disturbed/Violent Behaviour in Psychiatric In-patient Settings and Emergency Departments,* National Institute for Clinical Excellence clinical guideline 25, 2005

- *Promoting Safer and Therapeutic Services—Implementing the National Syllabus in Mental Health and Learning Disability Services—*The NHS security management service October 2005

This material does not form part of the Code. It is provided for assistance only.

---

**APPLYING THE PRINCIPLES**

This scenario is not intended to provide a template for decisions in applying the **4–145** principles in similar situations. The scenario itself is only illustrative and does not form part of the Code itself.

---

**SAFE AND THERAPEUTIC MANAGEMENT OF PATIENTS**

Abby is a 34 year old woman; she has been in hospital for ten days following her admission under section 2. Abby has been very distressed on the ward and has been verbally aggressive and threatening towards other patients and staff. The ward is very busy and staff are aware that Abby finds the environment difficult to cope with; they have tried to engage with Abby about ways in which they can support her on the ward and she has had several meetings with her primary nurse to discuss her care plan. Staff have also met with members of Abby's family including her husband and her mother. Abby's family are very concerned about her and visit every day.

Following an incident on the ward involving another patient, Abby's disturbed behaviour escalates; she becomes involved in a fight with another patient and tries to assault staff as they intervene in the incident. In order to prevent Abby from harming those around her and herself, Abby is restrained for a short period and placed in seclusion.

The ward staff need to decide whether Abby should remain in seclusion and how she should be looked after once out of seclusion. The ward staff apply the guiding principles of this Code, and among the things they might wish to consider in making a decision in these circumstances are the following.

**Purpose principle**
- What factors need to be considered in managing Abby's safety and wellbeing?

- To what extent is protecting other people an issue? How can other patients and staff be protected? What might be the best course of action for that?

- Can any risk presented by Abby only be managed by continuing to seclude Abby?
- Have any physical health factors been considered?

**Least restriction principle**

- What are the possible alternatives to the continued use of seclusion?
  — Increased levels of observation?
  — Giving Abby a chance to talk with someone at length?
  — Getting Abby and the patient with whom she had the fight to have a supervised talk?

**Respect principle**

- Does Abby have any views about why the incident occurred?
- Is Abby feeling particularly vulnerable, upset or excluded for some reason?
- Has anyone asked her why she is so distressed?
- Are there any cultural or gender matters that are prohibiting Abby from engaging with her team, eg would Abby prefer to discuss her care with a female nurse? Or are there any cultural issues that are prohibiting Abby from engaging with other patients, eg language barriers? Does Abby have the opportunity to attend a prayer room?
- Has Abby expressed any views, either now or previously, on what she would like to happen if she loses her temper or becomes aggressive?
- If a similar incident has occurred in the past, does Abby have any views about what has worked to help manage the situation and what has not and why not?

**Participation principle**

- Is Abby calm enough now to talk about what might happen next?
- What is the best way of discussing with Abby the need for seclusion, the process for reviewing its use and consideration of what might happen next?
- Can Abby give her interpretation of why she became so distressed?
- Has Abby been given an opportunity to talk to someone about her concerns?
- Have Abby's family expressed any views about what they think may help? What have her family said when they have visited?

**Effectiveness, efficiency and equity principle**

- Is there some way of reorganising things so that staff can spend more time with Abby without taking staff away from other patients' needs?

## 16. PRIVACY AND SAFETY

**4–146**    16.1 This chapter deals with privacy and safety in hospitals where patients are detained under the Act, including access to telephones and other equipment and the use of searches.

**Respect for privacy**

16.2 Article 8 of the European Convention on Human Rights requires public **4–147**
authorities to respect a person's right to a private life. This includes people
detained under the Act. Privacy and safety are therefore important constituents
of the therapeutic environment. Hospital staff should make conscious efforts to
respect the privacy of patients while maintaining safety. This encompasses the circumstances in which patients may meet or communicate with people of their
choosing in private and the protection of their private property.

**Private telephone calls and e-mail and internet access**

16.3 Hospitals should make every effort to support the patient in making and **4–148**
maintaining contact with family and friends by telephone and to enable such
calls to be made with appropriate privacy. Most wards contain coin-operated
and card-operated telephones. Hospital managers should ensure that patients
can use them without being overheard. Installing booths or hoods around them
may help to provide the necessary level of privacy.

16.4 The principle that should underpin hospital or ward policies on all telephone use is that detained patients are not, of course, free to leave the premises
and that individual freedom to communicate with family and friends should therefore be maintained as far as is possible. Any restrictions imposed should be the
minimum necessary, so as to ensure that this principle is adhered to.

16.5 Hospital managers should have a policy on the possession and use of
mobile phones by patients and their visitors.

16.6 When drawing up their policy on the use of mobile phones, hospital managers should bear in mind the following points:

- given that mobile phones provide a readily available means of communication with family and friends and are in widespread use, most detained
  patients are likely to have one. It is unlikely to be appropriate to impose a
  blanket ban on their use except in units specifically designed to provide
  enhanced levels of security in order to protect the public;

- different considerations will apply to different locations within the hospital.
  There may be valid reasons for banning or limiting the use of mobile phones
  in some parts of the premises to which detained patients have access, for
  example because of a perceived risk of interference with medical and
  other electronic equipment which could adversely affect the health of
  patients or because of intrusion into the lives of other patients or individuals
  in the community;

- it is necessary to recognise that each patient has a right to expect a peaceful
  environment, and that constant interruptions from ringing telephones have a
  potentially anti-therapeutic effect;

- it may be reasonable to require mobile phones to be switched off except
  where their use is permitted and to restrict their use to designated areas to
  which detained patients have access;

- many mobile phones have cameras and give access to the internet. This creates potential for the violation of the privacy and dignity of other patients,
  staff and visitors to the ward, and may constitute a security risk. It would
  therefore be appropriate to stipulate the circumstances in which

photographs and videos can be taken, for example only with specific permission from hospital staff;

- the difficulty in identifying when camera functions are being used may be an additional reason for restricting the areas in which mobile phones may be used;

- it is important to ensure that the hospital's policy on the use of mobile phones can be enforced effectively. For example, it may be appropriate in certain circumstances to confiscate phones from patients who consistently refuse to comply with the rules;

- any decision to prevent the use of cameras or to confiscate a mobile phone should be fully documented and be subject to periodic review;

- there should be rules on when staff and visitors can bring mobile phones into a secure setting;

- the normal rules governing the use of the hospital's power supply to charge mobile phones or other such electrical devices may need to be varied for detained patients (given the restrictions with which such patients are faced);

- staff need to be fully informed of the hospital's policy, and steps must be taken to communicate it to all patients and visitors; and

- the policy will need to be reviewed regularly and updated, where necessary, in the light of experience.

16.7 Managers should also have guidance on patients' access to e-mail and internet facilities by means of the hospital's IT infrastructure. This guidance should cover the availability of such facilities and rules prohibiting access to illegal or what would otherwise be considered inappropriate material.

**Private property**

**4–149**    16.8 Hospitals should provide adequate lockable facilities (with staff override) for the storage of the clothing and other personal possessions which patients may keep with them on the ward and for the secure central storage of items of value or which may pose a risk to the patient or to others, eg razors. Information about arrangements for storage should be easily accessible to patients on the ward. Hospitals should compile an inventory of what has been allowed and stored and give a copy to the patient. The inventory should be updated when necessary.

**Separate facilities for men and women**

**4–150**    16.9 All sleeping areas (bedrooms and bed bays) must be segregated, and members of one sex should not have to walk through an area occupied by the other sex to reach toilets or bathrooms. Separate male- and female-only toilets and bathrooms must be provided, as should separate day rooms. If in an emergency it is necessary to treat a patient in an environment intended for the opposite sex, senior management should be informed, steps should be taken to rectify the situation as soon as possible, and staff should protect the patient's privacy against intrusions—particularly in sleeping accommodation, toilets and bathrooms. Consideration should be given to the particular needs of transgender patients.

**Personal and other searches**

16.10 Hospital managers should ensure that there is an operational policy on **4–151** searching patients detained under the Act, their belongings and surroundings and their visitors. When preparing the policy, hospital managers should consider the position of informal patients.

16.11 The policy should be based on the following clear principles:

- the intention is to create and maintain a therapeutic environment in which treatment may take place and to ensure the security of the premises and the safety of patients, staff and the public;

- the authority to conduct a search of a person or their property is controlled by law, and it is important that hospital staff are aware of whether they have legal authority to carry out any such search;

- searching should be proportionate to the identified risk and should involve the minimum possible intrusion into the person's privacy; and

- all searches will be undertaken with due regard to and respect for the person's dignity.

16.12 The policy may extend to the routine and random searching without cause of detained patients, if necessary without their consent, but only in exceptional circumstances. For example, such searches may be necessary if the patients detained in a particular unit tend to have dangerous or violent propensities which create a selfevident pressing need for additional security.

16.13 Patients, staff and visitors should be informed that there is a policy on searching. Information about searches should be provided in a variety of formats to meet patients' and visitors' needs and should be readily available.

**Conducting personal and other searches**

16.14 The consent of the person should always be sought before a personal **4–152** search or a search of their possessions is attempted. If consent is given, the search should be carried out with regard to the dignity of the individual and the need to ensure maximum privacy.

16.15 Consent obtained by means of a threat, intimidation or inducement is likely to render the search illegal. Any person who is to be searched personally or whose possessions are to be searched must be informed that they do not have to consent.

16.16 A person being searched or whose possessions are the subject of a search should be kept informed of what is happening and why. If they do not understand or are not fluent in English, the services of an interpreter should be sought, if practicable. The specific needs of people with impaired hearing or a learning disability, and those of children and young people, should be considered.

16.17 A personal search should be carried out by a member of the same sex, unless necessity dictates otherwise. The search should be carried out in a way that maintains the person's privacy and dignity and respects issues of gender, culture and faith. It is always advisable to have another member of the hospital staff present during a search if it is not possible to conduct a same-sex search.

16.18 A comprehensive record of every search, including the reasons for it and details of any consequent risk assessment, should be made.

16.19 Staff involved in undertaking searches should receive appropriate instruction and refresher training.

16.20 In certain circumstances, it may be necessary to search a detained patient or their possessions without their consent.

16.21 If a detained patient refuses consent, their responsible clinician (or, failing that, another senior clinician with knowledge of the patient's case) should be contacted without delay, if practicable, so that any clinical objection to searching by force may be raised. The patient should be kept separated and under close observation, while being informed of what is happening and why, in terms appropriate to their understanding. Searches should not be delayed if there is reason to think that the person is in possession of anything that may pose an immediate risk to their own safety or that of anyone else.

16.22 If a search is considered necessary, despite the patient's objections, and there is no clinical objection to one being conducted, the search should be carried out. If force has to be used, it should be the minimum necessary.

16.23 The policy should set out the steps to be taken to resolve any disagreement or dispute where there is a clinical objection to a search.

16.24 Where a patient physically resists being personally searched, physical intervention should normally only proceed on the basis of a multi-disciplinary assessment, unless it is urgently required. A post-incident review should follow every search undertaken where consent has been withheld.

16.25 There should be support for patients and staff who are affected by the process of searching. This may be particularly necessary where a personal search has had to proceed without consent or has involved physical intervention.

16.26 Where a patient's belongings are removed during a search, the patient should be given a receipt for them and told where the items will be stored.

16.27 The exercise of powers of search should be audited regularly and the outcomes reported to the hospital managers.

## Hospital accommodation offering conditions of enhanced security

**4–153** 16.28 There are some detained patients who may be liable to present a particular danger to themselves or to others and who therefore need to be accommodated in wards or units specifically designed to offer enhanced levels of physical security. For patients detained under Part 3 of the Act, this may be a requirement of a court or of the Secretary of State for Justice, but in many cases the decision will lie primarily with the patient's responsible clinician.

16.29 When considering whether patients should be placed in, be moved to or remain in such a ward or unit, responsible clinicians should, in consultation with the multi-disciplinary team, ensure that:

- they have carefully weighed the patient's individual circumstances and the degree of risk involved; and

- they have assessed the relative clinical implications of placing the patient in an environment with enhanced physical security, in addition to or as opposed to providing care by way of intensive staffing.

16.30 Treatment in conditions of enhanced security should last for the minimum period necessary. Where responsible clinicians have taken the decision to transfer a patient within a hospital to a ward with enhanced security, they should ensure that arrangements are made to facilitate the patient's prompt return to a less secure ward when that enhanced security is no longer required.

16.31 Where responsible clinicians believe that patients no longer require conditions of enhanced security (or the current level of security), they should take steps to arrange their transfer to more appropriate accommodation. Where necessary, this may involve identifying another hospital that is willing and able to offer the patient suitable accommodation.

16.32 In the case of restricted patients, it will be necessary to seek the consent of the Secretary of State for Justice for a transfer to another hospital or, where the patient's detention is restricted to a particular unit, for a move within the same hospital.

16.33 Managers of hospitals offering accommodation with enhanced levels of security should ensure that:

• accommodation specifically designated for this purpose has adequate staffing levels; and

• they have written guidelines, setting out the categories of patient for whom it is appropriate to use physically secure conditions and those for whom it is not appropriate.

**Physical security in other hospital accommodation**

16.34 Hospital managers will need to consider what arrangements should be **4–154** put in place to ensure the safety of patients who are not subject to enhanced security.

16.35 Patients admitted to acute wards, whether or not they are formally detained there, will have complex and specific needs. In such an environment, ward staff must balance competing priorities and interests when determining what safety measures are necessary.

16.36 The intention should be to protect patients, in particular those who are at risk of suicide, self-harm, accidents or inflicting harm on others unless they are prevented from leaving the ward. Arrangements should also aim not to impose any unnecessary or disproportionate restrictions on patients or to make them feel as though they are subject to such restrictions. It may also be necessary to have in place arrangements for protecting patients and others from people whose mere presence on a ward may pose a risk to their health or safety.

16.37 It should be borne in mind that the nature of engagement with patients and of therapeutic interventions, and the structure and quality of life on the ward, are important factors in encouraging patients to remain in the ward and in minimising a culture of containment.

16.38 Locking doors, placing staff on reception to control entry to particular areas, and the use of electronic swipe cards, electronic key fobs and other technological innovations of this sort are all methods that hospitals should consider to manage entry to and exit from clinical areas to ensure the safety of their patients and others.

16.39 If hospitals are to manage entry to and exit from the ward effectively, they will need to have a policy for doing so. A written policy that sets out precisely what the ward arrangements are and how patients can exit from the ward, if they are legally free to leave and made available to all patients on the ward. The policy should be explained to patients on admission and to their visitors. In addition to producing the policy in English, hospitals may need to consider trans-lating it into other languages if these are in common use in the local area.

16.40 If managing entry and exit by means of locked external doors (or other physical barriers) is considered to be an appropriate way to maintain safety, the practice adopted must be reviewed regularly to ensure that there are clear benefits for patients and that it is not being used for the convenience of staff. It should never be necessary to lock patients and others in wards simply because of inade-quate staffing levels. In conjunction with clinical staff, managers should regularly review and evaluate the mix of patients (there may, for example, be some patients who ought to be in a more secure environment), staffing levels and the skills mix and training needs of staff.

---

**Related material**

● Using Mobile Phones in NHS Hospitals, May 2007

● The Safety and Security in Ashworth, Broadmoor and Rampton Hospitals Directions, 2000 (as amended)

This material does not form part of the Code. It is provided for assistance only.

---

## 17. WISHES EXPRESSED IN ADVANCE

**4–155**    17.1 This chapter gives guidance on statements by patients who are subject to compulsory measures under the Act about their preferences for what they would or would not like to happen if particular situations arise in future. This includes legally binding advance decisions to refuse treatment.

### Definitions
**4–156**    17.2 This chapter distinguishes between advance decisions to refuse medical treatment and other statements of views, wishes and feelings that patients make in advance.

17.3 An advance decision means a decision to refuse specified medical treat-ment made in advance by a person who has the mental capacity to do so. Advance decisions are a way in which people can refuse medical treatment for a time in the future when they may lack the capacity to consent to or refuse that treatment.

17.4 Advance decisions are concerned only with refusal of medical treatment. Other advance expressions of views, wishes and feelings may be about medical treatment or about any other aspect of a patient's care, and may be about what the patient wants to happen as much as about what they would prefer not to happen.

### Advance decisions under the Mental Capacity Act
**4–157**    17.5 The Mental Capacity Act 2005 (MCA) says that people who have the capacity to do so, and who are at least 18 years old, may make an advance decision to refuse specified treatment which will have effect at a time when they no longer have capacity to refuse or consent to treatment. If a valid and applicable advance

decision exists, it has the same effect as if the patient has capacity and makes a contemporaneous decision to refuse treatment.

17.6 Sometimes, the fact that a patient has made an advance decision refusing treatment for mental disorder will be one of the reasons why a decision is taken to detain them under the Mental Health Act. That may be the only way to ensure they get the treatment they need.

17.7 In certain circumstances, described in **chapter 24,** the Mental Health Act allows patients to be given medical treatment for their mental disorder without their consent and therefore even though they have made a valid and applicable advance decision to refuse the treatment. This only applies to patients who are detained under the Act and to patients on supervised community treatment (SCT). Furthermore, except in emergencies, it only applies to SCT patients if they have been recalled to hospital by their responsible clinician.

17.8 Even where clinicians may lawfully treat a patient compulsorily under the Mental Health Act, they should, where practicable, try to comply with the patient's wishes as expressed in an advance decision. They should, for example, consider whether it is possible to use a different form of treatment not refused by the advance decision.

17.9 Except where the Mental Health Act means that they need not, clinicians must follow all other advance decisions made by their patients which they are satisfied are valid and applicable, even if the patients concerned are detained under the Act or are on SCT. By definition, this includes all valid and applicable advance decisions made by detained and SCT patients to refuse treatment which is not for mental disorder.

17.10 Clinicians should always start from the assumption that a person had the mental capacity at the time in question to make the advance decision. However, if a clinician is not satisfied that the person had capacity at the time they made the advance decision, or if there are genuine doubts about its validity or applicability, they can treat the person without fear of liability, so long as they comply with the other requirements of the MCA, including the requirement to act in the patient's best interests.

17.11 For more information on what constitutes an advance decision, the effect they have and when they are valid and applicable (including specific additional requirements about the way advance decisions to refuse life-sustaining treatment must be documented), please refer to the Code of Practice to the MCA.

### Advance statements of wishes and feelings

17.12 There may be times when, because of their mental disorder, patients who **4–158** are subject to compulsory measures under the Mental Health Act are unable or unwilling to express their views or participate as fully as they otherwise would in decisions about their care or treatment under the Act. In such cases, patients' past wishes and feelings—so far as they are known—take on a greater significance.

17.13 Some patients will deliberately state their wishes in advance about a variety of issues, including their medical treatment, the steps that should be taken in emergencies and what should be done if particular situations occur. Such wishes should be given the same consideration as wishes expressed at any other time.

17.14 Encouraging patients to set out their wishes in advance will often be a helpful therapeutic tool, promoting collaboration and trust between patients and professionals. It is also a way in which effective use can be made of patients' expertise in the management of crises in their own conditions.

17.15 Whenever expressing a preference for their future treatment and care, patients should be encouraged to identify as precisely as possible the circumstances they have in mind. If they are saying that there are certain things that they do not want to happen—for example, being given a particular type of treatment, or being restrained in a particular way—they should be encouraged also to give their views on what should be done instead.

17.16 Patients should, however, be made aware that expressing their preference for a particular form of treatment or care in advance like this does not legally compel professionals to meet that preference.

17.17 Where patients express views to any of the professionals involved in their care about how they should be treated or about ways they would not wish to be treated in future, the professional should record those views in the patient's notes. If the views are provided in a written form, they should be kept with the patient's notes.

17.18 Whether the patient or the professional records the patient's views, steps should be taken, unless the patient objects, to ensure that the information:

- is drawn to the attention of other professionals who ought to know about it; and

- is included in care plans and other documentation which will help ensure that the patient's views are remembered and considered in situations where they are relevant in future.

17.19 Advance decisions to refuse treatment should also be recorded and documented in the same way.

17.20 If the professional to whom the wish is being expressed forms the opinion that the patient lacks capacity to understand the wish they are expressing, the professional should record their opinion, and their reasons for it, alongside the record of the patient's wish.

17.21 The fact that a patient has expressed their wishes about a particular matter in the past is not a substitute for seeking their views on it when the situation actually arises, even if they are no longer in a position to think about their views as clearly as they did when they expressed their wishes previously. Everyone has the right to change their mind. In particular, where patients have the mental capacity to express a clear wish in the present, that wish should always be assumed to have overtaken their previous wishes, even if it is significantly different.

17.22 Where patients lack the capacity to formulate and express their views on an issue on which they have given their views in advance, the professionals should record whether they make a decision under the Mental Health Act which is contrary to those previously expressed views. They should also record their reasons for the decision, just as they would if they were going against wishes that a patient was expressing in the present.

---

**Related material**

- Mental Capacity Act 2005
- *Mental Capacity Act 2005 Code of Practice,* TSO, 2007

This material does not form part of the Code. It is provided for assistance only.

---

## 18. CONFIDENTIALITY AND INFORMATION SHARING

18.1 This chapter deals with issues about confidentiality and information **4–159** sharing which arise in connection with the Act.

**General points**

18.2 Except where the Act itself says otherwise, the law on confidentiality is the **4–160** same for patients subject to the Act as it is for any other patients. The box below gives a brief summary of the most fundamental points of the general law. There are some additional considerations in relation to children and young people (see **chapter 36**).

---

**Confidentiality—a brief summary**

In common law, a duty of confidence arises when one person discloses information to another in circumstances where it is reasonable to expect that the information will be held in confidence. Certain situations, such as discussions with a health professional or social worker, are generally presumed to be confidential.

However, there are circumstances in which it is both justifiable and important to share otherwise confidential patient information with people outside the immediate team treating a patient.

If a person lacks the capacity to consent to the disclosure, it may nonetheless be acceptable and appropriate to disclose the information in the person's best interests.

Otherwise, confidential patient information should be disclosed outside the team only:

- with the person's consent (where the person has capacity to consent);
- if there is a specific legal obligation or authority to do so; or
- where there is an overriding public interest in disclosing the information.

The "public interest" is not the same as what might be of interest to the public. Where confidential patient information is involved, public interest justifications for overriding confidentiality could include (but are not limited to) protecting other people from serious harm and preventing serious crime.

The common law does not normally permit disclosure of confidential patient information solely in the person's own interests, where they have capacity to consent to the disclosure but refuse to do so.

---

> A person's right to have their privacy respected is also protected by Article 8 of the European Convention on Human Rights. The disclosure of confidential information may be a breach of that right unless it is a necessary and proportionate response to the situation.

18.3 Information sharing between professionals can contribute to the care and treatment of patients and help to protect people from harm. This includes information sharing as part of the Care Programme Approach (or its equivalent).

18.4 A range of public services is involved in the provision of services to patients who are subject to compulsory measures under the Act, including housing and social services. Patients must be consulted about what information it may be helpful to share with these services and when. Professionals should be clear about how the sharing of such information could benefit the patient or help to prevent serious harm to others and whether there are any potential negative consequences. Advocates and advice services can support patients in helping them decide what information should be shared.

18.5 Sharing information with carers and other people with a valid interest in the care and wellbeing of the patient can also contribute to and support their care and treatment. Where patients have capacity to agree and are willing to do so, carers and other people with a valid interest should be given information about the patient's progress to help them offer views about the patient's care. A patient's agreement to such disclosure must be freely given. In the case of patients detained under Part 3 of the Act, people with a valid interest may include victims and the families of victims (see **paragraphs 18.18–18.20**).

**Disclosure of confidential patient information for the purposes of the Act**

4–161    18.6 The Act creates a number of situations where confidential information about patients will need to be disclosed, even if the patient does not consent. These include:

- reports to the Tribunal when a patient's case is to be considered;

- reports to the Commission in relation to patients who have been treated on the basis of a certificate issued by a second opinion appointed doctor (SOAD); and

- reports to the Secretary of State for Justice on restricted patients.

18.7 The Act also gives certain people and bodies—including the Commission, SOADs and (in certain circumstances) independent mental health advocates[11]—the right to access records relating to patients.

18.8 In addition, where the Act allows steps to be taken in relation to patients without their consent, it is implicit that confidential patient information may be

---

[11] Independent mental health advocacy services under the Act are expected to be introduced in April 2009.

disclosed to the extent that it is necessary to take those steps. So, for example, confidential patient information may be shared to the extent that it is necessary for:

- medical treatment which may be given without a patient's consent under the Act;

- safely and securely conveying a patient to hospital (or anywhere else) under the Act;

- finding and returning a patient who has absconded from legal custody or who is absent without leave; or

- transferring responsibility for a patient who is subject to the Act from one set of people to another (eg where a detained patient is to be transferred from one hospital to another, or where responsibility for a patient is to be transferred between England and another jurisdiction).

18.9 Even though information may be disclosed in these cases, it is still necessary for people proposing to disclose the information to assure themselves that it is necessary in the circumstances, that the aim of the disclosure cannot reasonably be achieved without it, and that any breach of the patient's confidentiality is a proportionate response given the purpose for which the disclosure is being considered. Care must also always be taken to ensure that any information disclosed is accurate.

**Limitations on sharing information with carers, relatives and friends**
18.10 Simply asking for information from carers, relatives, friends or other **4–162** people about a patient without that patient's consent need not involve any breach of confidentiality, provided the person requesting the information does not reveal any personal confidential information about the patient which the carer, relative, friend or other person being asked would not legitimately know anyway.

18.11 Apart from information which must be given to nearest relatives, the Act does not create any exceptions to the general law about disclosing confidential patient information to carers, relatives or friends.

18.12 Carers, relatives and friends cannot be told a patient's particular diagnosis or be given any other confidential personal information about the patient unless the patient consents or there is another basis on which to disclose it in accordance with the law. But carers should always be offered information which may help them understand the nature of mental disorder generally, the ways it is treated and the operation of the Act.

18.13 Carers, relatives, friends and other people also have a right to expect that any personal information about themselves, or any information about the patient which they pass on to professionals in confidence, will be treated as confidential. Unless there is an overriding reason that makes it necessary and there is legal authority to do so, information they provide about patients should not be repeated to patients in a way that might reveal its source, unless the carer, relative, friend or other person was made aware that that could happen and has not objected to it.

**Sharing information to manage risk**
18.14 Although information may be disclosed only in line with the law, there is **4–163** no reason in practice why patient confidentiality should make it impossible for

professionals and agencies to share information needed to manage any serious risks which certain patients pose to other people.

18.15 Where the issue is the management of the risk of serious harm, the judgement required is normally a balance between the public interest in disclosure, including the need to prevent harm to others, and both the rights of the individual concerned and the public interest in maintaining trust in a confidential service.

18.16 Whether there is an overriding public interest in disclosing confidential patient information may vary according to the type of information. Even in cases where there is no overriding public interest in disclosing detailed clinical information about a patient's state of health, there may nonetheless be an overriding public interest in sharing more limited information about the patient's current and past status under the Act, if that will help ensure properly informed risk management by the relevant authorities.

### Recording disclosure without consent

**4–164**   18.17 Any decision to disclose confidential information about patients—for any reason—should be fully documented. The relevant facts should be recorded, along with the reasons for the decision and the identity of all those involved in the process of reaching it. Reasons should be given by reference to the grounds on which the disclosure is to be justified.

### Information for victims of crimes (Sections 35–45 of the Domestic Violence, Crime and Victims Act 2004)

**4–165**   18.18 The victims of certain mentally disordered offenders detained in hospital have rights under the Domestic Violence, Crime and Victims Act 2004 (DVCV Act) to make representations and receive information about that patient's discharge.

18.19 In other circumstances, professionals should encourage (but cannot require) mentally disordered offender patients to agree to share information that will enable victims and victims' families to be informed about their progress. Among other benefits, disclosure of such information can sometimes serve to reduce the danger of harmful confrontations after a discharge of which victims were unaware.

18.20 Professionals should be ready to discuss with patients the benefits of enabling some information to be given by professionals to victims, within the spirit of the Code of Practice for Victims of Crime issued under the DVCV Act.

---

**Related material**

- *Public Sector Data Sharing: Guidance on the Law,* Ministry of Justice, November 2003

- *Confidentiality: NHS Code of Practice,* Department of Health, November 2003

- Domestic Violence, Crime and Victims Act 2004

- *The Code of Practice for Victims of Crime,* Office for Criminal Justice Reform, October 2005

---

- *Guidance for Clinicians—Duties to Victims under the Domestic Violence, Crime and Victims Act 2004,* Home Office Mental Health Unit, 2005[12]
- Mental Capacity Act 2005
- *Mental Capacity Act 2005 Code of Practice,* TSO, 2007
- Data Protection Act 1998
- Human Rights Act 1998

This material does not form part of the Code. It is provided for assistance only.

## 19. VISITING PATIENTS IN HOSPITAL

19.1 This chapter covers visiting patients in hospital and those circumstances **4–166** where it may be necessary to consider the exclusion of visitors. The chapter also refers to particular considerations for child visitors.

### Arrangements for visits to patients
19.2 All patients have the right to maintain contact with and be visited by any- **4–167** one they wish to see, subject to carefully limited exceptions. The value of visits in maintaining links with family and community networks is recognised as a key element in a patient's care and treatment.

19.3 Visits should be encouraged and made as comfortable and easy as possible for the visitor and the patient. Reasonable and flexible visiting times, access to refreshment and pleasant surroundings will all contribute to a sense of respect for the patient's entitlement to be visited.

19.4 In addition to visits, every effort should be made to assist the patient, where appropriate, to maintain contact with relatives, friends and advocates in other ways. In particular, patients should have readily accessible and appropriate daytime telephone facilities (see **chapter 16**).

### People with a right to visit patients
19.5 The Act gives certain people the right to visit patients in private if they **4–168** wish. This includes second opinion appointed doctors (SOADs), independent doctors or approved clinicians appointed to examine the patient in relation to an application or reference to the Tribunal, people visiting on behalf of the Commission, and independent mental health advocates (IMHAs).[13]

19.6 Hospital managers must ensure that such visits can take place in private, if that is what the person concerned wants.

19.7 If there are particular concerns for the security of the visitor, they should be discussed with the visitor with a view to agreeing suitable security arrangements.

---

[12] Further guidance on hospital managers' new duties in respect of unrestricted patients is to be published shortly.
[13] Independent mental health advocacy services under the Act are expected to be introduced in April 2009.

19.8 Hospital managers should also ensure that patients can communicate with their legal representatives in private, and should facilitate visits by those representatives when they request them.

**Exclusion or restriction of visitors**

**4–169**    19.9 There are circumstances where hospital managers may restrict visitors, refuse them entry or require them to leave. Managers should have a policy on the circumstances in which visits to patients may be restricted, to which both clinical staff and patients may refer.

19.10 There are two principal grounds which could justify the restriction or exclusion of a visitor: clinical grounds and security grounds.

19.11 The decision to prohibit a visit by any person whom the patient has requested to visit or has agreed to see should be regarded as a serious interference with the rights of the patient. There may be circumstances when a visitor has to be excluded, but these instances should be exceptional and any decision should be taken only after other means to deal with the problem have been considered and (where appropriate) tried. Any such decision should be fully documented and include the reasons for the exclusion, and it should be made available for independent scrutiny by the Commission.

*Restriction or exclusion on clinical grounds*

**4–170**    19.12 From time to time, the patient's responsible clinician may decide, after assessment and discussion with the multi-disciplinary team, that some visits could be detrimental to the safety or wellbeing of the patient, the visitor, other patients, or staff on the ward. In these circumstances, the responsible clinician may make special arrangements for the visit, impose reasonable conditions or if necessary exclude the visitor. In any of these cases, the reasons for the restriction should be recorded and explained to the patient and the visitor, both orally and in writing (subject to the normal considerations of patient confidentiality).

*Exclusion on security grounds*

**4–171**    19.13 The behaviour of a particular visitor may be disruptive, or may have been disruptive in the past, to the degree that exclusion from the hospital is necessary as a last resort. Examples of such behaviour include:

- incitement to abscond;
- smuggling of illicit drugs or alcohol into the hospital or unit;
- transfer of potential weapons;
- unacceptable aggression; and
- attempts by members of the media to gain unauthorised access.

19.14 A decision to exclude a visitor on the grounds of their behaviour should be fully documented and explained to the patient orally and in writing. Where possible and appropriate, the reason for the decision should be communicated to the person being excluded (subject to the normal considerations of patient confidentiality and any overriding security concerns).

**Monitoring by hospital managers**

19.15 Hospital managers should regularly monitor the exclusion from the hos-  **4–172**
pital of visitors to detained patients.

19.16 Restricting visitors to informal patients who lack capacity to decide
whether to remain in hospital could amount to or contribute to a deprivation of
liberty and may indicate that an authorisation under the deprivation of liberty safeguards[14] of the Mental Capacity Act 2005 may need to be sought.

**Children and young people**

19.17 All hospitals should have written policies and procedures regarding the  **4–173**
arrangements for children and young people who visit patients in hospital and
for visits to patients who are children or young people. Policies should be
drawn up in consultation with local social services authorities and local safeguarding children boards.[15]

19.18 Local policies should ensure that the best interests and safety of the children and young people concerned are always considered and that visits by or to
children and young people are not allowed if they are not in their best interests.
However, within that overarching framework, hospitals should do all they can
to facilitate the maintenance of children's and young people's contact with friends
and family and offer privacy within which that can happen.

19.19 Information about visiting should be explained to children and young
people in a way that they are able to understand. Environments that are friendly
to children and young people should be provided where necessary.

19.20 Where a child or young person is being detained, it should not be
assumed simply because of their age that they would welcome all visitors, and
like adults their views should be sought.

## 20. INDEPENDENT MENTAL HEALTH ADVOCATES

20.1 This chapter explains the role of independent mental health advocates  **4–174**
(IMHAs) under the Act **(Reference Guide chapter 34)**.

**Purpose of independent mental health advocacy services**

20.2 Independent mental health advocacy services provide an additional safe-  **4–175**
guard for patients who are subject to the Act. IMHAs are specialist advocates who
are trained specifically to work within the framework of the Act to meet the needs
of patients.

20.3 Independent mental health advocacy services do not replace any other
advocacy and support services that are available to patients, but are intended to
operate in conjunction with those services.

**Patients who are eligible for independent mental health advocacy services**
**(qualifying patients) (Section 130C)**

20.4 Patients are eligible for support from an IMHA if they are:  **4–176**

---

[14] The deprivation of liberty safeguards are expected to be in force from April 2009.
[15] The Secretary of State for Health has issued directions which set out more detailed restrictions on
   visits by children to patients in high security psychiatric hospitals.

- detained under the Act (even if they are currently on leave of absence from hospital);
- conditionally discharged restricted patients;
- subject to guardianship; or
- supervised community treatment (SCT) patients.

20.5 For these purposes, detention does not include being detained:

- on the basis of an emergency application (section 4) until the second medical recommendation is received (see **chapter 5**);
- under the holding powers in section 5; or
- in a place of safety under section 135 or 136.

20.6 Other patients ("informal patients") are eligible if they are:

- being considered for a treatment to which section 57 applies ("a section 57 treatment"); or
- under 18 and being considered for electro-convulsive therapy or any other treatment to which section 58A applies ("a section 58A treatment").

20.7 The Act calls patients who are eligible for the support of an IMHA "qualifying patients".

**The role of independent mental health advocates (Section 130B(1) and (2))**

**4–177**     20.8 The Act says that the support which IMHAs provide must include helping patients to obtain information about and understand the following:

- their rights under the Act;
- the rights which other people (eg nearest relatives) have in relation to them under the Act;
- the particular parts of the Act which apply to them (eg the basis on which they are detained) and which therefore make them eligible for advocacy;
- any conditions or restrictions to which they are subject (eg as a condition of leave of absence from hospital, as a condition of a community treatment order, or as a condition of conditional discharge);
- any medical treatment that they are receiving or might be given;
- the reasons for that treatment (or proposed treatment); and
- the legal authority for providing that treatment, and the safeguards and other requirements of the Act which would apply to that treatment.

20.9 It also includes helping patients to exercise their rights, which can include representing them and speaking on their behalf.

20.10 IMHAs may also support patients in a range of other ways to ensure they can participate in the decisions that are made about their care and treatment.

20.11 The involvement of an IMHA does not affect a patient's right (nor the right of their nearest relative) to seek advice from a lawyer. Nor does it affect any entitlement to legal aid.

**Duty to inform patients about the availability of independent mental health advocacy services (Section 130D)**

20.12 Certain people have a duty to take whatever steps are practicable to **4–178** ensure that patients understand that help is available to them from IMHA services and how they can obtain that help, as set out in the following table. This must include giving the relevant information both orally and in writing.

*Duty to provide patients with information about advocacy services*

| Type of patient | Steps to be taken by | As soon as practicable after | **4–179** |
|---|---|---|---|
| **Detained patient** | The managers of the hospital in which the patient is liable to be detained | The patient becomes liable to be detained | |
| **Guardianship patient** | The responsible local social services authority | The patient becomes subject to guardianship | |
| **SCT patient** | The managers of the responsible hospital | The patient becomes an SCT patient | |
| **Conditionally discharged patient** | The patient's responsible clinician | The patient is conditionally discharged | |
| **Informal patient** | The doctor or approved clinician who first discusses with the patient the possibility of them being given the section 57 or 58A treatment in question | That discussion (or during it) | |

20.13 The relevant person must also take whatever steps are practicable to give a copy of the written information to the patient's nearest relative, unless the patient requests otherwise (and subject to the normal considerations about involving nearest relatives see **paragraphs 2.27–2.33**).

20.14 However, any information about independent mental health advocacy services should make clear that the services are for patients and are not advocacy services for nearest relatives themselves.

20.15 The duty to give information to nearest relatives does not apply to informal patients, nor to patients detained in hospital under Part 3 of the Act (although it does apply to those patients if they subsequently become SCT patients).

**Seeking help from an independent mental health advocate**

20.16 A qualifying patient may request the support of an IMHA at any time **4–180** after they become a qualifying patient. Patients have the right to access the independent mental health advocacy service itself, rather than the services of a particular IMHA, though where possible it would normally be good practice for the same IMHA to remain involved while the person's case stays open.

20.17 A patient may choose to end the support they are receiving from an IMHA at any time.

20.18 IMHAs must also comply with any reasonable request to visit and interview a qualifying patient, if the request is made by the patient's nearest relative, an approved mental health professional (AMHP) or the patient's responsible clinician (if they have one). But patients may refuse to be interviewed and do not have to accept help from an IMHA if they do not want it **(Section 130B(5))**.

20.19 AMHPs and responsible clinicians should consider requesting an IMHA to visit a qualifying patient if they think that the patient might benefit from an IMHA's visit but is unable or unlikely for whatever reason to request an IMHA's help themselves.

20.20 Before requesting an IMHA to visit a patient, they should, wherever practicable, first discuss the idea with the patient, and give the patient the opportunity to decide for themselves whether to request an IMHA's help. AMHPs and responsible clinicians should not request an IMHA to visit where they know, or strongly suspect, that the patient does not want an IMHA's help, or the help of the particular IMHA in question.

**Independent mental health advocates' access to patients and professionals**

**4–181**  20.21 Patients should have access to a telephone on which they can contact the independent mental health advocacy service and talk to them in private.

20.22 IMHAs should:

- have access to wards and units on which patients are resident;
- be able to meet with the patients they are helping in private, where they think it appropriate; and
- be able to attend meetings between patients and the professionals involved in their care and treatment when asked to do so by patients.

20.23 When instructed by a patient, the nearest relative, an AMHP or the responsible clinician, an IMHA has the right to meet the patient in private. IMHAs also have a right to visit and speak to any person who is currently professionally concerned with a patient's medical treatment, provided it is for the purpose of supporting that patient in their capacity as an IMHA **(Section 130B(3))**.

20.24 Professionals should remember that the normal rules on patient confidentiality apply to conversations with IMHAs, even when the conversation is at the patient's request. IMHAs have a right of access to patients' records in certain cases (described below), but otherwise professionals should be careful not to share confidential information with IMHAs, unless the patient has consented to the disclosure or the disclosure is justified on the normal grounds (see **chapter 18**).

**Independent mental health advocates' access to patients' records (Section 130B(3) and (4))**

20.25 Where the patient consents, IMHAs have a right to see any clinical or **4–182** other records relating to the patient's detention or treatment in any hospital, or relating to any after-care services provided to the patient. IMHAs have a similar right to see any records relating to the patient held by a local social services authority.

20.26 Where the patient does not have the capacity (or in the case of a child, the competence) to consent to an IMHA having access to their records, the holder of the records must allow the IMHA access if they think that it is appropriate and that the records in question are relevant to the help to be provided by the IMHA.

20.27 When an IMHA seeks access to the records of a patient who does not have the capacity or the competence to consent, the person who holds the records should ask the IMHA to explain what information they think is relevant to the help they are providing to the patient and why they think it is appropriate for them to be able to see that information.

20.28 The Act does not define any further what it means by access being appropriate, so the record holder needs to consider all the facts of the case. But the starting point should always be what is best for the patient and not (for example) what would be most convenient for the organisation which holds the records.

20.29 In deciding whether it is appropriate to allow the IMHA access, the holder of the records needs to consider whether disclosure of the confidential patient information contained in the records is justified.

20.30 The key consideration will therefore be whether the disclosure is in the patient's best interests. That decision should be taken in accordance with the Mental Capacity Act 2005 (MCA) (or, for children under 16, the common law), like any other decision in connection with the care or treatment of patients who cannot make the decision for themselves.

20.31 Record holders should start from a general presumption that it is likely to be in patients' interests to be represented by an IMHA who is knowledgeable about their case. But each decision must still be taken on its merits, and the record holder must, in particular, take into account what they know about the patient's wishes and feelings, including any written statements made in advance. (For further information on taking decisions in the best interests of people who lack capacity to make the decision themselves, please see the Code of Practice to the MCA.)

20.32 Records must not be disclosed if that would conflict with a decision made on the patient's behalf by the patient's attorney or deputy, or by the Court of Protection.

20.33 If the record holder thinks that disclosing the confidential patient information in the records to the IMHA would be in the patient's best interests, it is likely to be appropriate to allow the IMHA access to those records in all but the most exceptional cases.

---

**Related material**

- Mental Capacity Act 2005
- Mental Capacity Act 2005 Code of Practice, TSO, 2007

  This material does not form part of the Code. It is provided for assistance only.

---

## 21. LEAVE OF ABSENCE

**4–183**    21.1 This chapter provides guidance on leave of absence for detained patients under section 17 of the Act **(Reference Guide 12.39–12.56)**.

### General points
**4–184**    21.2 In general, while patients are detained in a hospital they can leave lawfully—even for a very short period—only if they are given leave of absence by their responsible clinician under section 17 of the Act.[16]

21.3 Responsible clinicians cannot grant leave of absence from hospital to patients who have been remanded to hospital under sections 35 or 36 of the Act or who are subject to interim hospital orders under section 38.

21.4 Except for certain restricted patients (see **paragraph 21.14**), no formal procedure is required to allow patients to move within a hospital or its grounds. Such "ground leave" within a hospital may be encouraged or, where necessary, restricted, as part of each patient's care plan.

21.5 What constitutes a particular hospital for the purpose of leave is a matter of fact which can be determined only in the light of the particular case. Where one building, or set of buildings, includes accommodation under the management of different bodies (eg two different NHS trusts), the accommodation used by each body should be treated as forming separate hospitals. Facilities and grounds shared by both can be regarded as part of both hospitals.

### Power to grant leave
**4–185**    21.6 Only the patient's responsible clinician can grant leave of absence to a patient detained under the Act. Responsible clinicians cannot delegate the decision to grant leave of absence to anyone else. In the absence of the usual responsible clinician (eg if they are on leave), permission can be granted only by the approved clinician who is for the time being acting as the patient's responsible clinician.

21.7 Responsible clinicians may grant leave for specific occasions or for specific or indefinite periods of time. They may make leave subject to any conditions which they consider necessary in the interests of the patient or for the protection of other people.

21.8 Leave of absence can be an important part of a detained patient's care plan, but can also be a time of risk. When considering and planning leave of absence, responsible clinicians should:

- consider the potential benefits and any risks to the patient's health and safety of granting or refusing leave;

- consider the potential benefits of granting leave for facilitating the patient's recovery;

- balance these benefits against any risks that the leave may pose in terms of the protection of other people (either generally or particular people);

---

[16] Patients will also lawfully be absent from hospital if they are being transferred or taken to another place under the Act, or under another piece of legislation. This would include, for example, patients being transferred to another hospital under s.19 of the Act, or patients who are required to attend court.

- consider any conditions which should be attached to the leave, eg requiring the patient not to visit particular places or persons;

- be aware of any child protection and child welfare issues in granting leave;

- take account of the patient's wishes, and those of carers, friends and others who may be involved in any planned leave of absence;

- consider what support the patient would require during their leave of absence and whether it can be provided;

- ensure that any community services which will need to provide support for the patient during the leave are involved in the planning of the leave, and that they know the leave dates and times and any conditions placed on the patient during their leave;

- ensure that the patient is aware of any contingency plans put in place for their support, including what they should do if they think they need to return to hospital early; and

- (in the case of mentally disordered offender patients) consider whether there are any issues relating to victims which impact on whether leave should be granted and the conditions to which it should be subject.

21.9 When considering whether to grant leave of absence for more than seven consecutive days, or extending leave so that the total period is more than seven consecutive days, responsible clinicians must first consider whether the patient should go onto supervised community treatment (SCT) instead. This does not apply to restricted patients, nor, in practice, to patients detained for assessment under section 2 of the Act, as they are not eligible for SCT (**Section 17(2A)**).

21.10 The requirement to consider SCT does not mean that the responsible clinician cannot use longer-term leave if that is the more suitable option, but the responsible clinician will need to be able to show that both options have been duly considered. The decision, and the reasons for it, should be recorded in the patient's notes.

21.11 One use of leave for more than seven days may be to assess a patient's suitability for discharge from detention. Guidance on factors to be considered when deciding between leave of absence and SCT is given in **chapter 28**.

21.12 Hospital managers cannot overrule a responsible clinician's decision to grant leave. However, the fact that a responsible clinician grants leave subject to certain conditions, eg residence at a hostel, does not oblige the hospital managers or anyone else to arrange or fund the particular placement or services the clinician has in mind. Responsible clinicians should not grant leave on such a basis without first taking steps to establish that the necessary services or accommodation (or both) are available.

**Restricted patients**

21.13 Any proposal to grant leave to a restricted patient has to be approved by **4–186** the Secretary of State for Justice, who should be given as much notice as possible and full details of the proposed leave (**Section 41(3)**).

21.14 Where the courts or the Secretary of State have decided that restricted patients are to be detained in a particular unit of a hospital, those patients require leave of absence to go to any other part of that hospital as well as outside the hospital.

21.15 Restricted patients are not eligible for SCT. The Secretary of State would normally consider any request for section 17 leave for a restricted patient to be in the community for more than a few consecutive nights as an application for conditional discharge.

### Short-term leave

**4–187**  21.16 Subject to the agreement of the Secretary of State for Justice in the case of restricted patients, responsible clinicians may decide to authorise short-term local leave, which may be managed by other staff. For example, patients may be given leave for a shopping trip of two hours every week to a specific destination, with the decision on which particular two hours to be left to the discretion of the responsible nursing staff.

21.17 The parameters within which this discretion may be exercised must be clearly set out by the responsible clinician, eg the particular places to be visited, any restrictions on the time of day the leave can take place, and any circumstances in which the leave should not go ahead.

21.18 Responsible clinicians should regularly review any short-term leave they authorise on this basis and amend it as necessary.

### Longer periods of leave

**4–188**  21.19 Longer-term leave should be planned properly and, where possible, well in advance. Patients should be fully involved in the decision and responsible clinicians should be satisfied that patients are likely to be able to manage outside the hospital. Subject to the normal considerations of patient confidentiality, carers and other relevant people should be consulted before leave is granted (especially where the patient is to reside with them). Relevant community services should also be consulted.

21.20 If patients do not consent to carers or other people who would normally be involved in their care being consulted about their leave, responsible clinicians should reconsider whether or not it is safe and appropriate to grant leave.

### Recording leave

**4–189**  21.21 Hospital managers should establish a standardised system by which responsible clinicians can record the leave they authorise and specify the conditions attached to it. Copies of the authorisation should be given to the patient and to any carers, professionals and other people in the community who need to know. A copy should also be kept in the patient's notes. In case they fail to return from leave, an up-to-date description of the patient should be available in their notes.

21.22 The outcome of leave—whether or not it went well, particular problems encountered, concerns raised or benefits achieved—should also be recorded in patients' notes to inform future decision-making. Patients should be encouraged to contribute by giving their own views on their leave; some hospitals provide leave records specifically for this purpose.

### Care and treatment while on leave

**4–190**  21.23 Responsible clinicians' responsibilities for their patients remain the same while the patients are on leave.

21.24 A patient who is granted leave under section 17 remains liable to be detained, and the rules in Part 4 of the Act about their medical treatment continue to apply (see **chapter 23**). If it becomes necessary to administer treatment without the patient's consent, consideration should be given to whether it would be more appropriate to recall the patient to hospital (see **paragraphs 21.31–21.34**), although recall is not a legal requirement.

21.25 The duty on local social services authorities and primary care trusts to provide after-care under section 117 of the Act for certain patients who have been discharged from detention also applies to those patients while they are on leave of absence (see **chapter 27**).

### Escorted leave (Section 17(3))

21.26 A responsible clinician may direct that their patient remains in custody **4–191** while on leave of absence, either in the patient's own interests or for the protection of other people. Patients may be kept in the custody of any officer on the staff of the hospital or any person authorised in writing by the hospital managers. Such an arrangement is often useful, for example, to enable patients to participate in escorted trips or to have compassionate home leave.

21.27 While it may often be appropriate to authorise leave subject to the condition that a patient is accompanied by a friend or relative (eg on a pre-arranged day out from the hospital), responsible clinicians should specify that the patient is to be in the legal custody of a friend or relative only if it is appropriate for that person to be legally responsible for the patient, and if that person understands and accepts the consequent responsibility.

21.28 Escorted leave to Scotland, Northern Ireland or any of the Channel Islands can only be granted if the local legislation allows patients to be kept in custody while in that jurisdiction.[17]

### Leave to reside in other hospitals

21.29 Responsible clinicians may also require patients, as a condition of leave, **4–192** to reside at another hospital in England or Wales, and they may then be kept in the custody of staff of that hospital. However, before authorising leave on this basis, responsible clinicians should consider whether it would be more appropriate to transfer the patient to the other hospital instead (see **chapter 30**).

21.30 Where a patient is granted leave of absence to another hospital, the responsible clinician at the first hospital should remain in overall charge of the patient's case.

If it is thought that a clinician at the other hospital should become the responsible clinician, the patient should instead be transferred to that hospital. An approved clinician in charge of any particular aspect of the patient's treatment may be from either hospital. (For further guidance on allocating responsible clinicians see **chapter 14**.)

### Recall from leave (Section 17(4))

21.31 A responsible clinician may revoke their patient's leave at any time if **4–193** they consider it necessary in the interests of the patient's health or safety or for the protection of other people. Responsible clinicians must be satisfied that

---

[17] When this edition of the Code comes into force, it is expected that escorted leave to Scotland will be possible—but that is subject to the Scottish Parliament.

these criteria are met and should consider what effect being recalled may have on the patient. A refusal to take medication would not on its own be a reason for revocation, although it would almost always be a reason to consider revocation.

21.32 The responsible clinician must arrange for a notice in writing revoking the leave to be served on the patient or on the person who is for the time being in charge of the patient. Hospitals should always know the address of patients who are on leave of absence.

21.33 The reasons for recall should be fully explained to the patient and a record of the explanation included in the patient's notes. A restricted patient's leave may be revoked either by the responsible clinician or by the Secretary of State for Justice.

21.34 It is essential that carers (especially where the patient is residing with them while on leave) and professionals who support the patient while on leave should have easy access to the patient's responsible clinician if they feel consideration should be given to return of the patient before their leave is due to end.

### Renewal of authority to detain
**4–194**  21.35 It is possible to renew a patient's detention while they are on leave if the criteria in section 20 of the Act are met (see **chapter 29**). But leave should not be used as an alternative to discharging the patient either completely or onto SCT where that is appropriate. **Chapter 28** gives further guidance on factors to consider when deciding between leave of absence and SCT.

### Patients who are in hospital but not detained
**4–195**  21.36 Patients who are not legally detained in hospital have the right to leave at any time. They cannot be required to ask permission to do so, but may be asked to inform staff when they wish to leave the ward.

---

**Related material**
- *Guidance for Responsible Medical Officers—Leave of Absence for Patients Subject to Restrictions,* Ministry of Justice Mental Health Unit

  This material does not form part of the Code. It is provided for assistance only.

---

## 22. ABSENCE WITHOUT LEAVE

**4–196**  22.1 This chapter gives guidance about action to be taken when patients are absent without leave (AWOL) or have otherwise absconded from legal custody under the Act.

### General points
**4–197**  22.2 Under section 18 of the Act, patients are considered to be AWOL in various circumstances, in particular when they:

- have left the hospital in which they are detained without their absence being agreed (under section 17 of the Act) by their responsible clinician;

- have failed to return to the hospital at the time required to do so by the conditions of leave under section 17;

- are absent without permission from a place where they are required to reside as a condition of leave under section 17;

- have failed to return to the hospital when their leave under section 17 has been revoked;

- are supervised community treatment (SCT) patients who have failed to attend hospital when recalled;

- are SCT patients who have absconded from hospital after being recalled there;

- are conditionally discharged restricted patients whom the Secretary of State for Justice has recalled to hospital; or

- are guardianship patients who are absent without permission from the place where they are required to live by their guardian.

### Detained patients (Reference Guide 12.57–12.64)

22.3 Detained patients who are AWOL may be taken into custody and returned **4–198** by an approved mental health professional (AMHP), any member of the hospital staff, any police officer, or anyone authorised in writing by the hospital managers.

22.4 A patient who has been required to reside in another hospital as a condition of leave of absence can also be taken into custody by any member of that hospital's staff or by any person authorised by that hospital's managers.

22.5 Otherwise, responsibility for the safe return of patients rests with the detaining hospital. If the absconding patient is initially taken to another hospital, that hospital may, with the written authorisation of the managers of the detaining hospital, detain the patient while arrangements are made for their return. In these (and similar) cases people may take a faxed or scanned copy of a written authorisation as evidence that they have the necessary authority without waiting for the original.

### Guardianship patients (Reference Guide 19.86–19.91)

22.6 Guardianship patients who are AWOL from the place where they are **4–199** required to live may be taken into custody by any member of the staff of the responsible local social services authority (LSSA) or by any person authorised in writing by the LSSA or by the private guardian (if there is one).

### SCT patients (Reference Guide 15.66–15.70)

22.7 SCT patients who are AWOL may be taken into custody and returned to **4–200** the hospital to which they have been recalled by an AMHP, a police officer, a member of staff of the hospital to which they have been recalled, or anyone authorised in writing by the managers of that hospital or by the responsible clinician.

### Other situations in which patients are in legal custody (Reference Guide chapter 31)

22.8 In addition, there are various situations in which patients are considered to **4–201** be in legal custody under the Act. These include, for example:

- the detention of patients in places of safety under section 135 or 136;

- the conveyance of patients to hospital (or elsewhere) under the Act, including where patients are being returned to hospital when they have gone AWOL; and

- where patients' leave of absence is conditional on their being kept in custody by an escort.

(See **chapters 10, 11** and **21** respectively.)

22.9 If patients who are in legal custody for such other reasons abscond, they may also be taken into custody and returned to the place they ought to be, in accordance with the Act (**Sections 137 and 138**).

**Local policies**

**4–202**    22.10 Hospital managers should ensure that there is a clear written policy about the action to be taken when a detained patient, or a patient on SCT, goes missing. All relevant staff should be familiar with this policy. Hospital managers should agree their policy with other agencies—such as the police and ambulance services—as necessary.

22.11 Policies in relation to detained and SCT patients should include guidance about:

- the immediate action to be taken by any member of staff who becomes aware that a patient has gone missing, including a requirement that they immediately inform the professional in charge of the patient's ward (where applicable), who should in turn ensure that the patient's responsible clinician is informed;

- the circumstances in which a search of a hospital and its grounds should be made;

- the circumstances in which other local agencies with an interest, including the LSSA, should be notified;

- the circumstances in which the police should be informed, who is responsible for informing the police and the information they should be given (this should be in line with local arrangements agreed with the police);

- how and when other people, including the patient's nearest relative, should be informed (this should include guidance on informing people if there is good reason to think that they might be at risk as a result of the patient's absence);

- when and how an application should be made for a warrant under section 135(2) of the Act to allow the police to enter premises in order to remove a patient who is missing; and

- how and by whom patients are to be returned to the place where they ought to be, and who is responsible for organising any necessary transport (see **chapter 11**).

22.12 LSSAs should have equivalent policies for the action to be taken when they (or a private guardian) become aware that a guardianship patient is AWOL from the place where they are required to live.

22.13 The police should be asked to assist in returning a patient to hospital only if necessary. If the patient's location is known, the role of the police should, wherever possible, be only to assist a suitably qualified and experienced mental health professional in returning the patient to hospital.

22.14 The police should always be informed immediately if a patient is missing who is:

- considered to be particularly vulnerable;

- considered to be dangerous; or

- subject to restrictions under Part 3 of the Act.

There may also be other cases where, although the help of the police is not needed, a patient's history makes it desirable to inform the police that they are AWOL in the area.

22.15 Whenever the police are asked for help in returning a patient, they must be informed of the time limit for taking them into custody.

22.16 Where the police have been informed about a missing patient, they should be told immediately if the patient is found or returns.

22.17 Although every case must be considered on its merits, patient confidentiality will not usually be a barrier to providing basic information about a patient's absence to people—such as those the patient normally lives with or is likely to contact—who may be able to help with finding the patient.

22.18 Where a patient is missing for more than a few hours, their nearest relative should normally be informed (if they have not been already), subject to the normal considerations about involving nearest relatives (see **paragraphs 2.32–2.33**).

22.19 It is good practice when a detained or SCT patient returns after a substantial period of absence without leave always to re-examine the patient to establish whether they still meet the criteria for detention or SCT. Where patients (other than restricted patients) have been AWOL for more than 28 days, section 21B of the Act requires such an examination to take place within a week of the patient's return (or else the patient's detention or SCT will end automatically).

22.20 Incidents in which patients go AWOL or abscond should be reviewed and analysed so that lessons for the future can be learned, including lessons about ways of identifying patients most at risk of going missing.

22.21 All instances of absence without leave should be recorded in the individual patient's notes. Where a patient has gone AWOL previously, it may be useful for the patient's care plan to include specific actions which experience suggests should be taken if that patient were to go missing again.

## 23. MEDICAL TREATMENT UNDER THE ACT

23.1 This chapter gives guidance on medical treatment for mental disorder **4–203** under the Act, especially treatment given without patients' consent. A summary of when treatment may be given under the Act is presented at the end of the chapter **(Reference Guide chapters 16 and 17)**.

**Definitions**

**4–204**   23.2 In the Act, "medical treatment" also includes nursing, psychological intervention and specialist mental health habilitation, rehabilitation and care **(Section 145(1))**.

23.3 The Act defines medical treatment for mental disorder as medical treatment which is for the purpose of alleviating or preventing a worsening of a mental disorder or one or more of its symptoms or manifestations **(Section 145(2))**.

23.4 This includes treatment of physical health problems only to the extent that such treatment is part of, or ancillary to, treatment for mental disorder (eg treating wounds self-inflicted as a result of mental disorder). Otherwise, the Act does not regulate medical treatment for physical health problems.

**Treatments to which special rules and procedures apply**

**4–205**   23.5 Sections 57, 58 and 58A of the Act set out types of medical treatment for mental disorder to which special rules and procedures apply, including, in many cases, the need for a certificate from a second opinion appointed doctor (SOAD) approving the treatment.

23.6 Guidance on sections 57, 58 and 58A is given in **chapter 24**, but in summary the treatments involved are as in the table below.

*Summary of treatments covered by sections 57, 58 and 58A*

| Section | Forms of treatment covered |
|---|---|
| Section 57 | Neurosurgery for mental disorder<br>Surgical implantation of hormones to reduce male sex drive |
| Section 58 | Medication (after an initial three-month period)—except medication administered as part of electro-convulsive therapy (ECT) |
| Section 58A | ECT and medication administered as part of ECT |

Note: it is possible that other forms of treatment may be added to any of these sections by regulations.

**Treatment of detained patients and supervised community treatment patients recalled to hospital ( Part 4 of the Act) (Sections 56–64; Reference Guide chapter 16)**

**4–206**   23.7 Part 4 of the Act deals mainly with the treatment of people who have been detained in hospital, including supervised community treatment (SCT) patients who have been recalled to hospital. They are referred to in this chapter as "detained patients".

23.8 Some patients detained in hospital are not covered by these rules, as set out in the table opposite. When this chapter talks about detained patients, these patients are not included. There are no special rules about treatment for these patients—they are in the same position as patients who are not subject to the Act at all, and they have exactly the same rights to consent to and refuse treatment.

*Meaning of detained patients in this chapter*

| In this chapter "detained patients" means | Exceptions | 4–207 |
|---|---|---|
| Patients who are liable to be detained in hospital under any section of the Act (including those on leave of absence or absent without leave) | Patients detained on the basis of an emergency application under section 4 unless or until the second medical recommendation is received | |
| | Patients held in hospital under the holding powers in section 5 | |
| | Patients remanded to hospital for a report on their mental condition under section 35 | |
| | Patients detained in hospital as a place of safety under section 135 or 136 | |
| | Patients temporarily detained in hospital as a place of safety under section 37 or 45A, pending admission to the hospital named in their hospital order or hospital direction | |
| | Restricted patients who have been conditionally discharged (unless or until they are recalled to hospital) | |
| SCT patients who have been recalled to hospital | — | |

23.9 Unless sections 57, 58 or 58A apply, section 63 of the Act means that detained patients may be given medical treatment for any kind for mental disorder, if they:

- consent to it; or

- have not consented to it, but the treatment is given by or under the direction of the approved clinician in charge of the treatment in question.

23.10 If sections 57, 58 or 58A apply, detained patients may be given the treatment only if the rules in those sections are followed (see **chapter 24**).

### Treatment of SCT patients not recalled to hospital (Part 4A of the Act) (Sections 64A–64K; Reference Guide chapter 17)

23.11 Part 4A of the Act sets out different rules for treatment of SCT patients **4–208** who have not been recalled to hospital by their responsible clinician. This includes SCT patients who are in hospital without having been recalled (eg if they have been admitted to hospital voluntarily).

23.12 For convenience, this chapter refers to SCT patients who have not been recalled to hospital as "Part 4A patients".

23.13 The rules for Part 4A patients differ depending on whether or not they have the capacity to consent to the treatment in question. For patients aged under 16, capacity means the competence to consent (see **paragraph 23.30** and **chapter 36**).

23.14 Part 4A patients who have the capacity to consent to a treatment may not be given that treatment unless they consent. There are no exceptions to this rule, even in emergencies. The effect is that treatment can be given without their consent only if they are recalled to hospital.

23.15 Part 4A patients who lack the capacity to consent to a treatment may be given it if their attorney or deputy, or the Court of Protection, consents to the treatment on their behalf.

23.16 Part 4A patients who lack capacity to consent to treatment may also be given it, without anyone's consent, by or under the direction of the approved clinician in charge of the treatment, unless:

- (in the case of a patient aged 18 or over) the treatment would be contrary to a valid and applicable advance decision made by the patient (see **chapter 17**);

- (in the case of a patient aged 16 or over) the treatment would be against the decision of someone with the authority under the Mental Capacity Act 2005 (MCA) to refuse it on the patient's behalf (an attorney, a deputy or the Court of Protection); or

- (in the case of a patient of any age) force needs to be used in order to administer the treatment and the patient objects to the treatment.

23.17 In this last case, force means the actual use of physical force on the patient. Where force needs to be used, it is up to the person proposing to give the treatment to decide whether a patient objects to the treatment. The question is simply whether the patient objects—the reasonableness (or unreasonableness) of the objection is irrelevant.

23.18 In deciding whether patients object to treatment, all the relevant evidence should be taken into account, so far as it reasonably can be. In many cases, patients will be perfectly able to state their objection, either verbally or by their dissenting behaviour. But in other cases, especially where patients are unable to communicate (or only able to communicate to a limited extent), clinicians will need to consider the patient's behaviour, wishes, feelings, views, beliefs and values, both present and past, so far as they can be ascertained **(Section 64J)**.

23.19 If there is reason to think that a patient would object, if able to do so, then the patient should be taken to be objecting. Occasionally, it may be that the patient's behaviour initially suggests an objection to being treated, but is in fact not directed at the treatment at all. In that case the patient would not be taken to be objecting.

23.20 Whether or not Part 4A patients consent to treatment, there are certain treatments they can only be given if they have been approved by a SOAD on a "Part 4A certificate". The Mental Health Act refers to this as the "certificate requirement", which is above and beyond the requirements described in **paragraphs 23.14–23.19** (the Act calls these the "authority" to give treatment). Broadly speaking, the certificate requirement applies to any treatment for which a certificate would be necessary under section 58 or 58A of the Act were the patient detained instead (see **chapter 24**).

*Emergency treatment under section 64G*

23.21 In an emergency, treatment can also be given to Part 4A patients who lack **4–209** capacity (and who have not been recalled to hospital) by anyone, whether or not they are acting under the direction of an approved clinician.

23.22 It is an emergency only if the treatment is immediately necessary to:

- save the patient's life;

- prevent a serious deterioration of the patient's condition, and the treatment does not have unfavourable physical or psychological consequences which cannot be reversed;

- alleviate serious suffering by the patient and the treatment does not have unfavourable physical or psychological consequences which cannot be reversed and does not entail significant physical hazard; or

- prevent the patient behaving violently or being a danger to themselves or others, and the treatment represents the minimum interference necessary for that purpose, does not have unfavourable physical or psychological consequences which cannot be reversed and does not entail significant physical hazard.

If the treatment is ECT (or medication administered as part of ECT), only the first two categories above apply.

23.23 Where treatment is immediately necessary in these terms, it can be given even though it conflicts with an advance decision or the decision of someone who has the authority under the MCA to refuse it on the patient's behalf.

23.24 In addition, force may be used (whether or not the patient objects), provided that:

- the treatment is necessary to prevent harm to the patient; and

- the force used is proportionate to the likelihood of the patient suffering harm and to the seriousness of that harm.

23.25 These are the only circumstances in which force may be used to treat SCT patients who object, without recalling them to hospital. This exception is for situations where the patient's interests would be better served by being given urgently needed treatment by force outside hospital rather than being recalled to hospital. This might, for example, be where the situation is so urgent that recall is not realistic, or where taking the patient to hospital would exacerbate their condition, damage their recovery or cause them unnecessary anxiety or suffering. Situations like this should be exceptional.

**Treatment of other patients**

23.26 The Act does not regulate treatment of any other patients, except that: **4–210**

- the special rules and procedures in section 57 apply to all patients (**Section 56(1)**); and

- the special rules and procedures in section 58A apply to all patients under the age of 18 (**Section 56(5)**).

(See **chapter 24**.)

**Capacity and consent**

**4–211**    23.27 The Act frequently requires healthcare professionals to determine:

- whether a patient has the capacity to consent to or refuse a particular form of medical treatment; and

- if so, whether the patient does in fact consent.

The rules for answering these questions are the same as for any other patients.

*Capacity to consent: people aged 16 or over*

**4–212**    23.28 For people aged 16 or over, capacity to consent is defined by the MCA (see box opposite). The principles of the MCA state (among other things) that:

- people must be assumed to have capacity unless it is established that they lack capacity;

- people are not be to be treated as unable to make a decision unless all practicable steps to help them do so have been taken without success; and

- people are not be to be treated as unable to make a decision merely because they make an unwise decision.

---

**4–213** | **What does the Mental Capacity Act 2005 mean by "lack of capacity"?**

Section 2(1) of the MCA states:
For the purposes of this Act, a person lacks capacity in relation to a matter if at the material time he is unable to make a decision for himself in relation to the matter because of an impairment of, or a disturbance in the functioning of, the mind or brain.

This means that a person lacks capacity if:

- they have an impairment or disturbance (eg a disability, condition or trauma) that affects the way their mind or brain works; and

- the impairment or disturbance means that they are unable to make a specific decision at the time it needs to be made.

Section 2(2) states that the impairment or disturbance does not have to be permanent. A person can lack capacity to make a decision at the time it needs to be made even if:

- the loss of capacity is partial;

- the loss of capacity is temporary; or

- their capacity changes over time.

A person may also lack capacity to make a decision about one issue but not about others.

---

Section 3(1) says that a person is unable to make a decision if they cannot:

- understand information about the decision to be made (the Act calls this "relevant information");
- retain that information in their mind;
- use or weigh that information as part of the decisionmaking process; or
- communicate their decision (by talking, using sign language or any other means).

The first three should be applied together. If a person cannot do any of these three things, they will be treated as unable to make the decision. The fourth only applies in situations where people cannot communicate their decision in any way.

For further information see the Code of Practice to the MCA.

23.29 When taking decisions about patients under the Mental Health Act, it should be remembered that:

- mental disorder does not necessarily mean that a patient lacks capacity to give or refuse consent, or to take any other decision;
- any assessment of an individual's capacity has to be made in relation to the particular decision being made a person may, for example, have the capacity to consent to one form of treatment but not to another;
- capacity in an individual with a mental disorder can vary over time and should be assessed at the time the decision in question needs to be taken;
- where a patient's capacity fluctuates in this way, consideration should be given, if a decision is not urgently required, to delaying the decision until the patient has capacity again to make it for themselves;
- not everyone is equally capable of understanding the same explanation— explanations should be appropriate to the level of the patient's assessed ability; and
- all assessments of a patient's capacity should be fully recorded in their notes.

### Competence to consent: children under 16
23.30 The MCA does not apply to medical treatment for children under 16. **4–214** Children who have sufficient understanding and intelligence to enable them fully to understand what is involved in a proposed treatment are considered to be competent (or "Gillick competent") to consent to it. The common law deals with cases where children are not capable of consenting. See **chapter 36**.

*Consent*

23.31 Consent is the voluntary and continuing permission of a patient to be **4–215** given a particular treatment, based on a sufficient knowledge of the purpose, nature, likely effects and risks of that treatment, including the likelihood of its success and any alternatives to it. Permission given under any unfair or undue pressure is not consent.

23.32 By definition, a person who lacks capacity to consent does not consent to treatment, even if they co-operate with the treatment or actively seek it.

23.33 It is the duty of everyone seeking consent to use reasonable care and skill, not only in giving information prior to seeking consent, but also in meeting the continuing obligation to provide the patient with sufficient information about the proposed treatment and alternatives to it.

23.34 The information which must be given should be related to the particular patient, the particular treatment and relevant clinical knowledge and practice. In every case, sufficient information must be given to the patient to ensure that they understand in broad terms the nature, likely effects and all significant possible adverse outcomes of that treatment, including the likelihood of its success and any alternatives to it. A record should be kept of information provided to patients.

23.35 Patients should be invited to ask questions and professionals should answer fully, frankly and truthfully. There may sometimes be a compelling reason, in the patient's interests, for not disclosing certain information. A professional who chooses not to disclose information must be prepared to justify the decision. A professional who chooses not to answer a patient's question should make this clear to the patient so that the patient knows where they stand.

23.36 Patients should be told that their consent to treatment can be withdrawn at any time. Where patients withdraw their consent (or are considering withdrawing it), they should be given a clear explanation of the likely consequences of not receiving the treatment and (where relevant) the circumstances in which the treatment may be given without their consent under the Mental Health Act. A record should be kept of the information provided to patients.

### Treatment without consent—general points

**4–216**   23.37 Although the Mental Health Act permits some medical treatment for mental disorder to be given without consent, the patient's consent should still be sought before treatment is given, wherever practicable. The patient's consent or refusal should be recorded in their notes, as should the treating clinician's assessment of the patient's capacity to consent.

23.38 If a patient initially consents, but then withdraws that consent (or loses the capacity to consent), the treatment should be reviewed. The clinician in charge of the treatment must consider whether to proceed in the absence of consent, to provide alternative treatment instead or to give no further treatment.

23.39 Clinicians authorising or administering treatment without consent under the Mental Health Act are performing a function of a public nature and are therefore subject to the provisions of the Human Rights Act 1998. It is unlawful for them to act in a way which is incompatible with a patient's rights as set out in the European Convention on Human Rights ("the Convention").

23.40 In particular, the following should be noted:

- compulsory administration of treatment which would otherwise require consent is invariably an infringement of Article 8 of the Convention (respect for family and private life). However, it may be justified where it is in accordance with law (in this case the procedures in the Mental Health Act) and where it is proportionate to a legitimate aim (in this case, the reduction of the risk posed by a person's mental disorder and the improvement of their health);

- compulsory treatment is capable of being inhuman treatment (or in extreme cases even torture) contrary to Article 3 of the Convention, if its effect on the person concerned reaches a sufficient level of severity. But the European Court of Human Rights has said that a measure which is convincingly shown to be of therapeutic necessity from the point of view of established principles of medicine cannot in principle be regarded as inhuman and degrading.

23.41 Scrupulous adherence to the requirements of the legislation and good clinical practice should ensure that there is no such incompatibility. But if clinicians have concerns about a potential breach of a person's human rights they should seek senior clinical and, if necessary, legal advice.

**Treatment plans**

23.42 Treatment plans are essential for patients being treated for mental dis- **4–217** order under the Mental Health Act. A patient's responsible clinician is responsible for ensuring that a treatment plan is in place for that patient.

23.43 A treatment plan should include a description of the immediate and long-term goals for the patient and should give a clear indication of the treatments proposed and the methods of treatment.

23.44 The treatment plan should form part of a coherent care plan under the Care Programme Approach (or its equivalent), and be recorded in the patient's notes.

23.45 Psychological therapies form an important part of modern mental health-care and are part of a holistic approach to an individual's care, which looks at the individual in the round.

23.46 Psychological therapies should be considered as a routine treatment option at all stages, including the initial formulation of a treatment plan and each subsequent review of that plan. Any programme of psychological intervention should form part of the agreed treatment plan and be recorded in the patient's notes as such. At no time should it be used as an isolated and spontaneous reaction to particular behaviour.

23.47 Wherever possible, the whole treatment plan should be discussed with the patient. Patients should be encouraged and assisted to make use of advocacy support available to them, if they want it. This includes, but need not be restricted to, independent mental health advocacy services under the Act. Where patients cannot (or do not wish to) participate in discussion about their treatment plan, any views they have expressed previously should be taken into consideration (see **chapter 17**).

23.48 Subject to the normal considerations of patient confidentiality, the treatment plan should also be discussed with their carers, with a view to enabling them to contribute to it and express agreement or disagreement.

23.49 Discussion with carers is particularly important where carers will themselves be providing care to the patient while the plan is in force. However, carers still have an important role to play even if the patient is to be detained in hospital. Plans should not be based on any assumptions about the willingness or ability of carers to support patients, unless those assumptions have been discussed and agreed with the carers in question.

23.50 For patients aged under 16 (and in some cases those aged 16 or 17), the plan should similarly be discussed with the people who have parental responsibility for them. Again, this is subject to the normal considerations of patient confidentiality for children and young people.

23.51 Treatment plans should be regularly reviewed and the results of reviews recorded in the patient's notes.

**Interface between Parts 4 and 4A of the Mental Health Act and section 28 of the Mental Capacity Act 2005**

**4–218**    23.52 Insofar as it deals with decisions about medical treatment for people aged 16 or over who lack capacity to consent to such treatment, the MCA applies to patients subject to the Mental Health Act in the same way as to anyone else, with exceptions set out in the following table. These exceptions apply only to medical treatment for mental disorder.

*Medical treatment of patients subject to the Mental Health Act—exceptions to the normal rules on treatment and consent in the Mental Capacity Act 2005*

**4–219**

| Situation | Exceptions to the normal rules in the MCA |
|---|---|
| Section 57 treatment (neurosurgery for mental disorder etc) | The MCA may not be used to give anyone treatment to which section 57 applies (see **chapter 24** for guidance on section 57). |
| Section 58A treatment (ECT and related medication) | The MCA may not be used to give detained patients (as defined in **paragraphs 23.7–23.8**) ECT or any other treatment to which section 58A applies. |
| Treatment for detained patients | The MCA may not be used to give detained patients (as defined in this chapter) any other medical treatment for mental disorder. Treatment must be given in accordance with Part 4 of the Mental Health Act instead (see **paragraphs 23.7–23.10**). |
| Treatment for SCT patients who have not been recalled to hospital (Part 4A patients) | The MCA may not generally be used to give these SCT patients any medical treatment for mental disorder, but attorneys, deputies and the Court of Protection may consent to such treatment on behalf of these SCT patients. |
| Advance decisions to refuse treatment (as defined in the MCA) | Where the Mental Health Act allows treatment to be given against the wishes of a patient who has capacity to consent, it also allows treatment to be given despite the existence of a valid and applicable advance decision made under the MCA (see **chapter 17**). |

| Situation | Exceptions to the normal rules in the MCA |
|---|---|
| | But note that, except in emergencies:<br><br>• treatment to which section 58A applies cannot be given contrary to a valid and applicable advance decision; and<br><br>• treatment cannot be given to SCT patients who have not been recalled to hospital (Part 4A patients) contrary to a valid and applicable advance decision. |
| Patients who have attorneys or court-appointed deputies under the MCA with authority to take decisions on their behalf about their medical treatment | Attorneys and deputies (acting within the scope of their authority under the MCA) may not:<br><br>• consent to treatment to which section 57 applies on behalf of any patient;<br><br>• consent to treatment to which section 58A applies— but note that (except in emergencies) they may refuse it on a patient's behalf; or<br><br>• consent to or refuse any other treatment on behalf of detained patients (as defined in **paragraphs 23.7– 23.8**).<br><br>But note that attorneys and deputies may:<br><br>• consent to treatment on behalf of SCT patients who have not been recalled to hospital (Part 4A patients), even if treatment is to be given forcibly; and<br><br>• except in emergencies, also refuse treatment on behalf of those patients. |

23.53 See **chapter 4** for guidance on the interface between detention under the Mental Health Act and the deprivation of liberty safeguards under the MCA. See **chapter 26** for the interface between the powers of guardians under the Mental Health Act and the MCA.

**The Court of Protection and other courts**
23.54 Although the Mental Health Act refers only to decisions of the Court of **4–220** Protection, other courts may, in certain circumstances, have the power to order that treatment must not be given. Should such an order be made, legal advice should be sought on the legal authority for continuing or starting any such treatment.

*Summary of when medical treatment for mental disorder may be given under the Mental Health Act*

**4–221**

| Type of patient (and relevant part of the Act) | When treatment can be given | Notes (for further detail see chapter 24) |
|---|---|---|
| Detained patient—see definition in **paragraphs 23.7–23.8** | If sections 57, 58 or 58A apply, treatment may be given only in accordance with those sections.<br><br>Otherwise, treatment may be given:<br><br>• with the patient's consent; or<br>• without the patient's consent under section 63, if the treatment is by or under the direction of the approved clinician in charge. | Neurosurgery for mental disorder and other treatments to which section 57 applies cannot be given without the patient's consent and must always be approved by a SOAD.<br><br>ECT and other treatments to which section 58A applies cannot be given to a patient who has capacity to consent but refuses to do so. They can be given to patients who lack capacity (or who are under 18) only if approved by a SOAD.<br><br>Medication to which section 58 applies can be given without the patient's consent, but only with the approval of a SOAD.<br><br>Sections 57, 58 and 58A do not apply in emergencies, where treatment is defined in section 62 as immediately necessary. |
| SCT patient who has not been recalled to hospital (Part 4A patient) | If section 57 applies, treatment can be given only with the patient's consent and if the other rules in section 57 are followed.<br><br>Otherwise, if the patient has capacity to consent, treatment may be given only with the patient's consent.<br><br>Or, if the patient lacks capacity to consent, treatment may be given: | Unless it is an emergency, if the treatment is one to which section 58 or 58A applies, it normally has to be approved by a SOAD on a Part 4A certificate as well. |

| Type of patient (and relevant part of the Act) | When treatment can be given | Notes (for further detail see chapter 24) |
| --- | --- | --- |
| | • with the consent of an attorney, deputy or the Court of Protection;<br><br>• without anyone's consent, provided that (i) the treatment is given by or under the direction of the approved clinician in charge; (ii) it is not inconsistent with a valid and applicable advance decision, or a decision of an attorney, deputy or the Court of Protection; and either (iii) no force needs to be used, or (iv) force does need to be used but the patient does not object;<br><br>• in an emergency only, if (i) the treatment is immediately necessary; and (ii) if force is to be used, the treatment is needed to protect the patient from harm and any force used is proportionate to the risk of harm. | |
| Other patients | Treatment is not regulated by the Act, except that:<br><br>• where section 57 applies, patients can be given treatment only if they consent and the other rules in section 57 are followed; and<br><br>• patients under 18 cannot be given ECT or other treatments to which section 58A applies, unless it is approved by a SOAD. (Sections 57 and 58A do not apply in emergencies.) | |

---

**Related material**

- Mental Capacity Act 2005
- *Mental Capacity Act 2005 Code of Practice,* TSO, 2007

This material does not form part of the Code. It is provided for assistance only.

---

## 24. TREATMENTS SUBJECT TO SPECIAL RULES AND PROCEDURES

**4–222**     24.1 This chapter gives guidance on the special rules and procedures in the Act for certain types of medical treatment for mental disorder **(Reference Guide chapters 16 and 17)**.

**Definitions**

**4–223**     24.2 In this chapter:

- "detained patients" means the same as in the previous chapter (see **paragraphs 23.7–23.8**);
- "SOAD" means a second opinion doctor appointed by the Commission to approve certain forms of treatment;
- "SOAD certificate" means a certificate issued by a SOAD approving treatment for a particular patient;
- "Part 4A patient" means a supervised community treatment (SCT) patient who has not been recalled to hospital; and
- "Part 4A certificate" means a SOAD certificate issued under Part 4A of the Act in respect of the treatment of an SCT patient.

**Clinician in charge of treatment**

**4–224**     24.3 This chapter frequently refers to the "clinician in charge of treatment". This means the clinician in charge of the particular treatment in question for a patient, who need not be the same as the responsible clinician in charge of a patient's case overall.

24.4 In many cases, for detained and SCT patients the clinician in charge of treatment must be an approved clinician, as set out in the following table.

*Summary of when the clinician in charge of treatment under the Act must be an approved clinician*

**4–225**

| Type of patient | When the clinician in charge of treatment must be an approved clinician |
|---|---|
| Detained patient | When the treatment is being:<br>• given without the patient's consent;<br>• given with the patient's consent, on the basis of a certificate issued under section 58 or 58A by an approved clinician (rather than a SOAD)—see **paragraphs 24.13 and 24.20;** or |

| Type of patient | When the clinician in charge of treatment must be an approved clinician |
|---|---|
|  | • continued with the consent of an SCT patient who has been recalled to hospital (including one whose community treatment order has then been revoked) to avoid serious suffering to the patient, pending compliance with section 58—see **paragraph 24.28.** |
| Part 4A patient | When the treatment is being given to a patient who lacks capacity to consent to it and without the consent of an attorney, deputy or the Court of Protection (unless it is immediately necessary and being given under section 64G—see **paragraphs 23.21–23.22**). |

24.5 Hospital managers should keep a record of approved clinicians who are available to treat patients for whom they are responsible and should ensure that approved clinicians are in charge of treatment where the Act requires it.

**Treatments requiring consent and a second opinion under section 57**
24.6 Section 57 applies to neurosurgery for mental disorder and to surgical **4–226** implantation of hormones to reduce male sex drive. It applies to all patients, whether or not they are otherwise subject to the Act.

24.7 Where section 57 applies, these treatments can be given only if all three of the following requirements are met:

- the patient consents to the treatment;

- a SOAD (and two other people by the Commission) certify that the patient has the capacity to consent[18] and has done so; and

- the SOAD also certifies that it is appropriate for the treatment to be given to the patient.

24.8 A decision to administer treatments to which section 57 applies requires particularly careful consideration, given their significance and sensitivity. Hospitals proposing to offer such treatments are strongly encouraged to agree with the Commission the procedures which will be followed to implement the requirements of section 57.

24.9 Before asking the Commission to put in hand the process of issuing a certificate, referring professionals should personally satisfy themselves that the patient is capable of giving valid consent and is willing to consent. The restrictions and procedures imposed by section 57 should be explained to the patient, and it should be made clear to the patient that their willingness to receive treatment does not necessarily mean that the treatment will be given.

---

[18] In fact, here and in ss.58 and 58A, the Act refers to the patient being "capable of understanding the nature, purpose and likely effects" of the treatment. However, for all practical purposes this can be understood to mean the same as the test of whether the patient has the capacity to consent (or, if under 16, the competence to do so).

**Treatments requiring consent or a second opinion under section 58**

**4–227**    24.10 Section 58 applies to the administration of medication for mental disorder. But it only applies once three months have passed from the day on which any form of medication for mental disorder was first administered to the patient during the patient's current period of detention under the Act ("the three-month period").

24.11 For these purposes, the patient's current period of detention continues even if the section under which the patient is detained changes. It also includes any time the patient has spent on SCT.

24.12 Section 58 does not apply to medication administered as part of electro-convulsive therapy (ECT). That is covered by section 58A instead (see **paragraphs 24.18–24.24**).

24.13 Section 58 applies only to detained patients. They cannot be given medication to which section 58 applies unless:

- the approved clinician in charge of the treatment, or a SOAD, certifies that the patient has the capacity to consent and has done so; or

- a SOAD certifies that the treatment is appropriate and either that:

  — the patient does not have the capacity to consent; or

  — the patient has the capacity to consent but has refused to do so.

24.14 Hospital managers should ensure that systems are in place to remind both the clinician in charge of the medication and the patient at least four weeks before the expiry of the three-month period.

24.15 Warning systems must be capable of dealing with the possibility that a patient may become an SCT patient, and may also have their community treatment order revoked, during the three-month period. A patient's move between detention and SCT does not change the date on which the three-month period expires.

24.16 Where approved clinicians certify the treatment of a patient who consents, they should not rely on the certificate as the only record of their reasons for believing that the patient has consented to the treatment. A record of their discussion with the patient, and of the steps taken to confirm that the patient has the capacity to consent, should be made in the patient's notes as normal.

24.17 Certificates under this section must clearly set out the specific forms of treatment to which they apply. All the relevant drugs should be listed, including medication to be given "as required" (prn), either by name or by the classes described in the British National Formulary (BNF). If drugs are specified by class, the certificate should state clearly the number of drugs authorised in each class, and whether any drugs within the class are excluded. The maximum dosage and route of administration should be clearly indicated for each drug or category of drugs proposed. This can exceed the dosages listed in the BNF, but particular care is required in these cases.

**Electro-convulsive therapy under section 58A**

**4–228**    24.18 Section 58A applies to ECT and to medication administered as part of ECT. It applies to detained patients and to all patients aged under 18 (whether or not they are detained).

24.19 The key differences from section 58 are that:

- patients who have the capacity to consent may not be given treatment under section 58A unless they do in fact consent;

- no patient aged under 18 can be given treatment under section 58A unless a SOAD has certified that the treatment is appropriate; and

- there is no initial three-month period during which a certificate is not needed (even for the medication administered as part of the ECT).

24.20 A patient who has capacity to consent may not be given treatment under section 58A unless the clinician in charge, or a SOAD, has certified that the patient has the capacity to consent and has done so. If the patient is under 18, only a SOAD may give the certificate, and the SOAD must also certify that the treatment is appropriate.

24.21 A patient who lacks the capacity to consent may not be given treatment under section 58A unless a SOAD certifies that the patient lacks capacity to consent and that:

- the treatment is appropriate;

- no valid and applicable advance decision has been made by the patient under the Mental Capacity Act 2005 (MCA) refusing the treatment;

- no suitably authorised attorney or deputy objects to the treatment on the patient's behalf; and

- the treatment would not conflict with a decision of the Court of Protection which prevents the treatment being given.

24.22 In all cases, SOADs should indicate on the certificate the maximum number of administrations of ECT which it approves.

24.23 For children and young people under 18, a SOAD certificate by itself is not sufficient to authorise the treatment, unless they are detained. Clinicians must also have the patient's own consent or some other legal authority, just as they would if section 58A did not exist (see **chapter 36**).

24.24 Whether or not section 58A applies, patients of all ages to be treated with ECT should be given written information before their treatment starts which helps them to understand and remember, both during and after the course of ECT, the advice given about its nature, purpose and likely effects.

**Part 4A certificates**

24.25 Part 4A patients may be given certain treatments for mental disorder only **4–229** if a SOAD has certified that the treatment is appropriate, using a Part 4A certificate. The requirement to have a certificate is in addition to the other rules governing treatment of SCT patients, described in **chapter 23 (Sections 64B, 64C, 64E and 64H)**.

24.26 A Part 4A certificate is needed for:

- treatments which would require a certificate under section 58 if the patient were detained—ie medication after an initial three-month period ("section 58 type treatment"); and

- ECT and any other types of treatment to which section 58A applies ("section 58A type treatment").

However, a certificate is not required for section 58 type treatment during the first month following a patient's discharge from detention onto SCT (even if the threemonth period in section 58 has already expired or expires during that first month).

24.27 When giving Part 4A certificates, SOADs do not have to certify whether a patient has, or lacks, capacity to consent to the treatments in question, nor whether a patient with capacity is consenting or refusing. But they may make it a condition of their approval that particular treatments are given only in certain circumstances. For example, they might specify that a particular treatment is to be given only with the patient's consent. Similarly, they might specify that a medication may be given up to a certain dosage if the patient lacks capacity to consent, but that a higher dosage may be given with the patient's consent.

**SCT patients recalled to hospital—exceptions to the need for certificates under section 58 or 58A (Section 62A; Reference Guide 17.33–17.44)**

**4–230**    24.28 In general, SCT patients recalled to hospital are subject to sections 58 and 58A in the same way as other detained patients. But there are three exceptions, as follows:

- a certificate under section 58 is not needed for medication if less than one month has passed since the patient was discharged from hospital and became an SCT patient;

- a certificate is not needed under either section 58 or 58A if the treatment in question is already explicitly authorised for administration on recall on the patient's Part 4A certificate; and

- treatment that was already being given on the basis of a Part 4A certificate may be continued, even though it is not authorised for administration on recall, if the approved clinician in charge of the treatment considers that discontinuing it would cause the patient serious suffering. But it may only be continued pending compliance with section 58 or 58A (as applicable)—in other words while steps are taken to obtain a new certificate.

24.29 As a result, SOADs giving Part 4A certificates need to consider what (if any) treatments to approve should the patient be recalled to hospital. They must also decide whether to impose any conditions on that approval. Unless they specify otherwise, the certificate will authorise the treatment even if the patient has capacity to refuse it (unless it is a section 58A type treatment).

24.30 The potential advantage of authorising treatments to be given on recall to hospital is that it will enable such treatments to be given quickly without the need to obtain a new certificate. However, SOADs should do so only where they believe they have sufficient information on which properly to make such a judgement.

24.31 The exceptions to the requirement to have a certificate under section 58 or 58A set out in **paragraph 24.28** continue to apply if the patient's community treatment order (CTO) is revoked, but only while steps are taken to comply with section 58 (where relevant). Responsible clinicians should ensure that steps are put in hand to obtain a new SOAD certificate under section 58 or 58A, if one is needed, as soon as they revoke a CTO.

**Urgent cases where certificates are not required (sections 62, 64B, 64C and 64E)**

24.32 Sections 57, 58 and 58A do not apply in urgent cases where treatment is **4–231** immediately necessary (section 62). Similarly, a Part 4A certificate is not required in urgent cases where the treatment is immediately necessary (sections 64B, 64C and 64E).

24.33 This applies only if the treatment in question is immediately necessary to:

- save the patient's life;
- prevent a serious deterioration of the patient's condition, and the treatment does not have unfavourable physical or psychological consequences which cannot be reversed;
- alleviate serious suffering by the patient, and the treatment does not have unfavourable physical or psychological consequences which cannot be reversed and does not entail significant physical hazard; or
- prevent patients behaving violently or being a danger to themselves or others, and the treatment represents the minimum interference necessary for that purpose, does not have unfavourable physical or psychological consequences which cannot be reversed and does not entail significant physical hazard.

If the treatment is ECT (or medication administered as part of ECT) only the first two categories above apply.

24.34 These are strict tests. It is not enough for there to be an urgent need for treatment or for the clinicians involved to believe the treatment is necessary or beneficial.

24.35 Urgent treatment under these sections can continue only for as long as it remains immediately necessary. If it is no longer immediately necessary, the normal requirements for certificates apply.

24.36 Although certificates are not required where treatment is immediately necessary, the other requirements of Parts 4 and 4A of the Act still apply. The treatment is not necessarily allowed just because no certificate is required.

24.37 Hospital managers should monitor the use of these exceptions to the certificate requirements to ensure that they are not used inappropriately or excessively. They are advised to provide a form (or other method) by which the clinician in charge of the treatment in question can record details of:

- the proposed treatment;
- why it is immediately necessary to give the treatment; and
- the length of time for which the treatment is given.

### Requesting a SOAD visit

**4–232**   24.38 If a SOAD certificate is required, the clinician in charge of the treatment in question has the personal responsibility of ensuring that a request is made to the Commission for a SOAD to visit.

24.39 Clinicians should not normally request a visit from a SOAD in order to obtain a certificate which they could issue themselves confirming that a patient has consented to treatment. They should request a visit for that purpose only if they are genuinely unable to determine for themselves whether the patient has the capacity to consent or whether the patient is in fact consenting.

### Arranging and preparing for SOAD visits

**4–233**   24.40 SOADs will visit detained patients in hospital. For SCT patients, hospital managers should ensure that arrangements are made for the SOAD to see the patient at a mutually agreed place, eg at an out-patient clinic or somewhere that the patient might visit regularly.

24.41 Attending hospital for examination by a SOAD is a condition of all CTOs. If SCT patients fail to attend when asked to do so, they may be recalled to hospital for the examination, if necessary. But that should only ever be a last resort. (See **paragraph 25.49**.)

24.42 The treatment proposal for the patient, together with notes of any relevant multi-disciplinary discussion on which it was based, must be given to the SOAD before or at the time of the visit. If a Part 4A certificate is being requested, the proposal should clearly indicate which (if any) treatments it is proposed should be authorised in the case of the patient's recall to hospital.

24.43 During a visit, SOADs should:

- satisfy themselves that the patient's detention or SCT papers are in order (where applicable); and

- interview the patient in private if possible. Others may attend if the patient and the SOAD wish, or if it is thought that the SOAD would be at significant risk of physical harm from the patient (and the SOAD agrees).

24.44 Hospital managers are responsible for ensuring that people whom the SOAD wishes to meet (including the clinician in charge of the treatment) are available in person at the time the SOAD visits.

24.45 The managers are also responsible for ensuring that all relevant documentation, including the patient's full clinical notes, are available for the SOAD's inspection.

24.46 SOADs have a right to access records without the patient's consent, if necessary, but only those records relating to the treatment of the patient in the hospital or other establishment in which they are examining the patient. If an SCT patient with capacity to do so refuses the SOAD access to records which the SOAD thinks are relevant, the examination should be arranged in a hospital where the relevant records would be available.

24.47 Where the proposed treatment includes medication, the SOAD's attention should be drawn specifically to any recent review of the patient's medication. Clinicians should consider seeking a review by a specialist mental health pharmacist before seeking a SOAD certificate, particularly if the patient's medication regimen is complex or unusual.

24.48 Approved clinicians should ensure that SOADs are informed if the hospital knows that the patient has an attorney or deputy who is authorised under the MCA to make decisions about medical treatment on the patient's behalf. Details of any relevant advance decisions, or advance statements of views, wishes or feelings, should already be recorded in the patient's notes. But if they are not, they should be drawn to the SOAD's attention.

### Statutory consultees (Sections 57(3), 58(4), 58A(6) and 64H(3))

24.49 SOADs are required to consult two people ("statutory consultees") **4–234** before issuing certificates approving treatment. One of the statutory consultees must be a nurse; the other must not be either a nurse or a doctor. Both must have been professionally concerned with the patient's medical treatment, and neither may be the clinician in charge of the proposed treatment or the responsible clinician (if the patient has one).

24.50 The Act does not specify who the statutory consultees should be, but they should be people whose knowledge of the patient and the patient's treatment can help the SOAD decide whether the proposed treatment is appropriate. People who may be particularly well placed to act as statutory consultees include the patient's care co-ordinator (if they have one) and, where medication is concerned, a mental health pharmacist who has been involved in any recent review of the patient's medication.

24.51 The statutory consultees whom the SOAD proposes to consult should consider whether they are sufficiently concerned professionally with the patient's care to fulfil the function. If not, or if a consultee feels that someone else is better placed to fulfil the function, they should make this known to the clinician in charge of the treatment and to the SOAD in good time.

24.52 Statutory consultees may expect to have a private discussion with the SOAD and to be listened to with consideration. Among the issues that the consultees should consider commenting on are:

- the proposed treatment and the patient's ability to consent to it;

- their understanding of the past and present views and wishes of the patient;

- other treatment options and the way in which the decision on the treatment proposal was arrived at;

- the patient's progress and the views of the patient's carers; and

- where relevant, the implications of imposing treatment on a patient who does not want it and the reasons why the patient is refusing treatment.

24.53 If the SOAD wishes to speak to the statutory consultees face to face, the hospital managers should ensure that the SOAD is able to do so.

24.54 Consultees should ensure that they make a record of their consultation with the SOAD, which is then placed in the patient's notes.

24.55 SOADs should also be prepared, where appropriate, to consult a wider range of people who are concerned with the patient's care than those required by the Act. That might include the patient's GP and, unless the patient objects, the patient's nearest relative, parents (where relevant), other family and carers, and any independent mental health advocate[19] (or other advocate) representing the patient.

### The SOAD's decision and reasons

**4–235** 24.56 The SOAD's role is to provide an additional safeguard to protect the patient's rights, primarily by deciding whether certain treatments are appropriate and issuing certificates accordingly. Although appointed by the Commission, SOADs act as independent professionals and must reach their own judgement about whether the proposed treatment is appropriate.

24.57 When deciding whether it is appropriate for treatment to be given to a patient, SOADs are required to consider both the clinical appropriateness of the treatment to the patient's mental disorder and its appropriateness in the light of all the other circumstances of the patient's case.

24.58 SOADs should, in particular:

- consider the appropriateness of alternative forms of treatment, not just that proposed;

- balance the potential therapeutic efficacy of the proposed treatment against the side effects and any other potential disadvantages to the patient;

- seek to understand the patient's views on the proposed treatment, and the reasons for them;

- give due weight to the patient's views, including any objection to the proposed treatment and any preference for an alternative;

- take into account any previous experience of comparable treatment for a similar episode of disorder; and

- give due weight to the opinions, knowledge, experience and skills of those consulted.

24.59 SOADs must provide written reasons in support of their decisions to approve specific treatments for patients. SOADs do not have to give an exhaustive explanation, but should provide their reasons for what they consider to be the substantive points on which they made their clinical judgement. These reasons can be recorded on the certificate itself when it is given, or can be provided to the clinician in charge of the treatment separately as soon as possible afterwards.

24.60 A certificate may be acted on even though the SOAD's reasons have yet to be received. But if there is no pressing need for treatment to begin immediately, it is preferable to wait until the reasons are received, especially if the patient is likely to be unhappy with the decision.

24.61 When giving reasons, SOADs will need to indicate whether, in their view, disclosure of the reasons to the patient would be likely to cause serious harm to the patient's physical or mental health or to that of any other person.

24.62 It is the personal responsibility of the clinician in charge of the treatment to communicate the results of the SOAD visit to the patient. This need not wait until any separate statement of reasons has been received from the SOAD. But when a separate statement is received from the SOAD, the patient should be

---

[19] Independent mental health advocacy services under the Act are expected to be introduced in April 2009.

given the opportunity to see it as soon as possible, unless the clinician in charge of the treatment (or the SOAD) thinks that it would be likely to cause serious harm to the physical or mental health of the patient or any other person.

24.63 Documents provided by SOADs are a part of—and should be kept in— the patient's notes. The clinician in charge of the treatment should record their actions in providing patients with (or withholding) the reasons supplied by a SOAD.

24.64 Every attempt should be made by the clinician in charge of the treatment and the SOAD to reach agreement. A generally sound plan need not be rejected as a whole because of a minor disagreement about one aspect of it.

24.65 If SOADs are unable to agree with the clinician in charge of the treatment, they should inform the clinician personally as soon as possible. It is good practice for SOADs to give reasons for their disagreement.

24.66 Neither the SOAD nor the approved clinician should allow a disagreement in any way to prejudice the interests of the patient. If agreement cannot be reached, the position should be recorded in the patient's notes by the clinician in charge of the treatment in question, and the patient's responsible clinician (if different) should be informed.

24.67 The opinion given by the SOAD is the SOAD's personal responsibility. There can be no appeal to the Commission against the opinion.

**Status of certificates under Part 4 and Part 4A**

24.68 A certificate issued by an approved clinician or by a SOAD is not an **4–236** instruction to administer treatment.

24.69 The fact that the SOAD has authorised a particular treatment does not mean that it will always be appropriate to administer it on any given occasion, or even at all. People administering the treatment (or directing its administration) must still satisfy themselves that it is an appropriate treatment in the circumstances.

24.70 They also need to take reasonable steps to assure themselves that the treatment is, in fact, authorised by the certificate, given what is said in the certificate about the patient's capacity and willingness to consent (see **paragraph 24.79**).

24.71 Original signed certificates should be kept with the documents which authorise the patient's detention or SCT, and copies should be kept in the patient's notes. As a matter of good practice, a copy of the certificate relating to medication should also be kept with the patient's medicine chart (if there is one) to minimise the risk of the patient being given treatment in contravention of the provisions of the Act.

**Review of treatment and withdrawal of approval (sections 61 and 64H)**

24.72 Although the Act does not require the validity of certificates to be **4–237** reviewed after any particular period, it is good practice for the clinician in charge of the treatment to review them (in consultation with the responsible clinician, if different) at regular intervals.

24.73 The clinician in charge of any treatment given in accordance with a SOAD certificate must provide a written report on that treatment and the relevant patient's condition at any time if requested to do so by the Commission under section 61 or 64H of the Act. This is in addition to the reports they are automatically required to provide periodically under those sections.[20] Copies of reports should be given to patients.

24.74 Under sections 61 and 64H, the Commission may also, at any time, direct that a certificate is no longer to approve either some or all of the treatments specified in it from a particular date.

24.75 However, where the Commission revokes approval in that way, treatment (or a course of treatment) which is already in progress may continue, pending a new certificate, if the clinician in charge of it considers that discontinuing it would cause the patient serious suffering.

24.76 This exception only applies pending compliance with the relevant requirement to have a certificate—in other words, while steps are taken to obtain a new certificate. It cannot be used to continue treatment under section 57 or section 58A against the wishes of a patient who has the capacity to refuse the treatment, because in those cases there is no prospect of obtaining a new certificate.

**Action where treatment is continued pending a new certificate**

**4–238** 24.77 Where treatment is continued to avoid serious suffering pending compliance with a certificate requirement, the clinician in charge of the treatment should immediately take steps to ask for a SOAD visit. This applies both to cases where certificates have been withdrawn by the Commission and to cases where the treatment of SCT patients is being continued pending a new certificate following their recall to hospital (see **paragraphs 24.28** and **24.31**). If the SOAD visits and decides not to give a certificate for treatment which requires one, the treatment must end immediately.

24.78 As with immediately necessary treatment given without a certificate, hospital managers should monitor the use of these exceptions. They should require clinicians to record details of why it was necessary to continue treatment without a certificate and how long it took to obtain a new certificate.

**Other circumstances when certificates cease to be effective**

**4–239** 24.79 There are a number of other circumstances in which a certificate will cease to authorise treatment (or a particular treatment). These are summarised in the following table. People administering treatment on the basis of a certificate should always take reasonable steps to satisfy themselves that the certificate remains applicable to the circumstances.

*Circumstances in which certificates cease to authorise treatment, even though they have not been withdrawn*

**4–240**

| Type of certificate | Circumstances in which the certificate ceases to authorise treatment |
|---|---|
| Certificate issued by approved clinician under section 58 or 58A | The clinician concerned stops being the approved clinician in charge of the treatment. |
| SOAD certificate under section 57 | The patient no longer consents to the treatment. |

[20] At the time of publication, the Mental Health Act Commission expects these reports to be submitted on form MHAC1 which it provides for the purpose.

| Type of certificate | Circumstances in which the certificate ceases to authorise treatment |
|---|---|
| | The patient no longer has capacity to consent to the treatment. |
| SOAD certificate under section 58 or 58A | The patient stops (even if only temporarily) being either a detained patient or an SCT patient—except in the case of section 58A certificates for patients aged under 18. |
| | The SOAD specified a time limit on the approval of a course of treatment, and the time limit expires. |
| | The certificate was given on the basis that the patient consented, but the patient no longer consents or has lost the capacity to consent. |
| | The certificate was given on the basis that the patient lacked capacity to consent, but the patient now has that capacity. |
| | (Section 58 only.) The certificate was given on the basis that the patient had capacity to consent but was refusing, and either the patient is now consenting or the patient has lost the capacity to consent. |
| | (Section 58A only.) The certificate was given on the understanding that the treatment would not conflict with an advance decision to refuse treatment, but the person giving the treatment becomes aware that there is such a conflict. |
| | (Section 58A only.) The certificate was given on the understanding that the treatment would not conflict with a decision of an attorney, a deputy or the Court of Protection, but the person giving the treatment becomes aware that there is such a conflict; or an attorney, deputy or the Court of Protection makes a new decision that the treatment should not be given. |
| Part 4A certificate | The patient stops (even if only temporarily) being either a detained patient or an SCT patient. (But note that a Part 4A certificate authorises section 58 type treatment for a patient whose CTO has been revoked only pending compliance with section 58 itself.) |

| Type of certificate | Circumstances in which the certificate ceases to authorise treatment |
|---|---|
|  | The SOAD specified a time limit on the approval of a course of treatment, and the time limit has expired. |

24.80 In all the circumstances listed in the table, treatment cannot be continued while a new certificate is obtained, unless no certificate is needed because the treatment is immediately necessary (see **paragraphs 24.32–24.35**).

24.81 It is not good practice to use a certificate that was issued to a patient when detained and who has since been discharged onto SCT to authorise treatment if the patient is then recalled to hospital, even if the certificate remains technically valid. A new certificate should be obtained as necessary.

24.82 Hospital managers should make sure that arrangements are in place so that certificates which no longer authorise treatment (or particular treatments) are clearly marked as such, as are all copies of those certificates kept with the patient's notes and medication chart.

---

**Related material**

• British National Formulary, British Medical Association and Royal Pharmaceutical Society of Great Britain

This material does not form part of the Code. It is provided for assistance only.

---

## 25. SUPERVISED COMMUNITY TREATMENT

**4–241**   25.1 This chapter gives guidance on supervised community treatment (SCT) (**Reference Guide chapter 15**).

**Purpose of SCT**

**4–242**   25.2 The purpose of SCT is to allow suitable patients to be safely treated in the community rather than under detention in hospital, and to provide a way to help prevent relapse and any harm—to the patient or to others—that this might cause. It is intended to help patients to maintain stable mental health outside hospital and to promote recovery.

25.3 SCT provides a framework for the management of patient care in the community and gives the responsible clinician the power to recall the patient to hospital for treatment if necessary.

**Who can be discharged onto SCT? (Section 17A)**

**4–243**   25.4 Only patients who are detained in hospital for treatment under section 3 of the Act, or are unrestricted Part 3 patients, can be considered for SCT. Patients detained in hospital for assessment under section 2 of the Act are not eligible. (See also **paragraphs 36.64–36.65** on children and young people.)

25.5 SCT is an option only for patients who meet the criteria set out in the Act, which are that:

- the patient is suffering from a mental disorder of a nature or degree which makes it appropriate for them to receive medical treatment;

- it is necessary for the patient's health or safety or for the protection of others that the patient should receive such treatment;

- subject to the patient being liable to be recalled as mentioned below, such treatment can be provided without the patient continuing to be detained in a hospital;

- it is necessary that the responsible clinician should be able to exercise the power under section 17E(1) of the Act to recall the patient to hospital; and

- appropriate medical treatment is available for the patient.

### Assessment for SCT

25.6 The decision as to whether SCT is the right option for any patient is taken **4–244** by the responsible clinician and requires the agreement of an approved mental health professional (AMHP). SCT may be used only if it would not be possible to achieve the desired objectives for the patient's care and treatment without it. Consultation at an early stage with the patient and those involved in the patient's care will be important.

25.7 In assessing the patient's suitability for SCT, the responsible clinician must be satisfied that the patient requires medical treatment for mental disorder for their own health or safety or for the protection of others, and that appropriate treatment is, or would be, available for the patient in the community. The key factor in the decision is whether the patient can safely be treated for mental disorder in the community only if the responsible clinician can exercise the power to recall the patient to hospital for treatment if that becomes necessary (see **paragraphs 25.47–25.53**).

25.8 In making that decision the responsible clinician must assess what risk there would be of the patient's condition deteriorating after discharge, for example as a result of refusing or neglecting to receive treatment.

25.9 In assessing that risk the responsible clinician must take into consideration:

- the patient's history of mental disorder; and

- any other relevant factors.

25.10 Whether or not a patient has previously had repeated admissions, the patient's history may be relevant to the decision. For example, a tendency to fail to follow a treatment plan or to discontinue medication in the community, making relapse more likely, may suggest a risk justifying use of SCT.

25.11 Other relevant factors will vary but are likely to include the patient's current mental state, the patient's insight and attitude to treatment, and the circumstances into which the patient would be discharged.

25.12 Taken together, all these factors should help the responsible clinician to assess the risk of the patient's condition deteriorating after discharge, and inform the decision as to whether continued detention, SCT or discharge would be the right option for the patient at that particular time.

25.13 A risk that the patient's condition will deteriorate is a significant consideration, but does not necessarily mean that the patient should be discharged onto SCT. The responsible clinician must be satisfied that the risk of harm arising from the patient's disorder is sufficiently serious to justify the power to recall the patient to hospital for treatment.

25.14 Patients do not have to consent formally to SCT. But in practice, patients will need to be involved in decisions about the treatment to be provided in the community and how and where it is to be given, and be prepared to co-operate with the proposed treatment.

### Action upon Tribunal recommendation (Section 72(3A))

**4–245**  25.15 When a detained patient makes an application to the Tribunal for discharge, the Tribunal may decide not to order discharge, but to recommend that the responsible clinician should consider whether the patient should go onto SCT. In that event, the responsible clinician should carry out the assessment of the patient's suitability for SCT in the usual way. It will be for the responsible clinician to decide whether or not SCT is appropriate for that patient.

### Care planning, treatment and support in the community

**4–246**  25.16 Good care planning, in line with the Care Programme Approach (CPA) (or its equivalent) will be essential to the success of SCT. A care co-ordinator will need to be identified. This is likely to be a different person from the responsible clinician, but need not be.

25.17 The care plan should be prepared in the light of consultation with the patient and (subject to the normal considerations of patient confidentiality):

- the nearest relative;

- any carers;

- anyone with authority under the Mental Capacity Act 2005 (MCA) to act on the patient's behalf;

- the multi-disciplinary team involved in the patient's care; and

- the patient's GP (if there is one). It is important that the patient's GP should be aware that the patient is to go onto SCT. A patient who does not have a GP should be encouraged and helped to register with a practice.

25.18 If a different responsible clinician is to take over responsibility for the patient, it will be essential to liaise with that clinician, and the community team, at an early stage. Where needed, arrangements should be made for a second opinion appointed doctor (SOAD) to provide the Part 4A certificate to enable treatment to be given (see **paragraphs 24.25–24.27**).

25.19 The care plan should set out the practicalities of how the patient will receive treatment, care and support from day to day, and should not place undue reliance on carers or members of the patient's family. If the patient so wishes, help should be given to access independent advocacy or other support where this is available (see also **chapter 20**).

25.20 The care plan should take account of the patient's age. Where the patient is under the age of 18 the responsible clinician and the AMHP should bear in mind that the most age-appropriate treatment will normally be that provided by child and adolescent mental health services (CAMHS). It may also be necessary to involve the patient's parent, or whoever will be responsible for looking after the patient, to ensure that they will be ready and able to provide the assistance and support which the patient may need.

25.21 Similarly, specialist services for older people may have a role in the delivery of services for older SCT patients.

25.22 Patients on SCT are entitled to after-care services under section 117 of the Act. The after-care arrangements should be drawn up as part of the normal care planning arrangements. The Primary Care Trust and local social services authority (LSSA) must continue to provide aftercare services under section 117 for as long as the patient remains on SCT. (See also **chapter 27**.)

25.23 The care plan should be reviewed regularly, and the services required may vary should the patient's needs change.

**Role of the AMHP**

25.24 The AMHP must decide whether to agree with the patient's responsible **4–247** clinician that the patient meets the criteria for SCT, and (if so) whether SCT is appropriate. Even if the criteria for SCT are met, it does not mean that the patient must be discharged onto SCT. In making that decision, the AMHP should consider the wider social context for the patient. Relevant factors may include any support networks the patient may have, the potential impact on the rest of the patient's family, and employment issues.

25.25 The AMHP should consider how the patient's social and cultural background may influence the family environment in which they will be living and the support structures potentially available. But no assumptions should be made simply on the basis of the patient's ethnicity or social or cultural background.

25.26 The Act does not specify who this AMHP should be. It may (but need not) be an AMHP who is already involved in the patient's care and treatment as part of the multi-disciplinary team. It can be an AMHP acting on behalf of any willing LSSA, and LSSAs may agree with each other and with hospital managers the arrangements that are likely to be most convenient and best for patients. But if no other LSSA is willing, responsibility for ensuring that an AMHP considers the case should lie with the LSSA which would become responsible under section 117 for the patient's after-care if the patient were discharged.

25.27 If the AMHP does not agree with the responsible clinician that the patient should go onto SCT, then SCT cannot go ahead. A record of the AMHP's decision and the full reasons for it should be kept in the patient's notes. It would not be appropriate for the responsible clinician to approach another AMHP for an alternative view.

**Making the community treatment order**

25.28 If the responsible clinician and AMHP agree that the patient should be **4–248** discharged onto SCT, they should complete the relevant statutory form and send it to the hospital managers. The responsible clinician must specify on the form the date that the community treatment order (CTO) is to be made. This date is the authority for SCT to begin, and may be a short while after the date on which the form is signed, to allow time for arrangements to be put in place for the patient's discharge.

**Conditions to be attached to the community treatment order (Section 17B)**

**4–249**    25.29 The CTO must include the conditions with which the patient is required to comply while on SCT. There are two conditions which must be included in all cases. Patients are required to make themselves available for medical examination:

- when needed for consideration of extension of the CTO; and

- if necessary, to allow a SOAD to provide a Part 4A certificate authorising treatment.

25.30 Responsible clinicians may also, with the AMHP's agreement, set other conditions which they think are necessary or appropriate to:

- ensure that the patient receives medical treatment for mental disorder;

- prevent a risk of harm to the patient's health or safety;

- protect other people.

25.31 Conditions may be set for any or all of these purposes, but not for any other reason. The AMHP's agreement to the proposed conditions must be obtained before the CTO can be made.

25.32 In considering what conditions might be necessary or appropriate, the responsible clinician should always keep in view the patient's specific cultural needs and background. The patient, and (subject to the normal considerations of patient confidentiality) any others with an interest such as a parent or carer, should be consulted.

25.33 The conditions should:

- be kept to a minimum number consistent with achieving their purpose;

- restrict the patient's liberty as little as possible while being consistent with achieving their purpose;

- have a clear rationale, linked to one or more of the purposes in **paragraph 25.30;** and

- be clearly and precisely expressed, so that the patient can readily understand what is expected.

25.34 The nature of the conditions will depend on the patient's individual circumstances. Subject to **paragraph 25.33,** they might cover matters such as where and when the patient is to receive treatment in the community; where the patient is to live; and avoidance of known risk factors or high-risk situations relevant to the patient's mental disorder.

25.35 The reasons for any conditions should be explained to the patient and others, as appropriate, and recorded in the patient's notes. It will be important, if SCT is to be successful, that the patient agrees to keep to the conditions, or to try to do so, and that patients have access to the help they need to be able to comply.

## Information for SCT patients and others

25.36 As soon as the decision is made to discharge a patient onto SCT, the **4–250** responsible clinician should inform the patient and others consulted of the decision, the conditions to be applied to the CTO, and the services which will be available for the patient in the community.

25.37 There is a duty on hospital managers to take steps to ensure that patients understand what SCT means for them and their rights to apply for discharge. This includes giving patients information both orally and in writing and must be done as soon as practicable after the patient goes onto SCT. Hospital managers' information policies should set out whether this information is to be provided by the responsible clinician, by another member of the professional team or by someone else. A copy of this information must also be provided to the nearest relative (subject to the normal considerations about involving nearest relatives—see **paragraphs 2.27-2.33**). (See also **paragraphs 18.18–18.20** and **30.29** on information to be given to the victims of certain Part 3 patients.) **(Section 132A.)**

## Monitoring SCT patients

25.38 It will be important to maintain close contact with a patient on SCT and to **4–251** monitor their mental health and wellbeing after they leave hospital. The type and scope of the arrangements will vary depending on the patient's needs and individual circumstances and the way in which local services are organised. All those involved will need to agree to the arrangements. Respective responsibilities should be clearly set out in the patient's care plan. The care co-ordinator will normally be responsible for co-ordinating the care plan, working with the responsible clinician (if they are different people), the team responsible for the patient's care and any others with an interest.

25.39 Appropriate action will need to be taken if the patient becomes unwell, engages in high-risk behaviour as a result of mental disorder or withdraws consent to treatment (or begins to object to it). The responsible clinician should consider, with the patient (and others where appropriate), the reasons for this and what the next steps should be. If the patient refuses crucial treatment, an urgent review of the situation will be needed, and recalling the patient to hospital will be an option if the risk justifies it. If suitable alternative treatment is available which would allow SCT to continue safely and which the patient would accept, the responsible clinician should consider such treatment if this can be offered. If so, the treatment plan, and if necessary the conditions of the CTO, should be varied accordingly (note that a revised Part 4A certificate may be required).

25.40 If the patient is not complying with any condition of the CTO the reasons for this will need to be properly investigated. Recall to hospital may need to be considered if it is no longer safe and appropriate for the patient to remain in the community. The conditions may need to be reviewed—for example, if the patient's health has improved a particular condition may no longer be relevant or necessary. The responsible clinician may vary conditions as appropriate (see **paragraphs 25.41–25.45**). Changes may also be needed to the patient's care or treatment plan.

## Varying and suspending conditions (Section 17B)

25.41 The responsible clinician has the power to vary the conditions of the **4–252** patient's CTO, or to suspend any of them. The responsible clinician does not need to agree any variation or suspension with the AMHP. However, it would not be good practice to vary conditions which had recently been agreed with an AMHP without discussion with that AMHP.

25.42 Suspension of one or more of the conditions may be appropriate to allow for a temporary change in circumstances, for example, the patient's temporary absence or a change in treatment regime. The responsible clinician should record any decision to suspend conditions in the patient's notes, with reasons.

25.43 A variation of the conditions might be appropriate where the patient's treatment needs or living circumstances have changed. Any condition no longer required should be removed.

25.44 It will be important to discuss any proposed changes to the conditions with the patient and to ensure that the patient, and anyone else affected by the changes (subject to the patient's right to confidentiality), knows that they are being considered, and why. As when the conditions were first set, the patient will need to agree to try to keep to any new or varied conditions if SCT is to work successfully, and any help the patient needs to comply with them should be made available. (See also **paragraphs 18.10–18.13**.)

25.45 Any variation in the conditions must be recorded on the relevant statutory form, which should be sent to the hospital managers.

### Responding to concerns raised by the patient's carer or relatives

**4–253**    25.46 Particular attention should be paid to carers and relatives when they raise a concern that the patient is not complying with the conditions or that the patient's mental health appears to be deteriorating. The team responsible for the patient needs to give due weight to those concerns and any requests made by the carers or relatives in deciding what action to take. Carers and relatives are typically in much more frequent contact with the patient than professionals, even under well-run care plans. Their concerns may prompt a review of how SCT is working for that patient and whether the criteria for recall to hospital might be met. The managers of responsible hospitals should ensure that local protocols are in place to cover how concerns raised should be addressed and taken forward. (See also **paragraphs 18.2–18.5**.)

### Recall to hospital (Section 17E)

**4–254**    25.47 The recall power is intended to provide a means to respond to evidence of relapse or high-risk behaviour relating to mental disorder before the situation becomes critical and leads to the patient or other people being harmed. The need for recall might arise as a result of relapse, or through a change in the patient's circumstances giving rise to increased risk.

25.48 The responsible clinician may recall a patient on SCT to hospital for treatment if:

- the patient needs to receive treatment for mental disorder in hospital (either as an in-patient or as an out-patient); and

- there would be a risk of harm to the health or safety of the patient or to other people if the patient were not recalled.

25.49 A patient may also be recalled to hospital if they break either of the two mandatory conditions which must be included in all CTOs—that is, by failing to make themselves available for medical examination to allow consideration of extension of the CTO or to enable a SOAD to complete a Part 4A certificate. The patient must always be given the opportunity to comply with the condition before recall is considered. Before exercising the recall power for this reason, the responsible clinician should consider whether the patient has a valid reason for failing to comply, and should take any further action accordingly.

25.50 The responsible clinician must be satisfied that the criteria are met before using the recall power. Any action should be proportionate to the level of risk. For some patients, the risk arising from a failure to comply with treatment could indicate an immediate need for recall. In other cases, negotiation with the patient—and with the nearest relative and any carer (unless the patient objects or it is not reasonably practicable)—may resolve the problem and so avert the need for recall.

25.51 The responsible clinician should consider in each case whether recalling the patient to hospital is justified in all the circumstances. For example, it might be sufficient to monitor a patient who has failed to comply with a condition to attend for treatment, before deciding whether the lack of treatment means that recall is necessary. A patient may also agree to admission to hospital on a voluntary basis. Failure to comply with a condition (apart from those relating to availability for medical examination, as above) does not in itself trigger recall. Only if the breach of a condition results in an increased risk of harm to the patient or to anyone else will recall be justified.

25.52 However, it may be necessary to recall a patient whose condition is deteriorating despite compliance with treatment, if the risk cannot be managed otherwise.

25.53 Recall to hospital for treatment should not become a regular or normal event for any patient on SCT. If recall is being used frequently, the responsible clinician should review the patient's treatment plan to consider whether it could be made more acceptable to the patient, or whether, in the individual circumstances of the case, SCT continues to be appropriate.

**Procedure for recall to hospital**

25.54 The responsible clinician has responsibility for coordinating the recall **4–255** process, unless it has been agreed locally that someone else will do this. It will be important to ensure that the practical impact of recalling the patient on the patient's domestic circumstances is considered and managed.

25.55 The responsible clinician must complete a written notice of recall to hospital, which is effective only when served on the patient. It is important that, wherever possible, the notice should be handed to the patient personally. Otherwise, the notice is served by delivery to the patient's usual or last known address. (See **paragraphs 25.57–25.58**.)

25.56 Once the recall notice has been served, the patient can, if necessary, be treated as absent without leave, and taken and conveyed to hospital (and a patient who leaves the hospital without permission can be returned there). The time at which the notice is deemed to be served will vary according to the method of delivery.

25.57 It will not usually be appropriate to post a notice of recall to the patient. This may, however, be an option if the patient has failed to attend for medical examination as required by the conditions of the CTO, despite having been requested to do so, when the need for the examination is not urgent (see **paragraph 25.49**). First class post should be used. The notice is deemed to be served on the second working day after posting, and it will be important to allow sufficient time for the patient to receive the notice before any action is taken to ensure compliance.

25.58 Where the need for recall is urgent, as will usually be the case, it will be important that there is certainty as to the timing of delivery of the notice. A notice handed to the patient is effective immediately. However, it may not be possible to achieve this if the patient's whereabouts are unknown, or if the patient is unavailable or simply refuses to accept the notice. In that event the notice should be delivered by hand to the patient's usual or last known address. The notice is then deemed to be served (even though it may not actually be received by the patient) on the day after it is delivered—that is, the day (which does not have to be a working day) beginning immediately after midnight following delivery.

25.59 If the patient's whereabouts are known but access to the patient cannot be obtained, it may be necessary to consider whether a warrant issued under section 135(2) is needed (see **chapter 10**).

25.60 The patient should be conveyed to hospital in the least restrictive manner possible. If appropriate, the patient may be accompanied by a family member, carer or friend. (See also **chapter 11**.)

25.61 The responsible clinician should ensure that the hospital to which the patient is recalled is ready to receive the patient and to provide treatment. While recall must be to a hospital, the required treatment may then be given on an out-patient basis, if appropriate.

25.62 The hospital need not be the patient's responsible hospital (that is, the hospital where the patient was detained immediately before going onto SCT) or under the same management as that hospital. A copy of the notice of recall, which provides the authority to detain the patient, should be sent to the managers of the hospital to which the patient is being recalled.

25.63 When the patient arrives at hospital after recall, the clinical team will need to assess the patient's condition, provide the necessary treatment and determine the next steps. The patient may be well enough to return to the community once treatment has been given, or may need a longer period of assessment or treatment in hospital. The patient may be detained in hospital for a maximum of 72 hours after recall to allow the responsible clinician to determine what should happen next. During this period the patient remains an SCT patient, even if they remain in hospital for one or more nights. The responsible clinician may allow the patient to leave the hospital at any time within the 72-hour period. Once 72 hours from the time of admission have elapsed, the patient must be allowed to leave if the responsible clinician has not revoked the CTO (see **paragraphs 25.65–25.70**). On leaving hospital the patient will remain on SCT as before.

25.64 In considering the options, the responsible clinician and the clinical team will need to consider the reasons why it was necessary to exercise the recall power and whether SCT remains the right option for that patient. They will also need to consider, with the patient, the nearest relative (subject to the normal considerations about involving nearest relatives), and any carers, what changes might be needed to help to prevent the circumstances that led to recall from recurring. It may be that a variation in the conditions is required, or a change in the care plan (or both).

**Revoking the CTO (Section 17F)**

25.65 If the patient requires in-patient treatment for longer than 72 hours after **4–256** arrival at the hospital, the responsible clinician should consider revoking the CTO. The effect of revoking the CTO is that the patient will again be detained under the powers of the Act.

25.66 The CTO may be revoked if:

- the responsible clinician considers that the patient again needs to be admitted to hospital for medical treatment under the Act; and

- an AMHP agrees with that assessment, and also believes that it is appropriate to revoke the CTO.

25.67 In making the decision as to whether it is appropriate to revoke a CTO, the AMHP should consider the wider social context for the patient, in the same way as when making decisions about applications for admissions under the Act (see **chapter 4**).

25.68 As before, the AMHP carrying out this role may (but need not) be already involved in the patient's care and treatment, or can be an AMHP acting on behalf of any willing LSSA. If no other LSSA is willing, responsibility for ensuring that an AMHP considers the case should lie with the LSSA which has been responsible for the patient's after-care.

25.69 If the AMHP does not agree that the CTO should be revoked, then the patient cannot be detained in hospital after the end of the maximum recall period of 72 hours. The patient will therefore remain on SCT. A record of the AMHP's decision and the full reasons for it should be kept in the patient's notes. It would not be appropriate for the responsible clinician to approach another AMHP for an alternative view.

25.70 If the responsible clinician and the AMHP agree that the CTO should be revoked, they must complete the relevant statutory form for the revocation to take legal effect, and send it to the hospital managers. The patient is then detained again under the powers of the Act exactly as before going onto SCT, except that a new detention period of six months begins for the purposes of review and applications to the Tribunal (see also **paragraph 24.31**).

**Hospital managers' responsibilities**

25.71 It is the responsibility of the hospital managers to ensure that no patient is **4–257** detained following recall for longer than 72 hours unless the CTO is revoked. The relevant statutory form must be completed on the patient's arrival at hospital. Hospital managers should ensure that arrangements are in place to monitor the patient's length of stay following the time of detention after recall, as recorded on the form, so that the maximum period of detention is not exceeded. (See also **paragraphs 2.8–2.15** on information for patients.)

25.72 The hospital managers should also ensure that arrangements are in place to cover any necessary transfers of responsibility between responsible clinicians in the community and in hospital.

25.73 If a patient's CTO is revoked and the patient is detained in a hospital other than the one which was the responsible hospital at the time of recall, the hospital managers of the new hospital must send a copy of the revocation form to the managers of the original hospital.

25.74 The hospital managers have a duty to ensure that a patient whose CTO is revoked is referred to the Tribunal without delay.

**Review of SCT**

**4–258**     25.75 In addition to the statutory requirements in the Act for review of SCT, it is good practice to review the patient's progress on SCT as part of all reviews of the CPA care plan or its equivalent.

25.76 Reviews should cover whether SCT is meeting the patient's treatment needs and, if not, what action is necessary to address this. A patient who no longer satisfies all the criteria for SCT must be discharged without delay.

**Discharge from SCT (Sections 23 and 72)**

**4–259**     25.77 SCT patients may be discharged in the same way as detained patients, by the Tribunal, the hospital managers, or (for Part 2 patients) the nearest relative. The responsible clinician may also discharge an SCT patient at any time and must do so if the patient no longer meets the criteria for SCT. A patient's CTO should not simply be allowed to lapse.

25.78 The reasons for discharge should be explained to the patient, and any concerns on the part of the patient, the nearest relative or any carer should be considered and dealt with as far as possible. On discharge from SCT, the team should ensure that any after-care services the patient continues to need under section 117 of the Act will be available.

25.79 If guardianship is considered the better option for a patient on SCT, an application may be made in the usual way.

---

**Related material**

● *Refocusing the Care Programme Approach,* Care Programme Approach guidance, March 2008

This material does not form part of the Code. It is provided for assistance only.

---

**APPLYING THE PRINCIPLES**

**4–260**     This scenario is not intended to provide a template for decisions in applying the principles in similar situations. The scenario itself is only illustrative and does not form part of the Code itself.

---

**RECALL OF A SUPERVISED COMMUNITY TREATMENT PATIENT TO HOSPITAL**

Mary has a long-standing bipolar disorder. She has been on SCT for the past 12 months following an initial two months' detention in hospital.

Mary's condition has been managed successfully by a care plan which includes oral medication. However, it has transpired that Mary has missed taking a significant amount of her medication over the past couple of weeks.

One of the conditions of Mary's CTO is that she regularly attends a named clinic to review her treatment and progress. For the first time since her discharge from hospital, she fails to attend.

---

The responsible clinician meets with members of the multidisciplinary team to decide whether Mary needs to be recalled to hospital for treatment.

**When the multi-disciplinary team members meet, they are required to consider the principles. Among the questions they might wish to consider in making a decision in these circumstances are the following.**

**Purpose principle**

- What are the risks to Mary and others if she does not receive her medication? How soon might those risks arise and in what circumstances?

- What will be best for Mary's wellbeing overall?

**Least restriction principle**

- What are the possible alternatives for managing Mary's care? For example, the multi-disciplinary team contacting Mary, or arranging a home visit to see her.

- Would varying the conditions of the CTO assist Mary to comply with her treatment programme?

- Might Mary be prepared to accept another treatment regime if there is an alternative which would be as clinically effective?

- Have alternative options been explored with Mary before?

**Respect principle**

- What is Mary's view of why she has stopped taking her medication?

- Is Mary's failure to attend clinic anything to do with a conscious decision to refuse medication, or is there some other reason? Have all possible reasons been considered?

- Are there any social, cultural or family-related factors, which may have led Mary to miss her appointment?

- Taking into account Mary's history and known past and present wishes, are there any particular reasons why Mary may not have presented at the clinic?

- Has Mary expressed any views about what she would like to happen if she stopped taking her medication?

**Participation principle**

- Is Mary willing to discuss what is going on?

- What might be the best way of approaching Mary to discuss the current situation?

- Are Mary's family or carers involved in her day-to-day care aware that she is on SCT, and if so should their views be sought on the best way to help Mary to re-establish contact with services?

- Does Mary's GP have any ideas about engaging Mary?

- What is Mary's view about her family being contacted?

> - Have Mary's family or carers expressed any views about what they think may help Mary?
>
> **Effectiveness, efficiency and equity principle**
>
> - Mary has said in the past that she enjoys her contact with the team's community psychiatric nurse (CPN)—would giving her more time with the CPN be an effective way of tackling the current situation? Could it be done without other patients with the same or greater clinical needs being disadvantaged?

## 26. GUARDIANSHIP

**4–261**    26.1 This chapter gives guidance on guardianship under the Act **(Reference Guide chapter 19)**.

**Purpose of guardianship**

**4–262**    26.2 The purpose of guardianship is to enable patients to receive care outside hospital when it cannot be provided without the use of compulsory powers. Such care may or may not include specialist medical treatment for mental disorder.

26.3 A guardian may be a local social services authority (LSSA) or someone else approved by an LSSA (a "private guardian"). Guardians have three specific powers as follows:

- they have the exclusive right to decide where a patient should live, taking precedence even over an attorney or deputy appointed under the Mental Capacity Act 2005 (MCA);

- they can require the patient to attend for treatment, work, training or education at specific times and places (but they cannot use force to take the patient there);

- they can demand that a doctor, approved mental health professional (AMHP) or another relevant person has access to the patient at the place where the patient lives **(Section 8)**.

26.4 Guardianship therefore provides an authoritative framework for working with a patient, with a minimum of constraint, to achieve as independent a life as possible within the community. Where it is used, it should be part of the patient's overall care plan.

26.5 Guardianship does not give anyone the right to treat the patient without their permission or to consent to treatment on their behalf.

26.6 While the reception of a patient into guardianship does not affect the continued authority of an attorney or deputy appointed under the MCA, such attorneys and deputies will not be able to take decisions about where a guardianship patient is to reside, or take any other decisions which conflict with those of the guardian.

**Assessment for guardianship (Section 7)**

**4–263**    26.7 An application for guardianship may be made on the grounds that:

- the patient is suffering from mental disorder of a nature or degree which warrants their reception into guardianship; and

- it is necessary, in the interests of the welfare of the patient or for the protection of other persons, that the patient should be so received.

26.8 Guardianship is most likely to be appropriate where:

- the patient is thought to be likely to respond well to the authority and attention of a guardian and so be more willing to comply with necessary treatment and care for their mental disorder; or

- there is a particular need for someone to have the authority to decide where the patient should live or to insist that doctors, AMHPs or other people be given access to the patient.

26.9 As with applications for detention in hospital, AMHPs and doctors making recommendations should consider whether the objectives of the proposed application could be achieved in another, less restrictive, way, without the use of guardianship.

26.10 Where patients lack capacity to make some or all important decisions concerning their own welfare, one potential alternative to guardianship will be to rely solely on the MCA—especially the protection from liability for actions taken in connection with care or treatment provided by section 5 of the MCA. While this is a factor to be taken into account, it will not by itself determine whether guardianship is necessary or unnecessary. AMHPs and doctors need to consider all the circumstances of the particular case.

26.11 Where an adult is assessed as requiring residential care but lacks the capacity to make a decision about whether they wish to be placed there, guardianship is unlikely to be necessary where the move can properly, quickly and efficiently be carried out on the basis of:

- section 5 of the MCA or the decision of an attorney or deputy; or

- (where relevant) the MCA's deprivation of liberty safeguards.

26.12 But guardianship may still be appropriate in such cases if:

- there are other reasons—unconnected to the move to residential care—to think that the patient might benefit from the attention and authority of a guardian;

- there is a particular need to have explicit statutory authority for the patient to be returned to the place where the patient is to live should they go absent; or

- it is thought to be important that decisions about where the patient is to live are placed in the hands of a single person or authority—for example, where there have been long-running or particularly difficult disputes about where the person should live.

26.13 However, it will not always be best to use guardianship as the way of deciding where patients who lack capacity to decide for themselves must live. In cases which raise unusual issues, or where guardianship is being considered in the interests of the patient's welfare and there are finely balanced arguments about where the patient should live, it may be preferable instead to seek a best interests decision from the Court of Protection under the MCA.

26.14 Where the relevant criteria are met, guardianship may be considered in respect of a patient who is to be discharged from detention under the Mental Health Act. However, if it is thought that the patient needs to remain liable to be recalled to hospital (and the patient is eligible), supervised community treatment is likely to be more appropriate (see **chapter 28**).

**Responsibilities of local social services authorities**

**4–264**  26.15 Each LSSA should have a policy setting out the arrangements for:

- receiving, scrutinising and accepting or refusing applications for guardianship. Such arrangements should ensure that applications are properly but quickly dealt with;

- monitoring the progress of each patient's guardianship, including steps to be taken to fulfil the authority's statutory obligations in relation to private guardians and to arrange visits to the patient;

- ensuring the suitability of any proposed private guardian, and that they are able to understand and carry out their duties under the Act;

- ensuring that patients under guardianship receive, both orally and in writing, information in accordance with regulations under the Act;

- ensuring that patients are aware of their right to apply to the Tribunal and that they are given the name of someone who will give them the necessary assistance, on behalf of the LSSA, in making such an application;

- authorising an approved clinician to be the patient's responsible clinician;

- maintaining detailed records relating to guardianship patients;

- ensuring that the need to continue guardianship is reviewed in the last two months of each period of guardianship in accordance with the Act; and

- discharging patients from guardianship as soon as it is no longer required.

26.16 Patients may be discharged from guardianship at any time by the LSSA, the responsible clinician authorised by the LSSA, or (in most cases) the patient's nearest relative **(Section 23)**.

26.17 Discharge decisions by LSSAs may be taken only by the LSSA itself, or by three or more members of the LSSA or of a committee or sub-committee of the LSSA authorised for that purpose. Where decisions are taken by three or more members of the LSSA (or a committee or subcommittee), all three people (or at least three of them, if there are more) must agree.

26.18 LSSAs may consider discharging patients from guardianship at any time, but must consider doing so when they receive a report from the patient's nominated medical attendant or responsible clinician renewing their guardianship under section 20 of the Act.

## Components of effective guardianship

*Care planning*

26.19 An application for guardianship should be accompanied by a comprehen- **4–265**
sive care plan established on the basis of multi-disciplinary discussions in
accordance with the Care Programme Approach (or its equivalent).

26.20 The plan should identify the services needed by the patient and who will
provide them. It should also indicate which of the powers that guardians have
under the Act are necessary to achieve the plan. If none of the powers are required,
guardianship should not be used.

26.21 Key elements of the plan are likely to be:

- suitable accommodation to help meet the patient's needs;

- access to day care, education and training facilities, as appropriate;

- effective co-operation and communication between all those concerned in
  implementing the plan; and

- (if there is to be a private guardian) support from the LSSA for the guardian.

26.22 A private guardian should be prepared to advocate on behalf of the
patient in relation to those agencies whose services are needed to carry out the
care plan. So should an LSSA which is itself the guardian.

26.23 A private guardian should be a person who can appreciate any special disabilities and needs of a mentally disordered person and who will look after the
patient in an appropriate and sympathetic way. The guardian should display an
interest in promoting the patient's physical and mental health and in providing
for their occupation, training, employment, recreation and general welfare in a
suitable way. The LSSA must satisfy itself that a proposed private guardian is
capable of carrying out their functions and it should assist them with advice
and other forms of support.

26.24 Regulations require private guardians to appoint a doctor as the patient's
nominated medical attendant. It is the nominated medical attendant who must
examine the patient during the last two months of each period of guardianship
and decide whether to make a report extending the patient's guardianship.
(Where the patient's guardian is the LSSA itself, this is done by the responsible
clinician authorised by the LSSA.)

26.25 It is for private guardians themselves to decide whom to appoint as the
nominated medical attendant, but they should first consult the LSSA. The nominated medical attendant may be the patient's GP, if the GP agrees.

*Power to require a patient to live in a particular place*

26.26 Guardians have the power to decide where patients should live. If **4–266**
patients leave the place where they are required to live without the guardian's permission, they can be taken into legal custody and brought back there (see **chapter
22**) (**Section 18(3)**).

26.27 This power can also be used to take patients for the first time to the place
they are required to live, if patients do not (or, in practice, cannot) go there by
themselves (**Section 18(7)**).

26.28 Patients should always be consulted first about where they are to be required to live, unless their mental state makes that impossible. Guardians should not use this power to make a patient move without warning.

26.29 The power to take or return patients to the place they are required to live may be used, for example, to discourage them from:

- living somewhere the guardian considers unsuitable;

- breaking off contact with services;

- leaving the area before proper arrangements can be made; or

- sleeping rough.

But it may not be used to restrict their freedom to come and go so much that they are effectively being detained.

26.30 The power to require patients to reside in a particular place may not be used to require them to live in a situation in which they are deprived of liberty, unless that is authorised separately under the MCA. That authorisation will only be possible if the patient lacks capacity to decide where to live. If deprivation of liberty is authorised under the MCA, the LSSA should consider whether guardianship remains necessary, bearing in mind the guidance earlier in this chapter.

*Guardianship and hospital care*

**4–267**   26.31 Guardianship does not restrict patients' access to hospital services on an informal basis. Patients who require treatment but do not need to be detained may be admitted informally in the same way as any other patient. This applies to both physical and mental healthcare.

26.32 Nor does guardianship prevent an authorisation being granted under the deprivation of liberty safeguards in the MCA, if the person needs to be detained in a hospital in their best interests in order to receive care and treatment, so long as it would not be inconsistent with the guardian's decision about where the patient should live.

26.33 Otherwise, guardianship should not be used to require a patient to reside in a hospital except where it is necessary for a very short time in order to provide shelter while accommodation in the community is being arranged.

26.34 Guardianship can remain in force if the patient is detained in hospital under section 2 or 4 of the Mental Health Act for assessment, but it ends automatically if a patient is detained for treatment as a result of an application under section 3. Regulations also allow a patient to be transferred from guardianship to detention in hospital under section 3. The normal requirements for an application and medical recommendations must be met, and the transfer must be agreed by the LSSA (**Section 6**).

**Patients who resist the authority of the guardian**

**4–268**   26.35 If a patient consistently resists exercise by the guardian of any of their powers, it can normally be concluded that guardianship is not the most appropriate form of care for that person, and the guardianship should be discharged. However, the LSSA should first consider whether a change of guardian—or change in the person who, in practice, exercises the LSSA's powers as guardian—might be appropriate instead.

## Guardianship orders under section 37 (Reference Guide 19.60–19.66)

26.36 Guardianship may be used by courts as an alternative to hospital orders **4–269** for offenders with mental disorders where the criteria set out in the Act are met. The court must first be satisfied that the LSSA or named person is willing to act as guardian. In considering the appropriateness of the patient being received into their guardianship, LSSAs should be guided by the same considerations as apply to applications for guardianship under Part 2 of the Act.

26.37 The guidance in this chapter on components of effective guardianship applies to guardianship order patients in

the same way as it applies to other guardianship patients. The main difference between applications for guardianship under Part 2 of the Act and guardianship orders is that nearest relatives may not discharge patients from guardianship orders. Nearest relatives have rights to apply to the Tribunal instead.

---

**Related material**

• Mental Capacity Act 2005

• *Mental Capacity Act 2005 Code of Practice,* TSO, 2007

• *Deprivation of Liberty Safeguards,* Addendum to the *Mental Capacity Act 2005 Code of Practice*

This material does not form part of the Code. It is provided for assistance only.

---

## 27. AFTER-CARE

27.1 This chapter gives guidance on the duty to provide after-care for patients **4–270** under section 117 of the Act **(Reference Guide chapter 24)**.

### Section 117 after-care

27.2 Section 117 of the Act requires primary care trusts (PCTs) and local social **4–271** services authorities (LSSAs), in co-operation with voluntary agencies, to provide aftercare to patients detained in hospital for treatment under section 3, 37, 45A, 47 or 48 of the Act who then cease to be detained. This includes patients granted leave of absence under section 17 and patients going onto supervised community treatment (SCT).

27.3 The duty to provide after-care services continues as long as the patient is in need of such services. In the case of a patient on SCT, after-care must be provided for the entire period they are on SCT, but this does not mean that the patient's need for after-care will necessarily cease as soon as they are no longer on SCT.

27.4 Services provided under section 117 can include services provided directly by PCTs or LSSAs as well as services they commission from other providers.

27.5 After-care is a vital component in patients' overall treatment and care. As well as meeting their immediate needs for health and social care, after-care should aim to support them in regaining or enhancing their skills, or learning new skills, in order to cope with life outside hospital.

27.6 Where eligible patients have remained in hospital informally after ceasing to be detained under the Act, they are still entitled to after-care under section 117 once they leave hospital. This also applies when patients are released from prison, having spent part of their sentence detained in hospital under a relevant section of the Act.

**After-care planning**

**4–272** 27.7 When considering relevant patients' cases, the Tribunal and hospital managers will expect to be provided with information from the professionals concerned on what after-care arrangements might be made for them under section 117 if they were to be discharged. Some discussion of after-care needs, involving LSSAs and other relevant agencies, should take place in advance of the hearing.

27.8 Although the duty to provide after-care begins when the patient leaves hospital, the planning of after-care needs to start as soon as the patient is admitted to hospital. PCTs and LSSAs should take reasonable steps to identify appropriate after-care services for patients before their actual discharge from hospital.

27.9 Where a Tribunal or hospital managers' hearing has been arranged for a patient who might be entitled to after-care under section 117 of the Act, the hospital managers should ensure that the relevant PCT and LSSA have been informed. The PCT and LSSA should consider putting practical preparations in hand for after-care in every case, but should in particular consider doing so where there is a strong possibility that the patient will be discharged if appropriate after-care can be arranged. Where the Tribunal has provisionally decided to give a restricted patient a conditional discharge, the PCT and LSSA must do their best to put after-care in place which would allow that discharge to take place.

27.10 Before deciding to discharge, or grant more than very short-term leave of absence to, a patient, or to place a patient onto SCT, the responsible clinician should ensure that the patient's needs for after-care have been fully assessed, discussed with the patient and addressed in their care plan. If the patient is being given leave for only a short period, a less comprehensive review may be sufficient, but the arrangements for the patient's care should still be properly recorded.

27.11 After-care for all patients admitted to hospital for treatment for mental disorder should be planned within the framework of the Care Programme Approach (or its equivalent), whether or not they are detained or will be entitled to receive after-care under section 117 of the Act. But because of the specific statutory obligation it is important that all patients who are entitled to after-care under section 117 are identified and that records are kept of what after-care is provided to them under that section.

27.12 In order to ensure that the after-care plan reflects the needs of each patient, it is important to consider who needs to be involved, in addition to patients themselves. This may include:

- the patient's responsible clinician;

- nurses and other professionals involved in caring for the patient in hospital;

- a clinical psychologist, community mental health nurse and other members of the community team;

- the patient's GP and primary care team;

- subject to the patient's views, any carer who will be involved in looking after them outside hospital, the patient's nearest relative or other family members;
- a representative of any relevant voluntary organisations;
- in the case of a restricted patient, the probation service;
- a representative of housing authorities, if accommodation is an issue;
- an employment expert, if employment is an issue;
- an independent mental health advocate, if the patient has one;
- an independent mental capacity advocate, if the patient has one;
- the patient's attorney or deputy, if the patient has one; and
- any other representative nominated by the patient.

27.13 A thorough assessment is likely to involve consideration of:

- continuing mental healthcare, whether in the After-care community or on an out-patient basis;
- the psychological needs of the patient and, where appropriate, of their family and carers;
- physical healthcare;
- daytime activities or employment;
- appropriate accommodation;
- identified risks and safety issues;
- any specific needs arising from, for example, co-existing physical disability, sensory impairment, learning disability or autistic spectrum disorder;
- any specific needs arising from drug, alcohol or substance misuse (if relevant);
- any parenting or caring needs;
- social, cultural or spiritual needs;
- counselling and personal support;
- assistance in welfare rights and managing finances;
- the involvement of authorities and agencies in a different area, if the patient is not going to live locally;
- the involvement of other agencies, for example the probation service or voluntary organisations;
- for a restricted patient, the conditions which the Secretary of State for Justice or the Tribunal has imposed or is likely to impose on their conditional discharge; and

- contingency plans (should the patient's mental health deteriorate) and crisis contact details.

27.14 The professionals concerned should, in discussion with the patient, establish an agreed outline of the patient's needs and agree a timescale for the implementation of the various aspects of the after-care plan. All key people with specific responsibilities with regard to the patient should be properly identified.

27.15 It is important that those who are involved are able to take decisions regarding their own involvement and, as far as possible, that of their agency. If approval for plans needs to be obtained from more senior levels, it is important that this causes no delay to the implementation of the after-care plan.

27.16 If accommodation is to be offered as part of the after-care plan to patients who are offenders, the circumstances of any victims of the patient's offence(s) and their families should be taken into account when deciding where the accommodation should be offered. Where the patient is to live may be one of the conditions imposed by the Secretary of State for Justice or the Tribunal when conditionally discharging a restricted patient.

27.17 The after-care plan should be recorded in writing. Once the plan is agreed, it is essential that any changes are discussed with the patient as well as others involved with the patient before being implemented.

27.18 The after-care plan should be regularly reviewed. It will be the responsibility of the care co-ordinator (or other officer responsible for its review) to arrange reviews of the plan until it is agreed that it is no longer necessary.

### Ending section 117 after-care services

**4–273**    27.19 The duty to provide after-care services exists until both the PCT and the LSSA are satisfied that the patient no longer requires them. The circumstances in which it is appropriate to end section 117 after-care will vary from person to person and according to the nature of the services being provided. The most clear-cut circumstance in which after-care will end is where the person's mental health has improved to a point where they no longer need services because of their mental disorder. But if these services include, for example, care in a specialist residential setting, the arrangements for their move to more appropriate accommodation will need to be in place before support under section 117 is finally withdrawn. Fully involving the patient in the decision-making process will play an important part in the successful ending of after-care.

27.20 After-care services under section 117 should not be withdrawn solely on the grounds that:

- the patient has been discharged from the care of specialist mental health services;

- an arbitrary period has passed since the care was first provided;

- the patient is deprived of their liberty under the Mental Capacity Act 2005;

- the patient may return to hospital informally or under section 2; or

- the patient is no longer on SCT or section 17 leave.

27.21 Even when the provision of after-care has been successful in that the patient is now well settled in the community, the patient may still continue to need after-care services, for example to prevent a relapse or further deterioration in their condition.

27.22 Patients are under no obligation to accept the after-care services they are offered, but any decisions they may make to decline them should be fully informed. An unwillingness to accept services does not mean that patients have no need to receive services, nor should it preclude them from receiving them under section 117 should they change their minds.

---

**Related material**

- *Refocusing the Care Programme Approach: Policy and Positive Practice Guidance*, March 2008

  This material does not form part of the Code. It is provided for assistance only.

---

## 28. GUARDIANSHIP, LEAVE OF ABSENCE OR SCT?

28.1 This chapter gives advice on deciding between guardianship, leave of **4–274** absence and supervised community treatment (SCT) as ways of supporting patients once it is safe for them to leave hospital.

### Deciding between guardianship, leave of absence and SCT

28.2 There are three ways in which an unrestricted patient may be subject to the **4–275** powers of the Act while living in the community: guardianship, leave of absence and SCT.

28.3 *Guardianship* (section 7 of the Act) is social care-led and is primarily focused on patients with welfare needs. Its purpose is to enable patients to receive care in the community where it cannot be provided without the use of compulsory powers. (See **chapter 26**.)

28.4 *Leave of absence* (section 17) is primarily intended to allow a patient detained under the Act to be temporarily absent from hospital where further in-patient treatment as a detained patient is still thought to be necessary. It is clearly suitable for short-term absences, to allow visits to family and so on. It may also be useful in the longer term, where the clinical team wish to see how the patient manages outside hospital before making the decision to discharge. However, for a number of patients, SCT may be a better option than longer-term leave for the ongoing management of their care. Reflecting this, whenever considering longer-term leave for a patient (that is, for more than seven consecutive days), the responsible clinician must first consider whether the patient should be discharged onto SCT instead. (See **chapter 21**.)

28.5 *SCT* (section 17A) is principally aimed at preventing the "revolving door" scenario and the prevention of harm which could arise from relapse. It is a more structured system than leave of absence and has more safeguards for patients. A key feature of SCT is that it is suitable only where there is no reason to think that the patient will need further treatment as a detained in-patient for the time being, but the responsible clinician needs to be able to recall the patient to hospital. (See **chapter 25**.)

28.6 Some pointers to the use of the three options are given in the following boxes.

*SCT or longer-term leave of absence: relevant factors to consider*

| 4–276 | Factors suggesting longer-term leave | Factors suggesting SCT |
|---|---|---|
| | Discharge from hospital is for a specific purpose or a fixed period. | • There is confidence that the patient is ready for discharge from hospital on an indefinite basis. |
| | • The patient's discharge from hospital is deliberately on a "trial" basis. | • There are good reasons to expect that the patient will not need to be detained for the treatment they need to be given. |
| | • The patient is likely to need further in-patient treatment without their consent or compliance. | • The patient appears prepared to consent or comply with the treatment they need—but risks as below mean that recall may be necessary. |
| | • There is a serious risk of arrangements in the community breaking down or being unsatisfactory—more so than for SCT. | • The risk of arrangements in the community breaking down, or of the patient needing to be recalled to hospital for treatment, is sufficiently serious to justify SCT, but not to the extent that it is very likely to happen. |

*SCT or guardianship: relevant factors to consider*

| 4–277 | Factors suggesting guardianship | Factors suggesting SCT |
|---|---|---|
| | • The focus is on the patient's general welfare, rather than specifically on medical treatment. | • The main focus is on ensuring that the patient continues to receive necessary medical treatment for mental disorder, without having to be detained again. |
| | • There is little risk of the patient needing to be admitted compulsorily and quickly to hospital. | • Compulsory recall may well be necessary, and speed is likely to be important. |
| | • There is a need for enforceable power to require the patient to reside at a particular place. | |

**Deprivation of liberty while on SCT, on leave or subject to guardianship**

28.7 Patients who are on SCT or on leave, and who lack capacity to consent to the arrangements required for their care or treatment, may occasionally need to be detained in a care home for further care or treatment for their mental disorder in circumstances in which recall to hospital for this purpose is not considered necessary. The same might apply to admission to a care home or hospital because of physical health problems.

28.8 If so, the procedures for the deprivation of liberty safeguards in the Mental Capacity Act 2005 (MCA) should be followed. Deprivation of liberty under the MCA can exist alongside SCT or leave of absence, provided that there is no conflict with the conditions of SCT or leave of absence set by the patient's responsible clinician.

28.9 Where patients on SCT or on leave who lack capacity to consent to the arrangements required for their care or treatment need to be detained in hospital for further treatment for mental disorder, they should be recalled under the Mental Health Act itself. The MCA deprivation of liberty safeguards cannot be used instead.

28.10 For guidance on the interface between guardianship and the deprivation of liberty safeguards, see **chapter 26** on guardianship.

## 29. DETENTION AND SCT: RENEWAL, EXTENSION AND DISCHARGE

29.1 This chapter gives guidance on how the procedures in the Act for renewing **4–278** detention and extending supervised community treatment (SCT) should be applied, and on responsible clinicians' and nearest relatives' power to discharge patients.

### Renewal of detention (Reference Guide 12.65–12.95)
29.2 Before it expires, responsible clinicians must decide whether patients' cur- **4–279** rent period of detention should be renewed. Responsible clinicians must examine the patient and decide within the two months leading up to the expiry of the patient's detention whether the criteria for renewing detention under section 20 of the Act are met. They must also consult one or more other people who have been professionally concerned with the patient's medical treatment.

29.3 Where responsible clinicians are satisfied that the criteria for renewing the patient's detention are met, they must submit a report to that effect to the hospital managers.

29.4 But before responsible clinicians can submit that report, they are required to obtain the written agreement of another professional ("the second professional") that the criteria are met. This second professional must be professionally concerned with the patient's treatment and must not belong to the same profession as the responsible clinician.

29.5 Apart from that, the Act does not say who the second professional should be. Hospital managers should determine their own local policies on the selection of the second professional. Policies should be based on the principle that the involvement of a second professional is intended to provide an additional safeguard for patients by ensuring that:

- renewal is formally agreed by at least two suitably qualified and competent professionals who are familiar with the patient's case;

- those two professionals are from different disciplines, and so bring different, but complementary, professional perspectives to bear; and

- the two professionals are able to reach their own decisions independently of one another.

29.6 Accordingly, second professionals should:

- have sufficient experience and expertise to decide whether the patient's continued detention is necessary and lawful, but need not be approved clinicians (nor be qualified to be one);

- have been actively involved in the planning, management or delivery of the patient's treatment; and

- have had sufficient recent contact with the patient to be able to make an informed judgement about the patient's case.

29.7 Second professionals should satisfy themselves, in line with the local policies, that they have sufficient information on which to make the decision. Whether that requires a separate clinical interview or examination of the patient will depend on the nature of the contact that the second professional already has with the patient and on the other circumstances of the case.

29.8 Before examining patients to decide whether to make a renewal report, responsible clinicians should identify and record who the second professional is to be. Hospital managers' policies may, if the hospital managers wish, say that the identity of the second professional is to be decided or agreed by a third party—such as a senior clinician or manager—but the Act does not require that.

29.9 Unless there are exceptional circumstances, the decision of the identified second professional should be accepted, even if the responsible clinician does not agree with it. If, in exceptional circumstances, it is decided that the agreement of a different second professional should be sought, that decision should be drawn to the attention of the hospital managers if, as a result, a renewal report is made.

**Extending supervised community treatment (Reference Guide 15.71–15.103)**

4–280    29.10 Only responsible clinicians may extend the period of a patient's SCT by extending the period of the community treatment order (CTO). To do so, responsible clinicians must examine the patient and decide, during the two months leading up to the day on which the patient's CTO is due to expire, whether the criteria for extending SCT under section 20A of the Act are met. They must also consult one or more other people who have been professionally concerned with the patient's medical treatment.

29.11 Where responsible clinicians are satisfied that the criteria for extending the patient's SCT are met, they must submit a report to that effect to the managers of the responsible hospital.

29.12 But before responsible clinicians can submit that report, they must obtain the written agreement of an approved mental health professional (AMHP).

29.13 This does not have to be the same AMHP who originally agreed that the patient should become an SCT patient. It may (but need not) be an AMHP who is already involved in the patient's care and treatment. It can be an AMHP acting on behalf of any willing local social services authority (LSSA). But if no other LSSA is willing, responsibility for ensuring that an AMHP considers the case should lie with the LSSA which is responsible under section 117 for the patient's after-care.

29.14 The role of the AMHP is to consider whether or not the criteria for extending SCT are met and, if so, whether an extension is appropriate.

**The responsible clinician's power of discharge (Reference Guide 12.113–12.116)**

29.15 Section 23 of the Act allows responsible clinicians to discharge most **4–281** detained patients and all SCT patients by giving an order in writing.

29.16 Because responsible clinicians have the power to discharge patients, they must keep under review the appropriateness of using that power. If, at any time, responsible clinicians conclude that the criteria which would justify renewing a patient's detention or extending the patient's SCT (as the case may be) are not met, they should exercise their power of discharge. They should not wait until the patient's detention or SCT is due to expire.

29.17 A decision by a second professional not to agree to the renewal of detention does not bring a patient's current period of detention to an end before it is otherwise due to expire. Similarly, a decision by an AMHP not to agree to the extension of a patient's SCT does not end the existing period of SCT. But in both cases, it would normally be a reason for responsible clinicians to review whether they should use their power to discharge the patient.

**The nearest relative's power of discharge (Reference Guide 12.101–12.112 (detention) and 15.104 –15.112 (SCT))**

29.18 Patients detained for assessment or treatment under Part 2 of the Act may **4–282** also be discharged by their nearest relatives.

29.19 Before giving a discharge order, nearest relatives must give the hospital managers at least 72 hours' notice in writing of their intention to discharge the patient.

29.20 During that period, the patient's responsible clinician can block the discharge by issuing a "barring report" stating that, if discharged, the patient is likely to act in a manner dangerous to themselves or others **(Section 25(1))**.

29.21 This question focuses on the probability of dangerous acts, such as causing serious physical injury or lasting psychological harm, not merely on the patient's general need for safety and others' general need for protection.

29.22 The nearest relative's notice and discharge order must both be given in writing, but do not have to be in any specific form. In practice, hospital managers should treat a discharge order given without prior notice as being both notice of intention to discharge the patient after 72 hours and the actual order to do so.

29.23 Hospital managers should offer nearest relatives any help they require, such as providing them with a standard letter to complete. The following box illustrates what a standard letter might look like.

**Illustrative standard letter for nearest relatives to use to discharge patients**

To the managers of [INSERT NAME AND ADDRESS OF HOSPITAL IN **4–283** WHICH THE PATIENT IS DETAINED, OR (FOR A SUPERVISED COMMUNITY TREATMENT PATIENT) THE RESPONSIBLE HOSPITAL.]

**Order for discharge under section 23 of the Mental Health Act 1983**

My name is [GIVE YOUR NAME] and my address is [GIVE YOUR ADDRESS]

*[Complete A, B or C below]*

A. To the best of my knowledge and belief, I am the nearest relative (within the meaning of the Mental Health Act 1983) of [NAME OF PATIENT].

OR

B. I have been authorised to exercise the functions of the nearest relative of [NAME OF PATIENT] by the county court.

OR

C. I have been authorised to exercise the functions of the nearest relative of [NAME OF PATIENT] by that person's nearest relative.

I give you notice of my intention to discharge the person named above, and I order their discharge from [SAY WHEN YOU WANT THE PATIENT DISCHARGED FROM DETENTION OR SUPERVISED COMMUNITY TREATMENT].

*[Please note: you must leave at least 72 hours between when the hospital managers get this letter and when you want the patient discharged.]*

Signed _____

Date _____

### Discharge by the hospital managers and the Tribunal

**4–284**  29.24 Patients may also be discharged by the hospital managers and by the Tribunal. See **chapter 31** and **chapter 32** respectively.

### Applying the Principles

This scenario is not intended to provide a template for decisions in applying the principles in similar situations. The scenario itself is only illustrative and does not form part of the Code itself.

**CONSIDERING RENEWAL OF DETENTION**

Adele is a middle-aged woman who has been detained in hospital for five months. Adele has a long-term history of mental disorder and has been in hospital for periods totalling five of the past 30 years. In the past, she has been readmitted to hospital on more than one occasion after her condition relapsed following her discharge.

Adele is being examined so that a decision can be taken about whether to renew her detention, which is due to expire in six weeks. This involves considering the alternatives to renewing detention. The responsible clinician and the second professional apply the guiding principles of this Code, and accordingly consider the following.

**Purpose principle**

- Why is Adele being detained? What is the risk posed by her mental disorder and to whom? Can any risk only be managed by continuing to detain Adele?

- What effect does being detained in hospital have on Adele's wellbeing generally?

- What are the risks to Adele if she stays detained?

**Least restriction principle**

- What are the possible alternatives to renewal, eg specific community-based care and treatment (with or without SCT or guardianship)?

- If detention does need to be renewed, could Adele nonetheless safely be given more freedom—such as more frequent or longer leave of absence?

**Respect principle**

- What are Adele's views on her current condition and treatment plan? Does she think treatment in hospital should continue and, if so, does she think she still needs to be detained?

- Does Adele have a view on the risk to herself or others, were she not detained in hospital? Has she any ideas on how those risks could best be managed?

- Has Adele expressed any views, either now or previously, on similar circumstances in the past and how they were managed? Does Adele have any views on what worked and what did not and why?

- What are Adele's individual characteristics, her needs, aspirations and values, and how could these be supported?

- If Adele were a young man rather than a middle-aged woman, would the decision be approached differently? Is any difference justified?

**Participation principle**

- What is the best way of informing Adele of the purpose and process for undertaking the examination and of communicating the outcome? What might be the best way of explaining the reasoning for any decision that is contrary to what Adele wants?

- Does Adele want someone present to support her during the examination? Are there any valid reasons for not following her wishes?

- Are there any paid or unpaid carers, family members and friends, or anyone else, whose views ought to be sought? What does Adele think about the idea of involving these people?

- Does Adele, or do any of the other people to be consulted, have any particular communication needs which need to be taken into account and addressed?

- Has Adele been reminded of her right to an independent mental health advocate (IMHA) to enable support through this process?

- Has the responsible clinician considered requesting an IMHA to contact Adele directly?

**Effectiveness, efficiency and equity principle**

- Are there resources in the community to safely help Adele manage her mental health?

- Based on the available evidence, how likely is a treatment programme to work? Would there be a benefit for Adele's condition and her general well-being and that of her family?

## 30. FUNCTIONS OF HOSPITAL MANAGERS

**4–285**    30.1 This chapter gives general guidance on the responsibilities of hospital managers under the Act, and on specific powers and duties not addressed in other chapters, including those in relation to transfers between hospitals, victims of crime, patients' correspondence and references to the Tribunal.

### Identification of hospital managers (Reference Guide 1.32–1.35)

**4–286**    30.2 In England, NHS hospitals are managed by NHS trusts, NHS foundation trusts and primary care trusts (PCTs). For these hospitals, the trusts themselves are defined as the hospital managers for the purposes of the Act. In an independent hospital, the person or persons in whose name the hospital is registered are the hospital managers.

30.3 It is the hospital managers who have the authority to detain patients under the Act. They have the primary responsibility for seeing that the requirements of the Act are followed. In particular, they must ensure that patients are detained only as the Act allows, that their treatment and care accord fully with its provisions, and that they are fully informed of, and are supported in exercising, their statutory rights.

30.4 As managers of what the Act terms "responsible hospitals", hospital managers have equivalent responsibilities towards patients on supervised community treatment (SCT), even if those patients are not actually being treated at one of their hospitals.

30.5 In practice, most of the decisions of the hospital managers are actually taken by individuals (or groups of individuals) on their behalf. In particular, decisions about discharge from detention and SCT are taken by panels of people ("managers' panels") specifically selected for the role.

30.6 In this chapter, unless otherwise stated, "hospital managers" includes anyone authorised to take decisions on their behalf, except managers' panels.

### Exercise of hospital managers' functions (Reference Guide 12.5–12.13 (detention) and 15.7–15.8 (SCT))

**4–287**    30.7 Special rules apply to the exercise of the hospital managers' power to discharge patients from detention or SCT. In broad terms, this power can be delegated only to managers' panels made up of people (sometimes called "associate hospital managers") appointed specifically for the purpose who are not officers or employees of the organisation concerned. For guidance on this power see **chapter 31.**

30.8 Otherwise, hospital managers (meaning the organisation, or individual, in charge of the hospital) may arrange for their functions to be carried out, day to day, by particular people on their behalf. In some cases, regulations say they must do so.

30.9 The arrangements for who is authorised to take which decisions should be set out in a scheme of delegation. If the hospital managers are an organisation, that scheme of delegation should be approved by a resolution of the body itself. Unless the Act or the regulations say otherwise, organisations may delegate their functions under the Act to any one and in any way which their constitution or (in the case of NHS bodies) NHS legislation allows them to delegate their other functions.

30.10 Organisations (or individuals) in charge of hospitals retain responsibility for the performance of all hospital managers' functions exercised on their behalf and must ensure that the people acting on their behalf are competent to do so. It is for the organisation (or individual) concerned to decide what arrangements to put in place to monitor and review the way that functions under the Act are exercised on its behalf—but many organisations establish a Mental Health Act steering or scrutiny group especially for that task.

## Specific powers and duties of hospital managers

*Admission*

30.11 It is the hospital managers' responsibility to ensure that the authority for **4–288** detaining patients is valid and that any relevant admission documents are in order. For guidance on the receipt, scrutiny and rectification of documents see **chapter 13.**

30.12 Where a patient is admitted under the Act on the basis of an application by their nearest relative, the hospital managers must request the relevant local social services authority (LSSA) to provide them with the social circumstances report required by section 14 **(Reference Guide 12.34–12.35).**

*Transfer between hospitals* **(Reference Guide chapter 13)**

30.13 The Act allows hospital managers to authorise the transfer of most **4–289** detained patients from one hospital to another in accordance with regulations. (For restricted patients, the consent of the Secretary of State for Justice is also required.) Decisions on transfers may be delegated to an officer, who could (but need not be) the patient's responsible clinician.

30.14 The managers do not have the power to insist that another hospital accepts a patient, nor to insist that a proposed new placement is funded by a PCT or anyone else. Decisions about funding should be taken in the same way as for any other patient.

30.15 People authorising transfers on the hospital managers' behalf should ensure that there are good reasons for the transfer and that the needs and interests of the patient have been considered. Transfers are potentially an interference with a patient's right to respect for privacy and family life under Article 8 of the European Convention on Human Rights, and care should be taken to act compatibly with the Convention when deciding whether to authorise a transfer.

30.16 Valid reasons for transfer might be clinical—the need, for example, for the patient to be in a more suitable environment or in a specialist facility. They could also be to move the patient closer to home. In some cases, a transfer may be unavoidable, because the hospital is no longer able to offer the care that the patient needs.

30.17 Wherever practicable, patients should be involved in the process leading to any decision to transfer them to another hospital. It is important to explain the reasons for a proposed transfer to the patient and, where appropriate, their nearest relative and other family or friends, and to record them. Only in exceptional circumstances should patients be transferred to another hospital without warning.

30.18 Among the factors that need to be considered when deciding whether to transfer a patient are:

- whether the transfer would give the patient greater access to family or friends, or have the opposite effect;

- what effect a transfer is likely to have on the course of the patient's disorder or their recovery;

- the availability of appropriate beds at the potential receiving hospital; and

- whether a transfer would be appropriate to enable the patient to be in a more culturally suitable or compatible environment, or whether it would have the opposite effect.

30.19 Detained patients may themselves want a transfer to another hospital—in order to be nearer their family or friends, for example. Or they may have a reasonable wish to be treated by a different clinical team, which could only be met by a transfer.

30.20 The professionals involved in their care should always be prepared to discuss the possibility of a transfer, and should raise the issue themselves with the patient if they think the patient might be interested in, or benefit from, a transfer.

30.21 Requests made by, or on behalf of, patients should be recorded and given careful consideration. Every effort should be made to meet the patient's wishes. If that cannot be done, the patient (or the person who made the request on the patient's behalf) should be given a written statement of the decision and the reasons for it.

30.22 Nearest relatives' consent to transfers is not a statutory requirement. But unless the patient objects, the patient's nearest relative should normally be consulted before a patient is transferred to another hospital, and, in accordance with the regulations, they must normally be notified of the transfer.

30.23 When a patient is transferred, the documents authorising detention, including the authority for transfer, should be sent to the hospital to which the patient is transferred. The transferring hospital should retain copies of these documents.

*Transfers to guardianship* (**Reference Guide 13.35–13.39 and 19.137–19.139**)

**4–290**    30.24 Regulations allow hospital managers to authorise the transfer of most detained patients into guardianship instead, with the agreement of the relevant LSSA. This is a procedural alternative to discharging the patient from detention and then making an application for guardianship. Again, this decision may be delegated to officers, including the patient's responsible clinician.

30.25 As with transfers between hospitals, people taking decisions on behalf of hospital managers and LSSAs should ensure that there are good reasons for any transfer and that the needs and interests of the patient have been considered.

*Transfer and assignment of responsibility for SCT patients* (**Reference Guide 15.45–15.54**)

**4–291**    30.26 The managers of a hospital to which an SCT patient has been recalled may authorise the patient's transfer to another hospital during the 72-hour maximum period of recall. These decisions may be delegated in the same way as other transfer decisions described above. The people exercising this power on the managers' behalf must ensure that the needs and interests of the patient are considered before a transfer is authorised, in the same way as when considering the transfer of a detained patient.

30.27 Hospital managers may also reassign responsibility for SCT patients so that a different hospital will become the patient's responsible hospital. The same considerations apply **(Reference Guide 15.128–15.134)**.

*Information for patients and relatives*

30.28 Sections 132, 132A and 133 of the Act and regulations require hospital **4–292** managers to arrange for detained patients, SCT patients and (where relevant) their nearest relatives to be given important information about the way the Act works and about their rights. For further guidance on the exercise of these duties see **chapter 2.**

*Duties in respect of victims of crime* **(Sections 35–45 of the Domestic Violence, Crime and Victims Act 2004)**

30.29 The Domestic Violence, Crime and Victims Act 2004 places a number of **4–293** duties on hospital managers in relation to certain unrestricted Part 3 patients who have committed sexual or violent crimes. This includes liaising with victims in order to:

- advise victims if the patient's discharge is being considered or if the patient is about to be discharged;

- forward representations made by victims to people responsible for making decisions on discharge or SCT and for passing information received from those people to the victim;

- informing victims who have asked to be told, if the patient is to go onto SCT and of any conditions on the community treatment order (CTO) relating to contact with them or their family, any variation of the conditions, and the date on which the order will cease; and

- informing responsible clinicians of any representations made by the victim about the conditions attached to the CTO.

30.30 These duties complement similar arrangements for restricted Part 3 patients, which are managed by the probation service rather than hospital managers.

30.31 Separate guidance on hospital managers' duties under the Domestic Violence, Crime and Victims Act 2004 is issued by the Ministry of Justice.

*Patients' correspondence* **(Reference Guide chapter 14)**

30.32 Section 134 allows hospital managers to withhold outgoing post from **4–294** detained patients if the person to whom it is addressed has made a written request to the hospital managers, the approved clinician with overall responsibility for the patient's case, or the Secretary of State that post from the patient in question should be withheld. The fact that post has been withheld must be recorded in writing by an officer authorised by the hospital managers, and the patient must be informed in accordance with the regulations.

30.33 The managers of high-security psychiatric hospitals have wider powers under section 134 to withhold both incoming and outgoing post from patients in certain circumstances.[21] Their decisions are subject to review by the Commission. The hospital managers of high-security psychiatric hospitals should have a written policy for the exercise of these powers.

*Duty to refer cases to Tribunals* **(Reference Guide 23.1–23.15)**

**4–295** 30.34 Hospital managers are under a duty to refer a patient's case to the Tribunal in the circumstances set out in section 68 of the Act, summarised in the following table.

*Hospital managers' duties to refer cases to the Tribunal*

**4–296**

| **Hospital managers must refer the following patients** | **When** |
|---|---|
| Patients who are detained under Part 2 of the Act, and patients who were detained under Part 2 but are now SCT patients | Six months have passed since they were first detained, unless:<br>• the patient applied to the Tribunal themselves after they became a section 3 patient;<br>• the patient's nearest relative applied to the Tribunal after the patient became a section 3 patient;<br>• the patient's case was referred to the Tribunal by the Secretary of State after the patient became a section 3 patient; or<br>• the managers have already referred the patient's case to the Tribunal because their CTO was revoked (see below).<br>(If the patient is still a section 2 patient pending the outcome of an application to the county court for a change in their nearest relative, there are no exceptions.) |
| Patients who are detained under Part 2 of the Act, or were detained under Part 2 but are now SCT patients | Three years have passed since their case was last considered by the Tribunal (one year if they are under 18). |

[21] The Secretary of State for Health has also issued directions requiring the managers of these hospitals to take similar action in respect of correspondence between patients within the hospital, phone calls and items brought in for patients from outside.

| Hospital managers must refer the following patients | When |
|---|---|
| Patients detained under hospital orders, hospital directions or transfer directions under Part 3 of the Act without being subject to special restrictions, or who were detained under Part 3 of the Act but are now SCT patients | Three years have passed without their case being considered by the Tribunal (one year if they are under 18). |
| People who were SCT patients but whose CTOs have been revoked | As soon as practicable after the responsible clinician the CDO. |

Note: for these purposes:

- detention under Part 2 of the Act does not include any time spent detained under the holding powers in section 5 (see chapter 12); and

- applications to the Tribunal do not count if they are withdrawn before they are determined.

30.35 Hospitals will be able to comply properly with these duties only if they maintain full and accurate records about:

- the detention and discharge of the patients for whom they are responsible;

- applications made by those patients to the Tribunal; and

- applications and references to the Tribunal made by other people in respect of those patients.

30.36 Hospital managers should ensure that they have systems in place to alert them (or the officers to whom the function is delegated) in good time to the need to make a reference. Officers exercising this function for the managers should be familiar with the relevant requirements of the Tribunal itself and the procedural rules by which it operates.

30.37 When hospital managers are required to refer the case of an SCT patient whose CTO is revoked to the Tribunal, this must be done as soon as practicable after the CTO is revoked.

30.38 Hospital managers should from time to time audit the timeliness with which they comply with their duties to refer patients to the Tribunal.

*References by the Secretary of State for Health* (**Reference Guide 23.16–23.22**)

30.39 The Secretary of State for Health may at any time refer the case of most **4–297** detained patients, and all SCT patients, to the Tribunal. Anyone may request such a reference, and the Secretary of State will consider all such requests on their merits.

30.40 Hospital managers should consider asking the Secretary of State to make a reference in respect of any patients whose rights under Article 5(4) of the European Convention on Human Rights might otherwise be at risk of being violated because they are unable (for whatever reason) to have their cases considered by the Tribunal speedily following their initial detention or at reasonable intervals afterwards.

30.41 In particular, they should normally seek such a reference in any case where:

- a patient's detention under section 2 has been extended under section 29 of the Act pending the outcome of an application to the county court for the displacement of their nearest relative;

- the patient lacks the capacity to request a reference; and

- either the patient's case has never been considered by the Tribunal, or a significant period has passed since it was last considered.

*Hospital accommodation for children and young people* (**Reference Guide 12.30–12.33**)

**4–298**     30.42 Section 131A of the Act puts a duty on hospital managers to ensure that any children or young people aged under 18 receiving in-patient care for mental disorder in their hospitals are accommodated in an environment which is suitable for their age (subject to their needs).[22] For guidance on this see **chapter 36.** The duty applies to children and young people admitted informally to hospitals, as well as those detained under the Act.

---

**Related material**

- *The Code of Practice for Victims of Crime,* Office for Criminal Justice Reform, October 2005

- *Guidance for Clinicians—Duties to Victims under the Domestic Violence, Crime and Victims Act 2004,* Home Office Mental Health Unit, 2005

This material does not form part of the Code. It is provided for assistance only.

---

## 31. HOSPITAL MANAGERS' DISCHARGE POWER

**4–299**     31.1 This chapter gives guidance on the exercise of hospital managers' power to discharge detained and supervised community treatment (SCT) patients (**Reference Guide 12.117–12.120 (detention) and 15.115–15.117 (SCT)**).

**The power to discharge**

**4–300**     31.2 Section 23 of the Act gives hospital managers the power to discharge most detained patients and all SCT patients. They may not discharge patients remanded to hospital under sections 35 or 36 of the Act or subject to interim hospital orders under section 38, and they may not discharge restricted patients without the consent of the Secretary of State for Justice.

---

[22] This duty is expected to be in force from April 2010.

**Exercise of power of discharge on behalf of managers**

31.3 The hospital managers—meaning the organisation or individual in charge **4–301** of the hospital—must either consider discharge themselves or arrange for their power to be exercised on their behalf by a "managers' panel".

31.4 A managers' panel may consist of three or more people who are:

- members of the organisation in charge of the hospital (eg the chair or non-executive directors of an NHS trust); or

- members of a committee or sub-committee which is authorised for the purpose **(Section 23(4))**.

31.5 In the case of an NHS foundation trust, a panel can consist of any three or more people appointed for the purpose by the trust whether or not they are members of the trust itself or any of its committees or sub-committees **(Section 23(6))**.

31.6 In NHS bodies (including NHS foundation trusts), none of the people on managers' panels may be employees (or, in the case of NHS trusts, officers) of the body concerned. (People do not become employees or officers simply because they are paid a fee for serving on managers' panels.) **(Section 23(5))**

31.7 In independent hospitals, managers' panels should not include people who are on the staff of the hospital or who have a financial interest in it.

31.8 In all cases, the board (or the equivalent) of the organisation concerned should ensure that the people it appoints properly understand their role and the working of the Act. It should also ensure that they receive suitable training to equip them to understand the law, work with patients and professionals, reach sound judgements and properly record their decisions. This should include training in how risk is assessed and how to comprehend a risk assessment report.

31.9 Appointments to managers' panels should be made for a fixed period. Reappointment (if permitted) should not be automatic and should be preceded by a review of the person's continuing suitability.

**When to review detention or SCT**

31.10 Hospital managers should ensure that all relevant patients are aware that **4–302** they may ask to be discharged by the hospital managers and of the distinction between this and their right to apply for a Tribunal hearing.

31.11 Hospital managers:

- may undertake a review of whether or not a patient should be discharged at any time at their discretion;

- must undertake a review if the patient's responsible clinician submits to them a report under section 20 of the Act renewing detention or under section 20A extending SCT;

- should consider holding a review when they receive a request from (or on behalf of) a patient; and

- should consider holding a review when the responsible clinician makes a report to them under section 25 barring an order by the nearest relative to discharge a patient.

31.12 In the last two cases, when deciding whether to consider the case, managers' panels are entitled to take into account whether the Tribunal has recently considered the patient's case or is due to do so in the near future.

31.13 It is desirable that a managers' panel considers a report made under section 20 or section 20A and decides whether to exercise its discharge power, before the current period of detention or SCT ends. However, the responsible clinician's report itself provides authority for the patient's continued detention or SCT, even if a managers' panel has not yet considered the case or reached a decision.

### Criteria to be applied

**4–303**   31.14 The Act does not define specific criteria that the hospital managers must use when considering discharge. The essential yardstick is whether the grounds for continued detention or continued SCT under the Act are satisfied. To ensure that this is done in a systematic and consistent way, managers' panels should consider the questions set out below, in the order stated.

31.15 For patients detained for assessment under sections 2 or 4 of the Act:

- is the patient still suffering from mental disorder?
- if so, is the disorder of a nature or degree which warrants the continued detention of the patient in hospital?
- ought the detention to continue in the interests of the patient's health or safety or for the protection of other people?

31.16 For other detained patients:

- is the patient still suffering from mental disorder?
- if so, is the disorder of a nature or degree which makes treatment in a hospital appropriate?
- is continued detention for medical treatment necessary for the patient's health or safety or for the protection of other people?
- is appropriate medical treatment available for the patient?

31.17 For patients on SCT:

- is the patient still suffering from mental disorder?
- if so, is the disorder of a nature or degree which makes it appropriate for the patient to receive medical treatment?
- if so, is it necessary in the interests of the patient's health or safety or the protection of other people that the patient should receive such treatment?
- is it still necessary for the responsible clinician to be able to exercise the power to recall the patient to hospital, if that is needed?
- is appropriate medical treatment available for the patient?

31.18 If three or more members of the panel (who between them make up a majority) are satisfied from the evidence presented to them that the answer to any of the questions set out above is "no", the patient should be discharged.

31.19 Where the answer to all the relevant questions above is "yes", but the responsible clinician has made a report under section 25 barring a nearest relative's attempt to discharge the patient, the managers should also consider the following question:

- would the patient, if discharged, be likely to act in a manner that is dangerous to other people or to themselves?

31.20 This last question provides a more stringent test for continuing detention or SCT (see **chapter 29**).

31.21 If three or more members of the panel (being a majority) disagree with the responsible clinician and decide that the answer to this question is "no", the panel should usually discharge the patient. However, the hospital managers retain a residual discretion not to discharge in these cases, so panels should always consider whether there are exceptional reasons why the patient should not be discharged.

31.22 In all cases, hospital managers have discretion to discharge patients even if the criteria for continued detention or SCT are met. Managers' panels must therefore always consider whether there are other reasons why the patient should be discharged despite the answers to the questions set out above.

**Procedure for reviewing detention or SCT**

31.23 The Act does not define the procedure for reviewing a patient's detention **4–304** or SCT. However, the exercise of this power is subject to the general law and to public law duties which arise from it. Hospital managers' conduct of reviews must satisfy the fundamental legal requirements of fairness, reasonableness and lawfulness. Managers' panels should therefore:

- adopt and apply a procedure which is fair and reasonable;

- not make irrational decisions—that is, decisions which no managers' panel, properly directing itself as to the law and on the available information, could have made; and

- not act unlawfully—that is, contrary to the provisions of the Act and any other legislation (including the Human Rights Act 1998 and relevant equality and anti-discrimination legislation).

*Conduct of reviews where detention or SCT is contested*

31.24 Reviews should be conducted in such a way as to ensure that the case for **4–305** continuing the patient's detention or SCT is properly considered against the questions set out above and in the light of all the relevant evidence. This means that managers' panels need to have before them sufficient information about the patient's past history of care and treatment, and details of any future plans. The main source of this is likely to be the patient's documentation and care plan under the Care Programme Approach (CPA) (or its equivalent). It is essential that panels are fully informed about any history of violence or self-harm and that a recent risk assessment is provided to the panel.

31.25 In advance of the hearing, managers' panels should be provided with written reports from the patient's responsible clinician and from other key individuals directly involved in the patient's care who they think are appropriate, such as the patient's care co-ordinator, named nurse, social worker, occupational therapist or clinical psychologist.

31.26 The patient should be provided with copies of the reports as soon as they are available, unless (in the light of any recommendation made by their authors) panels are of the opinion that disclosing the information would be likely to cause serious harm to the physical or mental health of the patient or any other individual. The patient's legal or other representative should also receive copies of these reports.

31.27 Reports should be provided in good time so that patients and their representatives can consider them and, where relevant, draw the panels' attention to any apparent inaccuracies. Any decision to withhold a report (in whole or part) should be recorded, with reasons.

31.28 The nearest relative should normally be informed when managers' panels are to consider a patient's case, unless the patient objects, subject to the normal considerations about involving nearest relatives (see **paragraphs 2.27–2.33**).

31.29 Panels should be prepared to consider the views of the patient's relatives and carers, and other people who know the patient well, either at the patient's request or where such people offer their views on their own initiative. Relatives, carers and any other relevant people may be invited to put their views to the managers' panel in person. If the patient objects to this, a suitable member of the professional care team should be asked to include the person's views in their report.

31.30 The report submitted by the responsible clinician should cover the history of the patient's care and treatment and details of their care plan, including all risk assessments. Where the review is being held because the responsible clinician has made a report under section 20, 20A or 21 B renewing detention or extending SCT, panels should also have a copy of the report itself before them. This should be supplemented by a record of the consultation undertaken by the responsible clinician in accordance with those sections before making the report. The written reports should be considered by the panel alongside documentation compiled under the CPA (or its equivalent).

31.31 Where relevant, panels should also have in front of them any order made by the responsible clinician under section 25 barring a patient's discharge by their nearest relative.

31.32 The procedure for the conduct of any hearing is for managers' panels themselves to decide, but generally it needs to balance informality against the rigour demanded by the importance of the task. Key points are:

- the patient should be given a full opportunity, and any necessary help, to explain why they should be no longer be detained or on SCT;

- the patient should be allowed to be accompanied by a representative of their own choosing to help in putting their point of view to the panel;

- the patient should also be allowed to have a relative, friend or advocate attend to support them; and

- the responsible clinician and other professionals should be asked to give their views on whether the patient's continued detention or SCT is justified and to explain the grounds on which those views are based.

31.33 It is also for hospital managers themselves to decide where hearings should take place. For SCT patients, and patients currently on leave of absence from hospital, the hospital itself may not be the most convenient or acceptable place for the patient. Hospital managers should be prepared to consider whether there are more appropriate locations which it would be feasible to use.

31.34 The patient and the other people giving views to the panel should, if the patient wishes it, be able to hear each other's statements to the panel and to put questions to each other, unless the panel believes that would be likely to cause serious harm to the physical or mental health of the patient or any other individual. Unless, exceptionally, it is considered too unsafe, patients should always be offered the opportunity of speaking to the panel alone (with or without their representative and anyone else they have asked to attend to support them at the hearing).

31.35 Members of managers' panels will not normally be qualified to form clinical assessments of their own. They must give full weight to the views of all the professionals concerned in the patient's care. If there is a divergence of views among the professionals about whether the patient meets the clinical grounds for continued detention or SCT, managers' panels should consider adjourning to seek further medical or other professional advice.

31.36 In considering the questions set out earlier in this chapter and deciding in the light of them whether or not to discharge the patient from detention, managers' panels need to consider very carefully the implications for the patient's subsequent care. Before a managers' panel considers a case, the responsible clinician, in consultation with the multi-disciplinary team, should have considered what services and other arrangements might be put in place for the patient if discharged and whether those arrangements would be sufficient to make continued detention or SCT (as the case may be) no longer necessary.

31.37 The presence or absence of adequate community care arrangements may be critical in deciding whether continued detention (in particular) is necessary. If managers' panels believe they have not been provided with sufficient information about arrangements that could be made were the patient discharged, they should consider adjourning and requesting further information.

31.38 If panels conclude that the patient ought to be discharged, but practical steps to put after-care in place need to be taken first, they may adjourn the panel for a brief period to enable that to happen before formally discharging the patient. Alternatively, they may order the patient's discharge from a specified date in the near future. They may not discharge patients provisionally but defer the final decision to discharge until certain conditions have been met.

*Uncontested renewals*

31.39 If a patient's detention or SCT is renewed or extended by their responsible clinician, the hospital managers must always decide whether the patient should be discharged anyway, even if the patient has indicated that they do not wish to challenge the renewal or extension. **4–306**

31.40 It is for hospital managers to decide whether to adopt a different procedure in uncontested cases. Some hospitals, as a matter of policy, do not differentiate between contested and uncontested cases.

31.41 Where a different procedure is used, patients should be interviewed by at least one member of the managers' panel considering their case, if they request it, or if the panel thinks it desirable after reading the renewal or extension report.

31.42 Otherwise, managers' panels may consider the case on the papers, if they wish. But they should hold a full hearing if they have reason to suspect that the patient may, in fact, wish to be discharged, or there are prima facie grounds to think that the responsible clinician's decision to renew detention or extend SCT is not correct. The mere fact that patients have not said they object to the renewal or extension should not be taken as evidence that they agree with it, or that it is the correct decision.

*Decisions*

**4–307**   31.43 Hospital managers have a common law duty to give reasons for their decisions. The decisions of managers' panels, and the reasons for them, should be fully recorded at the end of each review. The decision should be communicated as soon as practicable, both orally and in writing, to the patient, to the nearest relative (where relevant) and to the professionals concerned.

31.44 If the patient is not to be discharged, at least one member of the panel should offer to see the patient to explain in person the reasons for the decision. Copies of the papers relating to the review, and the formal record of the decision, should be kept in the patient's notes.

**NHS patients treated by independent hospitals (Reference Guide 12.121–12.122 (detention) and 15.118–15.119 (SCT))**

**4–308**   31.45 NHS bodies have the power to discharge:

- NHS patients who are detained in independent hospitals; and

- NHS SCT patients whose responsible hospital is an independent hospital.

This is in addition to the power of the managers of the independent hospitals themselves. The NHS body concerned is the one which has contracted with the independent hospital in respect of the patient.

31.46 NHS bodies may take the decision themselves, delegate it to a panel of three or more members of their board or of a committee or sub-committee which is approved for that purpose, or (in the case of an NHS foundation trust) delegate it to any three or more people appointed for the purpose. The members of the panel must not be employees of the body (or officers, if the body is an NHS trust).

31.47 As a general rule, NHS bodies are entitled to expect that the managers' panel arrangements in independent hospitals will be sufficient. They do not need to arrange a panel hearing of their own simply because they are requested to do so. But they (or a panel on their behalf) must consider whether there are any special circumstances which would make it unfair to a patient for them not to hold a hearing. As a result, NHS bodies contracting with independent hospitals should take steps to satisfy themselves that the independent hospital's own arrangements for taking discharge decisions are adequate to protect the rights of NHS patients.

## 32. THE TRIBUNAL

32.1 This chapter provides guidance on the role of the Tribunal[23] and related **4–309** duties on hospital managers and others.

### Purpose of the Tribunal (Reference Guide chapters 20 and 21)

32.2 The Tribunal is an independent judicial body. Its main purpose is to review **4–310** the cases of detained, conditionally discharged, and supervised community treatment (SCT) patients under the Act and to direct the discharge of any patients where it thinks it appropriate. It also considers applications for discharge from guardianship.

32.3 The Tribunal provides a significant safeguard for patients who have had their liberty curtailed under the Act. Those giving evidence at hearings should do what they can to help enable Tribunal hearings to be conducted in a professional manner, which includes having regard to the patient's wishes and feelings and ensuring that the patient feels as comfortable with the proceedings as possible.

32.4 It is for those who believe that a patient should continue to be detained or remain an SCT patient to prove their case, not for the patient to disprove it. They will therefore need to present the Tribunal with sufficient evidence to support continuing liability to detention or SCT. Clinical and social reports form the backbone of this evidence. Care should be given to ensure that all information is as up to date as possible to avoid adjournment. In order to support the Tribunal in making its decision all information should be clear and concise.

### Informing the patient and nearest relative of rights to apply to the Tribunal

32.5 Hospital managers and the local social services authority (LSSA) are **4–311** under a duty to take steps to ensure that patients understand their rights to apply for a Tribunal hearing. Hospital managers and the LSSA should also advise patients of their entitlement to free legal advice and representation. They should do both whenever:

- patients are first detained in hospital, received into guardianship or discharged to SCT;

- their detention or guardianship is renewed or SCT is extended; and

- their status under the Act changes—for example, if they move from detention under section 2 to detention under section 3 or if their community treatment order is revoked.

---

[23] At the time of publication, the Tribunal is the Mental Health Review Tribunal (MHRT). However, the MHRT is intended to be replaced in England by a new First-Tier Tribunal established under the Tribunals, Courts and Enforcement Act 2007. There is also intended to be a right of appeal, on a point of law, from that Tribunal to a new Upper Tribunal.

32.6 Unless the patient requests otherwise, the information should normally also be given to their nearest relative (subject to the normal considerations about involving nearest relatives see—**paragraphs 2.27–2.33**).

32.7 Hospital managers and professionals should enable detained patients to be visited by their legal representatives at any reasonable time. This is particularly important where visits are necessary to discuss a Tribunal application. Where the patient consents, legal representatives and independent doctors should be given prompt access to the patient's medical records. Delays in providing access can hold up Tribunal proceedings and should be avoided.

32.8 In connection with an application (or a reference) to the Tribunal, an independent doctor or approved clinician authorised by (or on behalf of) a patient has a right to visit and examine the patient in private. Those doctors and approved clinicians also have a right to inspect any records relating to the patient's detention, treatment and (where relevant) after-care under section 117. Where nearest relatives have a right to apply to the Tribunal, they too may authorise independent doctors or approved clinicians in the same way. The patient's consent is not required for authorised doctors or approved clinicians to see their records, and they should be given prompt access to the records they wish to see (**Sections 67 and 76**).

**Hospital managers' duty to refer cases to the Tribunal**

**4–312**    32.9 The hospital managers have various duties to refer patients to the Tribunal. They may also request the Secretary of State to refer a patient, and there are certain circumstances where they should always consider doing so. (See **chapter 31**.)

**Reports—general**

**4–313**    32.10 Responsible authorities (that is the managers of the relevant hospital or the LSSA responsible for a guardianship patient) should be familiar with the Tribunal's rules and procedures. The rules place a statutory duty on the responsible authority to provide the Tribunal with a statement of relevant facts together with certain reports.

32.11 It is important that documents and information are provided in accordance with the Tribunal's rules and procedures in good time for any Tribunal hearing. Missing, out-of-date or inadequate reports can lead to adjournments or unnecessarily long hearings. Where responsible clinicians, social workers or other professionals are required to provide reports, they should do this promptly and within the statutory timescale.

32.12 In the case of a restricted patient, if the opinion of the responsible clinician or other professional changes from what was recorded in the original Tribunal report(s), it is vital that this is communicated in writing, prior to the hearing, to the Tribunal office and the Mental Health Unit of the Ministry of Justice to allow them the opportunity to prepare a supplementary statement.

32.13 If a Tribunal panel feels that it needs more information on any report, it may request it, either in the form of a supplementary report or by questioning a witness at the hearing itself.

32.14 In some circumstances, the Tribunal will not sit immediately after receiving the report. In these cases, the report writers should consider whether anything in the patient's circumstances have changed and should produce a concise update to the report. This is especially important if the patient's status changes—for example, if a patient becomes an SCT patient or moves from detention under section 2 to section 3.

32.15 In those cases, the application will need to be considered under the new circumstances, and the report will need to provide a justification for continued detention or liability to recall under the new circumstances. The Tribunal may ask the author of the report to talk through it, so it is good practice for the authors to re-familiarise themselves with the content of any report before the hearing. If the author of the report is unable to attend, it is important that anyone attending in their place should, wherever possible, also have a good knowledge of the patient's case.

32.16 Hospital managers (or LSSAs in guardianship cases) should ensure that the Tribunal is notified immediately of any events or changes that might have a bearing on Tribunal proceedings—for example, where a patient is discharged or one of the parties is unavailable.

32.17 If the author of a report prepared for the Tribunal is aware of information they do not think the patient should see, they should follow the Tribunal's procedure for the submission of such information. Ultimately, it is for the Tribunal to decide what should be disclosed to the patient.

32.18 Reports should be sent to the appropriate Tribunal office, preferably by secure e-mail, otherwise by post.

32.19 The responsible authority must ensure that up-to-date reports prepared specifically for the Tribunal are provided in accordance with the Tribunal's rules and procedures. In practice, this will normally include a report completed by the patient's responsible clinician. Where the patient is under the age of 18 and the responsible clinician is not a child and adolescent mental health service (CAMHS) specialist, hospital managers should ensure that a report is prepared by a CAMHS specialist.

32.20 Where possible, reports should be written by the professionals with the best overall knowledge of the patient's situation.

32.21 The reports should be submitted in good time to enable all parties, including the Secretary of State in restricted cases, to fulfil their responsibilities.

**Medical examination**
32.22 A medical member of the Tribunal may want to examine the patient at **4–314** any time before the hearing. Hospital managers must ensure that the medical member can see patients who are in hospital in private and examine their medical records. It is important that the patient is told of the visit in advance so that they can be available when the medical member visits.

**Withdrawing the application**
32.23 A request to withdraw an application may be made by the applicant in **4–315** accordance with the Tribunal rules. The applicant may not withdraw a reference made by the Secretary of State.

32.24 An application will also be considered to be withdrawn if the patient is discharged. If this happens outside office hours, someone acting on behalf of the hospital managers (or the LSSA, if it is a guardianship case) should contact the Tribunal office as soon as possible, to inform them. For detained patients, this could be done by a member of the ward staff.

**Representation**

**4–316**　32.25 Hospital managers (or LSSAs, as the case may be) should inform patients of their right to present their own case to the Tribunal and their right to be represented by someone else. Staff should be available to help patients make an application. This is especially important for SCT patients who may not have daily contact with professionals.

**The hearing**

*Attendance at hearings*

**4–317**　32.26 Normally, a patient will be present throughout their Tribunal hearing. Patients do not need to attend their hearing, but professionals should encourage them to attend unless they judge that it would be detrimental to their health or wellbeing.

32.27 It is important that the patient's responsible clinician attends the Tribunal, supported by other staff involved in the patient's care where appropriate, as their evidence is crucial for making the case for the patient's continued detention or SCT under the Act. Wherever possible, the responsible clinician, and other relevant staff, should attend for the full hearing so that they are aware of all the evidence made available to the Tribunal and of the Tribunal's decision and reasons.

32.28 A responsible clinician can attend the hearing solely as a witness or as the nominated representative of the responsible authority. As a representative of the responsible authority, the responsible clinician has the ability to call and cross-examine witnesses and to make submissions to the Tribunal. However, this may not always be desirable where it is envisaged that the responsible clinician will have to continue working closely with a patient.

32.29 Responsible authorities should therefore consider whether they want to send an additional person to represent their interests, allowing the responsible clinician to appear solely as a witness. Responsible clinicians should be clear in what capacity they are attending the Tribunal, as they may well be asked this by the panel.

32.30 It is important that other people who prepare reports submitted by the responsible authority attend the hearing to provide further up-to-date information about the patient, including (where relevant) their home circumstances and the after-care available in the event of a decision to discharge the patient.

32.31 Increasingly, Tribunal hearings find it helpful to speak to a nurse, particularly a nurse who knows the patient. It is often helpful for a nurse who knows the patient to accompany them to the hearing.

32.32 Hospital managers should ensure that all professionals who attend Tribunal hearings are adequately prepared.

**Accommodation for hearings**

**4–318**　32.33 The managers of a hospital in which a Tribunal hearing is to be held should provide suitable accommodation for that purpose. The hearing room should be private, quiet, clean and adequately sized and furnished. It should not contain confidential information about other patients. If the room is also used for other purposes, care should be taken to ensure that any equipment (such as a video camera or a two-way mirror) would not have a disturbing effect on the patient.

32.34 The patient should have access to a separate room in which to hold any private discussions that are necessary—for example, with their representative—as should the Tribunal members, so that they can discuss their decision.

32.35 Where a patient is being treated in the community, the hospital managers should consider whether a hospital venue is appropriate. They may wish to discuss alternatives with the Tribunal office.

### Interpretation

32.36 Where necessary, the Tribunal will provide, free of charge, interpretation **4–319** services for patients and their representatives. Where patients or their representatives are hard of hearing or have speech difficulties (or both), the Tribunal will provide such services of sign language interpreters, lip speakers or palantypists as may be necessary. Hospital managers and LSSAs should inform the Tribunal well in advance if they think any such services might be necessary.

### Communication of the decision

32.37 The Tribunal will normally communicate its decision to all parties orally **4–320** at the end of the hearing. Provided it is feasible to do so, and the patient wishes it, the Tribunal will speak to them personally. Otherwise, the decision will be given to the patient's representative (if they have one). If the patient is unrepresented, and it is not feasible to discuss matters with them after the hearing, the hospital managers or LSSA should ensure that they are told the decision as soon as possible. Copies of the decision can be left at a hospital on the day of the hearing. All parties to the hearing should receive a written copy of the reasons for the decision.

### Complaints

32.38 Complaints from users about the Tribunal should be sent to the Tribunal **4–321** office. The Tribunal has procedures in place to deal with complaints promptly.

### Further information on the Tribunal

32.39 The Tribunal itself publishes further information and guidance about its **4–322** procedures and operations.

## 33. PATIENTS CONCERNED WITH CRIMINAL PROCEEDINGS

33.1 This chapter offers guidance on the use of the Act to arrange treatment for **4–323** mentally disordered people who come into contact with the criminal justice system **(Reference Guide chapters 3–11)**.

### Assessment for potential admission to hospital

33.2 People who are subject to criminal proceedings have the same rights to **4–324** psychiatric assessment and treatment as anyone else. Any person who is in police or prison custody or before the courts charged with a criminal offence and who is in need of medical treatment for mental disorder should be considered for admission to hospital.

33.3 Wherever possible, people who appear to the court to be mentally disordered should have their treatment needs considered at the earliest possible opportunity, by the court mental health assessment scheme where there is one.

Such people may be at greatest risk of self-harm while in custody. Prompt access to specialist treatment may prevent significant deterioration in their condition and is likely to assist in a speedier trial process, helping to avoid longer-term harm or detention in an unsuitable environment.

33.4 If criminal proceedings are discontinued, it may be appropriate for the relevant local social services authority (LSSA) to arrange for an approved mental health professional (AMHP) to consider making an application for admission under Part 2 of the Act.

33.5 A prison healthcare centre is not a hospital within the meaning of the Act. The rules in Part 4 of the Act about medical treatment of detained patients do not apply and treatment cannot be given there under the Act without the patient's consent (see **chapter 23**).

### Agency responsibilities
**4–325**   33.6 Primary care trusts (PCTs) should:

- provide the courts, in response to a request under section 39 of the Act, with comprehensive information on the range of facilities available for the admission of patients subject to the criminal justice process. In particular, PCTs should provide the courts with comprehensive information regarding child and adolescent mental health service (CAMHS) beds that are (or could be made) available for patients;

- appoint a named person to respond to requests for information; and

- ensure that prompt medical assessment of defendants is provided to assist in the speedy completion of the trial process and the most suitable disposal for the offender.

33.7 Section 39A requires an LSSA to inform the court, if requested, whether it, or any person approved by it, is willing to receive an offender into guardianship and how the guardian's powers would be exercised. LSSAs should appoint a named person to respond to requests from the courts about mental health services provided in the community, including under guardianship.

### Assessment by a doctor
**4–326**   33.8 A doctor who is asked to provide evidence in relation to a possible admission under Part 3 of the Act should bear in mind that the request is not for a general report on the defendant's condition but for advice on whether or not the patient should be diverted from prison by way of a hospital order (or a community order with a mental health treatment requirement under criminal justice legislation).

33.9 Doctors should:

- identify themselves to the person being assessed, explain who has requested the report and make clear the limits of confidentiality in relation to the report. They should explain that any information disclosed, and the medical opinion, could be relevant not only to medical disposal by the court but also to the imposition of a punitive sentence, or to its length; and

- request relevant pre-sentence reports, the Inmate Medical Record, if there is one, and previous psychiatric reports, as well as relevant documentation regarding the alleged offence. If any of this information is not available, the doctor's report should say so clearly.

33.10 The doctor, or one of them if two doctors are preparing reports, should have access to a bed, or take responsibility for referring the case to another clinician who does, if they propose to recommend admission to hospital. In the case of a defendant under the age of 18, the doctor should ideally have specialist knowledge of CAMHS and the needs of young people.

33.11 The doctor should, where possible, identify and access other independent sources of information about the person's previous history (including convictions). This should include information from GP records, previous psychiatric treatment and patterns of behaviour.

33.12 Assessment for admission of the patient is the responsibility of the doctor, but other members of the clinical team who would be involved with the person's care and treatment should also be consulted. A multidisciplinary assessment should usually be undertaken if admission to hospital is likely to be recommended. The doctor should also contact the person who is preparing a pre-sentence report, especially if psychiatric treatment is recommended as a condition of a community order.

33.13 In cases where the doctor cannot state with confidence at the time of sentencing whether a hospital order will be appropriate, they should consider recommending an interim hospital order under section 38 of the Act. This order provides for the person to be admitted to hospital for up to 12 weeks (which may be extended for further periods of up to 28 days to a maximum total period of 12 months) so that the court can reach a conclusion on the most appropriate and effective disposal.

**Independent medical assessment**

33.14 A patient who is remanded to hospital for a report (section 35) or for **4–327** treatment (section 36) is entitled to obtain, at their own expense, or where applicable through legal aid, an independent report on their mental condition from a doctor or other clinician of their choosing, for the purpose of applying to court for the termination of the remand. The hospital managers should help in the exercise of this right by enabling the patient to contact a suitably qualified and experienced solicitor or other adviser.

**Reports to the court**

33.15 Clinical opinion is particularly important in helping courts to determine **4–328** the sentence to be passed. In particular, it will help to inform the decision whether to divert the offender from punishment by way of a hospital order, or whether a prison sentence is the most suitable disposal.

33.16 A medical report for the court should set out:

- the material on which the report is based;
- how that material relates to the opinion given;
- where relevant, how the opinion may relate to any other trial issue;

- factors relating to the presence of mental disorder that may affect the risk that the patient poses to themselves or to others, including the risk of re-offending; and

- if admission to hospital is recommended, what, if any, special treatment or security is recommended and whether the doctor represents an organisation that is able to provide what is required.

The report should not speculate about guilt or innocence.

33.17 Section 157 of the Criminal Justice Act 2003 requires the court to obtain a medical report before passing a custodial sentence other than one fixed by law. Before passing such a sentence, the court must consider any information before it which relates to the offender's mental condition and the likely effect of such a sentence on that condition and on any treatment that may be available for it.

33.18 It may, therefore, be appropriate to include recommendations on the disposal of the case. In making recommendations for disposal, the doctor should consider the longer-term, as well as immediate, consequences. Factors to be taken into account include:

- whether the court may wish to make a hospital order subject to special restrictions;

- whether, for restricted patients, the order should designate admission to a named unit within the hospital;

- whether, in the event of the court concluding that a prison sentence is appropriate, the offender should initially be admitted to hospital by way of a hospital direction under section 45A; and

- whether a community order with a mental health treatment requirement may be appropriate.

33.19 Where an offender is made subject to special restrictions ("restricted patients"), the court, or the Secretary of State for Justice in some circumstances, may specify that the person be detained in a named unit within a hospital. This is to ensure an appropriate level of security.

33.20 A named hospital unit can be any part of a hospital which is treated as a separate unit. It will be for the court (or the Secretary of State, as the case may be) to define what is meant in each case where it makes use of the power. Admission to a named unit will mean that the consent of the Secretary of State will be required for any leave of absence or transfer from the named unit, whether the transfer is to another part of the same hospital or to another hospital.

33.21 The need to consider the longer-term implications of a recommended disposal is particularly important where an extended or indeterminate sentence for public protection is indicated under the Criminal Justice Act 2003. Either a hospital order under section 37 or attachment of a hospital direction to the prison sentence under section 45A is available to the court. Discretion lies with the court.

33.22 A hospital order, with or without restrictions, diverts the offender from punishment to treatment. There is no tariff to serve, and the period of detention will be determined by the disorder and the risk of harm which attaches to it.

33.23 A hospital direction, by contrast, accompanies a prison sentence and means that, from the start of the sentence, the offender will be managed in hospital in the same way as a prisoner who has been transferred to hospital subject to special restrictions under sections 47 and 49 of the Act (see **paragraph 33.34**). The responsible clinician can propose transfer to prison to the Secretary of State for Justice at any time before the prisoner's release date if, in their opinion, no further treatment is necessary or likely to be effective.

## Availability of places

33.24 If the medical evidence is that the person needs treatment in hospital, but **4–329** the medical witness cannot identify a suitable facility where the person could be admitted immediately, they should seek advice from the PCT for the person's home area. If the person has no permanent address, responsibility lies with the PCT for the area where they are registered with a GP or, if they are not registered with a GP, where the offence was committed for which sentence is being passed.

## Transport to and from court

33.25 For patients remanded to hospital under sections 35 or 36 of the Act, or **4–330** subject to a hospital order or an interim hospital order, the court has the power to direct who is to be responsible for conveying the defendant from the court to the receiving hospital. In practice, when remand orders are first made, patients are usually returned to the holding prison, and arrangements are then made to admit them to hospital within the statutory period.

33.26 When a patient has been admitted on remand or is subject to an interim hospital order, it is the responsibility of the hospital to return the patient to court as required. The court should give adequate notice of hearings. The hospital should liaise with the court in plenty of time to confirm the arrangements for escorting the patient to and from the court. The hospital will be responsible for providing a suitable escort for the patient when travelling from the hospital to the court and should plan for the provision of necessary staff to do this. The assistance of the police may be requested, if necessary. If possible, and having regard to the needs of the patient, medical or nursing staff should remain with the patient on court premises, even though legal accountability while the patient is detained for hearings remains with the court.

33.27 For further guidance on conveyance of patients under the Act, see **chapter 11**.

## Treatment without consent—patients remanded for report

33.28 The rules in Part 4 of the Act about medical treatment of detained patients **4–331** do not apply to patients remanded to hospital under section 35 for a report on their mental condition. As a result, treatment can be administered only with their consent, or, in the case of a patient aged 16 or over who lacks capacity to consent, in accordance with the Mental Capacity Act 2005 (see **chapter 23**).

33.29 Where a patient remanded under section 35 is thought to be in need of medical treatment for mental disorder which cannot otherwise be given, the patient should be referred back to court by the clinician in charge of their care as soon as possible, with an appropriate recommendation and with an assessment of whether they are in a fit state to attend court.

33.30 If there is a delay in securing a court date, consideration should be given to whether the patient meets the criteria for detention under Part 2 of the Act to enable compulsory treatment to be given. This will be concurrent with, and not a replacement for, the remand made by the court.

### Transfer of prisoners to hospital

**4–332**    33.31 The need for in-patient treatment for a prisoner should be identified and acted upon quickly, and prison healthcare staff should make contact immediately with the responsible PCT. Responsible NHS commissioners should aim to ensure that transfers of prisoners with mental disorders are carried out within a timeframe equivalent to levels of care experienced by patients who are admitted to mental healthcare services from the community. Any unacceptable delays in transfer after identification of need should be actively monitored and investigated.

33.32 Prisoners with a diagnosis of severe and enduring mental disorder who have given informed consent to treatment should also be considered for transfer to hospital for treatment if the prison environment is considered to be contributing to their disorder. An assessment of need and regular review should consider whether the prison healthcare centre is capable of providing for the prisoner's care if they are considered to be too unwell or vulnerable to return to residential wings.

33.33 Prisoners transferred to hospital under sections 47 or 48 should not be remitted to prison unless clinical staff from the hospital and prison have met to plan the prisoner's future care. This is often called a "section 117 meeting". Appropriate staff from the receiving prison should be invited to attend the review meeting prior to the prisoner's discharge back to prison.

### Patients transferred from prison subject to special restrictions

**4–333**    33.34 When a person is transferred from prison to hospital under sections 47 or 48 as a restricted patient, it is the responsibility of the hospital managers and the responsible clinician to ensure that the patient has received, and as far as possible has understood, the letter from the Ministry of Justice explaining the roles of hospital managers and responsible clinicians in relation to restricted patients.

33.35 When prisoners have been transferred under section 47 and remain detained in hospital after their release date, they cease to be restricted patients but remain detained as if on a hospital order without restrictions. The responsible clinician's options under the Act are modified accordingly, and the patient may, for example, be discharged onto supervised community treatment (SCT).

### Further guidance on the management of restricted patients

**4–334**    33.36 Professionals should approach the Mental Health Unit of the Ministry of Justice for more detailed guidance about the management of restricted patients.

---

**Related material**

- *Notes for the Guidance of Social Supervisors—Supervision and After-care of Conditionally Discharged Restricted Patients,* Home Office, 2007

- *Mental Health Act 2007—Guidance for the Courts and Sentencing Powers for Mentally Disordered Offenders,* March 2008

- Prison Service Instruction 3/2006, which gives comprehensive guidance on the transfer process, professional roles and timescales

- Criminal Justice Act 2003

- *Guidance for Supervising Psychiatrists—Supervision and After-care of Conditionally Discharged Restricted Patients,* Home Office, June 2006

  This material does not form part of the Code. It is provided for assistance only.

---

## 34. PEOPLE WITH LEARNING DISABILITIES OR AUTISTIC SPECTRUM DISORDERS

34.1 This chapter deals with issues of particular relevance to patients with **4–335** learning disabilities, autistic spectrum disorders or both.

### Learning disabilities

34.2 For the purposes of the Act, a learning disability is defined as "a state of **4–336** arrested or incomplete development of the mind which includes significant impairment of intelligence and social functioning" **(Section 1(4))**.

34.3 Although defined as a mental disorder in this way, learning disability shares few features with the serious mental illnesses that are the most common reason for using the Act. Relatively few people with learning disabilities are detained under the Act, and where they are, it is not usually solely because of their learning disability itself.

34.4 The identification of an individual with a learning disability is a matter for clinical judgement, guided by current professional practice. Those assessing the patient must be satisfied that they display a number of characteristics. The following is general guidance in relation to the key factors in the definition of learning disability for the purposes of the Act.

*Arrested or incomplete development of mind:* An adult with arrested or incomplete development of mind is one who has experienced a significant impairment of the normal process of maturation of intellectual and social development that occurs during childhood and adolescence. By using these words in its definition of learning disability, the Act embraces the general understanding that features which qualify as a learning disability are present prior to adulthood. For the purposes of the Act, learning disability does not include people whose intellectual disorder derives from accident, injury or illness occurring after they completed normal maturation (although such conditions do fall within the definition of mental disorder in the Act).

*Significant impairment of intelligence:* The judgement as to the presence of this particular characteristic must be made on the basis of reliable and careful assessment. It is not defined rigidly by the application of an arbitrary cut-off point such as an IQ of 70.

*Significant impairment of social functioning:* Reliable and recent observations will be helpful in determining the nature and extent of social competence, preferably from a number of sources who have experience of interacting with the person in social situations, including social workers, nurses, speech and language and occupational therapists, and psychologists. Social functioning assessment tests can be a valuable tool in determining this aspect of learning disability.

34.5 It is important to assess the person as a whole. It may be appropriate to identify learning disability in someone with an IQ somewhat higher than 70 if their social functioning is severely impaired. A person with a low IQ may be correctly diagnosed as having a learning disability even if their social functioning is relatively good.

**Abnormally aggressive and seriously irresponsible behaviour (Section 1(2A) and (2B); Reference Guide 1.12–1.15)**

**4–337**     34.6 An application for detention for treatment, or for reception into guardianship, on the basis of a learning disability without another concomitant mental disorder may be made only where it is associated with one or both of the following further features:

- abnormally aggressive behaviour; or

- seriously irresponsible conduct.

34.7 Neither term is defined in the Act, and it is not possible to state with any precision exactly what type of conduct could be considered to fall into either category. It will, inevitably, depend not only on the nature of the behaviour and the circumstances in which it is exhibited, but also on the extent to which that conduct gives rise to a serious risk to the health or safety of the patient or to the health or safety of other people, or both.

34.8 In assessing whether a patient's learning disability is associated with conduct that could not only be categorised as aggressive but as abnormally so, relevant factors may include:

- when such aggressive behaviour has been observed, and how persistent and severe it has been;

- whether it has occurred without a specific trigger or seems out of proportion to the circumstances that triggered it;

- whether, and to what degree, it has in fact resulted in harm or distress to other people, or actual damage to property;

- how likely, if it has not been observed recently, it is to recur; and

- how common similar behaviour is in the population generally.

34.9 Similarly, in assessing whether a patient's learning disability is associated with conduct that is not only irresponsible but seriously so, relevant factors may include:

- whether behaviour has been observed that suggests a disregard or an inadequate regard for its serious or dangerous consequences;

- how recently such behaviour has been observed and, when it has been observed, how persistent it has been;

- how seriously detrimental to the patient, or to other people, the consequences of the behaviour were or might have been;

- whether, and to what degree, the behaviour has actually resulted in harm to the patient or the patient's interests, or in harm to other people or to damage to property; and

- if it has not been observed recently, how likely it is to recur.

34.10 When assessing whether a patient with a learning disability should be detained for treatment under the Act, it is important to establish whether any abnormally aggressive or seriously irresponsible conduct identified stems from difficulties in communication. If, for example, the patient is displaying such conduct as their only way of drawing attention to an underlying physical health problem, it would be wrong to interpret the behaviour as an indication of a worsening of their mental disorder, and treatment under the Act would not be an appropriate response.

**Practice considerations**

34.11 Unless urgent action is required, it would not be good practice to diag- **4–338** nose a patient who has a learning disability as meeting either of these additional conditions without an assessment by a consultant psychiatrist in learning disabilities and a formal psychological assessment. Ideally, this would be part of a complete appraisal by medical, nursing, social work, speech and language therapy, occupational therapy and psychology professionals with experience in learning disabilities, in consultation with a relative, friend or supporter of the patient. Wherever possible, an approved mental health professional (AMHP) who assesses a patient with a learning disability under the Act should have training and experience in working with people with learning disabilities. The patient's person-centred plan and health action plan may also inform the assessment process.

34.12 All those involved in examining, assessing, treating or taking other decisions in relation to people with learning disabilities should bear in mind that there are particular issues that people with learning disabilities may face. These include:

- incorrect assumptions that they do not have capacity to make decisions for themselves and a tendency to be over-protective;
- over-reliance on family members, both for support and for decision-making. Although the considerable expertise that family members often have should be acknowledged, this may put them in the difficult position of having to take decisions inappropriately on behalf of the patient;
- a lack of appreciation of the potential abilities of people with learning disabilities, including their potential to speak up for themselves;
- being denied access to decision-making processes, not being included in meetings about them, information made inaccessible to them, and decisions being made in their absence;
- limited life experiences to draw on when making choices; and
- their learning disability being seen as the explanation for all their physical and behavioural attributes when there may, in fact, be an underlying cause relating to a separate issue of physical or mental health (diagnostic overshadowing).

34.13 Those working under the Act with people with learning disabilities should bear in mind the following general points:

- people with learning disabilities may use non-verbal communication rather than spoken language. This nonverbal communication may include behaviour, gestures, posture and body language, ways of moving, signing, noises and pointing. It is important to recognise people's communication in all its forms and to avoid assuming that people's behaviour is a symptom of their mental disorder, when it may be an attempt to communicate feelings or physical pain or discomfort.

- people with learning disabilities may find new environments, such as a medical setting, frightening. All "reasonable adjustments" (as required by the Disability Discrimination Act 1995) need to be made to adapt and respond to each individual's needs. This may mean offering a quiet space, for example, or having one link person assigned who speaks with the person.

- the most appropriate method of communication for each person with learning disabilities should be identified as soon as possible, and the help of a speech and language therapist should be sought wherever appropriate. It is helpful to identify a specific person who will undertake this task.

- some people with learning disabilities may prefer to have written material in simple language with images or symbols to assist, and this could be reinforced orally, through personal contact or other means. It can be helpful to repeat information and leave a record of the information that has been passed on, so that the person can consult it and ask others to clarify anything that is difficult to understand.

- it is important to set aside sufficient time for preparation of suitable information and for preparation before meetings. Meetings should be held in an environment that is not intimidating, in order to allow the patient every chance to understand the information given.

34.14 People with learning disabilities may also encounter problems in:

- understanding what is being explained to them and communicating their views (in situations that increase their levels of anxiety they may find it even more difficult to understand what is said to them); and

- in being understood, particularly where lack of spoken language makes it hard for them to provide explanations of pain or other symptoms that might aid diagnosis of physical or mental illness.

34.15 Where information relates to their right to have their case reviewed by the Tribunal, the information will need to be designed to help people with learning disabilities understand the Tribunal's role. They may well need support to make an informed decision about whether and when to make an application.

34.16 Where professionals taking decisions under the Act have limited expertise with people with learning disabilities, it is good practice to seek advice from the local specialist service, which can provide details of alternatives to compulsory treatment and give advice on good communication. But any problem with availability of such services should not be allowed to delay action that is immediately necessary. It is desirable that, during examination or assessment, people with learning disabilities have someone with them whom they know well and with whom they have good communication (subject to the normal considerations of patient confidentiality).

34.17 The potential of co-morbidity with mental illness and personality disorder should also be kept in mind, in order that the skills of clinicians and others with appropriate expertise can be brought into play at all points in the assessment, treatment and care pathway. The possibility of physical health problems underlying the presentation of abnormally aggressive or seriously irresponsible behaviour should similarly always be kept in mind.

### Autistic spectrum disorders

34.18 The Act's definition of mental disorder includes the full range of autistic **4–339** spectrum disorders, including those existing alongside a learning disability or any other kind   of mental disorder. While it is possible for someone on the autistic spectrum to meet the conditions for treatment under the Act without having any other form of mental disorder, even if it is not associated with abnormally aggressive or seriously irresponsible behaviour, this is likely to happen only very rarely. Compulsory treatment in a hospital setting is rarely likely to be helpful for a person with autism, who may be very distressed by even minor changes in routine and is likely to find detention in hospital anxiety provoking. Sensitive, person-centred support in a familiar setting will usually be more helpful. Wherever possible, less restrictive alternative ways of providing the treatment or support a person needs should be found.

34.19 Autistic spectrum disorders are disorders occurring from early stages in development in which the person shows marked difficulties with social communication, social interaction and social imagination. They may be preoccupied with a particular subject of interest.

34.20 These disorders are developmental in nature and are not mental illnesses in themselves. However, people with an autistic spectrum disorder may have additional or related problems, which frequently include anxiety. These may be related to social factors associated with frustration or communication problems or to patterns of thought and behaviour that are rigid or literal in nature. As with people with learning disabilities, it should be borne in mind that people with autistic spectrum disorders may also have co-morbid mental disorders, including mood disorders and, occasionally, personality disorders.

34.21 A person with an autistic spectrum disorder may have additional sensory and motor difficulties that make them behave in an unusual manner and that might be interpreted as a mental illness but are in fact a coping mechanism. These include sensitivity to light, sound, touch and balance and may result in a range of regulatory behaviours, including rocking, self-injury and avoidance, such as running away.

34.22 A person with an autistic spectrum disorder is likely to behave in ways that seem odd to other people. But mere eccentricity, in anyone, is not in itself a reason for compulsory measures under the Act.

34.23 There can also be a repetitive or compulsive element to much of the behaviour of people with autistic spectrum disorders. The person may appear to be choosing to act in a particular way, but their behaviour may be distressing even to themselves. It may be driven or made worse by anxiety and could lead to harm to self or others. Repetitive behaviour does not in itself constitute a mental disorder.

34.24 The examination or assessment of someone with an autistic spectrum disorder requires special consideration of how to communicate effectively with the person being assessed. Whenever possible, the people carrying out assessments should have experience and training in working with people with these disorders. If this is not possible, they should seek assistance from specialists with appropriate expertise, but this should not be allowed to delay action that is immediately necessary. Assessment should ideally be part of a complete appraisal—a multidisciplinary process involving medical, nursing, social work, occupational therapy, speech and language therapy and psychology professionals (as necessary) with relevant specialist experience.

34.25 Where appropriate, someone who knows the person with an autistic spectrum disorder should be present at an initial examination and assessment (subject to the normal considerations of patient confidentiality). Knowledge of the person's early developmental history and usual pattern of behaviour will help prevent someone with an autistic spectrum disorder from being wrongly made subject to compulsory measures under the Act, or treated inappropriately with psychopharmacological agents.

34.26 A person with an autistic spectrum disorder may show a marked difference between their intellectual and their emotional development, associated on occasion with aggressive or seriously irresponsible behaviour. They may be able to discuss an action intellectually and express a desire to do it (or not, as the case may be) but not have the instinctive social empathy to keep to their intentions. This should be understood and responded to by professionals, who should recognise that the nature of the communication problems may require specialist structured approaches to communication. However, when the person is unable to prevent themselves from causing severe harm to themselves or others, compulsory measures under the Act may become necessary.

34.27 If people with autistic spectrum disorders do need to be detained under the Act, it is important that they are treated in a setting that can accommodate their social and communication needs as well as being able to treat their mental disorder.

---

**Related material**

- *Valuing People—A New Strategy for the 21st Century* (Cm 5086), The Stationery Office, March 2001

- *Valuing People: A New Strategy for Learning Disability for the 21st Century: Planning with People towards Person Centred Approaches—Guidance for Partnership Boards,* Department of Health, 28 January 2002

- *Action for Health, Health Action Plans and Health Facilitation Detailed Good Practice Guidance on Implementation for Learning Disability Partnership Boards,* Department of Health, 6 August 2002

This material does not form part of the Code. It is provided for assistance only.

# APPLYING THE PRINCIPLES

This scenario is not intended to provide a template for decisions in applying the **4–340** principles in similar situations. The scenario itself is only illustrative and does not form part of the Code itself.

---

## AUTISM AND LEARNING DISABILITY

Albert is a 22 year old man with profound and multiple learning disabilities. He is six feet four inches tall and very powerfully built. As a child, he was also diagnosed with Kanner syndrome—a severe form of autistic spectrum disorder. He is unable to speak.

Albert lives in a residential care home. Following the recent death of a close friend, Albert became withdrawn and uncommunicative. His GP diagnosed depression and prescribed medication.

After a few weeks on this medication, Albert's mood changed. He was no longer withdrawn but began to display aggressive behaviour and, in particular, began banging the side of his head against the door handle. Staff at the group house felt he was becoming a risk to himself and to other people who came into contact with him and asked for a Mental Health Act assessment.

In considering whether admission to hospital under the Act is appropriate for Albert, the doctors and the AMHP should consider the principles and how they might be applied.

Among the things they might wish to consider in making a decision in these circumstances are the following.

### Purpose principle

- What factors need to be considered in assessing for Albert's safety and wellbeing?
- Have any physical health factors been considered?
- Are there any social, occupational, psychological or sensory issues that may be influencing Albert's behaviour?
- Are there any issues of risk? If so, is the risk to Albert or to other people? Or both?
- If Albert were to be detained, how may the resultant change of environment impact on his condition?

### Least restriction principle

- What are the possible alternatives to admission under the Act? Additional support to Albert in the residential care home? Further assessment, including investigation of possible underlying physical health problems?

### Respect principle

- Is any aspect of Albert's behaviour an attempt to communicate what is wrong or express any views about what he would want to happen?
- How has he communicated his views in the past?

---

- Given that Albert is young and strong, are any assumptions being made about the risk his behaviour poses and, if so, how might they be affecting the options being considered?

**Participation principle**

- What methods have been employed to try to ascertain Albert's view about his care and treatment?

- Have Albert's family been contacted?

- What do they know about Albert that might inform an evaluation of his condition and the likely effectiveness of the various possible responses?

- What do they want and what do they know about him that might inform what he might want?

- Have the staff at the residential care home been asked what they think Albert's behaviour might mean and whether they have any information that might inform an evaluation of his condition and the likely effectiveness of the various possible responses?

- Do the staff know what Albert might want?

- Does Albert have access to an advocate or other support mechanism that can help interpret his behaviour?

- Has Albert's GP been contacted? What is the GP's view about Albert's condition and what is their view about what Albert might want?

**Effectiveness, efficiency and equity principle**
- Is there someone with specialist knowledge of learning disability and autism available to be involved in the assessment? If so, given the circumstances, can the assessment wait until they can attend?

## 35. PEOPLE WITH PERSONALITY DISORDERS

**4–341**     This chapter deals with issues of particular relevance to people with a personality disorder.

**Personality disorders—general points**
**4–342**     35.1 The Act applies equally to all people with mental disorders, including those with either primary or secondary diagnoses of personality disorder.

35.2 Generally, people who have personality disorders present a complex range of mental health and other problems:

- many people may have a diagnosis of more than one personality disorder, and they may also have other mental health problems such as depression, anxiety or post-traumatic stress syndrome;

- suicidality, self-harm, substance misuse problems and eating disorders are also common in people with personality disorders;

- some individuals experience very severe, periodic emotional distress in response to stressful circumstances and crisis, particularly people with borderline personality disorder;

- some individuals can at times display a form of psychosis that is qualitatively different from that displayed by people with a diagnosis of mental illness;

- people with personality disorders usually have longstanding and recurrent relationship difficulties;

- people with personality disorders are more likely than other population groups to experience housing problems and long-term unemployment;

- a very small subgroup of people with personality disorders may be anti-social and dangerous;

- anti-social personality disorder is strongly associated with offending, and it is estimated that personality disorders have a high prevalence within offender populations.

### Personality disorders and mental health legislation

35.3 People with personality disorders who are subject to compulsory measures **4–343** under the Act may include individuals who:

- have a primary diagnosis of personality disorder and present a serious risk to themselves or others (or both);

- have complex mental disorders, including personality disorder, and present a serious risk to themselves or to others (or both);

- have a primary diagnosis of personality disorder or complex disorders including personality disorder and are transferred from prison for treatment in secure psychiatric or personality disorder in patient services;

- are transferred from prison or other secure settings for treatment within designated dangerous and severe personality disorder (DSPD) units in hospitals; and

- are personality disordered offenders who have completed in-patient treatment in DSPD units, or other secure settings, but who may need further treatment in the community.

### Practice considerations

*Assessment*

35.4 People with personality disorders may present and behave in very different **4–344** ways from those with other mental disorders. It is important that such behaviours and presentations are properly understood if the Act is to be used appropriately.

35.5 Especially in times of crisis, decisions about the use of the Act for people with personality disorders will often have to be made by professionals who are not specialists in the field. It is therefore important that approved mental health professionals and doctors carrying out initial assessments have a sufficient understanding of personality disorders as well as other forms of mental disorder.

35.6 Individuals who have historically been labelled by various local agencies as having a personality disorder may never, in fact, have had a thorough clinical assessment and formulation. A number of validated assessment tools enable a more precise identification to be made. Professionals will need to ensure that any treatment and after-care plans are shaped by appropriate clinical assessments conducted by suitably trained practitioners.

35.7 In emergency or very high-risk situations, where such an assessment has not already been carried out and an application for detention under the Act is being considered, then responding to the immediate risk to the health or safety of the patient or to other people is the first priority. However, achieving an appropriate clinical assessment and formulation should be an immediate aim of detention.

### Appropriate medical treatment

**4–345**    35.8 What constitutes appropriate medical treatment for a particular patient with a personality disorder will depend very much on their individual circumstances. First and foremost, that calls for a clinical judgement by the clinicians responsible for their assessment or treatment.

35.9 A proposed care plan will not, of course, meet the Act's definition of appropriate medical treatment unless it is for the purpose of alleviating or preventing a worsening of the patient's mental disorder, its symptoms or manifestations (see **chapter 6**).

35.10 Generally, treatment approaches for personality disorders need to be relatively intense and long term, structured and coherent. Sustainable long-term change is more likely to be achieved with the voluntary engagement of the patient.

35.11 People with personality disorders may take time to engage and develop motivation for such longer-term treatment. But even patients who are not engaged in that kind of treatment may need other forms of treatment, including nurse and specialist care, to manage the continuing risks posed by their disorders, and this may constitute appropriate medical treatment.

35.12 In the majority of cases, the primary model of intervention for personality disorders is rooted in a psycho-social model.

35.13 Patients who have been detained may often need to continue treatment in a community setting on discharge. Where there are continuing risks that cannot otherwise be managed safely, supervised community treatment, guardianship or (for restricted patients) conditional discharge may provide a framework within which such patients can continue their treatment in the community.

35.14 In deciding whether treatment under the Act can be delivered safely in the community, account should be taken of:

- where the specific model of treatment intervention can be delivered most effectively and safely;

- if management of personal and social relationships is a factor in the intervention, how the appropriate day-today support and monitoring of the patient's social as well as psychological needs can be provided;

- to what degree the psycho-social model of intervention requires the active participation of the patient for an effective and safe outcome;

- the degree to which the patient has the ability to take part in a psycho-social intervention that protects their own and others' safety;

- the degree to which 24-hour access to support will be required; and

- the need for the intervention plan to be supervised by a professional who is appropriately qualified in the model of intervention and in risk assessment and management in the community.

35.15 In the case of personality disordered offenders who may already have received long-term treatment programmes within secure or prison settings, treatment in the community may well still be required while they resettle in the community.

---

**Related material**

- *Personality disorder: No longer a diagnosis of exclusion. Policy implementation guidance for the development of services for people with personality disorder,*
Department of Health, January 2003

This material does not form part of the Code. It is provided for assistance only.

---

## 36. CHILDREN AND YOUNG PEOPLE UNDER THE AGE OF 18

36.1 This chapter provides guidance on particular issues arising in relation to **4–346** children (less than 16 years old) and young people (16 or 17 years old) **(Reference Guide chapter 36)**.

36.2 This chapter sets out some of the key factors that need to be borne in mind and their interconnections, including:

- some of the main concepts that need to be considered when dealing with patients who are under 18, such as who has parental responsibility, and the parental zone of control;

- when the Mental Health Act should be used and when the Children Act should be used;

- what it means for children and young people to be capable of consent;

- how to make decisions about ad year olds;

- how to deal with informal patients under 16 years old;

- how treatment for under 18s mission or treatment of informal patients of 16 or 17is regulated by the Mental Health Act;

- when an application to the court should be made;

- the need to provide age-appropriate services;

- applications and references to the Tribunal; and

- general duties concerning, for example, local authorities visiting children and young people in hospital.

### General considerations

36.3 The legal framework governing the admission to hospital and treatment of **4–347** children is complex, and it is important to remember a number of factors. Those responsible for the care of children and young people in hospital should be familiar with other relevant legislation, including the

Children Acts 1989 and 2004, Mental Capacity Act 2005 (MCA), Family Law Reform Act 1969, Human Rights Act 1998 and the United Nations Convention on the Rights of the Child, as well as relevant case law, common law principles and relevant codes of practice.

36.4 When taking decisions under the Act about children and young people, the following should always be borne in mind:

- the best interests of the child or young person must always be a significant consideration;

- children and young people should always be kept as fully informed as possible, just as an adult would be, and should receive clear and detailed information concerning their care and treatment, explained in a way they can understand and in a format that is appropriate to their age;

- the child or young person's views, wishes and feelings should always be considered;

- any intervention in the life of a child or young person that is considered necessary by reason of their mental disorder should be the option that is least restrictive and least likely to expose them to the risk of any stigmatisation, consistent with effective care and treatment, and it should also result in the least possible separation from family, carers, friends and community or interruption of their education, as is consistent with their wellbeing;

- all children and young people should receive the same access to educational provision as their peers;

- children and young people have as much right to expect their dignity to be respected as anyone else; and

- children and young people have as much right to privacy and confidentiality as anyone else.

### People with parental responsibility

**4–348**  36.5 Those with parental responsibility will usually, but not always, be the parents of the child or young person. Legally, under the Children Act 1989, consent to treat a child or young person is needed from only one person with parental responsibility, although it is good practice to involve both parents and others close to the child or young person in the decision-making process. However, if one person with parental responsibility strongly disagreed with the decision to treat and was likely to challenge it in court, it might be appropriate to seek authorisation from the court before relying on the consent of another person with parental responsibility.

36.6 It is essential that those taking decisions under the Mental Health Act are clear about who has parental responsibility and that they always request copies of any court orders for reference on the child or young person's medical or social service file. These orders may include care orders, residence orders, contact orders, evidence of appointment as the child or young person's guardian, parental responsibility agreements or orders under section 4 of the Children Act and any order under wardship. If the parents of a child or young person are separated, and the child or young person is living with one parent, the person responsible for the care and treatment of the patient should try to establish whether there is a residence order and, if so, in whose favour.

36.7 Once it is established who has parental responsibility for the child or young person, the person responsible for the care and treatment of the patient must determine whether a person with parental responsibility has the capacity, within the meaning of the MCA, to take a decision about the child or young person's treatment and whether the decision is within the zone of parental control (see **paragraphs 36.9–36.15**).

### Children looked after by the local authority

36.8 Where children or young people are looked after by the local authority (see **4–349** section 22 of the Children Act 1989), treatment decisions should usually be discussed with the parent or other person with parental responsibility who continues to have parental responsibility for the child. If a child or young person is voluntarily accommodated by the local authority, parents or other people with parental responsibility have the same rights and responsibilities in relation to treatment as they would otherwise. If the child or young person is subject to a care order, the parents (or others with parental responsibility) share parental responsibility with the local authority, and it will be a matter for negotiation and agreement between them as to who should be consulted about treatment decisions. However, local authorities can, in the exercise of their powers under section 33(3)(b) of the Children Act 1989, limit the extent to which parents (or others) may exercise their parental responsibility. (See also **paragraphs 36.80–36.82** for the duties of local authorities in relation to hospital patients.)

### Zone of parental control

36.9 People with parental responsibility may in certain circumstances (see **4–350** below) consent on behalf of a child under 16 to them being given medical treatment or being admitted informally for such treatment. Even in these circumstances, mental health professionals can rely on such consent only where it is within what in this guidance is called the "zone of parental control". This may also apply to young people of 16 or 17 years of age who are given medical treatment for mental disorder and who lack the ability to consent for themselves, and to decisions about such young people being admitted for such treatment informally if they lack capacity. The concept of the zone of parental control derives largely from case law from the European Court of Human Rights in Strasbourg.[24] It is difficult to have clear rules about what may fall in the zone, when so much depends on the particular facts of each case. Certain guidelines are set out below, but where there is doubt professionals should take legal advice so that account may be taken of the most recent case law.

36.10 In assessing whether a particular decision falls within the parameters of the zone of parental control, two key questions must be considered:

- firstly, is the decision one that a parent would be expected to make, having regard both to what is considered to be normal practice in our society and to any relevant human rights decisions made by the courts?; and

---

[24] For example *Nielsen v Denmark* (1989) 11 E.H.R.R. 175.

- secondly, are there no indications that the parent might not act in the best interests of the child or young person?

36.11 The less confident a professional is that they can answer both questions in the affirmative, the more likely it will be that the decision in question falls outside the zone.

36.12 The parameters of the zone will vary from one case to the next: they are determined not only by social norms, but also by the circumstances and dynamics of a specific parent and child or young person. In assessing where the boundaries lie in any particular case, and so whether a parent's consent may be relied upon, mental health professionals might find it helpful to consider the following factors:

- the nature and invasiveness of what is to be done to the patient (including the extent to which their liberty will be curtailed)—the more extreme the intervention, the more likely it will be that it falls outside the zone;

- whether the patient is resisting—treating a child or young person who is resisting needs more justification;

- the general social standards in force at the time concerning the sorts of decisions it is acceptable for parents to make—anything that goes beyond the kind of decisions parents routinely make will be more suspect;

- the age, maturity and understanding of the child or young person—the greater these are, the more likely it will be that it should be the child or young person who takes the decision; and

- the extent to which a parent's interests may conflict with those of the child or young person—this may suggest that the parent will not act in the child or young person's best interests.

36.13 For example, in a case where the parents had gone through a particularly acrimonious divorce, it might not be possible to separate the decision about whether to admit the child to hospital from the parents' own hostilities, and it might not be possible to treat the parents as able to make an impartial decision. It might also not be appropriate to rely on the consent of a parent in circumstances where the mental health of the child or young person has led to chronic battles over control in the home. In another case, there might be concerns about the mental capacity of the person with parental responsibility, and whether they have capacity to take a decision about the child's treatment.

36.14 It is also possible that a decision on treatment could be outside the zone of parental control simply because of the nature of the proposed treatment, eg where, like electroconvulsive therapy (ECT), it could be considered particularly invasive or controversial.

36.15 In any case where reliance could not be placed on the consent of a person with parental responsibility, or on that of the child or young person, consideration should be given to alternative ways to treat them. One way would be to apply to have the child or young person detained under the Mental Health Act, but this is available only where they meet all the criteria for such detention. In cases where they do not meet the criteria, it may be appropriate to seek authorisation from the court.

**Care for children whose liberty must be restricted—when might the Mental Health Act or the Children Act be appropriate?**

36.16 There is no minimum age limit for detention in hospital under the Mental **4–351** Health Act. It may be used to detain children or young people where that is justified by the risk posed by their mental disorder and all the relevant criteria are met.

36.17 However, where the child or young person with a mental disorder needs to be detained, but the primary purpose is not to provide medical treatment for mental disorder, consideration should be given to using section 25 of the Children Act 1989.

36.18 For example, if a child or young person is seriously mentally ill, they may require to be admitted for treatment under the Mental Health Act. But if they are behaviourally disturbed, and there is no need for them to be hospitalised, their needs might be more appropriately met within secure accommodation under the Children Act. Professionals who address these questions should:

- be aware of the relevant statutory provisions and have easy access to competent legal advice;

- keep in mind the importance of ensuring that the care and treatment of the child or young person are managed with clarity and consistency and within a recognisable framework (such as the child and adolescent mental health services (CAMHS) Care Programme Approach); and

- attempt to select the option that reflects the predominant needs of the child or young person at that time, whether that is to provide specific mental healthcare and treatment or to achieve a measure of safety and protection. In any event, the least restrictive option consistent with the care and treatment objectives for the child or young person should be adopted.

**Decisions on admission and treatment of under 18s**

36.19 The decision to admit a child or young person to hospital is inextricably **4–352** linked to the decision to treat them once they have been admitted. But they may need to be considered separately in light of the different provisions that are relevant to each decision.

36.20 At least one of the people involved in the assessment of a person who is under 18 years old, ie one of the two medical practitioners or the approved mental health professional (AMHP), should be a clinician specialising in CAMHS. Where this is not possible, a CAMHS clinician should be consulted as soon as possible. In cases where the child or young person has complex or multiple needs, other clinicians may need to be involved, eg a learning disability CAMHS consultant where the child or young person has a learning disability. See **chapter 4** for fuller information on the assessment process.

**Informal admission and treatment of 16 or 17 year olds**

36.21 The law about admission and treatment of young people aged 16 or 17 **4–353** differs from that for children under 16. But in both cases, whether they are capable of consenting to what is proposed is of central importance.

*Informal admission of 16 and 17 year olds with capacity to consent*

**4–354**   36.22 A decision about admission for informal treatment of a 16 or 17 year old who has capacity must be made in accordance with section 131 of the Mental Health Act. Section 131 of the Act provides that where a patient who is 16 or 17 years old has capacity (as defined in the MCA) to consent to being admitted to hospital for treatment of a mental disorder, they themselves may consent or not consent to being admitted, regardless of the views of a person with parental responsibility. This means that if a young person who is 16 or 17 years old, and who has the capacity to make such a decision, consents to being admitted for treatment, they can be treated as an informal patient in accordance with section 131, even if a person with parental responsibility is refusing consent.

36.23 Section 131 also applies to a patient who is 16 or 17 years old and has capacity but does not consent (for whatever reason, including being overwhelmed by the implications of the decision) or who refuses consent, so in these circumstances a person with parental responsibility cannot consent on their behalf. In such cases, consideration should be given to whether the patient satisfies all the criteria for detention under the Act. If those criteria are not satisfied, but treatment in hospital is thought to be in the patient's best interests, it may be necessary to seek authorisation from the court instead.

36.24 If the young person is admitted informally, the considerations set out in **paragraphs 36.27** onwards will apply to their treatment.

*Informal admission of 16 and 17 year olds who lack capacity to consent*

**4–355**   36.25 Different considerations apply to a decision to informally admit a young person aged 16 or 17 where the young person lacks capacity. Section 131 of the Act does not apply. The MCA may apply in the same way as it does to those who are aged 18 or over, unless the admission and treatment amounts to a deprivation of liberty. If there is a deprivation of liberty, admission of a 16 or 17 year old cannot be authorised under the MCA, and the legality of any such admission should be assessed under common law principles.

36.26 Common law principles allow a person with parental responsibility in these circumstances to consent, but only if the matter is within the zone of parental control. If it is outside the zone, then consideration should be given to whether the young person meets all the criteria for detention under the Mental Health Act. If the Act is not applicable, it may be necessary to seek authorisation from the court.

*Informal treatment of 16 and 17 year olds who are capable of consenting*

**4–356**   36.27 Special provision is made for the treatment of young people. By virtue of section 8 of the Family Law Reform Act 1969, people who are 16 or 17 years old are presumed to be capable of consenting to their own medical treatment and to any ancillary procedures involved in that treatment, such as an anaesthetic.

36.28 This test is different from that in section 131 of the Mental Health Act. A young person who has capacity to consent (within the meaning of the MCA) may nonetheless not be capable of consenting in a particular case, for example because they are overwhelmed by the implications of the relevant decision.

36.29 As would apply in the case of an adult, consent will be valid only if it is given voluntarily by an appropriately informed patient capable of consenting to the particular intervention. However, unlike in the case of an adult, the refusal by a person aged 16 or 17 to consent may in certain circumstances be overridden by a court.

36.30 Section 8 of the Family Law Reform Act applies only to the young person's own treatment. It does not apply to an intervention that is not potentially of direct health benefit to the young person, such as non-therapeutic research into the causes of a disorder. However, a young person may be able to consent to such an intervention if they have the understanding and ability to do so.

36.31 When assessing whether a young person is capable of consent, the same criteria should be used as for adults.

36.32 If the young person is capable of giving valid consent and does so, then it is not legally necessary to obtain consent from a person with parental responsibility as well. It is, however, good practice to involve the young person's family in the decision-making process, if the young person consents to their information being shared.

36.33 When a young person refuses consent, the courts in the past have found that a person with parental responsibility can overrule their refusal in non-emergency cases. However, there is no post-Human Rights Act decision on this, and the trend in recent cases is to reflect greater autonomy for under 18s in law. In the Department of Health's view, it is not wise to rely on the consent of a person with parental responsibility to treat a young person who refuses in these circumstances. Consideration should be given to whether the young person meets all the criteria for detention under the Mental Health Act. If they do not, it may be necessary to seek authorisation from the court.

36.34 In an emergency, where a 16 or 17 year old who is capable of consenting refuses to have treatment, it is likely that the young person's decision could be overruled and the clinician could act without anyone's consent if the refusal would in all likelihood lead to their death or to severe permanent injury.

*Informal treatment of 16 and 17 year olds who are not capable of consenting*

36.35 Different considerations also apply to a decision to treat a young person **4–357** aged 16 or 17 informally where the young person lacks capacity or is otherwise not capable of consenting. Where the young person lacks capacity, the MCA will apply in the same way as it does to those aged 18 and over, unless the treatment amounts to a deprivation of liberty.

36.36 If the treatment amounts to a deprivation of liberty, it cannot be authorised under the MCA for a 16 or 17 year old, and the legality of any such treatment should be assessed under common law principles.

36.37 Common law principles will also apply if the young person has capacity to consent (as defined in the MCA) but for some other reason is not capable of consenting, for example because they are overwhelmed by the implications of the decision. This means that a person with parental responsibility could consent on their behalf if the matter is within the zone of parental control. If it is not, then consideration should be given to whether the young person meets all the criteria for detention under the Mental Health Act. If they do not, it may be necessary to seek authorisation from the court.

### Under 16s

*What is Gillick competence?*

**4–358**   36.38 In the case of Gillick,[25] the court held that children who have sufficient understanding and intelligence to enable them to understand fully what is involved in a proposed intervention will also have the competence to consent to that intervention. This is sometimes described as being "Gillick competent". A child may be Gillick competent to consent to admission to hospital, medical treatment, research or any other activity that requires their consent.

36.39 The concept of Gillick competence is said to reflect the child's increasing development to maturity. The understanding required for different interventions will vary considerably. A child may have the competence to consent to some interventions but not others. The child's competence to consent should be assessed carefully in relation to each decision that needs to be made.

36.40 In some cases, for example because of a mental disorder, a child's mental state may fluctuate significantly, so that on some occasions the child appears to be Gillick competent in respect of a particular decision and on other occasions does not. In cases such as these, careful consideration should be given to whether the child is truly Gillick competent at any time to take a relevant decision.

36.41 If the child is Gillick competent and is able to give voluntary consent after receiving appropriate information, that consent will be valid and additional consent by a person with parental responsibility will not be required. It is, however, good practice to involve the child's parents, guardian or carers in the decision-making process, if the child consents to their information being shared.

*Informal admission and treatment of under 16s who are Gillick competent*

**4–359**   36.42 Where a child who is Gillick competent consents, they may be admitted to hospital as an informal patient. Where a child who is Gillick competent to do so has consented to being admitted informally, they may be given treatment if they are competent to consent to it and do consent. Consent should be sought for each aspect of the child's care and treatment as it arises. "Blanket" consent forms should not be used.

36.43 Where a child who is Gillick competent refuses to be admitted for treatment, in the past the courts have held that a person with parental responsibility can overrule their refusal. However, there is no post-Human Rights Act decision on this. The trend in recent cases is to reflect greater autonomy for competent under 18s, so it may be unwise to rely on the consent of a person with parental responsibility.

36.44 Consideration should be given to whether the child meets all the criteria for detention under the Mental Health Act. If they do not, it may be appropriate to seek authorisation from the court, except in cases where the child's refusal would be likely to lead to their death or to severe permanent injury, in which case the child could be admitted to hospital and treated without consent.

---

[25] *Gillick v West Norfolk and Wisbech Area Health Authority* [1986] A.C. 112.

*Informal admission and treatment of under 16s who are not Gillick competent*

36.45 Where a child is not Gillick competent, it will usually be possible for a **4–360** person with parental responsibility to consent on their behalf to their informal admission to hospital for treatment for mental disorder.

36.46 Before relying on parental consent in relation to a child who is under 16 years old and who is not Gillick competent, an assessment should be made of whether the matter is within the zone of parental control.

36.47 A child's views should be taken into account, even if they are not Gillick competent. How much weight the child's views should be given will depend on how mature the child is. Where a child has been Gillick competent to make a decision but then loses competence, any views they expressed before losing competence should be taken into account and may act as parameters limiting the zone of parental control. For example, if a child has expressed willingness to receive one form of treatment but not another while Gillick competent but then loses competence, it might not be appropriate to give the treatment to the child as an informal patient where the child has previously refused it, even if a person with parental responsibility consents.

36.48 If the decision regarding the admission and treatment of a child (including how the child is to be kept safely in one place) is within the zone of parental control, and consent is given by a person with parental responsibility, then the clinician may rely on that consent and admit and treat the child as an informal patient on that basis.

36.49 The fact that a parent or other person with parental responsibility has informally admitted a child should not lead professionals to assume that consent has been given to all components of a treatment programme regarded as "necessary". Consent should be sought for each aspect of the child's care and treatment as it arises. "Blanket" consent forms should not be used.

36.50 If the decision is not within the zone of parental control, or the consent of a person with parental responsibility is not given, the child cannot be admitted and treated informally on the basis of the parent's consent. An application can be made under the Mental Health Act if the child meets all the criteria for detention under the Act. If the criteria are not met, it may be necessary to seek authorisation from the court.

**Emergency treatment**

36.51 A life-threatening emergency may arise when a patient who is under 18 is **4–361** capable of consenting to a treatment but refuses to do so, or where a person with parental responsibility could consent but there is no time to seek their consent, or where they are refusing consent and there is no time to seek authorisation from the court. In such cases, the courts have stated that doubt should be resolved in favour of the preservation of life, and it will be acceptable to undertake treatment to preserve life or prevent irreversible serious deterioration of the patient's condition.

**Treatments for under 18s regulated by the Mental Health Act**

36.52 Treatment for mental disorder for under 18s is regulated by the Act when **4–362** the patient is:

- detained;

- on supervised community treatment (SCT); or

- for some treatments, an informal patient.

36.53 Even where treatment under the Act does not require consent, the safe-guards differ depending on whether the patient is able to and does consent, so it is important to know whether the patient is able to and does consent.

*Treatment requiring the patient's consent (section 57)*

**4–363**    36.54 Treatment covered by section 57 of the Act (primarily neurosurgery for mental disorder) cannot be given to a child or young person who does not person-ally consent to it, whether they are detained or not. These treatments cannot, therefore, be given to any young person or child who is not capable of consenting, even if a person with parental responsibility consents.

*Electro-convulsive therapy (section 58A)*

**4–364**    36.55 There is provision in the Act about treatment with ECT of patients who are under 18 which applies whether they are being informally treated or are detained under the Act.

36.56 Detained patients cannot be given ECT without their consent, if they are capable of consenting to the treatment, unless it is an emergency. If they are not capable of consenting, or if it is an emergency, they may be given ECT without their consent in accordance with rules described in **chapter 24**.

36.57 The same applies to SCT patients, except that, even in emergencies, if they have capacity or competence they may be given ECT without consent only if they have been recalled to hospital.

36.58 In addition, no child or young person under the age of 18 may be given ECT without the approval of a second opinion appointed doctor (SOAD), unless it is an emergency, even if they consent to it.

36.59 There is nothing in the Act itself to prevent a person with parental responsibility consenting to ECT on behalf of a child or young person who lacks the ability to consent for themselves and who is neither detained nor an SCT patient.

36.60 However, although there is no case law at present directly on this point, it would not be prudent to rely on such consent, because it is likely to lie outside the parental zone of control. Therefore, if a child under 16 who is not detained or an SCT patient needs ECT, court authorisation should be sought, unless it is an emergency. This should be done before a SOAD is asked to approve the treatment. In practice, the issues the court is likely to address will mirror those that the SOAD is required to consider.

36.61 This will also be the case for young people of 16 or 17 who are not detained or SCT patients and who lack the ability to consent for themselves, except where the MCA could be used to provide the necessary authority. The MCA can be used for this only where it is not necessary to deprive the young person of liberty.[26] As in cases where court authorisation is obtained, a SOAD certificate will still be needed, unless it is an emergency.

36.62 Children and young people who are not detained under the Act but may require ECT are eligible for access to independent mental health advocates.[27]

*Other treatment under the Act—detained and SCT patients only*

36.63 The Act itself sets out when detained and SCT patients (of all ages) can **4–365** be given other types of treatment for mental disorder, such as the requirement in section 58 for consent or a second opinion before medication can be given to detained patients after the initial period of three months. People with parental responsibility are not required to consent to such treatment on behalf of children and young people in this position.

## Supervised community treatment

36.64 There is no lower age limit for SCT. The number of children and young **4–366** people whose clinical and family circumstances make them suitable to move from being detained to having SCT is likely to be small, but it should be used where appropriate.

36.65 Parents (or other people with parental responsibility) may not consent on a child's behalf to treatment for mental disorder (or refuse it) while the child is on SCT. However, if SCT patients under the age of 18 are living with one or both parents, the person giving the treatment should consult with the parent(s) about the particular treatment (subject to the normal considerations of patient confidentiality), bearing in mind that if there is something that the parents would not accept, it would make it very difficult for the patient to live with their parents while on SCT. This dialogue should continue throughout the patient's treatment on SCT. If a parent is unhappy with the particular treatment or conditions attached to SCT, and the child is not competent to consent, a review by the patient's team should take place to consider whether the treatment and care plan, and SCT in general, are still appropriate for the child.

## Applications to the High Court

36.66 In certain situations where decisions about admitting a child or young **4–367** person informally or giving treatment need to be made, but the action cannot be taken under the MCA and it is not appropriate to use the Mental Health Act, the assistance of the High Court may be sought. Consideration will need to be given to whether an application should be made under the inherent jurisdiction or for a section 8 order under the Children Act 1989. This will depend on the facts of each case. Where a child is under 16, an application should be considered, in particular where the child:

- is not Gillick competent and where the person with parental responsibility cannot be identified or is incapacitated;

---

[26] The word "not" was accidentally omitted from the version of the Code presented to Parliament, making the sentence factually incorrect.

[27] Independent mental health advocacy services under the Act are expected to be introduced in April 2009.

- is not Gillick competent and where one person with parental responsibility consents but another strongly disagrees and is likely to take the matter to court themselves;

- is not Gillick competent and where there is concern that the person with parental responsibility may not be acting in the best interests of the child in making treatment decisions on behalf of the child, eg where hostility between parents is a factor in any decision making or where there are concerns as to whether a person with parental responsibility is capable of making a decision in the best interests of the child;

- is not Gillick competent and where a person with parental responsibility consents but the decision is not within the zone of parental control, eg where the treatment in question is ECT; or

- is Gillick competent or is a young person who is capable of making a decision on their treatment and is refusing treatment.

## Age-appropriate services[28]

**4–368**  36.67 Section 131A of the Act says that children and young people admitted to hospital for the treatment of mental disorder should be accommodated in an environment that is suitable for their age (subject to their needs).

36.68 This means that children and young people should have:

- appropriate physical facilities;

- staff with the right training, skills and knowledge to understand and address their specific needs as children and young people;

- a hospital routine that will allow their personal, social and educational development to continue as normally as possible; and

- equal access to educational opportunities as their peers, in so far as that is consistent with their ability to make use of them, considering their mental state.

36.69 Hospital managers should ensure that the environment is suitable, and in reaching their determination they must consult a person whom they consider to be suitable because they are experienced in CAMHS cases.

36.70 If, exceptionally, a patient cannot be accommodated in a dedicated child or adolescent ward, then discrete accommodation in an adult ward, with facilities, security and staffing appropriate to the needs of the child, might provide the most satisfactory solution, eg young female patients should be placed in single-sex accommodation. Where possible, all those involved in the care and treatment of children and young people should be child specialists. Anyone who looks after them must always have enhanced disclosure clearance from the Criminal Records Bureau and that clearance must be kept up to date.

36.71 In a small number of cases, the patient's need to be accommodated in a safe environment could, in the short term, take precedence over the suitability of

---

[28] This duty is expected to be in force from April 2010, but hospital managers should take all the steps they reasonably can to comply with the duty even before it comes into force. The Secretary of State recognises that some hospitals will not be able to do so fully immediately.

that environment for their age. Furthermore, it is also important to recognise that there is a clear difference between what is a suitable environment for a child or young person in an emergency situation and what is a suitable environment for a child or young person on a longer-term basis. In an emergency, such as when the patient is in crisis, the important thing is that the patient is in a safe environment. Once the initial emergency situation is over, hospital managers, in determining whether the environment continues to be suitable, would need to consider issues such as whether the patient can mix with individuals of their own age, can receive visitors of all ages and has access to education. Hospital managers have a duty to consider whether a patient should be transferred to more appropriate accommodation and, if so, to arrange this as soon as possible.

36.72 There will be times when the assessment concludes that the best place for an under 18 year old is an adult ward. This may happen when the young person is very close to their 18th birthday, and placing the young person on a CAMHS ward for a matter of weeks or days and then transferring them to an adult ward would be countertherapeutic. In some cases the young person may express a preference to be on an adult ward, such as when they are under the care of the early intervention psychosis team and they wish to go to the ward when the team rotates rather than to a unit with much younger children.

36.73 Where a young patient's presence on a ward with other children and young people might have a detrimental effect on the other young patients, the hospital managers need to ensure that the interests of other patients are protected. However, the needs of other patients should not override the need to provide accommodation in an environment that is suitable for the patient's age (subject to their needs) for an individual patient aged under 18.

36.74 Children and young people aged under 18 should also have access to age-appropriate leisure activities and facilities for visits from parents, guardians, siblings or carers.

### The responsible clinician and others caring for and treating under 18s

36.75 Where possible, those responsible for the care and treatment of children **4–369** and young people should be child specialists. Where this is not possible, it is good practice for the clinical staff to have regular access to and make use of a CAMHS specialist for advice and consultation.

### Rights to apply to the Tribunal

36.76 Children and young people who are detained under the Mental Health **4–370** Act have the same rights as other patients to apply to the Tribunal. It is important that children and young people are given assistance so that they get access to legal representation at an early stage. In addition, hospital managers should bear in mind that their duties to refer patients to the Tribunal are different in respect of patients who are under 18 years old. Where older patients must be referred after a three-year period without a Tribunal hearing, children and young people must be referred after one year.

### Education

36.77 No child or young person below the school leaving age should be denied **4–371** access to learning merely because they are receiving medical treatment for a mental disorder. Young people over school leaving age should be encouraged to continue learning.

**Confidentiality**

**4–372**   36.78 All children and young people have a right to confidentiality. Under 16s who are Gillick competent and young people aged 16 or 17 are entitled to make decisions about the use and disclosure of information they have provided in confidence in the same way as adults. For example, they may be receiving treatment or counselling that they do not want their parents to know about. However, there are circumstances when the duty of care to the patient might require confidentiality to be breached to the extent of informing those with parental responsibility.

36.79 The decision to disclose information to parents and others with parental responsibility is complex for this age group and depends on a range of factors, including:

- the child or young person's age and developmental level;

- their maturity;

- their ability to take into account the future as well as the present;

- the severity of the mental disorder and the risks posed to themselves and to others;

- the degree of care and protection required;

- the degree of the parents' involvement in the care of the child or young person;

- the closeness of the relationship with the parents; and

- the current competence of the child or young person to make a decision about confidentiality.

In addition, it should be noted that competence to take a decision about information sharing, as with treatment, may change over time.

**Duties of local authorities in relation to hospital patients**

**4–373**   36.80 Local authorities should ensure that they arrange for visits to be made to:

- children and young people looked after by them who are in hospital, whether or not they are under a care order; and

- children and young people accommodated or intended to be accommodated for three months or more by NHS bodies, local education authorities or care homes.[29] This is in addition to their duty in respect of children and young people in their care in hospitals or nursing homes in England and Wales as required by section 116 of the Act. Local authorities should take such other steps in relation to the patient while they are in hospital or a nursing home as would be expected to be taken by the patient's parent(s).

36.81 Local authorities are under a duty in the Children Act 1989 to:

---

[29] See the Review of Children's Cases Regulations 1991 (Statutory Instrument 1991/895 as amended) and ss.85 and 86 of the Children Act 1989.

- promote contact between children and young people who are in need and their families, if they live away from home, and to help them get back together (paragraphs 10 and 15 of Schedule 2 to the Children Act); and arrange for people (independent visitors) to visit and befriend children and young people looked after by the authority, wherever they are, if they have not been regularly visited by their parents (paragraph 17 of Schedule 2 to the Act).

36.82 Local authorities should be alerted if the whereabouts of the person with parental responsibility is not known or if that person has not visited the child or young person for a significant period of time. When alerted to this situation, the local authority should consider whether visits should be arranged.

---

- Children Act 1989 and guidance (particularly volumes 1, 4, 6 and 7)
- National Service Framework for Children, Young People and Maternity Services—Standard 9 (The Mental Health and Psychological Well-being of Children and Young People) issued by the Department for Education and Skills and the Department of Health in October 2004
- *Every Child Matters: Change for Children,* Department for Education and Skills, 2004
- *NHS Confidentiality Code of Practice,* Department of Health, 2003
- *Working Together to Safeguard Children,* HM Government, 2006

    This material does not form part of the Code. It is provided for assistance only.

---

The following flow charts are for information only and do not form part of the Code, and they should be read in conjunction with the text in this chapter.

**Informal admission and treatment of under 16s**

**4–374**

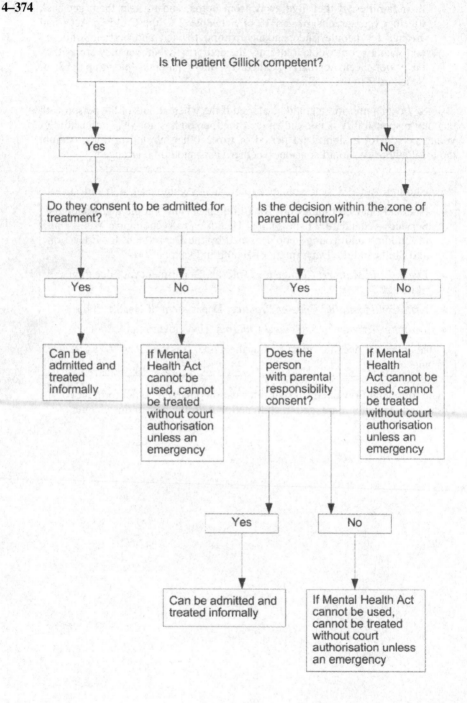

**Informal admission of 16 and 17 year olds**

4–375

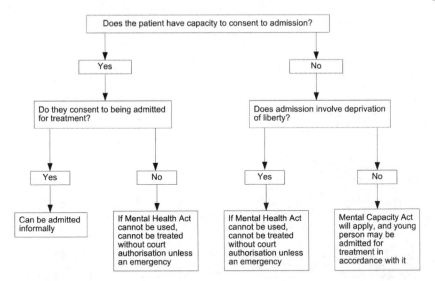

### Informal treatment of 16 and 17 years olds

4–376

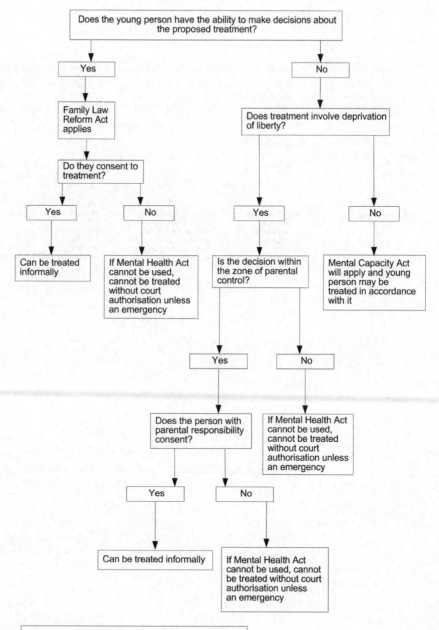

**Note:** A decision on treatment could be outside the zone of parental control simply because of the nature of the proposed treatment, eg where, like ECT, it could be considered particularly invasive or controversial (see **paragraphs 36.9-36.15**)

**Examples**

36.83 The following examples should be read in conjunction with the preceding **4–377** flow charts.

*Example A*

A 13 year old child is assessed as not being Gillick competent. The primary pur- **4–378** pose of the intervention is to provide medical treatment for mental disorder. The decision to authorise treatment falls within the zone of parental control, as what is proposed is fairly standard, but no person with parental responsibility consents. The child cannot be admitted informally under section 131(1) of the Mental Health Act. If the child meets the relevant criteria, the child could be admitted to hospital for assessment (section 2) or for treatment (section 3) under the Act.

*Example B*

A 14 year old girl is assessed as not being Gillick competent. The primary pur- **4–379** pose of the intervention is to provide medical treatment for mental disorder, but she is severely anorexic and this will involve force feeding. This is likely to take it outside the zone of parental control, so even though a person with parental responsibility consents, it is unlikely that the child can be admitted informally under section 131(1). If the child meets the relevant criteria, she could be admitted to hospital for assessment (section 2) or for treatment (section 3) under the Act.

*Example C*

A 15 year old child is assessed as being Gillick competent. The primary purpose **4–380** of the intervention is to provide medical treatment for mental disorder. The child does not consent to treatment in hospital. The child's parents are keen for the child to be admitted to hospital and give their consent. However, it is not considered safe to rely on the parents' consent where a Gillick-competent child is refusing. The child cannot be admitted informally under section 131(1). If the child meets the relevant criteria, the child could be admitted to hospital for assessment (section 2) or for treatment (section 3) under the Act.

*Example D*

A 16 year old young person is assessed as being able to make decisions about **4–381** the proposed intervention. The primary purpose of the intervention is to provide medical treatment for mental disorder. The young person consents to treatment in hospital (and they do not need to be detained). The young person should be treated as an informal patient.

*Example E*

A 17 year old young person is assessed as not having the capacity to make **4–382** decisions about the proposed intervention. The MCA could be used to authorise treatment if the criteria for its use are met.

*Example F*

**4–383**     A 15 year old is assessed as not being able to make decisions about the proposed intervention. The primary purpose of the intervention is not to provide medical treatment for mental disorder but to provide safety and protection. Consideration should be given to using section 25 of the Children Act.

## ANNEX A
## KEY WORDS AND PHRASES USED IN THIS CODE

| Term | Definition |
|------|-----------|
| **4–384 Absent without leave (AWOL)** | When a **detained patient** leaves hospital without getting permission first or does not return to hospital when required to do so. Also applies to **guardianship** patients who leave the place their guardian says they should live and to **SCT patients** and **conditionally discharged restricted patients** who don't return to hospital when **recalled,** or who leave the hospital without permission after they have been recalled. |
| **The Act** | Unless otherwise stated, the Mental Health Act 1983 (as amended by the Mental Health Act 2007). |
| **Advance decision to refuse treatment** | A decision, under the **Mental Capacity Act,** to refuse specified treatment made in advance by a person who has capacity to do so. This decision will then apply at a future time when that person lacks **capacity** to consent to, or refuse the specified treatment. |
| **Advocacy** | Independent help and support with understanding issues and assistance in putting forward one's own views, feelings and ideas. See also **Independent mental health advocate.** |
| **After-care** | Community care services following discharge from hospital; especially the duty of health and social services to provide after-care under **section 117** of the Act, following the **discharge** of a patient from detention for treatment under the Act. The duty applies to **SCT patients** and **conditionally discharged restricted patients,** as well as those who have been fully discharged. |
| **Application for detention** | An application made by an **approved mental health professional,** or a **nearest relative,** under **Part 2** of **the Act** for a **patient** to be detained in a hospital either for **assessment** or for **medical treatment.** Applications may be made under section 2 (application for admission for assessment), section 3 (application for admission for medical treatment) or section 4 (emergency application for admission for assessment). |
| **Appropriate medical treatment** | Medical treatment for mental disorder which is appropriate taking into account the nature and degree of the person's **mental disorder** and all the other circumstances of their case. |

| Term | Definition |
|------|------------|
| **Appropriate medical treatment test** | The requirement in some of the **criteria for detention,** and in the **criteria for SCT,** that **appropriate medical treatment** must be available for the **patient**. |
| **Approved clinician** | A mental health professional approved by the **Secretary of State** (or the **Welsh Ministers**) to act as an approved clinician for the purposes of **the Act**. Some decisions under the Act can only be taken by people who are approved clinicians. All **responsible clinicians** must be approved clinicians. |
| **Approved mental health professional (AMHP)** | A social worker or other professional approved by a **local social services authority (LSSA)** to carry out a variety of functions under **the Act**. |
| **Assessment** | Examining a **patient** to establish whether the patient has a **mental disorder** and, if they do, what treatment and care they need. |
|  | It is also used to be mean examining or interviewing a patient to decide whether an **application for detention** or a **guardianship application** should be made. |
| **Attorney** | Someone appointed under the **Mental Capacity Act** who has the legal right to make decisions (eg decisions about treatment) within the scope of their authority on behalf of the person (the donor) who made the power of attorney. Also known as a "donee of lasting power of attorney". |
| **Capacity** | The ability to take a decision about a particular matter at the time the decision needs to be made. Some people may lack capacity to take a particular decision (eg to **consent** to treatment) because they cannot understand, retain, use or weigh the information relevant to the decision. A legal definition of lack of capacity for people aged 16 or over is set out in section 2 of the **Mental Capacity Act** 2005. |
|  | See also **competence to consent.** |
| **Care Programme Approach (CPA)** | A system of care and support for individuals with complex needs which includes an assessment, a care plan and a care co-ordinator. It is used mainly for adults in England who receive specialist mental healthcare and in some CAMHS services. There are similar systems for supporting other groups of individuals, including children and young people (Children's Assessment Framework), older adults (Single Assessment Process) and people with learning disabilities (Person Centred Planning). |
| **Carer** | Someone who provides voluntary care by looking after and assisting a family member, friend or neighbour who requires support because of their mental health needs. |

| Term | Definition |
|---|---|
| **Child (and children)** | A person under the age of 16. |
| **Child and adolescent mental health services (CAMHS)** | Specialist mental health services for children and adolescents. CAMHS cover all types of provision and intervention—from mental health **mental health** promotion and primary prevention and specialist community-based services through to very specialist care, as provided by in-patient units for children and young people with mental illness. They are mainly composed of a multi-disciplinary workforce with specialist training in child and adolescent mental health. |
| **Children Act 1989** | A law relating to **children** and **young people** and those with parental responsibility for them. |
| **Commission** | The independent body which is responsible for monitoring the operation of **the Act**. At the time of publication, this is the Mental Health Act Commission (MHAC). However, legislation is currently before Parliament which will abolish the MHAC and transfer its functions to a new body, the Care Quality Commission, which is to establish a new integrated health and adult social care regulator, bringing together existing health and social care regulators into one regulatory body. Subject to Parliament, it is expected that the new Commission will be established in April 2009. |
| **Community treatment order (CTO)** | Written authorisation on a statutory form for **the discharge** of a patient from **detention** in hospital onto **supervised community order (CTO) treatment**. |
| **Competence to consent** | Similar to **capacity** to **consent,** but specifically about children. As well as covering a child's inability to make particular decisions because of their mental condition, it also covers children who do not have the maturity to take the particular decision in question. |
| **Compulsory measures** | Things that can be done to people under **the Act** without their agreement. This includes **detention** in hospital, **supervised community treatment** and **guardianship**. |
| **Compulsory treatment** | **Medical treatment for mental disorder** given under **the Act** against the wishes of the **patient.** |
| **Conditional discharge** | The **discharge** from hospital by the **Secretary of State for Justice** or the **Tribunal** of a **restricted patient** subject to conditions. The patient remains subject to **recall** to hospital by the Secretary of State. |
| **Conditionally discharged restricted patient** | A **restricted patient** who has been given a **conditional discharge.** |

| Term | Definition |
|---|---|
| Consent | Agreeing to allow someone else to do something to or for you. Particularly consent to treatment. Valid consent requires that the person has the **capacity** to make the decision (or the **competence to consent,** if a child), and they are given the information they need to make the decision, and that they are not under any duress or inappropriate pressure. |
| Convey and conveyance) | Transporting a patient under **the Act** to hospital (or anywhere else), conveyance) compulsorily if necessary. |
| Court of Protection | The specialist court set up under the **Mental Capacity Act** to deal with all issues relating to people who lack **capacity** to take decisions for themselves. |
| Criteria for detention | A set of criteria that must be met before a person can be **detained**, or remain detained, under the Act. The criteria are different in different sections of the Act. |
| Criteria for SCT | A set of criteria that must be met before a person can become an **SCT patient** or remain an SCT patient. |
| Criminal Records Bureau | An Executive Agency of the Home Office, which provides access to criminal record information through its disclosure service. |
| Deprivation of liberty | A term used in Article 5 of the **European Convention on Human Rights (ECHR)** to mean the circumstances in which a person's freedom is taken away. Its meaning in practice has been developed through case law. |
| Deprivation of liberty safeguards | The framework of safeguards under the **Mental Capacity Act** (as amended by the Mental Health Act 2007) for people who need to be deprived of their liberty in their best interests for care or treatment to which they lack the capacity to consent themselves. |
| Deputy or Court-appointed deputy) | A person appointed by the **Court of Protection** under section 16 of the **Mental Capacity Act** to take specified decisions on behalf of someone who lacks **capacity** to take those decisions themselves. This is not the same thing as the **nominated deputy** sometimes appointed by the **doctor** or **approved clinician** in charge of a patient's treatment. |
| Detained patient | Unless otherwise stated, a patient who is **detained** in hospital under **the Act**, or who is liable to be detained in hospital but who is (for any reason) currently out of hospital. In **chapters 23** and **24**, detained patients has a more specific meaning, explained in **paragraphs 23.7–23.8**. |
| Detention (and detained) | Unless otherwise stated, being held compulsorily in hospital under **the Act** for a period of **assessment** or **medical treatment**. Sometimes referred to colloquially as "sectioning". |

| Term | Definition |
| --- | --- |
| **Detention for assessment (and detained for assessment)** | The **detention** of a person in order to carry out an **assessment**. Can normally only last for a maximum of 28 days. Also known as "section 2 detention". |
| **Detention for medical treatment (and detained for medical treatment)** | The **detention** of a person in order to give them the **medical treatment for mental disorder** they need. There are various types of detention for medical treatment in **the Act**. It most often means detention as a result of an **application for detention** under section 3 of the Act. But it also includes several types of detention under **Part 3** of the Act, including **hospital directions, hospital orders** and **interim hospital orders**. |
| **Diagnostic over-shadowing** | A risk for everyone with a **mental disorder**, but a particular danger for people with **learning disabilities**, that behavioural problems may be misinterpreted as symptomatic of mental disorder when they are in fact a sign of an underlying physical health problem. |
| **Discharge** | Unless otherwise stated, a decision that a **patient** should no longer be subject to **detention, supervised community treatment, guardianship** or **conditional discharge.**<br><br>Discharge from detention is not the same as being discharged from hospital. The patient might already have left hospital on **leave of absence,** or might agree to remain in hospital as an **informal patient.** |
| **Displacement (or nearest relative)** | The provision under section 29 of **the Act,** under which the county court can order that the functions of the **nearest relative** be carried out by another person or by a **local social services authority**. |
| **Doctor** | A registered medical practitioner. |
| **Doctor approved under section 12** | A doctor who has been approved by the **Secretary of State** (or the **Welsh Ministers**) under the Act as having special experience in the diagnosis or treatment of mental disorder. In practice, **strategic health authorities** take these decisions on behalf of the Secretary of State in England.<br><br>Some medical recommendations and medical evidence to courts under the Act can only be made by a doctor who is approved under section 12. (Doctors who are **approved clinicians** are automatically treated as though they have been approved under section 12.) |
| **Electro-convulsive therapy (ECT)** | A form of **medical treatment for mental disorder** in which seizures are induced by passing electricity through the brain of an anaesthetised **patient**; generally used as treatment for severe depression. |

| Term | Definition |
|------|-----------|
| **Emergency application** | An **application for detention** for **assessment** made only one supporting medical recommendation in cases of urgent necessity. The patient can only be detained for a maximum of 72 hours unless a second medical recommendation is received. Also known as a "section 4 application". |
| **European Convention on Human Rights (ECHR)** | The European Convention for the Protection of Human Rights and Fundamental Freedoms. The substantive rights it guarantees are largely incorporated into UK law by the **Human Rights Act 1998**. |
| **GP** | A patient's general practitioner (or "family doctor"). |
| **Guardian** | See **guardianship**. |
| **Guardianship** | The appointment of a **guardian** to help and supervise patients in the community for their own welfare or to protect other people. The guardian may be either a **local social services authority (LSSA)** or someone else approved by an LSSA (a **private guardian**). |
| **Guardianship application** | An application to a **local social services authority** by an **approved mental health professional** or a **nearest relative** for a **patient** to become subject to **guardianship.** |
| **Guardianship order** | An order by the court, under **Part 3** of **the Act** that a **mentally disordered offender** should become subject to **guardianship**. |
| **Guiding principles** | The principles set out in **chapter 1** that have to be considered when decisions are made under the Act. |
| **Habilitation** | Equipping someone with skills and abilities they have never had. As opposed to **rehabilitation,** which means helping them recover skills and abilities they have lost. |
| **Health action plan** | A plan which details the actions needed to maintain and improve the health of an individual with a learning disability and any help needed to achieve them. It links the individual with the range of services and supports they need in order to have better health. It is part of their broader **person-centred plan**. |
| **Holding powers** | The powers in section 5 of **the Act** which allow hospital in-patients to be detained temporarily so that a decision can be made about whether an **application for detention** should be made.

There are two holding powers: under section 5(2), **doctors** and **approved clinicians** can detain patients for up to 72 hours; and under section 5(4), certain nurses can detain patients for up to 6 hours. |

| Term | Definition |
| --- | --- |
| **Hospital direction** | An order by the court under **Part 3** of **the Act** for the **detention for medical treatment** in hospital of a **mentally disordered offender.** It is given alongside a prison sentence. Hospital directions are given under section 45A of the Act. |
| **Hospital managers** | The organisation (or individual) responsible for the operation of **the Act** in a particular hospital (eg an **NHS trust**, an **NHS foundation trust** or the owners of an **independent hospital**). Hospital managers have various functions under the Act, which include the power to **discharge** a patient. In practice, most of the hospital managers' decisions are taken on their behalf by individuals (or groups of individuals) authorised by the hospital managers to do so. This can include clinical staff. Hospital managers' decisions about discharge are normally delegated to a **"managers' panel"** of three or more people. |
| **Hospital order** | An order by a court under **Part 3** of **the Act** for the **detention for medical treatment** in hospital of a **mentally disordered offender**, given instead of a prison sentence or other form of punishment. Hospital orders are normally made under section 37 of the Act. |
| **Human Rights Act 1998** | A law largely incorporating into UK law the substantive rights set out in the **European Convention on Human Rights**. |
| **Independent hospital** | A hospital which is not managed by the NHS. |
| **Independent mental health advocate (IMHA)** | An advocate available to offer help to patients under arrangements **mental health** which are specifically required to be made under **the Act**.[30] |
| **Independent mental health advocacy services** | The services which make **independent mental health advocates** available to **patients**. The Act calls patients who are eligible for these services "qualifying patients". |
| **Informal patient** | Someone who is being treated for a **mental disorder** and who is not **detained** under **the Act**. Also sometimes known as a "voluntary patient". |
| **Interim hospital order** | An order by a court under **Part 3** of **the Act** for the **detention for medical treatment** in hospital of a **mentally disordered offender** on an interim basis, to enable the court to decide whether to make a **hospital order** or deal with the offender's case in some other way. Interim hospital orders are made under section 38 of the Act. |

---

[30] These arrangements are not expected to be in force until April 2009.

| Term | Definition |
|---|---|
| **Learning disability** | In **the Act,** a learning disability means a state of arrested or incomplete development of the mind which includes significant impairment of intelligence and social functioning. It is a form of **mental disorder**. |
| **Learning disability qualification** | The rule which says that certain parts of **the Act** only apply to a **learning disability** if the learning disability is associated with **qualification** abnormally aggressive or seriously irresponsible behaviour on the part of the person concerned. |
| **Leave of absence** | Permission for a **patient** who is **detained** in hospital to be absent from the hospital for short periods, eg to go to the shops or spend a weekend at home, or for much longer periods. Patients remain under the powers of **the Act** when they are on leave and can be **recalled** to hospital if necessary in the interest of the patient's health or safety or for the protection of other people. |
| **Local social services authority (LSSA)** | The local authority (or council) responsible for social services in a particular area of the country. |
| **Managers** | See **hospital managers**. |
| **Managers' panel** | A panel of three or more people appointed to take decisions on behalf of **hospital managers** about the **discharge** of patients from **detention** or **supervised community treatment**. |
| **Medical recom- mendation** | Normally means a recommendation provided by a **doctor** in support of an **application for detention** or a **guardianship application.** |
| **Medical treatment** | In **the Act**, this covers a wide range of services. As well as the kind of care and treatment given by **doctors,** it also includes nursing, psychological therapies, and specialist mental health **habilitation, rehabilitation** and care. |
| **Medical treatment for mental disorder** | **Medical treatment** which is for the purpose of alleviating, or preventing a worsening of, the **mental disorder**, or one or more of its symptoms or manifestations. |
| **Mental Capacity Act** | The Mental Capacity Act 2005. An Act of Parliament that governs decision-making on behalf of people who lack **capacity,** both where they lose capacity at some point in their lives, eg as a result of dementia or brain injury, and where the incapacitating condition has been present since birth. |
| **Mental disorder** | Any disorder or disability of the mind. As well as mental illnesses, it includes conditions like personality disorders, autistic spectrum disorders and **learning disabilities**. |

| Term | Definition |
|---|---|
| **Mental Health Act Commission** | See **Commission**. |
| **Mental illness** | An illness of the mind. It includes common conditions like depression and anxiety and less common conditions like schizophrenia, bipolar disorder, anorexia nervosa and dementia. |
| **Mentally disordered offender** | A person who has a **mental disorder** and who has committed a criminal offence. |
| **Nearest relative** | A person defined by section 26 of **the Act** who has certain rights and powers under the Act in respect of a **patient** for whom they are the nearest relative. |
| **NHS** | The National Health Service. |
| **NHS commissioners** | **Primary care trusts (PCTs)** and other bodies responsible for commissioning NHS services. |
| **NHS trust and NHS foundation trust** | Types of NHS body responsible for providing NHS services in a local area. |
| **Nominated deputy** | A **doctor** or **approved clinician** who may make a report detaining a **patient** under the **holding powers** in section 5 in the absence of the **doctor** or approved clinician who is in charge of the patient's treatment. |
| **Part 2** | The part of **the Act** which deals with **detention, guardianship** and **supervised community treatment** for civil (ie non-offender) patients. |
| | Some aspects of Part 2 also apply to some patients who have been detained or made subject to guardianship by the courts or who have been transferred from prison to detenton in hospital by the **Secretary of State for Justice** under **Part 3** of **the Act.** |
| **Part 2 patient** | A civil patient—ie a patient who became subject to **compulsory measures** under **the Act** as a result of an **application for detention** or a **guardianship application** by a **nearest relative** or an **approved mental health professional** under **Part 2** of the Act. |
| **Part 3** | The part of **the Act** which deals with **mentally disordered offenders** and defendants in criminal proceedings. Among other things, it allows courts to **detain** people in hospital for treatment instead of punishing them, where particular criteria are met. It also allows the **Secretary of State for Justice** to transfer people from prison to detention in hospital for treatment. |

| Term | Definition |
| --- | --- |
| **Part 3 patient** | A patient made subject to **compulsory measures** under **the Act** by the courts or by being transferred to detention in hospital from prison under **Part 3** of the Act. Part 3 patients can be either "restricted" (ie subject to special restrictions on when they can be **discharged,** given **leave of absence,** and various other matters) or "unrestricted" (ie treated for the most part like a **Part 2 patient).** |
| **Part 4** | The part of **the Act** which deals mainly with the **medical treatment for mental disorder** of **detained patients** (including **SCT patients** who have been **recalled** to hospital). In particular, it sets out when they can and cannot be treated for their mental disorder without their **consent**. |
| **Part 4A** | The Part of the Act which deals with the **medical treatment for mental disorder** of **SCT patients** when they have not been **recalled** to hospital. |
| **Part 4A certificate** | A **SOAD certificate** approving particular forms of **medical treatment for mental disorder** for an **SCT patient**. |
| **Part 4A patient** | In **chapters 23** and **24** means an **SCT patient** who has not been **recalled** to hospital. |
| **Patient** | People who are, or appear to be, suffering from a **mental disorder**. This use of the term is not a recommendation that the term "patient" should be used in practice in preference to other terms such as "service users", "clients" or similar terms. It is simply a reflection of the terminology used in **the Act** itself. |
| **Person-centred plan** | An individual plan for each person with a **learning disability,** tailored to their needs and aspirations, which aims to help them to be a part of their community and to help the community to welcome them. |
| **Place of safety** | A place in which people may be temporarily detained under **the Act.** In particular, a place to which the police may remove a person for the purpose of assessment under section 135 or 136 of the Act. (A place of safety may be a hospital, a residential care home, a police station, or any other suitable place.) |
| **Primary care trust (PCT)** | The NHS body responsible, in particular, for commissioning (arranging) NHS services for a particular part of England. PCTs may also provide NHS services themselves. |
| **Private guardian** | An individual person (rather than a **local social services authority**) who is a patient's **guardian** under **the Act**. |
| **Qualifying patients** | Patients who are eligible for support from **independent mental health advocacy services**. |

| Term | Definition |
|---|---|
| **Recall (and recalled)** | A requirement that a **patient** who is subject to **the Act** return to hospital. It can apply to patients who are on **leave of absence,** who are on **supervised community treatment,** or who have been given a **conditional discharge** from hospital. |
| **Regulations** | Secondary legislation made under **the Act**. In most cases, it means the Mental Health (Hospital, Guardianship and Treatment) (England) Regulations 2008. |
| **Rehabilitation** | See **habilitation.** |
| **Remand to hospital (and remanded to hospital)** | An order by a court under **Part 3** of **the Act** for the **detention** in hospital of a defendant in criminal proceedings. Remand under section 35 is for a report on the person's mental condition. Remand under section 36 is for **medical treatment for mental disorder.** |
| **Responsible clinician** | The **approved clinician** with overall responsibility for a patient's case. Certain decisions (such as renewing a patient's **detention** or placing a patient on **supervised community treatment**) can only be taken by the responsible clinician. |
| **Responsible hospital** | The hospital whose managers are responsible for an **SCT patient**. To begin with, at least, this is the hospital in which the patient was detained before being discharged onto **supervised community treatment.** |
| **Responsible local social services authority (LSSA)** | The **local social services authority (LSSA)** responsible for a **patient** who is subject to **guardianship** under the Act. The responsible LSSA is normally the LSSA for the area where the patient lives. But if the patient has a **private guardian**, it is the LSSA for the area where the guardian lives. |
| **Restricted patient** | A **Part 3 patient** who, following criminal proceedings, is made subject to a restriction order under section 41 of **the Act**, to a limitation direction under section 45A or to a restriction direction under section 49. The order or direction will be imposed on an offender where it appears that it is necessary to protect the public from serious harm. One of the effects of the restrictions imposed by these sections is that restricted patients cannot be given **leave of absence** or be transferred to another hospital without the consent of the **Secretary of State for Justice,** and only the **Tribunal** can discharge them without the Secretary of State's agreement. See also **Unrestricted Part 3 patient.** |
| **Revocation (and revoke)** | Term used in **the Act** to describe the rescinding of a **community treatment order (CTO)** when an **SCT patient** needs further treatment in hospital under the Act. If a patient's CTO is revoked, the patient is **detained** under the powers of the Act in the same way as before the CTO was made. |
| **SCT patient** | A patient who is on **supervised community treatment.** |

| Term | Definition |
| --- | --- |
| **Second opinion appointed doctor (SOAD)** | An independent **doctor** appointed by the **Commission** who gives a second opinion on whether certain types of **medical treatment for mental disorder** should be given without the patient's **consent.** |
| **Secretary of State** | Cabinet ministers in the Government. In the Act, either of State for Health or the Secretary of State for Justice, depending on the context. |
| **Secretary of State for Health** | The **Secretary of State** who is responsible, among other things, for the NHS and social services for adults. The Secretary of State for Health is supported by the Department of Health. |
| **Secretary of State for Justice** | The **Secretary of State** who is responsible, among other things, for courts, prisons, probation, criminal law and sentencing. The Secretary of State for Justice is supported by the Ministry of Justice. |
| **Section 4 application** | See **emergency application. application**. |
| **Section 57 treatment** | A form of **medical treatment for mental disorder** to which the special rules in section 57 of the Act apply, especially neurosurgery for **mental disorder** (sometimes called "psychosurgery").[31] |
| **Section 58 treatment** | A form of **medical treatment for mental disorder** to which the special rules in section 58 of the Act apply, which means medication for **mental disorder** for detained patients after an initial three-month period.[31] |
| **Section 58A treatment** | A form of **medical treatment for mental disorder** to which the special rules in section 58 of the Act apply, especially **electro-convulsive therapy.**[31] |
| **Section 117** | See **after-care**. |
| **SOAD certificate** | A certificate issued by a **second opinion appointed doctor (SOAD) approving particular forms of medical treatment for a patient.** |
| **Strategic health authority (SHA)** | NHS body responsible for overseeing all NHS services in a particular region of England. |
| **Supervised community treatment (SCT)** | Arrangements under which patients can be discharged from detention in hospital under **the Act,** but remain subject to the Act in the community rather than in hospital. Patients on SCT are expected to comply with conditions set out in the **community treatment order** and can be **recalled** to hospital if treatment in hospital is necessary again. |

---

[31] It is possible that other forms of treatment may be added to s.57, s.58 or s.58A by regulations.

| Term | Definition |
| --- | --- |
| **Tribunal** | A judicial body which has the power to discharge patients from **detention, supervised community treatment, guardianship** and **conditional discharge**. |
| | At the time of publication, this means the Mental Health Review Tribunal (MHRT). However, subject to Parliament, the MHRT is intended to be replaced in England by a new First Tier Tribunal established under the Tribunals, Courts and Enforcement Act 2007. |
| **Unrestricted Part 3 patient** | A patient subject to a **hospital order** or **guardianship order** under Part 3 of **the Act,** or who has been transferred from prison to detention in hospital under that Part, who is not also subject to a restriction order or direction. For the most part, unrestricted patients are treated in the same way as **Part 2 patients,** although they cannot be discharged by their **nearest relative.** See also **Restricted patient.** |
| **Voluntary patient** | See **informal patient**. |
| **Welsh Ministers** | Ministers in the Welsh Assembly Government. |
| **Young person** | A person aged 16 or 17. |

# ANNEX B
## LIST OF POLICIES AND PROCEDURES

This annex contains a summary of the policies, procedures and guidance which the Code says should be put in place locally by hospital managers, local social services authorities (LSSAs) and others.

| Paragraph of Code | Policy, procedure or guidance | |
| --- | --- | --- |
| 2.44 | **Information policy** Hospital managers should have in place policies to ensure that all detained and supervised community treatment (SCT) patients and their nearest relatives are given information about their legal situation and rights in accordance with the legislation. | 4–385 |
| 4.46 | **Police assistance for people undertaking assessments with a view to applications under the Act** There should be locally agreed arrangements for the circumstances in which the police should be asked to provide assistance to approved mental health professionals (AMHPs) and doctors undertaking assessments. | |
| 8.16 | **Displacement of nearest relatives** LSSAs should provide clear, practical guidance to help AMHPs decide whether to make an application to the county court for the appointment of an acting nearest relative for a patient and how to proceed. | |
| 8.19 | **Displacement of nearest relatives** LSSAs should provide clear practical guidance to help AMHPs decide who to nominate when making an application to displace a nearest relative. | |
| 10.7 | **Warrants under section 135 of the Act** LSSAs should ensure that guidance is available to AMHPs on how and when to apply for a warrant under section 135 to permit the police to enter premises. | |
| 10.16 | **Sections 135 and 136 of the Act** LSSAs, NHS bodies, police forces and ambulance services should have an agreed local policy in place governing all aspects of the use of section 135 and 136 (police powers and places of safety). | |
| 11.9–11.12 | **Conveyance of patients under the Act** Relevant authorities, including NHS bodies responsible for hospitals, ambulance services and the police, should agree joint local policies and procedures for conveying patients under the Act, setting out clearly the respective responsibilities of the different agencies and service providers. | |

| Paragraph of Code | Policy, procedure or guidance |
| --- | --- |
| **13.8** | **Receipt of applications for detention**<br>Hospital managers should provide a checklist for the guidance of people delegated to receive detention documents. |
| **13.15** | **Receipt of guardianship applications**<br>LSSAs should prepare a checklist for the guidance of those delegated to receive guardianship applications on their behalf. |
| **14.3** | **Allocation of responsible clinicians**<br>Hospital managers should have local protocols in place for allocating responsible clinicians to patients. |
| **15.6** | **Management of disturbed or violent behaviour**<br>All hospitals should have a policy on the recognition and prevention of disturbed, challenging or violent behaviour, including the use of de-escalation techniques, enhanced observation, physical intervention, rapid tranquillisation and seclusion. |
| **15.21** | **Restraint and physical interventions**<br>Hospital policies on management of disturbed behaviour should include clear written policies on the use of restraint and physical interventions, including provisions for post-incident reviews. |
| **15.31** | **Mechanical restraint**<br>If any forms of mechanical restraint are to be used, there should be a clear policy in place governing their use. |
| **15.36** | **Training for staff exposed to aggression or violence**<br>All hospitals should have a policy on training staff who work in areas where they may be exposed to aggression or violence or who may need to become involved in the restraint of patients. |
| **15.42** | **Observation**<br>All hospitals should have clear written policies on the use of observation. |
| **15.47–15.59** | **Seclusion**<br>Hospital policies should include clear written guidelines on the use of seclusion and set requirements for recording, monitoring and reviewing the use of seclusion and any follow-up action. |
| **15.66** | **Longer-term segregation**<br>Hospitals proposing to allow long-term segregation should have a policy in place which sets out when it is to be used and how it is to be kept under review. |
| **16.5–16.6** | **Mobile phones**<br>Hospital managers should have a policy on the possession and use of mobile phones by patients and their visitors. |

| Paragraph of Code | Policy, procedure or guidance |
|---|---|
| 16.7 | **Internet access**<br>Hospital managers should have guidance on patients' access to e-mail and the internet using the hospital's own IT infrastructure. |
| 16.10 | **Searching**<br>Hospital managers should ensure that there is an operational policy on searching detained patients, their belongings and surroundings and their visitors. |
| 16.33 | **Accommodation with enhanced levels of security**<br>Hospitals offering accommodation with enhanced levels of security should have written guidelines, setting out the categories of patients for whom it is appropriate to use physically secure conditions and those for whom it is not appropriate. |
| 16.39 | **Entry and exit from wards**<br>Wards should have a written policy that sets out precisely what the arrangements are for entry to and exit from the ward. |
| 19.9 | **Visits to patients in hospitals**<br>Hospitals should have a policy on the circumstances in which visits to patients may be restricted. |
| 19.17 | **Visits by and to children and young people**<br>All hospitals should have written policies and procedures regarding the arrangements for children and young people who visit patients in hospital and for visits to patients who are children or young people. |
| 22.10 | **Patients absent without leave from hospital**<br>Hospital managers should ensure that there is a clear written policy about the action to be taken when a detained patient, or a patient on SCT, goes missing. This policy should be agreed with other agencies such as the police and ambulance services. |
| 22.12 | **Guardianship patients absent without leave**<br>LSSAs should have policies for the action to be taken when they, or a private guardian, become aware that a guardianship patient is absent without leave (AWOL) from the place they are required to live. |
| 25.46 | **Supervised community treatment—concerns of carers and relatives**<br>The managers of responsible hospitals should ensure that local protocols are in place to cover how concerns raised by carers or relatives about SCT patients' health or compliance with the conditions of their community treatment orders are addressed and taken forward. |

| Paragraph of Code | Policy, procedure or guidance |
| --- | --- |
| 26.15 | **Guardianship** Each LSSA should have a policy setting out the arrangements for the way in which it will discharge its responsibilities in relation to guardianship. |
| 29.5 | **Renewal of detention** Hospital managers should determine local policies on the selection of the second professional required to agree to the renewal of a patient's detention. |
| 30.33 | **Inspection and withholding of correspondence** The managers of high-security psychiatric hospitals should have a written policy for the exercise of their power to withhold both the incoming and outgoing post from patients in certain circumstances. |

# PART 5

# HUMAN RIGHTS ACT 1998

## (1998 C.42)

An Act to give further effect to rights and freedoms guaranteed under the **5–001** European Convention on Human Rights; to make provision with respect to holders of certain judicial offices who become judges of the European Court of Human Rights; and for connected purposes.

[9th November 1998]

$$* \quad * \quad * \quad *$$

GENERAL NOTE

This Part examines the Human Rights Act 1998 as it applies to the care and treatment of mentally disordered people.

*Introduction*

The Second World War and its associated horrors caused an upsurge in international con- **5–002** cern for human rights. The European Convention for the Protection of Human Rights and Fundamental Freedoms, commonly known as the European Convention on Human Rights ("the Convention"), emerged out of that concern. It was concluded under the auspices of the Council of Europe in 1950, was ratified by the UK in 1951 and entered into force in 1953. The European Union, which is a separate entity from the Council of Europe, is not a party to the Convention.

*The Commission and the Court*

One of the most distinctive features of the Convention has been the role played by two **5–003** organs, the European Commission on Human Rights ("the Commission") and the European Court on Human Rights ("the Court"), in building up a substantial body of case law in the course of deciding petitions brought by individuals. Until recently, such petitions have been required to pass through two hurdles. Initially, the case has been examined by the Commission to determine whether it is "admissible". In 1998 the role of the Commission was abolished and there are now only two European institutions, the Court (which can sit in Chambers and in a Grand Chamber) and the Committee of Ministers of the Council of Europe, that administer the Convention.

Larry Gostin has described how the Court operates:

"The Court can consider cases only after exhaustion of all domestic remedies and within a period of 6 months from the date when the final decision was taken (Article 35). The Court can hold an application 'inadmissible' if it is 'incompatible' with the Convention (e.g. the Convention does not apply), 'manifestly ill-founded' (e.g. the facts do not disclose a prima facie violation), or an 'abuse of the rights of petition' (e.g. politically motivated). If the Court finds the case 'admissible', it will investigate: it can secure a 'friendly settlement' (i.e. a negotiated agreement) or, after hearing, render a decision on the merits. If it finds a violation of the Convention, the Court has the power to afford

973

'just satisfaction' (i.e. damages and reimbursement of legal costs) (Article 41). A Chamber's judgment can be appealed to the Grand Chamber if it raises a serious issue affecting the interpretation of the Convention or of general importance (Article 43)" (L.O. Gostin, "Human Rights of Persons With Mental Disabilities: The European Convention of Human Rights", 23 Int. J. of Law and Psychiatry 134 (2000)).

*Interpreting the Convention*

**5–004**     The Court has said:

"Inherent in the Convention is a search for a fair balance between the demands of the general interest of the community and the requirements of the protection of the individual's fundamental rights" (*Soering v United Kingdom* (1989) 11 E.H.R.R. 439).

The Convention is "an instrument designed to maintain and promote the ideals and values of a democratic society (*Kjeldsen v Denmark* (1979–80) 1 E.H.R.R. 711 para.53). Its "very essence . . . is respect for human dignity and human freedom" (*Pretty v United Kingdom* (2002) 35 E.H.R.R. 1 para.65). The Convention is "intended to guarantee not rights that are theoretical and illusory but rights that are practical and effective" (*Marckx v Belgium* (1979–80) 2 E.H.R.R. 330 para.31) and is "directed to the protection of fundamental human rights, not the conferment of individual advantage or benefit" (*R. (on the application of Razgar) v Secretary of State for the Home Department* [2004] UKHL 27; [2004] 3 All E.R. 821 at para.4 per Lord Bingham). In interpreting the Convention, the Court takes account of generally accepted features of the legislation and government of the Member States (*James v United Kingdom* (1986) 8 E.H.R.R. 123 para.54). The meaning of the Convention cannot differ from Member State to Member State.

The Court has said that the Convention is a "living instrument" which must be interpreted in the light of present day conditions (see, for example, *Tyrer v United Kingdom* (1970) 2 E.H.R.R. 1). This approach was emphasised in *Selmouni v France* (2000) 29 E.H.R.R. 403, para.101, where the Court said that "the increasingly high standard being required in the area of protection of human rights and fundamental liberties correspondingly and inevitably requires greater firmness in assessing breaches of the fundamental values of democratic societies". The interpretation of Convention rights will therefore need to be subject to constant reappraisal in order for them to adapt to present day conditions. However, the Court has consistently declared itself to be slow to trespass on areas of social, political and religious controversy, where a wide variety of national and cultural traditions are in play and different political and legal choices have been made by members of the Council of Europe; see, for example, *Botta v Italy* (1998) 26 E.H.R.R. 241 at para.35. The Court has also said that in securing the rights protected by the Convention, the Contracting States, notably their courts, are obliged to apply the provisions of national law in the spirit of those rights. Failure to do so can amount to a violation of the Convention Article in question (*Storck v Germany* (2006) 43 E.H.R.R. 6; [2005] M.H.L.R. 211 para.93).

The Court has developed a standard approach when considering cases:

1. Has there been an interference with a Convention right, bearing in mind the need to construe the Convention broadly in order to give it practical effectiveness?

2. If there has been an interference with a non-absolute article, is it justified?

3. To be justified the interference must be: (a) lawful; (b) intended to pursue a legitimate aim (i.e. one of the aims listed in arts 8(2), 9(2), 10(2) or 11(2)); (c) necessary in a democratic society; and (d) not discriminatory.

With regard to 3, the Court has said that:

(a) Lawfulness involves more than merely formal authorisation. It requires that:

"the law must indicate the scope of any . . . discretion conferred on the competent authorities and the manner of its exercise with sufficient clarity, having regard to the legitimate aim of the measure in question, to give the individual adequate protection against arbitrary interference" (*Malone v United Kingdom* (1985) 7 E.H.R.R. 14, para.68).

(b) To be "necessary in a democratic society" the limitation or restriction must fulfil a pressing social need and be "proportionate to the legitimate aim pursued" (*Handyside v United Kingdom* (1976) 1 E.H.R.R. 737 para.49). This means that even if a particular policy or action that interferes with a Convention right pursues a legitimate aim this will not justify the interference if the means used to achieve the purpose are excessive. Proportionately must be assessed by the standards of a democratic society, characterised by "pluralism, tolerance and broadmindedness" (*Handyside* above). The striking of a fair balance lies at the heart of proportionality (*Sporrong v Sweden* (1983) 5 E.H.R.R. 35).

(c) The second principle that the Court has developed under 3(c) is the "Margin of Appreciation". This principle, which means the range of discretion open to national authorities without violating Convention provisions, is a reflection of the fact that national authorities, including national courts, "are in principle in a better position than the international judge to give an opinion on the exact content of" restrictions on Convention rights (*Handyside,* above, para.48). The margin of appreciation is particularly wide when the issues involve an assessment of the priorities in the context of the allocation of limited State resources (*Sentges v Netherlands* (2004) 7 C.C.L.R. 400).

*Extra-territorial effect*
In *R. v Special Adjudicato Ex p. Ullah* [2004] UKHL 26, the House of Lords answered **5–005** the following question in the affirmative:

"Whether any article of the European Convention on Human Rights other than Article 3 could be engaged in relation to a removal of an individual from the United Kingdom where the anticipated treatment in the receiving state will be in breach of the requirements of the Convention, but such treatment does not meet the minimum requirements of Article 3 of the Convention."

Their Lordships held that successful reliance on articles other than art.3 as a ground for resisting extradition or expulsion demands presentation of a very strong case. The Court has held that except in wholly exceptional circumstances, aliens who are subject to expulsion cannot in principle claim any entitlement to remain in the territory of a contracting state in order to benefit from medical, social or other forms of assistance provided by the expelling state (*Henao v The Netherlands*, App.No.13669/03, June 24, 2003).

*Human Rights Act 1998*
This Act is one of the most significant pieces of constitutional legislation enacted in the **5–006** UK. It incorporates provisions from the European Convention on Human Rights into UK law. The relevant provisions of the Convention are reproduced in Sch.1 to the Act, which is set out below. The Act is ultimately subject to the sovereignty of Parliament, in that:

1. It does not provide the courts with a power to strike down primary legislation that is inconsistent with the Convention.

2. It leaves Parliament free, if it chooses to do so, to enact and maintain legislation that is incompatible with the Convention.

3. The Act is not entrenched against repeal.

Within these constraints, the Act attempts to achieve the Government's aim to "bring rights home" (*Rights Brought Home: the Human Rights Bill*, Cm.3782 (1997)) by operating through three mechanisms:

1. Courts and tribunals are required to construe all legislation (past and future) "so far as it is possible to do so . . . in a way which is compatible with Convention rights" (s.3). When doing so the court or tribunal must take account of the case law of the Court and the Commission. This requirement means that domestic courts must search for a construction that would prevent the making of a "declaration of incompatibility".

2. All public authorities, including all courts and tribunals, and private providers who are exercising "functions of a public nature", are required to act in accordance with the Convention, within the scope permitted by primary legislation (s.6) and to have regard to European jurisprudence (s.2). An "act" includes a failure to act (s.6(6)). Approved mental health professionals, responsible clinicians, approved clinicians and nurses are public authorities for the purposes of the Convention when they perform functions under the Mental Health Act. Decisions made by a private hospital relating to the care or treatment of detained patients are decisions of a public nature. The hospital therefore becomes a public authority for the purposes of s.6 and its decisions are susceptible to judicial review (*R. (on the application of A) v Partnership in Care Ltd* [2002] EWHC 529; [2002] 1 W.L.R. 261).

3. The higher courts are able to make a "declaration of incompatibility" in respect of a provision of primary legislation, which the court considers to be incompatible with a Convention right (s.4). Such a declaration does not affect the validity, continued operation or enforcement of the provision in respect of which it is made (s.4(6)(a)) but it may lead to the correction of the legislation by Parliament making a "remedial order" which has the effect of bypassing the full legislative process (s.10).

Where it is not possible to interpret subordinate legislation so as to be compatible with the Convention, the courts have power to disapply it unless the primary legislation prevents removal of the incompatibility (s.4(4)(b)).

*Proceedings*

**5–007** Under s.7 of the Act, a person who claims that a public authority has acted (or proposes to act) in a way which is incompatible with a Convention right may (a) bring civil proceedings for damages against the authority under the Act or (b) rely on the Convention right concerned in any criminal or civil proceedings, but only if he is (or would be) a victim of the act. The great majority of cases have fallen within route (b). A public authority cannot be a "victim" for the purposes of the Convention (*Ayuntamiento de M v Spain* (1991) D&R 209). Reliance on a Convention right does not restrict other existing rights and freedoms under domestic law (s.11).

*Damages*

**5–008** The award of damages under the Act is governed by s.8. The question of when damages should be awarded and on what basis was considered by the House of Lords in *R. (on the application of Greenfield) v Secretary of State for the Home Department* [2005] UKHL 14; [2005] 2 All E.R.240 and by the Court of Appeal in *Van Colle v Chief Constable of Hertfordshire* Police [2007] EWCA Civ 325; [2007] 3 All E.R. 122.

SCHEDULE 1

THE ARTICLES

PART I

THE CONVENTION

RIGHTS AND FREEDOMS

Article 2

Right to Life

1. Everyone's right to life shall be protected by law. No one shall be deprived of his life intentionally **5–009**
save in the execution of a sentence of a court following his conviction of a crime for which this penalty
is provided by law.

2. Deprivation of life shall not be regarded as inflicted in contravention of this Article when it results
from the use of force which is no more than absolutely necessary:

(a)  in defence of any person from unlawful violence;

(b)  in order to effect a lawful arrest or to prevent the escape of a person lawfully detained;

(c)  in action lawfully taken for the purpose of quelling a riot or insurrection.

GENERAL NOTE

The Court has stated that this article "ranks as one of the most fundamental provisions in **5–010**
the Convention and, together with Article 3, enshrines one of the basic values of the democratic societies making up the Council of Europe" (*Cakici v Turkey* (2001) 31 E.H.R.R. 5
para.86).

This article is unconcerned with issues to do with the quality of living or what a person
chooses to do with his or her life. It cannot be interpreted as conferring the diametrically
opposite right, namely a right to die; nor can it create a right to self-determination in the
sense of conferring on an individual the entitlement to choose death rather than life
(*Pretty v United Kingdom* (2002) 35 E.H.R.R. 1 para.39). The object and purpose of the
Convention requires that this Article be interpreted and applied so as to make its safeguards
practical and effective (*McCann v United Kingdom* (1996) 21 E.H.R.R. 97 paras 146–147).

The Court has emphasised that persons in custody are in a vulnerable position and that
the authorities are under a duty to protect them. It is incumbent on the State to account for
any injuries suffered in custody, which obligation is particularly stringent where that individual dies (*Edwards v United Kingdom* (2002) 35 E.H.R.R. 19 para.56).

In *Osman v United Kingdom* (2000) 29 E.H.R.R. 245 para.115, the Court said that it was
common ground that the State's obligation under this article:

"extends beyond its primary duty to secure the right to life by putting in place effective
criminal law provisions to deter the commission of offences against the person backed up
by law-enforcement machinery for the prevention, suppression and sanctioning of such
provisions. It is thus accepted by those appearing before the Court that Article 2 of the
Convention may also imply in certain well-defined circumstances a positive obligation
on the authorities to take preventive operational measures to protect an individual whose
life is at risk from the criminal acts of another individual".

The Court said that for this positive obligation to be breached it must be established to the Court's satisfaction "that the authorities knew or ought to have known at the time of the existence of a real and immediate risk to the life of an identified individual or individuals from criminal acts of a third party and that they failed to take measures within the scope of their powers which, judged reasonably, might have been expected to take to avoid that risk" (para.116). The Court also said that, given the reality of resource allocation and the operational choices that have to be made, not every claimed risk to life can entail for the authorities a Convention requirement to take operational measures to prevent the risk from materialising and that the positive obligation "must be interpreted in a way which does not impose an impossible or disproportionate burden on the authorities" (*Osman* above). The positive obligation applies in the public-health sphere (*Dodov v Bulgaria* (2008) 47 E.H.R.R. 41 para.80). However, "where a Contracting State had made adequate provision for securing high professional standards among health professionals and the protection of the lives of patients, it cannot accept that matters such as error of judgment on the part of a health professional or negligent co-ordination among health professionals in the treatment of a particular patient are sufficient of themselves to call a Contracting State to account from the standpoint of its positive obligations under art.2 of the Convention to protect life" (*Powell v UK* (2000) 30 E.H.R.R. CD 362).

The *Osman* case places professionals who are performing functions under the Mental Health Act under a positive obligation to take appropriate preventative measures in respect of patients whom they know (or ought to have known) to be so dangerous as to be a threat to the lives of identified others. A positive obligation to save the life of a detained patient who is on hunger strike could also arise (see *X v Germany*, noted in art.3 under "degrading").

**5–011**    The *Osman* principle has been extended to self harm by people for whose welfare the state is responsible (*Keenan v United Kingdom* (2001) 33 E.H.R.R. 38; also see *Renolde v France* [2008] M.H.L.R. 331). The application of the principle to hospital patients who are detained under the Mental Health Act was examined by the House of Lords in *Savage v South Essex Partnership NHS Foundation Trust* [2008] UKHL 74; [2009] 1 All E.R. 1053 where it was held that it was not necessary for a claimant alleging a breach of this article to establish either gross negligence or anything more serious. The obligations of health authorities under this article were summarised by Lord Rodger at paras.68 to 72 of his speech:

"In terms of Art 2, health authorities are under an over-arching obligation to protect the lives of patients in their hospitals. In order to fulfil that obligation, and depending on the circumstances, they may require to fulfil a number of complementary obligations.

In the first place, the duty to protect the lives of patients requires health authorities to ensure that the hospitals for which they are responsible employ competent staff and that they are trained to a high professional standard. In addition, the authorities must ensure that the hospitals adopt systems of work which will protect the lives of patients. Failure to perform these general obligations may result in a violation of Art 2. If, for example, a health authority fails to ensure that a hospital puts in place a proper system for supervising mentally ill patients and, as a result, a patient is able to commit suicide, the health authority will have violated the patient's right to life under Art 2.

Even though a health authority employed competent staff and ensured that they were trained to a high professional standard, a doctor, for example, might still treat a patient negligently and the patient might die as a result. In that situation, there would be no violation of Art 2 since the health authority would have done all that the article required of it to protect the patient's life. Nevertheless, the doctor would be personally liable in damages for the death and the health authority would be vicariously liable for her negligence. This is the situation envisaged by *Powell* [*Powell v United Kingdom* (2000) 30 E.H.R.R. CD 362].

The same approach would apply if a mental hospital had established an appropriate system for supervising patients and all that happened was that, on a particular occasion, a nurse negligently left his post and a patient took the opportunity to commit suicide.

There would be no violation of any obligation under Art 2, since the health authority would have done all that the article required of it. But, again, the nurse would be personally liable in damages for the death and the health authority would be vicariously liable too. Again, this is just an application of *Powell.*

Finally, Art 2 imposes a further 'operational' obligation on health authorities and their hospital staff. This obligation is distinct from, and additional to, the authorities' more general obligations. The operational obligation arises only if members of staff know or ought to know that a particular patient presents a 'real and immediate' risk of suicide. In these circumstances Art 2 requires them to do all that can reasonably be expected to prevent the patient from committing suicide. If they fail to do this, not only will they and the health authorities be liable in negligence, but there will also be a violation of the operational obligation under art 2 to protect the patient's life. This is comparable to the position in *Osman* and *Keenan*. As the present case shows, if no other remedy is available, proceedings for an alleged breach of the obligation can be taken under the Human Rights Act 1998."

Subsequent to this finding, the daughter of the patient who committed suicide was identified as a "victim" for the purposes of s.7(7) of the 1998 Act and awarded compensation of £10,000 for non-pecuniary loss: see *Savage v South Essex Partnership NHS Foundation Trust* [2010] EWHC 865 (Q.B.), approved by the Court of Appeal in *Rabone*, below.

In *Rabone v Pennine Care NHS Trust* [2010], the Court of Appeal held that the "operational obligation" identified in *Savage* did not apply to voluntary patients, even where there is a "real and immediate" risk of death.

The provision of care to a detainee who is at risk of self harm could also give rise to issues under art.8.

The procedural element contained in this article:                    **5–012**

"imposes the minimum requirement that where a state or its agents potentially bear responsibility for loss of life the events in question should be subject to an effective investigation or scrutiny which enables the facts to become known to the public, and in particular to the relatives of any victim" (*Taylor, Campton and Gibson families v United Kingdom*, App. No. 23412/94; also see *McCann v United Kingdom* (1996) 21 E.H.R.R. 97, para.161).

Whatever form of investigation is employed, the authorities must act of their own motion, once the matter has come to their attention. They cannot leave it to the initiative of the next of kin either to lodge a formal complaint or to take responsibility for the conduct of any investigative procedures (*Edwards v United Kingdom*, above, para.69). The Court has said that the investigation must be independent, effective, and reasonably prompt, must have a sufficient element of public scrutiny, and the next of kin must be involved to the appropriate extent (*Jordan v United Kingdom* (2003) 37 E.H.R.R. 2 paras 106 to 109). In the *Edwards* case, the Court said at para.105:

"The essential purpose of such investigation is to secure the effective implementation of the domestic laws which protect the right to life and, in those cases involving State agents or bodies, to ensure accountability for deaths occurring under their responsibility. What form of investigation will achieve those purposes may vary in different circumstances".

The House of Lords reviewed the Strasbourg and domestic jurisprudence concerning the circumstances that give rise to the state's obligation to carry out an effective investigation into the death or near death of a person who was in the custody of the state and the requirements of the investigation in *R. (on the application of JL) v Secretary of State for the Home Department* [2008] UKHL 68. *JL* was followed in *R. (on the application of Allen) v HM Coroner for Inner North London* [2009] EWCA Civ 623, where the Court of Appeal held that an art.2 investigation was required in a case where it was *possible* that the death of patient who was detained in a psychiatric hospital was caused by the failure of the medical authorities to take general measures to save her.

*Paragraph 1*

**5–013**    EVERYONE'S LIFE SHALL BE PROTECTED BY LAW.    Apart from the law relating to abortion, the extent to which this article can be invoked to protect the life of an unborn child is uncertain: see the note on "The Human Rights Act 1998" under s.3 of the Mental Health Act.

INTENTIONALLY.    This word should be given its natural and ordinary meaning, and applies only to cases where the purpose of the prohibited action is to cause death (*Re A (Children) (Conjoined Twins: Surgical Separation)* [2004] 4 All E.R. 961 CA; also see *Association X v United Kingdom* (1978) 14 D. & R. 31).

*Paragraph 2*

USE OF FORCE.    This article covers not only intentional killing but also situations where it is permitted to "use force" which may result, as an unintended outcome, in the deprivation of life. The use of the term "absolutely necessary" indicates that a stricter and more compelling test of necessity must be employed from that normally applicable when determining whether state action is "necessary in a democratic society" under para.2 of arts 8 to 11 of the Convention. Consequentially, the force used must be strictly proportionate to the achievement of the permitted aims (*McKerr v United Kingdom* (2002) 34 E.H.R.R. 20 para.110).

In *Saoud v France*, October 9, 2007, the Court said that the authorities had a positive obligation to protect the health of persons who were in detention or police custody or who had just been arrested. A breach of this article was found in this case where an arrested person who suffered from schizophrenia and was very dangerous died from slow asphyxia after being held on the ground by the police for 35 minutes. The Court deplored the fact that no precise instructions had been issued to the police regarding this type of immobilisation technique.

ARTICLE 3

PROHIBITION OF TORTURE

No one shall be subjected to torture or to inhuman or degrading treatment or punishment.

GENERAL NOTE

**5–014**    This article, which enshrines one of the most fundamental values of democratic society (*T and V v United Kingdom* (2000) 30 E.H.R.R. 121 para.69), prohibits in absolute terms torture or inhuman or degrading treatment or punishment, irrespective of the circumstances and the victim's behaviour (see, for example, *Van der Ven v Netherlands*, (2004) E.H.R.R. 46 para.46). It is not subject to any saving clauses. One of its main purposes is to protect "a person's dignity and physical integrity" (*Tyrer v United Kingdom* (1978) 2 E.H.R.R. 1 para.33). Provided it is sufficiently real and immediate, a mere threat of conduct prohibited by this article may itself constitute a violation (*Campbell v Cosans v United Kingdom* (1982) 4 E.H.R.R. 293 para.26). In assessing evidence, the Court has adopted the standard of proof "beyond reasonable doubt". However, as applied by the Court, this term has an autonomous meaning. The role of the Court is not to rule on criminal guilt or civil liability, but on the responsibility of Contracting States under the Convention (*Mathew v Netherlands* (2006) 43 E.H.R.R. 23 para.156).

Although this article admits of no exceptions, logically the prohibition of inhuman and degrading treatment ought to have the same exceptions as those contained in art.2(2). The Court has acted on the assumption that this article is subject to such exceptions as long as any force used is strictly necessary and proportionate: see, for example, *RIVAS v France*, April 1, 2004, at paras 41, 42.

In *A v United Kingdom* (1999) 27 E.H.R.R. 611, the Court held that this article requires "States to take measures designed to ensure that individuals within their jurisdiction are not subjected to torture or inhuman or degrading treatment or punishment, including such ill-treatment administered by private individuals" (para.22). There is a particular need for states to take such measures in the context of psychiatric hospitals, where patients are typically in a position of inferiority and helplessness (*Wilkinson v United Kingdom* (1998) 26 E.H.R.R. CD131). A failure to take reasonably available measures which could have had a real prospect of altering the outcome or mitigating the harm is sufficient to engage the responsibility of the state (*E v United Kingdom* (2003) 36 E.H.R.R. 31 para.99). These measures "should provide effective protection, in particular, of children and other vulnerable persons and include reasonable steps to prevent ill-treatment of which the authorities had or ought to have had knowledge" (*Z v United Kingdom* (2002) 34 E.H.R.R. 3 para.73).

This article, like art.2, imposes an obligation to investigate (*Assenov v Bulgaria* (1999) 28 E.H.R.R. 652). The investigation "should be capable of leading to the identification and punishment of those responsible" (para.102). A failure to find state agents guilty of a crime of violence against a detainee under their control cannot absolve the state of its responsibilities under the Convention (*Afanasyev v Ukraine* (2006) 42 E.H.R.R. 52 para.64).

According to the Court, the ill-treatment that the person is subjected to:

"must attain a minimum level of severity if it is to fall within the scope of Article 3. The assessment of this minimum is, in the nature of things, relative; it depends on all the circumstances of the case, such as the duration of the treatment, its physical or mental effects and in some cases, the sex, age and state of health of the victim, etc." (*Ireland v United Kingdom* (1979) 2 E.H.R.R. 25 at para.162).

In *O'Rourke v United Kingdom*, June 26, 2001, para.60, the Court said that "it is quite impossible by a simple definition to embrace all human conditions that will engage Article 3". The Court provided the following guidance in *Pretty v United Kingdom* (2002) 35 E.H.R.R. 1 at para.52:

"As regards the types of 'treatment' which falls within the scope of Article 3 of the Convention, the court's case law refers to 'ill-treatment' that attains a minimum level of severity and involves actual bodily injury or intense physical or mental suffering. Where treatment humiliates or debases an individual showing lack of respect for, or diminishing, his or her human dignity or arouses feelings of fear, anguish or inferiority capable of breaking an individual's moral and physical resistance, it may be characterised as degrading and also fall within the prohibition of Article 3. The suffering which flows from naturally occurring illnesses, physical or mental, may be covered by Article 3, where it is, or risks being, exacerbated by treatment, whether flowing from conditions of detention, expulsion or other measures, for which the authorities can be held responsible".

In *Selmouni v France* (2000) 29 E.H.R.R. 403 at para.101, the Court said that it:

"has previously examined cases in which it concluded that there had been treatment which could only be described as torture. However, having regard to the fact that the Convention is a 'living instrument which must be interpreted in the light of present-day conditions', the Court considers that certain acts which were classified in the past as 'inhuman and degrading treatment' as opposed to 'torture' could be classified differently in future. It takes the view that the increasingly high standard being required in the area of the protection of human rights and fundamental liberties correspondingly and inevitably requires greater firmness in assessing breaches of the fundamental values in a democratic society".

This significant statement means that the concept of inhuman or degrading treatment will inevitably expand to encompass conduct that was previously outside the scope of this article. Note, however, that in *R. (on the application of DB) v Secretary of State for the Home Department* [2006] EWHC 659 (Admin) at para.45. Davis J. said that over-ready assertions of reliance on this article, "if not kept under proper restraint, can only operate to debase in the public perception what ought to be regarded as one of the most fundamental of rights enshrined in the Convention."

Paragraph 41 of the report of the European Committee for the Prevention of Torture and Inhuman or Degrading Treatment (August 2000) was "usefully" brought to the attention of the Court of Appeal in *R. (on the application of Wilkinson) v The Responsible Medical Officer Broadmoor Hospital* [2001] EWCA Civ 1545; [2002] 1 W.L.R. 419 at para.28. Paragraph 41 of the report states:

> "Patients should, as a matter of principle, be placed in a position to give their free and informed consent to treatment. The admission of a person to a psychiatric establishment on an involuntary basis should not be construed as authorising treatment without his consent. It follows that every competent patient, whether voluntary or involuntary, should be given the opportunity to refuse treatment or other medical intervention. Any derogation from this fundamental principle should be based upon law and only relate to clearly and strictly defined exceptional circumstances".

Although this article cannot be construed as laying down a general obligation to release prison detainees on health grounds (*Mouisel v France* (2004) 38 E.H.R.R. 34). However, this provision does require the state to ensure that prisoners are detained in conditions which arecompatible with respect for human dignity, that the manner and method of the execution of the measure do not subject them to distress or hardship of an intensity exceeding the unavoidable level of suffering inherent indetention and that, given the practical demands of imprisonment, their health and well-being are adequately secured by, among other things, providing them with the requisite medical assistance (*Kaprykowski v Poland,* February 3, 2009, para.69). The lack of appropriate medical treatment for such a person may amount to treatment contrary to this article (*Keenan v United Kingdom* (2001) 33 E.H.R.R. 38, para.110). *Keenan* was a case where the threshold of this article was reached where a serious disciplinary punishment involving segregation and additional detention was imposed on a mentally ill prisoner known to be a suicide risk without any effective monitoring or psychiatric care. A similar finding was made in *Renolde v France* (2009) 48 E.H.R.R. 969. The threshold was not reached in *Drew v United Kingdom* (2006) 43 E.H.R.R. SE2, where a prisoner was detained on a prison medical wing for eight days without access to effective psychiatric medication prior to his transfer to hospital. In *Brand v Netherlands* [2001] M.H.L.R. 275, the Court declared inadmissible an application that a lengthy detention of a mentally disordered person in prison pending a place being found for in a secure psychiatric institution constituted a breach of this article on the ground that there was no evidence that the applicant's mental health or the possibilities of treatment had suffered on account of the time spent in prison. This article has never been applied to merely policy decisions on the allocation of resources (*R. v North West Lancashire Health Authority Ex p. A* [2000] 1 W.L.R. 997 at 1000).

**5–015**   The assessment of whether a particular treatment or punishment is incompatible with the standards of this article has, in the case of mentally ill persons, to take into consideration their vulnerability and their inability, in some cases, to complain coherently or at all about how they are being affected by any particular treatment (*Keenan v United Kingdom*, above, para.110). In *Keenan* the Court said, at para.112, that:

> "in respect of a person deprived of his liberty, recourse to physical force which has not been made strictly necessary by his own conduct diminishes human dignity and is in principle an infringement of the right set out in Article 3. Similarly, treatment of a mentally ill person may be incompatible with the standards imposed by Article 3 in the

protection of fundamental human dignity, even though that person may not be able, or capable of, pointing to any specific ill-effects".

Case law on this article indicates that medical treatment only engages the article if the free and informed consent of the patient has not been forthcoming (*X v Denmark* (1983) 32 DR 282). The Court has been reluctant to categorise either psychiatric treatment (no matter how disagreeable (*Naumenko v Ukraine*, February 10, 2004)) or institutional conditions as "inhuman or degrading treatment". In *Herczegfalvy v Austria* (1993) 15 E.H.R.R. 437, the patient had been handcuffed to a security bed with a belt placed around his ankles. The Court, in holding that medical treatment could, in principle reach a level of severity sufficient to amount to "inhuman or degrading treatment" contrary to this article, said at paras 82, 83:

"The Court considers that the position of inferiority and powerlessness which is typical of patients confined in psychiatric hospitals calls for increased vigilance in reviewing whether the Convention has been complied with. While it is for the medical authorities to decide, on the basis of recognised rules of medical science, on the therapeutic methods to be used, if necessary by force, to preserve the physical and mental health of patients who are entirely incapable of deciding for themselves and for whom they are therefore responsible, such patients nevertheless remain under the protection of Article 3, the requirements of which permit no derogation . . . [H]owever, the evidence before the Court is not sufficient to disprove the Government's argument that, according to the psychiatric principles generally accepted as the time, medical necessity justified the treatment in issue".

Although these principles were advanced in relation to a patient who lacked capacity, in *Nevmerzhitsky v Ukraine* (2006) 43 E.H.R.R. 32, the Court applied them to a mentally capable applicant, who was not mentally ill, who complained that he had been force-fed while in criminal detention and that this had infringed this article. The Court held at para.94:

"[A] measure which is of therapeutic necessity from the point of view of established principles of medicine cannot in principle be regarded as inhuman or degrading. The same can be said about force-feeding that is aimed at saving the life of a particular detainee who consciously refuses to take food. The Convention organs must nevertheless satisfy themselves that the medical necessity has been convincingly shown to exist."

The *Bolam* test (see *Bolam v Friern Barnet Hospital* [1957] 1 W.L.R. 582) does not apply to the question of "medical necessity" under this article (*R. (on the application of N) v M and others* [2002] EWHC Admin 1911). The onus of justifying medical necessity is placed on the patient's approved clinician (*Bolam* above). This approach was approved by the Court of Appeal ([2002] EWCA Civ 1789; [2003] M.H.L.R. 157 at paras 17, 18) where the court said that the phrase "convincingly shown" is easily understood. Although the standard is a high one, it does not need "elaboration or further explanation". The factors that need to be addressed when forming a judgment as to whether the proposed treatment has been convincingly shown to be a medical necessity include:

"(a) how certain is it that the patient does suffer from a treatable mental disorder; (b) how serious a disorder is it; (c) how serious a risk is presented to others; (d) how likely is it that, if the patient does suffer from such a disorder, the proposed treatment will alleviate the condition; (e) how much alleviation is there likely to be; (f) how likely is it that the treatment will have adverse consequences for the patient; and (g) how severe may they be" (para.19).

**5–016** The court rejected a submission that, in a case where there is a responsible body of opinion that a patient is not suffering from a treatable condition, that the treatment is not in the patient's best interests and is not medically necessary, then it cannot be convincingly shown that the treatment proposed is in the patient's best interests or medically necessary (para.29).

The conclusion from *Herczegfalvy* is that forcible measures inflicted upon either an incapacitated or a capacitated patient which are not a medical necessity may constitute inhuman or degrading treatment. Conversely, a denial of treatment which has been found to be a medical necessity could also be claimed to be a violation of this article (*D v United Kingdom* (1997) 24 E.H.R.R. 423).

An admissibility decision of the Commission in *Grare v France* (1992) 15 E.H.R.R. CD 100, suggests that psychiatric treatment in the form of medication with unpleasant side-effects could involve a breach of this article if the side-effects were sufficiently serious: see O. Thorold "The Implications of the European Convention on Human Rights for United Kingdom Mental Health Legislation" [1996] E.H.R.L. 619–636, at 620. If the medication is therapeutically justified, an application on this ground would have little prospect of success unless it could be shown that there was alternative medication available which was equally efficacious and gave rise to significantly less serious side effects.

Although the courts will doubtless be reluctant to interfere in matters of pure clinical judgment, the Commission, in *Tanko v Finland*, App. No. 23634/94, said that it "does not exclude that a lack of proper care in a case where someone is suffering from a serious illness could be certain circumstances amount to treatment contrary to Article 3". In *X v Denmark* (1983) 32 D. & R. 282 at 283, the Commission held that "medical treatment of an experimental character and without the consent of the person involved may under certain circumstances be prohibited by Article 3" (cited in E. Wicks. "The Right to Refuse Medical Treatment under the European Convention on Human Rights" (2001) 9 Med. L.R. 17 at 22).

Although this article cannot be interpreted as laying down a general obligation to release a detainee on health grounds or to place him in a civil hospital to enable him to receive specific medical treatment (*Kalashnikov v Russia* (2003) 36 E.H.R.R. 34 para.95), the detention of persons of unsound mind in an unsatisfactory or non-therapeutic environment could amount to a violation of this article if the ill-treatment of the patient attains a minimum level of severity (*Aerts v Belgium* (2000) 29 E.H.R.R. 50). When assessing conditions of detention, account has to be taken of the cumulative effect of those conditions, as well as the specific allegations made by the applicant (*Dougoz v Greece* (2002) 34 E.H.R.R. 61 para.46). The effect of the decision in *Aerts* was explained by the Court in *Kudla v Poland* (2002) 35 E.H.R.R. 11 at para.94:

> "[Under Article 3] the State must ensure that a person is detained in conditions which are compatible with respect for his human dignity, that the matter and method of the execution of the measure do not subject him to distress or hardship of an intensity exceeding the unavoidable level of suffering inherent in detention and that, given the practical demands of imprisonment, his health and well-being are adequately secured by, among other things, providing him with the requisite medical assistance".

There are three particular elements to be considered in relation to the compatibility of an applicant's health with his stay in detention: (a) the medical condition of the prisoner, (b) the adequacy of the medical assistance and care provided in detention, and (c) the advisability of maintaining the detention measure in view of the state of health of an applicant (*Dybeku v Albania*, December 18, 2007, para.42.) In this case the Court said, at para.50, that "a lack of resources cannot in principle justify detention conditions which are so poor as to reach the threshold of severity for Art.3 to apply".

**5–017** In *Aerts* the Court held that, where the sole basis of detention is unsoundness of mind, an anti-therapeutic environment may contravene art.5(1), even if it is not severe enough to amount to inhuman and degrading treatment under this article.

Removal from association, such as the seclusion of a mentally disordered patient, does not normally amount to inhuman or degrading treatment, but it will depend upon the conditions, duration, purpose and the effects on the person concerned (*Koskinen v Finland* (1994) 18 E.H.R.R. CD 146 and *A v United Kingdom*, App. No. 6840/74). In *Dhoest v Belgium* (1987) 12 E.H.R.R. 97 at para.117, the Commission said that it had stated that:

"complete sensory deprivation, coupled with total social isolation, can destroy the personality and constitutes a form of treatment which cannot be justified by the requirements of security or for any other reason. It has moreover drawn a distinction between this and removal from association with other prisoners for security, disciplinary or protective reasons, and would not normally consider that this form of segregation from the prison community amounts to inhuman or degrading treatment. The same reasoning applies *mutatis mutandis* to persons who have been committed to a mental hospital in the framework of criminal proceedings".

A strip and intimate body search carried out in an appropriate manner with due respect for human dignity and for a legitimate purpose may be compatible with this article. However, where the manner in which a search is carried out has debasing elements which significantly aggravate the inevitable humiliation of the procedure, this article will be engaged. The requirement to submit to a strip search will generally constitute an interference under art.8(1) and require to be justified under art.8(2) (*Wainwright v United Kingdom* (2007) 44 E.H.R.R. 40 at paras 42, 43).

In *Vilvarajah v United Kingdom* (1992) 14 E.H.R.R. 248, the Court said at para.103 that:

"expulsion by a Contracting State of an asylum seeker may give rise to an issue under Article 3, and hence engage the responsibility of that State under the Convention, where substantial grounds have been shown for believing that the person concerned faced a real risk of being subjected to torture or to inhuman or degrading treatment or punishment in the contrary to which he was returned".

Having regard to the absolute nature of the right guaranteed, this article may extend to situations where the danger emanates not from the authorities of the receiving countries, but from persons or groups of persons who are not public officials, (*D v United Kingdom* (1997) 24 E.H.R.R. 423, para.49). The Court will assess the risk of inhuman or degrading treatment at the time of its own consideration of the case (*D v United Kingdom*, above, para.50). In *D* the Court said, at para.54, that "aliens . . . who are subject to expulsion cannot in principle claim any entitlement to remain on the territory of a contracting state in order to continue to benefit from medical, social or other forms of assistance provided by the expelling state during their stay". Since the judgment in *D.* the Court has never found a proposed removal of an alien from a Contracting State to give rise to a violation of this article on grounds of the applicant's ill-health: see *N v United Kingdom* (2008) 47 E.H.R.R. 39 para.34 where the Court said, at para.42, that the:

"decision to remove an alien who is suffering from a serious mental or physical illness to a country where the facilities for the treatment of that illness are inferior to those available in the Contracting State may raise an issue under Article 3, but only in a very exceptional case, where the humanitarian grounds against the removal are compelling. In the *D.* case the very exceptional circumstances were that the applicant was critically ill and appeared to be close to death, could not be guaranteed any nursing or medical care in his country of origin and had no family there willing or able to care for him or provide him with even a basic level of food, shelter or social support".

**5–018** The Court observed, at para.45:

> "that, although the present application . . . is concerned with the expulsion of a person with an HIV and AIDS-related condition, the same principles must apply in relation to the expulsion of any person afflicted with any serious, naturally occurring physical or mental illness which may cause suffering, pain and reduced life expectancy and require specialised medical treatment which may not be so readily available in the applicant's country of origin or which may be available only at substantial cost".

In *KH (Afghanistan) v Secretary of State for the Home Department* [2009] EWCA Civ 1354, para.43, the Court cited *N* and held that even-asylum seekers with mental illness who have no families cannot be regarded as "very exceptional" cases. In order for a case to fall into this category it would have to be exceptional inside the class of person without family support, perhaps a very young or very old person.

In *J v Secretary of State for the Home Department* [2005] EWCA Civ 629, the court held that, in deciding whether there was a real risk of a breach of this article in a case involving a risk of suicide on a person's enforced return to his country of origin, one question that had to be addressed was whether the fear of ill-treatment upon which the risk of suicide was said to be based, was objectively well founded. *J* was applied in *Y and Z (Sri Lanka) v Secretary of State for the Home Department* [2009] EWCA Civ 362, the first reported art.3 "foreign" claim based on the risk of suicide that has succeeded, where Sedley L.J., at para.15, said that a question of equal importance was whether any genuine fear, albeit without an objective foundation, is such as to create a risk of suicide if there is an enforced return.

Aspects of mental health practice that could be challenged under this article include:

(a) the placing of female patients with a history of sexual abuse by men in mixed sex wards;

(b) the automatic handcuffing of patients. In *Mouisel v France* [2004] 38 E.H.R.R. 34 at para.48, the Court held that handcuffing did not normally give rise to an issue under art.3 where it was imposed in connection with lawful detention and did not entail use of force or public exposure exceeding what was reasonably considered necessary. It was important to consider whether there was a risk that the person might abscond or cause injury or damage. The case law on this issue was considered in *R. (on the application of Graham and Allen) v Secretary of State for Justice* [2007] EWHC 2940 (Admin) and *R. (on the application of Faizovas) v Secretary of State for Justice* [2009] EWCA Civ 373, where the Court of Appeal considered *Unyan v Turkey*, January 8, 2009, and said, at para.22, that *Unyan* highlights the importance of separate consideration of the necessity for security measures at the treatment stage and that at that stage the authorities had to take account of not only the security risk but also the type of treatment which the prisoner had to undergo.

(c) the unjustified use of CS spray;

(d) the imposition of control and restraint techniques on a patient where neither the patient's history nor a current assessment justifies their use;

(e) forcible measures inflicted upon a patient which are not a medical necessity; and

(f) the forced feeding of a patient: see the note on "degrading" below.

If the treatment is not of sufficient severity to bring it within this article, it might be possible to bring an application under art.8 if the patient was mentally competent to refuse the intervention. The Court's case law does not exclude that treatment which does not reach the severity of treatment under this article may nonetheless breach art.8 in its private life aspect where there are sufficiently adverse effects on physical and moral integrity (*Costello-Roberts v United Kingdom* (1995) 19 E.H.R.R. 112). However it would be difficult, although not necessarily impossible, for a claimant who relies on health grounds to resist removal from the UK to fail under this article but succeed under art.8 (*R. (on the application of Razgar) v Secretary of State for the Home Department* [2004] UKHL 27; [2004] 3 All E.R. 821 para.59).

TORTURE. The Court has defined torture as "deliberate inhuman treatment causing very serious and cruel suffering" (*Ireland v United Kingdom* (1978) 2 E.H.R.R. 25 para.167).

INHUMAN. The Court has considered treatment to be "inhuman" because, inter alia, it was premeditated, was applied for hours at a stretch and caused either actual bodily injury or intense physical or mental suffering (*Kudla v Poland* (2002) 35 E.H.R.R. 11 para.92).

DEGRADING. Treatment may be considered degrading "if it is such as to arouse in its **5–019** victims feelings of fear, anguish and inferiority capable of humiliating and debasing them and possibly breaking their physical and moral resistance. Moreover, it is sufficient if the victim is humiliated in his or her own eyes (*Smith and Grady v United Kingdom* (2000) 29 E.H.R.R. 493 para.120). The Court will also have regard to whether the treatment adversely affects the victim's personality in a manner incompatible with this article (*Raninen v Finland* (1998) 26 E.H.R.R. 563 para.55). The fact that the object of treatment was not to humiliate or debase the person concerned cannot conclusively rule out a finding of violation of this article (*Price v United Kingdom* (2002) 34 E.H.R.R. 53 para.24).

The suffering and humiliation must go beyond the inevitable element of suffering or humiliation connected with a given form of legitimate treatment or punishment, as in, for example, measures depriving a person of their liberty (*Wainwright v United Kingdom*, above, para.41).

In *X v Germany* (1984) 7 E.H.R.R. 152, the Commission said that:

"the forced feeding of a person does involve degrading elements which in certain circumstances may be regarded as prohibited by Article 3 . . . Under the Convention the High Contracting parties are, however, also obliged to secure to everyone the right to life as set out in Article 2. Such an obligation should in certain circumstances call for positive action on the part of the Contracting Parties, in particular an active measure to save lives when the authorities have taken the person in question into their custody. When, as in the present case, a detained person maintains a hunger strike this may inevitably lead to a conflict between an individual's right to physical integrity and the High Contracting Party's obligation under Article 2 . . . a conflict which is not solved by the Convention itself".

*X* was applied in *Nevmerzhitsky v Ukraine* (2006) 43 E.H.R.R. 32, where the Court held, at para.94, that force-feeding that was aimed at saving the life of a detainee who consciously refused to take food could not in principle be regarded as inhuman and degrading. However, the medical necessity for such a procedure had to be convincingly shown to exist and the Court had to ascertain that the procedural guarantees for the decision to force feed had been complied with. Moreover, the manner in which an individual was subjected to force-feeding could not trespass the threshold of minimum severity envisaged by the case law on this article. Force feeding which was not a medical necessity was found to have breached this article in *Ciorap v Moldova*, June 19, 2007.

It is clear from these cases that a State may on occasions be justified in inflicting treatment which would otherwise be in breach of this article in order to serve the ends of art.2 (*R. (on the application of Pretty) v Director of Public Prosecutions* [2001] UKHL 61; [2002] 1 All E.R.1, per Lord Bingham at para.13).

In *NHS Trust A v NHS Trust B v H* [2001] 1 All E.R. 801, Butler-Sloss P. held that this Article "requires the victim to be aware of the inhuman and degrading treatment which he or she is experiencing or at least be in a state of physical or mental suffering" (para.49).

This surprising finding, which has the effect of removing the protection afforded by this article from a group of extremely vulnerable citizens, i.e. insensate patients, was criticised by Munby J. in *R. (on the application of Burke) v General Medical Council* [2004] EWHC 1879 (Admin); [2004] 2 F.L.R. 1121, who said at para.149:

> "In my judgment treatment is capable of being 'degrading' within the meaning of Article 3, whether or not it arouses feelings of fear, anguish or inferiority in the victim. It is enough if judged by the standard of right thinking bystanders—human rights violations obviously cannot be judged by the standards of the perpetrators—it would be viewed as humiliating or debasing the victim, showing a lack of respect for, or diminishing, his or her human dignity."

It is submitted that Munby J.'s obiter statement is to be preferred as it is consistent with Convention caselaw: see *Keenan v United Kingdom* (2001) 33 E.H.R.R. 913 para.112.

### ARTICLE 4

#### PROHIBITION OF SLAVERY AND FORCED LABOUR

**5–020**    1. No one shall be held in slavery or servitude.

2. No one shall be required to perform forced or compulsory labour.

3. For the purpose of this Article the term "forced or compulsory labour" shall not include:

(a) any work required to be done in the ordinary course of detention imposed according to the provisions of Article 5 of this Convention or during conditional release from such detention;

(b) any service of a military character or, in case of conscientious objectors in countries where they are recognised, service exacted instead of compulsory military service;

(c) any service exacted in case of an emergency or calamity threatening the life or well-being of the community;

(d) any work or service which forms part of normal civic obligations.

### ARTICLE 5

#### RIGHT TO LIBERTY AND SECURITY

**5–021**    1. Everyone has the right to liberty and security of person. No one shall be deprived of his liberty save in the following cases and in accordance with a procedure prescribed by law:

(a) the lawful detention of a person after conviction by a competent court;

(b) the lawful arrest or detention of a person for non-compliance with the lawful order of a court or in order to secure the fulfilment of any obligation prescribed by law;

(c) the lawful arrest of detention of a person effected for the purpose of bringing him before the competent legal authority on reasonable suspicion of having committed an offence or when it is reasonably considered necessary to prevent his committing an offence or fleeing after having done so;

(d) the detention of a minor by lawful order for the purpose of educational supervision or his lawful detention for the purpose of bringing him before the competent legal authority;

(e) the lawful detention of persons for the prevention of the spreading of infectious diseases, of persons of unsound mind, alcoholics or drug addicts or vagrants;

(f) the lawful arrest or detention of a person to prevent his effecting an unauthorised entry into the country or of a person against whom action is being taken with a view to deportation or extradition.

2. Everyone who is arrested shall be informed promptly, in a language which he understands, of the reasons for his arrest and of any charge against him.

3. Everyone arrested or detained in accordance with the provisions of paragraph 1(c) of this Article shall be brought promptly before a judge or other officer authorised by law to exercise judicial power and shall be entitled to trial within a reasonable time or to release pending trial. Release may be conditioned by guarantees to appear for trial.

4. Everyone who is deprived of his liberty by arrest or detention shall be entitled to take proceedings by which the lawfulness of his detention shall be decided speedily by a court and his release ordered if the detention is not lawful.

5. Everyone who has been the victim of arrest or detention in contravention of the provisions of this Article shall have an enforceable right to compensation.

GENERAL NOTE

In *McKay v United Kingdom* (2007) 44 E.H.R.R. at para.20, the court said: **5–022**

"Article 5 of the Convention is, together with Articles 2, 3 and 4, in the first rank of the fundamental rights that protect the physical security of an individual and as such its importance is paramount. Its key purpose is to prevent arbitrary or unjustified deprivations of liberty."

The protection that art.5(1) provides against a deprivation of liberty is absolute, subject only to the cases listed in sub-paragraphs (a) to (f). In *R. v Governor of Brockhill Prison Ex p. Evans (No.2)* [2000] 4 All E.R. 15 HL Lord Hope said at 29, 30:

"The jurisprudence of the European Court of Human Rights indicates that there are various aspects to Article 5(1) which must be satisfied in order to show that the detention is lawful for the purposes of that Article. The first question is whether the detention is lawful under domestic law. Any detention which is unlawful in domestic law will automatically be unlawful under Article 5(1). It will thus give rise to an enforceable right to compensation under Article 5(5), the provisions of which are not discretionary but mandatory. The second question is whether, assuming that the detention is lawful under domestic law, it nevertheless complies with the general requirements of the Convention. These are based upon the principle that any restriction on human rights and fundamental freedoms must be prescribed by law (see Articles 8 to 11 of the Convention). They include the requirements that the domestic law must be sufficiently accessible to the individual and that it must be sufficiently precise to enable the individual to foresee the consequences of the restriction (see *Sunday Times v United Kingdom* (1979) 2 E.H.R.R. 245; *Zamir v United Kingdom* (1983) 40 D. & R. 42 at 55 (paras 90–91)). The third question is whether, again assuming that the detention is lawful under domestic law, it is nevertheless open to criticism on the ground that it is arbitrary because, for example, it was resorted to in bad faith or was not proportionate (see *Engel v Netherlands (No.1)* (1976) 1 E.H.R.R. 647 (para.58); *Tsirlis and Kouloumpas v Greece* (1997) 25 E.H.R.R. 198 (para.56))."

In *Storck v Germany* (2006) 43 E.H.R.R. 6; [2005] M.H.L.R. 211, the Court held that:

1. The State has a positive obligation to protect the liberty of its citizens, and the State was therefore obliged to take measures providing effective protection of vulnerable persons, including reasonable steps to prevent a deprivation of liberty of which the authorities had or ought to have had knowledge (para.100).

2. The State could not completely absolve itself from its responsibility by delegating its obligations in this sphere to private bodies or individuals. Private psychiatric institutions, in particular those able to hold persons without a court order, need not only a licence, but a competent supervision on a regular basis of the justification of the confinement and medical treatment (para.103).

3. Detention in a private institution could engage the State's responsibility under the Convention in three ways; by the direct involvement of public authorities, such as police officers, in the applicant's detention; by the courts' failure to interpret the provisions of the civil law relating to her claim in the spirit of art.5; and by the violation of its positive obligations to protect the applicant against interferences with her liberty carried out by private persons (para.89).

This Article embraces the detention and release of the mentally disordered, but not a right to treatment (*Winterwerp v Netherlands*, below, at para.51 and *Ashingdane v United Kingdom*, below, at para.44). In *A (A Mental Patient) v The Scottish Ministers* [2001] UKPC D5; [2002] H.R.L.R. 6 PC at para.29, Lord Hope said that it followed from these cases that "the fact that [the patient's] mental disorder is not susceptible to treatment does not mean that, in Convention terms, his continued detention in a hospital is arbitrary or disproportionate".

*Paragraph 1*
The Court has said that:

". . . the list of exceptions to the right to liberty secured by Article 5(1) is an exhaustive one and only a narrow interpretation of those exceptions is consistent with the aim and purpose of that provision, namely to ensure that no one is arbitrarily deprived of his or her liberty" (*Quinn v France* (1996) 21 E.H.R.R. 529 at para.42).

Although the list in para.1 is exhaustive, "the applicability of any one ground does not necessarily preclude that of another; a detention may, depending on the circumstances, be justified under more than one sub-paragraph" (*Eriksen v Norway* (2000) 29 E.H.R.R. 328 para.76). There must be some relationship between the ground of permitted deprivation of liberty relied on and the place and conditions of detention (*Reid v United Kingdom* (2003) 37 E.H.R.R. 9).

Detention pursuant to this paragraph inevitably brings with it a restriction for the detained person of his private and family life. The Court has held that it is essential that the detaining authority helps that person to maintain contact with his close family (*Messina v Italy (No.2)*, September 28, 2000, para.41).

**5–023**   EVERYONE.   Including children (*Nielsen v Denmark* (1989) 11 E.H.R.R. 175 para.58).

SECURITY OF PERSON.   Little attention has been given by the Court to this aspect of art.5.

PROCEDURE PRESCRIBED BY LAW.   This expression and "in accordance with the law" in art.8(2) are to be understood as bearing the same meaning (*R. (on the application Gillan and another) v Metropolitan Police Commissioner* [2006] UKHL 12; [2006] 4 All E.R. 1041 para.31. The:

"domestic law must itself be in conformity with the Convention, including the general principles expressed or implied therein. The notion underlying [this term] is one of fair and proper procedure, namely that any measure depriving a person of his liberty should issue from and be executed by an appropriate authority and should not be arbitrary" (*Winterwerp v Netherlands* (1979) 2 E.H.R.R. 387 at para.45).

While it is normally in the first place for the national authorities, notably the courts, to interpret and apply domestic law, it is otherwise in relation to cases where, as under this paragraph, failure to comply with the law entails a breach of the Convention. In such cases the Court can and should exercise a certain power to review whether national law has been observed. Moreover, any deprivation of liberty must not only have been effected in conformity with the substantive and procedural rules of national law but must equally be in keeping with the very purpose of this article, namely to protect the individual from arbitrariness (*Gajcsi v Hungary* [2006] M.H.L.R. 322).

The domestic law, which can be written or unwritten (*Laumont v France* (2003) 36 E.H.R.R. 35 para.45), must be sufficiently precise to allow the individual (if need be, with appropriate advice) to foresee, to a degree that is reasonable in the circumstances, the consequences which a given action may entail (*Steel v United Kingdom* (1999) 28 E.H.R.R. 603 para 54; also see *Kawka v Poland*, January 9, 2001, para.49). This requirement does not mean that the common law cannot grow or shape itself to changing social conditions and perceptions (*SW and CR v UK* (1996) 21 E.H.R.R. 363). It means that "any such change must be principled and predictable"; per Sedley L.J. In *Re F (Adult: Court's Jurisdiction)* [2001] 2 F.L.R. 512 at 531, CA.

Where the issue of a person's liberty is at stake, states have to ensure that their courts remain accessible, even during a vacation period or a weekend, to ensure that urgent matters are dealt with speedily and in full compliance with a procedure prescribed by law (*Bik v Russia*, para.37, April 22, 2010).

Although it is generally useful to keep detailed records of what happens at hearings, neither this article nor any other provision of the Convention contains a requirement that an official record of a hearing be kept, whether verbatim or in summary form (*Nakach v Netherlands* [2006] M.H.L.R. 22 paras 35, 36). However, a failure to draw up an official record of a hearing as required by domestic law would breach para.1 of this article (*Schenkel v Netherlands* [2006] M.H.L.R. 27).

*Paragraph 1(a)*

CONVICTION. A mentally disordered offender who is convicted of a criminal offence **5–024** and ordered to be detained in a psychiatric hospital will be detained under both art.5(1)(a) and 5(1)(e) (*X v United Kingdom* (1981) 4 E.H.R.R. 188 para.39).

*Paragraph 1(c)*

The ordering of a psychiatric report in order to determine the mental state of a person **5–025** charged with an offence remains a necessary measure and one which protects individuals capable of committing offences without being in full possession of their mental faculties. However, the state authorities are required to make sure such a measure does not upset the fair balance that should be maintained between the rights of the individual, in particular the right to respect for private life, and the concern to ensure the proper administration of justice (*Worwa v Poland* (2006) E.H.R.R. 35 para.82).

*Paragraph 1(d)*

FOR THE PURPOSE OF EDUCATIONAL SUPERVISION. And not merely incidental to another **5–026** purpose. However, educational supervision need not be demonstrated to be the sole purpose of the detention (*Bouamar v Belgium* (1989) 11 E.H.R.R. 1 para.50).

*Paragraph 1(e)*

In *Witold Litwa v Poland*, below, the Court identified a link between all of the categories **5–027** of people noted in this sub-paragraph. The link is that all those persons:

"may be deprived of their liberty either in order to be given medical treatment or because of considerations dictated by social policy, or on both medical and social grounds . . . [A] predominant reason why the Convention allows the persons mentioned in paragraph 1(e) of Article 5 to be deprived of their liberty is not only that they are dangerous for public safety but also that their own interests may necessitate their detention" (para.60).

In *A v The Scottish Ministers* [2000] H.R.L.R. 450, the Lord President summarised the principles to be derived from the authorities on this paragraph:

"The admission and detention of a person of unsound mind must be in conformity with a procedure laid down in domestic law. The domestic law relating to the detention of such persons must conform to three criteria: a true mental disorder must be established before a competent authority on the basis of objective medical expertise; the mental disorder must be of a kind or degree warranting compulsory confinement; and the validity of the patient's continued detention depends upon the persistence of such a disorder. Moreover, Article 5(1)(e) does not require that the detention of persons of unsound mind be for the purpose of treatment, but it should be in a hospital, clinic or other appropriate institution authorised for the purpose. Detention under Article 5(1)(e) is justified where it is necessary to serve a legitimate social purpose, which may be the protection of the public".

In this case the court, having considered the reasoning of the European Court of Human Rights in *Witold Litwa v Poland* (2001) 33 E.H.R.R. 53 concluded that:

(i) detention under this paragraph can be justified on the ground of social policy, including the protection of the public, as long as the detention is necessary in the circumstances, and other measures are insufficient to achieve that end; and

(ii) it is lawful to continue to detain a mentally disordered person who is admitted to hospital on the satisfaction of a treatment condition and who now no longer satisfies that condition although he does satisfy another Convention condition, such as the protection of the public.

The individual's detention must be a proportionate response. In *Litwa*, the Court said, at para.78, that the detention of an individual is such a serious measure that it is only justified where other, less severe, measures have been considered and found to be insufficient to safeguard the individual or public interest which might require that the person concerned be detained. The deprivation of liberty must be shown to have been necessary in the circumstances. *Litwa* was applied in *Reid v United Kingdom* (2003) 37 E.H.R.R. 9, where the Court held, at para.51, that compulsory confinement:

"may be necessary not only where a person needs therapy, medication or other clinical treatment to cure or alleviate his condition, but also where the person needs control and supervision to prevent him, for example, casing harm to himself or other persons".

**5–028**   LAWFUL.   This paragraph does not require the initial detention to be authorised by a court or tribunal. The lawfulness under domestic law of a person's detention is not of itself decisive: it must also be established that the detention was in conformity with para.1, which is to prevent persons from being deprived of their liberty in an arbitrary fashion (*Withold Litwa v Poland*, above, paras 72, 73). A detention will be arbitrary where, despite complying with the letter of national law, there has been an element of bad faith or deception on behalf of the authorities or where the domestic authorities neglected to attempt to apply the relevant legislation correctly or where there was an excessive delay in renewing the patient's detention (*Mooren v Germany* (app.no.11364/03), July 9, 2009, paras.78 to 81)). Lawfulness implies "that the deprivation of liberty is in keeping with the purpose of the restrictions permissible under Article 5(1)" (*Bouamar v Belgium* (1989) 11 E.H.R.R. 1 para.50). A subsequent finding that a court erred under domestic law in making the order depriving a person of their liberty will not necessarily affect the validity of the intervening period of detention (*Benham v United Kingdom* (1996) 22 E.H.R.R. 293 para.42). *Benham* was applied in *R. (on the application of A) v Harrow Crown Court* [2003] EWHC 2020 (Admin) where Stanley Burton J. held that the detention of a patient on the authority of an irregular order did not infringe this Article because the detention was not arbitrary. However, there will be a breach of this article if the defect in the order amounts to "a gross and irregular irregularity" (*Mooren v Germany*, above, para.75).

A significant delay in the transfer of a mentally disordered person who needs psychiatric treatment from a penal establishment to a psychiatric hospital can constitute a violation of this paragraph (*Mocarska v Poland* [2007] M.H.L.R. 228; also see *Pankiewicz v Poland* [2008] M.H.L.R. 233).

DETENTION.    Whether a person's situation constitutes a "deprivation of liberty" for the purposes of para.1 is considered in Part 6.

In *Bollan v United Kingdom (dec)*, no.42117/98, May 4, 2000, the Court found that the **5–029** imposition of a more restrictive form of confinement in respect of a lawfully detained patient is regarded solely as a modification of the conditions of detention (cited in *Stojanovski v The Former Yugoslav Republic of Macedonia*, app.no.1431/03, October 22, 2009, para.29). It follows that the seclusion of a detained patient does not engage this Article because the seclusion affects the conditions of the patient's detention, it does not amount to detention as such (*R. v Mersey Care National Health Service Trust Ex p. Munjaz* [2005] UKHL 58; [2006] 4 All E.R. 736).

The Convention does not guarantee "for a person who has been ordered to undergo compulsory psychiatric treatment, the right to choose the place of his detention" (*Valle v Finland* [2000] M.H.L.R. 255).

PERSONS OF UNSOUND MIND.    In *Winterwerp v Netherlands*, above, the Court held that in order for a detention on the ground of unsoundness of mind to be lawful the Government has to be able to show by reliable medical evidence before a competent national authority that:

(i)   except in emergency cases, a true mental disorder has been established by objective medical expertise;

(ii)   the mental disorder is of a kind of degree warranting compulsory confinement; and

(iii)   the validity of continued confinement depends upon the persistence of such a disorder.

To this list must be added a fourth principle, that detention must be a proportionate response to the patient's circumstances (*Witald Litwa v Poland*, above, para.78).

Taking these requirements in turn:    **5–030**

(i)   The Court held that the term "persons of unsound mind" is "not one that can be given a definitive interpretation . . . it is a term whose meaning is constantly evolving as research in psychiatry progresses, an increasing flexibility in treatment is developing and society's attitude to mental illness changes, in particular so that a greater understanding of the problems of mental patients is becoming wide-spread. In any event, Art.5(1)(e) obviously cannot be taken as permitting the detention of a person simply because his views or behaviour deviate from the norms prevailing in a particular society" (at para.37). In *X v Federal Republic of Germany*, 6 D. & R. 182, the Commission found that the term "unsound mind" did not just mean mental illness, but must be understood in a wider sense to include abnormal personality disorder. The test under this paragraph has been described in the domestic courts as one of "whether it can 'reliably be shown' that [the patient] suffers from a mental disorder sufficiently serious to warrant detention" (*R. (on the application of H) v Mental Health Review Tribunal, North and East London Region* [2001] EWCA Civ 415, at para.29 per Lord Phillips M.R. at para.29).

Whether or not recovery from an episode of mental illness which justifies a patient's detention is complete and definitive or merely apparent cannot in all cases be measured with absolute certainty. It is the behaviour of the patient outside hospital which will be conclusive of this (*Stojanovski v The Former Yugoslav Republic of Macedonia,* app.no.1431/03, October 22, 2009, para.34).

The particular form and procedure for seeking the opinion of a medical expert:

"may vary depending on the circumstances. It may be acceptable, in urgent cases or where a person is arrested because of his violent behaviour, that such an opinion be obtained immediately after the arrest. In all other cases a prior consultation should be necessary. Where no other possibility exists, for instance due to a refusal of the person concerned to appear for an examination, at least an assessment by a medical expert on the basis of the file must be required, failing which it cannot be maintained that a person has reliably been shown to be of unsound mind" (*X v United Kingdom,* above).

Furthermore, the medical assessment must be based on the actual state of mental health of the person concerned and not solely on past events. A medical opinion cannot be seen as sufficient to justify deprivation of liberty if a significant period of time has elapsed between the deprivation and the provision of the opinion (*Varbanov v Bulgaria* [2000] M.H.L.R. 263, para.47). In *Winterwerp,* the Court said that a period of emergency detention which lasted for six weeks before a medical opinion was obtained from a general practitioner did not violate this Article.

The Commission has held that the medical evidence may come from a general practitioner rather than a psychiatrist (*Schuurs v The Netherlands* 41 D&R 186, 188–9).

(ii) In *Kolanis v United Kingdom* (2006) 42 E.H.R.R. 12, para.70, the Court rejected a submission that the decision of the Mental Health Review Tribunal that the patient could be discharged subject to conditions was tantamount to a finding that the second *Winterwerp* criterion was no longer fulfilled, with the result that any subsequent undue delay in release was in breach of art.5. The discharge of the patient was only regarded as appropriate if there was continued treatment or supervision necessary to protect her own health and the safety of the community. In the absence of that treatment, her detention continued to be necessary in line with the purpose of art.5(1)(e); see further the notes on s.73(7).

(iii) This requirement links to the review procedure provided for under para.4 of this article. In *Johnson v United Kingdom* (1999) 27 E.H.R.R. 296, the Court rejected the submission of the applicant, a restricted patient, that once there had been a finding by an expert authority, in this case the Mental Health Review Tribunal, that the mental disorder had ceased, he should as a consequence have been immediately and unconditionally released. The Court said at para.61:

"Such a rigid approach to the interpretation of that condition would place an unacceptable degree of constraint on the responsible authority's exercise of judgment to determine in particular cases and on the basis of all the relevant circumstances whether the interests of the patient and the community into which he is to be released would in fact be best served by this course of action. It must also be observed that in the field of mental illness the assessment as to whether the disappearance of the symptoms of the illness is confirmation of complete recovery is not an exact science".

A responsible authority is therefore entitled to exercise a:

"measure of discretion in deciding whether in the light of all the relevant circumstances and interests at stake it would in fact be appropriate to order the immediate and absolute discharge of a person who is no longer suffering from the mental disorder that led to his confinement" (para.63)

In *Aerts v Belgium* (2000) 25 E.H.R.R. 50, the applicant, who was an offender patient, was **5–031** placed in provisional detention in the psychiatric wing of a prison for seven months before a place became available in a psychiatric institution. The Court heard evidence that the wing was not regarded as an appropriate institution for persons of unsound mind, as there was no regular medical attention and it was not a therapeutic environment. The Court held that, in principle, the detention of a person of unsound mind will only be lawful for the purposes of this paragraph "if effected in a hospital, clinic or other appropriate institution authorised for that purpose" (para.44). In this context "for that purpose" must mean purpose of caring for the mentally disordered. The detention of the applicant violated this paragraph because the "proper relationship between the aim of the detention and the conditions in which it took place was . . . deficient" (para.49). This implies that there must be some therapeutic involvement with the patient. The Court further found that the conditions in which the applicant was detained were not sufficiently severe to lead to a finding of inhuman or degrading treatment under art.3. It follows that where detention is justified under this paragraph, complaints about the conditions in the patient's place of detention are better brought under this article rather than art.3. It is likely that the Court would need evidence that standards relating to the provision of services and/or the quality of conditions in the place of detention had fallen very low for it to be satisfied that this article had been violated; also see the note on s.47 under the heading "The Human Rights Act 1998"..

ALCOHOLICS.    Persons who are not medically diagnosed as "alcoholics", but whose conduct and behaviour under the influence of alcohol pose a threat to public order or themselves, can be taken into custody for the protection of the public or their own interests, such as their health or personal safety (*Withold Litwa v Poland*, above). This finding would equally apply to persons who were not medically diagnosed as drug addicts, but whose conduct and behaviour under the influence of drugs give rise to similar concerns.

### Paragraph 2
In the psychiatric context, the purpose of this paragraph is adequately to inform the **5–032** patient of the reason for his detention so that he may judge its lawfulness and take steps to challenge it if he thinks fit, thus availing himself of the right guaranteed by art.5(4) (*Conka v Belgium* (2002) 34 E.H.R.R. 54, para.50).

In *Van der Leer v Netherlands* (1990) 12 E.H.R.R. 567, para.27, the Court held that the term "arrest" extends beyond the realm of criminal law measures and embraces deprivation of liberty on the ground of unsoundness of mind. A patient who is detained under the 1983 Act must therefore be informed promptly, in language that he understands, of the reasons for his detention. The information provided must be sufficient to enable the patient to know why he is being detained: the mere recital of the legal basis for the detention is insufficient (*Fox, Campbell and Hartley v United Kingdom* (1991) 13 E.H.R.R. 157). Compliance with this requirement would therefore not be achieved by providing the patient with a copy of the application papers in the absence of an explanation of the circumstances that gave rise to the making of the application. It is likely that the Court would hold that information could be withheld if it might cause psychological harm to the patient. In this situation, the patient's legal representative should be provided with the relevant details.

PROMPTLY.    The information need not be provided in its entirety by the detaining officer at the very moment of the detention. Whether the content and promptness of the information were sufficient is to be assessed in each case according to its special features (*Conka v Belgium*, above). It is therefore possible to delay the giving of the information until the patient is mentally capable of understanding it.

### Paragraph 4
This paragraph and para.1 are "separate provisions and observance of the former does **5–033** not necessarily entail observance of the latter" (*Douiyeb v Netherlands* (2000) 30 E.H.R.R. 790, para.57). It:

"provides a crucial guarantee against the arbitrariness of detention, providing for detained persons to obtain a review by a court of the lawfulness of their detention both at the time of the initial deprivation of liberty and, where new issues of lawfulness are capable of arising, periodically thereafter" (*Benjamin and Wilson v UK* (2003) 36 E.H.R.R. 1, para.33).

It is not concerned with the details of detention, such as the place and conditions of the patient's detention (*Ashingdane v UK* (1985) 7 E.H.R.R. 528 paras 43, 49) and it cannot be invoked by a person who is lawfully released (*Stephens v Malta (No.1)* (app.no.33740/06), Sept.14, 2009, para.102).

A detained person is not required to show that on the facts of his case he stands any particular chance of success in obtaining his release (*Waite v UK* (2003) 36 E.H.R.R. 54 para.59). The role of the reviewing body is to identify whether the reasons which initially justified the detention continue to subsist, not to review the decision to detain (*X v UK* (1992) 14 E.H.R.R. 188 para.58. Although this paragraph does not guarantee a right to appeal against decisions on the lawfulness of detention, it follows from its aim and purpose that its requirements must be respected by appeal courts if an appeal lies against a decision on the lawfulness of detention (*Rutten v Netherlands*, July 24, 2001, para.53). This paragraph does not require the reviewing body to have any other control of the detention process, such as decisions regarding leave of absence (*Roux v UK* (1986) 48 D. & R. 263 at 268). Where a court initially orders detention, the review required by this paragraph is incorporated in that decision (*Winterwerp v Netherlands*, above, para.55).

The principles which emerge from the Court's case law on this paragraph as they apply to the detention of person of unsound mind were summarised in *Megyeri v Germany* (1993) 15 E.H.R.R. 584, at para.22. They include the following:

(i) A person of unsound mind who is compulsorily confined in a psychiatric institution for an indefinite or lengthy period is in principle entitled, at any rate where there is no automatic periodic review of a judicial character, to take proceedings "at reasonable intervals" before a court to put in issue the "lawfulness"—within the meaning of the Convention—of his detention (see *X v United Kingdom*, above, at para.52).

(ii) Article 5(4) requires that the procedures followed have a judicial character and give to the individual concerned guarantees appropriate to the kind of deprivation of liberty in question; in order to determine whether a proceeding provides adequate guarantees, regard must be had to the particular nature of the circumstances in which such proceedings takes place (see *Wassink v Netherlands*, September 27, 1990, Series A, No. 185–A, p.13, para.30).

(iii) The judicial proceedings referred to in art.5(4) need not always be attended by the same guarantees as those required under art.6(1) for civil or criminal litigation. None the less, it is essential that the person concerned should have access to a court and the opportunity to be heard either in person or, where necessary, some form of representation. Special procedural safeguards may prove called for in order to protect the interests of persons who, on account of their mental disabilities, are not fully capable of acting for themselves (see *Winterwerp v Netherlands*, above, at para.60).

(iv) Article 5(4) does not require that persons committed to care under the head of "unsound mind" should themselves take the initiative in obtaining legal representation before having recourse to a court (*Winterwerp*, above, para.60)

**5–034**    The Court went on to say at para.23 that it:

"follows from the foregoing that where a person is confined in a psychiatric institution on the ground of the commission of acts which constituted criminal offences but for which he could not be held responsible on account of mental illness, he should—unless there are special circumstances—receive legal assistance in subsequent proceedings relating to the continuation, suspension or termination of his detention. The importance of what is at stake for him—personal liberty—taken together with the very nature of his affliction—diminished mental capacity—compel this conclusion".

Where a tribunal finds that a patient's detention in hospital is no longer necessary and that she is eligible for release on conditions, new issues of lawfulness may arise where detention nonetheless continues, due, for example, to difficulties in fulfilling the conditions. It follows that such patients are entitled under this paragraph to have the lawfulness of that continued detention determined by a court with requisite promptness (*Kolanis v United Kingdom*, (2006) 42 E.H.R.R. 12, para.80).

In the *Winterwerp* case, above, the Commission said that the patient's lawyer had the right to examine the patient's file, but that it was not necessary for the patient to be informed of all the evidence or that he be allowed access to all of the information in his medical file. This approach was confirmed by the Court in *Nikolova v Bulgaria* [2001] E.H.R.R. 3 at para.58 where it was said that "[e]quality of arms is not ensured if counsel is denied access to those documents in the investigation file which are essential in order effectively to challenge the lawfulness of his client's detention".

EVERYONE.    Either personally or through some form of representation (*De Wilde, Ooms and Versyp v Belgium* (1971) 1 E.H.R.R. 373, paras 73–76).

TO TAKE PROCEEDINGS.    Until relatively recently, the Court accepted that an automatic review of the patient's case would satisfy this paragraph; see, for example, *X v United Kingdom* [1981] 4 E.H.R.R. 188. However a study of the Strasbourg jurisdiction reveal a shift of emphasis in recent years towards a greater stress on the requirement that a detained person should be able to take the initiative himself to start proceedings to challenge the lawfulness of his detention; see, for example, *Rakevich v Russia*, October 28, 2003. This shift is considered by Keene L.J. in *Secretary of State for Justice v Rayner* [2008] EWCA Civ 176; [2008] M.H.L.R. 115.

LAWFULNESS OF HIS DETENTION.    It is for the authorities to prove that an individual satisfies the conditions for compulsory detention, rather than the converse (*Reid v United Kingdom*, (2003) 37 E.H.R.R. 9 para.70). The review must encompass the lawfulness of the detention under this article as well as its lawfulness under domestic law (*Johnson v United Kingdom* (1999) E.H.R.R. 296 para.60). Detention lasts from the time when the detention is authorised to the time when it is officially lifted, even if the patient is not physically detained during the whole of this period, i.e. it covers periods of leave of absence and absence without leave (*Van der Leer v Netherlands*, above, para.35).

DECIDED.    It is not sufficient for the court to have merely advisory functions, it must have the power to order release if it finds the detention to be unlawful (*Benjamin and Wilson v United Kingdom*, above, para.34).

SPEEDILY.    Which is a less stringent requirement than arises with the tem "promptly" in para.3 (*E v Norway*, below, para.64). "In the Court's view, this concept cannot be defined in the abstract; the matter must . . . be determined in the light of the circumstances of each case" (*Sanchez-Reisse v Switzerland* (1987) 9 E.H.R.R. 71 at para.55). In practice, the Court has dealt with this issue on a case-by-case basis. It is the obligation of the state to organise its legal system to enable it to comply with convention requirements (*Bezicheri v Italy* (1989) 12 E.H.R.R. 210 para.25). The "excessive workload" of the judge assigned to a particular case cannot be prayed in aid. Nor can the fact that the judge is on holiday (*E v Norway* (1990) 17 E.H.R.R. 30, para.64). There is no general principle that "administrative necessity" excuses delay (*R. (on the application of Noorkoiv) v Secretary of State for the Home Department* [2002] EWCA Civ 770; [2002] 4 All E.R. 515 para.26). The

Commission has said that the authorities must take a patient's right to a speedy review "practical and effective" (*Luberti v Italy* (1982) App. No. 9019/80, para.69). Where there has been a delay in undertaking a review, the Court must determine whether the delay can be attributed to the authorities (*Luberti v Italy* (1982) E.C.H.R. Ser. A, No. 75 para.34). In proceedings concerning a review of a psychiatric detention, the complexity of the medical issues involved in a case is a factor which may be taken into account when assessing compliance with the requirements of this paragraph (*Musial v Poland* (2001) 31 E.H.R.R. 29 para.47). Where there are complex issues to be determined "the primary responsibility for delays resulting from the provision of expert opinions rests ultimately with the state" (*Musial* at para.46).

**5–035**     In *Cottenham v United Kingdom*, [1999] M.H.L.R. 97, the Court, in an admissibility decision, found that the tribunal could not be criticised for a delay of 10 months which had been caused by the patient's solicitor's request for an adjournment to obtain an independent psychiatric report. The Court said that it:

> "does not rule out that, given the particular problems of detained patients, where it appears that the legal representatives of such a person are acting negligently or in some way causing unjustified delay in the presentation of an application to a MHRT, the tribunal would be under a duty to make enquiries and to ensure that the application is proceeded with expeditiously".

Less urgency is required when the patient makes a further application in pursuance of his right to a periodic review of this detention. A delay of over four months in these circumstances has been held by the Court to be incompatible with this paragraph (*Koendjbiharie v Netherlands* (1990) 13 E.H.R.R. 820).

In *R. (on the application of C) v Mental Health Review Tribunal London South and West Region* [2001] EWCA Civ 1110; [2002] 1 W.L.R. 176, the Court of Appeal said that decisions of the Court such as *E v Norway*, above, where a delay of eight weeks between application and hearing was held to violate this paragraph, were not attempts to decide as of principle whether a particular practice or policy of setting a specified time for a hearing was in breach of this paragraph. What the Court had made clear was that each case was to be decided upon its own particular circumstances. The Court of Appeal held that this approach was not compatible with a policy of automatically listing cases for hearing eight weeks after the application had been made: see the note on r.37 of the Tribunal Procedure (First-tier Tribunal) (Health, Education and Social Care Chamber) Rules 2008.

COURT. This term has a much wider meaning under the Convention than in English law. In *X v United Kingdom* (1981) 4 E.H.H.R. 188, para.53, the Court said that it "is not within the province of the Court to enquire what is the best or most appropriate system of judicial review in this sphere, for Contracting States are free to choose different methods of performing their obligations". A body can be a court if it is independent of the executive and of the parties to the case and has a judicial character (*De Wilde, Ooms and Versp* (1971) 1 E.H.R.R. 373 para.76). The court must also be impartial (*DN v Switzerland* (2003) 37 E.H.R.R. 21 para.42). In *DN*, the Court said that "impartiality must be determined by a subjective test, that is on the basis of the personal conviction of a particular judge in a given case, and also by an objective test, that is ascertaining whether the judge offered guarantees sufficient to exclude any legitimate doubt in this respect" (para.44). The Court also said that:

> "any judge in respect of whom there is legitimate reason to fear a lack of impartiality must withdraw. In deciding whether in a given case there is a legitimate reason to fear that a particular judge lacks impartiality, the standpoint of the parties concerned is important but not decisive. What is decisive is whether this fear can be held to be objectively justified" (para.46).

A tribunal clearly qualifies as a court for the purposes of the Convention (*X v United Kingdom*, above). Hospital managers, when exercising their power to review the detention of a patient, are not a court because the managers are a party to the review (*De Wilde, Ooms and Versp*, above).

*Paragraph 5*

This paragraph requires an enforceable claim for compensation before a national court if **5–036** a breach of any of the other paragraphs in this article has occurred. The Court has held that ". . . there can be no question of 'compensation' where there is no pecuniary or non-pecuniary damage to compensate" (*Wassink v Netherlands*, above, para.38). In *R. (on the application of Wright) v Secretary of State for the Home Department* [2006] EWCA Civ 68; [2006] H.R.L.R. 23, the Court of Appeal held that the right under this paragraph is a domestic right and, as a matter of construction, a person could only be the victim of a detention in contravention of the provisions of this paragraph if there were a breach of paras 1 and/or 4 recognised by domestic law. This approach was followed by Collins J. in *TMM v London Borough of Hackney* [2010] EWHC 1349 (Admin) at para.52.

The current trend of authority in the Court is not to award pecuniary damages on a finding of a violation of this paragraph: see the cases cited in *Niedbala v Poland* ((2001) 33 E.H.R.R. 48 at para.88. Modest pecuniary damages have been awarded where the applicant has suffered damage resulting from a deprivation of liberty that he would not have suffered had this paragraph not been violated (*Niedbala* above).

The Strasbourg jurisprudence on compensation under this article was reviewed by Stanley Burnton J. in *R. (on the application of KB and others) v Mental Health Review Tribunal and another* [2003] EWHC 193 (Admin); [2003] 2 All E.R. 209. His Lordship held that:

1. In the absence of an analytic approach being taken by the Strasbourg Court to this matter, the domestic courts had to determine the principles that were to apply.

2. An award of damages under this paragraph depends on there being proof of damage (*Wassink*, above, followed).

3. There is no power to award exemplary damages (s.9(3) of the Human Rights Act 1998).

4. The distress and frustration felt by a patient because of the delay in the hearing of a Mental Health Act Tribunal would not always justify the award of damages. Such feelings had to be significant "of such intensity that it would in itself justify an award for non-pecuniary damage" (*Silver v United Kingdom* (1983) 5 E.H.R.R. 347 at para.10). An important touchstone of that intensity will be that the hospital staff considered it to be sufficiently relevant to the mental state of the patient to warrant its mention in the notes.

5. The domestic courts should take account of the scale of damages awarded by the Strasbourg Court but should be free to depart from it in order to award adequate, but not excessive, compensation in UK terms.

6. There was no justification for an award of damages being lower under the 1998 Act than for a comparable tort.

7. In assessing damages, the relevant period was that between the time when the tribunal should have determined a patient's application and the date when it was actually determined, i.e. the period of unlawful delay.

Stanley Burnton J.'s judgment was applied and praised by the Court of Appeal in *Anufrijeva v London Borough of Southwark* [2003] EWCA Civ 1406; [2004] 1 All E.R. 833 where the Court said, at para.66, that the remedy has to be "just and equitable" to afford "just satisfaction".

ARTICLE 6

RIGHT TO FAIR TRIAL

**5–037**   1. In the determination of his civil rights and obligations or of any criminal charge against him, everyone is entitled to a fair and public hearing within a reasonable time by an independent and impartial tribunal established by law. Judgment shall be pronounced publicly but the press and public may be excluded from all or part of the trial in the interest of morals, public order or national security in a democratic society, where the interests of juveniles or the protection of the private life of the parties so require, or to the extent strictly necessary in the opinion of the court in special circumstances where publicity would prejudice the interests of justice.

2. Everyone charged with a criminal offence shall be presumed innocent until proved guilty according to law.

3. Everyone charged with a criminal offence has the following minimum rights:

(a)   to be informed promptly, in a language which he understands and in detail, of the nature and cause of the accusation against him;

(b)   to have adequate time and facilities for the preparation of his defence;

(c)   to defend himself in person or through legal assistance of his own choosing or, if he has not sufficient means to pay for legal assistance, to be given it free when the interests of justice so require;

(d)   to examine or have examined witnesses against him and to obtain the attendance and examination of witnesses on his behalf under the same conditions as witnesses against him;

(e)   to have the free assistance of an interpreter if he cannot understand or speak the language used in court.

GENERAL NOTE

**5–038**   This article, which provides for the right to a fair hearing in civil or criminal proceedings in domestic law, "is concerned with standards of justice, the separation of powers and the rule of law" (*Matthews v Ministry of Defence* [2003] UKHL 4; [2003] 1 All E.R. 689 at para.25 per Lord Hoffman). In deciding whether or not there has been a breach of this Article the Court has to ascertain whether the proceedings considered as a whole, including the way in which the evidence was taken were fair (*Mantovanelli v France* [1997] 24 E.H.R.R. 370 para.34). A procedural failure will not lead to the proceedings being quashed or set aside unless substantial unfairness has occurred (*Sheridan v Stanley Cole (Wainfleet) Ltd* [2003] EWCA 1046; [2003] 4 All E.R. 1181 para.49). Under the Convention, art.13 is the guarantee of an effective remedy for breach of a Convention right, not para.1 of this article.

Although it had been the view of the Commission that the jurisprudence of the Court was to the effect that proceedings relating to the detention of a person of unsound mind did engage this article because they did not concern "civil rights and obligations" (*AR v UK* (1996) E.H.L.R. 324), the Court in *Aerts v Belgium* (1998) 29 E.H.R.R. 50, para.59, held that "the right to liberty . . . is a civil right". This article is therefore engaged when a tribunal reviews the detention of a patient. The lawfulness of the detention of patients can be challenged under art.5(4) and the Court, in its interpretation of that paragraph, has been prepared to borrow some of the concepts of fairness in judicial proceedings from this article: see *Shtukaturov v Russia* [2008] M.H.L.R. 238 para.66.

As Wachenfeld has stated: "Guardianship proceedings must comply with the standards of Article 6(1) because it involes the determination of a civil right. See for example, Commission Admissibility Decision *X, Y and Z v Switzerland*, App. No. 6916/76, 6 D. & R. 107, 112, 12 March 1976" (Margaret G. Wachenfeld, "The Human Rights of the Mentally Ill in Europe" (1991) 60 *Nordic Journal of International Law*, 109–292, at 224).

*Paragraph 1*

The right of access to a court guaranteed by this Article is "practical and effective", not **5–039** "theoretical or illusory" (*Del Sol v France* (2002) 35 E.H.R.R. 38 at para.21).

In *Ashingdane v UK* (1985) 7 E.H.R.R. 528, the Court found that the restrictions on bringing legal proceedings placed on patients by s.141 of the Mental Health Act 1959 (now see s.139 of the 1983 Act) did not transgress the patient's "right to a court" under this paragraph. The Court said at para.57:

"Certainly, the right of access to the courts is not absolute but may be subject to limitations; these are permitted by implication since the right of access 'by its very nature calls for regulation by the State, regulation which may vary in time and in place according to the needs and resources of the community and of individuals' (*Golder v UK* (1979) 1 E.H.R.R. 524, paragraph 38). In laying down such regulation, the Contracting States enjoy a certain margin of appreciation. Whilst the final decision as to observance of the Convention's requirements rests with the Court, it is no part of the Court's function to substitute for the assessment of the national authorities any other assessment of what might be the best policy in this field".

IN THE DETERMINATION. This phrase "refers not only to the particular process of the making of the decision but extends more widely to the whole process which leads up to the final resolution" (*R. (on the application of Alconbury Developments Ltd) v Secretary of State for the Environment, Transport and the Regions*) [2001] UKHL 23; [2001] 2 All E.R. 929 HL at para.152 per Lord Clyde).

CIVIL RIGHTS AND OBLIGATIONS. In *Pudas v Sweden* (1998) 10 E.H.R.R. 380, the Court said at para.35:

"According to the well established case law of the Court, the concept of 'civil rights and obligations' is not to be interpreted solely by reference to the respondent State's domestic law and Article 6(1) applies irrespective of the status of the parties, and of the character of the legislation which governs how the dispute is to be determined and the character of the authority which is invested with jurisdiction in the matter; it is enough that the outcome of the proceedings should be decisive for private right and obligations".

In *(R. (on the application of Wilkinson) v The Responsible Medical Officer Broadmoor Hospital* [2001] EWCA Civ 1545; [2002] 1 W.L.R. 419 at para.35, Simon Brown L.J. said that a decision to treat a patient forcibly will inevitably determine his civil rights. However, the right to state medical treatment is not a civil right falling within this article (*L v Sweden* (App. No. 10801/84)). Neither is the provision of services, such as social care services, which are dependent upon a series of evaluative judgments by the provider as to whether the statutory criteria are satisfied and how the need for it ought to be met (*Ali v Birmingham City Council* [2010] UKSC 8).

FAIR . . . HEARING. Among the rights that the Court and the Commission have ident- **5–040** ified as comprising the right to a fair hearing are: the right to adversarial proceedings, the right to have a hearing within a reasonable time, the right to equality of arms, the right to know the grounds on which a decision is based and access to information necessary to bring the case effectively: see further S. Grosz *et al., Human Rights: The 1998 Act and the European Convention* (2000), pp.244 et seq.

Whilst domestic courts enjoy a certain margin of appreciation when dealing with mentally ill persons, that should not be at the expense of a fair trial (*Shtukaturov v Russia*, above, para.68).

The right to have access to information can engage the art.8 rights of the subject of the information (*McMichael v United Kingdom* (1995) 20 E.H.R.R. 205). Although a party has a right to a fair trial under this article, that does not mean that he or she necessarily has an absolute and unqualified right to see all the documents (*Doorson v Netherlands* (1996) 22 E.H.R.R. 330 para.70; also see *Re B (Disclosure to Parties)* [2001] 2 F.L.R. 1017).

In proceedings before a court of first and only instance the right to a "public hearing" entails an entitlement to an oral hearing unless there are exceptional circumstances that justify dispensing with such a hearing (*Miller v Sweden* (2006) 42 E.H.R.R. 51 para.29). An individual has a right to participate effectively in a trial by, for example, being able to hear and follow the proceedings. In the case of a child, it is essential that he is dealt with in a manner which takes full account of his age, level of maturity and intellectual and emotional capacities, and that steps are taken to promote his ability to understand and participate in the proceedings (*SC v UK* (2004) 40 E.H.R.R. 10). Special procedural safeguards may prove called for in order to protect the interests of persons who, on account of their mental disabilities, are not fully capable of acting for themselves (*Winterwerp v Netherlands*, above, para.60).

In *R. (on the application of PD) v West Midlands and North West London Mental Health Review Tribunal* [2004] EWCA Civ 311, the Court of Appeal made reference to *Piersack v Belgium* (1982) 5 E.H.R.R. 169 where "the Court appears to have contemplated that the practical problems of finding properly qualified members of a Tribunal may be relevant when considering whether a member is disqualified on account of bias". The Court of Appeal said, at para.11, that it "would not exclude the possibility that such considerations might be relevant in an extreme case where it was impossible, or virtually impossible, to assemble a Tribunal free of connections that might give rise to apprehension of apparent bias".

Although there is no automatic right under the Convention for legal aid or legal representation to be available for an applicant who is involved in proceedings which determine his or her civil rights and obligations, this article may be engaged under two interrelated aspects. Firstly, para.(1) embodies the right of access to a court. A failure to provide the applicant with the assistance of a lawyer may breach this provision where such assistance is indispensable for effective access to court. Secondly, the key principle governed by the application of this article is fairness. In cases where an applicant appears in court notwithstanding lack of assistance of a lawyer and manages to conduct his or her case, the question may nonetheless arise as to whether the procedure was fair (*P, C and S v UK* (2002) 35 E.H.R.R. 31).

In the *Winterwerp* judgment, above, the Court held, at para.74, that the fact that the emergency confinement of the patient directed by the burgomaster did not afford the patient the opportunity of being heard, either in person or through a representative, did not satisfy the requirement of a "fair hearing".

**5–041** PUBLIC HEARING. A private hearing is possible. "[W]hile the need to protect professional confidentiality and the private lives of patients may justify holding proceedings in camera, such an occurrence must be strictly required by the circumstances" (*Diennet v France* (1996) 21 E.H.R.R. 554, para.34).

REASONABLE TIME. "The reasonableness of the length of proceedings is to be assessed in the light of the particular circumstances of the case, regard being had to the criteria laid down in the court's case-law, in particular the complexity of the case, the applicant's conduct and the conduct of the competent authorities" (*Pélissier and Sassi v France*, (2000) 30 E.H.R.R. 715 at para.67).

INDEPENDENT AND IMPARTIAL TRIBUNAL. This article guarantees to litigants an effective right of access to an independent and impartial court (*Golder v United Kingdom* (1975) 1 E.H.R.R. 524, para.26). The court must have "full" jurisdiction. In *Le Compte, Van Leuven and De Meyer v Belgium* (1982) 4 E.H.R.R. 1 at para.51, the Court defined the concept of access to a court of full jurisdiction in the following terms:

". . . Article 6(1) draws no distinction between questions of fact and questions of law. Both categories of question are equally crucial for the outcome of proceedings relating to 'civil rights and obligations'. Hence, the 'right to a court' and the right to a judicial determination of the dispute cover questions of fact just as much as questions of law".

In order to establish whether a tribunal is "independent" for the purposes of this paragraph, regard must be had, inter alia, to the manner of appointment of its members and their terms of office, the existence of safeguards against outside pressures and the question whether it presents an appearance of independence (*Incal v Turkey* (2000) 29 E.H.R.R. 449, para.65). As to "impartiality", in *Pullar v United Kingdom* (1996) 22 E.H.R.R. 391 at para.30, the Court said that there are two tests for assessing whether a tribunal is impartial within the meaning of this paragraph: the first consists in seeking to determine the personal conviction of a particular judge in a given case and the second in ascertaining whether the judge offered guarantees sufficient to exclude any legitimate doubt in this respect. The House of Lords has explained that "there is now no difference between the common law test of bias and the requirements under Article 6 of the Convention of an independent and impartial tribunal" (*Lawal v Northern Spirit Ltd* [2003] I.C.R. 856 at 862 para.14 per Lord Steyn); see further the notes on r.34 of the Tribunal Procedure (First-tier Tribunal) (Health, Education and Social Care Chamber) Rules 2008.

In *Kingsley v United Kingdom* (2001) 33 E.H.R.R. 288, the European Court said, at para.51, that, even if an adjudicatory body determining disputes over "civil rights and obligations" does not comply with para.1 of this Article, there is no breach of the Article if the proceedings before the body are subject to subsequent control by a judicial body that has full jurisdiction and does provide the guarantees of para.1. An appellate court having full jurisdiction would satisfy this requirement (*Runa Begum v Tower Hamlets LBC*, above) as would a court hearing an application for judicial review: see *Bryan v United Kingdom* (1996) 21 E.H.R.R. 342 and *Secretary of State for Health v Personal Representative of Christopher Beeson* [2002] EWCA Civ 1812, where Laws L.J. said at para.30:

"If there is no reason of substance to question the objective integrity of the first-instance process (whatever may be said about its *appearance*), it seems to us that the added safeguard of judicial review will very likely satisfy the Article 6 standard unless there is some special feature of the case to show the contrary".

### ARTICLE 7

#### NO PUNISHMENT WITHOUT LAW

1. No one shall be held guilty of any criminal offence on account of any act or omission which did **5–042** not constitute a criminal offence under national or international law at the time when it was committed. Nor shall a heavier penalty be imposed than the one that was applicable at the time the criminal offence was committed.

2. This Article shall not prejudice the trial and punishment of any person for any act or omission which, at the time when it was committed, was criminal according to the general principles of law recognised by civilised nations.

### ARTICLE 8

#### RIGHT TO RESPECT FOR PRIVATE AND FAMILY LIFE

1. Everyone has the right to respect for his private and family life, his home and his correspondence. **5–043**
2. There shall be no interference by a public authority with the exercise of this right except such as is in accordance with the law and is necessary in a democratic society in the interests of national security, public safety or the economic well-being of the country, for the prevention of disorder or crime, for the protection of health or morals, or for the protection of the rights and freedoms of others.

GENERAL NOTE

**5–044**     The purpose of this article "is to protect the individual against intrusion by agents of the state, unless for good reason, into the private sphere within which individuals expect to be left alone to conduct their personal affairs and live their persona lives as they choose" (*R. (on the application of the Countryside Alliance) v Attorney General* [2007] UKHL 52 at para.10). It was described by Stanley Burnton J. as "the least defined and most unruly of the rights enshrined in the Convention" in *R. (on the application of Wright) v Secretary of State for Health and Secretary of State for Education and Skills* [2006] EWHC 2886 (Admin) at para.60. In *R. (on the application of Wood) v Metropolitan Police Commissioner* [2009] EWCA Civ 414; [2009] 4 All E.R. 951 at paras 20–22, Laws L.J. said that the central value protected by this Article is the personal autonomy of every individual and that the:

"notion of the personal autonomy of every individual marches with the presumption of liberty enjoyed in a free polity: a presumption which consists in the principle that every interference with the freedom of the individual stands in need of objective justification. Applied to the myriad instances recognised in the Art.8 jurisprudence, this presumption means that, subject to the qualifications I shall shortly describe, an individual's personal autonomy makes him—should make him—master of all those facts about his own identity, such as his name, health, sexuality, ethnicity, his own image, of which the cases speak; and also of the "zone of interaction" (*Von Hannover v Germany* (2005) 40 EHRR 1, para.50) between himself and others. He is the presumed owner of these aspects of his own self; his control of them can only be loosened, abrogated, if the State shows an objective justification for doing so.

This cluster of values, summarised as the personal autonomy of every individual and taking concrete form as a presumption against interference with the individual's liberty, is a defining characteristic of a free society. We therefore need to preserve it even in little cases. At the same time it is important that this core right protected by Art. 8, however protean, should not be read so widely that its claims become unreal and unreasonable. For this purpose I think there are three safeguards, or qualifications. First, the alleged threat or assault to the individual's personal autonomy must (if Art.8 is to be engaged) attain "a certain level of seriousness". Secondly, the touchstone for Art.8(1)'s engagement is whether the claimant enjoys on the facts a "reasonable expectation of privacy" (in any of the senses of privacy accepted in the cases). Absent such an expectation, there is no relevant interference with personal autonomy. Thirdly, the breadth of Art.8(1) may in many instances be greatly curtailed by the scope of the justifications available to the State pursuant to Article 8(2)."

The "Strasbourg institutions have analysed Article 8 issues by asking the following questions: (1) does the subject matter fall within the scope of Article 8? (2) if so, has there been an interference by a public authority? (3) if so, was it 'in accordance with the law'? (4) if so, did it pursue a legitimate aim, i.e. one of those set out in Article 8(2)? (5) if so, was it 'necessary', i.e. did the interference correspond to a 'pressing social need' and was it proportionate to that need?" (S. Grosz, J. Beatson, P. Duffy, *Human Rights: The 1998 Act and the European* Convention, (2000), p.265).

In *Glaser v United Kingdom* (2001) 33 E.H.R.R. 1, the European Court of Human Rights said at para.63:

"The essential object of Article 8 is to protect the individual against arbitrary interference by public authorities. There may however be positive obligations inherent in an effective "respect" for family life. These obligations may involve the adoption of measures designed to secure respect for family life even in the sphere of relations between individuals, including both the provision of a regulatory framework of adjudicatory and enforcement machinery protecting individuals' rights and the implementation, where appropriate, of specific steps (see among other authorities, *X and Y v Netherlands* (1986) 8 E.H.R.R. 235, and, *mutatis mutandis, Osman v United Kingdom* (2000) 29 E.H.R.R. 245). In both the negative and positive contexts, regard must be had to the fair balance which has to be struck between the competing interests of the individual and the community, including other concerned third parties, and of the state's margin of appreciation (see, among other authorities, *Keegan v Ireland* ((1994) 18 E.H.R.R. 342)".

The reference to "relations between individuals" in *Glaser* demonstrates the link between the right to private life and the right to family life. If members of a family are prevented from sharing family life together, art.8(1) is likely to be infringed (*Anufrijeva v London Borough of Southwark* [2003] EWCA Civ 1406; [2004] 1 All E.R. 833 at para.12).

Positive obligations may exceptionally arise in the case of the handicapped in order to ensure that they are not deprived of the possibility of developing social relations with others and therefore developing their own personalities. In the case of the physically handicapped, positive obligations require appropriate measures to be taken, to the greatest extent feasible, to ensure that they have access to essential economic and social activities and to an appropriate range of recreational and cultural activities. A positive obligation will only be imposed where there is a direct and immediate link between the measures sought and the applicant's private life (*Botta v Italy* [1998] 26 E.H.R.R. 241).

The Court has applied the concept of positive obligation in a number of areas including requiring a state to enable the guardians of a mentally defective girl to lodge a complaint with a view to instituting criminal proceedings against a man who had sexually abused her (*X and Y v Netherlands*, above); to establish a fair system whereby the question of access to the personal files of a child in public care will be determined (*Gaskin v United Kingdom* (1990) 12 E.H.R.R. 36); and to take all reasonable steps to facilitate reunion between a child in public care and his parents (*Hokkanen v Finland* (1995) 19 E.H.R.R. 139). Positive obligations are not absolute. Before inaction can amount to a lack of respect for private and family life, there must be some ground for criticising the failure to act. There must be an element of culpability. Where the complaint is that there has been culpable delay in the administrative process necessary to determine and to give effect to an art.8 right, there will be no infringement of the article unless substantial prejudice has been caused to the applicant. There is a need to have regard to resources when considering the obligations imposed by a State by this article (*Anufrijeva v London Borough of Southwark*, above, paras 45–47).

With regard to medical treatment and care, this article cannot be considered applicable every time an individual's everyday life was disrupted but only in exceptional circumstances where the State's failure to adopt measures interfered with an art.8 right because of a special link between the inaction and the needs of the individual. Even then a fair balance has to be struck between the competing demands of the community as a whole and those of the individual (see *Glasser*, above). A particularly wide margin of appreciation was due where the issues involved an assessment of competing priorities for a limited state resource (*Sentges v Netherlands* (2004) 7 C.C.L.R. 400).

In *Passannante v Italy* (1998) 26 E.H.R.R. CD 153, a case where the applicant had waited five months to see a hospital specialist, the Commission stated that:

"where the State has an obligation to provide medical care, an excessive delay of the public health service in providing a medical service to which the patient is entitled and the fact that such a delay has, or is likely to have, a serious impact on the patient's health could raise an issue under Article 8(1) of the Convention."

Also see *Scialacqua v Italy* (1998) 26 E.H.R.R. CD 164, noted under art.2.

Under this Article the authorities:                                                                                    **5–045**

"must strike a fair balance between the interests of a person of unsound mind and the other legitimate interests concerned. However, as a rule, in such a complex matter as determining somebody's mental capacity, the authorities should enjoy a wide margin of appreciation. This is mostly explained by the fact that the national authorities have the benefit of direct contact with the persons concerned and are therefore particularly well placed to determine such issues" (*Shtukaturov v Russia* [2008] M.H.L.R. 238 at para.87).

The Commission has recognised that public authorities might have to take particular steps to protect the mentally disordered in order to fulfil their obligations under this article:

" The impossibility for the above category of persons [the mentally disabled] to form or express their will calls for protective measures on behalf of the authorities which go beyond what is required with regard to persons who are in full possession of their physical and mental capacities" (*X and Y v Netherlands* (1983) 6 E.H.R.R. CD311 at para.81).

Where a public authority commits acts which it knows are likely to cause psychiatric harm to an individual, those acts are capable of constituting an infringement of this article. Maladministration will not, however, cause such an infringement simply because it causes stress that leads to a particularly susceptible individual to suffer such harm in circumstances where this was not reasonably to be anticipated. No lack of respect for family life is manifested in such circumstances (*Anufrijeva v London Borough of Southwark*, above, para.143).

In "Protecting the Rights of People with Mental Disabilities: The European Convention on Human Rights", Oliver Lewis states that in the psychiatric setting, this article will be engaged by issues as diverse as:

"freedom of correspondence, right not to be in a crowded living space, access to non-pharmacological therapy, access to fresh air and exercise, privacy in washing and toileting, privacy of visits, confidentiality of medical records, rights to sexuality, right to be free from unwanted sexual advances, freedom from surveillance of daily life and searches of living space and of person" (European Journal of Health Law (2002) 9: 293–320, 308).

In *Ciliz v Netherlands* [2000] 2 F.L.R. 469 at 482, the Court said that whilst this article contains no explicit procedural requirements, the decision-making process leading to measures of interference must be fair and such as to afford due respect to the interests safeguarded by the article. It is therefore the case that a violation of this article is likely to occur if an application is made to detain a child under the Mental Health Act in circumstances where the parents of the child have not been offered the opportunity of being involved in the decision-making process. In *Glass v United Kingdom* (2004) 39 E.H.R.R. 15, the Court held that a failure to obtain the authority of the High Court to authorise the treatment of a child in a non-emergency situation where the child's parents objected to the treatment in question constituted a violation of this article.

Treatment that does reach the level of severity required by art.3 may nevertheless breach this article in its private life aspects where there are sufficiently adverse effects on a person's physical and moral integrity (*Costello-Roberts v United Kingdom* (1995) 19 E.H.R.R. 112). However it would be difficult, although not necessarily impossible, for a claimant who relies on health grounds to resist removal from the UK to fail under art.3 but succeed under this article (*R. (on the application of Razgar) v Secretary of State for the Home Department* [2004] UKHL 27; [2004] 3 All E.R. 821 at para.59).

In *Storck v Germany* (2006) 43 E.H.R.R. 6; [2005] M.H.L.R. 211, the Court held that the state's obligations under this article in respect of a person who has been detained in a private psychiatric clinic arises for the same reasons to those relevant to art.5.

*Paragraph 1*

RESPECT. "'Respect' means more than 'acknowledge' or 'take into account', it implies **5–046** some positive obligations on the part of the public authorities (*Campbell and Cosans v United Kingdom* (1982) 4 E.H.R.R. 293; *Valsamis v Greece* (1997) 24 E.H.R.R. 294)" (*Anufrijeva v Southwalk London Borough Council*, December 4, 2002 at para.104 per Newman J.). In *Sheffield and Horsham v United Kingdom* (1998) 27 E.H.R.R. 163, the Court said at para.52:

> "The Court reiterates that the notion of 'respect' is not clear cut, especially as far as the positive obligations inherent in that concept are concerned: having regard to the diversity of the practices followed and the situation obtaining in the Contracting States, the notion's requirements will vary considerably from case to case.".

PRIVATE . . . LIFE. In *Bensaid v United Kingdom* (2001) 33 E.H.R.R. 10, the Court said at para.47:

> "Private life is a broad term not susceptible to exhaustive definition. The Court has already held that elements such as gender identification, name and sexual orientation and sexual life are important elements of the personal sphere protected by Article 8. Mental health must be regarded as a crucial part of private life associated with the aspect of moral integrity. Article 8 protects a right to identity and personal development, and the right to establish and develop relationships with other human beings and the outside world. The preservation of mental stability is in that context an indispensable precondition to effective enjoyment of the right to respect for private life".

But, not "every act or measure which adversely affects moral or physical integrity will interfere with the right to respect to private life" (*Bensaid*, above, para.46). However, even a minor interference with the physical integrity of an individual must be regarded as an interference with the right to respect for private life if it is carried out against the individual's will (*Storck v Germany*, above, para.168).

In *Botta v Italy* (1998) 26 E.H.R.R. 241, the Court said that "the guarantee afforded Art.8 **5–047** is primarily intended to ensure the development, without outside interference, of the personality of each individual in his relations with other human beings" (para.32). In this case the Court's case law on the concept of private life was described being "based on a pragmatic, common-sense approach rather than a formalistic or purely legal one" (para.27). The rights invoked must not be "too wide and indeterminate" (*Zehnalova and Zehnal v Czech Republic*, May 14, 2002). In *Niemietz v Germany* (1992) 16 E.H.R.R. 97 at para.29, the Court said that

> "it would be too restrictive to limit the notion to an 'inner circle' in which the individual may live his own personal life as he chooses and to exclude therefrom entirely the outside world encompassed within that circle. Respect for private life must also comprise, to a certain degree, the right to establish and develop relationships with human beings" .

A person's private life may be concerned in measures effected outside his or her home or private property. It can include the publication of a person's photograph (*Sciacca v Italy* (2006) 43 E.H.R.R. 20). A person's reasonable expectation of privacy is a significant though not necessarily conclusive factor (*Perry v United Kingdom* (2004) 39 E.H.R.R. 3 para.37). The "ability to conduct one's life in a manner of one's own choosing may also include the opportunity to pursue activities perceived to be of a physically or morally harmful or dangerous nature for the individual concerned" (*Pretty v United Kingdom*, below at para.62).

In *Raninen v Finland* (1998) 26 E.H.R.R. 563 para.63, the Court acknowledged that the notion of physical and moral integrity of the person extends to situations of deprivation of liberty (which can involve the seclusion of a patient (*R. v Mersey Care National Health*

*Service Trust Ex p. Munjaz* [2005] UKHL 58; [2006] 4 All E.R. 736)). It also includes information about a person's mental condition (*Gaskin v United Kingdom* (1990) 12 E.H.R.R. 36 para.37). In *R. (on the application of H) v Ashworth Hospital Authority* [2001] EWHC Admin 872; [2001] M.H.L.R. 241, Sir Christopher Bellamy Q.C. said, citing *Guerra v Italy* (1998) 26 E.H.R.R. 357 and *Lopez Ostra v Spain* (1995) 20 E.H.R.R. 277, that there was support for the proposition that the notion of physical integrity identified in *X and Y v Netherlands* (1986) 8 E.H.R.R. 235, extends to the protection of a person's health (para.124). In order to succeed under this article the claimant would have to show that there was a real and immediate risk to his health from which the defendant has failed to protect him, and that the defendant had not taken such steps as were reasonably to be expected of it to obviate that risk (para.128). A failure to provide smoking facilities for psychiatric patients does not generally come within the ambit of this article, although there might be rare cases in which the stability of someone's mental health required smoking facilities (*R.(on the application of G) v Nottinghamshire Healthcare NHS Trust* [2008] EWHC 1096 (Admin); [2008] M.H.L.R. 150).

The "imposition of medical treatment, without consent of a mentally competent adult patient, would interfere with a person's physical integrity in a manner capable of engaging the rights protected by [this article]" (*Pretty v United Kingdom*, below, para.63). This article would not be breached if forcible treatment is given to a mentally incompetent detained patient in a situation where, "according to the psychiatric principles generally accepted at the time, medical necessity justified the treatment in issue": see *Herczegfalvy v Austria* (1993) 15 E.H.R.R. 437, paras 83, 86, noted under art.3. Where the patient is a child, any medical treatment (including the taking of a medical photograph) must be authorised by the person with parental responsibility for that child (*Glass v United Kingdom*, above, para.75). The forcible medical examination of a person in order to determine whether his mental capacity could be restored was found to be an interference with his right to respect for private life in *Matter v Slovakia* (2001) 31 E.H.R.R. 32.

With regard to action taken to prevent detainees harming themselves, the authorities:

". . . must discharge their duties in a manner compatible with the rights and freedoms of the individual concerned. There are general measures and precautions which will be available to diminish the opportunities for self-harm, without infringing personal autonomy. Whether any more stringent measures are necessary in respect of a prisoner and whether it is reasonable to apply them will depend on the circumstances of the case" (*Keenan v United Kingdom* (2001) 33 E.H.R.R 38, para.91).

In *R (on the application of N) v Secretary of Sate for Health* [2009] EWCA Civ 795; [2009] M.H.L.R. 266, the Court of Appeal held that this article did not protect the right for patients to smoke at Rampton Hospital: the prohibition of smoking in such an institution did not have a sufficiently adverse effect on a patient's physical or moral integrity.

In *Goodwin v United Kingdom* (2002) 35 E.H.R.R. 18, the issue before the Court was whether or not the UK government had failed to comply with a positive obligation to ensure the right of the applicant, a post-operative male to female transsexual, to respect for her private life, in particular through the lack of legal recognition given to her gender reassignment. In finding that there had been a breach of this article, the Court made reference to *Dudgeon v United Kingdom* (1982) 4 E.H.R.R. 149 at para.41, where the Court had said that it must be recognised that serious interference with private life can arise where the state of domestic law conflicts with an important aspect of personal identity. In the medical sphere, the refusal to accept a particular treatment might lead to a fatal outcome, yet the imposition of medical treatment without the consent of a mentally competent adult patient, would interfere with a person's physical integrity in a manner capable of engaging the rights protected under art.8(1). In *Pretty v United Kingdom* (2002) 35 E.H.R.R. para.63, the Court held that a person may claim to exercise a choice to die by declining to consent to treatment which might prolong life.

Restrictions placed on a male psychiatric patient's freedom to dress as a woman and to **5–048** assume the appearance of a woman constitutes an interference with his private life: see *R. (on the application of E) v Ashworth Hospital Authority* [2001] EWHC Admin 1089 para.40, where Richards J. held that the interference was justified under para.2 by virtue of therapeutic and security concerns that had been put forward in support of the hospital's approach. As a matter of domestic law, a hospital is entitled to give precedence to the interests of the patients as a whole over the interests of individual patients (*R. v Broadmoor Special Hospital Ex p. S, H and D* [1998] C.O.D. 199).

A person has a right under this article to have access to files concerning his own life. Any restriction on this right in domestic law must meet the requirements of para.2. In cases involving the disclosure of personal data, the Court has recognised that a margin of appreciation should be left to national authorities in striking a fair balance between the relevant public and private interests. The scope of this margin depends on such factors as the nature and seriousness of the interests at stake and the gravity of the interference (*Peck v United Kingdom*, (2003) 36 E.H.R.R. 41 para.77). The data subject is not required to specifically justify a request to be provided with a copy of their personal files; rather, it is for the authorities to show that there existed compelling reasons for refusing that facility (*KH v Slovakia* (2009) 49 E.H.R.R. 34, para.48). If a public authority is not able to secure the consent of a person who has contributed to the file to have that material disclosed, there must be an independent authority that can decide whether the material should be disclosed (*Gaskin v United Kingdom*, above and *MG v United Kingdom* (2003) 36 E.H.R.R. 3).

In *Z v Finland* (1997) 25 E.H.R.R. 3 at paras 95–97, the Court said that:

"the protection of personal data, not least medical data, is of fundamental importance to a person's enjoyment of his or her right to respect for private and family life . . . Respecting the confidentiality of health data . . . is crucial not only to respect the sense of privacy of a patient but also to preserve his or her confidence in the medical profession and in health services in general. [Disclosure must be justified by] an overriding requirement in the public interest".

At the same time, the Court accepted that "the interests of a patient and the community as a whole in protecting the confidentiality of medical data may be outweighed by the interest in investigation and prosecution of crime and in the publicity of court proceedings . . . where such interests are shown to be of even greater importance".

The confidentiality of a patient's medical records belongs to the patient. For the particular importance of confidentiality in psychiatric medical notes, see *Ashworth Hospital Authority v MGN Ltd* [2002] UKHL 29; [2002] 4 All E.R. 193 para.63; also see the note on the "rights and freedoms of others", below and Fenella Morris, "Confidentiality and the Sharing of Information" (2003) Journal of Mental Health Law, 9, 38–50.

Where the report of an independent inquiry into homicides committed by a mentally disordered person contains citations from his medical and other records, a claim that the publication of the report to the world at large would breach this article in that it was not necessary in the public interest must be the subject of a "very high intensity" review by a court. It is not enough to assert that the decision to taken was a reasonable one: a compelling case needs to exist to justify publication. In such a situation art.10 also comes into play if only because of the general corresponding right of the public to be free to *receive* information where it is sought to be published (*R. (on the application of Stone) v South East Coast Strategic Health Authority* [2006] EWHC 1668 (Admin); [2006] M.H.L.R. 288 at paras 31–33).

An enquiry by a patient's doctor addressed to a third party which is aimed at obtaining information about the patient rather than communicating it does not infringe this article (*R. (on the application of O'Reilly) v Blenheim Healthcare Ltd* [2005] EWHC 241 (Admin)).

The appointment of a guardian for a mentally disordered patient is an interference with that person's private life because the guardian is given power to make personal decisions on behalf of that person (*X v Federal Republic of Germany* (1980) 20 D. & R. 193). Although the Convention does not place any restrictions on the guardian's powers, the exercise of such powers must fall within one of the limitations set out in para.2.

**5–049**    The searching of a mentally disordered detained patient would violate this article in the absence of a justification under para.2. It has been stated that the Court:

> "has exercised particular judicial vigilance where the authorities are empowered under national law to order and effect searches without a judicial warrant. Very strict limits on such powers are called for in such cases in order to protect individuals from arbitrary interference by the authorities with the rights guaranteed under [this article (*Camenzind v Switzerland* (1999) 28 E.H.R.R. 458)]" (S. Grosz *et al.*, above, at p.285).

However, in *R. (on the application Gillan) v Metropolitan Police Commissioner* [2006] UKHL 12; [2006] 4 All E.R. 1041 at para.28, Lord Bingham said that he was:

> "doubtful whether an ordinary superficial search of the person can be said to show a lack of respect for private life. It is true that 'private life' has been generously construed to embrace wide rights to personal autonomy. But it is clear Convention jurisprudence that intrusions must reach a certain level of seriousness to engage the operation of the Convention which is, after all, concerned with human rights and fundamental freedoms, and I incline to the view that an ordinary superficial search of the person and an opening of bags, of the kind which passengers uncomplainingly submit at airports, for example, can scarcely be said to reach that level."

In *Wainwright v United Kingdom* (2007) 44 E.H.R.R. 40 para.43, the Court held that the requirement to submit to a strip search will generally constitute interference under this paragraph that would require justification under para.2.

The use of surveillance techniques, such as CCTV in hospitals and care homes may well involve art.8 rights. In *Khan v UK*, (2001) 31 E.H.R.R. 2000, a case involving the use of a covert listening device by the police, the Court said at para.26:

> "The Court recalls, with the Commission in the case of *Govell*, that the phrase 'in accordance with the law' not only requires compliance with domestic law but also relates to the quality of that law, requiring it to be compatible with the rule of law. In the context of covert surveillance by public authorities, in this instance the police, domestic law must provide protection against arbitrary interference with an individual's right under Article 8. Moreover, the law must be sufficiently clear in its terms to give individuals an adequate indication as to the circumstances in which and the conditions on which public authorities are entitled to resort to such covert measures".

Surveillance operations conducted by local authorities and NHS trusts must comply with the provisions of Pt II of the Regulations of Investigatory Powers Act 2000 which was passed partly as a result of the decision in *Khan*. The normal use of security cameras per se, whether in the public street or on premises, do not raise issues under this Article as long as they serve a legitimate and foreseeable purpose (*Perry v United Kingdom* (2004) 39 E.H.R.R. 3 para.40).

**5–050**    FAMILY . . . LIFE.   The State must act in a manner calculated to allow those concerned to lead a normal family life (*Z and E v Austria* (1986) 49 D. & R. 67). The existence or non-existence of "family life" is essentially a question of fact depending upon the reality in practice of close personal ties (*K and T v Finland* (2003) 36 E.H.R.R. 18 para.150). It is therefore the case that it is actual family life, rather than family life in the abstract that needs to be considered (*R. (on the application of Ahmadi) v Secretary of State for the Home Department* [2005] EWHC 687 (Admin) para.25). This article "makes no distinction between the 'legitimate and the illegitimate' family" (*Marckx v Belgium* (1979) 2 E.H.R.R. 330 para.31). The concept of family life embraces, even where there is no co-habitation, the tie between a parent and his or her child (*Boughanemi v France* (1996) 22 E.H.R.R. 228) including adoptive parent/child relationships (*X v Belgium and Netherlands* (1975) D.R. 75). When deciding whether a relationship between a couple can be said to amount to "family life", a number of factors may be relevant, including whether the couple live together, the length of their relationship and whether they have demonstrated their commitment to each other by having children together or by any other means (*Al-Nashif v Bulgaria* (2003) 36 E.H.R.R. 37 para.112). In *R. (on the application of L) v Secretary of State for Health* [2001] 1 F.L.R. 406, Scott Baker J. considered the jurisprudence on this article. He said:

"Family life it seems to me, is an elastic concept that depends very much on the facts of the individual case. In some cases the existence of family life will be immediately obvious; in others the reverse will be true. But the onus of establishing family life in each case is in my judgment on the applicant".

In *Messina v Italy (No.2)*, September 28, 2000, para.61, the Court said:

"The Court recalls that all lawful detention pursuant to Article 5 . . . naturally brings with it a restriction for the interested party of his private and family life. It is, however, essential in respect of his family life that the penitentiary administration helps the inmate to maintain contact with his close family".

With regard to the parent-child relationship, the Court has said that:

"a fair balance must be struck between the interests of the child and those of the parent and that in doing so particular importance must be attached to the best interests of the child, which depending on their nature and seriousness, may override those of the parent. In particular . . . the parent cannot be entitled under Article 8 . . . to have such measures taken as would harm the child's health and development" (*EP v Italy* (2001) 31 E.H.R.R. 17 at para.62).

There must be extraordinarily compelling reasons before a baby can be physically removed from its mother, against her will, immediately after birth as a consequence of a procedure in which neither she nor her partner has been involved (*P, C and S v United Kingdom* (2002) E.H.R.R. 31). In "judicial decisions where the rights under Article 8 of parents and of a child are at stake, the child's rights must be the paramount consideration" (*Yousef v Netherlands* (2003) 36 E.H.R.R. 20 at para.73).

In *Anderson and Kullman v Sweden* (1986) 46 E.H.R.R. DR 251, the Commission said that the:

"Convention does not as such guarantee the right to public assistance either in the form of financial support to maintain a certain standard of living or in the form of supplying day home care places, nor does the right under Article 8 of the Convention to respect for family life extend so far as to impose on a State a general obligation to provide for financial assistance to individuals in order to enable one of the parties to stay at home to take care of the children".

There is no Convention duty to provide support to foreign nationals who are in a position freely to return home (*R. (on the application of Kimani) v Lambeth LBC* [2003] EWCA Civ 1150; [2004] 1 W.L.R. 272), and the right to family life is not infringed because it must be conducted outside the United Kingdom in a country with a lower standard of living (*R. (on the application of Mahmood) v Secretary of State for the Home Department* [2001] 1 W.L.R. 840).

**5–051**    HOME.    Neither this article nor any other provision of the Convention guarantees housing of a particular standard or at all (*Chapman v United Kingdom* (2001) 33 E.H.R.R. 399,
para.99). However, a refusal of the authorities to solve a housing problem of an individual
suffering from a severe disease might in certain circumstances raise an issue under this
article because of the impact of such refusal on the private life of the individual
(*Marzari v Italy* (1999) 28 E.H.R.R. CD 175). Although not every breach of a local authority's duty to provide residential accommodation under s.21 of the National Assistance Act
1948 will result in a breach of this article, those entitled to care under s.21 are a particularly
vulnerable group. Positive measures have to be taken, by way of community care facilities,
to enable them to enjoy, so far as possible, a normal and family life. The question that needs
to be asked is what was the effect of the breach in practical terms on the claimant's family
and private life? (*R. (on the application of Bernard) v London Borough of Enfield* [2002]
EWHC 2282 (Admin); (2002) 5 C.C.L.R. 577). In *Anufrijeva v Southwalk London Borough
Council*, above, the Court of Appeal, in confirming the correctness of the approach adopted
in *Bernard*, said at para.43:

> "We find it hard to conceive, however, of a situation in which the predicament of an indi-
> vidual will be such that Article 8 requires him to be provided with welfare support, where
> his predicament is not sufficiently severe to engage Article 3. Article 8 may more readily
> engaged where a family unit is involved. Where the welfare of children is at stake,
> Article 8 may require the provision of welfare support in a manner which enables family
> life to continue".

In *Gomez v Spain (2005)* 41 E.H.R.R. 40, para.53, the Court stated:

> "A home will usually be the place, the physically defined area, where private and family
> life develops. The individual has a right to respect for his home, meaning not just the
> right to the actual physical area, but also to the quiet enjoyment of that area. Breaches
> of the right to respect of the home are not confined to concrete or physical breaches,
> such as unauthorised entry into a person's home, but also include those that are not con-
> crete or physical, such as noise, emissions, smells or other forms of interference. A
> serious breach may result in the breach of a person's right to respect for his home if it
> prevents him from enjoying the amenities of his home."

In *R (on the application of N) v Secretary of Sate for Health* [2009] EWCA Civ 795, the
Court of Appeal held that although Rampton Hospital was the patient's home, it was not
the same as a private home in that it was a public institution operated as a hospital
where supervision was intense for safety and security reasons. The degree to which a person
could expect freedom to do as he pleased, and engage in personal and private activity,
would vary according to the nature of the accommodation in which he lived. A patient
in a high security hospital did not lose all rights to a private life but the nature of that
life and the activities he may pursue were seriously restricted, and always supervised.

In *R. v North and East Devon Health Authority Ex p. Coughlan* [2000] 3 All E.R. 850, the
Court of Appeal held that the enforced move of a patient by an NHS Trust from accommodation that had been promised as her home for life, a move that would be both emotionally
devastating and seriously anti-therapeutic, was a breach of this Article that was not justified
by para.2.

CORRESPONDENCE.    A law which allows for state interference with correspondence
must not leave the authorities too much latitude. It must "indicate with reasonable clarity
the scope and manner of the exercise of the relevant discretion conferred on the public authorities" (*Domenichini v Italy*, (2001) 32 E.H.R.R. 4 para.33).

In *Klass v Germany* (1979) 2 E.H.R.R. 214, the Court held that this article protects telephone conversations as well as written correspondence. A similar finding would almost
certainly be made on other forms of communication, such as email.

*Paragraph 2*

The exceptions provided for in this paragraph must be interpreted narrowly, and the need **5–052** for them in any given case must be convincingly established (*Societe Colas Est v France* (2004) 39 E.H.R.R. 17 para.47). In *Re L (Care: Threshold Criteria)* [2007] 1 F.L.R. 1050 at para.51, Hedley J. said that "Art.8(2) . . . contemplate[s] the exceptional rather than the commonplace."

The principles which govern the court's approach in determining whether an interference with an art.8 right can be justified under this paragraph were identified by Newman J. in *R. (on the application of N) v Ashworth Special Hospital Authority and the Secretary of State for Health* [2001] EWHC Admin 339; [2001] M.H.L.R. 77 at para.9:

"(i) When considering whether an interference with a Convention right is proportionate the burden lies on the State to justify its actions.
 (ii) The interference must go no further than is strictly necessary to achieve its permitted purpose.
(iii) The more substantial the interference the more that is required to justify it.
(iv) The court should anxiously scrutinise a decision of the executive which interferes with human rights and should consider applying an objective test 'whether the decision maker could reasonably have concluded that the interference was necessary to achieve one or more of the legitimate aims recognised by the Convention'.
 (v) The mode of such objective review is more intrusive, or it could be said, more demanding than the convention *Wednesbury* test.
(vi) The court should give due deference or allow a margin of appreciation to the decision maker".

Where the interference is with an intimate part of an individual's private life, there must be particularly serious reasons to justify the interference (*Smith v United Kingdom* (2000) 29 E.H.R.R. 493 at para.89). However the state is entitled to control even seemingly consensual sexual acts in private where it is necessary to "safeguard . . . against exploitation and corruption . . . those who are specially vulnerable because they are young, weak in body or mind, inexperienced, or in a state of special physical, official or economic dependence" (*Dudgeon v United Kingdom* (1982) 4 E.H.R.R. 149 at para.49).

The common law and statutory powers of the police enter private premises to prevent a breach of the peace, which are preserved by s.17(6) of the Police and Criminal Evidence Act 1984, do not contravene this paragraph as they are "in accordance with law" and are pursued with the legitimate aim of the "prevention of disorder or crime" for the purposes of this paragraph. The use of this power by the police must be a proportionate measure in all the circumstances (*McLeod v UK* (1999) 27 E.H.R.R. 493).

PUBLIC AUTHORITY. If a state fails to secure the rights contained in this article, if necessary by domestic legislation, it incurs responsibility to its citizens under the Convention, irrespective of the status of the person or body under its jurisdiction which is infringing them (*Costello-Roberts v UK* (1995) 19 E.H.R.R. 112).

IN ACCORDANCE WITH THE LAW. See the note on "prescribed by law" in art.5(1). This expression:

"requires firstly that the impugned measure should have some basis in domestic law; it also refers to the quality of the law in question, requiring that it should be accessible to the person concerned, who must moreover be able to foresee its consequences for him, and compatible with the rule of law" (*Lambert v France* (2000) 30 E.H.R.R. 346).

This requirement is "directed to substance and not form. It is intended to ensure that any interference is not random and arbitrary but governed by clear pre-existing rules, and that the circumstances and procedures adopted are predictable and foreseeable by those to whom they are applied"; per Lord Bingham in *R. v Mersey Care National Health Service Trust Ex p. Munjaz* [2005] UKHL 58; [2006] 4 All E.R. 736 at para.34. His Lordship said that the "law" could be statute, binding ministerial regulations or ministerial guidance requiring institutions to have clear written guidelines which must be accessible, foreseeable and predictable. It can also include the common law (*Sunday Times v United Kingdom* (1979) 2 E.H.R.R. 245 at para.27).

The fact that the law confers discretion on a professional, such as a doctor, is not in itself inconsistent with the requirement of foreseeability, subject to the proviso that: "the scope of the discretion and the manner of its exercise are indicated with sufficient clarity, having regard to the legitimate aim of the measure in question, to give the individual adequate protection against arbitrary interference" (*Gillow v United Kingdom* (1989) 11 E.H.R.R. 335 at para.51). In *Petra v Romania* (2001) 33 E.H.R.R. 5, the Court said at para.37: "[W]hile a law which confers a discretion must indicate the scope of that discretion, it is impossible to attain absolute certainty in the framing of the law, and the likely outcome of any search for certainty would be excessive rigidity".

**5–053**   NECESSARY IN A DEMOCRATIC SOCIETY.   The:

> "notion of necessity implies that the interference corresponds to a pressing social need and, in particular, that it is proportionate to the legitimate aims pursued. In determining whether an interference was 'necessary in a democratic society' the Court will take into account that a margin of appreciation is left to Contracting States. Furthermore the Court cannot confine itself to considering the impugned facts in isolation but must apply an objective standard and look at them in the light of the case as a whole" (*Matter v Slovakia* (2001) 31 E.H.R.R. 32, para.66).

The word "necessary" is not synonymous with "indispensable", but it implies the existence of a pressing social need (*Sunday Times v UK* (1979) 2 E.H.R.R. 245 at para.59). In the context of similar wording in art.11(2), the Court has said that "the term 'necessary' does not have the flexibility of such expressions as 'useful' or 'desirable'" (*Chassagnou v France*, March 29, 1999 at para.112). The more serious the intervention, the more compelling must be the justification (*Johanssen v Norway* (1996) 23 E.H.R.R. 33).

ECONOMIC WELL-BEING.   A court should be slow to interfere with decisions which involve a balance of competing claims on the public purse in the allocation of economic resources (*R. v Criminal Injuries Compensation Board Ex p. P* [1995] 1 All E.R. 870 per Neill L.J. at 881). This approach has been reaffirmed in home closure cases since the coming into force of the 1998 Act. In *R. (on the application of Phillips and Rowe) v Walsall MBC* [2001] EWHC 789 (Admin), Lightman J. said at para.11:

> "I may add that if (contrary to my view) a move such as is presently contemplated could possibly constitute an interference with a fundamental right under Article 8, it could surely be justified as required for the economic well-being of the Council and of those in need of its services. Resources of public authorities are notoriously limited and it must be a matter for elected authorities such as the Council to have leeway in how they are husbanded and applied".

**5–054**   PROTECTION OF HEALTH.   The Court has not developed an equivalent test of "medical necessity" in relation to this article, as it has in the context of art.3.

In *R. (on the application of Razgar) v Secretary of State for the Home Department* [2004] UKHL 27; [2004] 3 All E.R. 821 at para.59, Baroness Hale made the following comments in a case where the applicant's health needs were being properly or at least adequately met in this country and the complaint was that they would not be adequately met in the county to which he is to be expelled:

"Although the possibility cannot be excluded, it is not easy to think of a foreign health care case which would fail under Art.3 but succeed under Art.8. There clearly must be a strong case before the Article is even engaged and then a fair balance must be struck under Art.8(2). In striking that balance, only the most compelling humanitarian considerations are likely to prevail over the legitimate aims of immigration control or public safety."

In *L v Sweden*, 45 D. & R. 181, the Commission held that a decision provisionally to release a patient who had been detained in a psychiatric hospital constituted an interference with his right to respect for family life under this article. However, the Commission went onto declare the application manifestly ill-founded as the decision was justified in the interests of the patient's health. The reason for not discharging the patient absolutely was that there were reasons to believe that she would stop taking her medication if this happened, and that this would lead to a deterioration in her health. This decision sanctions both the granting of leave to, and the conditional discharge of, a detained patient on condition that the patient continues to accept medication, as long as the terms of this paragraph are satisfied.

RIGHTS OF FREEDOM OF OTHERS. "Article 8.2 could have been, but is not, expressly limited to Convention rights and liberties"; per Stanley Burnton J. in *Craven v Secretary of State for the Home Department and the Parole Board* [2001] EWHC Admin 850 at para.35. In this case an exclusion zone attached to a prisoner's parole was upheld partly because "the respect for private life protected by Article 8 should include a victim's family right to go about their business with a minimum of anxiety, and without undue restriction on their own movements". Also note the statement of Hale L.J. in *Re W & B (Children)* [2001] EWCA Civ 757 at para.54, that the rights of the child to be taken into account in this paragraph are not confined to his Convention rights, and include his interests.

In *TV v Finland* (1994) 18 E.H.R.R. CD 179, the Commission held that the disclosure that a prisoner was HIV positive to prison staff directly involved in his custody and who themselves were subject to obligations of confidentiality was justified as being necessary "for the protection of the rights and freedoms of others". Similar considerations would apply to a patient who had been assessed as being a danger to other patients or to staff.

ARTICLE 9

FREEDOM OF THOUGHT, CONSCIENCE AND RELIGION

1. Everyone has the right to freedom of thought, conscience and religion; this right includes freedom **5–055** to change his religion or belief and freedom, either alone or in community with others and in public or private, to manifest his religion or belief, in worship, teaching, practice and observance.

2. Freedom to manifest one's religion or beliefs shall be subject only to such limitations as are prescribed by law and are necessary in a democratic society in the interests of public safety, for the protection of public order, health or morals, or for the protection of the rights and freedoms of others.

ARTICLE 10

FREEDOM OF EXPRESSION

1. Everyone has the right to freedom of expression. This right shall include freedom to hold opinions **5–056** and to receive and impart information and ideas without interference by public authority and regardless of frontiers. This Article shall not prevent States from requiring the licensing of broadcasting, television or cinema enterprises.

2. The exercise of these freedoms, since it carries with it duties and responsibilities, may be subject to such formalities, conditions, restrictions or penalties as are prescribed by law and are necessary in a democratic society, in the interests of national security, territorial integrity or public safety, for the prevention of disorder or crime, for the protection of health or morals, for the protection of the reputation or rights of others, for preventing the disclosure of information received in confidence, or for maintaining the authority and impartiality of the judiciary.

GENERAL NOTE

**5-057**    The courts "have frequently stated that in the field of freedom of speech there is no difference in principle between English law and [this Article]" (*Ashworth Security Hospital v
MGN Ltd* [2001] 1 All E.R. 991 at para.71 CA, per Lord Phillips M.R.).

Paragraph 1 of this article guarantees the right to freedom of expression. An interference
with this right entails a violation of the article if it does not fall within one of the exceptions
provided for in para.2. In *Handyside v United Kingdom* (1976) 1 E.H.R.R. 737, the Court
said at para.49:

> "Subject to Article 10(2), [this Article] is applicable not only to 'information' or 'ideas'
> that are favourably received or regarded as inoffensive or as a matter of indifference, but
> also to those that offend, shock or disturb the State or any sector of the population. Such
> are the demands of that pluralism, tolerance and broadmindedness without which there is
> no democratic society. This means, amongst other things, that every 'formality', 'con-
> dition', 'restriction' or 'penalty' imposed in this sphere must be proportionate to the
> legitimate aim pursued".

In *Goodwin v United Kingdom* (1996) 22 E.H.R.R. 123 at 137, the Court held that an
order requiring a journalist to identify his sources would only be justified by "an overriding
requirement in the public interest".

This Article will often overlap with an art.8 claim, especially with regard to a claim concerning access to information.

*Paragraph 2*

**5-058**    In *Kelly v BBC* [2001] 1 All E.R. 323, Munby J. said at 335:

> "Well-known jurisprudence of the European Court on Human Rights establishes: (i) that
> the exceptions in paragraph 2 must be narrowly interpreted; (ii) that if a restraint is to be
> justified under paragraph 2 it must be 'necessary in a democratic society'—that is to say,
> the necessity for any such restriction must be 'convincingly established' by reference to
> the existence of a 'pressing social need', and the restriction must be 'proportionate to the
> legitimate aim pursued'; and (iii) that the restriction must be 'prescribed by law'—that
> is, the law must be 'adequately accessible to the citizen' and must be 'formulated with
> sufficient precision to enable a citizen to regulate his conduct': see *Rantzen v Mirror
> Group Newspapers (1986) Ltd* [1993] 4 All E.R. 975 at 990, citing *Sunday Times v
> United Kingdom (No.1)* (1979) 2 E.H.R.R. 245 and *Sunday Times v United Kingdom
> (No.2)* (1992) 14 E.H.R.R. 229".

With regard to the question whether a detained patient should be allowed to have in his possession hardcore pornographic magazines, it is likely that the courts will adopt the
reasoning of Scott Baker L.J. in *R. (on the application of Morton) v The Governor of
Long Lartin Prison and the Secretary of State for the Home Department* [2003] EWCA
Civ 644, in respect of hospitals that detain patients whose mental disorder might be
adversely affected if they had access to such material. His Lordship said at para.22:

> "Because the prisoner lives in a small and enclosed community, the interests of others
> are concerned as well as those of the prisoner himself. That is why Article 10(2) bites
> in this case. It seems to me obvious that once material of the kind prohibited in this
> case is allowed in the hands of a prisoner, there is an obvious risk that it will reach
> the eyes and hands of others, with the consequential risk of abuse, exploitation, assault
> and so forth".

The interviewing of detained patients by journalists can be monitored without contravening
this article. Permission for the interview need not be forthcoming if it would place the
patient's well-being at risk or would have an adverse effect on other patients or on good

order or security in the hospital. Where national security is involved, the interview can take place within the earshot of an official and tape-recorded *(R. (on the application of A) v Home Secretary* [2003] EWHC 2846 (Admin)).

The provisions of s.134 of the Act, under which a patient's correspondence can be withheld, are likely to be held to be in accordance with this paragraph in that the restrictions in the section "are necessary in a democratic society, in the interests of . . . public safety, . . . for the protection of health or morals, [or] for the protection of the reputation or rights of others . . . ".

## ARTICLE 11

### FREEDOM OF ASSEMBLY AND ASSOCIATION

1. Everyone has the right to freedom of peaceful assembly and to freedom of association with others, including the right to form and to join trade unions for the protection of his interests.  **5–059**

2. No restrictions shall be placed on the exercise of these rights other than such as are prescribed by law and are necessary in a democratic society in the interests of national security or public safety, for the prevention of disorder or crime, for the protection of health or morals or for the protection of the rights and freedoms of others. This Article shall not prevent the imposition of lawful restrictions on the exercise of these rights by members of the armed forces, of the police or of the administration of the State.

## ARTICLE 12

### RIGHT TO MARRY

Men and women of marriageable age have the right to marry and to found a family, according to the national laws governing the exercise of this right.  **5–060**

GENERAL NOTE

This article "secures the fundamental right of a man and a woman to marry and to found  **5–061** a family. The second aspect is not however a condition of the first and the inability of any couple to conceive or parent a child cannot be regarded as *per se* removing their right to enjoy the first limb of this provision" *(Goodwin v United Kingdom* (2002) 35 E.H.R.R. 18 at para.98).

While this article is confined to legally formalised heterosexual relationships (as defined by gender, see *Goodwin,* above), art.8 is far broader in its scope. An interference with family life which is justified under art.8(2) cannot at the same time constitute a violation of this article *(X & Y v Switzerland* (1978) 13 D. & R. 105).

The Marriage Act 1983 places no restrictions on mentally disordered patients, whether detained or not, from marrying as long as they have sufficient mental capacity to contract a marriage (see the General Note to the Act under the heading "Marriage"). Any substantial interference with this right would violate this article. However, the Commission in *Hamer v United Kingdom* ((1982) 4 E.H.R.R. 139) left open whether it might, exceptionally, be possible to prohibit a patient's marriage on the grounds of special dangerousness, and the consequential risk posed to the partner: see O. Thorold, "The Implications of the European Convention on Human Rights for United Kingdom Mental Health Legislation", [1996] E.H.R.L.R. 619–636 at 634.

The Commission has considered the right to sexual relations in a number of cases. In *X v United Kingdom* (1975) 2 D. & R. 105, a long-term prisoner complained of being deprived both of his conjugal rights and of the exercise of his paternal rights. In giving its opinion, the Commission said:

"With a view to his family rights the applicant has also complained that he has been prevented from 'founding further family'. It is true that Article 12 of the Convention secures to everyone of marriageable age the right to found a family . . . Although the right to found a family is an absolute right in the sense that no restrictions similar to those in paragraph 2 of Article 8 of the Convention are expressly provided for, it does not mean that a person must at all times be given the actual possibility to procreate his descendants. It would seem that the situation of a lawfully convicted person detained in prison in which the applicant finds himself falls under his own responsibility, and that his right to found a family has not otherwise been infringed".

A similar finding was made by the Commission in *X & Y v Switzerland*, above, where, in an application founded on art.8, it was held that that article does not require conjugal visits, even if the husband and wife are detained in the same prison. The rationale of this finding was based on the need to prevent "disorder or crime".

Different considerations would apply to the position of mentally disordered detained patients, as they are not "responsible" for their hospitalisation. Thorold argues that conjugal visits:

"can help to preserve a patient's marital relationship and thereby improve longer-term mental health prognosis. Any limitation on sexual relationships between patients, or a patient and a spouse, would have to be strictly justified. A prohibition which was expressed in general terms would be in grave danger of breaching Art.12. It may therefore be necessary for a policy to be formulated which permits sexual relations subject to well-defined exceptions, of which danger to another person would clearly be one" (op. cit., at 635).

In *Secretary of State for the Home Department Ex p. Mellor* [2001] EWCA Civ 472, the Court of Appeal concluded that the qualifications on the right to respect for family life that are recognised by art.8(2) apply equally to rights under this article (per Lord Phillips M.R. at para.39). This means that justification for the exceptions referred to by Thorold must be found in art.8(2).

RIGHT TO MARRY. Even if there is no prospect of cohabitation (*Hamer v United Kingdom*, above).

ARTICLE 14

PROHIBITION OF DISCRIMINATION

**5–062**    The enjoyment of the rights and freedoms set forth in this Convention shall be secured without discrimination on any ground such as sex, race, colour, language, religion, political or other opinion, national or social origin, association with a national minority, property, birth or other status.

GENERAL NOTE

**5–063**    This article does not provide a free-standing prohibition on discrimination. It prohibits discrimination only in relation to enjoyment of rights and freedoms guaranteed by the Convention. In *Botta v Italy* (1998) 26 E.H.R.R. 241, the Court said at para.39:

"Article 14 complements the other substantive provisions of the Convention and its protocols. It has no independent existence, since it has effect solely in relation to 'the enjoyment of the rights and freedoms' safeguarded by those provisions. Although the application of Article 14 does not presuppose a breach of one or more of those provisions—and to this extent it is autonomous—there can be no room for its application unless the facts of the case fall within the ambit of one or more of the latter".

A tenuous link with another provision of the Convention is not sufficient to bring this article into play (*M v Secretary of State for Work and Pensions* [2006] UKHL 11; [2006] 4 All E.R. 929).

In *Pretty v UK* (2002) 35 E.H.R.R. 1, the Court said at para.88:

"For the purpose of Article 14 a difference in treatment between persons in analogous or relevantly similar positions is discriminatory if it has no objective and reasonable justification, that is if it does not pursue a legitimate aim or if there is not a reasonable relationship of proportionality between the means employed and the aim sought to be realised. Moreover, the Contracting States enjoy a margin of appreciation in assessing whether and to what extent differences in otherwise similar situations justify a different treatment. Discrimination may also arise where States without an objective and reasonable justification fail to treat differently persons whose situations are significantly different".

The approach that courts should adopt when applying this article was considered by the House of Lords in *R. (on the application of Carson) v Secretary of State for Work and Pensions* [2005] UKHL 37; [2005] 4 All E.R. 545.

*Abdulaziz v UK* (1985) 7 E.H.R.R. 471 is authority for the proposition that there may be a violation of this article considered together with another article (in that case art.8) in a case where there would be no violation of that other article taken alone.

ANY GROUND SUCH AS. The list that follows is illustrative, not exhaustive. In *R. (on the application of Pretty) v Director of Public Prosecutions* [2001] UKHL 61; [2002] 1 All E.R. 1 at para.105, Lord Hope held this article is capable of extending to discrimination in the enjoyment of Convention rights on the grounds of physical or mental capacity. Also note that in *B v Secretary of State for Work and Pensions* [2005] EWCA Civ 929 at para.25, Sedley L.J. said that mental capacity, "although not listed in [this article], is arguably at least as sensitive a personal characteristic, in relation to discrimination, as race or sex."

SEX. Very weighty reasons are generally required for differences of treatment based solely on gender (*Abdulaziz, Cabales and Balkandali v United Kingdom* (1985) 7 E.H.R.R. 471 at para.78).

OTHER STATUS. Which could include the status of a patient detained under the 1983 Act and a prisoner (*R (on the application of N) v Secretary of Sate for Health* [2009] EWCA Civ 795). This term has been held to include sexual orientation (*Salgueiro v Portugal* (2001) 31 E.H.R.R. 1055) and family status (*R. (on the application of L) v Manchester City Council* [2001] EWHC Admin 707 at para.91). In *R. (on the application of T and S (a minor, by her next friend T)) v Secretary of State for Health and Secretary of State for the Home Department* [2002] EWHC Admin 1887 at para. 86, Sir Edwin Jowitt said that "the word status is not to be construed narrowly but should be given a purposive construction".

### ARTICLE 16

#### RESTRICTIONS ON POLITICAL ACTIVITY OF ALIENS

Nothing in Article 10, 11 and 14 shall be regarded as preventing the High Contracting Parties from imposing restrictions on the political activity of aliens. **5–064**

### ARTICLE 17

#### PROHIBITION OF ABUSE OF RIGHTS

Nothing in this Convention may be interpreted as implying for any State, group or person any right to engage in any activity or perform any act aimed at the destruction of any of the rights and freedoms set forth herein or at their limitation to a greater extent than is provided for in the Convention. **5–065**

**5–066**   The restrictions permitted under this Convention to the said rights and freedoms shall not be applied for any purpose other than those for which they have been prescribed.

## PART II

## THE FIRST PROTOCOL

### ARTICLE 1

#### PROTECTION OF PROPERTY

**5–067**   Every natural or legal person is entitled to the peaceful enjoyment of his possessions. No one shall be deprived of his possessions except in the public interest and subject to the conditions provided for by law and by the general principles of international law.

 The preceding provisions shall not, however, in any way impair the right of a State to enforce such laws as it deems necessary to control the use of property in accordance with the general interest or to secure the payment of taxes or other contributions or penalties.

### ARTICLE 2

#### RIGHT TO EDUCATION

**5–068**   No person shall be denied the right to education. In the exercise of any functions which it assumes in relation to education and to teaching, the State shall respect the right of parents to ensure such education and teaching in conformity with their own religious and philosophical convictions.

### ARTICLE 3

#### RIGHT TO FREE ELECTIONS

**5–069**   The High Contracting Parties undertake to hold free elections at reasonable intervals by secret ballot, under conditions which will ensure the free expression of the opinion of the people in the choice of the legislature.

GENERAL NOTE

**5–070**    While this article is phrased in terms of the obligation to hold elections, the case law of the Court establishes that it guarantees individual rights, including the right to vote and to stand for election. In *Hirst v United Kingdom* (No.2) (2006) 42 E.H.R.R. 41, the Court held that although states enjoy a wide margin of appreciation in determining whether restrictions on prisoners' right to vote can be justified, it could not accept that s.3 of the Representation of the People Act 1983, which provides for absolute bar on voting by any serving prisoner in any circumstances, falls within an acceptable margin of appreciation. This ruling has required the Government to review the position of patients who are detained under the Mental Health Act and who are disenfranchised by virtue of the operation of s.3A of the 1983 Act: see the General Note to the Act under the heading "Voting".

PART III

THE SIXTH PROTOCOL

ARTICLE 1

ABOLITION OF THE DEATH PENALTY

The death penalty shall be abolished. No one shall be condemned to such penalty or executed.     **5–071**

ARTICLE 2

DEATH PENALTY IN TIME OF WAR

A state may make provision in its law for the death penalty in respect of acts committed in time of     **5–072**
war or of imminent threat of war; such penalty shall be applied only in the instances laid down in the
law and in accordance with its provisions. The State shall communicate to the Secretary General of the
Council of E]urope the relevant provisions of that law.

## PART 6

## DEPRIVATIONS OF LIBERTY – MENTAL HEALTH ACT 1983 OR MENTAL CAPACITY ACT 2005?

This Part considers the following question: if action taken, or about to be taken, **6–001** with respect to a mentally incapacitated person constitutes a deprivation of that person's liberty which Act should be invoked, the Mental Health Act ("the 1983 Act") or the Mental Capacity Act ("the 2005 Act")? This choice exists as a result of the Government's response to the finding of the European Court of Human Rights ("the ECtHR") in *HL v United Kingdom* (2004) 40 E.H.R.R. 761.

### *HL v United Kingdom (the "Bournewood case")*
In *HL,* Mr L alleged that he had been detained at the Bournewood Hospital as an **6–002** informal patient in violation of art.5(1) of the European Convention on Human Rights ("the Convention") which is designed to ensure that no one should be arbitrarily deprived of his liberty. He also claimed that the procedures available to him for a review of the legality of his detention did not satisfy the requirements of art.5(4), which provides a person who has been deprived of his liberty with a right to a speedy independent legal review of the detention. The facts of the case are remarkable. From the age of 13, for a period of over 30 years, Mr L, who had a profound learning disability, was autistic and lacked the capacity to consent or dissent from being in hospital, was a patient at the Bournewood Hospital. He was eventually discharged into the community to live with carers, Mr and Mrs E. Under their care Mr L flourished for three years until an incident occurred that led to his readmission to hospital. While attending a day centre, Mr L became particularly agitated and he could not be calmed. Mr and Mrs E, who had been able to deal with such incidents successfully, could not be contacted. A doctor attended and administered a sedative to Mr L. On the advice of Mr L's social worker, he was taken to the Bournewood Hospital by which time the effect of the sedative was beginning to wear off and he was becoming increasingly agitated. Mr L was assessed by a psychiatrist as requiring inpatient treatment. On Mr L's admission, his consultant psychiatrist considered whether it was necessary to detain him under the provisions of the 1983 Act but decided that this was not necessary because he appeared to be fully compliant and had not resisted admission to the hospital. He was therefore admitted informally. Mr and Mrs E made it plain that they wanted to take Mr L back into their care. Mr L's consultant psychiatrist was not prepared to countenance this and he remained in the hospital. Proceedings were commenced in the name of Mr L against the Bournewood NHS Trust for judicial review of the trust's decision to detain him and for a writ of habeas corpus to release him from detention. It was claimed that Mr L's detention was unlawful on the ground that the 1983 Act, which had not been invoked, was the only basis for the hospital's right to detain him. The hospital claimed that Mr L was not being detained, but if he was, the detention was authorised under the

common law doctrine of necessity. Subsequent to the decision of the House of Lords ([1998] 3 All E.R. 289) to dismiss Mr L's claim, an application was made to the ECtHR.

The decision of the ECtHR focused on the finding of the House of Lords that the detention of a compliant mentally incapacitated patient could be justified under the doctrine of necessity. The court held that:

1. In order to determine whether a person has been deprived of his liberty for the purposes of art.5(1) of the Convention, the starting point must be the specific situation of the individual concerned and account must be taken of a whole range of factors arising in a particular case such as the type, duration, effects and manner of implementation of the measure in question. The distinction between a deprivation of, and a restriction upon, liberty is merely one of degree or intensity and not one of nature or substance (para.89).

2. The correspondence between HL's carers and his psychiatrist reflected both the carers' wish to have HL immediately released to their care and, equally, the clear intention of the health care professionals to exercise strict control over his assessment, treatment, contacts and, notably, movement and residence: HL would only be released from the hospital to the care of his carers as and when the professionals considered it appropriate. It followed that HL was being deprived of his liberty because "professionals treating and managing [HL] exercised complete and effective control over his movements" in that he "was under continuous supervision and control and was not free to leave [to return to his carers]" (para.91). The fact that HL might have been on a ward which was not "locked" or "lockable" was not determinative (para.92). With regard to HL's compliance to his admission, the court observed that:

   "the right to liberty is too important in a democratic society for a person to lose the benefit of Convention protection for the single reason that he may have given himself up to be taken into detention, especially when it is not disputed that that person is legally incapable of consenting to, or disagreeing with, the proposed action" (para.90).

3. The court found "striking the lack of any fixed procedural rules by which the admission and detention of compliant incapacitated patients is conducted" when contrasted with "the extensive network of safeguards applicable to psychiatric committals covered by the 1983 Act" (para.120). This absence of procedural safeguards in the doctrine of necessity failed to protect HL against arbitrary deprivations of his liberty. His detention therefore violated art.5(1).

4. There had also been a violation of art.5(4) as HL did not have the opportunity to have the lawfulness of his detention reviewed by a court as neither judicial review nor other judicial remedies cited by the Government satisfied the requirements of art.5(4) (para.141).

The finding that HL was being deprived of his liberty because he "was under continuous supervision and control and was not free to leave" is not helpful as general guidance as virtually all patients with either advanced dementia or profound learning disabilities would be subject to the continuous supervision and control of staff because their clinical needs would demand that level of care. It is also the case that no mentally incapacitated person would be free to leave a hospital or care home in the sense of being allowed to wander out of the institution into the community. In this context, not free to leave must mean either not being allowed to leave following purposeful attempts by P to leave or not free to leave following a request by relatives and/or carers that P be discharged.

### What constitutes a "deprivation of liberty"?

Restrictions on a person's movements and freedom to chose his residence which **6–003** do not constitute a deprivation of liberty and which are necessary "for the prevention of crime, for the protection of health or morals, or for the protection of the rights and freedom of others" are allowed for under art.2 of Protocol 4 of the Convention, which has not been ratified by the United Kingdom. According to Lord Hope "Art.2 of Protocol 4 helps to put the ambit of [Art.5] into its proper perspective" (*Austin v Commissioner of Police of the Metropolis* [2009] UKHL 5; [2009] 3 All E.R. 455, para.15).

A deprivation of liberty can occur in either an institutional or a domestic setting, although with the latter there must be a significant element of confinement (*Re A (child) and Re C (adult)* [2010] EWHC 978).

In *Secretary of State for the Home Department v JJ* [2007] UKHL 45; [2008] 1 All E.R. 613 at para.57, Baroness Hale said:

> "My Lords, what does it mean to be deprived of one's liberty? Not, we are all agreed, to be deprived of the freedom to live one's life as one pleases. It means to be deprived of one's physical liberty . . . And what does this mean? It must mean being forced or obliged to be at a particular place where one does not choose to be . . . But even that is not always enough because merely being required to live at a particular place or to keep within a particular geographical area does not, without more, amount to a deprivation of liberty. There must be a greater degree of control over one's physical ability than that. But how much?"

The answer to the question posed by Baroness Hale is not easy to discern from the, occasionally inconsistent, case law. Moreover, as Lord Bingham said in *JJ* at para.17, there is no "bright line" separating deprivations of liberty from mere restrictions on liberty.

*HL v United Kingdom* was applied in *JE v DE and Surrey County Council* [2006] EWHC 3459 (Fam); [2007] M.H.L.R. 39, where Munby J. held, at para.77, that there are three elements relevant to the question of whether in the case of an adult there has been a deprivation of liberty engaging the state's obligations under art.5(1):

1. An objective element of a person's confinement in a particular restricted space for a not negligible length of time.
2. A subjective element, namely that the person has not validly consented to the confinement in question. Where a person has capacity, consent to their confinement may be inferred from the fact that they do not object. No such conclusion may be drawn in the case of a patient lacking capacity to consent.
3. The deprivation of liberty must be imputable to the state, i.e. the state is responsible for the deprivation.

Where a relative wished to take over the care of a resident of a care home (the same approach would apply to a hospital patient) and the resident was indicating a willingness to be discharged to such care, his Lordship said, at para.115, that the crucial question is not so much whether (and, if so, to what extent) the person's freedom or liberty was or is curtailed within the institutional setting. The fundamental issue is whether the person is deprived of his liberty to leave the care home where he was placed not in the sense of leaving for the purpose of some approved trip or outing, but rather "leaving in the sense of removing himself permanently in order to live where and with whom he chooses". If the person is not free to leave in this sense, those treating and managing the person exercise complete and effective control over the person's care and movement and he is therefore being deprived of his liberty for the purposes of art.5(1).

This decision is illustrative of the general approach that the courts have taken to the identification of a deprivation of liberty, which is to emphasise the need to establish the confinement of the person concerned. In *Secretary of State for the Home Department v E* [2007] UKHL 47; [2008] 1 All E.R. 699 at para.11, Lord Bingham said:

> "The matters which particularly weighed with the judge were not irrelevant, but they could not of themselves effect a deprivation of liberty if the core element of confinement, to which other restrictions (important as they may be in some cases) are ancillary, is insufficiently stringent."

Maurice Kay L.J. made the following comment on Lord Bingham's remarks in *AP v Secretary of State for the Home Department* [2009] EWCA Civ 731 at para.29:

> "If I may be permitted to put it metaphorically: for the purposes of Art.5, the other restrictions (including the degree of social isolation) are the tail; it is the core element of confinement that is the dog."

Both the ECtHR and the High Court have sometimes found that onerous restrictions on a person's liberty do not constitute a deprivation of liberty. For example, in *Ciancimino v Italy* (1991) 70 D.R. 103 the applicant was obliged to live in a nominated commune which he was not permitted to leave, was obliged to report to the police daily at 11 am and was subject to a curfew from 8 pm to 7 am, but this did not amount to a deprivation of liberty (cited in *JJ*, above, para.18). And in *Re A (child) and Re C (adult)*, above, the fact that A and C, who lived at home, were locked in their bedrooms at night for 10 to 12 hours was found to be a mere restriction upon their liberty because such action constituted a proportionate response to the effects of the rare genetic disorder from which they suffered. However, it should be noted that in *R. (on the application of Gillan) v Metropolitan Police Commissioner* [2006] UKHL 12; [2006] 4 All E.R. 1041 at para.23, Lord Bingham said that the jurisprudence of the ECtHR on what constitutes a deprivation of liberty "is closely focused on the facts of particular cases, and this makes it perilous to transpose the outcome of one case to another where the facts are different". A similar comment can be made of cases decided in domestic courts.

**6–004**    In *JE and Surrey County Council* and *HL v United Kingdom,* the following principle established by the ECtHR in *Guzzardi v Italy* (1980) 3 E.H.R.R. 33 at para.93 was applied:

> "The difference between deprivation of and restriction upon liberty is . . . merely one of degree or intensity, and not one of nature or substance. Although the process of classification into one or other of these categories

sometimes proves to be no easy task in that in some borderline cases are a matter of pure opinion, the Court cannot avoid making the selection upon which the applicability of Article 5 depends"

This passage was cited by Collins J. in *R. (on the application of G) v Mental Health Review Tribunal* [2004] EWHC 2193 (Admin) at para.20, as authority for the proposition "that there will be borderline cases when a decision either way cannot be said to be wrong in law". His Lordship said that it is important to bear in mind that the purpose of any measure of restriction, while a relevant consideration, must not be given too much weight. This consideration was identified by Keene L.J. in *Secretary of State for the Home Department v Mental Health Review Tribunal and PH* [2002] EWCA Civ 1868; [2003] M.H.L.R. 202 at para.16. This case, which is noted under s.73(2) of the 1983 Act, identified the principles established by the ECtHR which are applicable to the interpretation of art.5(1). One of the principles identified, that if the restrictions are taken principally in the interests of the individual they might not amount to a deprivation of liberty, is taken from *HM v Switzerland* (2004) 38 E.H.R.R. 17, where the ECtHR held that that an elderly mentally disordered patient who was required by a government order to reside in a care home which allowed freedom of movement and encouraged contact with the outside world was not being deprived of her liberty. The court concluded that:

"in the circumstances of the present case the applicant's placement in the [care] home did not amount to a deprivation of liberty . . . but was a responsible measure taken by the competent authorities in the applicant's interests" (para.48).

Although Munby J. has said that the purpose principle must be treated with "appropriate degree of caution" because it receives "absolutely no support from the subsequent decisions of the court in *HL v United Kingdom* and *Storck v Germany*" (*JE and DE v Surrey County Council,* above, para.70), in *Austin v Metropolitan Police Commissioner* [2007] EWCA Civ 989; [2008] 1 All E.R. 564 para.98, a case where the police contained members of the public who where involved in a demonstration, the court noted "that, although the decision in *HM v Switzerland* was distinguished in *HL v United Kingdom*, the ECtHR did not disagree with the principle." When *Austin* reached the House of Lords, Lord Hope said that it "would seem in principle that the more intensive the measure and the longer it is kept in force the greater will be the need for it to be justified by reference to the purpose of the restriction if it is not to fall within the ambit of [art.5]". A more robust approach was taken by Lord Walker who said that if "confinement amounting to deprivation of liberty . . . is established, good intentions cannot make up for any deficiencies in justification for the confinement" (*Austin v Commissioner of Police of the Metropolis,* above, paras 28 and 44). In *Secretary of State for the Home Department v JJ,* above, para.58, a case concerning the requirements of a control order, Baroness Hale cited *PH* and said that it "appears that restrictions designed, at least in part, for the benefit of the person concerned are less likely to be considered a deprivation of liberty than are restrictions designed for the protection of society". Baroness Hale's statement has a particular significance in the very different context of the care of individuals in hospitals and care homes because it would be claimed by those caring for such individuals that the vast majority of restrictions that occur are "designed, at least in part, for the benefit of the person concerned" in that they are in that person's best interests. As a consideration of the purpose of a restriction introduces a significant degree of uncertainty into the already difficult process of identifying whether a deprivation of liberty is occurring in a hospital or a care home, it is suggested that Munby J.'s cautious approach to this issue be followed; also see Parker J's analysis in *Re MIG and MEG* [2010] EWHC 785 (Fam) at paras 163–166.

6–005    In *JJ*, it was common ground between the parties that the concept of "deprivation of liberty" has an autonomous meaning: "that is, it has a Council of Europe-wide meaning for the purposes of the Convention, whatever it might or might not be thought to mean in any member state" (per Lord Bingham at para.13). It follows that a deprivation of liberty should not be equated with the domestic tort of false imprisonment.

Notwithstanding the decision in *HL v United Kingdom*, the deprivation of a patient's liberty for a short period in order to respond to an emergency does not constitute a violation of art.5(1) (*X v United Kingdom* (1982) 4 E.H.R.R.188 para.41; also see *Winterwerp v Netherlands* (1979–80) 2 E.H.R.R. 387 para.19). There will also be no deprivation of liberty if the confinement in question is for a negligible length of time (*Storck v Germany* (2006) 43 E.H.R.R. 6 para.74).

In order to comply with art.5(1) in the absence of an emergency, the authorisation of the deprivation must be obtained before someone is detained (*City of Sunderland v PS and CA* [2007] EWHC 623 (Fam); [2007] M.H.L.R. 196 para.23). A subsequent review of detention under art.5(4) cannot retrospectively authorise an unlawful detention (*HL v United Kingdom* para.123).

### Some guidelines

6–006   Bearing in mind that there is no definitive legal test for establishing what will amount to a deprivation of a person's liberty and that the core element of a deprivation of liberty is confinement (*Secretary of State for the Home Department v E*, above), an analysis of European and domestic case law suggests that the following circumstances would constitute a deprivation of liberty:

1. Force, threats or medication being used to overcome the patient's resistance to being taken to the hospital or care home. However, a deprivation of liberty will not occur if the force or medication used constituted restraint which is authorised by s.6 of the 2005 Act. The conveyance of the patient to the hospital or care home is considered below.

2. Subterfuge being used to ensure the patient's co-operation in being taken to the hospital or care home, e.g. the patient being misled into believing that he or she will return home the next day.

3. The decision to admit the patient to the hospital or care home being opposed by relatives and/or carers who either live with or are closely involved in caring for the patient or a request by them for the patient to be discharged to their care being denied. Given the judgments in *HL v United Kingdom* and *JE v DE and Surrey County Council,* the presence of this factor alone would usually lead to a conclusion that the person is being subjected to a deprivation of liberty. However, in *LLBC v TG, JG and HR* [2007] EWHC 2640 (Fam); [2007] M.H.L.R. 203, McFarlane J. accepted a submission of the Official Solicitor that the fact that some family members

opposed the placement of TG in a care home was not sufficient to change the character of circumstances which would not otherwise amount to a deprivation of liberty. The factors given the most weight by the court in coming to this conclusion were: (i) the care home in question was an ordinary care home with ordinary restrictions on liberty; (ii) the family were entitled to visit TG on a largely unrestricted basis and were entitled to remove him for outings; (iii) TG was compliant, happy and objectively content with his situation; and (iv) there was no occasion where TG was objectively deprived of his liberty.

4. Force or a locked door being used to prevent the patient from leaving the hospital or care home in a situation where the patient is making purposeful attempts to leave and he or she cannot be persuaded to desist. This is the case even though the patient might have a deluded reason for wishing to leave. Although restraint authorised by s.6 can be used to prevent isolated attempts by the patient to leave if such action is required to prevent immediate harm to the patient, it would not provide authority for preventing persistent attempts by the patient to leave.

5. An assessment concluding that the patient would make a purposeful attempt to leave the hospital or care home if he or she had the physical capacity to do so.

6. Medication being used for the primary purpose of preventing the patient from making an attempt to leave the hospital or care home.

7. Restrictions being placed on the patient's freedom of movement within the hospital or care home which are designed to prevent the patient from making an attempt to leave.

8. Threats being used to dissuade the patient from making an attempt to leave the hospital or care home.

9. A decision by the hospital or care home to deny or severely restrict access to the patient by relatives, carers and/or people with whom the patient enjoys a significant relationship.

10. The patient's access to the community being denied or severely restricted in a situation where the patient would be capable of benefiting from such access.

It is suggested that the following restrictions on a patient's liberty would not, by themselves, constitute a deprivation of liberty:

1. Restraint which is authorised by s.6 being used: (i) on a non-compliant patient during the patient's conveyance to the hospital or care home; (ii) to feed, dress or provide medical treatment for the patient; (iii) to prevent the patient from coming to harm.

2. The patient being treated or cared for in a locked environment.

3. The design of door handles or the use of key pads making it difficult for a confused patient to leave the hospital or care home.

4. Staff bringing a patient who has wandered back to the hospital or care home, using restraint authorised by s.6 if necessary.

5. The patient's behaviour or care needs requiring restrictions being placed on his or her movements within the hospital or care home and/or contact with others.

6. The fact that the patient does not have the mental capacity to decide whether to remain in the hospital or care home or not.

7. Dissuading a confused patient leaving the hospital or care home, using benign force (i.e. force that is not being used to overcome significant resistance) if necessary.
8. Restraint authorised by s.6 being used to prevent a purposeful attempt by the patient to leave if such action is required to prevent immediate harm to the patient; see further, point 4 on the previous list.
9. A refusal to allow a physically frail patient, a patient with no sense of road safety or a patient who is otherwise vulnerable from leaving the hospital or care home without an escort.
10. A temporary refusal to let the patient leave the hospital or care home for health or safety reasons or because of the unavailability of an escort.
11. The short term use of the statutory or common law powers set out in Appendix A to restrain the patient from causing harm to others or to property.
12. Placing reasonable limitations on the visiting of the patient by relatives or carers.
13. Preventing contact with a person who has been assessed as presenting a risk of harm to the patient.

**6–007** Although none of these restrictions, taken alone, would constitute a deprivation of the patient's liberty, the cumulative effect of a number of restrictions could have such an effect *(Guzzardi v Italy,* above, para.95) if, taken together, they have the effect of confining the patient in the hospital or care home *(Secretary of State for the Home Department v E,* above).

Phil Fennell argues that:

> "if the person lacks capacity and the decision-maker is assuming complete control over treatment to the extent that they are making decisions about the administration of strong psychotropic medication or even ECT to a patient, then that is assuming complete control over treatment and would be a factor tipping the balance firmly towards there being a deprivation of liberty requiring the use of the Mental Health Act 1983 or at the very least use of the protective care provisions such as those proposed to fill the Bournewood Gap" ("The Mental Capacity Act 2005, the Mental Health Act, and the Common Law", Journal of Mental Health Law, November 2005, p.167).

As the provision of any medical treatment to an incapacitated patient involves a clinician assuming complete control over that patient's treatment, it is submitted that the provision of the treatments mentioned by Fennell would not, on their own, lead to a finding that there has been a deprivation of liberty. The case law of the ECtHR does not support the contention that a finding of a deprivation of liberty can be made solely on the basis that a particular treatment is being proposed for the patient: a "whole range of factors arising in a particular case" must be taken into account *(HL v United Kingdom* at para.89). The Mental Health Act Commission doubted "that there is anything inherent in the procedure for ECT treatment that amounts to a deprivation of liberty" (MHAC, Twelfth Biennial Report 2005–2007, para.6.86).

**The response of the Government to the judgment in *HL v United Kingdom***
In order to remedy the breaches of art.5 identified by the ECtHR in *HL v United* **6–008** *Kingdom*, the Government undertook to provide additional procedural safeguards for incapacitated people who were not subject to the 1983 Act, but whose care and treatment involved a deprivation of liberty. Accordingly, a consultative document ("'Bournewood' Consultation: The approach to be taken in response to the judgment of the European Court of Human Rights in the 'Bournewood' case" (March 2005)) was issued by the Government. The following options were identified:
1. A new form of "protective care" which would consist of a new system to govern admission/detention procedures, reviews of detention and appeals.
2. Extending the use of detention under the 1983 Act to the *Bournewood* group of patients.
3. Using existing arrangements for guardianship under the 1983 Act (modified as necessary).

A report of the outcome of the consultation was published in June 2006. At the same time the Government announced its decision to proceed with the protective care option, which had been favoured by the majority of respondents to the consultation, with a view to new deprivation of liberty safeguards being introduced into the Mental Capacity Act 2005. The Mental Health Bill (now the Mental Health Act 2007) was identified as a suitable vehicle through which to amend the 2005 Act for this purpose. The new safeguards are located in Sch.A1 to the 2005 Act.

**Deprivations of Liberty under the Mental Capacity Act 2005**
Section 4A of the 2005 Act prohibits the deprivation of the liberty of a person **6–009** under that Act other than in the following situations:
 (i) where, in an order made under s.16(2)(a), the Court of Protection has authorised the deprivation;
 (ii) where the deprivation is authorised for life-sustaining or other emergency treatment while a decision is awaited from the Court (s.4B); or
 (iii) where the deprivation is authorised by Sch.A1.

As an authorisation under Sch.A1 can only apply to the deprivation of a person's liberty in a hospital or a care home, an application must be made to the Court of Protection if the deprivation takes place elsewhere. A deprivation of liberty authorised under the 2005 Act does not entitle the institution to do anything other than detain the patient or resident for the purposes of the order or authorisation.

The authorisation procedures set out in Sch.A1 (and the associated Sch.1A) are extremely complex and caused the Joint Committee on Human Rights to "question whether they will be readily understood by proprietors of residential care homes, even with the benefit of professional advice" (*Legislative Scrutiny: Mental Health Bill,* HL Paper 40; HC 288, para.90). A detailed examination of the authorisation procedure can be found in Pt 2 of the author's *Mental Capacity Act Manual* (2010). There are two types of authorisation: standard and urgent. A "managing authority" must request a standard authorisation when it appears likely that at some time during the next 28 days someone will be accommodated in its hospital or care home in circumstances that amount to a deprivation of liberty within the meaning of art. 5. The request must be made to the "supervisory body". Whenever possible, authorisation should be obtained in advance of the deprivation occurring. Where this is not possible, and the managing authority believes it is necessary to deprive someone of their liberty in their best interests before the standard authorisation process can be completed, the managing authority must itself give an urgent authorisation and then apply for a standard authorisation.

### Conveyance to the hospital or care home

6–010 The authorisation procedure contained in Sch.A1 does not provide authority for depriving people of their liberty when they are being conveyed from their home, or another location, to the hospital or care home specified in the authorisation, although an authorisation can be given before the person arrives there so that it can take effect on arrival. In *GJ v Foundation Trust* [2009] EWHC 2972 (Fam) at para.75(c), Charles J. said that "the gap which Parliament deliberately left by not providing that authorisations . . . covered taking a person to hospital or care home can be filled by the [Court of Protection] . . .". This issue was taken up by the Joint Committee on Human Rights which recommended that a "take and convey" power be added to an authorisation. The Government responded as follows:

> "We will reflect in the Code of Practice the importance of considering the impact of any transportation as part of assessing best interests. In practice, many people who will become subject to the . . . deprivation of liberty safeguards will already be accommodated in hospitals or care homes at the time that a change in their care regime brings them within the scope of the safeguards, so the conveying issue will not arise.
>
> We do accept, however, that, in a very few cases, there may be exceptional circumstances, for example where it is necessary to do more than persuade or restrain the person for the purpose of the conveyance, or perhaps if the journey was exceptionally long, where transportation may amount to a deprivation of liberty and it may be necessary to seek an order of the Court of Protection where additional consideration of the particular circumstances of the case would be an extra protection for the individual (or consider use of the 1983 Act). We do not therefore consider that it is desirable to extend authorisations to cover these rare cases, because we do not think it would strengthen the protections for the person concerned" ("The Government's response to the report of the Joint Committee on Human Rights", Department of Health, April 13, 2007, paras 80, 81).

The Joint Committee was not convinced by this response and remained of the view that in order to be compatible with art.5 it was necessary for the legislation "to provide a procedure which precedes detention in all cases" (*Legislative Scrutiny: Seventh Progress Report*, HL Paper 112; HC 555, para.1.29). The issue here is not solely one of strengthening the "protections of the persons concerned"; those involved in transporting the person to the hospital or care home require legal justification for their action. If the act of transporting the person merely involves restricting a person's liberty, the authorisation for the restriction is to be found in ss.5 and 6 of the 2005 Act. If, however, exceptional circumstances exist which amount to a person being deprived of his liberty during the transportation in a non-emergency situation, such as restraint being required to prevent harm to others, ss.5 and 6 would not provide the necessary authority and an application for an order authorising the deprivation would have to be made to the Court of Protection. However, there would be no need to seek an order from the court if the period of transportation would be "for a negligible length of time" (*Storck v Germany,* above). If the person is being transported to a care home, guardianship would provide the necessary authorisation as s.18(7) of the 1983 Act provides professionals with a power to take and convey the person to a specified place of residence.

**Schedule 1A—persons ineligible to be deprived of liberty by the Mental Capacity Act**
The 2005 Act cannot be used to deprive P of his liberty if P is "ineligible": see **6–011** s.16A of the 2005 Act for the Court of Protection and Sch.A1 paras 12(e) and 17 for the authorisation procedure. P is ineligible if he falls within Cases A to E of Sch.1A. These Cases identify when the 1983 Act takes precedence over the 2005 Act.

In *GJ v Foundation Trust* [2009] EWHC 2972 (Fam); [2010] M.H.L.R. 13, para.65, Charles J. said that decision makers under the 2005 and 1983 Acts must recognise the primacy of the 1983 Act and "take all practicable steps to ensure that that primacy is recognised and given effect to". Among the reasons given by his Lordship, for reaching this conclusion was that it is "in line with the underlying purpose of the amendments to the MCA 2005, to fill a gap namely the '*Bournewood Gap*'. This shows that the purpose was not to provide alternative regimes but to leave the existing regime under the MHA 1983 in place with primacy and to fill a gap left by it and the common law (para.60)." This case is considered in the notes to Case E.

In the following notes, "P" is used to denote a person who would otherwise satisfy the authorisation eligibility criteria set out in Sch.A1, and references to paragraph numbers are references to the paragraphs in Sch.1A.

*Case A (Patients detained under the Mental Health Act 1983)*
P is ineligible if he is subject to the "hospital treatment regime" and is detained **6–012** under that regime in either an independent or NHS hospital by virtue of being subject to a "hospital treatment obligation", i.e. he is detained under ss.2, 4, 3, 35, 36, 37, 38, 44, 45A, 47, 48 or 51 of the 1983 Act or under "another England and Wales enactment which has the same effect as a hospital treatment obligation", such as the Criminal Procedure (Insaniity) Act 1964 (paras 2, 8). The consequence of this is that if P is detained under the 1983 Act he is ineligible for detention under the 2005 Act, although he could be treated for any physical disorder under that Act.

*Case B (Patients on Leave of Absence or Conditional Discharge)*
This Case applies if P is subject to the "hospital treatment regime" (i.e. he is sub- **6–013** ject to a "hospital treatment obligation": see above) but is not detained in hospital under that regime. This covers patients who have been granted leave of absence under s.17 of the 1983 Act or who have been granted a conditional discharge under either s.42 or s.73 of that Act. P will be ineligible if:
  (i) the proposed course of action under the 2005 Act is "not in accordance with a requirement" which the 1983 Act imposes, such as a requirement as to where P is, or is not, to reside (para.3). This means that P would be ineligible if, for example, there is a conflict between where P is required to reside under the conditions of a conditional discharge and where he would be required to reside under a standard authorisation; or

(ii) the proposed care and treatment to be administered under the 2005 Act "consists in whole or in part of medical treatment for mental disorder in a hospital" (para.4). This means that an authorisation cannot be used as an alternative to the procedures for a patient's recall to hospital under the 1983 Act. However, the patient would be eligible if he required treatment in hospital for a physical disorder.

It is difficult to imagine circumstances when it might be necessary to have an authorisation in a case where the patient is on s.17 leave in that s.17(3) provides for the patient to be kept in custody during a period of leave of absence.

*Case C (Patients on a Community Treatment Order)*

**6–014** P is ineligible if:

(i) he is subject to a "community treatment regime", i.e. a community treatment order under s.17A of the 1983 Act, or "an obligation under another England and Wales enactment which has the same effect as a community treatment order" (para.9); and

(ii) either of the situations set out in paras (i) or (ii) of Case B, above, apply.

*Case D (Patients subject to Guardianship)*

**6–015** If P is subject to a guardianship application under s.7 of the 1983 Act, a guardianship order under s.37 of that Act, or an obligation under another England and Wales enactment which has similar effect (para.10), he will be ineligible if:

(i) the proposed course of action under the 2005 Act is not in accordance with a requirement imposed by the guardian, including any requirement where P is to reside (para.3). This means that P would be ineligible if, for example, there is a conflict between where P is required to reside by the guardian and where he would be required to reside under a standard authorisation; or

(ii) the standard authorisation would authorise P to be a mental health patient (i.e. a person accommodated in a hospital for the purpose of being given medical treatment for mental disorder (para.16)), P objects (or would be likely to object if he was in a position to do so) to being a mental patient or to being given some or all of the mental health treatment, and no valid consent has been given by a donee of a lasting power of attorney or a court deputy to each matter to which P objects: see the notes on Case E. If such consent is forthcoming, P becomes eligible. The donee and the deputy will be required to act in P's best interests when making their decision (s.4 of the 2005 Act). In determining whether P would be likely to object, regard must be had to all the circumstances, including P's behaviour, his wishes and feelings and his views values and beliefs, although circumstances from the past only need to be considered insofar as it is appropriate to consider them (para.5).

*Case E (Patients who are "within the scope" of the 1983 Act but are not subject to it)*

An establishment which is registered as a care home, but is neither registered as an independent hospital nor part of the NHS, is not a hospital for the purposes of Sch.1A. A person being cared for in such a home is therefore not a "mental health patient" for the purposes of this Case (see paras.5(3) and 16) and is not ineligible (*W Primary Care Trust v TB* [2009] EWHC 1737 (Fam); [2010] 2 All E.R. 331).

P is "within the scope" of the 1983 Act if an application under s.2 or s.3 of that **6–016** Act "could be made in respect of him" and P could be detained in a hospital in pursuance of such an application, were one made (para.12(1)). In making this determination it is to be assumed that the necessary medical recommendations are in place (para.12(3),(4)) and that the treatment referred to in s.3(2)(c) of the 1983 Act cannot be provided under the 2005 Act (para.12(5)).

If P comes within the scope of the 1983 Act, he would be ineligible if the situation set out in para.(ii) of Case D, above, applies, i.e. he objects (or would be likely to object if he was in a position to do so) to being admitted to hospital or to being treated for his mental disorder there and no valid consent has been given by a donee or a deputy. If a donee or deputy consents, P will be eligible. In determining whether P would be likely to object, regard must be had to all the circumstances, including P's behaviour, his wishes and feelings and his views, values and beliefs, although circumstances from the past only need to be considered insofar as it is appropriate to consider them (para.5, and see below).

In *GJ v Foundation Trust*, above, Charles J. said that as the test in s.3(2)(c) relates to treatment rather than assessment, "an assessment can be said to be outside paragraph 5(3) of Sch.1A to the MCA [para.5 of Sch.1A is set out below]. But, as the focus of this aspect of the authorisation scheme concerning eligibility is (a) on P being detained in a hospital or in a care home for the purpose of being given care or treatment (see paras 1(2) and 2 of Sch.A1 to the MCA), and (b) arises when an application under s.2 or s.3 MHA could be made in respect of P, in my judgment the provisions looked at as a whole have the result that the assessor under the MCA should also proceed on the assumption that assessment and treatment under s. 2 MHA 1983 cannot be provided under the MCA" (para.44). With regard to the interpretation of the term "could" in para.12(1) (a) and (b), his Lordship said that the decision maker should approach the issue "by asking himself whether in his view the criteria set by, or the grounds in, s.2 or s.3 MHA 1983 are met (and if an application was made under them a hospital would detain P)" (para.80).

His analysis of the legislation led his Lordship to reach the following conclusions:

"In my judgment, the MHA 1983 has primacy in the sense that the relevant decision makers under both the MHA 1983 and the MCA should approach the questions they have to answer relating to the application of the MHA 1983 on the basis of an assumption that an alternative solution is not available under the MCA.

[I]n my view this does not mean that the two regimes are necessarily always mutually exclusive. But it does mean . . . that it is not lawful for the medical practitioners referred to in ss.2 and 3 of the MHA 1983, decision makers under the MCA, treating doctors, social workers or anyone else to proceed on the basis that they can pick and choose between the two statutory regimes as they think fit having regard to general considerations (e.g. the preservation or promotion of a therapeutic relationship with P) that they consider render one regime preferable to the other in the circumstances of the given case" (paras.58–59).

As stated above, the fact that P is found to come within the scope of the 1983 Act does not, by itself, mean that P is ineligible; he or she must also satisfy the test in para.5. The first and second conditions in para.5 "are linked in that the objection required by the second condition is to being a mental health patient or to some or all of the treatment for a mental disorder . . . and thus the treatment given to such a patient" (para.81).

In determining whether the first condition is satisfied i.e. the relevant instrument "authorises P to be a mental health patient", the decision maker should adopt a "but for" test if P suffers from both a mental and a physical disorder (para.87). This means that the decision maker should ask (i) what treatment would P receive for his physical disorder which is unconnected to his mental disorder, and (ii) what treatment would P receive for his mental disorder (including treatment for a physical disorder or illness that is connected to his mental disorder and/or which is likely to directly affect his mental disorder). The decision maker should then ask whether, "but for" the need for P to have treatment for his physical disorder, should P be detained in hospital. If the answer is in the negative, P does not satisfy the test. Put another way, the test is not satisfied if the need for treatment for his physical disorder is "the only effective reason" for P's detention (para.89).

His Lordship said that the "objection" condition has to be looked at "without taking any fine distinctions between the potential reasons for the objection to treatment of different types, or to simply being in a hospital. As is recognised and provided for by para.5(6), this is because it is often going to be the case that the relevant person (P) does not have the capacity to make a properly informed and balanced decision. So what matters, applying the approach set out in paragraph 5(6), is whether P will or does object to what is proposed" (para.83). This statement establishes a low threshold for establishing whether P objects in that any non compliant behaviour by P is likely to constitute evidence of an objection.

The Code of Practice on the Deprivation of Liberty Safeguards, para.4.46, states that if there is reason to think that P would object if able to do so, then P "should be assumed to be objecting". It is not the role of the assessor to consider whether an objection is reasonable.

Paragraph 5 of Sch.1A reads:

**"P objects to being a mental health patient etc**

5.—(1) This paragraph applies in cases D and E in the table in paragraph 2.

(2) P is ineligible if the following conditions are met.

(3) The first condition is that the relevant instrument authorises P to be a mental health patient.

(4) The second condition is that P objects—

(a) to being a mental health patient, or

(b) to being given some or all of the mental health treatment.

(5) The third condition is that a donee or deputy has not made a valid decision to consent to each matter to which P objects.

(6) In determining whether or not P objects to something, regard must be had to all the circumstances (so far as they are reasonably ascertainable), including the following—

(a) P's behaviour;

(b) P's wishes and feelings;

(c) P's views, beliefs and values.

(7) But regard is to be had to circumstances from the past only so far as it is still appropriate to have regard to them."

## The 1983 Act or the 2005 Act?
*Deprivations of liberty in hospitals*
Schedule 1A sets out the circumstances that prevent a person who is being **6–017** deprived of his liberty from being the subject of a standard authorisation under the 2005 Act. If Sch.1A applies, the 1983 Act must be used. Given the ruling in *GJ v Foundation Trust*, above, that the 1983 Act should have primacy, the authorisation procedure should only be invoked for:
  (i)   compliant patients (i.e. patients who do not satisfy the objection test in para.5(4) of Sch.1A),
  (ii)  patients who require detention to enable their physical disorder to be treated (i.e. patients who are not mental health patients for the purposes of para.5(3) of Sch.1A), and
  (iii) patients who come within the scope of Case E but either (a) are patients with a learning disability who require detention under s.3 but whose disability is not "associated with abnormally aggressive or seriously irresponsible behaviour" (see s.1(2A),(2B),(4) of the 1983 Act) or (b) are being treated for their mental disorder in a hospital which does not accept patients detained under the 1983 Act.
Also see the guidance given in the *Code of Practice* at paras 4.16 and 4.18.


*Deprivations of liberty in care homes*
Paragraph 13.16 of the Code of Practice on the 2005 Act states that guardianship **6–018** cannot be used to deprive a person of their liberty. This is a commonly held opinion, but is it correct? Several legal commentators think that it is not: see Phil Fennell, below, and Michael Gunn, "Hospital Treatment for Incapacitated Patients", Med.Law Rev. 2009 17: 274–281. The 1983 Act provides the guardian of a mentally incapacitated person with the following powers:
  • a power to take the person to the place specified by the guardian, using force if necessary (ss.18(3), 137).
  • a power to require the person to reside at the specified place (s.8(1)(a)).
  • a power to return the person to the specified place if he leaves without authority, using force if necessary (ss.18(3), 137).
  • a power to take the person to a place where he will receive medical treatment under the authority of the 2005 Act (s.8(1)(b)).
Put bluntly, a person under guardianship can be forced to leave his home to go to a place where he does not want to go to, can be required to stay at that place, and can be returned to that place if he leaves without being given permission to do so. Given the interpretation that the ECtHR and the High Court have given to the meaning of a deprivation of liberty, how can it possibly be argued that a person

who is subject to the operation of such powers is not being deprived of his liberty? Such a person is clearly subject to the continuous control of the guardian and is not free to leave the specified place of residence (*HL v United Kingdom*, above, para.91). If the use of guardianship can have the effect of depriving a person of his liberty, is the deprivation authorised by the guardianship? The following points that suggest that it is:

1. As Phil Fennell has said, there "is nothing in the MHA 1983 to say that guardianship cannot authorise deprivation of liberty" (*Mental Health: the new law* (2007) para.6.104).
2. If the legitimate use of the guardianship provisions can have the effect of depriving a person of his liberty, it would be remarkable if the Act did not authorise what it allows for.

Does guardianship comply with the requirements of art.5? Guardianship is clearly a "procedure prescribed by law" for the purposes of art.5(1), and the House of Lords held in *R. (on the application of MH) v Secretary of State for Health* [2005] UKHL 60; [2005] 4 All E.R. 1311 that art.5(4), which provides that a person who has been deprived of his liberty must be entitled to take proceedings to challenge the lawfulness of the detention, is not breached by virtue of the fact that the person concerned lacks the mental capacity to institute such proceedings. It is also the case that the procedure for making a guardianship application under s.7 of the 1983 Act meets the substantive and procedural requirements for the lawful detention of persons of unsound mind which were established by the ECtHR in *Winterwerp v Netherlands*, above.

The Government could be faced with a compatibility issue under the Convention if a person who has been deprived of his liberty by virtue of the operation of the guardianship provisions makes an application to the tribunal. Subsequent to the decision of the Court of Appeal in *R. (on the application of H) v Mental Health Review Tribunal, North and East London Region* [2001] EWCA Civ 415, which declared that ss.72(1) and 73(1) of the 1983 Act were incompatible with arts 5(1) and 5(4) because they placed the burden upon the patient to prove that the criteria justifying detention no longer exist, Parliament passed the Mental Health Act 1983 (Remedial) Order 2001 (SI 2001/3712) which placed the burden of proof on the detaining authority. As this Order did not reverse the burden of proof in s.72(4), which deals with applications made by guardianship patients, the Government might have to make a further remedial order to ensure compatibility with art.5. The fact that the guardianship regime may not be fully compatible with the Convention does not prevent it being used if practitioners consider it to be the appropriate option.

**6–019**　　If guardianship, together with a requirement that the person reside at a particular place, can authorise the deprivation of that person's liberty, is it necessary for the deprivation also to be authorised by the procedure set out in Sch.A1? The Government's view is that both Acts would have to be used (Code of Practice on the 1983 Act, para.26.30). A care home is required by para.24 of Sch.A1 to request a standard authorisation if P is, or likely to be, a "detained resident in the care home". It follows that although guardianship can provide authority for authorising the deprivation of P's liberty during conveyance to the care home, and if P is required to be returned to the care home after having absconded, an authorisation under Sch.A1 will also be required if P is subject to a deprivation of liberty within the care home. Although in *DCC v KH*, Case No. 11729380, September 11, the Court of Protection held that the existence of a standard authorisation provided an implied authority to use restraint on P, amounting if necessary to a deprivation of liberty, if P refused to return to the care home where the deprivation of liberty was authorised, professionals might prefer to rely on the explicit power contained in s.18 of the 1983 Act.

Compared with guardianship, the authorisation procedure is Byzantine in its complexity, but this factor alone would not provide a "cogent reason" for departing from the guidance in the Code of Practice (*R. (on the application of Munjaz) v Mersey Care National Health Service Trust* [2005] UKHL 58; [2006] 4 All E.R. 736). The fact that there is a respectable argument in favour of the contention that the statement in para.13.16 of the Code of Practice that guardianship cannot be used to deprive a person of his liberty does not represent the true legal position provides such a reason. It is also the case that guardianship offers the following protections to P which are not present in the authorisation procedure:

- Unlike the authorisation procedure, guardianship provides explicit legal authority to deprive a person of his liberty during conveyance from that person's home to the specified place of residence (s.18(7)) and for the person to be returned to the specified place of residence in the event of that person absconding (s.18(3)).
- The responsible local social services authority must arrange for a person under guardianship to be visited at intervals of not more than three months, and at least one such visit in any year shall be by an approved clinician or a "section 12 doctor": see reg.23 of the English Regulations and reg.10 of the Welsh Regulations.
- The 1983 Act provides a patient's nearest relative with significant powers with respect to guardianship that are intended to protect the interests of the patient, including the power to discharge the patient from guardianship.

# APPENDIX A

## FURTHER POWERS TO RESTRAIN AND/OR DETAIN MENTALLY DISORDERED PATIENTS

Where a patient has been detained under the Mental Health Act 1983, there is an implied **A–001** power for staff to exercise a degree of control over the activities of the patient: see the note on "act purporting to be done in pursuance of this Act" in s.139(1). Both statute and the common law provide further powers that can be used to restrain and/or detain patients. They are:

1. In *R. (on the application of Munjaz) v Mersey Care NHS Trust* [[2003 EWCA Civ 1036; [2003] M.H.L.R. 362 at para.46 Hale L.J. said:

   "There is a general [common law] power to take such steps as are reasonably necessary and proportionate to protect others from the immediate risk of significant harm. This applies whether or not the patient lacks the capacity to make decisions for himself.".

2. If the patient is mentally incapacitated, s.6 of the Mental Capacity Act 2005 enables the patient to be restrained when: (1) the person using the restraint reasonably believes that its use is necessary to prevent harm to the patient; and (2) its use is proportionate both to the likelihood and seriousness of the harm and is in the patient's best interests; see further, the author's *Mental Capacity Act Manual* (2008), pp.41–44.

3. Under s.3(1) of the Criminal Law Act 1967 "a person may use such force as is reasonable in the circumstances in the prevention of crime, or in effecting or assisting the lawful arrest of offenders or suspected offenders or persons unlawfully at large". This provision, which could apply to both informal and detained patients, enables a member of staff to use reasonable force to either restrain the patient or to place him or her in seclusion in self-defence or in the defence of others or to protect property. It does not apply where the patient is insane within the meaning of the M'Naghten rules because such a person is deemed not capable of committing a crime. The test of insanity established by the House of Lords in the *M'Naghten* case [1843–60] All E.R. 229, is that:

   "it must be clearly proved that, at the time of the committing of the act, the party accused was labouring under such a defect of reason, from disease of the mind, as not to know the nature and quality of the act he was doing was wrong, or, if he did know it, that he did not know he was doing what was wrong".

Caselaw has established that "disease of the mind": (i) covers diseases of the body affecting the operation of the mind (*R. v Kemp* [1957] 1 Q.B. 399); and (ii) includes patients who suffer from epilepsy (*R. v Sullivan* [1983] 2 All E.R. 673) and diabetic patients who suffer from hyper-glycaemia because of a failure to take insulin (*R. v Hennessy* [1989] 2 All E.R. 9). "Defect of reason" does not cover patients who retain the power of reasoning but who in moments of confusion or absentmindedness fail to use their powers to the full (*R. v Clarke* [1972] 1 All E.R. 219) or who know that their actions are unlawful (*R. v Windle* [1952] 2 Q.B. 826).

An insane person may be may be restrained and detained under the common law if he or she is a danger to him or herself or others: see *Black v Forsey*, below.

4. The common law power to prevent a breach of the peace was summarised by Lord Bingham in *R. (on the application of the Laporte) v Chief Constable of Gloucestershire Constabulary* [2006] UKHL 55; [2007] 2 All E.R. 529 at para.29:

> "Every constable, and also every citizen, enjoys the power and is subject to the duty to seek to prevent, by arrest or other action short of arrest, any breach of the peace occuring in his presence, or any breach of the peace which (having occurred) is likely to be renewed, or any breach of the peace which is about to occur."

A breach, which can take place in public or on private property, involves "actual harm done either to a person or to a person's property in his presence or some other form of violent disorder or disturbance and itself necessarily involves a criminal offence" (ibid., per Lord Brown at para.111). Harm to property will constitute a breach only if done or threatened in the owner's presence because the natural consequence of such harm is likely to be a violent retaliation (*Percy v Director of Public Prosecutions* [1995] 3 All E.R. 124 DC). The power to prevent a breach of the peace would enable a nurse physically to restrain a patient whose words or behaviour are such that imminent violence is expected on a hospital ward. Detention under this power can only be justified for a short period. Prolonged detention must be authorised either by the Mental Health Act or by arresting the person concerned (see below) and bringing him or her before a magistrate.

**A–002**

If a person is arrested for a breach of the peace, that person should be informed of the reasons for the arrest and he or she should be taken before a magistrate or to a police station as soon as reasonably practicable (*John Lewis & Co Ltd v Tims* [1952] 1 All E.R. 1203). With regard to the use of this power, the Court of Appeal has held that: (i) there has to be a sufficiently real and present threat to the peace to justify the extreme step of depriving a citizen of his liberty when that citizen is not at that time acting unlawfully (*Foulkes v Chief Constable of Merseyside Police* [1998] 3 All E.R. 705); (ii) a breach can occur on private premises even if the only persons likely to be affected by the breach are inside the premises and no member of the public outside the premises is involved (*McConnell v Chief Constable of the Greater Manchester Police* [1990] 1 All E.R. 423); and (iii) where a person has been arrested for causing a breach of the peace, he or she can be detained to prevent a further breach only if there is a real (rather than fanciful) apprehension that, if released, he or she would commit or renew the breach within a short time (*Chief Constable of Cleveland Police v McGrogan* [2002] EWCA Civ 86). The European Court of Human Rights has held that the power to arrest a person for a breach of the peace does not violate art.5(1) of the European Convention of Human Rights (*Steel v United Kingdom* (1999) 28 E.H.R.R. 603).The fact that breach of the peace is treated as an offence for the purposes of art.5 does not mean that it is an "offence" within the meaning of the Police and Criminal Evidence Act 1984. The provisions of that Act do not apply to an arrest for a breach of the peace (*Williamson v Chief Constable of the West Midlands Police* [2003] EWCA Civ 337; [2004] 1 W.L.R. 14).

5. In *Black v Forsey*, 1987 S.L.T. 681, a case under the Mental Health (Scotland) Act 1984, the House of Lords confirmed that the common law confers upon a private individual power lawfully to detain, in a situation of necessity, a person of unsound mind who is a danger to him or herself or others. A person exercising the power must be able to justify his or her action, if challenged, by proving the mental disorder of the detainee and the necessity of detention. In the opinion of Lord Griffiths, the power is:

"confined to imposing temporary restraint on a lunatic who has run amok and is a manifest danger either to himself or to others—a state of affairs as obvious to a layman as to a doctor. Such a common law power is confined to the short period of confinement necessary before the lunatic can be handed over to a proper authority".

The combination of powers set out above provide sufficient authority for a mental health **A–003** professional or members of the public to act swiftly to prevent a mentally disordered person from causing harm to himself, to another person or to property as long as the force used is proportionate to the harm threatened. It must be emphasised that these powers only allow for an informal patient to be detained for a limited period and will fall away when the crisis has subsided; they cannot be used as an alternative to the procedures set out in the 1983 Act.

Apart from the powers noted above, the extent to which common law powers enable informal patients to be subject to the control of staff is unclear. In *Pountney v Griffiths* [1976] A.C. 314, the House of Lords noted that it had been conceded by counsel for a Broadmoor Hospital patient that hospital staff have "powers of control over all mentally disordered patients, whether admitted voluntarily or compulsorily, though the nature and duration of control varies with the category to which the patient belongs". The Report of the Committee of Inquiry into Complaints about Ashworth Hospital (Cm. 2028–1) considered, at p.196, that this statement "would be likely to receive the endorsement of the courts today ... see *R. v Deputy Governor of Parkhurst Prison and others Ex p. Hague* [1992] A.C. 58". The powers to control informal patients are clearly far less extensive that those that apply to detained patients. If a mentally capable informal patient is unable to accept the control and discipline that is considered by staff to be in his or her best interests and/or conducive to the good administration of the hospital, he or she should either be asked to leave or consideration should be given to using the powers of detention under the 1983 Act.

## VISITS BY CHILDREN TO ASHWORTH, BROADMOOR AND RAMPTON HOSPITALS DIRECTIONS 1999

[As amended by the Visits by Children to Ashworth, Broadmoor and Rampton Hospitals (Amendment) Directions 2000, 2001 and 2002]

GENERAL NOTE

Guidance on these Directions is attached to Health Service Circular 199/160. An amend- **B–001** ment to the guidance is contained in Health Service Circular 2000/027.

Local Authority Circular (99) 23 contains guidance on the steps to be undertaken by local authorities in receipt of a request by a high security hospital for advice on whether it is in the best interests of a child to visit a named patient. Amendments to this circular are made by Local Authority Circular (2000) 18.

These Directions were found to be lawful and not in breach of the European Convention on Human Rights in *R. (on the application of L) v Secretary of State for Health* [2001] 1 F.L.R. 406 where Scott Baker J. said:

"If there are special circumstances in which the patient has good reason for being visited by a child who is not within the permitted category relationship the remedy is to apply to the court for an order under the Children Act 1989."

The Secretary of State for Health, in exercise of the powers conferred upon him by section 17 of the National Health Service Act 1977 and all other powers enabling him in that behalf, hereby gives the following Directions:–

### Citation, commencement and interpretation

1.—(1) These Directions may be cited as the Visits by Children to Ashworth, Broadmoor **B–002** and Rampton Hospitals Directions and shall come into force on 1 September 1999.

(2) In these Directions–

"Chief Executive" means the chief executive of a hospital authority [or a person nominated by the chief executive to perform his functions under these Directions on his behalf.]

"child" means a person under the age of eighteen;

"clinical team" means the multi-disciplinary team of members of staff involved with a patient's treatment including the responsible medical officer in charge of the patient's treatment;

"Hospital" means Ashworth Hospital, Broadmoor Hospital or Rampton Hospital as the case may be;

["hospital authority" means, as the case may be, the National Health Service trust established by the Mersey Care National Health Service Trust (Establishment) Order, the National Health Service trust established by the Nottinghamshire Healthcare National Health Service Trust (Establishment) Order or the National Health Service trust established by the West London Mental Health National Health Service Trust (Establishment) Order;]

"nominated officer" means the officer nominated pursuant to paragraph 3(1)(a) of these Directions;

"parental responsibility" has the same meaning as in the Children Act 1989;

"relevant local social services authority" means the local social services authority in whose area the child resides;

"Schedule 1 offence" means an offence listed in Schedule 1 to the Sex Offenders Act 1997;

"the 17th September Directions" means the Directions about child visits to special hospitals given to the hospital authorities by letter dated 17th September 1998;

[and]

"ward area" includes the day rooms, patient bedrooms and any other rooms or areas including garden areas in the residential part of hospital premises to which patients have access as a matter of course.

(3) In these Directions, a reference to a numbered paragraph is a reference to the paragraph bearing that number in thee Directions and a reference in a paragraph to a numbered sub-paragraph is a reference to the sub-paragraph bearing that number in that paragraph.

### Visits

**B–003**
2.—(1) A hospital authority shall only permit a patient in a [hospital] to receive a visit from a child in accordance with these Directions.

(2) A hospital authority shall not permit a patient to receive a visit from a child unless–

(a) the authority has approved the child's visit in accordance with these Directions, and

(b) in the case of a patient who has a conviction for murder or manslaughter or a Schedule 1 offence or who has been found unfit to be tried, or not guilty by reason of insanity in respect of a charge of murder or manslaughter or a Schedule 1 offence, the patient–

   (i) is the parent or relative of that child; or
   (ii) has parental responsibility for that child; or
   (iii) was cohabiting with the parent of that child immediately prior to their detention under the Mental Health Act 1983 and the child was treated as a member of their household.

(3) In sub-paragraph (2) " parent" means the mother or father, the adoptive mother or father or the stepmother or stepfather of the child, and "relative" means a grandparent, brother, sister, uncle or aunt or cousin related to that child by blood (including half-blood) or marriage.

(4) Sub-paragraph (2) does not apply where an order made under the Children Act 1989 specifies that the child may visit the patient in the [hospital].

### Procedure for deciding on requests for visits

**B–004**
3.—(1) A hospital authority must–

(a) [nominate a senior Hospital manager who is a hospital authority officer, or a senior local social services authority officer who is engaged to provide services at the Hospital, to take responsibility] for overseeing the process of dealing with any request for permission for a child to visit a patient and for deciding whether to approve the visit; and

(b) ensure that the nominated officer discharges his responsibilities in accordance with these Directions.

(2) Any request for permission for a child to visit a patient in a [hospital] must be made in writing by the patient and must be forwarded to a nominated officer.

(3) Save in a case to which sub-paragraph (11) or (12) or (14) applies, the procedure set out in sub-paragraphs (4) to (10) shall apply.

(4) The nominated officer must arrange for the patient's clinical team to carry out an assessment as to whether, in their view, it would be appropriate for the visit to take place having regard to the patient's offending history (if any), their clinical history and present mental state and, in the event that a visit is recommended, any particular arrangements which would need to be made for a visit by that child to take place safely.

(5) Where following the assessment referred to in sub-paragraph (4)–

(a)  the nominated officer is satisfied that it would not be appropriate for the child to visit the patient, he must refuse the request for a visit, and

(b)  in any other case, the nominated officer must seek the advice of the relevant local social services authority as to whether it is in the best interests of the child to visit the patient and must send with that request for advice a copy of the assessment referred to in sub-paragraph (4).

(6) Subject to paragraph (7), on receipt of the advice from the relevant local social services authority, the nominated officer must decide whether to approve the visit having regard to that advice, the assessment referred to in sub-paragraph (4) and any other relevant information he has.

(7) The nominated officer may not approve a visit in any case where the advice from the relevant local social services authority is that it is not or may not be in the best interests of the child to visit the patient.

(8) In a case where the relevant local social services authority is unable to provide the advice mentioned in sub-paragraph (5)(b), the nominated officer–

(a)  must undertake such enquiries as he considers reasonable (including consultation with the child, if appropriate, and any person with parental responsibility, or caring, for the child) to enable him to assess, so far as possible, whether it is in the best interests of the child to visit the patient, and

(b)  must decide whether to approve the visit having regard to all available information including the assessment referred to in sub-paragraph (4).

(9) If no decision has been reached within six weeks of the date on which a request for a visit is received from a patient the nominated officer must inform the patient in writing of the reasons for the delay.

(10) The nominated officer must notify–

(a)  the patient,

(b)  the parent of the child and any other person with parental responsibility for the child or caring for child,

(c)  the child if he is of sufficient age and understanding, and

(d)  any relevant local social services authority,

of his decision and the reasons for that decision in writing.

(11) Subject to sub-paragraph (14), where the patient is a person described in paragraph 2(2)(b) and the child is not within the permitted categories of relationship set out in that paragraph, sub-paragraphs (4) to (8) shall not apply and the nominated officer must refuse the request for a visit and notify the patient accordingly.

(12) Subject to sub-paragraphs (13) and (14), where the person with parental responsibility for the child, or in the case of a child subject to a care order the designated local authority in whose care the child is placed under section 31(1)(a) of the Children Act 1989, has not agreed the child may visit the patient, sub-paragraphs (4) to (8) shall not apply and the nominated officer must refuse the request for the visit and notify the patient accordingly.

(13) Save in the case of a child subject to a care order, where there is more than one person with parental responsibility for the child, it is the person with parental responsibility with whom the child is living who must agree to the visit.

(14) Subject to paragraph 4(3), in any case where an order made under the Children Act 1989 specifies that the child may visit the patient in the [hospital] the nominated officer must allow the visit to take place.

**B–005**  4.—(1) Subject to sub-paragraph (3), any approval for the child to visit the patient shall be valid for a period of 12 months from the date on which it is given and may only be withdrawn in that period if the nominated officer is satisfied that there has been a relevant change of circumstances.

(2) If, after the period of 12 months referred to in sub-paragraph (1) has elapsed, the patient wishes to continue to have visits from the child, the nominated officer must review the permission in accordance with paragraph 3(3) to (8) and must notify the persons mentioned in paragraph 3(1) of his decision and the reasons for that decision in writing.

(3) Notwithstanding sub-paragraph (1), the nominated officer may at any time refuse to allow a visit to take place if there are concerns about the patient's mental state at the time of the proposed visit [or for any other reason he is satisfied that the visit should not take place on that occasion.]

**B–006**  5. A hospital authority must set up a procedure to enable a patient to make representations against any decision of the nominated officer not to approve a visit other than a refusal on the grounds set out in paragraph 3(11) or (12).

### Visits in exceptional circumstances
**B–007**  6.—(1) In exceptional circumstances and subject to any guidance given by the Secretary of State, the Chief Executive may give his written authority for a patient to receive a visit from a child pending a full assessment in accordance with paragraph 3.

(2) Sub-paragraph (1) shall not apply where the patient is a person described in paragraph 2(2)(b) and the child is not within the permitted categories of relationship set out in that paragraph.

### Arrangements to be put in place for visits
**B–008**  7.—(1) A hospital authority must ensure that–

(a)  during a visit the child has direct contact only with the patient for whom permission has been given for that child to visit,

[(b)  subject to sub-paragraphs (2) to (4), the child is accompanied by–

  (i)  a person with parental responsibility for him and with whom he is living, or a parent or relative of the child nominated by that person, or
  (ii)  such other person who has day to day care for him, or
  (iii)  where the child is subject to a care order, a person nominated by the designated local authority in whose care the child is placed under section 31 of the Children Act 1989, or
  (iv)  where the child is provided with accommodation pursuant to section 20 of the Children Act 1989, a person who has parental responsibility for him, or, with

the consent of the local authority which is accommodating the child, such other person (including a parent or relative of the child) as he may nominate.]

(c) a visit takes place in an appropriate setting and not in the ward area, and

(d) that there are sufficient staff of an appropriate grade and with requisite knowledge and understanding present to supervise a child's visit at all times.

(2) Sub-paragraph 1(b) shall not apply in the case of a child aged 16 or 17 where the nominated officer, having regard to the information he has received under paragraph 3, is satisfied that an unaccompanied visit is unlikely to prejudice the child's welfare.

[(3) The Chief Executive may, in exceptional circumstances, allow a visit to take place where the child is accompanied by a person other than as specified in paragraph 7(1)(b)(i), (ii) or (iv) where he considers that this is in the child's best interest in the particular circumstances of the case.

(4) In this paragraph "parent" and "relative" have the same meaning as in paragraph 2(3).]

**Annual report to the hospital authority**
8. The Chief Executive must submit an annual report to the hospital authority at the end **B–009** of each financial year providing details of–

(a) the number of patients visited by children in that year;

(b) any special arrangements put in place to ensure the safety of those children whilst visiting Patients, together with the Chief Executive's assessment of the appropriateness of such arrangements; and

(c) the Chief Executive's assessment of the continuing adequacy of the arrangements put in place by the hospital authority to ensure the safety of children whilst visiting patients.

**Transitional provisions**
9.—(1) Subject to sub-paragraph (5), where, in accordance with the 17th September **B–010** Directions, permission has been given for a child to visit a patient, the nominated officer must, within 6 months so far as is reasonably practicable, ensure that he reviews that permission in accordance with paragraphs 3(3) to (8) and must notify the person mentioned in paragraph 3(10) of his decision and the reasons for that decision in writing.

(2) Paragraph 5 shall apply in relation to any decision made under sub-paragraph (1).

(3) Subject to sub-paragraphs (4) and (6), where, in accordance with the 17th September Directions, permission has been given for a child to visit a patient, that child may continue to visit that patient pending the review under sub-paragraph (1) and the consideration of any representations, if any, made under paragraph 5.

(4) Subject to sub-paragraph (5), where the patient is a person described in paragraph 2(2)(b) and the child is not within the permitted categories of relationship set out in that paragraph, sub-paragraph (1) shall not apply and the nominated officer must withdraw permission for the child to visit that patient immediately.

(5) Subject to sub-paragraph (6), sub-paragraphs (1) and (4) shall not apply in any case where an order made under the Children Act 1989 specifies that the child may visit the patient in the [hospital] and in that event, the nominated officer must allow the visit to take place.

(6) Notwithstanding sub-paragraphs (3) and (5), the nominated officer may at any time refuse to allow a visit to take place if there are concerns about the patient's mental state at the time of the proposed visit.

**Revocations**

**B–011**   10. The 17th September Directions are hereby revoked.

# APPENDIX C

## THE SAFETY AND SECURITY IN ASHWORTH, BROADMOOR AND RAMPTON HOSPITALS DIRECTIONS 2000

[As amended by the Ashworth, Broadmoor and Rampton Hospitals Amendment Directions 2001, 2002, 2002 (No. 2), 2003 and 2009]

GENERAL NOTE

The Department of Health has published detailed Guidance Notes to supplement these **C–001** Directions.

In *Buck v Nottinghamshire Healthcare NHS Trust* [2006] EWCA Civ 1576; [2006] M.H.L.R. 351, the Court of Appeal held that the existence of these Directions and the failure to implement them could inform the court as to the content of the duty of care owned by Rampton Hospital to its nursing staff.

## Arrangement of Directions

36 Security audits

37 Revocation.

The Secretary of State for Health, in exercise of the powers conferred upon him by sections 16D, 17 and 126(4) of the National Health Service Act 1977, section 4(5) of the Regulation of Investigatory Powers Act 2000 and all other powers enabling him in that behalf, hereby gives the following Directions:–

## Citation and commencement

**C–003**  1.—(1) These Directions may be cited as the Safety and Security in Ashworth, Broadmoor and Rampton Hospitals Directions 2000.

(2) The Directions shall come into force on 30 November 2000 except for paragraph 29 which shall come into force at Broadmoor and Rampton Hospitals on 1 March 2001 and at Ashworth Hospital on 30 November 2000.

## Application

**C–004**  [2.—(1) These Directions are given to Mersey Care Health Service Trust established by Order in the year 2001, and to the Nottinghamshire Healthcare National Health Service Trust and the West London Mental Health Service Trust both established by Orders in the year 2000.

(2) [. . .]

## Interpretation

**C–005**  3.—(1) In these Directions–

"the 1983 Act" means the Mental Health Act 1983,

["the 2008 Regulations" means the Mental Health (Hospital, Guardianship and Treatment) (England) Regulations 2008],

"authorised member of staff" means a member of staff whom the hospital authority has authorised to discharge functions on its behalf under paragraphs 22 to 24 or 29 and different persons may be authorised to discharge different functions,

"clinical team" means the multi-disciplinary team of members of staff involved with a patient's treatment, including the patient's RMO,

"chief executive" means the chief executive of a hospital authority [or a person nominated by the chief executive to perform his functions under these Directions on his behalf],

"contractor" means a person other than a member of staff or of the emergency services who provides services to a Hospital on its premises or makes deliveries to those premises,

"ground access" means the permission granted to a patient by the ground access committee to move around the areas specified in that permission with the Hospital premises,

"ground access committee" has the meaning given in paragraph 32,

"Hospital" means Ashworth Hospital, Broadmoor Hospital or Rampton Hospital, as the case may be including all the premises forming part of the Hospital,

["hospital authority"] means as the case may be, the National Health Service trust established by the Mersey Care National Health Service Trust (Establishment) Order, the National Health Service trust established by the Nottinghamshire Healthcare National Health Service Trust (Establishment) Order or the National Health Service trust established by the West London Mental Health National Service Trust (Establishment) Order]

"Hospital keys" means keys giving access to the secure area of a Hospital,

"leave of absence" means the leave of absence which may be granted to a patient by an RMO under section 17 of the 1983 Act and includes, where relevant, any leave of absence which may be granted to a patient to whom any provision of Part III of that Act applies,

"medical director" means the medical director of a hospital authority and includes that person's deputy,

"member of staff" means–

    a) any person employed by a hospital authority in connection with the provision of high security psychiatric services at a Hospital and any person whose services are supplied by a third party to a hospital authority to assist in providing such services, and

    b) the chairman or any member or board director of a hospital authority with functions in respect of Hospital,

"patient", means a patient who is detained at a Hospital,

"patient area" means any part of a Hospital in the secure area to which a patient may have access as a matter of course,

"postal packet" has the meaning given in the 1983 Act, section 134(9),

"risk assessment has the meaning given in paragraph 30,

"rub-down search" means a personal search of a patient and any contents of the patient's pockets and does not include a strip search or an intimate body search,

"RMO" means the responsible medical officer for a patient as defined in section 34 or section 55 of the 1983 Act, as the case may be,

"secure area" means the part of a Hospital which is inside the secure perimeter of the Hospital,

"security department" means a group of members of staff with express responsibility for advising on, monitoring and, where relevant, implementing a hospital authority's security policy at a Hospital,

"security director" means the senior member of staff with responsibility for the security department,

"visiting child" means any person under the age of 18 in respect of whom entry into the secure area is proposed,

"visitor" means any person aged 18 or over, other than a member of staff, who proposes to enter the secure area and includes any member of the emergency services,

"ward area" means the day rooms, patients' bedrooms, corridors, toilets, bathrooms, ward kitchens and any other rooms or areas including garden areas in the residential parts of a Hospital in the secure area to which patients have access as a matter of course.

(2) In these Directions unless the context otherwise requires a reference to a paragraph is to the paragraph bearing that number in these Directions and in a paragraph a reference to a sub-paragraph identified by a number of letter is a reference to the sub-paragraph bearing that number or letter in that paragraph

## Conditions of safety and security

4. In order to promote conditions of safety and security in Ashworth, Broadmoor and **C–006** Rampton Hospitals each hospital authority is directed to exercise its functions in

connection with the provision of high security psychiatric services in accordance with these Directions.

### Arrangements for rub-down searches of patients

**C–007**    5. Each hospital authority shall ensure that all rub-down searches of patients authorised under these Directions are conducted as follows–

    (a) the patient's consent must be sought for each search and where this is given the search must be carried out with due regard for the patient's dignity and privacy and, unless there are exceptional circumstances, it must be carried out by members of staff who are of the same sex as the patient,

    (b) where a patient refuses to consent to being searched, that patient's RMO must consider whether the proposed search would harm the patient's mental health,

    (c) where in the RMO's view the search would harm the patient's mental health, but the members of staff authorised by the hospital authority to conduct the search consider that it should proceed, the matter must be referred for a decision by the Hospital's medical director and any delay which arises must be kept to a minimum,

    (d) in making a decision on the matter referred, the medical director shall take into account the RMO's view and the interests of security and safety of the individual and the Hospital,

    (e) while these matters are resolved the patient in question must be kept under observation and isolated from other patients and told what is happening and why in terms appropriate to his understanding,

    (f) if the medical director decides the search should proceed a further attempt should be made to obtain the patient's consent before proceeding with a search without consent and

    (g) if a search without consent proceeds it must be carried out with due regard for the patient's dignity and privacy and, unless there are exceptional circumstances, it must be carried out by members of staff who are of the same sex as the patient.

### Random and routine searches of patients and their rooms and lockers

**C–008**    6. Each hospital authority shall ensure that–

    (a) each patient's room, its contents and the patient's locker located outside his room are searched on a random occasion not less than once a month and on each such occasion the patient using the room is subjected to a rub-down search;

    (b) in addition to the searches in sub-paragraph (a), each patient is subjected to a rub-down search on a random occasion not less than once a month and that the patient's locker is searched at the same time;

    (c) each patient who receives a visitor is subjected to a rub-down search both immediately before and immediately after seeing the visitor except where the patient receives a visitor authorised to hold Hospital keys;

    (d) each patient who goes on leave of absence from the Hospital is subjected to a rub-down search before leaving the secure area and on returning from leave.

### Searches when patients move around the secure area

**C–009**    7.—(1) Each hospital authority shall ensure that on all occasions where more than one patient at a time moves from one patient area to another (such as from a workshop area to a ward area) a member of staff shall select randomly–

(a)  at least one patient from any group of up to 9 patients,

(b)  at least 10% of any group of 10 or more patients,

and any patient so selected shall be subjected to a rub-down search.

(2) Each hospital authority shall ensure that on all occasions when a single patient moves from one patient area to another the patient shall be subjected to a rub-down search.

## Searches of ward areas and other areas

8.—Each hospital shall ensure that–                                  **C–010**

(a)  all parts of the ward areas other than patients' rooms are searched not less than once a week, and

(b)  all therapy, workshop, recreation and leisure facility areas, and other non-ward areas which a patient may visit in the secure area, are searched not less than once every three months.

## Security of tools, equipment and materials

9. Each hospital authority shall prepare and issue written instructions for members of **C–011** staff for the control of tolls, equipment and materials in the secure area of the Hospital.

(2) Each hospital authority shall ensure that any patient needing to leave a workshop or occupational therapy area before the end of a session is first subjected to a rub-down search.

## Searches of members of staff

10.—(1) Each hospital authority shall ensure that searches of members of staff and of **C–012** any possessions they bring into or take away from the secure area are conducted in accordance with the following provisions of this paragraph.

(2) At least 10% of staff entering the secure area in a 24 hour period (calculated from midnight to midnight) must be selected randomly and subjected to a rub-down search.

(3) All bags, packages or other similar possessions accompanying a member of staff at the point of entry to the secure area must be x-rayed and, where necessary, physically inspected, before the member of staff in question is permitted to enter the secure area.

(4) All members of staff must pass through a staffed metal detection portal on entry to the secure area.

(5) At least 5% of members of staff leaving the secure area in a 24 hour period (calculated from midnight to midnight) must be selected randomly and subjected to a rub-down search and any of their bags, packages or other similar possessions may be x-rayed and where necessary, physically inspected.

(6) Where members of staff escort patients on leave of absence, before they leave the secure area they must be subjected to a rub-down search and any bags, packages or other similar possessions of theirs must be x-rayed and where necessary, physically inspected and where they return to the secure area while escorting patients they and their possessions must be searched and inspected similarly.

(7) Where any member of staff refuses to be searched or to permit his possessions to be searched the chief executive, or a deputy whom he nominates for the purpose, must be notified immediately and the chief executive or deputy shall have discretion to refuse entry to the secure area by that member of staff.

(8) All rub-down searches must be carried out with due regard for the member of staff's dignity.

(9) All rub-down searches are to be carried out by a person of the same sex as the member of staff unless there are exceptional circumstances.

### Searches of contractors, visitors and visiting children

C–013    [11.—(1) A hospital authority shall make arrangements to ensure that all contractors and visitors are aware that, unless one of the exceptions in sub-paragraphs (4), (5), (6), (7) or (8) is applicable, they and any visiting children will, with their consent, be subjected to a rub-down search and their possessions inspected before they are permitted to enter the secure area and that there may be similar searches or inspections on leaving the secure area.

(2) Searches shall be conducted as follows–

(a) where a rub-down search of a contractor, visitor or visiting child is carried out it is to be carried out with due regard for the dignity of the person being searched, and by a member of staff of the same sex as the person being searched except in exceptional circumstances and where the contractor or visitor agrees otherwise, including where a visitor agrees otherwise in respect of any visiting child with him for whom he is responsible,

(b) except where sub-paragraph (4), (5), (6) or (7) applies, all contractors, visitors and visiting children are to pass through a metal detection portal on entry to the secure area,

(c) except where sub-paragraph (4), (5), (6) or (7) applies, all contractors, visitors and visiting children are to pass through a metal detection portal on entry to the secure area,

(d) where a visiting child is of sufficient understanding to make an informed decision about being subject to a rub-down search and an inspection of any possessions, that child may consent to that search and inspection, and

(e) where a visiting child is of sufficient understanding to make an informed decision about being searched and that child refuses to consent to being subjected to a rub-down search or refuses to allow personal possessions to be inspected in accordance with sub-paragraph (b), as the case may be, any consent given on the visiting child's behalf by an adult who is responsible for the child shall not be relied on by any member of staff so as to permit a rub-down search without that child's consent.

(3) Subject to sub-paragraphs (4) to (8) where–

(a) a contractor refuses to be searched or refuses to allow his possessions to be inspected, or

(b) a visitor refuses–

(i) to be searched,

(ii) to allow any visiting children for whom he is responsible to be searched, or

(ii) to allow his own possessions or those of any visiting child for whom he is responsible to be inspected in accordance with sub-paragraph (2)(b),

Such contractor, or visitor and any visiting child, whether or not the child has consented to being searched in accordance with sub-paragraph (2)(d), shall not be permitted to enter the secure area on that occasion.

(4) If a decision is made to refuse entry to a visitor or visiting child into the secure area under sub-paragraph (3) the Hospital's chief executive shall, if the visitor so requests, review the decision and may, in exceptional circumstances, permit entry under specified conditions.

(5) A child, and any accompanying adult who is responsible for the child, shall not be refused entry under sub-paragraph (3) if an order has been made under the Children Act 1989 that the child may visit the patient in the Hospital but the visit may be subject to special safety and security conditions.

(6) Where–

(a) a visitor is a member of any of the emergency services and needs to enter or leave the secure area other than in a vehicle for the purpose of dealing with an emergency, or

(b) a contractor or visitor enters the secure area in a vehicle to which one of the exceptions in paragraph 12(2) applies, he shall not be subject to a rub-down search, monitoring by means of a metal detection portal or to inspection of his possessions on that occasion.

(7) A visitor who is authorised to have Hospital keys may be treated as a member of staff when entering or leaving the secure area so that he is subject to searches provided for under paragraph 10 instead of under this paragraph.

(8) Where a visitor is a member of a Mental Health Review Tribunal, and needs to enter the secure area in connection with performing his judicial function, he shall not be subject to a rub-down search on entering or leaving the secure area on that occasion unless–

(a) he will be carrying out an assessment of a patient in accordance with Rule 11 of the Mental Health Review Tribunal Rules 1983 whilst in the secure area,

(b) he activates the metal detection portal on passing through it and the reason for activation cannot be established by other means, or

(c) the chief executive considers that there is an exceptional reason why he should be subject to a rub-down search.

(9) Subject to sub-paragraph (10), no person shall be permitted to bring or send food for a patient into the secure area either for immediate or later consumption and any food provided when a visitor visits a patient should be obtained in the secure area.

[(10A) Catering and supply staff, authorised by the Chief Executive of the hospital authority, may be permitted to bring food for patients into a secure area in circumstances in which it is impracticable for a contractor to do so.

In this paragraph, "supply staff" means staff employed by the hospital authority supplies department and includes porters.]

(11) No person shall be permitted to bring or send tobacco or tobacco products for patients into the secure area.

(12) Nothing in sub-paragraphs (9) or (11) shall prevent a contractor working under a contract to supply a hospital authority with food, tobacco or tobacco products from being permitted to bring such products to the Hospital in accordance with that contract.

(13) All visits to patients shall be booked in advance.]

## Checks of vehicles

12.—(1) Each hospital authority shall prepare and issue instructions for members of staff **C–014** managing and escorting vehicles in the secure area of the Hospital.

(2) A hospital authority shall ensure that before any vehicle enters or leaves the secure area it is checked by a member of staff for the presence of any unauthorised persons or items, except where–

(a) the vehicle belongs to one of the emergency services and it is attending to deal with an emergency, or

(b) it is a vehicle in respect of which the chief executive, or a deputy whom he nominates for the purpose, has given a prior written dispensation from such a check.

### Contractors vehicles in patient areas

**C–015**    13. A hospital authority shall ensure that where any vehicle belonging to a contractor enters a patient area–

(a)  it is permitted to do so only for the purpose of loading or unloading tools or materials or supplies, or to permit access to the tools or materials it contains by the contractor.

(b)  a member of staff is present throughout the time the vehicle is in the patient area,

(c)  the vehicle is not left unattended at any time unless securely locked, and

(d)  a record of any tools or equipment taken from or returned to the vehicle is made by the member of staff.

### Testing patients for illicit substances

**C–016**    14.—(1) Each hospital authority shall make the following arrangements for testing patients at the Hospital for illicit substances.

(2) A member of staff shall request a sample–

(a)  each month from five per cent. of patients selected randomly on occasions and

(b)  from each patient at the time of admission of the Hospital.

(3) A member of staff may request a sample from a patient who is suspected of using illicit substances.

(4) A member of staff shall request the patient to provide a fresh sample, free from adulteration.

[(5) A patient requested to provide a sample shall be afforded such a degree of privacy for the purpose of providing a sample as may be compatible with the need to prevent or detect any adulteration of falsification of the sample; in particular a patient shall not be requested to provide a sample of urine in the sight of a person of the opposite sex.]

(6) in this paragraph–

"illicit substance" means–

(a)  any drug which is a controlled drug for the purposes of the Misuse of Drugs Act 1971 or

(b)  alcohol;

["sample" means–

(a)  a sample of urine;

(b)  a breath test for alcohol;

(c)  a swab taken from a person's mouth;

(d)  a sample of hair other than pubic hair.]

### Control of prescribed drugs

**C–017**    15. Each hospital authority shall prepare and issue written instructions to members of staff concerning the control of prescribed drugs within their Hospital, including–

(a)  the transportation of prescribed drugs from the Hospital pharmacy to the words,

(b)  the security of treatment rooms and medication storage units and

(c)  the arrangements for distributing prescribed drugs to patients and checking that patients take their medication when given it, except if patients have the express approval of a member of the clinical team to keep medication in their rooms.

## Written records of certain searches and tests

16. Each hospital authority shall ensure that a written record is kept of–   **C–018**

(a) all searches of patients, members of staff and their respective possessions;

(b) any search of a contractor, visitor, a visiting child or member of staff, or any search of those persons' possessions, which leads to any such person being refused entry to the secure area; and

(c) any taking of a sample from a patient to test for illicit substances and the outcome of the test or any refusal by a patient when requested to provide a sample.

## Security intelligence

17.—(1) Each hospital authority shall ensure that the security director establishes and   **C–019** maintains a security intelligence system and in particular the security director shall make and maintain–

(a) electronic records of security information relating to each patient; and

(b) electronic records of other security information relating to the Hospital.

(2) The security director shall ensure that the security intelligence system includes–

(a) the submission of general intelligence assessments to the hospital authority on a regular basis;

(b) instructions to the security department on collection, collation, evaluation and assessment of the reliability of security information;

(c) instructions to members of staff on what, and how, security information should be reported to the security department; and

(d) instructions to members of staff and members of the security department on sharing security information and data protection.

(3) For the purposes of this paragraph "security information" means information indicating a possible threat to the security or safety of the Hospital or people inside or outside the Hospital, including information on–

(a) plans for patients to escape from the Hospital;

(b) possible disturbances in the Hospital;

(c) arrangements for unauthorised items to be brought into the Hospital;

(d) matters which could threaten the wellbeing of a patient or a member of staff or other persons; and

(e) patient allegiances and behaviour which is the opinion of the security director may have security implications.

## Patients' possessions

18.—(1) A hospital authority shall ensure that–   **C–020**

(a) the number, volume and type of possessions permitted in each patient's room are subjected to a maximum limit;

(b) all possessions kept by patients in their rooms are listed in an inventory which the patient in question and a member of staff jointly keep updated; and

(c) the inventory is signed and dated by the patient and a member of staff when first compiled and on any occasion when it is updated.

(2) Subject to sub-paragraph (1), a hospital authority shall ensure that when patients request a member of staff in charge of a ward store or central stores to give them a personal possession from the store patients are able to retrieve the item within 48 hours, excluding week-ends and public or Hospital holidays.

### Items brought to Hospital premises for patients
C–021    19. Subject to [sections 134 and 134A(1) to (3)] of the 1983 Act and sub-paragraphs (8) to (10) of paragraph 11, each hospital authority shall ensure that any item brought to the Hospital for a patient, including any item brought by a visitor, is x-rayed, opened and inspected by a member of staff before being given to the patient and if any item is withheld–

(a) the hospital authority shall record the fact that the item has been withheld;

(b) the patient must be informed that the item is withheld, the reasons for withholding it and that he has the right to have the decision to withhold reviewed [by the Care Quality Commission];

[(c) the hospital authority shall comply with any direction given by the Care Quality Commission under regulation 2(2) of the Care Quality Commission (Additional Functions) Regulations 2009]; and

(d) [. . .].

GENERAL NOTE
C–022    Regulation 2 of the Care Quality Commission (Additional Functions) Regulations 2009 (SI 2009/410) reads:

**"Review of decision to withhold an item brought to a High Secure Hospital for a patient**
2.—(1) The Care Quality Commission shall review a decision made under paragraph 19 of the 2000 Directions (items brought to hospital premises for patients) to withhold an item if an application to review that decision is made by the intended recipient of the item within six months of that person receiving the information set out in paragraph 19(b) of those Directions.

(2) On an application under paragraph (1) the Care Quality Commission may direct that the item which is the subject of the application shall not be withheld."

### Patients' access to computer equipment etc
C–023    20. Each hospital authority shall ensure that–

[(a) patients have access to computer equipment, word processing facilities or game consoles that can be adapted as a computer, only where these are owned and controlled by the hospital authority.]

(b) no patient has access to any equipment which gives him access to the Internet.

### Patients' shops
C–024    21. Each hospital authority shall ensure that–

(a) no patient is permitted to have any responsibility for the running of a patients' shop but a patient may work in such a shop under the supervision of a number of staff and with the prior approval of the ground access committee after the committee has considered any recommendations made by a member of the patient's clinical team.

(b) no patient's shop is permitted in any ward area.

## Patients' incoming post

22. Subject to [sections 134 and 134A(1) to (3) of the 1983 Act and regulation 30 of the **C–025** 2008 Regulations], incoming postal packets addressed to a patient may be opened and inspected by an authorised member of staff and the contents recorded, except that any postal packet which indicates on the outside that it is sent by or on behalf of one of the persons or organisations referred to in section 134(3) of the 1983 Act may be opened only where this is necessary to confirm its origin and, where it is from such a person or organisation, it must be passed to the patient without further inspection.

## Internal Patient-to-patient post

23.—(1) An authorised member of staff may open and inspect internal patient-to-patient **C–026** post in the Hospital and may withhold the post, or an item included in the post, on one of the grounds specified in section 134(1) or (2) of the 1983 Act for withholding postal packets.

(2) If any patient-to-patient post, or item included in such post, is withheld–

(a) the hospital authority shall record the fact that the post or item has been withheld;

(b) the relevant patients must be informed that the post or item is withheld, the reasons for withholding it and that they have the right to have the decision to withhold reviewed [by the Care Quality Commission];

[(c) the hospital authority shall comply with any direction given by the Care Quality Commission under regulation 3(2) of the Care Quality Commission (Additional Functions) Regulations 2009]; and

(d) [. . .].

GENERAL NOTE

Regulation 3 of the Care Quality Commission (Additional Functions) Regulations 2009 **C–027** (SI 2009/410) reads:

**"Review of decision to withhold internal post in High Secure Hospitals**

3.—(1) The Care Quality Commission shall review a decision made under paragraph 23 of the 2000 Directions (internal patient-to-patient post) to withhold internal post or an item included in such post if an application to review that decision is made by the sender or the intended recipient of the post or item within six months of that person receiving the information set out in paragraph 23(2)(b) of those Directions.

(2) On an application under paragraph (1) the Care Quality Commission may direct that the post or item which is the subject of the application shall not be withheld."

## Patients' outgoing post

24.—(1) All outgoing postal packets from patients, other than letters or cards, shall be **C–028** packed and sealed by patients on their wards in the presence of an authorised member of staff.

(2) Subject to [sections 134 and 134A(1) to (3) of the 1983 Act and regulation 30 of the 2008 Regulations], letters and cards from patients may be opened and inspected from time to time by an authorised member of staff, except where the letter or card is addressed to one of the persons or organisations referred to in section 134(3) of the 1983 Act but any postal packet addressed to one of those persons or organisations may be opened solely to confirm its destination and, where it is to such a person or organisation, it may not be further inspected.

### Post of members of staff

**C–029**     25.—(1) Each hospital authority shall ensure that all postal packets coming into the secure area addressed to members of staff at the Hospital are x-rayed but no such postal packet may be opened and inspected for security reasons except with the consent of the addressee and with the addressee being present.

(2) Each hospital authority must warn members of staff that a postal packet addressed to them may be withheld and not allowed into the secure area if they refuse to allow it to be opened and inspected following an x-ray.

(3) If a postal packet is withheld under sub-paragraph (2) the member of staff must be informed of the reasons for withholding it and that he has the right to have the decision to withhold reviewed by the chief executive and the right to take the postal packet on leaving the secure area.

### Mobile telephones

**C–030**     26. Each hospital authority shall ensure that–

(a)  no patient has a mobile telephone in his possession or access to such a telephone,

(b)  no visitor carries a mobile telephone while in any part of the secure area, and

(c)  no member of staff carries a mobile telephone in the secure area unless the carrying of that telephone is essential for the carrying out of that member of staff's duties and has been previously authorised by the security director.

### Patients' outgoing telephone calls

**C–031**     27. Each hospital authority shall ensure that the following arrangements apply in respect of all outgoing telephone calls to be made by patients–

(a)  where a hospital authority maintains a telephone system whereby a patient can only dial numbers which have been pre-programmed into that system by a member of staff, a patient may make calls to any of those pre-programmed numbers;

(b)  patients may make telephone calls to any of the persons or organisations referred to in section 134(3) of the 1983 Act;

(c)  where sub-paragraph (a) applies the numbers of any persons referred to in section 134(3) of the 1983 Act to whom the patient wishes to make telephone calls shall be pre-programmed;

(d)  when patients are in a ward area they may have access to a telephone only at times between 8.00am and 10.00pm as determined by the authority and outside these hours they may have access only when expressly authorised by a member of staff on a particular occasion;

(e)  where the patient is not subject to the provisions of paragraph 29(1) and is assessed in accordance with paragraph 30 as presenting a high risk of escaping or organising action to subvert security and safety in collaboration with others, or where a telephone call is likely to cause distress to the person called or to the patient, a member of staff may listen to the patient making the call unless the call is to any of the persons or organisations referred to in section 134(3) of the 1983 Act;

(f)  where a decision is made to listen to a patient's telephone calls in accordance with sub-paragraph (e) the patient may have the decision reviewed by the chief executive; and

(g)  except where sub-paragraph (a) applies–

     (i)  subject to sub-paragraph (b), patients may only make telephone calls to the persons and numbers on a list approved for that purpose by the clinical team responsible for the patient in question;

    (ii)  where a patient wishes to make a telephone call to a person identified under sub-paragraph (b) or (g)(i) a member of staff is to dial the number in question, attempt to establish the identity of the person or organisation called and then pass the telephone to the patient; and

   (iii)  a member of staff shall observe the patient at all times during the telephone call.

## Patient's incoming telephone calls

28.—(1A) A hospital authority shall ensure that the following arrangements apply in **C–032** respect of all incoming telephone calls for patients–

(a)  a member of staff takes the call and then passes a message about the call to the patient in question, but

(b)  where the call is about an urgent or a compassionate matter the member of staff may permit the patient to speak to the caller.

(2) When a patient speaks to a caller in accordance with sub-paragraph (1)(b)–

(a)  a member of staff shall observe the patient at all times during the telephone call.

(b)  where the patient is not subject to the provisions of paragraph 29(1) and is assessed in accordance with paragraph 30 as presenting a high risk of escaping or organising action to subvert security and safety in collaboration with others, or where a telephone call is likely to cause distress to the person calling or to the patient, a member of staff may listen to the patient receiving the call; and

(c)  where a decision is made to listen to a patient's telephone calls in accordance with sub-paragraph (2)(b) the patient has the right to have the decision reviewed by the chief executive.

## Monitoring telephone calls

29.—(1) Subject to sub-paragraphs (4) and (5) if, following a risk assessment under para- **C–033** graph 30, a patient's clinical team decide, in consultation with a member of the security department–

(a)  that a patient presents a high risk of escaping or organising action to subvert security and safety in collaboration with others or

[(b)  in respect of any patient, if there is a need to protect the safety of the patient or others]

they shall consider including in the patient's risk management plan arrangements for authorised members of staff to record and monitor the patient's outgoing and incoming telephone calls while in progress.

(2) If a decision is made to record and monitor a patient's telephone calls under sub-paragraph (1)–

(a)  the decision must be reviewed when appropriate by the patient's clinical team in consultation with a member of the security department;

(b)  the patient must be informed of the reasons for the decision and that he has the right to have the decision reviewed by the [Care Quality Commission];

[(c) [(c) the hospital authority shall comply with any direction given by the Care Quality Commission under regulation 4(2) of the Care Quality Commission (Additional Functions) Regulations 2009]; and

(d) [. . .].

(3) Subject to sub-paragraph (4) and (5) and in addition to calls which are recorded and monitored under sub-paragraph (1), authorised members of staff may record a random 10 per cent. of the outgoing and incoming telephone calls of patients and may subsequently listen to the recorded calls.

(4) No person may record or monitor a telephone communication between a patient and any of the persons or organisations referred to in section 134(3) of the 1983 Act.

(5) Before a patient's outgoing or incoming telephone calls are recorded and monitored the hospital authority shall ensure that–

(a) where the telephone calls of a patient are recorded and monitored under sub-paragraph (1) that patient, and the persons to whom they are permitted to make calls, are warned that calls between them will be monitored and recorded and

(b) all patients other than those whose calls are recorded and monitored under sub-paragraph (1), and the persons to whom a patient is permitted to make calls, are warned of the provisions of sub-paragraph (3).

(6) Each hospital authority shall specify a limited period during which telephone call records made under sub-paragraph (1) and (3) may be stored and at the end of the specified period the records shall be destroyed unless a decision is made to store the records for further limited periods and the reason for such a decision is recorded.

GENERAL NOTE

**C–034**    In *R. (on the application of N) v Ashworth Special Hospital Authority and the Secretary of State for Health* [2001] EWHC 339 (Admin); [2001] M.H.L.R. 77, a patient challenged the legality of direction 29(3). In dismissing the application for judical review, Newman J. held that the provision of random monitoring of telephone calls, whilst constituting an interference with patient's rights under art.8 of the European Convention on Human Rights, is directed at a legitimate aim, namely the Secretary of State's duty under s.4 of the National Health Service Act 1977 (now the NHS Act 2006), and that the direction was a proportionate response to the permitted purpose of reducing the security risks at the three high security hospitals.

Regulation 4 of the Care Quality Commission (Additional Functions) Regulations 2009 (SI 2009/410) reads:

"**Review of decisions to record and monitor telephone calls in High Secure Hospitals**
**4.**—(1) The Care Quality Commission shall review a decision made under paragraph 29(1) of the 2000 Directions (monitoring telephone calls) to record and monitor a patient's telephone calls if an application to review that decision is made by the patient within six months of that person receiving the information set out in paragraph 29(2)(b) of those Directions.

(2) On an application under paragraph (1) the Care Quality Commission may direct that the recording and monitoring of the patient's telephone calls shall cease."

**Risk assessments**

**C–035**    30.—(1) Each hospital authority shall ensure that as soon as is practicable after this paragraph comes into force each patient has a risk assessment carried out by his clinical team provided he has not had an equivalent assessment in the previous three months, and every newly admitted patient shall have a risk assessment by his clinical team as soon as in practicable after admission to the Hospital.

[(2) The clinical team shall use the risk assessment to determine whether the patient presents a high risk of–

(a) immediately harming others;

(b) committing suicide or self-harming;

(c) being assaulted;

(d) escaping;

(e) subverting security and safety, or organising action in collaboration with others to subvert security and safety]

(3) When making or reviewing a risk assessment the clinical team shall decide on a risk management plan for the patient and that risk management plan shall, where appropriate, cover the matters set out in paragraphs 29(1) and 31.

(4) If the patient's clinical team decide that the patient presents a high risk

[(a) of escaping or of harming others; or]

(b) of organising action in collaboration with others to subvert security and safety the clinical team must consult a member of the security department before finalising a risk management plan for the patient.

(5) When the clinical team carries out a risk assessment they must–

(a) record their reasons for concluding that the patient presents any of the high risks specified in sub-paragraph (2);

(b) record the risk management plan for the patient, including any decision made on the matters specified in sub-paragraph (3);

(c) decide and record the date on which the risk assesment is to be reviewed; and

(d) decide and record the date on which any decision to monitor the patient's telephone calls while in progress, or lock the patient in his room at night, is to be reviewed.

(6) The clinical team shall review the risk assessment of each patient and the patient's associated risk management plan as necessary and at least once a year.

## Patients at night

31.—(1) Each hospital authority shall have a policy on the circumstances in which a **C–036** patient, considered to be at high risk of matters set out in sub-paragraphs 30(2) following a risk assessment under paragraph 30, can be locked up in his room at night.

(2) Where in accordance with its policy a hospital authority is minded to include locking up at night in a patient's risk management plan the patient's clinical team shall first consider whether

(a) there are medical grounds (which in the case of a patient assessed as at high risk of committing suicide or self harm will take into account that risk) for not locking the patient up at night and

(b) (following consultation with a member of the security department) there are other available measures which would be an effective alternative way to reduce the risk.

[(3) Where in accordance with a hospital authority's relevant policy, a patient meets the clinical and risk criteria for detention in a regime designated as suitable for those who are dangerous as a result of a severe personality disorder and consequently is accommodated in the hospital authority's Dangerous and Serious Personality Disorder ("DSPD") facility, he will be locked up in his room at night unless sub-paragraph (4) below applies.

(4) The hospital authority shall establish a process whereby the requirement to lock up a patient in the DSPD facility in his room at night, may be reviewed on any occasion if there are circumstances, for example the risk of suicide or self-harm, which would indicate that the locking up of the patient in his room at night on that occasion would be unsafe.]

## Patients' ground access

C–037   32. A hospital authority shall ensure that the following arrangements apply in respect of any requests for ground access–

(a)  it shall establish a committee to consider all requests for the granting of ground access to patients and the security director, or a member of the security department nominated by the director, shall be the chairman of the committee;

(b)  it shall ensure that the committee considers requests submitted by a member of the clinical team for the patient in question only where members of the team have already undertaken a risk assessment and where ground access is proposed as part of that patient's treatment plan;

(c)  it shall ensure that in making a decision the committee takes into account the interests of security and safety of the individual and the Hospital;

(d)  before the committee grants or refuses any such request the committee shall take into account all relevant issues, and, where appropriate, impose restrictions or conditions on any ground privilege it grants, including conditions or restrictions in respect of the area or areas of the hospital premises to which the ground access applies;

(e)  where in the view of the patient's RMO a decision not to grant ground access would impede a patient's eventual rehabilitation the decision must be referred for review by the medical director; and

(f)  before making a decision on the matter referred, the medical director shall consult the security director and the medical director shall take into account–

(i)  the RMO's view and
(ii)  the interests of security and safety of the individual and the Hospital.

## Leave of Absence

C–038   33. Each hospital authority shall ensure that before a patient is granted leave of absence under section 17 of the 1983 Act–

(a)  the RMO, in consultation with the members of the patient's clinical team including a member of the security department, undertakes a risk assessment and

(b)  the security director, or a member of the security department whom the security director authorises to act on his behalf, considers the request for leave of absence and makes recommendations to the RMO.

## Escorting patients

C–039   34. Each hospital authority shall–

(a)  identify and train members of staff who will take responsibility for escorting patients outside the secure area of the Hospital and

(b) prepare and issue written instructions to those members of staff on carrying out such escorting duties, including instructions on the appropriate use of handcuffs and escorting chains.

## Security of keys and locks

35. The security director of each hospital authority shall prepare and issue written **C–040** instructions to members of staff, and persons authorised by the hospital authority to hold Hospital keys, on the security of keys and locks relating to the secure perimeter of the Hospital.

## Security audits

[36. Centrally co-ordinated arrangements shall be made for each hospital authority to **C–041** invite the Prison Service Audit Team to visit each hospital annually to review the security of the secure area and the secure perimeter of the hospital and submit a report to the hospital authority.]

## Revocation

37. The Safety and Security in Ashworth, Broadmoor and Rampton Hospitals Directions **C–042** 1999 are revoked.

# APPENDIX D

# MENTAL HEALTH ACT 1983 APPROVED CLINICIAN (GENERAL) DIRECTIONS 2008

The Secretary of State for Health gives the following directions in exercise of the powers conferred by sections 7, 8 and 273 of the National Health Service Act 2006.

# PART 1

## Application, etc.

### Application, commencement and interpretation

**1.**—(1) These Directions apply to Strategic Health Authorities.                    **D–001**

(2) These Directions apply in relation to England.

(3) These Directions shall come into force on 3rd November 2008.

(4) In these Directions—

"the 1983 Act" means the Mental Health Act 1983;

"the 2006 Act" means the National Health Service Act 2006;

"approve" and "approval" include "re-approve" and "re-approval";

"approved clinician" has the meaning given by section 145(1) of the 1983 Act;

"approving Authority" means the Authority that has approved the person to act as an approved clinician;

"Authority" means a Strategic Health Authority continued in existence or established under section 13 of the 2006 Act;

"medical treatment" has the meaning given by section 145 of the 1983 Act;

"mental disorder" has the meaning given by section 1(2) of the 1983 Act;

"period of approval" means the period of time for which the approval is granted in accordance with direction 5;

"professional requirements" means the requirements set out at Schedule 1 to these Directions;

"relevant competencies" means the skills set out at Schedule 2 to these Directions;

"responsible clinician" has the meaning given by section 34(1) of the 1983 Act;

"responsible medical officer" means a person as defined in section 34(1) in relation to Part 2 of the 1983 Act and in section 55(1) in relation to Part 3 of the 1983 Act immediately before 3rd November 2008; and

"treatment" means medical treatment for mental disorder.

## PART 2

### Approvals: General

**Function of approval**

**D–002**   2. The Secretary of State directs the Authorities to exercise the function of approving persons to act as approved clinicians.

3. The function of approving persons to act as approved clinicians is a specified function that an Authority may direct a Primary Care Trust, any part of whose area falls within that Authority's area, to exercise in accordance with section 15(1) of the 2006 Act.

**Approval to act as an approved clinician**

**D–003**   4. An Authority shall only approve a person to act as an approved clinician where the Authority is satisfied that the person—

(a) fulfils at least one of the professional requirements;

(b) possesses the relevant competencies, and

(c) has—

    (i) completed a course for the initial training of approved clinicians within the previous two years, or

    (ii) been approved, or been treated as approved, to act as an approved clinician in England or Wales within the previous five years.

**Period of approval**

**D–004**   5. An Authority may approve a person to act as an approved clinician for a period of five years commencing with the date of approval.

**Conditions of approval**

**D–005**   6. When any approval is granted under these Directions, it shall be subject to the following conditions—

(a) the approved clinician shall undertake to cease to act as an approved clinician and to notify the approving Authority immediately if the clinician no longer meets any of the requirements set out in direction 4;

(b) the approved clinician shall undertake to cease to act as an approved clinician and to notify the approving Authority immediately if that clinician is suspended from any of the registers or listings referred to in the professional requirements, or if any suspension ends, and

(c) such other conditions as the approving Authority thinks appropriate.

**Suspension of approval**

**D–006**   7.—(1) If—

(a) at any time after being approved, or

(b) in the case of a person approved under Part 3 of these Directions, at the time of their approval or at any time thereafter,

the registration or listing of an approved clinician as required by the professional requirements is suspended, the approving Authority must suspend that clinician's approval to act as an approved clinician for as long as the approved clinician's registration or listing is suspended.

(2) Where an approved clinician's approval is suspended, that clinician may not act as an approved clinician unless and until the suspension of approval is ended by the approving Authority in accordance with paragraph (3).

(3) Where the approving Authority is notified that the suspension of the approved clinician's registration or listing has ended, the approving Authority shall, unless it is not satisfied the person possesses the relevant competencies or meets any conditions attached to their approval, end the suspension of approval.

(4) Where the suspension of approval has ended, the approval shall continue to run for any unexpired period of approval, unless the approving Authority ends it earlier in accordance with direction 8.

## End of approval

**8.**—(1) Except where paragraph (2) applies, the approval of an approved clinician shall **D–007** end at the end of the day on which their period of approval expires.

(2) The approving Authority shall end the approval of a person as an approved clinician before the expiry of the period of approval—

(a) in accordance with a request in writing by the approved clinician to do so, or

(b) except where direction 7 applies, if it is not satisfied that the approved clinician—

    (i) meets any condition attached to that clinician's approval;
    (ii) possesses the relevant competencies, or
    (iii) fulfils at least one of the professional requirements.

(3) Where an approving Authority ends the approval of an approved clinician under paragraph (2), that Authority must immediately notify that clinician in writing of the date of the ending of approval and the reason for the ending of approval.

## Records

**9.**—(1) The approving Authority must keep a record of each approved clinician it **D–008** approves which shall include—

(a) the clinician's name;

(b) the clinician's profession;

(c) the date of approval;

(d) the conditions attached to the clinician's approval;

(e) details of any period of suspension of approval under direction 7;

(f) details of the completion of any training referred to in direction 4(c)(i);

(g) details of any previous approvals referred to in direction 4(c)(ii), and

(h) the date of and reason for the ending of the approval, if applicable.

(2) The record referred to in paragraph (1) must be retained by the approving Authority for a period of five years commencing with the day on which the clinician's approval ended.

# PART 3

Transitional Arrangements

**Transitional Arrangements**

D–009    **10.** The Secretary of State directs that an Authority must approve as an approved clinician the persons referred to in this Part and that any approval under this Part is subject to directions 6 to 9.

**11.** An Authority shall approve to act as an approved clinician a person who—

(a)  has carried out the functions of a responsible medical officer under the 1983 Act within the period of twelve months ending on 2nd November 2008, and

(b)  is a registered medical practitioner approved by that Authority under section 12(2) of the 1983 Act.

**12.** A person to whom direction 11 applies shall be approved to act as an approved clinician for the period of twelve months commencing on 3rd November 2008, or until the end of their period of approval under section 12(2) of the 1983 Act, whichever is later.

**13.** An Authority shall approve to act as an approved clinician a person who—

(a)  has not carried out the functions of a responsible medical officer under the 1983 Act within the period of twelve months ending on 2nd November 2008, but

(b)  has been in overall charge of the medical treatment for mental disorder of a person within the period of twelve months ending on 2nd November 2008, and

(c)  is a registered medical practitioner approved by the Authority under section 12(2) of the 1983 Act.

**14.** Where direction 13 applies—

(a)  the person shall be approved to act as an approved clinician for a period of twelve months commencing on 3rd November 2008, and that period shall be extended for a further two years if during that period of twelve months the person completes a course for the initial training of approved clinicians, and

(b)  direction 4(c)(ii) shall not be satisfied by a person who has not completed a course for the initial training of approved clinicians within the period referred to in paragraph (a).

**15.** An Authority shall approve to act as an approved clinician a person who—

(a)  has not carried out the functions of a responsible medical officer under the 1983 Act within the period of twelve months ending on 2nd November 2008 and has not, within that period, been in overall charge of the medical treatment for mental disorder of a person, but

(b)  is a registered medical practitioner approved by an Authority under section 12(2) of the 1983 Act who has been appointed to the post of consultant psychiatrist in England within the period of eighteen months ending on 2nd November 2009.

**16.** Where direction 15 applies—

(a)  the person shall be approved to act as an approved clinician until 2nd November 2009, and

(b)  direction 4(c)(ii) shall not be satisfied by a person approved under that direction.

## PART 4

## Revocations

**17.** The Mental Health Act 1983 Approved Clinician Directions 2008 are revoked.     **D–010**

## SCHEDULE 1

PROFESSIONAL REQUIREMENTS

**1.** The professional requirements are that the person is—     **D–011**

    (a)  a registered medical practitioner;

    [(b)  a psychologist registered in Part 14 of the Register maintained under article 5 of the Health Professions Order 2001.]¹

    (c)  a first level nurse, registered in Sub-Part 1 of the Nurses' Part of the Register maintained under article 5 of the Nursing and Midwifery Order 2001, with the inclusion of an entry indicating their field of practice is mental health or learning disabilities nursing;

    (d)  an occupational therapist registered in Part 6 of the Register maintained under article 5 of the Health Professions Order 2001; or

    (e)  a social worker, registered as such with the General Social Care Council.

## SCHEDULE 2

RELEVANT COMPETENCIES

**1.** The role of the approved clinician and responsible clinician     **D–012**
**1.1.** A comprehensive understanding of the role, legal responsibilities and key functions of the approved clinician and the responsible clinician.

**2.** Legal and Policy Framework     **D–013**
**2.1.** Applied knowledge of—

    (a)  mental health legislation, related codes of practice and national and local policy and guidance;

    (b)  other relevant legislation, codes of practice, national and local policy guidance, in particular, relevant parts of the Human Rights Act 1998, the Mental Capacity Act 2005, and the Children Acts, and

    (c)  relevant guidance issued by the National Institute for Health and Clinical Excellence (NICE).

**2.2.** In the above paragraph "relevant" means relevant to the decisions likely to be taken by an approved clinician or responsible clinician.

**3.** Assessment     **D–014**
**3.1.** Demonstrated ability to—

    (a)  identify the presence of mental disorder;

    (b)  identify the severity of the disorder, and

---

¹ Para.1(b) substituted by the Mental Health Act 1083 Approved Clinician (General) (Amendment) Regulations 2009.

(c) determine whether the disorder is of a kind or degree warranting compulsory confinement.

**3.2.** Ability to assess all levels of clinical risk, including risks to the safety of the patient and others within an evidence-based framework for risk assessment and management.
**3.3.** Demonstrated ability to undertake mental health assessments incorporating biological, psychological, cultural and social perspectives.

**D–015**    **4.** Treatment
**4.1.** Understanding of—

(a) mental health related treatments, i.e. physical, psychological and social interventions, and

(b) different treatment approaches and their applicability to different patients.

**4.2.** Demonstrated high level of skill in determining whether a patient has capacity to consent to treatment.
**4.3.** Ability to formulate, review appropriately and lead on treatment for which the clinician is appropriately qualified in the context of a multi-disciplinary team.
**4.4.** Ability to communicate clearly the aims of the treatment, to patients, carers and the team.

**D–016**    **5.** Care Planning
**5.1.** Demonstrated ability to manage and develop care plans which combine health, social services and other resources, ideally, but not essentially, within the context of the Care Programme Approach.

**D–017**    **6.** Leadership and Multi-Disciplinary Team Working
**6.1.** Ability to effectively lead a multi-disciplinary team.
**6.2.** Ability to assimilate the (potentially diverse) views and opinions of other professionals, patients and carers, whilst maintaining an independent view.
**6.3.** Ability to manage and take responsibility for making decisions in complex cases without the need to refer to supervision in each individual case.
**6.4.** Understanding and recognition of the limits of their own skills and recognition of when to seek other professional views to inform a decision.

**D–018**    **7.** Equality and Cultural Diversity
**7.1.** Up-to-date knowledge and understanding of equality issues, including those concerning race, disability, sexual orientation and gender.
**7.2.** Ability to identify, challenge, and where possible redress discrimination and inequality in all its forms in relation to approved clinician practice.
**7.3.** Understanding of the need to sensitively and actively promote equality and diversity.
**7.4.** Understanding of how cultural factors and personal values can affect practitioners' judgements and decisions in the application of mental health legislation and policy.

**D–019**    **8.** Communication
**8.1.** Ability to communicate effectively with professionals, patients, carers and others, particularly in relation to decisions taken and the underlying reasons for these.
**8.2.** Ability to keep appropriate records and an awareness of the legal requirements with respect to record keeping.
**8.3.** Demonstrated understanding, and ability to manage, the competing requirements of confidentiality and effective information sharing, to the benefit of the patient and other stakeholders.
**8.4.** Ability to compile and complete statutory documentation and to provide written reports as required of an approved clinician.
**8.5.** Ability to present evidence to courts and tribunals.

# INDEX

## LEGAL TAXONOMY
### FROM SWEET & MAXWELL

This index has been prepared using Sweet and Maxwell's Legal Taxonomy. Main index entries conform to keywords provided by the Legal Taxonomy except where references to specific documents or non-standard terms (denoted by quotation marks) have been included. These keywords provide a means of identifying similar concepts in other Sweet & Maxwell publications and online services to which keywords from the Legal Taxonomy have been applied. Readers may find some minor differences between terms used in the text and those which appear in the index. Suggestions to *sweet&maxwell.taxonomy@thomson.com*.

# Index

# Index

## Index

# Index

# Index